Fishes of the World

Fishes of the World
An Illustrated Dictionary

Alwyne Wheeler

**Line Drawings by
Annabel Milne and Peter Stebbing**

**Photographs supplied by
Photo Aquatics**

**American Consultant
Editor: Thomas H. Fraser**

MACMILLAN PUBLISHING CO., INC.
NEW YORK

Macmillan Publishing Co., Inc.
866 Third Avenue, New York, N.Y. 10022

First American Edition 1975

This book was designed and produced by
George Rainbird Limited
Marble Arch House, 44 Edgware Road, London W2 2EH

House Editor : Curigwen Lewis
Designer : Jonathan Gill-Skelton

Printed and bound in England

Library of Congress Cataloging in Publication Data
Wheeler, Alwyne C.
Fishes of the World
1. Fishes – Dictionary.   2. Fishes – Pictorial
works.
I. Milne, Annabel.   II. Stebbing, Peter.
III. Title.
QL614.7.W47   1975   597   75.6972

ISBN 0 02 626180 4

Contents

Common names are fully cross-referred
in the dictionary section

Preface

The world of fishes presents the curious paradox that it is at once seemingly familiar but actually largely unknown. Fishes impinge on people's lives in many ways. Some keep them as pets, others derive pleasure and relaxation from catching, or trying to catch them, SCUBA swimmers are often satisfied just to watch them in their world, while many men earn their living catching them for food, and some few others in just studying them. Practically everyone eats fish at sometime in their lives. Yet despite all these associations between man and fish they remain in many ways unknown.

Preparing this book has been both a rewarding and a humbling task. Rewarding in the sense that it has given me the opportunity to write about these most fascinating of animals and to learn while further exploring their world. Humbling, because the more one learns about fishes the more one appreciates that our knowledge of their life styles and habits concerns only a minute proportion of the known species.

Every writer of such a survey of the fishes of the world must rely heavily on the published work of others in the field. My indebtedness to very many authors of books about fishes is great, too great to allow me to itemize them individually. To the unnamed authors of all, books and scientific papers, I would like to acknowledge their contribution to the advancement of ichthyological knowledge.

Users of this book will be aware of the very great contributions made to it by the artists and photographers whose work is here published. The artists, Peter Stebbing and Annabel Milne, have taken great pains to represent the fishes, some never before illustrated; their care and patience must be acknowledged. The photographers, who are too many to mention here by name but whose contribution is listed elsewhere, have produced what amounts to a unique record of the world of fishes. Some of the photographs have been taken of fishes in aquaria, but others have been taken underwater in conditions of discomfort, and even of some danger to the photographer; all but a very few show live fishes in the full range of their colour and body form. To all the photographers I offer my thanks for their help, patience, and immense contribution to this book.

I must also acknowledge my indebtedness to the British Museum (Natural History), London, where I have been given much freedom to study fishes, and generously allowed extra-mural facilities while writing this book.

Acknowledgments frequently end with a more or less formal note of thanks to the author's wife. This is no exception, except that it is not a formality. Cicely Wheeler has patiently collected, catalogued, sorted and selected several thousand colour photographs, has acted as agent between publisher, author, and the photographers. She has also kept track of the artists' work, acted as *advocatus diaboli*, inspirer, and goad to the author, and helped in every way. Expressing my thanks to her is no mere formality and it gives me pleasure to dedicate this book to her.

Alwyne Wheeler
Theydon Bois Essex

Introduction

This book is about the living fishes found in the waters of the earth. Water covers more than three quarters of the earth's surface and it is true to say that no considerable area of this water is naturally uninhabited by fishes. One kind or another is found in polar seas under the ice, in the tropical swamps of the equator, in the greatest depths of the ocean or at high altitudes in hill streams. In occupying this vast and three-dimensional living space fishes have evolved into a host of forms and inhabit a variety of habitats unattained by other vertebrate animals. Some of this great variety has been demonstrated in the following pages which contain examples of the recognized families of fishes, but very far from all species for it has been estimated that there are today some 22,000 different species of fishes including the sharks and lampreys. Although showing such diversity they all have certain fundamental features in common. To most people a fish is a water-living, scaly creature with fins; but some snakes have scales and live in water and many amphibians and squids have serviceable fins. The definition then must be more detailed, and concern itself with internal structures. Fishes and the fish-like vertebrates are animals which also have a supporting rod along the length of the body, respire by means of gills taking dissolved oxygen from the water in which they live; they also have a 2-chambered heart.

Some primitive kinds of fishes, for example the lampreys, the sharks, and rays, have only cartilaginous spinal columns as supporting rods in contrast to the bony fishes which have well-developed calcified vertebrae. The 32 known species of lamprey and the related hagfishes are the sole survivors of the agnathan fishes, a group of great diversity in the fossil record. They lack jaws and obtain their food by teeth set within a muscular, suctorial pharynx. They also have a single nostril in the mid-line of the head, and a series of separate gills in pouches behind the head but no trace of the gill covers found in the bony fishes. This series of gill openings on the anterior body is typical of another great class of fishes, the elasmobranchs (the sharks and rays), now known from relatively few living forms (500–600 species) but from numerous fossil remains.

Although it is true that the sharks and rays have certain primitive features, and are often spoken of as primitive fishes, it cannot be assumed that because of this they are in some way inferior. Indeed, their very survival as a group from the Devonian period, and their diversity today in the sea, suggest that they possess adaptive features of a high survival value, if lacking qualities for dynamic speciation.

Sharks and rays (Elasmobranchii) have well-developed jaws, and numerous teeth, the upper jaw is not fused to the cranium, and they have a series (5–7 sets) of gills, and gill-slits. Their skins are covered with tooth-like scales (denticles) and their fins at the edges are strengthened by hair-like cartilaginous supports. The ratfishes or chimaeras (Holocephali) have 4 pairs of gills, but these open into a single gill chamber each side. Their teeth too are few and specialized being rat-like incisors in front with grinding teeth in the sides of the jaws, and the upper jaw is fused to the cranium. All the sharks, rays, and chimaeras have cartilaginous skele-

tons. They all also have internal fertilization of the egg, the males possessing rather elaborate claspers associated with the pelvic fins which transfer sperm from male to female. Possibly herein lies the secret of their success, for many sharks are live-bearers, while others, and most rays, as well as the chimaeras, lay relatively few large-yolked, well-protected eggs. The production of a few, large ova with for each a good chance of survival may be the secret of the success of the elasmobranchs.

It is, however, the bony fishes (Osteichthys) which today dominate the waters of the world, and these are the recognizable fishes, with gill covers, scales, and bony-rayed fins. They are divided into 3 major groups, the tassel-fins (Crossopterygii), the lungfishes (Dipnoi) and the ray-fins (Actinopterygii). All 3 were distinct and well-separated as early as Devonian times but their fundamental similarities suggest an earlier common ancestor. The tassel-fins and the lungfishes are greatly outnumbered by the ray-fin fishes. The coelacanth, *Latimeria*, is the sole living representative of the crossopterygian fishes, a group of great abundance in the past history of the earth. Like its fossil relatives it has lobed fins, the second dorsal, anal, pectoral, and pelvic fins all being limb-like, and mobile, with fine rays at their tips. The tail fin is divided into upper and lower lobes with a smaller prominent lobe in the mid-line.

The lungfishes are found in freshwater (only 7 living species spread in Australia, South America, and Africa are known). All are well known as air-breathers, the Australian *Neoceratodus* having a single-chambered swimbladder lung, while the others have 2 chambers. All have tassel-fin fins although dorsal, tail, and anal fins are fused into one.

With the ray-fins (Actinopterygians) the greatest diversity of form is reached. Three major groups are recognized, of which the teleosts are the most abundant, and probably most recently evolved, first becoming dominant in the Cretaceous. These are the fishes with distinct rays or spines supporting their fins, their tails symmetrical, and not with the axis of the body upturned at its tip. The tooth-bearing bones of the jaws are attached to the anterior end of the snout. The other 2 groups, both small, are the Chondrostei, which includes the sturgeons (Acipenseridae) and the bichirs (Polypteridae), while the Holostei include the relatively few garpikes (Lepisosteidae) and the bowfin (Amiidae). In both groups the tail fin, although superficially symmetrical, has an asymmetrical skeleton, the terminal vertebrae being upturned, while the bichirs, bowfins, and gar pikes have heavy, smooth ganoid scales, and also have a swimbladder connected to the pharynx or gut, which can be used to breathe air. The sturgeons, alone amongst bony fishes, have retained the primitive heterocercal tail in which the last vertebrae are upturned and the tail fin is notably asymmetrical.

The teleosts or bony fishes have shown the greatest aptitude for exploiting the living spaces of the earth's waters. Some, such as the Homalopteridae have penetrated into Asiatic hillstreams to live in the torrential watercourses, adapted to be a living sucker forever clinging to rock faces to prevent themselves being swept downstream. This ability to evolve suction pads is shown by quite unrelated marine fishes, the clingfishes (Gobiesocidae) a few of which are found in freshwater, and the sea-snails (Cyclopteridae), both noted for their powerful pelvic suckers which in the littoral species are certainly used to stay put amongst the breaking surf. Both groups contain members which for one reason or another have lost their sucker discs, and abandoned or almost abandoned the bottom-hugging life style of their relatives.

The deep oceans too contain fishes of almost unimaginable variety and way of life. Small lantern fishes (Myctophidae) live in the upper layers of the ocean, equipped with flashing lights, the two sexes of the one species often with different patterns of light organs. On the ocean floor or close to it live the deep-sea cods (Eretmophoridae), halosaurs and spiny eels (Halosauridae and Notacanthidae), the last two equipped by their body form to swim in a head-down posture feeding on the invertebrates of the sea bed.

Tropical waters are well known for the abundance of their fish life. Coral reefs are famous for the colourful host of butterflyfishes and angelfishes (Chaetodontidae), wrasses (Labridae), parrotfishes (Scaridae), and triggerfishes (Balistidae), and others, all exploiting this rich and varied habitat. Some colourful tropical fishes also use their brilliance to advertise their services as pickers of parasites, as do certain wrasses, while others, like *Pterois* (Scorpaenidae), warn by colour of their venomous armament. Certain marine blennies (Blenniidae) are coloured to mimic the cleaner-wrasses, while young batfishes (Ephippidae) mimic floating mangrove leaves, and also possibly distasteful turbellarian flatworms. The best known leaf-mimics, however, are the freshwater Amazonian leaffishes (family Nandidae).

Away from the inshore waters the tropical seas are inhabited by a great variety of fishes. The tunas (Scombridae) range the open sea in far greater variety than they are found in temperate waters. Shoals of jacks (Carangidae), anchovies (Engraulidae), and herring-like fishes (Clupeidae), are abundant in the surface waters, and the 2 last are prey to a wide range of oceanic birds and fishes, including the jacks and tunas. Sharks too are more abundant in the warmer waters both in inshore situations and in the open sea, where the large sharks of the family Isuridae, and some Carcharhinidae are common.

Although the tropical waters are well known for the variety of fishes, and their abundance, the polar seas are far from being fishless. The Arctic Ocean has an abundance of codfishes (Gadidae), sculpins (Cottidae), and rockfishes or redfishes (Scorpaenidae), besides salmons (Salmonidae), and their relatives the capelin (Osmeridae). Few of these families are represented in Antarctic seas where the dominant group of fishes close to the polar ice are the Antarctic cods (Nototheniidae). They have their counterparts, however, as in the Bovichthyidae which in high southern latitudes occupy similar habitats to those occupied by some sculpins in the Northern Hemisphere, and the migratory 'southern trouts' (Galaxiidae) have a similar life history to the northern salmonids.

Freshwaters tend to contain rather fewer families, although often fully as many species as in any habitat of the sea. Amongst the abundant freshwater groups is the carp and minnow family (Cyprinidae) which is found across the whole of temperate and tropical Eurasia, Africa, and North America, but not, other than by introduction, in Australia or South America. Characins (Characidae), to which the cyprinids are related, are by contrast found only in Africa and in South and Middle America; in central South America they reach a peak of abundance (as witness the many tetras imported from South America to adorn, and often to languish and die, in tropical aquaria). Catfishes, of which numerous families are recognized, are likewise more common in South America than Africa, but also occur in large numbers in fresh water in tropical Asia and in North America; a few extend into other temperate waters. The spiny-finned fish order Perciformes also contributes several purely freshwater families, amongst them the very numerous species of cichlids (Cichlidae) in tropical America, Africa, and a few in Asia, as well as the perches and darters (Percidae) which are naturally found in the Northern Hemisphere, most numerously in North America.

This brief survey of the important or abundant groups of fishes has concentrated mainly on geographical or major habitat associations, and has omitted far more than it has listed. The world of fishes contains so many fascinating examples of adaptation of body form or behaviour that it is possible only to mention a few in passing, with the knowledge both of omissions and that many discoveries remain yet to be made (for as yet we know very little about the great majority of fish species already discovered). Within the limits of our present knowledge, however, many others will be found in the body of this book.

The wealth of fish life includes many such as the lungfishes, the gouramis, climbing perches, the reedfish, and the bichir which are capable of air breathing, and are thereby capable of living in swamps and marshes often devoid of dissolved oxygen, and even, especially in the case of the lungfishes, of enduring prolonged aestivation in waterless conditions. Other fishes have developed electrical organs, which in the electric catfish, the marine torpedos, and the electric eel, are powerful, and are used both offensively and defensively. Other fishes, many totally unrelated, have more subtle electrical powers. The mormyrids of Africa, and the gymnotids of South America both produce relatively weak electrical impulses, connected probably with navigation and as an early warning system in the often turbid waters they inhabit. The rays and skates have considerable electrical ability, involving not only the production of electrical discharges but probably reception as well, for how else do these bottom-living, cryptically coloured fish, which usually lie partially buried, recognize their own kind in their paired sexual encounters?

Nor is the world of fishes a silent one as was at one time popularly supposed. Many fish make noises, and make them by different methods. The carp family and herrings are said to produce a high-pitched squeak by expelling air from the swim-bladder into the gut. Other fishes, like certain an-chovies, make involuntary sounds when schools are actively veering in swimming. Numerous fishes produce other in-voluntary sounds, as when the lower pharyngeal teeth are grinding against the patch of teeth or hard tissue in the roof of the gullet to make rasping sounds which are amplified by the adjacent swim-bladder. In schooling fishes this will have survival value, for a single fish locating food will inevitably reveal its location by the noise made in enjoying the meal. There are two major methods of deliberate sound produc-tion, the rubbing together of parts of the bony skeleton to produce staccato sounds, and the use of the swimbladder as a resonance chamber to amplify sounds produced by special muscles.

Stridulators specialize in rubbing or clicking parts of the skeleton against adjacent bones; several catfishes of South America are well known for the creaks and groans so pro-duced. Other, smaller fishes, such as sea-horses and gobies can produce clicks by jerking their heads; the volume of sound produced is small but no doubt of value as a means of communication between one fish and another.

Sound producers with adapted swimbladders are al-together in a different class. Many of the drums (Sciaenidae) can be heard booming underwater by a reasonably acute human ear. The toadfishes (Batrachoidae) of the Atlantic coast of North America are another famous sonic group, uttering powerful fog-horn-like boops and grunts. The deep sea is also very likely an area of constant sound produced by fishes (although other animals such as whales and snapping shrimps also perform). The rat-tails (Macruridae) are the dominant family of fishes on the lower continental shelf and in the deep sea and many have a highly developed swim-bladder – it seems a justifiable inference to suspect them of being very able sonic fishes.

The uses of sound production to the fish are varied, and it is obvious that no animal will make sounds if it cannot hear them, or the reply, so hearing must be equally acute. Many sound producers live in heavily silted waters and use their sonic ability to keep contact with their own species. Others make sounds as part of an offensive or defensive performance, some use them as warnings of territorial rights, while many fishes become notably more loquacious as their spawning season approaches. Overall the evidence suggests that fishes like humans, use sounds for all the needs of communication within and between the species, be it making war or love, giving warnings or merely keeping in touch.

That some fishes have light organs and employ them to keep in touch with one another has already been mentioned. The deep sea is the major habitat of fishes with light organs. Especially amongst the mid-water species there is an array of light, from lanternfishes (Myctophidae), hatchetfishes (Sternoptychidae) to stomiatids, with neat rows of glowing lights on the underside. Most of the known species have distinct patterns visible to the human eye but certainly more meaningful to members of the same species. Searsids have a complicated shoulder organ, in effect a sac filled with luminescent cells in strands of tissue. When pressed the cells

are shot out into the water to burst with a cloud of blue-green sparks. Without doubt this process is voluntarily controlled by the fish, which, one may assume, when attacked by a predator simply disappears in a magician's cloud of sparks. Other fishes, notably the stomiatoids have large light organs on the cheek; whether this is some form of close-quarters search-light used when feeding, as it is tempting to assume, or simply a low-level light to adapt their own eyes against their own and other fishes' sudden brilliant light flashes is arguable, and as yet unproven.

More subtle uses of luminous organs are those employed by the ceratioid anglerfishes (Ceratiidae and other families) and star-eaters and black-dragonfishes (Astronesthidae and Melanostomiatidae). Members of these families have lighted lures with which they fish, mostly chin barbels with green or blue-green luminous tissue to entice prey within reach of their capacious jaws.

The light of these fishes is produced in special glandular cells, but others, including several shallow water forms, pro-duce the same result by means of cultures of symbiotic luminous bacteria in special organs. The East Indian *Photoblepharon* and its relatives (family Anomalopidae) have a broad organ containing bacteria beneath the eye. When active (they are mostly nocturnal) the light is flashed inter-mittently, although unlike the fully controlled light organs or photophores, the only way it can be blacked-out is by the blinking of a shutter or the rotation of the organ. These flashing lights surely are used to keep together in the predator-dense dark coral reef zones where they live? Other shallow-water fishes such as the pine-cone fish (Mono-centridae) and cardinalfishes (Apogonidae) have bacterial light sources.

This survey of some of the sensory abilities of fishes has so far omitted two of the major human senses, that of sight and smell. These being relatively familiar must be dismissed briefly, and it is sufficient to say that most fishes have vision which is quite adequate for their needs. This is even true of the blind fishes of caves and the deep-sea floor, in both of which natural light is absent and many species have drastic-ally reduced eyes, and virtually no sight. Their loss is more than compensated for by the development of the sensory pores typical of the lower vertebrates which form the lateral line and its branches over the head. This system serves as a distance-touch-sense. These series of sense organs, which respond to changes in local water pressure, such as flow patterns nearby, give warning of the approach of prey, or predator, or the nearness of a solid object. It is a sense difficult to understand in many ways (as humans lack it totally) but it acts almost like a close-quarters radar, feeding to the brain information on the surroundings without needing confirmation from other senses. With it, blinded trout for example, can live and thrive as ably as their fully sighted companions, and naturally sightless fish occupy caves or the unlit sea bed without undue disablement.

Odours spread through water as they do in air by diffusion, and the fish's nostrils are well equipped with a sensory lining linked to the brain by olfactory nerves. Odours are detected as the water is passed through the nostrils, each of which in most bony fishes has a double opening. The sharks have well developed nostrils, usually rather large and with a folded opening on the underside of the head; they also possess large olfactory lobes in the brain. Not surprisingly, scent plays a large part in the shark's daily life, as anyone will aver who has watched them attracted to, and milling around, a fishing boat where the catch is being gutted.

The development of olfactory organs in bony fishes is varied. Some, such as eels have highly developed nostrils and nasal sacs with abundant sensory lining tissue. Others, such as the pikes, flying-fishes and halfbeaks have reduced olfactory capacity. Eels are notoriously capable of scenting food from a distance, and many moray eels are believed to be nocturnal in their feeding forays where acute nasal perception would clearly be of value. Experimental studies of eels have shown that they are capable of detecting certain chemicals at a dilution which must mean that only a few molecules are passing through the nasal organs. If the detection of the home river by adult salmon returning from the sea is made by olfactory means, as seems most likely, then when approaching the river mouth the salmon are probably detecting only molecules of the 'home scent' in the great dilution of water and sea. Additionally, it has been demonstrated that fishes are able to detect by scent some chemical substances given off by the damaged skin of an injured fish. Thus the remainder of a shoal of minnows will scatter in panic when the alarm-substance (Schreckstoff) is detected from an injured member of the school.

The sense of taste is also well developed. The sensory cells that react to food or other substances are similar in form to the olfactory cells, but the system is less refined as physical contact is required. Taste buds are scattered widely round the lips, mouth, pharynx, and even gill arches of most fishes, or even on the general exterior surface. Those fish typically living close to the sea bed or in sedimented waters frequently have a greater elaboration of taste buds, and are equipped with barbels on the chin or around the snout, or even long sensitized pelvic fins. The barbels found amongst carps and catfishes are efficient food-finders and in the sea most of the cod family (Gadidae) have at least one, sometimes as many as five barbels, and the latter have elongate pelvic rays in addition. The gurnards or sea-robins (Triglidae) also have the lower pectoral fin rays separate from the fin and capable of considerable mobility so that they touch the sea floor like long bent fingers either side of the head; these too are well endowed with taste buds.

In their sensory abilities fishes can thus be seen to be extraordinarily well equipped for life in the many habitats offered by the sea and by fresh water. The variation in body form and life style that they have adopted to conform with the pressures of their environment are mentioned under the entries given for species. It must, however, be emphasized that our knowledge of the life history and habits of very many fishes is most imperfect; many gaps exist which only time and future exploration of their lives will fill. Ichthyology is still largely in the descriptive stage, where species previously undiscovered or unrecognized are being described, sometimes by the hundred each year. No survey of the wealth of fish life can be complete until this descriptive stage is past.

Additionally, the classification of living fishes is still in very fluid form. Producing a 'family tree' to the world of fishes can be compared to attempting to piece together a jigsaw puzzle with three-quarters of the pieces missing, half of the missing pieces being represented by the very incomplete fossil record of fishes and the remainder by those as yet undiscovered or whose anatomy is not yet adequately studied.

The difficulties inherent in attempting even to group genera into families and the relationship of one family to another is aptly illustrated by the tropical, freshwater characins, whose sheer volume of numbers has partly deterred advances in this field. As recently as 1972 Dr Jacques Géry, the noted French characo-phile, proposed a new re-alignment within this group in South America, which radically changed their classification. His classification was unfortunately published too late to be utilized in the present book which relies, in this and other groups, on the classification proposed in 1966 by P. H. Greenwood, Donn E. Rosen, Stanley H. Weitzman, and George S. Myers (*Bulletin of the American Museum of Natural History*, volume 131, pages 339–456), with some deletions and such additions as have been proposed, and seemed well founded, up to 1972.

The dictionary entries are arranged in alphabetical order, separate entries being made for families (cross-referenced to the genera included), and under the scientific name of the species of fish. Thus, the Atlantic salmon will appear under its scientific, Latinized name, *Salmo salar*, cross-referenced to the family Salmonidae, reference to which will lead to all the other members of the family included. Widely used vernacular names mostly in the English language are also given and cross-indexed.

The plates are arranged in systematic order of families, thus bringing the closest related groups together. Within each family the order is alphabetical except in certain cases where it has proved necessary to slightly interrupt the order for production reasons.

Credits for Photographs

Photo Aquatics

Gerald R. Allen   *Plates* 29, 46, 309, 383, 387, 394, 432.

T. Andrzejczyk   *Plates* 106, 140, 143, 155.

Heather Angel   *Plates* 15, 107, 122, 131, 151, 232.

J. Birkholz   *Plates* 30, 366, 379

M. Barrington Martin   *Plates* 188–9, 304, 406–7, 428, 467.

Adalbert Büttner   *Plates* 32, 76, 86, 94, 108, 145–6, 150, 164, 172–5, 302, 377–8, 405, 443, 462, 463, 486.

D. Corke   *Plate* 224.

Peter David   *Plates* 25–6, 39, 41–5, 47–8, 185–6, 191, 216, 225, 228, 452, 480, 497.

I. Everson   *Plate* 417.

Hans Flaskamp   *Plates* 22, 180, 221, 227, 267, 340, 348, 466, 470, 491.

S. Frank   *Plates* 49–51, 57–60, 64–5, 68–75, 83, 87–8, 91–2, 109, 113, 116–19, 133–4, 138, 177, 192, 195, 197–200, 203–5, 209, 212–14, 257, 423–4, 435, 454.

S. G. Giacomelli   *Plates* 1, 5, 7, 8, 181, 416, 422.

Herman J. Gruhl   *Plates* 2, 4, 11, 13, 19, 21, 24, 37–8, 40, 123, 141, 247, 262, 265–6, 283, 290, 293, 303, 306, 317, 322, 329, 332, 336, 351, 384–5, 399, 402, 413, 442, 444, 469, 478, 481, 485, 487–8.

Wolfgang Hackmann   *Plates* 23, 259, 263, 296, 299, 330, 343–4, 349, 391, 437, 499

Hilmar Hansen   *Plates* 10, 14, 16–18, 20, 33, 35–6, 53, 55, 61–2, 82, 85, 89, 93, 101–5, 110–11, 114–15, 121, 125–9, 135–7, 139, 142, 147–9, 152–4, 156–63, 165–7, 169–71, 176, 178–9, 182–4, 206, 210–11, 215, 219–20, 223, 229–31, 233, 235–46, 248, 252–4, 272, 286–7, 292, 295, 297–8, 301, 307, 310, 313–16, 319–20, 325–8, 333–5, 337–8, 350, 352–6, 358–65, 367–74, 376, 380–2, 386, 389–90, 395, 397–8, 400, 401, 403–4, 409, 411–12, 420–21, 425, 427, 430–31, 433, 436, 438–40, 445–50, 453, 455, 459–61, 464, 471–4, 477, 479, 482–3, 489–90, 492, 494–6, 498.

H. Honing   *Plate* 500.

E. Janss   *Plates* 255, 258, 392, 410, 429.

P. Kopp   *Plates* 3, 6, 9, 12, 249, 268, 331, 342, 345, 347, 396.

A. Losh   *Plate* 418.

R. Lubbock   *Plates* 28, 269, 273, 291, 321, 323–4, 475.

L. E. Perkins   *Plates* 79, 130, 226, 277, 294, 441.

J. Plaatsman   *Plate* 112.

John E. Randall   *Plates* 217, 222, 251, 305, 318, 476.

The Royal Society (Dr N. Locket)   *Plate* 501.

B. Schreiken   *Plates* 196, 234, 256, 465, 468.

P. Scoones   *Plates* 190, 312, 419, 426.

P. Solaini   *Plates* 250, 264, 288, 300, 339, 341, 346, 388.

Walt Starck   *Plates* 27, 218, 260–1, 270–1, 284–5, 311, 393, 408, 414–15, 484, 493.

Braz Walker   *Plates* 34, 52, 54, 66–7, 73, 77, 80–1, 84, 97–8, 100, 120, 132, 144, 193–4, 201, 207, 274, 278–9, 281–2, 289.

Alwyne Wheeler   *Plates* 187, 434, 451.

R. Zukal   *Plates* 31, 56, 63, 78, 90, 95–6, 99, 124, 168, 202, 208, 275–6, 280, 308, 357, 375, 456–8.

maxillary bone   preopercular   opercular   dorsal fin   adipose fin   caudal or tail fin   **Salmo salar**

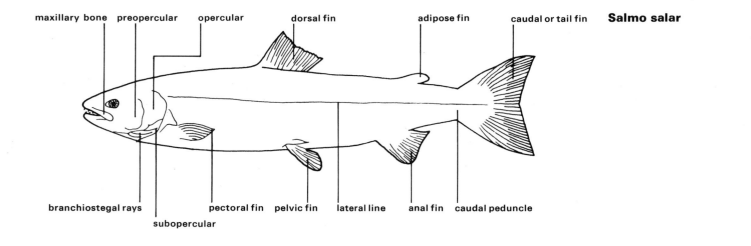

branchiostegal rays   pectoral fin   pelvic fin   lateral line   anal fin   caudal peduncle

subopercular

Squalus acanthias   spiracle   first dorsal fin   second dorsal fin   upper caudal lobe

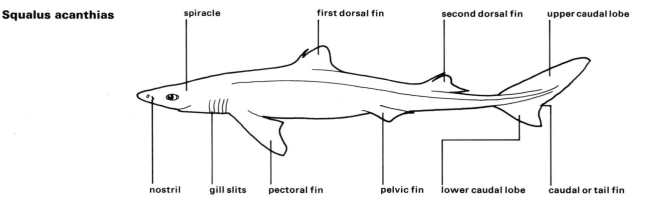

nostril   gill slits   pectoral fin   pelvic fin   lower caudal lobe   caudal or tail fin

preopercular   second or soft rayed dorsal fin   **Sarda sarda**

upper jaw   snout   opercular   first or spiny dorsal fin   dorsal finlets

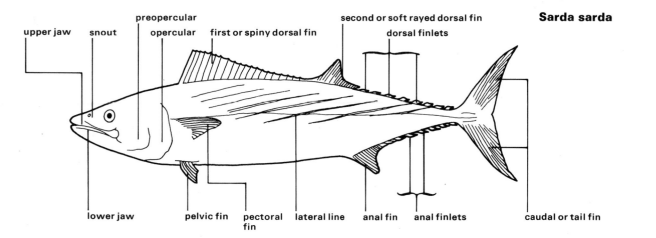

lower jaw   pelvic fin   pectoral   lateral line   anal fin   anal finlets   caudal or tail fin
                             fin

Glossary

Airbladder   See swimbladder.

Ammocoete   The larval form of lampreys, also known as prides.

Anadromus   Ascending rivers from the sea to spawn, e.g. salmon.

Bathypelagic   A rather arbitrary depth zone in the open sea, usually from 915–3658 m. (500–2000 fathoms). (See also pelagic and mesopelagic.)

Benthic   Bottom-living animals (*benthos*).

Branchiostegal rays   Bony rays supporting the membranes which close the gill cavity.

Bryozoans   A group of colonial animals which look plant-like – the moss animals.

Catadromus   Descending rivers to spawn in the sea, e.g. freshwater eels.

Caudal peduncle   The usually narrowing, tail end of the fish between the anal fin and the tail fin.

Cephalopods   The group of animals which includes squids and octopuses.

Cetaceans   The group of mammals which includes whales, dolphins, and porpoises.

Cloaca   Chamber at the end of the lower gut into which empty the urinary and reproductive tracts; thus, all have one common opening from the body.

Copepods   A group of small crustaceans.

Ctenoid   Of scales having on the posterior (free) margin small needle-like projections (see cycloid).

Ctenophones   A group of planktonic animals similar to jellyfish with oval or band-shaped bodies, e.g. sea gooseberry.

Cycloid   Of scales having smooth margins (see ctenoid).

Ecto-parasites   External parasites, e.g. the fish louse and leech.

Eutrophic   Enriched with organic matter and nutrients; an eutrophic lake will have dense vegetation, a heavy animal population and usually a soft organic, muddy bottom.

Ganoid   Of scales having an enamel-like substance, as seen in the garpikes (*Lepisosteus*).

Gasbladder   See swimbladder.

Gonopodium   Intromittent organ formed by modified anterior anal rays of male fish (as in live-bearing toothcarps).

Gorgonians   A group of marine colonial animals related to the hydroids, best known as sea-fans.

Gular plate   Bony plate or plates placed behind the chin, and between the lower jaws.

Heterocercal   Unequally lobed; applied to the tail fin where the upper lobe is longer than the lower, and the last vertebrae are turned upwards.

Holothurians   A group of animals known as sea-cucumbers; related to the star-fishes and sea-urchins.

Hydroids   Group name for small colonial animals (related to sea-anemones and jellyfish), sometimes known as sea-firs.

Illicium   Modified fin ray located on the head of anglerfishes and relatives; the 'fishing rod' of these fishes.

Interopercle   A bone of the lower part of the side of the head, part of the opercular series.

Intromittent organ   Organ for introducing spermatozoa into the body of the female (as in live-bearing toothcarps, sharks and rays).

Leptocephalus   A name originally applied to the larval stage of eels; now used for elongated laterally compressed, transparent larvae of eels and eel relatives. Plural – leptocephali.

Mesopelagic   Depth zone in offshore waters or open sea from 183–915 m. (100–500 fathoms). (See also pelagic and bathypelagic).

Neotenous   An animal which, although sexually mature, exhibits larval characters.

Opercle   The large rectangular bone of the gill cover.

Operculum   Gill cover, the bony covering over the gill cavity, composed of the series of preopercle, interopercle, subopercle, and opercle.

Ossicles   See Weberian apparatus.

Papilla   A small fleshy projection. Plural papillae.

Pelagic   Living in open water near the surface.

Pharyngeal   The region immediately behind the gills and anterior to the gut.

Pharyngeal bones   Bones behind the gills opposed to one another and usually bearing teeth.

Photophone   A light-producing organ, usually on head, sides or belly.

Planktonic   Life which drifts in the sea (e.g. plankton).

Preopercle   The most anterior bone of the opercular series, usually forming the cheek.

Pride   See ammocoete

Redd   Gravel nest of salmonid fishes.

Riffle	Part of stream or river where bottom is stony, the current fast, and the water shallow.
Rotifers	A group of very small, freshwater animals, known as the wheel animals.
Salps	Group name for free-swimming tunicates.
Scute	A bony or horny plate.
Substrate	Sea or river bed.
Sub-terminal	(Of the mouth), when the lower jaw is just shorter than the upper, hence the mouth is slightly ventral.
Supra-occipital	Unpaired bone at the back of the skull usually with a crest above.
Swimbladder	Tubular gas-filled sac lying in the abdomen beneath the backbone; its function is to give the fish buoyancy but in some groups of fishes it is associated with sound production. Known also as airbladder and gasbladder.
Tubificid	A group of aquatic worms, e.g. *Tubifex*.
Tunicates	Group name for animals which includes sea-squirts, usually jelly-like, sometimes colonial, with a 'tadpole' larval stage which is not unlike the early stages of some vertebrates.
Vomer	The anterior bone in the mid-line of the roof of the mouth.
Weberian apparatus	The modified first four or five vertebrae in the carp family and relatives that connect the swimbladder to the inner ear by a series of small bones or ossicles.

The Plates

Symbols used in the captions

♂   male
♀   female
∂   juvenile

The captions should be read from
left to right, not from top to bottom.

1
Lampetra planeri
2
Odontaspis taurus

3
Carcharhinus albimarginatus
4
Carcharhinus obscurus

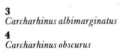

5
Scyliorhinus canicula
6
Sphyrna zygaena

7
Mustelus mustelus
8
Raja clavata

9
Dasyatis americana
10
Potamotrygon laticeps

11
Taeniura lymma
12
Manta birostris

13
Aetobatus narinari
14
Potamotrygon motoro

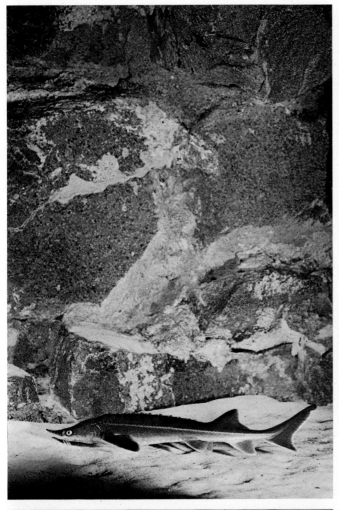

21
Muraena melanotis
22
Lycodontis tessellata

23
Taenioconger sp.

24
Muraena sp.

25
Nessorhamphus sp.
26
Derichthys sp.

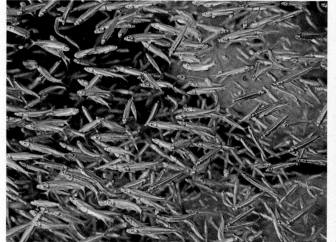

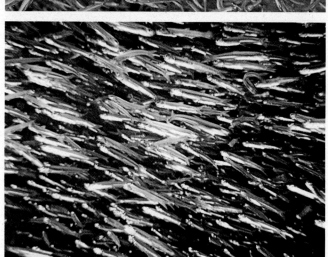

27
Jenkinsia lamprotaenia
28
Sardinella sp.

29
Stolephorus heterolobus
30
Osteoglossum bicirrhosum

31
Pantodon buchholzi
32
Xenomystus nigri

33
Gnathonemus petersi
34
Gnathonemus stanleyanus

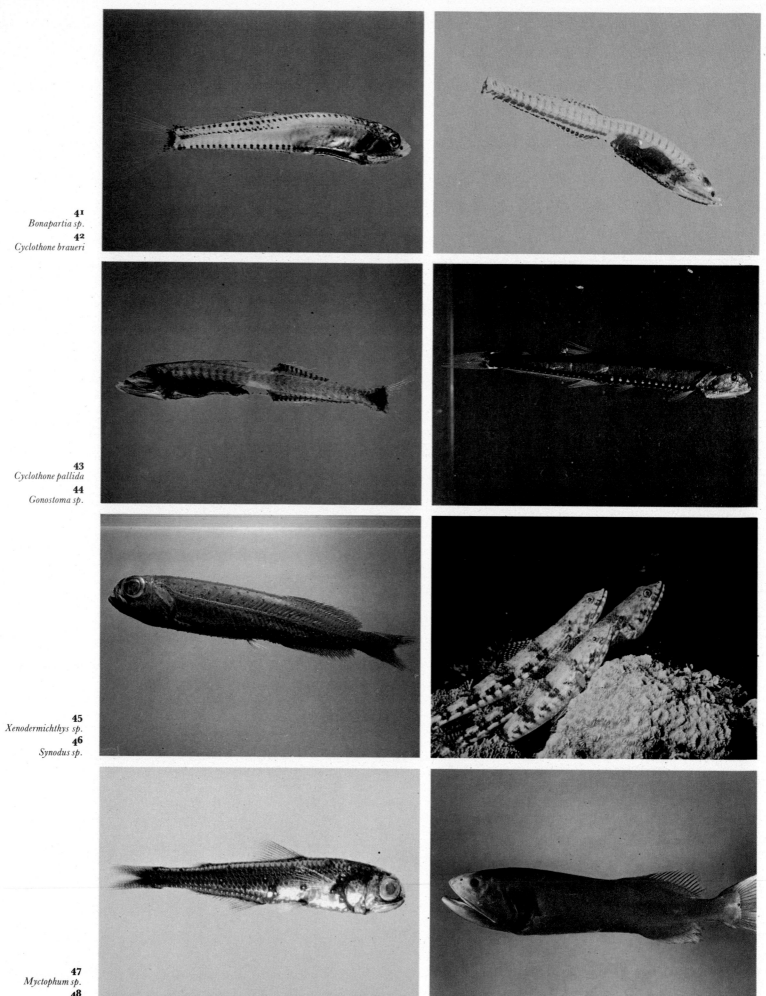

41
Bonapartia sp.

42
Cyclothone braueri

43
Cyclothone pallida

44
Gonostoma sp.

45
Xenodermichthys sp.

46
Synodus sp.

47
Myctophum sp.

48
Barbourisia rufa

49
Alestes longipinnis
50
Anoptichthys jordani ♀ + ♂

51
Arnoldichthys spilopterus
52
Astyanax mexicanus

53
Cheirodon axelrodi
54
Colossoma nigripinnis

55
Hemigrammus caudovittatus
56
Hemigrammus erythrozonus

57
Hemigrammus ocellifer ♀ + ♂
58
Hemigrammus pulcher

59
Hemigrammus rhodostomus ♂ + ♀
60
Hyphessobrycon bellottii

61
Hyphessobrycon callistus
62
Hyphessobrycon eos

63
Hyphessobrycon flammeus
64
Hyphessobrycon herbertaxelrodi ♂ + ♀

73
Metynnis maculatus
74
Micralestes acutidens ♂

75
Micralestes interruptus ♂ + ♀
76
Micralestes occidentalis

77
Moenkhausia oligolepis
78
Moenkhausia pittieri

79
Moenkhausia sanctaefilomenae
80
Myleus rubripinnis

81
Mylossoma argenteum
82
Nematobrycon palmeri

83
Petitella georgiae ♂ + ♀
84
Pristella riddlei

85
Pygocentrus piraya
86
Rooseveltiella nattereri

87
Thayeria boehlkei
88
Thayeria obliquua

89
Boulengerella lucius
90
Copeina guttata

91
Nannostomus beckfordi
92
Nannostomus trifasciatus♂ + ♀

Hemiodopsis vorderwinkleri

94
Gasteropelecus levis

95
Chilodus punctatus
96
Anostomus anostomus

97
Anostomus gracilis
98
Anostomus trimaculatus

99
Leporinus affinis
100
Leporinus nigrotaeniatus

101
Citharinus citharus

102
Nannocharax ansorgei
103
Nannocharax taenia

104
Electrophorus electricus
105
Apteronotus albifrons

106
Abramis brama
107
Alburnus alburnus

108
Barbus callipterus
109
Barbus conchonius ♂

110
Barbus filamentosus

111
Barbus holotaenia
112
Barbus macrops

113
Barbus nigrofasciatus
114
Barbus tetrazona

115
Barbus titteya
116
Blicca bjoerkna

117
Brachydanio albolineatus ♀ + ♂
118
Brachydanio nigrofasciatus

119
Brachydanio rerio ♂ + ♀
120
Campostoma anomalum

121
Carassius auratus
122
Carassius auratus

123
Cyprinus carpio
124
Danio devario

125
Danio malabaricus
126
Epalzeorhynchus kalopterus

127
Labeo bicolor
128
Labeo munensis

129
Leptobarbus hoevenii

130
Leuciscus idus
131
Leuciscus leuciscus

132
Notropis lutrensis
133
Rasbora borapetensis

134
Rasbora heteromorpha
135
Rasbora kallochroma

136
Rasbora lateristriata
137
Rasbora maculata

138
Rasbora vaterifloris ♂
139
Rasborichthys altior

140
Rutilus rutilus
141
Scardinius erythrophthalmus

142
Tanichthys albonubes
143
Tinca tinca

144
Carpoides carpio
145
Crossostoma sp.

146
Gastromyzon borneensis
147
Homaloptera orthogoniata

148
Botia berdmorei

149
Botia horae
150
Botia sidthimunki

151
Noemacheilus barbatulus

152
Noemacheilus sp.

153
Kryptopterus bicirrhis

154
Ompok bimaculatus

155
Silurus glanis

156
Schilbe sp.

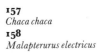
157
Chaca chaca
158
Malapterurus electricus

159
Synodontis alberti

160
Synodontis flavitaeniatus

161
Synodontis nigriventris

162
Amblydoras hancocki
163
Hassar orestis

164
Bunocephalus coracoideus

165
Plotosus lineatus
166
Pimelodus ornatus

167
Sorubim lima
168
Loricaria filamentosa

169
Loricaria parva
170
Otocinclus maculicaudata

171
Callichthys callichthys

172
Corydoras arcuatus
173
Corydoras julii

174
Corydoras melanistius
175
Corydoras pestaei

176
Corydoras punctatus
177
Corydoras schultzei ♂

178
Corydoras schwartzi

179
Dianema longibarbis
180
Sanopus splendidus

181
Lophius piscatorius

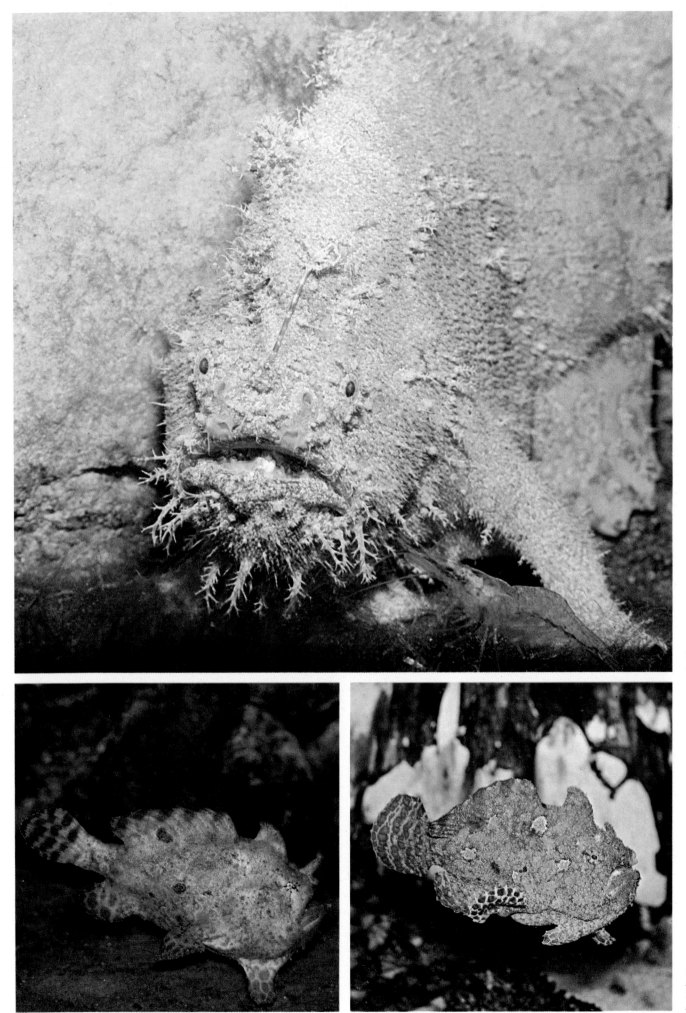

182
Antennarius hispidus

183
Antennarius oligospilos
184
Antennarius sp.

185
Oneirodes carlsbergi
186
Caulophryne jordani

187
Lota lota
188
Merlangius merlangus

189
Pollachius virens
190
Trisopterus luscus

191
Gadomus sp.
192
Dermogenys pusillus♂ + ♀

193
Strongylura marina
194
Adinia xenica

195
Aphyosemion australe ♂
196
Aphyosemion batesi ♀

197
Aphyosemion gardneri ♂
198
Aphyosemion lujae ♂

199
Aphyosemion walkeri ♂
200
Epiplatys fasciolatus ♂

201
Jordanella floridae
202
Nothobranchius guentheri

203
Pachypanchax playfairi ♂ + ♀
204
Pterolebias peruensis ♀

205
Roloffia liberiens ♂
206
Belonesox belizanus

207
Poecilia latipinna
208
Poecilia velifera

209
Poecilia reticulata ♂

210
Xiphophorus helleri
211
Xiphophorus xiphidium

212
Nematocentrus maccullochi
213
Atherina mochon pontica

214
Bedotia geoyi ♂

215
Telmatherina ladigesi ♂
216
Anoplogaster cornuta

217
Adioryx xantherythrus

218
Flammeo marianus
219
Holocentrus diadema

220
Holocentrus scythrops
221
Holocentrus rubrum

222
Myripristis amaenus

223
Myripristis murdjan
224
Zeus faber

225
Antigonia sp.
226
Gasterosteus aculeatus ♂ + ♀

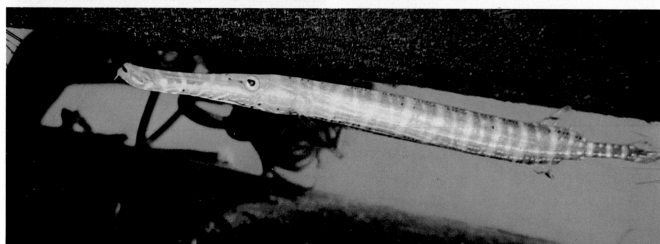

227
Aulostomus maculatus

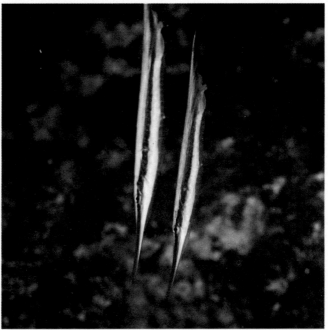

228
Macroramphosus gracilis
229
Aeoliscus strigatus

230
Doryrhamphus melanopleura
231
Dunckerocampus dactyliophorus

232
Entelurus aequoreus
233
Hippocampus kuda

234
Hippocampus hippocampus
235
Hippocampus ramulosus

236
Syngnathus pulchellus

237
Ophicephalus micropeltes
238
Ophicephalus obscurus

239
Ophicephalus striatus
240
Monopterus cuchia

241
Dendrochirus brachypterus

242
Dendrochirus zebra
243
Inimicus didactylus

244
Pterois antennata

245
Pterois radiata
246
Pterois russelli

247
Pterois volitans
(+ Labroides dimidiatus)

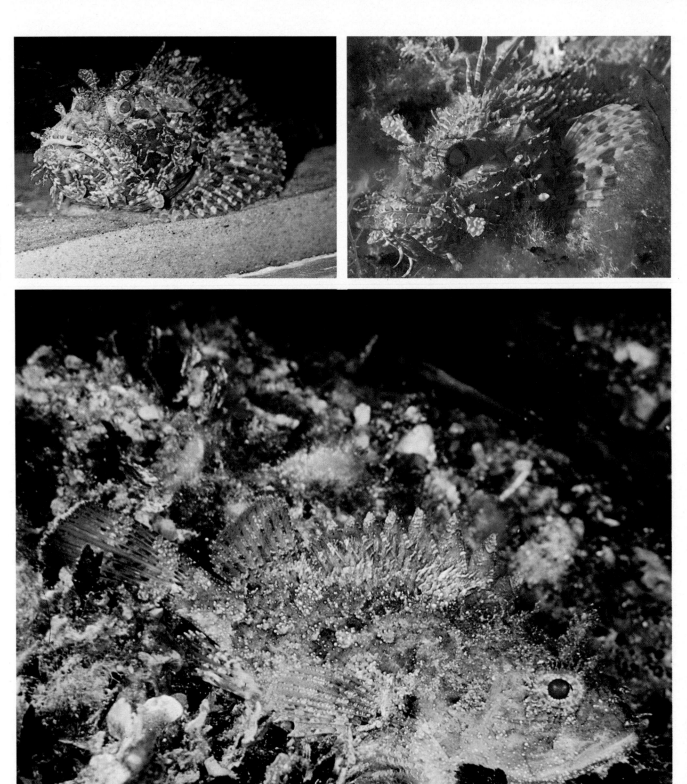

248
Scorpaena plumieri
249
Scorpaena scrofa

250
Scorpaena porcus

251
Scorpaenopsis diabolus
252
Trigla lucerna

253
Synanceia verrucosa

254
Platycephalus indicus
255
Artedius sp.

256
Cyclopterus lumpus
257
Chanda ranga

258
Alphestes sp.
259
Anthias squamipinnis

260
Anthias sp.
261
Anthias sp.

262
Anthias anthias

263
Plectropomus maculatus
264
Cephalopholis fulvus

265
Cephalopholis miniatus

266
Cephalopholis sp.

267
Epinephelus sp.
268
Plectropomus maculatus

285
Apogon lachneri
286
Apogon maculatus

287
Sphaeramia orbicularis
288
Cheilodipterus quinquelineata

289
Etheostoma spectabile
290
Echeneis naucrates

291
Alectis sp.
292
Alectis ciliaris

342
Pomacanthus arcuatus

349
Pomacanthus semicirculatus
350
Prognathodes aculeatus

351
Pygoplites diacanthus

352
Monocirrhus polyacanthus
353
Polycentropsis abbreviata

354
Aequidens duopunctata
355
Apistogramma ortmanni

356
Cichlasoma cutteri
357
Cichlasoma festivum

358
Cichlasoma severum

359
Cichlasoma octofasciatum
360
Geophagus australe

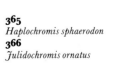

367
Lamprologus tetracanthus
368
Melanochromis vermivorus

369
Pelmatochromis sp.
370
Pelmatochromis buettikoferi

371
Pelmatochromis guentheri
372
Pelmatochromis 'camerunensis'

373
Petenia spectabilis
374
Petrotilapia tridentiger

375
Pseudotropheus auratus
376
Pseudotropheus zebra

377
Pterophyllum scalare
378
Symphysodon aequifasciata

379
Symphysodon discus
380
Tropheus moorii

381
Uaru amphiacanthoides
382
Abudefduf cyaneus

383
Abudefduf filifer
384
Abudefduf saxatilis

391
Oxycirrhites typus
392
Paracirrhites arcuatus

393
Paracirrhites sp.
394
Paracirrhites forsteri

395
Mugil saliens
396·
Sphyraena sp.

403
Halichoeres centriquadrus
404
Halichoeres margaritaceus

405
Larabicus quadrilineatus
406
Labrus mixtus ♂

407
Labrus mixtus ♀
408
Lachnolaimus maximus

409
Macropharyngodon pardalis
410
Pimelometopon darwini

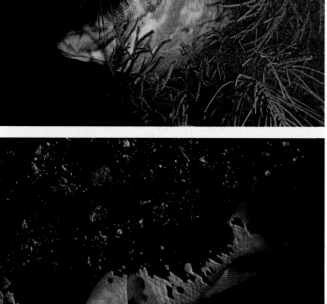

411
Thalassoma bifasciatum
412
Thalassoma lunare

413
Scarus sordidus

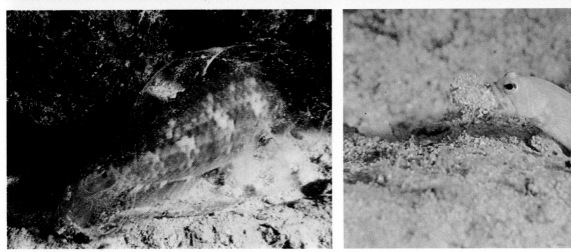

414
Scarus croicensis
415
Opistognathus aurifrons

416
Uranoscopus scaber

417
Harpagifer bispinis

418
Chaenocephalus aceratus

419
Blennius gattorugine

420
Blennius incognitus

421
Blennius nigriceps

422
Blennius ocellaris

423
Blennius sphinx

478
Pseudobalistes fuscus
479
Rhinecanthus assasi

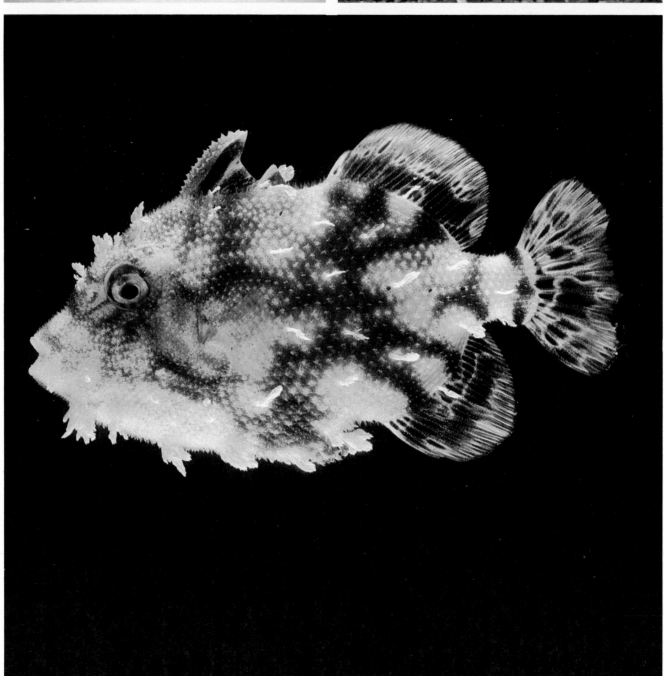

480
Xanichthys ringens ♂

481
Ostracion cubicus

482
Ostracion cyanurus
483
Ostracion meleagris

484
Ostracion lentiginosum
485
Ostracion tuberculatus

486
Tetrosomus gibbosus
487
Amblyrhynchotes diadematus

488
Arothron aerostaticus
489
Arothron hispidus

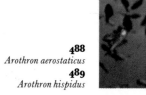

490
Arothron meleagris

491
Arothron sordidus
492
Canthigaster margaritatus

493
Canthigaster valentini
494
Tetraodon mbu

495
Tetraodon miurus

496
Chilomycterus schoepfi

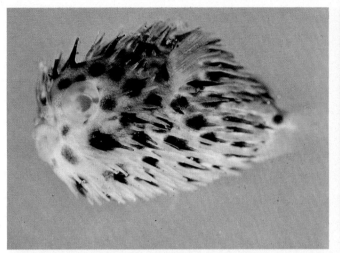

497
Diodon holocanthus ♂

498
Diodon holocanthus

499
Diodon sp.

500
Lophodiodon calori

501
Latimeria chalumnae

The Dictionary

A

Ablennes Belonidae
hians FLAT NEDDLEFISH, BARRED
LONGTOM 1·2 m. (4 ft)
Worldwide in the warmer parts of all the oceans. In the Atlantic it occurs from Bermuda and New England to Brazil, and from the Cape Verde Islands to Angola. It is widely distributed in the Indian and Pacific oceans.

It is easily distinguished from its relatives by its greatly compressed body, which is flattened from side to side. It also has distinctive dark vertical bars on its side, although the body is greenish above and silvery elsewhere, except for a dark tip to the lobe of the dorsal fin. Its bones are green.

It is mainly an offshore species, although found inshore on open ocean coasts. It is carnivorous, feeding on a wide variety of fishes.

Abramis Cyprinidae
brama BREAM, BRONZE BREAM 61 cm. (2 ft)
The bream is distinguished by its very deep, compressed body with a long many-rayed anal fin. Its head is comparatively small, and its mouth is ventral and very protrusible. Its colouring varies with age and the water in which it lives; large specimens are dark, olive-green on the back, bronze on the sides and belly with all the fins dark grey; young specimens are more silvery.

Bream prefers warm, slow-flowing or stagnant waters, and is most at home in lowland rivers, reservoirs, and lakes. It is always found in shoals, in summer close inshore in shallow water, in winter in deeper water. It spawns with much splashing of the water in late spring and summer at water temperatures between 13° and 15° C, usually at night in places where there is abundant weed growth. Spawning is later in the n., cooler parts of its range where it may spawn only every other year.

The long tube-like mouth of the bream suggests that it feeds close to the bottom. As an adult, its food is mainly bottom-living invertebrates, chiefly insect larvae, worms, and molluscs. Young bream often feed in middle waters, eating planktonic crustaceans.

The bream is widely distributed across Europe, from the British Isles, e. to the Danube, the Caspian basin, and the central U.S.S.R. To the N. it extends to n. Finland and the U.S.S.R. Its range to the S. is limited by the Alps and the mountains of central France.

The bream is a favoured angling fish and has been widely distributed in the British Isles in attempts to improve fishing waters. Elsewhere in Europe, especially inland areas, it is a valued food fish; its flesh is tasty and large specimens may weigh between 5–9 kg. (11–20 lb.). The fact that they live for some time out of water adds to their value in marketing and transporting what could otherwise be a highly perishable commodity. **106**

Abramites Anostomidae
microcephalus HEADSTANDER
13 cm. (5 in.)
A rather deep-bodied characin-like fish. In coloration it is attractive, being dark brown on the back, yellowish on the sides with a series of irregular dark brown bars across the body,

some complete, others narrow and incomplete. The pectoral and tail fins are light yellow, as is the anal fin which has a dark base and a dark margin. The pelvic fins are mainly dark.

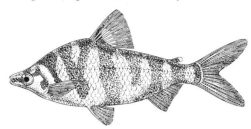

This fish is a native of the lower Amazon, although it is said to be uncommon there. Another, rather similar species, *A. solarii*, lives to the S. in the Rio Parana and possibly in the Rio Paraguay. Both have been kept as aquarium fishes and make very attractive, peaceable pet fish. Both typically adopt a head-down attitude. They feed on bottom-living organisms particularly plants.
A. solarii see under **A. microcephalus**

Abudefduf Pomacentridae
cyaneus 7·5 cm. (3 in.)
A damselfish which is well known in the w. Pacific and which has been found around Timor, New Guinea, the Philippines, Mariana Islands, and Samoa.

It is a brilliant little fish its colouring more or less entirely blue, with often a yellowish tail. In this species the scales run forward only onto the upper part of the head, the dorsal fin has no dark blotch on it, and the tail fin is almost square cut. **382**
A. filifer 6 cm. (2½ in.)
Originally described from the Kei Islands in Indonesia, this damselfish is very little known. It lives on and close to reefs in the sea.

It is distinguished by the pointed lobes of the soft dorsal and anal fins. **383**
A. melanopus BLUE AND GOLD DAMSELFISH
6 cm. (2½ in.)
A Pacific species, occasional around the coral reefs of N. Queensland. It is very active and forms small shoals. It is distinguished particularly by the bright golden yellow, pointed lobes of its tail fin.
A. saxatilis SERGEANT MAJOR, CORALFISH
23 cm. (9 in.)
Worldwide in distribution in warm water. In many areas, such as the West Indies, it is the most abundant inshore species, found on coral reefs but also inhabiting pier and wharf pilings, rocks, and sandy areas. The eggs, which are attached to solid surfaces cleared of algae, are guarded by the male.

This species is very distinctively barred. Two colour phases exist depending on the depth of water inhabited. In shallow water the body is yellowish with dark stripes, but in deeper water or shaded areas such as caves, it becomes deep blue with slightly lighter sides. **384**
A. sordidus CORALFISH 25 cm. (10 in.)
A widely spread Indo-Pacific species, found from the Red Sea and the e. coast of Africa as far S. as East London, to the islands of the central Pacific, including the Hawaiian Islands. The young are especially common as tide-pool inhabitants, but the adults tend to be rather solitary or found in small groups on the outer coral faces or beneath loose rock. It is particularly attracted to areas where the water is well

mixed and turbulent. It feeds on coral-living invertebrates and algae.

It is greyish brown with faint light and brown longitudinal stripes. There is a conspicuous light ringed black spot at the rear end of the

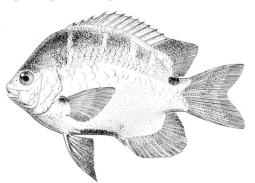

spiny dorsal fin, and a dusky saddle across the tail; the tail, second dorsal, and pelvic fins are clear.

Acanthaluteres Balistidae
guntheri TOOTH-BRUSH LEATHERJACKET
30 cm. (12 in.)
Widely distributed in Australian seas, and known from the coasts of New South Wales, Victoria, S. Australia, and Tasmania. It is reasonably common in the S. of this range, in shallow coastal waters down to depths of 37–55 m. (20–30 fathoms).

It is an elongate species with a smoothly rounded profile, small mouth with sharp teeth, the single barbed dorsal spine is placed just above the eye. The common name is due to the males having a long patch of stiff slender bristles along the lower sides. The body is mainly brownish yellow, with scattered blue lines and spots, but the lower part is bluish with small brown spots.

Acanthochaenus Stephanoberycidae
luetkeni 12 cm. (4¾ in.)
A small deep-sea fish known from fewer than 6 specimens from the w. N. Atlantic, and in the s.w. Indian Ocean. It is believed to live in mid-waters, close to the bottom, and has been caught only at depths of 2200–5300 m. (1203–2899 fathoms).

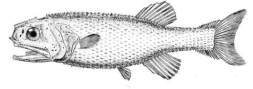

It is easily distinguished by its rough-edged scales, posteriorly placed pelvic fins, and lack of spines preceding the dorsal fin. It is dark above, greyish below.

ACANTHOCLINIDAE
A family of small Indo-Pacific fishes which are closely related to the Plesiopidae, Pseudochromidae, and other families, and are sometimes lumped with them into a single family. They are all distant relatives of the sea basses (Serranidae).

They are distinguished by having many dorsal and anal spines (19–20, and 8–10 respectively). Their pelvic fins have one spine and 2 rays. Most of the members of the family have 3 lateral lines, but some have only one. See **Acanthoplesiops**.

Acanthocybium   Scombridae
solanderi WAHOO, PETO 206 cm. (81 in.)
Worldwide in its distribution in tropical seas, the wahoo is apparently nowhere very abundant. It is a fast-swimming open ocean species, which is usually found singly or in small schools in offshore waters, or when close to reefs, always adjacent to open water. Its food consists of a wide range of fishes, squid, and cuttlefish, and as it is one of the fastest swimming of predators, few fish living in the same habitat are immune from attack.

Its relative scarcity means that other than locally it is not fished for commercially, but it is a prime angling fish. It is usually angled for from boats using a trolled spoon or bait fish and is one of the great fighting fish. Specimens weighing as much as 63 kg. (139 lb.) have been caught by angling.

It is distinguished by its body form, elongate and almost tubular, by its beak-like snout and the numerous spines (21–27) in the first dorsal fin. It is deep blue on the back, silvery on the sides and below, the 2 colours separated by a band of green. Running vertically across the back and sides are numerous dusky bands, many of them joined in pairs on the belly.

Acanthodoras   Doradidae
spinosissimus TALKING CATFISH
15 cm. (6 in.)
Distributed in the middle region of the Amazon basin. The talking catfish has enjoyed some popularity as an aquarium fish due to its ability to produce quite loud sounds, audible outside the aquarium. These sounds are apparently made by moving the pectoral spines, the noise being amplified by the swimbladder.

Its body form is typical of the family, the head and anterior body being flattened and covered with a bony shield. The body is enveloped in heavy scutes, especially spiny on the back; the dorsal and pectoral spines are large and equipped with thorns on the front and sides. Its back is deep brown with light patches; a white stripe on the side. Chiefly crepuscular, it is occasionally active in dim light.

Acanthopagrus   Sparidae
berda PIKEY or MUD BREAM 76 cm. (30 in.)
An Indo-Pacific species found from the Red Sea and E. African coast to India, the E. Indies and n. Australia. It is a very common species and is taken in inshore waters around wharfs, on reefs, and in sandy bays. It is also found in estuaries.

It is a good food fish, but in s. Africa is best known as an angling species, difficult to catch but fighting gamely once hooked.

It is grey to dull olive, ventrally light; the dorsal and anal fins have dark edges. It is distinguished by its very large second anal spine.

Acanthopegasus   Pegasidae
lancifer SCULPTURED SEA-DRAGON
9 cm. (3½ in.)
A species found in moderately deep water off the coasts of S. Australia, Victoria, and Tasmania. It has been dredged as deep as 44 m.

(24 fathoms) but as with most members of the family, is more usually seen as jetsam on the shore after a storm.

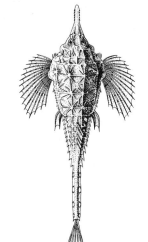

The whole head, body, and tail are enclosed in an armour of thorny bony rings, those on the head and body deeply sculptured with starlike pattern. It is brownish, with dark bands on the rings.

Acanthophthalmus   Cobitidae
kuhlii COOLIE LOACH 8 cm. (3 in.)
A popular and relatively common aquarium fish, although rather shy and retiring. Its body is flattened from side to side, almost wormlike. The eyes are covered with scaleless transparent skin. Its colouring is quite striking being yellowish to salmon pink with a series of dark brown to black transverse bars across the back and sides which are in turn partly divided by a light streak. These black bars, running from head to tail, number 12–15 in the subspecies *A. kuhlii sumatranus*, and 15–20 in *A. kuhlii kuhlii*.

The species is widely distributed in Sumatra and Java, and has been reported from Borneo, Singapore, and Thailand. It frequents streams, sometimes at high altitudes, living close to the bottom and concealed by dense weed growth.
A. semicinctus HALF-BANDED COOLIE LOACH
8 cm. (3 in.)
A strikingly coloured loach which comes from Indonesia and has achieved some popularity as an aquarium fish. It differs slightly in body form from other members of the genus, being somewhat deeper in the body, and having the pelvic and anal fin rather more forwardly placed. Its colouring is distinctive; the sides are a beautiful salmon-pink to golden red, with 12–16 dark brown or black saddles along them. Except for the front ones, these blotches do not extend below the middle of the side – hence 'half-banded coolie loach'.

Females are said to have smaller fins; males have a thickened pectoral fin ray.

Acanthoplesiops   Acanthoclinidae
indicus SCOTTIE 5 cm. (2 in.)
Found in the tropical Indian Ocean. This species was first described by Francis Day from Colombo (Sri Lanka), and later recorded by him from Madras, India. It has subsequently been found on many of the Indian Ocean

islands and along the E. African coast. It lives in shallow water, on reefs. Little is known of its life history and habits.

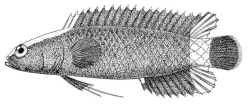

Its most obvious characters are the many spines in the dorsal and anal fins, and the much enlarged scales at the posterior end of the body.

Acanthopsis   Cobitidae
choirorhynchos 22 cm. (8¾ in.)
A very distinctive loach which is widely distributed in SE. Asia. In Burma, Thailand, Vietnam, Sumatra, Borneo, and Java it is common in rivers, especially clear, swift streams with sand or gravelly beds, but also found in slow-flowing muddied rivers. This fish adapts its colouring to match the bottom of the river in which it lives : in clear water it is visible only as a moving shadow. Those in currents lie with the head turned upstream, but when alarmed burrow with great rapidity.

This loach is distinguished by its long body and pointed slender snout. The eyes are small, placed high on the head, and a double pointed spine, concealed by skin, lies in front of each. It has 3 pairs of barbels on the snout or around the mouth.

The colouring is very variable, but it is usually peppered with small dark dots.

It has been kept as an aquarium fish, and is relatively undemanding, though rarely seen.

ACANTHURIDAE
The family of tangs or surgeonfishes, so called because most members of the family have on either side of the tail a movable compressed spine which resembles a surgeon's scalpel or lancet. The spines can be erected so that they point forward and form a formidable weapon when the tail is lashed from side to side. In one genus *(Naso)* fixed, forward-pointing spines replace the erectile spines.

Surgeonfishes are worldwide in distribution in tropical seas. The family is best represented in the Indo-Pacific; relatively few species occur in the tropical Atlantic and none in the Mediterranean. In general, they are deep-bodied, compressed fishes, often colourful, with a small mouth and fine, highly specialized chisel-like teeth with which they graze on algae. Some species have thick-walled, gizzard-like stomachs, presumably an adaptation to enable them to utilize the often large quantities of coral and sand ingested.

Surgeonfishes pass through a distinctive stage as planktonic larvae, in which scales are absent and long ridges form on the body. The drifting young eventually are swept inshore where they sink to the bottom and rapidly change into the juvenile form. So different are the young from juveniles and adults that they were formerly considered to be a distinct genus named *Acronurus*. See **Acanthurus, Ctenochaetus, Naso, Zanclus, Zebrasoma.**

Acanthurus   Acanthuridae
coeruleus BLUE TANG 30 cm. (12 in.)
The blue tang is an abundant reef fish in the

tropical w. Atlantic. It is distributed from New York and Bermuda s. to Brazil, including the Gulf of Mexico and the Central American coast. It is abundant in the W. Indies.

It feeds entirely on algae, and its teeth are adapted for browsing. It lives well clear of the bottom, and is typically seen in well lighted situations on coral reefs.

The adults are deep purplish blue, often with narrow lengthwise darker blue lines; the fins tend to be a lighter blue towards their edges. The area around the spines on the tail is conspicuously white. The young fish are bright yellow except for a blue crescent-spot above and below the pupil of the eye. Intermediate-aged specimens are often blue anteriorly with a bright yellow tail.

In body form it is much like any other surgeonfish, although it is deeper-bodied, with a more nearly vertical head profile than other w. Atlantic species. **437**

A. glaucopareius 20 cm. (8 in.)
This surgeonfish is found mainly in the Pacific Ocean; it has, however, been reported from the e. Indian Ocean at Christmas and Cocos-Keeling Islands. In the tropical Pacific it occurs in the E. Indies and Philippine Islands and most of the island groups, extending even as far to the E. as the Galapagos Islands, and the Revillagigedo Islands, Mexico. Yet, strangely, it is rare in Hawaii.

It is typically an inhabitant of the surge channels of coral atolls, although occasionally found in more sheltered waters. It is found at depths from 1–2 m. to 50 m. (27 fathoms). In the surge channel the water is very turbulent and is frequently white and bubbly, although shelter in the creviced reef is always close. This species browses on filamentous algae growing on rocks and coral. **439**

A. leucosternon 17 cm. (6¾ in.)
An Indian Ocean species which has been recorded from Zanzibar and Mauritius, Sri Lanka and India, e. to Sumatra. It is not well-known and does not seem to be very common anywhere in its range. **440**

A. lineatus 27 cm. (10¾ in.)
A strikingly marked and beautiful surgeonfish from the tropical Indo-Pacific. It is immediately distinguished from its relatives by the overall bluish tinge with alternating yellow and dark-bordered blue bands. These bands run lengthwise except on the head where they are oblique and on the tail where they turn vertically. The fins are deep blue, the dorsal and anal with blue lines on them. The colour pattern is very variable, however. The tail fin is deeply concave.

This species is distributed across the Indian Ocean and well into the Pacific. It ranges from E. Africa to the Central Pacific, although in places it may be locally scarce. **441**

A. monroviae 40 cm. (15¾ in.)
An e. Atlantic species of surgeonfish which is found only on the tropical W. African coast from isolated areas such as Liberia, Cameroon, Senegal, and the Cape Verde Islands. Its biology is little known, and the species has been reported to be relatively rare. It is found in shallow inshore water.

It is basically a dark-coloured fish with fine lengthwise blue lines along the body. There is a broad yellow patch around the tail spine, and, in some specimens at least, the yellow is bordered with a blue line. **442**

A. olivaceus ORANGE-SPOT SURGEONFISH 41 cm. (16 in.)
This surgeonfish ranges from the E. Indies to Oceania. It has been reported from Macassar and the Celebes, the tropical Australian coast, the Philippines, Hawaii, and most of the island groups of the Pacific.

This species is usually found in moderately deep water at about 9 m. (5 fathoms) and deeper. It typically lives in sand patches but close to rock or coral in which the fish takes refuge if threatened. It feeds by grazing on the diatoms and detritus of the sandy bottom and has a thick-walled, gizzard-like stomach.

It is quickly identified by the presence of a large, elongate, dark-edged bright orange patch on the shoulder. The body and head are otherwise soft brown. Young fish are wholly bright orange-yellow, changing at about 5 cm. (2 in.) to the adult colouring.

Old adults develop a convex forehead, which becomes a particularly prominent outgrowth in old males. **443**

A. sohal 27 cm. (10¾ in.)
A surgeonfish endemic to the Red Sea, and first described as long ago as 1775 by Pehr Forsskål, the Danish explorer of the Arabian coastline. Like other surgeonfishes it is very common in shallow water in the vicinity of rocks and reefs. Its food consists of various kinds of algae, especially green filamentous forms.

It is a very distinctive species with a deeply concave tail fin, the outer edges of which form elongate streamers and its coloration is distinctive in its native range. **444**

A. triostegus CONVICT TANG,
FIVE-BANDED SURGEONFISH 25 cm. (10 in.)
This is one of the most widely distributed of known surgeonfishes for it is found across the

whole of the tropical Indo-Pacific. In the W. it occurs on the E. African coast as far S. as Zululand and to the E. it reaches the Galapagos Islands and the Mexican coast. It is represented in the Hawaiian Islands by a subspecies *A. t. sandvicensis*. In many parts of its range it is the commonest species of the group.

An adaptable species found in almost all habitats around reefs and rocky areas but tends to be most common in the calmer waters of lagoons and below the surge regions. It feeds extensively on filamentous algae which are abundant on rocks and coral areas and may be encountered singly or in large schools.

Readily distinguished by its pale greenish brown background, with 5 black crossbars running across the sides. The tail spine is relatively small.

Acestrorhynchus Characidae
microlepis 30 cm. (12 in.)
The body shape of this characin, long and thin with a pointed head, recalls the pike-like chara-

cins of tropical Africa (*Hydrocynus* and *Hepsetus*). Like them it is a fish-eating predator, but is found in S. America, from the Amazon basin and Guyana.

Its mouth is large and has strong teeth; the scales are small, and the dorsal and anal fins are both close to the tail. Coloration varies according to age. Young fish are light brown, with lengthwise series of spots. The adults are greenish above, bluish green on the sides with a lengthwise series of dark spots, the most conspicuous being close to the head and the tail. The belly, dorsal fins and the upper part of the tail fin are described as brick red in large fish.

Although it has been kept in captivity, this fish does not adapt well to life in aquaria. Its diet of living fish creates added expense.

ACHIRIDAE
A family of sole-like flatfishes, with both eyes on the right side; strictly confined to the shores and streams of N. and S. America, where they almost completely replace the true, left-eyed soles (Soleidae) of the Old World. In N. America they are mostly marine; in S. America they abound in fresh as well as littoral waters. In the opinion of the chief investigators of the group, the achirids, or broad soles, originated independently of the soleids. See **Trinectes**.

Achoerodus Labridae
gouldii BLUE GROPER, GIANT PIGFISH 1·4 m. (4½ ft)
An Australian wrasse, known from most of the Australian States, and found on rocky shores,

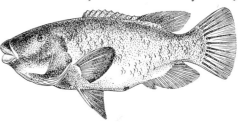

on reefs and around headlands, especially where the rock is honeycombed with caves. It appears to live in caverns or under rocky overhangs, feeding on molluscs and crustaceans, and rarely venturing far from its home territory except at flood tide. Well-known as a sporting fish, both to the angler and the spearfisherman. Large specimens weighing 36 kg. (80 lb.) have been reported. Its flesh, except when young, is not very palatable.

Males are purplish brown with orange lines, and blue stripes running along the sides. Females are dull brick red, lighter on the belly. At one time the 2 sexes were thought to represent distinct species.

Acipenser Acipenseridae
fulvescens LAKE STURGEON 2·7 m. (9 ft)
The lake sturgeon is widely distributed in freshwaters of e. N. America, from the Saskatchewan River in Alberta, e. to the lower St Lawrence, and s. to Alabama. It can be distinguished from the other American sturgeons by its numerous (about 36) bony plates along each side, and by the long barbels placed midway between tip of snout and mouth. It was formerly one of the most valuable commercial fishes in the Great Lakes (especially lakes Erie and Ontario) but was heavily fished and quickly became rare, a state which the later pollution of the lakes has worsened.

This sturgeon is found on clean gravel or sandy bottoms where there is an abundance of invertebrate life. It is found at times in remarkably shallow water for its size, no doubt in searching areas best populated by molluscs, crayfish, and insects, on which it feeds.

A. gueldenstaedti RUSSIAN STURGEON, OSETR 2·4 m. (8 ft)

The Russian sturgeon is the most important of the sturgeons to the fishing industries of the U.S.S.R. and Iran. It is caught in the sea with drift nets, while in rivers it is taken in seines. Like other sturgeons it takes a comparatively long time to reach sexual maturity, and the stocks have suffered from the industrial development of the lower regions of the rivers. Conservation measures have been partly successful in saving the fishery, and this species is one which is being raised in fish farms in the U.S.S.R.

Its range includes the basins of the Caspian Sea, the Sea of Azov and the Black Sea. It spawns in rivers running into these seas, on gravelly grounds where the eggs hatch in about 4 days. The larvae and young fish spread downstream, but generally stay close to the bottom or hide under stones. They feed on invertebrates, especially on insect larvae and small crustaceans. The larger fish eat a wide variety of marine invertebrates, such as worms and benthic fishes.

A. nudiventris SHIP, SHIP STURGEON 2 m. (6½ ft)

The ship is an anadromous sturgeon found in the Aral, Caspian, and Black Sea basins; it is the only sturgeon found in the Aral Sea. It is distinguished from the other European sturgeons by its continuous lower lip, and its fringed barbels.

Except in the Aral Sea, it is not a particularly important commercial fish, and there the stocks were seriously affected by a bacterial infection in the late 1930s. There, as elsewhere, the ship has also been affected by the development of rivers for hydro-electric power, pollution, and overfishing, but conservation measures have been taken and in the U.S.S.R. farms rear numbers of this species.

The ship spawns in rivers, usually on pebbly bottoms from early April to May. The eggs are about 3 mm. in diameter and take about 8 days to hatch at 12° C. Fecundity is high, large females containing up to 1¼ million eggs. Individual fish spawn once every 2–3 years. Like other sturgeons, the ship takes a long time to reach sexual maturity, 6–9 years for males, 12–14 years for females. Despite the considerable fishing pressure on the species specimens of 30 years of age are not uncommon.

A. oxyrinchus see under **A. sturio**

A. rutheneus STERLET *c.* 80 cm. (31½ in.)

A small sturgeon found in the Danube basin, around the n. coasts of the Black and Caspian seas and widely in e. Europe and the w. U.S.S.R. Like other sturgeons it migrates upstream to spawn in running water over a stony bottom. Adults and young frequently overwinter in deep water in rivers without running down to the sea. Males mature at 4–5 years and about 35 cm. (13¾ in.), females between 5 and 9 years at 41–46 cm. (16–18 in.).

It is a delicate-looking sturgeon with a narrow, pointed, upturned snout, and fringed barbels in front of the mouth. The small bony plates along the sides are light in colour.

This, being a small species, is the most common kept as an exhibit in public aquaria. It is fished for commercially in the rivers Don and Volga, and it is now raised in fish farms in the U.S.S.R. for stocking reservoirs and for restocking natural waters. It has also been crossbred with *A. gueldenstaedti* for use in fisheries as a fast growing form. Its eggs are used for caviar and the flesh is very well flavoured. **15**

A. stellatus SEVRUGA, STELLATE STURGEON *c.* 2 m. (6½ ft), and 77 kg. (170 lb.)

The sevruga, or stellate sturgeon, is confined to the Black Sea and Caspian Sea basins. It is an anadromous migratory form which spawns in freshwater in rivers, such as the Don, the Ural, and the Volga. Most of these rivers have winter and spring forms, one of which enters river mouths in autumn overwintering in freshwater, while others come into the river in spring; both spawn during the early summer. The winter form usually spawns further upstream.

This is a fast-growing sturgeon, the females of which attain a length of 1 m. (3¼ ft) in their sixth or seventh year, although the males are rather slower growing, and the rate of growth in both sexes varies according to local conditions.

The sevruga (the name most widely used in the U.S.S.R.) is a valuable commercial species. It is exploited both in the U.S.S.R. and in Iran and is the second most important sturgeon in the fisheries of these countries. The stock showed signs of decline in the 1930s, but due to conservation measures the Caspian population at least has recoverd remarkably in recent years.

A. sturio STURGEON, ATLANTIC STURGEON 3 m. (10 ft), 214 kg. (470 lb.)

The sturgeon is widely distributed around the European coastline, from Norway and the Baltic, S. to the Mediterranean, and in the Black Sea. On the e. American coastline a closely

related, if not identical sturgeon *(A. oxyrinchus)* ranges from the Gulf of Mexico to the St Lawrence River. Over the whole of its range the sturgeon is now an uncommon fish, pollution of river mouths, obstructions such as weirs and dams, and its vulnerability whilst in rivers to fishing pressure, have greatly reduced the populations. In w. Europe the only rivers to contain a breeding stock are the Guadalquivir (Spain), the Gironde (France), although some are found in Lake Ladoga (U.S.S.R.) and the e. Baltic Sea.

The sturgeon is anadromous, breeding in spring in rivers on pebbly bottoms in a moderate current. A very large number of eggs are produced (between 800,000 and 2,400,000 per female, depending on size). The young sturgeon lives in the river for up to 3 years and small fish up to 20 cm. (8 in.) can be caught near the spawning grounds. The adults return to the sea after spawning. Their food consists almost entirely of bottom-living invertebrates. Young fish eat insect larvae and crustaceans in the rivers, in the sea crustaceans, worms, and occasionally small fish.

The sturgeon has been exploited by man since at least the Mesolithic period (for the distinctive scutes have been found on sites of this age on the e. Scottish coast). Its flesh is of excellent quality, and the unshed eggs were widely used for caviare, but its present rarity throughout its range means that it is no longer caught for food. In Europe at least, the sturgeon is in urgent need of protection.

A. transmontanus WHITE STURGEON At least 4·6 m. (15 ft)

This is the largest of the American sturgeons, and indeed the largest fish found in freshwater in N. America. The biggest specimens recorded appear to have been a female of 816 kg. (1800 lb.) from British Columbia in 1897, and another in 1912 at Vancouver, Washington of 582 kg. (1285 lb.), while others of 4 m. (13 ft) in length and over 454 kg. (1000 lb.) in weight were recorded from the Snake River, Idaho. These very large specimens were all females (the males appear to be much smaller) and presumably they were old, for in the present century the largest specimens caught are rarely more than 136 kg. (300 lb.) in weight, suggesting that fishing pressure does not permit them to live long enough to grow to these great sizes.

The white sturgeon has been recorded from n. Baja California, in Mexico (where rare), to Cook Inlet, Alaska, and is apparently confined to the American Pacific coast rivers. It is not an anadromous species, although occasional specimens do wander out into the ocean. It does, however, migrate fairly regularly within the river systems. In winter the smaller specimens move upstream on a feeding migration, although the large ones retire to deeper water. In spring they return to the shallows where they spawn. Although the young sturgeon feed mostly on bottom-living invertebrates, the adults eat large quantities of fish.

The white sturgeon can be distinguished by the position of the barbels under its snout, closer to the tip of the snout than to the mouth. It also has fewer bony plates (11–12) along its back.

At one time the white sturgeon was heavily fished for its roe (for caviare production) and became greatly diminished in numbers (in the Sacramento River of California about 5000 per month were caught in 1872, practically none were taken in 1917). Conservation measures re-established a larger stock, and by 1954 limited catches could be allowed for sportfishing. The slow-growing nature of this and other sturgeons means there is always a great risk of over-exploiting the stocks.

ACIPENSERIDAE

The family of the sturgeons, a group of primitive fishes found only in the N. Hemisphere. There are some 25 species, in 4 genera, and the greatest number of species lies in central Eurasia. Some species are migratory, spawning in freshwater, but spending the greater part of their lives in the sea; others are confined to freshwater.

Their general features include a long spindle-shaped body, a heterocercal tail, several series of heavy bony scutes on the body, and fins lacking bony rays or spines. The mouth is ventral, with barbels in front of the fleshy lips. See **Acipenser, Huso, Pseudoscaphirhynchus, Scaphirhynchus**.

Acropoma   Acropomidae **japonicum** 17 cm. (6¾ in.)

This species has been found in deep water in the area to the S. of Japan, off the Philippines,

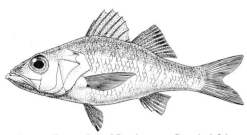

n. Australia, and the Natal coast, South Africa. It is found at depths of 238–457 m. (130–250 fathoms). Its biology is unknown.

It is light pink, becoming silvery below, with small black spots in lines on the lower belly and tail. This fish has a double tubular luminous organ which extends along the breast and belly between the pelvics.

ACROPOMIDAE

A family of small deep-water fishes found in the Indo-Pacific. Several species have been recognized, but there is a strong possibility that they are all one wide-ranging species.

It is an elongate fish with moderately large, rather fragile scales. Two well separated dorsal fins and a single anal fin with 3 slender spines, place it amongst the sea basses and cardinal fishes. However, there is considerable confusion about its true relationships. See **Acropoma**.

ADALAH see **Psettodes erumei**

Adinia Cyprinodontidae
xenica DIAMOND KILLIFISH 5 cm. (2 in.)
A killifish found in salt and brackish water on the Gulf coast of N. America from Florida to Texas. It is widely distributed and locally quite common.

It has a distinctively angular body shape, particularly on the back, which is somewhat trapezoidal. Body scales are moderately large, in fewer than 30 rows along the side of the body. From the side the body looks unusually deep and the back flattened. The back is dusky and the sides are crossed by a series of narrow vertical dark stripes, rather enlarged along the midline. **194**

Adioryx Holocentridae
vexillarius DUSKY SQUIRRELFISH
15 cm. (6 in.)
This species is widely distributed in the W. Atlantic and Caribbean from New Jersey and Bermuda s. to the Lesser Antilles; also in the Gulf of Mexico and along the Central American coast. It is the commonest squirrelfish in shallow water in the Caribbean—and in tide pools on rocky or coral bottoms, down to 15 m. (8 fathoms).

It is a rather deep-bodied squirrelfish, but possesses all the other characters of this group. It can be distinguished by the rather dark back; it has dull red lines alternating with light stripes on the body, the fins are pinkish except that the spiny dorsal fin membrane has dark stripes parallel to the spines, and large dark blotches between the first 4 spines.
A. xantherythrus 18 cm. (7 in.)
This is said to be the most widely distributed Hawaiian squirrelfish in depths of 6–15 m. (3–8 fathoms). It seems to be restricted to the outer side of the reef.

Physically this species closely resembles other members of the family, but it can be dis-

tinguished from some of them by its moderately short anal spine (which does not reach to the tail fin base). In coloration it is similar to other species, being mostly reddish, especially the spiny dorsal fin, but the lengthwise stripes on the body have a pinkish tinge, thus giving it a rather lighter appearance compared with other species.

The late Dr Earl S. Herald of the Steinhardt Aquarium, California, reported courting activity in this species in which the pairs, intermittently emitting sounds, pressed their tails together while the front of the body was turned away, thus forming a V or Y. **217**

ADRIANICHTHYIDAE

A small family of freshwater fishes found only in lakes in the interior of the Celebes, in the E. Indies. Three species only are recognized. All are small fishes, the largest attains about 20 cm. (8 in.)

They are rather elongate with compressed bodies, the head flattened and depressed, especially over the snout which appears almost duck-billed. The scales, all small, cover the body completely and extend onto the head. See **Xenopoecilus**.

Aeoliscus Centriscidae
strigatus SHRIMPFISH 15 cm. (6 in.)
Widely distributed in the Indo-Pacific but best-known on the Queensland coast of Australia. The genus *Aeoliscus* is distinguished by the movable spine at the tip of the body which is formed by the posterior end of the dorsal fin.

This fish adopts a peculiar head-down posture when active, swimming in a smooth glide by means of the anal and tail fins. It is greenish silvery with a lengthwise stripe along the back and each side. These stripes serve to mask the otherwise conspicuous eyes, and also closely imitate the long black spines of sea urchins, amongst which the shrimpfish is frequently found. The flat compressed shape also helps to conceal the fish amongst the spines.

Shrimpfishes have been reported swimming in small shoals in caves, working along the bottom, up the side, and across the roof in their 'head-down' posture. Little is known of their biology. **229**

Aequidens Cichlidae
duopunctata 10 cm. (4 in.)
A S. American cichlid which was first made known from specimens collected at Manáos, on the Amazon.

It is a rather deep-bodied form, with a large eye and steep head profile. The dorsal and anal fins end in long streamers which extend to about the tip of the tail fin. **354**

Aetapcus Pataecidae
maculatus WARTY PROWFISH
21 cm. (8¼ in.)
A deep-bodied compressed fish, with a high dorsal fin that originates above the snout and extends along the tail to unite with the tail fin. The body tapers from its greatest depth at the eye. The whole body, including the fins, is enveloped in a thick warty skin which is scaleless but covered with flat, wart-like protuberances.

Its coloration is olive, spotted on head and body with black, while the fins are blackish.

This prowfish is found on the coasts of W. Australia, S. Australia, and Tasmania. It is

relatively common in shallow water and is occasionally caught, although not deliberately, by anglers.

Aetobatus Myliobatidae
narinari SPOTTED EAGLE RAY
236 cm. (93 in.)
This large eagle ray is distributed throughout the tropical zones of the Atlantic, Pacific, and Indian oceans. In the Atlantic it ranges from around Angola on the African coast, n. to the Cape Verde Islands, and from s. Brazil to N. Carolina. It migrates seasonally outside these areas with summertime warming of the sea. Large shoals, sometimes numbering hundreds of specimens, have been seen at sea.

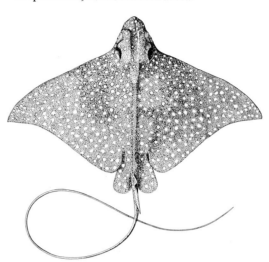

It is one of the largest eagle rays, often exceeding 2 m. (6½ ft) in width, and due to the thickness of its body its weight is relatively high, estimated up to 181–227 kg. (400–500 lb.).

It has relatively narrow, pointed pectoral fins, and a distinct head in advance of these fins. The long and whip-like tail bears close to its base a long serrated-edged spine. Its light brown back is conspicuously marked with white, or yellowish spots.

This eagle ray feeds heavily on the larger molluscs, especially clams and oysters, although some have been reported to eat octopuses, prawns, and marine worms. Where shellfish are cultured the damage caused by these rays can be very serious. They are also capable of inflicting serious wounds with their tail spines. **13**

AFRICAN
CHARACIN, ONE-STRIPED see
Nannaethiops unitaeniatus
GLASS CATFISH see **Physailia pellucida**
LEAFFISH see **Polycentropsis abbreviata**
LONG-FINNED EEL see **Anguilla mossambica**
MOTTLED EEL see **Anguilla nebulosa**
POMPANO see **Alectis crinitis**
SCAT see **Scatophagus tetracanthus**
SNAKE-HEAD see **Ophicephalus africanus**

Afronandus Nandidae
sheljuzhkoi 5 cm. (2 in.)
Found only in French tropical W. Africa, along the Ivory coast near Abidjan and Agboville. This relatively recently discovered and little-known fish lives in springs.

It is immediately distinguished by having only 4 anal spines, and by lacking any lateral

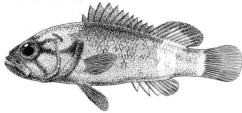

line. Its colouring is dark green. A juvenile is illustrated.

It has been kept in aquaria with some success after its original importation to Germany in 1952.

AGASSIZ'S DWARF CICHLID see
Apistogramma agassizi

AGENEIOSIDAE
A family of S. American catfishes found mostly in the NE. of that continent, although some species range as far S. as Argentina. They have scaleless skins, without bony plates or scutes. In this family the barbels on the upper jaw are slender, short and few; there are none on the lower jaw. An adipose fin is present but small, the dorsal fin is set well forward near the head, and the anal fin is long. The small swim bladder is enclosed in bony processes arising from the anterior vertebrae.

Some species have local value as food; others are exported as aquarium fish. See **Ageneiosus**.

Ageneiosus   Ageneiosidae
  brevifilis MANDUBA 55 cm. (21½ in.)
This catfish is widely distributed in ne. S. America, from Guyana through the Amazon basin to Peru, Uruguay, and Argentina. It is found especially in rivers, in over-grown backwaters, and where the current is slack. It feeds on small fishes and crustaceans, and is in turn esteemed for the fine flavour of its flesh. Specimens of 50 cm. (19½ in.) length weigh around 2 kg. (4¼ lb.), and are about 5 years old.

Males differ from females by having a shorter barbel and dorsal spine, they also lack the prolonged anterior anal fin lobe.

Dull coloured, greyish brown above with irregular spots on the head; sides and belly silvery.

AGONIDAE
These small fishes, the poachers or pogges, are found in the cooler regions of both N. Pacific and N. Atlantic oceans, as well as Arctic and Antarctic seas generally. The N. Pacific contains the greater number of species. They are very distinctive, having a body armour of several rows of overlapping plates, small fins and generally small mouths.

Most are coastal species, all are found on or close to the sea bed. See **Agonus, Aspidophoroides, Bathyagonus, Bothragonus, Leptagonus, Pallasina**

Agonus   Agonidae
  acipenserinus STURGEON POACHER
30 cm. (12 in.)
Widely distributed along the N. American Pacific coast from n. California to the Bering

Sea. This poacher is very common in moderately shallow water along at least the n. parts of its range. It is found in depths of 18–55 m. (10–30 fathoms) mostly on muddy bottoms; its food consists mainly of crustaceans and marine worms.

An aptly named species for the head has a very sturgeon-like appearance, except for the 4 turned-up spines at the tip of the snout, and clusters of branched barbels at the mouth. In other respects its body form is typical of the family.

A. cataphractus HOOKNOSE, POGGE
15 cm. (6 in.)
An abundant fish on the Atlantic coast of Europe, from the English Channel to n. Norway and Iceland. In the S. it comes inshore in the winter months, and is often caught in quite shallow water, but normally it lives in 10–200 m. (5–109 fathoms); it is said to have been found as deep as 500 m. (273 fathoms). It is usually encountered on sandy or muddy bottoms.

It spawns in early winter in shallow water, often on inshore sand banks, occasionally on the shore itself; the eggs are laid in clumps on the bottom and overwinter before hatching. The young are surface-living at first but take to the bottom around mid-summer at a length of about 2 cm. (¾ in.).

It is easily distinguished by its heavy scaly body, and by its hard head, which has 2 sharp, recurved hooks at the tip. The underside of the head is thickly equipped with short barbels.

Ahlia   Ophichthidae
  egmontis KEY WORM EEL 38 cm. (15 in.)
The key worm eel ranges from Florida and the Bahamas s. to Brazil and throughout the Gulf of Mexico; it is very common in the Bahamas. It is an elongate, almost worm-shaped eel, with low dorsal and anal fins, joining at the end into a distinct but short tail fin. The dorsal fin originates almost midway along the body, above the vent. This eel is usually uniformly pale in colour, sometimes light brown, and often has fine dark dots overall.

It lives most of the time buried in sand, and although it is common in sandy bays and on sand banks, it is also found in small sand pockets within coral reefs. However, when sexually mature this eel's habits change: it becomes pelagic, and nocturnally active, forming loose shoals and moving into deeper water to spawn. Externally too the eels change; they become silvery, the eye increases in size, and the pectoral fins become larger.

AHOLEHOLE see **Kuhlia sandvicensis**
AINAME see **Hexagrammos otakii**
AKAAMADAI see **Branchiostegus japonicus**

AKYSIDAE
A family of small catfishes, including some miniature species sexually mature when only 3 cm. long. Members of the family are confined to Asian freshwaters in Burma, Thailand, Java, Borneo, and Sumatra.

The family is characterized amongst Asian catfishes by the short dorsal fin with a sharp spine at its front, a distinct adipose fin, and a broad-based barbel developed on the posterior nostril. See **Akysis**.

Akysis   Akysidae
  leucorhynchus 4 cm. (1½ in.)

A small catfish found in the Meping River in Thailand. It is evidently a miniature species for specimens of 3 cm. have been found to be sexually mature and containing nearly ripe eggs. It is slender and has a rather stout dorsal spine, a distinct adipose fin, and longish, broad-based barbels.

The body is mostly whitish with 3 irregular black cross bands; the snout is white and between it and the first black band there is a patch of rich brown.

Alabes   Alabetidae
  rufus SHORE EEL 10 cm. (4 in.)
A common species on the s. coasts of Australia, in S. Australia, Victoria, New South Wales, Tasmania, and s. Queensland. It is found in intertidal areas hiding under stones and amongst seaweed in shallow rock pools.

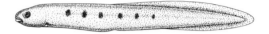

In life this long, eel-like fish is green with a series of dusky spots along the sides, but when placed in preservative it turns a dull red (hence the inappropriate name *rufus*).

ALABETIDAE
A small family of fishes found mainly in fresh and brackish water in Australia and India. The body form is eel-like with dorsal, tail, and anal fins continuous; the pectoral fins are absent and the pelvics are very small and 2-rayed.

Members of this family have a single gill slit beneath the throat, a feature they share with the synbranchiform fishes (see Synbranchidae) although their relationships seem to lie with the Blenniidae. See **Alabes**.

ALASKA BLACKFISH see **Dallia pectoralis**
ALBACORE see **Thunnus alalunga**
ALBACORE, FALSE see **Euthynnus alletteratus**

Albula   Albulidae
  vulpes BONEFISH, LADYFISH 91 cm. (3 ft)
The bonefish occurs worldwide in tropical seas and is common on both sides of the tropical Atlantic, especially around the Florida and Bahamas coasts. In the Indo-Pacific it is well known on the African coast, in the warmer Australian

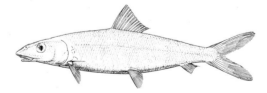

seas, and off Hawaii. It is a magnificent fighting fish for the angler, and although it is not very large, attaining a maximum weight of around 9 kg. (20 lb.), it is greatly appreciated wherever it occurs. However, it is not particularly well flavoured as a food fish.

The bonefish is silvery, becoming dark

green-blue on the back, but living specimens have a series of faint dark stripes on the sides. Its snout projects in unmistakable fashion beyond its relatively small mouth. When feeding, bone-fish keep in shoals, working their way over the bottom, head downwards, so that occasionally, in shallow water, their tails emerge above the surface. Their food consists almost entirely of bottom-living invertebrates, particularly clams, crabs, and shrimps, less often fishes.

ALBULIDAE

A small family of tropical marine fishes related to the tarpons and the tenpounder. Its members are herring-like in build, with an elongate body, a single dorsal fin, silvery scales, and a forked tail fin. As with its relatives the larvae are thin and transparent, like eel larvae. They metamorphose in shallow inshore water, decreasing in total length by more than half in the process.

The family contains several species, some of them from deep water, but the best known is the bonefish, *Albula vulpes*, worldwide in distribution in tropical seas. See **Albula**.

Alburnus   Cyprinidae
  alburnus BLEAK 20 cm. (8 in.)
The bleak is a gregarious shoaling fish, extremely common, excessively so in places, in lowland rivers of Europe, from the English rivers e. to the Caspian basin. It occurs n. through Sweden, Finland, and parts of the U.S.S.R.

It is a slender-bodied, highly compressed fish with a rather small oblique mouth. It has a moderately long, many-rayed anal fin. Its back is dark bluish green, its sides creamy silver, and its belly is bright silvery. The silvery guanin crystals are extracted from the silver scales and used as *essence d'orient* in the manufacture of artificial pearls. Many thousands of bleak may be used to produce a small quantity of essence.

It is usually found in open waters near the surface, and lives in shoals feeding on planktonic crustaceans, flying insects, and larvae. It is very much a surface feeder. Because of its abundance it forms an important link in the food chains of Europe's rivers, being eaten by many fish-eating birds, by perch, pike, zander, and trout. **107**

Aldrichetta   Mugilidae
  forsteri YELLOW-EYED or FRESHWATER
MULLET 38 cm. (15 in.)
A grey mullet found in the s. parts of Australia, especially S. Australia, Victoria, and Tasmania.

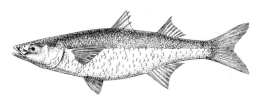

It is found mainly in estuaries in brackish water, but it frequently occurs in entirely freshwater. It is the most important commercial mullet in the s. states of Australia and is caught mainly in seine nets. It is also a popular angling fish and is said to readily take a bait.

It is distinguished by its rather long snout and pointed head with moderately large teeth on the jaws and tongue. It is olive-brown above, silvery to light yellow below, with a conspicuously yellow eye.

Aldrovandia   Halosauridae
  macrochir 65 cm. (25½ in.)
A long thin halosaur found in very deep water in the Atlantic Ocean, and reported from the s. Indian Ocean. It has been captured in many places in the N. Atlantic as well as off South Africa and is relatively common and widely distributed. Its depth range is from 1163–3166 m. (635–1731 fathoms), although it seems to be most abundant between 1800–2400 m. (984–1312 fathoms).

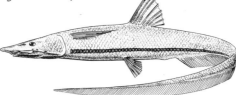

The eyes are moderate and protected by a thickish skin, no doubt to save them from damage while the animal is burrowing in the bottom mud. It is dull black in colour.

Alectis   Carangidae
A large genus of marine fish. Besides *A. ciliaris* the other species illustrated in colour has not been identified. **291**
A. ciliaris PENNANT TREVALLY
38 cm. (15 in.)
An Indo-Pacific species of wide distribution. The pennant trevally (its Queensland name) is found at least from Indian waters e. to Australia and Hawaii. It is particularly common in bays and shallow inshore waters.

It is distinguished from related species in this area by its deeper body, larger eye, and short, rounded snout. The first 4 or 5 rays of the dorsal and anal fins are produced into extremely long trailing streamers, which in young fish may be twice the body length. Their length decreases proportionally as the fish grows. **292**
A. crinitus AFRICAN POMPANO 91 cm. (3 ft)
A widely distributed fish in the tropical Atlantic which also occurs in the e. Pacific. In the Atlantic it occurs in the W. from Massachusetts to Brazil, and in the E. from the Canaries to Angola. It is an open-water fish found, when adult, on the outer reefs and offshore generally.

It grows to a moderate size and is in some favour as a sporting fish where it is locally common. Adults are rather slender bodied, with the upper profile of the head steep and the edges of the body angular. The front rays of the dorsal and the anal fin are long (about equal to the length of the body). It is silvery overall.

Young fish have rather deep, flattened bodies and their extremely long anterior dorsal and anal rays shorten notably with age. The young are dusky above with a dark edge to the tail fin, and silvery on the belly. It has been suggested that with these very long fin rays the young fish resemble jellyfish with long streaming tentacles, and thus gain some protection from predators.

ALEPISAURIDAE

A family containing very few species (probably only 2) found in the open sea in the Atlantic, Indian, and Pacific oceans. They are large, voracious mesopelagic fishes, which as adults have been caught mostly on deep-set lines laid for tuna. They are hermaphrodite.

Long slender fishes, with soft rather flaccid flesh, the lancetfishes have pointed snouts,

large jaws, very large dagger-like teeth on the palate, and smaller sharp teeth in the jaws. They have a high, sailfish-like dorsal fin, a forked and large tail fin, moderate curved pectoral and pelvic fins, and an adipose fin near the tail. See **Alepisaurus**.

Alepisaurus   Alepisauridae
  ferox LONGNOSE LANCETFISH
1·6 m. (63 in.)
Unmistakable on account of its body shape; in colour it is iridescent, darker on the back and shading through the most beautiful bronzy hues on the sides; its fins are black.

Although 1·6 m. is given above as a maximum size, larger specimens of lancetfish have been recorded, but not necessarily identified to species. Despite its length, it is not heavy, a fish of 1·6 m. weighing about 4·5 kg. (10 lb.), for the skeleton is reduced to almost paper thinness.

The lancetfish is widely distributed in the warmer waters of the Atlantic, Pacific, and Indian oceans, although occasional specimens are found in cooler, n. waters, even as far N. as Greenland.

It is a voracious predator feeding on a wide variety of fish, cephalopods, and crustaceans. To the marine biologist the stomach of a large specimen is often a treasure house in which lies many rare, and sometimes previously unknown animals. Quite striking tallies have been reported; for example a specimen caught about 480 km. (300 miles) off California contained 41 fish of 5 kinds, 3 cephalopods of 2 kinds, and other small invertebrates. Most large lancetfish have been taken on long lines, especially those mid-water lines set for tuna. They have been captured from the surface down to a depth of about 500 m. (273 fathoms) and below and these lower depths seem to be their more favoured region.

ALEPOCEPHALIDAE

A family of mostly small deep-sea fishes, characterized by their small mouths and weak teeth, a dorsal fin placed far back and no adipose fin on the back. Most have large, thin, cycloid scales, although some are scaleless; their heads are scaleless and covered with smooth skin – which gives them their common name of smooth-heads or slickheads.

There is considerable variation in body form within the family, and many species are known from only single specimens captured by research vessels. Some of the larger species are taken incidentally by deep fishing trawlers in the e. Atlantic, but they are not used as food. See **Alepocephalus, Leptoderma, Xenodermichthys**.

Alepocephalus   Alepocephalidae
  rostratus 70 cm. (28 in.)
This is a very distinctive smooth-head found in the w. Mediterranean and e. Atlantic from off sw. Ireland s. to the Cape Verde Islands. It is a rather short-bodied species with large scales

overall, but with the head naked and covered with blue-black skin. It is deep brown, with blackish fins. The eye is very large, and the dorsal and anal fins lie far back along the body, opposite one another. The snout is concave in profile.

It is found in deep water, mostly between 365 and 1000 m. (200–546 fathoms), although catches as deep as 3655 m. (2000 fathoms) are on record; however there is a distinct possibility that this fish was caught at a considerably shallower depth as the net was being hauled in. This fish is occasionally taken by commercial trawlers fishing in deep water for hake off SW. Ireland, but it seems to be rare there for never more than 1–2 are taken per haul.

Alestes   Characidae
  longipinnis LONG-FINNED CHARACIN
13 cm. (5 in.)
A characin found in tropical W. Africa, from Sierra Leone to the Congo. It is a beautiful little fish. Males have elongate dorsal fin rays, and the anal fin is rounded. They also have reddish tinted tail and dorsal fins. **49**
A. macrolepidotus 55 cm. (22 in.)
A large-scale African characin, usually with as few as 22–26 scales in the lateral line. It is moderately deep-bodied, the ventral profile rising sharply at the base of the anal fin to give a short but narrow caudal peduncle. The snout is pointed, and the head is flattened above so that the mouth is terminal and the eye rather lower in the head than usual for these fish. It is a silvery fish, bluish-grey on the back with a dark blotch above the pectoral base in young fish and a long, narrow streak along the flanks. All the fins have a pinkish tinge.

It is widely distributed in tropical Africa, in the basins of the Nile, Niger, Chad, Volta, and Congo rivers, as well as Lake Albert, and the Albert and Murchison Niles. It is found in the inshore regions of the lake, and widely in rivers. It feeds on small fishes, insects, and bottom debris.

It, with other *Alestes* species, is a valuable food fish in inland African waters.
A. nurse 25 cm. (10 in.)
This species is widely distributed in tropical Africa from the Nile to the Niger, Liberia and the Cameroons, also in Lake Albert in Uganda, and lakes Rudolf and Chad.

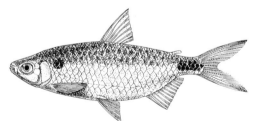

It is beautifully, if rather soberly, coloured; the body is yellowish brown to olive with a bright brassy iridescence, particularly on the lower sides and tail. The dorsal, pelvic, and anal fins are tinged with vermilion, and the tail-fin lobes are bright red. There are 2 indistinct dark blotches, one over the pectoral base, and the larger and more distinct on the tail.

The teeth in *Alestes* species are few and large; in the upper jaw they are in 2 series, each tooth with several cusps, and those in the inner row rather larger than those in the outer. The lower jaw has an outer row of massive, 3-cusped

teeth, and an inner series of 2 small curved teeth.

The attractive young, which are kept in aquaria, swim gracefully in small shoals.

ALEWIFE see **Alosa pseudoharengus**

Alfaro   Poeciliidae
  cultratus KNIFE LIVE-BEARER
9 cm. (3½ in.)
Found in small waters, pools, and streams in Costa Rico, Nicaragua, and on the Atlantic slope of Panama. Its body form differs in some noticeable ways from the normal poeciliid standard, especially in being greatly compressed. The tail has a knife-like edge ventrally, and the anal fin is placed before this keel. The female is considerably larger than the male (which rarely grows longer than 4 cm., 1½ in.). It is kept in aquaria.

The male is pale brown with shining blue sides, a narrow dark band along the posterior side, and fine black spots overall. The tail fin has a dark edge; the other fins are golden. The conspicuous gonopodium is golden yellow. The female is dull brown.

Allocyttus   Oreosomatidae
  verrucosus OX-EYE OREO, WARTY DORY,
ORE 38 cm. (15 in.)
A deep body, very large eye, and very protractile mouth all help distinguish this fish. The young are also set apart by the 2 rows of rounded, enlarged bumps on the lower sides, as well as normal small scales. The spiny dorsal fin is relatively short and the spines low but strong; the 2–3 anal spines are also small, but the pelvic spine is moderately large. It is dark brownish.

Specimens have been found off South Africa, W. and S. Australia, and in the N. Pacific. It is possibly widely spread throughout the deep oceans of the Indo-Pacific. It occurs at moderate depths down to 1646 m. (900 fathoms).

ALLIGATOR GAR see **Lepisosteus spatula**
ALLIGATORFISH see **Aspidophoroides monopterygius**
ALLISON TUNA see **Thunnus albacares**

Alopias   Alopiidae
  caudatus see **A. vulpinus**
  greyi see **A. vulpinus**
  vulpinus THRESHER SHARK 6 m. (19½ ft)
The thresher shark occurs in all oceans, although in Australian seas it is usually known under different scientific names (*A. caudatus* and *A. greyi*). It is a surface-living shark, mostly oceanic in habit, although not uncom-

mon in coastal waters at times. Around the British Isles a few are caught by sport fishermen each summer and autumn, and most records from the American Atlantic (where it is found as far N. as the Gulf of St Lawrence) are for the same seasons. In these areas it evidently makes an inshore (and n.) migration in the warm season.

The thresher gives birth to fully-formed live pups, which may be up to 1·5 m. (5 ft) in length. In compensation for the large size of the pups at birth the female bears only 2–4 in a litter. As young threshers of that size are frequently reported it seems that they are born throughout its range.

The use that the shark makes of its long tail is remarkable, for working alone, or more often in pairs, it herds a school of fish into a compact mass with its flailing tail before charging into the disordered and tight-packed shoal. Solitary fish are struck with the tail until disabled and captured. The time-honoured tale that in company with a swordfish the thresher will attack a whale is now regarded as nothing more than a myth.

Threshers seem nowhere to be as common as some other large sharks. Consequently they are not frequently encountered by sport fishermen, nor do they make much impact on commercial fisheries by their consumption of fish. They seem quite harmless to swimmers.

ALOPIIDAE
A small family of sharks, known from all the oceans of tropical and temperate areas. They are mostly oceanic in habit, but occasionally are found in inshore coastal waters. All are characterized by the tremendously long tail, often more than half the length of the body. See **Alopias**.

Alosa   Clupeidae
  aestivalis BLUEBACK, GLUT or SUMMER
HERRING 38 cm. (15 in.)
The blueback herring shares with other shads the habit of spending most of its life in the sea and returning to freshwater to spawn. It is closely similar to the alewife (*A. pseudoharengus*) but differs, when living, in the colour of its back, distinctly blue instead of green. The blueback's eye is rather smaller, and it is a slimmer fish, but they resemble one another so much that they are frequently confused. The only reliable quick means of identification is that the body cavity lining is sooty or black in the blueback.

It ascends the rivers to spawn later in the summer and breeds further downstream than the alewife. Spawning takes place at a water temperature of about 21°C, and the eggs, which are only 1 mm. in diameter, sink to the river bed and stick to whatever they touch. The young fish travel downriver in the autumn when they are often only about 5 cm. (2 in.) long.

The blueback is found from n. Florida to the New England coast in some abundance, and outside these limits rarely. It is still moderately common along the Atlantic coast, but evidently less so now than formerly. Particularly in the S. of its range, its periodic abundance in the rivers leads to its vernacular name of 'glut herring'.

A. fallax TWAITE SHAD 61 cm. (2 ft)
This shad is a large-headed, rather heavy-bodied herring-like fish. Like its relatives it is basically silvery, with large, easily detached scales; its back is bright blue, with deep yellow tints, almost bronze at times, on the head and sides. It has series of 5–7 rounded dark blotches along the sides immediately behind the head.

The twaite shad is widely found in European seas, distributed from Iceland (where it is rare), and in the Baltic, s. to the Mediterranean. It is an anadromous fish, living in inshore waters and entering rivers to spawn in freshwater. Like most fish with similar habits in European seas it has suffered greatly from pollution and obstructions in rivers which hinder its ascent.

It feeds mainly on small crustaceans and fishes. Spawning runs occur in the spring, and the shad is known as Mayfish in many European tongues for its appearance in the river in that month. It spawns at night in shallow reaches, with a great deal of splashing and leaping; the eggs are widely distributed in the gravel downstream of the spawning site.

In some lakes the twaite shad has lost its migratory habits, those in the Italian lakes Como, Maggiore, and Garda being non-migratory (as are those in Lake Killarney, Ireland – where they are known as goureen). They differ morphologically from the parent stocks in a number of ways.

A. mediocris HICKORY SHAD, FALL HERRING 61 cm. (2 ft)
The hickory shad is one of the several herring-like fish to inhabit the inshore waters of the w. N. Atlantic, along the American coastline from Florida to Maine. They probably spawn in spring. In the N. they become more common during the warmer months.

Their food consists very largely of fish, including sand eels, anchovies, herrings, and silversides, but they also eat squids, and crustaceans. They are much less dependent on plankton than are the other shads and, in consequence, the gill rakers are fewer and shorter.

Hickory shad are not important as food fish, being poorly flavoured and very bony. A moderate quantity are landed each year especially on the coasts of the s. states.

It is distinguished from its relatives by the fewer gill rakers, by its protruding lower jaw, and the forward position of the dorsal fin. Its colour is greyish green above shading gently into iridescent silver on the sides, the tips of the lower jaw and the tail fin are dusky. A dark spot on the shoulder with a line of smaller spots following it.

A. pseudoharengus ALEWIFE
38 cm. (15 in.)
The alewife is a fish of the American Atlantic seaboard, from the Gulf of St Lawrence and n. Nova Scotia, s. to N. Carolina. Like other shads it enters rivers to spawn and is thus frequently found in freshwater. Landlocked

races exist in certain lakes, notably Lake Ontario and its connections, and the Finger Lakes of New York. It has been introduced into the upper Great Lakes where it has increased inordinately, at times dying in such numbers as to be a major nuisance.

It is grey-green on the back, silvery on the sides and belly, with a dusky spot just behind the head. The sides often show iridescent streaks of green or violet in life. In general appearance it is like a deep-bodied herring, with the dorsal fin set well forward. The belly keel has strong serrations formed by the sharp edges of the scales which gives it its local name of sawbelly.

The alewife is still an abundant fish which feeds primarily on plankton, chiefly copepods and other crustaceans; it also eats young fish. However, they fast during their spawning migration upriver; this usually starts in April although some enter streams in March or as late as May. The earliest colonists evidently found the alewife in incredible quantities in the E. Coast rivers, but industrial development and pollution has barred many rivers to them, and their numbers have declined, as has their general range. In the last century they were subject to an important fishery, analysis of catches in 1896 amounting to a total of about 22 million fish for the year in the Gulf of Maine alone. Catches of this size are not made today, although the alewife is still captured commercially, particularly in the lower reaches of rivers where the migrating shoals are easily caught in seines and traps. The alewife is a very good food fish, and is marketed both fresh and salted.

It spawns in backwaters, in slow stretches of streams, never in fast water. Females shed from 60 to 100 thousand eggs according to size. After spawning the adults move downstream. The pinkish eggs stick to stones, brushwood, or any other solid matter. They hatch in about 6 days at 16° C. After about a month the young move downstream, reaching the sea at a length of about 10 cm. (4 in.).

A. sapidissima SHAD, AMERICAN SHAD
76 cm. (30 in.)
The shad is native on the Atlantic coast of N. America from the s. coast of Newfoundland and the St Lawrence River to the St John's and Appalachicola rivers in Florida. It was introduced to the Pacific coast at various times between 1871 and 1886 and quickly established itself in the N. American rivers and coastal waters where it now provides a healthy fishery.

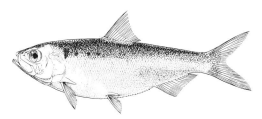

Externally it is typically herring-like with soft-rayed fins, and large, easily detached scales. It is dark bluish or greenish above, white and silvery on the sides and belly, with a dusky blotch close behind the head and several smaller ones behind that.

The shad spends a large part of its life in the sea but migrates into rivers to spawn, after

which it returns to the sea. They are schooling fish swarming in the surface of the sea often in thousands. Like other shads and herrings, they feed on plankton, mainly on the small copepod crustaceans so common at the surface. They also eat other crustaceans and fishes. Adult fish enter the rivers in spring or summer, generally later to the cooler N. In large rivers some migrate for distances as great as 320–480 km. (200–300 miles); others turn off into smaller streams where they find sandy or pebble beds suitable for spawning. The eggs are buoyant and roll about with the current, hatching in 12 to 15 days at 11° C. The young fish follow their parents downriver and enter the sea in late autumn at a length of 4–11 cm. ($1\frac{1}{2}$–$4\frac{1}{2}$ in.).

The shad was a fish of almost incredible abundance along the Atlantic coast in early colonial days, but the vast shoals were indiscriminately netted as they entered the rivers. River obstructions such as dams and weirs, and more recently pollution of the lower reaches of the rivers, have reduced the stocks still further. Today, while the shad is by no means rare along the Atlantic coast, its numbers are but a fraction of their former status.

Alphestes Serranidae
A variable genus belonging to the large family, Serranidae, of mainly marine fish. The species illustrated in colour has not been identified. **258**
A. afer MUTTON HAMLET 30 cm. (1 ft)
Found along the Atlantic coast of America from Bermuda, the Bahamas, and Florida to Argentina and the Falkland Islands. It is in places a common fish especially in areas of turtle grass, but it also occurs, although rarely, on reefs. It generally lives in water shallower than 3 m. (10 ft).

It is distinguished by the downturned spine on the angle of the preoperculum, but the narrow, pointed head with the eye far forward near the snout is equally characteristic. It is olive with heavy mottlings and orange patches. At night the colour pattern changes as 2 dark cross bands appear on the body.

Alticops Blenniidae
periophthalmus ROCK SKIPPER, HOPPER
15 cm. (6 in.)
An Indo-W. Pacific species of wide distribution, particularly abundant in shallow intertidal areas in rock pools, and can be seen to jump and skip agilely over the rocks.

It is distinguished by the almost vertical profile, with a tuft of cirri on the nostril and a small tentacle above the eye. Its dorsal fins are completely divided. It is rosy-green with several violet-brown cross bars, and 2 rows of pearly blue bars on the sides.

Aluterus Balistidae
scriptus SCRAWLED FILEFISH 91 cm. (3 ft)
A very distinctive filefish with a long, slender and compressed body, pointed snout, and long tail fin. Its colouring is also distinctive being olive-brown to greeny grey, with an irregular pattern of rather distinct blue dots and lines and scattered black spots.

This species is reported as occurring in tropical oceans around the world. In the Atlantic it occurs on both sides, off W. Africa, and around St Helena, and on the American coast from New England and Bermuda to Brazil. It

is occasionally seen by divers, drifting along at an odd angle, its nose down and propelled by its undulating dorsal and anal fins. Its food is varied but is all encrusting or bottom living, including hydrozoans, algae, gorgonians, sea grass, and sea anemones. The young fish live mainly in sea grass beds and mimic the fronds very well, usually by lying in line and swaying with water movements.

AMBERJACK,
  GREATER see **Seriola dumerili**
  KING see **Seriola grandis**
  SOUTH AFRICAN see under **Seriola grandis**

Amblyapistus   Scorpaenidae
  binotatus 20 cm. (8 in.)
An Indian Ocean species found only on the coast of e. Africa. It lives amongst weeds in moderately shallow water and is frequently encountered by inshore fishermen who fear its sharp, probably venomous, spines.

This and its Indo-Pacific relatives are very distinctive species, with a flattened compressed body, steep profile, smooth skin with scales deeply embedded, and rather smooth head. The first spines of the dorsal fin are stout and high, well separated from one another, but joined at the base by a thick membrane. Its colouring is usually dull but the light spot on the side is very noticeable.

Amblyceps   Amblycipitidae
  mangois 13 cm. (5 in.)
This interesting little catfish is found in rapid-running streams at the bases of hills in the region of the Himalayas, n. Burma, and Thailand. It lives in clear rapidly flowing water over pebble beds, among stones and rocks. With the seasonal dying out of the streams it buries itself deeper by wriggling between stones to hidden water or into pools. Its respiration is typical of other hillstream fishes, a series of rapid inhalations and then a period of quiescence which may last from 1–4 minutes.

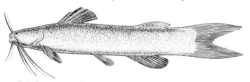

Living specimens are dull brown above, lighter below. The tail fin varies in shape from square cut to deeply forked.

AMBLYCIPITIDAE
A family of small loach-like catfishes found in the rivers of India, Burma, and Thailand. The family is close to the bagrid catfishes, but differs in certain features of the skeleton, notably in having the lateral extensions of the fourth vertebra expanded like an inverted cup in which the lateral lobes of the swim-bladder lie. See **Amblyceps**.

Amblycirrhitus   Cirrhitidae
  pinos REDSPOTTED HAWKFISH
  8 cm. (3 in.)
Widespread in the w. Atlantic from the

Bahamas and Florida, and in the Caribbean throughout the W. Indies. It lives on hard substrates, of coral heads and reefs, and is usually seen perched on a raised 'lookout' or hovering just above the bottom. Its depth range varies from 2–30 m. (1–16 fathoms).

A very distinctive fish in the area in which it lives. The elongate lower pectoral fin rays are

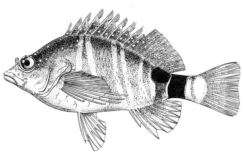

characteristic, as are the tufts on the membrane of the spiny dorsal fin, and on the edge of the nostril. The body is olive green, with darker green bars, and bright red spots anteriorly and on the dorsal fins. There is a black ring around the tail, and a dark spot at the base of the soft dorsal fin; the tail is light pinkish brown, white anteriorly.

Amblydoras   Doradidae
  hancocki 15 cm. (6 in.)
A thorny catfish widely distributed in ne. S. America, notably in the lowlands of the Amazon basin, Guyana, Bolivia, and Peru. In these areas it lives in ponds which are seasonally flooded during the rains, as well as in the creeks filled with fallen hardwood trees and their

branches. It is said to breed by depositing its eggs in a nest hollowed out of fallen leaves.

A strikingly heavy-bodied and thorny catfish, with the flattened head, 3 pairs of barbels round the mouth, and heavy spine on the gill cover, typical of the family. Sides with heavy, spiny scutes, dorsal fin high, adipose fin present. Brown with darker marks on the back, a light streak along the sides, and dull white on the belly.

Not a very active fish, usually close to the bottom and only active in the half-light. Occasionally kept in aquaria. **162**

AMBLYOPSIDAE
A small family of freshwater fishes confined to a region of the se. states of N. America. They are relatively slender fishes with a spindle-shaped body, a single dorsal fin, scaleless head, but irregularly arranged scales on the sides. Pelvic fins are small or absent.

Only 6 species are recognized, 4 of which live in limestone cave systems and are colourless and sightless. The other species have small eyes and live in swamps on the Atlantic coastal plain and inland.

In many ways they resemble the tooth carps. See **Amblyopsis, Chologaster, Typhlichthys**.

Amblyopsis   Amblyopsidae
  spelaea NORTHERN CAVEFISH
  10·5 cm. (4¼ in.)
Found only in the limestone caves of Indiana, and in Mammoth Cave, Kentucky. It is relatively common in the former State but in the Mammoth Cave it is now scarce. It is occasionally available as an aquarium fish.

Its body is slender, the dorsal fin is placed well back along the body, and the pelvics are small. The eyes are minute and covered by skin, but the head and body have many small papillae which are clearly vibration sensors, for the fish can detect the smallest displacement of water nearby. It is a pale yellowish pink overall in colour.

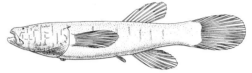

Parental care is accomplished by a curious method: the female carries the fertilized eggs in her capacious gill chamber for up to two months until they hatch.

Amblyrhynchotes   Tetraodontidae
  diadematus 30 cm. (12 in.)
A species endemic to the Red Sea from whence it was described by E. Rüppell as long ago as 1828. It is closely related to the Indo-Pacific species *A. nigropunctatus*, but like some Red Sea fish species, shows slight but distinct variation from the Indian Ocean form.

In the Red Sea it is the most common pufferfish to be seen in the area of the reef. It is distinguished by its plump, solid appearance and by the dense prickles over the whole body. The dorsal, anal and tail fins are short and rounded. A distinctive dark brown mask envelops the eyes and runs obliquely back and downwards to below the pectoral fin base; the lips are brown-ringed. **487**
A. honckenii 30 cm. (12 in.)
An Indo-Pacific species of wide distribution. It is well known on the African coast from the Cape to Zanzibar. The late Professor J. L. B. Smith, the noted S. African ichthyologist, reported it to be the most common African species of pufferfish, being found from the Cape to Natal in estuaries, and to be found in rock pools, and in coastal waters down to 110 m. (60 fathoms).

It is a rather slender-bodied pufferfish with no raised skin fold along the sides. The back and sides are almost prickleless but the belly is covered with small spines. The chin and lower jaw are prominent, and the teeth are large and sharp. Its coloration is variable, it has the ability to match its background colour to its surrounds and it often buries itself in soft sand or mud. Its back is greyish or sandy brown, often plain coloured, and the belly is yellowish or creamy. Its flesh is highly poisonous and it is not molested by predators including man.
A. nigropunctatus see under **A. diadematus**

AMERICAN
  CONGER see **Conger oceanica**
  EEL see **Anguilla rostrata**
  GOOSEFISH see under **Lophius piscatorius**
  JOHN DORY see **Zenopsis ocellata**

PLAICE see **Hippoglossoides platessoides**
SAND LANCE see **Ammodytes americanus**
SHAD see **Alosa sapidissima**

Amia Amiidae
calva BOWFIN, MUDFISH 91 cm. (3 ft)
The bowfin is confined to the freshwaters of e. N. America. It is perhaps best known from the Great Lakes region, all of which it inhabits except for Lake Superior; it also occurs from the Mississippi River system in Minnesota to the St Lawrence in Quebec, and from Florida to the Carolinas.

It lives in backwaters and quiet, still waters, often in densely overgrown and frequently oxygen-poor surroundings. It can utilize atmospheric oxygen by using its swim bladder as a lung. The males, which are usually smaller than females, can be distinguished by the spot at the upper base of the tail having a distinct orange border, which is lacking in the female (which also sometimes lacks the spot altogether). The male constructs a saucer-shaped hollow in shallow water in spring in which the eggs are laid. Between 20,000 and 70,000 eggs may be produced by a female; they take from 8–10 days to hatch, during which time the male guards them. The newly hatched larva has a large yolk sac which nourishes it while it remains attached, by the cement gland on its head, to the side of the nest. Until they attain a length of 10 cm. (4 in.), the young bowfins are herded and protected by the male.

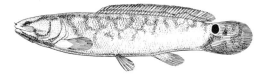

The bowfin is dull green, or greeny brown, becoming yellowish on the belly. It has little value as food or for sport, and as a predator it is usually regarded as a threat in angling waters.

AMIIDAE
Only one species of the family exists today, and it is often called a living fossil because its numerous fossil relatives were widespread for a long period. The sole living member of the family the N. American bowfin, *Amia calva*, is distinguished by its smooth, rounded cycloid scales, 2 bony plates under the throat – a primitive feature – and its heterocercal tail, the body axis turning upwards and making the upper part of the tail fin pronounced. The fossil relatives of the bowfin also possessed these features. See **Amia**.

Ammodytes Ammodytidae
This genus is widespread in the N. Hemisphere. The species illustrated has not been identified.
428
A. americanus AMERICAN SAND LANCE
21 cm. (8½ in.)
An inhabitant of the e. seaboard of America which occurs from Labrador S. to Cape Hatteras. It is closely related to the European sand eel *A. marinus*, as well as the Pacific *A. hexapterus*, and future research may show that all three are one variable species.

As with other sand eels, it lives on sandy bottoms both inshore and on offshore banks. It is a schooling fish which occurs in large shoals,

often burrowing into the sand. In common with the other species it is an important food fish for many of the commercially important species of the w. Atlantic.

Its body form is similar to that of the other members of the family; its distinction as a species depends on the number of vertebrae and fin rays, both rather variable features. It is brownish or blue-green above, silvery on the sides, and white on the belly.
A. hexapterus see under **A. americanus**,
    A. tobianus
A. marinus see under **A. americanus**,
    A. tobianus
A. tobianus SAND EEL 20 cm. (8 in.)
A European species, found from Iceland and Norway to s. Europe and in the Mediterranean. Its habitat is inshore waters from mid-tide level to a depth of 30 m. (16 fathoms) but it is frequently found on offshore banks within these depth ranges. It is always abundant on clean sandy bottoms in which it burrows with remarkable ability.

It is an important food fish for many of the valuable commercial species; herring, mackerel, and most gadoid fishes feed extensively on this sand eel. It is also fished for commercially as an industrial species, especially in the N. Sea.

It is closely related to the other European species, *A. marinus*, and to the N. Pacific *A. hexapterus*.

AMMODYTIDAE
The family of sand eels, or sand lances, a small group of marine fishes found widely in the N. Hemisphere. The members of the family are elongate thin fishes with pointed heads, the lower jaw being prominent, and long, soft-rayed dorsal and anal fins. All the species are superficially similar and uncertainty exists in the relationships and nomenclature of different populations of sand eels in various areas.

Although relatively few in number of species, the sand eels by their abundance make a vast contribution to the food chains of the oceans. They are eaten by many fishes and fish-eating birds, as well as themselves consuming large quantities of plankton. In some areas they are commercially exploited as a source of fish meal. See **Ammodytes**, **Hyperoplus**

Ammotretis Pleuronectidae
rostratus LONG-SNOUTED FLOUNDER
25 cm. (10 in.)
This species is widely distributed in s. Australian states – New South Wales, Victoria, S. Australia, Tasmania, and s. W. Australia. It is extremely common in parts of this range on soft bottoms, especially sand in relatively shallow water. It is the most important food fish amongst all the Australian flatfishes.

It is strikingly shaped, very similar to the soles, with the dorsal fin beginning right round in front of the mouth, on a hooked extension of the upper lip. The eyes are on the right side of the head, the pectoral fins are small and equal both sides, but the pelvic is much larger, and longer-based on the right (eyed) side than the left. It is dark brown without any particular markings.

Amphelikturus Syngnathidae
dendriticus PIPEHORSE 5 cm. (2 in.)
Found only in the tropical w. Atlantic at the islands of the Bahamas and Bermuda. Very few

specimens are known, and this fish is regarded as rare.

As its common name suggests it is half seahorse, half pipefish, for it has characters peculiar to both groups. Its tail is prehensile and can be curled round small anchorages, but it also has a tail fin. Its head is held at a slight angle to the body, less than in the seahorses but not straight as in pipefishes. In addition, the male's brood pouch is partially enclosed, another intermediate feature.

Its coloration varies from dark blotches on a light background to very dark. The most obvious distinguishing features of this species are the short snout and the tufts of branched skin on the head, back, and belly.

Amphichthys Batrachoididae
cryptocentrus SAPO BOCON 38 cm. (15 in.)
A toadfish of typically ugly appearance, which is found in the Caribbean and tropical Atlantic, from Panama, and Venezuela to Brazil, and in the Lesser Antilles. It is relatively common on rocky bottoms in shallow water.

It is dark brown, varying to yellowish brown in blotches above, whitish ventrally; rows of lateral line pores stand out as distinct pale dots. It has the body shape of a tadpole, with a flattened broad head and wide mouth, both fringed with loose flaps of skin. The body is stout in front, slender posteriorly, and quite scaleless. It is sold in the fish markets of the s. Caribbean.

AMPHILIIDAE
A family of small African catfishes, most of which live in fast-flowing rivers and rocky streams. The members of the family are distinguished by their scaleless bodies, short dorsal and anal fins, and a long, rather low, adipose fin. The dorsal fin does not have a sharp pointed bony spine; the first pectoral ray is thickened. The pectoral and pelvic fins are enlarged and broad. The head is broad and flattened, with 2 pairs of barbels on the lower jaw and one pair on the upper jaw. See **Amphilius**.

Amphilius Amphiliidae
platychir MOUNTAIN BARBEL 18 cm. (7 in.)
A small catfish found in the Zambesi River system and s. to the rivers of Natal. It is a hill-stream fish found at altitudes of 610–1829 m. (2000–6000 ft) above sea level, in rocky streams, where it feeds on insect larvae and other invertebrates. The broadened pelvic and pectoral

fins, with the flattened underside of the body, form a weak suction which helps the fish keep station in the running water. It lays eggs on the underside of stones, and the young at first look very like tadpoles.

This species is usually olive-yellow, spotted and blotched with darker brown.

Amphiprion Pomacentridae
biaculeatus SPINY-CHEEKED ANEMONE-FISH 16 cm. (6¼ in.)
Widely distributed in the tropical Pacific Ocean, and also found in the e. Indian Ocean. It is an attractive fish, in some areas rather common on reefs and coral grounds where it

lives in close association with sea-anemones. It is distinguished by the moderate development of 2 spines beneath the eye, and the very small scales on the body, a feature that was formerly considered sufficient to place it in a separate genus *Premnas*.

It is basically deep orange-brown with 3 vertical white black-edged bars, but the width and length of these bars varies considerably.
A. bicinctus ANEMONEFISH 10 cm. (4 in.)
A very distinctive Red Sea species. Records outside this sea are thought to be due to the former confusion of this species with *A. chrysopterus*, which is common in the Central Pacific.

It is bright orange except for 2 blue-white bars running across the sides, one just behind the eye, the other on the middle side. Some specimens have very dark areas on the head and upper sides, between the white bars.

It lives in the shallowest water close to the shoreline, the juveniles even in tidal areas. The association of this and other *Amphiprion* species with sea-anemones is well known. The copious mucus of their skin is thought to contain a substance that inhibits the discharge of the anemone's stinging cells. This species has a complex association with the anemone; the adults are stationary, living in pairs within one, or 2, anemones, which form the centre of their territory, even if the host moves over the rock. Juveniles, on the other hand, are found in groups within the shallow-water anemone *Radianthus koseirensis*, sometimes as many as 20 fish living together. They split up on reaching a length of 3–5 cm. (1¼–2 in.) and live singly or in pairs thereafter.

This anemonefish feeds on planktonic crustaceans and other small organisms which are taken during quick sorties from the shelter of the anemone. Its presence offers some protection to the anemone from predatory fishes, such as certain butterflyfishes, which are driven off by the anemonefish. **385**
A. chrysopterus see under **A. bicinctus**
A. melanopus 9 cm. (3½ in.)
An anemonefish which is confined to the e. region of the Indo-Australian archipelago and the islands of the w. Pacific. In this area it is relatively common and is found in association with the cluster-dwelling anemone *Physobrachia douglasi*. As with other *Amphiprion*-anemone associations both partners enjoy some form of protection from predators, but the fish feeds on a wide range of copepod and other crustaceans, algae, and marine worms. **386**
A. percula ANEMONEFISH 6 cm. (2½ in.)
A fish which is widespread in the w. and central Pacific, being found along the Queensland coast of Australia and commonly in Melanesia, including the Solomon Islands and New Guinea, as well as Micronesia and Polynesia.

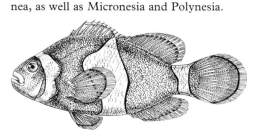

Its colouring is variable: the head, body and fins are bright orange to brownish, darker on the head and back than on the sides. The 3 white cross bands are narrowly edged with

black, and all the fins have white edges, with black bands.

It is an abundant fish on coral areas, living in association with the large sea-anemone *Stoichactis*. It spawns on the cleaned coral or rock close beside the anemone and both parents guard the eggs. **387**

Amphistichus   Embiotocidae
argenteus BARRED SURFPERCH
43 cm. (17 in.)
A Californian species found from Bodega Bay to Playa Maria, Baja California. As its name suggests, its typical habitat is the surf line along sandy beaches although occasionally it is found in deeper water offshore. It is known to feed mainly on small crustaceans and molluscs.

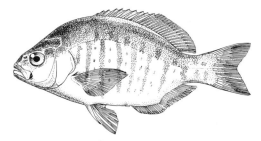

Like other surfperches it gives birth to living young. The adults mate in early winter or just before, and the young are born from March to July. The size of the brood varies with the size of the mother; one about 25 cm. (10 in.) long will produce about 25 young, but as many as 113 young have been reported.

It is a deep-bodied species, with light body colouring and golden or bronze bars running across the back and sides.

AMUR,
BLACK see **Mylopharyngodon piceus**
WHITE see **Ctenopharyngodon idella**
AMUR PIKE see **Esox reicherti**

ANABANTIDAE
The family of the climbing perches, a small group of freshwater fishes found in Asia (one species) and Africa (numerous species). Superficially looking like small perches, with numerous spines in both dorsal and anal fins, they differ in a number of ways, most notably in possessing an accessory respiratory organ above the gills in each gill chamber. The organ is much folded, labyrinthine even, and gives this group the popular name of labyrinth fishes.

For long this family was a hold-all for the whole group of labyrinth fishes which included the paradise fishes, the gouramis, and the fighting fishes, many popular aquarium species, but most have now been reallocated between the Belontiidae, Osphronemidae, and Helostomatidae, leaving only three genera in this family. See **Anabas**, **Ctenopoma**, **Sandelia**.

Anabas   Anabantidae
testudineus CLIMBING PERCH
25 cm. (10 in.)
A widely occurring Asiatic fish throughout the watercourses of S. China, the Philippines, throughout Indo-China, Malaysia, and the E. Indies to India and Sri Lanka.

It lives in all kinds of freshwater including large rivers but is most abundant in canals, ditches, lakes and ponds. Its supplementary respiratory organs, housed in a cavity above

the rather poorly developed gills, permit it to survive in anaerobic water. It is as likely to be found in stagnant swamps, where dissolved oxygen is minimal, as in open rivers. Its gills are so reduced in size that they are unable to obtain sufficient oxygen from the water – even in well-aerated water the fish must breathe air to survive.

Associated with its capacity for air breathing is its ability to progress over dry land. The habits of the climbing perch were first described as long ago as 1791 by a Danish naturalist Daldorff, who found one climbing the rough, much bracketed trunk of a Palmyra palm to a point 1·5 m. (5 ft) above ground and bathing in a stream of rainwater on the trunk. Since then the notion that it climbed trees as a way of life has been rooted. Various observers of the fish in its native habitat, while admitting the occasional possibility of this happening, have shown that its forté is to trek overland between one body of water and another. Numerous reports of *Anabas* being found well away from water, usually at night, and its wide distribution, show that this is its normal life style. Its mode of progression is chiefly by flexure of the tail against the ground while the pectoral fins and gill covers serve as props to support the body. On slopes it not infrequently tumbles downwards in undignified fashion, but its normal gait is jerky and uneven.

In many parts of Asia it is a widely used food fish. Its importance depends on several qualities, amongst them the hardiness of the fish, for they can be marketed alive if splashed with water from time to time. The flesh is of good edible quality.

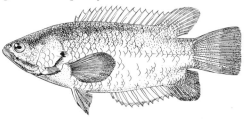

It is frequently kept in aquaria, although it does not make an especially good pet fish. It is often rather shy and pugnacious, requiring a large, well-planted aquarium and feeding indiscriminately on crustaceans, insects, and plant matter.

It is not conspicuously marked, adults being mostly greyish, or greenish-grey.

ANABLEPIDAE
A small family of live-bearing fishes from Central American and n. S. American freshwaters. Only 3 species are recognized in this family, none growing to exceed 30 cm. (12 in.).

All species exhibit one of the most remarkable adaptations seen in fishes. Each eye is divided across the centre by a band of opaque tissue which effectively divides the eye into 2 separate upper and lower 'eyes'. Not only is the cornea divided but the fish has separate retinas. This arrangement gives the fish simultaneous vision under water and in the air when it is cruising with the body just below, and the eye division just at, the water surface, as is its habit. The lens of the upper 'eye' is more rounded than that of the underwater 'eye', so that vision is as acute in air as in water.

The members of the family are rather slender-bodied, with a blunt head and terminal mouth. The dorsal and tail fins are rounded. The body is angled downward posteriorly, so that the far-backward dorsal fin and the tail fin remain below the water surface. This arrangement permits the fish to flit away at the slightest disturbance. Males have a modified anal fin which serves as an intromittent organ, for all species are live-bearers. See **Anableps**.

Anableps   Anablepidae
  anableps FOUR-EYES, FOUR-EYED FISH
30 cm. (12 in.)
Found in the coastal and estuarine waters of Central America and n. S. America, mainly in shallow, muddy coastal waters, estuaries, lagoons, and freshwater lakes. It lies near the surface of the water or partially covered by water on a muddy bank, watching for aerial and aquatic prey, and predators, by means of its unique double eyes.

The male tubular copulating organ, a modification of the anal fin, is able to be moved in any one fish to the left or to the right. The female's genital aperture is covered by an enlarged scale, free either on the left side or the right. It has been held that the consequence of this peculiarity is that only 'left-handed' males can mate with a 'right-handed' female. The dextral and sinistral ratios are nearly equal.

Its body colour is olive-green, paler on the belly. Four or 5 brownish stripes run along the sides.

It has been kept as a pet fish and has considerable interest on account of its habits. It requires a temperature of around 28° C, shallow water, and a high salinity. It has been bred in captivity producing at a time 1–5 young about 3–4 cm. (1¼–1½ in.) long at birth.

ANACANTHOBATIDAE
A small family of deep-water rays perhaps worldwide in their distribution in tropical waters but known only from the Gulf of Mexico, off South Africa, and in New Zealand waters. All have a long, pointed snout, the African and American species lack dorsal fins completely, while the New Zealand representative, *Arhynchobatis asperrimus*, has a single dorsal fin. For this reason it has been placed in a family on its own by some ichthyologists. See **Anacanthobatis, Springeria**.

Anacanthobatis   Anacanthobatidae
  americanus see under **A. marmoratus**
  longirostris see under **A. marmoratus**
  marmoratus 25 cm. (10 in.)
This deep-water ray was first described from off the Natal coast in 1924. It differs from other rays in that the pelvic fins are deeply divided into separate lobes. Its body is quite smooth, with small papillae on the upper surface. The snout is long and pointed; its tail short with a rudimentary fin, but no dorsal fins or spines are present along the tail. It is regarded as a rare fish.

Other species of *Anacanthobatis* have been recorded off the e. coast of tropical America. *A. americanus* from Guyana, Venezuela, and Panama, in depths of 183 to 732 m. (100–400 fathoms); *A. longirostris* from the Gulf of

Mexico and W. of the Great Bahama Bank, in 530–640 m. (290–350 fathoms). The latter species has a very long snout, and the eyes are placed about the centre of the disc; its tail is particularly short, and it is described as olivaceous or light purple on the back. Both are small rays, measuring up to 35 cm. (13 in.) and 50 cm. (19½ in.) respectively.

Anampses   Labridae
  caeruleopunctatus 30 cm. (12 in.)
A small wrasse which is found over a wide area of the tropical Indian Ocean and central Pacific. It was first described from the Red Sea, and occurs occasionally along the Indian Ocean coast of Africa but is, however, not abundant anywhere. It is sometimes found in the intertidal zone of reefs, but is more common in deeper water in lagoons.

The members of this genus are distinguished by the curious formation of the teeth: a single pair of enlarged teeth at the centre of each jaw point forward and jut out of the mouth, while above and below a pair of curved fang-like teeth point outwards. **397**

ANARHICHADIDAE
The family of sea catfishes or wolffishes, a group of mainly deepwater, supposed relatives of the inshore blennies (Blenniidae). They are found only in the temperate and boreal seas of the N. Hemisphere. They are long-bodied, rather large fishes, with a many rayed dorsal fin joined to the tail fin, and have a formidable array of pointed dog-like teeth in the front of the jaws, and blunt crushing teeth in the palate and sides of the jaw.

Some sea cats are fished commercially in the N. Atlantic but mainly as a side catch to more valuable food fish. Anglers occasionally catch one species or another, depending on the area, but they are hardly considered to be sporting fishes. See **Anarhichas, Annarhichthys, Lycichthys**.

Anarhichas   Anarhichadidae
  lupus CATFISH, WOLFFISH
120 cm. (47 in.)
A N. Atlantic species, found offshore from New Jersey and the Maine coast in the W., and the n. British coast in the E., and across the Atlantic at Iceland and Greenland. Mostly an inhabitant of moderately deep water, it is found at depths of 100–300 m. (55–164 fathoms), although to the N., young fish occur up to the shore zone.

It breeds in mid-winter, laying large clumps of eggs between stones and algae on the seabed. Its food consists mainly of echinoderms, crabs, and molluscs. It is locally fished for but is not an important food fish or commercially exploited species.

It is distinguished by its body form, and large dog-like teeth (a characteristic of the family). It is dark blue-grey, with a series of darker brownish bars along the back and sides.
A. minor SPOTTED CATFISH 2 m. (6½ ft)
A n. Atlantic species which occurs rarely as far S. as Scottish waters in the E., and to the Gulf of Maine in the W. It is distributed throughout the n. Arctic seas. It is found in water of moderate depth, most commonly from 100–250 m. (55–136 fathoms), although the extremes of its depth range are 25–460 m. (13–250 fathoms). It prefers muddy or fine sandy

bottoms. Breeding takes place in spring, the eggs being laid in clumps; the larvae after hatching are pelagic. Its food consists mainly of hard-shelled invertebrates, particularly echinoderms, crabs, and molluscs.

It is a moderately important commercial fish in n. waters, being taken both on lines and by trawling.

It is brownish yellow with large blackish brown spots on the back and sides.

Anarhichthys   Anarhichadidae
  ocellatus WOLF-EEL 2 m. (6½ ft)
A N. Pacific species found from s. California and along the coasts of Oregon, Washington, British Columbia to Alaska and the Aleutian Islands. In the N. of its range it lives in shallow water over rocky grounds, but to the S. it is found only in moderately deep water of 122 m. (70 fathoms).

It feeds on hard-shelled invertebrates, especially crabs, sea urchins, and occasionally molluscs. Small fishes have been found in its gut. Its maximum length is estimated at 2·4 m. (8 ft.), and weight in excess of 45 kg. (100 lb.); lengths of 2 m. have been confirmed. It spawns in the winter months, clumps of whitish eggs being laid in crevices in rocks, and guarded by the parents.

This wolf-eel is unmistakable in its area of distribution being long-bodied and slender, lacking pelvic fins, having the tail drawn out to a point without a distinct tail fin, and possessing massive teeth in the front of the jaws. Its colouring is variable, greys, brown or green with numerous large rounded black spots.

It is caught occasionally by anglers, and speared by divers off the Californian coast, but is not commercially exploited.

Anchoa   Engraulidae
  hepsetus STRIPED ANCHOVY 15 cm. (6 in.)
The striped anchovy is found in the w. Atlantic along the N. American coast from Nova Scotia and the Maine coast where it is rare, and abundantly from Chesapeake Bay s. to the W. Indies and Uruguay. It is abundant in shoals along coastal waters, being found as deep as 73 m. (40 fathoms), although mostly found in shallower water than this.

It spawns in spring. The eggs are pelagic and hatch within 48 hours at spring temperatures. As a young fish it eats copepods, but as it grows its diet changes and other small crustaceans, mollusc and worm larvae are eaten.

The striped anchovy is an important fish. A considerable number are marketed directly for food, but its greatest value is as a food staple for larger commercial fishes, such as the American seatrout. It is widely eaten by birds.

A typical anchovy in shape, rather elongate, with a large eye and protuberant snout, a large mouth with an underslung jaw. Its anal fin is rather short and its front lies beneath the end of the dorsal fin. It is a grey-green in colour, the back with dusky dots, but the most pronounced feature is the eye-wide brilliantly silvery stripe from head to tail.

A. lyolepsis DUSKY ANCHOVY 7·5 cm. (3 in.) This anchovy is widely distributed through the Caribbean and Gulf of Mexico, from the s. U.S. to Venezuela. Although taken in depths as great as 55 m. (30 fathoms), it is most often found close to the shore in shallow water. For this reason it is the most commonly encountered anchovy on Caribbean reefs. It is used locally as food, but is not heavily exploited; on the other hand it is an important forage fish for many of the larger commercial species of the area.

The dusky anchovy is rather slender, with a narrow head, and rather more pronounced snout than is usual in anchovies. Its back is olive-grey, and the sides have a distinct eye-wide silvery stripe from head to tail. The tip of the snout and the top of the head are dusky.

A. mitchilli BAY ANCHOVY 10 cm. (4 in.) The bay anchovy is found along the N. American Atlantic coast from Cape Cod, Massachusetts s. to Yucatan, Mexico. It occurs rarely in the Gulf of Maine. It is a typically inshore anchovy; although it may be found on open coasts at depths of 27–36 m. (15–20 fathoms), it is most abundant in estuaries and in sandy bays in much shallower water.

It spawns in early spring to summer; the eggs float at or near the surface. The bay anchovy, when young, feeds almost entirely on copepod crustaceans; as adult on copepods and large swimming crustaceans, but will then also eat young fish and other planktonic animals. In turn these anchovies are eaten by large numbers of other fishes, birds, and mammals, and are fished for to some extent by men for use as bait and for processing as food. Because of its abundance it is an important element in the food chains of these coasts.

Superficially it is much like other anchovies, with a large eye, and an enormous mouth, a protuberant snout and underslung jaw. Its dorsal fin is placed well along its back and its anal fin is long, originating in front of the dorsal fin. It is almost translucent, with a narrow silvery band between head and tail and dark spots on the back.

ANCHOVETA see **Engraulis ringens**
ANCHOVY see Engraulidae
ANCHOVY see **Engraulis encrasicolus**
ANCHOVY,
    AUSTRALIAN see **Engraulis australis**
    BAY see **Anchoa mitchilli**
    DUSKY see **Anchoa lyolepis**
    NORTHERN see **Engraulis mordax**
    STRIPED see **Anchoa hepsetus**
    TAPER-TAIL see **Coilia quadragesimalis**
    WISKERED see **Thrissocles setirostris**

Ancistrus Loricariidae
    cirrhosus VIEJA 14 cm. (5½ in.)
Widely distributed in n. S. America, from Trinidad, the Guyanas, through the Amazon region to Argentina (Rio de la Plata, and Rio Uruguay). This is a most striking fish, with heavy scute-like scales on the back and sides, the interoperculum (below the eye) freely movable and equipped with 11–13 curved spines. The anterior part of the head has many long fleshy barbels. The dorsal fin is high with a well developed roughened spine in front.

There are similar spines in the pectoral and pelvic fins; the adipose fin is distinct.

It is dark brown above with numerous whitish spots scattered over the head and body. The fins are dark-spotted, with a large blotch on the base of the anterior dorsal.

Occasionally kept as a pet fish.

ANEMONEFISH see Pomacentridae
ANEMONEFISH see **Amphiprion bicinctus, A. percula**
ANEMONEFISH,
    SPINY-CHEEKED see **Amphiprion biaculeatus**
ANGELFISH see Chaetodontidae
ANGELFISH see **Euxiphipops asfur, Heniochus acuminatus, Platax pinnatus, Pterophyllum scalare, Squatina squatina**
ANGELFISH,
    DEEP see **Pterophyllum altum**
    EMPEROR see **Pomacanthus imperator**
    FRENCH see **Pomacanthus paru**
    GREY see **Pomacanthus arcuatus**
    QUEEN see **Holacanthus ciliaris**
    ZEBRA see **Pomacanthus semicirculatus**
ANGELSHARK see Squatinidae
ANGELSHARK,
    ORNATE see **Squatina tergocellata**
    PACIFIC see **Squatina californica**
ANGLERFISH see Brachionichthyidae, Caulophrynidae, Centrophrynidae, Ceratiidae, Chaunacidae, Diceratidae, Gigantactinidae, Himantolophidae, Linophrynidae, Lophiidae, Melanocetidae, Neoceratiidae, Oneirodidae
ANGLERFISH,
    STRIPED see **Phyrnelox striatus**
    WARTY see **Sympterichthys verrucosus**

Anguilla Anguillidae
    anguilla EUROPEAN EEL 1·5 m. (5 ft.)
This eel is found along the whole of the European and N. African coastline, from the Arctic Circle to the Black Sea. It also occurs around and in island groups like the Canaries, Azores, Madeira, and Iceland. Throughout these areas it is known in freshwater of almost all qualities, except the most polluted, but much of the population lives in estuaries, and on the coast, especially to the N. of its range. When nearing sexual maturity the eels migrate to the sea and, it is believed, swim in the middle layers of the sea to the region of the Sargasso Sea in the central Atlantic. Here they spawn, and the adults die. After hatching, the young larvae drift in the surface waters back towards Europe, taking some 3 years to complete the journey. In coastal waters they undergo metamorphosis and transform to elvers, many of which then enter rivers to live in freshwater.

The eel larva is long and thin, rather like a willow leaf in shape, and transparent. Its head is pointed, the jaws strong with large teeth, and the eyes are large. The smallest observed larvae are 5 to 7 mm. in length; just before their arrival in continental waters they measure

from 60–80 mm. (2¼–3½ in.). These larvae have for long been known, and were originally thought to be adult fish which were placed in the genus *Leptocephalus*. Since the discovery that these fish are the larval forms of eels and certain related fishes, the name 'leptocephalus' has been used in a wider sense for larvae of the same general body form.

In freshwater the eel lives in a variety of habitats, mostly in rivers and smaller streams, but in still water also. It is mainly active in the night-time or twilight hours. It feeds on a very wide variety of insect and crustacean life, as well as many fishes. Large eels are reputed to eat ducklings and small aquatic mammals. There is little evidence that they harm trout and salmon, but occasionally estuarine eels feed on salmon smolts, and do compete in freshwater with the young of these fish for food and living space.

The eel is a valuable food fish in Europe, and weighs up to 9 kg. (20 lb.). It is fished for mostly in freshwater, particularly during the migration down river – the ripening, migrating adults are virtually never caught. Eels are often marketed alive, or smoked. The flesh is rich and nutritious. So valuable has the eel become that large quantities of elvers are exported from the w. coastline of Europe and used to stock inland waters which would be inaccessible. Nevertheless the potential eel stocks are as a whole underexploited in the British Isles.

A. australis SHORT-FINNED EEL 91 cm. (3 ft)
This eel is found in the coastal and fresh waters of New Zealand, s. Australia, and some of the islands N. of New Zealand. Freshwater eels are the same in general appearance the world over, but this species differs from most (and the other, larger New Zealand species, *A. dieffenbachi*) by having its dorsal fin placed further back, almost directly above the anal fin origin. It is brownish above, silvery beneath.

The short-finned eel is found in all freshwaters although the larger specimens prefer the deeper, slower rivers, and lakes. The young often hide under stones in the open river bed; larger specimens burrow into mud, or retreat under overhangs or obstructions. Like the other freshwater eels this species spawns in the sea, possibly over great depths in the ocean E. of Australia. The larvae are typical leptocephali which change in coastal waters into elvers which can be found in their millions at the mouths of large and small streams and rivers, as they begin their long ascent to freshwater. In S. Australia at least, development of weirs and barrages in the lower parts of rivers has seriously impeded this migration and here the short-finned eel has become relatively rare.

A. dieffenbachi see under **A. australis**
A. mossambica PALING, AFRICAN LONG-FINNED EEL 1·2 m. (4 ft) or more
A. mossambica is found in freshwaters along e. S. Africa, from the Cape to Mozambique, occasionally farther N. This eel is believed to breed in deep water in the w. Indian Ocean, somewhere off the Madagascar coast (as do the other E. African eels). During its larval life it

drifts inshore on the S. Equatorial Current, and later most of the larvae are carried S. of Madagascar to bring them along the continental coastline. Others stray and are swept n. outside the usual area for the species.

It is plain olive-brown to slate-grey, with a yellowish belly. Its plain colouring and long dorsal fin set it apart from its relatives in the area. It is the dominant eel in the lowland freshwaters of s. Africa.

Considerable confusion exists as to the maximum size this species attains. Some authors claim that 13·5 kg. (30 lb.) fish occur, and even credit specimens with 22·6 kg. (50 lb.) weight, while others cite a maximum of 4·5 kg. (10 lb.). There is little doubt that the larger fish are females, as the males of all freshwater eels are much the smaller.

A. nebulosa AFRICAN MOTTLED or INDIAN LONG-FINNED EEL 1·8 m. (6 ft)
This eel is found in the coastal waters of the Indian Ocean, and in the freshwaters of countries bordering that ocean. Two subspecies have been recognized, *A. nebulosa nebulosa* from the Indian sub-continent, and *A. n. labiata* from e. Africa and Madagascar. Both, however, are characterized by their olive-brown coloration, with pronounced darker brown mottling on the back and fins; the underside is yellowish. The dorsal fin origin is well in advance of the base of the anal fin, hence its name of long-finned eel.

This is an abundant eel throughout its range. The African subspecies has been found in Rhodesia, over 1610 km. (1000 miles) inland up river. It is the dominant eel of the warmer E. African freshwaters, and is found from the headwaters to the estuaries of the rivers. It is a large eel, females of 20 kg. (45 lb.) and more have been caught, and specimens up to 11·3 kg. (25 lb.) are common. It is believed to spawn in the deeps off the Madagascar coast, and that the leptocephalus larvae drift towards the Madagascar and E. African coast. The Indian subspecies breeds elsewhere in the Indian Ocean.

A. rostrata AMERICAN EEL 1·2 m. (4 ft)
The American eel is found along the coasts and rivers from W. Greenland and Newfoundland, s. along the Atlantic coast to the Gulf of Mexico and Panama. In the greater part of this range it is abundant in harbours, estuaries, river mouths, and coastal marshes, and upstream to the headwaters, except where barred by pollution or insurmountable obstructions.

In body shape it closely resembles the European eel; its lower jaw is longer than the upper, the pectoral fin is small and rounded, and the dorsal fin rises about one third of the way along the back. The only essential difference between this and the freshwater eel of Europe is that it has fewer vertebrae (usually 107) compared with the normal 114 or 115 in the European eel.

It is held to spawn in the w. central Atlantic, rather w. of the spawning area of the European eel. The larvae are typical leptocephali, but take only one year instead of 3 before they are drifted into inshore waters and undergo metamorphosis into elvers. They arrive on the Atlantic coast during spring and early summer.

The American eel has an affinity for still, muddy waters, although plenty are found on the coastline on rocky or even sandy bottoms. They are mainly nocturnal in habit, lying buried in the mud during the day. They feed on a wide variety of animal life, mainly crustaceans and fishes in estuarine waters, and on insect larvae as well in freshwater. The large eels scavenge for all kinds of refuse wherever they live. They attain a weight of 7·5 kg. (16½ lb.).

Although the American eel is as nutritious as the European eel it is not much appreciated as food. Except locally, it is not exploited commercially, and then only on a small scale.

ANGUILLIDAE
One of the best known of the families of eels, the anguillids comprise the freshwater eels of the world. They are widely distributed, and at some stages of their life history are found in all seas, except the polar seas and the e. Pacific. They all return to the sea to spawn.

All have a similar body shape, long and thin with a long dorsal fin which joins through the tail fin to the anal fin. Pectoral fins are present, but the pelvic fins are lacking. Females are usually much larger than males.

All the members of the family start life as thin transparent, leptocephalus larvae. See **Anguilla**.

ANISOCHROMIDAE
A small family of fishes known only from the w. Indian Ocean, along the coast of Kenya, and possibly occurring elsewhere in that area. Only a single, minute species is included.

It is closely related to the Pseudochromidae but differs in a number of ways, most notably in having only a single lateral line along the upper side, in lacking scales on the head, and in having the pelvic fins placed well forward, in front of the pectorals. It also has a total of 33 vertebrae, against 26 to 27 in Pseudochromidae. See **Anisochromis**.

Anisochromis   Anisochromidae
   kenyae 2·7 cm. (1 in.)
Known so far only along the coast of Kenya, from the Tanzanian border to about 3° S., 40° E., and at Pemba on the Tanzanian coast. It is abundant in pools in reefs around low-tide mark in some areas of this coastline. Its discoverer, the late Professor J. L. B. Smith, found females with 90–100 relatively large ripening eggs from October to December. He reported also that this species feeds on minute crustaceans.

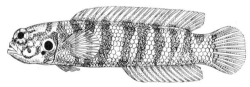

It is strikingly coloured, and the sexes are totally different in coloration. The females are mainly greenish, with lighter cross bars on the sides, and shining silvery spots. The adult males are mainly black with 10–11 lighter cross bars on the upper sides and many silvery spots. On top the head is orange-red, on the sides reddish with a silvery bar running from the eye. The dorsal and anal fins are red with a black edge, except that the front of the dorsal has a black blotch, edged ventrally with yellow.

Anisotremus   Pomadasyidae
   davidsoni SARGO 43·5 cm. (17¼ in.)
The sargo is the only member of the family on the Pacific coast of America N. of Mrxico. It ranges from Monterey Bay to Baja California and occurs in the n. Gulf of California. It has been introduced to the Salton Sea in California, where it is now an abundant gamefish.

In the coastal waters it occurs in kelp beds and on rocky and sandy bottoms in loose schools down to depths of 40 m. (22 fathoms). It feeds mostly on bottom-living crustaceans and molluscs.

It is distinguished in its area by the strong anal spines, the second spine being especially large, and particularly by its colour: a broad black bar extends from the front of the spiny dorsal fin vertically across the greenish blue back and the silvery sides.

The sargo is a popular sportfish on the Californian coast, taken mostly by anglers and spear-fishermen near shore. It is also landed by commercial fishermen, but is not an important market fish.

A. surinamensis BLACK MARGATE
61 cm. (2 ft)
Widely distributed from Florida and the Bahamas to Brazil, and found throughout the W. Indies and the Gulf of Mexico.

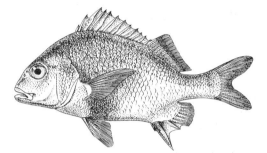

It is not commonly seen in definite schools, but rather in small groups in inshore waters on the larger patch reefs or steep-sloping rocky grounds. By day it is often found in caves; at night it forages for the crustaceans, fishes, and the long-spined sea urchins on which it feeds.

Silvery grey, with a dusky spot on each scale on the back apparently forming diagonal broken lines: lower anterior body dusky and the fins dark. The young fish have 2 black stripes and a dark spot at the base of the tail fin.

ANOMALOPIDAE
A small family of fishes related to the berycoids and pine-cone fishes. Like them they are rather deep-bodied, heavily scaled, and have a series of sharp spines in the dorsal and anal fins as well as branched rays.

The great interest in this family is the presence of a broad, elliptical bar beneath each eye, which shows dead white by daylight, but which at night glows brightly by means of luminous, symbiotic, primitive bacteria known as bacteroids. The means by which the light from these glands is controlled differs from species to species. They are often called lantern-eyes.

Two species occur in the seas of the E. Indies, and a third has been reported from the Caribbean. They are mostly small fishes. See **Anomalops, Photoblepharon**.

Anomalops   Anomalopidae
   kaptoptron 30 cm. (12 in.)
A fish found in the seas of the E. Indies, commonly in the area of the Island of Banda. Here it lives offshore in 4–5 m. (2–3 fathoms) of water, and is active at night, swimming in

shoals of 20–50 fish in open water just away from the reef.

Considerable interest centres around the curious light organ beneath each eye. This is an elongate, oval bar which shines deep white in daylight. Internally it is complex, filled with polygonal tubes richly supplied with blood vessels. The tubes contain symbiotic bacteria, which give off a bright light. Unlike luminous organs under the fish's control, bacteria-filled organs cannot simply be extinguished, so in this species the whole organ is rotated so that the luminous face is turned downwards and the black tissue of the back of the gland masks the light.

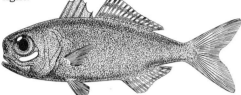

In life this fish swims around at night, mostly before the moon has risen, or on moonless nights, blinking its light rapidly as it swims. Whether the function of the light is to keep the members of the shoal in touch with one another, to attract prey, or simply to provide light to navigate by, is not known. The fishermen on the Island of Banda remove the luminous gland and use it as a lure on their hooks, apparently with good effect on their catches.

Anoplarchus   Stichaeidae
  purpurescens HIGH COCKSCOMB
20 cm. (8 in.)
Widely distributed along the w. coastline of N. America n. from California. It is found in the intertidal zone down to about 3 m. (10 ft) of depth. It feeds extensively on green algae supplemented with polychaete worms, crustaceans, and molluscs.

In late winter egg masses are laid along the shore between rocks or beneath shells, to be guarded and aerated by the female, which fans the eggs by constantly moving her body.

It is distinguished by a number of features, amongst them the absence of pelvic fins, the presence of a fleshy crest along the top of the head, and scales on the rear of the body only. Its coloration is variable, usually brownish, sometimes purple to black, with varied pattern of dark marks. The top of the head and belly in the male are yellowish. A light bar crosses the base of the tail fin.

Anoplogaster   Anoplogasteridae
  cornuta FANGTOOTH, OGREFISH
15 cm. (6 in.)
Widely distributed in the Atlantic and Pacific oceans in mid-water thought to be usually deeper than 610 m. (330 fathoms). Adults have been taken only in mid-water trawls, usually

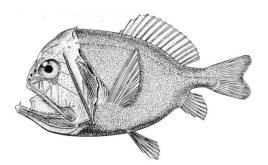

alive and trying to bite. It feeds on a variety of small fishes, squids, and crustaceans. It is uniformly dark brown to black. **216**

ANOPLOGASTERIDAE
A family which contains a single species of deep-water fish which is widely distributed in the Atlantic and Pacific oceans.

There is a considerable discrepancy between the body form of the juveniles and the adults. The adults have a big rounded head and rather deep body, with very large, fang-like teeth in the jaws, and a rough skin. The juveniles have several long spines on the head, lack fangs in the jaws, and have a triangular body section. At one time they were regarded as distinct types of fish, and the later described adults were long known as *Caulolepis longidens*. See **Anoplogaster**.

Anoplopoma   Anoplopomatidae
  fimbria SABLEFISH *c*. 1·2 m. (4 ft)
Distinguished by its coloration, slaty blue to black above, shading on the sides, with the lining of the gill cover conspicuously dark. Otherwise the slender body and the widely spaced dorsal fins are as characteristic as the rather small, broad mouth and blunt snout.

The sablefish ranges from the Bering Sea to Baja California, and is found as a bottom-living fish on the continental shelf, but the early stages are pelagic and are found in abundance near the surface far out in mid-ocean. Adults are usually rather sedentary, but some are known to make long migrations. Juveniles and adults are commonly found in a few metres of water in the N. of their range but to the S. they range down to 1463 m. (800 fathoms). They are usually found on bottoms of firm mud or blue clay.

The sablefish spawns in late winter and early spring.

It is a minor sporting fish along the Pacific coast, but only to the N. are large specimens found close inshore. All along the coast N. of s. California it is an important commercial species, caught mainly in otter trawls, sometimes on lines and in traps. The abundance of the species in deep water represents a still scarcely tapped resource. The flesh is fine-grained but very oily, and is thus usually smoked, though it is also tasty when fresh. The maximum size attained is arguable; record fish are said to attain 25 kg. (56 lb.), but most are around the region of 14 kg. (30 lb.).

ANOPLOPOMATIDAE
A family now regarded as comprising only the sablefish and the skilfish. They are related to the scorpionfishes and greenlings, and are distinguished from them by having the head without ridges or spines and by having only a single lateral line. They have 2 well separated dorsal fins.

The 2 members of this family are rather large fishes found only in the N. Pacific. The sablefish is of moderate commercial importance; the skilfish is seldom taken. See **Anoplopoma**, **Erilepis**.

Anoptichthys   Characidae
  jordani BLIND TETRA 8 cm. (3 in.)
This very interesting and totally blind fish is found in 3 caves of San Luis Potosi, Mexico, in streams and pools. It was first brought to notice in 1936 by a Mr Basil Jordan from specimens captured by local Indians. Its body shape is close to the genus *Astyanax* from which it differs most notably by having vestigial eyes, completely covered by skin and other tissue, and by the absence of pigment. Because of the exterior blood supply it is uniformly flesh coloured with a silvery sheen; the fins are slightly pink. Males are usually slimmer in build and more strongly coloured than females.

The blind tetra is a commonly kept aquarium fish and although it apparently prefers to live in poorly illuminated parts of the aquarium it does not need darkness. It is relatively easy to keep, being constantly on the move in search of food, but never bumping into the walls of the aquarium. It has frequently been bred in captivity, the pair spawning in usual characin fashion, with their ventral surfaces pressed together and shedding eggs near the surface, but which then scatter over the bottom. They hatch in 2–3 days at 26–27° C, and

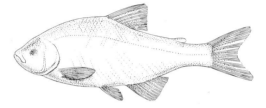

at first the fry have distinct and apparently normal eyes. After about 2 weeks the eyes become distorted, abnormal, and partially enclosed in tissue. Later in the growth of the young fish the rudimentary eyes shrink and become completely covered with tissue. In the mouth of one cave there have been found a few hybrids between this cavefish and the Mexican tetra, *Astyanax mexicanus*. **50**

ANOSTOMIDAE
This family is widely distributed in ne. S. America from Venezuela s. to the Argentine. Most of the known species are relatively small, and are best known to the public as aquarium fishes (the head-standers), but some attain a moderate size and are locally valued as food fishes.

Most of the members of the family are rather long-bodied with small heads and terminal mouths. Small mouths are a special feature, and they are variously specialized either with fleshy lips, minutely toothed, or with flattened scraping teeth in the lower jaw. Most are bottom-feeders: the majority feed on any small bottom-living organisms, although some are entirely plant eaters, and a very few are carnivorous. Many of the members of the family are head-standers, they feed, and spend most of their time, swimming obliquely head-downwards close to the bottom. Many species have lengthwise stripes. See **Abramites, Anostomus, Lemolyta, Leporinus**.

Anostomus   Anostomidae
  anostomus STRIPED ANOSTOMUS
14 cm. (5½ in.)
A very beautiful and attractive aquarium fish which is native to w. Guyana and in the upper

Amazon. Its coloration is distinctive with lengthwise dark stripes running from head to tail – one along the mid-line of the back, another from the mouth to the tail fin, passing through the eye, and a third from the throat to the tail fin. The bases of all the fins are reddish.

Its habit of swimming in small shoals in an oblique position with its head turned to the bottom leads to it being popularly classed with the headstanders. The shoal will glide in this position without effort, feeding on bottom-living organisms, or they lie still amongst roots and stems of plants near the surface where their lengthwise stripes render them nearly invisible. In Guyana these fish have been found living amongst the dense mass of fallen hardwood trees that lie in streams, to which habitat they appear to be very well adapted. **96**

A. gracilis 10 cm. (4 in.)
A slender-bodied fish which is found in the Amazon basin, having been reported from the Rio Guaporé and the Rio Negro. It does not appear to be very abundant and little is known about it.

In body form it is typical of the family, but its adipose fin is very small. **97**

A. trimaculatus THREE-SPOT ANOSTOMUS 20 cm. (8 in.)
This rather sturdy fish has a cylindrical but moderately deep body in front of the dorsal fin origin. The head is moderately pointed, but the tip of the snout is blunt. The body is covered with medium sized scales, and an adipose fin is present. It derives its name from the 3 rounded black blotches on the sides, one beneath the dorsal fin, another at the base of the tail fin, and the third mid-way between them.

This fish is native to the lower Amazon River and the rivers of Guyana. It has been imported as a pet fish but has not achieved great popularity. **98**

ANOSTOMUS,
STRIPED see **Anostomus anostomus**
THREE-SPOT see **Anostomus trimaculatus**

ANOTOPTERIDAE
A family containing only a single, widely distributed oceanic fish, *Anotopterus pharao*. The body is extremely elongate and slender, soft, and flexible, with extremely light bones. The head is large, with a long pointed snout, large jaws and many small teeth except in the palate where they are very large and directed forwards. Fins are greatly reduced except for the tail fin, and the dorsal fin is entirely lacking although it has a small adipose, rayless fin on the back near the tail. This family appears to be most closely related to the Alepisauridae and the Paralepididae. See **Anotopterus.**

Anotopterus   Anotopteridae
pharao DAGGERTOOTH, JAVELINFISH
107 cm. (42 in.)

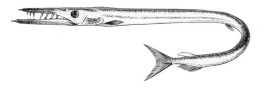

This rather fragile fish has an antitropical distribution, for it is found in temperate and sub-polar seas in both hemispheres but not in the tropics. It is distinguished by its large size, greatly elongate form, and pointed jaws, with the lower jaw especially long and tipped with a hard pointed process, and, particularly, by the lack of a rayed dorsal fin. It is dusky silver in colour with black fins; a sexually mature specimen has been described as blackish with a silvery belly.

The daggertooth is a predator living near the surface of the open seas. Most of the specimens for which data on capture are available were taken between 37–275 m. (20–150 fathoms) deep. However, relatively few have been captured by nets, most of the specimens known to science having been recovered from the gut of other fishes, amongst them tunas, salmons, and sharks – none of which are thought to forage in very deep water.

When mature, *Anotopterus* probably lives in much greater depths, but it is a measure of how little is known about this fish that only one sexually ripe fish has ever been described; it was caught in deep water off Madeira in 1961. Surprisingly for a fish which is renowned for its massive teeth, this mature daggertooth was actually toothless. It is suggested that the demands made on the fish by the ripening gonads mean that teeth are not replaced as they fall out, and that the whole skeleton becomes decalcified to some extent. The daggertooth is hermaphrodite, a condition found in a number of its deep-sea relatives.

It feeds on small fishes and appears to eat whatever is locally abundant, including its own young. When mature it seems to cease feeding.

ANSORGE'S CHARACIN see **Neolebias ansorgei**
ANTARCTIC COD see Nototheniidae
ANTARCTIC COD, GIANT see **Dissostichus mawsoni**

ANTENNARIIDAE
The family of frogfishes, an odd group of rather sedentary fishes, which have exchanged the ability to swim and manoeuvre swiftly for cryptic colouring and subtle feeding behaviour. Most species are bottom-living, lying amongst the rocks, coral, sea weeds, or attached animal growths, in perfect concealment. They entice their prey to within striking distance by means of a very effective small lure, with fleshy filaments, at the end of a detached ray on the snout.

They are widely distributed in tropical and warm seas throughout the world. All are stout-bodied and have a scaleless, gelatinous warty skin, which is loose and envelops the fins in loose folds. The pectoral fins project at an angle and have an elbow-like joint. These fins move around the bottom by crawling. One type *(Histrio)*, however, lives primarily in floating sargassum. See **Antennarius, Histrio, Phrynelox.**

Antennarius   Antennariidae
In addition to the 2 species illustrated in colour, an unidentified frogfish is shown. **184**
A. hispidus TOADFISH, FROGFISH, FISHING-FROG 20 cm. (8 in.)
Widespread in inshore waters in the Indo-Pacific, from s. Africa to the Philippines and Japan. In colour it is variable.

It is found from the shore-line down to depths of around 92 m. (50 fathoms). **182**

A. multiocellatus LONGLURE FROGFISH
15 cm. (6 in.)
This frogfish is found in the tropical w. Atlantic, and has been reported from Bermuda, the Bahamas and Florida, S. to the lesser Antilles and throughout the Caribbean. It is the most common frogfish in the W. Indies.

It is distinguished by the extreme length of the 'fishing rod' on the snout, which has a small tufted lure at its tip. The colouring is variable, from dark brown to drab yellow, with a light saddle behind the dorsal fin, and another across the nape. It has scattered white-ringed black spots on the back.

This frogfish has been described as gliding slowly over the bottom, and with its stout dorsal spines bent on opposite sides of its body. Its resemblance to a moving gastropod mollusc is noticeable, and may be due to deliberate mimicry. It feeds on small fishes and occasionally on crustaceans.

A. oligospilos 18 cm. (7 in.)
Occurs mainly in the tropical Indo-Pacific, but has been found as far W. as the se. coasts of Africa. It is a deep-bodied, portly frogfish with, on the snout, a long fishing rod tipped with a large much-branched lure. The second and third dorsal rays are long but enclosed in thick, gelatinous skin.

The distinguished S. African ichthyologist, the late J. L. B. Smith, reported a 15 cm. (6 in.) frogfish of this species which contained 2 10 cm. (4 in.) fish packed neatly side by side, head to tail inside its stomach; a mute testimony to its capacity for food and to the efficiency of its fishing lure. **183**
A. scaber SPLITLURE FROGFISH
11 cm. (4½ in.)
Widely distributed in the American Atlantic from New Jersey to s. Brazil, including the Gulf of Mexico. It occurs in shallow water on differing habitats including mud bottoms. In colour very variable, 2 main varieties, one almost entirely black, the other light brown with bold black streaks and spots. The latter colour phase is most common. The lure at the tip of the first dorsal spine is deeply forked.

This species has been reported to inflate itself by filling its stomach with air or water.

Anthias   Serranidae
A variable genus. Besides those mentioned below, two unidentified species are shown. **260, 261**
A. anthias 24 cm. (9½ in.)
Found in the Mediterranean, and in the Atlantic from Madeira and the N. African coast to Biscay. It is a moderately deep-water species found below 31 m. (17 fathoms) amongst rocks where small shoals hover just inside the entrances of crevices and caves. It feeds on small fishes and spawns in the spring. **262**
A. squamipinnis 10 cm. (4 in.)
A most strikingly beautiful Indo-Pacific fish. It is widely distributed in the Red Sea, and also occurs on the E. African coast and elsewhere in the central tropical Indo-Pacific. Mainly it frequents coral areas, where small shoals adopt a home range by a coral head, beneath which these fish find shelter when threatened. This species exhibits the phenomenon of sex change – the shoals are composed of female fish, and one large male fish. If the male dies, or is removed, the most 'senior' female, in terms

of dominance, then changes sex and in a week or two becomes a fully functional male. **259**

Antigonia Caproidae
A very widely distributed genus. The species illustrated is as yet unidentified. **225**
A. capros 17 cm. (6¾ in.)
An oceanic species widely distributed in the Atlantic and the Pacific oceans. Similar fishes belonging to this genus, and clearly closely related, are also known in these and the Indian Ocean. They are mostly found in depths of 55–914 m. (30–500 fathoms), and from the frequency that they are taken in bottom trawls they evidently live close to the sea bed.

It is a deep-bodied, reddish fish, with a small protrusible mouth and a moderate eye. The first dorsal fin is high with strong spines, the anal fin has 3 strong spines; the dorsal and anal fins are otherwise composed of numerous, rather low soft rays. Body scales are small, numerous, and rough-edged.

Antimora Eretmophoridae
rostrata BLUE HAKE 56 cm. (22 in.)
A N. Atlantic deep-sea cod found from the Gibraltar area in the E., and best known from s. Baffin Island to off Cape Hatteras. It has also been reported from the S. Atlantic, Pacific and Indian oceans, in part at least on the basis of related species. It is found between 550–1280 m. (300–700 fathoms), but has been reported at 2660 m. (1453 fathoms). It is believed to be one of the more plentiful fishes in waters of 640 m. (350 fathoms) and more off the American coast, but is less abundant elsewhere.

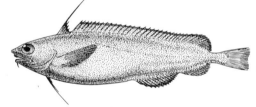

The species of this genus are quite distinctive owing to the long front ray in the first dorsal fin, and the sharply pointed rather flattened snout. It is deep violet or blackish brown above and below, with a dark mouth and gill chamber.

Aotea Aoteidae
acus Length not known
This species was described in 1926 from a single specimen taken from the stomach of a snapper in Cook Strait, New Zealand. It was assumed to be a marine fish and possibly a deep-water inhabitant. No further specimens seem to have

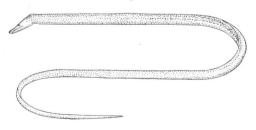

been recorded. The original specimen was much damaged with abrasions and swellings apparently caused by parasites; it had no fins. It was elongate with a cylindrical, scaleless body, pointed snout and wide mouth.

AOTEIDAE
A family erected to contain a single species based on a badly damaged specimen from New Zealand waters. It seems more than likely that this family is based on no more than a damaged and poorly preserved specimen of one of the less common Pacific eels. See **Aotea**

Apeltes Gasterosteidae
quadracus FOUR-SPINE STICKLEBACK
6 cm. (2½ in.)
Found only on the e. coastal region of N. America, from the Gulf of St Lawrence and Newfoundland s. to Virginia. It occasionally occurs in freshwater but is principally a marine fish. Its habits resemble those of other sticklebacks, spawning in late spring and early summer in a nest built and guarded by the male.

Identification is possible by the presence of 3 or 4 spines on the back, inclined alternately to left and right, and by the first spine of the main dorsal and the anal fin being joined to the soft rays. It is mainly olive-brown above, darker mottled, and silvery below; spawning males have bright red pelvic fins.

Aphanius Cyprinodontidae
dispar 8 cm. (3 in.)
A toothcarp widely distributed in the coastal regions bordering the n. E. African coast and the Indian Ocean coast of the Middle E. It has been recorded in Ethiopia, the Red Sea, S. Arabia, Iraq, and Persian Gulf, living in freshwater and saline pools near the sea. A population of this form is also found in pools near the Dead Sea.

A lively little fish which is widely kept in aquaria. It thrives best in a warm (20–25° C) slightly brackish milieu, and breeds freely, the eggs being deposited on plant leaves. They hatch in 10–14 days. The adults eat both live food and algae; the young feed on algae and diatoms.

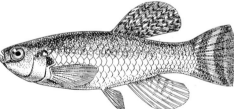

The male is brownish blue with numerous silvery blotches on the sides, and a row of vertical dark bars towards the tail and on the tail fin. The fins are bluish. The female is bluish grey with a similar row of dark bars on the sides.

Aphanopus Trichiuridae
carbo BLACK SCABBARD FISH
110 cm. (43 in.)
An elongate, dark-skinned fish which has long been known only in the N. Atlantic Ocean from the Canaries, Madeira, N. to Iceland, but has recently been found in California. Off Madeira, where it is one of the most important food fish, it is captured in quantity and regularly in a fishery employing long baited lines. It is also

commercially exploited off Portugal in deep water. To the N. of Biscay it has long been regarded as a rare fish, quite incorrectly, but it lives rather deeper than most of the commercial trawlers operate, and recent deep experimental trawling has produced numerous specimens.

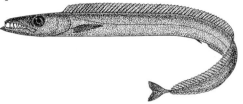

It is distinguished by its elongate, compressed body, with the dorsal fin running from near the head to the small tail fin. The relatively massive spine in front of the anal fin is usually depressed. When living it has a most beautiful coppery colouring, with iridescent sheen but, once stale, is dull black. Trawl-caught fish are usually stripped of their skin and are white.

It is a deep-water fish, usually found in 183–640 m. (100–350 fathoms), probably coming nearer to the surface at night. It does not live close to the sea bed and is usually found at least 100 m. (54 fathoms) off the bottom. It feeds on a wide range of fishes and squids, and occasionally eats shrimps.

APHREDODERIDAE
A family that contains a single species found on the Atlantic coast drainage of N. America. It is a slender-bodied fish, with a single, high and many-rayed dorsal fin, a rounded tail fin, and small anal. The body is covered with small toothed scales; the lateral line is usually incomplete.

The pirate perch shares with the Amblyopsidae the curious feature that the vent, placed near the anal fin origin in the young, moves forward to a position on the throat in the adult. See **Aphredoderus**

Aphredoderus Aphredoderidae
sayanus PIRATE PERCH 13 cm. (5 in.)
This small fish is found in the e. U.S., in freshwater along the coastal plain from New York to Texas, then n. through the Mississippi basin to the Great Lakes drainage of s. Michigan. It is the single known member of its family. Its high dorsal fin has 3 slender spines and 10–11 branched rays. It has rounded fins and a large oblique mouth.

It is olive-green to brownish, with dark spots and flecks that fall into broken lines on the sides. The underside is yellow-brown, and the tail has 2 small stripes across the base before the fin.

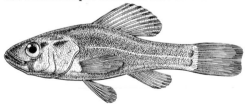

In nature this fish lives in ponds and lakes with deep organic mud and vegetation on the bottom. It feeds on insect larvae, crustaceans, and small fishes.

Aphyocharax Characidae
rubripinnis BLOODFIN 5 cm. (2 in.)
The bloodfin is a native of the Paraná River in

Argentina. It is a slim-bodied characin, yellowish silver in colour, with blood-red anal, pelvics, and lower lobe of the tail fin; to a lesser extent the dorsal fin is bright red. The males tend to be rather more brightly coloured than the females.

Deservedly popular as an aquarium fish, it is peaceful and undemanding, and swims in large, active shoals. It eats all kinds of aquarium fish food and can be bred in captivity in a large, well planted aquarium at a temperature close to 26° C. The eggs are shed at random over the bottom. The young hatch in about 30 hours and at first hang, inactive, near the surface on plants. They soon begin to feed on small animal food and grow quickly.

APHYONIDAE

A small family of ophidioid fishes (related to, and by some thought to be part of, the family Ophidiidae), mostly found in moderate to great depths in all the tropical and warm-temperature oceans. They are rather elongate, slender fishes with loose skin, and are so nearly transparent that the pigmented body cavity shows through. The eyes are small, usually weakly pigmented and often not visible through the outer skin, beneath which they lie. The members of the family are all viviparous, producing young almost fully formed. Many are bottom dwellers, some are believed to be pelagic. See **Barathronus**

Aphyosemion Cyprinodontidae
arnoldi ARNOLD'S LYRETAIL 6 cm. (2½ in.)
This lyretail originates in the general area of the Niger delta, W. Africa. Its rather wide range and variable colouring have lead to its being divided into a number of local races, and selective breeding in the aquarium has heightened many of the characters. It is one of the most brightly coloured species and is very popular as a pet fish. The males have well developed streamers from the outer rays of the tail fin, and their dorsal and anal fins are large.

Of the colour varieties described, one of the most common is brownish red on the back, steel blue on the sides with large blotches, the tail fin shading to greeny blue with red marks and submarginal red band. The female is brownish olive with red spots.

The males are quarrelsome in captivity, but pairs breed prolifically, producing 15–25 eggs per day during the season. These hatch in 35–40 days and are not greatly delayed by dry weather.

A. australe CAPE LOPEZ LYRETAIL
6 cm. (2½ in.)
Found in swamps and small ditches around Cape Lopez in the Gabon, and the Ogowe delta. This species has been imported to Europe as a pet fish several times and from the resulting stock numerous aquarists' varieties have been bred.

It is a very beautiful fish, the male being especially brightly coloured, red spotted on a reddish background. The dorsal and anal fins are large, and the tail fin is produced with 2 pointed lobes. The edges of the tail and anal fins are yellowish white. The fins of the female are not greatly expanded. **195**
A. batesi 5 cm. (2 in.)
Found in W. Africa, particularly in the wooded plateau of e. Cameroon and n. Gaboon. It seems to be restricted to swamps and similar

habitats, in conditions of mainly mud and minimal water.

As with other related cyprinodonts the males are brightly coloured, the females rather drab. The males have considerable red pigment irregularly distributed in spots, and thin vertical red lines. The fins are moderately elongate, the tail fin with 2 long streamers.

This species, despite its relatively attractive appearance, has not been introduced as an aquarium fish. **196**
A. calabricum see **Roloffia liberiensis**
A. gardneri STEEL-BLUE APHYOSEMION
5 cm. (2 in.)
This species is widely distributed in central W. Africa. Since it was first collected at Okwoga, the headwaters of the Cross River, it has been found in the lower Niger drainage in many places, although there has been some confusion about the limits of variability of this form.

It is a brilliantly coloured fish, the male especially so. It is basically greenish, the body with red spots and blotches. The dorsal, anal, and tail fins are heavily red-spotted and have a yellow outer stripe. The female is brownish.

It has long been popular as an aquarium species, and is lively and undemanding. The eggs are laid on the bottom and hatch after 20 days. It is described as a semi-annual species. **197**
A. lujae 5 cm. (2 in.)
A native species of the Congo, the original specimens having been collected at Kondue, Sankuru River, Kasai. Other specimens have been found in the forests of the Central Congo, but there seems to be some doubt as to whether this species is distinct from others in the area.

The male is brilliantly coloured, with rather high dorsal, anal and tail fins. The basic colour is pale green, with numerous carmine spots on the back and head, forming intense red stripes on the sides. The anal fin is red with a bright yellow edge. The female is dull green, with small, deep red spots on back, sides, and fins. **198**
A. walkeri 5 cm. (2 in.)
Found in w. Africa, originally in the Bokitsa Mine area of Ghana, and later in Ghana and the s. Ivory Coast. It lives in pools and swamps in the humid forests of this area. *A. walkeri* is one of the rivuline toothcarps which is almost an annual fish; the eggs do not hatch for some time after they are laid, an adaptation to dry season periods when the drought might kill off the adults. This is, however, even more marked in other related species.

The males in particular are beautiful fishes, with a rather high dorsal and anal fin and a long tail with elongate outer rays. **199**

APHYOSEMION, STEEL-BLUE see
Aphyosemion gardneri

Apistogramma Cichlidae
agassizi AGASSIZ'S DWARF CICHLID
7·5 cm. (3 in.)
Widely distributed in the Amazon basin s. to Bolivia.

It is a slender-bodied species with a long dorsal and anal fin, both with long streamer rays at the end of the fin, especially pronounced in the male. A dark stripe runs along the body, a second line runs from the mouth to the angle of the gill cover.

A popular aquarium fish although rather sensitive to poor conditions. It spawns under stones or inside cavities, the eggs are cherry-red, and the female undertakes the care of the eggs and young when they hatch. She leads them around the aquarium in a dense shoal in a very attractive fashion.
A. ortmanni ORTMANN'S DWARF CICHLID
8 cm. (3 in.)
A cichlid native in w. Guyana and the central Amazon Basin.

As with other members of the dwarf cichlid group, the body is rather slender and only moderately compressed, while the second dorsal, anal, and pelvic fins are elongate. The colouring is variable, but the markings of dark lengthwise stripes on the belly are said to be diagnostic. There is an elongate dark spot on the tail at the base of the fin, and a dark stripe through the eye onto the cheek.

This species has for long been a popular aquarium fish. **355**

Apletodon Gobiesocidae
microcephalus SMALL-HEADED
CLINGFISH 4 cm. (1½ in.)
A tiny clingfish found so far only in isolated localities on the w. Scottish and English Channel coasts, and from the Mediterranean. Its range is probably continuous in suitable habitats but it is rarely captured.

Found on the lower shore line, and below low-tide mark down to 25 m. (14 fathoms), it is usually encountered under stones or in the holdfasts of the large kelps. It breeds in the hollow 'root system' of these seaweeds, the eggs being laid inside the cavity, in spring and summer.

It is usually greenish, mottled with reddish brown; the males have a reddish spot on the dorsal and anal fins, and under the throat. The dorsal and anal fins are short (5–6 rays) and free of the tail fin.

APLOACTINIDAE

The fishes of this small family, which occur only in the southern Pacific, are distinguished by the relatively few rays in the pelvic fins, by the absence of scales (the skin being covered with velvety papillae or skin flaps), and by having few or no spines in the anal fin. The head bones bear knob-like ends, and the dorsal fin, which has sharp spines in front, is long and usually continuous. They are closely related to the stonefish family Synanceiidae. See **Aploactisoma**.

Aploactisoma Aploactinidae
milesii VELVETFISH 23 cm. (9 in.)
Well-known from the s. coasts of Australia and found as far n. as Victoria and New South Wales. It lives in shallow water, amongst weedy areas and is relatively common.

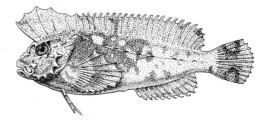

The velvetfish is basically dull brown with darker spots, and with the tips of the papillae on its skin reddish or orange. It can be easily recognized by the velvety appearance of these papillae, which cover the body skin. The dorsal fin is high in front, much like a cockatoo's crest, and the head is covered with bony knobs.

Aplocheilichthys   Cyprinodontidae
  pelagicus 5 cm. (2 in.)
A singularly interesting toothcarp which is found only in Lake Edward, Uganda. Most members of this genus, and the family, are inhabitants of small pools, streams, or the edges of larger waters where they are usually found close to the bottom or in vegetation. This species, however, is pelagic and inhabits the surface layers of the large, open lake and is even said to spawn in open water. Its food consists of small planktonic crustaceans and insect larvae.

It is a long slender fish with numerous small scales. Its coloration is described as bright yellow with a dark streak down the side; the tail fin is edged with black.

Aplocheilus   Cyprinodontidae
  blocki DWARF or GREEN PANCHAX
5 cm. (2 in.)
Found in Indian freshwaters, this fish has been reported from Cochin, Madras, and Sri Lanka. It lives in stagnant, shaded waters under the cover of trees. It is the smallest member of the group in Asiatic freshwaters.

The males are brightly coloured, yellowish green with rows of yellowish or red spots, the belly bright green. The fins are bright yellow with reddish spots. The female is less brightly coloured. In body form, this panchax is similar to other members of the family, but the dorsal fin has few rays and is high, whereas the anal fin is long-based and elongate at the tip.

It has been imported as an aquarium fish for many years, and thrives in a well-planted tank shielded from direct sunlight. Spawning is preceded by an attractive courtship, the male dancing and bobbing around the female. The eggs are laid on fine-leaved plants, and hatch in 12–14 days.
A. panchax BLUE PANCHAX 8 cm. (3 in.)
Widely distributed through India, Sri Lanka, Burma, Thailand, Malaya, and Indonesia. In this vast area numerous local populations exist, some of which are distinct in minor ways from populations elsewhere and have been given subspecific names; other names have been proposed for aquarium bred varieties. In India it is widely distributed and is found in the Indus, Ganges, and Bramaputra drainages; in Thailand it is equally widespread being found in brackish pools in coastal waters, and in the central regions in drains, ditches, and pools connected to rivers. In all these areas it is a valuable predator on the larvae of the malaria-bearing mosquito.

It is variably coloured, the males are bluish to grey-yellow, the back darker, the belly yellowish. The dorsal fin has a black patch in its centre base; the tail fin is whitish-edged.

It is a relatively popular aquarium species, undemanding and easily bred, but the males tend to be pugnacious. In Thailand they have been kept as second-rate fighting fishes.

Aplochiton   Aplochitonidae
  zebra TROUT 28 cm. (11 in.)
A widely-distributed trout-like fish found in the freshwaters of Patagonia and the Falkland Islands. This species was first collected by Charles Darwin in the latter islands from a freshwater lake close to the sea and connected to it by a small brook. To some extent it appears to be migratory as other specimens have been caught in the sea.

The most striking feature of this fish is the bold vertical, dark stripes running across the back and upper sides. These tend to fork or be interrupted towards the tail, but over the front half of the body are remarkably zebra-like. Its coloration is brownish green above, pale grey-green on the sides fading to silver ventrally. The head is orange-brown above, the gill covers pale yellow with an overlying silvery sheen. The body is scaleless.

It is said to be good eating, and in the Falklands is known as trout. There is reason to fear that the release of N. Hemisphere salmonids (*Salmo* spp.) into Falkland Island freshwaters may adversely affect this native species.

APLOCHITONIDAE
A small family confined to temperate waters in the S. Hemisphere. The species inhabit rivers and occasionally lakes, as well as coastal waters, in the s. tip of S. America, s. Australia including Tasmania, and New Zealand. Most are migratory, living in the sea and entering rivers to spawn.

They are all small fishes, mostly less than 30 cm. (12 in.) long, which superficially resemble the N. Hemisphere trouts. Like them, they have an adipose fin, moderately stout bodies with a blunt snout. Teeth in the jaws are very small, or absent. Some have scaleless bodies, others are fully scaled. See **Aplochiton, Prototroctes**.

APLODACTYLIDAE
A small family of moderate-sized fished found mostly on the coasts of s. Australia and New Zealand, although some occur in the e. S. Pacific off Chile and Peru. Probably represented by fewer than 5 species.

In many respects they resemble the hawk-fishes (family Cirrhitidae) and the morwongs (family Cheilodactylidae), notably in having thickened and unbranched lower pectoral fin rays. The members of the family have numerous spines in the dorsal fin, and from 16 to 21 soft rays. The jaw teeth are flattened incisors, or have 3 flattened cusps. They have little value as food or sporting fish. See **Dactylosargus**.

Aplodinotus   Sciaenidae
  grunniens FRESHWATER DRUM
1·2 m. (4 ft)
As its name indicates, this is one of the few members of the family that inhabits fresh water. It occurs in N. America from s. Saskatchewan and Ontario, through the Mississippi drainage to the Gulf of Mexico, and as far S. as Mexico and Guatemala. It is widespread in the Mississippi system.

A large fish, it attains a weight of 23 kg. (50 lb.) where conditions are favourable, but mostly weighs around 7 kg (15 lb.). It lives in deep pools of large streams, in the main channel of rivers, and in lakes and reservoirs. Spawning is in May and June, the adult fish gathering at the surface, often with their backs breaking the water, offshore in lakes. The eggs are small and pelagic and are quickly distributed through the water.

The freshwater drum feeds on bottom-living invertebrates, principally molluscs, but crustaceans and insect larvae are also eaten. It is said to move into shallow water to feed at night.

Often taken by anglers but the flesh is not of high grade, and is only eaten locally. It has a certain interest to anglers on account of its size, and because it is one of the few freshwater fishes that make audible sounds. Its earstones (otoliths) are often kept as curios, called 'lucky stones' (perhaps because they bear an L-shaped groove). These earbones are frequent in ancient habitation sites of American Indians, sometimes distant from the range of the species. Judging from the size of the bones, the species primevally must have attained a very much greater weight, estimated as high as 91 kg. (200 lb.). Such large size, plus the loud grunting noise, quite audible in a canoe, is thought to have induced legends by the aborigines.

Apodocreedia   Creediidae
  vanderhorsti 10 cm. (4 in.)
A little known fish found so far only at Inhaca Island, Delagoa Bay, on the Indian Ocean coast of s. Africa. It has been found buried in sand between tide marks.

Its body form is distinctive, the moderately large scales especially so, each scale being 3-lobed. The lateral line runs low along the body. It is silvery white.

Apogon   Apogonidae
  lachneri WHITESTAR CARDINALFISH
6 cm. (2½ in.)
Known from the Bahamas and Florida to Curaçao, British Honduras, and Mexico. It is a common fish in depths of 15–61 m. (8–33 fathoms), but is not found in shallower water often. **285**
A. maculatus FLAMEFISH 10 cm. (4 in.)
A common species in the w. Atlantic, where it occurs from Bermuda and New England s. to Brazil, and throughout the Caribbean and Gulf of Mexico. It is in places the most common of the W. Indian cardinalfishes.

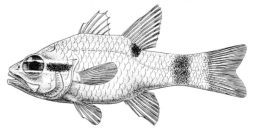

It is found from just below the shoreline to a depth of nearly 128 m. (70 fathoms). In daylight it keeps to shaded crevices, small caves, or under overhangs, but it becomes active around the reefs at night. The male carries the egg mass in its mouth (this is also true of other species in the family).

The flamefish is distinguished by its bright red colouring, with slim white lines running above and below the eye and onto the gill cover, and a broad black saddle across the tail. **286**

APOGONIDAE

A moderately large family of mainly marine fishes. Most are found in shallow tropical or subtropical areas, but some are found in deep water in temperate areas, while a few species live in fresh water. The greatest abundance of cardinalfishes is found in the Indo-Pacific and on reef areas they swarm, clearly playing an important role in the ecology of the reef.

Most are small fishes, brightly coloured, with two dorsal fins, the first of which is short and wholly spiny. Most members of the family have only 2 spines in the anal fin. The tropical cardinalfishes contain many species in which the males are mouth brooders of the eggs, and males are often distinguishable by their deeper, wider head shape. One species is said to pick up the egg clump only when danger threatens. See **Apogon, Astrapogon, Cheilodipterus, Epigonus, Phaeoptyx, Siphamia, Sphaeramia.**

Apristurus Scyliorhinidae
brunneus BROWN CATSHARK 61 cm. (2 ft)
The catsharks of the genus *Apristurus* are rather deep-water fishes found in the Atlantic, Pacific, and Indian oceans. The brown catshark is unusual in that it is found in relatively shallow water, from 137–347 m. (75–190 fathoms), along the Pacific coast of N. America from California to the Strait of Georgia (British Columbia). It is a bottom-living shark, frequently taken in shrimp trawls and on set lines.

Like the other members of the family, it lays eggs protected in a light brown case about 5 cm. (2 in.) in length, oblong, with tendrils at each of the 4 corners.

It is dark brown, becoming black on the edges of the fins, but is otherwise unmarked. These deep-water catsharks are usually dully coloured; they have poorly developed dorsal and pectoral fins, rather long tails and flattened snouts. They are one of the few groups of shark in abyssal depths. One species, the Indian Ocean *Apristurus indicus*, was captured at a depth of 1840 m. (1005 fathoms).
A. indicus see under **A. brunneus**

APTERONOTIDAE

A small family of S. American freshwater fishes, closely related to the knifefishes, Gymnotidae. They differ from their relatives by the possession of a distinct tail fin, and by having a long filamentous dorsal fin in the region of the middle back which can be depressed into a groove on the back. The most notable feature about these fishes is the very long anal fin that begins on the throat and runs to near the end of the tail. Most members of the family have a short blunt snout, but one species, *Sternarchorhynchus oxyrhynchus*, from the Amazon and Guyana, has a long, curved, trunk-like snout.

As in the knifefishes, the means of locomotion is the long anal fin which beats with a rhythmic wave motion. Most of the apteronotids are crepuscular or nocturnally active, navigating by means of electrical fields they generate in modified tissues. See **Apteronotus**.

Apteronotus Apteronotidae
albifrons TOVIRA CAVALLO 51 cm. (20 in.)
This fish is found in the Guianas, the Amazon and Orinoco, Rio Paraguay, and the Rio Parana. It feeds on fish, large crustaceans, and insect larvae. Small specimens also eat small crustaceans.

It has been kept in aquaria and because of its colouring is an interesting pet fish. In Guyana it is said to be regarded by the natives with superstition, being reputed to be inhabited by a ghost or an evil spirit. **105**

Aracana Ostraciontidae
ornata ORNATE COWFISH 15 cm. (6 in.)
Widely distributed on the coasts of s. Australia, mostly on shores of W. Australia, S. Australia, Victoria, and Tasmania, where it is a common species. Most members of this group (which were at one time placed in the family Aracanidae) are inhabitants of moderately deep water, but this species is found as shallow as 20 m. (11 fathoms).

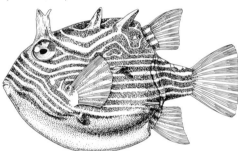

The most notable feature of this fish is the series of curved, blunt spines along the back and sides of the carapace. Males have a high bump on the snout; the female's snout is smoothly rounded. The colouring is also sexually dimorphic: males have blue spotting with a yellow network of lines surrounding the spots, but ventrally and on the tail the pattern is one of blue and yellow alternating lines. Females, overall, have blue and yellow lengthwise stripes, becoming wavy on the back.

Arapaima Osteoglossidae
gigas ARAPAIMA 4 m. (13 ft)
The arapaima is often claimed to be the largest freshwater fish in the world. Lengths of 4·5 m. (15 ft) have been reported, although these are as likely as not estimates. Specimens of 2–2·5 m. (7–8 ft) are, however, frequently encountered and measured. Similarly weights in this species have been recorded from 200 kg. (440 lb.) down to 90 kg. (200 lb.). The growth in large aquaria, as in Sea World, San Diego, is surprisingly rapid.

It is confined to the freshwaters of tropical S. America. Within that area it is widely distributed and known by the following names, paiche in Peru, pirarucu in Brazil; arapaima is the local name in Guyana.

The arapaima is a nest-builder, breeding in April or May in clear areas with sandy bottoms. Here it hollows out a nest of about 15 cm. (6 in.) depth, and 51 cm. (20 in.) width, in which the eggs are laid and guarded. Growth of the young fish is very rapid.

The arapaima is a valuable and high quality food fish. In Brazil it is said to be sun dried in long strips. It is showing alarming signs of depletion and in the Peruvian Amazon a poorly enforced 1 m. (3 ft) size limit has been set.

ARAPAIMA see **Arapaima gigas**
ARAWANA see **Osteoglossum bicirrhosum**
ARCHED CORYDORAS see **Corydoras arcuatus**
ARCHERFISH see Toxotidae
ARCHERFISH see **Toxotes chatareus, Toxotes jaculator**

Arcos Gobiesocidae
macrophthalmus TADPOLE CLINGFISH 9 cm. (3½ in.)
Widely distributed in the W. Indies and reported from the Bahamas, Tobago, Curaçao, Virgin Islands to Puerto Rico. As its common name suggests, it is very broad across the head and body with a small tapering tail; further distinguished by the jutting lower jaw with 4–6 protruding front teeth. Its colouring is mainly purplish, shading to brown posteriorly.

Found in shallow, inshore water, even in the surf, it intrudes its flattened body into the narrowest cracks in the reef. Its food consists of limpets, chitons, crabs, other crustaceans, and worms; the flattened front teeth are adapted for prising limpets and chitons off the rocks and coral.

ARCTIC
CHARR see **Salvelinus alpinus**
CISCO see **Coregonus autumnalis**
COD see **Boreogadus saida**
GRAYLING see **Thymallus arcticus**
LAMPREY see **Lampetra japonica**

Arctoscopus Trichodontidae
japonicus HATAHATA 26 cm. (10¼ in.)
A native species in the w. N. Pacific from Kamchatka s. to Japan and the e. coast of Korea. It is a coastal species, usually found in sand or mud, in which it buries, at depths down to 150 m. (82 fathoms). It spawns in the intertidal zone in depths of 1 m. (½ fathom) after an inshore migration in November. Each female deposits a spherical mass of eggs, usually around 800 in number, amongst algal fronds. The eggs, light crimson in colour, hatch in around 51 days, and the larvae are found in inshore waters until May.

It is an important food fish in Japanese waters. The adults are caught in shore seines in shallow water and are pickled in a mixture of salt and yeast, if not eaten fresh. The eggs, known as buriko, are also eaten, and it is said are 'the unavoidable item in the New Year dinner'.

In body form it is closely similar to the sandfish, *Trichodon trichodon*, but the mouth is more oblique and the fringed lips less pronounced.

Argentina Argentinidae
silus ATLANTIC ARGENTINE 56 cm. (22 in.)
This argentine is found on both sides of the Atlantic. In the E. from off sw. Ireland to Iceland and the Norwegian Sea, and on the American coast from the Gulf of Maine to Labrador.

In both areas it lives on the edge of the continental shelf in depths of 91–914 m. (50–500 fathoms), occasionally in shallower water.

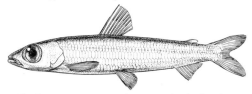

It does not seem to be a particularly abundant fish, although locally it may be common. It is fairly often caught in trawl hauls in appropriate depths incidentally to the catch of other species. It is not marketed, its flesh being rather soft and insipid.

This argentine feeds on small fishes, crustaceans, and squids, many of them mid-water animals. It spawns in summer; the eggs and larvae are planktonic.

The Atlantic argentine is pale greeny yellow with a silvery sheen, particularly marked on the sides.

ARGENTINE, ATLANTIC see **Argentina silus**
ARGENTINE PEARLFISH see **Cynolebias belotti**

ARGENTINIDAE
A small family of marine fishes, most rather small; worldwide in tropical and temperate oceans. Most of these fishes are taken near the bottom on the edge of the continental shelf, but some are found in mid-water and are pelagic, as are the young of all species in which the biology is known. Most have large lateral eyes, but those of *Xenophthalmichthys* are tubular.

All argentinids have scales, very large and bony in some species, small mouths, few teeth in the jaws, and most have an adipose fin. See **Argentina, Xenophthalmichthys**.

ARGUS see **Scatophagus argus**

Argyropelecus Sternoptychidae
aculeatus 7 cm. (2¾ in.) or more
This hatchetfish is widely distributed in the tropical and subtropical parts of all the oceans. It is a conspicuously silvery fish when living, although in some specimens the silver pigment is underlaid by black. Quite the most distinctive feature is the rows of oval, pale yellow or white light-producing organs on the underside. Arranged in characteristic clusters and numbers, these light organs are downwards turned, so that from beneath each species of hatchetfish should be able to recognize its own kind.

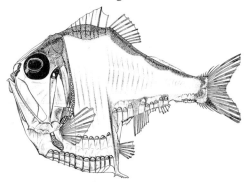

This species occurs in mid-water, during the day at depths of 200–550 m. (110–300 fathoms), but it migrates towards the surface each night so that it has not infrequently been taken in surface nets at night. It has also been found in the stomachs of a number of pelagic predatory fishes.

Argyrosomus Sciaenidae
antarctica see **Johnius antarctica**
regius MEAGRE, KABELJOU, SALMON
BASS, KOB 1·8 m. (6 ft)
This very large croaker is an inhabitant of the E. Atlantic and SW. Indian Ocean. It is found throughout the Mediterranean, S. to Senegal, and n. to the British Isles, where it is an occasional visitor.

It is catholic in its choice of habitat, being found indifferently from the shore line down to about 370 m. (200 fathoms), and enters estuaries freely, particularly when young. It is found particularly on sandy bottoms, and feeds principally on fishes.

Where it occurs commonly it is a very valuable food fish; off S. Africa it is one of the most important food fishes taken both by lines and by trawls. It has some value as an angler's fish but not much.

It is distinguished by its long slender body, rounded snout and very large jaws, although the teeth are small. The lateral line is very distinctive and has several branches to each tube; these scales also have a dull gold shine. It is silvery grey above, bronzy on the sides, and white on the belly. Inside the mouth is yellow.

It is closely related to, and is possibly identical with the Australian mulloway, *Johnius antarctica*.

Arhynchobatis asperrimus see under
Anacanthobatidae

ARIIDAE
Catfishes which with a few exceptions live in the sea and have a worldwide distribution in tropical and subtropical areas. They seem especially to favour estuaries. Active fishes, often schooling near the surface. Many species grow to a moderate size and are used for food locally, but are hazardous fish to handle on account of the wounds their sharp pectoral spines can inflict.

They all have an adipose fin, relatively short fins in general, and forked tails. They have 4–6 barbels around the mouth, and each pair of nostrils are close together. The lateral line has cross branches. Males of this family carry the eggs in their mouths until a little after hatching, fasting while doing so. See **Arius, Bagre, Tachysurus**.

Ariomma Nomeidae
bondi see under **A. melanum**
melanum BROWN DRIFTFISH
30 cm. (12 in.)
A little-known species found in the Gulf of Mexico, the Caribbean and n. to Cape Hatteras. It is a rather elongate species with 39–56 scales in the lateral line. Its coloration is uniform dusky brown. It is related to another species *A. bondi*, found in the same area but ranging as far N. as Cape Cod, which has smaller scales and is blue above, silvery below.

Members of this genus are mostly slender-bodied marine fishes with a forked tail, 2 dorsal fins, and well-developed fatty eyelids. They are bottom-living or near-bottom-living fishes of deep water when adult, although the young are pelagic and are taken in surface collections. Adults feed on crustaceans and probably other bottom-dwelling invertebrates. Like their relatives in the families Centrolophidae and Stromateidae they have a large sac in the pharynx lined with toothed papillae.

The ariommids live in deep water in the tropics and warm waters of the Atlantic and Indian oceans and have been reported also from a number of areas in the Pacific. In all probability they are worldwide in tropical seas. As a group they are close to *Nomeus* and were for long classified with that genus. Recently, however, Dr Richard L. Haedrich has placed them in a family of their own, the Ariommidae.

Ariosoma Congridae
bowersi 40 cm. (16 in.)
This species is found in the vicinity of the Hawaiian Islands and is quite common in shallow water over sand. It is a small silvery eel that burrows in sandy bottoms, and although it has a large eye this is completely covered by transparent tissue which protects the eye when the eel is burrowing. It differs from the other local conger eels in that its posterior nostril is close to the upper lip, by its large eyes, and by its colour.

Aristostomias Malacosteidae
scintillans SHINY LOOSE-JAW
22 cm. (8½ in.)
The shiny loose-jaw is widely distributed from off British Columbia to California and generally in the e. Pacific. It is essentially a deep-water fish, rarely caught in water less than 293 m. (160 fathoms) and often much deeper than that.

It is a black-skinned, rather elongate fish with dorsal and anal fins opposite one another. The jaws are freely movable and swing forward on the loosely attached head to attain a quite incredible gape. It has a moderately large light organ under and below the eye, a luminous tip to its long chin barbel, and groups of photophores along the sides.

Arius Ariidae
feliceps see **Tachysurus feliceps**
felis SEA CATFISH 30 cm. (12 in.)
A catfish found on the American Atlantic coast from Cape Cod to Panama, uncommon N. of Virginia, but very abundant to the S. Is reported from estuaries. An interesting fish in which the males incubate the eggs in their mouths, and for a time the young fish too, fasting in all for a period of 6 weeks. Spawning takes place usually in May to July in pairs. The female's pelvic fins are modified in shape by having on the inner side a thick flap which is believed to be used to hold the eggs temporarily before they are transferred to the male's mouth.

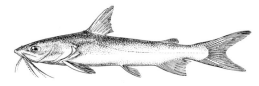

This fish frequents sandy-bottomed harbours, feeding mostly on crabs, shrimps, and occasional fishes. They move in large shoals which emit a considerable amount of noise by swim-bladder vibrations and clicking pectoral spines.

ARMORHEAD, PELAGIC see **Pentaceros richardsoni**

ARMOURED SEA ROBIN see **Peristedion miniatum**

Arnoglossus   Bothidae
  laterna SCALDFISH 19 cm. (7½ in.)
Widely distributed in European waters from the Norwegian coast s. to the Mediterranean. It is particularly common in shallow inshore waters on sandy bottoms and at depths of 10–60 m. (5–33 fathoms), although it is occasionally taken deeper, even as deep as 200 m. (109 fathoms). It is too small to have any commercial value, although in the Mediterranean it is sometimes sold for food.

The members of this genus are amongst the few flatfish species in which males are externally quite different from females; in the males the rays in the front part of the dorsal fin are much elongated.

It is sandy brown or greyish brown with faint dark speckles. The large scales are so fragile that when the fish is trawled, they are stripped off, so that the fish looks as if it has been scalded – hence the name.

ARNOLD'S LYRETAIL see **Aphyosemion arnoldi**

Arnoldichthys   Characidae
  spilopterus RED-EYED CHARACIN
7 cm. (2¾ in.)
This species is immediately distinguished from all other African characins by the differing size of its scales. Above the lateral line the scales are 2 or 3 times the size of those on the sides below and on the belly. The body is rather slim and the head and particularly the eye are large.

It is a beautiful fish with rather delicate colouring. Females are less brightly coloured, and have a lower anal fin.

This characin lives in tropical W. Africa, from Lagos to the Niger estuary. It has been kept in captivity, in acid, peaty water at temperatures of 24–27° C. **51**

Arothron   Tetraodontidae
  aerostaticus TOBY 20 cm. (8 in.)
A widespread tropical Indo-Pacific species which appears to be distributed from the Red Sea and E. African coast across to Hawaii, Japan, and the Philippines. It was first described by the Reverend Leonard Jenyns from a small specimen captured during Charles Darwin's voyage of the 'Beagle'. Unfortunately the coloration changes dramatically as this fish grows, and there are many synonyms in existence. Some authors consider this species to be the same as *A. stellatus*; others deny this.

The youngest specimens are black with white stripes all over the body, but the white areas on the belly widen with age, while the black stripes break into isolated black dots. As an adult this species is light greenish brown above, covered with rounded black blotches, and the belly is white.

It is a coral-haunting fish, especially when young, although large specimens are freeswimming. In many areas of the world it is eaten after careful preparation, for the liver and gonads contain a virulent poison which can kill within hours. **488**

A. hispidus TOBY, BLAASOP, TOADFISH
50 cm. (20 in.)
A widely distributed inhabitant of the tropical Indo-Pacific, ranging from the Red Sea, Zanzibar, and e. Africa to the Australian coast, the Pacific islands, Hawaii, and Japan. In many areas it is very common around reefs, but the young are found mainly in more open situations amongst sea grass beds, and in estuaries, often in very shallow water.

It inflates itself quickly when alarmed and most specimens in every net haul will be almost spherical, thus prickly and difficult to extract from the net.

It is a large pufferfish, with spines covering the whole body. Its back varies from greenybrown to dark brown. **489**

A. immaculatus see under **A. sordidus**

A. meleagris 30 cm. (12 in.)
A w. and central Pacific species which is widely distributed and reported from many Pacific island groups including the Hawaiian Islands, Tahiti, and the Marshall Islands, although apparently not common in any of these places.

It is distinguished by the rounded rather low dorsal and anal fins typical of the genus, and by its brown-coloured body, with the belly only slightly lighter than the back and covered overall with small, densely-packed white spots. Even the fins (except for their extremities) and the lips are brown with white spots. **490**

A. sordidus 30 cm. (12 in.)
First found and described from the Red Sea by the German explorer E. Rüppell in 1828. It appears to be confined to that sea, which has many such endemic forms only slightly different from Indian Ocean species. This species is closely related to *A. immaculatus* of the Indo-Pacific, but differs from it in usually lacking the characteristic dark markings on the body.

It is apparently not a common fish, but is always found in association with coral reefs. **491**

A. stellatus see under **A. aerostaticus**

ARRIPIDAE
A small family confined to the waters around s. Australia and New Zealand, containing only 2 species, the Australian salmons.

They are rather elongate fishes with cylindrical bodies, scaled completely including the head. The dorsal fin is long, its anterior, spiny portion is high but joined to the rest of the fin; the anal fin is short with 3 anterior spines. They are in no way related to the N. Hemisphere salmons but they are valuable food and sporting fishes. See **Arripis**.

Arripis   Arripidae
  georgianus RUFF, TOMMY RUFF
40 cm. (16 in.)
Very abundant along the coasts of all the s. states of Australia. It is closely related to *A. trutta*, and as far as its size allows is also an important food and game fish. In contrast, however, its flesh is marketed fresh as it is extremely tasty and tender.

It lives in shallow, inshore waters, often just beyond the surf zone, but can be found further offshore on open ocean areas.

It is distinguished from the Australian salmon by its larger head, and by the roughness of its scales, which are larger and have toothed edges. It is greenish above, silvery below; the young have yellowish vertical bars on the upper sides, turning to blotches in the adults.

A. trutta AUSTRALIAN SALMON 91 cm. (3 ft)
An abundant fish along the s. coasts of Australia, from W. Australia to New South Wales. It also occurs around Tasmania, Lord Howe and Norfolk islands, and in New Zealand, where it is known as kahawai, the Maori name. It is a large fish, averaging around 4·5 kg. (10 lb.) in weight, but with occasional specimens attaining 9 kg. (20 lb.).

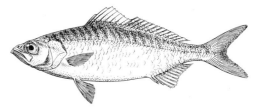

An important commercial fish, caught mainly in beach seines in shallow water. Little is eaten fresh, however, for the flesh is of poor quality, but large quantities are canned, which appears to improve the edibility. It is also highly regarded as a sporting fish; it takes a bait or lure readily and fights hard when hooked, leaping and swimming powerfully. Claimed by some to be the finest small game fish in Australian waters.

It is essentially an inshore species, being very common around the mouths of rivers, particularly when young. Shoals of all age groups are found just beyond the surf line. It feeds very heavily on crustaceans, particularly the shrimp-like euphausiids, and small fishes such as pilchards.

The Australian salmon is greenish above, lighter below; its pectoral fin is bright yellow. Young specimens are heavily spotted with black trout-like markings, and are sometimes called 'salmon-trout'.

ARROW
  BLENNY see **Lucayablennius zingaro**
  GOBY see **Clevelandia ios**
ARROW-TOOTH FLOUNDER see **Atheresthes stomias**

Artedius   Cottidae
The fish illustrated has not been specifically identified. **255**

A. harringtoni SCALYHEAD SCULPIN
10 cm. (4 in.)
A N. Pacific species ranging from central California to Alaska. It lives at moderate depths, usually amongst algae covered rocks, but is occasionally found in the lower shore zone.

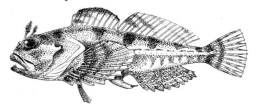

It is distinguished by the wide band of spiny scales bordering the dorsal fins on either side of the back, as well as on the upper part of the head. Mature males develop enlarged front teeth, and a much branched tentacle above the eye, as well as a distinctive colour pattern.

Aseraggodes   Soleidae
  macleayanus NARROW-BANDED SOLE
28 cm. (11 in.)
An Australian species which is found on the

coasts of New South Wales and s. Queensland. It is relatively common and is often caught in trawling in shallow water. It moves inshore in spring, and spawns in river mouths in summer. The young are particularly common in estuaries, even penetrating upstream above tidal limits. Both young fish and adults move into deeper water in winter.

Its body is lavender-grey with 32–36 narrow irregular brown cross-bars on the head and body.

Its flesh is of good quality, and it is potentially an important commercial fish in ne. Australia.

ASIATIC SMELT see **Osmerus dentex**
ASP see **Aspius aspius**

Aspasmogaster Gobiesocidae
   tasmaniensis TASMANIAN CLINGFISH
7 cm. (2¾ in.)
A clingfish found on the s. coasts of Australia, from W. Australia to Victoria, Tasmania, and Lord Howe Island. It is relatively common in rock pools along the coasts, usually associated with rocks to which it clings with its sucker.

The coloration has been described as dark green with numerous brownish vertical bars; other collectors have described it as uniform pink, almost transparent.

Aspidontus Blenniidae
   taeniatus 10 cm. (4 in.)
A widespread species in the Indo-Pacific. It is a slender-bodied blenny with a pointed snout and slightly ventral mouth; its lower jaw has 2 massive, curved teeth, forward-pointing when the mouth is open. Its coloration is conspicuous, being blue, becoming lighter with age, with a widening dark stripe running from tip of snout to tail fin.

In colouring it closely resembles the cleaner-wrasse, *Labroides dimidiatus* (**247**), a species which feeds on ecto-parasites of larger fishes and is generally immune from attack by predators. *Aspidontus* feeds on skin, scales, and pieces of fin, ripped out of larger fishes. It is clearly a mimic of the wrasse, using its resemblance to this harmless, tolerated fish to approach unsuspecting fishes before biting them. Observers have noted that it is mostly young fish which are attacked, larger specimens are presumed to have learned by experience to distinguish between the wrasse and the blenny.

Aspidophoroides Agonidae
   monopterygius ALLIGATORFISH
17 cm. (6¾ in.)
A slim-bodied poacher which is almost slender enough to be confused with the pipefishes. Its entire head and body are covered with bony plates, it has only one dorsal fin, placed about mid-way along the body, its eyes are large, and it has 2 curved spines on the tip of the snout.

It occurs from W. Greenland and the E. coast of Labrador s. to Cape Cod and New Jersey. It lives on sandy and shell bottoms, and also on soft mud, in water of 18–190 m. (10–104 fathoms). It has been found in the stomachs of cod, haddock, and halibut.

Aspius Cyprinidae
   aspius ASP 1·2 m. (4 ft)
The asp is a long-bodied, predatory fish found in Europe and Asia, from the Baltic Basin e. to the Caspian Sea rivers. It is greenish brown above, lighter on the sides, with each scale picked out by a darker blotch. Ventrally it is silvery-white, with dark reddish ventral fins. The mouth is large; the lower jaw is the longer and protrudes.

It lives in the slow-flowing parts of large lowland rivers, although often penetrating to swift-flowing shallows. In April to May it spawns in fast-flowing water on stones or gravel, the eggs dropping amongst the stones. The young fish, for a short while, eat invertebrates, but at a comparatively early age they begin to eat fish. Adults eat fish and occasionally take a frog or a duckling. It is a moderate fish; attaining weights up to 9 kg. (20 lb.)

It is an important commercial fish in the Black Sea region, and considerable quantities are taken annually. It is also a good sporting fish, taking a baited hook, or spinner. In Europe it needs to be conserved.

Aspredinichthys Aspredinidae
   tibicen 12 cm. (5 in.)
A small catfish of the rivers of the Guianas in ne. S. America. Its body form is typical of the family, having a short, flattened, almost triangular head and abdomen, and a very slender tail with a small forked tail fin. The anal fin is long, and runs the length of the tail.

The female incubates the eggs by carrying them attached to her body. The eggs are fastened to spongy tentacles that develop during the breeding season on the female's belly.

ASPREDINIDAE
A family of generally small catfishes, which because of their peculiar shape – flattened wide head and anterior body, and long tail – have been given the name of banjo catfishes. They live only in freshwater and estuarine habitats in n. S. America.

They are scaleless, although the head is covered with a bony armour, and members of one group have bony scutes along the sides. One pair of barbels on the upper jaw, 2 pairs on the chin. The gill openings are rather small. They lack an adipose fin.

Most members of the family are nocturnal and hide under leaves and vegetation during the day. See **Aspredinichthys**, **Buncocephalus**.

Aspro Percidae
   asper see under **A. zingel**
   streber see under **A. zingel**
   zingel ZINGEL 35 cm. (13¾ in.)
A fish native to the central European rivers like the Danube, Prut, and Dneister rivers, but other, closely related species (the strebers) occur in the Rhône (*A. asper*), and in the Danube (*A. streber*). They all live in rather shallow, rapidly running water, and their flattened bellies and rather streamlined shape are adaptations for life in running water. The zingel is an inactive, bottom-living species, which

lies quietly amongst the stones during the day, and becomes active at night when it seeks out the bottom-living invertebrates on which it feeds.

Its back is medium brown, with dark mottling and blotches; its sides and belly are yellowish.

ASSOUS see **Atherina breviceps**

ASTROBLEPIDAE
A moderately large, and rather confusing family of S. American catfishes, close to the Loricariidae in many ways but differing from them in certain respects. Like them, the head and body are depressed and flattened and there is an adipose fin, frequently with a stout spine. The teeth in the jaws are flattened, have 2 cusps, and lie in a narrow band.

Many of the known species are adapted to life in fast running, even torrential waters of the mountainous regions, and can cling to boulders. Most species are small. See **Astroblepus**.

Astroblepus Astroblepidae
   grixalvii PEZ NEGRO 30 cm. (12 in.)
A small catfish, although the largest member of the family. It is found in fast running rivers in the Central and E. Cordillera, in Colombia. In this area it has some economic importance as a food fish, but its range and abundance have greatly declined in recent years.

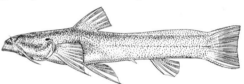

In body form it is typical of the family. A depressed head with ventral mouth and well-developed thick barbels. The fins are all well-developed, and have a strong anterior spine; the adipose fin is large and long, but has no spine as it does in some other species.

Astrodermella see under Luvaridae

Astronesthes Astronesthidae
   niger BLACK STAR-EATER 63 mm. (2½ in.)
This species appears to be confined to the Atlantic Ocean in the tropical and temperate zones. Within these areas it is the most common star-eater known, a number having been collected at the surface at night, while most have been caught in nets towed at about 100 m. (55 fathoms). Tows as deep as 1000 m. (547 fathoms) have produced specimens. Nothing is known of its habits except that one specimen had a lantern fish in its stomach.

This species is the only astronesthid in which luminescence has been observed. Freshly caught specimens flash intermittently with a violet-blue light when touched, but the luminous area appears to be the front of the back, the fins, and the barbel, which are sheathed in a thin whitish tissue. The photophores that are distributed on the head and body apparently have not been involved in this display of living light.

ASTRONESTHIDAE

This family of deep-sea fish has been called the star-eaters, and it is not an inappropriate name for fishes with 2 main rows of photophores on each side, and light organs before and behind the eye. In general they are small fishes, specimens longer than 15 cm. (6 in.) being rare. They are rather large-headed, black fish, with well developed fangs in the front of the jaws and a comb-toothed edge to the upper jaw bone. A barbel is attached to the underside of the chin, usually rather stout; in some species it is much branched and apparently luminous.

Members of the family have been found in all tropical and most temperate seas of the world. Some species have been taken only in water as shallow as 100 m. (54 fathoms), the larger species tend to live deeper to a limit of 1400 m. (765 fathoms). See **Astronesthes.**

Astropogon   Apogonidae
stellatus CONCHFISH 5 cm. (2 in.)
Distributed in the tropical w. Atlantic, from the Bahamas s. It lives in moderately shallow water of from 1–10 m. (3¼–33 ft), as a commensal in the mantle cavity of live individuals of the very large Caribbean snail, the queen conch *(Strombus gigas)*. Other members of this genus live in small cavities of rocks or in empty shells, but apparently not in live shells.

It is distinguished by its brown to black coloration, the edges of the scales pale, and three rows of dusky spots on the sides. The lower head and body are silvery.

Astyanax   Characidae
bimaculatus TWO-SPOT TETRA
15 cm. (6 in.)
The genus *Astyanax* differs from the other tetra genera *Hyphessobrycon* and *Hemigrammus*, in that it has a continuous lateral line (the latter genera usually have only a few anterior scales with lateral line pores). Members of the genus are distributed from New Mexico, s. Texas and s. through the whole of Central and S. America.

The two-spot tetra is found in ne. S. America, S. to the La Plata. Its coloration is light, rather brassy on the back and sides, with 2 very distinct black blotches, one just behind the head, the other at the base of the tail-fin. Males are rather larger than females but slimmer; also their vertical fins are slightly red-tinted.

It is kept in aquaria but is not a particularly popular fish.
A. fasciatus BANDED TETRA 17 cm. (6¾ in.)
A very widely distributed characin which occurs from Mexico and Central America s. to the Argentine. Through this vast range it forms a number of subspecies which vary largely in colouring, markings, and the size of the eye.

This species is typical of the genus, with a rather deep-bodied, thickset appearance, an adipose fin, forked tail, and a complete row of lateral line scales. It is gleaming silvery or brassy, the back slightly brown. A dark smudge on the shoulder (sometimes not very obvious), and a more pronounced dark mark near the tail fin are joined by a greenish silver stripe.

Several of the named subspecies of this *Astyanax* have been bred in captivity. The weakly adhesive eggs are shed at random amongst plants and over the bottom of the aquarium. The young hatch in 24–36 hours in 19–24° C; they hang attached to the weed for about 5 days, after which they begin to feed. It is a good aquarium fish although not widely kept.

A. mexicanus MEXICAN TETRA 8 cm. (3 in.)
A characin found, as its name suggests, in Mexico, and in the s. U.S. (Texas and New Mexico) s. to Panama. It is very closely related to the *A. fasciatus* group, and is by some authorities regarded as a subspecies, *A.f. mexicanus.*

Like other members of the genus this species is kept in aquaria, in which it is a peaceable and undemanding fish, and moderately easy to breed. However, it compares poorly with the brilliantly coloured tropical tetras and is not a particularly popular aquarium fish.

It has an additional interest in that it is the only *Astyanax* found in the U.S., and is the presumptive ancestor of the blind tetra *(Anoptichthys jordani)* of Mexican caves. **52**

ATELEOPIDAE

A family of deep-water fishes, containing 3 or 4 genera and perhaps 10 species. Most of the described species have been based on few specimens and, as they are very fragile, there is a strong possibility that some of the observed differences will prove to be due to individual variation and damaged material, and that the number of species will be reduced.

All have a very long body, the trunk being about equal to the head, and both together equalling half the tail length. They have a thread-like pelvic fin under the throat, a short dorsal fin, and a long anal fin which merges into the tail fin. The general resemblance is to a very soft, flabby rabbitfish which lacks spines in the dorsal and pectoral fins.

The ateleopids are widely distributed in all tropical and warm-temperate oceans, in moderately deep water 183–550 m. (100–300 fathoms). Their nearest relatives are the whalefishes, but the relationship is not close. Most ateleopids seem rare, or at least rarely taken. See **Ateleopus.**

Ateleopus   Ateleopidae
japonicus 61 cm. (2 ft)
This bizarre deep-water fish is widely distributed in the Indo-Pacific, from the waters of E. Africa to Japanese seas. Its body is very soft and seems formless, but it can be distinguished by the long pelvic fin filament under the throat, by the short-based dorsal fin, and by the long tail with an equally long anal fin which continues to the end of the body. It is greyish brown on the body and on the anal and tail fins, darker brown on the head, and black on the dorsal and pectoral fins.

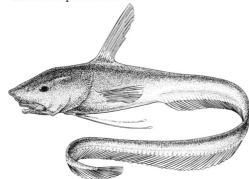

Most specimens have been found between depths of 183–550 m. (100–300 fathoms). Its body shape, and underslung mouth, with finely ridged lips and no teeth in the lower jaw, suggest that it is a bottom-living fish, which like the spiny-eels and halosaurs (Notacanthidae and Halosauridae), snake along at an angle to the sea bed feeding on benthic invertebrates. If specimens in museum collections are any guide this seems to be a rare fish, although as usual in such cases this is probably only a reflection of our relatively inefficient catching methods.

Atheresthes   Pleuronectidae
stomias ARROW-TOOTH FLOUNDER
84 cm. (33 in.)
An inhabitant of the N. Pacific Ocean from the Bering Sea s. to central California. Along the coast of Canada it is very abundant. Its depth range is from 730–915 m. (400–500 fathoms). It feeds indiscriminately on small crustaceans and fishes of numerous kinds as an adult, but the larvae eat only copepods and their larvae.

Although this is a moderate-sized fish it is not utilized for human food but is exploited on a small scale for animal feed.

It can be distinguished by having its eyes on the right of its head, by its very large jaws armed with large teeth, the longest arrow-shaped, and by the upper eye being placed on the extreme edge of the head. It is brown to olive-brown on the eyed side, the edges of the scales slightly darker. On the eyeless side it is white.

Atherina   Atherinidae
breviceps ASSOUS, WHITEBAIT
12 cm. (4¾ in.)
A S. African species found from the Atlantic coast round the Cape to Natal. Like some other species of its family, it is found only inshore and in the mouths of estuaries. Here they swim in large shoals near the surface, with their snouts almost breaking through. Many aquatic birds and other fishes feed on them, and locally they are rated good eating, if small.

It is a round-bodied silverside, rather slender, and with 2 well-spaced dorsal fins. Its scales are moderately small, about 46 in a lengthwise row, and the pectoral fin is moderately high. It has 13–14 dorsal rays. Body transparent except for the bold silvery lateral stripe.
A. mochon 12 cm. (4¾ in.)
Widely distributed in the Mediterranean and the Black Sea, where the population is regarded as a distinct subspecies, *A. mochon pontica*. It is almost indifferent to the salinity of the water in which it is living, being found in the full salinity of the sea, in brackish lagoons, and in almost fresh water. It reproduces in May and June; the eggs have long filaments by which they are anchored to algae. The larvae are pelagic, darting about in dense shoals at the surface of the water.

In the Black Sea this species is fished for commercially but the total weight of the landed catch is small, due in part to the smallness of the fish. **213**
A. presbyter SAND-SMELT 15 cm. (6 in.)
Widely distributed in the e. Atlantic from Scotland and Denmark, where it is rare, to the N. African coast and the Mediterranean. It is a gregarious schooling fish of inshore and coastal waters, which becomes more common to the N. in summer. It is found close inshore on

sandy bays, and in estuaries and sea inlets, and is occasionally trapped in intertidal pools where the shoal can be seen darting with perfect cohesion away from threatening danger. They spawn in high shore pools at mid-summer; the eggs have many long filaments which tangle in the algae, or with one another. The fry are about 7 mm. long at hatching and stay in the pool until they reach a length of at least 5 cm. (2 in.).

The sand-smelt feeds on small crustaceans and occasionally small fishes. It is frequently preyed upon by such fishes as bass, and caught by terns and other predatory birds. They can be eaten, but are not commercially exploited.

Its body form is typical of the family. It is a striking green on the back, olive on the sides with fine sooty spots fringing the edges of the scales. A brilliant silver line runs from head to tail; the belly is whitish.

ATHERINIDAE

A family of rather small fishes found in temperate and tropical seas, and less commonly in fresh water. They resemble the grey mullets in some features, notably in having an anterior dorsal fin composed of a few slender spines, and were for a long time thought to be closely related. Their affinities are now thought to lie with the toothcarps.

Most members of the family are relatively slender, but some are compressed, and others have cylindrical bodies. They have large eyes and terminal, almost always protrusible mouths. Their bodies are fully scaled with mainly cycloid, often fragile scales.

The silversides or sand-smelts are shoaling fishes of inshore seas. They are frequently found in large numbers and in places are fished for commercially. The eggs of most species have on their surface one to many short filaments by which they adhere on touch to aquatic plants, or flotsam. See **Atherina, Atherinomorus, Bedotia, Craterocephalus, Leuresthes, Menidia, Pranesus, Telmatherina.**

Atherinomorus   Atherinidae
stipes HARDHEAD SILVERSIDE 12 cm. (5 in.)
Widely distributed along the s. coasts of the U.S. from Florida and the Bahamas through the Caribbean to Brazil. It is the most abundant silverside in the W. Indian region. It frequently shoals with members of the round-herring genus *Jenkinsia*.

In body form it is typical of the family, having a rather elongate but cylindrical body, 2 dorsal fins, the first having only thin spines, a pectoral fin placed high on the side, and a large eye. Its colouring is variable: in life it is almost transparent during the day, only the narrow silvery stripe (which overlies a black streak) showing; at night, it becomes darker, with dusky back, tail fin, and the silver stripe obscured.

ATLANTIC
ARGENTINE see **Argentina silus**

BLUE-FIN TUNA see **Thunnus thynnus**
BONITO see **Sarda sarda**
CUTLASSFISH see **Trichiurus lepturus**
FLYINGFISH see **Cypselurus heterurus**
GUITARFISH see **Rhinobatus lentiginosus**
HALIBUT see **Hippoglossus hippoglossus**
MACKEREL see **Scomber scombrus**
MANTA see **Manta birostris**
MIDSHIPMAN see **Porichthys porosissimus**
NEEDLEFISH see **Strongylura marina**
POMFRET see **Brama brama**
SALMON see **Salmo salar**
SAURY see **Scomberesox saurus**
SEA RAVEN see **Hemitripterus americanus**
SILVERSIDE see **Menidia menidia**
STURGEON see **Acipenser sturio**
THREAD HERRING see **Opisthonema oglinum**
TOMCOD see under **Microgadus proximus**
TORPEDO see **Torpedo nobiliana**
Atopomycterus nichthemerus see **Diodon nichthemerus**

Atractoscion   Sciaenidae
aequidens TERAGLIN, CAPE SALMON, GEELBEK 127 cm. (50 in.)
Found around the coast of S. Africa, from the Cape to Natal, and in ne. Australia from Queensland and New South Wales. It is essentially an offshore species, living as deep as 110 m. (60 fathoms), usually on the open ocean coast. Young specimens, however, occur close to the shore, and even enter deep estuaries.

It is a highly esteemed food fish, mostly eaten fresh but sometimes cured. Much of the catch is taken by trawling in deepish water, but some by line. Because it haunts deep water it is not often taken by anglers. It attains a weight of 9 kg. (20 lb.).

It is bluish above, silvery on the sides and white below, with a yellowish flush on the cheeks and the inside of the mouth bright yellow. It is distinguished from the other large croakers in the areas in which it lives by the concave edge to its tail fin.

Atrophacanthus   Triacanthidae
danae 4·4 cm. (1¾ in.)
A curious small fish found only in the Celebes Sea during investigations by the Danish research vessel 'Dana', after which it was named. The first specimens to be captured were taken in estimated depths of 2500–3500 m. (1367–1913 fathoms) when over 150 were caught, although others were taken in 300–2000 m. (164–1093 fathoms). This seems to be a bathypelagic species which lives and breeds in midwater over considerable depths; it is the deepest-living plectognath fish.

It is rather slender-bodied, with a high dorsal fin composed of 3 slender spines (a fourth is usually not visible); the pelvic fins are represented by a long thin serrated spine on each side. The whole head and body are covered with long spiny scales, the lips are thick, the eye moderately large. It is pale, and mainly silvery below.

AUCHENIPTERIDAE
A family of catfishes which are distinguished by their scaleless bodies, and which often have a zig-zag lateral line with short branches at each

angle. The dorsal fin is short, and placed well forward, close to the head, a short adipose fin is present. Barbels are present around the mouth, usually the pair on the upper jaw are long, those on the chin (one or two pairs) are short. Gill openings are small.

The family contains a number of genera, all living in fresh water in South America from Argentina to Venezuela. See **Auchenipterus, Centromochlus.**

Auchenipterus   Auchenipteridae
nuchalis 18 cm. (7 in.)
A scaleless catfish found in the s. Amazon region and Paraguay. Barbels are rather long on the lower jaw, and the upper jaw barbels are longer than the head. The body is rather compressed and moderately deep; the dorsal fin is short, placed just behind the head; the adipose fin is very small, but the anal is long and well developed.

The back is greyish, the sides are silvery and the head region is distinctly silvery; there is a dusky spot on the head in the area of the nostrils; the tail fin is dusky.

Auchenoglanis   Bagridae
occidentalis 1 m. (39 in.)
Widely distributed in Africa from the Nile, Senegal, Niger, and Congo rivers, and in most of the Great Lakes of Africa. The adults are most common in the swamps in the flood plains of the rivers, but the young are found in the shallows of rivers and lakes. It is said to spawn during floods following the heavy rains. It is caught locally by fishermen, although it is said that in some areas they refuse to eat it on the ground that its flesh is poisonous. It is omnivorous, feeding on bottom-living animals and plant material; large specimens eat fishes.

Adults are deep brown on the back, often with large black spots that extend onto the fins. The young are more variably coloured, pale brown or olive with numerous spots and blotches, sometimes so many that it is better described as a dark fish with a network of light markings. The young are popular for aquaria.

AULOPIDAE
A small family of primitive myctophoid fishes containing at least 11 species. They occur in warm coastal waters on both sides of the N. Atlantic, across the Pacific, and in s. Australia. Closely similar to lizardfishes, with rather large heads, big jaws, and moderately slender bodies which are covered with rather large scales. The high dorsal fin contains numerous rays, of which the second one is especially elongate in the European and some other species; all have a small adipose fin close to the tail fin. The other fins are well developed. Only one genus is usually recognized in the family. See **Aulopus.**

Aulopus   Aulopidae
filamentosus 48 cm. (19 in.)
This fish is found in the e. Atlantic from Portugal to the Canary Islands, as well as widely in the Mediterranean. It lives on the bottom at depths from about 400 m. (218 fathoms) down to 1000 m. (546 fathoms). It is believed to breed throughout the year in the Mediterranean. It is carnivorous, but eats relatively small bottom-living organisms, for it has only small teeth in dense rows.

It is light brown, with the dorsal and tail fins dark spotted and the other fins pinkish. Some specimens, probably the males, are very distinctly marked with yellow.

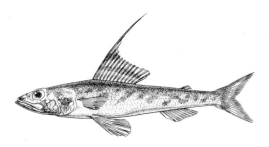

Its principal distinguishing feature is the elongate anterior dorsal fin ray, which is higher than the rest of the fin in females but is greatly extended, to about twice the height of the other rays in adult males.

A. purpurissatus SERGEANT BAKER 60 cm. (2 ft)
The Sergeant Baker is widely distributed along the coasts of Australia from S. Queensland through New South Wales, Victoria, and S. Australia to W. Australia. It is probably most common, and is certainly best known off the New South Wales coast. It is occasionally found on reefs, and always haunts rocky or coral areas from shallow water down to the lower continental shelf. Sometimes young occur in estuaries.

It is occasionally caught on hook and line by fishermen trying for the snapper, which lives on the same grounds. Occasionally catches are made by trawlers. Its flesh is said to be white, firm, and of good flavour, but the fish is too difficult to catch in quantity for it to be marketed regularly.

It is a beautifully coloured fish: the edges of the scales make a crimson tracery over the purple or scarlet back and sides; the belly is yellowish white; and the fins are yellowish with red spots in bands. The males are distinguished by the great lengthening of the second and third dorsal fin rays; in the females these rays are less extremely elongated. Except for the very small adipose fin, the fins are large.

The Sergeant Baker is said to have been named for a soldier of this name who first caught this fish in the New South Wales settlement, but it might be suggested that the colouring of the fish is similar to the uniforms worn by British troops of that period. (For the same reason most red-coloured fish are today known as 'soldiers' to the English fisherman.)

AULORHYNCHIDAE
The family of the tubenose or tubesnout, a marine stickleback found from s. Alaska to s. California. Only the single species is represented in the family.

The family is characterized by the extremely elongate head and body, almost cylindrical, and very slender towards the tail. The snout is slim with a very small mouth and hinged jaw. A row of about 25 small spines along the back forms the first dorsal fin, the second dorsal is small, and placed opposite the anal fin which is the same shape. Recent studies by Professor Carl L. Hubbs and his co-workers suggest that this family should be included within the Gasterosteidae. See **Aulorhynchus**.

Aulorhynchus   Aulorhynchidae
flavidus TUBESNOUT 16 cm. (6¼ in.)
Widely distributed along the Pacific coast of N. America from s. Alaska to Baja California, Mexico. It is a common shore and inshore fish along nearly all of its whole range, and is sometimes seen in dense shoals at the surface. The late Earl S. Herald recorded a school of literally millions of tubesnouts in 24 m. (44 fathoms) of water off California; they were densely packed for one quarter of a mile (400 m.) in diameter and for 12 m. (6½ fathoms) in depth.

It feeds on small plankton, principally crustaceans, and fish larvae, and is eaten in turn by many larger fishes. Like other sticklebacks it builds a nest of algae cemented together with fine mucous threads from the male's urogenital region. The nests are made in the mossy growths at the base of the kelp; the translucent

orange eggs are deposited in them by the female; and the whole is then guarded by the male. The eggs hatch in 2–3 weeks, and the young fish are herded by the male in a shoal at the bottom.

AULOSTOMIDAE
A small family found in tropical seas in the Atlantic, and Indo-Pacific. Superficially they resemble the cornetfishes (family Fistulariidae) and pipefishes (family Syngnathidae), sharing with these fishes an elongate shape, a rather long compressed snout, and certain internal features. The trumpetfishes have scales on their bodies and an underlying network of fine bones.

Only 3 species are recognized, all found in reef areas or in rocky inshore waters. They are not particularly active fishes, spending most of their time hanging vertically, or at an angle to the bottom, well concealed amongst branching coral or gorgonians. See **Aulostomus**.

Aulostomus   Aulostomidae
maculatus TRUMPETFISH 76 cm. (30 in.)
A widely distributed species of trumpetfish which is found from the coast of Brazil n. to the Bahamas and Bermuda. It is found throughout the Caribbean and the Gulf of Mexico, but although relatively common is not found anywhere in large numbers. It is typically a fish of the reefs seen drifting at odd angles or head down, frequently aligned with gorgonians and other underwater growths or obstructions. The young are often found floating in sargassum. At all ages its coloration is cryptic, and although it appears to be ungainly and slow it is a very efficient predator on small, often quick-moving, fishes such as blennies. **227**

A. strigosus TRUMPETFISH 86 cm. (34 in.)
An e. Atlantic trumpetfish which is found over a wide area from St Helena, Ascension Island, the Canaries, and Cape Verde Islands, the tropical W. African coast, and Madeira. Probably most of these populations are distinct and little interchange takes place between them. This species was relatively recently recognized as distinct from the w. Atlantic form, but its existence has been known for many years. Its abundance in Madeira is said to have increased in the late 1950s.

Its biology is little known but there is no reason to doubt that its habits are much the same as the Caribbean species *A. maculatus*.

It differs in having a slightly longer body, more scales from head to tail, and a series of large light spots and dark bars near the tail fin.

AUSTRALIAN
 ANCHOVY see **Engraulis australis**
 GRAYLING see **Prototroctes maraena**
 LUNGFISH see **Neoceratodus forsteri**
 MULLOWAY see under **Argyrosomus regius**
 PILCHARD see **Sardinops neopilchardus**
 SALMON see **Arripis trutta**
 SMELT see **Retropinna semoni**

Auxis   Scombridae
rochei see under **A. thazard**
thazard FRIGATE MACKEREL, PLAIN BONITO 61 cm. (2 ft)
In many respects the frigate mackerel is more of a mackerel than a tuna. Its small size supports this, as does the wide separation of first and second dorsal fins. However, it has more finlets (7 or 8) following both dorsal and anal fins, and has a well developed large-scaled corselet anteriorly. It grows to a weight of around 3 kg. (7 lb.).

It is widely distributed in the tropical waters of the Atlantic, Indian, and Pacific oceans, moving seasonally into temperate waters. It is typically a pelagic, schooling fish of the open seas although it comes inshore in warm seasons. Numbers are caught in fisheries for other tuna, but its flesh is not highly regarded. Some are caught by sportsfishermen but again it is not a particularly sought after fish.

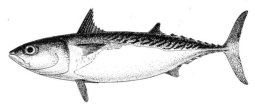

Like other members of the group, its food consists mainly of small fishes which live at the surface of the sea; some squids and crustaceans are also eaten.

Its coloration is distinctive, blue-green or dark blue on the back, silvery on the sides and belly. Rather indistinct wavy, dusky lines run obliquely across the back from the corselet upwards.

A closely related species, which differs mainly in having a wider corselet, *A. rochei*, has a similar range but appears to be found more often in inshore waters.

Avocettina   Nemichthyidae
infans SNIPE EEL 61 cm. (24 in.)
A widely distributed deep-sea eel found in the tropical and sub-tropical Atlantic, Pacific, and Indian oceans. It is a bathypelagic species, found in mid-water but not on the bottom, in the deep sea. It has been estimated that its centre of distribution depthwise is between

1400 and 2600 m. (765 and 1420 fathoms), although records exist of it captured as deep as 4575 m. (2500 fathoms).

It is similar in appearance to the other members of the family. In colour it is dusky brown, darker ventrally.

Little is known of its life history, and it is usually only captured by special deep-sea research expeditions, although one specimen was reported to have been taken tangled by its jaws in a submarine cable brought up for repair from 1464 m. (800 fathoms) depth.

AYU see **Plecoglossus altivelis**
AZZAZI see **Rhinecanthus assasi**

B

BADIDAE

A family containing the single species *Badis badis*, which was for long included within the Nandidae. However, it has been recently demonstrated that it is similar in courtship behaviour and the structure of its skeleton to the anabantoids (see Anabantidae and relatives) and is now aligned with the gouramis and others. See *Badis*.

Badis   Badidae
badis BADIS 8 cm. (3 in.)
Distributed widely in India and Burma in still and slowly flowing water. It is a popular aquarium fish, and can be kept in a community tank, although when kept with its own species it is quarrelsome. Males, especially, are strongly territorial and excavate lairs under rocks on soft substrates or bore into masses of algae; each defends its own territory, and uses its lair as a shelter in which to lurk, feeding mainly on small crustaceans and worms at which it darts.

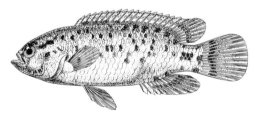

Breeding takes place within the male's lair, where the pair of fish perform a typical close embrace before the eggs are shed and fertilized. The eggs fall to the bottom of the lair, and are guarded by the male, who fans them, and removes spoiled eggs for the 48 hours or so until they hatch, keeping the larvae within cover for 5 or 6 days afterwards. One male may spawn with several females to make up the brood.

The coloration of *Badis* is very variable. Males, in particular, when being aggressive, spawning, or guarding the eggs become almost black. Colour changes at other times are continuous and very variable. **460**

Bagarius   Sisoridae
bagarius GOONCH 2 m. (6½ ft)
Widely distributed in India, Burma, Thailand,

and Vietnam, and also in Sumatra, Borneo, and Java. It lives in the larger rivers, apparently indifferent to the flow: in some areas it hides under logs and floating houses in slow-flowing rivers; elsewhere it inhabits rapids amongst boulders, often in the white water of the rapid. The goonch thus lives in the regions frequented by the mahseer and achieves great disfavour amongst fishermen angling for that species by taking their baits. It is a large fish which weighs up to 113 kg. (250 lb.).

Its body is greatly flattened, and appears slender from the side; the head is particularly depressed, and the eyes are small and placed on its upper surface. Its colour is variable: it is generally deep olive-green with darker blotches and numerous small dark spots; some specimens are blue-striped on the head.

The gooch is a predator on a wide variety of fishes and bottom-living invertebrates. It is locally a valuable food fish.

Bagre   Ariidae
marinus GAFFTOPSAIL CATFISH
61 cm. (2 ft)
A distinctive Atlantic coast catfish found from Cape Cod to Panama and common S. of Chesapeake Bay, particularly in the coastal and estuarine waters of Florida. It has only 2 barbels on its chin, and the upper jaw barbel is flat and ribbon-like; the dorsal and pectoral fins have long thin filaments, the high dorsal fin giving rise to its common name. A solitary species, sometimes found in small groups It feeds on crabs, shrimps and fishes.

Spawning takes place in summer; the male carries the eggs in his mouth until after hatching. A moderately 'noisy' fish, which makes distinctive yelps and sobs underwater by means of its swimbladder vibrations.

BAGRE ROSADO see **Hypophthalmus edentatus**
BAGRE SAPO see **Rhamdia sapo**

BAGRIDAE

A family of freshwater catfishes widely distributed in tropical Africa, s. and e. Asia as far N. as Japan. They are scaleless, usually slender-bodied fishes with a large adipose fin, and an almost ventral, curved mouth with toothed jaws. As with all catfishes, barbels are well developed on the head and around the mouth, and the one on the upper jaw is usually long. Most members of the family have small eyes, in some species covered over by skin. Pectoral spines are strong and serrated; the dorsal spine also is well developed.

Many bagrids grow to a large size and are locally important food fishes. Others are small and are sometimes kept as aquarium fishes. In general they are crepuscular or nocturnal, although species which live in heavily clouded water may be active in daytime. Some species are capable of making audible sounds. Most are voracious, bottom-living fish with quite unspecialized diet. See **Auchenoglanis, Bagrus, Clarotes, Leiocassius, Mystus, Pseudobagrus**.

Bagrus   Bagridae
docmac 1 m. (3¼ ft)
This catfish is widely distributed in Nigeria, Ghana, the Nile Basin, and the Great Lakes of Africa. It is quite a large fish; specimens weighing as much as 22·7 kg. (50 lb.) have been

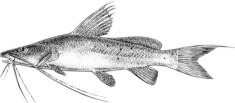

reliably recorded, while estimates of a maximum of 34 kg. (75 lb.) have been made. It is a valuable commercial fish wherever is it common. A predatory species, when large feeding on fishes, although young specimens eat insect larvae and crustaceans mainly.

Adults are dark grey, almost black above, and creamy-white on the belly; the young are lighter, being smoke-grey or olive-brown and golden underneath. The fins are yellowish to dusky, occasionally with dark spots. The young are rather attractive and are occasionally kept in aquaria. It is distinguished by its very long adipose fin, the very flattened head, long barbells, and the production of the upper lobe of the tail fin into a point.

BAIKAL COD see **Comephorus baicalensis**

Balistapus   Balistidae
undulatus 23 cm. (9 in.)
Widespread in the tropical Indo-Pacific, from the Red Sea, Zanzibar, and the E. African coast, to Sri Lanka and India, the E. Indies, and through a very large area of the w. and central Pacific. It was first described in 1797 by the explorer Mungo Park, who was later to explore, and die in, the region of Nigeria. It appears to be one of the most abundant triggerfishes in many parts of its vast range.

A very distinctively coloured fish, immediately distinguished by having 6–8 curved, forward-pointing spines on each side of the tail. It should be handled with great care as it can inflict a painful wound with these spines. Moreover, it may bite the hand that holds the head. **469**

Balistes   Balistidae
capriscus see **B. carolinensis**
carolinensis TRIGGERFISH, GREY
TRIGGERFISH 41 cm. (16 in.)
An Atlantic species found on both sides of the ocean, in the E. from the coast of W. Africa n. to Portugal (and throughout the Mediterranean), and in the W. from Argentina n. exceptionally to Nova Scotia. In European waters this fish is a summertime migrant into British seas, becoming in warm seasons (as in 1973) relatively abundant on the S. and SW. coasts. A similar n. migration is observed in the w. Atlantic.

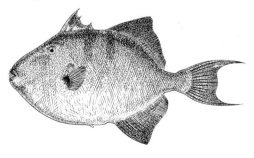

Its habit of moving n. with summertime warming of the sea suggests that it is essentially an open water inhabitant, not an inshore species. The young certainly are found in floating *Sargassum* weed, and their pelagic habit is probably the cause of its wide distribution.

Its body form is typical of the triggerfishes, being deep and compressed with a distinctive arrangement of the dorsal spines. Its teeth are orange, flattened incisors in the mid-line of the jaw. Coloration is variable, usually green or greyish brown, with the back darker than the sides; the fins often have blue lines.

Occasional specimens are captured by sea anglers in British waters, although never intentionally. It is not eaten except perhaps by way of experiment.

This species is also known by the name *Balistes capriscus*.

B. radula see **Melichthys ringens**
B. vetula QUEEN TRIGGERFISH, OLD-WIFE 56 cm. (22 in.)
A very distinctive triggerfish, especially by reason of the long streamers on the tail and dorsal fins. This fish always has 2 broad diagonal curved light blue bands on the lower face, the lower running from a blue ring around the mouth, the upper starting on the snout. The background varies from yellowish brown, with green sides, to deep brown.

It is reported as occurring throughout the tropical Atlantic but records of it in the e. Atlantic appear to need substantiating. In the w. Atlantic it ranges from New England s. throughout the Gulf of Mexico and the Caribbean Sea to Brazil. It is common on reefs and lives also over sandy or sea-grass-covered areas from the surface down to 46 m. (25 fathoms). It eats a wide variety of invertebrates but feeds most heavily on sea urchins of the genus *Diadema*, which it picks up in its jaws by holding a single spine, and turns it over until it can attack the unprotected ventral side.

This species is eaten locally in the Bahamas, where it is sometimes called 'turbot' in the fish market; on rare occasions its flesh has proved to be poisonous. **470**

Balistoides Balistidae
conspicillum BIG-SPOTTED TRIGGERFISH 33 cm. (13 in.)
A most strikingly patterned triggerfish which can be distinguished by the dark chocolate-brown colouring of the upper parts of the body contrasting with the bold yellow, rounded blotches on the belly.

It is widely distributed through the tropical Indo-Pacific, from the E. African coast to India, the E. Indies, n. Australia, to Japan. It is particularly common in rocky areas and around coral reefs. Although widespread it seems to be relatively uncommon. **471**

BALISTIDAE
The family of triggerfishes and filefishes, as here understood, includes all of the rather deep-bodied, compressed fishes with a spiny first dorsal fin, separate teeth in the jaws and no pelvic fins. Several previously recognized families (e.g. Aluteridae and Monacanthidae) are included in this group.

The balistids are usually found in tropical, shallow inshore waters, although a few species adopt an oceanic life style, and others occur seasonally in temperate seas. Some, possibly most, live amongst coral reefs or in shallow eel grass beds.

The triggerfishes are well-known for the interesting development of the dorsal spines. The first spine is very large and stout, and when erected the small second spine locks it into place. This spine acts as the trigger (hence triggerfish and *Balistes*) which must be released before the large spine can be depressed. When alarmed, or attacked, triggerfishes take refuge in a crevice in the coral or rock and raise their dorsal spine, effectively wedging themselves in, while still being able to snap with their rat-like teeth at an attacker.

Other members of the family rely on coloration and curious shape to frustrate predators by mimicking algae or plants, and they are usually cryptically coloured. Some of the triggerfishes, however, are brightly coloured and are conspicuous underwater.

By and large they are not important food fishes, although locally some species are eaten. Many others are suspected of being poisonous to man, at least on occasions, and many filefishes have bitter if not poisonous flesh. See **Acanthaluteres, Alutera, Balistapus, Balistes, Balistoides, Cantherhines, Chaetoderma, Melichthys, Meuschenia, Monacanthus, Navodon, Odonus, Oxymonacanthus, Pervagor, Pseudobalistes, Rhinecanthus, Stephanolepis, Xanichthys.**

BALLAN WRASSE see **Labrus bergylta**
BALLOONFISH see **Diodon holocanthus**
BALLYHOO see **Hemiramphus brasiliensis**
BAMBOOFISH see **Sarpa salpa**
BANDANG see **Chanos chanos**
BANDED
    BELLOWSFISH see **Centriscops humerosus**
    BREAM see **Tilapia sparrmanii**
    BUTTERFLYFISH see **Chaetodon striatus**
    CICHLID see **Cichlasoma severum**
    EPIPLATYS see **Epiplatys fasciolatus**
    FROGFISH see **Halophryne diemensis**
    HUMBUG see **Dascyllus aruanus**
    KNIFEFISH see **Gymnotus carapo**
    TETRA see **Astyanax fasciatus**
    TOADFISH see **Torquigener pleurogramma**
BANDFISH see **Rhamphichthys rostratus**
BANDFISH, RED see **Cepola rubescens**
BANDTAIL PUFFER see **Sphoeroides spengleri**
BANGOS see **Chanos chanos**
BANJO CATFISH see **Buncocephalus**

Banjos Banjosidae
banjos 30 cm. (12 in.)
Found fairly widely in the Sea of Japan, on the

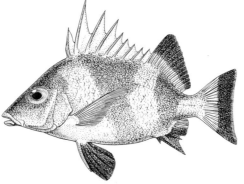

Pacific coast of Japan, in China along the S. China Sea, and in Taiwan.

A deep-bodied fish with high spiny dorsal fin, the membrane of which is deeply indented. It is dull green above, silvery on the sides and belly, but with the fins dark edged.

BANJOSIDAE
A family containing a single species found off the coasts of China, Taiwan, and Japan. It is a deep-bodied species with a laterally compressed body. The dorsal fin has 10 flattened, strong spines in its anterior section, the third ray being the longest; the anal fin has a very long, strong second spine. See **Banjos.**

BAR-FACED WEEVER see **Parapercis nebulosus**

Barathronus Aphyonidae
bicolor 16 cm. (6¼ in.)
This deep-water ophidioid fish is found in the Caribbean Sea and the Gulf of Mexico, at depths of 494–914 m. (270–500 fathoms), with one record from a depth of 1406 m. (768 fathoms). A rather large-headed species with an almost vertical mouth and protruding lower jaw. The body is oval in section in front, but compressed posteriorly; the fins are poorly developed. In most specimens examined the eyes are minute and poorly pigmented, in some they are unpigmented; to all intents *Barathronus* is blind. It is a pale coloured, almost transparent fish, with dark stripes along the belly and sides.

It is a viviparous fish which apparently gives birth to young at any time of the year. These are judged to be at least 1 cm. (⅖ in.) in length at birth and probably lead a planktonic life for a short while. Little is known of its food, except that copepods had been eaten by one specimen, but the size of the teeth in adults suggest that they eat largish prey. The adults are believed to be benthic.

BARB,
    BLACK-SPOT see **Barbus filamentosus**
    BLIND CAVE see **Caecobarbus geertsi**
    CHERRY see **Barbus titteya**
    CLOWN see **Barbus everetti**
    FIVE-BANDED see **Barbus pentazona**
    FLYING see **Esomus danrica**
    GLASS see **Oxygaster oxygastroides**
    HASSELT'S BONY-LIPPED see **Osteocheilus hasselti**
    INDIAN RIVER see **Cyclocheilichthys apogon**
    PURPLE-HEADED see **Barbus nigrofasciatus**
    RED see **Barbus conchonius**
    ROSY see **Barbus conchonius**
    SCHWANENFELD'S see **Barbus schwanenfeldii**
    SPOTTED see **Barbus binotatus**
    SUMATRA see **Barbus tetrazona**
    TIGER see **Barbus pentazona, Barbus tetrazona**
BARBEL see **Barbus barbus, Clarias mossambicus, Tachysurus feliceps**

BARBEL,
  BUTTER see **Eutropius depressirostris**
  MOUNTAIN see **Amphilius platychir**
  RIPPON FALL'S see **Barbus altianalis**
  SEA see **Tachysurus feliceps**
BARBER-EEL see **Plotosus lineatus**

Barbourisia   Barbourisiidae
  rufa *c.* 25 cm. (10 in.)
This brick red fish is typical of the colouring of many whalefishes, a group which are found in deep water in the open ocean. Its gill cavity is dark brown inside. Like other whalefishes, it is a great rarity in oceanographic collections.

It is distinguished from its relatives by possessing small but distinct pelvic fins, and by the skin of the head and body being covered with minute spines embedded in the loose and filmy skin. The huge jaws are covered with tiny, felt-like teeth. It is presumed that the specimen illustrated in colour is *B. rufa* but it was not examined. **48**

BARBOURISIIDAE
A family of whalefishes containing one species only, probably worldwide in the middle layers of the oceans. It shares with other whalefishes (see Cetomimidae and Rondeletiidae) their general features – a rather stout body shape, large head, minute eyes, and vast mouth; the dorsal and anal fins are placed far back near the tail. The only member of this family, however, has small but distinct pelvic fins. It also has a conspicuous lateral line. See **Barbourisia**.

BARBU see **Polydactylus virginius**
BARBUDO see **Polymixia nobilis**

Barbus versus **Puntius**
Many authorities place the small aquarium fishes known as barbs in the genus *Puntius*. The definition of this genus on a world basis (as opposed to local faunas) is not clear, and the whole group of fishes known as barbs, barbels, and mahseers requires revision.

For present purposes the catchall genus *Barbus* has been employed for the whole group, although further research may produce an acceptable subdivision in time.

Barbus   Cyprinidae
  altianalis RIPPON FALL'S BARBEL
  1 m. (39 in.)
This is a moderately stout-bodied barbel found widely in the Great Lakes of Africa and the Victoria Nile. Large specimens are deep-bodied and the lips may be very thick and fleshy, and the snout rather enlarged. The dorsal fin lies well back behind the mid-point of the body. The dorsal spine is relatively short – shorter than the length of the head. The fish is fully scaled with a complete lateral line. Large fishes are greeny-golden, lighter ventrally; the young are silvery.

This fish is particularly abundant in the Victoria Nile, especially in the turbulent, broken water of rapids and at the foot of waterfalls or dams, noticeably of the Rippon Falls

where large numbers of barbel could be seen at the foot of the falls, and some were leaping and attempting to jump the white water. In the lakes it is found in both open and shallow water.

Its food is varied and consists of molluscs, aquatic plants, insect larvae, and small fishes. It is believed to breed in the rivers and larger streams when they are in flood.

This barbel is one of the notable angling fishes of E. Africa. It fights well, and may weigh up to 8·5 kg. (19 lb.) although specimens of 18 kg. (40 lb.) have been reported.

B. barbus BARBEL 102 cm. (40 in.)
The barbel is the n. European representative of one evolutionary line of the carp family. Its rather slender body, with long head, fleshy lips and 4 long barbels around the mouth are as characteristic as the short-based dorsal fin with a heavy serrated-edged spine amongst its first rays. It is widely distributed across Europe from the British Isles, n. to the Danish border, and s. to the Pyrenees and the Alps, e. to Hungary. Related, possibly identical, forms are found in Spain, Portugal, and Italy.

They are typically fishes of running waters, usually in moderately deep and clear rivers, although they also thrive in silted lowland streams. They are usually found in shoals, keeping station against the current during the day and individually actively foraging at night. Their food is composed entirely of bottom-living invertebrates, especially insect larvae, molluscs, and crustaceans.

Barbel migrate upstream to spawn in running water during April, May, or June, depending on the water temperature. The eggs are shed in gravelly shallows; they adhere to or lodge between the stones, and hatch in 10–15 days.

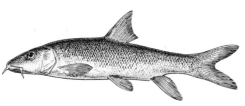

Barbel are fine sporting fish requiring considerable skill to catch and, at an upper weight of 6 kg. (13 lb.), they are a strong fish. The roe (unshed eggs) is poisonous and the flesh is bony and insipid and is not often used as food.

B. binotatus SPOTTED BARB 20 cm. (8 in.)
The spotted barb is widely distributed in the Indo-Australian archipelago and Malaya where it is often common in rivers, streams, and still water. In Thailand it is well distributed especially in mountain streams.

The spotted barb is rather deep-bodied with a moderately high dorsal fin, fully scaled body and 2 pairs of rather long barbels on the upper lip. It has an olive back, silvery sides with a bluish tinge, and several dark blotches, which vary with age although the one on the tail is constant. The dorsal and tail fins are pink with dark edges.

It is a very popular aquarium fish which can be easily bred. It rarely grows longer than 7 cm. (3 in.) in captivity.

B. callipterus 9 cm. (3½ in.)
A small African barb which is kept in aquaria, although not common or well known as a pet fish. Its native range is w. Africa from the Niger to the Cameroons, in running water.

It is a relatively slim fish, with the typically high, almost triangular dorsal fin of the barbs, and a deeply forked tail. It has 2 pairs of moderate barbels on the lips. It is modestly coloured. **108**

B. capensis CLANWILLIAM YELLOWFISH
1 m. (39 in.)
This is a popular angling fish of s. Africa and grows to a maximum weight of about 10 kg. (22 lb.). Its distribution is limited to the Olifants River in the sw. Cape, although the similar and closely related species, *B. holubi*, is found in the Orange River basin and has recently been introduced to the Olifants River. It is rather slender-bodied with the dorsal fin placed above the pelvic fins; it is completely scaled and has a continuous lateral line. Its head is naked, and the mouth has 2 barbels on each side of the upper lip. The lips are very variable in development; in some specimens they are thin, in others very thick and rubbery. Adults are olive-green on the back, golden on the sides and ventrally, but the young are silvery with irregular blotches and vertical bars on the sides.

It feeds on invertebrates, mostly bottom-living insect larvae, crustaceans, and molluscs, but the larger specimens are said to become fish eaters.

B. conchonius ROSY or RED BARB
14 cm. (5½ in.)
This is one of the most popular small barbs in the pet fish industry. It is hardy, and will survive low water temperatures, and is peaceful and relatively easy to breed.

It is native to the n. part of the Indian subcontinent, especially Bengal and Assam. A very beautiful fish. The colouring of the breeding male is deepened, the fins have black tips, but bright pink bases. The male is also slimmer than the female. **109**

B. everetti CLOWN BARB 13 cm. (5 in.)
The clown barb is found in Borneo and Sarawak. It is kept in aquaria and makes an attractive pet. Its body is relatively slim for a barb, but it has the typical 2 pairs of barbels around the mouth, the rear ones being long.

Its coloration is attractive; the back is reddish brown, the sides are golden with a rosy tinge. There are very large dark blue-black blotches on the sides – one across the nape, another on the dorsal fin base, and the third on the tail. There is also a very conspicuous large round blotch on the side and a small dark spot at the base of the tail with a light ring around it.

The clown barb has a reputation of being difficult to breed. It is recommended that the sexes are kept separate for some while, and fed well, before being introduced to a large well-planted aquarium standing in early morning sunlight.

B. filamentosus BLACK-SPOT BARB
15 cm. (6 in.)
An interesting barb found in sw. India, which has achieved some popularity as an aquarium fish where it is peaceable and easy to rear. Its interest centres around the changes in body form and colouring that take place with growth.

The young are brightly coloured with broad bars of deep black across the body, at the dorsal, anal, and tail fin bases. Their fins are deep red. Adults, however, are uniformly silvery with a distinct violet sheen, and a single dark blotch on the side just above the anal fin. Males have very elongate dorsal fin rays; the female's fin rays are short, and she is deep-bodied. This fish is one of the barbs which totally lacks barbels around the mouth. **110**

B. hexagonolepis BOKAR, KATLI 1·2 m. (4 ft)
The bokar is widely distributed in Assam and the region of the e. Himalayas (this name is used in the former area – katli is the Nepalese name). In this area it is the commonest of the large-scaled barbels, usually known as mahseers in India. Its habitat appears to be the lower reaches of the foot-hill rivers in which it is found in mid-stream, usually in the lee of boulders or other obstructions. Its diet is said to be mainly fallen leaves, fruits, and other plants, but it also eats animal matter to some extent.

Compared with the other mahseers, it is moderate in size, weighing at most 9·5 kg. (21 lb.), but more usually around 5·4 kg. (12 lb.). It is nevertheless a good angling fish.

It resembles other members of the genus, with a pair of long barbels on each side of the mouth, the lower lip separate from the jaw which has a hard cutting edge, and the snout covered with horny tubercles or pores. The head is relatively small. Scales on the body are large. It is olive-green on the back, with copper-coloured scales on the sides, ventrally shading to cream. The fins are dark grey.

B. holotaenia 12 cm. (4¾ in.)
An attractive small barb found in w. Africa in the tributaries of the Congo in the central Congo Basin, and n. to the Cameroons. It has been kept in aquaria but has not achieved great popularity, and it has not been bred in captivity.

It is shaped like a typical barb, being rather deep-bodied with a high dorsal fin. Both dorsal and ventral profiles are equally convex. It has a terminal mouth, with 2 pairs of small barbels. **111**

B. holubi see under **B. capensis**

B. macrops 10 cm. (4 in.)
A widespread small barb from W. Africa and the Chad basin, which extends in range into the Sahara, Portuguese Guinea, Ghana, and Liberia.

It is a beautifully coloured fish which lives in rivers, weedy lakes, and dams, and is very adaptable. Spawning takes place during the rainy season, in June–July. Most fish in the population apparently die at the age of one year. **112**

B. marequensis LARGE-SCALED YELLOW-FISH 60 cm. (2 ft)
This barbel is found in the rivers of s. Africa, and is especially common in the Limpopo and the Zambezi rivers. It is easily distinguishable by its large scales, which are longitudinally striated, and vary in number from 27-33 in the lateral line; the dorsal fin which is rather high originates in front of the pelvics. As in other barbels the form of the lips varies, some specimens have thick fleshy lips, others thin lips.

It frequents reaches where the river current is rapid, often being found in pools below rapids. It feeds on bottom-living invertebrates, as well as taking terrestrial insects which have fallen into the water. The larger fish are clearly piscivorous, and can be taken by anglers fishing with a spoon. It is a relatively small barbel, attaining a weight of about 3·2 kg. (7 lb.), but nevertheless gives good sport.

B. nigrofasciatus BLACK RUBY, PURPLE-HEADED BARB 5 cm. (2 in.)
This small barb is native to Sri Lanka where it is found in slow-flowing streams, in shaded areas or hiding under marginal vegetation. It is a popular aquarium fish and has for years been kept in captivity being peaceful and hardy and particularly suitable for the community tank.

Its colouring is very fine, although modest. Males have a dark dorsal fin, and reddish anal and pelvic fins. In the breeding season the male becomes brilliant red over the whole front part of the body, the dark bars have a greenish velvety tinge and rows of iridescent green light scale spots. This brilliant coloration is unfortunately ephemeral being lost after spawning, or on loss of condition. **113**

B. occidentalis 75 cm. (29 in.)
This is the only large barb in w. Africa, an area which supports large numbers of small species. It is common in the upper Niger.

It is a large-scaled species with a high dorsal fin, and 2 moderate barbels on the lips. It is silvery-grey, tinged with deep yellow, and the fins are all yellowish or deep gold.

It grows to a weight of 5 kg. (11 lb.), but makes poor eating for its flesh is full of tiny sharp bones. Large specimens are found in quiet water in the larger rivers, feeding on encrusting algae, and bottom-living invertebrates. However, towards the end of March and the beginning of the wet season, they move into the fast-running main stream, and migrate upstream in shoals to spawn. They are believed to spawn during the wet season in the flooded upper tributaries, and the young can be found in receding flood pools later in the year.

B. pentazona FIVE-BANDED OR TIGER BARB 5 cm. (2 in.)
A widely distributed small barb which is found in the Malay Peninsula, Sumatra, Borneo, and Singapore. Through this range it is rather variable and several subspecies have been described.

These differences are mostly based on the degree of development of the dark cross bars which run over the back and onto the sides, there being 5 or 6 major bars along the sides, the first of which passes through the eye. All these subspecies are beautifully coloured, the back reddish-brown, the sides bronzy and the underside yellowish. The scales on the black bars have greenish edges, and the bases of the fins are bright red. The female is fuller in body shape and rather more soberly coloured than the male.

It is a popular aquarium fish although rather shy and difficult to get to breed. Successful spawning, however, may produce as many as 300–400 eggs and as the fry are large at hatching, a large proportion of them survive.

B. putitora PUTITOR MAHSEER 2·7 m. (9 ft)
The putitor mahseer is one of several n. Indian barbels, known generally as mahseers, about which there is considerable nomenclatural confusion. Some authors also refer them to the genus, or subgenus *Tor*.

This mahseer is found all along the Himalayas, from Kashmir e. possibly to China. It is a large fish living in both clear, fast-flowing stony-bottom, and slowly-flowing rivers; the young are found in quieter waters in the lower tributary streams. It feeds on green algae, insect larvae, and molluscs, mostly bottom-living forms.

It is a long-bodied, torpedo-shaped fish with a broad deeply forked tail, and high dorsal fin. Its scales are large, and relatively few (25–28 in the lateral line). Its mouth has 2 pairs of slender, relatively small barbels, and the lips are variously developed from thin to enormously large folded flaps, apparently depending on the habitat frequented; those living in fast-flowing streams develop the largest lips. However it has been claimed that lip development is a sexual difference.

The adult putitor mahseer is an elegant olive-green on the back, shading through golden green to a yellowish belly. Each of the enormous scales is picked out by a central blotch of dull bronze.

It is one of the famous sporting fishes of India; large, old specimens reach vast weights and lengths, but at all sizes it is a fine angling fish.

B. schwanenfeldii SCHWANENFELD'S BARB 35 cm. (14 in.)
Schwanenfeld's barb is fairly frequently kept as a pet and it makes an especially fine fish for a large public aquarium. Its body is deep and strongly compressed, the dorsal profile being very high, especially in older fishes. The eye is large, and there are 2 pairs of rather long barbels.

It is silvery or golden yellow, the dorsal fin is red with a large black blotch at the tip, the tail fin is also blood-red or orange with a dark streak on each lobe. The other fins are orange or deep yellow.

This barb is a common and widespread native of Sumatra, Borneo, Malaya, and Thailand. It was named in honour of its discoverer in Sumatra, H. W. Schwanenfeld.

B. tambroides 70 cm. (28 in.)
A large freshwater fish, widely distributed in the bigger rivers in Java, Borneo, Sumatra, and Thailand which can best be described as the SE. Asian mahseer. It is barbel-like in general appearance with large scales (about 25 along the side of the body), a high dorsal fin, the first full-length ray of which is thick and spine-like. It has 2 pairs of barbels on the lips, and the lower lip has a flap in the mid-line.

Hugh M. Smith, the authority on the fishes of Thailand, reported that it enjoyed a high reputation as a food fish wherever it occurred in that country. It is to some extent migratory living in the upper reaches of rivers in the dry season, descending downstream with the floods from the rains, but shortly after returning upstream to spawn in July near the mouths of small tributaries which act as nurseries for the young. Local fishermen in Thailand catch this species on hooks baited with a cake made from the fruit of the sugar palm mixed with rice flour.

B. tetrazona SUMATRA OR TIGER BARB 7 cm. (2¾ in.)
The Sumatra barb, as its name suggests, is found in Sumatra, as well as Borneo. A closely related species from Cambodia and Thailand is regarded by some authorities as a subspecies, *B. t. partipentazona*. It is a very popular and successful aquarium fish, despite a susceptibility to disease and a rather aggressive temperament.

There are 4 black cross bands across the back and sides, the first through the eye, the second in front of the dorsal fin, the third over the anal fin base, and the last across the base of the tail fin. The subspecies *B. t. partipentazona* has an additional black bar on the back, running obliquely backwards from the front of the dorsal fin and ending less than half-way across the sides. The tail fin basal stripe is also narrower. 114

B. titteya CHERRY BARB 5 cm. (2 in.)
This is one of the most beautiful barbs, popular as aquarium fish. It is, however, rather timid and shy, although the males are pugnacious towards one another. It will thrive in a well planted rather shaded aquarium and has been bred in captivity.

The cherry barb is native to Sri Lanka and is found in shady streams, particularly in rills of foot-hill streams. Titteya is its local vernacular name.

The sexes are very different: the male is purple-brown on the back, silvery with a reddish tint on the sides and belly, and a deep brown stripe bordered by an iridescent streak runs lengthwise from the mouth to the tail fin. The fins are mostly bright red. The female is darker, more a light brown, with yellowish fins. 115

B. tor TOR MAHSEER 1·2 m (4 ft)
The tor mahseer is the most famous of Indian angling fishes, for although it is not so large as the putitor mahseer, *B. putitora*, it is more common and widely distributed. Its range includes the rivers of the foot-hills of the Himalayas from Bihar to Assam.

In this area it is an important local food fish. It lives in a variety of habitats from open, coloured and slow-flowing rivers to clear hill streams with stony beds. The young are found in the more sheltered tributary streams. It feeds on algae and water plants, as well as leaves which fall into the water, but a substantial amount of animal food, especially molluscs, is also taken.

A stoutly built mahseer, its colouring is striking: golden green on the back, golden on the sides fading to silvery on the belly; the fins are distinctly reddish orange except for the dorsal fin which is dark green-blue.

Barilius Cyprinidae
bola INDIAN TROUT 30 cm. (12 in.)
The Indian trout is native to India, but it is not a trout, although its body form and colouring suggest the European trout. It belongs to the carp family and is possibly closest to the rasboras.

It is a slender-bodied fish with small scales, a pointed head on which the bones beneath the eye cover most of the cheek. Its mouth is very large extending well beyond the eye. It is olive-green on the back, silvery on the sides with a pinkish flush. The fins are tinged with orange. In large specimens the sides are covered with small rounded dark spots; in the young these take the form of dark bars.

The Indian trout is found in the ne. areas of India, ranging from the Punjab to Assam and Burma. It is confined to the hilly regions, living in clear streams with rocky beds, and apparently preferring the rapids at the heads of pools, or the junction of 2 streams. It feeds on fishes when large, insects and young fish when young.

It is one of the prime sporting fishes of the Indian hills, taking a fly or spoon, and fighting furiously, leaping and turning in its struggle.

B. christyi 13 cm. (5 in.)
The genus *Barilius* is widely spread from China and Japan w. across Asia, into Africa. They are rather long-bodied, active, shoaling fishes looking almost herring-like, although have a barbel-like solidity as well.

B. christyi is found in the Congo region. Like its relatives it is torpedo-shaped, with a large mouth. It is essentially a silvery fish with a dark olive back; the sides have green tinges and a series of 16–18 vertical dark bars along the sides. The upper jaw has a reddish blotch, and there is a black mark at the base of the tail. The fins are yellowish.

Like its relatives it is a restless shoaling fish feeding on zooplankton and insect larvae. It is sometimes kept in aquaria, but requires a large tank with adequate space.

BARNDOOR SKATE see **Raja laevis**
BARRACOUTA see **Thyrsites atun**
BARRACUDA see Sphyraenidae
BARRACUDA,
   CALIFORNIA see **Sphyraena argentea**
   GREAT see **Sphyraena barracuda**
   PACIFIC see **Sphyraena argentea**
BARRACUDINA see Paralepididae
BARRACUDINA see **Paralepis-atlantica**
BARRACUTA see **Scomberomorus commerson**
BARRACUTA, KING see **Rexea solandri**
BARRAMUNDA see **Neoceratodus forsteri**
BARRAMUNDI see **Scleropages leichardti**
BARRAMUNDI, NORTHERN see **Scleropages leichardti**
BARRED
   CICHLID see **Cichlasoma festivum**
   CLINGFISH see **Tomicodon fasciatus**
   HAMLET see **Hypoplectrus puella**
   LONGTOM see **Ablennes hians**
   SURFPERCH see **Amphistichus argenteus**
BARRED-FACE SPINE-CHEEK see **Scolopsis temporalis**
BARREL-EYE see **Macropinna microstoma**
BARRELFISH see **Hyperoglyphe perciforma, Schedophilus medusophagus**
BASKING SHARK see **Cetorhinus maximus**
BASS see **Dicentrarchus labrax**
BASS,
   BLACK see Centrarchidae
   GIANT SEA see **Stereolepis gigas**
   LARGEMOUTH see **Micropterus salmoides**
   SALMON see **Argyrosomus regius**
   SMALLMOUTH see **Micropterus dolomieui**
   STONE see **Polyprion americanus**
   STRIPED see **Roccus saxatilis**
   WHITE SEA see **Cynoscion nobilis**
BASSLET, FAIRY see Grammidae
BASSLET, FAIRY see **Gramma loreto**
BASTARD
   GALJOEN see **Oplegnathus conwayi**
   MULLET see **Polynemus indicus**
   TRUMPETER see **Latridopsis forsteri**
BATFISH see Ephippidae, Ogcocephalidae
BATFISH see **Halieuta fitzsimonsi, Platax orbicularis, Platax pinnatus**
BATFISH,
   LONG-NOSED see **Ogcocephalus vespertillo**

PANCAKE see **Halieutichthys aculeatus**
ROUND see **Platax orbicularis**
SHORTNOSE see **Ogcocephalus nasutus**
SPINY see **Halieutichthys aculeatus**
SPOTTED see **Zalieutes elator**

Bathophilus Melanostomiatidae
flemingi 16·5 cm (6½ in.)
This scaleless dragonfish is found in the e. Pacific from the region of British Columbia to Mexico. It is, however, only taken off-shore over deep water. At night it has been captured between the surface and 183 m. (100 fathoms) and in daytime at around 1370 m. (750 fathoms).

It is a very distinctive fish in its natural area, with its large dorsal and anal fins opposite one another, its very long pelvic fins, and a chin barbel as long as its body. Its light organs are placed in pits on the sides.

Bathyagonus Agonidae
alascanus GRAY STARSNOUT 12·5 cm. (5 in.)
Found along the Pacific coast of N. America from n. California to the Bering Sea. It is particularly common on the coast of British Columbia in depths of 18–252 m. (10–138 fathoms). It lives mostly on sandy and muddy grounds.

Like most of the poachers it is brownish grey with a series of dark saddles across the back. It is distinguished by the erect many-spined rostral process, and the rather backward position of the anal fin.

Bathyclupea Bathyclupeidae
hoskynii 20 cm. (8 in.)
A species which is widespread in the Indian Ocean. It was first discovered during the exploratory surveys of R.I.M.S. 'Investigator', and described in the 1890s, being named for Commander R. F. Hoskyn, RN, Superintendent of the Marine Survey of India.

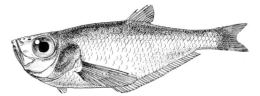

This species lives at considerable depths, having been taken as deep as 766 m. (419 fathoms), although evidently most abundant at around 366 m. (200 fathoms). It lives in mid-water but its biology is largely unknown.

It is silvery grey becoming black on the back.

BATHYCLUPEIDAE
A small family of deep sea fishes found both in the Caribbean Sea and the Indian Ocean. They are mid-water dwellers in depths of 366–766 m. (200–419 fathoms), silvery grey in colour, and physically very fragile.

The body is compressed and deep anteriorly, while the gape of the mouth is nearly vertical. The pectoral fins are long, the anal fin is low but long-based, and the eye large. The rather large scales are very fragile. This character and certain internal features led to it being regarded as a herring-like fish originally; today it is classed near the sweepers (Pempheridae). See **Bathyclupea**.

Bathydraco Bathydraconidae
scotiae DEEP DRAGONFISH 16 cm. (6¼ in.)

One of the least well known of the Antarctic dragonfishes. It has been found off Coats Land and on the opposite side of the continent between Queen Mary Land and Wilkes Land. It might be assumed to occur in intermediate areas at great depths for these specimens were captured at depths of 2650 and 2260 m. (1448 and 1235 fathoms).

Its coloration is pale brownish, ventrally rather darker, and has dusky fins.

The members of this genus are very thin elongate fishes, and fully scaled including the sides of the head.

BATHYDRACONIDAE

A family of Antarctic fishes restricted to the coasts of the continent and the Scotia Ridge n. to S. Georgia. One deep-water species is found around Kergulen. The members of the family are closely related to the Antarctic 'cods' (Nototheniidae) but they have flattened heads, and also lack the first dorsal fin. The group is diverse in appearance, some having long snouts, others large teeth in the jaws, and yet others few scales. See **Bathydraco, Prionodraco**.

Bathygobius   Gobiidae
soporator FRILLFIN GOBY 15 cm. (6 in.)
This goby is said to be widely distributed on both sides of the tropical Atlantic, but has been divided into several poorly defined subspecies which may be valid. It is best known, however, from the w. Atlantic where it ranges from Bermuda to s. Brazil, including the Gulf of Mexico and the W. Indies.

It is a very adaptable shallow-water goby, which is extremely common in most areas. It inhabits estuaries and can be found on muddy bottoms in low salinity, as well as tide pools on rocky shores. It is probably most common on mixed sand patches and turtle grass beds in depths of a few inches to 2·5 m. (8 ft).

It is a heavy-bodied goby with the body fully scaled, and the pelvic fin 'sucker' well developed. The upper rays of the pectoral fins are finely divided and much branched. Its colouring is drab, usually brown with darker bands and blotches on the back and upper sides. In some areas specimens have blue spots along the sides, most distinctly on the gill cover.

Bathylaco   Bathylaconidae
nigricans BONYTHROAT 28 cm. (11 in.)
This little-known fish has been found on a number of occasions in the Atlantic between the W. Indies and Madeira, as well as in the e.

Pacific. No doubt it will be discovered elsewhere in time. It has always been captured in the deep sea with nets at depths of from 640 to 4575 m. (350 to 2500 fathoms), except for one off Madeira which was taken from the stomach of a black scabbardfish.

It is dull brown in colour. Virtually nothing is known of its biology.

BATHYLACONIDAE

A family of doubtful affinities which contains only two little-known species, possibly of world-wide distribution in the deep sea (although only recorded in the Pacific and Atlantic oceans). Black fish, fully scaled except on the head, with large mouth and small pectoral fins placed low down on the belly. The most immediate distinguishing character is the flattened, plate-like nature of the branchiostegal rays in the throat. No other living fish possesses similar ones – the reason this family is regarded as distinct. It also suggests that 'bonythroat' is an appropriate name for these fish.

The teeth are very small, and there are no light organs save for a comma-shaped organ in front of the eye. See **Bathylaco**.

BATHYLAGIDAE

A small family of open ocean fishes distributed worldwide. In the Atlantic, species have been reported from the Davis Strait to Antarctica. They are relatively small fishes, rarely exceeding 18 cm. (7 in.) in length; many are much smaller. They have been reported (probably in error) from depths down to 3660 m. (2000 fathoms), and some, at least, migrate to nearer the surface at night.

The bathylagids or black-smelts, vary considerably in body shape; most are slender but several are rather deep-bodied. Most have very large eyes, directed to the sides, and small mouths; in some species the larvae have eyes on stalks. See **Bathylagus**.

Bathylagus   Bathylagidae
antarcticus 15 cm. (6 in.)
A small black-smelt found widely distributed in the S. Atlantic, and extending s. to the Antarctic seas. It is very slender, with a moderately large head, and very large eyes. The

mouth is moderate. Like many of its family it possesses an adipose fin. It is described as being a uniform blackish brown colour. It has been found in trawls hauled to depths of 1830–3660 m. (1000–2000 fathoms), but may have been found in shallower water. Nothing is known of its biology.

B. pacificus PACIFIC BLACK-SMELT
25 cm. (10 in.)
The body shape of the Pacific black-smelt is typical of the family. It has large eyes, a small mouth with small teeth. Its scales are large but easily dislodged, and few are found on specimens caught in nets. Its body is chocolate brown to black in colour.

It is found along the continental shelf of the Pacific coast of America from Alaska to California, in depths below 305 m. (166 fathoms). It is believed to spawn in spring. Like its relatives, it eats small crustaceans, and in turn is eaten in numbers by larger deep-water fish. A relative, B. stilbius is one of the commonest mid-water fishes off the Californian coast. This is similar in shape but has a pointed snout, and is iridescent in colour.

B. stilbius see under **B. pacificus**

Bathymaster   Bathymasteridae
signatus SEARCHER 30 cm. (12 in.)
A N. Pacific species, found from n. British Columbia to the Bering Sea, and along the Asian coast to the Commander Islands. It is a bottom-living inshore form, the biology of which is not well known. The young are planktonic and are found close inshore.

It is distinguished by its rather slender shape, its long dorsal fin of which only the first 3 rays are unbranched, by its moderate sized, toothed scales on the body and fins, and by the distinct pores on the head. It is brown in colour, darker on the back, with a distinct black patch on the front of the dorsal fin.

BATHYMASTERIDAE

A small family of marine fishes found in coastal waters of the N. Pacific. Eight or 9 species only have been recognized, all relatively slender with long dorsal fins, comprising a series of unbranched then branched rays. Small scales cover the body, occasionally the cheeks, and the bases of the fins.

All these fishes are small, few exceed 30 cm. (12 in.). See **Bathymaster, Ronquilus**.

Bathymicrops   Ipnopidae
regis 11 cm. (4½ in.)
This is a slender-bodied deep-water fish, with large jaws which bear small sharp teeth. The eyes are minute and only a vestige of them remains, covered by scales and skin. They are placed forward on the snout and are directed upwards. In colour it is greyish, but the areas over the belly and in the region of the eyes are darker.

Known from the Atlantic Ocean, between the Equator and 29° N., and in both e. and w. regions, it has always been found in the deepest areas, close to the bottom, in depths between 4255 and 5300 m. (2326–2898 fathoms). Related forms are known from the South Pacific and Indian oceans.

Bathyprion   Bathyprionidae
danae 39 cm. (15½ in.)
An elongate, superficially pike-like fish which has been found on only 3 occasions – 400 km. (250 miles) off Sydney, Australia, off Madeira, and in the se. Atlantic. Its appearance is quite distinctive. It is dark brown in colour.

The only known specimens have been taken at depths of about 2000–2700 m. (1093–1476 fathoms) over water much deeper than that. It is a deep-living bathypelagic fish, which, from its body form and fin pattern, probably lives a sedentary life hovering or cruising gently, with sudden darting movements to capture prey. It is probable that its food is mainly small, possibly young fishes and crustaceans, but not large or very active for its stomach is small.

While the teeth are large for a member of this group, they are fitted for gripping and are not the stabbing teeth of the active deep-sea predators.

BATHYPRIONIDAE

A family of deep sea fishes known only from

the single species, which has been taken 3 times in widely separated areas. In all probability it will be found widespread in all deep oceans.

This family was first described in 1966 and is placed close to the smooth-head family Alepocephalidae. Its resemblances include the anal and dorsal fins opposite and well down the body, pelvics on the belly, and small, low-placed pectoral fins. However the eyes are small and the maxillary and premaxillary bones have teeth along their length, the latter a feature of the searsid smooth-heads which are sometimes placed in a family of their own, the Searsidae. This group, however, has light organs on the shoulder which *Bathyprion* lacks. See **Bathyprion**.

BATHYPTEROIDAE

A relatively small family of deep-water, bottom-living fishes, which have rather slender bodies, and, most notably, elongated rays in various fins. Deep sea photographs have shown that at least one species uses the long rays in the pelvic and tail fins as a tripod by which it raises itself from the sea bed.

The members of the family have rather depressed heads, with minute eyes. All have distinct scales, most with a smooth edge. Most species also have curved hook-like rays on the lower edge of the tail fin. All species examined have proved to be hermaphrodites.

Representatives of the family are known from deep water in all tropical and temperate oceans, usually on soft muddy bottoms, but judging from records of captures their distribution is patchy. They range in depth from 475 m. (260 fathoms) to 5610 m. (2070 fathoms). See **Bathypterois, Benthosaurus.**

Bathypterois   Bathypteroidae
  dubius 26 cm. (10 in.)
This deep water fish is known only from the e. Atlantic and the Mediterranean. In this area it has been found on the sea bed at depths of 800 to 1805 m. (437–985 fathoms).

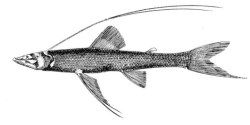

In body shape it is typical of its family, notably in the rather flattened head, and slender but rounded body. This species has an adipose fin, and a distinct notch beneath the anterior rays of the tail fin. The function of this notch is not known, nor is that of the long pectoral ray, although in view of its relative mobility, it may have a sensory function. The biology of this fish is virtually unknown.

Bathysauropsis   Chlorophthalmidae
  gracilis 25 cm. (10 in.)
A deep-water member of the family, its chief interest is that aspects of its anatomy suggest a relationship with the Ipnopidae, while others are clearly chlorophthalmid. *Bathysauropsis gracilis* has in particular the large eyes, and characteristic tooth pattern of the latter family. It lives mid-way between the middle level chlorophthalmids and the deep abyssal ipno-

pids, being found from 870 to 2600 m. (475–1425 fathoms).

It is a long-bodied slender fish with a flattened snout, moderately large eyes which are directed obliquely upwards. Its body is covered with scales, and it has well developed fins, including an adipose fin.

Bathysaurus   Synodontidae
  mollis DEEP-SEA LIZARDFISH
48 cm. (19 in.)
This is a deep-sea member of the family which has been found in the e. N. Atlantic, the Gulf of Mexico, and the Pacific Ocean, at great depths ranging from 2615 m.–4700 m. (1430–2570 fathoms).

It is a long, slim-bodied fish, with a compressed tail region; the head and anterior body are flattened. The jaws are very long, with numerous large curved, sometimes barbed, depressible teeth. All the fins are long, and this species has a small adipose fin between tail and dorsal fin. It is a bottom-living fish, which is colourless with the dusky body-cavity lining showing through. The top of the head is transparent and the brain can be seen through the bone. The eyes are light green.

Bathytyphlops   Ipnopidae
  marionae 28 cm. (11 in.)
Like the other members of its family, *B. marionae* is virtually eyeless. The eyes are very small and covered by skin, but not by scales, and although they are not pigmented, they have a small lens. It is a moderately slender fish, with large fins. Its mouth is relatively large, and has patches of minute teeth on the jaws and palate – apparently jaws not suitable for seizing hold of actively swimming prey. It is dark brown, with black gill regions.

It has been found in deep water from 869–2653 m. (475 to 1450 fathoms) in the Caribbean area and the Gulf of Mexico. Very few specimens are known, as is the case with its relative *B. sewelli*, known in the Arabian Sea at depths of 3840 to 3872 m. (2099–2117 fathoms).
B. sewelli see under **B. marionae**

Batrachocottus   Cottomephoridae
  nikolskii 24 cm. (9½ in.)
Found only in Lake Baikal in the central U.S.S.R. and there mainly confined to the immediate shore line, usually in 4–10 m. (2–5 fathoms) but extending down to 476 m. (260 fathoms). Unlike the other members of the family which eat mainly amphipod crustaceans, this sculpin feeds on insect larvae, chiefly caddis flies and chironomids.

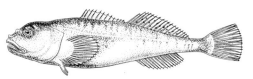

It is a rather commonplace looking sculpin. The body is mainly yellowish or grey, the fins colourless. Males are larger than the females, which rarely exceed 19 cm. (7 in.) in length.

BATRACHOIDIDAE
The toadfish family, a group of mainly bottom-dwelling, inshore fishes found in tropical and warm temperate seas. They have a rather short

thickset body, the head is wide and flattened, the eyes on top and looking upwards rather than laterally. The mouth is large, the lower jaw projecting, the jaws being well equipped with teeth. Gill openings are small, the pelvic fins are placed well forward on the throat.

A number of these fish are well-known producers of sound, some have light organs on the body, and others have venom spines. See **Amphichthys, Halophryne, Opsanus, Porichthys, Sanopus, Thalassophryne.**

BAY ANCHOVY see **Anchoa mitchilli**
BEACONFISH see **Hemigrammus ocellifer**
BEAKED
  CORALFISH see **Chelmon rostratus**
  LEATHER-JACKET see **Oxymonacanthus longisrostris**
  SALMON see **Gonorhynchus gonorhynchus**
BEARDED GHOUL see **Inimicus didactylus**
BEARDFISH, STOUT see **Polymixia nobilis**

Bedotia   Atherinidae
  geoyi 8 cm. (3 in.)
A freshwater silverside from the rivers and streams of Madagascar. It is very beautifully coloured and has met with some success as an aquarium fish. The male is more brightly coloured than the female, and is especially distinguished by having the outer edges of the tail coloured deep reddish brown; the female's tail is uncoloured.

It is peaceful and lively in the aquarium. They have bred in captivity, the male driving the female repeatedly. Eggs are shed in fine-leaved water plants over a period of several days. The parents are said to protect both eggs and young. **214**

BELLOWSFISH, BANDED see **Centriscops humerosus**

Belone   Belonidae
  belone GARFISH 94 cm. (37 in.)
A common fish in European seas, the garfish is found from Trondheim in Norway, s. Iceland, and the British Isles, s. to the Azores, Madeira and the Canary Islands, and throughout the Mediterranean and Black seas. It is a long slim fish with long, pointed, beak-like jaws which bear numerous sharp teeth. The dorsal and anal fins are long, but there are no finlets between them and the tail. It is gleaming silver, with a brilliant green or blue back; the belly and ventral fins have a yellowish tinge.

A surface-living fish found both in the open ocean and in inshore coastal waters where it spawns in early summer. The eggs are small and spherical and covered with numerous filaments, so that although they float at the surface, they also tangle in floating nets, flotsam, and algae. The young fish have jaws of unequal length, the lower jaw being very long, while the upper is short; in the past these young were described as species of halfbeaks.

It is an active fish which eats young fishes, especially herring, sprat, and sandeels, and also crustaceans. It is not an important food fish although small quantities are landed and sold. Its flesh is of excellent quality, although the bright green bones of the vertebral column are a little disconcerting. It is a fine sporting fish on light tackle, although not frequently fished for around the British coast.

Belonesox   Poeciliidae
  belizanus PIKE TOP-MINNOW
20 cm. (8 in.)
Found mainly in murky, muddied waters in river backwaters, marshes, and lakes in Central America from the Atlantic slope of Honduras, Guatemala, and Yucatan to s. Mexico. It is said to have suffered greatly from insecticides sprayed onto the water in mosquito control programmes.

The body shape is strikingly reminiscent of that of the pike, being elongate with long snout, and a large mouth. Its dorsal fin is also placed far back near the tail. In fact it feeds like a pike, lying amongst water plants and making a sudden sortie after passing prey.

They are kept in aquaria but, being rather large and predatory, only the specialist usually attempts to keep them. The female is the larger (males grow to only 10 cm., 4 in.) and is similarly coloured.

The young are born alive (15–25 mm. at birth) in broods of between 20 and 80, according to the size of the mother. **206**

BELONIDAE
The family of garfish, needlefish, or long-toms, a group of mainly marine, tropical and warm temperate fishes of distinctive shape but confusing similarity. All are long and slender, with moderately small dorsal and anal fins placed close to the tail, all the marine species have long beak-like jaws with many sharply pointed teeth.

In general they are schooling, surface living fishes. Some forms are found in the open sea, others are inshore species, often found close inshore around piers and wharf pilings, and on tidal flats. They are great jumpers, frequently leaping clear of the water when hooked, frightened, or startled by bright lights, although some seem to leap for the pleasure of doing so. Occasionally their leaps can have serious consequences, for fishermen in skiffs have been impaled by the beak.

Most needlefishes produce rather large, spherical eggs which are equipped with long filaments. These serve as floatation devices, and also become entangled in flotsam. In some species the young fish have curiously unequal jaws, the lower jaw being longer than the upper. The young of some of the inshore species also float passively at the surface mimicking floating twigs and eelgrass.

A few species of this family are found in freshwater. See **Ablennes, Belone, Belonion, Petalichthys, Strongylura, Tylosaurus, Xenetodon**.

Belonion   Belonidae
  apodion 5 cm. (2 in.)
This surprisingly minute needlefish is found in freshwater in S. America. It was first made known to Science as recently as 1966 by Dr B. B. Collette, and was discovered both in a lake in Bolivia, in the Rio Guaporé catchment, and in Brazil on the Madeira River, a tributary of the Amazon.

Despite the small size of the specimens described 31–50 mm. (1¼–2 in.), they are fully mature, and females of 24 mm. (1 in.) body length contain small eggs. They are remarkably slender, fragile little creatures, but are typical of the family Belonidae in general shape, except that the upper jaw is not produced into a beak;

only the lower jaw is long. This resembles the normal development of the jaws in most needlefish and this remarkable genus is considered to be neotenous, showing juvenile features although fully mature.

Belontia   Belontiidae
  signata COMB-TAILED PARADISEFISH
13 cm. (5 in.)
A rather small labyrinth fish. The tail fin is rounded in young fish but the central rays elongate with age. The back and upper sides are olive, with metallic reflections ventrally which in certain light show up reddish. Large fish have a reddish sheen overall. A round dark spot under the base of the soft dorsal, another on the pectoral base.

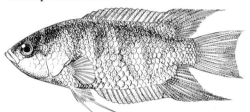

B. signata is found only in the freshwaters of Sri Lanka – it is widely distributed in hillstreams, ponds, tanks, and streams in the coastal plain. It is imported for the aquarium and although rather shy tends to be pugnacious and is likely to eat any much smaller fish.

BELONTIIDAE
The largest of the family groups within the labyrinth fishes, this family includes many of the aquarium fishes known as gouramis, paradisefish, and the Siamese fighting fish. Its members are found entirely in freshwaters of Asia ranging from China and the Philippines w. to India and including the major E. Indian islands.

It is closely related to the climbing-perch family but its members lack teeth on the prevomer (the most anterior bone in the roof of the mouth). They also have smoothly rounded opercular bones. Above the gills in the gill chamber on either side there is a much convoluted accessory breathing organ which enables the fish to breathe air at the surface; most members of the family live in still or slow-flowing waters often thickly vegetated and low or lacking in dissolved oxygen. See **Belontia, Betta, Colisa, Macropodus, Sphaerichthys, Trichogaster, Trichopsis**.

BELTED SANDFISH see **Serranus subligarius**
BELUGA see **Huso huso**

Bembrops   Percophididae
  caudimacula 25 cm. (10 in.)
Widely distributed in the Indian Ocean but, because of its relative scarcity due to the depths in which it lives, known only from scattered areas such as the Gulf of Aden, off Natal, and the Bay of Bengal. It is also reported from off Japan. It lives in depths of 366–640 m. (200–350 fathoms), on or close to the bottom of sandy or muddy grounds.

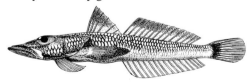

It is yellowish-brown, darker on the back, and the first dorsal fin has a dusky tip. It is distinguished by its prominent lower jaw and very large eyes. Its scales are also moderately large.

Benthobatis   Torpedinidae
  marcida DEEP-SEA ELECTRIC RAY
49 cm. (19¼ in.)
This electric ray has been found along the continental slope off S. Carolina and Florida, as well as off the N. Cuban coast, usually in depths of 640–914 m. (350–500 fathoms), although off Cuba young specimens are taken between 274 and 640 m. (150 and 350 fathoms) but not below.

Its smoothly rounded body contrasts with the rather triangular pelvic fin complex, and its body and skin are soft and limp. In colour it is a delicate fawn, with small whitish spots on the back; ventrally it is pure white or lightly brown-tinged. Its most interesting feature is the poor development of the eyes which are minute, covered entirely with skin and usually completely concealed. It is effectively blind.

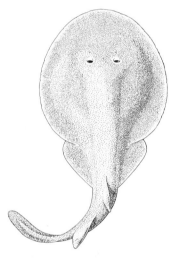

Little is known of its biology. At birth it is usually less than 81–87 mm. (3–3½ in.) long. It is believed to feed on crustaceans. A related species, *B. moresbyi*, lives off s. India and in the Arabian Gulf.
B. moresbyi see under **B. marcida**

Benthosaurus   Bathypteroidae
  grallator TRIPOD FISH 29 cm. (11½ in.)
This astonishing fish has been found mainly in the tropical Atlantic and the Gulf of Mexico in great depths, 2104–3375 m. (1148–1844 fathoms), but specimens are known from the Indian Ocean, and it is probably widely distributed. Its most immediate character is the extreme elongation of the first pelvic and lowest caudal rays. Deep water photographs of the sea bed have shown that the fish poses on the tips of these 3 rays, and apparently skips along on them like a cricket. Being a bottom-living species it would be at some advantage to raise itself up above the sea bed in this way.

Fresh tripod fish are dull brown or black in colour, but the tips of the dorsal, caudal, and some of the anal rays are pink, and the membranes of the pelvic fin are reddish. The eye is golden. The formation of the pectoral fin is distinctive for in all its relatives the pectoral fin is made up of 2 sections. Little is known of the biology of this fish.

Benthosema   Myctophidae
   glaciale 9 cm. (3½ in.)
This lanternfish is found widely across the N. Atlantic, from the Davis Strait to Cape Hatteras in the w. Atlantic, and from Spitzbergen to the Cape Verde Islands in the E. It also occurs in the Mediterranean. It is not, however, found near the coasts, but normally lives in the open sea from the surface down to 366 m. (200 fathoms). This is one of the relatively few lanternfish to be found in the far N. of the Atlantic. Like its relatives it is found at the surface at night, but at the lower levels of its vertical range in daylight. It spawns in spring and summer, feeds on planktonic crustaceans, and in turn is eaten by numerous larger fishes, such as cod in the N.

BERMUDA
   CHUB see **Kyphosus sectatrix**
   PEARLEYE see **Scopelarchus sagax**

BERYCIDAE
A family of mainly deep-sea fishes of cosmopolitan distribution. Some species are found in moderately shallow water, and the deep-sea forms are mid-water fish.

In general they are deep-bodied, rather compressed fish, with a large head, big eye, and strongly angled mouth. The head and body are covered with stout scales. Most species have rather prominent ridges and heavy spines on the head; this is particularly noticeable in the young. Their fins have heavy spiny rays and branched rays; the pelvics, which have many rays, have a heavy spine anteriormost.

Many of the berycoid fishes are bright red in colour. See **Beryx, Centroberyx**.

Beryx   Berycidae
   decadactylus 61 cm. (2 ft)
Found widely along the European Atlantic coast, in the Mediterranean, and S. along the N. African coast. It is usually captured in depths of 300–550 m. (164–300 fathoms), although it has occasionally been caught as shallow as 128 m. (70 fathoms). It lives close to the bottom, but probably is not a regular inhabitant of the sea floor. The young, which have singularly spiny heads, live in mid-water. All sizes feed on crustaceans, especially shrimps, and on fishes and squids.

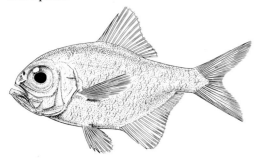

Its coloration is striking, a uniform orange-red which extends to the fins, while the body cavity has a purplish tinge. It is distinguished by its deep body, large head, eye, and oblique mouth.

Occasionally this fish is caught in numbers in British waters; although the flesh is of excellent quality it is not often marketed.

B. splendens ALFONCINO 63 cm. (25 in.)
Probably distributed worldwide, but best known in the N. Atlantic from Madeira to the Portuguese coast, where it is commercially exploited and known as Alfoncino, and in the N. Pacific off Japan. It is found occasionally as far N. as Iceland, and has been reported off the South African coast. It occurs in waters of 183–732 m. (100–400 fathoms).

It is a beautiful rose-red fish, slightly orange ventrally, but with all fins and the insides of the mouth and gill covers bright red. Its body form is similar to that of *B. decadactylus*, but it has a shallow body, and a shorter dorsal fin with 14–16 branched rays only.

Betta   Belontiidae
   splendens SIAMESE FIGHTING FISH
6 cm. (2½ in.)
The Siamese fighting fish is, as its name suggests, a native of Thailand or Siam. For many years it was confused with the Malayan species, *B. pugnax*, and was also carried around extensively so that its original distribution was obscured. In Thailand it is widely distributed in ponds, drainage channels, and sluggish rivers. Such areas are the haunt of numerous aquatic insects, most notably mosquitoes, the larvae of which form the main diet of this fish in the wild. Young fish tend to eat small crustaceans. The role of *Betta* as a controller of mosquito larvae is considerable, it was estimated by one scientist that each adult fish ate 10,000–15,000 larvae each year. In captivity mosquito larvae are the best food for this species which only willingly eats live, moving organisms.

This species lays its eggs in a bubble nest, produced mainly by the male. The mouth and pharynx give off a viscid mucous secretion which ensures a prolonged life for the bubbles blown into a tight mass at the surface. Eggs shed and fertilized are gathered as they sink and spat into the nest by either parent, although only the male guards them and produces new bubbles as the old ones break down. After hatching, the larvae remain in the nest until the yolk sac is absorbed; if they leave the nest the male picks them up in his mouth and spits them back. The function of the bubble nest is twofold, firstly ensuring that the young, during their sensitive early stages, are kept close to the well oxygenated surface waters, and secondly that they are kept together so that they can be adequately protected.

This fighting fish frequently lives in poorly oxgenated water and therefore breathes atmospheric oxygen at the surface, absorbing it in the accessory respiratory organs above the gills within the gill chamber.

The male is well known for its aggressive nature. In Thailand there is almost a cottage industry in breeding and keeping them to be staged in fish fights on which the owners and bystanders wager sums of money. Males need to be kept separate, both from females or other fishes which they will bully, and also from one another. They are usually isolated in individual jampots so that they can see one another and be stimulated to flash their fins and display. Put together the males immediately attack, tearing at fins and scales, and sometimes locking jaws. Much superficial damage is caused by the teeth in the jaws but death seldom results except from secondary fungal or bacterial infections.

This fish has a long history of domestication, originally as a fighting fish, latterly as a petfish. During several centuries of cultivation tremendous variety has been bred into the species. The wild fish is greyish brown or green with dusky lengthwise bands, but aquarium specimens are green, iridescent blue, wine red, and almost black. Many males develop very long fins. Females are generally yellowish brown with dusky cross bands; the fins are yellowish with a narrow red border. **454**

BIB see **Trisopterus luscus**
BICHIR see **Polypterus senegalus**
BICHIR, NILE see **Polypterus bichir**

Bidyanus   Theraponidae
   bidyanus SILVER PERCH 41 cm. (16 in.)
Found in the whole of the Murray-Darling river system of Australia, except in the highest reaches, and introduced into a few coastal streams in New South Wales. This was one of the most abundant freshwater fishes in this area, but its distribution and abundance have been adversely affected by dams and weirs. It lays planktonic eggs, spawning when the water level rises after rains, but the control of river levels has affected the survival of the fry, and spawning areas are much reduced.

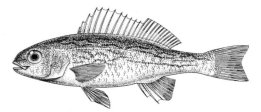

It is a good sporting fish, popular with anglers, and is tasty as well.

It is basically silvery, the upper surface lightly reticulated with brown.

This species was formerly placed in the genus *Therapon*.

BIG SKATE see **Raja binoculata**
BIG-EYE see Priacanthidae
BIG-EYE see **Priacanthus arenatus, Thunnus obesus**
BIG-EYE
   SCAD see **Selar crumenophthalmus**
   TUNA see **Thunnus obesus**
BIG-SCALED MACKEREL see **Gasterochisma melampus**
BIG-SPOTTED TRIGGERFISH see **Balistoides conspicillum**
BIGSCALE, CRESTED see **Poromitra crassiceps**
BILLFISH see Istiophoridae
BIRDWRASSE see **Gomphosus varius**
BISKOP, BLACK see **Cymatoceps nasutus**
BITTERLING see **Rhodeus amarus**
BLAASOP see **Arothron hispidus**
BLAASOP, BLUE see **Lagocephalus lagocephalus**
BLACK
   AMUR see **Mylopharyngodon piceus**
   BASS see Centrarchidae
   BISKOP see **Cymatoceps nasutus**
   BREAM see **Girella tricuspidata**
   CASCAROB see **Polycentrus schomburgkii**
   DOGFISH see **Centroscyllium fabricii**
   DRAGONFISH see **Idiacanthus fasciola**
   DRUM see **Pogonias cromis**
   GOBY see **Gobius niger**
   GROUPER see **Mycteroperca bonaci**
   HALIBUT see **Reinhardtius hippoglossoides**
   LOOSE-JAW see **Malacosteus niger**

BLENNIIDAE

A large family of mainly small and mostly marine fishes, distributed worldwide in tropical and temperate regions. A few species have penetrated into freshwater and live in lakes.

The blennies have scaleless skins, and numerous small, close-packed teeth in the jaws. Some blennies have relatively massive curved dagger-like, paired teeth in the sides of the jaws. They have 2 long rays in each pelvic fin. Tufts of skin and tentacles on the head are also features of the family, making recognition more positive.

Most blennies are found in shallow inshore waters living close to the bottom, their life-style being secretive and relying on obliterative coloration to survive. Many forms live in intertidal areas and some even jump across rocks from one pool to another, if provoked. A few blenny species are found when young as pelagic fishes and most forms have a brief planktonic juvenile stage. Most blennies breed, as they live, under stones, inside sea shells, or crevices, the eggs being deposited in clumps and guarded by one or both the adults.

Blennies are not exploited for food or put to other uses. Their abundance, and success as shore-living fishes, however, implies that they are important inhabitants of inshore communities in all seas. See **Alticops, Aspidontus, Blennius, Coryphoblennius, Ecsenius, Entomacrodus, Meiacanthus, Ophioblennius, Petroscirtes, Plagiotremus, Xiphasia.**

Blennius   Blenniidae
  gattorugine TOMPOT BLENNY
30 cm. (12 in.)
Found in European waters from n. Scotland and the Irish coast to W. Africa, and in the Mediterranean. It occurs amongst kelp on the lower shore but only becomes really common below low tide mark to depths of 8 m. (6 fathoms). It is most common on rocky grounds and amongst medium-sized boulders.

Like other blennies it spawns in spring in rocky crevices, the eggs being guarded by the male who also aerates them by fanning with his pectoral fins.

Identified by the rather stout body and single, much branched tentacle above each eye. **419**
B. incognitus 6 cm. (2½ in.)
A recently discovered blenny which was described only in 1968 from specimens found in the Mediterranean. It now appears that it is widespread throughout the Mediterranean, the Adriatic, Marmora Sea, and the Black Sea.

It is distinguished by the long tentacle above each eye, which is deeply branched from near the base. Its pectoral fins have 13–14 rays. As with most other blennies the 2 short spines in front of the anal fin in mature males are swollen and glandular; in this species the ray tip is broad and ridged – a diagnostic feature. **420**
B. nigriceps BLACK-HEADED BLENNY
4 cm. (1½ in.)
This little blenny is probably the most beautifully coloured of the family in European waters where it is found only in the Mediterranean Sea and the Adriatic.

It lives exclusively under rock overhangs and on the roof of small caverns and crevices, where the intensity of light is low and the surface encrusted with red algae, sponges, and other animal forms. It shares this habitat with the small scaled blenny, *Tripterygion minor*, which is identically coloured, and with which it is often found. The reason for this association is not known but some mimicry between the species is clear. **421**
B. ocellaris BUTTERFLY BLENNY
18 cm. (7 in.)
A European blenny, found through the Mediterranean and in the e. N. Atlantic from Scottish waters to Senegal. Its depth range varies from the shore down to 20 m. (11 fathoms) usually on shell or coralline algae covered grounds; in the Mediterranean it ranges down to 100 m. (54 fathoms). Its natural way of life is to live in crevices in rocks or mollusc shells, but not infrequently it is seen inhabiting discarded hollow crockery, broken bottles, or marrow bones on the sea bed. It lays its eggs in its natural rock crevice home, or unnatural alternatives, and they are guarded by the male.

Its most immediate distinguishing feature is the high dorsal fin, with the conspicuous black, white-ringed spot, not unlike the eye-spot on the wings of many butterflies, and presumably capable of performing a similar intimidating function. **422**
B. pholis SHANNY 16 cm. (6¼ in.)
The shanny is the most common and widely distributed blenny on the seashores of n. Europe. From Madeira and s. Portugal it ranges n. to the Orkney Islands and s. Norway. It is essentially an intertidal fish, and is often the most abundant shore fish both on rocky shores and in sandy pools which have algae attached to breakwaters or pier-piles. It occurs down to a depth of about 10 m. (5 fathoms).

Its diet is catholic; it eats filamentous green algae, barnacles, crustaceans of various kinds, and small fishes. The young feed mainly on the limbs of barnacles which protrude through the gaps in the crown of the shell and are neatly sheared off by the shanny's sharp teeth.

It spawns in summer, from April to early August; the eggs are laid on the underside of rocks and guarded by the male. After hatching, the larvae are pelagic but return to the shore by their first winter, as small light-coloured fish with dark heads and big boldly coloured pectoral fins (they look like small moths at the surface of the water).

The colouring varies with its habitat, but is always dull, browns and greens predominating.
B. sphinx 8 cm. (3 in.)
A Mediterranean species, which appears to occur throughout that sea, and the Adriatic. It lives in very shallow water on more or less seaweed-free bottoms. It spawns in early summer in rock crevices, the male displaying with heightened colouring before any passing female, and mating with those that respond.

This is a very distinctive blenny on account of the high dorsal fin, the male's being especially high and blue coloured. The profile of the face is steep, almost vertical, and behind the eye on each side is a conspicuous blue spot, red and black ringed. **423**

BLACK-HEADED see **Blennius nigriceps**
BUTTERFLY see **Blennius ocellaris**
CHECKERED see **Starksia ocellata**
EEL see **Peronedys anguillaris**
EEL GRASS see **Stathmonotus stahli**
HAIR-TAILED see **Xiphasia setifer**
HAIRY see **Labrisomus nuchipinnis**
MONTAGU'S see **Coryphoblennius galerita**
MOTTLED see **Tripterygion varium**
MUD see **Congrogadus subducens**
OYSTER see **Petroscirtes anolius**
PEARL see **Entomacrodus nigricans**
PYGMY BLACK-FACED see **Tripterygion minor**
RED SEA see under **Ecsenius gravieri**
REDLIP see **Ophioblennius atlanticus**
ROSY see **Malacoctenus macropus**
SCALED see Clinidae, Ophiclinidae
SNAKE see **Lumpenus lumpretaeformis**
SPOTTED EEL see **Notograptus guttatus**
THREE-FIN see Tripterygiidae
TOMPOT see **Blennius gattorugine**
VIVIPAROUS see **Zoarces viviparus**
WRASSE see **Hemiemblemaria simulus**

Blepsias   Cottidae
cirrhosus SILVER-SPOTTED SCULPIN
19 cm. (7½ in.)
A shallow-water sculpin found on the N. Pacific coast of America from n. California to the Bering Sea. It usually frequents eel grass beds and soft bottoms, and is frequently taken by shrimp trawls down to about 36·6 m. (20 fathoms). It spawns in the summer months, the light brown eggs being clustered on rocks in shallow water.

The silverspotted sculpin is distinguished by the series of silvery white spots on either side of the body, by the large skin tentacles on the snout and lower jaw, and by the very high rays of the second dorsal fin.

Blicca   Cyprinidae
bjoerkna SILVER or WHITE BREAM
30 cm. (12 in.)
A widespread European fish which occurs from the Caspian Sea w. to n. France, n. to Finland. It is a local fish in the British Isles found from the Thames to Yorkshire, although introduced elsewhere.

It is most abundant in shallow, eutrophic lowland lakes and slow-flowing rivers, being found usually amongst densely weedy shallows. It feeds on the larvae of insects, molluscs, and worms.

It closely resembles the common bream of Europe, *Abramis brama*, but has a larger eye, 22–26 rays in the anal fin, and has orange-red pectoral and pelvic fins with grey tips. Its back is bluish green; the sides and belly are conspicuously silvery.

It has no value as a sporting fish, and few anglers seem capable of identifying it correctly if they do catch it. It competes in mixed fisheries with bream and perch, both of which are considered more valuable as food or sporting fishes. **116**

BLIND
CAVE BARB see **Caecobarbus geertsi**
GOBY see **Typhlogobius californiensis**
SWAMP-EEL see **Ophisternon infernale**
TETRA see **Anoptichthys jordani**

BLOOD-RED SNAPPER see **Lutjanus sanguineus**
BLOODFIN see **Aphyocharax rubripinnis**
BLOODSNAPPER see **Lutjanus sanguineus**
BLOTCH-EYE see **Myripristis murdjan**
BLOTCHED PICAREL see **Maena maena**
BLUE AND GOLD DAMSELFISH see **Abudefduf melanopus**
BLUE
BLAASOP see **Lagocephalus lagocephalus**
BOBO see **Polydactylus approximans**
CATFISH see **Ictalurus furcatus**
CHROMIS see **Chromis cyaneus**
DISCUS see **Symphysodon aequifasciata**
GROPER see **Achoerodus gouldii**
HOTTENTOT see **Pachymetopon grande**
MARLIN see **Makaira nigricans**
HAKE see **Antimora rostrata**
MORWONG see **Nemadactylus valenciennesi**
PANCHAX see **Aplocheilus panchax**
PARROTFISH see **Scarus coeruleus**
PIKE see **Stizostedion vitreum**
POINTER see **Isurus oxyrinchus**
ROCK WHITING see **Haletta semifasciata**
SHARK see **Prionace glauca**
SPRAT see **Spratelloides robustus**
STREAK see **Labroides dimidiatus**
TANG see **Acanthurus coeruleus**
WHALER see **Prionace glauca**
WHITING see **Micromesistius poutassou**
BLUE-BANDED
HUSSAR see **Lutjanus kasmira**
SEA-PERCH see **Lutjanus kasmira**
BLUE-CHIN XENOCARA see **Xenocara dolichoptera**
BLUE-FIN
KILLIFISH see **Lucania goodei**
TOPMINNOW see **Lucania goodei**
TUNA see **Thunnus thynnus**
TUNA, ATLANTIC see **Thunnus thynnus**
TUNA, NORTH PACIFIC see **Thunnus orientalis**
TUNA, SOUTHERN see **Thunnus maccoyii**
BLUE-LINED SPINEFOOT see **Siganus virgatus**
BLUE-SPOT ROCK-COD see **Cephalopholis miniatus**
BLUE-SPOTTED
BOXFISH see **Ostracion tuberculatus**
CORNETFISH see **Fistularia tabacaria**
LONG-FIN see **Plesiops nigricans**
SUNFISH see **Enneacanthus gloriosus**
BLUE-STRIPED
GRUNT see **Haemulon sciurus**
PIPEFISH see **Doryrhamphus melanopleura**
BLUEBACK HERRING see **Alosa aestivalis**
BLUEBOTTLE FISH see **Nomeus gronovii**
BLUEFISH see **Pomatomus saltatrix**
BLUEGILL see **Lepomis macrochirus**
BLUEHEAD WRASSE see **Thalassoma bifasciatum**
BLUEMOUTH see **Helicolenus dactylopterus**
BLUETHROAT PIKE-BLENNY see **Chaenopsis ocellata**
BOARFISH see **Capros aper, Pentaceros richardsoni**
BOARFISH, BLACK-SPOTTED see **Zanclistius elevatus**
BOBTAILED SNIPE-EEL see **Cyema atrum**
BOCACCIO see **Sebastes paucispinis**
BOCÓN, SAPO see **Amphichthys cryptocentrus**

Bodianus   Labridae
pulchellus SPOTFIN HOGFISH
23 cm. (9 in.)
A w. Atlantic species which ranges from S. Carolina to Florida, and the Bahamas, the W. Indies with reports from islands off n. S. America and Ascension Island. It is a deepwater hogfish found mainly on the steepsloping reef faces at depths of 24 m. (13 fathoms) down to 110 m. (60 fathoms), and rarely shallower than this.

The young are believed to clean other fish of external parasites.

It is brightly coloured, the young mainly yellow with a black spot at the front end of the dorsal fin. As the fish grows the body becomes deep red, only the posterior, upper tail remaining yellow, while a central white patch runs down the sides. **398**
B. rufus SPANISH HOGFISH 61 cm. (24 in.)
Found in the tropical Atlantic Ocean, on the w. side from Bermuda, the Bahamas, and Florida through the Gulf of Mexico and the Caribbean to n. S. America. Elsewhere it has been reported from Ascension Island and St Helena in the S. Atlantic.

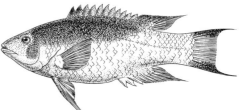

It is a beautifully coloured species, the upper part of the head and anterior body being blue (red in specimens from deep water), the lower parts of the head and body being yellow. Coloration in this species varies little with age and sex.

It is found on reefs from a depth of a metre or 2 down to 30 m. (17 fathoms). The adults feed on crabs, sea urchins, brittle stars, and molluscs, while the young are well known as cleaners of external crustacean parasites of other fishes.

BOGA see **Inermia vittata, Leporinus affinis**
BOKAR see **Barbus hexagonolepis**

Boleophthalmus   Gobiidae
The specimen illustrated in colour has not been identified. **431**
B. boddaerti MUD-HOPPER 13 cm. (5 in.)
A relatively small mud-hopper which does not have the head profile so steep, or the eyes so protuberant as its relatives the periophthalmid mud-skippers. It is widely distributed along the coasts of e. and s. Asia and the Malay

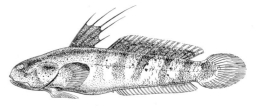

archipelago (related species occur on the Australian coast and the w. Pacific coastline generally). It is found chiefly in brackish water, sometimes occurring even in freshwater, but it is rarely found actually out of the water.

The nomenclature of this group is very confused and the precise limits of distribution and variation within the species are unknown. Most of the known forms are dark brownish with blue spots and oblique darker bands.

BOMBAY DUCK see **Harpadon nehereus**

Bonapartia Gonostomatidae
This genus was named for the distinguished Italian naturalist, Prince Charles Lucien Bonaparte, nephew of the emperor Napoleon Bonaparte. The species illustrated has not been identified. **41**
B. pedaliota 8 cm. (3 in.)
Bonapartia is a bathypelagic fish found in midwater between 500 and 1200 m. (273–656 fathoms). It has been recorded from the open sea on both sides of the Atlantic, from the Gulf of Guinea to Portuguese waters in the E., to Bermuda and the Caribbean.

It is a fragile little fish, rarely taken undamaged. When alive, it is light coloured and translucent, with silvery cheeks and iris and a single row of conspicuous light blue light organs on each side of the belly and tail.

BONEFISH see **Albula vulpes**
BONITO see **Katsuwonus pelamis, Sarda sarda**
BONITO,
  ATLANTIC see **Sarda sarda**
  OCEANIC see **Katsuwonus pelamis**
  PLAIN see **Auxis thazard, Orcynopsis unicolor**
BONNETHEAD SHARK see **Sphyrna tiburo**
BONNETMOUTH see **Inermia vittata**
BONY BREAM see **Nematalosa come**
BONY-LIPPED BARB, HASSELT'S see
  Osteocheilus hasselti
BONYTHROAT see **Bathylaco nigricans**

Boreogadus Gadidae
  saida ARCTIC or POLAR COD
46 cm. (15 in.)
A slender-bodied codfish which is found circumpolar in the Arctic regions of both N. Pacific and N. Atlantic, even to the edge of the polar icecap, at the surface amongst icefloes as well as at depths of 730 m. (400 fathoms). It is not commercially exploited, but it plays a vital role in the food webs of the Arctic for it is an

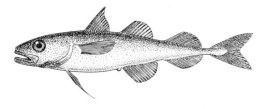

important food for seals, Arctic foxes, polar bears, birds, and cetaceans.

Borophryne Linophrynidae
  apogon 8 cm. (3 in.)
A small ceratioid angler fish found so far only in the Gulf of Panama in the e. Pacific, and in the vicinity of the Cocos Islands, in 914–1280 m. (500–700 fathoms). It is known from relatively few specimens.

The adult female is round-bodied, almost spherical except for the small tailfin and the small dorsal and anal fins. The mouth is large, the teeth fang-like; a short stout rod with a

rounded end, tipped with a branched lure is placed at the tip of the snout. The skin is black. Mature males are parasitic on the females; they are small (23 mm. (1 in.)) and dark skinned, with degenerate eyes, olfactory organs, and mouths. Free-living males are immature, almost transparent and toothless, but have well developed nostrils.

BOTHIDAE

A large group of flatfishes in which the eyes lie on the left side of the head, except in certain rare abnormal examples. They are often called left-eye flounders. The family is distinguished by having a dorsal fin beginning far round in front of the eyes, by all of the rays being segmented and none spiny, and by the pelvic fins having only branched rays. Unlike the turbots (family Scophthalmidae) the pelvic fins are short-based, although that on the coloured, eyed side is frequently longer than the other.

Most of the members of this family are small or relatively small flatfishes of little commercial importance. They are found throughout the tropical and temperate seas of the world, mostly in shallow water although some are found on the continental slope in several hundreds of metres of water. See **Arnoglossus, Bothus, Citharichthys, Engyprosopon, Lophonectes, Paralichthys, Pseudorhombus, Syacium**.

Bothragonus Agonidae
  swani ROCKHEAD 8 cm. (3 in.)
Found from California to British Columbia, in shallow water inshore and occasionally in tide pools. Its life style seems to be little known.

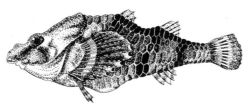

It is a very distinctive fish immediately recognizable by its deep body, the very broad head with a deep pit between the eyes.

Bothrocara Zoarcidae
  brunneum TWOLINE EELPOUT
61 cm. (2 ft)
A deep water eelpout found in the N. Pacific, from the Bering Sea to the area of San Francisco, mainly at depths of 640–1830 m. (350–1000 fathoms) on sand or muddy bottoms. It is essentially a bottom-dwelling fish, like other members of the family, and feeds on almost all small benthic organisms. It is occasionally captured by commercial fishermen, but more often by special deep trawling research vessels.

In body form it is typical of other members of the family; the head is wide and flattened, the mouth wide. Large cavities beneath the skin around the head. This species has 2 lateral lines.

Bothus Bothidae
  lunatus PEACOCK FLOUNDER
45 cm. (18 in.)
A left-eyed flounder found in the tropical w. Atlantic from Bermuda and Florida s. to Brazil and along the Central American and W. Indian coasts. It is relatively common in shallow water, down to a depth of 6 m. (3 fathoms), on a variety of sea beds, including sand and rock, sparse turtle grass patches, and in sand around coral. Like other members of the group it buries itself lightly in the sand and is rarely seen except when disturbed.

It is a colourful species and can be distinguished by this feature alone. The eyes are spaced well apart on the left side, the lower in advance of the upper; males have the eyes widely separated compared to females. **466**
B. mancus 35 cm. (14 in.)
An Indo-Pacific species of very wide distribution, from the E. African coast throughout the Indian Ocean coastline to the Malay Peninsula and thence through the Pacific Ocean to Hawaii and the Mexican W. coast. It is found in shallow water buried in sandy patches, and also on the flat pavement-like sections of the reef.

It is a very striking fish. The eyes are on the left side of the head, and set far apart. In adult

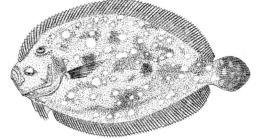

males the eyes are very widely spaced out and each is fringed with small fleshy flaps; the pectoral fin is very elongate, and the snout is covered with rough tubercles. The mouth is moderate. It is brownish overall with pale cream-coloured spots, light blue dots, and irregular orange-yellow blotches. The underside is creamy white.

Because of its abundance amongst the Pacific island groups this fish was one of the first flatfishes to be discovered by the earlier explorers. It was described in 1782 from specimens collected in Tahiti by Captain Cook's expedition.

Botia Cobitidae
  berdmorei 25 cm. (10 in.)
A native of Burma, and possibly also of Thailand, this distinctive loach is occasionally met with as a pet fish. Its elongate, but laterally flattened body, and particularly the pointed snout help to distinguish it, as does the deep caudal peduncle. As an aquarium fish it rarely grows longer than 10 cm. (4 in.). **148**
B. horae HORA'S CLOWN LOACH
10 cm. (4 in.)
A loach of wide distribution in Thailand which has been found in numerous rivers in that country since its first discovery in 1931. It is a small species which attains sexual maturity at a length of less than 9 cm. (3½ in.).

It is distinguished by its rather short-based dorsal fin which has only 8 branched rays, and by its coloration. This species has been kept in aquaria. **149**

B. macracantha CLOWN LOACH, TIGER BOTIA 30 cm. (12 in.)
This is one of the most strikingly coloured loaches of the genus *Botia*. It is characterized by having a bright orange-red basic colour, interrupted by 3 jet black wedge-shaped bars across the back and sides, the first over the head to include the eyes, the second in front of the dorsal fin, and the third across the tail just behind the dorsal fin. The fins are deep red. It has the deep, rather compressed body of the botias, with 4 pairs of barbels, and strong, curved spines beneath the eyes.

It is widespread in Sumatra and Borneo. It is a popular aquarium fish, if rather shy, and difficult to breed.

B. sidthimunki 4 cm. (1½ in.)
This, the smallest of the botia-loaches, is a very active and attractive aquarium fish. Like its relatives it has an erectile double spine beneath and slightly in front of each eye. Its body is more torpedo-shaped than most of its relatives, and the mouth is almost terminal. Its markings are very distinctive.

It is a native of Thailand. Aquarium stocks have been dependent on fresh introductions, for it has not been bred successfully in captivity. **150**

BOTIA, TIGER see **Botia macracantha**

Boulengerella Ctenoluciidae
lucius 61 cm. (2 ft)
A long slender pike-like fish found in n. S. America, in several of the larger rivers, the Rio Paraguay, e. Brazil, the lower Amazon, the Orinoco, and the Guianas and Venezuela. It runs upriver to spawn during the rainy season. It is entirely predatory and eats most of the available smaller fishes in open water.

Its body shape shows a marked resemblance to other predatory fishes, such as the N. American gars, and the pikes. The upper jaw terminates in a long cartilaginous tip, the jaw teeth are numerous, conical, curved, and sharp. Its body is elongate, and covered with scales. The dorsal fin is placed well back along the body, the anal fin is short, and the tail fin is forked. It is a bronzy green on the back, lighter on the sides, and silver on the belly; a faint dark stripe runs through the eye, and there is a small dark blotch on the tail fin rays. **89**

BOUNCE see **Scyliorhinus stellaris**

BOVICHTIDAE
A small family of marine fishes found in the S. Hemisphere, mostly just outside the Antarctic Convergence. Their distribution thus includes the s. tips of S. America, Australia, New Zealand, and oceanic islands such as Tristan da Cunha, Kergulen, and Macquarie Islands. They are not found in Antarctica proper.

They are closely related to the Antarctic cods (Nototheniidae) but differ mainly in having their gill cover membranes free from the throat, and by having teeth on the palate. See **Bovichtus, Pseudaphritis**.

Bovichtus Bovichtidae
diacanthus 25 cm. (10 in.)
Found exclusively in the Tristan da Cunha and Gough Island groups. Other closely similar species are found in s. seas, circumpolar in their distribution. They are found on intertidal shores inhabiting the rock pools and under stones in areas where algal cover is dense. The larval and juvenile stages of this fish are pelagic, blue-backed and silvery-sided, and form food for many of the sea birds in those areas.

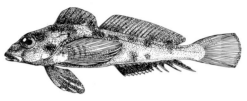

The head is triangular but depressed and has a conspicuous spine on the gill cover. Two dorsal fins, the first placed above the head; the pectoral fins are broad and the lower rays are thickened and free from the fin membrane. It is bluish grey with heavy brown mottling, and reddish bands on the fins.

BOWFIN see **Amia calva**
BOXFISH see Ostraciontidae
BOXFISH see **Lactoria diaphana, Ostracion lentiginosum, Tetrosomus gibbosus**
BOXFISH,
BLUE-SPOTTED see **Ostracion tuberculatus**
ROBUST see **Strophiurichthys robustus**

BRACHIONICHTHYIDAE
A small family of frogfishes, or anglers, found round the coasts of S. Australia. Its members are very similar in body shape to the Antennariidae, and have a long free first dorsal ray on the snout. The second and third rays are however, not free but form a small fin above the head. The gill openings lie behind the pectoral fins. They are small fishes. See **Sympterichthys**.

Brachydanio Cyprinidae
albolineatus PEARL DANIO 5 cm. (2 in.)
An elongate, slim-bodied fish with a deep ventral profile, and oblique jaws so that the mouth opening is dorsal. It can be distinguished from its relatives by its incomplete lateral line, which extends only to the base of the pelvic fins, and by the 2 pairs of moderately long barbels.

It is a beautiful fish, very popular for the aquarium. They are moderately easy to keep, requiring a sunny aquarium well planted with small-leaved plants, or algae. They spawn on the plants, the rather large eggs sticking to the leaves, and hatching in about 24 hours at temperatures of 26 to 28° C.

The pearl danio is widely distributed in e. India, Burma, and Sumatra. It has also been found in several parts of Thailand in mountain brooks, especially in the pools below waterfalls. **117**

B. nigrofasciatus SPOTTED DANIO 4 cm. (1½ in.)
The spotted danio is a very popular aquarium fish. It is native to the freshwaters of Upper Burma, being found in streams and lakes, often extremely small ones.

Females are deeper bodied than the males, and have a pale, yellowish belly; in the male it is orange. **118**

B. rerio ZEBRA DANIO 4·5 cm. (1¾ in.)
The zebra danio is native to the freshwaters of e. India. Its body shape is similar to that of other danios, rather elongate, with a deep belly, and almost straight back profile. Its dorsal fin is placed well along the back and is rather smaller than the anal. Its mouth is oblique and has 2 pairs of moderately long, but thin barbels. Its coloration is quite distinctive.

The zebra danio is a popular aquarium fish, peaceful and undemanding. It can tolerate a wide temperature range but needs about 24° C for spawning. It spawns readily, usually in the early morning, scattering its eggs amongst weeds. The adults tend to eat their eggs, so various expedients, such as dense algal growths or egg traps have to be relied upon to obtain successful hatching. **119**

Brachygobius Gobiidae
nunus BUMBLEBEE-FISH 4 cm. (1½ in.)
One of the most popular gobies available for the tropical aquarium, with its colouring of deep yellow and broad black or dark brown bands resembling that of a bumblebee. They often stay poised in the aquarium hanging on the glass surface, plants and rocks for long periods followed by short bursts of brisk activity. In shoals they are very attractive.

This species is widespread in SE. Asia, especially common in Thailand, the Malay Peninsula, Sumatra, Borneo, and Java. It occurs both in the sea and in estuaries, and also appears perfectly healthy in completely freshwater.

The short body and stocky build are as distinctive as the colouring and markings. There are, however, at least 2 other species which differ in only minor coloration details in s. Asia.

Brachyistius Embiotocidae
frenatus KELP PERCH 20 cm. (8 in.)
This surfperch is found from s. California to the Strait of Georgia, and confined to the coastal waters of the e. Pacific, typically around kelp-beds in shallow water and down to a depth of 27 m. (15 fathoms). It feeds on small crustaceans, and like other members of the family, is viviparous.

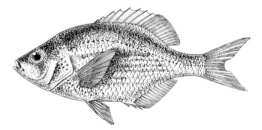

It is a moderately elongate fish, olive-brown above, each scale having a dark spot, and light coppery on the sides.

Brama Bramidae
brama RAY'S BREAM, BULLEYE, ATLANTIC POMFRET 76 cm. (30 in.)
Found in the N. Atlantic, and widely distributed from the N. African coast, along the Spanish and Portuguese coasts to Biscay. It also occurs in the Mediterranean, and less commonly in the w. Atlantic. In the S. Hemi-

sphere it is found off South Africa, New Zealand, Australia, and Chile.

In European waters this fish is commercially fished off n. Spain using longlines set at depths of 91–110 m. (50–60 fathoms). The flesh is sold fresh or canned for local consumption, and is said to be very good, white, firm and flaky. Ray's bream also features in occasional irregular irruptions into n. waters, possibly due to hydrographic conditions making the water off the British coast more suitable, although it is more likely to be due to a series of exceptionally good 'year classes' further S. Large numbers of these bramids enter the N. Sea in late summer and then are caught, or stranded along the coasts of Britain and Europe throughout the late autumn and early winter. The most recent and best documented of such occurrences were during the years 1969–1970 and again in 1973. It is not, however, a recent phenomenon for the first described specimen was reported by the great English naturalist John Ray from a specimen stranded on the E. coast of England in 1681.

It feeds on a wide range of fishes, cephalopods, and crustaceans.

It is a deep-bodied, compressed fish with a high forehead, a moderately large mouth, equipped with numerous strong teeth. Its colouring is dark brown above with gleaming coppery tints on the sides; the latter fade soon after death.

BRAMBLE SHARK see **Echinorhinus brucus**

BRAMIDAE
A family of moderate to large oceanic fishes, found in all but the polar seas of the world. Most are deep-bodied fishes with a single dorsal fin, the unbranched anterior spines forming a lobe in the fin. With one possible exception they are fishes of the high seas, living in moderate depths, but always in midwater. Young stages are pelagic, distinguished as members of the family by their spiny scales and somewhat spiny heads. The young not infrequently differ considerably from the adult in body and fin form and many have proved difficult to relate to the parent species.

In general, the bramids are poorly known, many of them are known from relatively few specimens, and the adults are difficult to catch. One or 2 species are used locally as food fishes. See **Brama, Pteraclis, Taractes.**

BRANCHIOSTEGIDAE
A small family of long-bodied, or if not elongate then laterally compressed marine fishes. They have a long, many-rayed dorsal fin with a few slender spines in the front; the anal fin is also long, with weak spines. The tilefishes are found in tropical and warm temperate seas. Some of them reach a considerable size and are valued food fishes. They are related to the Indo-Pacific whitings, family Sillaginidae.

Juveniles are pelagic, have spines on the head and spiny scales and are so different from the adult that they had been named as a separate genus *Dikellorhynchus*. They have been frequently found in the gut of the dolphin fish, *Coryphaena*. See **Branchiostegus, Lopholatilus, Malacanthus.**

Branchiostegus   Branchiostegidae
   japonicus 61 cm. (24 in.)

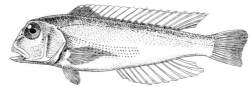

A rather compressed fish, with a relatively narrow slender body and deep head. The dorsal fin is moderately long, but has only 7 slender spines in its first part. It is dark red above, paler below; with 4 or 5 yellowish stripes on the sides; a silvery patch on the back of the head.

Widely distributed in Japanese waters, around the Philippines and in the E. China Sea, it is also reported from off se. Africa. It lives in depths down to 146 m. (80 fathoms). A popular food fish, which is commercially very valuable in Japan where it is known as akaamadai. It is eaten fresh, as well as canned or salted.

BREAM see **Abramis brama, Sarotherodon mosambicus**
BREAM,
   BANDED see **Tilapia sparrmanii**
   BLACK see **Girella tricuspidata**
   BONY see **Nematalosa come**
   BRONZE see **Abramis brama, Pachymetopon grande**
   GOVERNMENT see **Lutjanus sebae**
   MUD see **Acanthopagrus berda**
   PIKEY see **Acanthopagrus berda**
   RAY'S see **Brama brama**
   RED SEA see **Pagellus bogaraveo**
   SEA see Sparidae
   SEA see **Seriolella brama**
   SILVER see **Blicca bjoerkna, Rhabdosargus sarba**
   WHITE see **Blicca bjoerkna**
   YELLOW-FIN see **Rhabdosargus sarba**

Bregmaceros   Bregmacerotidae
   macclellandi 12 cm. (5 in.)
Widely distributed in the tropical Atlantic, Indian, and Pacific oceans. Seven very similar species are placed in the genus, all from tropical oceans. This species is found at the surface of the sea down to depths of 730 m. (400 fathoms), exceptionally to 4000 m. (2187 fathoms), and although mostly found in the open sea, it is occasionally cast ashore after prolonged winds and heavy storms.

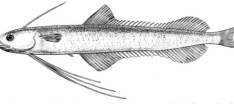

Its back is brownish above, with fine dark speckling; its sides and belly are silvery.

BREGMACEROTIDAE
A small family of marine fishes, related to the codfishes, but totally different in life-style and distribution. They are pelagic and inhabit the surface waters of tropical and sub-tropical oceans. They are slender-bodied, with a characteristic arrangement of fins. The dorsal fin consists of a single ray above the head, then a long, deeply divided fin, the front half high, the anal fin has a similar shape; both fins are separate from the tail fin. The pelvic fins are very long, and placed far forward near the throat. See **Bregmaceros.**

Brevoortia   Clupeidae
   tyrannus MENHADEN, POGY,
MOSSBUNKER 46 cm. (18 in.)
The menhaden is a wide ranging fish along the Atlantic coastline of N. America from Nova Scotia to e. Florida, and represented in the Gulf of Mexico by similar forms. It is an abundant marine fish found in shoals of hundreds of thousands at a time, sometimes seen in clear weather rippling the surface in a distinctive manner and breaking the surface with their snouts and fins.

The menhaden feeds on microscopic organisms, especially the minute plants (diatoms) in the plankton, which it strains out of the water with its fine-meshed gill rakers. The organisms are not selected deliberately, as the herring frequently does, but the menhaden swims with its mouth open and its gillcover wide spread filtering the water. It has been estimated that an adult filters between 24 and 28 litres (6–7 gallons) of seawater every minute when feeding.

The fat and oily menhaden is one of the most important commercial fish of the E. coast of the U.S., being used for the production of fishmeal, oil, and fertilizers. Although it is edible, it is too oily to appeal to man, but very many marine animals prey on it extensively. These include swordfish, tuna, shark, bluefish, cod, and other fishes, whales, dolphins, and many kinds of sea birds.

Menhaden are warm-water fish and thus make temperature-dependent migrations with the seasons. In spring and summer they move n. Their numbers change dramatically from year to year, sometimes in New England waters none are seen for several years, then for a while they are in great abundance. It has been suggested that especially warm years produce more diatom food and thus attract the fish, but the real reason probably lies in greater survival of the fry several years earlier during a particularly suitable year.

The buoyant eggs are shed in late autumn and early winter; they hatch after about 48 hours into larvae of 4·5 mm. (1¾ in.) long.

The adult menhaden is dark blue or green on the back, silvery on the sides. There is a conspicuous black spot behind the head, others irregularly on the sides. It is a very deep-bodied, herring-like fish with a large, scaleless head. The belly is keel-like and provided with sharp saw-tooth scales. The body scales have straight edges, and fine teeth along their free edge.

BRILL see Scophthalmidae
BRILL see **Eopsetta jordani, Scophthalmus rhombus**
BRILLIANT RASBORA see **Rasbora einthoveni**
BRISLING see **Sprattus sprattus**
BRISTLE-TOOTHED SURGEONFISH see **Ctenochaetus strigosus**
BRISTLEMOUTH see Gonostomatidae
BROAD-BILL SWORDFISH see **Xiphias gladius**
BROAD-SNOUTED SEVEN-GILLED SHARK see **Notorynchus maculatus**

Brochis   Callichthyidae
   coeruleus 8 cm. (3 in.)
A small catfish found in the upper Amazon near Iquitos. It is distinguished by having a

higher, more compressed body, and more rays in the dorsal fin than found in members of the genus *Callichthys*. The body appears very squat, and the bony plates covering the sides are very prominent. The snout is long, and the barbels are well developed.

Rather colourful for this group of fishes. The upper sides and back are dull green, ventrally turning to a shining green, underneath touched with deep yellow.

A peaceful and attractive aquarium fish.

BRONZE BREAM see **Abramis brama, Pachymetopon grande**
BROOK
    CHARR see **Salvelinus fontinalis**
    LAMPREY see **Lampetra planeri**
    LAMPREY, NORTHERN see **Ichthyomyzon fossor**
    STICKLEBACK see **Culaea inconstans**
    TROUT see **Salvelinus fontinalis**
BROTULID see Ophidiidae
BROWN
    BULLHEAD see **Ictalurus nebulosus**
    CATSHARK see **Apristurus brunneus**
    DISCUS see **Symphysodon aequifasciata**
    DRIFTFISH see **Ariomma melanum**
    MEAGRE see **Sciaena umbra**
    MUDFISH see **Neochanna apoda**
BROWN-BANDED CATSHARK see **Hemiscyllium punctatum**
BUENOS AIRES TETRA see **Hemigrammus caudovittatus**
BUFFALO, SMALLMOUTH see **Ictiobus bubalus**
BUFFALO
    SCULPIN see **Enophrys bison**
    TRUNKFISH see **Lactophrys trigonus**

Brosme   Gadidae
    brosme TORSK, CUSK 102 cm. (40 in.)
The torsk is found in the n. Atlantic on both the American and the European coasts. In the W. it is found from Newfoundland and Nova Scotia s. to Cape Cod, occasionally to New Jersey; in the E. from the coasts of N. Scotland to Iceland, along Norway to the Murman coast. It inhabits deep water, usually between 91–914 m. (50–500 fathoms), on hard bottoms. It spawns in spring and summer; the eggs, and later the larvae, float on the surface at first. The adults' food appears to be mostly bottom-living invertebrates.

It has some commercial importance and small landings are made from trawling and, more commonly, long-lining. Sea anglers catch them occasionally.

It is a very distinctive fish with a long chin barbel, long uniformly high dorsal and anal fins which abut to the rounded tail. It is usually reddish or brown, ventrally lighter; the vertical fins have a white edge and a dark submarginal band.

Buglossidium   Soleidae
    luteum SOLENETTE 13 cm. (5 in.)
This miniature sole is widely distributed, from the Danish N. Sea region and Scottish waters s. to Morocco, and throughout the Mediterranean. It is found on sandy bottoms usually only in offshore waters; it is very rare near the coasts. It is most common in depths of 9–37 m. (5–20 fathoms) but is occasionally taken as deep as 83 m. (45 fathoms).

The solenette is yellowish or light brown in

colour, attractively marked with a few scattered darker blotches. The dorsal and anal fins are regularly marked every fifth or sixth ray by a sharply differentiated black ray. The eyes on the right side of the head are very small and close together; in most other respects it resembles other members of the family.

Bulbometopon   Scaridae
    muricatus 1·2 m. (4 ft)
A very interesting species found widely in the central and w. Pacific Ocean and the Indian Ocean from the Red Sea, the E. African coast, and the Seychelles. Its coloration is unremarkable, being uniform brown; the young have whitish scales on the sides.

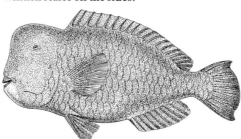

Adults are distinguished by the grotesque hump on the forehead, and even the young fish have a high profile. This hump is a gristly pad, not bone, and its front part is usually abraded suggesting that it is pressed against the coral or rock while the fish is browsing on algae. It is found in shoals in deep water but is very shy and not often captured. Adults grow to weights of at least 68 kg. (150 lb.); it is probably the largest parrotfish species known.

BULL
    HUSS see **Scyliorhinus stellaris**
    SHARK see **Carcharhinus leucas**
BULLEYE see **Brama brama**
BULLFISH see **Heniochus acuminatus**
BULLFISH, THREE-BANDED see **Heniochus permutatus**
BULLHEAD see Cottidae, Icelidae, Ictaluridae
BULLHEAD see **Cottus gobio**
BULLHEAD,
    BROWN see **Ictalurus nebulosus**
    SEA see **Taurulus bubalis**
BULLSEYE see **Epigonus telescopus**
BULLSEYE, COMMON see **Liopempheris multiradiata**
BUMBLEBEE-FISH see **Brachygobius nunus**
BUMMALO see **Harpadon nehereus**

Buncocephalus   Aspredinidae
    bicolor 15 cm. (6 in.)
Found in the w. Amazon basin to Ecuador,

this banjo catfish is occasionally imported for the aquarist.

It is a dull brown fish, variously mottled with darker and lighter patches, and strewn with small light spots. The ventral surface is pale.

B. coracoideus GUITARRITA 10 cm. (4 in.)
A banjo catfish, called guitarrita in Argentina, which is found in the Amazon region and the Rio Uruguay.

Its body form is typical of the family, the depressed head and anterior body being particularly noticeable. Its colouring is dull, greyish on the back, with pale clear fins, and spots. It is fairly commonly kept by aquarists, and is one of the few species to have bred in captivity. A hollow is excavated by the male in the bottom in a region clear of rocks and plants. The eggs are shed in the depression and guarded by the male. The young feed on rotifers, the adults on tubificid and other worms. **164**

BURBOT see **Lota lota**
BURNETT SALMON see **Neoceratodus forsteri**
BURRFISH see Diodontidae
BURRFISH see **Chilomycterus schoepfi**
BURRFISH, STRIPED see **Chilomycterus schoepfi**
BUTTER
    BARBEL see **Eutropius depressirostris**
    HAMLET see **Hypoplectrus puella**
BUTTERFISH see Stromateidae
BUTTERFISH see **Palunolepis brachydactylus, Peprilus triacanthus, Pholis gunnellus, Schilbe mystus, Stromateus fiatola**
BUTTERFISH,
    PACIFIC see **Peprilus simillimus**
    SOUTHERN see **Selenotoca multifasciata**
    SPOTTED see **Scatophagus argus**
BUTTERFLY
    BLENNY see **Blennius ocellaris**
    RAY see Gymnuridae
    RAY see **Gymnura natalensis**
    RAY, LESSER see **Gymnura micrura**
    RAY, SMOOTH see **Gymnura micrura**
BUTTERFLYFISH see Chaetodontidae
BUTTERFLYFISH see **Pantodon buchholzi, Pterois russelli, Pterois volitans**
BUTTERFLYFISH,
    BANDED see **Chaetodon striatus**
    FOUREYE see **Chaetodon capistratus**
    LATTICED see **Chaetodon rafflesii**
    LONGSNOUT see **Prognathodes aculeatus**
    RED-STRIPED see **Chaetodon lunula**
    SPOTFIN see **Chaetodon ocellatus**
    THREAD-FIN see **Chaetodon auriga**
    WHITE-SPOTTED see **Chaetodon kleinii**

C

CABEZON see **Scorpaenichthys marmoratus**

Caecobarbus   Cyprinidae
    geertsi BLIND CAVE BARB 10 cm. (4 in.)
A slender-bodied barbel-like fish found only in the cave system of Thysville in the former Belgian Congo. Like many other fishes living in caves, the adult's eyes are completely regressed and quite invisible. It is a pale silvery

pink colour with no dark pigment in the skin.

It is a small fish, the body covered in scales, but with the head naked. The lateral line scales are well developed and it has a complex sensory system on the head, and a pair of long barbels on each side of the mouth. It feeds on small crustaceans found living in the caves, and a certain amount of animal matter that is swept in from the outside.

Caesio   Lutjanidae
erythrogaster RED-BELLIED FUSILIER
35 cm. (14½ in.)
An Indo-Australian reef fish which is very common on the coasts of n. Australia. It is found in shoals always close to the coral. A good food fish.

It is dark blue above, lighter on the sides, rosy pink below. The tail fin is bright yellow and 2 violet bands run across the snout. The spiny dorsal fin is dark, the soft dorsal yellow with a bright red spot between the spines.

This species is representative of the more slender-bodied reef lutjanids which differ from the main snapper group.

CALABAR LYRETAIL see **Roloffia liberiens**

Calamoichthys   Polypteridae
calabaricus REEDFISH 90 cm. (35½ in.)
The elongate, snake-like form of the reedfish is quite distinctive. It is a beautiful olive-green, with pale sides and the yellowish underside; the pectoral fin has a dark blotch.

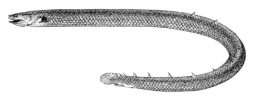

The reedfish is found in slowly flowing streams and still waters in W. Africa, essentially the Niger Delta, and the Cameroons. Like its relatives, the bichirs, it breathes atmospheric oxygen with its lung-like swim bladder, and can thus inhabit water of very low oxygen levels.

It swims slowly and eel-like over the bottom but can move rapidly on its side. In its natural habitat it lives in dense submerged vegetation. Its larva has external gills, one each side of the head, and looks remarkably like a newt tadpole.

Calamus   Sparidae
bajonado JOLTHEAD PORGY 61 cm. (2 ft)
A w. Atlantic species of seabream which ranges from New England and Bermuda to Brazil, including the Gulf of Mexico and the W. Indies. It is usually seen in clear water areas over or around reefs, but is occasionally found in tidal creeks. Its depth range extends to 45 m. (25 fathoms). It feeds heavily on sea urchins, molluscs, and crustaceans, and is an excellent food fish.

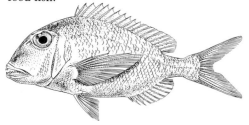

A distinctive species, mainly silvery with bluish centres to the scales. Around the eye, extending from the forehead to the underside of the head is brownish with brassy cheeks, and a prominent blue line beneath the eye; a bright orange patch at the corner of the mouth.

CALE, HERRING see **Olisthops cyanomelas**
CALIFORNIA
   BARRACUDA see **Sphyraena argentea**
   GRUNION see **Leuresthes tenuis**
   HALIBUT see **Paralichthys californicus**
   LIZARDFISH see **Synodus lucioceps**
   RAT-TAIL see **Nezumia stelgidolepis**
   SHEEPHEAD see under **Pimelometopon darwini**
CALIFORNIAN
   MONKFISH see **Squatina californica**
   PILCHARD see **Sardinops caeruleus**
CALLOP see **Plectroplites ambiguus**

CALLICHTHYIDAE

A family of S. American freshwater catfishes of remarkable appearance and great popularity as aquarium fishes. They are widely distributed in the tropical waters of n. S. America and Trinidad. They are immediately distinguishable by the wide, flat tile-like scales of the back and sides; the head is covered with bony plates. The body is usually rather deep, the upper profile of the head steep, the mouth small and nearly ventral with several well-developed barbels. The dorsal fin is high, an adipose fin is present with a stout spine in front; the other fins are usually moderate in size.

All are bottom-living fishes, adaptable to most conditions. Some live in swampy waters which become deoxygenated, then the fish can utilize atmospheric oxygen by gulping at the surface, the gas being absorbed in the hind-gut. They are reported to be able to travel overland for short distances. See **Brochis, Callichthys, Corydoras, Dianema, Hoplosternum**.

Callichthys   Callichthyidae
callichthys CASCARUDO 18 cm. (7 in.)
An armoured catfish of very wide distribution in the tropical regions of S. America, from the Guyanas to Paraguay, and Uruguay. It is a very distinctive fish, with a rather slender body, a somewhat pointed snout, and 2 paired barbels above and below the mouth. The body is covered with flat bony overlapping plates. The dorsal fin is relatively low.

Attractively, if soberly coloured, the males are rather brighter, showing a delicate blue or violet sheen on the sides. The females are a dull olive-green.

A popular aquarium fish, it is peaceful and relatively undemanding. It is most active in the half light, foraging on the bottom. Its spawning behaviour is interesting in that the parents deposit their eggs in a bubble-nest made amongst surface-floating plants. **171**

CALLIONYMIDAE

The family of the dragonets, a group of marine fishes found mostly in shallow inshore waters, although some are found at considerable depths. All have rather flattened depressed bodies, with broad pelvic fins placed almost beneath the head; gill apertures are restricted to a rounded opening either side of the head, in almost dorsal position. This is correlated with their habit of lying on the bottom, often par-

tially, sometimes wholly buried beneath sand and fine gravel.

A notable feature of the group is the sexual differences exhibited in almost all species known. Males, once sexually mature, are invariably brilliantly coloured and have larger fins than the usually drab coloured females and immature fish. In some species elaborate courtship displays at spawning have been described, and as sexual dimorphism is general, it may be inferred that such displays are also general. See **Callionymus, Synchiropus**.

Callionymus   Callionymidae
bairdi LANCER DRAGONET 11 cm. (4½ in.)
Found in the w. tropical Atlantic from Bermuda, the Bahamas, and Florida s. through the Gulf of Mexico and Caribbean. It is a shallow-water species usually associated with coral reefs and rubble, but also taken on rocky shorelines and on patch reefs surrounded by sand. It is often found buried in the sand.

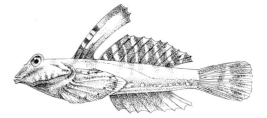

The male has high dorsal fins and its anal fin is larger than in the female; the male also has a bright yellow patch on the first dorsal fin, and blue spots round the eyes. Background coloration is a variably mottled brown, black and white. It is distinguished from the other shallow-water dragonet in the area by having 8 anal fin rays.

C. calauropomus COMMON STINKFISH
30 cm. (12 in.)
A common dragonet in the waters of s. Australia, and known off the W. Australian coast, along the s. coast, to New South Wales. It is frequently taken in commercial trawls over sandy bottoms in moderate depths.

The head is brownish above, orange below with blue spots on the cheeks; the body is pale orange with brown bands. Males are more brightly coloured than females, and their fins are relatively larger.

The vernacular name for this fish is due to the acrid smell of the body mucous, which is bitter (and possibly mildly poisonous) to taste. Few predatory birds will touch any species of dragonet.

C. lyra DRAGONET 30 cm. (12 in.)
A European species which is found from the s. coasts of Iceland and Norway – in both regions it is rare – s. to the Mediterranean. This is the largest of the 5 or 6 European species, and the males are particularly distinctive on account of the bright blue and yellow striped dorsal fins, and the blue spots on the head and back. Females are medium brown with darker saddles across the back.

It is found in shallow water down to a depth of 100 m. (55 fathoms), and is occasionally found in intertidal situations. It is confined to sand and shingle beds where it lives often buried in the bottom. It feeds on bottom-living invertebrates especially the smaller crustaceans and worms. Spawning takes place in spring following an elaborate display of highly coloured fins by the male. The eggs and early young are found at the surface.

Calloplesiops   Plesiopidae
altivelis 16 cm. (6¼ in.)
A fish found in the E. Indies, but for long known only from the island of Nias in Indonesia in shallow water around coral reefs.

It is distinguished from other members of the family in the area by the sharp angle of the preoperculum, and the relatively short upper jaw. It has only 11 spines in the dorsal fin. **272**

CALLORHINCHIDAE

One of the 3 families of chimaeroid fishes here recognized. Its members have cartilaginous skeletons, with a single gill opening each side covered by a flap of skin supported by cartilage, with 4 pairs of gill clefts. The body is elongate, with well-developed fins but no true fin rays. The eggs are fertilized internally, the males having a pair of copulatory claspers, and each is laid in a horny capsule. In several ways they (and other chimaeroids, e.g. Chimaeridae) appear to be intermediate between the bony fishes and the sharks.

The callorhinchids have a very elaborate, ploughshare-shaped tip to the snout which gives them their common name, elephantfish. They are restricted to the cool-temperate and cold regions of the S. Hemisphere; s. S. America, New Zealand, s. Australia, and the tip of s. Africa. Although several species have been described, they are possibly only local races of a single species. See **Callorhinchus**.

Callorhinchus   Callorhinchidae
milii ELEPHANT or GHOST SHARK
1 m. (3¼ ft)
The elephant shark is found in the cooler waters of s. Australia, and New Zealand. In places it is very abundant in depths down to 55 m. (30 fathoms) and in Tasmania it is said to enter harbours and river mouths. Its flesh is of excellent eating quality. Large specimens are heavy, fish up to 9 kg. (20 lb.) in weight having been recorded.

Its body is iridescent silvery with some brown markings on the back and on the gill cover. It is said to be faintly luminescent. Males have a small club-like, spine covered, process on the front of the head, as well as long claspers in the pelvic region. The snout is remarkable on account of its long trunk-like proboscis, shaped at its tip like a ploughshare.

CAMARÓN see **Homodiaetus maculatus**

Campostoma   Cyprinidae
anomalum STONEROLLER 10 cm. (4 in.)
Stonerollers are widely distributed in the freshwaters of the e. U.S. This species is found in the systems of the Mississippi, Missouri, and Ohio rivers, and ranges from Lake Ontario to Minnesota, s. to Georgia, Alabama, and parts of n. Mexico. Throughout the range several subspecies have been described.

The stoneroller is characteristically an inhabitant of clear brooks, creeks, rocky and sandy bedded streams, especially those in which there are numerous riffles.

The stoneroller is distinguished from the other N. American minnows by its short dorsal fin with relatively few rays, and by the distinct cartilaginous ridge of the lower jaw being separated from the lower lip by a deep groove. Internally its intestine is wound spirally round its swim-bladder. **120**

CANDIRU see **Vandellia cirrhosa**
CANDLEFISH see **Hemiramphus far**,
    Thaleichthys pacificus

Cantherines   Balistidae
ayraudi see **Navodon ayraudi**
pullus ORANGE-SPOTTED or TAIL-LIGHT FILEFISH 19 cm. (7½ in.)
Found in coastal waters throughout the tropical Atlantic, this species has been captured along the W. African coast, but is best known in the w. Atlantic where it ranges from Bermuda and New England, s. to Brazil. It is a common species in inshore waters down to depths of 7·6 m. (4 fathoms), but its juvenile stages (up to 5 cm., 2 in.) are open water forms, living pelagically and preyed upon by a great variety of active fishes, including the billfishes and tunas. As an adult it feeds on encrusting bottom growths especially sponges, algae, and bryozoans.

It is a very striking fish with a high dorsal fin, the second dorsal spine being rudimentary, a well-developed pelvic spine, and very finely toothed but rough scales. Its colouring is variable, but is basically brown overall with pale stripes on the head and body and orange dots with brown centres. Two white spots above and below the tail on each side are very prominent features.

Canthigaster   Tetraodontidae
margaritatus SHARP-NOSED PUFFER
15 cm. (6 in.)
An Indo-Pacific species of supposedly wide distribution, very common in the Red Sea, along the Arabian coasts, down E. Africa, and e. to the E. Indies, and the Pacific. However, there are a very large number of names available for the relatively few species of *Canthigaster*, and it is not possible to be certain that records of other 'species' do not in fact refer to this species, so it is difficult to be certain of its range. In reef areas it seems to be very common in tide pools, and over the shallow open reef.

The members of this genus have a sharply ridged back and a ridge along the belly; the skin along these folds is loose and can be inflated. This is most often seen as a form of territorial behaviour between males. *Canthigaster* species have a rather sharp snout and all are small. **492**

C. rostrata SHARPNOSE PUFFER
11 cm. (4½ in.)
An Atlantic species found on both sides of that ocean. In the W. it occurs from Bermuda, Florida, and the Bahamas S. to S. America, including the Caribbean and Gulf of Mexico. In the E. it is reported from St Helena, the W. African coast, Canaries, and Madeira.

It is a common fish, living in a variety of habitats, but possibly most abundant in sea grass beds. It is also found around coral reefs,

over sandy bottoms, and in tidal pools. Its depth range is from the shore line to 26 m. (14 fathoms). Diet for the fish is varied; Dr John E. Randall, who studied it in the Caribbean, recorded it eating manatee grass, sponges, crustaceans, polychaete worms, sea urchins, hydroids, and algae.

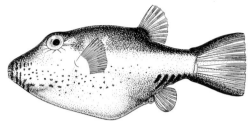

It is an attractive little fish with a ridge running along the mid-line of the back, a characteristic of this genus. The back is orange to purplish brown, the belly white to pale orange. The chin is decorated with small blue spots, blue lines radiate from the eye and run along the tail, and a set of vertical blue bars decorate the lower tail.

C. valentini 20 cm. (8 in.)
A widely distributed sharp-nosed pufferfish in the Indo-Pacific. It has been reported from the E. African coast to the Gulf of Aden, the Indian Ocean islands, thence e. to Queensland, Lord Howe Island, and Samoa.

It is a relatively distinct species, sharp-snouted, with a rough skin, and ridged on the back. Young fish have rounded blue and orange spots on their sides. **493**

CAPE
  GALAXIAS see **Galaxias zebratus**
  HAKE see **Merluccius capensis**
  KURPER see **Sandelia capensis**
  LOPEZ LYRETAIL see **Aphyosemion australe**
  SALMON see **Atractoscion aequidens**
CAPELIN see **Mallotus villosus**

CAPROIDAE

A small family of marine fishes, mostly found in moderate depths and, except locally, rarely abundant. Most of the known species are reddish in colour, some are bright red. All are small.

They are all rather deep-bodied and compressed, so that the body is very slim, and almost diamond-shaped with the strong dorsal fin spines on the upper angle, and pelvic fins (with a strong spine) at the lower angle. The snout is pointed, the jaws small, protractile, and with fine teeth. Scales cover the body, but they are small to minute and finely toothed.

Members of the family are found in all the deep oceans. See **Antigonia**, **Capros**.

Capros   Caproidae
aper BOARFISH 16 cm. (6¼ in.)
Found in the Mediterranean and the ne. Atlantic from the coast of Senegal to off SW. Ireland, but isolated specimens have been caught as far N. as s. Norway. It is normally a deep-water species, found between 100 to 400 m. (55–219 fathoms) on rocky and broken ground, and it has been suggested that it lives amongst the yellow or red encrusting growths of the rocks and crevices. Specimens taken away from rough ground may have been swept up from the deeper water by upwelling currents; they

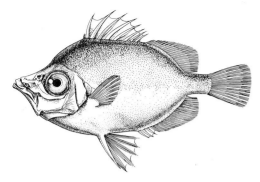

are occasionally caught in the w. English Channel in these circumstances.

It feeds mainly on crustaceans, especially small copepods, but also eats worms and molluscs. It breeds in springtime in the Mediterranean, the eggs and larvae being pelagic.

Specimens caught in deep water are brick red, sometimes with yellow bars. In shallow water they are a pale, straw colour.

CARACANTHIDAE
A family of rather obscure, small scorpion-fishes found only in the tropical Indo-Pacific. Their systematic status is a matter of some doubt, and their biology is little known.

Its members have deep rather compressed bodies, the skin without scales but densely covered with small skin flaps or papillae. The dorsal fin is single but the first rays are sharp and spiny. The pelvics are minute; all the other fins are small and are deeply embedded in the loose skin. See **Caracanthus**.

Caracanthus   Caracanthidae
  unipinna 5 cm. (2 in.)
This small scorpionfish is widely distributed in the Indo-Pacific, and has been recorded from the coast of e. Africa, Sri Lanka, and across to Hawaii. As it lives hidden in the interstices of coral on reefs, it is little known.

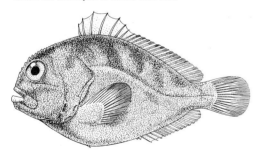

It is a variable greenish grey, lighter on the belly; the iris is golden yellow. It is distinguished by its deep, compressed head and body, scaleless skin, and minute pelvic fins.

CARANGIDAE
A large and important family of marine fishes, collectively known as jacks, scads, or pompanos, although many other names are in use. The family contains fishes of many divergent shapes, some are slender and cylindrical, others are deep-bodied, while a third group are compressed and almost plate-like. In addition the young are usually deeper-bodied than the adults of the same species.

Most carangids have a row of large, spiky scales along the side, best developed as scutes just in front of the tail. Most also have a characteristic sloping forehead, and 2 dorsal fins, although the first is sometimes composed of

separate and short spines. Many species also have detached small finlets behind the normal rayed dorsal and anal fins. All have 2 short anal spines in front of the anal fin, except that with age they are sometimes obscured by the body musculature.

Carangids are found in all the tropical, warm temperate, and temperate oceans of the world. Somewhat more than 200 species have been recognized, placed in numerous genera. They include many valuable food and game fish. See **Alectis, Caranx, Chorinemus, Elagatis, Naucrates, Oligoplites, Selar, Selene, Seriola, Trachinotus, Trachurus**.

Caranx   Carangidae
This genus belongs to a large and diverse family, Carangidae, and there is some confusion between species. Besides the illustrated *Caranx speciosus*, a second unidentified member of this genus is shown. **293**
C. hippos CREVALLE JACK 102 cm. (40 in.)
Possibly occurs in tropical regions around the world but this is not certain due to confusion between the many carangid species. It is certainly found on both sides of the Atlantic, in the w. Atlantic from Nova Scotia to Uruguay, and throughout the Gulf of Mexico. Young fish are common in shallow water, even in brackish areas in river mouths, and are usually found in schools ranging along and over the reefs. Large specimens are more solitary, but do form small

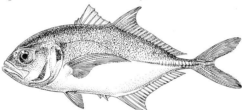

shoals. Adults are particularly common along the e. seaboard of the U.S. They are mainly fish-eaters, but shrimps and other invertebrates are also taken. It has often been alleged to be involved in ciguatera poisoning (the building up of toxic substances in the flesh) and the large specimens are poor eating anyway. They are, however, fine game fish and are taken by trolling and beach casting.

This species is metallic green to blue on the back, silvery on the sides, yellow below; the fins are yellowish.
C. latus HORSE-EYE JACK 76 cm. (30 in.)
A w. Atlantic carangid which ranges from Bermuda and New Jersey to the Brazilian coast and is common in the W. Indies. When young it is found in shallow inshore waters, often in brackish regions with muddy bottoms. Larger fish are found in deeper water, while the largest specimens are found in small schools on the outer reefs and in open water.

It is relatively slender-bodied with scutes along the tail, typical of the family. The upper profile of the head is smoothly rounded, and the eye is relatively large. Adults are silvery overall, the tail area is dusky, and the tail fin yellowish.

The horse-eye jack is a popular angling fish. Its flesh is palatable, but it is not commercially exploited to any great extent.
C. sexfasciatus GREAT TREVALLY, KING-FISH, CAVALLY 120 cm. (4 ft)
A trevally found widely in the Indo-Pacific, from the E. African coast, around India, n.

Australia, and into the w. Pacific, to Japan, Hawaii, and the Pacific islands. It is a large species which grows to a weight of about 18 kg. (40 lb.), and is particularly well known as a fine sporting fish. Throughout its range it is caught locally in some quantity for food.

The young are golden yellow and have 6 dark cross bars on the back and sides. Adults are silvery on the sides, bluish above; the top of the tail fin is blue, the lower lobe is bright yellow, as are the ventral fins.
C. speciosus KINGFISH, CAVALLA, GOLDEN TREVALLY 100 cm. (39 in.)
Widely distributed in the Indo-Pacific where it is found from the Red Sea and E. African coast to n. Australia. It is a large and handsome fish, found on the offshore reefs, although occasionally entering estuaries and appearing inshore.

The young fish is yellow on the sides and underneath, with a bluish back; 10-12 black cross bands run across the sides; the fins are yellow but the tail fin has a dark edge. The adult is very different: blue on the back, silvery on the sides, but without the dark cross bands.

It is a moderately popular angler's fish wherever it occurs. It is immediately distinguished by its lack of teeth. **294, 295**

CARAPIDAE
The family of pearlfishes, a small group of worldwide distribution in tropical and warm temperate seas, with a few species found in cooler waters. All are long and slender with a long well developed anal fin, a less well developed dorsal fin and a sharp pointed tail; pectoral fins are moderate in size (although in some species they are absent). In all species the pelvic fins are totally absent, and the anus is placed well forward on the throat.

They are secretive fishes which have adopted a life of near-parasitism, living inside the body cavities of sea cucumbers, clams, sea urchins, tunicates, and starfish. One species at least, lives inside the pearl shell and specimens have been found embedded in the shell wall – hence pearlfishes.

All pearlfishes are believed to pass through 2 larval stages after hatching from the pelagic egg. Both stages were at one time thought to be distinct groups of fishes and for this reason received individual names. The *vexillifer* stage, the first, is pelagic, and the larva has a long lobed filament from the front of the dorsal fin. As this structure is absorbed with growth, the larva becomes benthic in life style, and is known as a *tenuis*. Both stages are very elongate, the *tenuis* forms especially so. See **Carapus, Echiodon**.

Carapus   Carapidae
  acus 20 cm. (8 in.)
A pearlfish found only in the Mediterranean Sea and the Adriatic; records in the e. Atlantic are probably erroneous. It passes as a larva and juvenile through planktonic and benthic free-living stages, but as an adult lives a semi-parasitic life in sea cucumbers. Experiments have shown that the fish is attracted to elongate objects of the shape of the typical sea cucumber, especially when holothurian mucous is present on the object. The fish enters tail first through the anus, and lies inside the body cavity amongst the internal organs of mainly *Stichopus regalis* or *Holothuria tubulosa*. It does

considerable damage by feeding on the internal organs. It has also been found with small crustaceans in its gut.

Its body shape is similar to the other pearlfishes. It is translucent silvery white with reddish brown bars across the back.

Carassius   Cyprinidae
auratus GOLDFISH, PRUSSIAN or GIBEL CARP 30·5 cm. (12 in.)
The goldfish is distinguished from its relatives by the lack of barbels on the mouth, and by the strongly serrated front fin spines in both the dorsal and anal fins. The dorsal fin is long and many rayed, and the body is covered with moderately large scales.

Its natural distribution is hard to establish for certain but it seems that one form, the Asiatic goldfish, was native to e. Eurasia, including China. In the W. it was replaced by another form, the subspecies *C. auratus gibelio* (the gibel or Prussian carp), which was found in the w. U.S.S.R. and the Baltic states. Both have been kept and distributed either as food fish or for ornamental purposes, and one form or another is found throughout Europe, and in many other parts of the world.

It can tolerate water of relatively low oxygen level, and for this reason can be found in moderately polluted rivers. Normally it is an inhabitant of marshy pools, the backwaters of rivers, and lakes. The goldfish spawns amongst water plants in mid-summer when the water temperature reaches 20°C. Its numerous slightly sticky eggs, adhere to the water plants; they hatch in about a week. The young fish are golden-brown in colour, and even the progeny of pure gold parents do not become golden until aged about 18 months.

Many monstrous varieties have been bred by aquarists involving distortions of the head, fins, or coloration. **121, 122**

CARCHARHINIDAE

The largest family of living sharks with numerous species and worldwide range in tropical and temperate oceans. All are typical sharks, with a slim body shape, 2 dorsal fins, and a tail fin with the upper lobe much longer than the lower; all have 5 gill slits. Characteristically, they have large serrated triangular teeth in the upper jaw and pointed serrated ones in the lower. The members of the family vary greatly in maximum size, and some of the larger species are very dangerous to man. See **Carcharhinus, Galeocerdo, Galeorhinus, Negaprion, Prionace**.

Carcharhinus   Carcharhinidae
albimarginatus REEF WHITETIP SHARK *c.* 2·4 m. (8 ft)
A widespread shark in the tropical Indian and Pacific oceans, including the Red Sea. It is an active shark of inshore waters being particularly common along the edge of reefs, and coral atolls.

Although it has not been reported to attack man, its habit of living in inshore waters makes it potentially dangerous. Its normal diet would seem to be fish and squids, but it does scavenge around ships. A 1·8 m. (6 ft) specimen captured in Bikini Atoll had a 61 cm. (2 ft) long bone and joint it its stomach, the remains of a recent roast thrown overboard from a ship in the lagoon. **3**

C. gangeticus see under **C. leucas**
C. leucas BULL SHARK *c.* 3·6 m. (12 ft)
The bull shark is widely distributed in the tropical w. Atlantic, from s. Brazil to N. Carolina, and occasionally as far N. as New York. It is a sluggish shark, rarely seen at the surface, which lives in inshore waters and frequently penetrates up rivers. It is this species which is commonly found in the freshwater Lake Nicaragua, where it has been involved in several attacks on man. It is a dangerous shark throughout its range, both on account of its large size, and also because its inshore habits keep it in the area of the sea most frequented by man. Closely related if not identical sharks, *C. zambezensis*, known from the e. South African coast, and *C. gangeticus* from Indian seas, are similarly dangerous and share the bull shark's habit of ascending rivers.

The bull shark is grey-coloured above, white beneath, and when young its fins are dark tipped. It is rather stout-bodied and the first dorsal fin is placed well forward along the back. It eats a wide range of fishes, and squids, and is well known as a scavenger.

C. longimanus OCEANIC WHITETIP SHARK 3·5 m.(11½ ft)
This whitetip shark is a fish of the high seas, circumtropical in its distribution. It is probably the commonest large shark in the oceans. It is olive above and white below, and the tips of the dorsal, pectoral, and tail fins are characteristically white. The dorsal and pectoral fins are large and rounded.

Considered dangerous, but because it rarely comes into inshore waters it does not encounter humans frequently. On the other hand, it stubbornly follows fishing boats for long distances and is difficult to drive off. Despite its sluggish swimming, the whitetip feeds on some of the fastest swimming sea fishes – the tunas – as well as other fish species.

After a gestation period of one year, it gives birth to living young in litters of about 6, each 63–76 cm. (25–30 in.) long. They are born in early summer in tropical waters, in which area the gravid females are usually found. Non-breeding females and males migrate with the summer-time warming of the sea, within the 21°C. boundary.

C. obscurus DUSKY SHARK 3·6 m. (12 ft)
The dusky shark is found on both sides of the Atlantic, from the Mediterranean s. to S. Africa in the E., and s. Brazil to Massachusetts in the W.; also in the Pacific. It is more a pelagic open sea fish than many carcharinids, but it comes into shallow water frequently.

A moderately heavy-bodied shark with its first dorsal fin large and placed well forward, it is also distinguished by possessing a ridge along the mid-line of the back between the dorsal fins. It is one of the more active carcharhinid sharks and feeds on fishes. It is also a dangerous species which has several times been proved to have attacked men swimming. **4**

C. zambezensis see under **C. leucas**

Carchariidae see Odontaspidae

Carcharodon   Lamnidae
carcharias WHITE SHARK or POINTER, MAN-EATER 6·4 m. (21 ft)
The white shark, the most dangerous of all sharks on account of its size and aggressive nature, is found in temperate and tropical re-gions of all oceans. It is a fish of the open seas, but seasonally it comes into coastal waters where it may at times be common. On the European Atlantic coast it occurs as far N. as n. Spain (reports of it in British waters must be regarded as due to mistaken identifications). It occurs commonly in the Mediterranean, but is almost confined to the warmer, s. region and the Adriatic. On the coast of N. America, occasional specimens range as far n. as Nova Scotia, and it is fairly frequent in the Gulf of Maine; in Australian and S. African waters it is known to occur on all coasts. In all these areas its occurrence inshore is to some extent seasonal, certainly in the cooler temperate seas it appears as summer reaches its height and the water temperature rises.

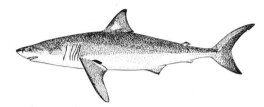

The white shark is not actually white. Its back varies in colour from slaty brown to dark grey; only the underside is white. It has a rather broad head, viewed from above, a high lunate tail, but its most characteristic feature is its teeth, large, triangular, with finely serrated cutting edges.

Its food appears to consist of almost any smaller aquatic animals; many species of fish are eaten, but seals, dolphins, and other sharks also feature in its diet. On the Californian coast a colony of the rare sea otter was attacked by white sharks and a number were killed. Attacks on men, particularly bathers and surf-board swimmers, are relatively frequent in tropical areas. Such attacks are usually unprovoked, and severe injuries and frequently death result; sometimes the victim completely disappears. The white shark will deliberately attack small boats, sometimes sinking them in the process, bathers have been attacked in knee-deep water, and many underwater swimmers have been followed by large sharks in a threatening manner. Many popular bathing beaches in Australia and South Africa have been fenced off at considerable cost to successfully prevent large sharks mingling with the bathers. In Australia particularly white sharks are caught by anglers.

The white shark is a large fish, a Cuban specimen of 6·4 m. weighed 3312 kg. (21 ft and 7302 lb.). Despite its relatively common appearance little is known of its life history beyond the fact that it bears living young, probably in broods of up to 9, and that it becomes mature sexually at a length of 3·3–4·3 m. (11–14 ft).

CARDINAL TETRA see **Cheirodon axelrodi**
CARDINALFISH see Apogonidae
CARDINALFISH,
    FRECKLED see **Phaeoptyx conklini**
    WHITESTAR see **Apogon lachneri**

Careproctus   Cyclopteridae
melanurus BLACKTAIL SNAILFISH 26 cm. (10¼ in.)
The blacktail snailfish ranges from n. British Colombia to Santa Catalina Island on the California coast, but it is not an inshore species. It lives near the bottom in depths of 91–1519 m.

(50–830 fathoms) and possibly much deeper. It is said to feed on worms, small crustaceans, and molluscs. It has been found in the guts of rockfish, arrow-toothed flounders, and hake.

It is distinguished by its slender, jelly-like body with a small suction disc on the underside of the head. The body is pinkish but the edges of the dorsal and anal fins, and the whole tail fin are blackish.

CARIBBEAN TONGUEFISH see **Symphurus arawak**

CARISTIIDAE

A small family of oceanic fishes, probably found in all the oceans of the world, but known from comparatively few specimens. It contains fewer than 5 species, and some of these are probably identical with one another.

They are all rather deep-bodied with a many-rayed, high dorsal fin, and a large anal fin; the pelvics are also well developed. The relationships of this family are not clear; it may well be closest to the bramids, but some authors suggest a placement close to the dories (Zeidae), or the stromateids (Stromateidae). See **Caristius.**

Caristius   Caristiidae
macropus MANEFISH, VEILFIN
33 cm. (13 in.)
The manefish is probably to be found throughout the oceans of the world but has been rarely taken in any of them; it is best known in the N. Pacific and N. Atlantic. Most have been taken in moderately deep water, 200–500 m. (109–273 fathoms); some specimens have been taken close to the sea bed, but the normal habitat is more probably in mid-water. It is believed to feed on small fishes and crustaceans, and young specimens have been found in the stomachs of several predatory fishes.

Its body is covered with small cycloid scales, which are easily rubbed off leaving the body uniform greyish brown, the fins being dark. When intact it is rather silvery brownish on the back.

Carnegiella   Gasteropelecidae
marthae BLACK-WINGED HATCHETFISH
3·5 cm. (1½ in.)
The black-winged hatchetfish is the smallest

species of the family. It is widely distributed in ne. S. America, Venezuela, Peru, and the Amazon, Orinoco, and Negro rivers. It is distinguished from its relatives by the middle part of the pectoral fins being distinctly black. The ventral outline of the fish is black pigmented, 2 dark lines run across the cheek, and it has a dark line along the side with a shining golden band above it; otherwise it is silvery.

It is a popular aquarium fish, made more so by its contrasting coloration. Like all hatchetfishes it can glide above the surface and is likely to jump out of an uncovered aquarium.

C. strigata MARBLED HATCHETFISH
4·5 cm. (1¾ in.)
This little hatchetfish is found in small forest pools in the Amazon and Guianas region. It can be distinguished from its nearest relatives by its markings, particularly the 3 dark irregular bars which run obliquely across the belly. It has a dark stripe along the side with a silvery upper edge, and the ventral profile is tinged a dusky yellow not black. The ground colour is yellowish with a distinct silvery sheen.

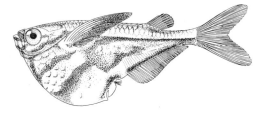

It is a popular aquarium fish, which has been bred in captivity. Reports of spawning activity indicate that after much splashing, and leaping, the eggs are shed and fertilized in a head to tail position. The small transparent eggs are shed over water plants.

Like other hatchetfishes it is a surface-living species, preferring to live in shaded surroundings, and because of its extremely narrow, compressed body and colouring, it is nearly invisible except when viewed side on.

CARP see **Cyprinus carpio**
CARP,
     GIBEL see **Carassius auratus**
     GRASS see **Ctenopharyngodon idella**
     PRUSSIAN see **Carassius auratus**
     SEA see **Dactylosargus arctidens**
     SILVER see **Hypophthalmichthys molitrix**
CARPET SHARK, COBBLER see **Crossorhinus tentacularis**

Carpiodes   Catostomidae
carpio RIVER CARPSUCKER 51 cm. (20 in.)
The river carpsucker is found in the central regions of the U.S. from the Montana plains to the Ohio River in Pennsylvania, in the Tennessee and Red River drainages. Its particular habitat is the larger silted rivers, and it is a relatively common fish.

It is a rather deep-bodied sucker, its body covered with large scales. The dorsal fin is many rayed and high in the front, although not greatly elongate. The snout is rounded, the mouth ventral, and the eye relatively small. **144**
C. cyprinus QUILLBACK 66 cm. (26 in.)
The quillback is widely distributed in the central and e. parts of the U.S., in the Mississippi system from w. Florida and Georgia to the Great Lakes and the St Lawrence drainage

system. It is confined mostly to lakes and large rivers.

It is a deep-bodied sucker, almost carp-like in general appearance, but with a ventral mouth, a blunt snout, and rather thick lips. Its dorsal fin is long and many-rayed, and its second ray is long, about twice the length of the other rays – hence quillback. Its body is covered with large scales.

A relatively large fish, good specimens may weigh up to 5·4 kg. (12 lb.). It is fished for commercially in Lake Erie, but elsewhere is not highly regarded as food.

CARPSUCKER, RIVER see **Carpiodes carpio**
CASCADURA see **Hoplosternum littorale**
CASCAROB,
     BLACK see **Polycentrus schomburgkii**
     KING see **Polycentrus schomburgkii**
CASCARUDO see **Callichthys callichthys**

Caspialosa   Clupeidae
kessleri BLACK-SPINED SHAD
51 cm. (20 in.)
This Caspian Sea shad is one of several species of shad-like fish endemic to the Caspian and Black seas, on the s. borders of the U.S.S.R. They differ from the shads found in the Mediterranean and Atlantic in having a larger mouth, and teeth on the vomer, a bone in the roof of the mouth, but are believed to have evolved from a common ancestor after the Black and Caspian seas became isolated from the Mediterranean in the Tertiary period. A closely related form, *C. kessleri pontica* is found in the Black Sea.

The black-spined shad is a large predatory fish which feeds mainly on smaller fishes when mature, although it feeds on planktonic crustaceans to some extent all its life. Most of the Caspian shads live the whole of their lives in the marine conditions offered by the sea and spawn there, but the black-spined shad runs into freshwater to spawn, chiefly into the Volga estuary. They spawn during June to late July, in eddies and places where the current is not too strong, and usually at night. The eggs float near the surface and develop while being carried downstream, and the larvae collect in backwaters, feeding on rotifers and copepods, later on insect larvae. In the Caspian Sea they migrate to the S. in winter, the adults returning to the n. coast and rivers to breed.

The black-spined shad is fished extensively in the n. Caspian, especially in the river mouths. It is an important food fish.

CASPIAN SPRAT see **Clupeonella delicatula**
CASTELNAU'S FISH see **Ompax spatuloides**
CASTOR-OIL FISH see **Ruvettus pretiosus**
CAT, MISSISSIPPI see **Ictalurus furcatus**
CATALUFA see **Priacanthus arenatus**
CATFISH see Ageneiosidae, Akysidae, Amblycipitidae, Amphiliidae, Anarhichadidae, Ariidae, Aspredinidae, Auchenipteridae, Bagridae, Callichthyidae, Cetopsidae, Chacidae, Clariidae, Cranoglanididae, Diplomystidae, Doradidae, Helogenidae, Heteropneustidae, Hypophthalmidae, Ictaluridae, Loricariidae, Olyridae, Pangasiidae, Pimelodidae, Plotosidae, Schilbeidae, Siluridae, Sisoridae
CATFISH see **Akysis leucorhynchus, Amblydoras hancocki, Anarhichas lupus, Clarias mossambicus**

CATFISH,
AFRICAN GLASS see **Physailia pellucida**
BANJO see **Buncocephalus**
BLUE see **Ictalurus furcatus**
CAVE see **Clarias cavernicola**
CHANNEL see **Ictalurus punctatus**
EEL see **Channalabes apus**
ESTUARY see **Cnidoglanis macrocephalus**
EUROPEAN see **Silurus glanis**
ELECTRIC see Malapteruridae
ELECTRIC see **Malapterurus electricus**
FLATHEAD see **Pylodictis olivaris**
FRESHWATER see **Tandanus tandanus**
MEKONG see **Pangasianodon gigas**
GAFFTOPSAIL see **Bagre marinus**
GLASS see **Kryptopterus bicirrhis**
JELLY see **Lycichthys denticulatus**
PUNGAS see **Pangasius pangasius**
SCALELESS see Mochokidae
SEA see **Arius felis**
SHOVEL-NOSED see **Sorubim lima**
SILOND see **Silonia silondia**
SPOTTED see **Anarhichas minor**
TALKING see **Acanthodoras spinosissimus**
TURKESTAN see **Glyptosternum reticulatum**
UPSIDE-DOWN see **Synodontis nigriventris**

Catlocarpio Cyprinidae
siamensis 3 m. (10 ft)
This is one of the largest members of the carp family known. Measured specimens of 2·5 m. (8¼ ft) length have been recorded, and reports of even larger specimens have been made.

It is common, and widespread in the larger rivers of Thailand, Cambodia, and probably elsewhere in Indo-China. It is particularly associated with large rivers but it enters the artificial water storage bungs, lakes, and canals. Little is known about its biology but it is probably seasonally migratory.

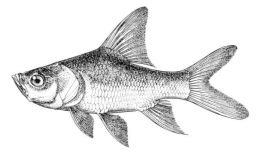

It is an important food fish in Thailand, and is frequently caught in nets in the region of Bangkok. Large specimens are caught on hooks baited with balls of cooked rice, and may be so powerful that they tow the fishermen's boat for several hours before tiring.

CATOSTOMIDAE
A relatively small family of freshwater fishes, best known from n. America, although represented in Asia by a few forms. In America they are generally known as suckers.

The family is close to the carp fishes (Cyprinidae) and like them they have the first 4 vertebrae modified into a Weberian apparatus. The swim bladder is divided into 2 or 3 lobes. They differ from the cyprinids in having a single row of very numerous pharyngeal teeth on the last gill arch. Members of the family

have thick, bristle-covered lips, very protrusible mouths, no jaw teeth, and no barbels. The body is covered with scales, and they have a single dorsal but no adipose fin.

Two main groups are recognizable. Members of one group are elongate and torpedo-shaped, usually inhabit flowing water, and feed on animal matter. The other group have deep bodies, are found in still water, and feed on algal and plant growths. See **Carpiodes, Catostomus, Chasmistes, Erimyzon, Ictiobus, Lagochila, Moxostoma, Xyrauchen.**

Catostomus Catostomidae
catostomus LONGNOSE SUCKER
63 cm. (25 in.)
The longnose sucker is widely distributed across N. America from Labrador and New Brunswick, s. to Pennsylvania, Minnesota, and Colorado, and w. to the Columbia River and Alaska. In Siberia it is found in the Arctic Ocean drainage rivers to the Yana River.

It is dark grey to black on the back and upper sides; the belly is white. Breeding males have well developed tubercles on the head and fins, and a bright red stripe along the sides.

It is found in both rivers and lakes, and is even said to occur in brackish water at the mouths of rivers. Its food, when adult, is entirely bottom-living invertebrates, but young feed on planktonic invertebrates and diatoms. It is found indifferently in swiftly flowing streams with stony bottoms and in lakes deeper than 15 m. (8 fathoms).

Breeding takes place after the snow and ice have disappeared, from April to June, in swift sections of gravelly rivers and in the inlet streams to lakes. The young stay buried in the gravel for a while after hatching.

In Arctic Canada this sucker is a food fish of some importance. In Siberia it is not appreciated.

C. commersoni WHITE SUCKER
63 cm. (25 in.)
This is a very widely distributed sucker in N. America, from Labrador and Nova Scotia, S. to Georgia and New Mexico, and w. to the upper Fraser River. It is not found along the Pacific coastal plain, or in Alaska and the far N. of Canada.

It is a slim-bodied fish, fully scaled with moderately sized scales. The snout is short and blunt, the lips thick. It is bronzy black on the back, silvery on the sides, with a dark stripe along the sides.

The white sucker is very tolerant of varying conditions and is found in most small to large streams and lakes, although in the N. it is found mostly in the warmer shallows. It is a bottom-living fish, feeding, when well grown, entirely on midge larvae, amphipods, and molluscs. The fry feed on planktonic organisms. It spawns on gravel shallows in lake margins or inlet streams.

Its flesh is said to be good to eat, and was particularly important as food to the Indians and early fur traders in N. America.

CATSHARK,
BROWN see **Apristurus brunneus**
BROWN-BANDED see **Hemiscyllium punctatum**
FALSE see **Pseudotriakis microdon**
VARIED see **Parascyllium variolatum**
CAUDO see **Phalloceros caudimaculatus**
Caulolepis longidens see under Anoplogasteridae

Caulophryne Caulophrynidae
jordani 20 cm. (8 in.)
A striking deep-sea angler found in the 3 major oceans at depths of 10 to 1500 m. (5–820 fathoms).

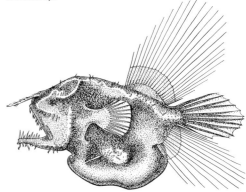

Adult females are rounded and the body is dark with small flaps of skin. The mouth is huge and the jaws are armed with sharp teeth. The young males and females are round-bodied with long fins; only the females develop the fishing rod illicium (the lure at the tip of a long ray on the head). Males are parasitic on the female when mature. They are rather slender, have small mouths, and, prior to attaching themselves, large nostrils and small eyes. **186**

CAULOPHRYNIDAE
Deep-sea anglerfishes found in the Pacific, Indian and Atlantic oceans. Although several forms have been described there seems to be only one well founded genus, and one species (which the Danish ichthyologist, Dr E. Bertelsen, divides into several subspecies).

It is distinguished by the very greatly elongate fins, especially the pectorals which are almost fan-like. Adult females are rather short-bodied and plump, but the males are slender and parasitic. See **Caulophryne**

CAVALLA see **Caranx speciosus**
CAVALLO, TOVIRA see **Apteronotus albifrons**
CAVALLY see **Caranx sexfasciatus**
CAVE
BARB, BLIND see **Caecobarbus geertsi**
CATFISH see **Clarias cavernicola**
CAVEFISH,
NORTHERN see **Amblyopsis spelaea**
SOUTHERN see **Typhlichthys subterraneus**
CELEBES
MEDAKA see **Oryzias celebensis**
RAINBOWFISH see **Telmatherina ladigesi**
CENTRAL MUDMINNOW see **Umbra limi**

CENTRARCHIDAE
An entirely N. American family of freshwater fishes and one of the characteristic groups of that fauna. It includes the black basses and sun-

fishes which are popular with sports fishermen and cold water aquarium keepers the world over. Many centrarchid species have been introduced to other parts of the world, rarely with beneficial results.

Most of the sunfishes have a thick-set, strongly compressed deep body. The dorsal fin is composed of stout spines and soft rays which together form a continuous fin, notched between the portions in some species. The body is fully scaled, the lateral line complete in most species. The family is distinguished as nest-builders; the male excavates a small depression in the sand, by flicking with his tail, in which the eggs are laid and jealously guarded. See **Elassoma, Enneacanthus, Lepomis, Micropterus, Pomoxis.**

CENTRISCIDAE
A small family of very distinctive marine fishes found only in the tropical Indo-Pacific. Like their relatives, the snipefishes (Macroramphosidae), they are elongate, and compressed, with a long, flattened snout. Instead of having scales the body is encased in thin bony shields which meet to form a sharp edge on the belly. The spiny dorsal fin has one long spine, and is placed at the end of the body, the true tail fin being displaced below the tail.

These are mostly small fishes of shallow seas which have no commercial value. See **Aeoliscus, Centriscus.**

Centriscops   Macroramphosidae
  humerosus BANDED BELLOWSFISH
23 cm. (9 in.)
A deep-bodied, long-snouted fish found in Australian waters. It has been recorded mainly off the S. of the continent, and a similar, perhaps identical species, *C. obliquus,* has been reported off South Africa. It has been taken in depths as great as 823 m. (450 fathoms).

It is a very distinct form with a heavy dorsal spine, serrated on its hind edge. The body is covered with rough-toothed scales. It is orange-pink, with 5 dark oblique bands across the body.
C. obliquus see under **C. humerosus**

Centriscus   Centriscidae
  scutatus RAZORFISH 15 cm. (6 in.)
Widely distributed in the Indian Ocean, and Indo-Australian Archipelago, this species was the earliest described of all the members of the family. It has the typical body shape, laterally compressed with a knife-edged belly, and only slightly rounded back. The snout is long, and the body covered with thin bony plates. The dorsal spine which terminates the tail is not movable.

Its biology is little known. It has been reported to swim in a 'head up' position, but by analogy with the shrimp fishes it is more likely to adopt their head down attitude normally, varying the posture on occasions. It is silvery with a conspicuous dark lateral band; the belly is golden with 6–8 cross-bars.

Centroberyx   Berycidae
  affinis NANNYGAI, REDFISH 45 cm. (18 in.)
Widely distributed in Australian waters in the s. half of the continent, from S. Queensland to W. Australia and Tasmania. It occurs to the N. as a rare wanderer. It appears to be a bottom-living species found on the continental shelf in 18–128 m. (10–70 fathoms).

Its body is deep and fully scaled. The head is large, with a large eye and a wide mouth, and has a series of rough, exposed bones and heavy scales. It is reddish on the head and sides, the centre of each scale bearing a red spot; the lower sides and belly are light orange. The fins are all orange-red.

The nannygai is commercially exploited along the New South Wales and S. Australian coasts. Its flesh is said to be of excellent quality, and large quantities were landed by seiners and trawlers. The catches declined after a short while, however, which suggests that this species is too slow in growing and replacing its numbers to support heavy exploitation.

The name nannygai is the aboriginal name in the Sydney area; redfish is the name coined to promote sales.

Centrolabrus   Labridae
  exoletus ROCK COOK, SMALL-MOUTHED WRASSE 15 cm. (6 in.)
A small wrasse found in the waters of n. Europe from Spain to n. Scotland and Norway. It is found very rarely in intertidal pools, but is more common in the immediately sublittoral zone from 2–20 m. (1–11 fathoms), amongst algae and eel grass. Its distribution appears to be local.

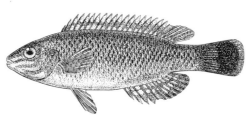

It feeds on small crustaceans in the plankton, and recent observations by Dr G. W. Potts of the Plymouth Laboratory have shown that some of its diet is composed of parasitic crustaceans from the skin of other fishes.

It is distinguished by its small mouth, by its 5 strong anal spines, and by the broad crescent-shaped dusky mark across the tail. This conspicuous marking is thought to be a distinguishing 'guild' mark for other fishes to identify a harmless cleaner-fish.

CENTROLOPHIDAE
A moderately large family of pelagic and bathypelagic fishes found on the high seas and over the continental shelf of mainly temperate oceans. A few species are found in shallow, inshore waters, and a number occur in tropical seas.

They are related to the family Stromateidae and Nomeidae and like both families possess the characteristic pouch in the pharynx, lined with papillae which are well equipped with small teeth. Most blackfishes are elongate-bodied when adult, but deeper-bodied when young. They are usually compressed, with very weak, flabby skeletons, although in some (e.g. *Seriolella*) spines are present in the dorsal

fin and the skeleton is well calcified. Many of the species have fine teeth in the jaws.

In common with their relatives the blackfishes are often found as young fishes in association with jellyfishes. In some species the adults certainly feed on medusae, and although young fish may also do so the association seems more for protection in their case. Several members of the family are locally exploited for food. See **Centrolophus, Hyperoglyphe, Icichthys, Schedophilus, Seriolella.**

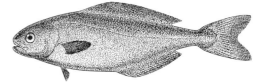

Centrolophus   Centrolophidae
  niger BLACKFISH, BLACK RUFF 1 m. (3¼ ft)
Although several species of *Centrolophus* have been described they are all considered to be synonyms of this species by the latest authority on the group. The blackfish is thus widely distributed in the Atlantic, the Mediterranean, off Australia, and New Zealand; it is probably worldwide in distribution. It is one of the largest members of the family.

Adult fish are moderately common in the N. Atlantic, especially in the E. It is occasionally taken in the nets of deep-water trawlers fishing over the edge of the continental shelf, but it seems to be a mid-water and bathypelagic fish rather than a bottom-living species. Adults feed on fishes, crustaceans, and jellyfish; young specimens feed on medusae, and have been found living with jellyfishes at the surface of the ocean. The young are distinctively marked with 3 or 4 dark vertical bands; the adults are dark greyish brown with a slaty tint over the body cavity.

It appears to be too rarely captured to be of any value as a commercial fish, although on occasions schools have been captured. The flesh is soft and although white has little flavour and that mostly unpleasant.

Centromochlus   Auchenipteridae
  aulopygius 8 cm. (3 in.)
This little catfish is found in ne. S. America in the Amazon basin, n. to Venezuela. It is strikingly coloured, chocolate brown above with oval light blotches; the dorsal and tail fins are similarly coloured, but ventrally they are lighter, as is the underside.

A thickset fish, with the dorsal fin far forward on the body. The anal fin is very short, but slightly longer than the base of the adipose fin. The tail fin is forked. Several pairs of barbels round the mouth, those on the upper jaw very long, 2 pairs on the chin short.

Occasionally imported as an aquarium fish; its biology is little known.

Centrophorus   Squalidae
  squamosus 142 cm. (56 in.)
A deep-water shark, best known in the n. E.

Atlantic from Iceland and the Scottish coast to Madeira, although it has also been found off South Africa and New Zealand. It lives in depths of 400 to 1500 m. (219–820 fathoms) and in the e. Atlantic is one of the most common of the squaloid deep-water sharks.

It is a form found close to the bottom and it feeds on a wide range of fishes and deep water crustaceans. It is rather broad-bodied and the snout and underside are flattened, the dorsal fins are large with very distinct spines. The teeth are oblique and sharp with a single cusp which, especially in the lower jaw, is acutely sloping.

Centrophryne   Centrophrynidae
  spinulosa 5 cm. (2 in.)
The only species represented in the family, it has been found from a number of widely spaced stations in the Indian and Pacific oceans, but is known from very few specimens. The maturing female has a wide, deep head and tapering body. The illicium (rod on the snout)

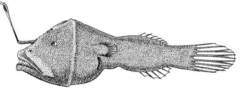

is angled and has a swollen, light coloured tip; a small barbel is present on the throat. The gape is large, the jaws equal in length, the lower jaw with a spine at the tip. Mature males are unknown, but those changing from larvae are small, brown, and are losing their teeth. Specimens of this species have been taken in depths of 30–2500 m. (16–1370 fathoms), the youngest nearer the surface.

CENTROPOMIDAE
A small family of deep-sea angler fishes which contains the single genus. It is close to the linophrynid angler fishes, and has, like them, a barbel on the throat but in the present group it is small and finger-like.

The members of this family have been found in the Pacific and Indian oceans, from the Gulf of Panama, the New Guinea area, and the Mozambique Channel. See **Centrophryne**.

CENTROPOMIDAE
A family of rather divergent fishes of the great order Perciformes. Like other members of the order they have strong spines in the dorsal and anal fins, in the former comprising a separate wholly spiny fin. The body is covered by scales, and the lateral line runs from just behind the head to the tail.

The family is composed of several natural groups, the American Pacific and Atlantic snooks or robalos, the glassfishes from Asia and the Australian seas and freshwaters, and the freshwater perches of Africa and Australia. Further study of these groups will probably demonstrate that each represents a separate family. Some are large and valued sporting and food fishes, others are minute and popular with aquarists. See **Centropomus, Chanda, Lates.**

Centropomus   Centropomidae
  undecimalis SNOOK 1·40 m. (55 in.)
A popular sporting fish, which is also highly regarded as a food fish, the snook is widely

distributed throughout the Caribbean, ranging exceptionally as far N. as the Bahamas and S. Carolina, and s. to Brazil. The young especially are found inshore in shallow coastal streams and lagoons, but adults are also found in mangrove sloughs, river mouths, and on inshore reefs. It can tolerate almost fresh water.

It is olive-green above, the sides are silvery, the lateral line is black. Large specimens may weigh as much as 23·5 kg. (52 lb.), and are prime sporting fish. The flesh is delicately flavoured, white, and flaky.

Centroscyllium   Squalidae
  fabricii BLACK DOGFISH 84 cm. (33 in.)
This is a deep-water shark of the n. N. Atlantic, found in the Davis Strait, off w. Greenland, the slopes of the Grand Bank and Georges Bank, Iceland, the Faroes, and Shetland. It is a deep brown to black above, almost black below. It can be distinguished from the other deep-water sharks by the large size of its eye, by the deeply-grooved dorsal fin spines, and the backward position of the pelvic fins.

The black dogfish has been caught near the surface but mostly it is taken in trawls in depths of 183–1500 m. (100–820 fathoms). Although it is considered to be relatively uncommon, a catch of over 100 specimens, some of which were only 15 cm. (6 in.) long, was reported off Nova Scotia in 1949. It is presumably an ovoviviparous shark, as are the other members of the family. It is known to feed on squid, pelagic crustaceans, and jellyfishes, but details of its diet ate scanty.

Centroscymnus   Squalidae
  coclolcpis PORTUGUESE SHARK
114 cm. (45 in.)
The Portuguese shark, so called because it was once fished for commercially off the coast of Portugal, is a common species along the continental shelf of Europe. On the N. American Atlantic coast it seems rather uncommon. It is one of the most common sharks in deep water, 600–1000 m. (328–547 fathoms), and down to about 2700 m. (1476 fathoms) from se. Iceland and the Faeroes s. to Madeira. This is one of the deepest living sharks known.

It is dark coloured, with a spine before each dorsal fin, which, however, only just project through the skin. The dorsal fins are small but of approximately equal size. It bears living young, females containing up to 16 embryos have been reported.

Cephalopholis   Serranidae
A large and variable genus; an unidentified *Cephalopholis* species is shown. **266**
C. fulvus CONEY 30 cm. (12 in.)
Found on the American east coast from Bermuda, s. Florida, the Bahamas, throughout the Caribbean and Gulf of Mexico, to Brazil. This is one of the most common W. Indian groupers in reef areas from the shore line to depths of about 46 m. (25 fathoms), although it has been

reported in deeper water. It feeds largely on crustaceans.

A number of colour phases of this species occur; one is yellowish, others range to deep red, usually in deep-water forms. The body is spotted with small, usually blue spots, but it always has 2 dark blotches on the top of the tail, and 2 smaller spots on the chin. **264**
C. miniatus CORAL TROUT, BLUE-SPOT
ROCK-COD 46 cm. (18 in.)
Widespread in the Indo-Pacific from the Red Sea and E. African coast to Australian waters and the w. Pacific. It is associated mainly with coral reefs, and in many areas is very abundant.

It is distinguished mainly by its colouring, basically scarlet above, lighter on the sides, covered with small black-edged blue spots. The posterior fins have dark blue borders. The tail fin is rounded in outline. **265**

Cephaloscyllium   Scyliorhinidae
  ventriosum SWELL SHARK 91 cm. (36 in.)
The swell shark is found on the Californian coast of America, particularly from Monterey Bay to Lower California. It is found in inshore waters, in the beds of the giant kelp seaweeds, and is often caught in lobster pots.

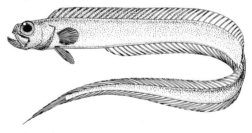

As a defence mechanism when brought to the surface it can swallow air so that it balloons up, the centre of the body swelling to at least twice its natural size.

Each egg is shed encased in an almost transparent light tan oblong capsule with tendrils at its corners which anchor it in the kelp beds until the young shark hatches out.

The swell shark is light brown with darker blotches and spots, which are particularly intense towards the tail. Its mouth is wide, and the teeth although small, are sharp and very effective at catching fishes.

Cepola   Cepolidae
  rubescens RED BANDFISH 70 cm. (27½ in.)
Found in the Mediterranean and e. N. Atlantic, as far N. as w. Scottish waters. In British seas it has for long been regarded as a rare fish, but there is reason to suppose that to the S., in the English Channel it is relatively common although its habit of lying buried in stiff mud makes it difficult to capture. Most specimens are caught after storms when, presumably, they have been driven out of their burrows.

Its coloration is distinctive; the back and sides are red or orange-pink, the belly and the fins are bright orange.

It feeds mainly on planktonic crustaceans and other small invertebrates.

CEPOLIDAE
A small family of marine fishes, represented by at most 6 species. All are extremely elongate,

almost eel-like in body form with long-based dorsal and anal fins which are continuous with the tail fin. The body is covered with minute scales.

The members of the family are found on European coasts, off New Zealand and s. Australia (genus *Cepola*), and more widely in the Indo-Pacific (genus *Acanthocepola*). Most are reddish in colour, live in shallow, inshore waters some amongst rocks others living in burrows in the sea bed. See **Cepola**.

Ceratias   Ceratiidae
   holboelli 120 cm. (47 in.)
The largest of the deep-sea anglers, and the first known, for it was first discovered stranded on the Greenland coast by the Danish navigator Lt Commander Holbøll some time before 1844.

Adult females are quite unmistakable being heavy-bodied, flabby fish with rather a long tail, short, stout fin rays in the dorsal and anal fins (4 in each) and in the tail. The body is darkly pigmented and covered with large conical spikes. The eyes are small, and the fishing rod on the snout long.

Larval females and males are pelagic, round-bodied fishes with loose skin, but on maturing the male becomes slender, and eventually attaches himself to a mature female, becoming parasitic on her. His eyes, mouth and gut degenerate, while his skin becomes rough like that of the female. Parasitic males measure up to 6 cm. (2½ in.).

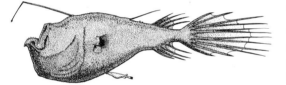

The adults are captured in depths of 121 to 1000 m. (66–546 fathoms). Occasional specimens of the large females, sometimes with one or more attached males are captured by commercial trawlers fishing in deep water in the N. Atlantic; at least one other was taken from the stomach of a sperm whale in Antarctic waters.

CERATIIDAE
A family of deep-sea angler fishes, the members of which are relatively large, although only 2 species are well known. They are set apart from the other ceratioids by having 2 or 3 globular, gland-like structures on the back in front of the dorsal fin, and short-based dorsal and anal fins with 4 or 5 rays. Females have a long slender fishing rod with a globular tip. The skin is rough and prickly. Males are parasitic as adults.

Members of the family are found in all the deep-water oceans. See **Ceratias, Cryptopsarus**.

CERATODONTIDAE
The family of the Australian lungfish, the single species known. It shows some affinities with the African and South American lungfishes (Protopteridae and Lepidosirenidae), notably in lacking properly calcified centra in its vertebrae, and having teeth fused into a number of distinctive bony plates. It differs from them fundamentally, however, in having a single lung in the mid-line of the body situated above the gut with which it communicates. Its pectoral and pelvic fins are broad, paddle-like in appearance, and the body is covered with large, solid scales. See **Neoceratodus**.

CERO see **Scomberomorus regalis**
CERO MACKEREL see **Scomberomorus regalis**

CETOMIMIDAE
The family to which most of the described bathypelagic whalefishes belong. Typically they are relatively small, few more than 15 cm. (6 in.) long, rather stout-bodied, with large heads and especially large jaws. They lack scales, and pelvic fins; they have small to minute eyes, and very distinctive lateral lines essentially consisting of a wide hollow tube with large openings, and between the openings small papillae. They also have a network of luminous tissue along the bases of the dorsal and anal fin and around the vent; the luminous tissue is not in the form of light organs but is a soft and fleshy mass. It probably glows reddish orange in life. Many whalefishes are themselves brick red in colour, others are dull brown.

They are found in deep water in all the oceans. Twenty or more species have been described, many of which are known from single specimens only. They are also very fragile and are rarely caught without considerable damage to the soft fleshy body, and often diaphanous skin. See **Cetomimus.**

Cetomimus   Cetomimidae
   indagator 14 cm. (5½ in.)
This is in some ways slightly atypical for a whalefish, for the head is relatively narrow and pointed, and the anal fin is elongate, but with a short constricted base. Typically for a whalefish, however, it has a long head, with enormous jaws, each of which are lined with irregular series of tiny, conical teeth; teeth are also present in the palate. The lateral line is distinctive, being a broad tube with 12 large pores. The anal fin rays have at their bases a web of luminous tissue which extends onto the body. The skin is very thin and fragile. It is probably reddish, but the original life colour has not been recorded.

The only known specimen of this species was captured by the Danish Deep-sea Expedition of 1950–52, E. of South Africa at a depth of about 2000 m. (1092 fathoms).

CETOPSIDAE
A small family of S. American catfishes confined mainly to the ne. region of the continent. Its members are scaleless, the skin smooth and without any bony plates or scute-like scales; the adipose fin is also lacking. They are streamlined fishes, the body cylindrical, the head somewhat flattened. Three pairs of barbels, 2 on the lower jaw, one on the upper jaw. The eyes are small and partially concealed under the skin. The dorsal fin is small and triangular, without heavy spines, and placed well forward just behind the head. See **Pseudocetopsis**.

CETORHINIDAE
The single member of this family is the basking shark, *Cetorhinus maximus*, an enormous shark of worldwide distribution outside the tropics. It is the second largest fish known, and is distinguished by its very wide gill slits, minute teeth, and long bristly gill rakers. See **Cetorhinus**.

Cetorhinus   Cetorhinidae
   maximus BASKING SHARK
   10·4 m. (34 ft)
The basking shark is a veritable giant amongst fishes, large specimens weighing considerably in excess of 6048 kg. (6 tons). Yet for all its size it is quite harmless, such incidents as upsetting small boats in which it has been involved,

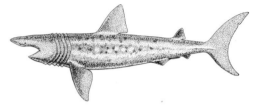

being more accidental than due to malice. Because its food is entirely composed of zooplankton, the minute, floating animals of the sea's surface, the inside of the shark's throat is lined with stiff dark bristles on the gill arches which act as filters to catch the plankton as it passes in the water from mouth to gill slit. To capture sufficient food the basking shark merely swims slowly around with its mouth wide open. Its jaw teeth are minute. In some areas the gill rakers drop-off in winter and the shark grows new ones each year, presumably lying dormant on the seabed whilst unable to feed, but in warm water areas these sharks are active all year round.

The basking shark is common in both the N. Atlantic and the Pacific, as well as in the S. Hemisphere. It is an oceanic shark found only occasionally close inshore. Its name refers to its habit of sluggishly swimming at the surface as if basking in the sun, for which reason in Ireland it is also called the sunfish. Formerly in the N. Atlantic it was harpooned for the sake of its liver oil, and meal made from its flesh, but this fishery has now almost died out.

Chaca   Chacidae
   chaca 20 cm. (8 in.)
The grotesque, tadpole-like shape of the head and body of this species is quite unmistakable. The head is broad and flattened; the eyes are widely spaced and dorsally placed. The wide mouth is fringed with short barbels, a pair of stub-like barbels at the angles of the mouth. The tail fin is singular in that it extends well onto the back. It is a dull brown with many black and pale spots on the back and sides.

Widely distributed through India, Burma, Sumatra, and Borneo, this fish lies in concealment in lowland streams and pools in flood plains. It is entirely bottom-living, extremely well concealed, and even when touched does not abandon its cryptic behaviour. It is catholic in its choice of food.

It has been kept in aquaria in Europe. **157**

CHACIDAE
A family of very curiously shaped catfish found widely in India, Burma, Sumatra, and Borneo. It contains one species. See **Chaca**.

Chaenocephalus   Channichthyidae
aceratus ICEFISH 60 cm. (23½ in.)
An Antarctic species found commonly in the area of S. Georgia, the S. Orkneys, and S. Shetland. This icefish is one of the so-called 'bloodless fishes' which lack the oxygen-carrying, iron-based haemoglobin in their blood. Their pale appearance and almost clear blood were well-known to the whaling crews before such phenomena were accepted as possible by scientists. Like other members of its family its head is pointed with an almost duck-billed snout and stout spines on the gill cover.

It lives in moderately shallow water of 5–340 m. (2·5–190 fathoms). **418**

Chaenogobius   Gobiidae
isaza FRESHWATER GOBY 8 cm. (3 in.)
A Japanese species which is locally a valued food fish despite its small size. In body form it is a typical goby, rather long-bodied with a large head and big mouth. Two short dorsal fins, the first composed of weak spines. The body scales are small (about 60 in a lengthwise row). It is light brown with many darker spots.

It is found in Lake Biwa, Japan and in the rivers entering the lake. It spawns in spring when the fish are found around the shores. It is captured later in the year in trap nets in very large numbers, and its flesh is said to be tasty, eaten either fresh or pickled in a sweet sauce.

CHAENOPSIDAE
The pike-blennies are closely related to the scaled-blennies (Clinidae) and some authors prefer to lump the 2 groups together. They do differ in a number of ways, notably in their extremely long eel-like shape, long jaws, a single long dorsal fin, and lack of scales.

They are found on both coasts of tropical America. Most are small fishes, often living in holes or in invertebrate tubes from which only the head projects. The males defend their territories with a great show of mouth gaping and threatening postures. See **Chaenopsis, Hemiemblemaria, Lucayablennius**.

Chaenopsis   Chaenopsidae
ocellata BLUETHROAT PIKE-BLENNY
12 cm. (4¾ in.)
Found in the Caribbean, and on the Florida and Bahamas coasts. It is an inhabitant of old worm tubes in sea grass beds, although it also occurs on sand and marsh bottoms in shallow water. It is a solitary, strongly territorial fish, defending its home tube with a great display of threat in which the large jaws are gaped at an intruder. The males have a bright orange spot on the front of the dorsal fin, and this and the conspicuous blue throat and gill cover supports are flashed in threat at an attacker or trespasser.

This species can be distinguished from its nearest relatives by having 13 pectoral fin rays,

and in the breeding male by its blue throat and gill cover membranes. Immature males and females are light brownish with dusky cross bars on the body; they lack the orange spot on the dorsal fin and the ventral blue of the male's head.

Chaetoderma   Balistidae
pencilligera PRICKLY LEATHER-JACKET
25 cm. (10 in.)
Found in the area between Singapore, Penang, and the n. coast of Australia. It is relatively common on the Queensland coast and around New Guinea, in shallow water with abundant algal growth.

It is a brownish grey in colour, with irregular wavy brown or blue lines on the body, and brown spots on the fins. The pectoral fin is conspicuously yellow. The whole of the head, body, and tail have densely branched filaments. The body scales are rather large and coarse, those in front arranged in cross rows, the posterior ones lengthwise. This is a typical filefish, very compressed in body form, with a high dorsal spine, and a deep flap beneath the belly supported by a curved spine. **473**

Chaetodipterus   Ephippidae
faber SPADEFISH 91 cm. (3 ft)
Found from New England and Bermuda (where it was introduced) to s. Brazil, including the Caribbean and the Gulf of Mexico. It grows to a large size, weights of up to 9 kg. (20 lb.) having been recorded, but specimens over 46 cm. (18 in.) are exceptional. Adults are found in small to large schools in water deeper than 9 m. (5 fathoms) usually swimming strongly well above the bottom, or all resting quietly, head towards the current. Smaller specimens are found close inshore around pier pilings, wrecks, and close to the water's edge.

It is a distinctive species, very small individuals being black overall, except for the marginal fins which are transparent. Larger fish are usually greyish silver with a series of pronounced vertical bars along the head and body, although sometimes totally black specimens are encountered. Very large adults are silvery grey with only 1–2 faint bars.

The black young fish have the habit of drifting at the water's edge, inclined to one side and swaying in the waves, looking much like black gastropods or the seed pods of the red mangrove, which are both found in these regions. Even larger dark specimens occasionally drift on their sides close to the bottom and resemble blackened plant debris.

The spadefish feeds on a wide range of invertebrate plant matter. Its flesh is said to be well-flavoured and firm. It takes a baited hook readily.

Chaetodon   Chaetodontidae
auriga THREAD-FIN BUTTERFLYFISH
23 cm. (9 in.)
A wide-ranging tropical Indo-Pacific species which is found from the Red Sea and e. coast of Africa, the Indian and E. Indian coast, n. Australia, through the w. and central Pacific islands and N. to Hawaii, the Philippines, and s. China. It is one of the best known and most

common of the butterflyfishes throughout its range. A single long ray extends from the top edge of the dorsal fin. **315**
C. capistratus FOUREYE BUTTERFLYFISH
15 cm. (6 in.)
Found from Massachusetts s. through the Caribbean and Gulf of Mexico. This is the most common of the butterflyfishes in the W. Indies, found mostly on reefs but also occurring on rocky, and occasionally sandy areas.

The white-ringed black spot at the rear end of the body is distinctive; the young of this species have a second spot on the second dorsal fin base which fades with age. The black band, narrowly edged with yellow, running through the eye is presumed to conceal the eye from predators while the eye-spot near the tail is presumed to heighten the confusion as to which is the front end of the fish.
C. collare 18 cm. (7 in.)
A widely distributed tropical Indo-Pacific species which has been reported from the Red Sea, India, the E. Indies, Formosa, China, and Japan. It is an inshore species found around reefs and rocky areas to a depth of 15 m. (8 fathoms), although the very young are often found in tidal pools in only inches of water.

It is distinguished by its yellowish brown coloration with faint dark lines following the scale rows and lighter on the belly. **316**
C. fasciatus 13 cm. (5 in.)
An endemic species in the Red Sea despite a few records, probably misidentifications, from elsewhere in the Indian Ocean.

It is distinguished by having a broad white band behind the black stripe through the eye. It is close to *C. lunula* but the dark band at the base of the soft dorsal does not cross the tail. **317**
C. fremblii 13 cm. (5 in.)
A native species to Hawaii and apparently found only around this island group. It is a relatively common shallow-water species there.

It is distinguished immediately by its colour pattern, especially in the lack of any dark stripe through the eye. It has a dark patch on the upper side at the base of the first dorsal spines, and a large dark blotch filling the area of the posterior side between soft dorsal and anal fins. The blue, lengthwise lines along the back and sides are equally distinctive. **318**
C. guttatissimus 13 cm. (5 in.)
A little-known Indian Ocean species, first found in Sri Lanka, then later off Zanzibar. It has also been reported from Mauritius, the E. coast of Africa (Delagoa Bay), the Red Sea, and India. A beautifully coloured butterflyfish. **319**
C. kleinii WHITE-SPOTTED BUTTERFLYFISH
13 cm. (5 in.)
Widespread in the tropical Indo-Pacific and found from the E. African coast (Zanzibar to Durban), the Indian Ocean islands, the E. Indies, India, n. Australia, Melanesia, and the Philippines. In parts of the range it is very common. **320**
C. larvatus 13 cm. (5 in.)
A species endemic to the Red Sea and the Gulf of Aden and found very commonly in this area.

It is a deep-bellied species with dark coloration, dark brown on the back paler on the head and lower sides. **321**
C. luciae 6·5 cm. (2½ in.)
This is one of the few species of butterflyfish to be found along the w. coast of Africa, in marked contrast to their abundance in the Indian

Ocean. It is found from the Cape Verde Islands, and from Senegal to Angola.

Its markings are distinctive in the area in which it lives. It is pale brown in general, lighter below. A broad dark band runs from the nape through the eye to the cheek; a second band runs from the second dorsal spine to the base of the pectoral fin. A dusky band covers the base of the soft dorsal fin and the anal fin. **322**

C. lunula RED-STRIPED BUTTERFLYFISH 20 cm. (8 in.)
Widely distributed in the Indo-Pacific. This species ranges from the coast of e. Africa, around Sri Lanka, the E. Indies, the n. coasts of Australia to the w. Pacific and Hawaii. It is found in shallow water, and is often the most common of the inshore butterflyfishes.

It is one of the most beautiful of this very brightly coloured group, its distinguishing feature being a broad dark bar from the upper edge of the pectoral base curving upwards to the dorsal spines. **323**

C. mesoleucos 10 cm. (4 in.)
A species apparently found only in the Red Sea, although there have been unreliably documented reports of it from Japan. This was another of the many species made known to science by the Danish explorer Pehr Forskål, who was the first man to describe the tropical fishes of the Red Sea.

It is distinguished from the other butterflyfishes by the front half of the body being whitish, the posterior half dark brown and marked with thin dark lines. **324**

C. meyeri 16 cm. (6¼ in.)
This butterflyfish is known only from the E. Indies, and has been recorded as locally common in the waters of the Moluccas, Celebes, Java, and the Philippines. It is a very strikingly marked species which, where it occurs, is not likely to be misidentified. **325**

C. ocellatus SPOTFIN BUTTERFLYFISH 20 cm. (8 in.)
A w. Atlantic species which is recorded from New England s. to Brazil, including the Gulf of Mexico. It is a common reef and inshore fish in the W. Indies.

In daylight the body is whitish with the fins bright yellow, a bright yellow-margined black band passes through the eye from the first dorsal spines, and a yellow bar runs along the edge of the gill cover. A small but prominent triangular black spot at the outer edge of the soft dorsal fin, which has a dusky blotch at its base. At night-time this dusky spot becomes black and the body develops dark bars. Like other butterflyfish it is active in the light, and rests in crevices, 'sleeping' at night. **326**

C. pictus 10 cm. (4 in.)
A species found only in the Red Sea, although often confused with the closely allied *C. vagabundus*. It was first described by Pehr Forsskål in an account published in 1775, but many later authors regarded it as the same species as *C. vagabundus*. Other students of the Red Sea fish fauna, however, have listed it as a variety of that species. **327**

C. rafflesii LATTICED BUTTERFLYFISH 15 cm. (6 in.)
A butterflyfish restricted in its destribution to the E. Indies, Melanesia, Polynesia, and the Philippines. It has been reported on the Queensland coast of Australia.

This species is named in honour of Sir Thomas Stamford Raffles, of the East India Company and founder of Singapore, who first collected it during his exploration of Sumatra. **328**

C. semilarvatus 20 cm. (8 in.)
An abundant butterflyfish in the Red Sea but found only there, in inshore waters around reefs and in the clear patches between corals. It is a very distinctive species. **329**

C. speculum see under **C. zanzibarensis**

C. striatus BANDED BUTTERFLYFISH 15 cm. (6 in.)
Widely distributed in the Atlantic; in the E. from W. Africa and the Cape Verde Islands, in the W. from New Jersey to s. Brazil including the Gulf of Mexico and the Caribbean. It is common around the reefs of the W. Indies.

A distinctively marked species with 4 bold dark bars, a white body tinged with yellow on the back, and the pelvic fins black with the exception of the fin spine. Young fishes have a white-ringed dark spot on the second dorsal fin until they reach a length of about 5 cm. (2 in.). **330**

C. trifasciatus 15 cm. (6 in.)
A very abundant coral reef species in the tropical Indo-Pacific, found from the Red Sea, Zanzibar and the e. coast of Africa, across the Indian Ocean to the E. Indies, n. Australia, Melanesia, Micronesia, Polynesia, and Hawaii.

Throughout this very large range it shows little variation in colour pattern which varies only slightly with growth. Its body is yellow, darker on the central region of the back, with thin greyish lines running obliquely across the body. Three major dark stripes across the face and head with yellow interspaces; orange areas on the soft dorsal, anal, and tail fins margined with black; the tip of the tail fin white.

C. vagabundus see under **C. pictus**

C. zanzibarensis 14 cm. (5½ in.)
A beautifully coloured butterflyfish found around the coast of Zanzibar. It is closely similar to, and has by some workers been regarded as identical with another widely distributed tropical Indo-Pacific species, *C. speculum*. Its most immediate distinguishing feature is the black oval blotch on the upper side beneath the soft dorsal fin. **331**

CHAETODONTIDAE

The family of butterflyfish and angelfishes, a well known and spectacular group on account of their brilliant coloration. All are inhabitants of tropical and warm temperate seas, particularly associated with coral reefs, where their apparently gaudy coloration blends, often perfectly, with the background hues.

All the members of the family are deep-bodied, with particularly high backs, thin, with rather small heads, small mouths with tiny teeth (the family name means literally 'bristle-teeth'). The dorsal and anal fins are heavily scaled, and the dorsal is continuous from strong spines anteriorly to branched rays posteriorly.

Two main divisions can be discerned within the family, the angelfishes which have a spine at the lower angle of the gill cover, and the butterflyfishes which lack this spine. According to some authors this, and other features are sufficient to require their placement in separate families, the angelfishes being placed in the Pomacanthidae.

Colour patterns can vary markedly in the group, some butterflyfishes have nocturnal patterns different from their active daytime pattern, while the angelfishes, when young, are often very differently coloured from the adults of the same species (see *Pomacanthus imperator*).

Although not valued as food fishes, both butterflyfish and angelfish have become very popular as pet-fish in marine aquaria. See **Chaetodon, Chelmon, Euxiphipops, Forcipiger, Hemitaurichthys, Heniochus, Holacanthus, Prognathodes, Pomacanthus, Pygoplites.**

CHAIN
DOGFISH see **Scyliorhinus retifer**
PICKEREL see **Esox niger**

Chalcalburnus   Cyprinidae
chalcoides DANUBE BLEAK, SHEMAIA
30 cm. (12 in.)
This cyprinid is found in the Danube and the rivers flowing into the Black Sea, the Sea of Azov, and the Caspian and Aral seas. It extends s. to Iran and the basins of the Tigris and Euphrates. Through this range it shows some variation, and has been divided into a number of subspecies.

It is slim-bodied, covered with medium sized scales, greenish blue on the back and brilliantly silver on the sides and ventrally. The populations living in the Russian seas are migratory. The Black Sea stock enters rivers in the autumn and overwinters well upstream to spawn in the spring. They shed their eggs on gravelly shallows in a rapid current at night. The eggs stick to the stones at first, but are usually dislodged to fall between the stones where they continue their development. The Caspian Sea populations spawn in inflowing rivers, but those in the Aral Sea are not migratory.

These very abundant shoaling fish are of considerable economic importance. Most of the stocks are fished for during the spawning migration when the fish are fat. They are caught in seines and trap-nets in very large quantities and when cured are regarded as a high quality food product. The Black Sea population has shown signs of exhaustion and special conservation measures have been enforced to preserve it.

Chalceus   Characidae
macrolepidotus PINK-TAILED CHARACIN
25 cm. (10 in.)
This very attractive, if modestly coloured, aquarium fish is distinguished by the noticeably pink to red tail fin. It is also unusual in

having very large scales on the back and upper sides of the body in contrast to those on the underside. It has a dark greyish back, lighter sides and a distinct greenish band along the mid-side. It is an elongate-bodied characin with rather small fins, the adipose fin being especially minute.

It is a lively shoaling fish which can jump well. It is easy to keep and not at all fussy about the food it is offered. Its native habitat is the Guianas, S. America.

Chalcinus   Characidae
  elongatus 20 cm. (8 in.)
This fish, which by some authorities is placed in the genus *Triportheus*, is found in ne. S. America in the Orinoco, Amazon, and Negro rivers. In body form it clearly has many resemblances to the hatchetfishes (Gasteropelecidae) but the similarity is probably due to convergence rather than relationship, that is, as a result of adopting the same life-style it has evolved a similar body shape. The deep-bodied keeled breast, long pectoral fins, and rather upturned mouth with protuberant lower jaw are similar to those in hatchetfishes. However, this fish is easily distinguished by the elongation of the middle rays of the tail fin.

Its coloration is modest. The back is brown to olive, the sides are silvery with a green sheen and a narrow dark line from head to tail fin, where it becomes wider.

It is a very attractive and lively fish in the aquarium, best kept at a temperature of 24–27°C.

Chamsocephalus   Channichthyidae
  esox 34 cm. (13½ in.)
An icefish which is found in the region of Patagonia, around the Falkland Islands, and in the Straits of Magellan. It is the only member of this family which occurs outside the strictly Antarctic area. It occurs in moderately shallow water from 25–130 m. (13·5–70 fathoms), and is evidently migratory to some extent as it is reported to be more common around the Falklands from January to March than at other times of the year. It is a good food fish, and is locally known as 'pike'.

Its distinctive features are the long snout and rather pike-like form, 2 dorsal fins, the first of which is spiny. It is light brown, marked with greyish black and iridescent purple.

Champsodon   Champsodontidae
  capensis 10 cm. (4 in.)
A w. Indian Ocean form reported from the Cape of Good Hope to Natal, although possibly identical to that known from off Hawaii, as *C. fimbriatus*, in which case it might occur elsewhere between these areas. It is found in

the open sea in depths down to 457 m. (250 fathoms), living in large shoals and rising to the surface at night. Commonly stranded on shore after storms.

The sharp preopercle spine, slender rays in the first dorsal, double lateral line with branches above and below are all distinctive. It is mainly silvery.
C. fimbriatus see under **C. capensis**

CHAMPSODONTIDAE
A small family of deep-water fishes found only in the Indo-Pacific. They have a number of peculiar features, for example a large curved spine on the lower edge of the preoperculum, 2 lateral lines with connecting lines between them, and a large mouth with slender teeth on the jaws; teeth are present also on the palate. All members of the family are small; relatively few species are known. See **Champsodon.**

Chanda   Centropomidae
  commersoni COMMERSON'S GLASSFISH
  10 cm. (4 in.)
The range of this glassfish is very wide, virtually in all coastal waters and brackish areas between the Red Sea and N. Australia. It is found in E. Africa and the Philippines. In many areas it is found in entirely fresh water.

It is a popular aquarium fish, rather more slender-bodied than *C. ranga*, to which it is otherwise similar. It is almost transparent except for the silvery layer over the body cavity.

The male is a pale yellow, the fins a deeper colour, even orange, except for the tips of the tail fin and dorsal which are black. Females are yellowish without black-tipped fins.

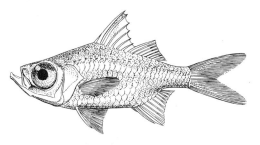

Although kept in freshwater aquaria the addition of sea salt is necessary to bring this fish into spawning condition. Its many eggs are shed amongst fine-leaved plants.
C. ranga INDIAN GLASSFISH 7 cm. (2¾ in.)
Widely distributed in India, Burma, and n. Thailand in both fresh and brackish water. Although locally captured and used for food, this little fish is best known as an aquarium pet fish.

Its body is deep and rather thickset, but is almost glass-like in its transparency. The first dorsal fin is high but its tip is rounded. The male glassfish is yellowish, with iridescent flanks in certain lights, and a lengthwise violet stripe runs from gill cover to tail. The fin rays are distinctly coloured although the membrane is clear. The female is usually more soberly coloured. **257**

CHANIDAE
The family of the large herring-like fish found widely in the Indo-Pacific region. Only one species is known, the valuable food-fish and occasional angling prize, the milkfish, *Chanos chanos*. It is distinguished by the following combination of characters: the pelvic fins are far back and beneath the dorsal fin which is high with prolonged anterior rays, the mouth is small, the lower jaw shorter than the upper, both lacking teeth, and by the presence of a distinct lateral line. The eyes are covered with transparent adipose tissue. Its nearest relatives are not the herring-like fishes (Clupeidae) but the family Gonorhynchidae. See **Chanos.**

Channa   Channidae
  asiatica 30 cm. (12 in.)
Found in se. Asia especially in S. China. This snake-head has achieved some popularity as an aquarium fish in Europe, and is one of several species used as food in its native range.

It has the typical body shape of the family, in particular the broad head with protuberant lower jaw, and the long dorsal and anal fins. It is the only snake-head to completely lack pelvic fins.

It is brown above, paler below, with white flecks on the body and a series of dark saddles across the back. There is a conspicuous black spot with a light ring near the base of the tail.

Channalabes   Clariidae
  apus EEL CATFISH 30 cm. (12 in.)
A catfish of strikingly different form from the remainder of the family. It is slender and eel-like, with pectoral fins greatly reduced, pelvic fins absent, and dorsal, tail, and anal fins joined to form a low fringing fin. The head is slightly flattened, and the barbels are well developed. It is found in Angola and the Congo Basin, inhabiting swampy and marsh conditions.

It has rarely been imported for exhibition as an aquarium fish.

CHANNEL
  CATFISH see **Ictalurus punctatus**
  FLOUNDER see **Syacium micrurum**

CHANNICHTHYIDAE
A small family of mainly Antarctic and cold-water S. Hemisphere fishes related to the Antarctic cods (Nototheniidae). They can be recognized by their total lack of scales, and by having an anterior spiny dorsal fin; most species have a flattened snout and very large, often spiny, head.

Their most interesting feature is that they lack the oxygen-carrying pigment haemoglobin in their blood, which appears pale whitish. Members of the family are gelatinous and pallid, with colourless gills. Oxygen is transported within the body by physical solution in the plasma, although this can carry very little in comparison with red-blooded fishes. Most icefishes are sedentary, rather inactive animals, living close to the sea bed and feeding on fishes and crustaceans. See **Chaeno-cephalus, Champsocephalus.**

CHANNIDAE

A family of freshwater fishes found only in tropical Africa and Asia. The body is cylindrical in front, rather compressed towards the tail, but the head is broad, with a deeply angled mouth and heavy scales; these features give the group their name of snakeheads. The dorsal and anal fins are long, many rayed and of an even height; the pectorals are moderate and rounded, the pelvic fins small (in one species absent).

All the snakeheads have an accessory respiratory organ in the upper part of the gill chamber which allows them to breathe air when living in de-oxygenated water, and also means they can travel overland in time of drought. They vary in length from 15 cm. (6 in.) to 1 m. (39 in.). The larger species are valued food fishes in parts of Asia. Some are kept as aquarium fish in Europe. See **Channa, Ophicephalus.**

Chanos Chanidae
chanos MILKFISH, SALMON HERRING, BANDANG, BANGOS 1·8 m. (6 ft)
The milkfish is a large, swift-swimming, active, brilliantly silver fish, with a high dorsal fin, and deeply forked tail. It lives in the open sea for most of the year, but comes into inshore waters, estuaries, and lagoons at about the spawning season. At this time large shoals can be seen from the shore, the powerfully built fish often cruising with their upper fin tips breaking the surface. It freely enters rivers even into freshwater and spawns, in the area of the Philippines, from March to May, a single fish producing as many as 6 million eggs. Spawning takes place in shallow sandy areas especially where the salinity is reduced.

In SE. Asia and the Philippines the natives have specialized in culturing the milkfish in a unique manner. The transparent and needle-like fry, measuring about 1 cm. in length, are collected from pools in the fringing reefs and estuarine backwaters and carried to brackish rearing ponds. They are grown on in these small ponds and other fish fry are removed before they are again transferred to larger lakes, including freshwater lakes where they are grown to a marketable size. The milkfish is purely a plant eater, in its earliest stages feeding on the dense blooms of blue-green algae that develop in still brackish waters. Later they feed on other and larger plants which thrive in the ponds often enriched by sewage. They are also often artificially fed. Milkfish are also able to survive in much higher temperatures than most other marine fishes could tolerate. Its value as a food fish in SE. Asia is enormous. Elsewhere the large free-swimming adults are not much fished for except by anglers who appreciate a hard-fighting and difficult quarry. Despite its many bones, its pinkish flesh is of very good quality.

Although superficially herring-like in appearance, the milkfish is only distantly related. It differs from the herrings by the rearward placing of the pelvic fins, by the 4 branchiostegal rays each side beneath the throat, and by the possession of a lateral line.

CHARACIDAE

A large family of freshwater fishes externally similar to the carp family (Cyprinidae) but differing in a number of important features. The characins lack barbels around the mouth, the mouth is not protractile, jaw teeth are always present fixed firmly to the bone and some parts of the dentition are often very strongly developed. Most characins have an adipose fin, placed on the back close to the tail. Their bodies are covered with cycloid scales, and a lateral line is present running along the side usually below the mid-line.

Most characins are carnivores, a few eat plants or plants and animals indiscriminately. They include those notable flesh-eaters, the S. American piranhas, placed in some classifications in the family Serrasalmidae.

The characins are related to the cyprinids and the catfishes, and like them have a chain of small bones or ossicles (the Weberian apparatus) between the inner ear and the swimbladder. Many of them are small fishes, often beautifully coloured, and these are familiar to the aquarist; others are very large and used as food fishes or are highly regarded by the angler in tropical freshwaters.

The family is represented by very many species in S. and Central America (as far N. as Texas) and in the greater part of Africa. See **Acestrorhynchus, Alestes, Aphyocharax, Arnoldichthys, Anoptichthys, Astyanax, Chalceus, Chalcinus, Charax, Cheirodon, Colossoma, Corynopoma, Creagrutus, Creatochanes, Crenuchus, Exodon, Gymnocorymbus, Hemigrammus, Hydrocynus, Hyphessobrycon, Luciocharax, Megalamphodus, Metynnis, Micralestes, Mimagoniates, Moenkhausia, Myleus, Mylossoma, Nematobrycon, Paracheirodon, Petitella, Pristella, Prochilodus, Pygocentrus, Rhapiodon, Roeboides, Rooseveltiella, Salminus, Serrasalmus, Thayeria.**

Characidium Hemiodontidae
fasciatum DARTER CHARACIN, TRITOLO
10 cm. (4 in.)
The darter characin is widely distributed in S. America from the Orinoco region s. to the Argentine rivers, the Rio de la Plata included. It is slender-bodied, almost loach-like in its appearance and behaviour. It lives on the bottom, especially on small stones with occasional larger hiding places, resting on the bottom on its pectoral and pelvic fins and darting in a jerky fashion when fed or disturbed. As a pet fish it is interesting but not spectacular, but it is relatively easy to breed, requiring only a moderate temperature, 18·5–24°C. The eggs are shed on the bottom quite indiscriminately and hatch in 30–40 hours.

Its coloration is variable, but basically is dull brown above, pale on the belly. It has a conspicuous dark band from the tip of the snout to the base of the tail fin, broadening irregularly where it is crossed by a varying number of dark cross bands. The end of the

lengthwise band has a conspicuous expanded dark blotch.

Charax Characidae
gibbosus HUMP-BACKED HEAD-STANDER
15 cm. (6 in.)
This so-called head-stander is found in rivers in the middle and lower Amazon, Rio Paraguay, and the Guianas. It receives its name from its habit of swimming at an angle to the bottom, with its head downwards. It feeds on bottom-living invertebrates. Like many other fishes which have adopted a head-down posture, it has a very elongate anal fin which forms its chief organ of propulsion.

It is also almost transparent, so that the gut and skeleton are clearly visible against the light. The back has a yellowish tinge, the sides are silvery, but the upper part is sprinkled with metallic spots which reflect light. It has a dark rounded elongate blotch on the shoulder.

It has been kept and bred in captivity for many years, and it is a peaceful aquarium inhabitant.

Chasmistes Catostomidae
cujus CUI-UI 61 cm. (2 ft)
A very striking heavy-headed sucker which has one of the most restricted ranges of any N. American freshwater fish, for it is found only in Pyramid Lake, and its affluent Truckee River in Nevada. It is a plump, robust fish, with a large head, blunt snout, and small eye; the lips are thin and with an almost terminal mouth make an atypical sucker.

At one time the cui-ui (the name is derived from the Indian vernacular) was extremely abundant in the lake, and migrated annually in spring up the Truckee River to spawn. The spawning run especially attracted large numbers of Pahute Indians to the vicinity to catch the close-packed fish, some of which were sun-dried and stored for later use. Its flesh was greatly esteemed.

However, increased use of the Truckee River water for irrigation has meant that the flow is greatly reduced, and the level of Pyramid Lake has fallen. The cui-ui has been seriously diminished in numbers, most notably in the interruption of its regular spawning migrations. It does, however, spawn in the margins of the lake during mid-May.

It feeds on small animal plankton and algal filaments, both found on or near rocky surfaces on the lake bed, as well as mid-water plankton.

Chaudhuria Chaudhuriidae
caudata 5 cm. (2 in.)
This curious little fish lacks the dorsal spines of its relations, the mastacembelid spiny eels, also lacks scales, and has a rounded snout. It is found in Lake Inlé in Burma. The original specimens were trapped in native fishing baskets filled with peat and aquatic vegetation, and sunk in the open lake; others have been caught in the floating vegetation which borders this very shallow lake. Despite its small observed maximum size, it is fully grown at 5 cm., and sexually mature fish of 2·6 cm. (1 in.) have been found.

The back and upper sides are dark purplish brown, sometimes mottled, while ventrally the body is yellow white. The fins are white with dark fine lines on either side.

CHAUDHURIIDAE
A small family, believed to contain only a single species, an eel-like fish found in the freshwater Lake Inlé in Burma. Originally described as a new kind of eel, its affinities are today recognized to lie with the spiny eels (family Mastacembelidae). See **Chaudhuria.**

CHAULIODONTIDAE
A small family of deep sea fishes, found throughout the Indian Ocean, N. Atlantic and Mediterranean and also in various parts of the S. Atlantic and Pacific oceans. Often referred to as viperfishes, they are mostly less than 30 cm. (12 in.) in length, and distinguished by the extreme length of the fangs in the jaws. Internally their anatomy is modified to put these fangs to good use: the first neck vertebra is very long, and is believed to act as a shock absorber against the impact and struggles of the prey. In addition the head is very mobile and can be tilted back, and the lower jaws drop open to form an angle of more than 90°. In doing so the delicate respiratory membranes of the gills and the heart and major blood vessels are pulled forward so that they are well clear of any struggles.

Only 6 species of viperfish are recognized today. Each appears to show a distinct preference for water masses of a certain salinity and temperature range, and they are thus rarely taken together. See **Chauliodus.**

Chauliodus Chauliodontidae
danae 15 cm. (6 in.)
This viperfish is distinguished from its relatives by the rearward position of the dorsal fin, and by the regular arrangement of small light organs between the major rows of larger light organs on the sides and belly. It is a dull coloured fish, usually dark brown on the back, lighter on the sides; the fins are pale. The sides are marked with 5 rows of hexagonal areas,

each of which is covered by a large, though fragile scale in life.

C. danae is found in the waters of the Caribbean and N. Atlantic, from n. Cuba across to the African coast, and in a similar region S. of the equator. This species is believed to be typical of water masses of moderate warmth (15°C at 150 m. (82 fathoms) appears to be the lower boundary), and of at least 50 per cent oxygen saturation. Like most of its relatives it makes vertical migrations daily, during daylight it is found at from 500–3500 m. (273–1900 fathoms) but at night it can be caught between the surface and 500 m. Only the young fish come near the surface.

C. sloani SLOANE'S VIPERFISH 30 cm. (12 in.)
Sloane's viperfish is worldwide in its distribution in tropical and temperate deep oceans, although there are many areas where it has not been reported. One such area is the region in which *C. danae* is found, and it has been suggested that the latter species is perhaps better adapted to the oxygen and temperature levels there. *C. sloani* has been found in deep water along the N. American and European Atlantic continental shelves. It appears to be most common between 1000–1800 m. (546–983 fathoms), but at night rises to between 50–800 m. (27–437 fathoms).

This viperfish is distinguished by the forward position of the dorsal fin, the first ray of which is long and equipped with a light organ used as a lure to bring prey close.

This species was named for the physician Sir Hans Sloane, whose collection formed the foundation of the British Museum. The original specimen was found off Gibraltar and presented to Sloane by Mark Catesby, author of *The Natural History of Carolina . . .* (1731–43). It is still preserved in the British Museum (Natural History).

CHAUNACIDAE
A family of deep-water angler fishes of moderate size, found first in the Atlantic but subsequently captured in the Indian and Pacific oceans. A few species only are recognized. See **Chaunax.**

Chaunax Chaunacidae
pictus 46 cm. (18 in.)
The first member of the family recognized, *Chaunax pictus* has been found in depths of 183–550 m. (100–300 fathoms) in all the oceans. It appears to be confined to muddy bottoms in which it probably burrows. Most specimens have been taken by deep trawling; a few have been washed ashore.

It is very distinctive; round-bodied with a big head, wide jaws with moderate teeth. The pectoral fins are angled, the gill opening is

small and placed well along the side. The skin is very loose, flabby, and rough. The single dorsal ray on the snout has a small lure at its tip, and can be withdrawn into a groove on the snout.

CHECKERED BLENNY see **Starksia ocellata**

Cheilinus Labridae
trilobatus 46 cm. (18 in.)
Widely distributed in the tropical Indo-Pacific, from the coast of Africa to n. Australia, the Central Pacific, and Japan. It is an abundant species in shallow reef areas and the deeper waters of lagoons, wherever algae and coral are abundant.

Its coloration is variable, the background purplish brown to olive, the head and each scale on the body with bright red streaks. The fins are reddish orange to yellow.

In large adults the soft rays of the dorsal and anal fins are very elongate, and the outer and central tail fin rays become long, giving this fin a 3-lobed appearance. **399**
C. undulatus HUMP-HEADED MAORI or GIANT WRASSE 2·3 m. (7½ ft)
The largest species of wrasse known to science, it is widespread in the tropical Indo-Pacific. In Australian waters, where it occurs on the Queensland coast, it is known as the humpheaded Maori wrasse, and a specimen as long as 2·3 m. weighing 190 kg. (420 lb.) was once captured. Specimens almost as large have been taken on the African coast. The large fish live in the deeper waters around the edges of the reefs; small fish occur in the shallows.

Very large specimens develop a big fleshy crest or bump on the forehead. Smaller specimens are remarkably beautifully coloured. Basically it is greenish overall with the centre of each scale deep blue, the fins and throat region are dark blue, and the head is yellowish.

CHEILODACTYLIDAE
A family of moderately large marine fishes found mostly in the S. Hemisphere around the s. coasts of Australia, and New Zealand, S. Africa, Tristan da Cunha, the Atlantic and Pacific coasts of s. S. America. One genus is found around the Hawaiian Islands, China and Japan.

In general they are slender-bodied elongate fishes with small to moderate scales. A single dorsal fin, about equally divided between spiny and soft rays, and slightly notched at the junction. Adults have very elongate unbranched rays in the lower pectoral fin, which are said to be used as feelers in detecting food.

The Australian members of the family, usually called morwongs, have some value as food and sporting fishes. See **Nemadactylus, Palunolepis, Psilocranium.**

Cheilodipterus Apogonidae
quinquilineatus FIVE-STRIPED PERCELLE 12 cm. (5 in.)
Widely distributed in the Indo-Pacific, from the E. African coast to Australia, and the islands of Polynesia and Micronesia. It is a common fish amongst the reefs and on rocky grounds throughout its range.

This group of cardinalfishes is distinguished by the presence of long caniniform teeth in the jaws, although in this species they are confined to the sides of the lower jaw. **288**

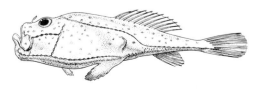

CHEIMARRICHTHYIDAE

This family contains a single species found in mountain streams of New Zealand.

It appears to be related to the sandperches (Mugiloididae) and weevers (Trachinidae) but differs from them in numerous ways. Its pelvic fins are greatly broadened and set well forward of the pectorals. The spiny dorsal fin is composed of 2–4 short, separate spines, but the second dorsal is long. See **Cheimarrichthys**.

Cheimarrichthys   Cheimarrichthyidae
 forsteri TORRENT FISH 13 cm. (5 in.)
Found in New Zealand's larger streams and rivers. In places it is relatively common, by day in the fastest flowing streams, even in torrent areas, although it seems to be inactive. It is believed to move into still water pools by night to feed, its daytime haunts of fast water being generally safer from predators.

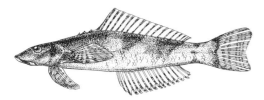

It is also migratory, moving downstream in the autumn to spawn, although exactly where it spawns is not certainly established. The youngest fish are found nearest the sea so spawning probably takes place in the sea; this would seem likely in view of the marine nature of its closest relatives.

At one time the torrent fish was especially favoured by the Maori, and it was prepared and cooked with great ceremony. Its aboriginal name is papanoko.

It is dull brown with darker irregular cross bars, lighter ventrally. The expanded pelvic fins and flattened anterior body are adaptations for its life in torrents.

Cheirodon   Characidae
 axelrodi CARDINAL TETRA 4 cm. (1½ in.)
The cardinal tetra is found in forest pools in the Upper Rio Negro, and tributaries of the Orinoco. It is a beautiful little fish, similar to the neon tetra in form and colour, and like it a popular aquarium fish. It seems, however, to be more red than that species. It breeds much as the neon tetra does, but is not particularly easy to get to breed or to rear and tends to be rather delicate. **53**

Chela   Cyprinidae
 mouhoti 6 cm. (2½ in.)
A member of a group widely distributed in streams and ponds in Asia, this species is confined to Thailand. Its body is very deep and flattened from side to side with a knife-like edge to the belly. The dorsal fin is set well along the back, but is shorter than the many-rayed anal fin. The pectorals are long. The lateral line runs parallel to the belly. It is a uniform bluish silver in colour, with a rounded black spot behind the gill cover.

The general appearance of this fish is so similar to the S. American characin hatchet-fishes, that it is not surprising to find that it can jump well clear of the surface. It has attained some regard as an aquarium species, but is not especially popular.

Chelidonichthys   Triglidae
 kumu RED GURNARD 61 cm. (24 in.)
An Indo-Pacific species of wide distribution, which is found from s. Africa, all Australian states, New Zealand and N. Japan and China. In s. Australia it is very abundant in both deep and shallow water and is commercially exploited on a small scale. It is excellent eating.

Its colouring is striking, reddish above and white ventrally, with the outer surface of the very long pectoral fins red while the inner surface is green with a black blotch in the centre on which there are a number of bright white spots. The function of this bright coloration is not known but might serve as a menacing coloration flashed quickly at the approach of danger and then disappearing again as the fish closes its fins.

Some authors place this species in the genus *Trigla*.

Chelmon   Chaetodontidae
 rostratus BEAKED CORALFISH
20 cm. (8 in.)
A common and widely distributed fish in the tropical Indo-Pacific which is found from E. Africa, India, Mauritius, the E. Indies, n. Australia to Japan and the Philippines. It is most common in reef areas, or around rocks in shallow water and is very distinctive by virtue of its long snout, which is drawn out into a beak with a moderate sized mouth at the end.

This species was for years attributed with the ability of spitting water at insects near the edge of the water, an attribute of *Toxotes* species. **333**

CHERRY BARB see **Barbus titteya**

Chiasmodon   Chiasmodontidae
 niger BLACK SWALLOWER
18 cm. (7 in.)
A deep-water fish found in the Atlantic, originally described from Madeira but subsequently captured elsewhere in that ocean, S. to the latitudes of the Cape. It is always taken in great depths, its bathymetric range being 550–2745 m. (300–1500 fathoms) although the shallower of these are mostly night-time records when it comes nearer the surface.

Teeth are very long, those in the front of the jaws longest and overlapping the lips when the mouth is closed. The jaws are capable of great extension and the stomach can accommodate prey larger than the fish itself, as shown in the illustration. It is black in colour.

CHIASMODONTIDAE

A family of deep-sea fishes found in all the major tropical and temperate oceans. They are slender-bodied fishes with large heads and huge jaws, equipped with long teeth. Several genera and species are recognized but many of them are based only on single specimens, suggesting that they are rather uncommon in the deep sea.

Members of the family are often called 'swallowers' due to the way the lower jaws practically disarticulate to permit large fishes to be swallowed. Their stomachs and body walls are equally elastic. See **Chiasmodon, Kali.**

Chilodontidae see under Curimatidae

Chilodus   Curimatidae
 punctatus SPOTTED HEAD-STANDER
7 cm. (2¾ in.)
This very attractive aquarium fish is widely distributed in n. S. America, in the upper Amazon basin rivers, and the Orinoco and Rio Negro. It is found in shallow, rather marshy

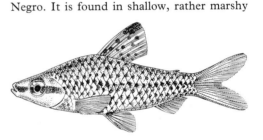

waters, often low in dissolved oxygen. Its fourth gill arch is greatly expanded and must serve as an additional breathing organ in times of stress. It has the curious habit of swimming restlessly in a head-down posture.

In colour it is unremarkable, the back is brownish, the sides yellow-brown, and the throat silvery; each of the scales on the back and sides has a dark centre giving the fish a spotted appearance. A rather distinct dark, sometimes interrupted line runs from the mouth to the tail. **95**

Chilomycterus   Diodontidae
 schoepfi STRIPED BURRFISH, BURRFISH
25 cm. (10 in.)
A w. tropical Atlantic species which is found from se. Brazil, n. through the Caribbean and Gulf of Mexico to Florida, occasionally straying as far N. as Cape Cod and Massachusetts Bay. In some areas of the American coast, particularly along the coast of the Carolinas and Florida, it is extremely abundant.

This small burrfish has triple-rooted spines fixed in an upright position, its teeth are fused into a single beak in each jaw, and the dorsal and anal fins are small and round.

This species has been demonstrated to jet-propel itself through the water by means of strong jets blown from the small gill openings. Its other means of propulsion is a gentle sculling movement with the pectoral, dorsal, and anal fins. **496**

Chimaera   Chimaeridae
   monstrosa RATFISH, RABBITFISH
1·5 m. (5 ft)
The ratfish is well distributed in the e. N.
Atlantic, from n. Norway and Iceland s. to
Morocco and the Azores, as well as in the w.
Mediterranean. It also occurs in S. African
waters.

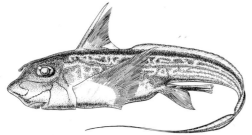

It is a deep-water fish, occasionally found in
100 m. (55 fathoms), but more commonly from
300–500 m. (164–273 fathoms). Deep-water
trawlers catch it in considerable numbers W.
of the British Isles and it is very common at
times. These catches frequently consist of only
one sex, and it seems that the ratfish migrates
in unisexual shoals, large females being found
in shallower water in spring and summer at
which time their eggs are deposited. The egg
cases are long and tapering, about 177 × 25
mm. (7 × 1 in.), and are thought to stick into
the sea bed by the pointed end.

Its body is creamy, or light brown, dark
mottled on the back with a metallic sheen; its
eyes shine with a yellowish glow when it is
alive. Males have a club-like appendage on the
head as well as pelvic claspers.

Its name rabbitfish, refers to its rabbit-like
incisor teeth, while ratfish is in reference to its
very long tail. Ratfish or 'rat' is the name used
at sea by British fishermen – rabbit being a
forbidden word.

CHIMAERA, LONG-NOSED see **Harriotta
   raleighana**

CHIMAERIDAE
The family of the ratfishes and rabbitfishes,
marine fish found mainly in the cooler regions
of the N. Atlantic, and the Indian and Pacific
oceans. They are long-bodied, cartilaginous
fishes, shark-like in many respects but with a
single gill opening on each side behind the
head, covered by a cartilaginous gill cover. The
males have copulatory claspers, and fertilization of the egg is internal; the egg is laid in a
very distinctive capsule.

This is the most numerous family of chimaeroids (the others are Callorhinchidae and
Rhinochimaeridae), but even then the number
of recognized species is fewer than 30. Two
genera are recognized: *Chimaera* from the
temperate Atlantic, the Caribbean, and N.
Pacific has a distinct anal fin separated from
the tail by a gap; *Hydrolagus*, from the N.
Atlantic, N. and S. Pacific, and off the Natal
coast of South Africa, completely lacks an anal
fin. See **Chimaera, Hydrolagus.**

CHINAMAN LEATHERJACKET see **Navodon
   ayraudi**
CHINAMANFISH see **Lutjanus
   nematophorus**
CHINESE
   GUITARFISH see **Platyrhina sinensis**

PADDLEFISH see **Psephurus gladius**
PERCH see **Siniperca chuatsi**
CHINOOK SALMON see **Oncorhynchus
   tshawytscha**

CHIROCENTRIDAE
A family, related to the herring-like fishes, containing one genus and possibly only one species.
It differs from the herrings by its dramatic
size, to 3·7 m. (12 ft) in length, and by the presence of large fang-like teeth in the mouth. It is
long-bodied, and strongly compressed, with a
sharp keel along the belly. The dorsal fin is
short and set far back, above the longer anal
fin. The lower intestine has a spiral structure
reminiscent of the spiral valve in the gut of
sharks and their relatives.

This family is confined to the tropical and
warm-temperate regions of the Indo-Pacific.
See **Chirocentrus.**

Chirocentrus   Chirocentridae
   dorab WOLF HERRING, DORAB
3·7 m. (12 ft)
The wolf herring is externally similar to a
gigantic herring, but has large fang-like teeth
in both jaws, as well as smaller teeth on its
tongue and the roof of the mouth. Its pectoral
fins are set low on the body and are moderately
well developed; the pelvic fins are minute. It is
deep bluish green above, intensely silvery on
the sides and ventrally, with a golden stripe
along the sides separating the major colour
areas.

It is widely distributed in the Indo-Pacific,
from the Red Sea and E. Africa across to the
Australian coasts. It is found in shallow water
from the shore down to about 110 m. (60 fathoms), although clearly most common in the
surface waters of the sea. In s. Africa it is commonly caught in shore-line fish traps.

Despite its size it is of little value as a food
fish, for its flesh is full of small bones. It is also
a dangerous fish to handle for it struggles
actively and snaps at anything, its large fangs
inflicting serious wounds. Its leaping powers
are legendary, large specimens springing clear
out of the water; this in turn shows that it is a
strong and powerful swimmer.

The name 'dorab' is the Arabic vernacular;
it was used on the Red Sea coast when the first
specimens were described by Pehr Forsskål, the
eighteenth-century Danish zoologist-explorer.

Chirolophis   Stichaeidae
   polyactocephalus DECORATED WAR-
BONNET 42 cm. (16½ in.)
A N. Pacific species which is found from
Washington, throughout the coast of British
Columbia to the Aleutian Islands and Bering
Sea. It lives in depths of 18–91 m. (10–50 fath-
oms) close to the sea bed.

It is distinguished by the striking development of the tentacles above the eye, with smaller

ones over the back of the head, and long
branched tentacles on the first dorsal rays. It is
pale brown above with whitish markings; dark
bars run across the back and sides.

CHIRONEMIDAE
A small family of marine fishes found on the
coasts of Australia and New Zealand. The
family is very close to the hawkfishes (family
Cirrhitidae) and the morwongs (family Cheilodactylidae), and contains 5–6 species at most.
Its members differ from the hawkfishes in
having a greater number of dorsal spines and
fin rays; the teeth in the jaws are small and
conical and they have teeth on the vomer, a
bone in the roof of the mouth. The lower pectoral rays are elongate and unbranched. See
Threpterius.

CHLAMYDOSELACHIDAE
A primitive shark family with only one living
representative, although the family is well
known from the fossil record. Amongst other
anatomical features of a primitive nature, the
upper jaw is loosely attached to the cranium.
Only the first 3–4 vertebrae are calcified. The
living shark is long, thin, and snake-like, with
broad fins placed close to the tail. The teeth are
3-pointed, and arranged in well spaced rows.
See **Chlamydoselachus.**

Chlamydoselachus   Chlamydoselachidae
   anguineus FRILLED SHARK 2 m. (6½ ft)
The frilled shark is the sole living member of
the family Chlamydoselachidae, although judging from fossil teeth, closely similar species
were living some 12–20 million years ago. It is
one of the most primitive living sharks – literally a living fossil.

It has been found in deep-water in the e. N.
Atlantic (Madeira to the Hebrides, and once n.
Norway), off S. Africa, and most commonly
in Japanese waters. The snake-like appearance
of this shark, is emphasized by the wide gill
slits, the first of which is continuous under the
throat, while the remaining 5 are larger than in
other sharks. The gill covers are prominent,
and give the neck region the appearance of a
ruffle or frill – hence its names.

Little is known of the life history. Most
specimens have been caught in depths of 200–
1000 m. (109–546 fathoms); the remains of
fishes have been found in their stomachs. It
bears living young, and in Japanese waters
females have between 6–12 pups in a litter,
each being about 61 cm. (2 ft) at birth. They
are born between April and June.

Chlidichthys   Pseudoplesiopidae
   johnvoelckeri 5 cm. (2 in.)
A beautifully coloured, but little-known fish
from the coast of se. Africa. Its colouring is
remarkable; the body is violet overall, the dorsal and anal fins are deep green except that
along the edge and at the extremity they are
pinkish. The tail fin has a deep purple spot with
a light edge.

It is distinguished by the lack of fin spines in
the dorsal fin, the first rays being simple and
unbranched, and in lacking a lateral line. The
only known specimens were described by the
late Professor J. L. B. Smith, the distinguished

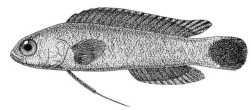

S. African ichthyologist, and were twice obtained from the mouth of the rare grouper, *Cephalopholis rogaa*, from deep reefs off the African coast.

CHLOROPHTHALMIDAE

A small family of bottom-living, mainly deep-water fishes. Most recognized species live in water of from 183–732 m. (100–400 fathoms), one lives in water of greater depth than 1829 m. (1000 fathoms). On the whole they are small, usually under 30 cm. (12 in.), and slender-bodied, with a large eye placed rather high on the head. Their eyes are iridescent green in life. They all have an adipose fin.

The members of the family occur in temperate and tropical regions of all the oceans. See **Bathysauropsis, Chlorophthalmus**.

Chlorophthalmus   Chlorophthalmidae
  agassizi SHORTNOSE GREENEYE
16 cm. (6¼ in.)
The shortnose greeneye is widely distributed in the tropical and warm temperate Atlantic and in the Mediterranean. It lives on the edge of the continental shelf, close to the bottom in areas of mud or fine sand. It eats invertebrates especially small crustaceans and squids. Its depth range is from 200–1440 m. (109–790 fathoms). The eggs and young are believed to be pelagic. The adults are hermaphrodite.

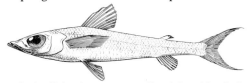

It is light brown or yellowish with dark points of colour; the eyes are conspicuous pale green.

CHOCOLATE GOURAMI see **Sphaerichthys osphronemoides**

Chologaster   Amblyopsidae
  cornutus RICEFISH, SWAMPFISH
5 cm. (2 in.)
This fish is found in ditches, small ponds and swamps of the s. Atlantic coastal states of the U.S. It is widely distributed in the lowlands of Georgia, the Carolinas, and Virginia. It does not live in brackish waters.

Unlike other members of the family the 2 *Chologaster* species have small but functional eyes, although experiments have shown that they can survive very well when deprived of sight; they are also pigmented. This species is brown above, paler below the middle of the body, and the belly is white. Three distinct lengthwise bands, the middle one of which is broken towards the tail.

It has been imported to Europe as an aquarium fish.

Chondrostoma   Cyprinidae
  nasus NASE 51 cm. (20 in.)
A freshwater fish of central Europe found in

the Rhine and Danube basins; it does not extend as far as the British Isles. It is slim-bodied with a blunt, rather protuberant snout. Its mouth is curved, the lips small, but horny and sharp-edged. In colour it is olive green to grey, the sides and belly distinctly silvery; the ventral fins slightly tinted.

It lives entirely in rivers and streams and browses on algae, particularly those growing on the stones on the river bed, although it also eats higher plants and some animal matter. It breeds in spring in large shoals in small streams at the foot of gravel-bottomed riffles. Young specimens make excellent cold-water aquarium fishes. Large specimens are fished in nets and traps and along the Danube are smoked to form a local delicacy.

Chorinemus   Carangidae
  lysan QUEENFISH, TALANG, LARGEMOUTH LEATHERSKIN 1·2 m. (4 ft)
An Indo-Pacific species, found across the whole Indian Ocean from E. Africa to Australia, and to the w. Pacific. It is common along the open ocean sides of reefs but comes into inshore waters on occasions.

A very popular game-fish with anglers in Australia and s. Africa, it grows to a weight of 11 kg. (25 lb.), and is caught by trolling, or with baited hooks in deeper water. In some areas it is caught in nets and exploited as food, but opinions differ as to its eating quality.

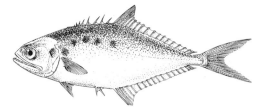

It is handsomely coloured, the back and upper sides greenish olive, the sides and belly yellowish to gold with 6–8 indistinct large greyish blotches on the sides.

Chorisochismus   Gobiesocidae
  dentex ROCK-SUCKER 30 cm. (12 in.)
This is the largest of the whole family of cling-fishes, and it is one of the very few members of the family found on the coast of s. Africa, where its range extends from the Cape to Natal. It is often found in tide pools, and below low tide mark clinging to stones by means of the powerful sucking disc. It is said to be occasionally stranded but survives exposure to air for a long time.

It is dull greenish brown, flecked on the sides with cream which becomes lighter ventrally. The dorsal and anal fins are small; the head and body very small and flattened. Readily takes a bait, but is rarely landed; its flesh is reputed by some to be poisonous.

Chriodorus   Exocoetidae
  atherinoides HARDHEAD HALFBEAK
25 cm. (10 in.)
An interesting halfbeak which in fact lacks the most typical halfbeak character, the great prolongation of the lower jaw. In this species both jaws are equal, and short. It looks superficially like a sand smelt (family Atherinidae) but can be distinguished by having only a single dorsal fin.

It is translucent green above with dark dots

on the edges of the scales; silvery below with an intense silvery stripe along the sides.

It is a surface-living, schooling fish which leaps readily when disturbed. In the Bahamas it is found in the freshwater Lake Forsythe where it feeds on the alga *Batophora* and the diatoms and other minute organisms living amongst the algae. It is known from the Bahamas, Florida, and Cuba to Yucatan in the Gulf of Mexico. Its life history is not well known.

CHROMIDE, GREEN see **Etroplus suratensis**

Chromis   Pomacentridae
  chromis DAMSELFISH 15 cm. (6 in.)
Widely distributed in the tropical e. Atlantic from Portugal to Angola, throughout the Mediterranean and around the Atlantic island groups, e.g. Cape Verde Islands, Madeira, and Azores. The damselfish is found in great abundance in many areas, and is one of the most common fishes in the s. Mediterranean. It is usually found in shoals near rocky coasts but keeps in mid-water. It spawns in mid-summer in flat depressions or on rocks which have been cleaned of algal growth. The male displays close to the chosen spawning site by flicking his tail fin, and making jerky swimming movements in front of the female. The eggs are guarded by the male until they hatch, and the young fish inhabit sheltered crannies in small groups during the late summer.

A distinctive small fish by reason of its body shape and behaviour. The young have brilliant blue stripes running down their sides. **388**
C. cyaneus BLUE CHROMIS 13 cm. (5 in.)
A w. Atlantic species found from Bermuda, the Bahamas, Florida and the W. Indies. It is an abundant fish over the deep open reefs and patch reefs at depths of 3–55 m. (2–30 fathoms), and clouds of this lovely fish can be seen on the edge of the reef picking at the planktonic crustaceans floating by in the current.

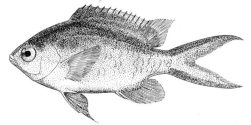

It is a particularly distinctive fish on account of its coloration – brilliant blue overall with a black edge to the spiny dorsal fin, and dark outer rays on the tail. The front rays of the anal fin are also dark.

CHROMIS, BLUE see **Chromis cyaneus**

Chrysophrys   Sparidae
  auratus SNAPPER, REDBREAM, SQUIRE, COCKNEY 130 cm. (51 in.)
A Pacific species found widely around the coasts of Australia, Lord Howe Island, and New Zealand. Adults are bottom dwellers living over rocky reefs or on shell or gravel bottoms in depths to 183 m. (100 fathoms), although they come into shallower water in summer. The young are found in sheltered bays and inlets along the coasts in shallow water. They occur in large schools but the very large adults are more solitary.

The many names applied to this species are

used for the growth stages, adult to young as given. Very old specimens develop a large hump on the forehead, and the snout and lips become fleshy – these are usually known as 'Old Man Snapper'.

Throughout its range it is a valuable food-fish, most being captured on long-lines, although locally it is taken in traps and occasionally netted. It is also a valued sporting fish which takes a wide range of bait, fights well, and may be exceptionally heavy; fish of 20 kg. (43 lb.) have been recorded.

The young are delicate pink with dark transverse bands across the body. Adults are reddish overall, paler on the belly, with small blue spots on the back, sides and fins.

CHUB see **Leuciscus cephalus**
CHUB,
  BERMUDA see **Kyphosus sectatrix**
  SEA see Kyphosidae
  SEA see **Ditrema temmincki**
CHUB MACKEREL see **Scomber japonicus**
CHUBSUCKER, LAKE see **Erimyzon sucetta**
CHUM SALMON see **Oncorhynchus keta**

Cichlasoma   Cichlidae
  cutteri CUTTER'S CICHLID 13 cm. (5 in.)
A native of Honduras, but a popular aquarium fish and for this reason readily available in captivity despite its relatively restricted distribution. It is a peaceable aquarium fish, only occasionally given to uprooting plants in the breeding season when it digs pits in the bottom.

It is a typical cichlid in shape with a rounded body, slightly compressed and deep. Males have deep red fins, females have pink fins, the male's throat is also bright red in the spawning season. **356**

C. festivum BARRED or FLAG CICHLID 15 cm. (6 in.)
Found in the Amazon basin and w. Guiana where it lives in the slower rivers and back-

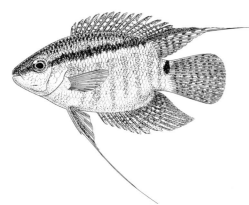

waters amongst tangled roots and thick vegetation.

It is a very distinctive species with a deep body and rather large fins, the pelvics in particular being long. This cichlid is beautifully coloured. **357**

C. octofasciatum EIGHT-BANDED CICHLID 20 cm. (8 in.)
A distinctive aquarium species which as its name suggests has several (usually 8) dark cross bars running over the back and sides. It is generally brownish grey, with a blue tint on the sides. Three distinct dark blotches, ringed with gold, one on the gill cover, a second on the mid-side, and the third on the tail.

It prefers to live in thickly weeded areas, probably eating algae. Its native range is Honduras, Guatemala, and s. Mexico. **359**
C. severum BANDED CICHLID 20 cm. (8 in.)
Found in the n. Amazon basin and the Guianas. It is distinguished when young by a series of 8–9 black bands on the sides; as it grows these bands fade and as adults only one on the tail persists. It merges with a dark ocellus with a yellowish outer ring on the rays of the posterior dorsal and anal fins.

It is a popular aquarium fish, and is generally a peaceful and successful inhabitant. In the breeding season it becomes a compulsive uprooter of vegetation, and the tank bottom is cleaned repeatedly. Up to 1000 eggs are laid in a single spawning. **358**

CICHLID,
  AGASSIZ'S DWARF see **Apistogramma agassizi**
  BANDED see **Cichlasoma severum**
  BARRED see **Cichlasoma festivum**
  CUTTER'S see **Cichlasoma cutteri**
  EIGHT-BANDED see **Cichlasoma octofasciatum**
  FLAG see **Cichlasoma festivum**
  GALILEE see **Sarotherodon galilaeus**
  GRAHAM'S see **Sarotherodon grahami**
  MOZAMBIQUE see **Sarotherodon mossambicus**
  ORTMANN'S DWARF see **Apistogramma ortmanni**
  RING-TAILED PIKE see **Crenicichla saxatilis**

CICHLIDAE
A large family of freshwater fishes found in S. America (except for the cool, temperate S.), Central America, and N. to Texas, in Africa, Madagascar and Asia Minor, and around the coastal regions of India and Sri Lanka. As a family it is remarkably successful having developed into a variety of forms and ways of life which allow various species to fill most of the living space available. In the African Great Lakes they are particularly abundant and many endemic genera have evolved in each lake.

The body is normally perch-like, usually slightly compressed, occasionally very flattened as in the angelfishes. It and most of the head are covered with scales, the dorsal and anal fins have a series of spines in their front section continuous with the soft rays. The most obvious distinguishing feature amongst freshwater fishes is the single nostril on each side of the head.

In general cichlids prefer still or slow flowing water with many hiding places; some are pronouncedly territorial. Most are generalized predators, but some, particularly in the Great Lakes, have specialized diets, for which their teeth and jaws are variously adapted for these diets. The cichlids exhibit many interesting variations in body-form to exploit their habitats. Some species are plankton-eaters, others

feed on fish, invertebrates, algae and plant matter, while some specialize in eating molluscs or cichlid eggs, or scales from other fishes. One species even habitually bites the eyes out of living fishes.

Their breeding habits exhibit many refinements. Many species are territorial, breeding in a cleaned nest which is guarded by one or both parents. Mouth brooding of eggs and young is the habit of many other forms, while several species nourish their young on the mucus secreted from the parental skin.

Many are popular aquarium fishes; in the areas in which they are abundant some are valuable food fishes. See **Aequidens, Apistogramma, Cichlasoma, Crenicichla, Etroplus, Geophagus, Haplochromis, Julidochromis, Lamprologus, Melanochromis, Pelmatochromis, Petenia, Petrotilapia, Pseudotropheus, Pterophyllum, Sarotherodon, Symphysodon, Tilapia, Tropheus, Uaru.**

Ciliata   Gadidae
  mustela FIVE-BEARDED ROCKLING 20 cm. (8 in.)
A slender, small fish, with a slippery small-scaled skin, 5 barbels around its mouth, including one on its chin, and a specialized dorsal fin of a slender ray and a series of small hair-like rays, in front of a more normal dorsal fin. It is dark brown, sometimes black or reddish, slightly lighter ventrally.

A most abundant fish on the shore and in the shallow sea of Europe, ranging from the vicinity of Lisbon to Iceland and Norway. It is frequently found on rocky shores in tide pools, and under stones – and is one of the most successful shore fish in Europe. It breeds in winter and spring offshore; the eggs and young are pelagic. The young are blue and silvery below, very active at the surface until they drift inshore. These so-called mackerel-midges were thought to be a distinct species of fish which was named *Couchia*, after the Cornish naturalist Jonathan Couch (1789–1870).

The five-bearded rockling is not exploited in any way, but it plays an important role as predator and prey on the n. European coast.

CIRRHITIDAE
A family of mainly Indo-Pacific fishes, which is also represented by a single species in the tropical w. Atlantic.

They are somewhat elongate fishes, fully scaled on head and body, with a spiny dorsal fin joined to the soft dorsal, and 3 well-developed spines in front of the anal fin. Members of the family have small tufts of cirri from the membrane of the dorsal fin, and they have a fringe on the rear edge of the anterior nostril. The lower rays of the pectoral fin are elongate and well separated from one another.

Most are relatively shallow water, small fishes, which live on rough grounds of rocks or coral, perching distinctively on a coral head but darting for cover if disturbed. See **Amblycirrhitus, Oxycirrhites, Paracirrhites**

CISCO see **Coregonus artedii**
CISCO,
  ARCTIC see **Coregonus autumnalis**
  EUROPEAN see **Coregonus albula**
  LAKE see **Coregonus artedii**
  LEAST see **Coregonus sardinella**

Citharichthys Bothidae
sordidus PACIFIC SAND-DAB 41 cm. (16 in.)
As its common name suggests this is a native
species in the Pacific, found along the American coast from Baja California to Alaska,
mainly in depths of 37–91 m. (20–50 fathoms),
although occasional specimens occur in shallower water and, especially to the N. of its
range, in water as deep as 306 m. (167 fathoms).

It feeds as an adult on a wide range of small
fishes, squids, crustaceans, and other invertebrates. Spawning takes place during summer
and early autumn, each female probably
spawning more than once.

In California it is a moderately important
commercial fish, considerable quantities being
taken in otter trawls. It is also a popular sea
anglers' fish, being taken from skiffs.

The sand-dab is dull brown or tan, irregularly mottled darker and black on the fins;
males have orange spots when living. It is
otherwise distinguished by having the eyes on
the left of the body, the lower eye being longer
than the snout and possessing a bony ridge
above it.

CITHARIDAE
A small family of flatfishes found in the
Atlantic, Indian, and w. Pacific oceans. The
family contains relatively few (probably only
5) species, and most of its members are small,
around 25 cm. (10 in.) in length.

They are distinguished from other flatfishes
by their large mouths, by having moderate and
equal sized pelvic fins, each of which contains
one spine and 5 branched rays. Two groups are
contained within the family: the sub-family
Citharinae which have branched rays only in
dorsal and anal fins, and have the eyes on the
left side of the head; and the Brachypleurinae
which have eyes and pigment on the right side,
and only the last few elements in the dorsal and
anal rays branched. The member of the latter
sub-family are Indo-Pacific in distribution;
the citharinids are found in the e. Atlantic, off
s. Africa, and in the ne. Pacific. See **Citharus.**

Citharidium Citharinidae
ansorgei 36 cm. (14 in.)
A deep-bodied fish found only in the River
Niger in Africa. Its body form is much like that
of *Citharinus*, although it is not quite so deep-
bodied, nor are the fins so elongate. It has a
long, scale-covered adipose fin, a straight
lateral line, and a small mouth with fine teeth.
It is a striking golden yellow with a dark head,
and 2 distinct but irregular dark, blue-black
bands running obliquely from the dorsal and
adipose fins downwards.

Within the Niger this fish is not rare, but it
is usually found where the current is slow and
in lakes. It breeds during the rainy season on
flooded ground, the young being common in
pools and lakes in the dry season.

CITHARINIDAE
A family of African freshwater fishes of wide
distribution in that continent, except for the
extreme S. and the desert areas. Many of them
are large, deep-bodied fishes, but others are
strikingly slender, almost pike-like in appearance. Most have small scales, but some have a
few large scales; all have a straight lateral line.
Most also have an adipose fin, although in some
forms it is minute or absent.

These fishes show as great a diversity of life
style as of body form. Some are peaceful plant-
eaters, others are entirely carnivorous; some
live in lakes, others live in running water. See
**Citharidium, Citharinus, Nannaethiops,
Neolebias.**

Citharinus Citharinidae
citharus 76 cm. (30 in.)
A strikingly deep-bodied fish with high and
well developed fins, and a concave profile to the
head. This species has a very large, square-cut
adipose fin, and long rays in the front of the
dorsal and anal fins. The coloration is silvery
basically, the base of the adipose fin grey, the
pelvics, anal, and the lower lobe of the tail fin
are flushed with red.

Citharinus citharus is widely distributed in
tropical Africa, having been reported in the
Nile, Niger, Volta, Senegal, and Gambia
rivers, as well as Lake Albert.

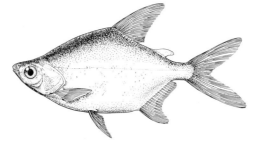

It feeds on the upper layer of bottom mud,
especially on diatoms and crustaceans inhabiting the bottom. Adults are found over muddy
areas, usually in shallow water. In some rivers
breeding has been observed to take place in
swampy areas covered by seasonal floods, and
the young are very abundant in pools during
the dry season. They are very much more
slender than the adults.

It is an important commercial fish on many
rivers and lakes in its area. **101**

Citharus Citharidae
macrolepidotus 25 cm. (10 in.)
Found throughout the Mediterranean and
along the e. Atlantic coast of Africa s. to
Angola. In this area it is moderately common
in depths of 100–300 m. (55–165 fathoms),
living on the sea bed in fine mud and sand. It
feeds on small crustaceans and occasionally
small fish.

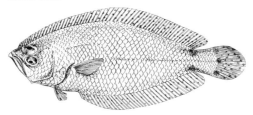

This species is warm brown in colour, with
dusky marks around the head, 2 dark blotches
on the tail at the base of the dorsal and anal fins,
and dusky patches on the dorsal and anal fin
bases. It is sinistral, that is the eyes are both on
the left side of the head.

CLANWILLIAM YELLOWFISH see **Barbus
capensis**

Clarias Clariidae
cavernicola CAVE CATFISH 15 cm. (6 in.)
Found in the Aigamas Cave, W. of Grootfon-

tein in S.W. Africa. It is a true cave dweller
with small, degenerate eyes, and quite colourless, but this apart it has all the appearances
externally of the clariid catfishes so widespread
in Africa. It is a dwarf form by comparison,
however, due no doubt to the relatively poor
living conditions offered by the cave.

With minor exceptions, when occasional
living insects are swept in, its main source of
food is the excreta of the baboons which frequent the cave. Nothing is known of its breeding biology, nor of its origin, for the history of
the river systems in the area is little known.
C. gariepinus see under **C. mossambicus**
C. mossambicus CATFISH, BARBEL 120 cm.
(47 in.)
Widely distributed in the rivers and lakes of E.
Africa, in the Blue Nile, and the Zambezi.
Another species, *C. gariepinus*, thought by
some workers to be identical, is found to the S.
in the rivers of Natal and S. to the Orange
River system. It is a long-bodied fish, greyish
black above, creamy-white below, and it has
a moderately distinct blackish stripe either
side of the lower head. The young are mottled
olive-brown.

This very large fish may attain a weight of
over 45 kg. (100 lb.), but such large specimens
become relatively rare under fishing pressure.
Its economic importance is not great, but its
flesh is tasty and good eating.

It consumes a wide variety of animal life, but
is especially a predator on small fishes, in
particular when it is mature. It is found in open
water but is most common in shallow marginal
areas. It breeds in small temporary streams
into which it penetrates during the season of
high floods. This catfish is renowned for its
habit of living in poorly oxygenated water, and

also for leaving the water completely in search
of food, or partially when ascending to breeding sites. Young specimens are kept in aquaria.

CLARIIDAE
A large family of catfishes found in the freshwaters of Africa, Syria and S.E. Asia. They
are elongate, rather eel-like with flattened
broad bony heads, and a broad transverse
mouth, with 4 pairs of long barbels around it.
The dorsal fin is long and many-rayed, but
lacks a spine; the anal fin is long. A few species
have a distinct adipose fin.

Superficially many of these forms are very
similar and dissection is needed to identify
them from anatomical features. This is true
of the accessory air-breathing organs, either
extending backwards internally from the gill
chamber, or developed as arborescent organs
at the back of the gill cavity. These accessory organs enable clariids to exist in oxygen-
poor environments, even to survive for a
long time out of water, and make overland
excursions in search of food. See **Channalabes, Clarias, Heterobranchus.**

Clarotes Bagridae
laticeps 71 cm. (28 in.)
A common catfish in the rivers of central

Africa, especially the Niger, Senegal, Volta, Nile, and Tchad. It inhabits rivers and swamps, and is omnivorous, feeding on fishes, insects, molluscs, and vegetable refuse. It breeds in July and August (in the Niger) during the season when the rivers are in flood.

It is a moderately important food fish locally, and is caught in nets, traps, and on longlines.

The genus *Clarotes* can be distinguished from other W. African catfishes by the presence of a slender spine and segmented rays weakly formed in the adipose fin. The bony ridges and ornamentation on the head show through the skin. It is brown or grey on the back, white ventrally.

CLEANER WRASSE see under **Aspidontus taeniatus**
CLEANERFISH see **Labroides dimidiatus**

Cleidopus   Monocentridae
gloriamaris KNIGHT-FISH, PORT-AND-STARBOARD-LIGHT FISH 23 cm. (9 in.)
An Australian species which has been found off the coasts of S. Queensland, New South Wales, and W. Australia. It is moderately common in deep water, but for long was known only from specimens found in the jetsam after storms. Trawling in moderate depths, however, produced many specimens.

It is a very distinctive fish with a rounded, deep body totally encased in large, heavy, spiny-edged scales, and the head armoured with large solid bones. The dorsal fin spines are large and sharp, but the pelvic spines are massive. Beneath the chin, and on either side, there are 2 open pits containing luminous, symbiotic bacteria, which glow coldly in the dark.

Its coloration is as remarkable as its extraordinary body form. The scales are bright yellow with a black edge on the back; the lips, chin, and parts of the jaws are jet black. The lower jaw has a scarlet stripe bordered by the intense white light gland, and the fins are all rose-pink or bright scarlet.

Some authorities place this fish in the genus *Monocentris*.

Clevelandia   Gobiidae
ios ARROW GOBY 5 cm. (2 in.)
A N. Pacific goby found along the coast of America from California, through Oregon and Washington to British Columbia. It lives in sheltered bays and estuaries and is often found in areas where the water is diluted by river water. Ordinarily it is very active, but at low tide, or when alarmed it seeks shelter in the burrows of ghost shrimps and mud shrimps. The fish co-exist with the crustaceans, and use the burrow as a refuge from which to seize passing planktonic organisms. They are said to place pieces of food too large to be swallowed near to a crab and to consume the debris when the crab tears it apart.

Unlike most gobies, the arrow goby does not guard its eggs; once laid they sink to the bottom and lie there unprotected.

It can be distinguished by its typical gobioid pelvic fins joined together to form a cup, by its slender body and large mouth which reaches back to behind the level of the eyes. It is pale grey or greenish with black and orange speckling, and iridescent spots on the sides.

CLIMBING PERCHES see Anabantidae
CLIMBING
  PERCH see **Anabas testudineus**
  PERCH, SPOTTED see **Ctenopoma acutirostre**
  PERCH, TAIL-SPOT see **Ctenopoma kingsleyae**
CLIMBINGFISH see **Periophthalmus koelreuteri**
CLINGFISH see Gobiesocidae
CLINGFISH see **Opeatogenys gracilis**
CLINGFISH,
  BARRED see **Tomicodon fasciatus**
  FLATHEAD see **Gobiesox maeandricus**
  SHORE see **Lepadogaster lepadogaster**
  SMALL-HEADED see **Apletodon microcephalus**
  TADPOLE see **Arcos macrophthalmus**
  TASMANIAN see **Aspasmogaster tasmaniensis**

CLINIDAE

The scaled blennies, a very varied group with numerous genera and species, are widespread in tropical and temperate seas. In general shape they resemble the comb-toothed blennies (Blenniidae), especially in having the pelvic fins placed forward on the throat, and comprising only a few slender rays. The clinids are, however, fully scaled over their bodies, and usually have more slender spines in the anterior part of the dorsal fin than rays in the posterior section.

They are mostly small bottom-dwelling fishes found in inter-tidal and inshore situations. In some regions, such as S. Africa and Australia, they have evolved into a large number of species and become the dominant element of the inter-tidal fish fauna. Some species give birth to living young; most lay eggs. See **Clinus, Cristiceps, Fucomimus, Gibbonsia, Labrisomus, Malacoctenus, Stathmonotus, Starksia.**

Clinostomus   Cyprinidae
elongatus REDSIDE DACE 10 cm. (4 in.)
A slender-bodied N. American cyprinid found in clear gravelly creeks and streams. It is widely distributed, if not evenly spread, in the ne. parts of the U.S., from Minnesota and Wisconsin, e. to Ohio and New York, and s. Canada in the Great Lakes drainages.

It is a slim fish with a narrow head and pointed snout, and large jaws which extend as far as the front of the eye. Its scales are very small. It is olive brown above, silvery on the sides and belly, with a distinct dark line along each side of the tail.

Clinus   Clinidae
superciliosus KLIPFISH, ROCKY 30 cm. (12 in.)
An abundant clinid along S. African shores, a region where this group has developed into a vast array of differing species. This is probably the most abundant species in the area, found in tide pools, under stones, amongst algae on the shore, and below low tide mark.

Its colouring varies with its habitat but is tinted to match its surroundings. It always has a series of dusky blotches on the sides, and mostly a single mark on the gill cover; background ranges from green, through reds to deep brown.

CLOWN
  BARB see **Barbus everetti**
  LOACH see **Botia macracantha**
  LOACH, HORA'S see **Botia horae**

Clupea   Clupeidae
harengus HERRING 41 cm. (16 in.)
A moderately deep-bodied fish, with the pectoral fins placed low on the sides, and a single dorsal fin well along the back, but with its origin in front of the pelvic fins. The body is moderately compressed but only in young fish is the belly keel-like. Herrings are brilliant blue on the back, silvery white on the belly with golden or brassy tints; a beautiful fish when alive, but rather dull by the time it reaches the fish shop.

It is widely distributed in the N. Atlantic, on European coasts from Iceland and the White Sea s. to the area of Gibraltar, and in the W. Atlantic from n. Labrador and w. Greenland s. to Cape Hatteras. These are the extreme limits of its occurrence; the herring is only sufficiently abundant in the n. areas to be commercially valuable. Within these areas there are a number of local races which are distinguished physically by features such as the number of vertebrae, as well as biologically by period of spawning and growth rates.

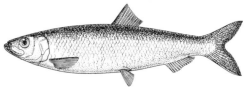

In general, herring spawn in the warmer months of the year, although each race has its own period of spawning. Most spawn on shallow banks inshore, in depths of 15–40 m. (8–22 fathoms), although some oceanic races spawn on offshore banks in deeper water, sometimes as deep as 200 m. (110 fathoms). When laid the eggs form a dense carpet on the sea bed, often many eggs deep. The young, however, are pelagic, swimming at the surface, and at times being extremely common in inshore waters.

Throughout their lives herring feed on plankton, especially the small copepod crustaceans, but other crustaceans are eaten in quantity, as well as young fishes, and other surface-living invertebrates. The herring is in its turn preyed upon by most of the larger species of fishes, such as cod, salmon, tuna, as well as by warm-blooded animals like dolphins, seals, and sea birds, especially gannets, and when the fish are young by terns and puffins. The herring is a basic element in the food chains of many marine animals living at or near the surface of the sea.

Its importance to man as a food is very great, and indeed the herring played a great role in the history of the development of the maritime nations of Europe. It is today fished in its adult stages throughout the N. Atlantic, although the heaviest exploitation is in European waters. Here, especially in the North Sea, the herring fishing has in recent years fluctuated greatly and there are grave fears for the future of the stocks unless conservation measures are adequate.

Herring are sold for human consumption fresh, and preserved in various ways – smoked as kippers, bloaters, or red herring, salted as cured herring, vinegar-cured as rollmops or soused herring. Many are tinned in sauces, especially in tomato or wine sauces. It is also used as a valuable source of fish meal and oil. In their first year they are caught and sold as whitebait.

C. pallasi PACIFIC HERRING 35 cm. (13¾ in.)
The Pacific herring is widely distributed in the N. Pacific from San Diego on the Californian coast N. to Alaska; along the Asian coast it is found from the Kurile Islands s. to Japan and Korea. It forms more or less isolated races in this area, but spawns throughout its range, each race on its local grounds and seasons. Its biology is much like that of its near relative, the Atlantic herring, feeding on planktonic crustaceans, fish, fish larvae, and invertebrates at the surface of the sea.

The Pacific herring is very important commercially to the Pacific coastal countries, the Japanese and Soviet Union fisheries being particularly important, and in Japan the annual herring catch exceeded for a long time any other fish species. They are also an important element in the diet of other animals in the area, including salmon, seals, cetaceans, and sea birds.

According to some authorities the Pacific herring is so closely related to the Atlantic form that it should be regarded only as a sub-species (*C. harengus pallasi*). It differs in having fewer vertebrae, sharp scales along the belly only behind the pelvic fins, and having less well developed teeth in the roof of the mouth.

CLUPEIDAE

A vast family containing the commercially important herrings, sardines, and their relatives. Mostly they are abundant in the coastal waters of the oceans, usually near the surface, in temperate and tropical regions. Most of them have small fine teeth, but long and complex gill rakers, for they feed on plankton. Many species are found in estuarine conditions, and in Africa particularly some representatives live in freshwater.

The majority of members of the herring family are small, few reaching a maximum of 1 m. (39 in.). Generally they are silvery-sided, darker on the back; their fins lack spines, and they are laterally compressed and thus have a sharp keel along the belly. The dorsal fin is situated around the mid-point of the body, the pectorals are placed close behind the head but low on the body, and the tail fin is deeply forked. Scales are usually large, thin, and easily shed.

As well as providing a valuable food resource for man, the family are essential elements in the food chains of many marine animals, including seabirds, cetaceans, and fishes, See **Alosa, Brevoortia, Caspialosa, Clupea, Clupeonella, Etrumeus, Harengula, Hilsa, Jenkinsia, Nematalosa, Opisthonema, Pomolobus, Sardina, Sardinella, Sardinops, Spratelloides, Sprattus.**

Clupeonella   Clupeidae
   delicatula CASPIAN SPRAT 17 cm. (6¾ in.)
This herring-like fish is typical of closely related species found in the Black and Caspian seas, on the s. borders of the U.S.S.R., which evolved in isolation when these seas were cut off from the Mediterranean. With the shads of the genus *Caspialosa*, they are part of the distinctive fauna of those seas. Superficially they are very similar to the sprat of w. Europe and have a sharply keeled throat and belly; the last rays of the anal fin are slightly prolonged.

They are very important commercial fishes in both seas, being caught with seine nets, and by being lured towards the net by bright lights. In addition they are the main food of the large shads of the Caspian and Black seas, themselves valuable food fish, as well as of numerous other fishes and birds.

The Caspian sprat is found in shallow water, but is more common to the S. in winter. It spawns in late winter and spring in shallow water and on inshore banks. It is a shoaling fish which during daytime forms enormous shoals usually to be found in slightly deeper water, but which at night split up and feed actively close inshore. It mainly eats planktonic crustaceans, the larvae of molluscs and fishes, while in river mouths it feeds on insect larvae.

This sprat is found in the Caspian Sea, the Black Sea, and the Sea of Azov; the Caspian population is recognized as a distinct sub-species *C. delicatula caspia*.

Cnesterodon   Poeciliidae
   decemmaculatus TEN-SPOTTED LIVE-BEARER 4 cm. (1½ in.)
An inhabitant of S. America, in s. Brazil, Uruguay, and Argentina to the La Plata. It is found in small quiet streams, and muddy ditches in which the water temperature is high.

The males have violet or bluish green colouring on their sides, pale greeny-grey on their backs. There are 6–12 vertical dark bars on the sides, which fade when the fish is quiescent. The female is coppery in colour and also has dark bars on the sides, which do not fade at any time. The male has a long gonopodium with a hooked tip.

An attractive aquarium fish which is, however, not very easy to breed in captivity. A brood of from 15–40 is usual.

This is one of the few live-bearing toothcarps to occur to the S. of the Amazon region in S. America.

Cnidoglanis   Plotosidae
   macrocephalus ESTUARY CATFISH
91 cm. (3 ft)
A widespread species apparently found on the coast of all Australian states, in some areas very common. Mostly found on muddy bottoms, it is typically found in estuaries, but also lives in sandy bays and in inshore waters.

A most hideous fish in appearance, its flesh is said to be good eating. Its head is broad and flattened, the body long and slender. Eight barbels surround the very capacious mouth. A long fin runs from just behind the vent, round the tail, to the mid-point of the back. The pectoral and dorsal spines can inflict serious, and very painful wounds. A conspicuous branched appendage lies before the vent; its function is not known.

It is uniform blackish brown above, whitish on belly, flecked with darker spots.

COALFISH see **Pollachius virens**
COBBLER CARPET SHARK see **Crossorhinus tentacularis**
COBIA see **Rachycentron canadum**

COBITIDAE

The family of the loaches; mainly small, rather slender-bodied fishes found only in Europe and Asia, and a restricted part of N.E. Africa. They attain their greatest abundance and diversity in s. Asia and the Malayan region. Most species are elongate, and rather flattened or at least have flattened bellies suggesting their bottom-living habits. Almost all species have a ventral mouth fringed with a number of pairs of barbels.

One group of loaches have distinct spines projecting rearwards below the eyes – said to be protection against predators. Loaches have invaded a variety of habitats from swiftly running hill streams to slow and still waters; one group is even capable of utilizing atmospheric oxygen by swallowing bubbles of air, the ensuing exchange taking place in the lower intestine.

Many kinds of loach are kept in aquariums. See **Acanthophthalmus, Acanthopsis, Botia, Cobitis, Lepidocephalus, Misgurnus, Noemacheilus.**

Cobitis   Cobitidae
   taenia SPINED LOACH 11 cm. (4½ in.)
A very widely distributed species found from e. England, across Europe, and Asia to China and Japan. In this vast range, numerous subspecies have been described, and the rather sedentary habits of this animal evidently lead to isolation and the formation of distinct races.

It lives in clear lakes, and slow flowing rivers, usually those with a muddy bottom, although sometimes found on sand. In the aquarium it buries quickly and easily and lies hidden with only its head showing; in the wild it evidently buries in a similar way and its presence is extraordinarily difficult to detect, but it also hides in the dense growths of blanket-weed algae that form in summer. It feeds on small crustaceans, and rotifers which inhabit the bottom mud. Breeding takes place in spring, the eggs being scattered over the roots of plants and algae.

The spined loach is often kept in unheated aquaria.

COCKNEY see **Chrysophrys auratus**
COCKSCOMB, HIGH see **Anoplarchus purpurescens**
COD see **Gadidae**
COD see **Gadus morhua**
COD,
   ANTARCTIC see Nototheniidae
   ARCTIC see **Boreogadus saida**
   BAIKAL see **Comephorus baicalensis**
   CULTUS see **Ophiodon elongatus**
   DEEP SEA see Eretmophoridae
   GIANT ANTARCTIC see **Dissostichus mawsoni**
   JUMPING see **Lobotes surinamensis**
   LUNAR-TAILED ROCK see **Variola louti**
   MURRAY see **Maccullochella macquariensis**
   POLAR see **Boreogadus saida**
   RED see **Physiculus bachus**
CODLING see **Gadus morhua**
COELACANTH see **Latimeria chalumnae**

COHO SALMON see **Oncorhynchus kisutch**

Coilia Engraulidae
quadragesimalis TAPER-TAIL ANCHOVY
25 cm. (10 in.)
This anchovy, like the other members of the genus *Coilia* is found in the Indo-Australian region. It is common on the Sri Lankan and Indian coasts. Although it retains the typical anchovy feature of a pronounced snout and an underslung lower jaw with a very large gape, it has an enormously long, almost rat-tailed body with a very small tail fin at the end. The anal fin is equally long, running almost the whole length of the tail fin.

It is silver-sided, light brown on the back, with 2 rows of pearl-like spots along the sides. It is most common in inshore waters especially in estuaries and harbours.

Colisa Belontiidae
fasciata GIANT GOURAMI 13 cm. (5 in.)
An inhabitant of the muddy waters of India and Burma, and possibly also found elsewhere in SE. Asia.

It is a well known and attractive aquarium fish. It differs from the gouramis of the genus *Trichogaster* by its long-based dorsal and anal fins. The pelvic fins are elongate but not as long as the body.

Variable in coloration, females are duller coloured and with rounded edges to the dorsal and anal fins. **455**
C. labiosa THICK-LIPPED GOURAMI
8 cm. (3 in.)
A gourami with a rather restricted distribution being found only in s. Burma. It is a popular aquarium fish and very colourful.

Like other *Colisa*-gouramis its dorsal and anal fins are of almost equal length; both have numbers of spines in the anterior section. This species is particularly distinguished by its thick lips, especially in the male. The pelvic fins are long and reddish in the male, clear in the female.

As with other gouramis this fish produces a dense nest of glutinous bubbles for the eggs and early young. **456**
C. lalia DWARF GOURAMI 5 cm. (2 in.)
This species is found only in India, according to Professor G. Sterba, the German ichthyologist, especially Bengal and Assam. It inhabits densely weeded waterways, tanks, slow streams and the backwaters of larger rivers. It produces a rather small but deep bubble nest in which the eggs develop.

It is a popular aquarium fish, if rather difficult to keep and sensitive to disease. It is a rather deep-bodied species, compressed, with typically long-based dorsal and anal fins. The fins are bright red in the male, paler in the female. **457**

COLLARED EEL see **Kaupichthys nuchalis**

Cololabis Scomberesocidae
saira PACIFIC SAURY 38 cm. (15 in.)
A schooling fish of the open ocean found in the N. Pacific where it is said to be one of the most abundant fishes. On the N. American coast it is found from the region of Alaska to Baja California, but it is not common in inshore waters. The spawning area is to the S. of its range across the Pacific, and here adults, larvae and young can be found. Juveniles are

carried n. by the ocean currents and may be found as far N. as Alaska, but the n. part of its range is a feeding area occupied seasonally and to varying extent depending on the year's climate and strength of currents.

It feeds almost exclusively on small surface-living crustaceans. In its turn it is eaten by squids, tuna, and marlins; sharks also take a heavy toll.

It is also fished for extensively by Japanese and Russian fishing boats. One method is to attract them to the surface by bright electric lights and to catch them by means of dip-nets. They are sold fresh, canned, and at times processed for fish meal and pet food. Occasional attempts have been made to utilize the resource off California.

The Pacific saury is similar in general appearance to the skipper, *Scomberesox saurus*, but has a relatively short snout, the jaws being only slightly produced.

COLORADO SQUAWFISH see **Ptychocheilus lucius**

Colossoma Characidae
nigripinnis PACU 70 cm. (28 in.)
This large deep-bodied characin is rather similar in body form to the piranhas, but its habits are entirely different. It is deep-bodied, with a rather large head, small eye, and small mouth. The adipose fin is rather large, and the anal fin is long and convex. It is grey-green on the back, the sides and anal fin are wholly black, and under the throat and anterior belly it is silvery. The black area appears to increase with age.

It is found in ne. S. America, where it is generally distributed in rivers. In the wild its natural food is ripe fruit. The pacu has been imported to Europe as an aquarium fish, but it is relatively uncommon in aquaria. **54**

COMB SCULPIN see **Icelinus borealis**
COMB-TAILED PARADISEFISH see **Belontia signata**
COMBFISH, LONGSPINE see **Zaniolepis latipinnis**

COMEPHORIDAE
Very aberrant freshwater sculpins confined to the central Russian Lake Baikal. They are distinguished by the lack of spines on the head, and the cavernous bones of the head which is covered by very thin transparent skin. The pelvic fins are absent. The body is long and slender, the dorsal and anal fins are many-rayed and run the length of the body. Two species only are known. See **Comephorus.**

Comephorus Comephoridae
baicalensis BAIKAL COD, LIVEBEARING
SCULPIN 19 cm. (7½ in.)
Confined to deep water in Lake Baikal, U.S.S.R., it is usually found at considerable depths during daylight, but comes up to within 10 m. (5 fathoms) of the surface at night. It feeds on pelagic crustaceans.

Both this and the other member of the

family, *C. dybowskii*, are viviparous. This species gives birth in summer, in July to August, the females coming up to the surface water to produce their young, after which they die. It is reported that only 3 per cent of the adult population are males – a remarkable sex ratio.

The Baikal cod is very fat, but is not exploited for food or other purposes.
C. dybowskii see under **C. baicalensis**

COMMERSON'S GLASSFISH see **Chanda commersoni**
COMMON
BULLSEYE see **Liopempheris multiradiata**
HARDYHEAD see **Pranesus ogilbyi**
HATCHETFISH see **Gasteropelecus sternicla**
PUFFERFISH see **Tetraodon cutcutia**
SAW SHARK see **Pristiophorus cirratus**
SKATE see under **Raja whitleyi**
STINGAREE see **Urolophus testaceus**
STINKFISH see **Callionymus calauropomus**
TOAD see **Sphoeroides hamiltoni**
CONCERTINAFISH see **Drepane punctata**
CONCHFISH see **Astrapogon stellatus**
CONEY see **Cephalopholis fulvus**

Conger Congridae
conger CONGER EEL 2·7 m. (9 ft)
The conger is a very large eel; records exist of specimens of over 2·7 m. (9 ft) and weighing 65 kg. (143 lb.), although such large fish are uncommon. Naturally enough, such a large eel is a powerful, and at close quarters, a dangerous fish, and although they are not especially aggressive they become so if provoked. In common with other members of the family it lacks large fangs in its jaws, but its teeth are cone-like, close packed and stout. Its food is varied and includes fish of many kinds; it also eats a large amount of crustaceans, chiefly crabs and lobsters, and cephalopods like the octopus.

Conger eels live in shallow water, the small ones are common in tidal pools on rocky shores, and offshore. It is almost always found in, or close to cover, mostly rocks or rockfaces, pier, and jetty pilings. Wrecks of sunken ships frequently house large congers.

In shallow water the conger is dark brown to black on the back, a light golden colour or white on the belly. Specimens from deep water are frequently fawn in colour. The conger is otherwise distinguished by the presence of pectoral fins, the lack of scales, and by the jaw shape, the upper jaw overlapping the lower. It is believed to spawn after a migration into deep water, the larvae have the typical leptocephalus form of eel larvae. The conger is found along the coasts of n. Europe, and in the Mediterranean. Its range is believed to extend s. to S. African waters, but there is a possibility that 2 species are involved in this range.

The conger is an excellent food fish. As it lives under cover on rough grounds, it can only be caught by lines – the total catch is thus

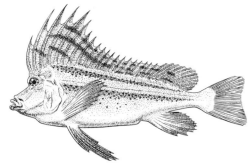

low. Anglers, however, especially in the U.K., catch large quantities and they are rated as good sporting fish, although nimbleness is at a premium in avoiding a large conger loose in a small boat.

C. oceanica AMERICAN CONGER 1·5 m. (5 ft)
The American conger is found on the continental shelf of the Atlantic coast from Cape Cod s. along the American coast. A similar if not identical species occurs off the coast of S. America. Larval forms are found further to the N. of Cape Cod, even as far as Nova Scotia. These are presumed to be accidental occurrences, larvae having been carried passively by ocean currents, for this conger, like its European relative spawns in deep water offshore. In this case it is said to spawn in the region of the W. Indies. The conger spawns only once in its life.

It is bluish grey to brown on the back, sometimes tinged with red, but dingy white below. Reputed to grow up to 2·1 m. (7 ft) in length, the great majority are much smaller than this; a weight of 10 kg. (22 lb.) was recorded as the heaviest along the coast of Maine.

It is found in shallow water (once passed its larval stages) down to a depth of about 260 m. (142 fathoms), but is believed to move offshore in winter. Its food consists principally of fish, such as butterfish, herring, and eels, but also it preys on shrimps and small molluscs. It is distinguished from other American eels by the forward position of its dorsal fin, its scaleless skin, narrow pointed head, and strong but conical teeth. It also has many more vertebrae than the common eel *(Anguilla rostrata)*, a point of some importance in distinguishing the transparent leptocephalus larvae; it has fewer than the European conger.

CONGER,
AMERICAN see **Conger oceanica**
RIBBON see **Taenioconger chapmani**
CONGER EEL see **Conger conger**
CONGER-PIKE see **Muraenesox arabicus**
CONGER-PIKE, COSTA'S see **Cynoponticus ferox**

CONGIOPODIDAE
The fishes of this family are often known as pigfishes on account of their rather protuberant snout. The body is deep and rather compressed, the skin without scales although sometimes warty. One long dorsal fin the greater part of which is composed of strong spines.

The pigfishes are related to the scorpionfishes and flatheads, but form a small rather distinctive group in the cooler seas of the S. Hemisphere. See **Congiopodus, Perryena.**

Congiopodus Congiopodidae
torvus RACEHORSE, HORSEFISH
80 cm. (32 in.)
Found only in the seas around S. Africa from

the Cape to Pondoland. It lives in moderately deep water and has been found down to 146 m. (80 fathoms), at times considerable numbers are taken by trawlers but it is not a commercially valuable species. Many others have been thrown ashore after storms.

Its coloration is variable but is usually plain brown, darkening with age. Its skin is rough in the young but becomes smooth in the adult.

CONGO TETRA see **Micralestes interruptus**
CONGOLLI see **Pseudaphritis bursinus**

CONGRIDAE
A family of marine eels which contains a number of genera and many species. Most are rather heavy-bodied, typically eel-like, with scaleless skins, and pectoral fins. The jaws are moderate, with strong teeth but no fang-like canines in the jaws. Most are found in shallow water to moderate depths inshore, but a few are found in the deep sea, and others in estuaries. They inhabit the temperate and tropical regions of the Atlantic, Indian and Pacific oceans. See **Ariosoma, Conger, Gnathophis, Nystactichthys, Taenioconger.**

CONGROGADIDAE
A small family of blenny-like fishes, all remarkably eel-like in appearance. All have a long thin body, long many-rayed dorsal and anal fins, either joined completely or nearly, to the tail-fin base.

Found scattered throughout the Indo-Pacific there are 5–6 genera and perhaps a dozen species. Most are small and burrow in sandy mud, or amongst rocks. See **Congrogadus, Halidesmus.**

Congrogadus Congrogadidae
subducens MUD BLENNY 38 cm. (15 in.)
A Pacific species which is found in the E. Indies, New Guinea, and along the Australian coast from W. Australia and the N. Territory. It inhabits muddy areas in shallow water but is occasionally found in rock-pools, presumably where it can bury itself.

It is a long slender fish, with dorsal and anal fins joined to the tail. Its head is short and its mouth moderate in size. Olive-green in colour, with rusty blotches on the back and sides and light bluish white dots on the belly. A blue-black spot, white ringed, on the upper gill cover.

CONVICT TANG see **Acanthurus triostegus**
COOK, ROCK see **Centrolabrus exoletus**
COOLIE
LOACH see **Acanthophthalmus kuhlii**
LOACH, HALF-BANDED see **Acanthophthalmus simicinctus**

Copeina Lebiasinidae
arnoldi SPRAYING CHARACIN 8 cm. (3 in.)
This beautiful little fish is known from the lower Amazon, Rio Parà. It has a slender body with rather long fins, those of the male being particularly long. The scales are large, each with a dark edge, thus forming a lacy pattern over the body. The back is yellowish brown, the sides lighter, and the belly almost white. A dark band runs through the mouth and across the eye. The fins are reddish, the dorsal fin being particularly noticeable with a yellowish base, a dark rounded spot, and a red tip. Males

in particular are brightly coloured, and have longer fins than the females.

The spraying characin's breeding habits have been often described. The eggs are actually deposited out of water, on the underside of a leaf, or overhanging object. With bodies close together the pair leap simultaneously from the water to deposit a few eggs on the leaf, and this is continued until 60 or more eggs have been deposited in a close clump. The male returns every 20–30 minutes to splash the eggs with water. The eggs hatch in 2–3 days and the fry fall into the water.

Copeina lives in swampy backwaters where oxygenation of the water is often poor, sometimes nil. The adult fish keep at the very surface of the water by habit, and their interesting spawning habits are probably a device to permit successful breeding in what would otherwise be impossible conditions.

It has, however, recently been suggested that this breeding habit, so often attributed to *Copeina arnoldi*, is in fact that of a species of *Copella*, possibly *C. nattereri*.

C. guttata RED-SPOTTED COPEINA 15 cm. (6 in.)
This fish is widely distributed in the middle Amazon, and its tributaries. It has been kept as an aquarium species for many years, and is very suitable as a pet fish for it is hardy, peaceable, and easy to breed. It lays its eggs in shallow pits excavated in the sand.

It is moderately slender, with large scales, and save for the tail which is forked, it has rounded fins. It has no adipose fin. The sexes are similar except that the female is usually paler coloured, while the upper lobe of the tail fin is elongated in males. **90**

COPEINA, RED-SPOTTED see **Copeina guttata**
Copella nattereri see under **Copeina arnoldi**
COPPER SWEEPER see **Pempheris schomburgki**

CORACINIDAE
A small family containing 2 species found around the s. coast of Africa. Their affinities appear to lie with the rudderfishes (Kyphosidae). They are deep-bodied, with a rounded head, small mouth with strong curved, incisor teeth and large flattened molars in the sides of the jaw. See **Coracinus.**

Coracinus Coracinidae
capensis GALJOEN, HIGHWATER, BLACKFISH, BLACK BREAM 70 cm. (27 in.)
A native of S. Africa and found only from Walfish Bay round the Cape to Natal, in shallow water and even in the surf. It is frequently found over rocky shores, and comes inshore at high tide foraging for the mussels and other molluscs and crustaceans on which it feeds.

It is a fine sporting fish which takes a bait eagerly and fights well. It grows to a weight of

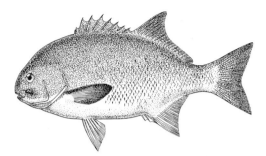

7 kg. (16 lb.) although on average it is around 1·4 kg. (3 lb.).

It is deep-bodied, with a steep profile, and a distinct spiny dorsal fin, joined to the second dorsal which, however, has a high front lobe in adults. On rocky grounds it is almost black above, grey on the sides; on sand it is mainly silvery.

CORAL
  SPINEFOOT see **Siganus corallinus**
  TROUT see **Cephalopholis miniatus**
CORALFISH see **Abudefduf saxatilis, Abudefduf sordidus**
CORALFISH, BEAKED see **Chelmon rostratus**
CORB see **Sciaena umbra**
Coregonidae see under Salmonidae

Coregonus Salmonidae
  albula VENDACE, POLLAN 46 cm. (18 in.)
This whitefish, which is sometimes known as the European cisco, is well distributed in Europe, from the British Isles e. through the Baltic Sea basin to the central U.S.S.R. In the British Isles it is known as vendace in Loch Maben and lakes Derwentwater and Bassenthwaite, and as pollan in several Irish loughs.

It is mainly found in lakes throughout its range although to the N. semi-migratory stocks are found, as in the Gulf of Finland. Most of the year it is found in moderately deep water, but in the autumn it is encountered in shallows on the gravelly spawning beds. It feeds principally on the small planktonic crustaceans, and in summer tends to be found near the surface at night where these animals congregate. It also eats insect larvae, molluscs, and incidentally young fishes.

This whitefish can be distinguished within its range by its prominent lower jaw, rather upturned mouth, and pointed head. It has many gill rakers on the first gill arch. Otherwise it is a silvery, herring-like fish with an adipose fin.

In e. Europe, parts of Scandinavia and the U.S.S.R. it is a moderately valuable food fish which has been to some extent cultivated by translocation to new waters.

C. artedii CISCO, LAKE CISCO 53 cm. (21 in.)
The lake cisco is widely distributed in n. N. America, from the upper Mississippi and Great Lakes n. to Labrador and the Mackenzie river system. Through this range many populations exist in isolated lakes, most of which have at some time or another been named as

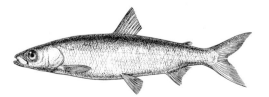

distinct forms but essentially only identifiable by their geographical location.

This whitefish is found mainly in lakes, often in large shoals and in deep or shallow water. It spawns in autumn over gravelly shallows, the adults returning to deeper water over winter. In spring they again migrate to the shallow shelf, this migration apparently being for the richer food in shallow water. They eat mainly plankton and crustaceans.

The lake cisco, or lake herring, is a valuable food fish wherever it occurs near to human populations. In the Great Lakes the fishery was mainly during their appearance in shallow water. In the far n. it has traditionally been the mainstay of man and dogs during winter.

C. autumnalis ARCTIC CISCO 64 cm. (25 in.)
The Arctic cisco is a typical whitefish in appearance, relatively long-bodied, with moderate scales, and a large adipose fin. Its number of gill rakers (26–31) on the lower limb of the first gill arch, and its habits and distribution help to distinguish it from its relatives.

It is found in w. Arctic Canada, and N. Alaska, and across the Arctic Ocean region of the U.S.S.R. w. to European Russia. A subspecies, *C. autumnalis migratorius*, lives in the Russian Lake Baikal, and attains a large size (up to 7 kg. (15 lb.)). It lives in the coastal areas of the lake and migrates to river mouths to spawn. The Arctic form both in Eurasia and N. America is also migratory, being frequently found in coastal waters and estuaries and spawning in the lower reaches of rivers. It is a typically estuarine fish, feeding on small crustaceans and the fry of fishes. In the larger rivers, however, it may migrate as far as 1000 km. (620 miles) upstream to spawn. It spawns in late summer and autumn, the eggs being shed loosely in the gravel.

The Arctic cisco is an important food fish especially in Siberia and the n. parts of European Russia. It is captured chiefly as it migrates up-river, when it is very fat. Eaten fresh, it is said to be very rich and good. It is also dried and stored as winter food for man and dogs.

C. clupeaformis HUMPBACK or LAKE WHITEFISH 1 m. (39 in.)
The humpback whitefish is widely distributed in n. America from the Bering Strait to Labrador and s. to the Great Lakes. Because of its food value it has been introduced outside its natural range. It is closely related to the Eurasian whitefish, *C. pidschian*, and may even be identical with it but the taxonomy of the whitefishes is confused.

It is large, occasionally attaining a weight of 19 kg. (42 lb.), although usually not more than 10 kg. (22 lb.). Distinguished by its thick upper lip, which projects, and by the flat-sided heavy body, it is very herring-like in general appearance.

Throughout its range it is an important food fish. Gill net fisheries have existed for many years exploiting this species in the Great Lakes, and more recently they have been developed in lakes in the far N. of Canada from which they must be flown out to market. The product commands a sufficiently high price for this to be economic.

The humpback whitefish feeds on a variety of organisms. Populations with many gillrakers feed on plankton, chiefly crustaceans, but the others are mainly bottom-feeders on molluscs, insect larvae, and shrimps. It is

typically a lake-dwelling whitefish although some occur in large rivers. It spawns in late autumn, the small eggs being scattered over the gravel bed in shallows in lakes and the mouth of tributary rivers. The eggs overwinter to hatch in spring, but are frequently greatly diminished in number by numerous egg-eating fish, crayfish, and birds. Growth rates are fast in the S. of its range, but to the N. are much reduced, although it may vary from lake to lake. In some Arctic lakes it may take 9 years to attain a weight of 1·5 kg. (3 lb.), and the larger fish may be as old as 28 years.

C. lavaretus HOUTING 51 cm. (20 in.)
This whitefish is widely distributed in n. Europe and the n. regions of the U.S.S.R. e. to Siberia. Within this range it exhibits many local variations of body form or gill raker structure and the relationships of some of these local populations have not been closely studied. Due to its wide distribution it has many local names: in Great Britain, the powan of the Scottish lochs, skelly or schelly of the Lake District lakes, and the gwyniad of N. Wales. A migratory form found in the Baltic, and formerly in the s. N. Sea (in the latter it is believed to be extinct now) was known as the houting. This form had a long rather protuberant snout, the other populations have a sub-terminal mouth.

Most of the lake populations feed on planktonic crustaceans, but some supplement this diet with bottom-living organisms. River-dwelling whitefish feed more on benthic organisms, crustaceans, molluscs, and insect larvae. There is great variability in spawning seasons and habits; Scottish powan spawn in mid-winter on gravelly shallows, while the migratory forms in Russian rivers spawn in summer.

This whitefish is very important locally as a food source. It is tolerant of warm water, and even moderate pollution, and it is widely bred and introduced in reservoirs in the U.S.S.R. and e. Europe for its fishery value.

C. pidschian see under **C. clupeaformis**
C. sardinella LEAST CISCO 41 cm. (16 in.)
The least cisco is a very variable species widely distributed across the n. Eurasian landmass, and also found in w. N. America (Alaska, and the N. W. Territory of Canada). Within this range it is found both as a lake-dwelling freshwater fish and as a migratory species. Not surprisingly, many populations differ considerably from one another and have in the past been named as distinct species, and are currently referred to as '*C. sardinella* complex'.

The least cisco is one of the more important fishes in n. Siberia and Arctic U.S.S.R. being captured by gill nets and seines. In Alaska and the Yukon it is caught locally and forms an important subsistence fishery.

Where it is found it is often extremely abundant, the migratory populations ascending rivers in great shoals. The migratory fish live mainly in estuaries feeding on crustaceans, and migrate during the summer to spawn in the autumn, laying their eggs on gravel or sand in the river. The eggs overwinter to hatch in the spring, while the adults return to the sea after spawning. Non-migratory populations are more common to the S. where the less rigorous winter conditions allow them to survive overwinter.

The least cisco is distinguished by its relatively small size and its protruding lower jaw. It is a rather slim fish.

Coris   Labridae
angulata 1·2 m. (4 ft)
This species is the largest member of the genus, most of whose representatives are not more than 15 cm. (6 in.) in length.

It is widely distributed in the Indo-Pacific from the e. coast of Africa across to the central Pacific islands. Small specimens are commonly taken in the shallow waters of reefs but the larger specimens are found only in considerable depths.

It is greatly variable in colour, the young being light or tan with numerous red spots on the head and anterior body, 2 orange areas on the dorsal fin with prominent black centres. The adults are dark green, almost black with narrow white edges to the fins. Adults develop a conspicuous bump on the forehead. **400**
C. formosus see **C. gaimardi**
C. gaimardi 38 cm. (15 in.)
Widely distributed in the Indo-Pacific from the E. African coast to the Hawaiian islands. Throughout its range it shows a great variety of colour patterns and markings; one such was formerly known as *C. formosus*. It is found in moderately deep water just off the reefs; it is rare in tidal pools. **401**
C. julis RAINBOW WRASSE 25 cm. (10 in.)
A s. European wrasse which is widespread and very common in the Mediterranean as well as occurring in the e. Atlantic from the Gulf of Guinea to n. Spain. It is mostly found amongst algal-covered rocks and sea grass beds from the surface down to depths of 120 m. (66 fathoms). It is active only during the day, probably burrowing into the sand at night. Its food is varied and at times it feeds heavily on surface plankton; young specimens act as cleaner fishes.

This is one of the several species of wrasse in which sex reversal has been proven. Functional females often become males, complete with change of coloration, with increasing age.

It is a very distinctive species with a long slender body, sharp snout, and pointed teeth. Females are usually dark olive-brown, the male has an orange zig-zag stripe down its side. **402**

CORNETFISH see Fistulariidae
CORNETFISH, BLUE-SPOTTED see **Fistularia tabacaria**
CORNISH
  BLACKFISH see **Schedophilus medusophagus**
  SUCKER see **Lepadogaster lepadogaster**
CORNISH-JACK see **Mormyrops deliciosus**

Corydoras   Callichthyidae
arcuatus ARCHED CORYDORAS 5 cm. (2 in.)
Found in the Amazon basin near the town of Tefflé, Brazil.

A typical member of the family with a short dorsal fin and small adipose fin, supported by a small spine, heavy scute-like scales overlapping one another and forming an apparent seam along the mid-sides. The broad dark band which originates at the mouth, runs through the eye and along the back profile, then turns downwards at the base of the tail to run along its lower margin. This marking is distinctive. A common aquarium fish. **172**
C. hastatus DWARF CORYDORAS 3 cm. (1¼ in.)

This miniature armoured catfish is native to the Amazon basin, near Villa Bella in Brazil. It makes a very attractive pet fish, living in shoals and frequently swimming clear of the bottom, is relatively easy to keep.

Its size and colouring help to distinguish it from the other *Corydoras* species. Its back is olive-green, sides yellowish, ventrally almost white, sprinkled with small spots. A black line runs from the head along the mid-line to the base of the tail where it expands into a blotch set in a clear yellow patch.
C. julii LEOPARD CORYDORAS 6 cm. (2½ in.)
A very attractive aquarium fish which originates in the small tributaries of the lower Amazon in Brazil.

Its coloration is quite distinctive. **173**
C. melanistius BLACK-SPOTTED CORYDORAS 6 cm. (2½ in.)
Found fairly widely distributed in ne. S. America, this armoured catfish has been reported from Venezuela, Bolivia (the Orinoco), and Guyana (the Essequibo).

In body form it is typical of the genus, but it can be distinguished by its markings. **174**
C. pestaei 5 cm. (2 in.)
Found only in the smallest tributaries of the Amazon. A remarkably colourful member of a family chiefly characterized by drab colours, and for this reason fairly popular as an aquarium fish.

It is less flattened ventrally than many members of the family, with an almost streamlined body outline, and with short, rounded fins. **175**
C. punctatus 6 cm. (2½ in.)
Widely distributed in n. S. America, from the Orinoco in Bolivia and Venezuela, through the Guyanas, to the Amazon basin. A rather high-backed armoured catfish with a steep profile and rounded dorsal fin; the mouth barbels are well developed. A popular aquarium fish. **176**
C. schultzei 6·5 cm. (2¾ in.)
Found in the smaller Amazon tributaries of Brazil, this fish was first described in 1940 from specimens imported to Germany for the aquarium trade. It is relatively brightly coloured. **177**
C. schwartzi 5 cm. (2 in.)
A small catfish found in the Rio Purus, Brazil and only relatively recently recognized as distinct from the many other *Corydoras* species. It has since been imported to Europe as an aquarium fish.

In body form it is typical of the genus with a high, rather squat head and body, with rather long barbels on the lips. The body is covered laterally by 2 rows of large overlapping scales. **178**

CORYDORAS,
  ARCHED see **Corydoras arcuatus**
  BLACK-SPOTTED see **Corydoras melanistius**
  DWARF see **Corydoras hastatus**
  LEOPARD see **Corydoras julii**

Corynopoma   Characidae
riisei SWORDTAIL CHARACIN 7 cm. (2¾ in.)
A slender characin with an almost straight back, strongly curved belly, and a compressed body. It is immediately distinguished by the form of the gill-cover; in the female it ends in a short rather stiff spine, in males it is elongate (half as long as the body), spoon shaped, with a black tip. Males also have much longer fin rays.

Its colour is essentially greeny brown on the back, and silvery on the belly, but the body is translucent so that these tints are fugitive with differing lighting.

The swordtail characin is found in Trinidad and n. Venezuela. It is kept in aquaria. Its breeding habits are particularly interesting for this is one of the comparatively few characins in which fertilization of the egg is internal. Their breeding display is very striking, the male strokes the female with the long gill-cover appendage, deep black at the tip and milky white on its stem. The female darts at the black tip as if it were food thus bringing her close to the male, whereupon a small black spermatophore is transferred from male to female. The spermatophore, contains sperm enough to fertilize a succession of ripening eggs, indeed it may last the female for her lifetime. The close resemblance between the tip of the gill-cover extension and the spermatophore suggests that the former plays an important part in conditioning the female to pick up the spermatophore in her mouth to later transfer it to the cloaca. The eggs are laid on plant leaves and hatch after 24–36 hours. They are guarded by the female.

Coryphaena   Coryphaenidae
equisetis POMPANO DOLPHINFISH
51 cm. (20 in.)
Apparently worldwide in its distribution, but relatively poorly known on account of earlier confusion with the larger species. It is widely distributed in the tropical Atlantic including the Gulf of Mexico and Caribbean; it has also been found in the Indian and Pacific oceans. Adults appear to be confined to the surface waters of tropical seas, and are rarely caught, but the young fish are common, and frequently attracted to lights at night.

The pompano dolphinfish is a relatively small fish (the maximum length given is doubtful), it is also brightly coloured but with more silvery tints and more distinct dark spots on the sides. It also has from 48–55 fin rays in the dorsal fin.
C. hippurus DOLPHINFISH, DORADO
1·5 m. (5 ft)
Widely distributed in all tropical and warm temperate oceans but usually found only in the open sea. The dolphinfish has the habit of swimming in small schools around floating patches of kelp, logs, or flotsam, and frequently is attracted to rafts and slowly drifting ships.

It is a fish-eating predator, feeding on a wide range of surface-living forms, a number of them fishes which live in floating weed. Dolphinfishes also eat squids and crustaceans. They are reputed to feed extensively on flying fishes, and to be a cause of many of their 'flights' while hunting, but relatively few have been found in studies of the stomach contents of the dolphinfish.

It is an exquisitely beautiful fish, brilliant turquoise blue or green above, silvery below, with yellowish ventral fins, but the colour changes on being hauled from the water. It can be identified by its body form, long dorsal fin (with 55–65 fin rays). Males have very high, almost vertical, foreheads with increasing age; they also grow much larger than females.

Dolphinfish are famed sporting fish; large specimens weigh over 23 kg. (50 lb.), and 41 kg. (90 lb.) specimens have been heard of. They fight well, and swim strongly; they are also excellent food fish. The commercial fishery for this species is locally valuable.

The use of dolphinfish as a name is a preferable, if cumbersome way of avoiding confusion with the more widespread cetacean dolphins. Dorado is used in Portuguese or Spanish speaking areas.

CORYPHAENIDAE

The family of the dolphinfishes, 2 species only are recognized both probably cosmopolitan in tropical seas. Considerable confusion between them has taken place and it is not easy to distinguish to which species various biological data apply.

They are both open sea fishes, with long bodies and small scales, a long dorsal fin and a deeply forked tail fin. Beautifully coloured when living, the colours are fugitive in death. The dolphinfish is a popular game fish; both species are excellent eating. See **Coryphaena.**

Coryphaenoides   Macrouridae
  rupestris 91 cm. (3 ft)
A N. Atlantic rat-tail, found in the E. from N. Norwegian waters to Biscay, and in the W. from Greenland, the Grand Bank, Labrador S. to Cape Hatteras. It occurs over a wide depth range from 183–2200 m. (100–1200 fathoms), but the shallower depths appear to be in the N. of its range. It is a bottom-living fish eating crustaceans and other invertebrates.

It is distinguishable by its blunt, rounded snout, and the position of the mouth which is almost terminal. The scales are moderately large with 5 spines on them so that the head and body feel rough to the touch. Medium-brown with darker fins.

Coryphoblennius   Blenniidae
  galerita MONTAGU'S BLENNY 8 cm. (3 in.)
Occurs in the NE. Atlantic as an intertidal fish between w. Ireland and S. Wales to N. Africa; is also found in the Mediterranean and Adriatic. Its especial habitat is in rather bare tidal pools which have low algal growth, or encrusting growths on the bottom. Even small, handbasin size, rock pools are inhabited.

It feeds on small crustaceans and the appendages of barnacles. Breeding takes place in early summer, the eggs being attached to the 'roof' of a small crevice and guarded by the male.

It is distinguished by the unmistakable fringed crest running across the forehead. Males have a distinct orange edge to this crest,

as well as orange on the rear end of the upper lip. **424**

COSTA'S CONGER-PIKE see **Cynoponticus
  ferox**

COTTIDAE

A large family of mostly marine fishes found in the N. Hemisphere. They are particularly well represented in the N. Pacific, whence the Atlantic forms are believed to have been derived. They also occur in freshwaters across the n. landmasses, but the variety of species is less than in the marine habitats.

The bullheads and sculpins have heads flattened from above with generous spines; the body is stout to elongate. Scales are absent, but many forms have minute skin spines, and others have spined bony plates along the sides.

Most species inhabit rather shallow inshore waters, some are found intertidally. Few of the members of the family are large fish, nor are they commercially valuable. See **Artedius, Blepsias, Cottus, Enophrys, Hemilepidotus, Hemitripterus, Myoxocephalus, Nautichthys, Oligocottus, Oncocottus, Scorpaenichthys, Taurulus.**

COTTOCOMEPHORIDAE

A moderate sized family of sculpin-like fishes which are confined to the central Russian Lake Baikal and some of its tributary rivers. Physically they are close to the sculpin family Cottidae but differ in certain respects of head skeleton; they also have teeth on the jaws and the vomer while in the Cottidae teeth are confined to the jaws.

Some species are of commercial importance in the area of Lake Baikal. They are also interesting on account of the manner in which they have evolved to take advantage of most of the available habitats in the lake. See **Batrachocottus, Cottocomephorus.**

Cottocomephorus   Cottocomephoridae
  comephoroides LONGWING SCULPIN
19 cm. (7½ in.)
Confined to Lake Baikal in the central U.S.S.R., and inhabiting that lake from the surface to 1000 m. (546 fathoms). It is a pelagic species living in shoals in the summer at depths between 150 and 1000 m. (82–546 fathoms) but in winter living in shallower water and closer to the lake bed. It spawns in February to April in shallow water near the shore, the males guarding the spawn until hatching when they follow the females back to the deep water.

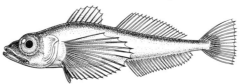

Its food in summer is mainly planktonic crustaceans which it follows towards the surface at night-time. In winter bottom-living organisms are found in their stomachs.

It has a very distinctive form.

COTTUNCULIDAE

A small family of sculpin-like fishes mostly found in moderately deep water and although best known in the N. Atlantic also found off S. Africa and elsewhere.

The body is covered in loose skin and is wholly covered with fine spines. The dorsal fin is included within the skin, but is low, of uniform height and not divided into 2. See **Cottunculoides, Cottunculus.**

Cottunculoides   Cottunculidae
  inermis 30 cm. (12 in.)
A deep water member of the family which has been found in the SE. tropical Atlantic, and off the Cape in S. Africa. Its normal depth range is in the region of 366–1098 m. (200–600 fathoms). Its biology is unknown.

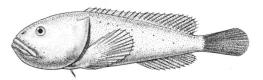

It is distinguished by the loose granular skin, single dorsal fin, the first rays being low. The head is smooth and it has 17–19 rays in the dorsal fin.

Cottunculus   Cottunculidae
  microps POLAR SCULPIN 20 cm. (8 in.)
A deep water species found in the N. Atlantic on both sides. It has been recorded from the Gulf of St Lawrence to New Jersey, off Greenland, Iceland, and in the Norwegian Sea. Its depth range is between 200–898 m. (110–490 fathoms). It feeds on mysiid and euphausiid crustaceans.

In the area in which it is found it is distinguished by its pallid brown colour, soft fleshy appearance and loose, rather prickly, skin.

Cottus   Cottidae
  asper PRICKLY SCULPIN 30 cm. (12 in.)
A freshwater sculpin found along the Pacific slope of N. America from California to Alaska including Queen Charlotte and Vancouver islands. Its habitat is in pools and quiet areas in clear coastal streams and lakes. Some populations live in brackish water, and in coastal areas the adults move to brackish water to breed.

It breeds in early spring; the small orange eggs are stuck on the roof of the 'nest', under a rock where they are fanned and guarded by the male. It feeds on aquatic insects and bottom-living invertebrates, occasionally small fishes, and seasonally salmon eggs. It is a cryptic species usually lying hidden and is mainly active by day. It is distinguished by its long many-rayed anal fin.

C. cognatus SLIMY SCULPIN 12 cm. (4¾ in.)
Widely distributed in freshwater in e. Siberia and in N. America s. from Manitoba and the Great Lakes to Virginia.

It lives in rivers and streams in cool running water over sandy and rocky bottoms. Some populations occur in cool clear lakes to a depth of 10 m. (5 fathoms). It spawns in spring in hollows excavated under rocks and stones; the

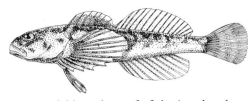

eggs are laid on the roof of the 'nest' and are guarded and fanned by the male.

The slimy sculpin is distinguished by having a double pore on the chin, and by its incomplete lateral line. The anal fin has only 10–13 rays.

C. gobio MILLER'S THUMB, BULLHEAD
10 cm. (4 in.)
A widely distributed European freshwater bullhead. It is found from the Caspian Sea area to England and Wales, and from the margins of the Baltic to the Alps and Pyrenees. It is very adaptable and lives in small streams, large rivers and lakes, but its typical habitat is clear flowing water on a pebbly bottom. In lakes it lives down to 9 m. (5 fathoms).

It spawns in spring, in a shallow hole excavated by the male under a stone. The eggs are shed onto the roof of the 'nest' and are guarded by the male until they hatch. The adults are found hiding under stones or in dense weedbeds; they only become really active at night. The bullhead eats bottom-living invertebrates, mostly crustaceans and fishes.

It is identified by its small size, broad flattened head, and by the light coloured pelvic fins, the inner ray of which is shorter than the outer ray. Its colouring is very variable.

Couchia see **Ciliata mustela**
COW SHARK see **Hexanchus griseus**
COW-NOSED
  RAY see Rhinopteridae
  RAY see **Rhinoptera bonasus**
COWCOD see **Sebastes levis**
COWFISH see Ostraciontidae
COWFISH see **Lactoria diaphana**
COWFISH,
  ORNATE see **Aracana ornata**
  SCRAWLED see **Lactophrys quadricornis**
CRAB-EATER see **Rachycentron canadum**
CRACKER, MUSSEL see **Sparodon durbanensis**

CRANOGLANIDAE
A family of Asiatic catfishes distinguished by the rather thin elongate body, and heavily armoured head region, fine teeth on the jaws but none on the palate. It resembles the genus *Pseudobagrus*. See **Cranoglanis**.

Cranoglanis Cranoglanidae
sinensis 28 cm. (11 in.)
A rather peculiar catfish described originally from freshwater in Hong Kong, but apparently really collected at Wuchow, Kwangsi Province in China. It occurs in abundance in the West

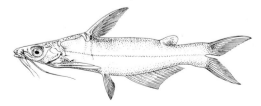

River and its tributary the Fu River at Wuchow. It grows to a maximum weight of about

2·2 kg. (5 lb.). It is a long slender fish, greenish above, silvery beneath; the fins are dusky.

Crapatulus Leptoscopidae
arenarius SANDFISH 9 cm. (3½ in.)
An Australian species which has been found on the coasts of W. Australia, S. Australia, New South Wales and Queensland, in shallow water on sandy flats. It burrows into the sand with wriggling movements of its body and can disappear within seconds. Because of this habit it is very rarely captured and it is little known in general.

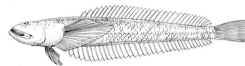

Its body is sandy coloured above and white below. Its most characteristic features are the large scales, eyes placed on the top of the head, and fringed lips.

CRAPPIE, WHITE see **Pomoxis annularis**

Craterocephalus Atherinidae
eyresii LAKE EYRE HARDYHEAD
9 cm. (3½ in.)
A species found in the freshwaters of S. Australia in the internal Lake Eyre drainage system. A number of other members of this genus are found in isolated freshwaters of Australia.

It is small and elongate, with a rounded body, the mouth is small, the eye moderately large. Its colouring is yellowish above, white below, with the 2 colour areas separated by an intense silvery line overlain by dark dots.

Creagrutus Characidae
beni GOLD-STRIPED CHARACIN
9 cm. (3½ in.)
An attractive characin, with silvery sides and belly flecked with yellow, and a brilliant red-gold band along the sides from the head to the tail, divided into 2 by a black stripe half way along the body; a dark and conspicuous shoulder blotch, and another blotch on the dorsal fin. The dorsal and anal fins are mainly reddish, the other fins are yellow tinted. The male is said to be duller coloured than the female, with yellowish fins.

The gold-striped characin is widely distributed in ne. S. America from the upper Amazon to Venezuela and also in s. Brazil. It is a pleasant aquarium fish, although not widely kept.

It is interesting on account of its breeding habits. The pair mates some days before the eggs are laid, the male's sperm being stored in the maternal oviducts where fertilization takes place. The eggs are finally laid on water plants, between 40–70 at a time. The young hatch in 24–28 hours at 26° C, and cling to the water plants for 24 hours, but are free-swimming after this period although usually found hiding on the bottom.

Creatochanes Characidae
affinis ORANGE-FINNED CHARACIN
13 cm. (5 in.)
Very widely distributed in S. America, including the Amazon basin, Paraguay, and n. to Guyana. It is a slender-bodied fish, with a high dorsal fin and large eyes, an adipose fin is

present, and the lateral line is downcurved and continues from head to tail.

Although the adult fish is modestly coloured the young are very bright. The back is grey-brown, the sides silvery with a greenish tint, while lower down the sides there is a broad shining stripe of rainbow hues. The fins are yellowish, except that the dorsal fin has a reddish base, and the tail fin lobes are dark.

Despite its attractive coloration this is hardly an ideal aquarium fish for it is an avid predator. It will eat live foods of all kinds but it clearly prefers smaller fishes, and is thus not practical as a pet in the mixed aquarium.

CREEDIIDAE
A small family of Indo-Pacific fishes found from the coast of Africa to Australian waters. They are all small and elusive animals and no doubt with more intensive collecting in the correct habitats members of the family will be found extensively.

They are slender, almost eel-like fishes with moderately large scales; the eyes are small and close together, and the head is pointed. See **Apodocreedia**.

Crenicichla Cichlidae
alta see under **C. saxatilis**
saxatilis RING-TAILED PIKE CICHLID
36 cm. (14 in.)
A widely distributed cichlid in S. America which is found in the whole of the Central Amazon basin, from Venezuela to Paraguay and Uruguay. It has been reported from Trinidad but recent work suggests that it is the related *C. alta* that occurs there.

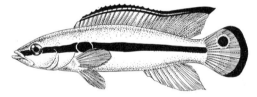

This is a large cichlid, and very distinctive on account of its long body shape. The colour is brown with a black line running from the tip of the snout to the tail; the tail fin has a dark border with a rounded blotch on the upper rays surrounded by a yellowish ring. Males have acutely pointed dorsal and anal fins, females have rounded fins.

Crenimugil Mugilidae
labrosus THICK-LIPPED MULLET
66 cm. (26 in.)
The most common and widespread of European grey mullets, this species is found from the Black Sea, throughout the Mediterranean, and the Atlantic coast as far as Scotland. It is rarely found as far N. as Norway and s. Iceland.

It is a common inshore and estuarine fish which penetrates into rivers and may be found in almost fresh water. It is usually found in small schools which can be seen dimpling the water surface as they cruise in close formation at the surface; at other times they can be seen browsing on rocks, pier pilings, and over the sea bed in a head-down posture. Its food consists mainly of filamentous algae, minute animals living in the muddy bottom, and detritus.

It is fished for commercially in the s. parts of its range and is taken in seine nets and fixed nets from the shore. In British waters its chief value is as a sporting fish – but it is difficult to catch on a hook.

Its most obvious distinguishing feature amongst mullets in the European area is the extremely thickened lips.

Crenuchus Characidae
spilurus SAILFIN CHARACIN 6 cm. (2½ in.)
The sailfin characin originates from the middle region of the Amazon and its tributaries, and w. Guyana. It is slender-bodied, although the well-developed fins give it an appearance of great depth. Its back and upper sides are reddish brown, the belly is yellowish, a faint dark band runs from head to tail with a yellow streak above it, and there is a very distinct dark blotch at the root of the tail. The dorsal and anal fins, and to a lesser extent the tail fin, have a most striking mottling of red-brown and orange colours. The pelvic fins are orange. The male has very high dorsal and anal fins with very long rays; the female has lower fins and is less well coloured.

It is a very decorative fish but seems rather delicate and difficult to keep in the aquarium.

CRESCENT PERCH see **Therapon jarbua**
CRESTED
  BIGSCALE see **Poromitra crassiceps**
  FLOUNDER see **Lophonectes gallus**
  WEEDFISH see **Cristiceps australis**
CRESTFISH see Lophotidae
CREVALLE JACK see **Caranx hippos**
CREVICE KELPFISH see **Gibbonsia montereyensis**
CRIMSON-SPOTTED RAINBOWFISH see **Melanotaenia fluviatilis**

Cristiceps Clinidae
australis CRESTED WEEDFISH
23 cm. (9 in.)
An Australian species which is widely distributed along the coasts of W. Australia, S. Australia, Victoria, New South Wales, and Tasmania. It lives amongst algae and sea grass in intertidal regions down to a depth of 3 m. (10 ft). Locally it is very common.

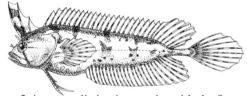

It is a very distinctive species with the first 3 rays of the dorsal fin separate from the remainder and very high. The rest of the dorsal fin is of uniform height except for the last branched rays which form a short lobe.

Its body is light green with broken dark bars, and in some specimens silvery markings. A dark stripe through the eye.

This species gives birth to live young.

CROAKER see Sciaenidae
CROAKER see **Pelates quadrilineatus**
CROAKING GOURAMI see **Trichopsis vittatus**

Crossorhinus Orectolobidae
tentacularis COBBLER CARPET SHARK
1 m. (3¼ ft)
A shallow-water carpet shark of w. and s. Australia. It is brown above, yellowish below with scattered round black spots; the young are

banded. It feeds on small fishes and invertebrates and is harmless to man.

Crossostoma Homalopteridae
The genus *Crossostoma* is a group of small loach-like fishes found in the freshwaters of China and Formosa. They are all slender-bodied with numerous, but often small barbels around the mouth. The pectoral and pelvic fins are broad and project outwards, leaving the belly and underside flat; most of these fish live in running water and are so adapted that they offer least resistance to the water. **145**
C. davidi 9 cm. (3½ in.)
This species has been recorded from Fukin where it was first found by the French missionary-explorer Père A. David. It has subsequently been captured in other regions around Fukin.

CROWNED SOLDIERFISH see **Holocentrus diadema**

Cryptopsarus Ceratiidae
couesi WARTED SEADEVIL 46 cm. (18 in.) female, 5 cm. (2 in.) male
This is the anglerfish which is best represented in oceanographic research collections, and may therefore be one of the most common in the oceans. It has been found in the Atlantic, Indian, and Pacific oceans, and seems to be an inhabitant of moderate depths between 1000–2000 m. (550–1100 fathoms). It was first captured on the Californian coast, in relatively shallow water in Monterey Bay.

Adult females are distinguished by their rather deep, rounded and moderately long bodies, with 3 swollen lumps on the back near the dorsal fin. The mouth is moderate, the illicium is long and slender but the lure at the tip is rounded; the fins are all relatively small.

Males and females are planktonic and free-swimming when larvae, but when mature the male becomes parasitic on the female, its mouth fusing to her skin. They look like dark-coloured, slender outgrowths of the female. Females have dark skin with heavy spiny covering.

CRYSTAL GOBY see **Crystallogobius linearis**

Crystallogobius Gobiidae
linearis CRYSTAL GOBY 5 cm. (2 in.)
The crystal goby is a European species found from the Lofoten Islands, Norway and the Faeroes, s. to Gibraltar, and in the Mediterranean. It differs from the vast majority of gobies in its habitat, for it is a pelagic species found at the surface of the sea, usually on open coasts, and often in depths of 400 m. (220 fathoms). During the breeding season (May to August) the males live close to the bottom and guard the eggs which are deposited in the inside of the tubes of bottom-dwelling worms. All the evidence suggests that these fishes live for at most one year, literally annual fishes.

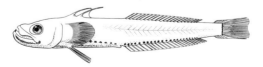

It is distinctive in the sense that it is completely transparent in life, the body is clear and

jelly like, only the dark pupils, the silvery swimbladder, and a line of dark specks along the base of the anal fin being visible. Males are distinguishable from females by having a well developed dorsal fin, and pelvic fins (both absent in females), and 2 large teeth on the lower jaw.

Ctenochaetus Acanthuridae
strigosus BRISTLE-TOOTHED SURGEON FISH, KOLE 28 cm. (11 in.)
Widely distributed in the tropical Indian and Pacific oceans, this surgeonfish has been reported from E. Africa across to Australia, and through the Pacific including the Hawaiian Islands. It is locally common throughout this range, especially around coral reefs in rather calm water. It feeds by grazing over rocks and dead corals picking up fine detritus, diatoms and other small algae. The teeth in this and other *Ctenochaetus* species are well adapted to this feeding regime, being very tiny, elongate and movable.

Its coloration is dull, reddish brown to chocolate-brown with numerous light blue lengthwise lines running from the bases of the dorsal and anal fins. There are small blue spots on the head, and a bright yellow ring around the eye.

CTENOLUCIIDAE
A small family of S. American freshwater fishes, related to one of the major families of fishes in that continent, the characins. The family is distinguished by the elongate body, with both dorsal and anal fins far back and close to the tail. They have pike-like jaws, and a pointed snout, with numerous conical teeth in a single row in the jaws. Some members of the family have a prolonged tip to the snout, others have a flap of skin on the sides of the lower jaw. They are typical predatory inhabitants of the larger rivers. See **Boulengerella, Ctenolucius**.

Ctenolucius Ctenoluciidae
hujeta HUJETA 30 cm. (12 in.)
A widely distributed species in n. S. America, found from the Pacific slope of Panama and Colombia as well as in the Maracaibo and Magdalena river basins in Venezuela. These populations have been divided into subspecies on the basis of the varying number of scales along the body, and coloration.

It is a predatory river-fish, with a long slim body, pointed head and long jaws. Its teeth are numerous, sharp and curved, but in a single series along each jaw. It has several sharp teeth in the roof of the mouth. The front sides of the lower jaw has a large flap of skin. The body is covered with scales, the dorsal and anal fins are placed far back along the body and are almost opposite. It is generally brownish on the back, sometimes with distinct wavy, brown streaks on the body.

Ctenopharyngodon Cyprinidae
idella GRASS CARP, WHITE AMUR
1 m. (39 in.)
The grass carp is native to the lowland rivers of China and the middle and lower reaches of the River Amur. Because of its value as a food fish it has been widely spread by introduction through SE. Asia, and for its qualities of aquatic weed control into e. Europe, the U.S.S.R.,

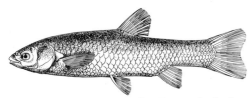

the U.S., and even parts of w. Europe including England. It is a very large fish growing at times to a maximum of 32 kg. (70 lb.). Its body is cylindrical, with a broad head, and a large mouth; it has large scales, and its fins are usually short-based and rounded. In colouring it is light; grey-green on the back shading to silvery on the sides.

In its natural habitat it is essentially a river fish; it spawns in the river, usually in summer when the flow is high. The eggs are pelagic and are carried downstream while they develop and the young fish can be found in quiet meanders and backwaters of the main river. After the larva has absorbed the yolk from the yolksac it feeds on small insect larvae and crustaceans, but at a relatively early age it changes to an herbivorous diet. It eats the larger water weeds in the river, which are crushed in the heavy pharyngeal mill of throat teeth.

It is a valuable commercial species in China and se. Asia not least because it can be fed on green vegetable waste like lawn cuttings, and the waste from green crops. This is directly converted to fish flesh which is available for food, rather than, as with most farmed fish, the conversion taking place through the intermediary agency of invertebrates and smaller fishes. It only grows well in warm temperatures and spawns in running water at temperatures of 27 to 29° C., so in most fish ponds it does not breed.

Considerable use is made of its vegetation-browsing habits in the U.S.S.R. and e. Europe for keeping down unwanted plant growth in reservoirs and canals. In warm waters it appears to be satisfactory, and the fact that it is only likely to breed in a few rivers makes it less damaging to the native fauna of these regions. Experimental stocking has been attempted in some waters in England but it is doubtful if the grass carp is appealing as a vegetation control to the river engineer. In addition, there is a considerable possibility of introducing parasites not native to the fauna with imported stock.

Ctenopoma   Anabantidae
  acutirostre SPOTTED CLIMBING PERCH
15 cm. (6 in.)
Native to the Middle and Upper Congo Basin, this climbing perch is frequently imported to Europe as an aquarium fish and is one of the most satisfactory species for this purpose.

It is very deep-bodied, the head being almost pointed, while the profiles are steep back to the pelvic and dorsal fins. Its background colouring is variable but a black blotch with a yellow or orange margin near the tail base is distinctive. **453**
C. kingsleyae TAIL-SPOT CLIMBING PERCH
20 cm. (8 in.)
An African climbing perch which is widely

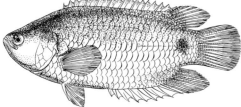

distributed from Senegambia to the Congo Basin. It lives in grassy swamps and forest streams feeding mainly on insects. In N. Nigeria considerable numbers of ripe and spawning fish have been found gathered in a stream where it joined a swamp in August. Locally throughout its range it is used as a food fish, and it is often also caught for the aquarium fish trade.

The scales are large and toothed, giving the body a rough feel. It is greenish brown, with a large dark blotch on the sides close to the tail fin.

This species was first made known to science from specimens collected by Miss Mary Kingsley who made expeditions to the W. African hinterland in the 1890s. It was appropriately named in her honour when formally described.

Ctenotrypauchen   Trypauchenidae
  microcephalus 18 cm. (7 in.)
A curious goby-fish which is widely distributed in the tropical Indo-Pacific. It ranges from s. Africa and the Persian Gulf e. around India and se. Asia to the Philippines. On many occasions it has been found in estuaries but it is also found in fully marine conditions in the sea. It lives in burrows made by itself in muddy or shingle bottoms in water of up to 27 m. (15 fathoms) deep.

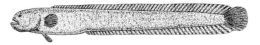

Its body form is quite distinctive, especially the obliquely angled mouth which has sharp teeth. It is pinkish overall.

CUBBYU see **Equetus acuminatus**

Cubiceps   Nomeidae
  gracilis 90 cm. (35 in.)
An open ocean fish of the e. Atlantic and Mediterranean. It is moderately common in the surface waters around the Azores and Madeira and is taken occasionally as far N. as Biscay (and once off Ireland). Closely related species are found in tropical waters in all the major oceans, and future research may show some of them to be identical with the Atlantic species.

Young specimens are often captured at the surface and taken under jellyfishes with which they live in association. Large specimens are free-living mesopelagic fishes which are occasionally captured on long-lines and in drift nets. Adults are a medium brown in colour.

CUCHARON see **Sorubim lima**
CUCHIA see **Monopterus cuchia**
CUCHILLA see **Sternopygus macrurus**
CUCKOO
  RAY see **Raja naevus**
  WRASSE see **Labrus mixtus**
CUI-UI see **Chasmistes cujus**

Culaea   Gasterosteidae
  inconstans BROOK STICKLEBACK
6·5 cm. (2½ in.)
A wholly N. American stickleback, it is found from the E. of the Rocky Mountains to New Brunswick, and from the headstreams of the Mississippi and Missouri river systems, N. to Great Slave Lake. It usually lives in slow streams and shallow lakes, amongst dense vegetation. Except in the breeding season it is found in large shoals, but in spring the males construct nests from plant fragments and fibres gummed together with mucus secreted by the kidneys.

They feed on insect larvae, small crustaceans, ostracods, and molluscs, and occasionally fish eggs. They are valuable forage for larger fishes such as pike and walleye.

Its body form is typical of the sticklebacks, being elongate and spindle-shaped with a short head. There are 5–7 closely set small spines along the mid-line of the back, as well as a small dorsal fin. Adults are dark olive-green above, mottled on the sides, and pale ventrally. In the breeding season males have a jet black belly; the females become light brown with speckles.

CULTUS COD see **Ophiodon elongatus**

Curimata   Curimatidae
  argentea 15 cm. (6 in.)
Members of this genus are widely distributed in S. and Central America; numerous species have been described. This species is found in Venezuela, Colombia, and Trinidad, and can be distinguished from its relatives by the very distinctive oblong, blackish blotch on the side of the tail close in front of the fin and barely extending onto the rays. It also has a dark streak along the base of the dorsal fin. Its colouring is otherwise rather silvery, upper side olive-green, and the sides with a bluish shine. The fins are yellow, but with a pinkish tinge at the base.

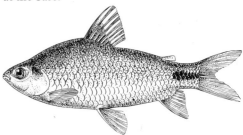

Curimata argentea has a small mouth, no teeth in the jaws or lips, but, as have the other members of the genus, a palate covered with folds of skin and raised papillae. The great part of its diet is vegetation; as might be expected its gut is very long and coiled.

CURIMATIDAE
A family of Central and S. American freshwater fishes related to the characins. According to some authorities the family, as here treated, is a composite of 3 distinct families, Curimatidae, Prochilodontidae, and Chilodontidae. The relationships of these groups are not well known.

Many of the species belonging to this family are popular as aquarium fishes, others important food fish in their native areas. As a group they resemble the characins in having scaly bodies and adipose fins, but they differ in lacking the elaborate dentition of these fishes. See **Chilodus, Curimatopsis, Curimata, Prochilodus, Pseudocurimata, Tylobranchus.**

Curimatopsis   Curimatidae
  saladensis ROSE-COLOURED
CURIMATOPSIS 15 cm. (6 in.)
A deep-bodied characin-like fish, found in S. America in the Rio Salado, at Sante Fe, and possibly the Rio Parana and Rio Paraguay as well. It differs from the characins in having completely toothless jaws, a long tongue, and the roof of the mouth ridged with skin. It possesses an adipose fin, and is covered with large scales although the lateral line is short.

The sexes differ in coloration, the females being duller. The males are greeny brown on the back, the sides silvery green, suffused with red. A dark line runs from head to tail. Fins are bright yellow to red, except for the pectorals.

It is a fairly popular aquarium fish, easy to keep and to breed, given temperatures between 20–30°C., and a well planted aquarium. The eggs hatch in 26–32 hours.

CURIMATOPSIS, ROSE-COLOURED see
  Curimatopsis saladensis
CURIMBATA see **Prochilodus platensis**
CUSK see **Brosme brosme**
CUSK EEL, DUSKY see **Parophidion**
  schmidti
CUSK-EEL see Ophidiidae
CUSK-EEL, SPOTTED see **Otophidium**
  taylori
CUTLASSFISH see Trichiuridae
CUTLASSFISH, ATLANTIC see **Trichiurus**
  lepturus
CUTTER'S CICHLID see **Cichlasoma cutteri**
CUTTHROAT TROUT see **Salmo clarki**
CUTTHROAT TROUT, YELLOWSTONE see
  Salmo clarki

Cyclocheilichthys   Cyprinidae
  apogon INDIAN RIVER BARB 25 cm. (10 in.)
A deep-bodied, rather compressed fish found through India and the Malay Archipelago. Its back is distinctly humped, the head large, and the mouth rather oblique. The dorsal fin is high. It is olive-brown, the sides are silvery with an iridescent sheen, and towards the tail it has a purplish tinge. Several rows of small dark dots on the sides, one to each scale, and a distinct round black blotch behind the gill cover, with another and larger one at the root of the tail. The fins are bright red, as is the iris.

When young it is an excellent aquarium fish – active, very beautifully coloured, and peaceful. It particularly likes well shaded aquariums. It is more or less omnivorous in its diet. In its native area it is a valuable food fish.

CYCLOPTERIDAE
A family of generally deep, heavy-bodied fishes found mainly in cool temperate and polar seas, and in the deep sea. Two main groups are recognizable, the lumpsuckers with 2 separated dorsal fins, although the first may be only a series of spiny plates, and a well developed sucker disc under the belly, and the sea snails, which are generally smaller, have 2 fins united into a single dorsal fin, and have a loose jelly-like skin. The inshore and bottom living sea snails have a sucker disc on the belly, but the bathypelagic species either lack the sucker, or have a very small one. See **Careproctus, Cyclopterus, Eumicrotremus, Liparis, Rhodichthys.**

Cyclopterus   Cyclopteridae
  lumpus LUMPSUCKER, LUMPFISH, SEA HEN 61 cm. (2 ft)
Widely distributed in the n. Atlantic, in the E. from s. England to the Arctic, around Iceland and Greenland, and in the W. along the Newfoundland coast to New Jersey. It is primarily a bottom-living fish, found from low-water mark to depths of 300 m. (164 fathoms) and sometimes more. Its general build, and in particular the powerful sucker disc on the belly, all imply an entirely benthic life, living close to, if not attached to the sea bed, yet many specimens are caught by mid-water nets; also it is fed on extensively by sperm whales around Iceland, which suggests that in n. seas a substantial part of its life is spent in mid-water. It does, however, spawn on the sea bed, often at low tide level on the shore; the large spongy masses of spawn are guarded and continuously aerated by the male. The young are at first pelagic, but later they attach themselves to seaweed, and occasionally floating driftwood and are then widely distributed.

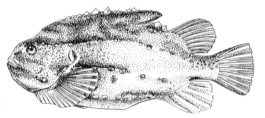

Its food consists of a wide range of invertebrates, amongst them crustaceans and jellyfishes, with occasional fish. It is eaten by sperm whales, seals, and the Greenland shark *Somniosus microcephalus*, and in n. Europe and the U.S.S.R is exploited as a food fish. Its flesh is salted, or more often smoked, and the salted, unfertilized eggs make a form of caviare. **256**

Cyclothone   Gonostomatidae
  braueri 5 cm. (2 in.)
The bristlemouths of the genus *Cyclothone* are worldwide in their distribution, found over deep water in all oceans except the Arctic, although they are found in the Antarctic region. They are all very fragile and consequently their precise identification, and thus the ranges of the individual species are a matter of some doubt. *C. braueri* has been described as living in the Atlantic Ocean and Mediterranean; it may well be cosmopolitan.

This species is whitish in colour, with a dusky patch over the abdominal region and with minute light organs along the belly. It is found from 200–1000 m. (109–546 fathoms), although the centre of its abundance is around 500 m. (273 fathoms). In general the light coloured species of *Cyclothone* live in less deep water than the dark ones, but most migrate vertically each day.

C. braueri is extremely abundant and forms an important forage fish for the larger predators living in the same depths. **42**
C. microdon 6 cm. (2½ in.)
Cyclothone microdon is cosmopolitan in its distribution, and is found in all oceans except for the polar seas. It is a deep-water species found down as deep as 2500 m. (1366 fathoms), and it was probably this species which was observed from a bathyscaphe at 2210 m. (1208 fathoms) in the Mediterranean. On this occasion they were seen within a few metres of the sea floor, so although the species is mainly midwater in habit it may be found down to the sea bed. The Mediterranean population is stunted, attaining sexual maturity at a length of about 2 cm. (¾ in.) and rarely growing longer than 3 cm. (1¼ in.) – it has been regarded as a distinct subspecies, *C. microdon pygmaea*.

C. microdon is uniformly dark, brownish black or jet-black. It is a very fragile fish which is rarely recovered entire. Like other bristlemouths it has extremely long jaws, the upper jaw overlapping the lower, and along the edges are set many sharply pointed and close packed teeth. *C. microdon* has teeth of a more or less uniform size interspaced at regular intervals with a larger fang. All *Cyclothone* species lack adipose fins.

This species is extremely abundant. Although not much is known about its biology it forms the food of many fish and may live in dense shoals in mid-water and near the sea bed. Many thousands have been taken in nets trawled at the appropriate depths. It must make a great contribution to the food chains of the deep sea.
C. pallida 5 cm. (2 in.)
This *Cyclothone* is brownish, with the abdominal region black, and the area in front of the anal fin transparent and colourless. It has been found in the Atlantic Ocean in some numbers, and is probably cosmopolitan in its distribution. In the Bermuda area where Dr William Bube made an intensive study of a column of deep sea, he found this species to be relatively uncommon (505 specimens) when compared with the related *C. microdon* (57,512 specimens). **43**

Cyema   Cyemidae
  atrum BOBTAILED SNIPE-EEL 15 cm. (6 in.)
This small eel is worldwide in its distribution in the deep, tropical oceans. Its general appearance is very distinctive, being dart-like, with long thin beak-like jaws. Its eyes are minute, but evidently functional as they have a wide pupil and perfectly formed lens. At the depths at which it mostly lives, between 1000–3000 m. (546–1640 fathoms), only minimal sunlight will penetrate the upper levels, and, except for the flashes of light from luminescent animals, it is a dark environment. No doubt the eyes of the bobtailed snipe-eel are suited to detect such light.

It is a bathypelagic fish, the adults of which have been captured down to 5100 m. (2787 fathoms). Larvae, which are semi-transparent, deep-bodied and leaf-like leptocephali, live in somewhat less extreme depths. They change to the adult form at a length of about 8 cm. (3 in.). In the e. Pacific spawning is said to take place in spring and early summer, but information is not available from other areas. Much remains to be discovered of the natural history of this eel.

CYEMIDAE

A family of deep-sea eel, containing only one species which is distributed in all the major oceans in tropical and warm temperate regions. It is a very distinctive species with an elongate, thin body, elongate jaws, and dorsal and anal fins beginning halfway along the body and then abruptly ending, almost as if the tail end had been chopped off. Its general shape is that of a dart. See **Cyema**

Cymatoceps   Sparidae
nasutus MUSSELCRACKER, BLACK BISKOP or STEENBRAS 127 cm. (50 in.)
A species endemic to S. Africa and found only from the Cape of Good Hope to Natal, mostly in rocky areas, often in very shallow water; it is not uncommon.

It is one of the famous sea-angler's fishes of S. Africa, taking almost any bait and fighting doggedly. Young specimens make better eating than the large ones whose flesh is rather coarse, although the head muscles are regarded as a delicacy. It attains a weight of 45 kg. (100 lb.).

Distinguished by its dentition, it has strong canine-like teeth in the front of both jaws, 4 in the upper jaw, 4–6 in the lower jaw, and a double series of rounded molars in the sides of the jaws. Large adults develop a fleshy lump on the snout.

Cymatogaster   Embiotocidae
aggregata SHINER PERCH
20 cm. (8 in.)
Native to the e. Pacific, and found from se. Alaska to s. California. It is abundant through most of this range, and in some areas is the dominant fish, both in numbers and in body volume.

In summer it is found in inshore waters in schools, often in harbours and around wharf pilings; in winter it is said to retire to deep water at least in the n. parts of its range. It is viviparous, internal fertilization of the eggs within the female being aided by the modified anal fin rays of the male. The young are born between April and July, broods varying according to the mother's size from 8–36 young.

It is a relatively slender-bodied surf-perch with a long and slender tail. Its coloration is silvery, dusky above, dusky bars running along the sides interspersed with yellow lines, and 3 broken vertical bars on the sides.

Locally it is used for food.

CYNOGLOSSIDAE

The tongue-soles, a family of flatfishes found in tropical seas. Like other flatfishes, as juvenile and adult they rest on one side of the body with both eyes lying close together on the upper side, although they too pass through a larval stage when the eyes are lateral (in the normal position for larval fish). The tongue-soles are especially well adapted to life on the bottom. Their pectoral fins are absent, the pelvic on only one side is developed, and dorsal and anal fins unite with the tail. Some forms have several lateral lines, others have none. The mouth is placed slightly at the side and has a mildly cynical curve about it; the eyes are on the left side of the body.

Many members of the family are important local food fishes, especially in the Indian Ocean where numerous species are found. See **Cynoglossus, Paraplagusia, Symphurus.**

Cynoglossus   Cynoglossidae
joyneri RED TONGUE-SOLE 30 cm. (12 in.)
A Japanese species which is also found to the S. in the w. Pacific. The red tongue-sole is a highly esteemed food fish and large quantities are caught in shore seines. Its flesh is said to be superior to all other soles in the area.

Its body form is similar to other species of tongue-sole, but its colour is distinctive being deep reddish brown with darker edges on the fins. On the blind right side it is white overall.
C. lingua LONG TONGUE-SOLE 43 cm. (17 in.)
Widely distributed in the Indo-Pacific, from the e. coast of Africa to India and Sri Lanka, and thence to the w. Pacific. It is found in coastal waters and estuaries on fine sand and sandy mud, frequently buried with only its eyes showing. It is rarely found deeper than 20 m. (11 fathoms).

This tongue-sole is distinguished by the extreme narrowness of its body. The jaws open on the lower side, and the dorsal fin origin lies right round the snout. It has 2 lateral lines on the left (eyed) side, one on the right; the scales of the eyed side have toothed edges, those on the blind side are smooth. It is greyish or pale brown usually without darker marks except that the region over the gills is dusky.

Exploited locally as a food fish but not especially valued for, despite its length, its extreme thinness reduces the yield of flesh per fish.
C. senegalensis 70 cm. (27½ in.)
A large tongue-sole which is found in the estuaries and in freshwater in the larger rivers of W. Africa. It is very elongate and narrow-bodied, with the mouth set askew on the lower side of the head and the dorsal fin running right round the snout. It has a complex lateral line system around the head with 2 lateral lines running the length of the body. It lives close to, or more usually buried in the muddy bottom; it is sometimes found on sand. It is yellowish brown on the eyed (left) side, white on the blind side.

Its flesh is of excellent quality and it is commercially fished on a small scale, frozen fish even being brought into the London fish-market. It is locally exploited throughout the W. African coastal and riverine regions.

Cynolebias   Cyprinodontidae
belotti PAVITO, ARGENTINE PEARLFISH 8 cm. (3 in.)
Widely distributed in the basin of the La Plata in Argentina; this fish has been much exported for the aquarium trade.

It lives mainly in the ephemeral pools, often small, shallow, and of high temperature, left at the margins of the rivers. Occasionally it is found in running water. It feeds on small crustaceans, aquatic insects and insect larvae.

It is a rather thickset, deep-bodied tooth-carp, with dorsal and anal fins opposite and evenly curved in outline. Males have a dark blue back, paler blue sides, with brilliant pale spots. The fins are brownish or green, the anal with a dark edge. A dark bar runs diagonally through the eye. The female is smaller than the male, yellowish with rows of faint dark bars across the body.

Cynoponticus   Muraenesocidae
ferox COSTA'S CONGER-PIKE 2 m. (6½ ft)
An uncommon inhabitant of the Mediterranean, where it was originally discovered, but now known to be common along the Atlantic coast of W. Africa to the Gulf of Guinea. In this region it is found commonly in depths of 30–70 m. (16–38 fathoms), although its absolute depth range seems to be around 100 m. (55 fathoms), and the largest specimens are always found near this lower limit. It is most common on the continental shelf on sandy or mud and sandy bottoms. The teeth of this eel, in contrast to some of its relatives, are relatively blunt and strong; only a patch near the front of the lower jaw are fang-like, and as might be expected from its dentition, its diet appears to be varied; many small to moderate sized fish are eaten, also crustaceans, and even molluscs.

It is generally grey, with green or brown tints, lighter ventrally and on the sides. The fins are clear, but the pectoral fins are black with a dull grey base.

Cynoscion   Sciaenidae
nobilis WHITE SEABASS 1·8 m. (6 ft)
This large fish is found on the Pacific coast of N. America from Alaska (but not common N. of British Columbia) to Baja California, as well as the n. Gulf of California.

It is distinguished partly by its size, but certainly by the short anal fin and long second dorsal; its mouth is terminal, and it has a low but distinct raised ridge along the mid-line of the belly. Adults are bluish above, silvery white below; young fish have 4–5 dusky bars across the back and sides, all sizes have a black blotch at the base of the pectoral fin.

The white seabass is an important game fish along the Californian coast. It is also landed by commercial fishermen in some quantities mostly caught in gill nets. It is eaten fresh and is of excellent flavour. The seabass grows to 34 kg. (75 lb.) and more.

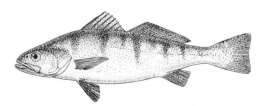

It is found indifferently in shallow water or deep, but the majority of large fish are found in depths of 23–45 m. (13–25 fathoms). The young are typically found in inshore quiet water. It feeds extensively on fishes, especially sardines, anchovies, and small mackerel, as well as on squids.
C. regalis WEAKFISH, SEA TROUT, SQUETEAGUE 1·2 m. (4 ft)
An inhabitant of the e. coast of N. America, the weakfish is found from Florida to Massachusetts, with occasional specimens straying to Nova Scotia. In the N. of this range they are summer migrants, moving in schools along

the inshore waters. During the summer they inhabit shallow water over sandy bottoms, but in winter they move into deeper water of up to 100 m. (55 fathoms).

It is a bottom-feeding fish, eating crabs, shrimps and other small crustaceans, molluscs, and a wide variety of fishes.

It is a popular food fish where it is abundant, although to the N. of its range it is too variable in quantity to be commercially important. It is also a good sporting fish and numbers are caught from the shore by anglers. It reaches a weight of 5·4 kg. (12 lb.) commonly, but specimens of 13·6 kg. (30 lb.) have been reported.

Distinguishing characteristics are size, the lack of barbel on the chin, its slender body and pointed head. It is dark olive-green on the back, silvery on the sides but with a bronzy sheen, and faint darker oblique lines.

CYPRINIDAE

This family belongs to the dominant group of freshwater fishes, the Cypriniformes. It is widely distributed, its members being found in N. and Central America, Europe, Asia, and Africa. The only regions in which they do not naturally occur are Madagascar, Australia, New Zealand, and S. America, to most of which areas they have been introduced by man!

Members of the family have toothless jaws but possess a grinding mill of pharyngeal teeth, characteristic to each species, set on the pharyngeal bones behind the gill chamber. These teeth crush the food taken. The cyprinid fishes have a bony linkage between the double-chambered swim-bladder and the inner ear, which gives them very sensitive hearing. Some cyprinids make sounds, others may use their enhanced hearing to avoid predators or to keep in touch with shoals of their own kind.

Considerable variation in body form exists, but most cyprinids conform to a familiar 'fish shape' with scales, lacking an adipose fin, and with a single dorsal fin. Spines are not usually present in their fins except that some species have a spine fronting the pectoral, dorsal, and anal fins. Many members of the family have barbels round the mouth, forming highly sensitive organs. See **Abramis, Alburnus, Aspius, Barbus, Barilius, Blicca, Brachydanio, Caecobarbus, Campostoma, Carassius, Catlocarpio, Chalcalburnus, Chela, Chondrostoma, Clinostomus, Ctenopharyngodon, Cyclocheilichthys, Cyprinus, Danio, Elopichthys, Engraulicypris, Epalzeorhynchus, Esomus, Garra, Gobio, Hemibarbus, Hypophthalmichthys, Labeo, Leucaspius, Leptobarbus, Leuciscus, Morulius, Mylocheilus, Mylopharyngodon, Notropis, Oreodaimon, Osteocheilus, Oxygaster, Pelecus, Phoxinus, Pimephales, Ptychocheilus, Puntius** (see **Barbus**), **Rasbora, Rasborichthys, Rhinichthys, Rhodeus, Richardsonius, Rutilus, Scardinius, Schizothorax, Semotilus, Tanichthys, Tinca, Vimba.**

Cyprinodon   Cyprinodontidae
milleri 4·4 cm. (1¾ in.)
A recently described pupfish from the arid Death Valley system of e. California and sw. Nevada; it was named in 1973 in honour of the distinguished American ichthyologist Dr R. R. Miller who has made a special study of the cyprinodonts in that region.

It lives in a relatively restricted area, Cottonball Marsh, in Death Valley, in what is said 'may be the most extreme fish habitat in North America in terms of temperature and salinity'. The lakes lie 80 m. (260 ft) below mean sea level, and in summer they dry to isolated shallow pools with salt depositing out around the fringes. This fish has been kept in water containing 78 p.p.m. salt (normal sea water is around 35 p.p.m.).

It is closely related to another species living in salt pools, *C. salinus*, but differs in having larger, 3-cusped jaw teeth, a shorter dorsal fin, and differences in head pores. Both may have evolved from a common, more widespread ancestor in at most a few thousand years.
C. salinus see under **C. milleri**
C. variegatus SHEEPSHEAD MINNOW
7·5 cm. (3 in.)
Found on the e. coast of the U.S. from Cape Cod to Texas, and Mexico, in brackish as well as salt water. Like the mummichog (*Fundulus heteroclitus*) it is found in shallow bays, inlets, and harbours, often in brackish water on salt marshes.

It breeds during the summer months, the males fighting furiously with one another, and chasing the females. Spawning takes place with the male clasping his dorsal and anal fins around the tail of the female while eggs and milt are extruded. The eggs sink in a mass to the bottom to which they adhere by means of long threads.

This fish is strikingly deep-bodied, and 'chubby' in appearance. The back is arched high, and the rounded dorsal fin at its highest point adds to its appearance. The tail is square cut. Most of the year both males and females are olive-green above with yellowish bellies. In the breeding season the male becomes brightly coloured, steel blue above, greenish on the back, and salmon red on the belly, while the fins are orange.

Has been kept in aquariums most successfully, and will spawn if given slightly saline cool water.

CYPRINODONTIDAE

A very large family of small, mainly freshwater fishes found in tropical and warm-temperate regions throughout the world except for the Australian region. They are often known by the catch-all name toothcarps, which indicates both their resemblance to the carp fishes and their main difference from them, the possession of fine teeth along the edges of the jaws and lack of a Weberian apparatus. Also known as top-minnows.

Members of the family have a rather flattened head, with a wide, terminal mouth, opening rather obliquely and being protrusible. The dorsal fin is usually set around the mid-point of the back. They do not have an adipose fin, or lateral line organs. Their bodies are almost always fully scaled, the scales being mostly large and cycloid.

As a group they are adaptable little fishes, able to tolerate extremes of heat, salinity, and drought which would be fatal to most other groups of fishes. One group, the rivulins, contains several so-called 'annual fishes' which live in pools in flood plains of rivers formed during the rainy season. The pools dry out in the dry season and the adults die, but not before they have buried fertilized eggs in the

mud bottom of the pool. These hatch out with the first rains and start a new generation.

Many of the egg-laying toothcarps are popular aquarium fishes. Most of them are brightly coloured, and show considerable sexual dimorphism, the males usually being larger and more brightly coloured than the females. See **Adinia, Aphanius, Aphyosemion, Aplocheilus, Aplocheilichthys, Cynolebias, Cyprinodon, Epiplatys, Fundulus, Jordanella, Lucania, Nothobranchius, Pachypanchax, Pterolebias, Rivulus, Roloffia, Valencia.**

Cyprinus   Cyprinidae
carpio CARP 1 m. (39 in.)
The carp is one of the most widely distributed cyprinid fishes largely due to man's capacity for interfering with nature. It is found across Europe, N. America, S. America, parts of Asia, Africa, Australia, and New Zealand. Its original home was in the rivers of the Black Sea and Aegean basins, notably the Danube. Its importance as a food fish to man has led to its wholesale introduction, although latterly redistribution has often been carried on to 'improve' sport fishing in parts of the world. Some of this redistribution took place very early on (for man has for years eaten carp), and studies of fish bones from early sites in Greece and Romania has revealed carp bones in quantity.

It is a deep-bodied fish, in its wild state fully scaled, although by controlled breeding artificial varieties have been produced such as mirror carp – with rows of few large scales, or leather carp – which lack scales completely. The mouth is large, protrusible and with 4 barbels (2 each side on the upper lip and the corners of the mouth). Its dorsal fin is long, and in front has a strong serrated spine.

Carp live best in pools and lakes, quiet backwaters of lowland rivers, and occasionally in slow-flowing rivers. They prefer warm conditions and densely weedy waters. They are very resistant to low oxygen levels and can survive where other fishes would die. Their diet is catholic: when young they eat minute bottom-living crustaceans and insect larvae; as larger fish they forage in search of molluscs, insect larvae, and larger crustaceans and, in summer especially, they eat a considerable amount of aquatic vegetation.

They breed in summer at temperatures around 23–24°C. Their eggs are shed on vegetation in shallow water, often with much splashing and rolling on the part of the adults. The small yellowish eggs hatch in 5–8 days at 23–24°C. The breeding success of carp in some of the cooler areas to which they have been introduced, such as the British Isles, is often poor; in many years the young do not survive. Carp are relatively long-lived – in the wild they may attain an age of 20 years, and in captivity up to 40–50 years, but reports of aged carp of a century or more are not substantiated by fact.

It is a valuable food fish in many parts of the world, its quick growth, large size, and ability to tolerate high temperatures contribute to making it an ideal species for farming. Carp farming is an important industry, and a valuable source of food in many countries, especially in e. Europe and Israel. Elsewhere it is often highly regarded as an anglers' fish.
123

Cypselurus   Exocoetidae
    heterurus ATLANTIC FLYINGFISH
43 cm. (17 in.)
Known from a wide area of the tropical and warm temperate Atlantic Ocean, and the Mediterranean Sea. In the w. Atlantic it has occurred from s. Canada to se. Brazil including the Gulf of Mexico; in the E. it is found from the Danish coast S. to Angola. The extremes of this range are only inhabited seasonally by a few fishes.

It is a well distinguished species with large pectoral and pelvic fins, both of which are dark, marked with a triangular bar across the edge of the fin. The dorsal fin is low and unpigmented. In other respects it is a typical flying fish with large eyes, fully scaled body, dorsal and anal fins far back near the tail, the lower lobe of which is the longer.

This species, like most flyingfishes, lays large spherical eggs with long adhesive filaments by which they become attached to clumps of floating seaweed or other flotsam. The young have a pair of short barbels on the chin. In tropical seas the young may be found close inshore; the adults also frequently occur in coastal waters, and seem to be confined to the coastal belt of some 640 km. (400 miles) of sea.

Cyttus   Zeidae
    australis SILVER DORY 41 cm. (16 in.)
The commonest member of the family in S. Australian waters, it is widespread in the cooler waters of that continent, being found from New South Wales to Tasmania and W. Australia. It is excellent eating but is not regularly fished for.

In life it is silvery with a metallic lustre and light reddish fins. In body form it is much like other members of the family with a relatively deep body; the mouth is moderate and greatly extensible. The body is covered with small scales.

D

DAB see **Limanda limanda**
DAB,
    LONG ROUGH see **Hippoglossoides**
        platessoides
    RUSTY see **Limanda ferruginea**
DACE see **Leuciscus leuciscus**
DACE,
    LONGNOSE see **Rhinichthys cataractae**
    NORTHERN REDBELLY see **Phoxinus eos**
    PEARL see **Semotilus margarita**
    REDSIDE see **Clinostomus elongatus**

Dactylobatus   Rajidae
    armatus 32 cm. (12½ in.)
A little known, bizarre species of ray which is found only on the w. Atlantic coast of N. America, off S. Carolina, Georgia, and Florida. The only recorded specimens have been captured in moderate depths of between 340–500 m. (185–273 fathoms), presumably the depth and the small size of this ray making it rather difficult to capture. The first catches were by the 'Albatross' Expedition in 1885 and 1886 but were not described until 1909. Nothing is known of its life history.

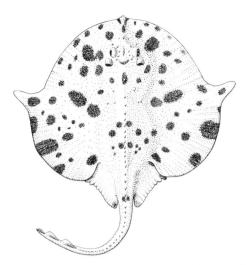

This is the only known ray in which several median rays of the pectoral fin are elongated to form a narrow lobe each side of the disc. Colour dorsally ashy grey with sooty spots and blotches; ventrally yellowish white.

DACTYLOPTERIDAE
A family of marine fishes, the flying gurnards, which bears some resemblance to the sea robins. They differ from them, however, in the arrangement of the head bones, by having a single or double spine placed well forward on the back just behind the head, and by the enormous enlargement of the pectoral fins. The head is covered with hard bone. Although related to the sea robins (Triglidae) the relationship is not thought to be particularly close.

They are tropical in habit, although a few species are found in warm temperate zones. Their ability to fly is to be questioned. See **Dactylopterus, Daicocus.**

Dactylopterus   Dactylopteridae
    volitans FLYING GURNARD 32 cm. (12½ in.)
Found on both sides of the Atlantic in warm temperate and tropical areas. In the w. Atlantic it ranges from Bermuda and Massachusetts to Argentina as well as throughout the Caribbean, while in the Atlantic it is found from Portugal s. to W. Africa and in the Mediterranean.

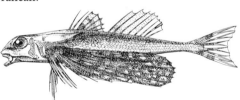

It is essentially a bottom-living fish found in relatively shallow water on sandy bottoms. Adults have been seen 'walking' along the sea bed on the pelvic fins, stirring up the sand with the short anterior pectoral rays as if searching for food. Its food appears to be composed almost entirely of bottom-living crustaceans and occasional fishes.

When alarmed, this fish spreads its huge pectoral fins, displaying a startling array of brilliant blue spots on the reddish background. To the observer not knowing what to expect, this flash of colour and the apparent increase in width of the fish is usually quite sufficient warning not to touch. Despite the heavily armoured head, with long spines on the operculum, the flying gurnard is quite harmless.

Although the young fish is often attracted to the surface by lights at night, there is no evidence that the adults ever leave the water and 'fly' or glide in spite of its name and the many accounts of its aerial ability.

Dactylosargus   Aplodactylidae
    arctidens SEA CARP 44 cm. (17¼ in.)
A fish which is widely distributed on the coasts of W. Australia, S. Australia, Victoria, and Tasmania. It is relatively rarely found and its biology is little known. It is known, however, that it feeds almost exclusively on algae.

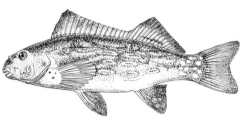

It is dark green above, lighter on the sides; 4 dark blotches on the back and light mottling on the lower sides and tail.

DACTYLOSCOPIDAE
The sand stargazers, a family of marine fishes related to the stargazers (Uranoscopidae), similar to the latter in many respects but generally more slender and smaller; they also have only 3 segmented rays in the pelvic fins.

The sand stargazers spend most of the lives buried in sand with just the eyes and the top of the head showing. They are carnivorous. Some species are known to guard their eggs by the male carrying them in 2 balls, one under the axilla of each pectoral fin.

The group is confined to the shallow warm waters of the New World. One species is found off Chile. See **Dactyloscopus, Gillellus, Myxodagnus.**

Dactyloscopus   Dactyloscopidae
    tridigitatus SAND STARGAZER
10 cm. (4 in.)
Known from Bermuda, the Bahamas and Florida, s. through the Gulf of Mexico and Caribbean, to Brazil. It is the most common member of the family in the W. Indies. It lives buried in bare, exposed sandy beaches from the surge zone around 3 m. (1½ fathoms) down to 15 m. (8 fathoms). This species has been observed to carry its eggs in a small ball tucked behind each pectoral fin.

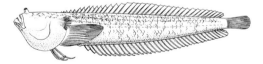

Its colouring is obliterative and almost an exact match for the sand in which it lives. The sides and belly are whitish. It is most immediately distinguished by its protuberant eyes, themselves very small, but placed on a stalk so that vision is unimpaired and all round even when the fish is buried.

DAGGERTOOTH see **Anotopterus pharao**

Daicocus   Dactylopteridae
    peterseni FLYING GURNARD 30 cm. (12 in.)
This striking looking fish is widely distributed

in the Indo-Pacific, although it was for long only known in the area of Japan. In Japanese waters it is common, and is employed as a food fish.

The head is covered with heavy bone, and is almost quadrangular in cross-section, as is the body which is covered with keeled scales. There is a long filament-like spine on the nape of the neck, while the pectoral fin-rays are enormously developed into lateral fans. The body is reddish above, white beneath, while the pectorals are pale brown with darker brown spots on them.

Dalatias   Dalatiidae
licha DARKIE CHARLIE 1·8 m. (6 ft)
This deep water shark is found along the lower continental slope in the e. N. Atlantic from Scottish waters s. to the Canary Islands, as well as in the Mediterranean. It is most common in depths of 350–650 m. (191–355 fathoms) although occasionally found down to 900 m. (492 fathoms). It is a live-bearing shark, the young being born at a length of about 30 cm. (12 in.). Litters of between 10–16 pups have been reported.

It is a dark brown with a black-tipped tail fin; the lips and spiracle are conspicuously white. The rather stout, rounded body has broad but not very large fins; it lacks an anal fin. Its teeth are sharply pointed, triangular in the lower jaw, dagger-shaped in the upper jaw. They meet in a very effective bite, and are capable of biting large chunks out of the backs of large fishes like hake and blue whiting. Smaller fishes and squids are eaten entire.

It is relatively common to the W. of the British Isles and is often caught by deep fishing trawlers. It is not, however, of any fisheries value.

DALATIIDAE
A small family of sharks mostly found in the open sea and in deep water. All are rather stout-bodied and have relatively small fins; they lack an anal fin, and have no spines before the dorsal fins, in contrast with the related family Squalidae which have spines but lack anal fins. Members of the family are worldwide in distribution. This family includes the smallest known sharks. See **Dalatias, Euprotomicrus, Isistius, Somniosus, Squaliolus.**

Dallia   Umbridae
pectoralis ALASKA BLACKFISH
20 cm. (8 in.)
The Alaska blackfish is a small fish well distributed in coastal regions of Alaska, and in rivers running to the Arctic coast, as on the Chukotsk Peninsula, Siberia. It is found in

weed-choked lowland brooks, lakes and marshes and is most common in the tundra regions although it can be found in forest pools. It is not an active species for it stalks its prey slowly by sculling movements of its pectoral fins before making a sudden dart forwards. Its food consists of insect larvae, small crustaceans, and snails.

Virtually nothing is known about the spawning behaviour. They are believed to spawn in July amongst dense vegetation; the eggs are adhesive, but no observations have been made in the wild.

The ability of this fish to withstand the Arctic winter is well known. They can survive the almost zero oxygen levels beneath the ice and snow, and are frequently reported as surviving being frozen into the ice. Such freezing is not necessarily lethal, provided the body fluids are not frozen. They are not often used for food although at one time they were apparently exploited for human and dog food.

Its scales are small, and it is dark brown above with 4–6 dark bars along the sides; ventrally it is pale.

DAMSELFISH see Pomacentridae
DAMSELFISH see **Chromis chromis**
DAMSELFISH,
    BLUE AND GOLD see **Abudefduf melanopus**
    THREE-SPOT see **Eupomacentrus planifrons**
    YELLOW see **Eupomacentrus planifrons**
    YELLOWTAIL see **Microspathodon chrysurus**

Danio   Cyprinidae
devario 10 cm. (4 in.)
Found in the nw. areas of India in the N. W. Provinces, Orissa, Bengal, and Assam. It is a rather deep-bodied member of the genus with a strongly convex ventral profile, long-based dorsal and anal fins, and a relatively large mouth.

Occasionally kept in the aquarium; it is not strikingly coloured. **124**
D. malabaricus GIANT DANIO 13 cm. (5 in.)
The great danio is found in freshwater on the W. coast of India, and from Sri Lanka. It lives in clean, swiftly flowing streams, ponds, and tanks. It is a moderately deep-bodied fish, the ventral profile being distinctly convex; the head is pointed with a terminal mouth on which there are 2 pairs of barbels, only the front ones of which are well developed. The lateral line is complete.

Beautifully and strikingly coloured. The sexes can be distinguished by the slimness of the male; the female has the golden side stripes more broken than in the male, and the middle blue stripe turns upwards at the tail fin.

The giant danio is a popular aquarium fish, peaceful and easy to keep. **125**

DANIO,
    GIANT see **Danio malabaricus**
    PEARL see **Brachydanio albolineatus**
    SPOTTED see **Brachydanio nigrofasciatus**
    ZEBRA see **Brachydanio rerio**
DANUBE BLEAK see **Chalcalburnus chalcoides**
DARA see **Polynemus indicus**
DARKIE CHARLIE see **Dalatias licha**
DART see **Trachinotus russelli**
DARTER,
    IOWA see **Etheostoma exile**
    ORANGE-THROATED see **Etheostoma spectabile**
    RAINBOW see under **Etheostoma spectabile**

DARTER CHARACIN see **Characidium fasciatum**
DARTFISH see **Myxodagnus belone**
DARWIN'S ROUGHY see **Gephyroberyx darwini**

Dascyllus   Pomacentridae
aruanus BANDED HUMBUG 9 cm. (3½ in.)
An Indo-Pacific species found from the Red Sea and E. African coast across to Australia and the central Pacific islands. It is very widely distributed in all areas where coral growths occur and may be seen in shoals numbering hundreds around coral heads. Its depth range extends to about 15 m. (8 fathoms), and is limited by the extent of the *Stylophora* coral colonies with which it associates.

It is essentially a territorial animal, while the shoal occupies a coral head, each fish, especially the males, has its own territory on the head and recognizes its neighbours' boundaries. In spawning, the eggs of one female are shed in patches on branches of the coral but they may overlap neighbouring territories. The males guard the eggs until they hatch. **389**

DASYATIDAE
The long-tailed stingrays are in general distinguished by their rather rectangular body shape, by their long, whip-like tails, and by the absence of both dorsal and tail fins. These rays have a long dagger-like spine on the anterior end of the tail, sometimes supplemented by 1–2 replacement spines in close proximity. These spines have serrated edges, and the grooves running their length on the lower side are filled with venom-secreting tissue. Although the spine cannot be moved by itself, the tail of these rays is so mobile that they can be lashed around sometimes powerfully enough to drive the spines through the planking of a small boat. The wounds caused can be very dangerous – death has resulted in men stabbed by the spines – and are always excruciatingly painful. Fatalities are frequent amongst victims who stand on the ray, which thrusts its spine upwards over its back with frightening rapidity and accuracy.

The dasyatids are primarily warm-water rays, found in shallow tropical seas, although they penetrate into temperate waters with seasonal warming of the sea. All are bottom-living, usually seen lightly buried in sand or mud, although they can swim well and powerfully on occasions.

Their economic value is slight. Some species are eaten, or at least the fleshy pectoral fins are; locally, oil is extracted from their livers. Some aboriginal natives in the Indo-Pacific used their tail spines as weapons, either as spear tips or daggers. On the other hand, where they are common, stingrays do tremendous damage to cultivated shellfish beds, their flattened teeth being well suited for crushing tough shelled molluscs, as well as the larger crustaceans. See **Dasyatis, Taeniura.**

Dasyatis   Dasyatidae
americana SOUTHERN STINGRAY
1·5 m. (5 ft) wide
The southern stingray is found in coastal waters of the American Atlantic and Caribbean, from Rio de Janeiro, Brazil, n. to New Jersey. In much of its range and especially in the Caribbean it is the most common stingray.

Its disc is quadrangular, the front edges being straight and the snout blunt. The eyes and spiracles are large and placed close to one another. There is a row of bony tubercles along the back; the tail lacks these but has a long, sharp, toothed spine near its base. The back is a dark greeny brown but the colour varies with the colour of the bottom on which it is lying; its lower surface is white.

The stingray is ovoviviparous; broods of 3–5 young have been recorded. They are about 18 cm. (7 in.) broad at birth. It feeds on a variety of crustaceans, molluscs, worms, and fishes. Always found in shallow water, usually buried in sand, in n. waters this stingray is found mainly in the summer months having evidently migrated n. as the water warms.

Because of its abundance, its habit of living in shallow water, and its size, the southern stingray must be regarded as a dangerous fish for its venom supplied spine can inflict very severe wounds. **9**

D. brevicaudata STINGRAY 4·3 m. (14 ft) long
This stingray is recognized by its rather pointed snout tip, its disc being wider than long, and by its relatively long tail which is about 1½ times the body length. Its tail tip is roughened, and the tail spines are sited about a third of the way along its length. It is dull grey to purplish brown above, white below.

It is widespread in the Indo-Pacific from s. Africa to Australia and New Zealand. In shallow sandy areas, and in the vicinity of reefs, it may be very common, and it has been known to enter estuaries.

This is the largest known stingray, and on account of its size the most dreaded by fishermen. It grows to 4·3 m. (14 ft) long and 1·8–2·1 m. (6–7 ft) wide, specimens this size having been estimated to weigh 340 kg. (750 lb.). The tail spine of a specimen of this size measures in excess of 41 cm. (16 in.) and is a dangerous weapon at close quarters. Human fatalities attributed to this species have been recorded in Australia.

D. pastinaca STINGRAY 2·6 m. (8½ ft) long
The stingray is found in European inshore waters from n. Scotland to Madeira and throughout the Mediterranean. In the n. parts of this range, as round the British Isles, it is found mostly in late summer and autumn, evidently the result of a n. migration.

Found in shallow water, it is especially common over sand, shingle, or mud bottoms. It feeds on bottom-living organisms, mostly

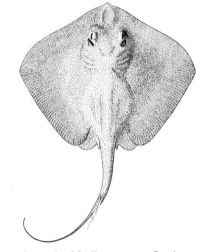

molluscs and crabs, but it eats some fish species. Like its relatives, its young are born fully formed having been nourished by secretions from the uterine wall before birth.

It has one, sometimes 2, long serrated spines near the base of the tail.

Datnoides Lobotidae
quadrifasciatus 30 cm. (12 in.)
Widely distributed in the lower reaches of rivers and coastal lakes between the Ganges, Burma, Thailand, Malaya, and the Indo-Australian archipelago. Although mostly found in freshwater, it also is taken in estuarine conditions.

It spawns in freshwater in the autumn when the adults move into still water. It is a valuable food fish throughout its range.

The body is deep and rather compressed, the head pointed with a large, terminal mouth. The dorsal fin is continuous, the anterior portion composed of sharp strong spines. The young have 8–10 dark crossbands, some of which are incomplete, and some of which merge with age. A dusky patch on the gill cover.

Some authors believe that this species may belong to the family Nandidae.

DAWN TETRA see **Hyphessobrycon eos**
DEALFISH see Veliferidae
DEALFISH see **Trachipterus arcticus**

Deania Squalidae
calceus see under **D. quadrispinosa**
quadrispinosa LONG-SNOUTED DOGFISH 1·2 m. (4 ft)
This deep-water shark is found off the s. coasts of Australia, and probably New Zealand. It has been trawled in depths of 155–550 m. (85–300 fathoms).

Its most obvious feature is the very long, flattened snout. It is dull grey above, lighter below.

Very little is known about the biology of this group of sharks for they are rarely captured. It is possible that this species is identical with *D. calceus,* of the e. N. Atlantic (s. Iceland to the Mediterranean). The latter species gives birth to living young.

DECORATED WARBONNET see **Chirolophis polyactocephalus**
DEEP
ANGELFISH see **Pterophyllum altum**
DRAGONFISH see **Bathydraco scotiae, Prionodraco evansii**
DEEP-PITTED POACHER see **Bothragonus swanii**
DEEP-SEA
EEL, KAUP'S see **Synaphobranchus kaupi**
ELECTRIC RAY see **Benthobatis marcida**
FLATHEAD see **Rhinhoplichthys haswelli**
LIZARDFISH see **Bathysaurus mollis**
TREVALLE see **Hyperoglyphe antarctica**

Delolepis Stichaeidae
gigantea GIANT WRYMOUTH 117 cm. (46 in.)
A N. Pacific species which occurs from n. California, to Unalaska Island, and the Bering

Sea. It has been taken offshore on the coasts of Oregon, Washington, and British Columbia, usually between 33–128 m. (18–70 fathoms). It seems possible that at some stage of its life history it lies buried in the sea bed. Its biology is little-known.

It is distinguished by the adult's size (this is the largest member of the family), by lacking pelvic fins, by the large projecting lower jaw, and scales on the posterior part of the body only. It is pale brown, tinged with yellow and violet, lighter below.

Dendrochirus Scorpaenidae
brachypterus SCORPIONFISH 18 cm. (7 in.)
An Indo-Pacific species which is found from the Red Sea, Zanzibar, and E. Africa to the Philippines, Samoa and Hawaii.

It is superficially similar to the firefishes *(Pterois)* but lacks their very bold colouring. The dorsal fin spines are long but not extremely so and are free of the membrane at their tips. The pectoral fin is entire, each ray sheathed in membrane to the tip, but this fin is short and does not reach as far back as the tail fin. Body scales are large, about 45 in a row.

Like its relatives this fish has venom producing tissue on the spines of the dorsal fin; wounds can be very painful. **241**

D. zebra ZEBRA FIREFISH, SCORPIONFISH 20 cm. (8 in.)
A beautiful but dangerous inhabitant of the Indo-Pacific. It is found from the E. African coast, India to Australia, Fiji, and the Hawaiian Islands.

The members of this genus resemble the firefishes of the genus *Pterois,* but the pectoral fin is shorter and does not reach the tail fin, the fin membrane is divided only at the tips but the rays are not otherwise free. The dorsal fin spines are comparatively short, free from the membrane, and are venom laden; wounds from them are intensely painful.

It frequents reef areas in shallow inshore waters including estuaries. **242**

Dentex Sparidae
dentex DENTEX 1 m. (39 in.)
A seabream of s. Europe, found from Senegal and the Canary Islands to Biscay, rarely venturing to British waters, and throughout the Mediterranean. It is a rather deep-water fish, the adults found from 30–200 m. (16–110 fathoms), although the young can be found in shallower water. It usually occurs over rocky ground and feeds on squids and fishes. It is a valued food fish but is never abundant enough to be regularly fished for.

Its most noticeable feature are the 4–6 large canine-like teeth in the front of the jaw. Males have a huge fleshy bump over the forehead. Large specimens are a uniform dull red, slightly lighter ventrally.

D. rupestris see **Petrus rupestris**

Denticeps Denticipitidae
clupeoides 5 cm. (2 in.)
Found only in medium sized alkaline streams of several river systems in sw. Nigeria, this little fish lives in shoals in mid-stream where the current is at its strongest. This, and its small size, are presumably the reason it escaped notice until 1959 when it was first described, for the rivers of w. Africa had been fairly well explored.

It is believed to spawn in September, which is when sexually ripe specimens have been caught, and the young are taken in November.

In life it is silvery, white on the belly and yellowish green above, with a faint golden stripe along the sides overlying a narrow, but distinct dark line. This line ends as a diamond-shaped spot near the tailfin. The fins are colourless, except for a fine black line at the base of the anal fin.

At first sight *Denticeps* is an unremarkable looking fish, but close examination of its head and anterior body shows them to be covered in small teeth. This is a very rare feature in the fish world.

DENTICIPITIDAE

A small, relatively recently discovered family of small herring-like fishes found in freshwater in w. Africa. Its only known member is remarkable in that its head, parts of its pectoral girdle, and the anterior lateral line scales possess a covering of small tooth-like denticles, dense in places. The lateral line system is extended by several major sensory canals across the gill covers. Most of its other features suggest the close affinity these fish have with the clupeoid fishes.

The family was first described from specimens found in rivers in sw. Nigeria. This account was published in 1959, almost contemporaneously with the discovery of fossil remains of the same family in Tanganyika. The fossil fish were so similar that they were considered to be no more than generically distinct, and they were described as *Palaeodenticeps tanganikae*. See **Denticeps**.

DERICHTHYIDAE

A small family of slender-bodied eels found in tropical seas, some in deep water but others in moderately shallow seas. They are scaleless eels with a distinct lateral line and large eyes. See **Derichthys**.

Derichthys   Derichthyidae
A genus of eels found in tropical and warm temperate seas. The species illustrated in colour has not been identified. **26**
D. serpentinus NECK EEL 26 cm. (10¼ in.)
An easily distinguished small, mid-water eel found in tropical and warm temperate seas throughout the world. Its most immediate feature is the constriction behind the head which gives it a neck-like appearance, but there are also very distinct large pores on the head and anterior body.

It does not seem to be abundant, and relatively few adult specimens have been caught. This is to some extent due to the difficulty of catching a small, slender, active fish which lives in deep water, between 457–1829 m. (250–1000 fathoms). It is a tawny-olive to mouse grey in colour, with a bluish sheen on the neck. It appears to feed on crustaceans.

Dermogenys   Exocoetidae
pusillus 7 cm. (2¾ in.)
This most striking small fish is widely distributed in Thailand, the Malaya Peninsula, Singapore, the Sunda Islands. It is found in fresh water, and in slightly saline water, where it is said to occur in vast numbers.

It is an attractive fish, slender bodied with a broad rounded tail, and dorsal and anal fins placed far back. It is a typical halfbeak in appearance, the lower jaw being twice as long as the upper. Its colour is variable, but males have a bright red blotch on the dorsal fin, and also the front part of the anal fin elongate and modified as an intromittent organ.

This species gives birth to living young. Mating occurs after some display and nudging by the male; the fertilized eggs take some 8 weeks to hatch. Brood sizes of 12–20 young, each about 1 cm. (½ in.) long, are usual.

The males are extremely quarrelsome and engage one another in protracted battles, wrestling with locked jaws until exhaustion renders the weaker incapable of further resistance. In Thailand the males are kept captive in earthenware jars, and carefully bred to ensure increased pugnacity, for they are matched at exhibition contests. Rarely do they severely injure one another, but the contest may go on for as long as 20 minutes until one retires.

The species is too small to be used for food, but it is a valuable controller of mosquito larvae which are its main diet. **192**

Desmodema   Trachipteridae
polystictum POLKA-DOT RIBBONFISH
1 m. (39 in.)
Distributed worldwide in tropical and warm temperate seas, but apparently nowhere common, and little known.

It is a long, thin ribbonfish with a high, curved back, and a very long rat-like tail. The long dorsal fin runs from the head to the tail tip, and the rays are longer and the fin deeper than the body. Its body is silvery, but the fins are crimson in life, except for the rear end of the dorsal which is dusky.

It lives in depths of 152–304 m. (83–167 fathoms) mainly, feeding on a variety of small fishes, squids, and crustaceans. The juveniles are moderately frequently found in the gut of larger predatory fishes. Some of the known specimens have been secured in this way, others have been found stranded, but most have been captured in deep fishing nets, either of commercial fishermen or of research vessels.

DEVIL RAY see Mobulidae
DEVIL RAY see **Mobula mobular**
DEVIL RAY,
   GIANT see **Manta birostris**
   PYGMY see **Mobula diabolus**
DEVILFISH see **Synanceia verrucosa**

Diademichthys   Gobiesocidae
lineatus 5 cm. (2 in.)
A fascinating small clingfish, which is quite different physically and in behaviour from the other species. It is very long and slender, and hardly compressed at all; the snout is long, longer in the female than in the male. Coloration is black with bright white lines, one running along the back, sides, and belly respectively.

This striking colouring and body shape are an adaptation to life in association with the long-spined, hat-pin sea urchin, *Diadema savignyi*, which has slender black spines. The clingfish lives between the spines, hovering head downwards. It clearly is well protected in this habitat, but also derives some food from the sea urchin shearing off and eating the tiny tube-feet of its host.

It is widely distributed in the Indo-Pacific, from New Caledonia to Mauritius, n. to the Java Sea and the Philippine Islands.

DIAMOND KILLIFISH see **Adinia xenica**
DIAMONDFISH see **Monodactylus argenteus**

Dianema   Callichthyidae
longibarbis 8 cm. (3 in.)
A very flat-headed catfish related to the genus *Corydoras*, but unlike them having a pair of extremely long barbels from the corner of the mouth reaching to beyond the pectoral fin. It has additionally 4 pairs of shorter barbels from the lower lip.

This species is found in the Amazon basin. It is apparently widely distributed and occurs in the Rio Ampiyacu, Peru, as well as the Rio Xingu, and other tributaries.

The tail fin is forked but is not marked with lengthwise black stripes as is the only other species, *D. urostriata*, from Manãos, Brazil. **179**
D. urostriata see under **D. longibarbis**

Diaphus   Myctophidae
metopoclampa 10 cm. (4 in.)
This lanternfish is very conspicuous on account of the large patch of luminous tissue in front of the eye covering the whole snout region. It also has 4 distinct light organs at the lower base of the tail fin. It is a short, deep-bodied species with a large head, and a wide mouth.

It is found in the temperate N. Atlantic and the Mediterranean, living from 100–800 m. (55–440 fathoms) of depth but like all lanternfishes rising to near the surface at night-time.

Dicentrarchus   Serranidae
labrax BASS 1 m. (39 in.)
A European species of relatively restricted distribution, found from n. England s. to N. Africa and throughout the Mediterranean and Black Sea. It is a strikingly handsome fish, with long athletic lines. It is principally blue-grey on the back, intensely silvery on the sides and white ventrally.

It is a predatory species feeding mainly on small pelagic fishes such as sardines, sprats, sand smelts, but also sand-eels and other bottom-living species, crustaceans and squids. Young fishes eat more invertebrates than do the older specimens.

It is typically an inshore species being found in the surf zone, around outcrops of rock, and off the beach on almost any kind of ground. It is capable of surviving in estuaries in almost fresh water, and no doubt could adapt to life in fresh water if acclimatized slowly. In British waters it is migratory, approaching inshore in spring and summer (when it also wanders far N.), and moving into deeper water in late autumn. It spawns in spring in inshore areas.

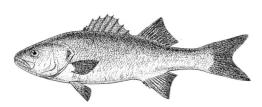

The bass is a renowned sporting fish which is rated by British sea anglers as their best fighting fish. It is also exploited commercially on a small scale throughout its range. Unfortunately it is a very slow growing species which can be over-exploited with only a little fishing effort.

DICERATIDAE
A small family of deep-sea anglerfishes found in both the Indian and Atlantic oceans, but best represented in the former. The group is known from very few specimens indeed and most of these are larvae. The family is distinguished by having 2 well developed rays on the head. See **Diceratias.**

Diceratias   Diceratidae
bispinosus 14 cm. (5½ in.)
A small deep-sea angler known from only 4 specimens, 2 being larvae; the males are as yet undescribed. It is found in the Indian Ocean, off the Malabar coast, off Banda, and in the Celebes Sea. Larvae have been taken in depths of 100 m. (54 fathoms), near the surface, the larger females in much deeper water.

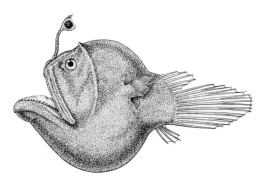

The larvae are almost spherical with loose, flabby skin, the mouth is small, the eyes moderate, and 2 short rays are present on the head.

DICK, SLIPPERY see **Halichoeres bivittatus**
Dikellorhynchus see under
     Branchiostegidae
DIMINUTIVE GOBY see **Lebetus scorpioides**

DIODONTIDAE
A small family of tropical marine fishes which includes the porcupine fishes or burrfishes. Superficially they are like the pufferfishes (family Tetraodontidae) to which they are related, but they differ in having the teeth fused in each jaw to form a sharp, parrot-like beak, and in having long, heavy-based spines over the whole body.

Porcupinefishes can inflate themselves into a nearly spherical shape causing the spines in

Diodon spp. to rise from their normal flat position; other genera carry their spines erected at all times. Inflated, a porcupinefish must be an impossible proposition for any predator, but some species also have a convincing bluff in the shape of marks on the back which on inflation turn into glaring 'eyes'.

Porcupinefishes are found in all tropical seas, but relatively few species are recognized, according to some authorities as few as 15. In some areas their flesh, especially their gonads, is considered poisonous. They are possibly most familiar to dwellers in temperate lands as grotesque lamp shades, the skin inflated and dried, and hanging from timbered ceilings as decorations in bars! In shallow water, in sandy bays, or over reefs they are often very abundant and attractive members of the fauna. See **Chilomycterus, Diodon, Lophodiodon.**

Diodon   Diodontidae
A genus of pufferfish found in tropical waters. In addition to the illustrated *D. holocanthus* a further member of this genus is shown, which has not been identified. **499**
D. holocanthus BALLOONFISH, SPINY PUFFER 51 cm. (20 in.)
Worldwide in tropical waters, and very versatile in its choice of habitats, being found in the creek waters of mangrove swamps, on reefs, and on sandy bays, in shallow water, rarely deeper than 6 m. (3 fathoms). It feeds on hard-shelled invertebrates, especially crabs, sea urchins, and gastropod molluscs.

In the Atlantic it does not range so far N. as its congener *(D. hystrix)* and is found from Florida and the Bahamas to Brazil; it also occurs in the Gulf of Mexico and throughout the Caribbean.

It is distinguished from some other pufferfishes by its double-based long spines, which normally lie flat and are only erected when the body is inflated. The spines on the forehead are longer than those above the pectoral fins. **497, 498**
D. hystrix PORCUPINEFISH 91 cm. (3 ft)
The porcupinefish is cosmopolitan in warm seas, found in the tropical Pacific, Indian and Atlantic oceans. In the last it ranges from Massachusetts to s. Brazil, and through the Gulf of Mexico and the Caribbean.

It is one of the largest members of the family and although most reference books give 36 inches as its maximal length, the largest authenticated specimen reported was 56 cm. (22 in.). It is moderately common throughout its range especially in shallow water over turtle grass beds or sandy flats. It feeds on sea urchins, gastropod molluscs, crabs, and hermit crabs, whose hard shells it easily crushes in its strong teeth.

In this genus the spines on the body are long, 2-rooted, and lie back when the body is not inflated. It is olive-green on the back, brownish on the sides, and clear white on the belly; with small black spots over all the head, body and fins.

Diplobatis   Torpedinidae
ommata see under **D. pictus**
pictus 16·5 cm. (6½ in.)
This small ray is known from the tropical w. Atlantic from the mouth of the Amazon to the Gulf of Venezuela. It was first described from Georgetown, Guyana in 1950, but has subsequently been found to be relatively common in depths of 16–119 m. (9–65 fathoms) along the e. coast of n. S. America.

It is a beautifully marked ray, with a light brown ground colour overlaid with darker brown blotches and white spots. There is a series of brown blotches along the edge of the disc. The degree of development of this pattern varies considerably between individuals. It is rather elongate in body shape, looking intermediate between the typical electric rays and the guitarfishes. A related species *D. ommata* is found on the Pacific coast of America from the Gulf of California to Panama.

Diplomystes   Diplomystidae
viedmensis OTUNO 23 cm. (9 in.)
A catfish found in the Rio Negro, Rio Aluminé, and Rio Yaucha basins of the Argentine. It is dull grey above, with small black spots on the back and sides; the belly is whitish. It is scaleless with a large head flattened from above, and a pronounced single barbel each side of the upper jaw; the mouth is wide.

Little appears to have been recorded of the biology of this fish.

DIPLOMYSTIDAE
A family of S. American freshwater catfishes, containing only 2 species in the single genus. It is regarded as one of the most primitive living groups of catfish, and its members are the only catfish with teeth in the upper jaw bones. They are scaleless fishes with a moderately long barbel on the upper jaw, a short dorsal fin and a very large adipose fin between the dorsal fin and the tail.

One species, *Diplomystes papillosus*, lives in rivers in Chile, the other, *D. viedmensis*, in the Argentine. See **Diplomystes.**

DIRETMIDAE
A family containing only a single genus and possibly 2 species. The species described here seems to be a rare fish but it is widely distributed through the Atlantic, and is found elsewhere in moderately deep water.

It is deep-bodied, almost circular in outline; its body and most of the head covered with rough-edged scales. The pelvic fins are distinctive with 5 rays and one long, heavy blade-like spine. The eye is large, and the mouth is large and oblique. See **Diretmus.**

Diretmus   Diretmidae
argenteus SPINYFIN 40 cm. (15¾ in.)
An oceanic fish, first found in deep water off Madeira, but subsequently caught in many places in the N. Atlantic. It lives in depths of 640–5000 m. (350–2700 fathoms), but is believed to be bathypelagic. From the number

of captures of this species it appears to be rare, and as most of the known specimens were under 10 cm. (4 in.) in length, it suggests that most of the information about the species is based on juvenile fish. A 40 cm. specimen was caught off the W. coast of s. Africa.

Its colouring is silvery, the back with a tinge of blue; adults are brownish black.

Disceus laticeps see **Potamotrygon laticeps**
DISCUS see **Symphysodon aequifasciata, S. discus**
DISCUS,
BLUE see **Symphysodon aequifasciata**
BROWN see **Symphysodon aequifasciata**
GREEN see **Symphysodon aequifasciata**

Dissostichus Nototheniidae
mawsoni GIANT ANTARCTIC COD
1 m. (3¼ ft)
A widely distributed Antarctic fish which has been found at numerous places close to the Antarctic continent. It lives in depths of 20–220 m. (11–120 fathoms).

It is a long-bodied Antarctic cod differing from most of its relatives in having a projecting lower jaw, and very large teeth. Like most members of the family it has 2 lateral lines, the upper one parallel to the back, running to the end of the dorsal fin; the lower one starts immediately below, runs to the tail along the side of the body.

It is uniformly brownish, with 4 irregular dark cross-bars and some dark spots. The first dorsal fin is blackish.

DISTICHODONTIDAE
A large family of tropical African characin-like freshwater fishes. They are distinguished externally from the true characins mainly by the lateral line which in these fishes runs from the upper gill opening to the tail in a straight line; their scales are also ctenoid (toothed on the free edge). Most members of the family have deep, rather compressed bodies, with a long dorsal fin, a large and scaled adipose fin, naked head with a rather blunt snout and almost ventral jaws. Teeth in the lower jaw are large, if slender and loosely set in the jaw bone; their cutting edges have 2 cusps.

Many of the members of the family attain a large size and are valuable food fishes in parts of Africa. The smaller species, and the young of the large ones, have been kept successfully in aquaria. See **Distichodus, Nannocharax.**

Distichodus Distichodontidae
mossambicus N'KUPE 70 cm. (27½ in.)
This species is found in s. tropical Africa, especially in the Zambezi system and Lake

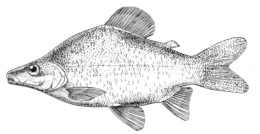

Kariba; it is reported in the Lower Sabi river in Mozambique.

Young fish are silvery, light olive-green on the back with a series of 8 dark bars across the back and upper sides. Older fish are dark olive-green on the back and sides and the bars fade into this coloration.

A powerful fish with considerable potential value to the angler, as it takes a meat or fish bait readily. It is also captured in some numbers in nets being locally important as a food fish.

Ditrema Embiotocidae
temmincki SEA CHUB 25 cm. (10 in.)
Widely distributed in Japanese waters, and found both in the Yellow Sea, the Sea of Japan, and the Okhotsk Sea. It is a shore fish, found in the surf and close inshore generally. Like other members of the family it is viviparous, the females giving birth to their young (12–40 in a brood) during spring and summer; the young fish are about 5 cm. (2 in.) long at birth.

It is a rather deep-bodied fish, with a low spiny dorsal fin, continuous with the soft dorsal, and a forked tail. Its coloration is very variable, either rusty blue or coppery red, with 2 blackish stripes through the eye to the mouth, and a double dot on the lower preopercle of the same colour.

It is considered to be a delicious food fish.

DIVER, SAND see Trichonotidae
DIVER,
GRAVEL see **Scylatina cerdale**
SAND see **Synodus intermedius**
DOCTOR, FISH see **Gymnelis viridis**
DOG, SANDY see **Scyliorhinus canicula**
DOG-TOOTH TUNA see **Orcynopsis unicolor**
DOGFISH see **Scyliorhinus canicula**
DOGFISH,
BLACK see **Centroscyllium fabricii**
BLACK-MOUTHED see **Galeus melastomus**
CHAIN see **Scyliorhinus retifer**
LARGE-SPOTTED see **Scyliorhinus stellaris**
LESSER-SPOTTED see **Scyliorhinus canicula**
LONG-SNOUTED see **Deania quadrispinosa**
SMOOTH see **Mustelus canis**
SPINY see **Squalus acanthias**
WHITE-SPOTTED see **Squalus kirki**

Dolichopteryx Opisthoproctidae
longipes 13 cm. (5 in.)
A representative of the group of opisthoproctids which are slender-bodied and thin. Like its relatives, its eyes are tubular, raised on short stalks to the dorsal surface of the head,

each with a large globular lens. It seems certain that this fish must have binocular vision above its head, but to what extent the eyes are mobile in life and thus enable it to see sideways is not known.

It is distinguished by its body shape, by its short pectoral and long pelvic fins, a pronounced snout, and a small mouth. Its skin is very soft and gelatinous.

It has been found in water around 1000 m. (546 fathoms) in depth in the tropical Atlantic, from off Morocco to off Bermuda, and in the e. Pacific from around the Galapagos and off California.

DOLLARFISH see **Peprilus triacanthus**
DOLLY VARDEN see **Salvelinus malma**
DOLPHINFISH see Coryphaenidae
DOLPHINFISH see **Coryphaena hippurus**
DOLPHINFISH, POMPANO see **Coryphaena equisetis**
DORAB see **Chirocentrus dorab**

DORADIDAE
A group of S. American freshwater catfishes most of which are rather distinctive in body shape and some of which are kept in aquaria. In general the thorny catfishes are broad-headed, and fat-bodied, with heavy bony plates on the head often distinctly rough. A heavy toothed spine running back from the shoulder; the dorsal and pectoral spines are also toothed. The sides and back are often covered with strong spiny scutes. Barbels round the mouth are long and numerous.

They are rather sluggish, bottom-dwelling and burrowing catfishes, active mainly in the half-light. Some, probably all, can make grunting sounds of quite audible proportions. See **Acanthodoras, Amblydoras, Hassar.**

DORADO see **Coryphaena hippurus, Salminus maxillosus**

Dormitator Gobiidae
maculatus FAT SLEEPER 46 cm. (18 in.)
A w. Atlantic species found commonly from the Bahamas and N. Carolina s. to Brazil including the Gulf of Mexico. It is found in intertidal areas usually on muddy bottoms but is only really common where the water is brackish. It is abundant in freshwater or slightly saline coastal pools and river mouths throughout its range.

It is distinguished by its rather short, but thickset body. It is fully scaled, the dorsal fins are large and rather high, as is the anal. The pelvic fins are separate from one another. It is usually dark brown above with lighter bluish spots; the dorsal and anal fins are reddish, and there is a distinct black-edged, dark blue spot behind the upper edge of the gill-cover.

In many parts of its range the sleeper is regarded as a food fish.

DORY,
AMERICAN JOHN see **Zenopsis ocellata**
JOHN see **Zeus faber**
MIRROR see **Zenopsis nebulosus**
SILVER see **Cyttus australis**
SPIKY see **Neocyttus rhomboidalis**
WARTY see **Allocyttus verrucosus**

Doryichthys Syngnathidae
deokhatoides 18 cm. (7 in.)

A widely distributed Asiatic freshwater pipe-fish which is found in Thailand, the Malaysian peninsula, Sumatra, and Borneo. It lives in lakes, streams, and rivers. It has for long been imported to Europe and makes an interesting pet-fish.

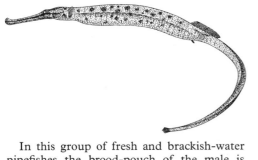

In this group of fresh and brackish-water pipefishes the brood-pouch of the male is entirely abdominal, and the rather large eggs, which are held in individual pockets of the belly skin, are protected but not enclosed by the folds of skin. It is greenish in colour, darker ventrally, with dark spots on the dorsal fin and a black stripe along the side of the head.

Doryrhamphus   Syngnathidae
   melanopleura BLUE-STRIPED PIPEFISH
6 cm. (2½ in.)
A miniature species which may be mature at a length of as little as 25 mm. (1 in.), although it does grow somewhat longer. This is probably the smallest known pipefish species. It is widely distributed in the Indo-Pacific being found from the Pacific coast of the Americas to Mauritius in the Indian Ocean and from Australia N. to Japan.

Its body form is very distinctive, being short-bodied, rather stout and thickset with the edges of the body rings prominent and ending in a spine on the rear edge. The tail is conspicuously shorter than the body, and the tail-fin is large. **230**

DOVER SOLE see **Microstomus pacificus,
   Solea solea**
DRAGON, WINGED see **Pegasus volitans**
DRAGONET see Callionymidae
DRAGONET see **Callionymus lyra**
DRAGONET, LANCER see **Callionymus
   bairdi**
DRAGONFISH see Stomiatidae
DRAGONFISH,
   BLACK see **Idiacanthus fasciola**
   DEEP see **Bathydraco scotiae,
   Prionodraco evansii**
   SNAKE see **Stomias colubrinus**

Drepane   Ephippidae
   punctata CONCERTINAFISH, SICKLEFISH
40 cm. (15¾ in.)

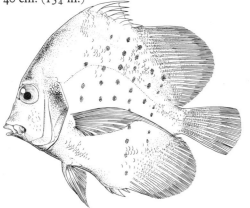

An Atlantic and Indo-Pacific species, widely distributed on both the W. and E. African coasts and e. to India, the E. Indies and n. Australia. The body is bright silvery, greyish above, with faint rows of dusky spots; the young have these dusky spots forming bars down the sides.

Found in shallow water, usually on sandy or muddy bottoms, frequently entering estuaries. It is an abundant fish in many parts of its range and a valuable food fish.

Drepanidae see Ephippidae
DRIFTFISH, BROWN see **Ariomma
   melanum**
DRUM see Sciaenidae
DRUM,
   BLACK see **Pogonias cromis**
   FRESHWATER see **Aplodinotus grunniens**
DRUMMER see Kyphosidae
DRUMMER see **Kyphosus sydneyanus**
DRUMMER, SILVER see **Kyphosus
   sydneyanus**
DUCK, BOMBAY see **Harpadon nehereus**

Dunckerocampus   Syngnathidae
   dactyliophorus 16 cm. (6¼ in.)
Widely distributed in the Pacific Ocean, and well known from such areas as Java, the Celebes, Philippines, and the Solomon Islands. It is mainly found just below the low tide mark, and has been taken at depths of 9 m. (5 fathoms). It frequents the lower sides of overhanging coral heads.

It is most striking when it is alive, for the background colour is whitish, with regular rings of bright vermilion around the whole length of the head and body. The tail fin is also vermilion. These colours fade after death to black and white bands. **231**

DUSKY
   ANCHOVY see **Anchoa lyolepis**
   CUSK EEL see **Parophidion schmidti**
   FLATHEAD see **Platycephalus fuscus**
   MORWONG see **Psilocranium nigricans**
   SEA PERCH see **Rhacochilus vacca**
   SHARK see **Carcharhinus obscurus**
   SQUIRRELFISH see **Adioryx vexillarius**
DWARF
   CICHLID, AGASSIZ'S see **Apistogramma
   agassizi**
   CICHLID, ORTMANN'S see **Apistogramma
   ortmanni**
   CORYDORAS see **Corydoras hastatus**
   FLOUNDER see **Trinectes maculatus**
   GOURAMI see **Colisa lalia**
   HERRING see **Jenkinsia lamprotaenia**
   PANCHAX see **Aplocheilus blocki**
   PENCILFISH see **Nannostomus
   marginatus**
   SEAHORSE see **Hippocampus zosterae**
   SHARK see **Squaliolus laticaudus**
   SUNFISH see **Elassoma evergladei**
   TOPMINNOW see **Heterandria formosa**

Dysommina   Dysomminidae
   rugosa 20 cm. (8 in.)
This species was first described from a speci-

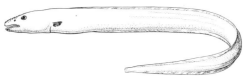

men collected off Cumberland Island, Georgia, by the pioneer marine expeditions of the 'Albatross' in 1886. It is a small eel, in colour almost uniformly yellowish, the fins lighter.

DYSOMMINIDAE
A small family of eels, allied to the family Nettodaridae, and close to Myrocongridae and Xenocongridae. Its members are represented in the warmer waters of the American Atlantic coast, and the Caribbean but are relatively little known. See **Dysommina.**

Dyssoma   Dyssomidae
   bucephalus 28 cm. (11 in.)
A strange looking eel, with a rather large and heavy head, Its eyes are small and apparently covered by skin. It is greyish brown, paler beneath, and with the fins edged in white.

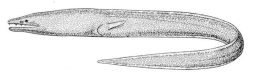

It was first discovered in the 1880s during the trawling surveys of the Indian survey ship 'Investigator', in the Bay of Bengal at depths of 205–440 m. (112–240 fathoms). Subsequently it has been found off the s. coast of Africa, and it is probably widely distributed in the w. Indian Ocean, although specimens are hard to obtain by normal fishing methods. Related forms occur in the Indian Ocean and N. Pacific.

DYSSOMIDAE
A small family of little studied, deep-water eels which have an elongate compressed body, dorsal and anal fins united with the tail fin. The jaws are not particularly well developed and the teeth are small.

Several species have been described and allocated to this family from the Indian Ocean in deep water, and the S. African coast. See **Dyssoma, Nettodarus.**

E

EAGLE
   RAY see Myliobatidae
   RAY see **Myliobatis aquila, Myliobatis
   australis**
   RAY, SPOTTED see **Aetobatus narinari**
EASTERN MUDMINNOW see **Umbra
   pygmaea**

ECHENEIDAE
The family of remoras or shark suckers, a group of marine fishes of unmistakable appearance and distinctive on account of their close association with larger fishes and even whales. They are all rather slender fishes, with a unique sucking disc on the top of the head, formed it is believed from a modified spiny dorsal fin. With the oval disc pressed flat onto the body of its host it is virtually impossible to dislodge. Attached in this way the fish can travel with its host wherever the latter wanders. Presumably it derives some protection from this arrangement, and some species at least act

as cleaners, picking parasites from the host's body.

Not surprisingly a rich crop of odd facts and fancies surround a fish with such strange habits. The larger species have been used to capture turtles by fishermen who attach a line to the tail. Mythology credits remoras with holding back sailing ships by attaching themselves to the ship's bottom.

There are 8 wide-ranging species some of which are specifically associated with only one kind of host. See **Echeneis, Phtheirichthys, Remora.**

Echeneis Echeneidae
naucrates SHARKSUCKER, SUCKERFISH
92 cm. (36 in.)
Widely distributed in the tropical oceans of the world with the exception of the e. Pacific. It rarely accompanies any fish but truly tropical species, and is thus not found in temperate seas. It attaches itself to a wide range of sharks, also large rays, sea turtles, and many kinds of large fish; it is also observed free-living.

This species of remora is used by the Torres Straits islanders to capture turtles at sea. Released as near to the turtle as the native boat can safely approach, the sharksucker makes straight for the turtle which is then hampered by the fish and the line attached to its tail. It is one of the commonest as well as the largest of the family.

This species is easily distinguished by its very elongate shape. It is brownish above and below; the sides have a black length-wise stripe running from jaw tip to tail, and bordered with white. **290**

Echidna Muraenidae
zebra ZEBRA EEL 127 cm. (50 in.)
The zebra eel is one of the most distinctive eels of the central tropical Indo-Pacific, for its black body is encircled with numerous (42–75) narrow white interspaces. The dorsal fin is not well developed and the anal fin origin is back near the tail. Its relatively deep body,

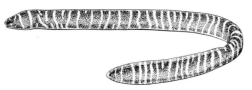

and blunt head with short jaws are typical of this group of eels. Like other echidnid eels it has short, blunt teeth; it is said to feed mainly on molluscs and crustaceans. It is not particularly common in the shallow tidal regions, and becomes noticeably more common in crevices in reefs below the tidal zone.

Echinomacrurus Macrouridae
mollis 37 cm. (14½ in.)
A very deep water rat-tail found originally at a depth of 5396 m. (2950 fathoms) in the e. Atlantic *c.* 31°N. 24°W. Subsequently it was captured rather more to the N. (43°N. 18°W.), but still in depths in excess of 5000 m. (2734 fathoms). Other specimens have been captured more recently in similar depths.

It is a striking-looking rat-tail with a very distinctive bulbous head, almost spongy in

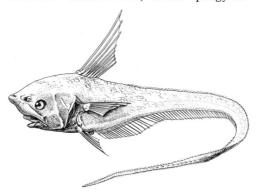

appearance, the outer surface being a soft tissue. The biology of this fish is unknown.

ECHINORHINIDAE
A small family of sharks which contains 3–4 possibly nominal species in temperate and tropical waters of the Atlantic and Indo-Pacific. These sharks are heavy-bodied with small fins except for the tail which is large, they have no anal fin, and their skin is studded with small plate-like spines. See **Echinorhinus.**

Echinorhinus Echinorhinidae
brucus BRAMBLE SHARK 3 m. (10 ft)
This is a heavy-bodied shark found in deep water in the tropical Atlantic and ranging N. to the British Isles and Cape Cod as a rarity. It is usually found in depths of 400–900 m. (220–490 fathoms) but also occurs in much shallower water. Considering its size very little is known about its natural history; it is probably a live bearing shark, and feeds on crabs, fishes, and spiny dogfish.

In colour it is unprepossessing, being a dull grey or brown with reflections of silver or yellow. It can be immediately identified by its rough skin, for its back bears numerous spiky thorns set in plates buried in the skin. These give it the name bramble shark.

Very similar sharks have been found off s. Africa, in Australasian waters, and in the N. Pacific. Although named as separate species there is every likelihood that only one world-wide species is involved.

Echiodon Carapidae
dentatus see under **E. drummondi**
drummondi PEARLFISH 30 cm. (12 in.)
This pearlfish is a n. European form which is found in deepish water off the continental shelf from Norway, and Scotland s. to Portugal. It is replaced in the Mediterranean by a related species *E. dentatus.* It is found mainly in depths of 146–275 m. (80–150 fathoms) but seems to be nowhere common along the European

coasts. Occasionally it is caught in trawls which contain the reddish sea cucumber *Stichopus,* which leads to the suggestion that it lives in association with this holothurian.

Like other pearlfishes it is long and slender, has no pelvic fins, and has the anus under the throat region. In colour a silver tinted pink, dusky bars on the back and sides.

It is one of the largest pearlfishes known.

Echiostoma Melanostomiatidae
barbatum 37 cm. (14½ in.)
This scaleless dragonfish is widely distributed in the tropical and warmer regions of the Atlantic Ocean, from the Gulf of Mexico and the Caribbean across to Madeira and as far S. as Cape Town. It has been taken from near the surface (at night) down to depths of nearly 2000 m. (1093 fathoms).

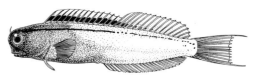

This is one of the very few deep sea fishes which has briefly been kept alive by zoologists in aquaria. It was described as a strong vigorous swimmer, snapping actively until a short while before it died. When the barbel was touched the fish reacted by trying to bite at the source of the sensation. When living it is a dull purplish black to blackish brown, the fin rays are brown or reddish. The chin barbel is black with the swollen part brown, pinkish or green and the tips pink or purple. The fish is said to be able to control the luminescence given off by each set of light organs; at times the organ behind the eye glows pink, at other times greenish white. The small light organs along the sides give off a rosy or red light, directed downwards. In addition, the whole body gives off a greenish white glow.

The development of the chin barbel in this fish is interesting on account of the variations in the shape of the filaments between young and sexually mature fish, and between the sexes. It would be surprising if such differences observable by the human eye were not of at least equal significance to the fish.

Ecsenius Blenniidae
gravieri 7 cm. (2¾ in.)
A blenny native to the Red Sea and the Gulf of Aden, as well as the lesser gulfs of Suez and Aqaba. It is found in shallow water on the coral reefs at the mouth of tube-like holes and around *Diadema,* the pin-cushion sea urchin.

It has the habit of perching on the coral, and making occasional forays in the close vicinity, feeding primarily on small crustaceans and algae.

It is blue-grey on the head and anterior body, with a yellowish body and tail; a thin dark line runs along the upper side ending in a series of spots. Its colouring is almost identical to the Red Sea blenny *Meiacanthus nigrolineatus,* which having formidable venom-injecting fangs in its lower jaw is almost immune from fish predators. There is little doubt that it derives protection from this resemblance, for it lives in close association with its model for mimicry.

EEL see Anguillidae, Congridae, Cyemidae, Derichthyidae, Dysomminidae, Dysso-midae, Heterenchelidae, Macrocephen-chelyidae, Muraenesocidae, Muraenidae, Myrocongridae, Neenchelyidae, Nessor-hamphidae, Nettastomatidae, Nettodari-dae, Ophichthidae, Serrivomeridae, Simenchelyidae, Synaphobranchidae, Xenocongridae

EEL,
   AFRICAN LONG-FINNED see **Anguilla mossambica**
   AFRICAN MOTTLED see **Anguilla nebulosa**
   AMERICAN see **Anguilla rostrata**
   COLLARED see **Kaupichthys nuchalis**
   CONGER see **Conger conger**
   DUSKY CUSK see **Parophidion schmidti**
   ELECTRIC see **Electrophorus electricus**
   EUROPEAN see **Anguilla anguilla**
   FACCIOLA'S see **Nettodarus brevirostris**
   GARDEN see **Nystactichthys halis, Taenioconger digueti**
   INDIAN LONG-FINNED see **Anguilla nebulosa**
   KAUP'S DEEP-SEA see **Synaphobranchus kaupi**
   KEY WORM see **Ahlia egmontis**
   LONG-TAILED see **Thyrsoides macrura**
   MORAY see **Lycondontis tessellata**
   NECK see **Derichthys serpentinus**
   RICE see **Monopterus alba**
   ROCK see **Squalus acanthias, Scyliorhinus canicula**
   SHARPTAIL see **Myrichthys acuminatus**
   SHORE see **Alabes rufus**
   SHORT-FINNED see **Anguilla australis**
   SLIME see **Simenchelys parasiticus**
   SMALL-EYED see **Pythonichthys microphthalmus**
   SNAKE see Ophichthidae
   SNIPE see Nemichthyidae
   SNIPE see **Avocettina infans, Nemichthys scolopaceus**
   SNUB-NOSED see **Simenchelys parasiticus**
   SPINY see Lipogenyidae, Mastacembelidae, Notacanthidae
   SPINY see **Mastacembelus frenatus, Notacanthus chemnitzii**
   SPOTTED SNAKE see **Ophichthus ophis**
   SURF see **Sphagebranchus ophioneus**
   THREAD see **Serrivomer parabeani**
   WORM see Moringuidae, Ophichthidae
   WORM see **Moringua macrochir**
   ZEBRA see **Echnida zebra**

EEL
   BLENNY see **Peronedys anguillaris**
   BLENNY, SPOTTED see **Notograptus guttatus**
   CATFISH see **Channalabes apus**
   EELGRASS BLENNY see **Stathmonotus stahli**
   EELPOUT see Zoarcidae
   EELPOUT see **Lota lota, Zoarces viviparus**
   EELPOUT,
   BLACKMOUTH see **Lycodes diapterus**
   ESMARK'S see **Lycodes esmarki**
   TWOLINE see **Bothrocara brunneum**
   EGG-LAYING TOPMINNOW see **Tomeurus gracilis**

Eigenmannia   Rhamphichthyidae
   virescens GREEN KNIFEFISH 46 cm. (18 in.)
This knifefish is distributed throughout n. S. America, from Venezuela to the Argentinian La Plata. In this vast area several distinct forms have been described which may have taxonomic status. It is long, slender and compressed, possessing only pelvic fins and the very long anal fin typical of these fishes, although the last part of the tail is free of the fin.

Its colour is variable. In some lights it appears to be a delicate flesh colour, the head end rather yellowish, with iridescent bluish stripes running lengthwise. The tail end of the fish tends to show as greenish. It is in effect translucent except for the coloured head and greenish tints. Specimens living in clear water often are more boldly striped than those from muddy water.

This is a moderately important food fish to the native peoples of the lowlands of tropical S. America. It is found abundantly in small streams flowing through the open savannas, as well as in drainage ditches and canals around plantations. Young specimens have been imported to keep as aquarium fish.

EIGHT-BANDED CICHLID see **Cichlasoma octofasciatum**

Elagatis   Carangidae
   bipinnulata RAINBOW RUNNER, RUNNER
   1·2 m. (4 ft)
Recorded from warm waters around the world. It is widespread in the tropical Atlantic and Indo-Pacific but is rarely found inshore, being more an inhabitant of the surface of the open sea.

It is a famous game fish, fighting well on a line and moreover being excellent eating. Specimens of up to 14 kg. (31 lb.) have been caught by sports fishermen.

The rainbow runner is so called for the beauty of its colouring, the back is bluish green, with 2 broad blue stripes on the sides separated by a deep yellow line. Another yellow line runs along the lower side while the belly is white. The fins are greeny-yellow. It is distinguished by its colouring, and by its slender shape, the tail lacking the bony scutes on the sides, but having a small dorsal and anal finlet behind the main fin.

Elassoma   Centrarchidae
   evergladei EVERGLADES PYGMY SUNFISH,
   DWARF SUNFISH 3·8 cm. (1½ in.)
This well-named miniature sunfish is found in the se. U.S., Alabama, Florida extending n. to N. Carolina. It is found in the well-weeded, swampy areas there, but is relatively adaptable and takes well to life in ponds and aquariums. It has become a popular cold-water aquarium fish in Europe, as it is in America.

It has a moderately elongate body, with a short, rounded dorsal fin containing 2–4 spines. It lacks a lateral line. Both sexes are greenish grey with silvery and black scattered scales; in the spawning season the male be-

comes velvet black with shining green scales. This miniature sunfish becomes sexually mature at a length of 2·2 cm. (⅞ in.). **275**

ELECTRIC
   CATFISH see Malapteruridae
   CATFISH see **Malapterurus electricus**
   EEL see **Electrophorus electricus**
   RAY see Torpedinidae
   RAY see **Torpedo nobiliana**
   RAY, DEEP-SEA see **Benthobatis marcida**
   RAY, LESSER see **Narcine brasiliensis**
   RAY, PACIFIC see **Torpedo californica**

ELECTROPHORIDAE
The family to which the electric eel belongs. It is confined to ne. S. America in pools and deeply shaded streams and creeks.

It is an eel-like fish, cylindrical and rather thickset and heavy at the head end although tapering in width, if not depth towards the tail. Its anal fin is long, beginning close behind the head and running along the body to turn upwards at the end to form a false tail fin. The skin is scaleless. Its nearest relatives are the knife-fishes (Gymnotidae) which inhabit the same regions. Its electrical powers are legendary. See **Electrophorus**.

Electrophorus   Electrophoridae
   electricus ELECTRIC EEL 2·4 m. (8 ft)
The electric eel is native to ne. S. America, including the Guyanas, the Orinoco, and the middle and lower Amazon basin. It is a long-bodied fish with a heavy broad head, its body is cylindrical anteriorly becoming compressed towards the tail. The vent is placed in front of the pectoral fins, and the anal fin origin is only just behind these fins; it lacks dorsal, tail, and pelvic fins. The snout is heavy and broad, the mouth wide, lower jaw protruding, with a single row of small teeth; the eye is small.

Its coloration is a uniform dull olive to almost black, the underneath of the head and throat are yellowish to orange.

The electric eel is best known for its extraordinary electrical ability. The large electric organs occupy four-fifths of the sides of the body, and may take up to half its bulk. These organs are composed of columns of wafer-like electroplates arranged in numerous rows. The electroplates are mostly connected in series, and their individual charges, small though they may be, add up to a considerable voltage. When electrically active they produce brief bursts of pulses, several to the second. The total shock amounts to as much as 500 volts, and at times as much as 1 ampere.

The effect of a full charge can severely shock a man, on smaller fishes it is lethal, and this is clearly how the electric eel obtains some of its food. Its electric power is, however, also a defensive device.

This fish can also produce much less intense electrical pulses, surrounding itself with a field which enables it to navigate as well as find food. It lives in pools and deeply shaded streams and creeks, often in very turbid water in which its rather small eyes are relatively impaired. Young fish eat mainly bottom-living invertebrates, the adults eat fishes, the size of the prey increasing with the size and power of the electric eel.

Electric eels are frequently kept in public aquariums where they live satisfactorily, if mostly in hiding, when not called upon to exercise their electrical power too frequently. In S. America it is occasionally used for food. It has also been the subject of numerous medical experiments, such as in the treatment of rheumatism. **104**

ELEPHANT SHARK see **Callorhinchus milii**
ELEPHANT-SNOUT FISH see **Mormyrus kannume**
ELEPHANTFISH see Callorhinchidae

Eleutheronema Polynemidae
tetradactylum GUCHHIA, SAWAL, GIANT THREADFIN 1·8 m. (6 ft)
A species found in inshore waters around India, the E. Indies, China, the Philippines, and n. Australia. It is best known, however, in Indian waters where it attains its greatest abundance and is common in estuaries and low salinity lakes.

In Indian waters it is a moderately valuable commercial species, caught mostly in gill nets, less often in trawls. Because of its habits of living close inshore and in estuaries it is captured by many local methods.

The youngest age group feed mainly on planktonic organisms especially crustaceans. Larger specimens eat prawns and crabs, and fishes of various kinds. They feed as much in mid-winter as on the sea bed.

It is distinguished by having only 4 free pectoral filaments and the lower lip developed only at the corner of the jaw. Its colouring is silvery green, yellowish-white on the belly. A dark patch on the upper part of the gill cover.

ELFT see **Pomatomus saltatrix**

Elopichthys Cyprinidae
bambusa 2 m. (6½ ft)
A very interesting and unusual cyprinid fish, the biology of which is little known. It inhabits the waters of the Amur River and some of the larger rivers of China. It is distinguished by its large size, its cylindrical body, a large non-protrusible mouth, and the lack of a spiny ray in the dorsal fin.

It is wholly predatory in its habits; during the first few months of its life it eats invertebrates, for the remainder it eats fishes only. It is a very active mid-water fish. It spawns in the channel of the rivers during June and July, the newly hatched young migrate to backwaters in their first months, but over-winter in the mainstream with the adults.

It is a fish with some commercial value, caught with seines and floating nets. The largest specimens are, however, rarely taken as they tend to break out of, or jump over the nets.

ELOPIDAE
A family containing the moderate sized, superficially herring-like, tenpounder or giant herring *Elops saurus*. Although several species have been described it is possible that there are only 4 species, all found in tropical seas. The family can be distinguished by the presence of a singular gular bone under the throat, and by numerous teeth in the jaws. See **Elops.**

Elops Elopidae
saurus LADYFISH, TENPOUNDER, GIANT HERRING 1·2 m. (4 ft)
The tenpounder is a much favoured game fish for the angler in tropical seas. It is perhaps best known where game fishing is taken most seriously, off the American, S. African, and tropical Australian coasts. Despite its size its chief attraction is the way in which it leaps and fights to escape, for its flesh is poor and very bony.

In colour it is silver blue above, brilliantly silvery on the sides. The back and tail fins are dusky. The eyes are sheathed by a transparent tissue. Although the adults and young live close inshore and in estuaries, the tenpounder is believed to spawn up to 160 km. (100 miles) offshore. The young larvae is thin and transparent, and closely resembles an eel leptocephalus, except that it has a well-developed forked tail. It drifts inshore to metamorphose into a miniature of the adult, although losing up to half its length in the process.

The young fish is common in mangrove swamps, sheltered bays and salt marshes. They are also found in estuaries. Adults are frequently found in the surf in shoals having presumably come inshore to feed on fishes and crustaceans.

EMBIOTOCIDAE
A very distinctive and interesting family of fishes found only in the N. Pacific and mainly in coastal waters. The one exception to this distribution is the tule perch, *Hysterocarpus traski,* found exclusively in fresh water in the delta of the Sacramento River, California.

Members of the family, usually known as surfperches or seaperches, are rather deep-bodied, oval fishes, their bodies covered with smooth-edged scales which extend to form a sheath at the base of the dorsal fin. The dorsal fins are continuous, the front portion with spines which gradually increase in height and the soft rays follow on. The anal fin has 3 anterior spines; in males the anterior portion of the anal fin is often modified into an intromittant organ, for the surfperches are live-bearers, fertilization is internal and the young develop nourished by the ovarian fluid which envelopes them.

In general the surfperches range in size from 7·5 to 45 cm. (3–18 in.). Several species are valuable as sporting or commercially exploited fish. See **Amphistichus, Brachyistius, Cymatogaster, Ditrema, Rhacochilus.**

EMERALD SHINER see **Notropis atherinoides**

EMMELICHTHYIDAE
A small family of rather slender, torpedo-shaped fishes found mainly in moderately deep water in the Atlantic and the Indo-Pacific. They are only found in tropical and warm-temperate seas.

Their bodies are covered in small scales which extend onto the head and form a scaly sheath on the fins. The jaws are protrusible, with small teeth. The dorsal fins may be separate or continuous, with the spiny first dorsal joined to the base of the second.

They are related to the Australian salmon family Arripidae. See **Emmelichthys, Inermia, Maena.**

Emmelichthys Emmelichthyidae
nitidus RED SEA-HARDER, REDBAIT 61 cm. (2 ft)
Best known from the offshore waters of the s. States of Australia (where it is known as redbait), but has also occurred off s. Africa occasionally. It might be expected to occur throughout the s. Indian Ocean. It has been taken in depths of 110–457 m. (60–250 fathoms) off S. Africa, but in S. Australia it is taken in shallower water, occasionally amongst pilchards.

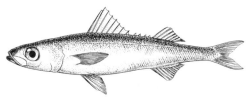

The redbait is a slender-bodied fish, with a short spiny first dorsal fin followed by a series of disconnected spines, then a soft-rayed fin. It is silvery with pale bluish tints on the back and upper sides.

EMPEROR see Lethrinidae
EMPEROR,
LONG-NOSED see **Lethrinus miniatus**
RED see **Lutjanus sebae**
SPANGLED see **Lethrinus nebulosus**
SWEETLIP see **Lethrinus chrysostomus**
EMPEROR
ANGELFISH see **Pomacanthus imperator**
TETRA see **Nematobrycon palmeri**

Enchelynassa Muraenidae
canina c. 2·4 m. (8 ft)
This moray is one of the more dangerous of the eels of the tropical Pacific, through which ocean it is well distributed extending as far N. as Hawaii. It commonly grows to 1·5 m. (5 ft), and in the Phoenix Islands it is said to reach a length in excess of 2·1–2·4 m. (7–8 ft).

It lives in a wide variety of habitats, among corals and crevices in rocks. The larger specimens are found in deep water. In colour it is plain brown without any markings. Its teeth are long, numerous and fanglike, so long in fact that when the tips of the hooked jaws are brought together there is a wide gap between the sides of the jaws. This genus is also distinguished by the long, flaplike appendage on the front nostrils. It is believed to eat fishes.

ENGLISH SOLE see **Parophrys vetulus**

Engraulicypris Cyprinidae
argenteus 8 cm. (3 in.)
The small cyprinids of the genus *Engraulicypris* are confined to Africa, and are mostly found in the larger lakes. They are shoaling fishes of the upper water layers; *E. argenteus* is found in Lakes Victoria, Nabugabo, Kyoga, and the Victoria Nile. It is a long-bodied fish,

with a strongly compressed body and large scales. Its lateral line runs low along the body, parallel to the ventral profile. The mouth is large, terminal and oblique. In colour it is brilliantly silvery with a pearl-like iridescence; the tail fin only is yellow.

It is found in surface water both inshore and over considerable depths, it tends to avoid weeded areas, and in rivers is found in swiftly running reaches.

Its breeding biology is distinctive, for unlike most members of its family, it simply sheds its eggs in the lake, and they float in mid-water. It produces a great number of eggs which hatch very quickly.

This species feeds mainly on planktonic crustaceans. In turn it is eaten by many birds and numerous fishes endemic to the lakes. By its very abundance it is an important fish in the economy of some African freshwaters.

ENGRAULIDAE

This is the family of the anchovies, relatives of the herring-like fishes (Clupeidae), but differing from them mainly in the shape of the head. The snout is prominent in the anchovies, and the jaw bones very large, framing an absolutely huge mouth. They also are rounded in body cross-section, lacking the sharp keel of the herrings.

Anchovies are distributed around the world in all tropical, subtropical, and temperate seas although most abundant in species in the Indo-Pacific. Most are relatively small, shoaling fishes of the sea's surface in coastal waters. Not a few are found in estuarine and low salinity habitats.

All anchovies feed on planktonic organisms in the sea sifted from the water through elaborate and closely-packed gill rakers on the gill arches. All also feature in the food chains of the sea, and some are important forage fish for commercially important fishes like tuna. They also form very valuable fisheries all around the world, although possibly most are under-exploited, compared with the sardine stocks. See **Anchoa, Coilia, Engraulis, Stolephorus, Thrissocles.**

Engraulis   Engraulidae
  australis AUSTRALIAN ANCHOVY
13 cm. (5 in.)
This anchovy is widely distributed in Australian waters especially to the S., off Tasmania, and off New Zealand. It is extremely abundant in bays and estuaries, although the larger fish are usually found a little offshore. In the s. parts of its range the greater part of the population moves offshore in winter. It spawns mainly in bays and inlets along the coast, but in the warmer waters it tends to spawn offshore. Like most anchovies it becomes sexually mature at the end of its first year, when it is about 7 cm. (2¾ in.) long.

The Australian anchovy is very similar to the European species; like most anchovies it is slender-bodied and rounded in cross-section, the snout is prominent and the lower jaw undershot. The jaws are very long.

This anchovy is very common in places and is fished for with hoop nets, beach seines, and by attracting the fish by light to the nets. Exploitation is local, however, and there is no doubt that like the sardine, the anchovy is another of Australia's little exploited marine

resources which will assume great importance in time.

E. encrasicolus ANCHOVY 20 cm. (8 in.)
The anchovy is widely distributed in European seas from n. Scotland s. to the N. African coast, throughout the Mediterranean and Black seas. The anchovy is a shoaling fish often found in large schools in inshore waters and particularly estuaries in summer, although in winter they move into deeper water. In n. European waters spawning is confined to the summer months, but to the s. of its range spawning goes on intermittently during most of the year.

The anchovy feeds on planktonic organisms, chiefly the young stages of crustaceans, including barnacles, which it sifts out of the water using its long gill rakers as a sieve.

Its back is a clear olive-green and the sides have a prominent silvery stripe along them from head to tail.

Although occasional captures of anchovies are made in n. waters, especially in the English Channel they are not particularly valuable commercial fish, but in the S. of their range, off Spain, Portugal and in the Mediterranean they equal the pilchard in importance. It is equally important to the Russian fishing industry in the Black Sea. It is captured chiefly in coastal seine nets, and purse seines often operated with attracting lights. The fish are rarely marketed fresh, most are processed salted, canned, or as pastes. The basic preparation is to pack the anchovies into barrels in salt, and to allow them to ripen for 3 months at temperatures up to 30°C., until the whole fish is red tinted. They are sold canned in oil or presented in other ways. The basic manner of treating them is as old as civilization itself, the ancient Greeks prepared their famous relish *garum* in much the same way.

E. mordax NORTHERN ANCHOVY
18 cm. (7 in.)
Externally the northern anchovy is a typical member of its family, with an overhanging snout and undershot chin, large jaws fringing a capacious mouth. It is relatively slender-bodied.

The northern anchovy is an e. Pacific fish, found from British Columbia to Cape San Lucas in Lower California. It is the most important commercial anchovy of this coast. A large quantity is exploited for processing for fish meal and oil, more is used for human consumption or processed into pet food, but the best known use of this anchovy is for bait for larger fish or as chum to attract the predators to the bait.

The northern anchovy is found in dense shoals, the young especially so, while the adults live rather more offshore and in smaller shoals. This shoaling is mainly a daytime habit; at night they separate into smaller units and feed near the surface. They eat all kinds of planktonic life, filtering minute crustaceans, fish eggs and larvae through their fine gill-raker meshes. The anchovy also forms a staple diet for many of the larger fish-eating fishes, mammals, and birds of the Pacific coast. Man too

has eaten them for many years for their remains have been detected in coastal Indian middens.

E. ringens ANCHOVETA 18 cm. (7 in.)
The anchoveta is native to the coastal region of Peru, although it ranges as far N. as the coast of s. California on occasions. In body form it is similar to other anchovies, with a prominent snout, large mouth, and slender body. It can be distinguished from its e. Pacific relatives by the way that the gill covers are joined to each other in the throat region.

The anchoveta is of enormous economic importance to the countries fishing along the Pacific coast of S. America. It is the most important resource of Peru. Its abundance depends essentially on the Humboldt current, a stream of enriched water flowing n. along the coast which is especially notable for its rich zooplankton, on which the anchoveta feeds. In the past, its value was indirect in that the great guano deposits of this coast were formed by the droppings of swarms of sea birds which fed on anchoveta. More recently, the fish has been directly exploited for fish meal, oil, and fresh food, and has become of great importance. However, the stocks are possibly susceptible to heavy fishing, and have begun to fluctuate, while they are certainly affected by climatic changes such as the submersion every few years of the cold Humboldt current by warm water from the N. These factors mean that the fishery is liable to great fluctuations over the years.

Engyprosopon   Bothidae
  grandisquama SPOTTED-TAIL FLOUNDER
13 cm. (5 in.)
A very distinctive left-eyed flounder which, as its name suggests, has scales rather larger than usual in this group; they are also easily dislodged. It is distinguished by the widely spaced eyes, which are further apart in males than females, by having both pectoral and pelvic fins on the eyed side larger than those on the blind side. It is light brown with darker mottlings which extend onto the fins, and 2 distinct dark spots on the tail fin.

This species is widely distributed in the tropical Indo-Pacific and ranges from the E. African coast to India, Australia, and up to the China Sea and Japan. It is found on sandy bottoms in shallow water of 9–55 m. (5–30 fathoms). In Japan, and locally elsewhere it is considered to be a good food fish, although not subject to important fisheries.

Enneacanthus   Centrarchidae
  chaetodon BLACK-BANDED SUNFISH
10 cm. (4 in.)
Found from New Jersey to Florida in ponds, lakes, and river backwaters, but not in running water. This is a miniature sunfish, very popular as a cold-water aquarium fish in Europe and N. America; it becomes sexually mature at only 5 cm. (2 in.).

It is a decorative little fish, rather deep-bodied with rounded dorsal fins, the first spiny fin clearly distinct from the second. Its banded colouring is typical; the females are said to become brighter in the spawning season. **280**
E. gloriosus BLUESPOTTED SUNFISH
8 cm. (3 in.)
A common species through the e. and s. areas

of the U.S., from about New York to Florida and Alabama. It is restricted to the coastal drainages of this area. It is a popular species amongst aquarists although frequently confused by them with *E. obesus*.

It is a dwarf species, sexually mature at about 5 cm. (2 in.). It is distinguished from its close relatives by the small black blotch on the fleshy extension to the gill cover. It is brightly coloured, the male in particular having lines of iridescent spots on the sides. **276**
E. obesus see under **E. gloriosus**

Enneanectes Tripterygiidae
pectoralis REDEYE TRIPLEFIN 4 cm. (1½ in.)
A Caribbean species found in Florida and the Bahamas, s. through the W. Indies to Venezuela. It is a shallow water form, found on hard bottoms, limestone boulders and patch reefs in depths up to 11 m. (6 fathoms). Like other 3-fin blennies, they dart around in shadowed and concealed areas with frequent pauses resting, raised up from the bottom on their pelvic fins.

This species is fully scaled and has a very distinct tentacle over each eye. The body is light brown with brown bars running across the back and sides. The last bar is very conspicuous. The anal fin, however, is unmarked with bars.

Enophrys Cottidae
bison BUFFALO SCULPIN 30 cm. (12 in.)
A N. Pacific species found on the American coast from Baja California to the Gulf of Alaska. It is distinguished from the numerous other sculpins in that area by the extreme development of the long, rough, upper preopercular spines, and the large, raised, bony scales on the lateral line.

The buffalo sculpin is very common along the entire coast and is frequently found in shallow water. It breeds in early spring; the orange brown eggs are laid in small clusters. It feeds on crustaceans, mussels, and young fishes, and readily takes a baited hook, although its sporting value is low.

ENOPLOSIDAE
A small family containing a single species of fish found only on the coasts of Australia. Its body form is similar to that of the butterflyfishes (Chaetodontidae), but it differs in several respects from them. Most notably, it has 2 well developed dorsal fins, the first with several long spines. The pelvic fins are also long and large with a strong spine. The body is deep and compressed, the head and snout pointed. See **Enoplosus.**

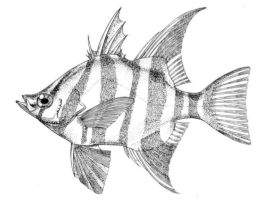

Enoplosus Enoplosidae
armatus OLD WIFE 23 cm. (9 in.)
An Australian species, common on the coasts of S. Australia, Tasmania, and New South Wales, and straggling into Queensland waters. It lives in moderately shallow water usually, although it has been trawled down to depths of 88 m. (48 fathoms), but as its usual habitat is rocky areas it is not often taken by this means. It occasionally takes a bait, and its flesh is said to be very good to eat, but it is not systematically exploited.

Its body form is very distinctive. Its coloration is equally so being silvery white with 8 dark brown bands; the fins are pinkish red.

Entelurus Syngnathidae
aequoreus OCEAN or SNAKE PIPEFISH 61 cm. (2 ft)
A long, slender-bodied pipefish, with the body rings inconspicuous, the skin smooth and rounded. In European waters it is also distinguished by its size, by having a small tail fin, by totally lacking any pectoral fins.

This is an Atlantic pipefish which is captured rather infrequently at the surface of the sea, but is only taken rarely in inshore waters. Some have been caught floating amongst loose algae which suggests that it may live amongst the deeper water kelps but almost nothing is known about the life history of this fish. Males with eggs fastened on the abdomen have been found in July, newly hatched young in August. The males do not have a fleshy brood pouch. **232**

Entomacrodus Blenniidae
nigricans PEARL BLENNY 10 cm. (4 in.)
A w. Atlantic species which is found from Bermuda, the Bahamas, and Florida, through the Caribbean and Gulf of Mexico to Brazil. A related form, *E. textilis* occurs on Ascension and St Helena in the S. Atlantic. It is a shallow water species occurring in tidepools down to a depth of 6 m. (3 fathoms) on rocky or boulder-strewn bottoms. It feeds mainly on algae.

This blenny is distinguished within its range by its coloration, olivaceous in general with paired dusky bars, and distinctive bluish-white, pearl-like spots on the sides. The dorsal fins are separated by a deep notch.
E. textilis see under **E. nigricans**

Entosphenus Petromyzonidae
tridentatus PACIFIC LAMPREY 76 cm. (30 in.)
Rivers and inshore waters of the sea along the Pacific coast of N. America from California to Alaska, and Japan. This lamprey is similar in its life history to the other members of the family. It spawns in riffles where the adults excavate a shallow hollow in the gravel about 46 cm. (18 in.) long. Individuals newly changed from their larval form have bright silvery sides and blue backs and migrate to the sea, where they feed parasitically on other fishes. Some non-migratory races of this species have evolved which are not parasitic as adults.

Eopsetta Pleuronectidae
jordani PETRALE SOLE, BRILL 70 cm. (27½ in.)
A right-eyed flatfish found widely on the Pacific coast of N. America. It is distributed from n. Baja California to the Gulf of Alaska

and the Bering Sea. It is found in water of a few fathoms, down to 550 m. (300 fathoms), although most abundant in 73–128 m. (40–70 fathoms), deeper in winter.

It is a valuable commercial fish along the Pacific coast, its large size and deep body making good fillets of excellent quality.

It is distinguished from other e. N. Pacific flatfishes by its wide body, large mouth with teeth in two rows in the upper jaw. The scales are small, and the lateral line is almost straight. It is uniform olive brown on the eyed side, white on the other sometimes with a pinkish flush.

It feeds on a wide range of fishes once it is adult but also eats numerous crustaceans and small bottom-living invertebrates.

Epalzeorhynchus Cyprinidae
kalopterus 14 cm. (5½ in.)
The genus *Epalzeorhynchus* contains a very distinctive group of Asiatic fishes, in which the body is elongate and cylindrical, with a ventral mouth, pronounced fringed upper lip, and 2 pairs of barbels.

This species is found in Sumatra and Borneo, where it is not rare in rivers. It has also been found in Thailand. It is a bottom-living fish found in pools and rivers, its habit of resting on its downturned pectoral fins on the bottom or on plants is characteristic. It feeds on encrusting algae and any contained small animals.

It is kept in aquaria quite commonly and although unspectacularly coloured, it is a peaceful and interesting aquarium fish. **126**

EPAULETTE FISH see **Glaucosoma scapulare**

EPHIPPIDAE
A small family of very deep-bodied fishes found in tropical seas, some species entering warm temperate waters. Probably as few as 10 species belong to this family. They live in inshore waters amongst reefs and on rocky bottoms, many of them feeding on molluscs.

Two main groups are discernible, the spadefishes (the family Ephippidae or Drepanidae according to some authors) which have a separate spiny dorsal fin, and the batfishes (formerly in the family Platacidae) in which the dorsal spines form a fin continuous with the soft-rayed dorsal which in this group is very well developed. They are related to the butterflyfishes (Chaetodontidae).

Many of the members of the family, notably the batfishes, when young are skilled mimics of floating leaves, or distasteful marine invertebrates.

Large specimens of batfishes often possess enormously swollen bones in the axial skeleton including the head bones, a condition known as hyperostosis. The swollen bone is oil-filled, and frequently persists long after the remainder of the skeleton has been dispersed, to be found on the shore, and later in the curio cabinet as a 'fossilized mouse' or some other fanciful name. See **Chaetodipterus, Drepane, Platax.**

Epigonus Apogonidae
telescopus BULLSEYE 76 cm. (30 in.)
Found in deep water in the Atlantic. In the N. it lives in depths of 183–914 m. (100–500

fathoms) and has been taken as far N. as the Shetland Islands. It also occurs in the S. Atlantic at depths of 914–1280 m. (500–700 fathoms) off the W. coast of S. Africa.

It is not a bottom-living fish but appears to be mostly found somewhat off the bottom perhaps 91–183 m. (50–100 fathoms) above the sea bed.

It is a deep brown colour, but is rather fragile, and many scales are knocked off in capture showing light skin beneath. Its fins are fragile; the anal fin with only 2 weak spines. Its eye glows dully when first caught, a pale greeny yellow reflection, and with its large size earns it its fisherman's name of bullseye.

Epinephelus   Serranidae
A large genus of groupers. The specimen illustrated in colour has not been identified. **267**
E. adscensionis ROCK HIND 61 cm. (2 ft)
A wide-ranging species in the tropical Atlantic having been reported from the Canary Islands, the Azores, Ascension Island, and S. to the Cape of Good Hope. In the w. Atlantic it is found from Massachusetts and Bermuda S. through the Bahamas, the W. Indies, to Brazil. It is found in inshore waters, and on reefs down to a depth of 30·5 m. (16 fathoms). It is particularly abundant on rocky bottoms and amongst rocks, and on wrecks, having a home

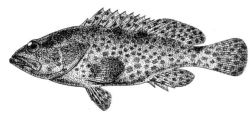

territory, usually a hole or crevice into which it retires when disturbed.

It is a very distinctive species by reason of its colouring and markings. It is light olive with intense dark spotting over the head and body. Several large dark brown spots are placed on the mid-line of the back, and on the top of the tail before the fin.
E. itajara JEWFISH 2·4 m. (8 ft)
This is one of the American groupers which is found on both the Atlantic and Pacific coasts. In the Atlantic it is known from Bermuda, the Bahamas, Florida, and the W. Indies.

It is a huge fish, which grows to a weight of at least 318 kg. (700 lb.); an angler captured a 308 kg. (680 lb.) specimen off Florida. It is a fine sporting fish, and is highly esteemed as food. It lives around sunken wrecks, between pilings, under coral ledges and in caves. It feeds on crustaceans, including large spiny lobsters, fishes, and even hawksbill turtles.

This species is one in which sex reversal has been suggested, males becoming functional females late in life.

Apart from its enormous size, it can be recognized by the broad, flat head, and coloration. This is generally dark brown with dark

spots on head and fins and 5 irregular broken bands running across the sides.
E. lanceolatus GROPER, GARRUPA
3·7 m. (12 ft)
A huge species which is found widely in the Indo-Pacific from the E. African coast to Australian waters and the w. Pacific. It is one of the largest groupers known and weighs up to at least 272 kg. (600 lb.) although most such weights are estimated. It also has the reputation of being a dangerous fish; the disappearance of divers in waters haunted by large groupers has been associated with attacks on man. They also follow launches for hours keeping in the wash behind the ship.

Although it is found mostly in the sea, in open water and around caves in coral reefs, it also enters estuaries.

This grouper is a well known sporting fish, it takes a baited hook readily and its vast size is an added attraction.

It is very variable in colour with age. Adults are uniform brown or dark brown with fins rather yellow; the young are golden-yellow with broad brown cross bands. The body is robust and very heavy, the head broad and the space between the eyes particularly wide.

Epiplatys   Cyprinodontidae
fasciolatus BANDED EPIPLATYS
8 cm. (3¼ in.)
A species which is widely distributed in W. Africa, especially in the regions of Liberia, Sierre Leone, and Nigeria. It has been introduced to Europe for many years as an aquarium fish, and is deservedly popular on account of its coloration, although it is rather a delicate species.

The male is very colourful, having a reddish brown back, the sides greenish red, paler on the belly. Each scale has a small bright red spot; 6–8 darkish oblique, parallel bands on the side. The throat and head are marked with red. The tail fin is large, and to a less extent the dorsal and anal fins are elongate. Many colour varieties have been found in nature, or have been developed by aquarists. **200**

EPIPLATYS, BANDED see **Epiplatys fasciolatus**

Eptatretus   Myxinidae
burgeri HAGFISH 61 cm. (2 ft)
This hagfish is common along the Pacific coast of Japan, and in the Sea of Japan to s. Korea. It lives in shallow water, 5–7 m. (3–4 fathoms) in depth, and is most active at night when it frequently attacks fishes caught in nets or on lines. It is also said to attack living uninjured fishes, boring into the body through the gill opening or vent and eating the flesh from within. Like other hagfishes it is very slimy.

It breeds from mid-August through October, each female laying up to 36 eggs. In Japan this hagfish is used for food as well as bait for better fish.
E. stouti see **Polistotrema stouti**

Equetus   Sciaenidae
acuminatus CUBBYU, HIGH-HAT
23 cm. (9 in.)
A W. Indian species found from Florida and the Bahamas s. to Brazil; probably also from Bermuda. It is an inhabitant of rocky areas, either found in small groups hiding under rock ledges, over sand or in turtle grass with rocks nearby. It is a shallow water species rarely found below 12 m. (7 fathoms). In many areas it is very common.

The fish is silvery with conspicuous dark brown lengthwise stripes, the most dominant down the side. The first dorsal fin is dark, except that the leading edge, as in the other fins is light.
E. lanceolatus JACKKNIFEFISH 23 cm. (9 in.)
Found in the w. Atlantic from Bermuda and the Carolinas s. through the Gulf of Mexico and the Caribbean to Brazil. It lives in moderately deep water, down to 18 m. (10 fathoms) although the young are found in shallow waters. It is usually found in rocky or coral habitats.

This is a strikingly marked species with a very high first dorsal fin which is dark brown to black in front, the colouring flowing in a curve across the body to the end of the tail, a second broad dark stripe from nape to pelvic fins, and a third through the eye, each dark stripe edged with white. The body is whitish silver elsewhere.

ERETMOPHORIDAE
The family of deep-sea cods, a group of worldwide distribution, which were formerly placed in the family Moridae. Most species are found in deep water, close to the ocean bottom or in mid-water. About 70 species are known placed in some 17 genera. Many of these forms are known from very few specimens and apart from a very few species their biology is unknown.

Their body-form is similar to the cods, they have 1–2, and occasionally 3 dorsal fins, mostly a single anal fin, and a characteristic tail fin. The swim bladder is connected to the auditory capsules in the cranium, and it is reasonable to suppose that these fish make meaningful noises and hear them clearly. See **Antimora, Mora, Physiculus, Saliota.**

Eridolychnus   Linophrynidae
schmidti 8 cm. (3¼ in.)
A deep-sea anglerfish found in all the tropical and temperate oceans and known from a number of specimens, males, females, and larvae. The mature females are stout almost globular in body form with spines above the eyes and behind the mouth. They differ from other ceratioids in that the teeth in the jaws are small and numerous, the fishing lure is set on the snout as a rounded lump without a long illicium, the skin is unpigmented.

One adult female of 8 cm. had 3 parasitic males attached to her underside each 18 mm. ($\frac{3}{4}$ in.) long. The adult males are colourless, their teeth, jaws, eyes and olfactory organs

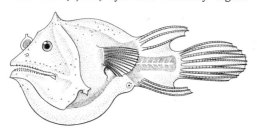

degenerated. The non-parasitic (immature) males have rather rounded bodies, large nostrils and moderate sized mouths. They are similar to larval females.

Erilepis   Anoplopomatidae
  zonifer SKILFISH 1·8 m. (6 ft)
A little-known N. Pacific fish which is found widely throughout that Ocean. It has been recorded in the E. from Japanese waters, and in the W. from se. Alaska to California.

Coloration is variable, usually dark green or blue above, fading on the sides with large white blotches on the body and fins.

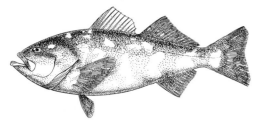

In Japan it is of commercial importance. The flesh is very oily, but is especially appreciated in winter.

Erimyzon   Catostomidae
  sucetta LAKE CHUBSUCKER 25 cm. (10 in.)
A widely distributed catostomid in s. Canada and the central region of the U.S. It is found from the Great Lakes s. to s. Alabama and e. Texas. It is a typical inhabitant of oxbow lakes, and the quieter, low gradient streams.

It is an elongate fish with a flattened belly but a rather high back, and a rather short (fewer than 20 rays) dorsal fin. The head is blunt, the lips thick, and the mouth terminal. The chubsuckers differ from the other N. American catostomids by lacking a lateral line at all ages. Only the first year young have any conspicuous markings and they are barred across the sides.

ERYTHRINIDAE
A group of S. American freshwater fishes related to the characins but differing in a number of features in the skeleton. In general they are rather elongate, but with rounded bodies, and short heads. The body is closely scaled, but the head is naked. The mouth is large, with curved conical teeth both in the jaws and on the palate. They all have rather short based, rounded fins, but lack the adipose fin of their relatives. See **Erythrinus, Hoplerythrinus, Hoplias.**

Erythrinus   Erythrinidae
  erythrinus 20 cm. (8 in.)
This fish is widely distributed in n. and central

S. America, from Venezuela s. across Brazil. It is a long-bodied predator, with rather pike-like behaviour, living amongst weeds or close to the bottom in wait of prey. It becomes more active at night than it is during the daytime. Its food consists of insect larvae and young fishes when young, and of larger fishes when adult. It often lives in ephemeral pools in river beds, which are frequently poorly supplied with oxygen, and it can utilize atmospheric oxygen by means of its specialized swimbladder.

Its body is cylindrical in front, flattened posteriorly, the fins are rounded, and it has no adipose fin. Its coloration varies, being light brown with a green sheen on the back. The sides have a dark lengthwise stripe ending in a pale-margined black spot; the head often has several dark streaks radiating from the eye. Its fins are usually yellowish, sometimes tinged with red.

Erythrinus has been kept in captivity, but due to its diet it is not a popular fish except in large public aquariums.

ESCOLAR see Gempylidae
ESCOLAR see **Lepidocybium flavobrunneum, Ruvettus pretiosus**
ESMARK'S EELPOUT see **Lycodes esmarki**

ESOCIDAE
This is a small family, containing only 1 genus *Esox*, and 5 species – the pikes. They are distributed in freshwater across the temperate regions of the N. Hemisphere and attain their greatest abundance of species in N. America. Physically they are all closely similar, long-bodied fish with a pointed snout, rather flattened from above. All are fully scaled, except on the head, and have a single dorsal fin placed opposite the anal fin and both far along the body near the tail. As one would expect from such active predatory fishes they have very many, and large teeth in their mouths. See **Esox.**

Esox   Esocidae
  americanus REDFIN or GRASS PICKEREL 33 cm. (13 in.)
Esox americanus inhabits the e. side of the N. American continent, and is divided into 2 subspecies the ranges of which are separated by the Appalachian Mountains. On the e. seaboard from the St Lawrence and Hudson rivers s. to Georgia lives the redfin pickerel (*E. a. americanus*), while inland the grass pickerel (*E. a. vermiculatus*) is found from the lower Great Lakes through the Mississippi drainage to Louisiana and central Texas. The subspecies hybridize in the s. regions, as does the redfin pickerel with the chain pickerel along the e. coast. Identification of these hybrids can be difficult.

It is a small species, living in sluggish streams, backwaters of larger rivers, lakes, ponds and even large ditches. It is always found amongst dense vegetation. Like other pikes and the chain pickerel its diet changes with age; as a young fish it feeds entirely on small insect larvae and crustaceans, later graduating to a mixture of fishes and invertebrates. They appear to live to a maximum age of about 7 years, but few survive for more than 3 years.

Neither of these pickerels is valued as game

fish, although occasionally enthusiasts will fish for them with light tackle.

E. lucius PIKE, NORTHERN PIKE 1·5 m. (5 ft)
The pike is circumpolar in its distribution, for it is found from the British Isles, e. across n. Europe, throughout the U.S.S.R., Alaska, Canada, and the n. U.S. to the Missouri and the Hudson River. Typically it is a fish of shallow lakes and quiet rivers, particularly backwaters and oxbow lakes. It is usually found close to the shore, and close to vegetation where its barred and mottled coloration blends with the background so as to be hardly noticeable. Its habits of lurking in concealment and then springing powerfully at a passing fish is clearly associated with this concealing coloration. It hunts by sight not by scent, and for this reason is rarely found in heavily silted water, nor very deep. As a young fish (up to 8 cm. ($3\frac{1}{4}$ in.)) it lives in densely weeded situations and feeds entirely on invertebrates, especially crustaceans, and insect larvae. As the pike grows it graduates on to young fish, tadpoles and newts, until as a mature fish there are very few fishes that it will not attempt to eat, including its own species, salmon, and trout. Large pike also take water birds, aquatic mammals, and amphibians.

Accounts of the pike's dietary oddities are a frequent temptation for the story teller, as particularly are stories of its size. The account of the 16th century Swiss polymath, Conrad Gessner, of a 5·2 m. (17 ft) long pike caught after 267 years of liberty, the skeleton of which was preserved in the Cathedral of Mannheim, is now discounted as fraud or exaggeration. But the pike does grow large. In the U.S.S.R. definite reports of weights up to 34 kg. (75 lb.) have been made, and less positive accounts of pike of 65 kg. (143 lb.) exist. There is no doubt, however, that in a good pike water specimens up to 22·7 kg. (50 lb.) can be produced.

In N. America its value is highest as a sporting fish and many large specimens are taken annually. In the U.S.S.R and e. Europe it is highly regarded as an angler's fish but its greatest value is as a commercially exploited food fish. In w. Europe it is avidly fished for the pot, and in places is sufficiently rare for restocking with artificially raised fry to be required. Throughout the world there seems to exist a curiously ambivalent attitude towards pike, many so-called sportsmen killing all pike they catch as dangerous freshwater 'sharks', while others attempt to maintain the stock of pike to cull smaller unwanted fishes.

The pike spawns in early spring, usually directly the snow water floods have covered watermeadows in the lower reaches of rivers. Sometimes they actually spawn in flooded grasslands, more usually along the banks of rivers. The females are always larger than the males. At spawning each female is usually accompanied by 2 or more males, shedding eggs by the thousand amongst the vegetation. Growth after hatching depends on water temperature and sex; the females grow faster than males, and in warm areas the young fish may be 20–30 cm. (8–12 in.) in the first year, but in the far north only 10 cm. (4 in.). **40**

E. masquinongy MUSKELLUNGE 2·4 m. (8 ft)
This is the largest of all the pikes, in the past giant specimens of 2·4 m. (8 ft) and weighing 45 kg. (100 lb.) were recorded, but today specimens of 27–32 kg. (60–70 lb.) are considered

large and rare. It is of restricted distribution for it is found only in the Great Lakes region of n. America. In addition to the lakes themselves and their feeder streams it occurs in the upper St Lawrence River and the Ohio. However, its range has greatly shrunk over the years, and the muskellunge is a rather scarce fish today, except very locally, where once it was common.

It is a highly favoured sporting fish, at least for its size if not for its fighting qualities. It is typically a fish of large lakes and rivers, being found in densely weeded areas. Like the northern pike it is wholly predatory and feeds on smaller fishes with an occasional water bird or mammal taken incidentally. Such a large fish requires large quantities of food, for it is estimated that to gain one unit of weight between 3 and 5 units of food must be eaten, in addition to the large quantity required for energy fuel.

The muskellunge is very similar to the northern pike (and occasionally interbreeds with it). It is usually best distinguished by the very greatly reduced size of the sensory pores on the head, and by the partially scaled cheek, only the top part being covered with scales, while the northern pike has a fully scaled cheek.

E. niger CHAIN PICKEREL 79 cm. (31 in.)
The chain pickerel is the largest of the N. American pickerels (the group of small pikes found only in the New World). It is distributed from Nova Scotia S. on the Atlantic slope, E. of the Appalachian Mountains to Texas, and in the Mississippi River system to s. Missouri and the Tennessee River in Alabama. It lives in quiet weedy waters, particularly in lakes, rather than in streams and smaller lakes.

It grows to a length of 79 cm. (31 in.) when it weighs over 4 kg. (9 lb.), so it is not a particularly large fish. It grows relatively slowly (figures for Massachusetts chain pickerel suggest a length of 58 cm. (23 in.) at 7 years, and a maximum age of 9 years although the normal individual maximum age in the population is nearer 3 or 4 years).

As a young fish the chain pickerel eats invertebrate food, particularly small crustaceans and insect larvae. As it grows it eats increasing numbers of fish (and of increasing size) but it is never wholly fish-eating as are the larger pikes.

The chain pickerel is a moderately well regarded sporting fish, although, as it does not attain a great size, it is less sought after than the pikes.

E. reicherti AMUR PIKE 114 cm. (45 in.)
The Amur pike, as its name suggests, is confined to the basin of the Amur River in the e. parts of the U.S.S.R. It differs from the pike in coloration, as an adult being silvery in colour

with numerous black spots each about the size of the pupil of the eye. The young, however, are very similar to young pike in colour, and physical resemblances are close.

It is said to live in the open waters of rivers and lakes, and to be much less restricted to weedy areas. The adults are to some extent migratory, living in rivers overwinter and moving into lakes and canals to spawn as soon as they are free of ice in spring.

It is a valuable food fish in the e. U.S.S.R.; in the Amur basin it is one of the most important commercial freshwater fishes. Its sporting value is probably very high but little has been recorded on this aspect of its utilization.

Esomus Cyprinidae
danrica FLYING BARB 15 cm. (6 in.)
An interesting fish, widely distributed in India and Sri Lanka, and reported from Singapore, which frequents the surface of ponds, tanks, and ditches. It is said to be able to survive in very muddy, shallow pools during droughts.

It is a slender fish with rather pointed fins, the pectorals being particularly long and well developed. The back profile is almost straight, the belly is deeply convex, and the head is pointed with 2 very long barbels from the upper jaw, and a second pair of shorter ones on the snout. The back is olive-green with an iridescent sheen, the sides silvery with a pinkish tinge. A dark brown band runs from the mouth to the end of the tips of the pectoral fins, then fades, but expands and darkens to form a large dark spot at the base of the tail.

This fish is often kept in aquaria in which it makes a peaceful and interesting pet. It has a habit of leaping from the surface so the tank must be covered.

ESTUARY
CATFISH see **Cnidoglanis macrocephalus**
PERCH see **Percalates colonorum**

Etelis Lutjanidae
carbunculus 91 cm. (3 ft)
Very widely distributed in the Indo-Pacific. Found from the Japanese coasts, the Philippines, Hawaii, and in the w. Indian Ocean off E. Africa, Mauritius and the Seychelles.

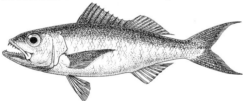

It is most common offshore and in rather deep water, and is caught mostly on long lines. It is a fine food fish; in Hawaii, where it is called onaga, it is the most important of the commercial fishes.

It is beautifully coloured, pink all over, reddish on the back, silvery below, the fins and inside the mouth deep red.

Etheostoma Percidae
caeruleum see under **E. spectabile**
exile IOWA DARTER 5 cm. (2 in.)
Widely distributed in s. Canada, and the n. parts of the U.S. It is in many ways typical of the N. American darters, a large group of small fishes of the perch family. The back and upper sides are light green finely blotched with dark brown, a series of dark brown patches along the sides alternating with reddish blotches.

In the breeding season (May to July), the males are brilliantly coloured, the first dorsal

fin with an orange band bordered with dark purple, ventrally it is yellow, and the fins are red.

It is found both in lakes and rivers, particularly those with a slow current and a hard, gravelly bottom. They also occur on muddy bottomed lakes amongst vegetation. This darter feeds on aquatic insects, crustaceans, and molluscs.

Its small size precludes any value as a food or sporting fish although it presumably has some value as forage for larger predators.

E. spectabile ORANGE-THROAT DARTER 8 cm. (3¼ in.)
A widely distributed N. American darter which is found in a very large area of the central U.S. virtually throughout the whole of the Mississippi-Missouri system.

It is distinguished, as the name suggests, by the deep orange colour of the throat and breast of the male in the breeding season. Non-breeding males, and females are pale under the throat.

The orange-throat darter lives in small to moderate sized streams of low gradient with riffles around 13 cm. (5 in.) deep on sand and gravel bottoms. It also tolerates turbid waters and silted bottoms. This species competes for living space with other darters, notably the rainbow darter (*E. caeruleum*) which prefers cleaner bottoms and faster flowing water, but appears to prevent the orange-throat darter from moving into such habitats. As with so many other freshwater fishes these nice ecological distinctions become obscured by human interference such as drainage and impoundment schemes. **289**

Etmopterus Squalidae
spinax VELVET-BELLY 53 cm. (21 in.)
The velvet-belly is a very common species in deep water in the e. Atlantic from Norway and Iceland s. to N. Africa, and in the Mediterranean. In colour it is dark brown, with a black stripe on each side towards the tail. The skin is covered with denticles, tooth-like structures, which are so fine that they feel like velvet, hence its common name.

It is a live-bearing species, the young being about 12·5 cm. (5 in.) at birth. They are born in litters of upwards of 6 after a gestation period of about 6 months.

The velvet-belly is found over the continental shelf in depths of 219–695 m. (120–380 fathoms). It feeds on crustaceans and fishes. This is one of the few sharks to possess luminous organs.

Etropiella Schilbeidae
debauwi 8 cm. (3¼ in.)
A small catfish found generally in the Congo basin. It makes a most interesting aquarium

fish on account of its continuous movement in small shoals. Isolated specimens do not thrive, and a shoal of the same species is necessary for survival.

It is distinguished by the presence of a small adipose fin, and especially by the dorsal fin being inserted far forward only just behind the head. Otherwise it is a typical member of the family with long anal fin, forked tail, compressed body, and 3 pairs of short barbels. It is translucent, but has a silvery throat and belly, and 3 distinct blue stripes lengthwise along the sides.

Etroplus Cichlidae
maculatus see under **E. suratensis**
suratensis GREEN CHROMIDE
41 cm. (16 in.)
Found in brackish water in Sri Lanka, and particularly common in river mouths and saline lagoons. It can tolerate freshwater for a short while, but is in best condition when kept in salt water.

It is a rather deep-bodied fish, greenish grey on the back and sides, with dusky vertical bands and the scales on the sides with greenish spots. Said to be banded with bright crimson and black in the breeding season.

Although this fish has been kept in aquaria it does not thrive. The related *E. maculatus* spawns in a hollow under a rock or cavity, and the parents guard the eggs. When they hatch the fry are moved to shallow pits and still protected for 5–6 days after which they become free-swimming. They keep in tight schools around the parents feeding off the mucus secreted by the skin of the adults.

Etrumeus Clupeidae
teres ROUND HERRING 25 cm. (10 in.)
The round herring is found in inshore waters along the Atlantic coast of N. America from the s. edge of the Bay of Fundy to n. Florida, and in the Gulf of Mexico. It is the only representative of the genus in the Atlantic, although others occur in the Pacific Ocean including the Californian coast.

It is a very slender, herring-like fish with a rounded body, totally lacking the sharply scaled keel along the belly so typical of the herrings. The anal fin is small, as are the pelvics; the scales are moderately large, very thin and so easily dislodged that it is difficult to catch a specimen with its scales in place. When alive it is olive-green on the back, silvery on the sides and belly. In the n. parts of its range, as along the coast of Massachusetts, the round herring is found inshore in summer, although its occurrence and abundance are sporadic. To the S. however, it is rarely found close to the shore, and appears to live at about 36 m. (20 fathoms) depth.

Eucinostomus Gerreidae
gula SILVER JENNY 18 cm. (7 in.)
A w. Atlantic species found from New England and Bermuda s. to Argentina. It is found in the Gulf of Mexico and in parts of the Caribbean.

The silver jenny is a shallow water fish found in depths around 1 m. (½ fathom), and occasionally down as deep as 9 m. (5 fathoms). It is mostly found in mangrove-lined tidal creeks, only occasionally in turtle grass beds. Like most members of the family it prefers sandy or sand and mud bottoms. It is a silvery

fish, bluish above with the fins dusky; young fishes have a series of dusky blotches across the upper sides and back.

EULACHON see **Thaleichthys pacificus**

Euleptorhamphus Exocoetidae
viridis OCEANIC HALFBEAK
46 cm. (18 in.)
World wide in its distribution, this distinctive halfbeak is found from the Pacific coast of America to Japan, Australia and across the Indian Ocean to the Red Sea and Madagascar. In the Atlantic it is found from the Caribbean to the W. African coast. Its range seems to be confined to the 25°C. isotherm, so it is found mostly in the tropics.

Its reported occurrence in isolated places suggested in the past that it was a sparsely distributed fish, but by using specially developed fishing nets towed at speed at the surface, it has been found to be common and widespread. It is, however, wholly pelagic and thus not often captured.

Eumicrotremus Cyclopteridae
orbis PACIFIC SPINY LUMPSUCKER
12·5 cm. (5 in.)
Found on the N. Pacific coast of America from Washington to the Bering Sea. It lives from low-tide level to depths of 146 m. (80 fathoms), usually on or close to rocky bottoms. It is occasionally captured in shrimp trawls and also encountered on the shore at low-tide mark. Specimens have been recorded from the gut of the lancetfish *Alepisaurus ferox*, a mainly

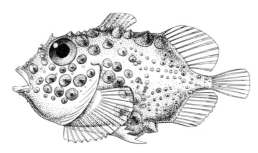

mid-water predator which suggests that at times the lumpsucker can be found well off the sea bed.

It is usually light green, sometimes brown, lighter on the undersurface.

Eupomacentrus Pomacentridae
planifrons YELLOW or THREE-SPOT
DAMSELFISH 13 cm. (5 in.)
A Caribbean and w. Atlantic species which is found from Bermuda, the Bahamas and Florida s. to the Lesser Antilles.

The young fish are bright yellow with a large black spot at the junction of the spiny and soft dorsal fins, a second spot on the top of the tail, and a small spot at the base of the pectoral fin. They tend to be solitary in their habits and to be seen around coral heads; they may pick parasites off other fishes. Adults are brownish with a yellow tinge, and lose the dark dorsal spot. It is a wide ranging damselfish found from depths of 1·5–26 m. (1–14 fathoms) on coral, rock, sand, shell, or sea grass beds.

Euprotomicrus Dalatiidae
bispinatus PYGMY SHARK
26·5 cm. (10½ in.)
The pygmy shark is one of the smallest of all known sharks; it is sexually mature at a length of less than 23 cm. (9 in.) (females) and 17 cm. (6¾ in.) (males), and the largest known specimen weighed only 70 g. (about 2½ oz). It has been found in the central water masses of the Pacific, S. Indian, and S. Atlantic oceans. It is known only from specimens taken at the surface of the sea (usually at night) in depths of 2000 to 10,000 m. (1094–5468 fathoms) of water. In these depths the pygmy shark is believed to migrate deeper during daylight hours for its food consists mainly of bathypelagic squids and fishes. It forms part of the mass of animal life migrating towards the surface as night falls.

The pygmy shark is luminescent, emitting a blue-green glow from thousands of minute light organs on the ventral surface. It also bears living young in litters of 8 – 4 in each oviduct. The young are born at a length of about 60 mm. (2⅜ in.).

Its colour varies from light brown to almost black.

EURASIAN WHITEFISH see under **Coregonus clupeaformis**
EUROPEAN
    CATFISH see **Silurus glanis**
    CISCO see **Coregonus albula**
    EEL see **Anguilla anguilla**
    HAKE see **Merluccius merluccius**
    MUDMINNOW see **Umbra krameri**
    SAND-EEL see under **Ammodytes americanus**
    SEAHORSE see **Hippocampus ramulosus**

Eurypegasus Pegasidae
draconis SEA MOTH 5 cm. (2 in.)
Widely distributed in the Indo-Pacific from the E. African coast, along the coasts of India, Indonesia, tropical Australia to Japan.

This is one of the more common sea moths, and it has long been known as a natural history curiosity, some of the earliest described reach-

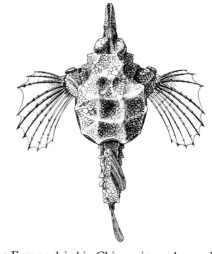

ing Europe dried in Chinese insect boxes. Not surprisingly, they represented something of a zoological puzzle. Brownish in colour.

EURYPHARYNGIDAE

One of the 3 nominal families of gulper-eels, deep sea relatives of the eels which were formerly placed in an order of their own, Lyomeri, although now placed with the eels in Anguilliformes. The other families are Saccopharyngidae and the nominal Monognathidae. The eurypharyngids are highly distinctive, with enormous jaws, and an elongate body. The dorsal fin originates well forward on the head. The head region is so greatly developed that the gill opening is closer to the vent than to the tip of the snout. See **Eurypharynx.**

Eurypharynx   Eurypharyngidae
    pelecanoides GULPER, GULPER-EEL
61 cm. (2 ft)
The only species recognized in this family is found in tropical and warm temperate oceans of the world, although most commonly reported from the Atlantic Ocean. It is found in deep water, its centre of vertical distribution being between 1400–2800 m. (765–1531 fathoms), although it has been found as shallow as 549 m. (300 fathoms) and as deep as 7625 m. (4000 fathoms). It is, however, found in mid-water at these depths, not on the bottom.

From the body shape and fragile build the gulper is judged as a poor swimmer, and yet they are obviously carnivores, eating on occasions quite sizeable fishes. How such a poor swimmer can manage to catch an active fish remains a mystery, but as most of the prey have been swallowed head first it is clear that they have not been caught by pursuit. Rather it is thought that the gulper swims slowly with its

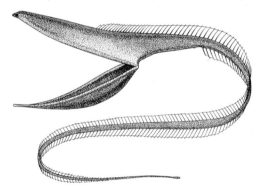

enormous jaws swung open until prey literally swims into its mouth, or perhaps the prey is enticed in some manner towards its open jaws. A small luminous organ at the tip of the tail may serve in this way, if the fish is able to dangle its tail in front of its mouth, or to swim in tight circles. It has a black scaleless skin.

EUTAENIOPHORIDAE

This family is little known except that its closest relatives are with the other 'wonderful-finned fishes' (families Kasidoridae and Mirapinnidae). They are thin, elongate fishes, with a smooth, naked skin, and dorsal and anal fins opposite to one another. The pelvic fins are narrow and wing-like in form, and placed on the throat. The juvenile and larval fish of this family have the skin of some rays of the tail fin produced into a long fleshy streamer, which may be 2 or more times the length of the body. This streamer seems to be lost with age although only relatively small fish have so far been found.

Members of the family are found worldwide as inhabitants of the tropical open oceans. See **Taeniophorus.**

Euthynnus   Scombridae
    affinis see under **E. alletteratus**
    alletteratus LITTLE TUNA, FALSE
ALBACORE 91 cm. (3 ft)
A common species in the tropical and warm temperate Atlantic which occurs also in the Mediterranean. In the w. Atlantic it ranges from New England and Bermuda to Brazil; in the e. it occurs from s. Africa to Biscay, occasionally to Britain. It is a common schooling species found in the inshore water over the continental shelf, and forming tight compact groups which prey on schools of smaller fishes, very often clupeoids. The presence of a school of little tuna is often betrayed by the sight of flocks of wheeling, diving sea birds which feed on the disturbed prey fish. It also feeds on squids and crustaceans.

Its flesh is very palatable and it has considerable commercial importance. It is also a favourite tuna amongst anglers even though its maximum weight is only 9 kg. (20 lb.).

Apart from its size this tuna can be identified by its coloration, dark steel blue above shading to silvery below. A series of oval dusky spots on the lower side and belly are distinctive although variable in size and number, for no other Atlantic tunny has dusky spots on the belly. The closely related Indo-Pacific form *E. affinis* has similar colouring.

Eutrigla   Triglidae
    gurnardus GREY GURNARD 41 cm. (16 in.)
This is the commonest and most widely distributed of the European gurnards; it is found from Norway and Iceland s. to the Mediterranean and Black Sea. It is relatively common in offshore, shallow water habitats but seems to be most abundant from the shore line down to 40 m. (22 fathoms). Its preferred habitat is sandy or muddy bottoms, but it is also common on rough bottoms.

It is a bottom-living species which feeds on crustaceans of all kinds, as well as benthic fishes. It spawns in the spring and summer, the eggs being pelagic, but the young fish are found close inshore at an early age.

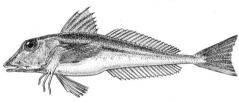

It is distinguished by its colouring which is grey with a pinkish tinge on the back, liberally sprinkled with white spots.

Eutropius   Schilbeidae
    depressirostris BUTTER BARBEL
30 cm. (12 in.)
A moderate sized catfish from S. Africa, found from Kenya s., which is closely related to the Nile species, *E. niloticus*. It grows to a moderate weight, large specimens attaining 1·4 kg. (3 lb.), and is a locally valuable angling and food fish.

It is very slender, but has a broad depressed head, a very long anal fin and a forked tail. Like other members of the genus it has a short, but

rather high dorsal fin, and a small adipose fin. It has 4 pairs of barbels.

It is silvery green with dark markings on the back, pale yellow on the belly, except for a dusky band at the base of the anal fin.

E. niloticus see under **E. depressirostris**

Euxiphipops   Chaetodontidae
    asfur 42 cm. (16½ in.)
An angelfish which is found in the Red Sea and the Gulf of Aden; it may also occur as far S. as Zanzibar, so its range could well include the nw. Indian Ocean.

It is distinguished by the cross-wise white band from the last dorsal spines to the vent, but which lies in front of the anal spines, and as the fish grows rounds off as a whitish blotch. Both the soft dorsal and the anal fin are pointed in outline. **332**

EVERGLADES PYGMY SUNFISH see **Elassoma evergladei**

Evermannella   Evermannellidae
    balbo 17 cm. (6¾ in.)
This fish has distinctly well developed telescopic eyes, which point upwards, and have large lenses; the feature is made more noticeable by the large 'glistening spot' on the side of the eye. This is a conspicuous greeny-white and is probably a light reflector, although its function is not known for certain. *E. balbo* is otherwise silvery with a pale pink tint, and fine black dots on the back.

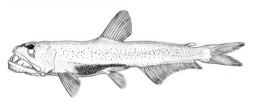

It is fairly well known as a Mediterranean fish and apparently inhabits that sea from end to end, but in the Atlantic it has only been found in deep-water off Bermuda. It is found in the open oceans from near the surface to depths of 1463 m. (800 fathoms). It must be presumed to be an active predator, and in view of the sparseness of adult fish in collections, too active to be caught by most types of fishing gear.

EVERMANNELLIDAE

A family containing a relatively few species, all rather short-bodied fishes, slender but with apparently disproportionately large heads. All the members of the family are quite small (up to 16 cm. (6¼ in.)), and live in mid-water depths of the 3 major oceans, including the Mediterranean.

All the sabre-toothed fishes have a very thin, papery skeleton, and are rather fragile, their scaleless skins rarely being intact. They have no luminous organs, but they have a conspicuous greeny-white glistening spot on the side of each eye which has been said to be luminous but probably acts as a light reflector. The eyes are slightly telescopic, and directed upwards. See **Evermannella.**

Evermannichthys   Gobiidae
    metzelaari ROUGHTAIL GOBY
3 cm. (1¼ in.)
Widely distributed in the Caribbean region

from the Bahamas to Curaçao, this goby is one of the well known sponge-living species. It is moderately common in the large loggerhead sponge *Spheciospongia vesparia* in depths of 1·2–26 m. (1–14 fathoms), living in the crevices and tubes of its host.

It is immediately distinguished by its very long, narrow body, the first and second dorsal fins widely spaced, and very characteristic, toothed scales on the lower side of the tail. These have been said to possibly help the goby move by giving it a grip on the walls of the sponge's tubes. The colouring is variable, but it is usually pale with dark markings, often forming bands across the body.

EXOCOETIDAE

The family of flyingfishes and halfbeaks which have in the past been usually treated as 2 families. Halfbeaks are like slender flyingfishes usually with the lower jaw prolonged into a beak, their pectoral fins are small (except for one species). They are schooling, surface-living fishes with the habit of skittering along the surface; some leap clear out of the water. Most are relatively small fishes (up to 46 cm. (18 in.)) of warm coastal areas, one lives in the open ocean, and a few species are specialized freshwater fishes.

Flyingfishes can conveniently be classed into two groups, one with large pelvic and pectoral fins and a long lower lobe to the tail and the other with only enlarged pectoral fins. Neither group actually flies; both use their large fin areas to give themselves lift to glide following active swimming below the surface. The double finned group with a long tail lobe increase their speed by rapid sculling at the surface and are capable of more sustained and controlled flight than the single-winged species which glide erratically. Flyingfishes are distributed worldwide in tropical and warm temperate regions with some occurring seasonally outside their normal range. See **Chriodorus, Cypselurus, Dermogenys, Euleptorhamphus, Exocoetus, Hemirhamphodon, Hemiramphus, Hirundichthys, Parexocoetus.**

Exocoetus   Exocoetidae
volitans FLYINGFISH 30 cm. (12 in.)
Widespread in tropical and seasonal in semitropical seas of all oceans. In the Atlantic it may be looked for in the region bounded by the Bahamas to the Canary Islands and from Rio de Janeiro to s. Angola. It also occurs in the Mediterranean. It is widely distributed in the Indian and Pacific oceans. It is typically an oceanic species.

This is one of the 2-winged species of flyingfishes; only the pectorals are greatly enlarged and if laid flat along the body they reach the tail fin. It is bluish above, silvery on the sides, white below; the pectorals are bluish brown.

Exodon   Characidae
paradoxus 15 cm. (6 in.)

Although when large this fish is a uniform greyish yellow with inconspicuous markings, as a young fish its colouring is quite remarkable. The background colour is a pale yellow, with very distinct iridescent streaks along the sides; the belly is silvery. Two large black blotches on the sides, one just behind the head, the other at the base of the tail often have pale margins. The fins are bright red, except for a yellowish tinge near the base.

It is an active, lively aquarium fish, fond of leaping from the surface, but one which needs a large, rather sparsely planted tank. It is not easy to rear, although it has been bred in captivity.

It is also not a good companion for smaller fishes for it attacks them and eats their scales. Its major single food source is the scales of other fishes which are removed by quick, stabbing jerks of the head at the free edge of the scale. Its peculiar teeth are well suited to this feeding method.

Exodon paradoxus is found in ne. S. America, in the Rio Branco, Rio Araguaia, and Rio Rupununi.

EYE-BITER, MALAWI see **Haplochromis compressiceps**
EYED SKATE see **Raja ocellata**

F

FACCIOLA'S EEL see **Nettodarus brevirostris**
FAIRY BASSLET see Grammidae
FAIRY BASSLET see **Gramma loreto**
FALL HERRING see **Alosa mediocris**
FALSE
    ALBACORE see **Euthynnus alletteratus**
    CATSHARK see **Pseudotriakis microdon**
    FEATHERBACK see **Xenomystus nigri**
    SHOVELNOSE STURGEON see **Pseudoscaphirhynchus kaufmanni**
FANFISH see **Pteraclis velifera**
FANGTOOTH OGREFISH see **Anoplogaster cornuta**

Farlowella   Loricariidae
gracilis 19 cm. (7½ in.)
A catfish of limited distribution in S. America, apparently found only in the Rio Caquetá, in s. Colombia.

This species is greyish on the back and sides with irregular dark blotches, the belly is pale.

Fins lightly spotted, a dark band along the upper edge of the tail.

Occasionally imported for the pet fish trade; they make engaging aquarium fish. The resemblance of these fish to twigs and leaf stalks is striking and they obviously gain some protection from it, living as they do in the leaf litter of rivers.

FAT SLEEPER see **Dormitator maculatus**
FATHEAD MINNOW see **Pimephales promelas**
FEATHER-FIN BULLFISH see **Heniochus acuminatus**

FEATHERBACK see Notopteridae
FEATHERBACK see **Notopterus chitala**
FEATHERBACK, FALSE see **Xenomystus nigri**
FIDDLE SHARKS see Rhinobatidae
FIDDLER RAY see **Trygonorhina fasciata**
FIFTEEN-SPINED STICKLEBACK see **Spinachia spinachia**
FIGHTINGFISH, SIAMESE see **Betta splendens**
FILEFISH see Balistidae
FILEFISH see **Stephanolepis auratus, Stephanolepis cirrhifer**
FILEFISH,
    ORANGE-SPOTTED see **Cantherhines pullus**
    SCRAWLED see **Aluterus scriptus**
    SLENDER see **Monacanthus tuckeri**
    TAIL-LIGHT see **Cantherhines pullus**
FINGERFISH see **Monodactylus argenteus**
FIREFISH,
    RED see **Pterois volitans**
    ZEBRA see **Dendrochirus zebra**
FIREWORKSFISH see **Pterois russelli**
FISH DOCTOR see **Gymnelis viridis**
FISHING-FROG see **Antennarius hispidus**

Fistularia   Fistulariidae
petimba FLUTEMOUTH 1·5 m. (5 ft)
Widely distributed in the Indo-Pacific from E. Africa and the Red Sea, to Japan, Hawaii, and n. Australia, particularly on the New South Wales and Queensland coasts.

It is immediately distinguishable by its long tail filament. It is greenish brown, light below with 2 blue stripes running along the back; some specimens have bright orange fins.

It is most common in inshore waters and estuaries. It is an active fish but has been reported as stalking shoals of fish by mimicry of a floating stick, floating straight and motionless at the surface until drifted by the tide close to the shoal. Then with astonishing suddenness it darts into the shoal to seize a fish. Single specimens have been observed to repeat this process several times on the same shoal.
F. tabacaria BLUE-SPOTTED CORNETFISH 1·8 m. (6 ft)
Widely distributed in shallow water on both sides of the tropical Atlantic but best known from the w. Atlantic where its range extends

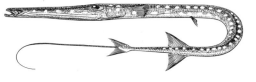

from New England and Bermuda to s. Brazil. It is widely distributed in the Caribbean and Gulf of Mexico.

It is brightly coloured, the back light brown, the sides pale, with 3 lengthwise rows of pale blue spots which fuse towards the tail to form a stripe. Despite this bright colouring the fish are extremely difficult to distinguish when they are hiding in sea grass beds, a favourite habitat, and in obscured, cloudy water even large specimens are well hidden by their coloration. They are active predators on small fishes.

FISTULARIIDAE

A small family of tropical marine fishes, usually known as cornetfishes or flutemouths, on account of their long narrow (flute-like) snout.

The family is well distributed in the tropical Atlantic, especially the Caribbean, and the Indo-Pacific.

They are common fishes around reefs and on turtle grass beds, actively darting singly, or in small shoals when young, at the surface or in a few feet of water.

They are easily distinguished by their extremely elongate shape, a narrow snout, head, and body ending in a whip-like extension to the tail. The body is scaleless, and there are no dorsal fin spines, in which they differ from their nearest relatives the trumpetfishes (family Aulostomidae). See **Fistularia**.

FIVE-BANDED
   BARB see **Barbus pentazona**
   SURGEONFISH see **Acanthurus triostegus**
FIVE-BEARDED ROCKLING see **Ciliata mustela**
FIVE-STRIPED PERCELLE see **Cheilodipterus quinquilineatus**
FLAG
   CICHLID see **Cichlasoma festivum**
   TETRA see **Hyphessobrycon heterorhabdus**

Flagellostomias   Melanostomiatidae
  boureei 32 cm. (12½ in.)
A long-bodied scaleless dragonfish found in the tropical and sub-tropical waters of the Atlantic Ocean, including the Caribbean Sea. It is distinguished from its relatives by its long anal fin, and by the detached lowest pectoral fin ray which is elongate and has luminous tissue on it. Its chin barbel is long, between half and three-quarters the length of the body, and depending on the age of the fish has a swollen tip with long filaments attached.

Luminous organs are well developed on the head in males, but are absent in females. Both sexes have pale-yellow luminous tissue on the barbel, the pectoral ray, and along the sides and belly. The colouring is otherwise brownish black.

FLAGFISH see Kuhliidae
FLAGFISH see **Jordanella floridae, Kuhlia taeniurus**
FLAGTAIL see Kuhliidae
FLAGTAIL see **Kuhlia taeniurus**
FLAKE see **Squalus acanthias, Mustelus antarctica, Pristiophorus cirratus, Scyliorhinus canicula**
FLAME TETRA see **Hyphessobrycon flammeus**
FLAMEFISH see **Apogon maculatus**

Flammeo   Holocentridae
  marianus LONGJAW SQUIRRELFISH 20 cm. (8 in.)
An easily recognized Caribbean species which has a long snout and projecting lower jaw, and the third anal spine very elongate, reaching to the tail fin base when depressed. It is widely distributed along the American coast from the Bahamas and the Carolinas, s. to the Lesser Antilles. It lives in moderately deep water, being found mainly below 15 m. (8 fathoms) but only becomes really common at 30–60 m. (16–33 fathoms); it is rare in shallow water, unlike the other squirrelfishes. **218**

FLAT
   HERRING see **Hilsa kelee**

NEEDLEFISH see **Ablennes hians**
FLATFISH see Achiridae, Bothidae, Citharidae, Cynoglossidae, Pleuronectidae, Psettodidae, Scophthalmidae, Soleidae
FLATHEAD see Platycephalidae
FLATHEAD,
  DEEP-SEA see **Rhinoplichthys haswelli**
  DUSKY see **Platycephalus fuscus**
  ROCK see **Thysanophrys cirronasus**
  TASSEL-SNOUTED see **Thysanophrys cirronasus**
FLATHEAD
  CATFISH see **Pylodictis olivaris**
  CLINGFISH see **Gobiesox maeandricus**
  MULLET see **Mugil cephalus**
FLOTSAMFISH see **Psenes pellucidus**
FLOUNDER see **Platichthys flesus**
FLOUNDER,
  ARROW-TOOTH see **Atheresthes stomias**
  CHANNEL see **Syacium micrurum**
  CRESTED see **Lophonectes gallus**
  DWARF see **Trinectes maculatus**
  LARGE-TOOTHED see **Pseudorhombus arsius**
  LONG-SNOUTED see **Ammotretis rostratus**
  PEACOCK see **Bothus lunatus**
  SAND see **Scophthalmus aquosus**
  SMOOTH see **Liopsetta putnami**
  SPOTTED-TAIL see **Engyprosopon grandisquama**
  STARRY see **Platichthys stellatus**
  SUMMER see **Paralichthys dentatus**
  WINTER see **Pseudopleuronectes americanus**
  WITCH see **Glyptocephalus cynoglossus**
  YELLOWTAIL see **Limanda ferruginea**
FLUTEMOUTHS see Fistulariidae
FLUTEMOUTH see **Fistularia petimba**
FLYING
  BARB see **Esomus danrica**
  GURNARDS see Dactylopteridae
  GURNARD see **Dactylopterus volitans, Daicocus peterseni**
HATCHETFISH see Gasteropelecidae
FLYINGFISH see Exocoetidae
FLYINGFISH see **Exocoetus volitans**
FLYINGFISH,
  ATLANTIC see **Cypselurus heterurus**
  BLACKFIN see **Hirundichthys rondeletii**
  SAILFIN see **parexocoetus brachypterus**
  SHORT-FINNED see **Parexocoetus brachypterus**

Forcipiger   Chaetodontidae
  longirostris 18 cm. (7 in.)
The 2 known species of the genus *Forcipiger* are distinguished by the extreme prolongation of the snout into a snipe-like bill, with a small mouth at the tip. They are also exceptionally deep-bodied, compressed fishes with high spiny dorsal rays. They are found only around reefs and rock formations.

This species was first discovered during Captain James Cook's third voyage round the world (1776–1780) at the Hawaiian Islands, (the original specimen still exists in the collection of the British Museum (Natural History), London). It was not again seen in Hawaiian waters until 1966 when the distinguished American ichthyologist John E. Randall captured one, while others were found by him in 1969. He discovered that this species exists in 2 colour phases, one basically yellow in colour, with black or brown on the head and

upper snout, and a dark round mark on the anal fin; the other is overall dark. Specimens of the dark form can change colour to the light; these are usually found in shallower water.

F. longirostris is widely distributed in the tropical Indo-Pacific from the Hawaiian Islands to the E. Indies, and the Comoro Islands in the w. Indian Ocean. **334**

Formio   Formionidae
  niger GERMANFISH 61 cm. (2 ft)
Found in the Sea of Japan and the Yellow Sea, from the Hawaiian Islands to n. Australia and thence to the Persian Gulf and e. Africa. Small scales cover the body and the posterior part of the lateral line is made up of a series of pointed, tube-bearing scales. Its colour is silvery grey.

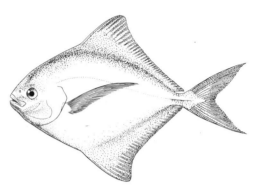

It is said to be an excellent food fish, and is used as such in many regions, but in places is too rare to be regularly caught. It is also said to swim in shoals on its side a few feet below the surface of the water.

FORMIONIDAE
A family of Indo-Pacific marine fishes the only member of which is superficially very similar to the jacks and crevalles. It differs from them by lacking free spines in front of the anal fin, and by having a lateral line of scales the size of normal body scales, and not having a series of bony scutes, although the scales are flat and spiky. See **Formio**.

FOUR-BEARDED ROCKLING see **Rhinonemus cimbrius**
FOUR-EYED FISH see **Anableps anableps**
FOUR-EYES see **Anableps anableps**
FOUR-HORNED SCULPIN see **Oncocottus quadricornis**
FOUR-SPINE STICKLEBACK see **Apeltes quadracus**
FOUR-EYE BUTTERFLYFISH see **Chaetodon capistratus**
FOX-FACE see **Lo vulpinus**
FRECKLED CARDINALFISH see **Phaeoptyx conklini**
FRENCH
  ANGELFISH see **Pomacanthus paru**
  GRUNT see **Haemulon flavolineatum**
  SOLE see **Pegusa lascaris**
FRESHWATER
  CATFISH see **Tandanus tandanus**
  DRUM see **Aplodinotus grunniens**
  GOBY see **Chaenogobius isaza**
  MULLET, YELLOW-EYED see **Aldrichetta forsteri**
FRIGATE MACKEREL see **Auxis thazard**
FRILLED SHARK see **Chlamydoselachus anguineus**

FRILLFIN GOBY see **Bathygobius soporator**
FROGFISH see Antennariidae,
    Brachionichthyidae
FROGFISH see **Antennarius hispidus,**
    Sympterichthys verrucosus
FROGFISH,
    BANDED see **Halophryne diemensis**
    LONGLURE see **Antennarius**
      multiocellatus
    SPLITLURE see **Antennarius scaber**
FROSTFISH see Trichiuridae
FROSTFISH see **Lepidopus caudatus**

Fucomimus   Clinidae
  mus KLIPFISH, WEEDFISH 10 cm. (4 in.)
One of the very many species of klipfish or
scaled blennies to be found on the S. African
coastline. This species is very abundant
amongst algae at and below low tide mark, and
is found between False Bay and Kei River, in
S. Africa. It is said to be a strangely lethargic
species which makes little effort to escape when
captured but just writhes slowly in the hand.

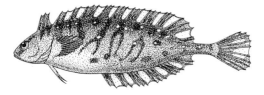

It is a very striking form, with the first 3
dorsal rays separate, and the succeeding rays,
as well as those of the anal and tail fins grouped
with gaps between every few rays, forming
'windows' in the fins. It is reddish, green, or
brown with silvery flecks.

FUGU see Tetraodontidae

Fundulus   Cyprinodontidae
  heteroclitus MUMMICHOG 13 cm. (5 in.)
A toothcarp native to e. N. America, the mummichog has been found between w. Newfoundland to Texas, and even Mexico, and offshore
at Bermuda. It is found along sheltered shores
where the tide flows over beds of eel grass, on
tidal flats in the occasional pools and creeks,
as well as in the estuarine regions of rivers and
streams. It is a very adaptable fish able to withstand low levels of dissolved oxygen and high
temperatures in tidal pools, as well as surviving
partially buried in mud.
    It is an omnivorous feeder, eating plant and
animal material, as well as scavenging on drifting refuse. They spawn in summer, the
brightly coloured male chasing the female
and at the moment of spawning clasping her
with his pelvic and dorsal fins. The eggs are
sticky and clump together in a yellowish mass
on sand or gravel.

The male has larger dorsal and anal fins than
the female, and the anal rays are thickened.
The male is dark green or steel blue, with

white and yellow spots and narrow silvery bars
on the sides. The colours become heightened at
spawning time. Females are plainer olive-
green, darker above than below.
    It is frequently kept as an aquarium fish, has
some value as an angler's bait, and is also a
favourite fish to keep for biological experiments on fishes.

FUSILIER, RED-BELLIED see **Caesio**
  erythrogaster

G

GADIDAE

The cods, a family of marine fishes (one is
found in freshwater) found principally in the
cooler waters of the N. Hemisphere, relatively
few having penetrated into the S. Hemisphere.
Most are fishes found on the continental shelf,
a few are found in the deep sea, while others
are littoral fish found between tide marks.
They have pelagic eggs and larval stages.
    They are soft-rayed fishes, lacking spines in
their fins, and possessing 2–3 dorsal and 1–2
anal fins. Most have a barbel on the chin, many
have barbels on their snouts. Scales are small,
well attached and cycloid.
    All the cod family is predatory, eating inver-
tebrates and other fishes; many species are
important food fish for man and other marine
animals. It is one of the most commercially
important fish families. See **Boreogadus,
Brosme, Ciliata, Gadus, Lota, Melanogrammus, Merlangius, Microgadus, Micromesistius, Molva, Pollachius, Rhinonemus, Theragra, Trisopterus, Urophycis.**

Gadomus   Macrouridae
A genus of rat-tails. The *Gadomus* illustrated
has not been specifically identified. **191**
G. longifilis 29 cm. (11½ in.)
A moderately deepwater rat-tail found on both
sides of the Atlantic, and with close relatives
in the Indo-Pacific. The e. Atlantic captures
from off Portugal, Morocco, the Canaries, and
the Azores, were made in depths of 1097–
2158 m. (600–1180 fathoms), those from the
w. Atlantic between 631–1351 m. (344–637
fathoms).
    This is a typical rat-tail in body form, but it
is distinctive in having a long chin barbel, and
extremely long streamers on its pectoral and
pelvic fins. Its eye is relatively small. It is unusual in that the lateral line system, usually
very well developed in rat-tails, is poorly
developed, and evidently the long barbel and
rays are used as sensory organs in place of an
acute lateral line system.

GADOPSIDAE

A family of freshwater fishes confined to the s.
rivers of Australia, especially Tasmania. A
single species only is contained in this family, a
rather slender-bodied fish with a long dorsal
fin, the first part of which is composed of spines
which increase evenly in size from front to
back. The body, head, and fin bases are covered
with small scales. The pelvic fins are placed far
forward, beneath the rear of the head and are
composed of a single, long ray on each side.
See **Gadopsis.**

Gadopsis   Gadopsidae
  marmoratus BLACKFISH, SLIPPERY
61 cm. (2 ft)
Found in the rivers of Tasmania, New South
Wales, Victoria, s. Queensland, and S. Australia. Formerly it was an abundant fish in many
of the rivers in these states, and was particularly common in the upstream tributaries and
smaller branches. It was a popular angling
species, and relatively easy to catch; it was reported to attain a weight of 5 kg. (11 lb.) in
suitable rivers. Now, for a variety of reasons,
its range and its numbers are much reduced.
The reasons for this decline that have been
advanced include introduction of exotic
species, especially trout, the silting up of
rivers due to clearance of the vegetation and
drainage, and in places water extraction and
pollution. There seems to be evidence of competition with trout, for the blackfish eats
caddis larvae and insects.

It is dark olive-brown, with black blotches;
the sides are yellowish.

Gadus   Gadidae
  morhua COD, CODLING 120 cm. (47 in.)
A N. Atlantic species of great economic importance. The cod is distinguished by a number of features especially its colouring for it has
a light coloured lateral line, the background
colour is greenish, grey, or even reddish green
(depending on the habitat in which it is living),
freckled with many rounded lighter spots. The
cod can grow very large but fishing pressure is
heavy and very large specimens are rarely
caught these days. The average weight is probably as low as 4·5 kg (10 lb.), with a fair number of captures up to 11 kg (25 lb.). Records of
fish of 90 kg. (200 lb.) date from the end of the
last century when some fishing grounds were
still relatively untouched.

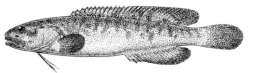

The cod ranges the coastal waters of the
whole N. Atlantic. In the E. it is found from
Biscay to the Barents Sea, and into the high
Arctic. A race in the Baltic is named as *G.
morhua callarias,* but differs in only minor
ways. The Atlantic cod is found around Iceland, s. Greenland, and in the w. Atlantic from
Hudson Bay to Cape Hatteras, N. Carolina.
The most prolific fishing grounds are in the n.
parts of its range, its occurrence to the S. in
numbers usually being due to winter-time
migration.
    The cod makes extensive migrations, in the
winter it tends to move s., but some populations in the N. move inshore in spring and into
deeper water during the winter. Migrations
tend to be variable with the particular population. Spawning takes place over a wide area of
the continental shelf, in water of 110–183 m.
(60–100 fathoms), mainly between February
and April. The surface-drifting eggs and larvae

are widely distributed by ocean currents. Young cod feed on surface-living small copepods and copepod eggs. Later they live closer to the bottom and feed on crustaceans, small fishes, and worms. As they grow they depend more and more on fishes, feeding particularly on herrings, sprats, capelin, sand-eels, and other species, but crustaceans are commonly eaten also.

The cod is caught in otter trawls, seine nets, and on lines. It is an extremely important commercial fish throughout its range, much of the catch being marketed fresh or frozen, while the waste is used for extensive by-products. Cod are also salted and dried for export to s. Europe and elsewhere. It has been a food of man since at least the Mesolithic, for coastal sites of this period have contained cod bones.

GAFFTOPSAIL CATFISH see **Bagre marinus**

Galaxias　　　　　　Galaxiidae
brevipinnis LOWLAND GALAXIAS
20 cm. (8 in.)
This galaxiid is found widely in the lower reaches of coastal streams on the w. coast of both islands of New Zealand. It is found in small streams with pools and shingle rapids, but with no falls or obstructions between them and the sea. Its habitat suggests that it may spend the earlier stages of its life in the sea.

Its general colouring is dull greeny-brown densely marked with darker brown.

G. maculatus JOLLYTAIL, INANGA
20 cm. (8 in.)
This species is the most widespread of the galaxiids in New Zealand, Tasmanian, and Australian waters. It also occurs in s. S. America. Due to this and its variability in differing conditions it has a large number of synonyms both in scientific and local nomenclature.

It is a rather slim fish with a small head, and rounded fins, the dorsal and anal fins being close to the tail. It is also dark mottled on a silvery background. In New Zealand the young of this fish, with others, form the whitebait, a delicacy widely appreciated in the springtime. In their whitebait stage they are even more slender than the adult, quite transparent, and live in large shoals.

Shoals of mature inanga collect in the estuaries of large and small rivers, following a downstream migration, particularly at the time of new moon. They spawn amongst vegetation flooded at the water's edge during the high tides immediately following the new moon's spring tides. The eggs are stranded by the receding tide and stay attached to the vegetation usually trapped low down in the moist base of the plants until they are covered by the next spring tide, 28 days later, when they hatch. If the succeeding tide fails to reach them they will apparently survive in the egg until the next spring tide. After hatching the young are swept out to sea, where they spend the winter before returning to freshwater.

At a year old they are mostly mature and migrate downstream to spawn, although some will stay for 2 more years in freshwater before

spawning. In freshwater they are shy fish, hiding under banks although small shoals can sometimes be seen in backwaters.

Studies of the jollytail in enclosed lakes in sw. Victoria show that even when denied access to the sea this fish remains migratory. Here, however, they live in the freshwater lake and migrate up into small streams when they are in flood following rain. The eggs lie in the vegetation on the flood plain until covered by the next spate, which may follow anytime between 2 and 6 weeks later depending on rainfall.

G. zebratus CAPE GALAXIAS 7·5 cm. (3 in.)
This species is found at the s. tip of Africa in the S. coastal regions from the Olifants River catchment E. to Kaaimans River. It is a very variable fish in both body shape and colour, and this in the past led to confusion as to the number of species of *Galaxias* found in S. Africa. However these differences are now regarded as being due to local environmental conditions, for example those fish found in peat-stained mountain streams are golden brown with many dark brown vertical bars, while in clearer streams the colouring is confined to a finer speckling of dark spots.

It is a slender fish, with a blunt rounded head. Its fins are rounded, the dorsal and anal being close to the tail. Like other galaxiids it is quite scaleless.

It is a very hardy fish capable of surviving wide changes of temperature and of oxygen levels. It feeds on smaller aquatic organisms including young fish. It is believed to spawn in freshwater.

GALAXIAS,
CAPE see **Galaxias zebratus**
LOWLAND see **Galaxias brevipinnis**

GALAXIIDAE

A family of rather distinctive fishes found only in the S. Hemisphere. Most are small (the largest attains a length of 71 cm. (28 in.)) and spawn in freshwater, although many are migratory spending at least part of their lives in the sea. They are found in the s. tip of S. America, in S. Africa, New Caledonia, s. Australia, including Tasmania, and in New Zealand in which islands they form the greater part of the native freshwater fish fauna.

Some are rather slender-bodied fishes, but the majority are thickset, almost plump, with a moderately large head. All have rounded dorsal and anal fins set opposite one another and far back near the tail. None of them have an adipose fin (a distinction from their nearest relatives the S. Hemisphere smelts – Retropinnidae), nor do they have scales.

The galaxiads are still a 'difficult' group for correct naming. During the thousands of years of isolation in their various areas of occurrence they have evolved in different ways, consequently understanding their relationships has been a matter of difficulty. The wide but disjunct distribution of the family is also of zoogeographical interest. See **Galaxias, Neochanna.**

Galeocerdo　　　　　　Carcharhinidae
cuvier TIGER SHARK 5·5 m. (18 ft)
The tiger shark is found far out to sea or close inshore and ranges through all tropical and subtropical seas. It wanders outside its normal

range during summer, with seasonal warming of the sea and in the Atlantic has been recorded as far N. as Iceland and the Massachusetts coast at this season. It is common in Australian waters. It is rated as one of the oceans' most aggressive sharks and has been involved in many fatal attacks on humans, both along Australian coasts, off Florida and elsewhere.

Up to a length of 2 m. (6½ ft) the back is brownish with a conspicuous colour pattern of dark stripes, which gives it its name – tiger shark. Larger specimens are grey or brownish and usually are not patterned.

As a game fish it is well regarded and specimens up to 807 kg. (1780 lb.) have been caught by anglers. It feeds on an astonishing variety of marine life, including sea turtles, large conch shells, horseshoe crabs, porpoises, and a great variety of fish. It also scavenges a great deal and strange food items like cans of salmon, leather wallets, and copper wire have been found in its gut.

It gives birth to living young, reputedly as many as 80, from 51–75 cm. (20–30 in.) long in a litter.

Galeorhinus　　　　　　Carcharhinidae
australis SCHOOL SHARK, TOPE
2 m. (6½ ft)
The school shark is found in inshore waters of all Australian states, but is most abundant in s. waters. It is greyish to brown above, lighter below, rather slender-bodied with large dorsal and pectoral fins and a well-developed tail. Its teeth are relatively small and oblique, and have a large central cusp with coarse serrations at the base.

Like other *Galeorhinus* species it gives birth to living young. In this species the average litter is 28, but the litter size may vary from 17 to 41; the pups are 30 cm. (12 in.) long at birth. Gestation lasts 6 months, but only half the mature females bear young each year. Sexual maturity is reached at 8 years (males) and 10 years (females). This combination of low reproductive rate, and late maturity has made the school shark particularly vulnerable to overfishing, and as it was heavily exploited in the s. waters of Australia stocks declined severely. Conservation measures, including a close season for fishing, have recently helped to stabilize the population levels of this valuable Australian foodfish.

G. galeus TOPE, TOPER, SWEET WILLIAM
2 m. (6½ ft)
The tope is a slender-bodied, greyish coloured shark which is common in the e. Atlantic, especially around the British Isles. It is a rather solitary shallow-water fish, occasionally found in small shoals, and close inshore especially in summer.

It feeds indiscriminately on shoaling fishes and particularly bottom-feeding forms, such as flatfishes. It gives birth to living young in summer, and litters of between 20 and 40 have been recorded (the number depends on the size of the mother). The young at birth measure 40–45 cm. (15½–17 in.).

The tope is well favoured by British sea

anglers and specialist 'tope-clubs' exist in a number of places. As it grows to a weight of 34 kg. (75 lb), it offers moderate sport but is not commercially exploited.

It is a shark with a number of vernacular names; toper being perhaps an allusion to the rather heavy snout (often flushed after capture), while the origin of its name 'sweet william' remains an enigma.

G. zyopterus SOUPFIN, OIL SHARK
2 m. (6½ ft)
A slender-bodied shark with the first dorsal fin considerably larger than the second. Its colour is dark bluish to dusky grey on the back, pale underneath, the larger fins have dark leading edges. It is found on the Pacific coast of N. America where it is common from s. California to British Columbia. In the n. parts of this range the males outnumber females, in the S. the position is reversed, while off central California the ratio between the sexes is approximately equal.

This active shark feeds on a wide variety of fishes and squid. It lives in water 50–400 m. (27–219 fathoms) deep, the males usually living in the greater depths.

During the 1940s this shark was subject to a very valuable fishery, its liver oil being exceptionally rich in vitamin A. It is also much prized by the Chinese in w. America for the preparation of shark fin soup, the dorsal and pectoral fins particularly being stewed while fresh, or sun-dried for later preparation.

Galeus   Scyliorhinidae
melastomus BLACK-MOUTHED DOGFISH
76 cm. (30 in.)
The black-mouthed dogfish is a common inhabitant of deep water along the European coastline. It is found from Norway to n. Africa and in the Mediterranean, although as it lives most abundantly between 180–730 m. (100–400 fathoms) it is rarely caught except by offshore trawlers.

It lays eggs in slender cases which lack tentrils at the corners. Breeding takes place in the summer months in British waters but in the Mediterranean is said to continue all year round. It feeds on fishes and crustaceans, and although mainly a bottom-living shark takes some mid-water fish species.

Its common name refers to the conspicuous black lined mouth. The body is a dark brown along the back conspicuously patterned with a light zig-zag line dividing a series of blotches on the sides.

GALILEE CICHLID see **Sarotherodon galilaeus**
GALJOEN see **Coracinus capensis**
GALJOEN, BASTARD see **Oplegnathus conwayi**

Gambusia   Poeciliidae
affinis MOSQUITOFISH 6 cm. (2¼ in.)
Naturally distributed along the e. and s. states of the U.S., from New Jersey to Texas, and S. to n. Mexico (*G. affinis holbrooki*). A sub-species (*G. affinis affinis*) occurs in the river

systems of San Antonio and Guadelupe in Texas. This fish (mostly *holbrooki*) has been distributed far and wide throughout the tropical and warm temperate zones of the world, as a controller of the larvae of malaria

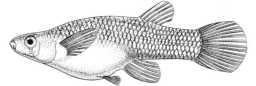

carrying mosquitos. It is even established as far away as Australia, is common in Italy, and s. France. Its reputation as a mosquito eater is great; it is said that it can eat its own weight daily, and in the enthusiasm for biological control of mosquitos it was carried throughout the world. Unfortunately it also preys on many species of native fishes, some of which are equally efficient mosquito predators, and in some places the survival of the native fish is threatened by the now uncontrollable exotic species.

It is very adaptable, being found in clear ponds, brooks, marshes, and streams. It also tolerates brackish water, and temperatures as high as 30°C. It is easy to keep in the aquarium but is aggressive, and is better placed (in warm climates) in outdoor ponds. The gestation period is 5–8 weeks, and from 40–60 young are produced in a brood.

It is a modestly coloured fish. The male is brownish grey with a blue sheen on the sides, a dark bar through the eye, and black spots on the sides. The female, which is the larger (males grow to 3 cm. (1⅛ in.)), is similarly coloured.

GAR see Lepisosteidae
GAR,
    ALLIGATOR see **Lepisosteus spatula**
    LONGNOSE see **Lepisosteus osseus**
    SHORTNOSE see **Lepisosteus platostomus**
    SILVER see **Strongylura marina**
GARDEN EEL see **Nystactichthys halis, Taenioconger digueti**
GARFISH see Belonidae
GARFISH see **Belone belone**
GARFISH,
    BLACK-BARRED see **Hemiramphus far**
    SHORT-NOSED see **Hemiramphus quoyi**
GARPIKE see Lepisosteidae

Garra   Cyprinidae
johnstonii 11 cm. (4½ in.)
This fish is found in the Victoria Nile and Lake Victoria. It is especially abundant in the turbulent running water of the river, and along the wave washed shores of the lake, a habitat in which it is well-equipped to survive with its broad sucker-disc beneath the head. This is a characteristic of the genus which is found in ne. Africa, and s. Asia. The lips are thickened and on the chin there is a large almost circular flat disc, with 2 small barbels either side of the mouth.

It is a small fish, dark grey-brown or bronze above, creamy below, with greyish fins, and 2–4 black spots at the dorsal fin base. Males have orange-tipped fins. Its food consists of algae and insect larvae which it presumably scrapes from the rocks.

GARRUPA see **Epinephelus lanceolatus**

Gasterochisma   Scombridae
melampus BIG-SCALED MACKEREL
165 cm. (65 in.)
A most distinctive member of the family, which is known from relatively few specimens. The pelvic fins (very large in young specimens) fit into a deep groove on the belly which runs back almost to the anus. The head profile is high like a dolphinfish.

It is bluish-black above, silvery below, the head blue, the tail fin and pelvic fins are black.

It is a rare oceanic tuna which has been recorded from off Argentina, South Africa, Australia, New Zealand, and in the s. Indian

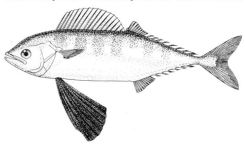

Ocean. Its biology is virtually unknown. A juvenile is illustrated.

GASTEROPELECIDAE
A very distinctive small family of tropical New World freshwater fishes. They have a deep, strongly compressed body, the upper profile being almost straight, while the profile of the belly sweeps down in a semicircular arc, curving back to the tail from the origin of the anal fin. This deep body is principally composed of an enlarged and specialized shoulder girdle and comparatively large musculature. The pectoral fins are long and set at an angle, level with the head.

These fishes can fly. The heavy pectoral muscles can move the long, rather broad pectoral fin so fast that the fish can leave the surface of the water and fly, in a straight line. In captivity the pectorals can be heard to make a buzzing sound as the fish leaves the water. (The marine flyingfishes, see Exocoetidae, glide on rigid wings, and do not fly in the strict sense).

The flying hatchetfishes live near the surface of the water feeding on insects and small crustaceans. They are distributed from Panama to La Plata. They are popular aquarium fishes, related to the tetras and characins (family Characidae). See **Carnegiella, Gasteropelecus, Thoracocharax**.

Gasteropelecus   Gasteropelecidae
levis SILVER HATCHETFISH 6 cm. (2¼ in.)
A typical flying hatchetfish in body form, with an almost straight dorsal profile, shallowly arched towards the back fin, but deeply curved on the belly forming a deep keel. This species closely resembles, and is often confused with, the more common *G. sternicla*.

The silver hatchetfish is found in the lower Amazon region in shaded pools. Like others of its family it feeds on insects, including small winged forms fallen into the water, as well as surface living insect larvae, and crustaceans. It has been kept in aquaria with some success.

94
G. sternicla COMMON HATCHETFISH
6·5 cm. (2½ in.)
This is probably the best known of the hatchet-

fishes, and certainly is the oldest known for it was first described by the Dutch ichthyologist, Laurens Gronovius in 1756 from a specimen captured in Surinam. Its range is the Amazon region and the Guianas.

It possesses the typical deep body and long pectoral fins of all members of the family. This species also has an adipose fin just before the tail fin. Its background colouring is yellowish to silver, and the fish appears to be mainly silvery when seen under bright lights. It is otherwise unmarked except for a lengthwise dark stripe, narrowly edged by lighter bands above and below. The fins are colourless.

It is a popular aquarium fish, relatively easy to keep, although usually habitually hanging still near the surface. It is capable of flying for a few inches across the surface of the water.

GASTEROSTEIDAE

The family of the sticklebacks, well-known fishes abundant in the waters of the N. Hemisphere. Some species are confined to marine habitats, others are found entirely in freshwater, but the majority can live in fully saline or fresh water (according to latitude) and are not unduly inconvenienced by change from one to the other.

Most of the species are small, their bodies slightly elongate, more usually torpedo shaped, and scaleless even if covered with bony plates. They have small but protractile jaws, with fine teeth, although some forms have a long snout. A typical feature of the group is the presence of a series of separate sharp spines along the back, and a sharp spine in the pelvic fins. Other fins are mostly small and have branched rays.

Care of eggs and young is characteristic of the family; males build the nest and guard it and the young. See **Apeltes, Culea, Gasterosteus, Pungitius, Spinachia.**

Gasterosteus   Gasterosteidae
  aculeatus THREE-SPINE STICKLEBACK
10 cm. (4 in.)
Widely distributed throughout the N. Hemisphere. In Europe it is found in freshwaters from the Mediterranean basin, n. to the Arctic Circle, and in the sea around n. Europe. It is distributed across n. Eurasia, and in the countries bordering the N. Pacific from the Bering Strait S. to Korea and California, and in freshwater in Canada and the n. U.S. In the S. of its range it is a freshwater fish, to the N. it is increasingly found in the sea.

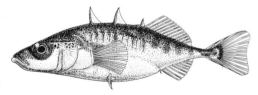

The three-spine stickleback is a small fish, usually less than 6 cm. (2¼ in.) long; the largest specimens are found in the sea, and to the N. It is ubiquitous, living in the smallest of freshwaters, ditches, and ponds as well as lakes and rivers. Usually it is confined to the shallow inshore region in open or lightly weeded habitats. In the sea it is found in pools amongst algae, and sublittorally although never at any great depth. It is occasionally found well offshore at the surface.

Its food preferences are catholic, almost any small animal, vertebrate or invertebrate is liable to be eaten. In the s. U.S.S.R. in the Black Sea region it is said to be a serious predator on, and competitor with the young of commercially valuable fishes, and control of the stickleback has been attempted. In its turn it is an important food for many larger fishes, large trout and perch, and pike of all except the smallest lengths, eat sticklebacks. Many birds feed on them; in some areas they are almost exclusively eaten by the kingfisher, and other birds eat them in greater numbers than any other fish. They have no commercial value, but locally the stickleback has been exploited for oil, forage, meal, and even used as a fertilizer.

Its spawning habits are well known. The male constructs a nest on the bottom from plant fragments and strips of algae, cementing it together with mucus from the urogenital apperture. His coloration is heightened, the back and sides become brighter green, the belly brilliant red, and the eyes blue. By conspicuous display he entices a series of females to his nest to lay their eggs, and guards and aerates the eggs and later the young throughout a period of several weeks. Adult males are highly territorial and drive off all other males and even threaten larger fishes.

Sticklebacks are not long-lived. In the wild few survive to 3 years; probably the life expectancy of a young fish can be measured in weeks rather than months. They become sexually mature at the end of the first year.

This species is well known for the variety of parasites it harbours. The most striking are the large cestode worm, *Schistocephalus solidus,* which causes the belly to become greatly swollen, and the sporozoan, *Glugea anomala* which produces white nodules on the sides. The former requires to be eaten by a bird to achieve its full life cycle. **226**

Gastromyzon   Homalopteridae
  borneensis 9 cm. (3½ in.)
This species, as its name suggests, is found on the island of Borneo. It is best known as an inhabitant of the mountainous regions of central and nw. Borneo, but has also been found at low altitudes near the coast of e. N. Borneo.

It is probably found throughout these regions wherever the local topography causes rapids to form in streams. It clings by its well developed sucker disc to rocks in the fastest currents, grazing on the encrusting algae and diatoms on the rocks.

Its most notable feature is the flattened anterior region of the body, and the enormous development of pectoral and pelvic fins to form an adhesion pad on the belly; the pelvic fins are united posteriorly with one another. **146**

Gaterin   Pomadasyidae
  diagrammus SILVER-BANDED SWEETLIPS
51 cm. (20 in.)
Widespread in the Indian Ocean from the E. African coast, to the Indian coast and the E.

Indies. In the central parts of its range it is common in coastal waters.

It is rather slender-bodied but with the high curved anterior body typical of the group. Its colouring is variable. **299**
G. gaterinus 41 cm. (16 in.)
Found in the Red Sea and along the e. coast of Africa as far S. as Delagoa Bay. It is a common and conspicuous fish along the edges of the reefs and in sandy bays, although it becomes rare to the S.

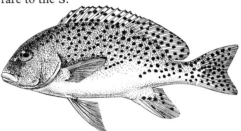

The juvenile has much the same colour as the adult but the dark spots form broken lines. **300**

GEELBEK see **Atractoscion aequidens**

GEMPYLIDAE

A small family of moderately large marine fishes found widely distributed in the tropical and temperate oceans of the world. Most of them are mesopelagic species, although some are found in moderately deep water. All are active, fast-swimming predatory fishes the biology of which, and even the distribution, being not well known due to the difficulty of catching sufficient numbers for study.

The gempylids, which are also known as snake mackerels, snoek, and escolars, are superficially like elongate tuna (Scombridae), but lack the keels on the sides of the body, and possess large to massive teeth in the jaws and palate. Most of the gempylids have 2 dorsal fins, some have secondary finlets behind the major fins.

Some are commercially exploited locally and are well esteemed as food fish. Other species are said to have flesh too oily to be palatable. See **Gempylus, Lepidocybium, Nesiarchus, Rexea, Ruvettus, Thyrsites.**

Gempylus   Gempylidae
  serpens SNAKE MACKEREL 152 cm. (5 ft)
Worldwide in its distribution, the snake mackerel is found in all tropical and occasionally in warm temperate oceans. Most of the early specimens captured were single specimens picked up at the ocean surface, often at night whence they seem to be attracted to light. The trans-Pacific expedition on 'Kon Tiki' captured one by this means. It is by no means so rare as was then thought, however, for numerous specimens have been captured at depths of several hundred feet below the surface on drifting long lines. It presumably swims too fast to be caught in nets for it is rarely taken in that way.

Its remarkable dentition shows it to be an active squid- and fish-eater. Young specimens are frequently found in the stomach of larger predatory fishes.

Its body form is remarkably elongate, almost eel-like but flattened from side to side. The first dorsal fin is composed of rather high spines; the second dorsal and anal are followed by a series of finlets. The head is long and pointed, the jaws large, the lower longer, and the teeth massive.

Genypterus   Ophidiidae
  blacodes LING 91 cm. (3 ft)
A species of cusk-eel found on the s. coasts of Australia, and around New Zealand. It is found in the states of S. Australia, Victoria, and Tasmania most abundantly. Although it is quite common it is not sufficiently abundant to be of great commercial importance but specimens are marketed, and it is said to be good eating (especially the liver).

In colour it is pinkish above with irregular dark mottling on the back and sides; ventrally it is almost white.

'Ling' is also used in Australia for the gadoid, *Lotella callarias,* neither should be confused with the N. Atlantic lings, *Molva* spp.
G. capensis KINGKLIP 1·5 m. (5 ft)
Found solely round the s. tip of Africa, from Walvis Bay to Algoa Bay in 54–456 m. (30–250 fathoms). It is an important commercial fish in Cape seas, taken mostly by trawl but also on lines. Its flesh is considered to be a great delicacy, and the liver is said, by the late Professor J. L. B. Smith, to be of a delicacy and flavour unsurpassed by even chicken liver.

It is a long slender fish with 2 slender pelvic fins under the throat, a long dorsal and anal fin, united at the tail. The head is flattened, the mouth is large. In colour it is dull brown above, medium brown on the sides with lighter mottling, and lightish ventrally. It is closely related to the New Zealand species, *G. blacodes.*

Geophagus   Cichlidae
  australe 18 cm. (7 in.)
Found in freshwater in the Argentine, around Buenos Aires and Santa Fe in lakes, and in the Rio de La Plata. It is a slender-bodied fish with a long snout and a straight profile.

This species, like others of the genus, can be kept in aquaria. It is troublesome, however, in that it likes to dig up the bottom of the tank, uprooting plants in the process. **360**
G. surinamensis 24 cm. (9½ in.)
Found in ne. S. America. It is a rather deep-bodied cichlid with a strongly arched head and nape. The pelvic and second dorsal and anal fins are very elongate.

Its coloration is variable, but males when spawning have a reddish breast and the fins develop blue spots. **361**

Geotria   Petromyzonidae
  australis POUCHED LAMPREY, PIHARAU, KOROKORO 60 cm. (23½ in.)
Found in rivers and coastal waters of s. Australia, Tasmania, and New Zealand. Adults enter river mouths in winter and move into the head waters to spawn. The larva is brown and wormlike, and lies buried in muddy sand in the river for several years, but at a length of about 7·5 cm. (3 in.) develops teeth in its mouth (previously having fed on filtered micro-organisms from the mud) and migrates to sea. As an adult it feeds parasitically sucking the

blood of fishes. The male, while migrating upstream to spawn, develops the characteristic pouch under its head, which gives it the name pouched lamprey.

Gephyroberyx   Trachichthyidae
  darwini DARWIN'S ROUGHY 46 cm. (18 in.)
A rare deep water fish probably of world-wide distribution. It was first found in deep water off Madeira, but has been taken in the w. Atlantic from off New Jersey to Panama, off the Natal coast of s. Africa, N. to the Red Sea and off w. and s. Australia and Japan. It is found in depths of 274–823 m. (150–450 fathoms).

It is deep-bodied, rather compressed, with a massive head. The eye is rather small, but the mouth is large. A series of strong spines in front of the dorsal fin rays. The scales are rather small but rough-edged and the belly has a line of large sharp scutes – this roughness gives it the above Australian name. It is reddish brown above, silvery beneath. It appears to feed on shrimps and small fishes.

GERMANFISH see **Formio niger**

Gerres   Gerreidae
  cinereus YELLOW-FIN MOJARRA 38 cm. (15 in.)
Found in both Atlantic and Pacific coasts of tropical America, in the w. Atlantic occurring from Bermuda and Florida to s. Brazil. It is evidently an adaptable fish found in many habitats, from mangrove lined tidal creeks, sandy bays, and clear reef areas. It has also been found in brackish water. It always lives in shallow water, often being taken in the surf zone. A bottom feeder, it preys on a wide variety of invertebrates by picking at the sea bed with an open mouth, expelling sand and sediment through the gill covers.

Its sides are silvery with 7 faint pinkish bars; the pelvic fins are yellow.
G. oyena LINED SILVER-BIDDY 25 cm. (10 in.)
Widely distributed in the Indian Ocean, this little fish is found from the Red Sea and E. African coast, as far S. as Durban to Sri Lanka, and the E. Indies to Japan. It is essentially a shallow-water species, found on sandy bottoms close to reefs and in the surf zone; it penetrates into estuaries. In body form it is typical of the family.

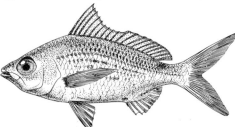

Its colouring is silvery, greyish blue on the back with individual scales picked out darker.

GERREIDAE
A family of small fishes widely distributed in most tropical seas. They are compressed bodied, silvery little fishes, fully scaled on head and body. They are distinguished by their tremendously protrusible mouths, the upper jaw hinging downward when the mouth is opened, to form a tube. The shape of the head and mouthparts is distinctive, the profile of the lower jaw is concave when the mouth is shut.

They are particularly well represented in the tropical American seas, where they are usually known as mojarras, and in E. Indian waters (Australian name silver-bellies).

Few of the group are considered edible. See **Eucinostomus, Gerres.**

GHOST
  PIPEFISH see Solenostomidae
  PIPEFISH see **Solenostomus cyanopterus**
  SHARK see **Callorhinchus milii**
GHOUL, BEARDED see **Inimicus didactylus**
GIANT
  ANTARCTIC COD see **Dissostichus mawsoni**
  DANIO see **Danio malabaricus**
  DEVIL RAY see **Manta birostris**
  GOURAMI see **Colisa fasciata**
  HERRING see **Elops saurus**
  PERCH see **Lates calcarifer**
  PIGFISH see **Achoerodus gouldii**
  SEA BASS see **Stereolepis gigas**
  THREADFIN see **Eleutheronema tetradactylum**
  TIGERFISH see **Hydrocynus goliath**
  TOAD see **Lagocephalus sceleratus**
  WRASSE see **Cheilinus undulatus**
  WRYMOUTH see **Delolepis gigantea**

GIBBERICHTHYIDAE
A family which was created to contain a single species of deep-water fish found in the tropical N. Atlantic, the Caribbean, and w. S. Pacific. Its closest relatives are the stephanoberycoids (see Stephanoberycidae), and the melamphaeids.

It is distinguished by its relatively deep body and very large head, short-based dorsal and anal fins with between 5–7 short spines in front of the dorsal fin. See **Gibberichthys.**

Gibberichthys   Gibberichthyidae
  pumilus 11 cm. (4¼ in.)
A deep-sea fish found in the tropical w. N. Atlantic and also in the S. Pacific near the

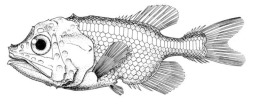

Samoan Islands. It is believed to live in the mid-water in the deep-sea. It is a small species for the 11 cm. specimen, which is the largest known, was sexually mature.

A remarkable looking fish known from very few specimens. The fishes described in the family Kasidoridae are now believed to be the larval stage of this species.

Gibbonsia   Clinidae
  montereyensis CREVICE KELPFISH 10 cm. (4 in.)
A common inhabitant of tidepools and intertidal kelp beds along the Pacific coast of N. America. It is found from Baja California along

the Californian coast, and from British Columbia, but has not been found between. It has been divided into 2 subspecies, one *C. montereyensis montereyensis* which is found on open ocean, exposed shores, and the other *C. montereyensis vulgaris* found on sheltered shores.

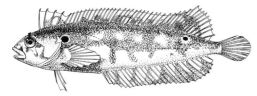

The long-based dorsal fin is divided anteriorly and posteriorly by 'windows', although the fin membrane is continuous. It is variable in colour, sometimes reddish, at others green with dark and silvery bars. A dark spot above the pectoral fin, others scattered on the body.

GIBEL CARP see **Carassius auratus**

GIGANTACTINIDAE
A small family of deep-sea anglerfishes found in all 3 major oceans and represented by only 2 genera.

Most of the distinctions between the families of ceratioid anglers are based on internal anatomy, but adult females are rather long-bodied and slender, and have a conspicuously long, whip-like fishing rod (illicium). Immature specimens are rounded with loose skin enveloping the body. Males are free-living, toothless when mature, with very well developed nostrils. See **Gigantactis.**

Gigantactis　　　　Gigantactinidae
　macronema 13 cm. (5 in.)
A widely distributed species which has been captured in the Atlantic as well as the e. Pacific

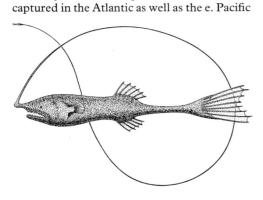

oceans. Closely related, and possibly identical species have been described from these, and the Indian Ocean.

Adults, both male and female, are relatively uncommon but the larvae, round-bodied with inflated loose skins, are more common. However, most specimens have been collected using special fishing gear on oceanographic research vessels. The most striking features of the females of this species are their enormously long fishing rod (illicium), slender tail, and dark spiny skin. They have been taken from near the surface down to 1646 m. (900 fathoms). Adult females apparently eat a wide range of deep water fish life.

Gigantura　　　　Giganturidae
　chuni see under **G. vorax**
　vorax 15 cm. (6 in.)
This telescope-eyed fish is known only from

the tropical w. Atlantic and Gulf of Mexico. A related species *(G. chuni)* occurs off the W. African coast. Most known specimens have been taken between depths of 293–3155 m. (160–1725 fathoms), but relatively few have been captured.

It is a brilliantly silvery fish, but the body cavity and inside of the mouth are jet black in colour and this tends to tint the overlying skin colour. The eyes are its most conspicuous feature, facing forwards they are virtually telescopic in appearance.

The giganturids clearly have very specialized, binocular vision, presumably of greatest value to the fish in finding prey. From the little biological information that is available they appear to be entirely fish-eaters, often ingesting prey such as viperfishes longer than themselves in body length. The stomach and body walls are very distensible to allow for the

size of the prey. Swallowing such large prey must be a lengthy and difficult process and it has been suggested that the dense black lining of mouth, throat, and stomach is intended to blackout the flashing light organs of the eaten fish so that the eater can remain undetected.

GIGANTURIDAE
A small family of mesopelagic fishes found in tropical, and warm temperate waters of the Atlantic, Indian, and Pacific oceans. Several species are known, all have been found in water of great depth although they themselves probably live in the middle regions down to 3658 m. (2000 fathoms).

They are very distinctive in that they have apparently telescopic eyes, the lenses placed forward looking at the end of a short tube. They all have a very large mouth, with sharp, depressible teeth in the jaws, large fan-like pectoral fins, and the lower rays of the tail fin very elongate. All are small fishes, few specimens longer than 15 cm. (6 in.) have been described.

Their relationships have long remained a puzzle, for they lack many bones that appear essential to other fish. They have no pelvic fins or pelvic girdle, parts of the gill complex are missing, and they have no scales. In addition they have a jelly-like tissue beneath the skin. These, and other features have led some workers to the conclusion that they are to some extent neotenous (retaining larval features through their adult lives), and certainly have not helped in aligning them with their relations. See **Gigantura.**

Gillellus　　　　Dactyloscopidae
　rubrocinctus SADDLE STARGAZER
6 cm. (2¼ in.)
Found in the tropical w. Atlantic, from the Bahamas and Florida to the 'hump' of Brazil. It lives in depths of 3–15 m. (10–50 ft), occasionally even shallower. Like its relatives it lives on sand, in which it burrows, but it is only found in sandy patches close to coral reefs, rocks or limestone outcrops; it does not occur on open beaches.

It is pale brown with 4 major reddish saddles across the back turning to brown on the sides.

Several red spots or lines around the eye, and reddish marks elsewhere on the head. In this stargazer the lateral line is strongly arched over the pectoral fin.

Ginglymostoma　　　Orectolobidae
　cirratum NURSE SHARK 4·3 m. (14 ft)
Found on both sides of the tropical and subtropical Atlantic from Brazil to Rhode Island in the W., and off the African coast in the E.; also along the Pacific coast of Central America. The nurse shark is broad-headed, with distinct barbels at each nostril, and large broad fins. It is yellowish to dull brown, paler beneath; the young have widely scattered small black spots. It is common in shallow water and can be frequently seen lying on the sea bed close to reefs. Not especially aggressive, when stepped upon or provoked by divers it bites and hangs on with bulldog tenacity. The nurse shark is ovoviviparous, that is the young are born alive after having developed from eggs in the mother's uterus.

Girardinus　　　　Poeciliidae
　metallicus GIRARDINUS 8 cm. (3¼ in.)
Found only on the island of Cuba (which also contains several other members of this genus), it is common in small rivers and ditches. Its body form is much as in other members of the family, but the dorsal fin is large, the mouth opening nearly vertical, and the male's gonopodium is especially long with 2 appendages at its tip.

It makes a pleasant aquarium fish, the male being yellowish brown above with a metallic reflection on the sides, and a line of curved bars from head to tail. The female lacks these bars.

It is a peaceful, hardy livebearer which produces between 10–100 young in a brood depending on the mother's size.

GIRARDINUS see **Girardinus metallicus**

Girella　　　　Kyphosidae
　nigricans OPALEYE 64 cm. (25 in.)
Native to the Californian coast, it is found from San Francisco to Cape San Lucas. It lives on rocky shores close to the bottom especially amongst kelp beds, and ranges in depth from 1·8–20 m. (1–11 fathoms). Like other members of the family it feeds on algae of various kinds, and eel grass, but the animal food amongst the plant matter is a vital constituent of its diet.

It is an important game fish, caught mostly from the shore and fights gamely. It is also exploited to a considerable extent by commercial fishermen, the catch being sold fresh.

It is a deep-bodied, solid looking fish, with a rather high spiny dorsal fin, the head is small and rounded. Its back is olive green, the sides silvery, and the eyes are bright blue.
G. tricuspidata LUDERICK, BLACKFISH, BLACK BREAM 71 cm. (28 in.)
An Australian species, found in the coastal

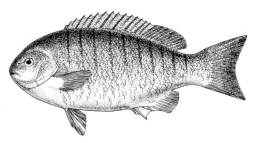

waters and estuaries of Queensland, New South Wales, S. Australia, and W. Australia, as well as Tasmania and New Zealand. It is found in shoals, often around rocky headlands and weed covered reefs; it feeds extensively on algae and the animals living on them.

It is a good sporting fish, baits used being green algae or tunicates. It is also an important food fish in New South Wales and is marketed fresh, often as black bream.

It is brown above with 10–12 narrow dark brown bands on the back and upper sides; the belly is greyish.

GLASS
  BARB see **Oxygaster oxygastroides**
  CATFISH see **Kryptopterus bicirrhis**
  CATFISH, AFRICAN see **Physailia pellucida**
  TETRA see **Moenkhausia oligolepis**
GLASS-CHARACIN, GUATEMALA see
  Roeboides guatemalensis
GLASSFISH see Centropomidae
GLASSFISH see **Salangichthys microdon**
GLASSFISH,
  COMMERSON'S see **Chanda commersoni**
  INDIAN see **Chanda ranga**
GLASSY SWEEPER see **Pempheris schomburgki**

Glaucosoma   Glaucosomidae
  scapulare PEARL PERCH, EPAULETTE
FISH 61 cm. (2 ft)
Found only on the e. coast of Australia in the waters of Queensland and New South Wales. It is usually found in the vicinity of sunken reefs, and offshore. It is mostly caught by fishermen using handlines and fishing for snapper (*Chrysophrys guttulatus*).

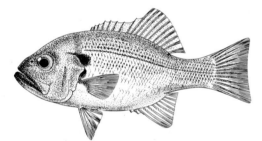

It is silvery greenish-brown, silvery below with many indistinct golden-brown spots. Above the end of the gill cover is an extra soft bony flap covered with jet black skin. This is easily abraded leaving the pearl-like bone exposed – hence its common name.

The pearl perch is rated one of the finest food fishes of Australian waters, although it is not available in large quantities.

GLAUCOSOMIDAE

A small family of moderately large fishes found only in the Pacific. They are best known in Australian waters where 2 members of the family are important food and game fish.

They are deep-bodied, robust fishes with a large head and big mouth. The dorsal fin is composed of short strong spines, and longer soft rays, but the spiny section is always low. The head and body are fully scaled. See **Glaucosoma.**

GLOWLIGHT TETRA see **Hemigrammus erythrozonus**
GLUT HERRING see **Alosa aestivalis**

Glyptocephalus   Pleuronectidae
  cynoglossus WITCH, WITCH FLOUNDER
63 cm. (25 in.)
Found on both sides of the N. Atlantic in moderately deep water. In the w. Atlantic it is found from the Gulf of St Lawrence and the s. Grand Bank s. to Cape Hatteras. In the E. it occurs around Iceland, s. to the mouth of the English Channel and n. to n. Norway.

It is found on muddy grounds and muddy sand in depths of 50–300 m. (27–164 fathoms), although it is also found deeper than this. It feeds on bottom-living invertebrates such as small crustaceans, starfishes, molluscs, and worms.

Despite its thin body and often small size, for it seems to grow very slowly, the witch has some commercial value. Its flesh is of very fine quality. It is fished for extensively in n. Europe and by U.S. fishermen and although the catch is not very large it is of considerable value.

The witch is identified by having the eyes on the right side of the head; these are relatively large, and the mouth is small. The body is narrow, and the lateral line is straight. It is a uniform light grey-brown with fine darker dots on body and fins; the end of the pectoral fin on the coloured side is dusky.

Glyptosternum   Sisoridae
  reticulatum TURKESTAN CATFISH
25 cm. (10 in.)
Found only in the mountainous regions of s. Turkestan and ne. Afghanistan, living in rivers with very rapid currents, hiding under rocks and clinging to the bottom. Its body is very flattened, and the anterior part of the pectoral fin is expanded to form a sucker by which it adheres to the rocks in the rapid current. The pelvic fins are also swollen and with the flattened lower body surface help in the adhesion.

The barbel at the edge of the gape is very broad based and long: the eyes are small and high on the head, all the fins are rounded. It feeds on invertebrates, mainly insect larvae.

Gnathodentex   Pentapodidae
  aureolineatus 46 cm. (18 in.)
Widespread in the Indo-Pacific, and found from the E. African coast to the E. Indies and the islands of the w. Pacific. It is found in moderately deep water in surge channels along the outer edges of reefs, and elsewhere in similar conditions. At night it forages in shallow water and is then found over the reef and inshore.

It is distinguished by having no scales on the anterior head or between the eyes, 4 small canine-like teeth in the upper jaw and an outwardly turned fang at each side of the lower jaw. Its coloration is pinkish above with lengthwise streaks of golden yellow, the fins orange, the lips and iris yellowish.

Gnathonemus   Mormyridae
  petersi 23 cm. (9 in.)
This mormyrid is found in w. tropical Africa, in the Cameroons, the Niger, and the Congo region. Its colouring is very distinctive and it has a long, movable finger-like projection on the point of the chin and a small mouth.

It is a popular aquarium fish, its peaceful habits making it particularly suitable for the fish tank, although like other mormyrids it is

more active at night than it is by day. **33**
G. stanleyanus 40 cm. (15¾ in.)
An elephant-snout or mormyrid which is found in the Congo and Gambia rivers. This genus is the most common of the mormyrids in W. Africa, its members have 3–10 small, conical notched teeth in the mid-line of each jaw, but they have a terminal mouth rather than an underslung one. They usually live in deep rocky pools in large rivers.

This species is distinguished by being very slender-bodied. **34**

Gnathophis   Congridae
  mystax 30 cm. (12 in.)
This deep water conger eel is found in the Mediterranean and e. Atlantic from Portugal to St Helena. It is probably common along the whole continental slope in suitable depths, although not often found. It is most often found at depths of around 400 m. (220 fathoms). Distinguished by its large eye, and the dorsal fin placed just above the pectoral fin, it also has rounded, blunt teeth in the roof of the mouth. The upper jaw is distinctly longer than the lower. It is a light grey in colour, white on the underside, and the long fins edged with black.

In the Mediterranean it spawns in the autumn, the eggs measure between 2·5 and 3 mm. in diameter, and hatch in about 4 days to produce a larva 6 mm. (¼ in.) long. The larvae are of typical leptocephalus form, but have a pointed snout, a rounded tail, and attain 12 cm. (4¾ in.) before metamorphosis to the young eel.

GO-HOME FISH see **Rhabdosargus globiceps**
GOATFISH see Mullidae
GOATFISH see **Pseudupeneus barberinus, Pseudupeneus fraterculus**
GOATFISH,
  GOLDEN-BANDED see **Pseudupeneus auriflamma**
  SPOTTED see **Pseudupeneus maculatus**

GOBIESOCIDAE
The clingfishes, a group of mainly marine, tropical and temperate fishes distinguished by a very powerful sucking disc on the ventral surface. They are worldwide in distribution. Most are small fishes, although the largest are about 30 cm. (12 in.) long. Most are found in shallow water, clinging to rocks or the substrate, some species are found intertidally, a few are found in freshwaters in Central America and the Galapagos Islands.

They are ventrally flattened, usually with a depressed almost triangular head, wide mouth, and dorso-lateral eyes. The pelvic fins form the front part of the sucking disc. Their bodies are scaleless, fins without spiny rays, usually low and not well developed. See **Apletodon, Arcos, Aspasmogaster, Chorisochismus, Diademichthys, Gobiesox, Lepadogaster, Opeatogenys, Tomicodon.**

Gobiesox   Gobiesocidae
  maeandricus FLATHEAD CLINGFISH
15 cm. (6 in.)
A Pacific coastal species found from British Columbia s. to Puget Sound, Washington, and San Diego, California. It clings to the rocks in the intertidal zone, feeding on small molluscs and crustaceans.

It is distinguished by its smooth skin, broad

flat head, also smooth. The dorsal and anal fins are low and joined to the tail fin base. Light olive brown to dull red, marked with orange and black flecks, a light bar through the eye.

GOBIIDAE

In terms of numbers of species and quite frequently individual numbers the gobies and sleepers are amongst the most successful fish groups of temperate and tropical regions. They are very abundant in inshore, coastal, and intertidal areas of the sea in all tropical and temperate zones; they also enter freshwater, and numerous freshwater species have evolved. The gobies are characterized by possessing united pelvic fins to form a single, cup-like fin, while the eleotrids or sleepers have separated pelvics. This difference was at one time sufficient for them to be placed in separate families (the sleepers were in Eleotridae). In other respects they are closely similar; both groups are mostly rather thickset little fishes with tapering tails, broad fins, and 2 dorsal fins (the first weakly spiny). Most have ctenoid (toothed) scales, at least over part of the body.

The gobiids are in general small, most live in crevices or close to the bottom, although some have adopted a pelagic life style. Few species exceed 30 cm. (12 in.) in length, most are 2–5 cm. (1–2 in.) when fully adult. The world's smallest fishes, and vertebrates, *Eviota, Mistichthys* and *Pandaka* are gobies. See **Bathygobius, Boleophthalmus, Brachygobius, Chaenogobius, Clevelandia, Crystallogobius, Dormitator, Evermannichthys, Gobiosoma, Gobius, Ioglossus, Lebetus, Nemateleotris, Neogobius, Pandaka, Periophthalmodon, Periophthalmus, Pomatoschistus, Proterorhinus, Risor, Stigmatogobius, Typhlogobius.**

Gobio   Cyprinidae
gobio GUDGEON 20 cm. (8 in.)
The gudgeon is a European freshwater fish widely distributed from Ireland, England and Wales, across Europe (including s. Sweden), to Asia. Its body is long, and rather cylindrical, with a longish head, a ventral mouth with a barbel at each corner. Its body is fully scaled, and the scales are fairly large.

A gregarious species, it is usually found in shoals, and as common in deep rivers as it is in shallow streams, pools, lakes, and marshes. It seems to prefer clean gravelly bottoms, however, and is always found on the bed of the river. Its food consists mainly of bottom-living insect larvae, crustaceans, and molluscs; young fish, eat quantities of small copepod crustaceans.

The gudgeon is an attractively coloured fish, greeny brown on the back, shading to yellow on the sides, lighter under the belly. It has a series of dark, rounded blotches along its sides.

It is too small to present much sport to the angler (although it takes a bait readily). In parts of Europe it is eaten, and as it has excellently flavoured flesh it is something of a gourmet's dish.

Gobioides   Gobioididae
broussonetti VIOLET GOBY 51 cm. (20 in.)
A long, compressed, eel-like goby which is found on the tropical e. coast of America, from Florida, and the Gulf of Mexico, through the Caribbean including the mainland coast, and

S. to Brazil. It is found on muddy and sandy sea beds, and seems especially abundant in estuaries. Observations on its natural history seem to be few but there is little doubt that it burrows in the substrate.

Its coloration is pinkish grey, lighter ventrally, the back and upper part of head with dusky brown blotches which sometimes form a weak chevron pattern. It is distinguished by its slender shape.

GOBIOIDIDAE

A family of goby-like fishes which have very elongate bodies, a long many-rayed dorsal fin which is joined to the tail fin, or at least closely approximated to it. Like most gobioids they have the pelvic fins united together to form a weak sucker disc. Members of the family inhabit shallow inshore water often in estuaries burrowing in mud or sand and mud bottoms. They are distributed throughout tropical seas. Numerous species have been described; no doubt there are others as yet undiscovered due to their secretive habits.

In a recent revision of the classification of the gobioid fishes this group has been placed in a subfamily (Gobionellinae) of the family Gobiidae. See **Gobioides, Taeniodes.**

Gobiosoma   Gobiidae
evelynae SHARKNOSED GOBY 4 cm. (1½ in.)
A Caribbean species found from the Bahamas to the Venezuelan coastline. It is one of at least 12 closely related members of the genus in the w. Atlantic. It is distinguished by its rather sharply pointed snout and under-slung jaws (hence sharknosed), as well as its coloration, a dark stripe runs from the snout through the eye, and broadening, covers the lower part of the body and tail. Above this the body is yellow, with a black mid-dorsal stripe.

This colouring is almost identical to that of the shallow water species, *G. genie* which is found in the same area. Both species are active cleaner-fish feeding on the external parasites of other larger fishes. Sharknosed gobies are often seen in pairs resting on a prominent coral head which is visited by fishes needing cleaning. The gobies slip over the body of the client by means of their pelvic fin which exerts a weak suction. They occasionally enter the mouth and gill cavities of the client fish, which have been observed to form a queue while waiting for attention. *G. evelynae* is found at depths of 7·5–26 m. (4–14 fathoms).
G. genie see under **G. evelynae**
G. horsti see under **Kaupichthys nuchalis**

Gobius   Gobiidae
niger BLACK GOBY 18 cm. (7 in.)
This is one of the larger gobies to be found in European seas, and it is the most frequently seen of the group in fish markets, especially in the Mediterranean. Its distribution includes both the Mediterranean and Black Sea, and the e. Atlantic coast from N. Africa to Norway, including the North Sea and the Baltic. It is found in shallow water at depths of 1–75 m. (½–41 fathoms) on sandy or muddy bottoms, and amongst eel grass. It is the only large goby to occur regularly in estuaries, where it is often found in low salinity conditions.

It breeds in spring and summer; the eggs are deposited under loose rocks and in bivalve shells, where they are guarded by the male.

In addition to its large size and thickset appearance this goby is readily identified by its large scales, the short finely-branched upper rays of the pectoral fin, and in the males at least the great height of the dorsal fins. Despite its name it is not conspicuously black; more usually it is dusky grey or brown with light mottling.

GOBLIN SHARK see **Mitsukurina owstoni**
GOBY see Gobiidae
GOBY,
    ARROW see **Clevelandia ios**
    BLACK see **Gobius niger**
    BLIND see **Typhlogobius californiensis**
    CRYSTAL see **Crystallogobius linearis**
    DIMINUTIVE see **Lebetus scorpioides**
    FRESHWATER see **Chaenogobius isaza**
    FRILLFIN see **Bathygobius soporator**
    HOVERING see **Ioglossus helenae**
    MOTTLED BLACK SEA see **Proterorhinus marmoratus**
    PAINTED see **Pomatoschistus pictus**
    PYGMY see **Pandaka pygmaea**
    ROUGHTAIL see **Evermannichthys metzelaari**
    SHARKNOSED see **Gobiosoma evelynae**
    SMALLMOUTH see **Risor ruber**
    SPIKE-FINNED see **Nemateleotris magnificus**
    TUSKED see **Risor ruber**
    VIOLET see **Gobioides broussonetti**
GOGGLE-EYE see **Priacanthus hamrur**
GOGGLE-EYE JACK see **Selar crumenophthalmus**
GOLD-EYE see **Hiodon alosoides**
GOLD-STRIPED CHARACIN see **Creagrutus beni**
GOLDEN
    PENCILFISH see **Nannostomus beckfordi**
    PERCH see **Plectroplites ambiguus**
    SARDINE see **Sardinella aurita**
    TREVALLY see **Caranx speciosus**
GOLDEN-BANDED GOATFISH see **Pseudupeneus auriflamma**
GOLDEN-STRIPED SOAPFISH see **Grammistes sexlineatus**
GOLDFINCH, WATER see **Pristella riddlei**
GOLDFISH see **Carassius auratus**

Gomphosus   Labridae
varius BIRDWRASSE 25 cm. (10 in.)
A small wrasse which appears to be widely distributed in the central Indo-Pacific, and is found as far to the W. as the African coast. Although it is widespread and moderately common it is not caught in any numbers. It is found in rocky areas and amongst reefs in shallow as well as moderately deep waters.

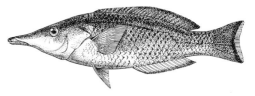

Members of the genus are quite distinctive on account of the long bird-like bill, with a moderately large mouth at its end. Its colouring is variable, often pinkish anteriorly, purple at the back.

Gonichthys   Myctophidae
   coccoi 6 cm. (2¼ in.)
This lanternfish is one of the slender-tailed species, found worldwide in tropical oceans, but represented by several species within the genus *Gonichthys*. It is a slender fish, with a slightly pointed snout, a long anal fin, and the tail, behind the anal fin, slender and at least as long as the head. Like other lanternfishes it has abundant light organs on the body.

It is widely distributed in the w. Mediterranean and the Atlantic Ocean in which it is found in the tropical and warm-temperate regions. Its vertical distribution extends from near the surface to a depth of 1500 m. (820 fathoms). Like other lanternfishes it moves towards the surface at night, and to deeper water in daylight.

It is dull silver on the back with brilliantly silvery sides which possess striking iridescence.

GONORHYNCHIDAE
A family of Indo-Pacific marine fish containing a single species. Its closest relatives appear to be the African freshwater fishes of the families Kneriidae and Phractolaemidae, and the marine Indo-Pacific Chanidae.

The Gonorhynchidae are distinguished by a number of characteristic, and unique features. The mouth is on the underside of the pointed snout, with a single barbel or whisker in the mid-line between mouth and snout tip. The pectoral fin is set low down on the body, the pelvics are beneath the dorsal fin, and both fins are far back along the body. The body is long, thin and almost eel-like, circular in cross-section, and is covered with small, rough scales. See **Gonorhynchus.**

Gonorhynchus   Gonorhynchidae
   gonorhynchus RATFISH, BEAKED
SALMON, MOUSEFISH, SAND-EEL
46 cm. (18 in.)
This unique fish is widely distributed in the Indo-Pacific, from s. Africa to Australia, and New Zealand, and from Japanese and Hawaiian waters. It is most common in the temperate areas, and is uncommon where the water is very warm.

Its body form is distinctive, as are the rough-edged scales which cover the entire body. In colour it is equally remarkable; inside the mouth and the gill chamber are purple, the underside is reddish, the scales on the sides are purplish blue, on the back darkening to brown. The tail fin has a black base but the tips of each lobe are pink.

This fish frequents sandy bottoms usually in shallow water although it is found commonly on sand offshore. It burrows in the sand, and feeds on bottom-living and small burrowing invertebrates. Although it is said to have well flavoured, firm flesh it is apparently not often marketed and only eaten occasionally.

There is much about its biology that is still unknown. It is thought to breed offshore, and the young are very slender, almost rod-like

and found near the surface of the sea. They are widely distributed whilst juveniles.

Gonostoma   Gonostomatidae
This is a genus of bristlemouths. The species illustrated in colour has not been identified. **44**
G. bathyphilum 20 cm. (8 in.)
This bristlemouth is known from both N. and S. Atlantic; in the E. from Scottish waters to the Canaries, and in the W. from Nova Scotia to the Caribbean. It is also found off S. Africa and s. It is a deep-water fish found commonly only from 900 m. downwards to 2500 m. (492–1367 fathoms), although young specimens have been taken nearer the surface. Its habits and life history are virtually unknown.

In colour it is black, with the light organs along the underside in a single row, very small and inconspicuous. It is very long and thin, and rather fragile but its mouth is large and heavily lined with thin, longish teeth.

GONOSTOMATIDAE
A family of bathypelagic fishes, widely distributed in the oceans of the world, but probably least abundant in the polar seas. The great majority of the members of the family are small to moderate sized fishes, but what they lack in stature they make up in number, for these are the most abundant of mid-water fishes. The genus *Cyclothone* in particular is overwhelmingly abundant in the open ocean at depths, and as a predator on invertebrates and prey for many larger fishes is of great importance to the economy of the deep sea.

Most gonostomatids, or bristlemouths, as they are often known, are slender and fragile. Their mouths are large, with long jaws each of which is equipped with many thin sharp teeth, usually in a single row. Most of the species are well provided with light organs on the underside of the body. See **Bonapartia, Cyclothone, Gonostoma, Maurolicus, Polymetme, Vinciguerra, Yarrella.**

Goodea   Goodeidae
   gracilis 9 cm. (3½ in.)
Found in the tributaries of the upper Rio Panuco, in Central Mexico. It has been kept in aquaria for a number of years, and is moderately hardy.

The male is distinguished from the female by slight colour differences, and by having the first rays of the anal fin short and modified as a form of gonopodium. Like other goodeids this species is a live bearer, giving birth to broods of up to 20; the young are about 20 mm. (¾ in.) at birth.

The male is olive-coloured with bright blue flecks, and a dark line running along the side; the female is less brightly coloured. The gut

of this species is very long and much coiled, suggesting that it is best adapted to eating plant food.

GOODEIDAE
A small family of freshwater fishes found in the

highland regions of Mexico and n. Central America. Most of the known species live in small streams and lakes which during the rainy season become flooded but at other times are almost dry. Some have been imported for aquarium keeping but in general they are rather delicate and not easy to maintain.

Systematically the goodeids belong amongst the toothcarps. They are physically similar to such familiar aquarium fishes as the guppy and the platties, lacking spines in their fins, being relatively small with fully scaled bodies, a flattened head, broad mouth with fine teeth on the jaws. The members of the family are viviparous. The males have the first 6–8 rays of the anal fin fused close together, shortened, and simplified to form a specialized gonopodium with which sperm is conveyed to the female's genital opening. The fertilized eggs develop in the maternal oviduct, and each brood is the result of a single mating (for unlike the poeciliid toothcarps, the sperm is not contained in a spermatophore which is retained to fertilize several broods). At a late stage in their development the embryos are nourished by a connection with the mother, and they are born fully developed, without a yolk sac, and active. See **Goodea, Neotoca.**

GOONCH see **Bagarius bagarius**
GOOSEFISH see Lophiidae
GOOSEFISH, AMERICAN see under **Lophius piscatorius**
GOURAMI see **Osphronemus goramy**
GOURAMI,
   CROAKING see **Trichopsis vittatus**
   DWARF see **Colisa lalia**
   CHOCOLATE see **Sphaerichthys osphronemoides**
   KISSING see **Helostoma temminckii**
   GIANT see **Colisa fasciata**
   MOONLIGHT see **Trichogaster microlepis**
   PEARL see **Trichodon trichodon**
   TALKING see **Trichopsis vittatus**
   THICK-LIPPED see **Colisa labiosa**
   THREE-SPOT see **Trichogaster trichopterus**
GOUREEN see **Alosa fallax**
GOVERNMENT BREAM see **Lutjanus sebae**
GRAHAM'S CICHLID see **Sarotherodon grahami**

Gramma   Grammidae
   loreto FAIRY BASSLET 8 cm. (3 in.)
This lovely little fish is widely kept for marine aquaria. Its colouring is spectacular, the front

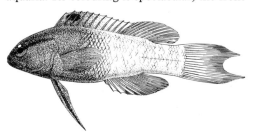

of the body being violet, the posterior half yellow, 2 golden streaks on the head and a black spot on the dorsal fin.

Its range extends from Bermuda and the Bahamas, throughout the Caribbean to Venezuela. It is found at depths of 1·8–61 m. (1–33 fathoms), and is usually seen in caves or beneath ledges, or hiding in small holes. Small shoals of 2–3 fish up to a dozen are normal.

They orientate themselves to be pressed against the substrate so that in caves or under ledges they frequently lie against the roof or overhang, belly upwards.

This fish has been reported to pick parasites off other, larger fishes. **271**

GRAMMICOLEPIDAE

A small family of apparently rare deep-sea fishes, related to the dories (family Zeidae). They resemble the dories in their very compressed body form, and by the combination of spines and soft rays in the dorsal and pelvic fins. They differ in having most extraordinary long scales which run as parchment-like ridges vertically across the body; also the mouth is small and nearly vertical.

The members of this family are little known, and rare in museum collections (although this does not mean they are rare in nature). They have been found in the Caribbean Sea, off Hawaii, South Africa, and the Philippines. Probably only 2 species exist although many scientific names have been proposed on the basis of single, imperfect specimens. See **Xenolepidichthys.**

GRAMMIDAE

A small family of very beautiful tropical marine fishes found especially in the W. Atlantic and Caribbean region, but also around Hawaii and tropical Australia. The basslets or fairy basslets as they are called, are related to the seabasses (Serranidae) but differ from them by having an interrupted lateral line, or none at all, and by having a single continuous dorsal fin with 11–13 spines and soft rays. The pelvic fins have one spine and 5 rays. See **Gramma.**

Grammistes Grammistidae
sexlineatus GOLDEN-STRIPED SOAPFISH
25 cm. (10 in.)
The soapfish is widely distributed in the Indo-Pacific, from E. Africa to the e. Pacific islands, including the N. Australian coast. It is a boldly patterned fish, in the young with 3 pale yellow stripes on a brown background, but as the fish grows the stripes break and additional yellow lines appear, and eventually the yellow is a series of dashes.

This strikingly coloured fish has been observed to swim around coral heads, usually alone, sometimes in pairs or trios, darting into crevices if disturbed. Its behaviour is relatively bold, and its colouring a warning, for the skin secretes large quantities of toxic mucus. Experiments to study the effectiveness of this defence have shown that large predators fed on small *Grammistes* quickly spit them out. The mucus has a distinctive bitter taste to man, and if the live fish is confined in an aquarium it liberates so much toxin that other fishes die.

GRAMMISTIDAE

A small family of perch-like fishes, known popularly as soapfishes from the soapy, slimy feel of the copious mucus on their skins, made more noticeable because if kept alive in a confined volume of water it becomes frothy. Its members are found in all tropical seas, the genus *Rypticus* in the Atlantic, Caribbean, the Gulf of Mexico and the e. Pacific has a number of species, while a number of single-species genera are found in the Indo-Pacific.

Its members are in general rather stout-bodied, with large heads and moderate jaws. Their scales are usually small. They all have a series of short, stout spines in the dorsal fin, and most (all except for *Rypticus*) have 2–3 stout anal spines. In general, the soapfishes look superficially like rather stout sea-perches with short spines.

All the members of the family produce copious mucus in their skins which is toxic to large predators. It tastes bitter in man (as does the flesh of some species), and experimentally the toxin has been shown to kill small mammals. Large predatory fish will refuse to eat soapfishes which often are brightly coloured to warn of their unappetizing qualities. See **Grammistes, Rypticus.**

GRASS
  BLENNY, SEA see **Stathmonotus stahli**
  CARP see **Ctenopharyngodon idella**
  PICKEREL see **Esox americanus**
GRAVEL DIVER see **Scytalina cerdale**
GRAYLING see Salmonidae
GRAYLING see **Thymallus thymallus**
GRAYLING,
  ARCTIC see **Thymallus arcticus**
  AUSTRALIAN see **Prototroctes maraena**
  NEW ZEALAND see **Prototroctes oxyrhynchus**
GREAT
  BARRACUDA see **Sphyraena barracuda**
  HAMMERHEAD SHARK see **Sphyrna mokarran**
  PIPEFISH see **Syngnathus acus**
  TREVALLY see **Caranx sexfasciatus**
GREATER
  AMBERJACK see **Seriola dumerili**
  SAND-EEL see **Hyperoplus lanceolatus**
  SAWFISH see **Pristis pectinata**
  WEEVER see **Trachinus draco**
GREEK MORAY see **Muraena helena**
GREEN
  CHROMIDE see **Etroplus suratensis**
  DISCUS see **Symphysodon aequifasciata**
  KNIFEFISH see **Eigenmannia virescens**
  PANCHAX see **Aplocheilus blocki**
  SUNFISH see **Lepomis cyanellus**
GREENEYE, SHORTNOSE see **Chlorophthalmus agassizi**
GREENLAND
  HALIBUT see **Reinhardtius hippoglossoides**
  SHARK see **Somniosus microcephalus**
  TURBOT see **Reinhardtius hippoglossoides**
GREENLING see Hexagrammidae
GREENLING, KELP see **Hexagrammos decagrammus**

Gregoryina Gregoryinidae
gygis 6 cm. (2¼ in.)
Found once in the Hawaiian islands on Laysan Island. The only known specimen was captured by a white tern *(Gygis alba)* and brought to its nest. This species has been tentatively accepted by ichthyologists but grave doubt exists as to its distinctness.

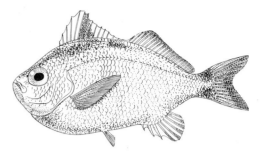

It seems to be well distinguished by its keeled chest and abdomen, the dorsal fin with 15 spines and 24 rays, of which the fourth and fifth spines are longest, those posterior being low.

GREGORYINIDAE

A family erected to contain not only a single species but a single specimen! It is tentatively recognized as being close to the flagfish family Kuhliidae, and it is similar to these fishes except that its chest is sharply keeled, the mouth is small, and there are only 7 branched rays in the anal fin. See **Gregoryina.**

GRENADIER see Macrouridae
GRENADIER, ROUGH-HEAD see **Macrourus berglax**
GREY
  ANGELFISH see **Pomacanthus arcuatus**
  GURNARD see **Eutrigla gurnardus**
  MULLET see Mugilidae
  NURSE see **Odontaspis arenarius**
  SNAPPER see **Lutjanus griseus**
  STARSNOUT see **Bathyagonus alascanus**
  TRIGGERFISH see **Balistes carolinensis**
GRILSE see **Salmo salar**
GRINNER, SPOTTED-TAILED see **Saurida undosquamis**
GROPER see **Epinephelus lanceolatus**
GROPER, BLUE see **Achoerdus gouldii**
GROUPER, BLACK see **Mycteroperca bonaci**
GRUNION, CALIFORNIA see **Leuresthes tenuis**
GRUNT see Pomadasyidae
GRUNT,
  BLUE-STRIPED see **Haemulon sciurus**
  FRENCH see **Haemulon flavolineatum**
GRUNTER,
  PIGNOSE see **Lithognathus lithognathus**
  SILVER see **Pomadasys hasta**
GUAGUANCHE see **Sphyraena guachancho**
GUATEMALA GLASS-CHARACIN see **Roeboides guatemalensis**
GUCHHIA see **Eleutheronema tetradactylum**
GUDGEON see **Gobio gobio**
GUABINE, LEAPING see **Rivulus hartii**
GUITARFISH see Rhinobatidae, Rhynchobatidae
GUITARFISH,
  ATLANTIC see **Rhinobatus lentiginosus**
  CHINESE see **Platyrhina sinensis**
  SPOTTED see **Rhinobatus lentiginosus**
GUITARRITA see **Buncocephalus coracoideus**
GULPER see **Eurypharynx pelecanoides**
GULPER, WHIPTAIL see **Saccopharynx ampullaceus**
GULPER-EEL see Eurypharyngidae, Saccopharyngidae

GULPER-EEL see **Eurypharynx pelecanoides**
GUMMY SHARK see **Mustelus antarctica**
GUNNEL see Pholidae
GUNNEL see **Pholis gunnellus**
GUNNEL,
  ROCKWEED see **Xererpes fucorum**
  SADDLEBACK see **Pholis ornata**
GUPPY see **Poecilia reticulata**
GURNARD see Triglidae
GURNARD,
  FLYING see Dactylopteridae
  FLYING see **Dactylopterus volitans, Daicocus peterseni**
  GREY see **Eutrigla gurnardus**
  RED see **Chelidonichthys kumu**
  TUB see **Trigla lucerna**
  YELLOW see **Trigla lucerna**
GURNET see **Trigla lucerna**
GURRY SHARK see **Somniosus microcephalus**
GWYNIAD see **Coregonus lavaretus**

Gymnachirus   Soleidae
  melas ZEBRA or NAKED SOLE 23 cm. (9 in.)
A w. Atlantic sole which is found from Massachusetts to Florida and the Bahamas, and along the coast of the Gulf of Mexico. It ranges from the shoreline down to 183 m. (100 fathoms) but is most abundant in depths of 30–45 m. (16–25 fathoms), and is usually found on clean sand.

It is distinguished amongst other soles in the area by its loose, scaleless skin and by the very restricted gill opening on the eyed side. Compared with most European soles its body is very broad and thickset. Its eyed side is usually light brown with a series of dark crossbands not sharply defined, and differing in number, width and intensity from individual to individual.

The young are frequently melanistic, that is wholly dark on the eyed side with the bands showing faintly as black lines on a near-black background. They are most frequently seen thus in well lighted areas of white sand in which they do not burrow but if prodded they move away in peculiar fashion their fins undulating along their length. Their resemblance in colour and locomotion to a large flatworm (which are often distasteful to predators) is probably not accidental.

GYMNARCHIDAE

A family containing a single species of African freshwater fish, which is somewhat similar, and related to the mormyrids. Its principal external characteristics lie in the reduction of the fins, only the dorsal and pectorals being present. The body is very elongate, and ends in a relatively sharp point with no tail fin. Its scales are very small. Its other interesting feature is that it has been long known for its electrical properties. See **Gymnarchus**.

Gymnarchus   Gymnarchidae
  niloticus 90 cm. (35 in.)
Gymnarchus niloticus, a relative of the Mormyridae and possessing some features of that family, is found in tropical African freshwaters, from the upper Nile, w. Africa, Senegal, Niger, and the Chad basin. Its compressed body with a long dorsal fin, and a finger-like tail tip to the body are quite distinctive. It lives in swamps, oxbow lakes, and still water condi-

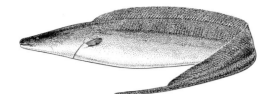

tions. In these often turbid waters it is able to detect prey, predators, and its own species by means of the electric field it generates in 4 elongate organs near the end of the tail on each side of the body. The fish is very sensitive to disturbances to the electric field it produces around itself in pulses or short bursts. In addition, as *Gymnarchus* swims by gently undulating its dorsal fin, and as often swims backwards as forwards, its electric sensitivity will help it avoid obstacles in its path.

Its breeding habits are most interesting. Prior to spawning it constructs a floating nest of plant fibres in which the 1000 or so eggs, each about 4 mm. in diameter, are laid. The parents guard the nest for the 3–4 days before hatching. The newly hatched young have long gill filaments and an elongate yolk-sac. They are reported to come to the surface for air. Young fish feed on insects and other invertebrates; adults eat fishes almost entirely.

Gymnarchus niloticus is often kept in laboratories for study of its electrical powers, and also in large aquaria. Locally it is of some value as a food fish, but its flesh is said to be strong flavoured and oily.

Gymnelis   Zoarcidae
  viridis FISH DOCTOR 22 cm. (8½ in.)
Found in the high arctic regions from the Barents Sea, the n. Atlantic, and the N. Pacific and Bering Sea. In the Atlantic it is found off Alaska, Labrador, and s. Greenland.

It is a slender-bodied fish which has a large mouth, thick lips, and large eyes. The dorsal and anal fins are well developed and united round the tail; it lacks pelvic fins. It is pale brown or greenish, occasionally with pale bars.

It is usually found in coastal waters down to a depth of 100 m. (55 fathoms) on muddy bottoms. It spawns in the autumn. It has no commercial value.

Gymnocephalus   Percidae
  cernua RUFFE, POPE 25 cm. (10 in.)
Found in Europe, from e. England, and the Baltic basin, across the Eurasian landmass to Siberia. It is a small fish, unusual in this family for having the 2 dorsal fins continuous, and also for having deep canals under the surface of the skin on the head.

It is found in both still and slow-flowing water in which it forms large shoals. It is essentially a fish of lowland rivers and inhabits the reaches of rivers and lakes in the flood plain, yet in distribution it is often rather local. Its food consists mainly of aquatic insects and crustaceans. It is favoured neither by anglers

nor for food, and in inland areas of Europe where freshwater fisheries are valuable it is a direct competitor with more valuable food fishes.

Its colouring is greeny brown above, with numerous dark flecks, the sides and belly are yellowish.

Gymnocorymbus   Characidae
  ternetzi BLACK TETRA, BLACKAMOOR 7·5 cm. (3 in.)
This very striking aquarium fish comes originally from the Mato Grosso region of Rio Paraguay and the Rio Negro. As young fish they swim in dense shoals, turning altogether and giving a distinct impression of military precision. The larger fish tend to live in smaller shoals and as they are less distinctly marked do not give the same impression.

Its body is rather deep and the anal fin is long-based and many-rayed, the dorsal fin is high. The most notable feature about this fish is its colouring; there are 2 vertical dark bars across the body and the whole of the rear half of the body is darkly coloured. In young fish this colouring is black, adults have less dense colouring and the males are merely greyish. Males also have clear white pin-points on the tail, and if viewed against the light have a tapering rear end to the body cavity.

Gymnosarda nuda see **Orcynopsis unicolor**
G. unicolor see **Orcynopsis unicolor**

Gymnothorax   Muraenidae
  moringua SPOTTED MORAY 1·2 m. (4 ft)
The spotted moray is the most common species in shallow water in the West Indian region. It ranges from Brazil to Florida, including the Gulf of Mexico, and has been reported from St Helena and Bermuda. In body form it is a typical moray, and lacks both pectoral and pelvic fins. Its jaws are liberally provided with sharp teeth, and it has needle-like, depressible canine teeth in the front of the jaws. Its coloration is pale yellow, whitish beneath, with a dense covering of darker (brown to purplish black) confluent spots all over the body.

It is a retiring species usually glimpsed hiding in crevices in the rock or reef. Most abundant in water up to 3 m. (1·5 fathoms) deep, and rarely found deeper than 15 m. (8 fathoms). It is often caught and used for food in the W. Indies.

G. pictus PAINTED MORAY 76 cm. (30 in.)
Widespread in shallow water in the Indo-Pacific from E. Africa to the islands of e. Oceania. In body form it is typical of the family Muraenidae, lacking both pectoral and pelvic fins and having a restricted gill opening.

In contrast with most morays which are nocturnally active, this eel feeds actively during daytime. It is frequently encountered cruising around in shallow water along the edge of the sea, over reefs. During low tide periods and at night it takes refuge in holes and crevices in tidal pools, usually on the landward side of reefs. These eels are territorial for if pursued they directly return to their original pool. Its food consists to some extent of fishes but the most important constituent is crustacean. Crabs of several kinds are eaten, including the very active grapsoid crabs of the reef. As might be expected for an eel which eats hard-shelled animals, its teeth are blunt and heavy, a contrast to the usual fangs of morays.

GYMNOTIDAE

A small family of S. American fresh-water fishes generally known as knifefishes. Only one genus is recognized, but 2 species have been accepted, both widely distributed. The knifefishes are long-bodied and eel-like with an enormously well developed anal fin running from beneath the throat to the tip of the tail. The pectoral fins are large but no other fins are present. They are very compressed from side to side, and the forward development of the anal fin has resulted in the body cavity being modified so that the anus is close to the throat.

The principal means of propulsion is the anal fin which moves with a regular wave motion in both directions, this resulting in the fish being able to move backwards as well as forwards. In general, they are slow-moving, even sluggish fishes, active in low light intensities either at night or in clouded water. Although not so well developed as in the electric eel (a close relative) they have considerable electrical ability, by which they can navigate and find their prey. Their visual ability is poor.

In their native range the knifefishes are caught and eaten; they are also often kept as aquarium fish. See **Gymnotus**.

Gymnotus   Gymnotidae
 carapo BANDED KNIFEFISH 61 cm. (2 ft)
The banded knifefish was the first member of the family to be known to science. It is widely distributed from Guatemala in Central America, s. to the Rio de la Plata in Argentina, and from the coast to the Andes. It is a lowland species found in shaded creeks and drainage channels in slow and still water. It is particularly common where the water is peat stained. When small it feeds on small crustaceans and insect larvae, as it grows its diet changes and insect larvae and larger crustaceans (such as shrimps) are eaten. When fully grown its diet is composed of shrimps and fishes (very occasionally young specimens of its own species). It is a crepuscular fish which forages when the sun is down, its considerable ability to detect food in the dark, or in cloudy water is fascinating, as is the ease with which it avoids obstacles by means of its electrical pulses.

The knifefish is eel-like in body shape, with a blunt head, and extending to a fine point at the tip of its tail. Its most noticeable feature is the anal fin which originates close behind the head and continues to the tip of the tail. It has no dorsal, tail, or pelvic fins, and the long anal fin is the only means of propulsion, it undulates gently moving the fish smoothly forward, or backwards.

In colouring it is very variable, from flesh coloured to pale grey, with numerous blue or green markings, giving the fish a purplish or olive-green tint. The fins are translucent, mottled with dark in adult specimens, and always with deep blue pigment on the anal fin. The dark bands become increasingly narrow towards the tail.

Gymnotus carapo has been kept successfully in large aquaria. In its native range it is eaten and fished for fairly intensively.

Gymnura   Gymnuridae
 micrura LESSER or SMOOTH BUTTERFLY RAY 86 cm. (34 in.)
This butterfly ray is found in the warm temperate regions of the w. Atlantic, from Brazil n. to Chesapeake Bay, and occasionally n. to New York and s. New England. It is relatively common along the coasts of the s. U.S. although to the N. it is a warm season migrant. It prefers a sandy bottom, and shallow water, and is often found over the tide-covered sand flats presumably foraging for food. It eats a variety of invertebrates, crabs, shrimps, even small crustaceans such as copepods, molluscs, and fishes.

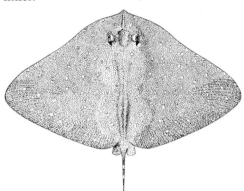

Like its relatives the lesser butterfly ray is viviparous, the young embryo being enclosed in a thin, yellowish membrane from which it hatches in the uterus, and while still equipped with external gills and a supply of yolk. After liberation the embryo is nourished by this yolk and by a secretion from glandular tissue of the maternal uterus. This maternal tissue extends into the spiracles of the embryo, and possibly its mouth as well, supplying the young with nutritive 'milk'. Usually only one embryo develops in each oviduct, occasionally 2 or 3 have been found. The young are between 15–22 cm. (6–8½ in.) at birth.

Females have rather rounded, blunter snouts than males. In colour this ray varies from grey, through brown to purplish, dotted densely with pale and dark spots, the tail has several dark crossbars. The lower surface is whitish with greyish edges to the disc. This ray can adapt its colour quite quickly to match its background.

G. natalensis BUTTERFLY RAY 2·4 m. (8 ft)
This butterfly ray has been recorded only from the waters of South Africa from Mossel Bay to Delagoa Bay; it may well be identical with other species in the Indo-Pacific. It is very variable in colour, changing its markings and background colour very quickly to suit its surroundings, it is usually greyish and mottled above, light underneath.

It shows a remarkable change in body form as it grows. When new-born it is almost triangular in shape but as it grows the pectoral fins become well developed and as an adult its disc is more than twice as wide as it is long. These rays have no dorsal fin, but possess a serrated tail spine. They feed mainly on shellfish, but eat other bottom-living invertebrates and fishes as well. This butterfly ray is not uncommon in shallow inshore waters.

GYMNURIDAE

The butterfly rays are a small family of worldwide distribution in tropical and warm temperate coastal waters including estuaries and river mouths. They are related to the long-tailed dasyatid rays but differ from them in a number of features amongst which are the greater width of the pectoral fins, and the shortness of the tail. Some butterfly rays have spines in their tails similar to, but smaller than those of the sting rays. One group has a single dorsal fin, the other lacks this fin.

Many of the butterfly rays are small but some grow up to a width of 2 m. (6½ ft). None are of commercial importance, the spineless species are harmless and even those with tail spines are much less dangerous than the long-tailed sting rays. According to some authors this family should be included within Dasyatidae. See **Gymnura.**

GYRINOCHEILIDAE

A small family of freshwater fishes found in se. Asia, mainly Thailand, Cambodia, and Borneo. Although related to the cyprinid fishes, the gyrinocheilids are quite distinct, and are set apart by their mouth structure, the lips being very well developed with rasp-like, roughened inner surfaces. In addition, they lack pharyngeal teeth, and have an unique gill region in that above the normal opening of the gill cover there is a second, inhalent, opening on each side.

This interesting feature is an adaptation to their life style of continuous suction onto solid surfaces both while feeding on encrusting algae and while living in running water. Normal respiration is thus precluded, and these fish both inhale and exhale through the gill openings. They respire very rapidly and usually live in oxygen-rich water, although one member of the family at least has attained some popularity as an aquarium fish. See *Gyrinocheilus.*

Gyrinocheilus   Gyrinocheilidae
 aymonieri 25·4 cm. (10 in.)
An interesting inhabitant of the mountainous regions of Thailand which shows remarkable adaptations to its life as an algae-browser usually in running water. It is a strict vegetarian which scrapes encrusting algae off rocks and hard surfaces with the rasp-like folds on the inner sides of the lips. Its gut is very long and coiled. Although this fish is perhaps best known as an inhabitant of swiftly running water, it is found, often in large numbers, in still waters and lowland rivers. It is widely distributed in Thailand.

It has achieved some popularity as a pet fish and is rated as one of the best cleaners of algae for the aquarium. Its habit of sucking onto the sides of the glass or rocks by its mouth lends it additional interest.

Its colouring is not spectacular, although young fish are strongly marked. A dark band runs from the tip of the snout to the tail fin, with a series of transverse bars arising from it above and below. The back is dark brown, the lower sides yellowish. Large specimens, rarely seen in captivity, are uniformly brown.

H

HAARDER see **Heteromugil tricuspidens, Mugil cephalus**
HADDOCK see **Melanogrammus aeglefinus**
Haemulidae see Pomadasyidae

Haemulon   Pomadasyidae
  album MARGATE 63 cm. (25 in.)
A w. Atlantic grunt which has been found from
Bermuda and Florida, throughout the W.
Indies to Brazil. It is most common in clear
water on open sea areas of sand, turtle grass
beds, and coral rubble. It is frequently found
around wrecks and coral reefs in small groups.
Its food is mainly bottom-living invertebrates
and it noses into the sea bed to find them; it
also eats fishes. Actively feeds by day and by
night.

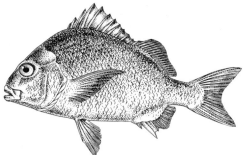

It is greyish overall, the soft dorsal and the
tail fin being abruptly dark, but each scale on
the back and sides has a dark centre. The colour
varies a great deal.

This is the largest of the grunts in the w.
Atlantic and is an important food fish.
H. flavolineatum FRENCH GRUNT
30 cm. (12 in.)
Known along the Atlantic coast of America
from Bermuda and Carolina to Brazil including the Caribbean and the coast of Central
America. It is one of the most common grunts
on Floridan and W. Indian reefs, in daylight
hours found in small shoals. At night they dis-
perse to feed on adjacent flats. Its depth range
is from the shoreline to about 15 m. (8 fathoms).

This is one of the grunts which has been
observed in face to face display with their
mouths pressed together. It is not known
whether this is courtship or territorial display.
301
H. sciurus BLUE STRIPED GRUNT
46 cm. (18 in.)
This is one of the most common and colourful
of the grunts found on the coral reefs of the W.
Indies. Its range extends from S. Carolina and
Bermuda to s. Brazil, including the Gulf of
Mexico and the Central American coast.
Young fish are found in shallow inshore waters
but the adults are typically reef fishes, forming
small schools.

The blue-striped grunt is brightly coloured
and has alternating blue and yellow stripes
along the head and body. The soft-rayed dorsal
and anal fins and the tail fin are dusky.

HAGFISH see **Eptatretus burgeri, Myxine
glutinosa**
HAGFISH, PACIFIC see **Polistotrema stouti**
HAIMARA see **Hoplias malabaricus**
HAIR-TAILED BLENNY see **Xiphasia setifer**
HAIRBACK HERRING see **Nematalosa come**
HAIRTAIL see Trichiuridae
HAIRTAIL see **Trichiurus lepturus**
HAIRY BLENNY see **Labrisomus
nuchipinnis**
HAKE see Merlucciidae
HAKE see **Merluccius merluccius, Rexea
solandri**
HAKE,
  BLUE see **Antimora rostrata**
  CAPE see **Merluccius capensis**
  EUROPEAN see **Merluccius merluccius**
  PACIFIC see **Merluccius productus**
  RED see **Urophycis chuss**
  SQUIRREL see **Urophycis chuss**
  WHITE see **Urophycis tenuis**

Haletta   Odacidae
  semifasciata BLUE ROCK WHITING
41 cm. (16 in.)
A long slender wrasse-like fish with a pointed
snout, large mouth with thick lips and teeth in
both jaws fused to form cutting edges. It is a
bright royal blue above, lighter below, the body
covered with pale gold lines, and with 10 brown
bars on the back and sides.

It is a common fish in weedy and rocky areas
in shallow inshore waters on the coasts of W.
Australia, S. Australia, Victoria, and Tasmania.
Sometimes found in moderate depths. It is not
considered to be good eating.

HALF-BANDED COOLIE LOACH see
  Acanthophthalmus semicinctus
HALFBEAK see Exocoetidae
HALFBEAK,
  HARDHEAD see **Chriodorus atherinoides**
  OCEANIC see **Euleptorhamphus viridis**
HALIBUT see **Hippoglossus hippoglossus**
HALIBUT,
  ATLANTIC see **Hippoglossus
    hippoglossus**
  BLACK see **Reinhardtius
    hippoglossoides**
  CALIFORNIA see **Paralichthys
    californicus**
  GREENLAND see **Reinhardtius
    hippoglossoides**
  PACIFIC see **Hippoglossus stenolepis**
  QUEENSLAND see **Psettodes erumei**

Halichoeres   Labridae
  bivittatus SLIPPERY DICK 23 cm. (9 in.)
Found from Bermuda and N. Carolina to
Brazil, and throughout the Caribbean. It is the
most common member of its genus in the W.
Indies in shallow reef and sandy areas, and is
catholic in its habitat preferences. It feeds
mainly on small crabs, sea urchins, worms,
molluscs and brittle stars, while large specimens eat fishes.

It is brightly coloured, adult males being
bright green on the back, yellow on the sides
with two dark lengthwise bars running along
the sides. The corners of the tail fin are dark.

This species is well known for its habit of
sleeping buried in sand, and has been observed
to make rapid eye movements (REM) during
sleep. Rapid eye movements amongst higher
vertebrates are associated with dreaming sleep.
H. centriquadrus 30 cm. (12 in.)
A fish native to the Red Sea and w. Indian
Ocean, from Mauritius, Madagascar, and the
E. African coast S. to Delagoa Bay. It lives
mainly in shallow water in and about coral
reefs.

It is clearly distinguished from the numerous
other members of the genus by having scales
on the upper edge of the gill cover, and patches
of scales above, behind, and below the eye. It
is most strikingly marked. **403**
H. margaritaceus 13 cm. (5 in.)
An Indo-Pacific species which is distributed
from Japan and the central Pacific, through
the E. Indies, and across the Indian Ocean to
Zanzibar, and the e. coast of Africa. It is a
shallow-water reef fish found commonly in
intertidal areas where good growths of algae
and coral occur, as well as down to depths of
13 m. (7 fathoms).

It is a diminutive wrasse, females of which
are sexually mature at 5 cm. (2 in.) body length.
Its colouring is variable, usually yellowish or
gold. **404**

Halidesmus   Congrogadidae
  scapularis SLANGETJIE 18 cm. (7 in.)
Found only along the coast of South Africa
from the Cape to Natal. It lives on the shore
line down to depths of 91 m. (50 fathoms). It
is said to be an agile small fish which, if pursued, leaves the water and swiftly wriggles
across land to escape.

It has 3 lateral lines. The body is greenish
black with a white-ringed, black spot just behind the head.

Halieuta   Ogcocephalidae
  fitzsimonsi BATFISH 36 cm. (14 in.)
Found only off the South African coast in
moderately deep water, 18–110 m. (10–60
fathoms). It is said to be not uncommon between Plettenberg Bay and East London. It is
greatly flattened, with an almost circular, disc-
like body and head, a short compressed tail.
The eyes are dorsally placed. The body is enveloped in a hard covering with many, regular
double spines on the back and sides. The pelvics are minute and placed well forward on the
belly. It is a dull reddish brown in colour.

Halieutichthys   Ogcocephalidae
  aculeatus SPINY or PANCAKE BATFISH
10 cm. (4 in.)
Round-bodied in outline when viewed from
above, this very distinctive batfish is found
from the Carolinas on the American Atlantic
coast s. through the Caribbean and Gulf of
Mexico. In addition to its round outline the
body is heavily ridged, with numerous, rather
blunt but prominent spines; the pectoral fins
are very large. It is grey-brown above with a
network of brown lines on the back, light ventrally. The pectorals are dark barred.

This fish is very common in moderately deep

water of 82–119 m. (45–65 fathoms). It lives on a bare sandy bottom, usually partially buried in the sand, and is reputed to be mainly nocturnally active. It is said to be able to swim freely and well.

Halophryne Batrachoididae
diemensis BANDED FROGFISH
26 cm. (10¼ in.)
Widely distributed in the Indo-Australian region, from sw. India to New Guinea, the N. and W. coasts of Australia, and off Queensland. It lives on many kinds of sea bed, is most often seen on mud in which it burrows, but is also found on coral reefs.

It is very variably coloured from purplish-black to violet above, and greyish below, darker irregular bands across the back and sides and on the anal fin. It has the typical toadfish shape, a flattened head, wide mouth, with many flaps of skin around it. Spines on the gill covers are large but without venom glands, although they can still inflict a painful wound.

HALOSAURIDAE
A small family of deep fishes, found in all oceans, and which live near the sea floor. They are elongate fishes, closely related to the Notacanthidae, the spiny eels, but differ from them in having a single, short dorsal fin which has no spines. They have a pair of pelvic fins placed well along the belly and a long, many-rayed anal fin which extends from the vent to the tip of the tail, although they have no caudal or tail fin. The mouth is placed ventrally and the snout is produced to form a long probing organ. The larvae are an elongate leptocephalus type thus confirming their general relationship to the eels. See **Aldrovandia, Halosauropsis.**

Halosauropsis Halosauridae
affinis 53 cm. (21 in.)
A long, thin-bodied halosaur widely distributed in the Indo-Pacific, from South Africa, off Zanzibar, and near the Maldive Islands, as well as in the Timor Sea and S. of Japan. It has been found on the sea bed in considerable depths, from 883 to 1789 m. (482–979 fathoms).

Its elongate snout, with ventral mouth, very slender body and long anal fin are typical of the family. The head and body are covered with scales, but the lateral line scales are large and conspicuous. Its eye is moderate in size, but protected by a transparent layer of skin. In colour it is black.

HAMLET,
  BARRED see **Hypoplectrus puella**
  BUTTER see **Hypoplectrus puella**
  MUTTON see **Alphestes afer**
HAMMERHEAD SHARK,
  GREAT see **Sphyrna mokarran**
  SMOOTH see **Sphyrna zygaena**

Haploblepharus Scyliorhinidae
edwardsi SKAAMOOG 61 cm. (2 ft)
A shark of s. Africa, found only in shallow water from Port Nolloth to Natal. Its body form is typical of the dogfishes. Its background coloration is yellow brown, with darker mott-

lings and warm brown bands on the back and sides to give a bold pattern.

Haplochromis Cichlidae
compressiceps MALAWI EYE-BITER
20 cm. (8 in.)
This species is found only in Lake Malawi. It is a very distinctive form having a rather slender body, long head and particularly long snout with steeply-angled, well-toothed jaws. Its most obvious feature, however, is its extremely compressed, laterally flattened head and body.

Its feeding habits are equally distinctive. It is a general predator which obtains much of its food by catching smaller fishes, usually stalked slowly, head-on from the cover of weeds. It has the unusual habit of swallowing its prey tail first. The native fishermen of Lake Malawi also reported that this fish fed on the eyes of other live fishes. This has since been confirmed in aquarium kept specimens, which have been observed to launch themselves directly at the eye of the prey, snapping with the lower jaw (which has specialized cutting teeth) and leaving behind an empty eye socket. Eyes are supplemented in its diet by insect larvae and small fishes. **362**
H. desfontainesi 15 cm. (6 in.)
Found widely in n. Africa in lakes and rivers and occurring in oases and artesian wells. It has been kept in aquaria but the males in the breeding season are pugnacious unless there is ample space.

It has a rather blunt head with a large mouth, the body is somewhat elongate. This species is a mouth brooder. **363**
H. livingstonii 20 cm. (8 in.)
A species of cichlid which is found only in Lake Nyassa and the Upper Shire River. It was named to commemorate the famous explorer of that region Dr David Livingstone.

It is a rather distinctively marked species with a slightly concave tail fin, long snout, and large mouth. **364**
H. sphaerodon 20 cm. (8 in.)
A species found only in Lake Malawi in s. Africa. It is characterized by its very distinctive marking, a wide, oblique dark stripe running from just in front of the dorsal fin to the lower base of the tail fin.

It is occasionally imported as an aquarium fish but is not well known. **365**

HARDHEAD
  HALFBEAK see **Chriodorus atherinoides**
  SILVERSIDE see **Atherinomorus stipes**
HARDYHEAD,
  COMMON see **Pranesus ogilbyi**
  LAKE EYRE see **Craterocephalus eyresii**
HARELIP SUCKER see **Lagochila lacera**

Harengula Clupeidae
humeralis RED-EAR SARDINE
21 cm. (8½ in.)
A sardine found in the Caribbean Sea from Venezuela n. to Florida, the Bahamas, and Bermuda. It is a rather deep-bodied herring-like fish with a distinctly large eye, the scales are large but easily detached, and there are pointed teeth in the roof of the mouth. The fish gets its name from the prominent orange spot at the upper edge of the gill opening. Otherwise the body is generally silvery, with brassy stripes along the darker back, the snout is also dusky yellow.

This sardine is the largest member of the genus. They are shoaling fish, feeding on plankton, and frequently found close to the coast and often in estuaries. They are thus easily available for local fisheries with beach seines and cast nets, and are used as food in the W. Indies. Here and elsewhere they are also used as bait for larger fishes.

HARLEQUIN SMILER see **Merogymnus eximius**
HARLEQUINFISH see **Rasbora heteromorpha**

Harpadon Harpadontidae
nehereus BUMMALO, BOMBAY DUCK
41 cm. (16 in.)
This fish is best known as Bombay duck, when it is split open and sun-dried without preservative, and used as an accompaniment for curries. Fresh it is usually sold under its Bombay name of bummalo or bummalow. On parts of the Indian Ocean coast it is a valuable commercial species and is particularly caught in the low salinity areas near the mouths of large rivers. It is captured in a series of large nets anchored to posts across the tidal flow. It appears to be a migratory species which lives well offshore for part of the year and then moves inshore during the monsoon period. It has been suggested that this migration is a response to the cold, well oxygenated rain water lowering the salinity of the sea in such areas as the mouths of the Ganges and the Irrawaddy where the major fisheries exist. There is also a suggestion that the bummalo are attracted by the large numbers of small fish and crustaceans that inhabit these areas, for it feeds on these organisms.

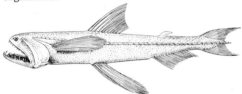

It is essentially a fish of the n. Indian Ocean, and although it is found on the Arabian coast S. of Karachi to well S. of Bombay, it is most abundant in the Bay of Bengal. It does not occur round the s. tip of India nor in Sri Lanka waters. On the Bombay coast it breeds far out to sea during February and March. The inshore fisheries take place in water of 11–18 m. (6–10 fathoms), but the fish has been caught offshore in deeper water.

Its body is cylindrical, pale and almost translucent when alive but with soft, flaccid flesh. It spoils quickly after capture which, no doubt, is one reason for drying the major part of the catch.

HARPADONTIDAE
A small family of marine fishes found in the Indian Ocean from E. Africa across to w. Australia. There are 4–5 species. They are closely similar to the lizardfishes of the family Synodontidae. The body is elongate, with a blunt rather short head; the snout is short, the eyes being placed near the end of the head, but the jaws are extremely long, and very well armed with long curved teeth of varying sizes. The pelvic and pectoral fins are very long, and the tail is deeply forked with the middle rays over-

laid by scales of the lateral line making a third, median tailfin lobe. Scales of the body are thin and easily dislodged, and are present only on the rear half of the body.

These fish have a glassy, transparent, rather gelatinous appearance, but their most notable feature are the numerous small barbed teeth on the edges of the mouth. See **Harpadon.**

Harpagifer Nototheniidae
bispinis PLUNDERFISH 10 cm. (4 in.)
This interesting little fish is distributed all around the borders of the Antarctic Convergence although it is not found in the high Antarctic region. It is found on the shores and very shallow water of Prince Edward, Crozet, Kerguelen, Macquarie islands, and on the s. tip of S. America, as well as the Falklands, S. Shetlands, and S. Orkneys. It is mainly a littoral species living in tide pools, and under stones at low tide, or sheltering in algal beds.

Its body form is short and broad, and is extraordinarily reminiscent of that of the sculpins and bullheads (Cottidae) which occupy similar habitats in the N. Hemisphere. Its coloration is very variable.

This species has been divided into a number of subspecies, each inhabiting a separate geographical region, but none is strikingly distinct from one another. They represent an interesting case of the effect of physical isolation on the evolution of different forms from an ancestral line. **417**

Harriotta Rhinochimaeridae
raleighana LONG-NOSED CHIMAERA
1 m. (3¼ ft)
This deep-water rabbitfish has been found on both sides of the N. Atlantic, off New York, Chesapeake Bay, Georges Bank, and Nova Scotia, as well as off w. Scotland and the Canaries. All these specimens were taken in depths of between 686 and 2603 m. (375–1422 fathoms) and the shallower of these depths refers only to the capture of an egg capsule. Relatively few specimens have ever been caught and its biology is virtually unknown. The egg capsule is dark brown, elongate, and has ribbed flanges along each side which are a pale amber in colour; it measures about 165 mm. (6½ in.) in length. The young are believed to hatch in summer.

This species is very distinctive with its enormously long pointed snout, otherwise it is a typical chimaeroid with an elongate tail, 2 dorsal fins, the first of which is high and has a long spine in front, the second is low and long. It lacks a separate anal fin. Mature males have a club-like organ on the forehead, densely spiny on the underside. In colour it is a uniform chocolate brown above and below, the fins are lighter, and live specimens have a pale green iris.

HART'S RIVULUS see **Rivulus hartii**
HARVESTFISH see **Peprilus alepidotus,**
    Peprilus triacanthus

Hassar Doradidae
orestis 28 cm. (11 in.)
A S. American catfish which has been found in Brazil mainly in the Amazon and its larger tributaries.

Members of this genus are found in n. S. America and are distinguished by having the snout and lower gill covers covered with skin, the bony plate behind the pectoral fin blunt and rounded, and most notably by having the anterior scutes of the lateral line very small although the posterior ones are large and thorny. It is further recognized by the black spot on the first 3 rays of the dorsal fin. The eyes are very elongate. **163**

HASSELT'S BONY-LIPPED BARB see
    Osteocheilus hasselti
HATAHATA see **Arctoscopus japonicus**
HATCHETFISH see Sternoptychidae
HATCHETFISH,
    BLACK-WINGED see **Carnegiella marthae**
    COMMON see **Gasteropelecus sternicla**
    FLYING see Gasteropelecidae
    MARBLED see **Carnegiella strigata**
    SILVER see **Gasteropelecus levis**
HAUSEN see **Huso huso**
HAWKFISH see **Oxycirrhites typus,**
    Paracirrhites arcatus
HAWKFISH, RED-SPOTTED see
    Amblycirrhitus pinos
HEAD, SLIME see **Hoplostethus**
    mediterraneus
HEAD-AND-TAIL-LIGHT FISH see
    Hemigrammus ocellifer
HEADSTANDER see **Abramites**
    microcephalus
HEADSTANDER,
    HUMP-BACKED see **Charax gibbosus**
    SPOTTED see **Chilodus punctatus**
HEDGEHOG SKATE see **Raja erinacea**

Helicolenus Scorpaenidae
dactylopterus BLUEMOUTH, BLACKBELLY
ROSEMOUTH 46 cm. (18 in.)
A deep water scorpaenid which is found widely on both sides of the N. Atlantic, in European waters extending from Norway S. to Madeira and in the w. Mediterranean. It is normally found in depths of 200–800 m. (109–436 fathoms) but is occasionally found inshore when young.

It is wholly predatory, feeding on small fishes, crustaceans, and squids. Although it is caught abundantly in deep trawls it is not utilized for food in n. Europe, but in the Mediterranean it finds a ready sale.

In colour it is rose pink on the back and sides lighter ventrally; the inside of the gill covers and mouth is a dark blue. It is distinguished by its very spiny head, large spines in the dorsal fin, and by the lower 9 pectoral fin rays being free from the fin membrane at their tips.

Helogenes Helogeneidae
marmoratus 10 cm. (4 in.)
A small catfish found only in the region of the e. Amazon basin and the Guianas. It is a nocturnal fish which frequents heavily overgrown river backwaters and pools, and particularly the tangle of roots and fallen trees.

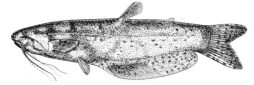

It is dull brown above with a reddish tinge and lighter mottlings, ventrally pale brown, with dark spots. Occasionally imported to Europe for aquaria.

HELOGENEIDAE
A family of S. American catfish found only in the Amazon basin and to the N. of the Amazon. It is known only from the single species.

The single member is a small, naked catfish, with a long anal fin, small dorsal and adipose fins, and a forked tail. It has 3 pairs of moderately long barbels, and small skin-covered eyes which are said to shine in the dark. It is nocturnal in its habits. See **Helogenes.**

Helostoma Helostomatidae
temminckii KISSING GOURAMI
30 cm. (12 in.)
The range of the kissing gourami extends from Java, Borneo, Sumatra, and Malaysia to well into central Thailand. Introduced to Sri Lanka. In these countries it is found in sluggish streams, swamps, ponds, and lakes, in which it inhabits well vegetated areas which often are deficient in oxygen. Like other labyrinth fishes it has an accessory respiratory organ above the gills in each gill chamber so its ability to thrive in areas where dissolved oxygen in the water is low is ensured.

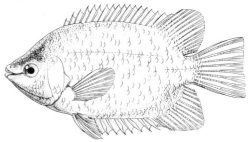

In inland areas in which it lives it is a valued food fish. In Europe and America it is well known as an aquarium fish. The habit of facing one another with their wide, fleshy lips closely adpressed gives rise to the popular name, kissing gourami. In fact this behaviour is more probably a threat display than a demonstration of affection. This fish is a peaceful but rather timid aquarium fish; it feeds on a wide variety of plant and animal food.

It is distinguished from its relatives by its compressed, oval body and pointed head with thick lips. **461**

HELOSTOMATIDAE
A family within the group of labyrinth fishes which also includes the climbing perches (Anabantidae) and gouramis (Belontiidae). A single species is known inhabiting the freshwaters of se. Asia.

It can be distinguished from its relatives by the long, many-spined dorsal and anal fins, by the small mouth with a horizontal gape and protrusible, broad lips. There are no teeth in the jaw, but there are movable teeth on the lips. See **Helostoma.**

Helotes Theraponidae
sexlineatus STRIPED PERCH, SIX-LINED
PERCH 28 cm. (11 in.)
A common fish in the Indo-Australian region and found especially on the warmer waters of Australia.

It is distinguished by the 6–8 narrow lengthwise dark brown stripes along the sides, which are otherwise silvery grey. The back is bluish grey. The first dorsal fin is well developed with high spines, and almost separated from the second fin.

Hemibarbus   Cyprinidae
  maculatus 41 cm. (16 in.)
The genus *Hemibarbus* is in many ways intermediate between the barbels (*Barbus* sp.) and the gudgeons (*Gobio* sp.). They have a cylindrical body, flattened ventrally, with a powerful spine in the front of the dorsal fin. Barbels are present at the corner of the mouth but are not very long.

H. maculatus is rather deep-bodied, with a high dorsal fin. Its snout is pointed and long and its lips are thin. It is distributed in the rivers of n. China and the central and lower reaches of the River Amur. It is a bottom-living fish of the quieter reaches of rivers, feeding on insect larvae, and to some extent on molluscs.

It is one of the few cyprinids in which the mature males are larger than the females. It spawns in summer on vegetation and the eggs hatch in about 4 days. The larva lacks an adhesive disc but has large pectoral fins so instead of hanging on the vegetation after hatching (as do the larvae of most cyprinids), it takes to the bottom directly supporting itself on its fins.

Locally it is a moderately valuable fish being captured by seines.

Hemiemblemaria   Chaenopsidae
  similus WRASSE BLENNY 10 cm. (4 in.)
Native to the coasts of Florida and the Bahamas. It lives in shallow water at depths of 6–15 m. (20–50 ft), usually inhabiting the burrow of a dead, boring mollusc in which it lies with only its head protruding. Its chief interest is its mimicry of the bluehead wrasse, *Thalassoma bifasciatum*, a peaceful and acceptable inhabitant of the reefs due to its parasite picking habits. The blenny is coloured to match the 3 main colour phases of the wrasse as it grows, its physical resemblance is remarkable, and it has adopted the smooth swimming style of the wrasse, chiefly propelled by its pectoral fins, in place of the darting, jerky swimming normal to blennies.

Using its close resemblance to the wrasse it enjoys relative freedom from predation and can approach close to small fishes on which it preys.

Its colouring varies but a lengthwise black stripe down the side, sometimes broken into separate blocks is constant.

Hemigrammus   Characidae
  caudovittatus BUENOS AIRES TETRA
8 cm. (3 in.)
This interesting characin is one of the largest members of the genus *Hemigrammus*. It is moderately popular as an aquarium fish except that its eats vegetation, including carefully cultured aquarium plants. It should be kept at temperatures of 24°C, and is easy to breed, the female scattering her adhesive eggs amongst the plants.

The colour of this fish is striking. Males are slimmer than females, and their anal fin is brick red, brighter than in the female.

As the popular name suggests, this fish is

found in the La Plata basin, Argentina, within which is Buenos Aires. **55**

H. erythrozonus GLOWLIGHT TETRA
4·5 cm. (1¾ in.)
Known originally from the rivers of Guyana, the glowlight tetra is now a relatively common fish in captivity. Its popularity with aquarists is deserved, for it is beautifully coloured. Males appear to be no more colourful than females and the only difference between the sexes is the slightly plumper body of the female.

It is moderately difficult to get to breed, and requires rather acid water and a temperature of 28°C for success. The spawning pairs are very active, darting in close spirals around the weed; the female often lays her eggs whilst upside down. The young hatch after 24 hours, but do not actively feed for several days. **56**

H. ocellifer HEAD-AND-TAIL-LIGHT FISH,
BEACONFISH 4·5 cm. (1¾ in.)
This beautiful aquarium fish originated in the area of Guyana and the Amazon basin. It is well-known and a common fish in captivity. Its popular names are in reference to the brilliant red and golden spot near the base of the tail fin, and the similar colours on the upper part of the eye.

Males differ from females in their slimmer build, and the easy visibility of the swim-bladder when viewed against the light. It is also said that males have a shining white spot on the anal fin.

This characin is easily bred. Ripe pairs being put into a well planted tank, at 23–25°C, in slightly acid water, will usually spawn in the evening with considerable activity, the eggs falling between stones on the bottom or into plant fronds. The eggs hatch in 30–36 hours, and the fry hang passively on the vegetation for several days before they begin feeding.

A subspecies *H. ocellifer falsus* has been described which differs notably in its slimmer shape. It too is quite common as an aquarists' fish. **57**

H. pulcher PRETTY TETRA 6 cm. (2¼ in.)
This aptly named tetra is a rather deep-bodied species although it has the characteristic form, high dorsal fin, and dorsal adipose fin of the tetras. Its original habitat was the middle Amazon region. It is brilliantly coloured.

Males are distinguishable from females by their slimmer shape, and the easily visible swim-bladder in the body cavity; in females it is obscured. The general consensus of opinion is that it is a rather difficult species to breed. **58**

H. rhodostomus RED-NOSED TETRA,
RUMMY-NOSED TETRA 4 cm. (1½ in.)
This tetra is very conspicuously coloured. In captivity the reddening of the head is seldom very noticeable, but fish in exceptionally good condition are occasionally seen and then the snout is very distinctly red. It is native to the lower part of the Amazon basin. **59**

Hemilepidotus   Cottidae
  hemilepidotus RED IRISH LORD
51 cm. (20 in.)
Found on the N. American Pacific coast from the Bering Sea to n. California. The red Irish lord is very common on the coast in the N. of its range in shallow water and on the shore and is often caught in shore seines. It has little or no value as a food fish. It spawns on rocky

shores in early spring, laying large masses of pinkish eggs often in the intertidal zone. Its food consists mostly of crustaceans and molluscs.

It is distinguished by the stepped outline of the spiny dorsal fin, by the 4 rows of spiny scales each side of the dorsal fins, and by its generally reddish colouring with brown spots.

HEMIODONTIDAE
A family of characin-like fishes widely distributed in Central and S. America (except for the S.). All are fully scaled and possess an adipose dorsal fin. Most of the members of the family are slender, round-bodied fishes. The family is distinguished from the true characins (Characidae) most notably by the dentition, or rather by the lack of dentition, for many of the hemiodonts have no teeth in the lower jaw, and those that possess teeth have only small teeth in the jaw.

Some of these fishes are kept as aquarium fish. See **Characidium, Hemiodopsis, Hemiodus.**

Hemiodopsis   Hemiodontidae
  quadrimaculatus see under **H. vorderwinkleri**
  vorderwinkleri 6·5 cm. (2½ in.)
A species found widely in the ne. region of S. America. It had long been confused with a related species, *H. quadrimaculatus,* and was only distinguished adequately in 1964 by the French ichthyologist Dr Jacques Gery. It has been found in the region of the Upper Amazon on the Brazilian-Colombian boundaries, and in several localities in Guyana.

Its body form is similar to other members of the family. **93**

Hemiodus   Hemiodontidae
  semitaeniatus 20 cm. (8 in.)
This fish is widely distributed through n. S. America especially in the lower Amazon, its s. tributaries, and n. to Guyana. In the latter region it is found in the relatively still waters of creeks leading from rivers, and in pools in the upper rivers isolated during the dry season. It is a swift swimming, agile, shoaling fish.

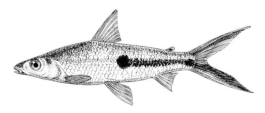

In colour it is bright silvery, the back light brown, the sides with greenish or bluish tints. A distinct rounded black spot on the side midway between the dorsal fin and the adipose fin is separate from the long stripe running along the sides of the tail and turning downwards along the lower lobe of the tail fin, where it broadens out. It is an attractive fish for the large aquarium.

Hemiramphus Exocoetidae
brasiliensis BALLYHOO 45 cm. (18 in.)
A common inshore species in the tropical Atlantic best known off the American coast from New England to Brazil and throughout the Gulf of Mexico and the Caribbean. It is also reported from tropical W. Africa.

It is a typical halfbeak but in this species the pectoral fin is comparatively short, and the upper lobe of the tail fin is orange. Otherwise it is dark green or blue above, silvery elsewhere, the tip of the lower jaw is orange.

It is a surface-living schooling fish which feeds on floating pieces of sea grass and small clupeid fishes. It is fed upon by larger fishes and terns, and some quantities are seined for human consumption.

H. far BLACK-BARRED GARFISH, NEEDLE-FISH, CANDLEFISH 67 cm. (26 in.)
Widely distributed in the Indo-Pacific this halfbeak is found from the Red Sea to Mozambique and South Africa, and e. to New Guinea and Queensland, and into the Pacific. In Australia it is known as black-barred garfish, in s. Africa needlefish or candlefish.

Its body shape is typical of the halfbeaks with a long lower jaw and a short upper jaw, the tail fin is deeply forked the lower lobe being the longer, and the dorsal fin base is twice that of the anal. This species has a series of 4–9 large black blotches down the sides, its back is light greenish brown, the sides silvery, the upper tail fin lobe bright yellow, the lower bright blue.

A surface-living, schooling fish which darts along near the surface in shallow water and even enters estuaries. It is reported to spawn in estuaries in summer in s. Africa.

It is a good food fish, caught mostly by seining or by dipnetting at night under a light.

H. quoyi SHORTNOSED GARFISH 35 cm. (14 in.)
A widely distributed species along the Australian coast especially W. Australia, Queensland, and New Guinea. It is a surface-living, schooling fish, of some commercial importance. It is frequently captured in seine nets on the open shores and commands a ready sale as it is a good quality food fish.

In body form it is very distinctive possessing the typical long lower jaw of the halfbeaks, which, however, is relatively short, around twice the length of the upper jaw measured from the eye. In colour it is yellowish green, dark above, silvery on the belly, and a silvery lengthwise band. The beak is orange-yellow in colour.

Hemirhamphodon Exocoetidae
pogonognathus 20 cm. (8 in.)
A freshwater halfbeak found in the Malay Peninsula, Sumatra, Borneo, and elsewhere in the E. Indies. It is characteristically found in shaded, forest streams and does not occur in brackish waters, nor is it so abundant as *Dermogenys,* another freshwater halfbeak of the area.

It is a long slender fish with a long lower jaw which has numerous fine teeth on it, and the tip of which ends as a stout barbel. The upper jaw is short and curved. It is an olive-brown above with shining silvery sides; the gill cover has a red blotch. The female has a larger anal fin than the male. This species is a live-bearer.

Hemiscyllium Scyliorhinidae
punctatum BROWN-BANDED CATSHARK
1·05 m. (41 in.)
This catshark is widely distributed in the Australasian region and is well-known on the Australian coast of S. Queensland to the Torres Strait and the N. Territory. It is common in shallows and on offshore banks and is often taken by line as well as seine net. Its flesh is said to be excellent as food, of firm texture and well flavoured.

In colour, the adults are uniformly reddish-brown or fawn, with variable dark spotting. The young are banded with 10 or more broad dark bars. The egg cases, and less frequently the young, are often cast up on the warmer coasts of Australia after heavy storms.

H. variolatum see **Parascyllium variolatum**

Hemitaurichthys Chaetodontidae
zoster 18 cm. (7 in.)
An Indo-Pacific butterflyfish with a curiously discontinous distribution. It was first discovered in the waters of Mauritius, and later found in the E. Indies, the Philippines, and Hawaii. Whether it occurs in intermediate areas and has not been captured, or its range is truly discontinuous is not known.

The genus is distinguished from *Chaetodon* by its small scales and teeth, and fewer dorsal rays. The colouring is very variable. **335**

Hemitripterus Cottidae
americanus ATLANTIC SEA RAVEN
62 cm. (25 in.)
A very striking inhabitant of the American Atlantic coastline from Chesapeake Bay n. to Newfoundland and Labrador. It inhabits rocky grounds from 2 m. (1 fathom) down to 91 m. (50 fathoms). It feeds on bottom-living invertebrates, especially crustaceans, as well as fishes. Breeding takes place in autumn and early winter, the eggs being deposited in clumps on the bases of certain sponges.

It has the surprising ability of inflating its belly with water when it will float helplessly at the surface.

It is distinguished by having numerous skin flaps on the head, and by the fin membrane of the spiny dorsal being deeply emarginate, giving it a ragged appearance. Its entire skin is notably prickly.

HEN, SEA see **Cyclopterus lumpus**

Heniochus Chaetodontidae
acuminatus ANGELFISH, FEATHER-FIN BULLFISH 25 cm. (10 in.)
The most widely distributed of all the species in this genus, and probably the most abundant. It is found from the Red Sea and the e. coast of Africa, S. to Durban, around the Indian Ocean islands, India, n. Australia, Polynesia, the Philippines, and Hawaii. It is a shallow water reef fish, common down to a depth of 30 m. (17 fathoms), and is a familiar sight in

the clear water swimming either singly or in a small school.

It is distinguished by the great development of the fourth dorsal spine, which forms a long filament in the adult at least as long as the body. It is distinctively patterned. **336**

H. monoceros 23 cm. (9 in.)
Found in the tropical Indo-Pacific, but not well known and only reported from isolated areas such as Mauritius, Java, Samoa, Tahiti, and elsewhere in the Polynesian region. It occurs in the Philippines, and possibly also in Hawaii. It is believed to be a rather deep water form which is only rarely collected in shallow reef areas.

This species is distinguished by its body form and coloration. It has the elongate fourth dorsal fin spine, a conical, bony prominence in the mid-line on the nape, and a small spine above each eye. **337**

H. permutatus THREE-BANDED BULLFISH
18 cm. (7 in.)
An Indo-Pacific species found from the E. Indies, n. Australia, Melanesia, Micronesia, Polynesia, and the Philippines. It is a reef-dwelling species which is found mostly in deeper water around coral heads; for this reason it is not so well known or so often seen as the shallow water *Heniochus* species.

This species has the elongate fourth dorsal spine which is typical of the genus, but it is only as long as the head, the fifth spine is longer than the others. **338**

HEPSETIDAE
A family closely related to the characins (Characidae) and containing only one species. In general appearance it is similar to several of the larger African characins, although its chief resemblance is to the pikes (Esocidae) of the N. Hemisphere, a group to which it is not related.

Its body form is elongate with the dorsal and anal fins far back along the body, and a rather high adipose fin close to the tail. The body is closely scaled, with the lateral line running parallel to the ventral profile. The head is elongate with large jaws which contain numerous teeth, in the lower jaw in 2 well separated rows at the sides, the inner row being short, but sharply pointed, while those in the outer row are unequal in size with many long and fang-like. Large fangs are present in the front of both jaws. See **Hepsetus.**

Hepsetus Hepsetidae
odoe PIKE CHARACIN, PIKE, KAFUE PIKE
36 cm. (14 in.) at least
The pike characin is found in central Africa, from Senegal and the Congo basin, to the Upper Zambezi and the Kafue River to the se. It is famed for its voracious appetite and fish-eating habits, one reason it is much prized by anglers who fish for it with a small spoon, plug or fly, and on light tackle it is a very game fighter. It grows to a weight of about 1·8 kg. (4 lb). It is also occasionally exhibited in aquaria, although in view of its piscivorous habits it is not recommended for the mixed aquarium! It also has the reputation of being rather delicate.

Its dorsal and anal fins are far back near the tail. In colour it is dull browny olive, breaking into indistinct vertical brown bars across the sides, the fins are yellowish with brown spots, and a series of dark stripes radiate from the eye. Coloration, however, varies with age and condition. The adipose fin is reddish.

The pike characin spawns in a manner unique for the group. The spawning pairs (females are usually larger than males) make nests of floating foam in which the eggs are deposited. The nest is guarded by one or both parents until the young fish leave the nest.

Heptranchias Hexanchidae
dakini see **H. perlo**
perlo SEVEN-GILLED SHARK, PERLON
2·1 m. (7 ft)
The seven-gilled shark is widely, but discontinuously distributed in temperate seas. It is common in the Mediterranean and in the Atlantic off Spain and Portugal, and also off Cuba; it is also found off Japan and off s. Australia (where it is known as the 'one-finned shark', *H. dakini*). It is found in deep water, usually near the bottom, but occasionally comes into shallow coastal seas. It is a dull grey on the back, lighter beneath, often with dusky tips to the fins. It can be recognized by its narrow tapering head and snout, the many cusped teeth in the lower jaw, and the 7 wide gill slits. The young are born alive, but are said to be quite small (about 23 cm., 9 in.) at birth.

The seven-gilled shark is not a dangerous species in that it seldom encounters man in the depths in which it lives. It is, however, a voracious feeder on hake, and other valuable food fishes. Locally it is fished for and eaten by man.

HERRING see Clupeidae
HERRING see **Clupea harengus**
HERRING,
  ATLANTIC THREAD see **Opisthonema oglinum**
  BLUEBACK see **Alosa aestivalis**
  DWARF see **Jenkinsia lamprotaenia**
  FALL see **Alosa mediocris**
  FLAT see **Hilsa kelee**
  GIANT see **Elops saurus**
  GLUT see **Alosa aestivalis**
  HAIRBACK see **Nematalosa come**

LAKE see **Coregonus artedii**
PACIFIC see **Clupea pallasi**
ROUND see **Etrumeus teres**
SALMON see **Chanos chanos**
SUMMER see **Alosa aestivalis**
WOLF see **Chirocentrus dorab**
HERRING CALE see **Olisthops cyanomelas**
HERRINGBONE RIVULUS see **Rivulus strigatus**

Heterandria Poeciliidae
formosa DWARF TOPMINNOW,
MOSQUITOFISH 3·5 cm. (1½ in.)
Apparently confined to the states of S. Carolina and Florida in the U.S. and encountered in small streams, ponds, ditches and swamps where dense vegetation offers cover.

Adult males measure only 2 cm. (¾ in.), the females only slightly larger. This is one of the smallest toothcarps known to science, and one of the smallest known vertebrate animals.

It is a slender little fish, yellowish brown above, silvery white below. A lengthwise zigzag dark line runs from the snout to the tail. The fins are pale brown, the male's dorsal fin has an orange edge. The female is similarly coloured.

A pleasant, lively aquarium fish, which can be aggressive towards its own kind, and is said to eat its own young. Its breeding habits are of some interest. After mating the eggs develop a few at a time and are fertilized internally as they develop. The young are born continuously, 2 or 3 every day over a period of 6–10 days.

HETERENCHELIDAE
A small group of eels which are best known in the tropical Atlantic and Mediterranean, although recently discovered in the e. Pacific Ocean. None is particularly large, most being less than 1 m. (3¼ ft) in length. All are long, slim-bodied eels lacking pelvic and pectoral fins, and with the dorsal and anal fins sheathed in thick skin. The tail is usually twice the length of the body, the head is small, the eyes often minute and covered with skin. Most of these adaptations are related to their habit of burrowing in sand. All have blunt, flattened teeth. See **Panturichthys, Pythonichthys.**

Heterobranchus Clariidae
longifilis 1 m. (39 in.) and more
Widely distributed through Africa, from the basins of the Nile, Niger, Congo, and Zambesi, and their associated lakes. It is a very large fish which attains a weight of over 45 kg. (100

lb.), usually the largest specimens coming from large, deep pools. It is usually found in creeks and swamps, although it has been recorded in areas like the turbulent water below the Murchison Falls.

Its colour varies with its habitat, but is usually brownish olive above, white on the belly, with yellowish fins.

HETERODONTIDAE
A small family of rather primitive sharks,

found only in shallow waters of the Indo-Pacific. Probably only 4 species known; all rather similar, with large, heavy heads, an eyebrow ridge over each eye, large, flattened teeth in the sides of the jaws, and a large spine in front of each dorsal fin. All species feed on hard shelled animals, crabs, molluscs, and sea urchins. See **Heterodontus.**

Heterodontus Heterodontidae
francisci HORN SHARK 1·2 m. (4 ft)
The horn shark is found on the Californian coast and S. along the coast of Mexico, as well as in the Gulf of California. Along these coasts it is found from tidepool level down to 25 m. (14 fathoms) frequently lying with its head wedged into a crevice. It is a sluggish species, feeding on hard shelled animals, and is quite harmless, except when molested by skin-divers when it will turn to bite.

It is an egg-laying shark, the eggs being protected by a dark brown horny case with a spirally twisted edge. These eggs are wedged between rocks and take 8–9 months to hatch, the young shark being only 10–13 cm. (4–5 in.) at hatching. The adults breed readily in captivity, the egg cases being deposited singly during February and March. Mating in these sharks begins with the male biting the female, frequently on her pectoral fin, and inserting one of his claspers into the female's genital opening. In all matings observed only one of the 2 claspers is used.

H. philippi PORT JACKSON SHARK
1·5 m. (5 ft)
This is a shallow water shark of s. Australian seas, particularly common off S. Australia. It is a small species and quite harmless. Its teeth are sharp in the front of the jaws, but to the sides they are broad, and rounded. Teeth such as these suggest that hard shelled animals such as crustaceans, molluscs, and sea urchins are eaten.

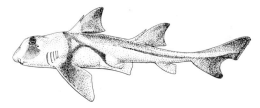

The Port Jackson shark is light brown in colour with dark marks on the head and across the body. It is an egg-laying species, producing an egg case with a double spiral flap. These egg cases are familiar objects on the Australian sea shore after storms.

Heteromugil Mugilidae
tricuspidens HAARDER, SPRINGER
76 cm. (30 in.)
A grey mullet apparently found only in South African waters where it occurs from Mossel Bay to Durban. It is found especially on mud banks in inshore waters and estuaries.

Its describer, the late Professor J. L. B. Smith, reports that it it renowned for its leaping abilities, large fishes being able to spring a clear 2·5 m. (8 ft) high and 12 m. (40 ft) long. It is especially difficult to catch in a seine net because of its jumping ability. It is occasionally hooked by anglers and fights magnificently; large specimens may weigh about 4 kg. (9 lb.)

Heteropneustes Heteropneustidae
fossilis 70 cm. (27½ in.)
Widespread throughout tropical Asia, from India, Sri Lanka to Vietnam and Thailand. It lives in ponds, ditches, swamps, and marshes, and less often in muddy rivers. Its elongate air-breathing sacs in the back musclature permit it to inhabit very oxygen-poor localities and it can tolerate conditions fatal to most fishes. It breeds during the rainy season, the yellowish eggs being laid in depressions hollowed out by the parents who guard them until hatching and the young for a long time afterwards.

This fish is edible, but the sharp, allegedly envenomed, pectoral spines are greatly feared by fishermen. It is occasionally kept in aquaria. It is a uniform grey brown in colour, sometimes almost black, with 2 narrow yellowish bands along the sides. The eye is distinctly yellow.

HETEROPNEUSTIDAE
A family of Asiatic catfishes close to the Clariidae. The 2 recognized species are slender-bodied, with a small dorsal fin, no adipose fin, but a very long many-rayed anal fin. Barbels are long, and numerous. They also have 2 long, hollow cylindrical cavities from the gill cavity through the muscles of the back which serve as accessory breathing organs, and allow the fish to use atmospheric oxygen – a necessary adaptation for fishes living habitually in stagnant pools and swamps. See **Heteropneustes.**

Heteroscarus Scaridae
acroptilus RAINBOWFISH 23 cm. (9 in.)
A species of parrotfish found in the waters of s. Australia. It is found in rocky areas in deep water off the coasts of W. Australia, S. Australia, and New South Wales.

In body form it is much like other parrotfishes, but the first 3 spines of the dorsal fin are greatly elongated in males only. The male coloration is greenish with 2 dusky bars on the sides, the cheeks are pinkish with blue lengthwise streaks. The fins are greenish, with blue and orange markings. The female is a dusky brown without any of the male's bright colouring.

Heterotis Osteoglossidae
niloticus 91 cm. (3 ft)
Heterotis is the tropical African representative of the family. It is widely-spread in the Upper Nile, and the rivers of Chad, Niger, Senegal,

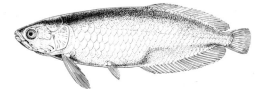

and Gambia. It is a nest builder, breeding in still waters close to the river, and excavating a nest some 1·2 m. (4 ft) in diameter with thick walls of vegetation and mud. Within this the

eggs are laid and protected by the parents; the eggs are large (about 2·5 mm. (0·1 in.) in diameter) and hatch in 2 days. The newly hatched larvae have external gills.

Its gill chamber contains a curiously modified fourth gill-arch in spiral form which was thought to be an accessory respiratory organ, but is now known to help in feeding by filtering fine organisms, especially minute plant plankton out of the water. Trapped in mucus covering the filter, this microscopical food is then swallowed. It is probably a particularly important item of diet in the dry season, when shrunken rivers prevent much active movement and feeding.

HEXAGRAMMIDAE
A family of N. Pacific marine fishes found on the N. American coast from California to the Arctic as well as on the Asian coast to Japan. This family, known generally as greenlings, includes several commercially important species in the Far E.

They are related to the scorpionfishes but lack the very obvious spines and ridges on the head. Most species have more than one lateral line, and the dorsal fin is single and continuous although the anterior rays are spiny and divided by a notch from the remainder of the fin. See **Hexagrammos, Ophiodon.**

Hexagrammos Hexagrammidae
decagrammus KELP GREENLING
53 cm. (21 in.)
Widely distributed along the Pacific coast of N. America from La Jolla, California, to Alaska. In the n. parts of its range it is abundant along rocky shores, reefs, and amongst kelp beds and is found literally in a few feet of water. To the S., however, it is only taken in deep water on rocky habitats at depths of 45 m. (25 fathoms).

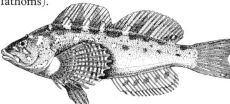

Spawning takes place in the autumn and early winter with pale blue eggs laid in large clumps amongst rocks. Young fish are common in the plankton in the open sea. The adult's food consists of worms, crustaceans, and small fishes. In turn they are eaten by steelhead trout, salmon, lingcod, and sharks, as well as birds and sea lions.

It is an important food fish in the N. of its range, but its use is local. Elsewhere it is regarded as a good sporting fish for anglers fishing in rocky areas.

It is distinguished by the presence of 5 lateral lines on each side, and by its singular coloration, the males having blue spots on the head and back each surrounded by a rust-brown ring; the females are covered with orange to brownish spots.

H. otakii AINAME 41 cm. (16 in.)
This is the commonest of the greenlings on the Asian coast of the N. Pacific, and it is found from n. Japan to Korea. It has 5 lateral lines each side, the first of which extends only half-way down the second dorsal fin. Its coloration is varied from brownish red to dark purple.

It spawns in winter, attaching its eggs in large clumps to the base of seaweed stems.

It is of commercial importance in Japan. The flesh is said to be tasty and is eaten raw or prepared in a variety of ways.

HEXANCHIDAE
A family of rather primitive sharks of world wide distribution, rather common in deep water. In general their life history is little known. All are rather elongate in body form and have either 6 or 7 long gill slits (most sharks have 5 only). They also have only 1 dorsal fin, have rather long tail fins, and the teeth in the lower jaw each have several parallel cusps giving them a comb-like appearance. See **Heptranchias, Hexanchus, Notorynchus.**

Hexanchus Hexanchidae
griseus SIX-GILLED SHARK, COW SHARK
4·9 m. (16 ft)
The six-gilled shark is world-wide in distribution; however, it is best known from the N. Atlantic and Mediterranean. Although it is usually found in the open sea, it ventures into inshore waters perhaps more than any other deep sea shark, and has been frequently seen and caught close to land. It is a dull grey, or brown in colour, with a broad head, wide mouth and 6 large gill slits.

It gives birth to live young, and litters of 40 pups have been found in large families. The newly born young are between 40 and 66 cm.

(15¾–26 in.) long. The six-gill appears to be a sluggish shark which feeds on a wide variety of fishes, and on account of its size can tackle most large marine creatures. In European waters it has been found to eat hake, rays, electric rays, and crustaceans and one had half a seal in its stomach. Elsewhere it has been known to eat dolphin fish, swordfish, and marlin. It is not known to be dangerous to man, and being a deep-water shark it rarely comes in contact with swimmers, but being a large and powerful shark it is probably best avoided wherever possible.

HICKORY SHAD see **Alosa mediocris**
HIGH COCKSCOMB see **Anoplarchus purpurescens**
HIGH-HAT see **Equetus acuminatus**
HIGHWATER see **Coracinus capensis**

Hilsa Clupeidae
kelee FLAT HERRING 30 cm. (12 in.)
A typically herring-like fish, but with a highly compressed and flattened body. Its outline is rather deep, and the keel along the belly is sharp. Its back is greenish, the sides and belly brilliantly silver, with a series of dark blotches along each side, slightly above the level of the eye.

It is an Indo-Pacific species, which ranges from China to the E. African coast usually in shallow inshore waters. In places it is extremely abundant and forms the basis for local fishing industries. In s. Africa it is well regarded by anglers as a bait fish. It is also eaten salted or smoked.

HIMANTOLOPHIDAE

A family of deep-sea anglerfishes reported from the Atlantic and Pacific oceans. They are rather round bodied ceratioids with short based dorsal and anal fins. The skin is spiny in males, but females have flattened bony plates in patches. The males are free-living and not parasitic on the females when adult; their jaws are small and toothless, but their olfactory organs are well developed. See **Himantolophus.**

Himantolophus   Himantolophidae
  groenlandicus 61 cm. (24 in.)
A striking looking deep-sea angler, the female is very rotund with a deep brown, smooth skin studded with large buckler-like plates. The modified ray rising from the anterior head between the eyes is thick and ends in a massive branched lure.

Most adult female specimens have been captured in the N. Atlantic, between Gibraltar, New England, and Greenland; others have been taken in South African waters and off Japan. Observations on their diet show that they eat fishes.

This species is one of the few deep-sea anglers to be occasionally encountered by deep water trawlers on the Icelandic and Faeroes grounds. A number have been captured in depths of 100–300 m. (55–164 fathoms); the young live in greater depths, down to 3000 m. (1640 fathoms) although they may also be found near the surface.

HIND, ROCK see **Epinephelus adscensionis**

Hiodon   Hiodontidae
  alosoides GOLD-EYE 51 cm. (20 in.)
The gold-eye is widely distributed through N. America, in the Mississippi basin from Louisiana n., and in the rivers of the Great Plains, N. to the Mackenzie Great Slave Lake.

The colour is silvery with a bluish back, and a conspicuously golden coloured iris to the eyes. Its herring-like appearance, with a long anal fin and dorsal fin far back near the tail make it distinctive.

The gold-eye lives in turbid waters, in large lakes and muddy rivers, occasionally in swift current. It feeds on a wide variety of organisms, principally insects and their larvae, and small fishes. They are believed to be mainly nocturnal in habit. Their eyes are particularly well adapted structurally for the fish to see in the dark, and in the dim light of turbid waters.

Gold-eye spawn in late spring on gravelly shallows of tributary streams. Their eggs are about 4 mm. in diameter, and are semi-buoyant

even after hatching for the oil globule in the yolk buoys up the newly hatched 7 mm. larvae.

It is a good game fish but its chief value is as a local delicacy, oak smoked as Winnepeg gold-eye. This has been rated as the most flavoursome of all fish in Canada.

Their name derives from the golden colour of the retina, which also glows brightly at night under artificial light.

H. tergisus MOON-EYE 43 cm. (17 in.)
The moon-eye is characterized by its silvery herring-like appearance, its long anal fin, dorsal fin far back along the body, and above all by its large silvery eye.

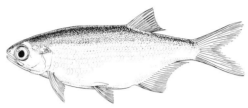

It is usually found in clear water of large lakes and streams. Its food is said to be mainly insects, their larvae and small fish. Occasionally they are caught by anglers and locally it is exploited for food.

This is the only representative of the family in the Great Lakes region of N. America, in which it is found only to the S. It occurs from the Hudson Bay tributaries to the St Lawrence, and s. to Alabama and Arkansas.

HIODONTIDAE

A small family of superficially herring-like fishes. The moon-eyes are confined to the freshwaters of e. N. America where there are 2 well-known species. They are silvery, deep-bodied fishes with blunt snouts, many teeth, a long anal fin, and a dorsal fin placed well back towards the tail.

Both species have a reputation as game fish, and one, the gold-eye is locally much valued as food. See **Hiodon.**

Hippocampus   Syngnathidae
  europaeus see under **H. hippocampus**
  hippocampus SHORT-SNOUTED SEAHORSE
16 cm. (6½ in.)
A European seahorse which is found widely in the Mediterranean Sea, and along the Portuguese and Spanish Atlantic coasts. It is found in shallow water, usually on muddy grounds amongst algae and underwater growths. It breeds during the summer months between April and October.

This seahorse is distinguished by its short snout and very high posterior region of the head. The Atlantic form has been recognized as a distinct species *H. europaeus* but there is no evidence that this separation is necessary. **234**
H. kuda SEAHORSE 30 cm. (12 in.)
This is one of the largest of the seahorses and is the species which is most widely kept in saltwater aquariums. It is widely distributed in the Indo-Pacific from the E. African coast to N. Queensland, and beyond Australia. It is probably the commonest of the Indo-Pacific seahorses.

In body form it is close to the European *H. ramulosus*, with rather inconspicuous body rings, moderately long snout, and a low crown to the head. It also has few (15–18) rays in the dorsal fin. **233**

H. ramulosus EUROPEAN SEAHORSE
16 cm. (6¼ in.)
This is the more common of the two European seahorses, and it is found as an occasional wanderer in British waters, chiefly the S. and SW. coasts, on the coast of Holland, and s. to the Mediterranean and N. African coasts. It is found throughout the Mediterranean and Black seas. In each of these major areas it has evolved distinctive populations, each of which has been named as a subspecies.

It lives in shallow inshore water amongst eel grass and *Posidonia* beds, fastening itself to the vegetation by curling its tail around the stems. It breeds in summer, usually May to August, when the male's brood pouch is very swollen and enlarged.

It is distinguished from the other species in the area by its relatively long snout, and by the rather narrow head. **235**
H. zosterae DWARF SEAHORSE 4 cm. (1½ in.)
This is the smallest species of seahorse, being fully grown when only 4 cm. in length. It is widely distributed from Bermuda, Florida, throughout the Gulf of Mexico to Campeche, and the Caribbean to Cuba. It is a shallow water fish, tolerant of wide changes in salinity and temperature and for these reasons popular as an aquarium fish.

This species breeds from mid-February to late-October. The observations of Dr Kirk Strawn in Florida show males have up to a maximum of 55 young in the brood pouch, although the female produces rather more eggs than this. At temperatures of about 29°C males probably average 2 broods per month, the young of which grow rapidly and are mature at 2–3 months. At least 3 generations are produced each year, but the life span rarely exceeds one year.

This seahorse is distinguished by its size and by the small dorsal fin which has only 11 to 13 rays.

Hippoglossoides   Pleuronectidae
  platessoides LONG ROUGH DAB,
AMERICAN PLAICE 61 cm. (24 in.)
A widely distributed N. Atlantic fish which is found in the e. Atlantic from n. Norway down to the Scottish coast and as far W. as Iceland, while in the w. basin it occurs from s. Labrador, W. Greenland and S. to off Rhode Island. It is a relatively deep-water species which lives at depths of between 37 and 183 m. (20–100 fathoms) although found on the shore line (in the far N.) down to 713 m. (390 fathoms). It lives on fine sand or muddy bottoms in cold water and is capable of tolerating low salinity in the N.

Adults feed on a wide range of the bottom-living fauna. They eat sea urchins, brittle stars, and crustaceans; occasionally they eat small fishes. The pelagic fry eat diatoms and small copepod crustaceans, but once living on the bottom they feed as do the adults if not on the same species then on smaller forms.

It is extremely abundant in suitable depths and is the subject of a profitable commercial fishery, especially along the American coast-line. They are mostly taken in otter trawls and Danish seines, although a few are taken by long-line. Their flesh is moderately successful as a food fish either frozen or fresh.

It is distinguished by having the eyes on the right side of the head. They are large and elongate, and the mouth is also large. The body scales are rather large and rough edged (hence its English name). Its colouring is a uniform russet-brown without any distinctive markings.

Hippoglossus   Pleuronectidae
   hippoglossus HALIBUT, ATLANTIC
HALIBUT 2·4 m. (8 ft)
The halibut is the largest Atlantic flatfish and is exceeded in size by only a few bony fishes (for example swordfish, tuna) or sharks. The maximum weight recorded is around 316 kg. (700 lb.) and a specimen of 266 kg. (588 lb.) was landed at a British fishing port only a few years ago. Such huge fish are, however, exceptional and must be very old (probably at least 40 years) for the average weight is closer to 45 kg. (100 lb.).

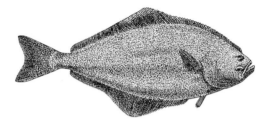

It is a valuable commercial fish throughout its range and it is captured by means of long-lines and otter trawls. It is marketed fresh or frozen and makes a consistently good price, although few are landed at a time. The flesh is of good quality and texture. Substantial numbers are captured by anglers but it is a specialized sport requiring heavy tackle and good seamanship.

The halibut is widely distributed in the N. Atlantic, being resident in the cold Arctic waters and penetrating in deep water far to the S. Its range extends from off SW. Ireland n. to the Barents Sea, around Iceland, w. Greenland, s. to Nova Scotia, Virginia and New Jersey. It is not, however, an inhabitant of the extremely cold, near-freezing Arctic water as is the Greenland halibut, *Reinhardtius hippoglossoides*. It lives on sand, gravel, and clay bottoms, and occasionally amongst rocks, although then it is usually found in the soft bottomed gulleys between rock faces. Its depth range is from 109–1460 m. (60–800 fathoms), but these deeper records are to the S. of its range where it overwinters in deep water.

The halibut is an active predator for a flatfish. Large specimens evidently make considerable forays into mid-water to feed. When young they feed on crustaceans and small fishes including sand-eels. At a length of about 70 cm. (27 in.) they feed almost entirely on fishes and there are few common fish species in the N. Atlantic which have not been found in halibuts' guts.

It spawns in late winter and early spring in depths of over 183 m. (100 fathoms), in European waters as deep as 1000 m. (547 fathoms). The eggs drift just below the surface to hatch in about 16 days at 6°C. Halibuts are enormously fecund, a 90 kg. (200 lb.) female will produce over 2 million eggs.

The halibut is distinguished by its large size, its concave edge to its tail, and its rather large mouth. The colour of its eyed (right) side is variable, often greenish-brown, sometimes

dark brown; the belly is always white. It can be distinguished from the Greenland halibut by the colour of its blind side, by the curve in the lateral line, and by the upper eye being sited well inboard of the head outline.

H. stenolepis PACIFIC HALIBUT
2·67 m. (8¾ ft)
The Pacific halibut is widely distributed in the N. Pacific. It is found from s. California n. along the American coast to Alaska, in the Bering Sea, and off the e. coast from Kamchatka, the Okhotsk Sea, and s. to n. Japan. It is found down to 1100 m. (600 fathoms), but is most common between 55 and 412 m. (30–225 fathoms).

It breeds in wintertime from November to January in 275-412 m. (150–225 fathoms), the eggs and larvae being pelagic although floating some way beneath the surface. At about 3–5 months of age the young fish rise towards the surface and float inshore on surface currents, becoming bottom-living at an age of about 6 months. Juveniles live inshore in relatively shallow water, gradually moving into deeper water as they grow. Females become mature at about 12 years of age, males considerably younger. The species has a high fecundity, females producing between 2 and 3 million eggs annually. Only females grow to the very large sizes recorded, the maximum length of males is around 140 cm. (55 in.).

The Pacific halibut is a voracious and active predator. Its food consists mainly of fishes, but squids, crabs, and clams are eaten.

It is an extremely valuable commercial fish which is captured by long-lines. Originally a staple fish of the aboriginals of the N. Pacific, once the area was developed the stocks quickly became overexploited and catches declined dramatically in inshore waters and later in the deep sea. In 1932 the fishery was regulated by the International Fisheries Commission and by imposing catch quotas in various areas, and with a vigorous programme of research and management, the stocks have been rebuilt. Recently Canadian and U.S. fishermen have been taking annual catches amounting to 50 million pounds, and similar catches are made by Russian, Japanese, and Korean vessels in the w. areas.

The Pacific halibut is very similar to its Atlantic counterpart. Its body is rather narrow but thickset, the head is large, as are the jaws which have conical teeth. The tail is slightly forked. Its colour is dark brown or grey on the eyed (right) side; white on the other side.

HIRAME see **Paralichthys olivaceus**

Hirundichthys   Exocoetidae
   rondeletii BLACKWING FLYINGFISH
25 cm. (10 in.)
A cosmopolitan flyingfish which is found in the warm temperate regions of all the oceans but is not found in the warmest tropical seas. In the Atlantic it occurs between the 30° and 42°N. latitudes and is very common in the Mediterranean where a somewhat dwarf race occurs.

In body form it is a typical flyingfish. In this genus both the pectoral and pelvic fins are enlarged, and the former when depressed reaches to the tail fin. The first 4 rays of the pectoral fin are stout and unbranched.

It is a surface living form found both on the high seas and close inshore; it feeds extensively

on animal plankton. In the Mediterranean its occurrence seems to be controlled by the 20°C. isotherm, within which it keeps.

Histiopterus   Pentacerotidae
   spinifer 36 cm. (14 in.)
Occurs on the Indian Ocean coast of Africa from Mossel Bay to the Red Sea in 45–450 m. (25–250 fathoms).

It is an extremely deep-bodied fish with a rather long, pointed snout. The dorsal fin spines are strong and high. Adults are dusky brown with narrow vertical bars across the body. The young are light brown with dark rounded blotches over the fins and body, and curved spines on the head.

Its biology is virtually unknown.

Histrio   Antennariidae
   histrio SARGASSOFISH 19·5 cm. (7¾ in.)
World-wide in its distribution, and recorded from the tropical regions of the Atlantic, Indian, and Pacific oceans. In the w. Atlantic it has been recorded from Bermuda, and New England to s. Brazil. It is a pelagic species found in the floating *Sargassum* weed of the ocean's surface. It crawls through the clumps of weed by means of its prehensile pectoral fins actually clasping the clumps of weed in the process.

Its coloration is impossible to describe so much does it vary. Inevitably it is a perfect match for the weed it inhabits. Its surface is well endowed with small lappets of loose skin. The snout has 2 long rays covered with small wisps of skin.

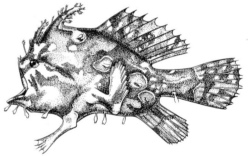

It feeds on a wide variety of planktonic creatures, particularly those that seek shelter in the *Sargassum* weed. Its eggs are shed as a floating egg raft amongst the weed or near by it, while the young fish are pelagic, floating at the surface until they make contact with suitable weed clumps. **184**

HOGCHOKER see **Trinectes maculatus**
HOGFISH see **Lachnolaimus maximus**
HOGFISH,
   SPANISH see **Bodianus rufus**
   SPOTFIN see **Bodianus pulchellus**
HOGSNAPPER see **Lachnolaimus maximus**

Holacanthus   Chaetodontidae
   africanus 25 cm. (10 in.)
This is the only species of angelfish to be found on the tropical W. African coast. It lives in relatively shallow water on rocky coasts but seems to be nowhere common.

It is immediately distinguished from other deep-bodied fishes in the tropical e. Atlantic by having a heavy spine on the lower edge of the preoperculum, as well as by the series of short spines in front of both dorsal and anal fins. It is also distinguished by the black mark

on the edge of the gill cover, by its light body with dusky head and tail, including the tail fin. **339**
H. ciliaris QUEEN ANGELFISH 46 cm. (18 in.)
A tropical w. Atlantic species restricted in its range from Florida and the Bahamas to Brazil, including the Gulf of Mexico, Dr James E. Bohlke and Mr Charles Chaplin, authorities on the fishes of the Bahamas, report that although the colouring of this fish may look startling it is not very conspicuous when drifting about among the corals and swaying sea growths and that it is a good colour match for the purple sea fans so common there.

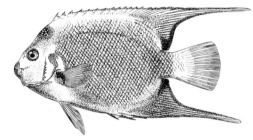

Young fish have 4 narrow, curved, light-blue stripes on a greenish background, except for a dusky bar through the eye. **340**
H. tricolor ROCK BEAUTY 30 cm. (12 in.)
Widely distributed in the w. Atlantic from Georgia and Bermuda, the Bahamas and Florida throughout the W. Indies, to se. Brazil. It is said to be the most common species of the genus of W. Indian reefs, but despite that it is not very abundant.

It is very distinctively coloured. Young fish are entirely orange-yellow with a blue edged black spot on the side beneath the second dorsal fin. This dark spot increases disproportionately in size as the fish grows, to eventually occupy the whole side. **341**

HOLOCENTRIDAE
Widely distributed in tropical and warm temperate seas, this family, the squirrelfishes or soldierfishes, are familiar especially on rocky or coral reef areas. Despite its wide distribution there are relatively few members of the family.

Most of them are brightly coloured, reds predominating but striped patterns are numerous. They all have heavy, rough-edged scales, large eyes, stout dorsal and anal spines, and spiny heads. One genus, *Holocentrus*, has a heavy spine at the corner of the gill cover.

Most of them are entirely nocturnal, lying up in rock crevices or caves during the day, and only venturing out at night to feed on the reef. They are also noisy fishes, apparently all having the ability to click, grunt, or creak loudly underwater. See **Adioryx, Flammeo, Holocentrus, Myripristis.**

Holocentrus   Holocentridae
ascensionis SQUIRRELFISH, LONGJAW
SQUIRRELFISH 61 cm. (2 ft)
Widely distributed in the tropical Atlantic, especially on the w. side. This squirrelfish is found from se. Brazil and Venezuela throughout the Caribbean and the Gulf of Mexico to Bermuda and exceptionally to New York. It is also found (as its scientific name suggests) around the S. Atlantic islands of Ascension and St Helena.

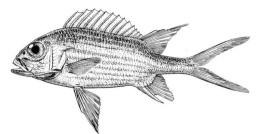

In the Bahamas it is found to be common on the offshore patch reefs, from the shoreline to 15 m. (8 fathoms) deep. Confined to rocky or coral areas, and mainly nocturnal in activity; like others of its family it feeds mainly on crustaceans.

It is distinguished by having the upper lobe of the tail fin usually longer than the lower. Its coloration is bright with red and white stripes running along the body, the front edges of the fins are white.

H. diadema CROWNED SOLDIERFISH
23 cm. (9 in.)
Widely distributed in the tropical Indo-Pacific from the Red Sea, and the African coast as far S. as Durban, and across to Hawaii. In Australian waters it has been found on the Queensland coast but is apparently rare. It is the commonest squirrelfish on the E. African coast. **219**
H. rubrum RED SOLDIERFISH 29 cm. (11½ in.)
Widely distributed in the tropical Indo-Pacific, it is found from the E. African coast to the Indo-Australian region where it is the most abundant of the family. In Australian waters it is found on the coasts of Queensland, N. Australia, and w. Australia. It lives in moderately deep water at depths of 27 m. (15 fathoms) and more. Like other members of the family it is mainly nocturnal. **221**
H. scythrops 25 cm. (10 in.)
Found around the Hawaiian islands where it is apparently restricted to rather deep water. Like others of the family it is mainly nocturnal in activity spending daylight periods under overhangs, in caves, or in crevices.

Its colouring, however, differs from the usual in the family; the sides are plain or only faintly striped and there is no prominent silvery bar on the cheek. It has 2 moderately large spines on the gill cover but they are less than half as long as the preopercular spine. It has large jaws, the upper jaw bone extending back to the middle of the eye, and the longest anal spine reaches back to the base of the tail fin. **220**

Holohalaelurus   Scyliorhinidae
regani SKAAMOOG 1·2 m. (4 ft)
The skaamoog, or skaamhaai as it is sometimes known, is found on the South African coast from Port Nolloth (SE. coast) to Natal. It has been recorded from depths of 110–457 m. (60–250 fathoms), and is relatively common in this area.

The spectacular markings, resembling some hieroglyphic code, are most pronounced in the larger fishes. The young are more soberly mottled with a warm brown on a reddish brown background. The body is very broad, with large rounded pectoral fins, the eyes are spaced far apart.

When captured and still living it has the habit of folding its tail round over its eyes as if hiding them; its name 'skaamoog' means 'shy eye'.

Homaloptera   Homalopteridae
orthogoniata 13 cm. (5 in.)
A homalopterid loach which is known only in a few rivers in S. and central Borneo; it has been reported in the Upper Kapuas, Makakam River, and the Baram River.

In body form it is typical of the family, the belly flattened, the head rounded, and pectoral and pelvic fins spread out laterally. The colouring of this species is very distinctive. **147**
H. smithi 7 cm. (2¾ in.)
This little fish is widespread in Thailand, where it was first found in 1928 in the Tadi River. It was named for its discoverer the late Hugh M. Smith. It is relatively common in waterfall streams in hilly country in Thailand.

It is distinguished from its local relatives, of which there are several, by the rearward position of the dorsal fin, behind the pelvics, and by the rather large scales, from 37 to 39 in the lateral line. The pectoral rays are long and overlap those of the pelvic fins. In colour it is a dull brown with about 6 black saddle-shaped bands, all the fins are flecked with dark brown.

HOMALOPTERIDAE
A small family of highly adapted freshwater fishes found in streams in se. Asia (India, s. China, the Malayan Peninsula, and the nw. Malayan Archipelago). All are small fishes with the front part of the body very flattened, and with the pectoral and pelvic fins expanded laterally so that the greater part of the underside forms a flat suctorial disc. The mouth is ventral but excluded from the disc and has several barbels.

These fishes mostly live in torrential hill streams, the disc-like body enabling them to stick to rocks in the rushing water. Some adaptation of the respiratory organs has taken place, for they inhale water through the side of the mouth, the gill openings are small and can be closed at will. These fish are noted for their habit of suspending normal respiratory movements for short periods, and it is evident that their oxygen requirements are low despite the fact that they live in highly oxygenated water. See **Crossostoma, Gastromyzon, Homaloptera.**

Homodiaetus   Trichomycteridae
maculatus CAMARÓN 6 cm. (2¼ in.)
Found widely in the rivers of Argentina especially the Rio de la Plata, the middle and lower reaches of the Rio Parana and River Uruguay. It is a slim-bodied fish, with a depressed head, short-based fins, 2 pairs of short rather stout barbels, and the gill covers with thorn-like spines. Yellowish-brown in colour, with a line of rounded darkish spots on the sides and other irregular rows above this. A dark bar across the base of the tail.

A catfish which requires well oxygenated water. It is found in well weeded parts of rivers, but is probably a parasite on the large pati catfish, *Luciopimelodus pati,* which occurs in the same habitats. It probably enters the gill chamber of the host to feed on blood from the gills.

HOOKNOSE see **Agonus cataphractus**

Hoplias Erythrinidae
malabaricus TIGERFISH, TARARIRA, HAIMARA 63 cm. (25 in.)
The tigerfish is widely distributed through n. and central S. America, from Venezuela, Colombia, and the Guianas, s. through Brazil, to Argentina, Peru and Bolivia. Through this range it is often very common and abundant. It is a predatory species which feeds on a wide variety of freshwater fishes and shrimps. Its typical habitat seems to be the shallow, often stagnant pools which remain after the rainy season, both in the plains and in drying out river-beds. It spawns in shallow, densely weeded pools in which it constructs a nest, and in which it is said to guard its young.

It is a very valuable, commercially exploited fish in many parts of S. America. It has also been kept in aquaria in Europe and elsewhere, but although colourful when young is not particularly popular. The young have reddish brown backs, fading to yellowish on the belly, red bands across the head, and a greenish band along the sides. Adults are dull green.

Like its relatives, this fish is able to utilize atmospheric oxygen – a useful attainment in view of the stagnant water in which it often lives.

Hoplerythrinus Erythrinidae
unitaeniatus JEJÚ, YARAU 30 cm. (12 in.)
A freshwater fish widely distributed in S. America from Venezuela and the Guianas, s. to Paraguay and n. Argentina. It is a round-bodied fish, moderately elongate, and with a heavy scaleless head. Its body is completely covered in large scales. The fins are rounded, most especially the tail, and dorsal fins. It is dull coloured on the back, being greyish brown with 3 dark lines from the eye across the gill cover, and a dark spot behind the gill cover.

This is one of the very abundant fishes found in pools in the savannas, which are isolated except during the floods of the rainy season. This species may be very common in pools which eventually dry out. No doubt its abundance in such habitats is due in part to its ability to utilize atmospheric oxygen; it comes to the surface every few minutes to gulp air. This fish spawns at the commencement of the rainy season when the pools in which it mainly lives are flooded.

HOPLICHTHYIDAE
A family of Pacific Ocean fishes found only in deep water, and as a consequence they are little known. In general build they are close to the flatheads (Platycephalidae) and like them have very flat expanded heads, a broad anterior body but a tapering tail. The body is scaleless, but the lateral line is armed with a row of heavy spines which anteriorly form a bony plate. See **Hoplichthys, Rhinhoplichthys.**

Hoplichthys Hoplichthyidae
acanthopleurus 18 cm. (7 in.)
Found only in the tropical w. Indian Ocean in

deep water. It has been taken off the coast of s. Africa (Natal and Zululand) in depths of 109–274 m. (60–150 fathoms).

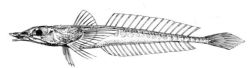

Its body form is typical of the flatheads. It is scaleless except for the line of 27 spiny scales on each side. In colour it is greenish above, pale pink on the sides; ventrally and on the second dorsal fin it is yellowish.

Hoplosternum Callichthyidae
littorale CASCADURA 20 cm. (8 in.)
Widely distributed in ne. S. America from Venezuela, the Guianas, and Trinidad, to the Peruvian Andes and Argentina. It is very common in the larger rivers, marshes, and swamps, even those in the coastal regions and is in places fished for commercially. Small specimens are exported for the aquarium trade in Europe and North America.

It is a very distinctive fish with a very heavy, thickset body, dark coloured, greeny-black above, the sides greyish, paler on the belly.

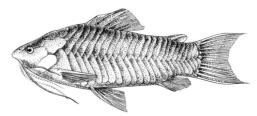

A most interesting fish which feeds on aquatic plants. In oxygen-poor surroundings it can absorb oxygen through the gut by gulping at the surface. The eggs are laid in a bubble nest formed by the parents amongst floating weed, and are guarded by the male both while unhatched and as young fish. The nest is a large structure, sometimes attaining a diameter of 36 cm. (14 in.).

Hoplostethus Trachichthyidae
mediterraneus SLIME HEAD 30 cm. (12 in.)
Widely distributed in the Atlantic Ocean, and it has been suggested cosmopolitan, in deep water. It is found mainly in 366–914 m. (200–500 fathoms) and in places is extremely abundant. From the frequency with which it is caught in bottom trawls it evidently lives close to the sea bed, at least in daytime.

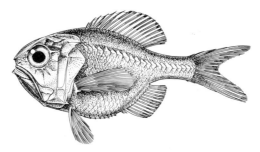

Its colouring is essentially silvery with a rose pink tinge.

HOPPER see **Alticops periophthalmus**
HORA'S CLOWN LOACH see **Botia horae**

HORAICHTHYIDAE
A family which contains a single genus and species found in brackish and freshwaters in sw. India. It is a slender fish, compressed laterally, but with a flattened head. Its body is covered with thin, cycloid scales, which extend on to the head. The mouth is moderately large, with sharp teeth in a single row. The dorsal fin is placed far along the body near the tail, it is short and with few rays; the anal is long and many-rayed. Males have a intromittent organ formed from the first rays of the anal fin.

This fish has many superficial resemblances to the S. American toothcarp *Tomeurus*. See **Horaichthys.**

Horaichthys Horaichthyidae
setnai 2·4 cm. (1 in.)
This fascinating little fish is found in the backwaters and tanks of the w. coast of India in the vicinity of Bombay. It is found within tidal areas but has not been found in the sea or flowing water, although it tolerates saline conditions and may be caught in small puddles of evaporating flood water after the monsoon season is over. It is a surface-living fish, found in vast numbers amongst floating vegetation. It feeds on copepod crustaceans, diatoms, and larvae at the surface, as well as small wind-drifted insects which fall onto the pools. It is transparent in life.

It spawns the whole year round, although the peak of the breeding season is July and August. The eggs are laid on the marginal weeds in clumps, they are covered with short filaments, and hatch in 8–10 days.

The first rays of the anal fin in the male are separated from the remainder of the fin, being elongate and greatly modified. These rays form a gonopodium by means of which the spermatophore is transferred to the genital pore of the female. Females have several modifications associated with the genital opening. In most females the opening is on the left side, sometimes it lies on the right or on the midline, most females have a moderate sized left

pelvic fin and no, or a greatly reduced, right pelvic fin; females also have large glandular pads round the genital opening. These highly modified organs are unusual in fishes, but similar specializations are found in some South American cyprinodonts, for example *Tomeurus,* and *Anableps.*

HOUTING see **Coregonus lavaretus**
HOVERING GOBY see **Ioglossus helenae**
HUCHEN see **Hucho hucho**

Hucho
Salmonidae
hucho HUCHEN 1·5 m. (5 ft)

The huchen is an elongate silver-bodied sal-monid, with a greenish back and coppery sheen on the sides. It is found only in the basin of the River Danube, and occasionally in lakes within that system, although various mis-guided attempts to introduce it elsewhere have been made in the past, and it is estab-lished in some French rivers.

It is not migratory, and only makes a short spawning migration (often downstream) to deeper water over a stony bed. Here the female digs a spawning redd and the eggs are covered with gravel. Spawning usually takes place in March or April.

The huchen is entirely predatory. Its young feed on the fry of other fish, and as an adult there are few fish species which do not appear in its diet. It is highly regarded as a game fish, and as specimens of 52 kg. (114 lb.) have been recorded it is a large and powerful fish.

It is, however, susceptible to pollution, and the lower Danube and its tributaries have been developed for various industrial uses, as well as receiving inadequately treated sewage dis-charges from many cities and towns. The stocks of the huchen's food fishes have also been depleted. The huchen is now a relatively rare fish, and its future survival is doubtful.

H. taimen TAIMEN 2 m. (6½ ft)

The taimen is the Siberian and e. form of the European huchen. It is widely distributed in e. Asia where it is fished for extensively with lines and nets and forms a locally important food fish. Its chief impact on the fisheries of the region, however, is as a predator on white-fishes which are themselves more valuable to fisheries.

It is a large species, attaining a weight of 70 kg. (154 lb.), living in large rivers with mod-erate to fast current. It spawns in small streams, on gravel beds in spring. Even when young it feeds on fishes, and when full grown there are few species which it does not eat. Growth is rapid in most rivers in which it lives.

It is a long slender fish, with large jaws and many teeth. At the spawning season its usual greeny-silver colour is modified by reddish tail and anal fins. It is distinguished from the huchen by its fewer (11–12) gill rakers.

HUMANTIN see under **Oxynotus paradoxus**
HUMBUG, BANDED see **Dascyllus aruanus**
HUMP-BACK SALMON see **Oncorhynchus gorbuscha**
HUMP-BACKED HEAD-STANDER see **Charax gibbosus**
HUMP-HEAD, INDIAN see **Kurtus indicus**
HUMP-HEADED MAORI WRASSE see **Cheilinus undulatus**
HUMPBACK
SUCKER see **Xyrauchen texanus**
WHITEFISH see **Coregonus clupeaformis**

HUJETA see **Ctenolucius hujeta**
HUMUHUM see **Rhinecanthus aculeatus**

Huso
Acipenseridae
dauricus KALUGA 5·5 m. (18 ft)

The kaluga is one of the largest freshwater fishes known, large specimens weighing at least one ton (1020 kg.) having been recorded. It is confined to the Amur River basin in Siberia (the Amur forms the e. border between China and the U.S.S.R.), and it does not migrate out to sea in the manner of the European beluga *(Huso huso)*. With that species it is distin-guished from the other sturgeons by the way the branchiostegal membranes are free from the throat, and particularly by the wide mouth which occupies the whole of the width of the underside of the head. A wide mouth like this suggests a more active mode of feeding than that used by the other sturgeons with their small extensible mouths, and the *Huso* stur-geons are predators of fishes from early in life. The kaluga feeds almost entirely on fishes, Pacific salmon when they are migrating, and carp-like and other fishes at all times of the year.

Although the kaluga is not migratory to the sea it moves downstream into the main channel of the Amur to overwinter in deep water. Many move as far as the estuary where they con-gregate in hollows. They return to the higher reaches to spawn in May and June on sandy and gravel bottoms, but individual fish spawn only every other year. Large females may con-tain up to 4 million eggs, which when shed are 3·2–4 mm. in diameter.

In common with other sturgeons the history of the exploitation of kaluga by man is one of reckless overfishing. Small, immature fish were caught indiscriminately, and large gravid females were captured simply for the eggs they contained. Regulation of the fishery has to some extent remedied the decline in numbers, and the kaluga is no longer threatened with extinction, but large specimens are fewer now and the species is less abundant than it was formerly.

H. huso BELUGA, HAUSEN 5 m. (16 ft)

The huge size of the beluga places it almost in the class of legendary fish. Indeed the maxi-mum weight of 1½ tons (1524 kg.) recorded dates from 1827 and the Volga-Caspian region, and has a suspicious roundness about it, but as specimens of up to 1200 kg. have been weighed and documented, it seems that the former may well be within the weight attained by the species. In 1922 a female beluga of 1220 kg. (2690 lb.) was caught in the mouth of the Volga, its head alone weighed 288 kg. (635 lb.), and its eggs 146 kg. (322 lb.); another in 1924 weighed 1228 kg. (2707 lb.), contained 246 kg. (542 lb.) of eggs, estimated to number 7¾ millions.

The beluga is a migratory sturgeon found in the basins of the Caspian and Black seas, the Sea of Azov, and the Adriatic. It travels up the larger rivers and some spawn far upstream, while others spawn downstream, depending whether they entered the river in winter or spring. They spawn on rocky bottoms in late

spring, the young hatching in about 8 days at 13°C. After hatching, the fry immediately start moving downstream to the sea. In the lower river its food consists mainly of inverte-brates, but once the fish begins to grow, it increasingly eats fishes. The adults eat fishes to the exclusion of other foods, mainly clupeid and cyprinid fishes; large specimens have been found to have eaten young Caspian seals on occasions.

The beluga is not of great importance to commercial fisheries, but considerable num-bers are taken in the Caspian Sea. Like other sturgeons it has suffered from pollution of the lower courses of rivers, from hydroelectric schemes, and to some extent over-fishing. A species which takes from 14 years (males) to 18 years (females) to become sexually mature can sustain much less fishing pressure than one which breeds in its second or third year. Added to which the fishery for sturgeon was concentrated on the mature, migrating fe-males for the sake of their ripening eggs for use as caviar. The stock was thus not replenished sufficiently. Not surprisingly beluga are now relatively uncommon where once they were abundant.

HUSS, BULL see **Scyliorhinus stellaris**
HUSSAR, BLUE-BANDED see **Lutjanus kasmira**

Hydrocynus
Characidae
goliath GIANT TIGERFISH 1·8 m. (6 ft)

This is the largest species of tigerfish found in African freshwaters. It is relatively restricted in its distribution being known only from the Congo basin and Lake Tanganyika, although reports of huge tigerfish in Lake Albert may refer to this species. It shares the body shape of other tigerfishes, being elongate, and heavily scaled. Its fins are all rather long and pointed, and the tail fin is especially well developed. Its teeth are long and fang-like, although rela-tively few in number and arranged in a single row in each jaw (although smaller, partly grown replacement teeth lie behind the main row). They interlock closely when the mouth is closed, but are clearly visible even in the closed jaws.

It is an avid predator on smaller fishes, and in view of its size most other fishes are smaller. Specimens have been reported weighing 57 kg. (125 lb.), and such huge fish are dangerous to handle when alive. Few specimens of this species have been caught by angling but with the other members of the genus they add weight to the tigerfish legend; exact measure-ments are rarely available for lengths and weights, but it may attain as much as 69 kg. (150 lb.).

H. vittatus TIGERFISH 1 m. (39 in.) and more

This is the celebrated tigerfish of African freshwaters, of which many anglers have written and which has been claimed to be one of the greatest sporting fishes of the world. It is a predator and will take a live bait or an arti-ficial lure, both on a wire trace, for it has sharp interlocking teeth. Specimens of 2·3–4·5 kg. (5–10 lb.) are said to be the strongest fighters, but the fish grows to around 18 kg. (40 lb.) at a maximum. The building of the Kariba dam on the Zambezi had a considerable effect on this species for instead of specimens up to 9 kg. (20 lb.) being exceptional in the lake they are now taken to 17·7 kg. (39 lb.). The change is undoubtedly due to the (possibly temporary) increases in numbers of prey fish. Its food consists entirely of fishes.

The tigerfish is widespread in Africa, for it is found from the Nile, Niger, Volta, and Congo basins to the Zambezi and Limpopo Rivers, also in lakes Albert and Tanganyika.

The fish is basically silvery with a bluish back, the dorsal and adipose fins are greyish but the other fins, most notably the lower lobe of the tail are flushed with pink. It has a rather distinct longitudinal dark line along each row of scales. The teeth in this fish are large and fang-like, in a single row except that a row of replacement teeth lies behind them; the outer teeth are so large as to be visible when the mouth is shut.

Hydrolagus Chimaeridae
 colliei RATFISH, 91 cm. (3 ft)
The ratfish is found in the e. N. Pacific, from Lower California to w. Alaska. It occurs offshore, and in places is so abundant that many hundreds may be taken in a trawl haul. It is found in depths of 92–913 m. (50–499 fathoms). It is a rather elongate species, dark brown on the back with lighter spots, and silvertinted sides, nearly white ventrally and on the fins, which are, however, dusky at their edges. Males have prominent claspers at the pelvic fins, with a divided tip; also a club-like organ on the forehead with a finely spiny tip.

The ratfish, like all the chimaeroids, has a long dorsal spine. It is saw-toothed along its rear edge, and grooved, the groove connecting with a venom gland at the base of the spine. Wounds from it are excruciatingly painful.

The vernacular name ratfish refers to its long tail, but the incisor teeth could be described as rat-like as well, only much broader. The first specimen of this fish to be examined was caught off Monterey, California during Captain Beechey's voyage on H.M.S. *Blossom* of 1825–28 in the Pacific. It was described and dissected by Mr Collie, a naturalist on board, for whom it was later named.

Hyperoglyphe Centrolophidae
 antarctica DEEP-SEA TREVALLE
1·36 m. (4½ ft)
A species which is found in temperate and cool temperate seas in the S. Hemisphere. It has been recorded (under different scientific names) from the S. Atlantic (Tristan da Cunha), off South Africa, off s. Australia, and New Zealand.

In contrast to the N. Atlantic species *(H. perciforma)* its young stages are little known, but adults are more frequently captured. It lives in schools at depths of up to 824 m. (450 fathoms) and is occasionally taken in deep water trawling or on long lines. Its flesh is considered to be delicious, and this species may well represent an untapped food resource in s. waters, as a relative *(H. japonica)* is already used in the N. Pacific.

It is distinguished by its large mouth and patch of scales on the top of the head. Its colouring is said to be steel-blue above, lighter below.

H. japonica see under **H. antarctica**
H. perciforma BARRELFISH, LOGFISH
91 cm. (3 ft)
The barrelfish owes its common names to its habit of congregating around floating wood, planks, or wreckage, and on occasions drifting inside boxes in flotsam. This is essentially a habit of the young fish 5–10 cm. (2–4 in.) in length, which are also found under gulf weed *(Sargassum)*. The young feed on hydroids, tunicates, salps, ctenophores, and barnacles as well as young fishes of various kinds. Adults are deep-water bathypelagic fishes, found in schools often close to the seabed but not often captured.

It is widely distributed along the e. coast of N. America from Florida to Nova Scotia. Young fish drift widely with ocean currents and this no doubt is the cause of their summer time abundance off the coast of New England. Occasional specimens have even drifted across the Atlantic to be captured on the British coast.

It is distinguished by its rather deep body with a blunt head and rounded snout. The first dorsal fin is composed of 6–8 short stout spines. Pelagic specimens are dark green above fading laterally to white. The adults are dark brown or nearly black with only a slightly lighter belly.

Hyperoplus Ammodytidae
 lanceolatus GREATER SAND-EEL
32 cm. (12½ in.)
A European species which is confined to the Atlantic coastline, from n. Spain to Norway and Iceland, and in the adjacent seas such as the s. Baltic and N. Seas.

It shares the habit of its relatives of swimming in large shoals, often at an oblique angle to the bottom, and if threatened, darting into the sandy sea bed. Young specimens are occasionally found on sandy shores between tide marks, but mostly this species is found from low tide mark to 150 m. (82 fathoms).

It feeds on animal plankton, including small fishes, and is itself eaten in quantities by sea birds, fishes, and even cetaceans.

Its body form is that of other members of the family, and its coloration, bluish green on back and sides, silvery on the belly, is likewise common to all species. It can be distinguished by the dusky smudge on the snout, and by its size, for it is one of the largest sand-eel species.

Hyphessobrycon Characidae
 bellottii 3·4 cm. (1½ in.)
A small characin from the Amazon region

which is occasionally imported as a pet-fish. It appears to be rather rare.

This is a slender silvery fish with in some cases an intense dark spot in a lighter circle or oval just above the lateral line. The tips of the dorsal, anal, and tail fins are conspicuously light. **60**
H. bifasciatus YELLOW TETRA 5 cm. (2 in.)
Found in the coastal regions of se. Brazil, the yellow tetra is a good aquarium fish, easy to breed and peaceable although rather outshone by some of its more colourful relatives. In coloration it is yellowish but translucent, two dark bars behind the head of which the first is shorter and more pronounced, a line of chevron marks along the sides. The fins are clear and uncoloured, but in young fish (half-grown) the bases of the fins are distinctly reddish and far more colourful than the adults.

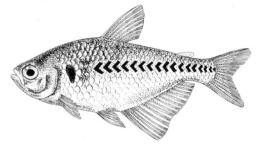

Males have a slightly reddish anal fin with a rounded free edge, they are also slimmer than the female.

It is a relatively easy tetra to breed provided it has a well-planted aquarium with slightly acid water.

H. callistus JEWEL TETRA 4·5 cm. (1¾ in.)
The jewel tetra is one of a group of species of mainly red coloured characins, hence known as blood characins, found in the waters of the middle Amazon and n. Paraguay. By some ichthyologists these species, which include the rosy tetra *(H. rosaceus)*, the Serpa tetra *(H. serpae)*, and the present species, are thought to be at most subspecies of one widely distributed form.

The jewel tetra is distinguished from its relatives by a very distinct and elongate black shoulder spot, immediately above the pectoral fin, by having the black blotch on the dorsal fin extending to the tip of the fin, and by having a broad black edge along the rear part of the anal fin.

It makes a very pleasant aquarium fish when small, although large specimens tend to attack other fish. **61**
H. eos DAWN TETRA 4·5 cm. (1¾ in.)
A tetra found in w. Guyana, which has been kept in aquaria for some years, although it is not yet known to have been bred in captivity. It is a rather slender species with the typical adipose fin, high dorsal fin and a moderately long anal fin. The lateral line is short and is composed of only 7–10 tubed scales. **62**
H. flammeus RED TETRA, FLAME TETRA
4·5 cm. (1¾ in.)
The red tetra (or red tetra from Rio, as it has been named) is found in the area around Rio de Janeiro, in brown swampy waters at temperatures of around 22°C.

It is a strikingly beautiful fish. Males have a very much deeper red colour on the anal fin with a wide black edge, while in females the dark edge is reduced or absent.

It breeds readily in captivity in well planted

peaty water. After much driving by the male, the pair take up a side by side position and up to ten eggs are deposited on plant leaves or gravel. This is repeated until 100 or more eggs are laid. The eggs are attached to plants and hatch in 36 hours. The adults must be removed from the spawning tank for, like most characins they will eat their eggs and young. **63**

H. herbertaxelrodi BLACK NEON TETRA 3·5 cm. (1½ in.)
A relatively newly discovered aquarium fish found first at Coxin on the River Taquary in sw. Brazil. It is slender-bodied with the rather high dorsal and anal fins common to the tetras. Its colouring is singularly beautiful. It has been bred in captivity and is popular with aquarists.

This species has been named for Dr Herbert Axelrod, to commemorate his distinguished services to aquarium science and ichthyology. **64**

H. heterorhabdus FLAG TETRA 5 cm. (2 in.)
The flag tetra is found in the Amazon basin in the Rio Tocantins. It is a popular and commonly kept aquarium fish, although it is not easy to maintain. Its colouring is very attractive, but the fish has to be in good condition for its full colouring to be seen.

Males are slimmer than the females, and the silvery coloured body-cavity is rather pointed. Males have fine hooks on the anal fin but they are too small to be seen with the naked eye. **65**

H. innesi see **Paracheirodon innesi**

H. ornatus 4 cm. (1½ in.)
A beautiful aquarium fish which is found in the lower Amazon and Guiana. It has for a long time been kept as an aquarium fish in Europe.

Its body form is typical of the tetras, rather compressed and deepest at the base of the dorsal fin. The anal fin is very long based, the dorsal short. Males have very long dorsal rays, making the fin high and sickle shaped, with the end dusky but the tip and front edge white. The female's dorsal fin has a black blotch but is relatively low; her body is more robust. **66**

H. pulchripinnis LEMON TETRA 5 cm. (2 in.)
A common and popular aquarium fish which comes from ne. S. America, although the exact river-system in which it was taken is not known. It is a striking fish, almost transparent so that the backbone can be clearly seen, but with a yellowish tinge. The upper half of the eye is conspicuously red; and the anal and dorsal fins are dark edged. The high dorsal fin is characteristic of this group of square-finned characins.

Males have a more intense and broader black stripe to the anal fin than have females. **67**

H. rosaceus ROSY TETRA, BLACK-FLAG TETRA 4 cm. (1½ in.)
This tetra was found originally on Gluck Island in the River Essequibo in W. Guiana. It is a fish which has suffered a long history of misidentification and taxonomic confusion. According to some students it is a subspecies of *H. callistus*; others have suggested that the relationships of these very similar species have been confused by hybridization. It is also variable in coloration.

The back is a reddish brown, the sides pale yellow to silvery, but the body is translucent and thus the colour changes with the lighting. There is a red stripe along the spinal column, and the pelvics, anal, and tail fin lobes are red-

dish. The dorsal fin has a very distinct black blotch high up on the fin, which is white edged. Males are notably more boldly coloured and have very high dorsal and anal fins. **68**

H. rubrostigma 9 cm. (3½ in.)
A very beautiful characin described originally from Colombia. Its body is rather deep and compressed with a high dorsal fin, and a long, many-rayed anal fin. Like most characins it has a small adipose fin and a forked tail. Males have the greater height and crescent shape of the dorsal fin. Its colour is striking.

This fish is regarded as being closely related to the group of blood characins which includes the jewel tetra *(H. callistus)* and the Serpa tetra *(H. serpae)*. **69**

H. serpae SERPA TETRA 4·5 cm. (1¾ in.)
The Serpa tetra was originally discovered in the Middle Amazon region, and southwards to Paraguay; it is named for the town of Serpa on the Amazon. Males are distinctly brighter in colour than females.

Although the Serpa tetra has been bred in captivity, it tends to be a difficult fish to keep and is subject to many diseases.

It is sometimes referred to as a subspecies of *H. callistius* along with a number of other red coloured tetras. **70**

Hypnos Torpedinidae
monopterygium NUMBFISH 61 cm. (2 ft)
Found in Australian seas from S. Queensland, along the New South Wales coast to S. Australia and W. Australia, the numbfish is one of the oddest looking electric rays. Its body is thick and fleshy, with rounded disc and pelvic fins, and a disproportionately short tail with small dorsal and tail fins. In colour it is dark brown to reddish brown, and it has been described as looking 'like a shapeless mass of raw beef in life', while after death the body becomes bloated and swells to thrice its normal thickness thus defying the earlier attempts of naturalists to describe it accurately. It was first described in 1795 as an anglerfish.

It is common on sandflats, even in estuaries, and its depth range extends down to about 219 m. (120 fathoms). It normally lies partly buried in sand or mud, and is said to eat a wide range of small crustaceans and fishes which are stunned by its electrical discharge. It produces severe electrical shocks, being well-named as the numbfish, or occasionally cramp-fish – both names used for other large electric rays.

Hypomesus Osmeridae
olidus POND SMELT 20 cm. (8 in.)
The pond smelt is widely distributed in Asia, from n. Japan to Siberia, and on the Arctic Ocean coastline. It is also found in Arctic Canada and Alaska. In the n. parts of its range it lives mainly in freshwater, but to the S. it is migratory, spawning in the lower reaches of rivers in April and in May. Landlocked populations of the pond smelt breed in streams tributary to the lake in which they live, and in common with similar populations of other smelts are smaller at sexual maturity, shorter lived and less fecund.

The pond smelt is a fragile little fish with a small mouth, large teeth, and large scales. It is a light olive-green on the back, silvery white on the belly, with a pronounced silvery stripe along its sides. Like the European smelt, its

flesh has a strong odour of cucumbers. It is a delicious food fish and locally exploited as food.

Hypophthalmichthys Cyprinidae
molitrix SILVER CARP, TOLSTOL 1 m. (39 in.)
The silver carp is a large cyprinid of distinctive body form. It is rather deep-bodied with a heavy head, and eyes set low on the side (below the level of the mouth). The gill rakers are attached to one another and thus form a unique sieve. In addition, the intestine is very long, in adults it is 15 times as long as the fish's body. It feeds entirely on the minute plant plankton, so rich in eutrophic waters.

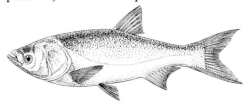

It is a native to China and the Amur basin in the E. of the U.S.S.R., but has been introduced into many parts of S.E. Asia and also, more recently, the U.S.S.R. It is a valuable commercial fish throughout its native range, and its ability to live on plant plankton which is often an embarrassment in enclosed waters such as reservoirs is welcomed. In China it is reared on special farms, the larvae being trapped and transferred when partly grown to waters enriched with organic matter to encourage the plant plankton to grow. Its flesh is said to be very tasty, but spoils quickly after death unless the fish is gutted.

In its native rivers it lives in the lowland reaches, migrating upstream to spawn behind sand bars and islands in swift water. Fecundity is very high and the eggs are pelagic. The young after hatching drop downstream to the floodplain and feed on zooplankton, changing to plant matter later as they grow.

The silver carp has the curious and exhilarating habit of leaping clear of the water when disturbed. Not infrequently they land on the deck of the intruding boat, occasionally (it is said) sinking it in the process.

HYPOPHTHALMIDAE
A family of South American catfishes found between the Guianas and Argentina. They are scaleless, lacking scutes or body armour, with a rather depressed head and compressed body. The anal fin is very long commencing on the belly immediately behind the pelvic fins; both the adipose fin and the dorsal fin are small. The gills have numerous long rakers forming a close sieve and these fishes are clearly plankton feeders. The eyes are small and laterally placed. See **Hypophthalmus**.

Hypophthalmus Hypophthalmidae
edentatus BAGRE ROSADO, MANDUVÉ 46 cm. (18 in.)
Well distributed in s. America from the Gui-

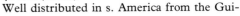

anas, through the Amazons to Argentina. It is a silvery fish, slate grey on the back with darker spots, silvery on the sides and belly; the fins have a dark margin. The jaws are toothless.

Hypoplectrus Serranidae
puella BUTTER or BARRED HAMLET
15 cm. (6 in.)
Widely distributed in the Caribbean and on the American coast of Florida, and as far N. as Bermuda. It is the most abundant hamlet in shallow water in the W. Indies, frequently seen, although not often closely approached, on shallow reefs. It ranges down to depths of 23 m. (12½ fathoms).
Several members of this genus occur in the Caribbean, all superficially very similar. This species can be distinguished by the broken bars on the body (the central one largest) and by the delicate blue lines running over the head.

Hypopomus Rhamphichthyidae
artedi MOTTLED KNIFEFISH 18 cm. (7 in.)
A very slender knifefish, with an eel-like, strongly compressed body. As in other species of the genus it has no dorsal, tail, or pelvic fins, and the anal fin is long, extending from just behind the head to within a head's length of the tail tip. In this species the posterior nostril is close to the eye which is very small and covered by skin; the jaws are toothless.
In coloration it is mainly light brown, the back with several short bars of rather bright brown fading out on the sides. The sides of the body and head have numerous dark brown mottlings, but the anal fin is clear.
It is found in the ne. region of S. America, from the Guianas, the Amazon, and Parana. Its food is composed entirely of bottom-living invertebrates, when young, insect larvae and worms, and when it is larger both these with the addition of small crustaceans. It has been kept as an aquarium fish.

HYPOPTYCHIDAE
A family which contains a single species, found in the e. N. Pacific, in the Sea of Japan and elsewhere.
Superficially it resembles a sand-eel (family Ammodytidae) being long and rather thin, and it was for years grouped with these fishes. They are probably its closest relatives. See **Hypoptychus.**

Hypoptychus Hypoptychidae
dybowskii 9 cm. (3½ in.)
Locally distributed in the e. N. Pacific and recorded at a number of places in the Sea of Japan and the Sea of Okhotsk. It is essentially an inshore and seasonally even an intertidal species, which is found at depths of 5–20 m. (3–11 fathoms). It breeds in June and July in the tidal region, the eggs being deposited on algae.

Its long slender body form is reminiscent of the related sand-eels, but it differs notably in having a dorsal fin only about as long as the anal. The eye is also larger, and although the

mouth is moderately large, the lower jaw does not protrude as in the sand-eels.

Hypostomus Loricariidae
watwata 30 cm. (12 in.)
A loricariid catfish of restricted distribution in the lowland reaches of rivers on the coast of Surinam and w. to the Demerara region of Guyana. It is confined to the coastal plain being found in the lower reaches of rivers and even semi-salt conditions on muddy or sandy bottoms.

Like other members of this genus the body armour is not continuous on the underside of the belly. The large bony scales on the back are, however, well developed. The dorsal fin is high and rather large, the first ray (and that of the pectoral fin) being massive. The body is dull brown or grey with distinct dark spots all over including the belly.

Hystricinella see under Luvaridae.

I

ICEFISH see Channichthyidae
ICEFISH see **Chaenocephalus aceratus**

ICELIDAE
A small family of sculpins or marine bullheads found only in the Arctic region and best represented in the N. Pacific. They are mostly small fishes inhabiting both shallow and deep seas. Superficially they resemble the bullheads (Cottidae) but are distinguished by their rather slender, elongate bodies, and by having the gill cover membrane united under the throat.
They also have a series of small bony plates running along the sides. See **Icelinus.**

Icelinus Icelidae
borealis NORTHERN or COMB SCULPIN
10 cm. (4 in.)
The northern sculpin is a shallow water inhabitant of the American coast of the N.

Pacific. It ranges from Washington to the Bering Sea, and is found in depths of 18–110 m. (10–60 fathoms).
It is a small fish distinguished by the numerous spiny branches on the upper preopercular spine, just behind the eye.
Its colouring is dark olive-brown above, creamy below, with darker saddles of brown

across the back. Males have black blotches on the spiny dorsal fin.

ICHTHYOBORIDAE
A small family of characin-like fishes found in w. tropical Africa in rivers and lakes. They are long-bodied fishes, with long jaws; some of them having large teeth. Most are predatory on fishes, although the smaller species moderate this diet with insect larvae and crustaceans.
Their bodies are fully covered with scales, and the lateral line is straight and usually complete. An adipose fin is usually present. The members of the family are distinguished from the Citharinidae and Distichodontidae, their nearest relatives, by the long body, and by the large teeth, in 1–2 rows in the jaws. In some species the upper jaw can swing open upwards. See **Phago, Phagoborus.**

Ichthyomyzon Petromyzonidae
fossor NORTHERN BROOK LAMPREY
15 cm. (6 in.)
This lamprey is restricted to the Mississippi River drainage in Wisconsin and n. Indiana, and the Great Lakes basins of Michigan and s. Ontario. It lives in creeks and small rivers, buried in sandy-muddy patches on the bottom, where it feeds on fine organic matter. It passes several years in the ammocete stage, transforming into an adult in late summer and autumn, and passing the winter without feeding before it spawns the next spring on stony riffles in the river.
This species thus differs from many lampreys as it neither migrates to the sea after metamorphosis nor is parasitic. Other species are known both in N. America and Europe (the American brook lamprey, *Lampetra lamottenii*, and the European brook lamprey, *Lampetra planeri*, are examples) which have similar life histories.

Ichthyscopus Uranoscopidae
lebeck STARGAZER 64 cm. (25 in.)
A stargazer found in both Indian and Pacific oceans, in the latter best known from the coasts of Queensland and New South Wales.

It is not uncommon in muddy estuarine areas, but has also been taken in trawls down to 137 m. (75 fathoms). Its habit of burrowing in sand or sandy mud makes it difficult to catch.
Its colouring is in harmony with its habitat, the back usually being brownish, although some specimens have rounded or oval light blotches well developed on the head and sides. The fins are yellowish; the belly is creamy yellow in colour.

Icichthys Centrolophidae
lockingtoni MEDUSAFISH 46 cm. (18 in.)
The medusafish is widely distributed in the cool temperate waters of the N. Pacific, occurring from off the coast of California to Alaska and s. to Japanese waters. Young specimens up

to 10 cm. (4 in.) are commonly found swimming close to or beneath jelly fishes. The young are widely known and appear to be common. They are thought to feed on the trailing tentacles of their host as well as deriving protection from their association. The juveniles are rather deep-bodied, have a rounded snout, and are a pinkish colour.

Adults, however, are dusky and relatively slim. They are characterized by having small scales over the body and cheeks, a long low dorsal fin, and characteristically soft flabby bodies; their skeletons are barely calcified. Adults live in the middle and near-surface waters of the open sea, but relatively few specimens have been caught so that the life-style of the adult is still almost unknown.

ICOSTEIDAE
The family contains a single species, the N. Pacific ragfish, *Icosteus aenigmaticus*. It is distinguished most particularly by the lack of calcification in the bones which are mostly cartilaginous; this gives the ragfish its peculiarly floppy appearance.

The young are deep-bodied, compressed fishes with rather high dorsal and anal fins. The pelvic fins are moderate in size, the pectorals large. Adults, which grow to a large size (up to 2·1 m. or about 7 ft) are slender-bodied, and lack pelvic fins completely. So great are the superficial differences that adult and young were regarded until quite recently as 2 species. See **Icosteus.**

Icosteus   Icosteidae
   aenigmaticus RAGFISH 2·1 m. (7 ft)
A North Pacific species found in both deep water and inshore from California n. to Alaska, and on the Asian coast S. to Japan. Young fish have been found in inshore waters near the surface, but the larger specimens seem to be pelagic or bathypelagic in habit and probably range across the whole N. Pacific. Large specimens have been taken from the stomachs of sperm whales on several occasions. In turn they are reputed to eat small fishes, squids, and octopuses.

The young fish is brown and yellow in colour with numerous rounded purplish spots; the fins are dusky. Adults are an overall chocolate

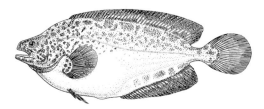

late brown colour. The extreme limpness of the body is as good a distinguishing character as any.

ICTALURIDAE
The family of the N. American catfishes, freshwater fishes found from Canada to Guate-

mala, but only by later introduction elsewhere in the world. In most respects they are 'typical' catfishes, with long whisker-like barbels round the mouth, large adipose fin on the back, and a sprong spine in the front of the dorsal and pectoral fins. Their bodies are smooth and scaleless.

They fall into 2 main groups, the catfishes and bullheads, some of which are large (up to 45 kg. (100 lb.) in weight), and the mostly small madtoms, all of which have venom glands at the base of the pectoral fin spines. Wounds from these can be very painful. They are mostly bottom-living, omnivorous fishes which have successfully colonized many habitats. Some have even taken to life in caves and have become blind and unpigmented. See **Ictalurus, Noturus, Pylodictis, Satan.**

Ictalurus   Ictaluridae
   furcatus BLUE CATFISH 1·5 m. (5 ft)
The blue catfish (or Mississippi cat as it is sometimes called) is one of the largest catfishes in N. America. It is distributed through the Mississippi system and in the larger rivers and lakes of the Gulf States, and is often moderately common. It grows to a large size, specimens up to 36·3 kg. (80 lb.) being relatively common, although last century giant specimens of up to 68 kg. (150 lb.) were recorded, fishing pressures are such now that it rarely attains its full potential. It is an important commercial fish throughout its range. Fishing is usually carried out with long lines using live or dead fish as bait near the bottom. It offers good sport to the angler.

It is a slender-bodied catfish, with a short-based adipose fin, a long anal fin which has a straight free edge, and a deeply forked tail fin. In colour it is a dull blue, or olive-blue, whitish below, with dark barbels.

I. nebulosus BROWN BULLHEAD
46 cm. (18 in.)
The brown bullhead was originally distributed in e. America, from s. Canada and N. Dakota, e. to New England and Virginia, and s. to the Carolinas, Florida, and Alabama. Two subspecies are recognized, *I. nebulosus marmoratus* being found in the latter, s. states. More than any other catfish this fish has been distributed wholesale. It is now established in w. N. America, New Zealand, and much of Europe as far E. as Russia. In most of these areas the introduction appears to have been effected by the release of pet fish, or to 'diversify' the local fauna and nowhere, except in some Russian lakes, is the bullhead fished for apart from casually by anglers.

It is essentially a bottom-living fish, found in muddy-bottomed well weeded ponds and slow-flowing rivers. It feeds on most of the common invertebrates of the region in which it lives.

These fishes are noted for their parental care of the young. They spawn in shallow hollows scooped in the mud, the male staying to guard the eggs. After hatching the young fish swim in dense schools accompanied by one or both parents which actively attack any intruder.

In colour it is dull, yellowish brown, occasionally almost black but always heavily blotched darker on the sides; the belly is a dull yellow-green.

I. punctatus CHANNEL CATFISH 1·2 m. (4 ft)
Widely distributed in e. N. America from the

Prairie Provinces and Hudson Bay areas in Canada s. through the Great Lakes, the Mississippi Valley to Florida and n. Mexico. It has been introduced to many areas both within and outside this area, and has successfully established itself. It is one of the most valuable catfishes in N. America, its flesh being palatable and firm; it also has some angling interest, large specimens weighing as much as 26 kg. (57 lb.), although weights of 11·3 kg. (25 lb.) are more usual.

It is a typical catfish in shape, long-bodied, scaleless, with a flattened head and long barbels around the mouth. It has a moderately large adipose fin, separate from the tail fin, a rounded outline to the anal fin and a deeply forked tail. Large specimens have less deeply forked tails.

It is deep slaty brown on the back, silvery on the sides, usually with dark spots which are lost with increasing age. The young are lighter and attractive enough to have been imported to England as pet fish for the garden pond (without intimation of the possibility of a 4 ft long pet!).

Ictiobus   Catostomidae
   bubalus SMALLMOUTH BUFFALO
91 cm. (3 ft)
This buffalo fish is probably the best known of the group, and is common and widespread in central Canada and the U.S. It is found from the Hudson Bay drainage, throughout the Mississippi system to the Gulf coast and the ne. rivers of Mexico. It is found in almost all large rivers and lakes in this region, characteristically in the main channels, and always close to the bottom.

It is a large, powerful fish which may weigh up to 16 kg. (35 lb.). In body form it is almost carp-like, its body fully scaled, the dorsal fin long and many rayed with the first rays rather higher than the remainder. Its mouth is relatively small with thick lips and is placed ventrally. The head is blunt and the eye moderate in size. This species is distinguished from the bigmouth sucker, *I. cyprinellus*, by the latter's large, oblique and terminal mouth, and its more slender pharyngeal teeth.

I. cyprinellus see under **I. bubalus**

IDE see **Leuciscus idus**

IDIACANTHIDAE
A small family of perhaps no more than 6 species, found in tropical and warm temperate waters in all the deep oceans. The family is closely related to the members of the family Melanostomiatidae, but differs from them in its extraordinary larval development and sexual dimorphism, as well as the structure of the dorsal and anal fin rays each of which has short spines at its base.

Adult females are long, slender-bodied, with long dorsal and anal fins. They have long pelvic fins, a long chin barbel, and teeth in the jaws, all of which males lack. The females grow to about 40 cm. (15¾ in.), the males to 7 cm. (2¾ in.). The larvae are very distinctive, being very thin and colourless, with their eyes at the ends of long stalks, each about half the length of the body. The larvae have pectoral fins, which both sexes lack as adults. See **Idiacanthus.**

Idiacanthus Idiacanthidae
fasciola BLACK DRAGONFISH
40 cm. (15¾ in.)
The black dragonfish appears to be widely distributed in the oceans of the world. In the Atlantic it has been found in the warmer, N. equatorial region essentially from the Caribbean Islands and Florida across to Gibraltar and the Cape Verde Islands. It has also been found in the e. Indian Ocean and w. tropical Pacific. It is found from the surface to 2000 m. (1094 fathoms), but there is considerable variation in depth at which the larval stages and mature adults are found.

The larvae are well known as transparent stalk-eyed young fish, from deep water when small, but near the surface as they grow. These fish eat diatoms and minute crustaceans. Adult females are elongate, thin-bodied, with well

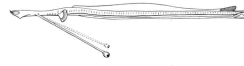

developed dorsal, anal, and pelvic fins, they also have a long chin barbel, with a branched and swollen tip. The female is black or very dark brown, with white fins, and luminous organs along the sides, and a pink light-organ behind the eye. The fins are lined with luminous material, and the tail is a deep yellow in life with luminous tissue.

Mature males are so totally different that they might be thought to be a different fish.

They are small, rarely reaching 7 cm. (2¾ in.), they lack pelvic fins, chin barbel, and teeth in the jaws, but they do have a large luminous organ behind the eye. The gut of the male is shrunken and useless, and this, with the lack of teeth in the jaws, has led to the belief that the males do not feed once they have attained maturity. The body cavity is, moreover, completely filled with large testes. Their mature life probably only extends for a month or 2, when they migrate to deep water to join the mature females. Mature females feed on a vatiety of smaller fishes, and probably survive for several spawning seasons.

IDOL, MOORISH see **Zanclus cornutus**

Ilyophis Synaphobranchidae
brunneus 57 cm. (22½ in.)
A very deep water eel which, although first captured in the Pacific near the Galapagos Islands, has subsequently also been found in the Atlantic Ocean. In both oceans it was taken in depths of over 1000 m. (546 fathoms) and the deepest captured specimen was taken in 2615 m. (1430 fathoms).

It is an elongate brownish eel, with a pointed head, and many fine teeth in the jaws. The chief external difference between this and

the other members of its family seems to be that the mouth does not extend so far behind the eyes. Gill openings are close together and ventral.

INANGA see **Galaxias maculatus**
INCONNU see **Stenodus leucichthys**
INDIAN
GLASSFISH see **Chanda ranga**
HUMP-HEAD see **Kurtus indicus**
LONG-FINNED EEL see **Anguilla nebulosa**
RIVER BARB see **Cyclocheilichthys apogon**
TROUT see **Barilius bola**

INDOSTOMIDAE
A family which contains a single species found in Upper Burma and Thailand.

Its slender body with small second dorsal fin placed opposite the similarly shaped anal fin, and a series of 5 short spines along the back, are remarkably reminiscent of the sticklebacks of the genera *Aulorhynchus* and *Spinachia*. The hard external plates which envelop the body are superficially similar to those found in the pipefishes (see Syngnathidae). For these reasons this curious little fish was previously aligned with these families. Recently, however, it has been shown that *Indostomus* is sufficiently distinct to deserve placement in a separate order the Indostomiformes, and that its nearest relatives are probably the clingfishes (Gobiesocidae). See **Indostomus.**

Indostomus Indostomatidae
paradoxus 3 cm. (1¼ in.)
A very small, bizzare shaped fish found originally in 1926 in Lake Indawgyi, a large shallow lake in Upper Burma, and subsequently in 1956 in a stream running to the lake within Thailand. It lives in shallow, heavily weeded water, and feeds entirely on animal food but only small live animals. In the aquarium it will feed on tubificid worms, turning as it approaches close, making a sudden dart to seize the worm, and then wriggling violently backwards to extract the worm from its tube.

It is a quiet, slow-moving fish when undisturbed propelling itself by rapidly fluttering the pectoral fins, although it can move very fast when necessary, using its tail fin for propulsion.

Despite the presence of the bony plates covering the body it is very flexible and can bend into an almost complete circle. It is also one of the few fish which can move its head up and down on the body.

Inactivity is habitual in this fish, most of its time is spent in shaded areas, lying flat on the bottom or resting in a head-up position at a steep angle to the bottom. This cryptic habit is reinforced by the colouring which is dusky brown, with indistinct darker bars on the fins, and light brown rectangles on the back.

Inermia Emmelichthyidae
vittata BOGA, BONNETMOUTH
23 cm. (9 in.)

Found in the w. tropical Atlantic from Bermuda, the Bahamas, and the W. Indies. It is commonly found in schools at depths of 15 m. (8 fathoms) or more on the open ocean side of reefs. They are active constantly moving fishes which feed on small planktonic animals, which they snap up individually with the aid of the extensible mouth.

It is a slender-bodied fish, with a long spiny dorsal fin joined at the base to the second dorsal; the tail fin is forked. It is blue above, silvery on the sides with 3 narrow dark, lengthwise stripes on the back, and a fourth diffuse stripe on the side; the snout is yellowish.

Inimicus Scorpaenidae
didactylus BEARDED GHOUL 33 cm. (13 in.)
A strikingly grotesque fish, depressed on the top until it is almost level, with the eyes raised up and the tip of the snout upturned. The head is well supplied with small fleshy flaps which also appear on the fins, although the body is smooth. The pectoral fins are large, the lowest 2 rays detached from the main fin. The spines of the dorsal fin are very sharp and for most of their length detached from the membrane.

It is widely distributed in the e. Indian and Pacific oceans, and is well known from the Andaman Islands, n. Australia, China, and the Philippines.

It lives in moderately deep water and is frequently caught by prawn trawlers, and on lines. It is greatly feared on account of its sharp, stinging spines, and not least because of its resemblance to the very venomous stonefishes (*Synanceia* sp.). Its rugged shape and colouring have obvious protective value when living amongst coral and marine growths. **243**

Ioglossus Gobiidae
helenae HOVERING GOBY 9 cm. (3½ in.)
A Caribbean species found around the islands of the W. Indies, notably Jamaica, Virgin Islands, Barbados, Tobago, and Puerto Rico. It is an attractively coloured species, light bluish grey, with yellow fins edged with blue. There is a yellow stripe under the gills and blue lines on the gill cover.

The hovering goby lives in 'U'-shaped burrows in sandy and silty bottoms. It is believed to excavate the burrow itself (not sharing an invertebrate burrow as so many other gobies do). Usually seen in pairs, they hover above the burrow entrance feeding on animal plankton. At the approach of danger they dart into the burrow, often using both entrances, although occasionally following one another down the same hole, which they enter head first.

They are mainly seen in sandy areas close to reefs in depths of 12–61 m. (7–33 fathoms), although juveniles are common over sand and coral rubble in depths less than this.

IOWA DARTER see **Etheostoma exile**

IPNOPIDAE
A family of slender bottom-living fishes found in the deep and abyssal sea, which have undergone the most remarkable modifications. Most are small fish (up to 45 cm., 17¾ in. maximum) with rounded bodies but rather flattened heads. In all the eyes are strikingly modified, being blind in the normal sense; the eyes of *Ipnops* are lensless light receptors, and in the

other genera the eyes are degenerate or covered with skin. All members of the family have large scales and a well-developed lateral line system.

Members of the family have been found in all the major oceans of the world. See **Bathymicrops, Bathytyphlops, Ipnops.**

Ipnops   Ipnopidae
  murrayi 15 cm. (6 in.)
This most remarkable fish is immediately distinguished by the shape of the head and body. The head is flattened from above, and the lower jaw protrudes, while the body is thin

and rounded. The most striking feature is the pair of flattened pale yellow structures on top of the head. These are modified eyes, light-sensitive but differing from the usual fish eye by the smallness of the rods, and the lack of a lens. *I. murrayi* appears to be confined to the Atlantic, from Tristan da Cunha and South Africa to the Gulf of Mexico. It has been found on the bottom at depths of 1463–3477 m. (800–1900 fathoms).

It is a dark brown or black in colour, save for the eye regions. Its biology is virtually unknown. Related species are found in the Pacific Ocean.

IRISH LORD, RED see **Hemilepidotus hemilepidotus**

Isistius   Dalatiidae
  brasiliensis 51 cm. (20 in.)
This small pelagic shark is found in the open seas of the tropical Atlantic, Pacific, and Indian oceans. Its most remarkable feature is its luminescence, the ventral surface of head and body giving off a vivid and greenish phosphorescent light. It has been taken far out in the ocean usually at night near the surface, which suggests that, like its relatives, it lives in deep water during daylight hours migrating towards the surface at night.

Apart from its luminous qualities it is an unremarkable brown colour, with a darkish band around its neck and whitish lips. Its principal food is squid, but it also eats fishes and crustaceans. Some of the squid found in the stomach of this shark were as large as the captor in bulk and it seems that the shark must be considerably more agile than its body shape suggests. It has a very large gape, which with its sharp teeth, presumably allows it to tackle large prey.

Iso   Isonidae
  natalensis SURF SARDINE 8 cm. (3 in.)
Found only on the Indian Ocean coast of s. Africa from Beira in Portuguese E. Africa S. to Knysna, near Port Elizabeth. It is abundant in the surf of the open beaches and also occurs in quieter bays, but despite its commonness very little is known about its biology.

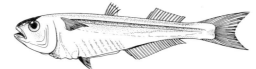

The scales which cover the rear of the body are very thin and fragile. In colour it is light olive on the back, transparent elsewhere except that the silvery stripe along the sides is very conspicuous; it is practically invisible in water.

ISONIDAE
A small family of fishes closely related to the silversides or sand-smelts, Atherinidae. Like them they are relatively slender-bodied but they are compressed laterally and have a sharp keel to the belly; the body is relatively deep. Two dorsal fins, the first one small composed of 4–6 slender spines; the anal fin is moderately long. The pectoral fins are set high upon the sides close behind the head. The members of the family are all transparent with a narrow, intense silver stripe down each side.

Inshore, surf-living fishes found on the e. coast of South Africa, s. Australia, and Japan. See **Iso.**

ISTIOPHORIDAE
The billfish family which includes some of the world's most famous sporting fish as well as several of value as food fish. The 10 or so members of the family are spread throughout tropical seas with some represented in warm temperate waters. Most are surface-living fishes of open seas which are rarely found very close inshore, and then usually only on coasts open to the ocean. Several of the known species are migratory.

The members of the family can be distinguished by their elongate bodies with a long, pointed snout forming the bill. This is rounded in cross-section (in contrast to the swordfish's flattened bill). Billfishes also have 2 keels either side of the tail just before the fin. The tail fin is narrow but rigidly spread, the dorsal fin is usually long with a high anterior lobe, and in the sailfishes is very well developed.

The billfishes are amongst the world's most active and fastest swimming fishes. The high aspect ratio of the tail fin, the streamlined shape, and concealed scales all being external pointers to swift movement. In addition the spine is composed of vertebrae all elaborately interlocked with bony process, this giving a rigidity to the body against which the musculature can exert great pressure.

All species are fish-eaters and are thought to use their long bill to stun prey-fish before eating them. See **Istiophorus, Makaira, Tetrapturus.**

Istiophorus   Istiophoridae
  albicans see **I. platypterus**
  americanus see **I. platypterus**
  gladius see **I. platypterus**
  orientalis see **I. platypterus**
  platypterus SAILFISH 3·6 m. (12 ft)
Widely distributed throughout the Atlantic, Indian and Pacific oceans. Its range encompasses the whole of the tropical Atlantic and these regions from the E. African coast to the Pacific coast of America, and from Arabia to South Africa, and Japan to Austra-

lia. It is highly migratory, undertaking coastwise movements along coastlines governed by seasonal weather, and from cooler to more tropical regions seasonally. It is a surface living fish, often found quite close to the shore. Its food consists mainly of fishes and squids and it appears to eat whatever species is locally abundant.

Its weight is only moderate when compared to the marlins. It attains a weight maximum of about 125 kg. (275 lb.), but the average weight of commercially caught fish is only around 32 kg. (70 lb.).

The sailfish is well known as a sporting fish. Although its weight is not high its fighting capacity and spectacular leaps make it a highly popular angler's fish. It is also exploited for food, although landings are rarely heavy. It is well regarded as a food fish although it seems generally accepted that it is inferior to the marlins.

When adult it is immediately distinguishable amongst its relatives by the very high dorsal fin. Generally dark steel blue above fading to white or silver below; the dorsal fin is a bright cobalt blue with round or oval black spots. The sides often have pale vertical bars or rows of spots.

This species has also been known as *I. albicans, I. americanus, I. orientalis,* and *I. gladius.*

Isurus   Lamnidae
  oxyrinchus MAKO, SHORTFIN MAKO,
SHARP-NOSED MACKEREL SHARK, BLUE
POINTER 3·5 m. (11½ ft)
The mako is a large oceanic shark, which occasionally is found close inshore. It is found in the Atlantic, Pacific, and Indian oceans (although the Pacific form is distinguished as *I. paucus*). It is a deep blue on the back, white below.

This is one of the sharks favoured by anglers, for it struggles bravely when hooked, and often leaps clear of the water in the process. As it may weigh up to 454 kg. (1000 lb.) this is an impressive occurrence. It is also a dangerous shark, being particularly frequently involved in attacks on small boats. It feeds on fishes and squids, often large ones, for a 327 kg. (720 lb.) mako caught off the Bahamas had a 50 kg. (110 lb.) swordfish in its stomach. That

it can capture such fast-swimming prey is not surprising for the mako is one of the most powerful, streamlined sharks in the sea. It is also one of the few fishes to have a body temperature higher than the water that surrounds it.

I. paucus see under **I. oxyrinchus**

ITOYORI see **Nemipterus virgatus**

J

Jenkinsia   Clupeidae
lamprotaenia DWARF HERRING
6·5 cm. (2½ in.)
The dwarf herring is apparently the most abundant small schooling fish in inshore waters in the Caribbean. Around the W. Indies it is particularly abundant feeding on the animal plankton at the surface, and can be seen in large compact shoals. It is a prime food source for many of the predatory fishes of the area, as well as sea birds. Thus although it is not directly exploited for food it has considerable indirect economic importance.

This little fish has a slender and compressed body, but with a rounded belly lacking the keel of the true herrings. The scales are very thin and easily dislodged. Its mouth is small and the jaws appear weak; the eye is moderately large. **27**

Jenynsia   Jenynsiidae
lineata ONE-SIDED LIVEBEARER
12 cm. (4¾ in.) females, 4 cm. (1½ in.) males
Widely distributed in e. S. America, from s. Brazil, Uruguay, Argentina and the mouth of La Plata. It was in the latter area that it was first collected by Charles Darwin on the voyage of the *Beagle*, to be described by the Rev. L. Jenyns, for whom the genus was later named.

It lives in small streams and rivers, but not in still waters, mainly in the lowland areas. Although it will feed on algae, its preferred food is small insects, insect larvae, and crustaceans.

Males have a long curved gonopodium, or copulatory organ, which can be moved either to right or left. The females similarly have a genital opening which opens on one side only.

A male that has a gonopodium moving to the right can therefore only mate with females that have the genital opening on the left. It is a moderately slender species with rounded fins; pale grey to olive-green above, a metallic sheen on the sides, and 3–6 brownish streaks on the sides.

It is occasionally imported as an aquarium fish but is rather quarrelsome. It can be bred successfully at temperatures up to 25°C, the number of young being produced being from 10–80.

JENYNSIIDAE
A small family of live-bearing toothcarps found in the general region of e. S. America. They are freshwater fishes mainly found in rivers and streams.

The body form is much like that of other toothcarps, relatively slender, with a broad head, and a wide mouth. The body is wholly scaled, the fins are rounded and lack spines, but the anal fin of the male is modified into a copulatory tube-like organ. The young are born alive. See **Jenynsia.**

Johnius   Sciaenidae
antarctica MULLOWAY, JEWFISH
1·8 m. (6 ft)
An Australian coastal species, found on the coast of S. Australia, Tasmania, Victoria, New South Wales, and s. Queensland. It is an extremely common fish in inshore waters, in the bays, river mouths, and estuaries. They seem to congregate in estuaries, and are alleged to attack the spawning shoals of grey mullet causing considerable losses to them. It is an active, fast-swimming and voracious fish which is particularly popular with anglers who catch large quantities annually.

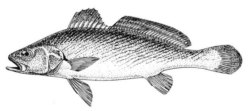

Its flesh makes good eating when young but large specimens are coarse and tasteless. It grows to a weight of at least 59 kg. (130 lb.).

It is greyish blue above, lighter on the belly, the young with narrow, oblique greyish lines; a dark patch in the pectoral fin base.

This species is very similar to the South African kabeljou, *Argyrosomus regius*. Both are placed, probably correctly, in the genus *Argyrosomus* by some authors.

Jordanella   Cyprinodontidae
floridae FLAGFISH 6 cm. (2¼ in.)
A most distinctive and very beautiful fish found only in ponds and marshes in Florida. Its body is stocky, plump, and rather thickset, and both the dorsal and anal fins are long-based, but the males have a much higher fin.

The males are especially colourful, olive to brown-green on the back, and on the sides each scale is light centred so that by reflected light the body gleams iridescent green or blue. The fins are yellowish with rows and bands of reddish spots. The female is a yellowish brown and again has light centred spots on the sides; it also has a dark blotch behind the pectoral base.

This has been a popular aquarium fish although the colours tend to fade in captivity. They are easy to spawn and the male herds the young fry and guards them for a while after hatching. **201**

Julidochromis   Cichlidae
ornatus 13 cm. (5 in.)
A species found in Lake Tanganyika. The members of this genus are all slender-bodied fish with a long many-rayed dorsal fin, 21–24 of which are thin spines. This species is strikingly coloured.

Within recent years this species has been several times imported for the aquarium trade, and is now more commonly seen as a pet fish than it was at one time. **366**

K

Kali   Chiasmodontidae
indica see under **K. normani**
macrodon see under **K. normani**
normani NEDDLETOOTH SWALLOWER
15 cm. (6 in.)
A small deep-sea fish found in the e. Pacific off California. Related species have been found in the Indian Ocean (*K. indica* and *K. macrodon*) at depths of around 2000 m. (1094 fathoms). It is probably a bathypelagic fish which moves up in the water column at night for individuals have been taken at 457 m. (250 fathoms) below the surface.

Like other members of the family the jaws and stomach are capable of accommodating large prey, sometimes even in excess of the fish's length. Its food consists mostly of fishes and crustaceans. It is distinguished by its slender shape, 2 dorsal fins, and huge jaws which because of the long back teeth cannot be closed.

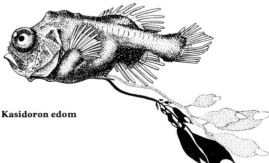

Kasidoron edom

KALUGA see **Huso dauricus**
KAMLOOPS see **Salmo gairdneri**

KASIDORIDAE

A family described as containing only 2 species of small extraordinary oceanic fishes. They have been captured in the surface waters of the w. Atlantic and w. Indian Ocean, but relatively few specimens are known. All have a most remarkable development of the pelvic fins, which form a much-branched and expanded tree-like organ. Recent research has shown that kasidorids are the larval stages of *Gibberichthys*. See **Kasidoron.**

Kasidoron   Kasidoridae
edom SIPHONOPHOREFISH 3 cm. (1¼ in.)
This remarkable species has so far been captured only in the w. Atlantic in an area between 240 km. (150 miles) E. of Cape Canaveral, Florida and NE. of Bermuda. It has been caught at between 2 and 50 m. (1 to 27 fathoms) at night, but it has been suggested that in daytime it lives between 150 and 500 m. (82–273 fathoms) deep. It is believed to be bathypelagic.

In colour it is described as black on the head and body in life, but it is enclosed in a transparent skin which is covered with small papillae giving the fish a velvety appearance. The pelvic fins are the most striking feature of this fish, they each consist of 6 rays all of which, except for the third, are short, but the exception has a long rounded stalk at the end of which hollow, leaf-like sacs cluster. The sacs are collectively greater in bulk than the fish's body, and being black coloured with a white tip are a very obvious feature. The clear part of the sac may have a luminous function, but this has not been proven. It has been suggested that the elaborate pelvic tree may be a protective device because of its resemblance to the jelly-fish like siphonophores or other coelenterates.

Kathetostoma   Uranoscopidae
averruncus SMOOTH STARGAZER
31 cm. (12¼ in.)
Found on the Pacific coast of America from California to Panama in depths of 18–244 m. (10–135 fathoms). The adults are essentially bottom-living fishes; larvae and young fish spend part of their lives at the surface and may be spread in this way beyond the normal range of the species. Adults feed mainly on smaller fishes; octopus has also been found in the gut.

In body form it is very similar to the other stargazers described. Its colouring is sandy brown with light blotches on the upper back and sides.
K. laeve STARGAZER 66 cm. (26 in.)
An Australian species which has been found off the coasts of W. Australia, S. Australia, Tasmania, Victoria, and New South Wales. It shares the family habit of burying itself in sand with only the eyes and tip of the mouth exposed.

In this species the head is extremely broad, and the eyes are placed far apart. The upper surface of the head is finely sculptured into ridges. Its coloration is sandy brown above with 2 broad dark patches on the back and another on the tail.

KATLI see **Barbus hexagonolepis**
KATONKEL see **Scomberomorus commerson**

Katsuwonus   Scombridae
pelamis SKIPJACK TUNA, BONITO, OCEANIC BONITO 100 cm. (39 in.)
A small tuna which is worldwide in its distribution in tropical waters and seasonally common in temperate seas. In the N. Atlantic it ranges to Massachusetts quite commonly and in the e. to the British Isles and Scandinavia. It is found in both small and large schools mostly offshore and on ocean coasts; it is not often found in inshore waters or estuaries. In many areas, such as the Queensland coast of Australia and the Caribbean it is extremely abundant and vast numbers are caught by commercial and sports fishermen. It is one of the mainstays of the Californian tuna fishery – most of the produce being canned. It attains a weight of 22·7 kg. (50 lb.).

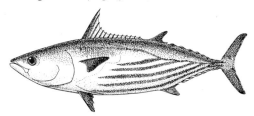

Herring-like fish, young scombroids, and lanternfish and euphausiid shrimps are the main diet, with crustaceans also being important.

Because of its oceanic habits it was this species which most of the early explorers of the world's oceans encountered. The journals of Captain Cook, for example, contain numerous references to bonito being captured.

The front part of the body is covered with moderately large scales forming a distinct corselet, the rear is scaleless. Its back is deep blue, the sides and belly silvery with 4–5 dusky lengthwise bands running along the lower sides. The fins are all dusky.

KAUP'S DEEP-SEA EEL see
    Synaphobranchus kaupi

Kaupichthys   Xenocongridae
nuchalis COLLARED EEL 14 cm. (5½ in.)
A brownish purple eel, paler underneath, with a dusky dorsal fin. A broad pale band across the head just behind the eye gives it its name. It is found in the Caribbean region from the Bahamas and the W. Indian islands to Curaçao. It lives at depths of between 1·6–15 m. (1–8 fathoms) on coral reefs, but burrows within sponges in company with the goby *Gobiosoma horsti*.

KELP
    GREENLING see **Hexagrammos decagrammus**
    PERCH see **Brachyistius frenatus**
KELPFISH, CREVICE see **Gibbonsia montereyensis**
KEY WORM EEL see **Ahlia egmontis**
KILLIFISH see Cyprinodontidae
KILLIFISH see **Pterolebias peruensis**
KILLIFISH,
    BLUE-FIN see **Lucania goodei**
    DIAMOND see **Adinia xenica**
KING
    AMBERJACK see **Seriola grandis**
    BARRACUTA see **Rexea solandri**
    CASCAROB see **Polycentrus schomburgkii**

MACKEREL see **Scomberomorus cavalla**
SALMON see **Oncorhynchus tshawytscha**
KING-OF-THE-HERRINGS see **Regalecus glesne**
KINGFISH see **Caranx sexfasciatus, Caranx speciosus, Scomberomorus cavalla**
KINGFISH,
    NORTHERN see **Menticirrhus saxatilis**
    YELLOWTAIL see **Seriola grandis**
KINGKLIP see **Genypterus capensis**
Kishinoella tonggol see **Thunnus orientalis**
KISSING GOURAMI see **Helostoma temminckii**
KITEFISH see **Monodactylus argenteus**
KLIPFISH see **Clinus superciliosus, Fucomimus mus**

Kneria   Kneriidae
auriculata 7·5 cm. (3 in.)
This small fish is well distributed in the upstream reaches of rivers in Rhodesia, Mozambique, and Transvaal. It is a slender, loach-like fish with a pointed head, rather large eyes, and a ventral mouth. It is covered with small scales, its fins are rounded, especially the pectorals, which are broad and form a flattened pad just at the front of the belly. It is dull coloured, the back mottled with dark blotches and with a few similar blotches along the end of the tail.

The mature male has a moderately large cup-shaped process on the rear edge of each operculum.

Kneria auriculata is an air-breathing species which is sometimes found in stagnant pools where only aerial respiration is possible. It is more common in streams, both on the lowveld and in mountainous regions at considerable altitudes. It is also a remarkably good climber, and has been seen to leave the water in an attempt to climb the damp concrete apron of a dam. In addition, it has been found in streams at an altitude of 1170 m. (3800 ft) which can only have been reached by fish in the past negotiating a series of waterfalls some 154 m. (500 ft) in total height. It is thought that the mouth and the pectoral fins may provide enough suctorial power to allow the fish to climb slowly.

KNERIIDAE

A small family of primitive freshwater fishes found in tropical and se. Africa. The members of the family are small, and slender bodied, with very small scales. The mouth is ventral in position, and is protractile, but it has no barbels around it. The fins are all small, but the pectorals are rather broad and placed ventrally.

They live in running water, often fast running water, and their flattened bellies and sucker-like pectoral fins and mouths are obvious adaptations to this habitat. See **Kneria.**

KNIFE LIVE-BEARER see **Alfaro cultratus**
KNIFEFISH see Gymnotidae, Rhamphichthyidae

KNIFEFISH,
  BANDED see **Gymnotus carapo**
  GREEN see **Eigenmannia virescens**
  MOTTLED see **Hypopomus artedi**
KNIFEJAW see **Oplegnathus conwayi**
KNIGHTFISH see **Cleidopus gloriamaris**
KOAYU see **Plecoglossus altivelis**
KOB see **Argyrosomus regius**
KOKANEE see **Oncorhynchus nerka**
KOLE see **Ctenochaetus strigosus**

Kraemeria Kraemeriidae
  samoensis 2·5 cm. (1 in.)
Widely distributed in the tropical and w.
Pacific and in the Indian Ocean. It has been
recorded from Samoa, the Marshall Islands,
the Seychelles, and elsewhere, living in loose
coral sand where the wave action is severe. It
burrows in the sand, helped presumably by

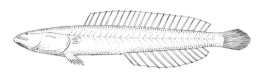

the strong projecting lower jaw acting as a
cutter. It is translucent in colouring.

KRAEMERIIDAE
A little-known family of tropical Indo-Pacific
fishes, whose precise relationships with other
groups have been for long a matter of doubt.
They are now firmly allied with the gobies
(family Gobiidae) on the basis of skeletal
characters, and in his most recent work (1973)
the distinguished goby specialist Dr P. J.
Miller relegates it to subfamily status within
the Gobiidae.

Most of the members of the family are
slender-bodied, scaleless fishes with the lower
jaw projecting and the chin enlarged. According to some authors some members of the
family have small scales embedded in the skin.
See **Kraemeria.**

KRØYER'S BARRACUDINA see **Paralepis
  atlantica**

Kryptopterus Siluridae
  bicirrhis GLASS CATFISH 10 cm. (4 in.)
The glass catfish is a popular aquarium species
the natural range of which is the Malay-Indo-
nesian region. It is one of the exceptions to
the general rule that catfishes are nocturnal
and bottom-living, for it lives in small shoals
active in daylight in mid-water. In the aquarium they adopt an oblique stance, with the
body held at an angle to the bottom, the lower
lobe of the tail fin touching the bottom. It is
a peaceful and interesting pet-fish.

Its body is excessively compressed, and
even the head is not greatly expanded. Its anal
fin is long, the tail fin forked, and the dorsal
fin reduced to a single ray. Its colouring is pale,
the back and upper side iridescent, the fins
dark, but the body appears to be almost translucent. **153**

Kuhlia Kuhliidae
  sandvicensis AHOLEHOLE 30 cm. (12 in.)
Found only around the Hawaiian islands, in
daytime in holes in the reef or in wrecks

between 1·5–15 m. (1–8 fathoms), but is
probably most active at night. It appears to
feed on algae, but in freshwater it snaps up any
insects fallen into the water.

It is a highly esteemed food fish, being captured mainly at night with baited hooks, although the young are taken in nets. The young
are found close inshore, even in intertidal
pools, and both young and old enter rivers and
can be found in freshwater.

It is a slender-bodied, fully-scaled fish with
a high anterior spiny portion to the dorsal fin,
and a sharp dip before the branched rays. Its
body colouring is essentially silvery.
  K. taeniurus FLAGTAIL, FLAGFISH
20 cm. (8 in.)
An Indo-Pacific species found from the E.

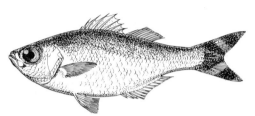

African to the Australian region. It is abundant
in most of this great range, in shallow water,
tide pools, and estuaries almost to the limit
of freshwater. The young are especially common in tide pools.

It is a distinctive species, with 5 dark bars
on the tail, one in the middle, 2 slender lines
running diagonally across the base of the tail,
and the outer lobes conspicuously black. The
tips are light coloured. Its back is greyish green
the sides silvery.

KUHLIIDAE
A family of mostly marine fishes of the tropical
Indo-Pacific. The flagfishes or flagtails, which
usually have their tails conspicuously dark
barred, are rather similar in body build to the
American freshwater basses (Centrarchidae).
Although the majority are marine fishes some
are found in freshwater.

The members of the family are rather
slender-bodied with moderate sized, toothed
scales, covering the head and body. The dorsal fin spines are strong and separated from
the second, soft-rayed fin by a deep notch. See
Kuhlia, Nannoperca.

KURPER, CAPE see **Sandelia capensis**

KURTIDAE
A small family of tropical Indo-Pacific dis-
tribution, ranging from India to New Guinea
and n. Australia and thence as far N. as China.
Two species only are recognized, one of which,
Kurtus gulliveri, is found only in freshwater
and brackish rivers of New Guinea and N.
Queensland.

Both members of the family are distinguished by the great depth anteriorly of an
otherwise compressed body. The anal fin is
very long, composed of many rays, the tail fin
is forked.

For long the affinities of these fishes was a
matter of doubt. In some respects they resemble berycoid fishes (see Berycidae), in
others they appear closer to the true spiny-
finned fishes such as the surgeonfish family
Acanthuridae. See **Kurtus.**

Kurtus Kurtidae
  gulliveri see under Kurtidae and
    K. indicus
  indicus INDIAN HUMP-HEAD 13 cm. (5 in.)
An abundant fish in the estuaries of rivers from
India to China, and particularly common in
the E. Indies. This fish often forms huge
shoals in rivers and estuaries, occasionally
penetrating almost into freshwater; it is
locally very abundant.

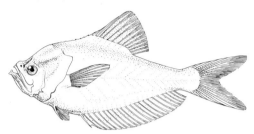

Its distinctive body form is quite unmistakable. Male hump-heads have a prominent
hook on the nape formed by skin covering
the supra-occipital crest. In the related *K.
gulliveri* it was discovered that the male carries the eggs in strings attached to the hook, it
may be assumed that both species do this. The
eggs form a distinct mass on the nape and are
presumably carried until they hatch.

KYPHOSIDAE
A family of worldwide distribution in tropical
and warm temperate seas. Most of the not very
numerous species live in shallow water in
rocky habitats or on reefs, and feed on algae.
The young, however, are found in the ocean's
surface amongst floating *Sargassum* weed, and
large adults are also found at sea sometimes
in association with driftwood, or following
ships. They are often called rudderfishes on
this account; sea chubs or drummers seem
better names.

In general most are deep-bodied, dark coloured fishes, with a small rounded head, and
small jaws. A moderate spiny dorsal fin is
joined to the soft dorsal, the anal fin has 3
spines. See **Girella, Kyphosus.**

Kyphosus Kyphosidae
  sectatrix BERMUDA CHUB 76 cm. (30 in.)
An Atlantic species found in the e. Atlantic
along the African coastline and in the W. from
Massachusetts and Bermuda, throughout the
Caribbean and Gulf of Mexico to Brazil. It is
very common in parts of the Caribbean in
shallow water on turtle grass beds, rocky bottoms and around patch reefs, but large specimens may be found in deep water in small
schools. It is mainly a plant-eater, but it also
consumes quantities of small invertebrates.

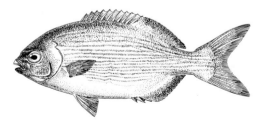

It is said to be a game fish which fights well,
and in some areas it is used as a food fish.

It is rather variable in coloration, but basically is dull grey with narrow lengthwise

stripes along the body, and wider yellowish marks on the head; the upper edge of the gill cover is dark.

K. sydneyanus DRUMMER, SILVER DRUMMER 76 cm. (30 in.)

An Australian coastal species found from W. Australia s. to Queensland, but most common on the s. coasts. It lives especially in the region of algae-covered rocks and reefs, and it eats plant matter almost exclusively. It is occasionally taken on a line or speared by an underwater swimmer but its flesh is of a poor flavour.

It is distinguished by the rather low second dorsal fin, the rays being lower than the spines in the dorsal. It is dark silvery, with rows of lengthwise light lines, and 2 dark stripes across the head.

L

Labeo Cyprinidae
bicolor RED-TAILED BLACK SHARK 12 cm. (4¾ in.)

Native of Thailand, this fish is said to be the commonest member of the genus in that country. It is, however, found only in the central regions, its centre of abundance being the Menam Chao Phya basin. It has been found around Bangkok.

It is a very beautiful fish, flat-bellied with well developed lips, which are modified internally to form a sucking organ while the edges of the jaws are hard and horny. It has 1–2 pairs of barbels on the lips.

These 'sharks' have earned this name by having a high dorsal fin; they are not related to the true sharks.

It is a hardy aquarium fish, thriving in rather peaty water, when given a shaded position. It effectively cleans the aquarium sides, bottom, and plants of algae, and can be fed on lettuce as well as the growing plants. **127**

L. munensis 12 cm. (4¾ in.)

A little known member of the so-called 'sharks'. Its native range is e. Thailand, the first known specimens being collected in the Mun River. It has since been brought to Europe as an aquarium fish and is as suitable for the tank as its better-known relatives from which it is distinguished by its colour.

It is a large scaled species with well-developed barbels on lips and snout. **128**

L. victorianus NINGU 41 cm. (16 in.)

A rather slender-bodied fish from African freshwaters, the ningu can be distinguished by the fairly high and large dorsal fin, and the blunt snout with a flap of skin in front of the upper lip. In this species the eyes are moderate and clearly visible from above and below.

It is an olive-green above, lighter, creamy coloured below; the dorsal, anal, and pelvic fins are often tipped with orange. It is found in lakes Victoria and Kyoga, the Victoria Nile, and the main rivers running into Lake Victoria. It feeds on mud, and plant debris, and has been observed grazing on the fungal and other growths on the bodies of other fishes. It spawns in temporary streams and flood pools, in the area of Lake Victoria at least.

This fish is the basis of an important fishing industry on Lake Victoria; much of its product is sold smoked.

Labracoglossa Labracoglossidae
argentiventris 25 cm. (10 in.)

A common fish of Japanese waters, being found both in the Sea of Japan and along the Pacific coast from central Honshu s. to the Philippines. It is a common fish on the Tokyo market, where it is sold as takabe; its flesh is said to be tasty. It spawns from August to October, the eggs having a distinctive black pigment.

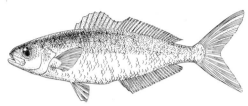

Its coloration is distinctive; bluish green above, light grey below with a clear stripe of yellow running from the eye to the tail fin and following the profile of the back.

LABRACOGLOSSIDAE

A family containing only 2 genera, each probably with only one species of marine fish. It is found in the Pacific Ocean.

The members of the family are slender-bodied, the mouth very protractile but with small teeth. The dorsal fins are continuous, the spiny rays numbering 10 being slender and joined to the second dorsal fin. See **Labracoglossa.**

LABRIDAE

The family of the wrasses, a group of marine fishes found in tropical, sub-tropical, and temperate seas the world over. Members of the family are characterized by having a single dorsal fin, the spiny part of which is considerably larger than the soft rayed part. Most have thick lips and well developed caniniform teeth in the jaws as well as large crushing teeth in the pharynx.

As a group, the wrasses are usually colourful, the juveniles and females differing markedly from adult males in coloration, and sometimes body form. As a consequence some species have been named several times, some names being bestowed on sexual or age differences, and the total of 600 or so known wrasse species is probably inflated unduly. Sex changes from active female to male have been observed in some species with accompanying change in coloration.

Wrasses are usually relatively small. Most species are within the 30 cm. (12 in.) length range, but some attain a maximal length of 10 cm. (4 in.). Members of the Indo-Pacific genus *Cheilinus* however, may grow to 3 m. (10 ft). Except locally, few wrasses are regarded as food fish, nor is their value as sporting fish high.

Many species of wrasse have been found to act as cleaner fishes, picking external parasites off other fishes at recognized stations. This has even been reported in the temperate waters of England and New Zealand, although best known amongst tropical species. Wrasses also show most interesting breeding behaviour, the differential colouring of males and females leading to elaborate pre-spawning displays. Some species construct nests out of plant material which are guarded, once the eggs are

deposited, by the male. As a group they are well known for their habit of sleeping at night, either buried in the sand of the bottom or wedged between rocks. Observation on sleeping wrasses in the Bermuda Aquarium have shown that they go through a period of rapid eye movement (REM) which, in higher vertebrates, is usually associated with dreaming. It thus suggests that some wrasses dream. See **Achoerodus, Anampses, Bodianus, Centrolabrus, Cheilinus, Coris, Gomphosus, Halichoeres, Labroides, Labrus, Lachnolaimus, Larabicus, Macropharyngdon, Pimelometopon, Thalassoma.**

Labrisomus Clinidae
nuchipinnis HAIRY BLENNY 20 cm. (8 in.)

Reported to occur on both sides of the tropical Atlantic, in the E. along the tropical African coast, and on the American Atlantic coast from Bermuda, the Bahamas, and Florida S. to Brazil. It is found throughout the Gulf of Mexico and the W. Indies where it is the most abundant member of the family.

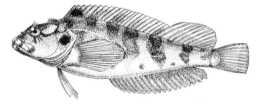

It lives in various habitats on sand and turtle grass beds, and on algal covered rocks, usually in water less than 3 m. (1½ fathoms) deep. It feeds on small crabs, other crustaceans, molluscs, brittle stars, worms, and small fishes.

It is distinguished by the much branched tentacles above the eye and on the nape, by the pronounced, white-ringed black spot on the gill cover, and by a dark spot at the front of the dorsal fin. Its colouring is variable, mainly olive with dusky bars and dots; males tend to be reddish ventrally.

Labroides Labridae
dimidiatus BLUE STREAK, CLEANERFISH 10 cm. (4 in.)

A beautiful, slender-bodied wrasse which is widely distributed in the Indo-Pacific, from the Red Sea and E. African coast to the tropical central Pacific. It is extremely common on parts of reefs, sometimes in tide pools, more usually below tidal level.

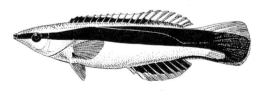

Its distinctive habit of acting as a cleaner fish picking parasites off larger, often predatory species is well known. Each fish adopts a routine area in which it holds territory and displays, soliciting for custom. Larger fishes come to these cleaning stations where the wrasse removes both external and internal gill parasites. In some areas this wrasse has been observed to change sex, the largest, most dominant specimen in the area being the only functional male, while all the subordinate specimens are female.

Important as these fish may be in controlling external parasites, they are not essential to the health of a community of fishes. Experimental removal of all specimens in the area does not result in other fishes quitting the area, or in becoming particularly unhealthy.

Its striking coloration is closely mimicked by the blenny *Aspidontus taeniatus*. The cleaner-fish is shown cleaning *Pterois volitans*. **247**

Labrus   Labridae
  bergylta BALLAN WRASSE 51 cm. (20 in.)
The largest and most widely distributed of European wrasses; this species is found in the Mediterranean, and in the e. Atlantic from the Canary Islands n. to Norway and n. Scotland. It is confined to rocky shores and off-shore reefs, the young occurring in low tidal pools although large specimens are usually found in 2–10 m. (1–5½ fathoms). Sometimes larger specimens are found in schools, but they are usually solitary.

It feeds mainly on crustaceans, especially crabs, but molluscs and barnacles are eaten also. The hard shells of these animals offer little protection against the strong, pointed jaw teeth, or the crushing mill of the pharyngeal teeth.

The ballan wrasse builds a nest of loose strands of algae wedged into a crevice and bound together with mucus threads. The eggs are laid within, and guarded by the male, but the fry are planktonic.

Because of its size the ballan wrasse is a moderately popular angling species. It grows to a weight of 5 kg. (11 lb.) and more. Its flesh is coarse and rather sweet, and is not usually enjoyed except by the most ravenous.

L. mixtus CUCKOO WRASSE 35 cm. (13¾ in.)
A moderately common European wrasse, which is found in the Mediterranean and e. Atlantic from Senegal to Norway and n. Scotland. Despite its wide range its biology is little known.

It is found on rocks and rough ground in depths of 37–183 m. (20–100 fathoms), although young fish may be found in shallower water than this. It feeds mainly on crustaceans, (squat lobsters, crabs), and molluscs, but is often caught in lobster pots apparently scavenging for food.

Males are conspicuously different in coloration from females and juveniles, the latter being invariably orange in colour with 3 brownish blotches on the back. Males are an indescribable blue and orange colouring, which may vary with breeding activity. Spawning is accompanied by an elaborate display on the part of the male. It is a nest-building species; after spawning is completed the male protects the eggs, although the young are planktonic. **406, 407**

Lachnolaimus   Labridae
  maximus HOGFISH, HOGSNAPPER
91 cm. (3 ft)
An inhabitant of the w. Atlantic where it ranges from Bermuda and N. Carolina to the S. American coast. It is found throughout the W. Indies and the Gulf of Mexico. It is widely distributed on reefs, especially on open bottoms where gorgonians are abundant. It feeds mainly on molluscs, crabs, hermit crabs, and sea urchins.

It grows to a considerable size, specimens up

to 11 kg. (25 lb.) having been reported. It is an excellent food fish, and is easily speared under-water, and on account of this and fishing pressure large specimens have become scarce, in the W. Indies at least.

It is a very deep-bodied wrasse, immediately distinguishable by the very long, thickened first 3 spines of the dorsal fin. Coloration is variable. Large males have a well defined dark maroon patch on the head and nape. **408**

LACTARIIDAE
A small family of Indo-Pacific fishes containing a single genus, and one, or at the most 2 species. They are rather deep-bodied, small fish, closely related to the trumpeter whiting (Sillaginidae), and distantly to the cardinal-fishes (Apogonidae). The mouth is large and oblique; the first dorsal fin is short based, with 7–8 weak spines, and quite separate from the second dorsal fin. The bases of both the second dorsal fin and the anal fin are covered with scales. See **Lactarius.**

Lactarius   Lactariidae
  lactarius WHITEFISH 28 cm. (11 in.)
Widely distributed in the Indo-Pacific but rather local in its abundance. It occurs N. to Taiwan in the Pacific, and is moderately common off s. India and Sri Lanka. It is found in coastal waters and on trawling grounds.

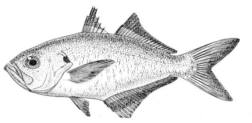

Its coloration is unremarkable being greyish above, silvery on the sides, a narrow black spot on the gill cover. The dorsal and tail fins have a dusky edge; the other fins are yellowish.

Lactophrys   Ostraciontidae
  guineensis see under **L. quadricornis**
  quadricornis SCRAWLED COWFISH
46 cm. (18 in.)
A w. Atlantic species found from Massachusetts and Bermuda to Brazil, including the Gulf of Mexico and the Caribbean. Reports of its occurrence on the South African coast may be due to confusion with the closely related tropical e. Atlantic species, *L. guineensis*.

It is a very common species in the Caribbean, found mainly in seagrass beds at depths down to 12 m. (6 fathoms), although there are records of it at 73 m. (40 fathoms). It feeds on a wide range of bottom-living invertebrates (including sponges, tunicates, crustaceans) and plants. It seems to be more abundant along the coasts of the continent and the larger islands, than around the offshore islands.

This species is distinguished by having a pair of spines jutting forwards from the eyes (hence cowfish), and others backward pointing at the rear end of the ventral carapace. The carapace is continuous behind the dorsal fin. It is pale greenish or brown with dark broken stripes, mainly horizontal on the cheeks but forming lines of dots on the sides; there is a conspicuous dark stripe above the eye and another along the lower edge of the carapace.

L. trigonus TRUNKFISH, BUFFALO
TRUNKFISH 45 cm. (17¾ in.)
Widely distributed in the w. Atlantic, from Massachusetts and Bermuda to Brazil, including the Caribbean and the Gulf of Mexico. It is basically an inhabitant of sea grass beds, but ranges along reefs in depths down to 6 m. (3 fathoms), although there is a record of it at 37 m. (20 fathoms) off Brazil. It feeds on bottom-living invertebrates and plants.

This species is alleged to make loud grunting noises when removed from the water. Locally it is regarded as an excellent food fish.

It is distinguished in its home range by having a short curved spine at the lower rear corners of the carapace, but none on the fore-head. Its colouring is variable, but is usually olive with small white spots, and patches behind the pectoral fin and on the side where the hexagonal plates are dark edged. Large specimens become marked overall with a chain-like marking dark on pale green.

L. triqueter SMOOTH TRUNKFISH
30 cm. (12 in.)
Native to the w. Atlantic, this species is found from Massachusetts and Bermuda to s. Brazil, including the Gulf of Mexico. It lives in shallow water round reefs, mostly down to 6 m.

(3 fathoms) occasionally deeper, feeding on a variety of bottom-living invertebrates such as worms, crabs, shrimps, and tunicates. On occasions it will blow a jet of water from its mouth into the sand in order to expose a food item.

In its native range it is distinguished by its small size, by lacking all spines at the corners of the carapace, and by its high arched back. It is yellowish in colour with the polygonal plates picked out in black and dark bases to the dorsal, tail and anal fins, as well as the mouth.

Lactoria   Ostraciontidae
  diaphana COWFISH, BOXFISH
25 cm. (10 in.)
An Indo-Pacific species which is widespread in tropical waters between the African coast, Australia, S. China, and Hawaii. It is distinguished by its relatively deep body, the carapace with a forward-pointing spine above each eye, another rather small curved spine at the lower hind corners of the carapace, and a small, short compressed spine in the centre of the back. In this species the ventral part of the carapace is translucent, and the young seem to be almost translucent overall. It has a zig-zag black line along the lower side of the body.

This species is placed in the genus *Ostracion* by some authors.

LADYFISH see **Albula vulpes, Elops saurus, Trachinotus russelli**

Lagocephalus   Tetraodontidae
  lagocephalus PUFFERFISH, OCEANIC
PUFFER, TOBY, BLUE BLAASOP 61 cm. (2 ft)
An Atlantic species which is known from n.

Europe to South Africa and throughout the Mediterranean. It is the only pufferfish to occur on the British coast, which it does rarely, and then usually only after a long, hot summer. It has also been reported from the Indian and Pacific oceans.

Unlike most pufferfishes which are shallow-water species, this appears to be a pelagic open-sea fish. Records of its occurrence confirm this, as does its deep blue coloured back and white belly, typical features of a surface-living fish. In general, its biology is little-known, but fishes and crustaceans have been found in its gut, and squid beaks also occur, while the fish's body is sometimes marked with squid sucker claws.

It can be distinguished by having a lateral line which is a raised fold of skin running along the lower side, the forked tail, and high dorsal and anal fins. Spines in this species are confined to the belly pouch.

L. sceleratus GIANT TOAD, SILVER TOADFISH 76 cm. (30 in.)
Widely distributed in the tropical Indo-Pacific and known from the Red Sea and E. African coast to Australia, the Philippines and Japan.

It is a long slender fish (when not inflated) with 2 lateral lines, the lower of which is a raised ridge, while the dorsal and anal fins are high, rather angular in outline, and the tail fin is forked. In this species the tail is flattened from above, and just before the fin is wider than deep. Its colouring is greenish above with well-spaced dark spots on the back, a broad silvery band down the sides, and white ventrally. The body anteriorly has small, densely packed spines, ventrally on the belly the spines are less crowded.

It appears to live in more open waters than most pufferfishes, possibly in deep water but also nearer the surface. It is virulently poisonous, its recorded history of toxic nature extending back to Captain Cook's second voyage round the world when, in 1774, the famous navigator ate some of a specimen caught on the Australian coast and narrowly escaped death. The toxin is particularly concentrated in the liver, gonads, gut, and possibly blood, but the flesh can be contaminated either by contact with these organs or if the fish is not drained of blood while fresh. Nevertheless it is eaten occasionally when properly prepared with no harmful results; a culinary form of Russian roulette!

Lagochila Catostomidae
lacera HARELIP SUCKER 25 cm. (10 in.)
The harelip sucker was first described in 1877 from specimens taken from a river in Georgia, U.S. It was later found to be moderately common in clear streams from the Maumee River in Ohio, a tributary of Lake Erie, s. to the Tennessee River system. At about the turn of the century, this sucker, which had been widely distributed throughout the Tennessee and Ohio rivers, virtually disappeared. Some specimens were captured in 1895 but none since, and the species is now believed to be extinct.

It was a moderately slender-bodied sucker with distinctive mouth parts, in particular the upper lip is not protractile while the lower lip was split into 2 distinct lobes.

LAKE ALBERT PERCH see **Lates albertianus**
LAKE EYRE HARDYHEAD see **Craterocephalus eyresii**
LAKE
  CHUBSUCKER see **Erimyzon sucetta**
  CISCO see **Coregonus artedii**
  HERRING see **Coregonus artedii**
  STURGEON see **Acipenser fulvescens**
  TROUT see **Salvelinus namaycush**
  WHITEFISH see **Coregonus clupeaformis**

Lamna Lamnidae
ditropis see under **L. nasus**
nasus PORBEAGLE, MACKEREL SHARK 3 m. (10 ft)
The porbeagle is a large active shark most common in the open oceans, but coming close to coastal waters on occasions. It is found in the N. Atlantic from Iceland S. to n. Africa, and in the Mediterranean, also in the w. Atlantic from Newfoundland to S. Carolina. Related species occur in the N. Pacific (*L. ditropis*) and off Australia (*L. whitleyi*).

It feeds on a wide range of surface-living fishes and squids, but occasionally eats bottom-living animals. It is not an aggressive shark, although dangerous at close quarters in a small boat, and numbers are caught by sport fishermen off the British coast. Norwegian commercial fishermen take large numbers on long lines but the meat (which is of good flavour and texture) is exported mainly to Italy.

The porbeagle gives birth to live young, usually in litters of up to 4, the young being about 50 cm. (19½ in.) long at birth. Newly born young, and the unborn, have a very swollen belly due to their having swallowed the unfertilized eggs in the maternal uterus. This yolk-filled stomach nourishes them for several weeks after birth.

The porbeagle is one of the highly developed swimmers in the ocean and its body tissues are usually warmer than the surrounding sea, an unusual feature in fishes.

L. whitleyi see under **L. nasus**

LAMNIDAE
A small family of large, dangerous, or potentially dangerous, sharks. All have stout muscular streamlined bodies, with a characteristic 'new moon' shaped tail, and a strong keel each side of the body before the tail fin. They all have large teeth.

This family is worldwide in its distribution in tropical, warm temperate, and even temperate seas. It includes the man-eater, several anglers' sharks, and at least one species eaten by man. See **Carcharodon, Isurus, Lamna.**

Lampanyctus Myctophidae
crocodilus 30 cm. (12 in.)
This lanternfish is found in the N. Atlantic and Mediterranean. It is widely distributed, and is found in depths of 400 to 800 m. (218–437 fathoms), although coming nearer the surface at night. It feeds on small bathypelagic invertebrates and fishes, and in turn it has been found in numbers as adult and young in the stomachs of tuna, especially the albacore.

It is a long, slender lanternfish with a dis-

tinctly pointed snout. Its fins, especially the pectoral fins are well developed. Its jaws are long, and its eye is only moderate in size and placed near the end of the snout. Scales are large on the body, although absent on the head. Light organs are well-developed and this species has a very distinct luminous patch on the front of the adipose fin. It is blackish brown on the back with very distinctly silvery sides and belly.

LAMPERN see **Lampetra fluviatilis**

Lampetra Petromyzonidae
fluviatilis LAMPERN 50 cm. (19 in.)
Lives in rivers, and coastal waters of the British Isles and nw. Europe. The lampern is a migratory fish which spawns, and spends a prolonged larval life in freshwater, before migrating to the sea. As an adult it is parasitic, sucking the blood from fishes, such as shad, sea trout, and houting, and many freshwater species. It stays in coastal and even estuarine waters for much of its adult life migrating into freshwater in the autumn. Spawning takes place well up rivers on gravelly river beds in spring, the adults excavating a shallow nest in the gravel in which the eggs are laid. The larvae, or prides, after hatching, bury themselves in soft mud downstream of the nesting site, where, being blind and toothless, they feed by filtering micro-organisms from the mud. This larval life lasts for up to 5 years.

The lampern has suffered greatly from pollution and obstructions in many of the larger rivers of its range. At one time it was a valuable food fish and was fished for commercially, for food and bait, in such rivers as the Thames. Fisheries still exist in other rivers, such as the Severn, but they are now of minor importance.

L. japonica ARCTIC LAMPREY 62 cm. (24½ in.) (parasitic form); 18 cm. (7 in.) (non-parasitic form)
Widely distributed from Lapland across the Arctic landmass of the U.S.S.R. along the n. Pacific coasts s. to Japan and Korea, and the w. N. American continent. This lamprey is mainly a migratory species along the Pacific coastal rivers, spawning in the upstream reaches of rivers; the larvae after a period of development in freshwater migrate to the sea where the adults feed parasitically on fishes. There are, however, numerous populations throughout its range which omit the migratory stage and are not parasitic as adults; in fact they do not feed after metamorphosis from the larva until they die following spawning. Both sexes help in clearing a shallow pit on the gravel of the river bed, picking up stones with their oral sucker and moving them. During spawning the male attaches himself to the female's head with his sucker and, their bodies twined together, the eggs are shed and fertilized to fall into the gravel. After hatching the young bury themselves in nearby muddy areas of the river.

This species was at one time raked out of the Yukon River by sticks under the ice in their thousands for food. It is today little eaten, although smoked lampreys are sold in Japan in numbers. Like the other lamprey species the young are often used for bait by anglers.

L. lamottenii see under **Ichthyomyzon fossor**

L. planeri BROOK LAMPREY, PLANER'S
LAMPREY 16 cm. (6¼ in.)
A species native to w. Europe and found
around the Baltic basin to the Pyrenees, but
not to the S., or S. of the Alps. It occurs
throughout the British Isles. The brook lamprey, as its name suggests spends its whole life
in streams and the upper reaches of rivers. It
spawns in the river without a sea-going phase
in its life. It also differs from most lampreys by
not being parasitic as an adult; its life is a prolonged larval stage followed by metamorphosis, breeding and death.

It is very similar to small specimens of the
European lampern (*Lampetra fluviatilis*) but
differs in its blunt teeth and by having the dorsal fins almost contiguous. Many workers consider it to be merely a non-migratory form of
the lampern; similar pairs of species of lamprey are found elsewhere. **1**

LAMPREY see **Petromyzon marinus**
LAMPREY,
　AMERICAN BROOK see under
　　Ichthyomyzon fossor
　ARCTIC see **Lampetra japonica**
　BROOK see **Lampetra planeri**
　NORTHERN BROOK see **Ichthyomyzon
　　fossor**
　PACIFIC see **Entosphenus tridentatus**
　PLANER'S see **Lampetra planeri**
　POUCHED see **Geotria australis**
　SEA see **Petromyzon marinus**

LAMPRIDAE
A family which contains only the single, mesopelagic, deep-water opah or moonfish. It is
widely distributed, being found in all oceans
except for the high Antarctic, it is probably
most common in tropical seas.

The family is closest to the ribbonfish and
the dealfishes, and shares with them a distinctive arrangement of the jaws to form a protrusible mouth. Otherwise it is totally dissimilar from its relatives, having a deep body,
a well developed anal fin and large tail and pectoral fins. It has no spiny rays in its fins. See
Lampris.

Lampris　　　　　　　　　Lampridae
　guttatus OPAH, MOONFISH 152 cm. (5 ft)
Worldwide in distribution; especially common in warm temperate and tropical seas. It is
best known in the n. Atlantic, and n. Pacific,
both from the Japanese and N. American
coastlines. It is a mid-water fish of the deep
seas, mostly found in depths of 100–400 m.
(55–218 fathoms). Until recently, midwaters at
these depths were relatively unexplored and
most of the specimens known had been acci-

dental strays in shallow water or had been
found floating at the surface. Relatively little
is known even now about the biology of this
species.

Its food consists mainly of mid-water fish
and squids, the fishes including, in the Pacific,
hake, rockfish, and lancetfish, and in the Atlantic, blue whiting and silvery pout *(Gadi-
culus argenteus)*. Despite its size, apparently
cumbersome shape, and toothless mouth, it is
evidently a very efficient predator on actively
swimming fishes and squids.

It is a relatively huge fish, specimens of
1·5 m. (5 ft) in length being over 1 m. (3¼ ft)
deep, and weighing around 50 kg. (110 lb.).
Reports of fish of 227–272 kg. (500–600 lb.)
have been recorded but the maximum measured weight seems to be around 73 kg. (160
lb.). Its flesh is excellent, if dry, but because
of the relative rarity of capture it is not
commercially exploited.

The coloration of this fish is remarkable;
deep blue on the back shading to silvery on
the belly with abundant white spots, and crimson fins. This alone makes it unmistakable.

Lamprologus　　　　　　　　　Cichlidae
　tetracanthus 18 cm. (7 in.)
A cichlid which is endemic to Lake Tanganyika. It lives in shallow inshore parts of the
lake, especially in rocky areas although also
found on sand. It feeds on a wide variety of
molluscs and small fishes, but its diet has not
been systematically studied.

It is a rather slim-bodied species, with a
short snout and small eyes. The jaws are rather
small but have numerous rows of sharp teeth.

This species has some value as a food fish
locally; it has also been imported to Europe
as an aquarium species. **367**

LANCE, SAND see Ammodytidae
LANCER DRAGONET see **Callionymus bairdi**
LANCETFISH see Alepisauridae
LANCETFISH, LONGNOSE see **Alepisaurus
　ferox**
LANTERNFISH see Myctophidae
LANTERNFISH see **Myctophum punctatum**

Larabicus　　　　　　　　　Labridae
　quadrilineatus 7·5 cm. (3 in.)
A small wrasse found in the Red Sea, although
it has also been recorded from the Indian
Ocean and Samoa these reports seem to have
been based on misidentifications. It is rather
similar in body shape to the wrasses of the
genus *Labroides* but differs from them in having a completely scaly head, in lacking a notch
in the lower lip, and in having a tail fin which
is slightly concave. Its bold colour pattern of
4 lengthwise stripes is quite distinctive.

Like other members of this genus, this fish
acts as a cleaner fish to other fishes in the coral
reef community. It also feeds on coral polyps,
and may locally pick the coral bare. **405**

LARGE-SCALED YELLOWFISH see **Barbus
　marequensis**
LARGE-SPOTTED DOGFISH see **Scyliorhinus
　stellaris**
LARGE-TOOTHED FLOUNDER see
　Pseudorhombus arsius
LARGEMOUTH
　BASS see **Micropterus salmoides**
　LEATHERSKIN see **Chorinemus lysan**

Lasiognathus　　　　　　　　　Oneirodidae
　saccostoma 7·5 cm. (3 in.)
One of the most striking looking of the deep-
sea anglers. It is known only from a single
female specimen captured in the Caribbean

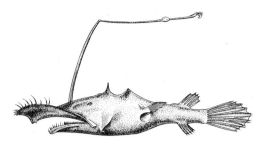

Sea in a depth of around 2500 m. (1370
fathoms). It is wholly black in colour.

Lates　　　　　　　　　Centropomidae
　albertianus LAKE ALBERT PERCH
1·8 m. (6 ft)
Found only in Lake Albert, and the Albert and
Murchison Niles. It is said to be largely restricted to the shallow inshore water of the lake,
and the shallower parts of the rivers, but occasionally it is found in deep water. It is abundant
in shallow bays round the lake.

In its range it is a very important food fish,
being captured in gill-nets and seines. It is also
a good sporting fish. It grows to a weight of at
least 163 kg. (360 lb.).

As a young fish it feeds on insect larvae and
crustaceans, but as it grows it becomes increasingly a fish-eater.

Its coloration is dark grey above, silvery on
the sides, and white below.

L. calcarifer GIANT PERCH, PALMER
1·8 m. (6 ft)
This huge and valuable fish is widely distributed along the Indian Ocean coastline,
from the Persian Gulf to N. Australia, and
from thence to the Philippines and China. It is
found both in the sea and in freshwater rivers,
into which it is said to run to spawn.

Throughout its range it is a valuable food
fish. Caught mostly on baited hooks it fetches a
high price and its firm white flesh is very good
eating. It grows to a considerable size, the
average marketable weight being between 1·4–
14 kg. (3–30 lb.) and the maximum around
41 kg. (90 lb.). Giant perch caught in freshwater are said not to have the flavour of sea
caught fish.

It is a moderately slender-bodied fish, with
a flattened, even concave, head profile. The
first dorsal fin has strong spines, the body is
covered with toothed scales and the mouth is
large. Adults are greenish grey above, silvery
on the sides and white below, the dorsal fin
membranes dusky although the spines are
light. The eyes are brilliant red.

L. niloticus NILE PERCH 2 m. (6½ ft)
An African freshwater fish of wide distribution, the Nile perch is found in the Nile
system, the Congo, Volta, Niger and in Lake
Chad. It has been introduced into Lake Victoria. Many man-made lakes and reservoirs in
Africa have been stocked with this species
which is fished for commercially as well as by
sportsmen.

It is as a sporting fish that the Nile perch is
best known. Usually fished for with small fish
as bait, it is a good fighter and generally makes

several leaps out of the water when first hooked. Large specimens can attain a weight of 40 kg. (88 lb.) in even moderate sized waters, while a good weight is around 80 kg. (176 lb.). It is also a highly prized food fish wherever it occurs, and in many areas of Africa it is the most important single food fish. It is caught in gill nets, on set lines, and by spearing at night with a light (their eyes are said to glow red in the torchlight). Amongst the ancient Egyptians it was equally esteemed, and at one time worshipped by a cult. Many mummified *Lates* have been found in burial grounds at Esneh on the Upper Nile.

The Nile perch is a voracious carnivore but feeds mostly on fishes. When young they are often found in quiet backwaters but the adults live in rivers, for preference amongst fallen trees or in the lee of boulders in the bed.

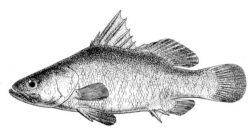

Its colouring is silvery or greyish on the sides, brownish green on the back, and light on the belly.

LATES, LEAF see **Belontia signata**

Latimeria   Latimeridae
    chalumnae COELACANTH 1·9 m. (6 ft)
The coelacanth is found only in the tropical w. Indian Ocean. The first specimen was captured near East London, South Africa, in December 1938; it was captured in a commercial trawler's net off the mouth of the River Chalumna at a depth of 67 m. (37 fathoms). Strangely, this fish must have strayed many hundreds of miles from its home waters for later captures were made around the Comoro Archipelago, a group of islands NW. of Madagascar. Since the second one was captured here in December 1952, intensive publicity has produced nearly a hundred specimens, all caught on lines at depths of 150–400 m. (82–218 fathoms) by native fishermen, even though costly and imposing international expeditions have spent weeks attempting to capture one.

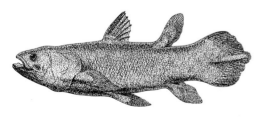

Latimeria is dark brown to blue in colour, with occasional light flecks on the scales. It is a heavy-bodied carnivorous fish, growing to a weight of about 90 kg. (200 lb.), most of the specimens captured by fishermen being taken on hooks baited with *Ruvettus*, the escolar or oil-fish. The body is excessively slimy, and contains copious quantities of oil, both in the body musculature and in the head.

Considerable controversy has existed amongst palaeontologists as to whether the fossil forms produced live young or laid eggs. Fossils containing the remains of young fish within their outline were held to be proof of viviparity, or in the opponent's view of cannibalism. It is not known how *Latimeria* breeds, but in January 1972 a large female of 1·93 m. (6 ft) was captured with 19 large eggs in the right ovary (the left is not developed). These eggs were 9 cm. (3½ in.) in diameter, and each weighed 320 gr. (11¼ oz.), they were wine red in colour and each was a spherical mass of yolk. Because there was no sign of a shell and only a thin membrane covered the egg it was suggested that the egg is probably laid in this condition and guarded by a parent. It seems, however, too much to believe that the coelacanth-line could have survived for so long with such low fecundity, and such an inefficient way of protecting the developing young. Because the male has no intromittent organ it has to be assumed that fertilization of the egg is external – but this is only assumption.

The coelacanth appears to live in the much creviced, nearly vertical rock and coral faced slope around the Comoros. The few living (or dying) fish that have been studied – none has yet succeeded in surviving capture by more than a few hours – are neutrally bouyant and make gentle sculling movements with their pectoral, pelvic, dorsal and anal fins. The pectoral fins are very mobile and the limbs on which the fin is placed enable them to twist, as well as move on their axes through 180°. No doubt when healthy the coelacanth uses these fins for precise manoeuvring while sprinting, as necessary, by sweeps of the large paddle-like tail. **501**

LATIMERIIDAE
The family that contains one species – the coelacanth *Latimeria chalumnae*, the only surviving species of the crossopterygian fishes. The coelacanths were once a very diverse and widespread group in both marine and freshwater habits. Fossil remains are known from rocks laid down in the Devonian (300 million years ago) through to the Upper Cretaceous (90 million years old) when they seemed to become extinct.

Latimeria is very like its fossil relatives. Except for the first dorsal, the fins are all set on a muscular, scale-covered limb, each with a solid skeletal base; the fin rays are set into the muscular lobe and are very different in appearance and structure from the normal rayed fin. There is a pair of bony gular plates between the halves of the lower jaw. The scales are large, overlap, and have very roughened surfaces. Internally its anatomy is of great interest. As had been deduced from fossil forms, the skull is hinged in 2 parts, but the notochord extends forward as far as the anterior section to which it is attached and for which it provides a supple joint to the cranium. The heart is of a very simple structure, the kidneys are ventral in position, while the intestine possesses a complex spiral valve. The swimbladder is not very large and is filled with fatty tissue, but it has an opening to the lower surface of the gullet, as in some lungfishes – its nearest living relatives. The centra, which in bony fishes make up the vertebral column, are absent and the only support for the body

is the large, gristly notochord which runs from the front of the head to the tail fin lobe. See **Latimeria.**

LATRIDAE
A small family of fishes found in the cool temperate seas of the S. Hemisphere. Most are moderate in size, and are potentially valuable food-fishes although only exploited locally at present.

In general, they are rather compressed, oval-bodied, with a long-based spiny dorsal fin which also contains many rays (over 23), and a many-rayed anal fin. Their closest relatives are the morwongs (family Cheilodactylidae) but they differ in having slender, but not elongate, unbranched rays in the lower pectoral fin. See **Latridopsis, Latris.**

Latridopsis   Latridae
    forsteri BASTARD TRUMPETER
61 cm. (2 ft)
An Australian species found on the coasts of S. Australia, Victoria, New South Wales, and Tasmania. It is found mainly offshore, but it is not very abundant in any one area, although occasional specimens are captured in nets when it comes inshore to spawn. Its flesh is rated as delicious.

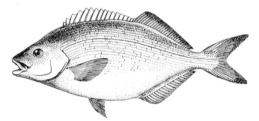

Its body is dark olive-green above, silvery below with a thin light yellow band along each row of scales.

It differs from the true Tasmanian trumpeter, *Latris lineata*, by having the upper pectoral rays longest and lacking teeth on the vomerine bone in the roof of the mouth.

Latris   Latridae
    lineata TASMANIAN TRUMPETER
102 cm. (40 in.)
Most abundant in Tasmanian waters, it also occurs in the offshore waters of S. Australia, Victoria, New South Wales, and New Zealand. It is found mainly along offshore reefs at considerable depths, but young fishes are caught in bays and estuaries.

It is considered to be one of the finest food fishes in Australian seas, and is fished for commercially in many areas. Large specimens may attain a weight of 27 kg. (60 lb.).

It is a silvery fish on the sides, with 3 lengthwise dark stripes on the back and upper sides, continuing forward on the head in broken lines and blotches.

LATTICED BUTTERFLYFISH see **Chaetodon rafflesii**
LEAF LATES see **Belontia signata**
LEAFFISH see Nandidae
LEAFFISH see **Monocirrhus polyacanthus**
LEAFFISH,
    AFRICAN see **Polycentropsis abbreviata**
    SCHOMBURGK'S see **Polycentrus schomburgkii**
LEAFY SEADRAGON see **Phycodurus eques**

Lebetus   Gobiidae
  scorpioides DIMINUTIVE GOBY
4 cm. ($1\frac{1}{2}$ in.)
The diminutive goby, as its name suggests, is a very small fish when adult, and has the distinction of being the smallest fish found in British seas. It ranges from the n. Bay of Biscay to Norway, the Faeroes, and s. Iceland, although it is known only from isolated areas within this range. It is found in a wide range of depths from 2–375 m. (1–206 fathoms), but is usually found offshore on coarse grounds especially those with calcareous algae coating the sea bed.

It is distinguished by its small size, by lacking an anterior membrane to the pelvic fins, and by the indentation of the rear margin of the pelvic disc.

Males are conspicuously different from females, the first dorsal fin being greatly enlarged, and dusky yellow edged with white, while the second dorsal fin has an intense black edge and yellow and white bands. Males are yellowish to brown, with reddish tinges ventrally. Females are greyish brown overall.

Lebiasina   Lebiasinidae
  bimaculata TWO-SPOT LEBIASINA
20 cm. (8 in.)
A slender-bodied freshwater fish found in the rivers, and pools of Peru, Ecuador, W. of the Andes. It is slim, with a rounded body anteriorly, rather small, rounded fins (except for the tail fin which is forked), and large scales. It has no adipose fin, although in some specimens a vestigial fin can be seen. It is delicately coloured, olive to light brown on the back, the sides light brown with a faint violet sheen, and the belly yellowish. The scales are reddish with darker edges. Two bright red spots, one on the shoulder and the other near the tail are distinctive.

It is a predatory fish, first eating insect larvae, but fishes only when adult. Despite this it is kept in captivity, but with larger fishes for company. It has a specially adapted swimbladder by which it can use atmospheric oxygen in the oxygen-depleted waters in which it lives.

LEBIASINIDAE
A group of mostly small fishes found in the freshwaters of Central and n. S. America. Most are rather slender-bodied, with rounded fins, and bright, usually striped, colour patterns. In general terms they are similar to rather elongate characins (Characidae) without the characteristic adipose fin (although a few members of the family have a minute adipose fin).

In their natural habitat they are surface-living fishes of small, slow-flowing or still, heavily weeded waters. They feed on surface-living insects, and most breed on leaves of plants only just submerged. One member actually lays its eggs on overhanging leaves and splashes them to keep them moist. Others are so wedded to the surface film that they hang at an angle in the water.

Many species in the family are popular aquarium fishes but despite this interest, the relationships within the family, and of the family to its relatives are not clearly understood. See **Copeina, Lebiasina, Nannostomus, Pyrrhulina.**

Leiocassius   Bagridae
  siamensis 18 cm. (7 in.)
An attractively coloured catfish from the rivers and streams of Thailand. It is widely distributed in that country and is occasionally captured low down rivers in brackish water. It is distinguished by its colouring which is dark brown with light, irregular cross-bands, one behind the head, another behind the dorsal fin, the third behind the adipose fin. The tail is clear, except that towards the end of each lobe there is a dark spot or bar.

In other respects it is a typical bagrid catfish with a large adipose fin, slender serrated spines in the pectoral and dorsal fins, a naked skin and moderate barbels. It is known to make a croaking sound, repeated several times, both when the fish is free as well as when captured. It is occasionally kept in aquaria.

LEIOGNATHIDAE
A family of rather small Indo-Pacific marine fishes which sometimes enter brackish or even fresh water in rivers.

They are deep-bodied, rather compressed fishes, and have extremely protrusible jaws which can be extended into a downward opening tube; the jaw teeth are usually small. The scales are minute and poorly developed over the head and breast; the skin gives off liberal quantities of mucus and these fishes are notoriously slimy (they are known as slimies or soapies in s. Africa).

Some members of the family have paired luminous glands at the base of the oesophagus, filled with light-producing bacteria. The body cavity is covered with silvery white tissue and reflects the light from these organs, so that the entire underside of the body glows. See **Leiognathus, Secutor.**

Leiognathus   Leiognathidae
  equula SLIMY, SOAPY 30 cm. (12 in.)
Widely distributed in the Indo-Pacific from the Pacific coast of Japan, the Philippines, the S. China Sea, the Indo-Australian archipelago to the Red Sea and the coast of E. Africa. It is very abundant throughout most of this range, and is widely used for food. It shoals in shallow inshore water and is thus relatively easy to catch in numbers.

The mouth, when closed is small and hori-

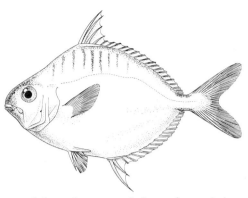

zontal, but when opened shoots forwards into a long downward-pointing tube. It is a silvery-sided fish, the back light brown, the fins grey.

Lemolyta   Anostomidae
  taeniata 25 cm. (10 in.)
A slender-bodied characin-like fish, with a small mouth, pointed head, rather cylindrical body, and a distinct anal fin. The mouth is tilted, so that it opens on the upper surface of the snout, an obvious adaptation to its habit of feeding on bottom-living organisms while swimming in a head-down attitude. The middle teeth of the lower jaw are flattened and sharp, and form a cutting edge.

Above it is deep brown, the sides lighter and yellowish brown on the belly with a bluish sheen. A dark brown stripe runs along the length of the fish from the tip of the snout to the base of the caudal fin, and 4 indistinct dark bars cross the back and run down to the lower sides. The fins are colourless.

It has been kept in captivity but it is not well-known as a pet fish. Its native range is in the middle Amazon basin in S. America.

Lepadogaster   Gobiesocidae
  lepadogaster SHORE CLINGFISH
6·5 cm. ($2\frac{1}{2}$ in.)
A relatively large clingfish found in the European coast from Scotland s. to the Mediterranean, the Canary Islands and Dakar on the African coast. It is distinguished by the rather pointed, 'duck-billed' snout, and by the deep body.

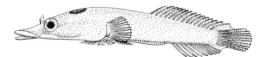

It is a bright rose pink, even reddish, although then usually brown blotched, with deeper red blotches on the snout and lips. There is a pair of deep blue eye spots with red margins on the back of the head.

The fish is locally abundant between tide marks, and is usually found clinging to the underside of rocks and boulders. It is most common near low-water mark, although also found below tide level. It spawns in summer, the rich golden eggs being fastened to the underside of a boulder, and guarded by one of the adults.

The power of adhesion of this fish's ventral sucker is remarkable considering its size. It can be quite difficult to dislodge, requiring considerable force on a straight pull. It was formerly known as the Cornish sucker.

Lepidocephalus   Cobitidae
thermalis 8 cm. (3 in.)
A loach which is found in the coastal districts of Malabar, India, and Sri Lanka. It inhabits slow flowing and still waters which are moderately shallow and have a soft bottom. In Sri Lanka it is found in pools up to an altitude of 490 m. (1600 ft), and also in pools fed by warm springs (hence its name – *thermalis*). It is frequently found buried in the bottom.

It is a slender-bodied loach, with a rather compressed body more so towards the tail. Its snout is blunt and rounded, and it has 4 pairs of longish barbels on the snout and around the mouth. The eyes are minute, covered with skin, and there is a small bifid spine beneath each eye.

This loach and other members of this Asiatic genus have been occasionally kept in aquaria.

Lepidocybium   Gempylidae
flavobrunneum ESCOLAR 1·8 m. (6 ft)
A curious fish, for long thought to be a rare scombroid but now placed amongst the gempylids. It was first described by Dr Andrew Smith (one of the earliest explorers of the South African fauna) in 1848. For many years it was thought to be confined to South Africa, but subsequently it has been reported from the N. Atlantic, the N. Pacific, and the S. Pacific, and is fairly certainly worldwide in tropical and warm temperate seas.

It is a torpedo-shaped fish with a short, low first dorsal fin, rather long second dorsal and anal, each succeeded by a series of finlets. It is a large fish attaining a weight of at least 45 kg. (100 lb.). Its biology is little known but it is presumed to live in mid-water, feeding actively on small fishes and squids. Its flesh is very oily. Light brown in colour when young, with age the escolar becomes almost black in colour.

Lepidopsetta   Pleuronectidae
bilineata ROCK SOLE 61 cm. (2 ft)
A species complex which in total lives in the N. Pacific from Korea and the Sea of Japan, the Okhotsk Sea, the Bering Sea, and down the e. coast from the Gulf of Alaska to s. California. Through this area several subspecies have been recognized. It lives in relatively shallow water, from a metre or two down to 183 m. (100 fathoms) but is most abundant between 37 and 73 m. (20–40 fathoms). It moves into deeper water in winter.

Its food consists of bottom-living invertebrates, sometimes exclusively the protuberant siphons of molluscs, and clams, shrimps, small crabs, brittle stars, and sand-eels. It is a rather slow-growing species taking 7 years to reach 28 cm. (11 in.). The oldest recorded fish was a female of 22 years at 52 cm. (20 in.); males live to 15 years and remain smaller (41 cm., 16 in.).

It is a highly prized food fish, and is the most important of all the small N. Pacific species.

It is commercially exploited throughout its range.

It is distinguished by its rough-edged scales on the eyed (right) side of the body, by the sharp curve in the lateral line, with a second branch running forward to the eyes and branching there.

Lepidopus   Trichiuridae
caudatus SCABBARDFISH, RIBBONFISH, FROSTFISH 203 cm. (80 in.)
Probably worldwide in distribution, although numerous synonyms exist for local populations. It is well known in the N. Atlantic in European waters and is commercially exploited off the Portuguese coast and s. It seems to be most abundant from the surface down to depths of 400 m. (219 fathoms). Locally where upwelling of deep water occurs this species is found in inshore waters and is sometimes stranded in numbers on the coast. This occurs seasonally in cool weather, the fish presumably becoming disorientated by the cold and stranding themselves; in New Zealand and South Africa it is often known as the frostfish for this reason.

Like its relatives it is long-bodied, with a pointed head and large teeth in the jaws. The dorsal fin is long, originating just behind the eyes and running to the tail fin, which is small but well developed. It is a brilliant silver in colour; large specimens have dark colouring on the dorsal fin and nape.

Its flesh is very good eating.

Lepidorhombus   Scophthalmidae
whiffiagonis MEGRIM, SAILFLUKE, WHIFF 61 cm. (2 ft)
The megrim is found along the Atlantic coast of Europe from s. Iceland, the Faeroes, and Scandinavia s. to Morocco, and in the w. Mediterranean. It is found in moderately deep water in depths of 50–300 m. (27–164 fathoms) although occasionally found in shallower water than this. It is most abundant on soft muddy bottoms. It feeds on a wide range of smaller fishes and crustaceans.

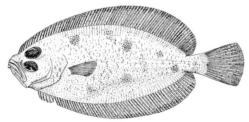

On the Atlantic coast of Europe it is very abundant and is fished for commercially. The flesh is palatable but rather dry, and inferior to that of the prime flatfishes.

Its curious scientific name commemorates a little-known Cornish naturalist of the 17th century, George Jago, who first described it as the whiff, Jago's whiff having been latinized as *whiffiagonis*. Its name sailfluke although little used today was given from the misapprehension of 19th century writers that this fish erected its tail vertically and using it as a sail allowed itself to be driven before the wind.

Lepidosiren   Lepidosirenidae
paradoxa SOUTH AMERICAN LUNGFISH 1·25 m. (50 in.)
Native to the region of central S. America, the

lungfish is found throughout much of the Paraná and Amazon river systems, but is most characteristic of the great swamps of the Chaco. It is typical of the shallow water swamplands and thickly weeded margins to lakes and rivers, areas which are seasonally flooded then become dry and parched.

The lungfish aestivates in these conditions, firstly by driving a deep burrow downwards at an angle into the mud of the swamp. As the water recedes the fish lives within the burrow gulping air at the surface, but with further fall in level it plugs the passage with pieces of mud, curls up with its tail over its head, and secretes a mucus covering around itself. Its body activities slow down but it continues to breathe air at a reduced rate. When rain falls and the area is again flooded it awakens, pushes out the mud plugs and becomes active again.

The ability to breathe atmospheric air also enables it to live in the often oxygen-deficient water of the swamps.

It spawns during the first weeks of the rainy season in a burrow in the swamp made by the male. The eggs are 6·5–7 mm. in diameter and are guarded by the male during incubation and after hatching. At this time the pelvic fins of the male develop much-branched, tree-like projections along their length, and they are richly supplied with blood vessels. This suggests that they have a respiratory function, but it has been argued that it could be needed to supply oxygen to the male during incubation, as well as to supply oxygen from the parent fish's bloodstream to the developing young. Clearly either could be possible, but the second suggestion sounds more probable.

The young have 4 pairs of feathery external gills just behind the head. The newly-hatched lungfish also has an adhesive ventral cement-gland by which it hangs suspended from vegetation. Both larval features are lost within 6–8 weeks, and at a length of about 4 cm. (1½ in.) the young fish can breathe air.

Lepidosiren is occasionally kept in aquaria, but its chief interest is zoological – it is hardly a showy fish. Its body is dark greyish brown, paler ventrally, occasionally with black spots. Young fish are dark brown to black in colour.

LEPIDOSIRENIDAE

The family containing a single species, the South American lungfish. The eel-like fish is found over a large area of the Amazon and Paraná basins in central S. America living mainly in the swamps and densely weeded areas. As it name suggests, it possesses a pair of lung-like sacs beneath the oesophagus but connecting with it. Living as it does in poorly oxygenated water, the lung-fish supplements the oxygen obtained through its gills by gulping air every minute or so at the surface.

Like other lungfishes it has a mainly cartilaginous skeleton, the nostrils are ventral, one of each pair opening on the inside of the lip, while the teeth are fused into a number of sharp bony plates.

The South American lungfish is related to the African species (which were formerly put in this family). It is, however, more elongate and eel-like, the body cylindrical anteriorly, compressed towards the tail. The scales are very small, and the pectoral and pelvic fins short and like stubby feelers.

The occurrence of related lungfishes in both S. America and Africa (as well as other groups such as characins, cichlids, etc.) is one of the pieces of evidence suggesting that the 2 continents were at one time joined together. See **Lepidosiren.**

LEPISOSTEIDAE

A family of N. American freshwater fishes which are often spoken of as 'living fossils' as the group was clearly more widely distributed at one time, and the living representatives show many primitive features. They are distinguished by their very elongate bodies, and thick, almost diamond-shaped ganoid scales. All have long beak-like jaws well endowed with teeth, the dorsal and anal fins are placed well back near the tail, and the tail-fin is heterocercal (the body turning upwards to form the upper lobe). The members of the family are usually called gars or garpikes. See **Lepisosteus.**

Lepisosteus   Lepisosteidae
osseus LONGNOSE GAR 1·5 m. (5 ft)
The longnose gar is found in freshwater from Quebec to Florida, and in the W. from the Great Lakes to n. Mexico. Adults are frequently found in brackish water in the S. of its range, and are less often found in the sea.

It is distinguished from the other gars by its very long, narrow snout. In colour it is generally olive-brown above and white below, but often has dark blotches on the body and fins. The young are relatively brightly coloured with a broad brown band along the sides and a reddish brown or cinnamon interrupted stripe above it. They also have a similar dark stripe along the back.

Like all gars, the longnose gar hangs still in the water hidden by vegetation, and waits for its prey to come within striking distance. Then with a sudden thrust it takes its prey crosswise in its mouth, often holding it that way for several minutes. It feeds on a large variety of fishes as well as crustaceans. Its predatory habits make it an unloved fish amongst fishermen generally, and it incidentally causes a good deal of damage to nets if it becomes entangled in them. Although its flesh can be eaten, it is not much favoured now, but the eggs are poisonous.

The longnose gar, like the other gars, spawns in freshwater in the late spring. Each female is accompanied by up to 4 males, and large numbers congregate in the shallows, splashing in the water. The eggs are sticky and adhere to the substrate, weeds or stones. Development is completed quickly, but the newly hatched young at first attach themselves to objects on or above the bottom by means of an adhesive sucker on the ventral surface of the snout. Once the yolk sac is absorbed, however, they become very active predators on the smaller crustaceans. **18**

L. platostomus SHORTNOSE GAR
76 cm. (30 in.)
A garpike which is widely distributed in the larger rivers of the Mississippi drainage and is thus present through most of the e. central states of the U.S. from the Gulf of Mexico n. but not on the Atlantic coast. It is most abundant in lowland lakes, oxbows, and backwaters of rivers, but some live in the still waters of pools in rivers. It tends to live in clear water, although sometimes found in silty areas, but it does not usually inhabit densely weeded areas.

It is olive-brown or yellowish above with a little mottling on the body, and but few dark spots which are confined to the tail and tail fin.

It is distinguished by its elongate shape, smooth scales, long snout, and moderately large teeth. It differs from other gars by having a broad snout and in lacking dark spots on the underside of the body. **18**
L. tristoechus see under **L. spatula**
L. spatula ALLIGATOR GAR 3 m. (10 ft)
The alligator gar is frequently found in salt, or semi-saline water from Florida along the coast of the Gulf of Mexico. It also occurs in freshwater in these regions and in the Mississippi River from the Ohio and Missouri rivers s.

It is a voracious predator eating large numbers of fishes, including several of commercial and sporting value, and large specimens are credited with taking ducks and waterfowl at the surface. It is itself commercially exploited in local fisheries around New Orleans, and its scales were used by Indians for jewelry.

It spawns in April through to June in the Louisiana region, but little is known about the development and growth of this species. It was at one time believed to occur in the Caribbean islands of Cuba, but recent studies have shown that the population in the freshwaters of that island belong to a separate species, *L. tristoechus*.

The alligator gar is distinguished by its large size, and broad, short snout. In colour it is usually a dark olive-brown, white to yellowish beneath. According to their size they have a variable number of spots on the fins, back, and sides.

Lepomis   Centrarchidae
cyanellus GREEN SUNFISH 20 cm. (8 in.)
Widely distributed through central N. America from s. Canada and N. Dakota to the Atlantic coast, and s. to Mexico and Georgia. It typically inhabits the smaller creeks, brooks and ponds of this area. In addition, it has been widely introduced in America outside its natural range.

It spawns in late spring and early summer between patches of vegetation on sand or fine gravel bottoms. Males and females pair off and excavate a 30 cm. (12 in.) wide depression, 6–8 cm. (2¼–3 in.) deep. In this the eggs are laid and stoutly defended by the male. Fishes

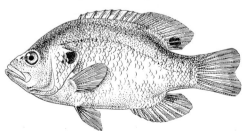

of this species feed mostly on aquatic insects, but will also eat young fishes.

A rather deep-bodied little fish with a dark spot on the bony edge of the gill cover. A dusky spot on the hind end of the soft dorsal fin.

L. gibbosus PUMPKINSEED 20 cm. (8 in.)
Found in N. America from s. Canada, the Great Lakes, and N. Dakota, E. to the Atlantic coast, and S. to Texas and Florida. It has been introduced to many parts of N. America including rivers on the W. Coast. Similarly it has been introduced to Europe, and is firmly esablished in central and w. Europe; a few isolated populations exist in England.

Its brilliance accounts for its popularity as an aquarium fish; this, in turn, has led to its wide distribution throughout Europe. As an angling species it is too small to have much appeal, except to the juvenile angler. It attains a weight of about 312 g. (11 oz.).

It is typically an inhabitant of quiet clear water, in brooks and ponds, especially those with an abundance of vegetation. It eats mostly snails and aquatic insects but is likely to eat almost any small water-living animal, including the fry of more valuable (to the angler) species.

It spawns in late spring, between patches of vegetation where the bottom is sandy in shallow water. The male builds a shallow nest about 30 cm. (12 in.) in diameter and 5–7 cm. (2–3 in.) deep in the middle in which the eggs are laid. He defends and guards the eggs and fry, until the latter are. well grown and can scatter. **277**

L. gulosus WARMOUTH 20 cm. (8 in.)
A small sunfish which is widely distributed in freshwater in the e. states of the U.S., from the Great Lakes s. to Georgia, Texas, and Alabama, and W. to Iowa and Kansas. It is a shallow-water species found on muddy bottoms in ponds, lakes, and slow-flowing lowland streams and is known locally as the mud sunfish.

Although it will take a baited hook freely, and will fight well, it is not an angler's fish, nor is it much used for food. It makes an attractive, though modestly coloured, aquarium fish. The large head and particularly the mouth are distinctive. **274**
L. macrochirus BLUEGILL 36 cm. (14 in.)
Found in the central part of N. America, from the Great Lakes s. through the Mississippi River basin to n. Mexico, and from the Carolinas W. to the Dakotas and Colorado. It is widely distributed and found in all lakes, ponds and quiet streams, with abundant vegetation. Its food consists mainly of aquatic invertebrates particularly insects; the larger specimens also eat small fishes.

They breed from May to July, the male building a saucer-shaped nest 23–30 cm. (9–12 in.) wide in a firm bottom close to the shore at a depth of 0·3–1·2 m. (1–4 ft). The eggs are adhesive, stick to the exposed stones, and they and later the fry are guarded by the male. Females may spawn at several nests.

It has the typical deep body of the sunfishes, covered with moderately large scales. Adults are olive-green above, the sides bluish, the belly white (males in spawning season are yellowish or rosy). Dark bars across the sides. The gill covers and cheeks are bluish, and the flap on the gill cover is intense black.

The bluegill is a good sporting fish despite its relatively small size (maximum weight about 1 kg., 2½ lb.). It is also a good food fish. The combination has resulted in its being widely distributed both within and outside its native range. It now is found in Rhodesia and s. Africa. **278**

L. megalotis LONGEAR SUNFISH 20 cm. (8 in.) Widely distributed in central N. America, from Canada to n. Mexico; it is found from Michigan and Minnesota s. to S. Carolina. It is found in most small streams and especially clear brooks.

Its colouring is very variable. The most notable feature is the large 'ear-flap' at the upper edge of the gill cover, which in adults is very long, the centre deep black and the edges golden green.

A popular aquarium fish in both America and Europe. Small specimens are most suitable, the large ones being rather quarrelsome. **279**

Leporinus   Anostomidae
   affinis BOGA 25 cm. (10 in.)
Leporinus affinis is widely distributed in n. S. America from the Rio Paraná, through the Amazon Basin, the Paraguay system, and the Orinoco. It is one of the typical headstanders, usually found adopting a near-vertical head-down attitude in the aquarium.

Its most striking character is the pointed head, with extensible jaws, but a small mouth and very few teeth. The lips are fleshy. Its coloration is very distinctive.

It is a fish of gravelly bottomed, rather slow-flowing streams. It is a plant-eater, and a peaceful aquarium fish. **99**

L. nigrotaeniatus MIERI 20 cm. (8 in.) A widely spread species in Guyana and the neighbouring parts of S. America. This species lives in rivers, particularly inhabiting rock pools and areas around rocks in fast-flowing reaches.

As an adult it is a rather plainly coloured fish. The young are boldly marked with dark bars across the back, a line of intense spots along the side from the head back to the level of the pelvic fins, and a dark line on the midline of the tail. Its body form is typical of this group, being slender, with a small mouth and minute adipose fin. **100**

Leptagonus   Agonidae
   decagonus 21 cm. (8¼ in.)
A poacher which is circumpolar in its distribution although best known in the N. Atlantic around Greenland, n. Iceland, and the Norwegian and White Seas. It has been reported in the Arctic N. Pacific. It is found in moderately deep water, from 120–350 m. (66–191 fathoms) and in the far N. to 915 m. (500 fathoms). It inhabits muddy or sandy-mud bottoms, where it feeds on small crustaceans and worms. Bathypelagic copepod crustaceans are also said to be eaten, which suggests that it rises above the sea bed to feed on occasions.

It is distinguished by its deep water habits, by the extreme slenderness of its body and the long tail.

Leptobarbus   Cyprinidae
   hoevenii 51 cm. (20 in.)
A river fish of Sumatra and Borneo, it is also widely distributed in the great central plain of Thailand, and the Mekong basin.

Its coloration is modestly beautiful. Young fish have a distinct dark line running along the sides from head to tail.

Young fish make excellent aquarium fish, being peaceful and relatively easy to keep. In Thailand it has achieved some fame as an angler's fish, being taken on baits such as prawn, paste, or simply vegetation, and fighting when hooked. As a food fish it is not highly esteemed, although occasionally eaten, but at times its flesh is said to be poisonous. The Thais know it as *pla ba* (mad fish) for when the fruit of the chaulmoogra-tree (*Hynocarpus*) ripen and fall into the streams, they are avidly eaten by the fish which is said to become intoxicated and behave in a peculiar fashion. **129**

Leptocephalus see under Anguillidae,
   Conger conger
Leptocephalus telescopicus see
   Nettodarus brevirostris

Leptoderma   Alepocephalidae
   macrops 19·5 cm. (7¾ in.)
This is a very long, slender-bodied smooth-head, with a long anal fin, and a rather shorter dorsal fin. The snout is short, the eye large, and the mouth is rather small. It is scaleless, the body being covered with a smooth, velvety black skin which is very fragile and usually badly torn when captured by nets.

It has been found only in the e. Atlantic, from off N. Africa, the Canary Islands, and the Biscay area, mainly at depths of 1000–2000 m. (546–1092 fathoms). It has, however, been captured as deep as 2330 m. (1272 fathoms). Its biology is little known.

LEPTOSCOPIDAE

A family of small fishes found in the cooler waters of Australia and New Zealand. The family contains only 3–4 species. They are all rather slender-bodied with broad, blunted heads and wide lateral mouths, the lips being fringed with small skin flaps. Scales are present over the whole body and long-based dorsal and anal fins. See **Crapatulus.**

LESSER
   BUTTERFLY RAY see **Gymnura micrura**
   ELECTRIC RAY see **Narcine brasiliensis**
   SPOTTED DOGFISH see **Scyliorhinus
      canicula**
   WEEVER see **Trachinus vipera**

Lestidium   Paralepididae
   atlanticum *c.* 19 cm. (7½ in.)
This elongate fish is typical of its family in general body shape. It is long, and very slender with a moderately long head. Its fins are small, except for the anal fin which has many rays; it has a distinct adipose fin. The teeth in the upper jaw are small to moderate, but the lower jaw has a number of very strong, long, straight teeth as well as some shorter curved ones. In life it is believed to be translucent. It has a single, elongate, internal luminous duct running along the belly.

This species is found in the open sea, from the surface down to 100 m. (55 fathoms) al-

though it has been found deeper. It is probably the most common of the barracudinas in the open ocean. It is circumtropical in the 3 major oceans, although least common in the e. Pacific and Atlantic oceans.

Like its relatives it is an active predator.

LETHRINIDAE

A relatively small family containing some 20 species of marine fishes found in the tropical Indo-Pacific, with a single species on the W. coast of Africa. They are very abundant on coral reefs and inshore waters, and the larger species are important food fishes.

In general the scavengers or emperors, as they are known, resemble the grunts (Pomadasyidae). They have 10 strong spines in the first dorsal fin which is continuous with the second, and 3 spines in the anal. They are most easily distinguished by their long snouts and deep scaleless cheeks, with moderate canine-like teeth in the front of the jaws. See **Lethrinus.**

Lethrinus   Lethrinidae
   chrysostomus SWEETLIP EMPEROR
91 cm. (3 ft)
A very abundant fish on the n. coast of Australia, and the commonest emperor of the Great Barrier Reef. It is found mainly on the coral on patches between reefs, small fishes in schools, the large ones being solitary. It is a valuable food and sporting fish, large numbers being taken on lines. It grows to a weight of 9 kg. (20 lb.). It is said to be one of the finest food fishes in the area.

Its coloration is very striking; the back is dark brown, the sides light grey but barred by extensions of brown from the back colouring. There is an intense blood red patch between and around the eyes, and a scarlet line from the corner of the mouth. The fins are mostly deep red. It has the typical long, scaleless snout and cheeks of the family.

L. miniatus LONG-NOSED EMPEROR,
SCAVENGER, MATA-HARI 91 cm. (3 ft)
Widely distributed throughout the Indian Ocean from the Red Sea and E. African coast to India and the E. Indies. Also found in the Pacific on the N. Australian coast and the w. Pacific islands. It is common on coral reefs down to a depth of 30 m. (17 fathoms), and is captured mainly on hook and line. It is a valuable food fish throughout its range.

It is a distinctive species, long-bodied with a long, pointed snout and deep cheeks. The mouth is moderate with sharp canine-like teeth in the sides of the jaws. Its colouring is olive-green, a reddish brown blotch on the edge of the gill cover, inside of the mouth orange. Fins pinkish with light bands.

L. nebulosus SPANGLED EMPEROR,
SCAVENGER, MATA-HARI 76 cm. (30 in.)
A wide-ranging fish in the Indo-Pacific from the Red Sea and E. African coast, India, the E. Indies, n. Australia, and the w. Pacific

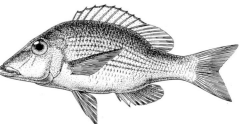

islands. It lives equally abundantly on and around coral reefs and more open waters. It is an extremely valuable food fish throughout its range being captured mostly on lines, but also in gill nets and trawls.

It is also a beautifully coloured fish, basically greeny brown on the back, fading to silvery on the belly, with each scale picked out with a pale blue spot forming regular but broken rows. The head is dull violet, the cheeks with blue spots and 3 light-blue bands radiating from the eye. The fin membranes are pink with scattered pale blue spots; the pelvic fins are yellowish.

Leucaspius   Cyprinidae
delineatus MODERLIESCHEN 12 cm. (5 in.)
The moderlieschen is widely distributed across central and e. Europe from the German and Danish rivers to the Caspian Sea. It is a small, very silvery fish with a distinct iridescent line along its sides. Its mouth is oblique and its eye large; it is distinguished from the bleak, *Alburnus alburnus,* which it closely resembles, by having a short anal fin and an incomplete lateral line of 7–13 scales.

It is a shoaling fish found in rivers, ponds, and small lakes, in which it feeds on planktonic organisms, flying insects, and it is said, algae. It spawns in summer, the female winding her string of eggs spirally around the stems of water plants. It is said that the male guards the eggs.

It is a particularly suitable fish for the aquarium and achieves some popularity in Europe for this purpose. Its scales have been used in the preparation of artificial pearls.

Leuciscus   Cyprinidae
cephalus CHUB 61 cm. (2 ft)
The chub is an European freshwater fish found mainly in rivers and streams. It is widely distributed from British rivers, across Europe to the w. Caspian Sea. It is found in rivers along the European Mediterranean seaboard. It is a shoaling fish when young, but medium and large specimens are very shy and solitary. Although it is found mostly in rivers, the chub will live and even thrive in lakes; in the Baltic it tolerates water of low salinity.

Its food is composed of insect larvae, worms, molluscs, and much plant material. Larger chub eat larger food items including fishes, crayfish, and even occasional items like frogs.

It breeds from April to June, at which time males have small white tubercles scattered over their heads. The eggs are relatively small and stick to weeds and stones amongst which they are shed.

The chub is a heavy-looking fish, elongate but cylindrical in form, and with a large broad head. In colour it is dark greeny grey on the back, silvery on the sides with each scale edged darker giving it a network appearance. The underside is off white; the ventral fins pinkish.

The chub is a fine sporting fish. The size and the immense caution of large specimens making them a prize for only the finest angler. As if to compensate for this they are so incredibly bony that they are impossible to eat.

L. idus IDE, ORFE 60 cm. (2 ft)
The ide is widely distributed in Europe, from Germany, Denmark and the Baltic basin across almost to Siberian rivers. It extends s. to the region of the n. Black Sea and Caspian Sea

basins. It lives mainly in rivers, although some populations live in large lakes, and frequently is found in brackish water near the river mouth.

Its food consists mainly of insect larvae, adult insects, and bottom-living invertebrates such as snails and crustaceans. Large specimens are fish eaters. It is found in shallow water, but large fish frequent deep areas; most of the population migrates to deep water in winter. It spawns in stony beds in March to April, in shallow water, with a great deal of splashing and leaping. The eggs are adhesive and stick to vegetation and stones, to hatch in 10–20 days; the adults migrate into deep water as soon as spawning is finished.

Orfe are noted for their golden colour, and are particularly popular as ornamental fish in garden ponds and public park lakes. They are susceptible to very cold weather. The normal silvery form especially in e. Europe and the U.S.S.R. is a valuable commercial fish, being caught in seines, and floating gill nets. It is said to be tasty to eat. **130**

L. leuciscus DACE 30 cm. (12 in.)
The dace is widely distributed through the freshwaters of n. Europe and n. Asia; its range extends virtually from Ireland (where it was introduced) across to Siberia, and from Swedish rivers to the S. of France. It is essentially a river fish, living in cool running water, and less often lakes. It spawns in streams just below a riffle on sandy or pebbly bottoms from March to May, and is one of the earliest spawning of European cyprinids. The shoals of mature fish gather on the spawning beds a few days before they spawn, and the eggs are washed down into the gravel when they are shed.

It feeds on a wide range of insect larvae, crustaceans, worms, and plants, and takes many flying insects. This habit makes it susceptible to the angler's fly, and dace can give good sport on the right tackle. It is a shoaling fish although the larger specimens tend to be rather solitary.

It is a slender-bodied fish which in some respects resembles both the roach and the chub. The most certain means of distinguishing it from a chub of the same size is by the free edge of the anal fin, concave in the dace, convex in the chub. **131**

Leuresthes   Atherinidae
tenuis CALIFORNIA GRUNION
18 cm. (7 in.)
Found only along the coast of California from Monterey Bay to San Juanico Bay, Baja California. It is found in inshore waters usually in shallows, but at spawning time it is actually found on the shore. The spawning begins in

February or March and continues to late August or early September. The females spawn between 4–8 times a season. The spawning fish strand themselves on the high spring tides at night on sandy shores high up the intertidal zone burying the fertilized eggs in the moist sand, and being carried back to the sea on the next high wave. The eggs remain buried in the sand for 10 days or so when the next high

tides uncover them and they hatch out, the young being swept into the water. The eggs will remain viable for up to a month, should the first spring high tide fail to cover them.

The spawning is communal and an impressive sight. The spawning grunion attract predators to the shore, and throughout their lives remain prey to a variety of larger animals, including man. Sport fishermen are permitted to catch grunion only by hand which limits catches but clearly adds to the spice of the occasion, undertaken as it is at night by the light of the moon and a torch.

The grunion is a slender fish with a conspicuous silvery stripe down each side. Its jaws are toothless.

LEVOVANGAN see **Monotaxis grandoculis**

Limanda   Pleuronectidae
aspera YELLOWFIN SOLE 45 cm. (17¾ in.)
Native to the N. Pacific, the yellowfin sole is found in the Okhotsk Sea and along the Asian coast, in the Bering Sea and on the American coast s. to British Columbia. In the Bering Sea it is the most abundant flatfish. Here, as elsewhere, it lives from 20–90 m. (11–50 fathoms) although occasionally found deeper.

It is distinguished, like other members of this genus, by its strongly arched lateral line above the pectoral fin, and by the toothed scales on the body. It is light brown with darker mottling and faint dark streaks on the fins on the right (eyed side), while the blind side is white.

In the Bering Sea, and along the Asian coast this fish is fished for commercially. On the N. American coast it is not so exploited (possibly because it is less common), but its flesh is of good quality.

L. ferruginea YELLOWTAIL FLOUNDER,
RUSTY DAB 60 cm. (2 ft)
A w. N. Atlantic species which is confined to the continental shelf between Labrador, the Gulf of St Lawrence, the Newfoundland banks to Chesapeake Bay. It is most abundant in depths of 37–73 m. (20–40 fathoms), but occurs between 9 and 109 m. (5–60 fathoms), and is always found on sandy, or mixed sand and mud bottoms. It feeds mainly on small crustaceans, molluscs, worms, and occasionally small fishes.

It is a relatively valuable commercial fish, large numbers being taken off the Canadian coast in otter trawls and marketed fresh or frozen. Its flesh is tasty.

Like other members of the family, its eyes are on the right side of the head. The body is oval and the head is small, with moderately small terminal mouth. Like the European dab, *L. limanda,* the lateral line is arched over the pectoral fin and the scales on the eyed side are distinctly rough to the touch.

It is brownish olive with many irregularly spaced reddish spots, the left (blind) side is white with yellow marks at tail and fins.

L. limanda DAB 38 cm. (15 in.)
A European species of flatfish, the dab is widely distributed from the White Sea s. to Biscay, around Iceland and in the w. Baltic Sea. It is enormously abundant in inshore waters on sandy bottoms, although it is also found on mud and fine gravel. It is found from the shore line down to depths of about 150 m. (82 fathoms) although it is probably most

abundant in 20–40 m. (11–22 fathoms). It also migrates seasonally, the larger fish moving inshore in spring and summer, and offshore with the first frosts of autumn. It spawns in spring, the eggs being planktonic, and the larvae drift widely in surface currents until they change to the adult form and life style at about 2 cm. (¾ in.).

The dab's food is very varied but crustaceans form the greatest quantity, although worms, molluscs, and fishes are eaten.

It can be distinguished from all other European flatfishes by having both eyes on the right side of the head, a relatively small mouth, a lateral line which is strongly curved above the pectoral fin. The scales are small, but those on the eyed side are finely toothed and always feel rough. The underside is white.

The dab is an important commercial fish in Europe. Although its small size is a disadvantage and its rough scales mean it has to be skinned to be eaten, its flesh (when fresh) is the sweetest of all flatfishes. It is mainly captured by local inshore trawling and shore seines. **467**

LIMNICHTHYIDAE

A family of small tropical Indo-Pacific fishes. They are little known in general.

The members of the family have long, slender bodies with large scales, long dorsal and anal fins placed about mid-way along the body. The snout is acute, fleshy and overlaps the lower jaw.

According to some authors this family could well be lumped with the Creediidae, Trichonotidae, and others. See **Limnichthys.**

Limnichthys   Limnichthyidae
fasciatus 3 cm. (1¼ in.)
Known only from the coasts of New South Wales and Lord Howe Island. This small fish is very likely to be a burrower in sand but its biology has not been recorded.

It is distinguished from *L. donaldsoni*, its only congener by having more rays in the dorsal fin (25–26) and anal fin (27–29) than that species.

LINED SILVER-BIDDY see **Gerres oyena**
LING see **Genypterus blacodes, Molva molva**
LINGCOD see **Ophiodon elongatus**

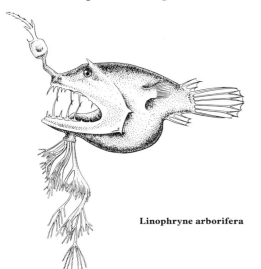

Linophryne arborifera

Linophryne   Linophrynidae
arborifera 7 cm. (3 in.)
A striking anglerfish with a quite unmistakable much-branched, long chin barbel. The illicium on the snout which bears the luminous lure is swollen and branched at its tip. The stout, rounded body, huge jaws and big teeth are also characteristic. Larval females are rounded, covered in a loose skin with moderately large jaws. Larval males have been rarely described, those that have are rather slender, with smaller jaws, and very large nostrils. Adult males are unknown, but are believed to be parasitic.

This angler has been captured in the Atlantic, Pacific, and Indian oceans; a relatively small number of specimens have been captured in depths of 100–3000 m. (54–1660 fathoms).

LINOPHRYNIDAE

A large family of deep-sea anglerfishes. Most have stout, rounded bodies, are dark coloured, have a distinct illicium (fishing rod with a lure) on the snout, many have a well-developed chin barbel. Jaws are large and teeth big and fanglike. Adult males are parasitic on the females, their eyes and olfactory organs degenerating. The members of this family have the anus displaced from the midline to the left side.

Worldwide in their distribution in the major deep oceans. See **Borophryne, Eridolychnus, Linophryne.**

Liopempheris   Pempheridae
multiradiata COMMON BULLSEYE
20 cm. (8 in.)
An Australian species found in the waters of all states and very common in many places. It lives mainly in shallow water close to rocky reefs and is found in large shoals.

Its body form is typical of the family, deep in front and compressed, with a large eye, moderate oblique mouth, and very long anal fin. The body is covered with large, fragile, smooth-edged scales. It is purplish or metallic blue above, silvery below, with numerous lengthwise light stripes running along the sides.

Liopsetta   Pleuronectidae
putnami SMOOTH FLOUNDER
30 cm. (12 in.)
The smooth flounder is found on the e. coast of N. America. It occurs from Ungava Bay, along the Labrador and Newfoundland coasts, s. to Maine and Providence, Rhode Island. It is a coastal and inshore species, often found in estuaries and river mouths, almost always on soft muddy bottoms. Found from the shoreline, it lives as deep as 27 m. (15 fathoms). Its range, both geographical and bathymetric, means that it is exposed to temperatures below freezing in winter.

Its small mouth dictates a diet of small, bottom-living organisms. It is known to feed on amphipods and small molluscs, small crabs, shrimps, and also worms.

It is not heavily exploited by commercial fisheries. Its habit of living in shallow water means that most of the catch is made by local, shore-seine fisheries. Its flesh is said to be of excellent quality, but it grows only to a weight of about 0·7 kg. (1½ lb.).

Liparis   Cyclopteridae
liparis SEA SNAIL 18 cm. (7 in.)
Found in the E. Atlantic, from the English Channel n. to the Arctic (including the Baltic), and around Iceland. A related species, often named as *L. liparis*, occurs in Greenland, from Alaska and the Arctic Ocean down the Canadian coast to the region of Virginia. It lives in the immediately sub-tidal region to depths of 183 m. (100 fathoms); in northern parts of its range it is found on the shore line. It breeds in mid-winter, the eggs being laid amongst hydroid growths on the sea bed, and on stony ground. Its food is mainly small crustaceans, particularly shrimps, but occasionally small fishes are eaten.

Its skin is loose and gelatinous. Its colour varies remarkably, usually the background colour is greenish or brown, with individual variations of stripes, spots, and bars.

LIPOGENYIDAE

A family of spiny eels, differing from the notacanths and the halosaurs sufficiently to be recognized as a distinct family. Only one species is known and that found in the w. N. Atlantic at considerable depths. Basically possessing the same body shape as its relatives, it has a long body with a long anal fin running from vent to tail tip, and composed of spines and soft rays. The dorsal fin, however, is composed of 10 elements, the first 5 spines, each longer than the last, and all joined together and to the succeeding 5 soft rays. See **Lipogenys.**

Lipogenys   Lipogenyidae
gillii 43 cm. (17 in.)
This fish is similar, and clearly closely related to the halosaurs. It was described in 1896 from a specimen captured at a depth of 1582 m. (865 fathoms) in the n. W. Atlantic by the U.S. research steamer *Albatross*.

The small toothless mouth with thick lips, and short dorsal fin with 5 graduated spines in the front of the fin set it apart from its relatives. The mouth parts are particularly noteworthy appearing to be suctorial with roughened contractile lips, flanked by wing-like flaps. Its colour is a uniform light brown, while the underside of the gill covers are dark. Nothing is known of its biology.

Lithognathus   Sparidae
lithognathus WHITEFISH, WHITE STEENBRAS, PIGNOSE GRUNTER 1·8 m. (6 ft)
A fish confined to the seas of South Africa and found on all coasts in the area. It haunts sandy areas, going into shallow lagoons in search of food buried in the sand. The late Professor J. L. B. Smith reported that when they enter such shallow water their tails could be seen waving above the surface as they rooted for animals in the sand. Feeds by blowing a jet of

water onto burrows to expose the animals inside.

This very large seabream is a prized sporting fish; it takes most baits, fights vigorously and swims at great speed. It weighs 14 kg. (30 lb.) and more, and is a fine food fish.

It is a rather slender-bodied fish, with a distinctive long snout which gives the head a pointed look. The lips are very thick. The body silvery with 7 wide cross-bars in juveniles.

LITTLE
    SCULPIN see **Myoxocephalus aeneus**
    SKATE see **Raja erinacea**
    TUNA see **Euthynnus alletteratus**
LIVEBEARING SCULPIN see **Comephorus baicalensis**
LIVEBEARER,
    KNIFE see **Alfaro cultratus**
    ONE-SIDED see **Jenynsia lineata**
    ONE-SPOT see **Phalloceros caudimaculatus**
    TEN-SPOTTED see **Cnesterodon decemmaculatus**
LIZARDFISH see Synodontidae
LIZARDFISH see **Saurida undosquamis, Trachinocephalus myops**
LIZARDFISH,
    CALIFORNIA see **Synodus lucioceps**
    DEEP-SEA see **Bathysaurus mollis**
    RED see **Synodus synodus**

Lo   Siganidae
  vulpinus FOX-FACE 23 cm. (9 in.)
A widely distributed species in the w. Pacific, having been recorded from the E. Indies, the Queensland coast of Australia, the Philippines, and parts of the Central Pacific.

This species is externally the most surgeon-fish-like of all the rabbitfishes and differs from the latter most notably in having the snout elongated into a short tube. The front of the head is concave. Its colouring is distinctive; the upper part of the body, the dorsal and tail fins and the anal fin are deep orange, while the remainder of the body is clear yellow. A black band runs from the dorsal fin forwards to cover most of the face and breast to the pelvic fins.

It is locally common in some areas browsing on algae at the base of coral formations.

Some authors place this species in the genus *Siganus* on the grounds that *S. corallinus* is intermediate between *vulpinus* and other *Siganus* species. However, the external appearance of *L. vulpinus* is so strikingly different from the numerous *Siganus* species that it is best distinguished from them.

LOACH see Cobitidae
LOACH see **Acanthopsis choirorhynchos**
LOACH,
    CLOWN see **Botia macracantha**
    COOLIE see **Acanthophthalmus kuhlii**
    HALF-BANDED COOLIE see **Acanthophthalmus semicinctus**
    HORA'S CLOWN see **Botia horae**
    POND see **Misgurnus fossilis**
    SPINED see **Cobitis taenia**
    STONE see **Noemacheilus barbatulus**
LOACH-GOBY see **Rhyacichthys aspro**

Lobotes   Lobotidae
  surinamensis TRIPLE-TAIL
100 cm. (39 in.)

Worldwide in tropical and warm temperate seas. In the Atlantic it is found from New England and Bermuda to Argentina, including the Caribbean and the Gulf of Mexico, also in the Mediterranean and adjacent Atlantic S. to s. Africa.

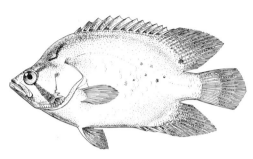

Throughout this large range it seems to be nowhere common. The adults are described as sluggish fishes frequenting coastal waters and entering muddy creeks. They grow to a large size, and a maximum weight of around 14 kg. (30 lb.). However, when trapped in a net it is said to jump wildly which may have led to its being locally known as 'jumping cod', in parts of the Australian coast.

Young triple-tails, by contrast, are relatively common and well known. They are found in shallow water inshore where they have been seen to mimic floating mangrove leaves, drifting at the surface in a gently curved posture with the head slightly lower than the tail. They are also frequently found in floating sargassum weed, which suggests that they are common offshore.

Its coloration is very variable. It is usually dull brown overall, but occasional pale specimens have been reported. Young fishes have pale margins to the vertical fins.

The name triple-tail refers to the very large lobes of the dorsal and anal fins, making it appear to have 3 tails.

LOBOTIDAE

A small family of tropical marine fishes which contains 2 genera with 1 and 2 species. Some doubt exists as to whether the second of these, *Datnoides*, is not in fact a member of the families Theraponidae or Nandidae.

The triple-tail, the only other member of the family, is a large sea-bass-like fish with a broad heavy body, covered with small scales. The dorsal fin is continuous and has 12-13 strong spines; the anal fin has 3 spines. See **Datnoides, Lobotes.**

LOGFISH see **Hyperoglyphe perciforma**
LONG
    ROUGH DAB see **Hippoglossoides platessoides**
    TONGUE-SOLE see **Cynoglossus lingua**
LONG-FIN, BLUE-SPOTTED see **Plesiops nigricans**
LONG-FINNED
    CHARACIN see **Alestes longipinnis**
    EEL, AFRICAN see **Anguilla mossambica**
    EEL, INDIAN see **Anguilla nebulosa**
    TUNNY see **Thunnus alalunga**
LONG-JAWED MACKEREL see **Rastrelliger kanagurta**
LONG-NOSED
    BATFISH see **Ogcocephalus vespertillo**
    CHIMAERA see **Harriotta raleighana**
    EMPEROR see **Lethrinus miniatus**

LONG-SNOUTED
    DOGFISH see **Deania quadrispinosa**
    FLOUNDER see **Ammotretis rostratus**
LONG-TAILED
    EEL see **Thyrsoides macrura**
    STINGRAYS see Dasyatidae
LONGEAR SUNFISH see **Lepomis megalotis**
LONGFIN, PERUVIAN see **Pterolebias peruensis**
LONGJAW SQUIRRELFISH see **Flammeo marianus, Holocentrus ascensionis**
LONGLURE FROGFISH see **Antennarius multiocellatus**
LONGNOSE
    DACE see **Rhinichthys cataractae**
    GAR see **Lepisosteus osseus**
    LANCETFIAH see **Alepisaurus ferox**
    SUCKER see **Catostomus catostomus**
LONGSNOUT BUTTERFLYFISH see **Prognathodes aculeatus**
LONGSPINE COMBFISH see **Zaniolepis latipinnis**
LONGTOM see Belonidae
LONGTOM, BARRED see **Ablennes hians**
LONGTOOTH SALMON see **Otolithes ruber**
LONGWING SCULPIN see **Cottocomephorus comephoroides**
LOOKDOWN see **Selene vomer**
LOOSE-JAWS see Malacosteidae
LOOSE-JAW,
    BLACK see **Malacosteus niger**
    SHINY see **Aristostomias scintillans**

LOPHIIDAE

A small family, the anglers or goosefishes, which is represented by a few species in the Pacific, Indian, and Atlantic oceans. All have a greatly flattened head, and body, with remarkably wide, well-toothed jaws. The first ray of the dorsal fin is long, placed near the snout, and has a fleshy lure near the tip, with which the fish entices its prey. The pectoral fins are broad, and angled out from the body on an elbow-like limb; the gill opening lies in the axil of the pectoral fin. See **Lophius.**

Lophius   Lophiidae
  americanus see under **L. piscatorius**
  budegassa 53 cm. (21 in.)
An anglerfish which appears to be best known in the Mediterranean, although it has been found in numbers off the N. African, Spanish, and Portuguese coasts and occurs as far N. as w. Scottish coast. Its habits are believed to be the same as those of *L. piscatorius*, although they have not been closely studied.

It is very similar to *Lophius piscatorius*, but differs in having fewer vertebrae, a paler skin, the skin continuous, though unpigmented

over the eyes, and most usefully, dark skin on the inside of the body cavity and plain-coloured pale pelvic fins.

L. piscatorius ANGLERFISH 1·5 m. (5 ft)
Widely distributed along the European coast from the Barents Sea s. to N. Africa, to the Mediterranean and Black Sea. It is a quite unmistakable fish, having an enormous wide head, a capacious mouth, and slender, though rounded in section, tail. The paddle-like pectoral fins, set on 'arms' are distinctive, as are the small pelvic fins beneath the belly. In coloration it is dull greeny brown, blotched with black, the belly is creamy white; the pelvic fins have dark edges.

This fish is found from shallow inshore water down to considerable depths, 1000 m. (546 fathoms) and more. It is essentially a bottom-living form which lies partially buried in sand, shingle, or mud. The small lappets of skin which fringe its head and body help to break up the outline of the fish so that it merges perfectly with the bottom. Its habit of angling with the fleshy lobe at the end of the first dorsal ray, luring smaller fish to within striking distance of its jaws is well known. The jaws and mouth are lined with numerous strong conical teeth, although the bony skeleton is light and in places paper-thin in contrast.

The anglerfish feeds on a wide range of fishes, and has occasionally been recorded as capturing seabirds, mostly the diving species. In European seas it is a moderately important food fish, even though the wastage of the huge head is tremendous. The flesh of the tail is white and faintly reminiscent of scampi in texture.

The angler's eggs are surface-floating. They are laid in the form of long ribbon-like veils of mucus, each egg taking a hexahedron shape. They and the larvae float at the surface, and are found only over deep water.

The American goosefish, *Lophius americanus*, is very closely related. It appears to spawn indifferently in shallow and deep water, and is found from the Newfoundland coast to N. Carolina, and possibly further S. still. **181**

Lophodiodon   Diodontidae
calori PORCUPINEFISH 51 cm. (20 in.)
A species found only along the e. coast of Africa from Knysna n.

It is a distinctive-looking fish distinguished by its colour and by having movable 2-rooted spines on its head and fixed 3-rooted spines on its body. **500**

Lopholatilus   Branchiostegidae
chamaeleonticeps TILEFISH
108 cm. (42½ in.)
Found along the Atlantic coast of N. America on the outer edge of the continental shelf from Nova Scotia to s. Florida, as well as in the Gulf of Mexico. It is a bottom-living fish found in the n. parts within a very restricted depth-range of 82-183 m. (45-100 fathoms). At these depths it lives in a layer of rather warm water, varying in temperature only between 8° and 12°C, but is apparently very common in this distinct water layer.

It feeds on a wide variety of bottom-living invertebrates, chiefly crabs, but also squid, shrimps, and molluscs, with occasional fishes. It spawns in July, and although fish estimated to be a year old have been found in deep water,

its growth rate and developmental stages are not well known.

The tilefish was first discovered off the E. Coast in 1879, and quickly became an important food fish. Within 3 years of its first discovery, however, a natural disaster believed to have been the upwelling of cold water from the deep Atlantic into its warm-water habitat apparently wiped-out the whole n. population. Throughout March and April 1882 millions of tilefish were found floating on the surface dead. None were caught for many years, but by 1915 the populations had partly recovered and small landings were being made. Since then it has continued to be exploited commercially on a small scale, although the potential supply is greater than the demand.

Its flesh is said to be excellent, both fresh and smoked. It also grows to a large size; it is said to attain a weight of 23 kg. (50 lb.), although the maximum recorded length of 108 cm. was for a 16 kg. (35½ lb.) fish.

It is brilliantly coloured, blue or green on the back with rose or yellow on the sides. The back and upper sides are dotted with small yellow spots. The dorsal fin is dark except that it has yellow spots and a pale edge. Its rather slender, but deep body, the eye high up and the mouth large and the loose skin flaps on the top of the head, and smaller flaps at the angles of the jaws, are distinctive.

Lophonectes   Bothidae
gallus CRESTED FLOUNDER 20 cm. (8 in.)
An Australian and New Zealand species which is found off the e. and s. seaboard of Australia and around Tasmania. It is a moderately deep-water species which is mainly found between 73–220 m. (40–120 fathoms). Most known specimens have been taken by research vessels; it has no commercial importance.

It is a very distinctive species with the eyes on the left of the head, close together, and a small mouth. Males have the first rays of the dorsal fin greatly elongated and have small tubercles on the snout and on the lower jaw. Its colour is brownish with 3 indistinct darker blotches along the mid-line of the side. The pelvic fin on the blind side is dusky in colour.

Lophotes   Lophotidae
fiskii 1·27 m. (50 in.)
A most striking fish, whose body form is difficult to believe. The most remarkable elongation of the forehead, which is steeply sloped in other members of the family, actually projects horizontally forward in this species, is characteristic.

This species has been found off the Japanese coast, and once off the South African coast. It is obviously widely distributed, but difficult to catch, so it is regarded as a rare fish.

It is silvery in colour with a reddish dorsal fin and dusky stripes.

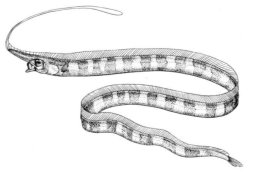

LOPHOTIDAE
A small family of fishes comprising 2–3 widely distributed species in temperate seas, although many more names have been proposed on supposed differences due to damaged specimens or geographical isolation. The crestfishes are related to the ribbonfishes and deal-fishes, and possess like them, a characteristic jaw structure. They are superficially similar to these fishes, being very elongate and ribbon-like with a long-based dorsal fin, no anal fin, and small pectoral fins.

They are very rarely encountered and their biology is little known. The crestfishes have an internal ink sac which produces liberal quantities of dark brown ink, similar to that of squids. They are believed to live in the upper layers of the mesopelagic zone.

See **Lophotes.**

Loricaria   Loricariidae
filamentosa 25 cm. (10 in.)
Found in the Rio Magdalena, Colombia, and from Venezuela. Its most characteristic distinguishing feature is the very elongate outer fin ray in the upper tail. Precise details for identification demand counts of the bony plates on the sides and belly. Around the mouth in this species there are 4 moderate-sized fleshy barbels in front of the upper jaw, and a large series around the outside of the lower jaw.

A frequently imported aquarium fish. **168**
L. parva VIEJA 13 cm. (5 in.)
A catfish found fairly widely in S. America in the middle reaches of the Rio Paraná, the Rio Paraguay, and rivers on the Mato Grosso, Brazil. It is widely imported for aquarium keeping and has been bred in captivity. Breeding takes place at a temperature between 22° and 25°C, yellowish eggs being produced which adhere to the substrate. Like the other members of the genus this is an algae eater, the minute plants being scraped off rocks and other plants with the fine comb-like teeth.

It has the typical 'armour plated' appearance of all loricariids, but has a conspicuously long pectoral fin, the outer rays of the tail fin are greatly elongate into long filaments. **169**

LORICARIIDAE
A large family of very distinctive catfishes from n. and central S. America, of the rivers of which continent they are characteristic and very abundant. They are typically heavily armoured, their heads and bodies enclosed in a hard case in one group, although another group have the ventral surface free of bony plates. The latter have an adipose fin.

Most members of the family are bottom-living with flattened ventral surfaces, and ventral, rounded sucking mouths with broad fringed lips.

Many are popular aquarium fishes, although as a group they are not highly coloured. See **Ancistrus, Farlowella, Hypostomus, Loricaria, Otocinclus, Plecostomus, Stoneiella, Xenocara.**

Lota   Gadidae
lota BURBOT, EEL-POUT 1 m. (39 in.)
The only freshwater member of the cod family, the burbot is distributed in lakes and rivers from e. England across Eurasia and N. America to the E. coast. In England it is very rare and is now verging on extinction. The

American forms have been claimed to be sub-specifically distinct.

It is very distinctive amongst freshwater species, being long and slender with 2 dorsal fins, the second being very long, a single anal fin and a barbel on the chin and raised rims round the nostrils looking like short barbels. Its scales are extremely small and are embedded. Its colouring is variable.

The burbot lives mainly on the bottom of clear lakes and rivers under rocks, roots, or in holes in the bank; it is crepuscular, only really active in the half-light of dawn and dusk. It spawns in winter, is very prolific, a large female may contain as many as 3 million eggs. The eggs lie on the bottom after fertilization. Young burbot feed on invertebrates mainly, especially small crustaceans and insect larvae. Larger fish eat mainly bottom-living fishes and larger crustaceans.

Although it was at one time used for food in w. Europe it is little used today, in the n. U.S.S.R. however, it is commercially important. Its flesh is as good eating as that of the cod. **187**

LOUVAR see **Luvarus imperialis**
LOWLAND GALAXIAS see **Galaxias brevipinnis**

Lucania Cyprinodontidae
goodei BLUE-FIN TOPMINNOW or
KILLIFISH 6 cm. (2½ in.)
An endemic Florida toothcarp which has enjoyed some popularity as an aquarium fish. It is relatively easy to keep in captivity, requiring a well planted aquarium, and live food, especially mosquito larvae. It spawns after vigorous driving by the male, which can be provoked by the addition of fresh water daily. The female lays 3–8 eggs at a time over a period of 5 weeks.

The male especially is strikingly coloured being greenish brown above with a brassy tint and a pale network of marks on the scales. A black stripe runs from nose-tip to tail, and a shorter stripe runs below this. The dorsal and anal fins are orange at the base with a black streak, and a beautiful deep blue tip. This colour fades in captive animals.

Lucayablennius Chaenopsidae
zingaro ARROW BLENNY 4 cm. (1½ in.)
Known from the Bahamas, the Cayman Islands, and Barbados, and found at moderate depths of 11–23 m. (6–12 fathoms) on patch reefs. It is not apparently widely distributed nor very common.

Its body form is distinctive. Of the scaleless pikeblennies in the Caribbean, this is the only species to have a protruding fleshy tip to the lower jaw. Its body is reddish, grey-mottled posteriorly while the prominent black blotches towards the tail have white rings round them. The dorsal fin of the male is dark; the female's fin is dark at the base only.

Lucifuga Ophidiidae
dentatus see under **L. spelaeotes**
spelaeotes 11 cm. (4½ in.)

A most interesting newly discovered fish which is known only from a small pool in the Bahamas. It was discovered in the Mermaid's Pool, a small freshwater sink in the limestone region near Nassau, in 1967, and described as new to science in 1970.

It is a very distinctive shape with a broad, flattened head, wide mouth with thick lips, a high back and a narrow tapering tail. The eye is well developed, although small and has a protruding lens and a window slit of clear tissue around it. The head has a conspicuous system of sensory cavities and canals, and the sensory papillae of the lateral line system are well developed. Most of the head is naked the remainder of the body has small scales covering it. The fish is a rich walnut brown, but the skin on the mucous chambers of the head, and parts of the fins are white.

The closest relatives of this species are believed to be a somewhat similar fish, *L. dentatus*, a native of the caves of Cuba, but it is also similar to some of the marine w. Atlantic brotulids. The Cuban species is ovoviviparous, and gives birth to live young.

At the time of its discovery only 2 specimens were captured, and the area around Mermaid's Pool was in danger of being developed for building. The survival of this fish may thus be in doubt.

LUCIOCEPHALIDAE
A family which contains a single species of labyrinth fish found only in the Malayan region, in Borneo, Sumatra, and the larger E. Indian islands. It lives in freshwater. While it has the characteristic feature of the other members of the group (e.g. Belontiidae, Osphronemidae, etc.) of an accessory respiratory organ each side of the head above the gills, it differs from the remainder in a variety of ways. It lacks a swimbladder, its body is elongate and almost rounded, the accessory breathing organ is simple, and the mouth is highly protrusible. See **Luciocephalus**.

Luciocephalus Luciocephalidae
pulcher PIKE-HEAD 18 cm. (7 in.)
A very distinctive fish with a long snout and deeply cleft mouth which has a system of folds enabling it to be extended into a long funnel.

The pike-head is found in the E. Indies and Malaysia living in running water, either drifting motionless with the current, snapping up insect prey at the surface, or lurking amongst vegetation in spots where counter currents accumulate drifting prey. It is wholly predatory, feeding on aquatic insects and their larvae, crustaceans, and smaller fishes. Its biology is little known, there are suggestions that it mouth broods its eggs but these have yet to be substantiated. It is kept in aquaria but not always successfully.

This interesting fish is modestly coloured, yellowish to red-brown above with a broad dark lengthwise band, pale edged on either side. Rows of fine spots on the upper sides, the fins are generally yellowish but the tail fin has dark brown spots on it.

Luciocharax Characidae
insculptus 70 cm. (28 in.)
This very interesting predatory characin resembles in appearance the garpikes of N. America.

In colour it is olive-brown on the back, yellow on the sides, and silvery ventrally. A round black spot at the base of the tail fin with a yellow margin is very characteristic.

This fish is found in the Rio Magdalena basin in S. America. It is entirely predatory, eating only small fishes. It has been kept in large aquaria but tends to be shy and timid, and frequently injures itself particularly its beak in trying to escape.

Luciopimelodus Pimelodidae
pati PATI, PIRACATINGA 41 cm. (16 in.)
Widely distributed in Argentina, found in the Rio Paraguay, Rio Paraná, Rio Uruguay, and the Rio de la Plata. It is a riverine species, most common where the water is turbid and deep, and the current moderate. It is frequently taken on lines in the lower reaches of these rivers.

Like other pimelodid catfishes the head is flattened and depressed while the body is laterally compressed. The mouth is large and wide, the eyes small, the paired barbel on the upper jaw reaches as far back as the middle of the adipose fin, the chin barbels are shorter. Coloration: silvery with dark spots and blotches especially on the back.

LUDERICK see **Girella tricuspidata**

Lumpenus Stichaeidae
lumpretaeformis SNAKE BLENNY
42 cm. (16½ in.)
Widely distributed in the N. Atlantic. The European populations range from the Irish

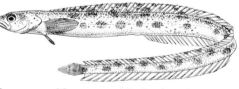

Sea n. to n. Norway, and Iceland, and are considered to be a subspecies *L. l. lumpretaeformis* differing from the American populations *L. l. serpentinus*, which is found from Massachusetts Bay to Labrador.

It is found in moderately shallow water, from 40–150 m. (22–82 fathoms), on muddy and soft bottoms into which it is believed to burrow. It feeds on small crustaceans, starfishes, and molluscs. Very little is known about its biology.

It is easily distinguished by its very long eel-like shape, with a long pointed tail. Its body is pale brown shading to blue with irregular greenish yellow spots on the sides. The belly is greenish yellow.

LUMPFISH see **Cyclopterus lumpus**
LUMPSUCKER see Cyclopteridae
LUMPSUCKER see **Cyclopterus lumpus**
LUMPSUCKER, PACIFIC SPINY see
    Eumicotremus orbis
LUNAR-TAILED ROCK COD see **Variola
    louti**
LUNGFISH see Ceratodontidae, Lepidosiren-
    idae, Protopteridae
LUNGFISH see **Protopterus aethiopicus,
    Protopterus annectens**
LUNGFISH,
   AUSTRALIAN see **Neoceratodus forsteri**
   QUEENSLAND see **Neoceratodus forsteri**
   SOUTH AMERICAN see **Lepidosiren
    paradoxa**

LUTJANIDAE

The family of snappers, tropical fishes of the world's seas, widely distributed with the exception of the e. Pacific. The typical members of the family are very distinctive, having in profile a long, almost triangular head, distinctly large canine-like teeth in the front of the jaws, and the upper jaw freely movable upwards but under the preorbital when the mouth is closed. Some members of the family do not have the triangular head, and are slender, open water fishes. All are fully scaled on the body and most of the head, the dorsal fin is continuous, the front part spiny and no more than notched to distinguish it from the branched rays.

The family is very abundant in tropical waters and contains several important food fishes. Some of these in certain areas are known to cause ciguatera, the often serious form of fish poisoning affecting man, and passed through food chains from one fish to another starting with fish which browse on poisonous algae.

Some 300 species belong to this family. See **Caesio, Etelis, Lutjanus, Ocyurus.**

Lutjanus   Lutjanidae
   analis MUTTON SNAPPER 76 cm. (30 in.)
Found in the w. Atlantic from New England and the Bahamas, s. to Brazil, including the Caribbean and the Gulf of Mexico. It is wide ranging within this area, found in tidal creeks with mangroves, in shallow bays with turtle grass on the seabed, and in more open water on a sandy bottom. It feeds on fishes and crustaceans, and in turn is a fine food fish; it may grow to a weight of 11 kg. (25 lb.).

It is distinguished by the black blotch on the side below the second dorsal fin, and 14 dorsal rays. Its coloration is variable, greenish

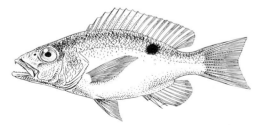

blue above, pinkish on the sides with red ventral fins.
L. apodus SCHOOLMASTER 61 cm. (2 ft)
Said to be found on both sides of the tropical

Atlantic but best known along the American coast from New England and Bermuda to Brazil. It is found throughout the Caribbean and the Gulf of Mexico.

Dr John E. Randall, the authority on Caribbean fishes reports that this is the most common snapper on W. Indian coral reefs, particularly amongst stands of elkhorn coral. It is also found commonly amongst mangroves, and in tidal pools, and turtle grass areas, but always in shallow water.

It is a rather deep-bodied species, usually greyish brown in colour, with light crossbars. The fins are orange to yellow.

It is a good food and sporting fish which grows to 3·6 kg. (8 lb.).
L. argentimaculatus RIVER ROMAN, RED SNAPPER, ROCK SALMON, MANGROVE JACK 91 cm. (36 in.)
Widespread in the tropical Indo-Pacific, and found from the Red Sea and E. African coast to n. Australia and the w. Pacific islands. This is one of the few snappers which lives in freshwater; it penetrates river mouths from the sea far up into freshwater. In n. Australia it is well-known as a river fish, a favourite haunt being amongst mangrove roots, hence one of its names.

It is a good sporting fish, and has considerable commercial importance as a food fish throughout its range. Like others of the family it convulsively snaps its sharply toothed jaws, hence the popular name 'snapper'.
L. griseus GREY SNAPPER 91 cm. (3 ft)
Found on both sides of the tropical Atlantic, but best known in the W. where it occurs from New England and Bermuda (where it was introduced) to the Gulf of Mexico, the Caribbean to s. Brazil. It is a common inshore fish, abundant in mangrove covered creeks, and common around rocky areas, reefs, and even into freshwater. It is an important food fish throughout its range. It also gives good sport and may weight up to 9 kg. (20 lb.).

It is a slender-bodied snapper with the typical long snout profile of the genus. It is usually grey overall with a reddish head and orange-red on the scales; the fins are orange. The colour is very variable.
L. kasmira SNAPPER, TANDA-TANDA, BLUE-BANDED SEA-PERCH, BLUE-BANDED HUSSAR 38 cm. (15 in.)
Widely spread in the tropical Indo-Pacific, from the E. African coast, the Red Sea, e. to Australia and the E. Indies, and the w. Pacific n. to the Philippines and Japan. It is very abundant in deepish water down to a depth of 30 m. (100 ft).

It is a strikingly colourful fish, although the colouring can be variable. **296**
L. nematophorus CHINAMANFISH 91 cm. (36 in.)
The Chinamanfish is an Indo-Australian species, found around the islands of e. Asia

and the N. Australian coast. It is very common on the Barrier Reef and other reefs in depths of 14–45 m. (8–25 fathoms). It grows to a large size, and a weight of some 15·5 kg. (34 lb.), and in many areas is captured and landed in large quantities.

In some areas and at certain times of the year it is never eaten for it has caused many cases of fish poisoning of a severe nature. In Queensland it appears to be more poisonous during the months of June, July and August.

As a young fish it is rosy in colour, light below with yellow tinges with a number of blue bands which run on to the head. It also has long thread-like extensions on the dorsal fin rays. Adults are crimson, darker above, with transverse spots and bands; the head has yellowish lines on it, including a ring around the eye.
L. sanguineus BLOODSNAPPER, BLOOD-RED SNAPPER, SADDLE-TAILED SEA PERCH 91 cm. (36 in.)
A widely distributed snapper in the tropical Indo-Pacific. Its range extends from the e. coast of Africa, around India and the E. Indies, and the coasts of Queensland and N. Australia. Its choice of habitats is very variable, frequently found closely associated with reefs; it also is found in mangrove swamps, and inshore bays. It also lives in moderate depths.

It is distinguished by its bright rose-pink colour overall with a zone of deep scarlet between the eyes.

It is a valuable food fish wherever it occurs in sufficient numbers. **297**
L. sebae RED SNAPPER, GOVERNMENT BREAM, RED EMPEROR 100 cm. (39 in.)
Widely distributed in the Indo-Pacific, from the coast of E. Africa, around the Indian and E. Indian coasts to n. Australia and the w. Pacific, n. to Japan. It is in most of this area an abundant fish, found on reefs and over sandy and rocky grounds.

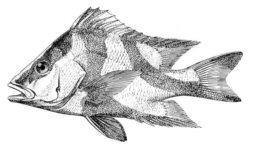

It is an important food fish everywhere, and is a fine sporting fish ever-ready to take a bait and fighting with fury once hooked. It is a large species, big specimens weighing as much as 22 kg. (48 lb.), but large or small its flesh is equally good for food.

Its coloration is always reddish; as adult salmon pink with a white spot on each scale, with whitish edged fins. Young fish up to about 30 cm. (12 in.) are a pale pink with 3 vivid red bands forming a central bar, with 2 inwardly pointing bars on the head and tail. This resembles a broad arrow, and accounts for its Australian local name of government bream.
L. vaigiensis SNAPPER, WAIGEU SNAPPER, YELLOW-MARGINED SEA PERCH 61 cm. (24 in.)
Originally found very widely in the Indo-Pacific, from E. Africa, around India and Sri Lanka, to Australia and the w. Pacific. It has

been introduced to Hawaiian waters as those islands had hitherto none of the shallow-water snappers so abundant in the islands of the S. Pacific.

In many areas extremely abundant on the reef and on sandy bottoms adjacent to the reef. It is locally exploited for food, without being particularly valuable in any one area.

The coloration is very variable. **298**

LUVARIDAE

A family containing the single species *Luvarus imperialis*. This species is cosmopolitan in tropical and warm temperate seas, but is little known and almost everywhere is regarded as an exceptionally rare fish. Many of the specimens reported have been stranded or cast ashore, most of them (as in the British Isles) at the extreme limit of its range. Purse-seine fisheries in offshore waters (as in California) have taken others moderately frequently which suggests that their natural habitat is in the upper 1000 m. (547 fathoms) of the open sea.

The adult is totally different in body form from the young. This has lead to the single species being described under several scientific names. The *Hystricinella* post-larva from 7–26 mm. (¼–1 in.), has a huge head almost vertical in profile, the eye being placed far back in the head. The pelvic and pectoral fins are large. The *Astrodermella* juvenile (up to 40 cm., 15¾ in.) has the body form of the adult but rather slender, however the dorsal and anal fins are high, and sail-like, as well as being heavily pigmented. See **Luvarus.**

Luvarus   Luvaridae
  imperialis LOUVAR 1·88 m. (74 in.)
A most striking and immediately distinctive marine fish, found throughout the tropical and warm-temperate seas and straying seasonally into cool temperate waters. It occurs occasionally in European waters as far N. as Norway, although it is moderately common, and breeds in the Mediterranean. It is possibly best known on the Californian coast where many specimens have been captured in the purse-seine tuna fishery.

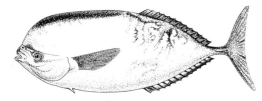

Its affinities clearly lie with the tunas (family Scombridae) and it has the typical tail fin form and keels on the sides of the tail. Its coloration is brilliant, a pale pink body, blue above and fading to silver after death. The fins are scarlet, although the tail fin is darker blue with reddish tinges.

The louvar must be assumed to be an open sea fish found in moderate depths. It feeds mainly on salps, medusae, and ctenophores, a jelly-like diet with which its toothless jaws can clearly cope. The interior of the stomach is lined with elongate projections very similar to those found in the blackfishes (family Centrolophidae) and the leathery turtle, both also medusa eaters.

It grows to a considerable weight. Specimens of 140 kg. (309 lb.) have been reported.

Lycichthys   Anarhichadidae
  denticulatus JELLY CAT, NORTHERN WOLFFISH 122 cm. (4 ft)
An inhabitant of the high Arctic Atlantic Ocean, found in the Barents Sea, the Norwegian Sea, around Greenland, and on the Nova Scotia banks. It lives on the bottom, usually on mud or fine sand where the water temperature is close to 0°C, in depths of 300–1000 m. (164–546 fathoms). Like its relatives it feeds mostly on hard-shelled invertebrates, especially sea urchins and brittle stars, and molluscs.

It is known as the jelly cat because its flesh is soft and watery, almost jelly-like. Although commonly caught by deep trawling, this rules out use of its flesh for food. Its colouring is dark chocolate brown with darker spots forming bars on the sides.

Lycodes   Zoarcidae
  diapterus BLACKMOUTH EEL POUT 15 cm. (6 in.)
Widely distributed in the e. and N. Pacific Ocean, from the Bering Sea to the Gulf of Panama. To the N. it has been found in moderate depths, between 120–640 m. (65–350 fathoms) off British Columbia, but in the S. of its range it is found in deeper water, even down to 1968 m. (1076 fathoms).

The skin is loosely attached to the body and translucent. Its coloration is described as pearly, dusted with fine black spots; the inside of the mouth and gill chamber is jet black.
L. esmarki ESMARK'S EELPOUT 74 cm. (29 in.)
This is the largest of the lycodid eelpouts in the N. Atlantic. It is common in the n. seas, the Barents Sea, off n. Norway, Iceland, e. Greenland, and found off Newfoundland, the Grand Bank, and Le Havre Bank.

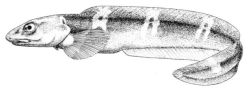

It is found in moderately deep water usually 275–460 m. (150–250 fathoms) although to the S. it is found as deep as 550 m. (300 fathoms). It is one of the lycodids which is commonly caught by British trawlers. It feeds mainly on starfish, sea urchins, and crinoids, and is clearly a bottom-living fish.

Its coloration is yellowish white on the belly and lower head, back and sides brownish with 5–9 transverse bands of whitish yellow. These bands become broken into loops and spots as the fish becomes older.

Lycodontis   Muraenidae
  tessellata MORAY EEL 1·5 m. (5 ft)
An inhabitant of the tropical Indo-Pacific of wide distribution in those oceans. It is found in shallow water and around coral reefs, while off s. Africa it is often found around wrecks. Large specimens can be aggressive and very dangerous if disturbed.

It is distinguished by its colour pattern of dark brown irregular polygonal marks surrounded by a yellowish network over head,

body, and fins. It has large depressible caniniform teeth in the front of the jaws and 1 or 2 series of teeth in the sides and roof of the mouth. **22**

LYRETAIL,
  ARNOLD'S see **Aphyosemion arnoldi**
  CALABAR see **Roloffia liberiens**
  CAPE LOPEZ see **Aphyosemion australe**

M

MAASBANKER see **Trachurus trachurus**
MCCULLOCH'S RAINBOWFISH see
  Nematocentrus maccullochi

Maccullochella   Serranidae
  macquariensis MURRAY COD
1·8 m. (6 ft)
The Murray cod is the largest and most important food fish of Australian freshwaters. It is widespread, found in the entire Murray-Darling system, in the headwaters of the Richmond and Clarence rivers in New South Wales, as well as the Dawson and Mary rivers of Queensland. It has been introduced into a number of reservoirs.

It is a very large fish; specimens of 90 kg. (198 lb.) have been reported, and fish of 30 kg. (66 lb.) are fairly common. They are a good sporting fish and make good eating, although the flesh of large specimens is rather tough and oily.

The Murray cod spawns when the water temperature reaches 20°C. and a flood of fresh water intervenes. Most often they spawn in the hollow trunks and on the branches of gum trees which have fallen into the water. The eggs are small and adhesive. Once past the fry stages this fish eats crustaceans and fishes.

It is usually dark green with bluish mottlings on the back and especially the sides.

Macdonaldia   Notacanthidae
  rostrata SHORTSPINE TAPIRFISH
43 cm. (17 in.)
An elongate, slender-bodied spiny eel with a series of short stout spines along the back varying in number from 28–31, but each free of any connecting membrane. The anal fin has 42–53 similar spines, but connected to one another and the following fin rays by a membrane. The head and body are covered with small scales. The mouth is ventral, beneath a rather pointed snout. The fish is a dull brown, with mouth and fins rather darker.

This spiny eel is best known from the w. N. Atlantic, but it has been captured in the e. Atlantic and off South Africa. In the w. Atlantic it has been taken on the edge of the continental shelf, along the edge of the Grand Bank, off Newfoundland, and off Martha's Vineyard, Massachusetts. It has been found in depths of 420–1757 m. (230–960 fathoms). Its biology is virtually unknown.

MACRISTIIDAE

A small family proposed in 1911 on the basis of a single specimen, and thought at that time to be related to the Alepocephalidae. Later, specimens became available which differed from the original specimen but they were all small, and the family was tentatively aligned with the Cretaceous fossil fishes known as ctenothrissids.

All the known specimens had very elongate fins, particularly the pectoral and pelvic fins (this is not unusual in many groups of fish in larval stages). In most of them the pelvics were placed well forward under the pectorals. However, recent studies have indicated that the small fishes which had been placed in this family are probably no more than larval, and juvenile stages of Bathysauridae and Ipnopidae, deep sea fishes whose developmental stages have not been studied. See **Macristium.**

Macristium   Macristiidae
  chavesi Known at 11cm. (4½ in.)
Macristium chavesi was described from a specimen of small size (11 cm.) caught in the region of the Azores. Subsequently a second specimen was reported from the Bay of Biscay, but this time only 33 mm. (1¼ in.) in length. Both fish have extremely long pelvic, pectoral, and anal rays and the smaller one has singularly long dorsal rays. Both possess many features

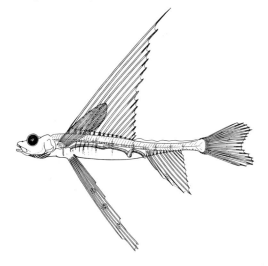

indicating that they were juvenile or post-larval fish.

MACROCEPHENCHELYIDAE

A little known family of eels, apparently related to the congers, but differing in the very blunt, short snout. Its representative is a typical eel, elongate and thin with rather high dorsal and anal fins. The pectoral fins are moderately long but the gill opening is restricted.

Only one member of the family is known. See **Macrocephenchelys.**

Macrocephenchelys Macrocephenchelyidae
  brachialis 49 cm. (19 in.)
This eel was described in 1934 from specimens collected in deep water in the Macassar Strait in 1909 by the U.S. research vessel *Albatross*. Two specimens were captured in a depth of around 670 m. (367 fathoms). It is a light coloured eel, pale brown on the back with the fins lighter and the long fins dusky on their edges.

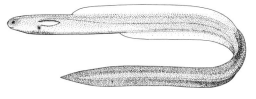

The moderately long pectoral fins are pale, with the upper edge dark.

Macrognathus Mastacembelidae
  aculeatus 38 cm. (15 in.)
An Asiatic spiny eel of very wide distribution, its range extends from India and Sri Lanka to Burma, throughout Thailand, Indo-China, Malaysia and Borneo, Sumatra, Java, and the Moluccas. It is found both on the coast in estuaries, lagoons, and the deltas of large rivers, and far inland in lakes, swamps, canals, and ditches.

It is a slender-bodied eel-like fish with a long, pointed, fleshy snout, a series (14–22) of separated spines in the dorsal fin, with a moderately long soft dorsal fin posteriorly. The anal fin is similarly shaped with only 2 spines visible anteriorly. The tail fin although small is separate and distinct. Adult specimens are rather deep-bodied. This genus is distinguished from the related *Mastacembelus* by the very long concave, curlew-billed snout, which is striated or finely ridged on the underside. Its background colouring is variable. **462**

Macropharyngodon Labridae
  pardalis 13 cm. (5 in.)
A small wrasse found in the Central Pacific, and recorded from a number of localities including Fiji, Samoa, and the Marshall Islands. It is abundant in tidal areas of the reefs and in lagoons in water as deep as 9 m. (30 ft).

It is a curiously shaped species, the dorsal and ventral profiles being equal. The jaw teeth point sharply forward in the centre of the jaws, while the outer teeth are curved outwards, and down (in the upper jaw) or up (in the lower jaw). **409**

Macropinna Opisthoproctidae
  microstoma BARREL-EYE 4 cm. (1½ in.)

A most striking inhabitant of the e. Pacific, found from Alaska to California, in depths around 183–914 m. (100–500 fathoms). It is stout-bodied, with a large head, rather protruding, flattened, shovel-like snout, and eyes protruding and mounted on a turret-like base. The eyes point upwards, and the lens actually protrudes above the outline of the back.

It is dark brown, although the young are light coloured with distinctive vertical dark bars. Its fins are rather long, the pelvics being particularly developed; it has a moderately large adipose fin.

Macropodus Belontiidae
  opercularis PARADISEFISH 9 cm. (3½ in.)
A native of Korea, China, Taiwan and Vietnam, where it thrives in the drainage ditches and paddy fields which cover much of the lowland plains. Like other labyrinth fishes it possesses accessory breathing organs in the gill chambers on each side of the head, and can live in very poorly oxygenated water. The male constructs a bubble-nest by blowing thick mucus-covered bubbles, usually under floating weed, and later, after considerable display, transfers the fertilized eggs to the nest.

It was one of the first aquarium fishes brought to Europe and has been kept in captivity for over a century. It is very undemanding but can be pugnacious to both its own kind and other species. On the other hand it is hardy and very colourful. All the fins are elongate, especially in males.

During the years that this fish has been bred by aquarists (and it has a long history of domestication in the Far East before it became available in Europe) many changes have been induced in coloration and fin form. **458**

MACRORAMPHOSIDAE

A small family of marine fishes found most commonly in tropical and temperate seas. Worldwide in distribution they are mostly pelagic or bathypelagic. None has any commercial value.

All have the same general body form, a compressed, deep body with a long snout and small mouth set at the tip. The body is covered with small, toothed scales, the eye is large, the fins in general small, except for a relatively massive first dorsal spine, and rather smaller second and third spines are placed at the mid-point of the back. See **Centriscops, Macroramphosus.**

Macroramphosus Macroramphosidae
  gracilis SLENDER SNIPEFISH
12·8 cm. (5 in.)
Widely distributed in the Mediterranean and e. Atlantic from off Portugal to s. Africa, and reported to occur in the Indian Ocean.

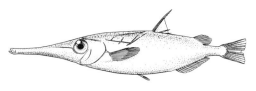

It is a fish of the middle-waters in depths of 100–300 m. (55–164 fathoms). Little is known of its biology, but it is believed to feed entirely on small planktonic animals, especially crustaceans. **228**

MACROURIDAE

A family of fishes of worldwide distribution living mainly in deep-water, in mid-water and near the bottom. They are very varied in details of body structure although they all have the basic body shape of a relatively large head, short body (if measured to the vent) and very long tail. The long tapering, scaled tail earns for them the name rattails; they are also called grenadiers. Few are well enough known to have individual vernacular names.

They are related to the codfish family and most forms have a distinct chin barbel as do the cods. They differ in not having a tail fin, and many species have a spine in the first dorsal fin.

The rattails are specialized noise producers, the males of some kinds can make sounds of surprising volume with their drumming swimbladder muscles; others have luminous organs on the belly, in some kinds enclosed in a distinct gland, or contained behind a clear lens on the belly. Both hold luminous bacteria. See **Coryphaenoides, Echinomacrurus, Gadomus, Macrourus, Nezumia, Trachyrhynchus.**

Macrourus   Macrouridae
berglax ROUGH-HEAD GRENADIER
91 cm. (3 ft)
A rattail widely distributed in deep water on both sides of the N. Atlantic. Along the continental slope from Nova Scotia and Newfoundland in the w. Atlantic S. to Georges

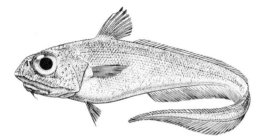

Bank, around Greenland, Iceland, off Spitzbergen and Norway in the E. It does not occur S. of the Faeroes-Shetland ridge. It is taken usually in water between 183–1240 m. (100–677 fathoms) deep. It is evidently a bottom feeder.

It is a very distinctive species, with a strongly ridged head, especially below the eye, and large rough, toothed scales; the mouth is entirely ventral, the eye large. Grey above and below, darker on the back; the fins sooty.

Macrozoarces   Zoarcidae
americanus OCEAN POUT 93 cm. (36½ in.)
Found in the w. N. Atlantic from near Labrador to Delaware and possibly to N. Carolina. It is a bottom-living fish which can be found from the intertidal zone to depths of 183 m.

(100 fathoms); it is most common on hard or semi-hard bottoms. It is said to migrate offshore in autumn into deeper water.

Unlike the European eelpout, which produces living young, this species lays eggs. They are large, about 6 mm. in diameter, yellowish,

and laid in masses clumped together with gelatinous mucus. It spawns in the autumn, the eggs hatch after 2–3 months.

This is a relatively stout-bodied eelpout, but typical of the group in every way. It is usually greeny-brown, darker mottled on the back and sides, lighter on the belly.

MACRUROCYTTIDAE

A small family of deep-water fishes, superficially resembling, and related to, the dories (family Zeidae). Its members are little known, relatively slim-bodied, with a large eye and a relatively large mouth. See **Macrurocyttus.**

Macrurocyttus   Macrurocyttidae
acanthopodus 15 cm. (6 in.)
A small species first described from the waters of the Philippine Islands. The original specimen was taken by the U.S. research vessel

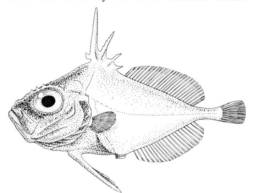

Albatross off the E. coast of Luzon in 878 m. (480 fathoms). Very few specimens have ever been captured.

The body is covered with fine, thin scales which are mostly shed on capture. It is brown generally, the body and fins being dark.

MADTOM, TADPOLE see **Noturus gyrinus**
MADTOMS see Ictaluridae

Maena   Emmelichthyidae
maena BLOTCHED PICAREL 24 cm. (9½ in.)
A species native to the Mediterranean and found from the coast of Portugal to the Canary Islands in the Atlantic.

It is a very beautifully coloured, and highly variable fish, but it always has a rectangular black patch high on the side. It is usually blue

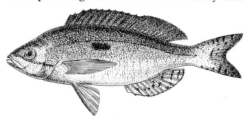

on the back, silvery on the sides and belly, with a yellow pectoral fin. The fin membranes are dark grey with blue lines. In adult males, this blue marking is pronounced and the head and body are covered with broken blue lines.

It is an abundant fish in the w. Mediterranean, found in moderate depths usually over a sandy or muddy bottom. It feeds mainly on planktonic crustaceans, but also eats young fishes. It breeds in late autumn in depths of 10–20 m. (5–11 fathoms), the male excavating a circular depression in sand in which the eggs are shed. This fish is a protogynous herma-

phrodite (female first, male later); the smaller specimens are mostly females, in samples of larger fish more males are found, and the largest fishes are all males.

It is locally used as a food fish but is not especially important.

MAFUGU see **Sphoeroides rubripes**
MAHSEER,
   PUTITOR see **Barbus putitora**
   TOR see **Barbus tor**

Makaira   Istiophoridae
indica BLACK or WHITE MARLIN
3·7 m. (12 ft)
A billfish which ranges virtually throughout the whole of the warmer parts of the Indian and Pacific oceans although it seems to be particularly abundant in certain areas such as off the Australian and n. New Zealand coasts, off Peru, New Guinea, and Hawaii (where it is often known as the white or silver marlin).

It is a very important commercial fish throughout its range; many are captured and the white flesh commands a high price. It is also a popular game fish for the angler fishing with surface gear and using fish or squid for bait. Large specimens are believed to attain 907 kg. (2000 lb.) but most specimens average less than half that. It is one of the 2 largest members of the group.

Distinguished immediately by its pectoral fins which are set quite rigidly at right angles to the sides of the body and literally cannot be folded against the body. It is a heavy-bodied species, deep in the belly and with flattened sides. The first dorsal fin is comparatively low. Its coloration is variable but usually dark slaty-blue above, changing abruptly to white or silvery below. It gets the confusing alternative name, white marlin, on account of the whitish haze over the body after death.

Like its relatives it is essentially a fish eater, with squid forming a secondary item of diet. Amongst its prey are smaller tunas and other schooling fish. Its occurrence throughout its range is seasonal but its migrations are not known in detail.

M. mazara see **M. nigricans**
M. nigricans BLUE MARLIN 4·6 m. (15 ft)
or more
The blue marlin is worldwide in its distribution in tropical and warm temperate seas. It is well known throughout the warmer Atlantic Ocean, from the s. Caribbean islands n. to the Bahamas, Florida, and Texas coasts. It occurs further N. even to the Gulf of Maine. In the e. Atlantic it occurs plentifully along the African coast and around the Canary Islands but is relatively less well-known. In the Pacific it is widely distributed around n. Australia, Hawaii, s. Japanese waters, and s. California and the Mexican coast.

It is one of the most important commercially exploited billfish. In the Pacific around Japan, Taiwan, and Hawaii the catch is especially high and annually totals over 454,000 kg. (1 million lb.). The sport-fishing for this species is equally important in Hawaii and in the tropical w. Atlantic. The average weight for rod-caught marlin is around 180 kg. (400 lb.) and maxima of 317–454 kg. (700–1000 lb.) are possible.

The blue marlin is a fish-eater with squid of secondary importance. This species is one of the few predators on the fast-swimming smaller tunas (*Katsuwonus* being particularly frequently eaten), but almost any shoaling fish are caught. It is migratory and becomes more common seasonally in off-shore waters at the cooler extremities of its range.

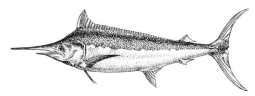

The blue marlin is dark steely blue on the back, fading to silvery white ventrally; the sides are usually marked with lightish bars but they are not prominent. It is distinguished from other marlins by its rather low lobed dorsal fin. The lateral line is complex forming a chain-like pattern over the body, but is not often visible in fresh fish.

Some authors regard the Atlantic and Indo-Pacific populations as distinct either at sub-species or species level. In the latter case they use the name *M. nigricans* for the Atlantic species; *M. mazara* for the Indo-Pacific species. Numerous synonyms for both names exist.

MAKO see **Isurus oxyrinchus**
MAKO, SHORTFIN see **Isurus oxyrinchus**

Malacanthus   Branchiostegidae
plumieri SAND TILEFISH 61 cm. (2 ft)
Recorded from Bermuda and S. Carolina to Brazil and throughout the Gulf of Mexico and the Caribbean. It has also been found at the S. Atlantic island of Ascension.

This tilefish lives on sandy bottoms and around the margins of turtle grass beds, in shallow water. It makes a burrow in the sand, often very extensive, and when alarmed it enters the burrow headfirst. Normally it is seen hovering near its burrow entrance. It feeds on many kinds of small fishes and crustaceans.

Its colouring is subdued, often as light as the sand in which it burrows; the head has lavender and yellow markings and the tail fin has orange lobes.

Malacoctenus   Clinidae
A genus of scaled blennies. The species illustrated has not been identified. **429**
M. macropus ROSY BLENNY 5·5 cm. (2¼ in.)
Widely distributed in the Caribbean, and known from Bermuda, the Bahamas, and Florida, s. to the Central American coast and through the W. Indies. It is probably the most abundant member of the family in the area and occurs from the shoreline down to 7·6 m. (4 fathoms). It lives on varied strata but is most common on bottoms of mixed marl, sand, and turtle grass. It feeds on copepods and small crustaceans in general.

This species is variable in colour. The male has a broad dark stripe along the upper part of the body, with whitish blotches, and the

sides are liberally sprinkled with red. Females are greyish brown with no red visible.

MALACOSTEIDAE

The malacosteids are usually known as loose-jaws on account of their striking family character of lacking a membrane between the sides of the lower jaw. In effect, they have no floor to their mouths. The jaw muscles are enclosed in a sheath of tissue and form a slender band. The jaws are extremely long and tremendously capacious, and, due to the specialized nature of the neck vertebrae, the head is movable vertically in a manner unusual for fishes.

In general they are slender fishes, with scaleless dark coloured skins. Most have light organs scattered over the head and body, usually minute but those on the head are often large. Most loose-jaws are small, the largest, *Malacosteus niger,* possibly grows to 30 cm. (12 in.). They are found in all the major oceans, except for polar seas, from the surface to a depth of up to 4000 m. (2186 fathoms). See **Aristostomias, Malacosteus.**

Malacosteus   Malacosteidae
niger BLACK LOOSE-JAW 30 cm. (12 in.)
This loose-jaw is worldwide in its distribution in tropical, temperate, and cooler waters. It has not, however, been found in the Mediter-

ranean, although well distributed in the adjacent Atlantic. Some specimens have been taken at the surface, but the species seems to be most abundant at around 915–1830 m. (500–1000 fathoms).

It is in many respects typical of the family, but is rather shorter-bodied than most. Black in colour, the light organ beneath the eye dark red, that behind the eye bright green. The head and body have numerous tiny scattered white or violet photophores.

MALAPTERURIDAE

The family containing the electric catfish. Characterized by its heavy flabby shape, lack of a dorsal fin with rays, and the presence of an adipose fin; all other fins being short and rounded. Three pairs of long, fleshy barbels around the lips. Well developed electrical organs occupy most of the body.

Widely distributed in the freshwaters of tropical Africa, from the Nile to the Zambezi, and through most of central and w. Africa. See **Malapterurus.**

Malapterurus   Malapteruridae
electricus ELECTRIC CATFISH
120 cm. (47 in.)
The electric catfish is immediately distinguished by its heavy build, scaleless, rather bloated appearance, by the complete absence of a rayed dorsal fin, although it has a well developed adipose fin. Its coloration is distinctive too, being greyish brown, the sides flesh-coloured and the belly dead white, covered irregularly with rounded black blotches. The young have a pale band around the tail fin base.

This fish is well known for its powerful electrical abilities. Even small ones are capable of inflicting a strong shock when handled. Large ones, if stood upon, can give a stunning jolt, even on occasions rendering fishermen unconscious. The shock is short and

sharp, and clearly voluntarily controlled for one can (sometimes) handle a specimen without it discharging its electrical power only to be surprised seconds later by a shock. Successive discharges are weaker. The electrical properties are possessed by muscle blocks beneath the skin, occupying most of the sides of the body. These electrical properties are probably as much defensive as used in obtaining prey, but it is widely believed that it stuns smaller fishes before eating them. It is certain that the electric catfish is not of the athletic build required for catching active fishes.

It is widely distributed in tropical Africa, through the whole of the Nile system, the rivers of W. Africa, the Chad, and Lake Rudolf basins, and the Zambezi system. It lives mostly in swamps, occasionally in rivers, and then only in the reed beds flanking the flowing water. They are large fish, a well-grown specimen weighing up to 15 kg. (33 lb.). The flesh is white and reported to be well flavoured.

It is surrounded by great mystique for the electric properties are clearly special. From the number of representations of the fish in ancient Egyptian pictographs it was obviously of high regard. In n. Nigeria today it is used by some fishermen for making magic, some organs being a veritable panacea. **158**

MALAWI EYE-BITER see **Haplochromis compressiceps**

Mallotus   Osmeridae
villosus CAPELIN 23 cm. (9 in.)
The capelin is a very distinctive smelt-like fish found in the N. Atlantic, from Spitzbergen to Oslo Fjord and the Faeroes in the E. around Iceland, and in the W. from Greenland and Labrador s. to the Gulf of Maine. A closely related form (usually regarded as a subspecies *M.v. catervarius*) is found in the N. Pacific, and adjacent parts of the Arctic Ocean.

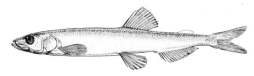

It is similar to a smelt, with moderately large jaws and an adipose fin, but it has much smaller, and more firmly attached scales. It is translucent in life, olive-green on the back, whitish on the belly, but with a distinct silvery stripe along each side. The sexes differ considerably in appearance, males having a strongly arched base to the anal fin, and very elongate scales along the sides and on the belly, giving an almost furry look. A female is illustrated.

Capelin are exceedingly abundant in coastal waters and are fed upon by almost all fish-eating birds, mammals, and fishes of the Arctic seas. Seals, finback and white whales, a host of n. sea birds, and such fish as salmon, charr, cod, and halibut all prey on the capelin at times. They are thus basic to many of the food chains of the n. seas. Man too eats them in quantity, and at one time they were a basic item in the diet, and winter food for the native Greenlanders and their dogs.

Capelin spawn in late spring and early summer, in vast shoals on the bottom close inshore. Although most spawn in water of 2–5 m. (1–3 fathoms), some are found on the shore, riding up the beach on the crest of a wave in pairs, or 2 males either side of a female, to deposit their spawn or milt in the gravel. The adults wriggle back to the water, or are swept away by a succeeding wave. The eggs are soon buried in the shifting gravel, and hatch in 2–3 weeks. Although most spawning takes place at night or in cloudy weather, the mortality amongst the adult fish is very high during their brief exposure to predators.

MAN-EATER see **Carcharodon carcharias**
MAN-O'-WAR FISH see **Nomeus gronovii**
MANDARINFISH see **Synchiropus splendidus**
MANDUBA see **Ageneiosus brevifilis**
MANDUVÉ see **Hypophthalmus edentatus**
MANEFISH see **Caristius macropus**
MANGROVE JACK see **Lutjanus argentimaculatus**

Manta Mobulidae
birostris GIANT DEVIL RAY, ATLANTIC MANTA At least 6·7 m. (22 ft)
This is the largest of the living rays, a giant amongst fishes. The greatest width recorded was 6·7 m. (22 ft) and the length of this specimen caught in the Bahamas was 5·2 m. (17 ft) but its tail was partly missing. This fish weighed in excess of 1360 kg. (3000 lb.). The giant devil ray is rarely captured and very few specimens have been examined adequately owing to their size, because those which do become available are taken by chance often in inaccessible places. There is therefore no reason to doubt that larger specimens will in time be reported.

It is distinguished from the other large devil rays by the position of its mouth which extends across the front of its head, and by the absence of teeth in its upper jaw. Like its relatives its pectoral fins are long and pointed; its tail is short, and its dorsal fin is small. Its head region is very wide with large, mobile, cephalic fins either side of the mouth. They can be rolled spirally when the fish is swimming, and extended vertically when feeding, it is suggested, to form a scoop or funnel leading to the mouth.

Internally these rays have a complex filter system on their gill arches through which flows all the water taken in during respiration. Small planktonic animals are trapped in this filter and are swallowed. The mantas thus feed on the smallest of prey, although they also engulf shoaling fishes and larger crustaceans. It is an interesting parallel that the largest of rays and sharks (*Cetorhinus* and *Rhincodon*), and cetaceans (blue whale) all feed on small animals filtered from the water masses.

The *Manta* (its name derives from the supposed resemblance of its wide shrouded form to a loose cloak) is found in inshore waters as well as offshore in the open sea. They are frequently seen swimming steadily at the surface, presumably feeding, but one supposes that they as often feed lower in the plankton-bearing sea, and may even rest on the bottom. They are quite harmless to man, despite popular stories of their enveloping divers with their fins! They have however, frequently been known to overturn small boats after being harpooned.

Mantas occur in all tropical seas. *M. birostris* is known from the Atlantic, in the W. from Brazil to the Carolinas, in the E. from Madeira and W. Africa. Closely related, if not identical, forms occur in the tropical Indo-Pacific. 12

MANTA, ATLANTIC see **Manta birostris**
MAORI WRASSE, HUMP-HEADED see **Cheilinus undulatus**
MARBLED HATCHETFISH see **Carnegiella strigata**

Marcusenius Mormyridae
isidori 10 cm. (4 in.)
This small mormyrid is found only in the lower regions of the Nile delta. It is very distinctive in body shape, although typically mormyrid in appearance, for it is very stocky, the body depth being only just under half its length. Its forehead and snout are rounded, with the mouth rather ventrally placed.

Its colouring is dull, brown or greyish brown on the back, lightening on the sides, with the belly pale grey or silvery. Frequently the fish is seen to have a violet sheen to the back. It is a peaceful species, forming small shoals, and thus makes an ideal aquarium fish.

MARGATE see **Haemulon album**
MARGATE, BLACK see **Anisotremus surinamensis**
MARINKA see **Schizothorax argentatus**
MARLIN,
    BLACK see **Makaira indica**
    BLUE see **Makaira nigricans**
    STRIPED see **Tetrapturus audax**
    WHITE see **Tetrapturus albidus**

MASTACEMBELIDAE
The family of freshwater spiny eels, a group of wide distribution in S. and SE. Asia, tropical Africa, and the Euphrates region. Most are rather long-bodied, eel-like fishes with compressed tails, and a row of sharp spines along the back, followed by a normal soft-rayed fin. The pelvic fins are absent. The snout is produced into a long fleshy proboscis, with tubular anterior nostrils at the sides. All members of the family are scaled.

In the wild most spiny eels are found in densely vegetated water or on soft muddy ground, either hidden in the plants or buried in weed. Some are found in low salinity estuarine areas.

In many regions these fishes are valuable food fish, their flesh is of good flavour, and some grow quite large. The smaller species are often kept in aquaria, their bright coloration and relative hardiness making them suitable as pet fish. See **Macrognathus, Mastacembelus.**

Mastacembelus Mastacembelidae
armatus 75 cm. (29½ in.)
Widely distributed in fresh, and less often brackish water, from India and Sri Lanka, through Burma, Thailand, to China, and the Malayan peninsula, SE. Asia to Sumatra, Java, and Borneo. It is found in well weeded waters and swamps, but the larger specimens are also found in open water in large rivers and lakes. It feeds on a wide variety of bottom-living insects, crustaceans, and large specimens eat small fishes.

Throughout its range this spiny eel is of some importance as a food fish. However, Hugh M. Smith, an authority on Thailand fishes, wrote 'on account of its shape, slippery skin, powerful muscles, and activity it is difficult to handle, and its short, sharp, stout spines can inflict painful wounds'. Small specimens are regularly imported and kept as aquarium fish.

It is distinguished by its warm brown coloration with a very dark, broken band running from eye to tail fin, with branches extending to the dorsal and anal fins. The belly is yellowish. 463

M. maculatus 46 cm. (18 in.)
An Asiatic species which has a rather restricted range, being found in Thailand, the Malaysian region, Sumatra, Java, and Borneo. It is a freshwater spiny eel found in swamps and well-weeded areas in lakes, ditches and large rivers.

It is distinguished by lacking spines on the preopercular bone, and also by having a sharp spine in front of the eye. Its colouring is also distinctive, the body being a warm brown with darker blotches, the dorsal and anal fins have light, yellowish edges, and there is a row of black spots along the base of the dorsal fin.

This species is often imported for keeping as an aquarium fish.

M. pancalus 20 cm. (8 in.)
An Indian spiny eel which is found in the large rivers and coastal plain of e. India and Bangladesh. It lives in estuarine conditions as well as in freshwater.

It is a deep-bodied species, although having the same basic body shape of the other members of the genus, it is more compressed. Females are deeper-bodied than males.

This spiny eel is often kept in aquaria. 464

Masturus Molidae
lanceolatus SUNFISH, TRUNKFISH, SHARPTAIL MOLA 3 m. (10 ft)
This sunfish appears to be worldwide in its distribution having been positively identified in the Atlantic off Florida, N. Carolina, and the Canary Islands, in the Red Sea, off s. Africa, and in the Pacific. A second species (*M. oxyuropterus*) is recognized by some authors and has a similar range; in all probability it is based on growth stages of the present species.

Masturus is recognized by its general resemblance to *Mola mola*, a huge deep-bodied fish, with small mouth, moderate eye, small gill slits and tiny pectoral fins. The body is considerably more elongate, being longer than high, with the lower jaw prominent; the upper middle rays of the 'tail fin' are long, giving the posterior outline a pointed lobe just above the centre point.

It is an inhabitant of the open ocean, probably most abundant from the surface to 200–300 m. (109–164 fathoms), but most of the specimens that have been examined were washed ashore, harpooned, or run-down by ships at the surface and therefore probably sick or dying.

The young stages of this fish have been well described; they pass through a series of nearly spherical body form growth stages with very long spines (which being common at times in oceanic plankton were thought to be a distinct genus of fishes – *Molacanthus*). By a length of 2·5 cm. (1 in.) the adult body-form has been assumed, and the spines are reduced to small studs, but the fish is still planktonic and has a small swim-bladder (which adults lack).

Masturus is a large fish, specimens of 7–10 ft (2·1–3 m.) have been reported, but the maximum weight attained is uncertain.

M. oxyuropterus see under **M. lanceolatus**

MATA-HARI see **Lethrinus miniatus, Lethrinus nebulosus**

Maurolicus   Gonostomatidae
  muelleri PEARLSIDES 65 mm. (2½ in.)
Pearlsides is a name bestowed in England on a fish which is probably cosmopolitan in the open sea. It is found in the Atlantic, from N. Norway and Iceland to S. of the Equator, in the S. Atlantic and in the Pacific Ocean. It is one of the most frequently encountered bristle-mouths, for it is found at the surface often close to land, and is not infrequently stranded both singly and in shoals.

When living it is very beautiful, greenish blue on the back, brilliantly silvery on the sides and belly, with gleaming pale blue light organs on the belly and below the tail. The light organs are moderate and arranged in close order.

Although it is often found at the surface it is probably mainly as a result of night-time migration from deeper water. It often is attracted to lights at night, but has been taken down to 300 m. (164 fathoms). Possibly it spends part of its life close to the sea floor. On account of its great abundance, pearlsides is a staple diet for very many of the larger bathy-pelagic predators. It is also very commonly found in the stomachs of tunnyfishes, as well as members of the cod family and the hake. It is clearly a very important forage fish. In its turn it feeds on small crustaceans and planktonic animals generally.

MAYFISH see **Alosa fallax**
MEAGRE see **Argyrosomus regius**
MEAGRE, BROWN see **Sciaena umbra**
MEDAKA,
  CELEBES see **Oryzias celebensis**
  JAPANESE see **Oryzias latipes**
MEDUSAFISH see **Icichthys lockingtoni**

Megalamphodus   Characidae
  megalopterus BLACK-PHANTOM TETRA
4 cm. (1½ in.)

This aquarium fish is found in the Mato Grosso region of S. America. It is a very attractive fish with a moderately slender body but notably high dorsal and anal fins, the latter fin is many rayed and with a long base. Males in particular have the dorsal fin elongate and rather broader towards the tip. A long black shoulder blotch extends vertically behind the head. Females have reddish dorsal and pelvic fins; in the males these are greyish. **71**
M. sweglesi RED-PHANTOM TETRA
4 cm. (1½ in.)
A very beautiful aquarium fish from the region of Colombia. It is a rather slender-bodied characin, with a long, and high anteriorly, anal fin. The dorsal fin is also high and pointed. It is delicately coloured, almost translucent when viewed against the light, orange tinted on the back and sides when not.

Males have a higher dorsal fin than females, and the latter have a white tip to the dorsal fin. It is said to be a difficult fish to keep in the aquarium. **72**

MEGALOPIDAE
A small family comprising 2 species of large tropical marine fish. Superficially they resemble giant herrings, with which fishes they were formerly grouped, with their silvery sides, single dorsal fin with flexible rays, and forked tail. Like the family Elopidae they have a single, large bony plate under the throat and many small teeth in the jaws. Also like that family their larvae are small, transparent leptocephali, resembling typical eel larvae. See **Megalops, Tarpon.**

Megalops   Megalopidae
  cyprinoides OX-EYE or PACIFIC TARPON
1·5 m. (5 ft)
The ox-eye tarpon is the Indo-Pacific relative of the Atlantic tarpon. It is widely distributed in these oceans from the African coast e. to Guam. Like its Atlantic relative, the adult is found in coastal waters or in the open ocean but the young fish frequent mangrove swamps and estuaries. It can supplement the sometimes sparse dissolved oxygen in the water by breathing air through a direct connection between the gullet and the specially adapted swimbladder.

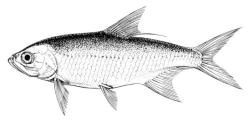

It is bluish green above, the sides silvery, and white below. The fins have a tinge of yellow to them. Although it is a moderately large fish it rarely grows longer than 1·2 m. (4 ft). It is a good sporting fish to the angler, leaping clear of the water when hooked. Its flesh, however, is very insipid, and bony, but despite this in Java it is reared in freshwater ponds from larvae taken at the coast. Like its relatives its larvae are thin and transparent, remarkably like eel-larvae except that they have forked tails. **20**

MEGRIM see **Lepidorhombus whiffiagonis**

Meiacanthus   Blenniidae
  nigrolineatus 7 cm. (2¾ in.)
A blenny which occurs only in the Red Sea and the Gulf of Suez and Aqaba. It has been observed on coral reef areas and adjacent sandy and plant-covered flats in depths to 45 m. (25 fathoms). It feeds primarily on small invertebrates and worms that it obtains from the sand around the coral formation.

Its colouring is striking, blue to blue-grey on the head, pale yellow on the posterior part of the body. Frequently it has a narrow black lengthwise stripe along the body. It is involved in a fascinating complex of mimicry with two other Red Sea blennies, *Ecsenius gravieri* and *Plagiotremus townsendi* which have adopted its general coloration and even behavioural patterns.

This species has large canine teeth in the lower jaw, grooved at the sides, and venom-producing tissue at the base. Experiments have shown that predators in the general area in which it lives have learned to avoid eating this fish, which can retaliate with a painful bite, and it is usually left alone by larger fishes. Its 2 mimics appear to profit from this immunity from predators.

MEKONG CATFISH see **Pangasianodon gigas**

Melamphaes   Melamphaeidae
  nigrescens 8 cm. (3¼ in.)
Widely distributed and possibly cosmopolitan in its range, but positively reported in the Atlantic, Indian Ocean (including the Arabian Sea), and in the W. Pacific. It is a mid-water

fish found at depths of 1098–4000 m. (600–2180 fathoms). Its chief depth of occurrence is around 2000 m. (1092 fathoms).

It is a black fish; the head is noticeable for its protruding thin bones and deep cavernous hollows.

MELAMPHAEIDAE
A family of small fishes of bathypelagic habit cosmopolitan in tropical and temperate seas. They are most common below a depth of about 1000 m. (546 fathoms) and some species are found down to depths of 4000 m. (2185 fathoms). Relatively few specimens have been taken and those only in special deep-water nets. Considerable confusion exists as to the number of valid species which is certainly many fewer than the number of forms described.

They are all rather deep-bodied, rounded, with moderately large heads which have paper-thin bones, prominent ridges and deep hollows. Most are dark and covered with large, paper-thin rounded scales which are easily detached. See **Melamphaes, Poromitra.**

MELANOCETIDAE

A family of rather small deep-sea anglerfishes represented by about 8 species found in the Atlantic, Pacific, and Indian oceans. They are distinguished from all other ceratioids by having a long-based dorsal fin, with between 12–17 rays, and a short anal fin (with 4 rays). As with other deep-sea anglers there is considerable discrepancy between the sizes of males and females, the latter being much the larger. The males are free-living and do not become parasitic. Most have rather rounded bodies with loosely attached skin; most species are uniformly black. See **Melanocetus.**

Melanocetus Melanocetidae
johnsonii 13 cm. (5 in.)
Found in all 3 major oceans of the world from near the surface to depths of 2288 m. (1250 fathoms). Most have been taken by midwater trawls and plankton nets during oceanographic expeditions, only the young are normally found near the surface.

The females are larger than the males, which grow to about 4 cm. ($1\frac{3}{4}$ in.). They are dark brown to black with clear fins. The dorsal ray, which acts as a fishing rod with a lure at its tip, is also clear. The females have capacious jaws, and very long dagger teeth. The males, after metamorphosis from larvae, are free-living, light brown in colour, with small toothless jaws, small eyes, but large olfactory organs.

M. murrayi 11 cm. ($4\frac{1}{2}$ in.)
Distributed in deep water in the Atlantic, Indian, and Pacific oceans, as well as the Caribbean Sea.

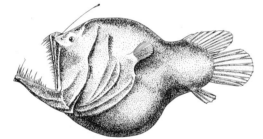

It is a round-bodied angler, the females larger than the males. Adult females are rounded with large jaws and fang-like teeth. Dull brown or black in colour with light fins, and a light 'fishing rod' on the snout. The tip of the lure is usually unpigmented.

Most specimens of adult females have been taken at depths of 1000–2000 m. (546–1100 fathoms). Food remains of copepods, arrowworms, and fishes have been found in the gut of juvenile specimens.

Melanochromis Cichlidae
vermivorus 10 cm. (4 in.)
A species of cichlid found only in Lake Malawi in s. Africa. It is confined almost exclusively to rocky habitats within that lake.

It is a beautifully coloured species which has attained some degree of popularity as an aquarium fish. The male is dark blue-black in colour with a lengthwise stripe from nosetip to tail and another on the upper side, both of pale blue.

Like other members of the genus it eats invertebrates but in this case its diet is relatively specialized and is composed solely of aquatic worms. **368**

Melanogrammus Gadidae
aeglefinus HADDOCK 80 cm. ($31\frac{1}{2}$ in.)
The haddock is found in coastal water on both sides of the N. Atlantic, from Biscay to the Barents Sea, around Iceland, and in the w. Atlantic from Newfoundland s. to Cape Cod. In wintertime it tends to move s. and may then occur more commonly than at other times of the year.

Its coloration is distinctive, purplish grey on the back, silvery grey on the sides and white on the belly. The lateral line is black, and there is a rounded black blotch on the sides between the dorsal and pectoral fins.

It is found mainly at depths between 40–300 m. (22–164 fathoms), but comes inshore into shallower water in the S. of its range. It spawns on the N. European coasts from February to June, the larvae being pelagic and floating near the surface. Young haddock are often found living in association with large jellyfishes, sheltering under the float amongst the trailing tentacles. After the pelagic stages are past, haddock become bottom-living, feeding almost entirely on benthic organisms such as brittle stars, worms, and molluscs, with some small fishes. Occasionally they will feed on sponges and the flesh of the haddock may have a tainted flavour as a result of this diet.

It is a valuable commercial fish on both sides of the Atlantic. Much of the catch is taken by bottom trawl, some by seine, and a small amount by line. The catch is marketed fresh, frozen, or is smoked. Its flesh is rated very highly.

Melanostigma Zoarcidae
atlanticum 14 cm. ($5\frac{1}{2}$ in.)
A deep water eelpout which was originally described from a specimen caught in the N. Atlantic (c. 57°N., 11°W.) at a depth of 1853 m. (1012 fathoms). Subsequently, specimens have been captured in the e. Atlantic, the Gulf of St Lawrence, off Newfoundland, and in deep water off New Jersey. Its depth range is from 673–1172 m. (368–640 fathoms). A closely related species has been found in the S. Atlantic in the Straits of Magellan and off S. Georgia.

M. atlanticum is distinguished by the total absence of pelvic fins, by its moderate sized pectorals, and longer teeth. The skin enveloping the body is loose and seems to be separated from the body by gelatinous fluid. It is purplish grey above, almost black near the tail, inside the mouth and gill-cover blackish. Males have relatively huge teeth.

MELANOSTOMIATIDAE

A moderately large family of modest sized fishes found in the upper layers of the deep oceans of the world, except for the polar seas. They are always taken in water of great depth, the maximum depth seems to be 4500 m. (2459 fathoms) although most species live between the surface and 1000 m. (546 fathoms) depth.

Most are slender-bodied fishes with relatively small heads, but have large tooth-filled jaws. They are scaleless, black or dark with a number of rows of small light organs along their sides, and usually with a larger light organ behind the eye. All members of the family have a chin barbel, often with a swollen tip and variously branched. Males and females of the same species often have a differently shaped barbel. See **Bathophilus, Echiostoma, Flagellostomias, Pachystomias.**

Melanotaenia Melanotaeniidae
fluviatilis CRIMSON-SPOTTED RAINBOW FISH, PINKEAR 9 cm. ($3\frac{1}{2}$ in.)
A widely distributed freshwater fish in e. Australia, it is found in the states of S. Australia, New South Wales, and Queensland in the Murray River system.

It is beautifully coloured, with pink fins, and silvery sides.

It lays its eggs in early summer during a protracted spawning season. The eggs bear fine threads by which they are fastened to water plants; they hatch in about 9 days at 20°C.

This fish has become popular as an aquarium species.

MELANOTAENIIDAE

A small family of freshwater fishes found mainly in Australia although 1–2 species are found in New Guinea as well. Probably also represented in Madagascar. They are closely related to the silversides or sand smelts (family Atherinidae) and resemble them to some extent, especially in having a first dorsal fin composed of several unbranched rays. They are in general, deeper bodied than most atherines, and rather more colourful. Most are known as rainbowfish. See **Melanotaenia, Nematocentrus.**

MELBOURNE SKATE see **Raja whitleyi**

Melichthys Balistidae
ringens BLACK TRIGGERFISH
51 cm. (20 in.)
Apparently well distributed in both the Indian and Pacific oceans between the s. African coast, Zanzibar, the Seychelles, the Philippines, and China. Its exact distribution is not certain due to taxonomic confusion; some authors regard this species as correctly named *Balistes radula*.

It is very distinctive, its head, body, tail, and fins being totally black, the base of the dorsal and anal fins are bluish white, while the outer tips to the tail fin rays are also white. **472**

Mene Menidae
maculata MOONFISH 20 cm. (8 in.)
Found from the coast of E. Africa, the Indian

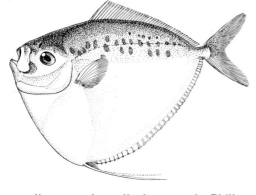

coastline, to n. Australia thence to the Philippines, Japan and the Hawaiian Islands. It lives in the deeper coastal waters off reefs but sometimes enters estuaries. It is said to be used as a food-fish on the Indian coasts.

Its body form is quite distinctive and its colouring is equally characteristic. The body is silvery-white overall becoming green on the back, and with a few greeny-grey patches on the upper sides. The pelvics and tail fin are dusky.

MENHADEN see **Brevoortia tyrannus**

MENIDAE

A family of Indo-Pacific distribution which is found from Hawaii and Japan w. to the E. African coast. Only a single species is recognized.

Its body form is quite striking, compressed into a flat disc, the dorsal profile being nearly straight, the ventral outline strongly curved and razor-edged. The dorsal and anal fins are low, but have numerous rays; the pelvics have a long, flattened and curved first ray.

This species is thought to be related to the jacks (Carangidae) but differs from them in a number of ways. See **Mene.**

Menidia   Atherinidae
  menidia ATLANTIC SILVERSIDE
14 cm. (5½ in.)
A long slender fish with a rounded body and short head, both covered with large scales; the eyes are large. Two dorsal fins, the first short with from 3–7 spines, the second only a little longer based; the anal fin long. The body is translucent, pale green above speckled along the edges of the scales with dark marks; a conspicuous silver band flanked by a black line runs along the side.

This species is native to the e. coastline of the U.S. and Canada. It is found from the Gulf of St Lawrence and Nova Scotia s. to Chesapeake Bay; a closely related form occurs to the S. of this area.

It is a schooling fish found in the inshore tidal regions in bays and estuaries and venturing with the high tide over flooded salt marshes. In the N. of the range they are found in estuaries. They spawn in May, June and July, in schools at about low water mark on sandy bottoms. The eggs have a bunch of sticky filaments on one spot, and cling to one another and the vegetation in strings and singly. The young are 12–15 mm. in length at hatching.

The silverside is an important forage fish for many of the larger, predatory fishes of the area. It is very good eating when treated like whitebait but is not commercially exploited.

MENPACHI see **Myripristis amaenus**

Menticirrhus   Sciaenidae
  saxatilis NORTHERN KINGFISH, WHITING
42 cm. (17 in.)
Found on the w. Atlantic coast of N. America from Florida n. to Cape Cod, and to Maine as a rare wanderer. It is an excellent food and game fish, and is caught in numbers by beach anglers fishing in the surf along the e. seaboard.

To the N. of its range it is a summer visitor, appearing in spring and vanishing around autumn. It is found in schools, keeping close to the hard or sandy sea bed that it prefers, and feeding widely on bottom-living invertebrates, chiefly crustaceans, and small fishes.

The kingfish is one of the few sciaenids to have no swimbladder; it is thus a silent fish by comparison with its sonic relatives.

It is distinguished in the area in which it lives by having a single barbel on the chin, a prominent and rounded snout with the mouth ventral and, in adults, the very long third dorsal fin spine. It is greyish blue above, silvery ventrally with a series of oblique, forward-running dusky bars on the back and sides.

Merlangius   Gadidae
  merlangus WHITING 70 cm. (28 in.)
Widely distributed in European waters from the N. coast of Norway, and Iceland s. to the Mediterranean and the Black Sea. It is particularly common in shallow waters of the continental shelf, and found down to a depth of 200 m. (110 fathoms).

A predator, it feeds most actively during daylight in midwinter or just off the bottom, eating when young, crustaceans and young fish, and when older, larger fishes such as sand-eels, sprats, as well as crustaceans. It is particularly abundant in relatively shallow, sandy bottomed areas, and the young can be caught in a few feet of water. The very young fish are frequently found living in association with large jellyfishes, darting in and out of the mass of trailing tentacles.

The whiting is a slender-bodied codfish with a small barbel and a prominent snout. The dorsal and anal fins are closely placed, the first anal being very long. Its colouring varies. **188**

MERLUCCIIDAE

The family of true hakes, a group of cod-like fishes which are found in moderate to deep water on the continental shelf of most temperate seas. Several species are recognized, but they are not very clearly differentiated except by geographical isolation, and their physical characters tend to overlap. They include the European hake *Merluccius merluccius,* the South African hake, *M. capensis,* a species in New Zealand, *M. australis,* the N. American Atlantic form, *M. bilinearis,* the e. Pacific *M. productus,* and the S. American forms, Pacific coast *M. gayi,* and the Atlantic coast *M. hubbsi.* Most are valuable commercial species.

They are distinguished by a rather elongate body shape, with 2 dorsal fins, the first short and triangular, and the second shaped like the anal, long with a pronounced dip in outline towards the end. The head is large, jaws long with strong teeth, the chin barbel is absent. Scales are moderate in size. All the hakes have a bluish grey back, silvery underneath. See **Merluccius.**

Merluccius   Merlucciidae
  capensis STOCKFISH 122 cm. (48 in.)
A typical hake in body form, and clearly closely related to the European species. It occurs off the coasts of S. Africa, n. to Angola on the W. coast of which it is most abundant, around to the vicinity of East London on the E. coast. Found in depths of 37–914 m. (20–500 fathoms), moving inshore in summer and into deeper water in winter. Its biology is similar to the European form.

The Cape hake, or stockfish is the most important commercial fish of the region. Great quantities are taken by trawl and line, and the fresh fish has excellent flesh, although like other hakes it becomes insipid on keeping.

M. merluccius HAKE, EUROPEAN HAKE
1 m. (39 in.)
The hake is found on the continental shelf of Europe from Norway and Iceland (where it is only seasonally common) to the Mediterranean and N. Africa. It is found mainly in deep water, 165–550 m. (90–300 fathoms), in winter, in summer it is found inshore, and young fish are commonly encountered in shallow water.

The hake is an important commercial fish in European waters, the most important fishing grounds lying to the W. of the British Isles, in Biscay, and off the Portuguese coast. The hake is, however, a slow-growing fish and the stocks have declined dramatically over the years. Large 'jumbo' hake, weighing up to 11·3 kg. (25 lb.) are rarely, if ever, caught now where they were moderately common at one time. The average maximum weight today is around 4·5 kg. (10 lb.).

The hake feeds principally on fish; in deep water they eat blue whiting and small hake, as well as squids, but when they are inshore they eat a large range of shoaling fishes. They are mid-water fish, although found near the bottom during daytime.

In body form it is much like other hakes, distinguished by its geographical range as much as differences in number of scales, or gill rakers. It is slate-grey or blue above, lighter ventrally, with the inside of the mouth dark.

M. productus PACIFIC HAKE 90 cm. (35 in.)
This hake ranges from n. Alaska to Magdalena Bay in California, and offshore along the continental shelf. It is found in depths of 183–914 m. (100–500 fathoms). Like other hakes it is a schooling fish which migrates vertically each day feeding nearer the surface as night approaches. It also migrates offshore in the winter.

It feeds mainly on fishes, but eats squids and crustaceans; the young fish eat small crustaceans mainly. In turn it is eaten by many marine animals especially small whales, porpoises, seals, and sea lions, swordfish, sharks, and halibut. Its flesh is rated as insipid and soft if kept, although very fresh it is good. Much of the hake caught was used for pet food and the manufacture of fish meal, but of recent years fisheries for it have been expanded by Russian ships.

Merogymnus Opistognathidae
eximius HARLEQUIN SMILER
36 cm. (14 in.)

An Australian jawfish which is known only from the waters of Queensland, although it has been found as far N. as the Capricorn group. Its biology is presumed to be similar to other members of the family.

It is golden or golden brown above, the sides have large oval golden blotches separated by blue connecting bands. The tail and the belly are violet with greenish tinges, and the head is lilac with violet spots. The ventral fins are bluish.

Metynnis Characidae
maculatus SPOTTED SILVER-DOLLAR
18 cm. (7 in.)

The characins belonging to the genus *Metynnis* are mostly deep-bodied and externally similar to the piranhas. They are, however, very different in their habits, for they are peaceful plant-eaters instead of carnivorous fish.

This species is found widely in ne. S. America, from the Guianas, the Amazon basin, and Rio Paraguay. Its habit of forming large shoals, and living in densely weeded backwaters is typical of the genus. With other plant-eating characins it plays a role in keeping the waterways clear of dense vegetation.

The adipose fin is very long-based in these fishes. The males have slightly longer anterior rays in the anal fin than the females. It is a favourite fish for the aquarist. **73**

Meuschenia Balistidae
hippocrepis HORSESHOE LEATHERJACKET
51 cm. (20 in.)

An Australian species which is widely distributed and apparently found off all the s. states. It is found in shallow water in rocky and weedy situations often close to the coast. It is occasionally taken on hand-lines, but it is not eaten.

It is an elongate species with a high, forward curved dorsal spine. The mouth is terminal with flattened and pointed teeth in the jaws. Its colouring is brilliant but variable, olive-green above, lighter below with broken blue lines on the body profile and blue around the mouth. The side of the body behind the pectoral fin has a distinct, and distinctive, black horseshoe-shaped mark.

MEXICAN TETRA see **Astyanax mexicanus**

Micralestes Characidae
acutidens SILVER MINNOW 7·5 cm. (3 in.)

A characin widely distributed through the rivers of tropical Africa, from the Nile to the Niger basin and s. to the Zambezi. It is extremely abundant in many rivers and is found in large shoals, being an important fodder fish for many of the larger predators.

The females are usually larger than the males which have a very pronounced lobe to the anal fin, giving the outer edge a strongly convex outline. The outer edge of the female's fin is slightly convex.

It is occasionally imported as an aquarium fish. **74**

M. interruptus CONGO TETRA 8 cm. (3· in.)
This species is found in the Congo basin. It is a singularly beautiful and attractive fish, and in the aquarium makes a very pleasing show. Its normal behaviour is to swim in small shoals.

The males are the larger, females rarely grow longer than 6 cm. (2½ in.). The female is usually less well coloured and has only slightly elongate dorsal and tail fin rays; these in the male are a notable feature, the dorsal rays in particular being long and almost streamer-like, while the middle rays of the tail fin are produced into a central lobe. This species has a very large adipose fin.

The colouring of this fish varies a good deal with condition and lighting but a healthy specimen will be light olive on the back, golden towards the tail, while on the sides a muted rainbow of colours gleams. It has a light blue blotch behind the gill covers.

This species has been bred in captivity. Pairs breed on sunny days; the large light brown eggs are shed indiscriminately over the bottom. A female will lay 300 or more eggs at one spawning; they hatch after 6 days at 25–26°C. **75**

M. occidentalis 6·5 cm. (2½ in.)
A small African characin which is found only in the rivers of W. Africa, from Ghana to the Ivory Coast.

Its body form is much like that of other members of the genus. The teeth are well developed, sharp with several cusps and there is an internal row behind the outer teeth. Like other members of the group it is probably an active predator on smaller fishes and invertebrates. **76**

Microchirus Soleidae
variegatus THICKBACK SOLE
23 cm. (9 in.)

A European sole of wide distribution. Its range extends from the w. English Channel s. to Morocco (and possibly also to Senegal), and throughout the Mediterranean. It is found as a rare fish along the British W. coast as far N. as Scotland.

It is an offshore species occurring most abundantly in 37–92 m. (20–50 fathoms), and exceptionally as shallow as 18 m. (10 fathoms) or as deep as 293 m. (160 fathoms). It is usually found on coarse sand.

Throughout its range wherever it is abundant it is fished commercially, although usually as a by-product of trawling for other species. Its name suggests its most obvious physical feature, its body being very thick by comparison with other soles. Its flesh is delicious. Its colouring is also characteristic being warm brown on the eyed (right) side with variable, mainly wide, cross bands of darker brown over the body. Ventrally it is creamy white.

MICRODESMIDAE

A small family of little-known fishes which are widely distributed in the tropical Indian and Pacific oceans, and along the w. Atlantic and Caribbean coast-line. Most of the genera assigned to this family are small, rather elongate fishes, some being eel-like in appearance. They are usually known as wormfishes. Most are scaleless or have minute embedded scales; the lower jaw projects, and the dorsal and anal fins are long-based and joined to the tail fin.

The small size of these fishes has for long made difficulties in placing them correctly in the systematic order of fishes. Various members have, at times, been grouped with the gobies, the eleotrids, and the blennies. They are now aligned with the first of these groups. Many of the species described and assigned to the family are known from single specimens and their apparent rarity has added to the confusion about their relationships. The biology of very few microdesmids has been studied. See **Microdesmus, Pholidichthys.**

Microdesmus Microdesmidae
dipus 11 cm. (4½ in.)

A little known species which is found on the Pacific coast of Central America, originally from Panama, known now to occur in Baja California and elsewhere. Its biology is virtually unknown.

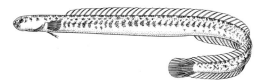

Presumably like other wormfishes it is a burrowing species inhabiting coarse sand or rubble and living mainly under cover. Its coloration is plain, olive-brown, the tail brownish, all other fins plain and translucent.

Microgadus Gadidae
proximus PACIFIC TOMCOD
25 cm. (10 in.)

A Pacific Ocean codfish found from Alaska to Point Sal, California. It is relatively small, but exhibits the features characteristic of the family – 3 well-spaced dorsal fins and 2 anal fins. The pelvic fins are long and reach almost to the vent. The chin barbel is small.

It is very common along the coasts of Washington, Oregon, and California, in depths of 27–91 m. (15–50 fathoms) on sandy or muddy bottoms. At times it is found in the surf zone. It offers fair sport to anglers on piers or even on the shore, and small quantities are caught in trawls for use as fresh fish and reduction to pet food. The tomcod feeds mainly on crustaceans and smaller fishes, and is eaten by many kinds of larger fishes and mammals.

It is closely similar to the Atlantic tomcod *Microgadus tomcod*, a fish found from s. Labrador to Virginia in the w. Atlantic only.

M. tomcod see under **M. proximus**

Microglanis Pimelodidae
parahybae 8 cm. (3 in.)

A small member of a family of catfishes which have rather short and thickset bodies, the head being flattened but the body laterally compressed. The dorsal and pectoral fins have stout spines, those on the pectoral being particularly strong and serrated. Barbels in 3 pairs, only moderately long. Usually brown, but varying from yellowish to chocolate brown. Three dark patches on sides.

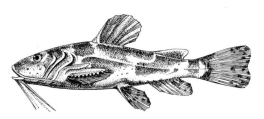

This species is found only in the Rio Paraiba basin in s. Brazil. It is moderately commonly kept as an aquarium fish, and is undemanding.

Micromesistius   Gadidae
poutassou BLUE WHITING 41 cm. (16 in.)
A pelagic, mainly oceanic fish found in vast numbers in the e. N. Atlantic from the Barents Sea s. to the Mediterranean and Adriatic. It is

found around Iceland, but has only rarely been reported on the American Atlantic coast. It is very rarely found inshore, but forms enormous shoals in the open sea from the surface down to 400 m. (219 fathoms).

It is medium blue on the back, fading to silvery on the sides and belly, although it quickly assumes a dull grey tinge after death.

Although not directly exploited for food, the blue whiting has considerable indirect economic importance both as competitor for food and as a fodder for other species. It has considerable potential as an industrial fish, used for the manufacture of fish meal, and oil.

A related species occurs in Antarctic seas.

Micropterus   Centrarchidae
dolomieui SMALLMOUTH BASS
68 cm. (27 in.)
A native of N. America from Quebec and n. Minnesota, s. to S. Carolina, Alabama, and Oklahoma, though widely redistributed in N. America, and now found in many areas outside its original range. It has been introduced on a number of occasions to England, but has failed to establish itself. It occurs in many European countries, and is particularly well-established in France. It has also been established in s. and e. Africa.

Its popularity with sports fishermen is the reason for its wide dispersal, for it is rated as one of the most game of North American freshwater fishes. This has led to it being introduced quite uncritically into many waters which are unsuitable for it, and to the detriment of the local fauna.

It is wholly predatory, eating mainly fishes of a suitable size, but also amphibians and invertebrates. When young it preys especially upon crustaceans and insect larvae.

Like all centrarchids it breeds in shallow water, often digging its nest close to a sunken log or boulder on the lake bed. The male hollows out the nest in sand or fine gravel by vibrating his pectoral fins and tail, and guards the eggs and fry. The eggs are adhesive and stick to the small stones in the nest.

It is dark green above, lighter on the sides, with several dusky vertical bars.

M. salmoides LARGEMOUTH BASS
81 cm. (32 in.)
A native of e. N. America, from the Great Lakes s. to Florida, Texas, and Mexico, and

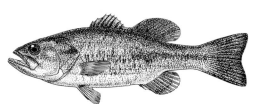

inland to Nebraska and Kansas through the Mississippi Valley. Outside this area it has been widely spread by sportsmen, and it is today found in Europe and s. Africa, reproducing freely. It occurs in one locality in s. England.

Its sporting qualities have assured its being cultured and introduced, and it is one of the important game fish of N. America. It grows to a weight of 11·3 kg. (25 lb.), but the average maximum is 2·3–6·8 kg. (5–15 lb.). In warm-water areas it grows fast, attaining a length of 35 cm. (14 in.) in 3 years, although its growth is slow in cooler areas.

The largemouth bass is a voracious predator and the larger specimens eat fishes mostly, including the young of their own species and other game fishes. When young they feed mainly on aquatic invertebrates.

It matures between 3–5 years of age, and spawns in spring and early summer, requiring a temperature of above 10°C. for successful spawning. The male excavates a nest in the sand or gravel in a depth of water about 1·8 m. (1 fathom). The nest is about 30 cm. (12 in.) in diameter; in it the eggs are laid. The female leaves the nest and the male assiduously guards both eggs and young.

This bass is distinguished by its dorsal fins being almost divided, and by the size of the mouth, the angle of the jaw bone being behind the eye level. **281**

Microspathodon   Pomacentridae
chrysurus YELLOWTAIL DAMSELFISH
11 cm. (4½ in.)
A very distinctive fish when adult, the front part of the body being deep brown to black, with scattered blue spots on the head and dorsal fin, and a bright yellow tail fin, the change being abrupt. The young fish are dark blue with brilliant metallic blue spots overall.

It is found in the w. Atlantic from Bermuda, the Bahamas and Florida to the n. coast of S. America, including the Gulf of Mexico. It has also been reported in the e. Atlantic. It is a common fish on coral reefs, and is rarely taken deeper than 15 m. (8 fathoms). It feeds mainly on algae from coral surfaces but also eats coral polyps and other invertebrates. The young are frequently seen amongst the branches of the yellow stinging coral (*Millepora*) and are parasite pickers.

Microstomus   Pleuronectidae
kitt LEMON SOLE 66 cm. (26 in.)
The lemon sole is a common European fish found on the continental shelf from the White Sea and n. Norway, Iceland, the Faeroes, s. to s. Biscay. Although young specimens can be found quite commonly in shallow inshore waters (especially to the centre and N. of its

range) it is mainly a fish of offshore banks. It is particularly common in depths of 40–200 m. (22–109 fathoms).

Its food is rather specialized. Polychaete worms are most often found in its diet, but large specimens also eat numerous crustaceans and bite off the protruding siphon and mantle of molluscs. They also eat brittle stars. Their diet is rigorously restricted by the small size of the mouth which is a distinctive feature of this fish.

In other ways it is distinguished by its dull brown colouring with a patchwork of mahogany, yellow, and green blotches. The body is smoothly oval, the eyes rather large and level with one another, and the head is comparatively small. Scales on the body are small and smooth edged, and the body has a soft slimy feel to it different from the other common European flatfishes.

It is an important food fish in n. Europe caught mainly by trawls and Danish seines. The most important grounds lie close to Scottish coasts, around the Faeroes, and off Iceland.
M. pacificus DOVER SOLE 71 cm. (28 in.)
This e. Pacific fish is the counterpart of the lemon sole of European seas; neither is a true sole, and the present species's common name is potentially a source of confusion with the Dover sole of English restaurants (see *Solea solea*). This species ranges from n. Baja California to the Bering Sea. It lives on mud bottoms and has been caught at depths of 30–1100 m. (16–600 fathoms). They feed on soft-bodied invertebrates, particularly worms.

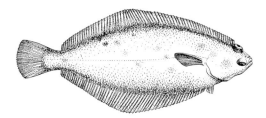

This species has a prolonged pelagic life history; postlarvae of 5 cm. (2 in.) have been found at the surface, as are young fish up to 10 cm. (4 in.) in length. Both larvae and young are food for many larger fishes, but the species no doubt owes its wide distribution to their drift at the surface of the sea.

Throughout its range it is heavily fished by trawling and considerable quantities are marketed both fresh or frozen as fillets. It is one of the more important small flatfish species on the Pacific coast.

It is closely similar to the European lemon sole (*M. kitt*). And like it has a small mouth, small head, straight lateral line, and an exceptionally smooth, slimy skin.

Mimagoniates   Characidae
barberi 4·5 cm. (1¾ in.)
This tetra is a close relative of the croaking tetra (*M. inaequalis*), well known for its accessory breathing organ from which croaking

noises can be produced. *M. barberi* is found in Paraguay and the n. Argentine. It is a slim-bodied fish with a long anal fin, and the dorsal fin far back and high rayed. It is very elegantly coloured with yellowish sides, tinted iridescent green, and a deep blue lengthwise band from the eye to the lower lobe of the tail fin, flanked above by a copper-red stripe. The fins are reddish. The male has a rather higher dorsal fin with a wider lower lobe to the tail fin.

Although it has not been bred very frequently in captivity this species exhibits a most intricate nuptial ritual. The male darts towards the female making a figure-of-eight turn ceaselessly beside her. Eventually, the male comes closer to the female, encircles her body and discharges a spermatophore beside her cloaca. The female picks this up in her cloaca and it later breaks down, the contained sperm fertilizing eggs in the oviduct days and even weeks after mating. The female later deposits the eggs onto the underside of leaves of aquatic plants from which they hatch in 24–30 hours.

M. inaequalis see under **M. barberi**

MINNOW see **Phoxinus phoxinus** and
 under **Campostoma anomalum**
MINNOW,
  FATHEAD see **Pimephales promelas**
  SHEEPSHEAD see **Cyprinodon
   variegatus**
  SILVER see **Micralestes acutidens**
  WHITE CLOUD MOUNTAIN see
   Tanichthys albonubes

Mirapinna   Mirapinnidae
 esau *c*. 5·5 cm. (2¼ in.)
This most remarkable fish appears to be known from a single specimen, 40 mm. in body length, captured at the surface in mid-Atlantic in June 1911 about 880 km. (550 miles) N. of the Azores. Its strange pelvic fins,

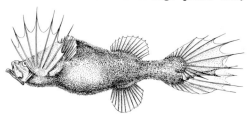

reduced pectorals, and singular overlapping double tail are distinctive features. In addition, the skin of the head, body, and fins is covered with a dense pile of hair-like outgrowths, unlike anything found in other fishes. The 'hairs' of the skin are well equipped with glandular cells, and it has been suggested that these may produce a poisonous or distasteful substance as a form of protection for the fish. Virtually nothing is known of its biology except that the original specimen had eaten small copepod crustaceans.

MIRAPINNIDAE

A family which contains at present only one species, *Mirapinna esau*, found in the tropical Atlantic. In appearance it is strikingly different from any other fish, although the internal structure suggests a placement near the Kasidoridae and Eutaeniophoridae.

Several features make this fish distinctive, most notably the wide-based and upwardly turned pelvic fins and the double tail fin with the lower rays of the upper lobe overlapping the upper part of the lower lobe. These features are recognized in the name Mirapinnidae – the wonderful-finned fishes. See **Mirapinna.**

MIRROR DORY see **Zenopsis nebulosus**

Misgurnus   Cobitidae
 fossilis WEATHERFISH, POND LOACH
30 cm. (12 in.)
A dull coloured loach, dark yellow-brown to

dull brown, with lengthwise dark bands running from head to tail.

The weatherfish is found in Central and e. Europe in shallow ponds and small lakes with muddy bottoms. It survives well in these often swampy conditions where oxygen levels may be low, for it gulps air at the surface, swallowing a bubble, which passes through the intestine and out of the vent, gaseous exchange taking place in the lower gut on the folded mucous lining. Its gills also function as a normal respiratory unit. It can survive short periods of drying up during warm weather by burying itself in the mud and reducing its body activities.

Its food is entirely bottom-living invertebrates. Spawning takes place in spring and early summer, the eggs being shed on water plants. At hatching, the larvae have long thread-like external gills.

The weatherfish is so called because of its alleged sensitivity to changes in atmospheric pressure; it becomes very restless shortly before a thunderstorm. It is occasionally kept in aquaria, and makes an interesting if generally inactive pet.

MISSISSIPPI CAT see **Ictalurus furcatus**

Mitsukurina   Mitsukurinidae
 owstoni GOBLIN SHARK 3·4 m. (11 ft)
The goblin shark has been captured off Portugal and S. Africa occasionally, but frequently off Japan. The distinctive teeth of this species have been found in a submarine cable in the Indian Ocean, so evidently it occurs in that ocean also. It is a deep-water shark, found in depths around 500 m. (273 fathoms) although in Sagami Bay, S. of Tokyo, where females are mostly caught, it is taken in waters as shallow as 33 m. (18 fathoms).

The remarkable head region of this shark, with its protruding shovel-like 'forehead' and protruding teeth, suggests a fish with specialized feeding habits, but little is known of its natural history. It is believed to bear living young.

MITSUKURINIDAE

A single species of deep-water shark with a grotesque pointed snout is the sole living representative of this family. It is, however, known from fossil remains from Syria, some 90–140 million years ago. The family name was bestowed in honour of the Japanese zoologist, Professor Kakichi Mitsukuri, who first drew attention to it. See **Mitsukurina.**

Mobula   Mobulidae
 diabolus PYGMY DEVIL RAY, OX-RAY
1·8 m. (6 ft) wide
Widely distributed in the Indo-Pacific, where within the tropical regions it is frequently common. It is often seen in small shoals of up to 5, in shallow water close inshore, and will jump repeatedly out of the water. It is described, however, as timid and difficult to approach. It is particularly common in the Great Barrier Reef area of Australia, on the E. African coast, and Red Sea.

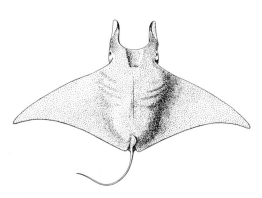

Like other members of its family it feeds on planktonic animals and small shoaling fishes. It is described as greyish-brown above, lighter below.

M. hypostoma see under **M. mobular**
M. mobular DEVIL RAY 5·2 m. (17 ft) wide
This devil ray seems to be confined to the e. Atlantic, from n. Spain and Portugal to the W. African coast. A single occurrence of a small specimen on the s. coast of Ireland in the early nineteenth century must have been due to accidental wandering on the part of that specimen. It occurs in the Mediterranean.

It shares the body shape of all devil rays, with long, rather pointed pectoral fins, the eyes and spiracles being lateral and 2 cephalic fins (movable fleshy flaps either side of the snout, which are the devil's horns implied by its common name). It has a small dorsal fin, and a moderately long tail, with a serrated spine. The mouth is on the lower surface of the head and this genus has very small, multi-cusped teeth in both jaws.

It is a giant when compared with its w. Atlantic relative, *M. hypostoma*, which grows to a width of about 1·2 m. (4 ft), for *M. mobular* commonly exceeds 4·55 m. (15 ft) in width. The largest recorded seems to have been a 5·2 m. (17 ft) specimen from Algeria, while a Spanish specimen of 4·55 m. (15 ft) weighed 358 kg. (788 lb.).

MOBULIDAE

The devil rays are a small family with relatively few species confined to tropical and warm temperate oceans. They are surface or near-surface living forms which have abandoned the bottom-hugging habits of most other rays, and feed on small planktonic organisms and schooling fishes.

These are the giants among rays, some of them reaching a width of 6 m. (20 ft) and a weight in excess of 1300 kg. (2866 lb.), others are more modest in size. All are viviparous, the embryos being nourished with a secretion from the maternal uterine tissue in the later stages of development.

These giant rays have a distinctive body shape with a broad disc composed mainly of the powerful pectoral fins which are rather pointed at their tips. The front edge of each pectoral fin forms a separate, nearly vertical, movable lobe, one each side of the mouth (the 'horns' or head fins). They have a long tail which lacks a tail fin, but do have a small dorsal fin and some species have a serrated spine at the base of the tail. See **Manta, Mobula.**

MOCHOKIDAE

Scaleless catfishes widely distributed in the freshwaters of Africa, except for the desert regions. Members of the family usually have a rather thickset body, the sides slightly compressed and the head flattened, but covered with bony plates which extend on to the back. Dorsal fin short but with a sharp spine, pectoral fins with a large spine. The pectoral fin, when moved in its socket, makes a low grunt, which earns these fish the name of 'squeakers' in s. Africa.

Most are active in twilight, and live in shoals in slow-flowing rivers and swamps. They are omnivorous. Some species swim on their backs, and show a reversal of the usual cryptic coloration. They have little commercial importance but many kinds are imported to Europe and America as they are very interesting fish to keep in captivity. See **Synodontis.**

MODERLIESCHEN see **Leucaspius delineatus**

Moenkhausia   Characidae
  oligolepis GLASS TETRA 12 cm. (4¾ in.)
This peaceful and popular aquarium fish is found widely distributed in the Amazon basin and the Guianas. It is most abundant in small pools and sluggish backwaters of rivers. It feeds on a wide variety of food.

It is a relatively deep-bodied characin with a long anal fin. Males have rather longer rays in the fins, and the first anal fin rays are especially longer than the others. **77**

M. pittieri 6 cm. (2½ in.)
This tetra is found only in Lake Valencia, Venezuela. It is a fine fish, which enhances any aquarium with its silvery sheen and active behaviour.

Its most notable feature is the height of the fins, the dorsal and anal fins being especially prolonged. Mature males tend to be brighter in colour and have much longer dorsal fin rays than females, so that the fin has a pennant-like appearance.

It is a moderately easy fish to keep, and has been bred in captivity. It requires ample space and thrives best if fed on zooplankton. **78**

M. sanctaefilomenae 8 cm. (3 in.)
A characin from the Paraguay River system and the basin of the River Paranahiba. Like the other members of this genus, the upper part of the eye is bright red.

It is a very lively and beautiful aquarium fish which has become deservedly popular. Females have a rather deeper body profile, males have slightly longer rays in the anterior portion of the anal fin, but sexual dimorphism is not marked. **79**

Mola   Molidae
  mola SUNFISH, OCEAN SUNFISH,
TRUNKFISH 4 m. (13 ft)
The sunfish is quite unmistakable, its body form being unlike any other fish except its immediate relatives. It differs from *Ranzania* by having an almost circular body, and from *Masturus* in lacking the small produced 'tail' on the rear edge. Its body is deep blue above, silvery on the sides, but after death it fades to an unattractive grey-brown.

Mola is found in all temperate and tropical seas of the world; nowhere is it common, but it seems less uncommon in the warm temperate areas. Many of the specimens examined have been floating inactively at the surface and gaffed, harpooned, or lifted into boats, others have been rammed, and many more are just sighted. These occurrences have given rise to the belief that the fish basks in the sun, hence its name (sunfish is also used for the basking shark off the W. coast of Ireland for the same reason). To what extent this basking behaviour is normal and whether these fish are sick or disabled is not known, but the latter seems more probable.

Sunfishes are most common in the open ocean, and probably range from the surface to 183–366 m. (100–200 fathoms) in midwater. Specimens caught in such depths have been feeding on jellyfishes, ctenophores (comb-jellies), crustaceans, and young fish. There are reports of it eating the leptocephalus larval stage of eels. In inshore waters odd specimens have been found with seaweed, and larger fishes in their gut, and a number of specimens have been accidentally caught by anglers – which suggests that they are unselective in their choice of food. Most *Mola* stomachs have been empty when opened.

While the average size of sunfish caught or seen is around 91 cm. (3 ft) and weights of up to 45 kg. (100 lb.) are normal, it can grow very large. Unfortunately most figures for maximal size have a suspicious 'roundness' about them, but the largest of recent 'guesstimates' is of a fish struck by a ship in the Tasman Sea which

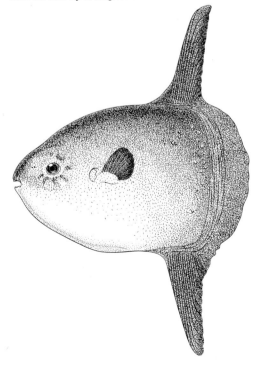

was 4 m. long (13·1 ft) and weighed more than 1500 kg. (3300 lb.). An 1865 report of a fish from off Argentina gave its weight as 1197 kg. (2640 lb.). Indisputable lengths and weights for this fish are much to be desired.

Despite its size and wide distribution its biology is little known. One female specimen of 1·24 m. (4½ ft) was estimated to contain 300 million eggs, yet neither fertilized eggs nor young larvae have ever been found. Later larvae are round bodied and equipped with short 'thumb-tack' spines on their skins, like the adults they have a high dorsal and anal fin.

Sunfishes are not deliberately fished. Their flesh is soft and insipid, although some people find them a delicacy. They are usually also infested with numerous external crustacean parasites and a complete fauna of intestinal and encysted parasitic worms. These tend to deter culinary curiosity.

MOLA, SHARPTAIL see **Masturus
  lanceolatus**
Molacanthus see **Masturus lanceolatus**

MOLIDAE

The family of marine sunfishes, giant inhabitants of the open seas, found worldwide in tropical and temperate oceans, with occasional specimens in cooler waters.

As is so often the case the larger species of fish are the least known and considerable doubt exists as to the number of species. Three genera are recognized containing 3–5 species. Similarly little is known about the biology of any species.

All are plectognath fishes, relatives of the triggerfishes (Balistidae) and pufferfishes (Tetraodontidae), and like them have well-developed teeth. In the sunfishes or trunkfishes the teeth are fused into a single unit above and below, making a strong, sharp beak. For the size of the fish (some species may weigh several thousand of pounds) the mouth is small. Their most striking feature, however, is the apparent absence of a tail, both dorsal and anal fins are short-based and high and placed at the ends of the truncate body. Such tail fin as exists is a line of lobes joining these 2 vertical fins along the rear of the body. See **Masturus, Mola, Ranzania.**

MOLLY see **Poecilia sphenops**
MOLLY, SAILFIN see **Poecilia latipinna,
  Poecilia velifera**

Molva   Gadidae
  molva LING 2 m. (6½ ft)
A gadoid found mainly in the e. Atlantic, although occasional specimens have been captured off the e. Canadian coast. In European waters it occurs from n. Norway to central Biscay, and off s. Iceland. It is abundant N. of the Channel. It is essentially a deep-water fish most commonly found in 300–400 m. (164–219 fathoms) although young fish are found in shallower, inshore water.

It is a long-bodied, large fish, growing to weights of 20 kg. (45 lb.) and more. It grows relatively rapidly attaining an average maximum age of 10 years for males, and around 14 years for females. It is an active predator, feeding principally on fishes, gadoids, herring, and occasionally flatfishes. Some crustaceans and even starfishes are eaten.

The ling is an important commercial fish, caught mainly in trawls, and lines in the n. parts of its European range. It is also caught locally by anglers.

Monacanthus Balistidae
tuckeri SLENDER FILEFISH 8·5 cm. (3½ in.)
Essentially a W. Indian species, this little file-fish occurs between the Carolinas, Florida, and the Lesser Antilles. Its choice of habitats is varied for it is sometimes seen hiding amongst gorgonian fronds, in sea grass beds, on coral reefs, and over mixed rock and sandy bottoms. It is only found in shallow water.

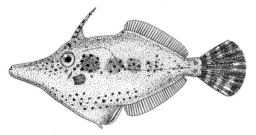

Its coloration is varied, basically shades of brown with rows of dark dots scattered on the body. The mid-line of the side is dark, the belly is silvery, while a pale reticulation of of lines runs over the whole body.

This small species has 2 spines either side of its tail and is much more slender than other filefishes found in the area.

MONKFISH see **Squatina squatina**
MONKFISH, CALIFORNIAN see **Squatina californica**

MONOCENTRIDAE
A most remarkable family of marine fishes, often known as pine-cone fishes. Two species are known, both found in the Indo-Pacific.

Both are plump and rounded, the head blunt and covered with hard bone, while the body is encased by heavy scales uneven in size, to form a rough, body armour. These heavy overlapping scales give it the name of pine-cone fish. The dorsal spines are large, and sharp, and lie alternately to left and right, while the pelvic spines are massive. Both the known species are small, growing to about 23 cm. (9 in.) long. See **Cleidopus, Monocentris.**

Monocentris Monocentridae
japonicus PINE-CONE FISH 12·7 cm. (5 in.)
Widely distributed in the Indo-Pacific from Japan, where it is common, to the s. tip of S. Africa. It lives in schools close to the bottom in deep water at depths of 37–183 m. (20–100 fathoms).

In Japan it is common enough to be ex-

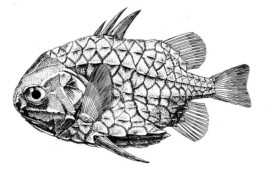

ploited commercially, and is eaten fried or roasted, with vinegar. It is also commonly kept in marine aquaria. It has a pair of small luminous organs under the lower jaw which contain symbiotic bacteria.

Monocirrhus Nandidae
polyacanthus LEAFFISH 10 cm. (4 in.)
Native to the ne. region of S. America, the leaffish is found in the basins of the Amazon and the Rio Negro. It is well-known for its remarkable mimicry of floating leaves, its body is deeply compressed, the head pointed and the lower jaw prominent with a short, stiff barbel at its tip. Its coloration is variable, but is usually brownish, mottled lighter and darker, although when living in an aquarium amongst green plants it is often greenish. Its habit of drifting near the surface, in a head-down posture leads it to look remarkably like a brown leaf floating, the chin barbel heightening the resemblance by appearing to be the leaf stalk. Its remarkable mimicry no doubt has some protective function. but its chief value is to allow the fish to approach prey by stealth. Its jaws are very protrusible, and shoot forward to seize small fishes with lightning rapidity. It feeds almost entirely on fishes, often up to half its own size.

It is a popular aquarium fish, but not suitable for a mixed community tank on account of its predatory habits. It spawns on large plant leaves or stones. The eggs are few and large and are laid directly on the leaf, the male usually guards and fans them until they hatch

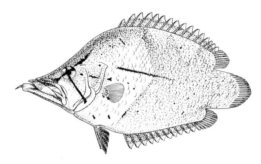

in 3–4 days, at a temperature of 22–25°C. The young grow rapidly and are predatory from hatching, at first feeding on crustaceans, later on fishes. 352

MONODACTYLIDAE
A small family of mainly inshore and estuarine fishes which are found around the Atlantic and Indian ocean coasts of Africa and around the Indian Ocean and w. Pacific shores.

Its members, of which there are about 6, are extremely deep-bodied, with compressed bodies, silvery in colour, small scales which extend onto the fins. Fin spines much reduced in size and pelvic fins rudimentary. See **Monodactylus.**

Monodactylus Monodactylidae
argenteus DIAMONDFISH, FINGERFISH, MOONFISH, KITEFISH 23 cm. (9 in.)
A native of the Indo-Pacific and widely distributed from Australian seas, around the coasts of the E. Indies and India, to the Red Sea and e. Africa. It is very common in most of its range, swimming in small schools in bays and river mouths. It is often found in fresh-water. It is said to be good to eat but is rather

small; on the other hand, it has proved to be a popular pet fish in the salt- or brackish-water aquarium. **308**
M. sebae 20 cm. (8 in.)
An African fish found along the coast of w. Africa from Senegal to the Congo. It is very common in inshore waters of the sea but enters estuaries and is found occasionally in fresh-water.

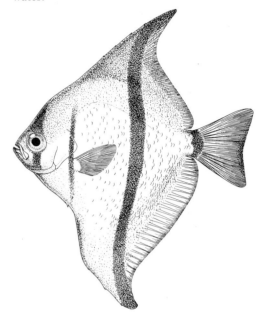

M. sebae has been imported to Europe for many years as a pet fish; it makes a striking sight in the marine or brackish aquarium.

Its body is excessively high, from the tip of the anal to the tip of the dorsal lobe almost twice as high as it is long. Its colouring is silver, light brown on the upper half of the body, with dark vertical bands running through the eye, behind the head, from the tip of the dorsal to the anal, and across the tail fin base.

MONOGNATHIDAE
A small, rather enigmatic group apparently related to the gulper-eels, formerly placed in the order Lyomeri. The monognathids were first described in 1936 from material collected by the Danish oceanographic expeditions of the early 1930s. Its members were distinguished from the other gulper-eels by the lack of an upper jaw and pectoral fins, and by differences in skeletal structure. They also have fewer vertebrae than their relatives. There are, however, some grounds for suggesting that they may be no more than growth stages of one or the other well-known gulper-eels.

All the specimens studied have been small, maximum 11 cm. (4¼ in.). They have been captured in the tropical e. Atlantic, as well as in the China Sea. They are bathypelagic in habit. See **Monognathus.**

Monognathus Monognathidae
taningi About 57 mm. (2¼ in.)
This small gulper-eel was recorded in the

Atlantic, S. of the Cape Verde Islands in moderately deep water of 120–1200 m. (66–656 fathoms).

Its general appearance is said to be like other gulper-eels. The stomach and body walls are evidently capable of being widely stretched by large food organisms. The upper jaw bone does not seem to be developed. Specimens are almost transparent.

Monopterus Synbranchidae
alba RICE EEL 91 cm. (3 ft)
This synbranchid eel is found widely distributed in Asia from n. China and Japan to Thailand and Burma. It is also found in the Philippines, and is said to have been introduced to the Hawaiian Islands. It is found in a variety of habitats, rivers, ponds, ditches, and swamps, and has colonized the rice-fields very successfully. During the dry season they take refuge in the deepest parts of the drainage ditches, burrowing in the mud in which they will survive, provided the skin is kept moist, until the next inundation.

They form an important food fish in inland regions, caught by probing the deeper muddy patches for aestivating fish. As they survive out of water for a long time, they can be transported for long distances. Small specimens are also captured for export as pet fish.

This fish spawns from July onwards (in Thailand) the eggs being spat into a bubble nest made by the male in shallow water. The rafts of eggs are not anchored by vegetation but float freely, guarded by the male, which apparently also guards the young at first.

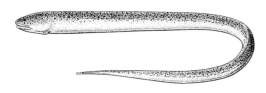

Large fish are olive-brown, the underside pale; younger fishes are pale brown with dark brown spots overall. A dark line runs from snout to the eye.

M. boutei see under **Ophistosternon infernale**
M. cuchia CUCHIA 70 cm. (28 in.)
Widely distributed in India in the states of Bengal, Orissa, the Punjab, and in Assam and Burma. It lives in swamps, backwaters of rivers, and ditches and lagoons, often in areas which become totally deficient in dissolved oxygen, and many of which dry up in summer. Two lung-like sacs that arise from the roof of the gill chambers constitute a very efficient air breathing system by which it can long survive out of water. Most of its life is spent buried in the bottom; it becomes active only at night.

Locally it is an important food fish. Young specimens are also imported to Europe as aquarium fish but they are relatively poor pets on account of their general inactivity and their predatory habits.

Their life coloration is very variable but they are usually dull green with yellowish dots and streaks, while ventrally they are yellowish.
240.

Monotaxis Pentapodidae
grandoculis LEVOVANGAN 76 cm. (30 in.)
An Indo-Pacific species found from the Red Sea (where it was first discovered by Pehr Forsskål, the eighteenth century Danish explorer) and the E. African coast, to India and the E. Indies, and the w. Pacific islands to Hawaii. It is found in moderately deep water along the edges of reefs close to open water. Below 3 m. (10 ft) it becomes common. In places it is very abundant and is a valuable food fish throughout its range.

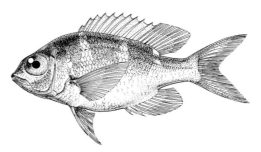

As an adult it is very distinctive, the massive broad and deep head, and large eye being characteristic. They are silvery grey above, lighter on the sides, with red or deep yellow fins. It has 6 canine-like teeth in the upper jaw, and 4–6 in the lower jaw, but all the teeth in the sides of the jaws are rounded molars.

MONTAGU'S BLENNY see **Coryphoblennius galerita**
Monocentris gloriamaris see **Cleidopus gloriamaris**
MONOCLE-BREAM, WHITE-CHEEKED see **Scolopsis vosmeri**
MOON WRASSE see **Thalassoma lunare**
MOON-EYES see Hiodontidae
MOON-EYE see **Hiodon tergisus**
MOONFISH see Lampridae
MOONFISH see **Lampris guttatus, Monodactylus argenteus, Trachinotus russelli**
MOONLIGHT GOURAMI see **Trichogaster microlepis**
MOORISH IDOL see **Zanclus cornutus**

Mora Eretmophoridae
mora 51 cm. (20 in.)
A deep water cod-like fish found in the Mediterranean and ne. Atlantic from the Canary Islands n. to the Faeroe Islands. It is confined to the deep sea, between 60–1400 m. (33–765 fathoms) but is only taken in the shallower depths to the S.

It is relatively slender-bodied with 2 dorsal fins, the first of which is short and slightly higher than the very long second dorsal. There are 2 anal fins, small but long-rayed pelvics, and a forked tail. A short chin barbel is present. The back is greenish black, the sides and belly lighter; the mouth and inside the gill covers are black.

MORAY see Muraenidae
MORAY see **Muraena helena**
MORAY,
GREEK see **Muraena helena**
PAINTED see **Gymnothorax pictus**
SPOTTED see **Gymnothorax moringua**
MORAY EEL see **Lycodontis tessellata**

Moridae see Eretmophoridae

Moringua Moringuidae
macrochir WORM EEL
About 46 cm. (18 in.)
This worm eel is widespread in the tropical Pacific, having been found from the E. Indian Archipelago to the Hawaiian Islands. Most of its life is spent buried in loose sand and fine gravel; it buries itself head first. It is yellowish when young, with minute, rudimentary eyes, and worm-like in appearance. However, upon attaining sexual maturity this eel becomes black above and silvery below, and the eyes and fins develop. With this change of body form there is a change in the habits of the eel; it becomes free-swimming and can be taken at the surface.
M. raitaborua c. 45 cm. (17¾ in.)
This worm eel was described from the mouth of the River Ganges, and it has been recorded elsewhere in Indian seas. Little appears to be known of its life history except that it shares the family trait of a juvenile burrowing phase, followed by a pelagic mostly nocturnal habit when sexually mature. The body form and coloration change greatly with maturity, the pectoral fins develop, as do the rather distinctive anal and dorsal fins, and the eye increases

greatly in size. In common with other members of the family there are considerable differences in body shape between the sexes.

MORINGUIDAE
The family of worm eels, characterized by their slender, but cylindrical body shape, by having the anus far behind the mid-point of the body. The dorsal and anal fins are poorly developed, although in some species the mature female develops moderate fins.

The greatest number of species of the family are found in the Indo-Pacific; it is also represented in the Caribbean. See **Moringua**.

MORMYRIDAE
A family of exclusively African freshwaters. Many of its members are of strange appearance, those with elongate trunk-like snouts and blunt-snouted forms intermingling. All have certain features in common: rather small mouths and eyes, dorsal and anal fins similarly shaped and placed near the rear of the body; most have forked tails. They are thick-skinned, slimy fishes.

Many species have electric organs in the sides of the rear body. These give off weak electrical pulses which aid in the detection of prey, predators, one another, and obstructions in the water. A relative of the mormyrids, *Gymnarchus*, has more elaborate and well-studied electric organs of a similar structure. See **Gnathomeus, Marcusenius, Mormyrus, Mormyrops, Petrocephalus.**

Mormyrops Mormyridae
deliciosus CORNISH-JACK 1·5 m. (5 ft)
The Cornish-jack (its S. African name) is a rather slender mormyrid, with narrow head, and terminal mouth; it is one of the few members of the family not to have a prolonged

snout. The dorsal fin is small, the anal long, and the scales are small. Its coloration is variable but it usually dark grey to bronze on the back, silvery on the belly.

It is a predatory fish feeding on small fishes, insects and crustaceans. It is believed to spawn in early summer, as the young fish are then most common in the weeded shallows. Males have a rather higher anal fin and are usually larger than females.

This species is found in the Lower and Middle Zambezi, as well as in the Congo basin and the rivers of W. Africa. It is replaced by a related species in the Nile.

A valuable food fish on account of its size alone, for it may weigh up to 18 kg. (40 lb.). Occasional specimens are taken by anglers.

Mormyrus Mormyridae
kannume ELEPHANT-SNOUT FISH
80 cm. (31½ in.)
This mormyrid is widely distributed in the River Nile system including the Victoria and Murchison Niles, and in many of the great African lakes, amongst them Victoria, Albert, Edward, and George. It is typical in body shape for a mormyrid, dull bronze above, lighter below.

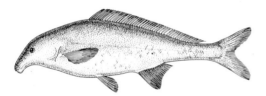

The elephant-snout fish has a considerable electrical capacity, producing a continuous stream of electrical impulses, relatively few when the fish is at rest but greatly increased if it is disturbed. By means of this electrical field it can receive warnings of obstacles or approaching predators in the rather murky water in which it lives. Like others of its family it has a very well developed brain especially the hind brain, supposed to be associated with the co-ordination of the sensory organs detecting disturbances in its electrical field.

It is found widely in shallow and offshore waters in the lakes, and has even been suggested to spawn in the rocky, wave-washed areas. Its food is predominantly bottom-living insect larvae, especially those of midges (Chironomidae).

This is one of several species of fish frequently represented in ancient Egyptian art, and it evidently held a special place in their lives. In many areas it is commercially exploited and makes a substantial contribution to fisheries.

M. proboscyrostris 57 cm. (22½ in.)
A mormyrid, or elephant-snout fish which is found only in the Upper Congo River, Africa. Its biology is little known, and relatively few specimens have ever been reported.

In many respects it is typical of the family, slender-bodied with a very long-based dorsal fin, and rather small, forked, tail fin. The snout is long and curved into a trunk, with small mouth, lower jaw projecting and thick lips. It is usually pinkish brown, sometimes with a bluish-grey stripe running along each side of the body and tail. **35**

Morone Serranidae
americana WHITE PERCH 38 cm. (15 in.)
The white perch, also known as the sea perch, is found along the Atlantic coast of N. America from Nova Scotia and the Gulf of St Lawrence to S. Carolina. It breeds in fresh or brackish water and is found landlocked in many freshwater lakes and their tributary streams.

It is an important sporting and commercial fish, the former in both fresh and salt water.

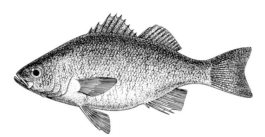

It is in fact more of a freshwater fish found in estuaries and lowland streams and ponds than a sea fish. It is essentially a shallow-water species, retiring into deeper water in winter. Fish form its main diet at all lengths, but crustaceans are eaten to some extent.

It is olive-grey on the back, shading to silvery green on the sides and white on the belly. The fins are dusky except that the pelvics are pink-tinged. Young fish have pale lengthwise stripes but these fade with age.

Morulius Cyprinidae
chrysophekadion BLACK SHARK
60 cm. (2 ft)
This species is widely distributed in Thailand, Cambodia, Java, Borneo, and Sumatra. It is a large fish when fully grown, often weighing in excess of 2 kg. (4.4 lb.), and forming an important fishery in places. Small specimens are suitable for the aquarium and are often available from importers.

A striking species being a uniform black, or blue-black, each scale on the sides with a distinct yellowish or reddish spot. The fins are velvety black.

Like its relatives of the genus *Labeo*, it feeds almost entirely on plants, especially encrusting algae, as well as higher plants. It is a useful fish in the aquarium for its alga-cleaning habits.

Like the *Labeo* species it is flat-bellied with a rather humped back, and a high dorsal fin. Its lips are relatively thick and folded with 2 pairs of barbels. In Thailand it has been reported to breed in swampy conditions in times of flood.

MORWONG see Cheilodactylidae
MORWONG see **Nemadactylus morwong**
MORWONG,
    BLUE see **Nemdactylus valenciennesi**
    DUSKY see **Psilocranium nigricans**
MOSQUITOFISH see **Gambusia affinis,**
        Heterandria formosa
MOSSBUNKER see **Brevoortia tyrannus**
MOTH, SEA see Pegasidae
MOTTLED
    BLACK SEA GOBY see **Proterorhinus**
        marmoratus
    BLENNY see **Tripterygion varium**
    EEL, AFRICAN see **Anguilla nebulosa**
    KNIFEFISH see **Hypopomus artedi**

MOTTLEFIN PARROTFISH see **Scarus**
    croicensis
MOUNTAIN BARBEL see **Amphilius**
    platychir
MOUSEFISH see **Gonorhynchus**
    gonorhynchus
MOUTH-BROODER, NILE see **Sarotherodon**
    niloticus

Moxostoma Catostomidae
macrolepidotum NORTHERN or SHORT-
HEAD REDHORSE 61 cm. (2 ft)
Widespread in central and e. Canada, from Montana and the Great Lakes region e. to the Hudson River in New York, and s. to Arkansas and Kansas. This redhorse is most often found in rivers and streams, although it also inhabits lakes. It spawns in the spring after an upstream migration to smaller streams or tributaries.

It is reputed to be one of the most important fishes of the genus, in the upper Mississippi system especially providing a local fishery.

The redhorse suckers are distinguished from their relatives by their very protractile upper lip, and the broad and undivided lower lip. The northern redhorse has an elongate, closely scaled body, a short dorsal fin, and when viewed from beneath the posterior margin of the lower lip has the form of a straight line. It is olive-green on the back, shading through bronze to yellowish on the belly. The tail and ventral fins are orange tinged.

MOZAMBIQUE CICHLID see **Sarotherodon**
    mossambicus
MUD
    BLENNY see **Congrogadus subducens**
    BREAM see **Acanthopagrus berda**
    SKATE see **Rhina ancylostomus**
    SUNFISH see **Chaenobryttus gulosus**
MUDFISH see **Amia calva, Protopterus**
        annectens
MUDFISH,
    BROWN see **Neochanna apoda**
    BLACK see under **Neochanna apoda**
MUDHOPPER see **Boleophthalmus**
        boddaerti, Periophthalmus
        koelreuteri, Periophthalmodon
        schlosseri
MUDMINNOW,
    CENTRAL see **Umbra limi**
    EASTERN see **Umbra pygmaea**
    EUROPEAN see **Umbra krameri**
MUDSKIPPER see **Periophthalmodon**
    schlosseri

Mugil Mugilidae
argenteus TIGER MULLET, JUMPING
MULLET 45 cm. (18 in.)
A grey mullet which is widely distributed in Australian waters, and is found also around Samoa. It is a valuable food fish, common in estuaries and in inshore waters, and taken mainly in shore seines. Some are captured by anglers, but they are difficult to catch. Its habit of leaping over nets gives it the S. Australian name of jumping mullet. Its aboriginal name in Queensland is tygum.

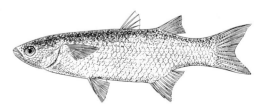

It is steel blue above, silvery on the sides and white below. The scales on the back have lengthwise darker streaks and golden tints. There is a dark patch on the inside of the pectoral fin and a golden patch in front of it.

M. cephalus STRIPED MULLET, HAARDER, FLATHEAD MULLET 91 cm. (3 ft)
A very widely distributed mullet which is found in the tropical and warm temperate waters of the world, both in the open sea and inshore waters, estuaries and almost freshwater. It is believed to spawn offshore in deep water. The juveniles are silvery planktonic creatures much preyed upon by predatory fishes and sea birds. Adults are found far up rivers. Throughout its range it provides important, if local, commercial fisheries, and in some areas is considered to be a good sporting fish.

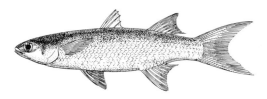

Like other grey mullets it is usually found in small schools. It feeds on diatoms, algae, and minute animal material found amongst the bottom mud; it also browses filamentous algae off pier pilings and rocks.

It is a heavy-bodied, blunt-headed fish with pronounced clear adipose eye-lids. Its back is grey-blue with dark stripes; its belly is silvery.

M. curema WHITE MULLET 91 cm. (3 ft)
An American mullet which is found both in the e. Pacific and along the Atlantic coast from New England and Bermuda to s. Brazil. In the Caribbean and the Gulf of Mexico it is the most abundant species of grey mullet.

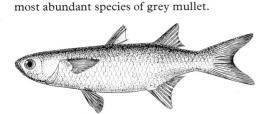

It is caught commercially in areas where it is common, including the Florida coast. Like other members of the family, it is found mainly in inshore waters, but also occurs in estuaries, and low-salinity pools.

It is dark olive above with bluish reflections and a dusky blotch on the pectoral fin base; a golden patch on each cheek.

M. saliens 30 cm. (12 in.)
A species of grey mullet found mainly in the Mediterranean from the Aegean Sea to Gibraltar, and in the e. Atlantic from Portugal s. to W. Africa. It has been reported off S. Africa but this was possibly a result of confusion with a related species.

It is commercially exploited locally and is especially common in saline lagoons where it is captured in surface nets. Its flesh is not so highly esteemed as some of the large grey mullets of the area. **395**

MUGILIDAE
The family of mullets or grey mullets, a large group of mainly marine fishes of closely simi-

lar physical appearance and thus presenting difficulties of identification. The body is usually thick, rather compressed posteriorly, and with a large, blunt-snouted head. The lips are set at an angle to one another, forming an inverted V from the front, are often thick, and lined with fine teeth. The dorsal fins are short-based, the first consisting of only 4 strong spines. The body is heavily scaled.

Grey mullets have a thick-walled gizzard-like stomach and a very long intestine. They feed on fine algal material and bottom detritus sucked up and filtered through the gill-raker sieve, and crushed in the muscular stomach. At any time examination of the gut contents of mullets will show more sand and mud than any other material.

In many areas grey mullets are valuable food fishes. Their habit of living in inshore waters, estuaries, and even freshwater makes them easily accessible.

The nomenclature of the grey mullets is very confused particularly as regards the generic limits. See **Aldrichetta, Crenimugil, Heteromugil, Mugil.**

MUGILOIDIDAE
A small family of Indo-Pacific fishes found in tropical waters. They are known as sand perches, weevers, and smelts, the latter names in Australia and S. Africa respectively, where the true weevers and smelts do not occur.

The members of the family are elongate with rather stout bodies covered with small scales. The head is large as are the jaws. Two dorsal fins joined at the base, the first being short-based and rather low.

They are rather small fishes, found in shallow inshore waters. They usually burrow in sand or hide under stones or coral blocks. See **Neopercis, Parapercis.**

MULLET see Mugilidae
MULLET,
    BASTARD see **Polynemus indicus**
    FLATHEAD see **Mugil cephalus**
    GREY see Mugilidae
    JUMPING see **Mugil argenteus**
    RED see Mullidae
    RED see **Mullus surmuletus,**
      Pseudupeneus barberinus
    STRIPED see **Mugil cephalus**
    THICK-LIPPED see **Crenimugil labrosus**
    TIGER see **Mugil argenteus**
    WHITE see **Mugil curema**
    YELLOW-EYED FRESHWATER see
      Aldrichetta forsteri
MULLEY see **Wallagonia attu**

MULLIDAE
The family of goatfishes or red mullets, worldwide in distribution in tropical and warm-temperate seas.

All the members of the family conform to the same general body plan, rather elongate with a steeply curved dorsal profile, and flattened belly. They have 2 widely separated, but short, dorsal fins, and the anal fin is also short; it has 2 spines in it. Their most obvious feature, however, is the pair of long barbels on the chin, delicate organs used to probe the sea bed in search of the benthic invertebrates on which they prey.

Young goatfishes are pelagic, swimming near or at the surface, and attracted to lights

at night. They are silvery in colour with dark blue backs.

The total number of described valid species of goatfish is probably around 60. See **Mulloidichthys, Mullus, Pseudupeneus.**

Mulloidichthys   Mullidae
    auriflamma see **M. flavolineatus**
    flavolineatus 30 cm. (12 in.)
A widely distributed red mullet in the Indo-Pacific, which has been found from the Red Sea and the e. coast of Africa e. through the E. Indies, the Philippines, and the islands of the Pacific to Hawaii. It is an abundant fish on sandy and muddy-sand bottoms in many parts of this range, and is locally a valuable food fish.

This species was formerly known as *M. auriflamma*. **305**

MULLOWAY see **Johnius antarctica**
MULLOWAY, AUSTRALIAN see under
    Argyrosomus regius

Mullus   Mullidae
    surmuletus RED MULLET 40 cm. (15¾ in.)
Widely distributed in the Mediterranean and e. Atlantic from England s. to the Canaries. It is found in small groups, less often schools of up to 50, in depths of 3–90 m. (2–50 fathoms), usually on sand and sandy-mud. They forage over the bottom, sensing with their barbels for buried invertebrates, and burrowing after them once located.

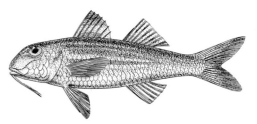

They are brilliantly colourful fish, in shallow water they are often reddish-brown, but deeper they become red overall. In daylight a lengthwise brownish streak runs along the side, with yellow lines above and below. At night these lines are broken into patches. Colour thus varies with time of day but also varies when the fish is disturbed or frightened.

The red mullet is a delicious food fish, and in the s. parts of its range it is caught in large numbers in trawls and seines.

MUMMICHOG see **Fundulus heteroclitus**

Muraena   Muraenidae
A genus of moray eels. The species illustrated in colour have not been identified. **19, 24**
M. helena MORAY, GREEK MORAY
1·3 m. (4¼ ft)
This moray is found in the Mediterranean and the e. Atlantic from the Cape Verde Islands and the Azores, n. to Biscay, although exceptionally specimens have been found in s. British waters. It is dark brown, with varied mottling of yellow or cream, finer and irregular anteriorly, but becoming more regular and heavy towards the tail. The head is usually dark with an intense black spot around the gill opening.

The moray is typically seen in deep cracks and crevices in rocky areas with only its head protruding. Even this relatively small species can be remarkably vicious when captured. It feeds on fishes mostly but also eats crustaceans and occasionally squids and cuttlefish. It breeds in July to September, the eggs, which are rather large, float at the surface.

After hatching the young larva measures about 10 mm. at 7 days, is typically flattened with a sharp, pointed snout and rounded tail, and in its early stages, small pectoral fins.

M. melanotis 80 cm. (32 in.)
A species of moray eel which is widely distributed along the W. African coast. It is found in shallow water on rocks and broken ground usually well hidden in crevices.

It is distinguished by having a large dusky patch around the gill slits, and by its coloration of yellow spots, small on the back, larger on the sides which densely cover the head and body and are separated by narrow chocolate brown network of lines. **21**

MURAENESOCIDAE
A moderately large family of eels, related to the Congridae, and like them with scaleless skins, well developed pectoral fins, and large muscular bodies. The muraenosocids, however, have elongate heads, narrow strong jaws with large, sharp, canine-like teeth. They are found in most tropical and warm temperate seas, and are best represented in the Indo-Pacific. Some little-known species have been found in deep water, but most are known as inhabitants of shallow seas, and in places estuaries. See **Cynoponticus, Muraenesox.**

Muraenesox   Muraenesocidae
   arabicus CONGER-PIKE, PIKE-EEL
About 2·1 m. (7 ft)
This eel is widely distributed in the Indo-Pacific, from the Red Sea and E. African coast to India, China and Australia. It is mainly silvery, with a grey or yellow sheen on the back; the dorsal and anal fins have a broad black margin. The head is narrow and the jaws are long, and well equipped with long fangs in the front and along the sides of the upper jaw.

It is found in inshore waters, in estuaries, and even in fresh water on occasions. Its flesh is said to be excellent eating but capturing it is

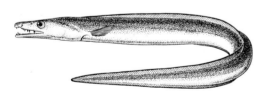

hazardous, as it is aggressive and vicious. Attacks by large specimens are much feared by the local fishermen where it is common.

MURAENIDAE
The most abundant and widely distributed family of eels, the morays are found in the tropical and warm temperate areas of all the oceans. Many of them are boldly patterned,

and distinctively coloured, others are plain in colour. Some species are very large, morays of 3 m. (10 ft) having been recorded, and many of the large species can be dangerous and even aggressive when provoked. Most, however, grow to a maximum of less than 1 m. (3¼ ft).

The morays are typically eel-like in body shape, long and thin with well developed dorsal and anal fins. They all lack both pelvic and pectoral fins. Other important distinguishing features include the dentition, the shape and placing of the nostrils, and a general reduction in the size of the gill opening. See **Echidna, Enchelynassa, Gymnothorax, Lycodontis, Muraena, Thyrsoidea.**

MURAENOLEPIDAE
A small family of fishes found in Antarctic seas which are related to the codfish family. They differ most obviously in having the rays of the dorsal and anal fins joined to the tail fin; also the pectoral fin supports have more basal bones than in the codfishes. See **Muraenolepis.**

Muraenolepis   Muraenolepidae
   microps 19 cm. (7½ in.)
An Antarctic fish of wide distribution close to the polar ice and also ranging as far to the

N. as the Patagonian mainland and the Falkland Islands. It is found in inshore conditions, a depth range of 18–830 m. (10–453 fathoms) having been recorded.

MURRAY COD see **Maccullochella macquariensis**
MUSKELLUNGE see **Esox masquinongy**
MUSSELCRACKER see **Cymatoceps nasutus, Sparodon durbanensis**

Mustelus   Triakidae
   antarctica GUMMY SHARK 1·5 m. (5 ft)
The gummy shark is common on the s. coasts of Australia and off New Zealand. It is a uniform grey in colour with minute white spots

on the back, and has a slender body with well developed fins. Like other members of the family, its teeth are arranged mosaic-like in both jaws, they are rounded and are clearly suited for crushing hard-shelled prey. Its vernacular name refers to its characteristic teeth.

It is very common in water 2–220 m. (1–120 fathoms) and has over the years come to take an important place in the commercial fishery landings in s. Australia. It is marketed as 'flake'. Immediately before and during the Second World War its oil-rich liver provided a major source of Vitamins A and D.

M. asterias SMOOTH HOUND 120 cm. (4 ft)
The smooth hound is widely distributed in European seas, being found from n. Scotland s. to N. Africa and in the Mediterranean. It is a relatively small sluggish shark which lives on the bottom in depths of less than 165 m. (90 fathoms) and frequently as shallow as 5 m. (3 fathoms).

It is dull grey on the back with a cream coloured underside, but the back and sides are liberally spotted with small white spots. A related European species, *M. mustelus*, is grey without such light spots.

This is a live-bearing species, the young sharks being born in litters of up to 28 (20 is usual), and at a length of about 30 cm. (12 in.)

M. canis SMOOTH DOGFISH 1·5 m. (5 ft)
The smooth dogfish is found in the w. Atlantic from Cape Cod to Uruguay, occasionally straying n. in summer to the Bay of Fundy. It is found in coastal waters where it feeds on crustaceans, and a wide variety of bottom-living invertebrates, squids and fishes.

This shark is viviparous, litters of 10–20 young being born in the spring or summer after a gestation period of about 10 months. The young are between 28 and 35 cm. (11–14 in.) when born. In summer time the smooth dogfish migrates n. and becomes noticeably more abundant in the n. parts of its range. Off the New England coast it is the second most numerous shark, second to the spur dog (*Squalus acanthias*), but it is the most destructive of all predators to the commercially important crabs and lobsters of the area.

M. mustelus SMOOTH HOUND 122 cm. (4 ft)
A small shark found in European waters from Scottish and Danish waters s. to the Mediterranean, and Madeira. It is a common shark throughout this area except for the particular extremities, usually found close to the bottom in relatively shallow water, 165 m. (90 fathoms) deep, or less. Its food is mostly hard-shelled crustaceans including hermit crabs, often complete with their adopted mollusc shell and its epiphytic fauna.

This species is uniformly grey on the back; some specimens have small black dots on the body. The belly and underside are creamy white. It is further distinguished by giving birth to living young. Up to 15 young are born at a time, depending on the size of the mother; they are nourished before birth by a specialized yolk-sac placenta. **7**

MUTTON
   HAMLET see **Alphestes afer**
   SNAPPER see **Lutjanus analis**

Mycteroperca   Serranidae
   bonaci BLACK GROUPER 1·2 m. (4 ft)
A very large grouper found in the w. Atlantic from New England and Bermuda to Brazil, including the Gulf of Mexico and the Caribbean. It frequently attains a weight of 23 kg.

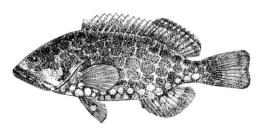

(50 lb.), but the maximum reported weight was 82 kg. (180 lb.). It is a sport fish of considerable importance. Its diet is mainly small fishes and crabs.

Its colouring is variable, from pale grey with dark blotches, to dark reddish grey with dark streaks. The black blotches are rather large and regular in shape, and the pectoral fin has an orange margin.

MYCTOPHIDAE

The family of lanternfishes, one of the best known, most abundant, and most often seen groups of deep sea fish. There are numerous species worldwide in their distribution and even penetrating into the polar seas. The name lanternfish is given for the numerous bright light organs clustered along the belly and the sides in discrete and characteristic rows and clusters for each species. They are relatively familiar to the seafarer because at night they come close to the surface, and can be attracted alongside by a ship's lights, and are often washed aboard in heavy weather. Although they may be found right at the surface at night-time, during daylight the same fishes will be caught 700–1000 m. (383–546 fathoms) deep. Most lanternfish are small, usually less than 15 cm. (6 in.) in length, blunt-headed, with large eyes, usually a small adipose fin, and many light organs. See **Benthosema, Diaphus, Gonichthys, Lampanyctus, Myctophum, Symbolophorus.**

Myctophum   Myctophidae
The species illustrated in colour has not been identified. **47**
M. punctatum 10 cm. (4 in.)
This lanternfish is widely distributed in the Mediterranean and N. Atlantic. The under surface and lower sides are liberally provided with small rounded light organs, arranged in distinct rows especially noticeably over the base of the anal fin. In this species males and females differ in the arrangement of light

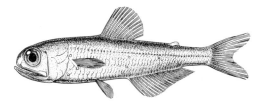

organs; the males have 3, close-clustered organs on the upper side of the tail, while females have from 2–6 well spaced light organs beneath the tail. These, like others on the body, give a clear, pale blue light. The body is otherwise silvery brown, darker on the back.

This lanternfish is known to breed in the Mediterranean from April through to July. The larvae have eyes on short stalks, but by a length of 2 cm. (¾ in.) the young fish assumes the adult form and the light organs begin to appear.

It is a schooling fish, often caught in large numbers, but always in moderately deep water and well offshore.

Myleus   Characidae
   rubripinnis 36 cm. (14¼ in.)
A species of deep-bodied characin which is widespread and abundant in Guyana and the

neighbouring areas of S. America. It is found in creeks and the main-stream of rivers.

It is plate-like in body form with a small head and broad tail. Its jaws have 2 series of teeth, the lateral rows flattened and molar like, the front ones incisors – it eats fruit and plant matter.

This species is imported to Europe as an aquarium fish. **80**

MYLIOBATIDAE

The eagle rays are widespread in tropical and warm temperate regions of the 3 great oceans, and their smaller seas. The pectoral fins are rather long and pointed but join the head at eye level, leaving the head region distinct. The eyes and spiracles are large and placed on the sides of the head. The tail is longer than the disc; it has a small dorsal fin, but no caudal fin. Some species have the tail spine typical of the stingrays. The teeth are flat and pavement like.

Many eagle rays are large fish, some species grow to 2·1–2·4 m. (7–8 ft) in breadth, and a weight of 362 kg. (800 lb.) has been reported.

They are more active than the long-tailed stingrays, swimming freely in mid-water with a flying motion of the pectoral fins, graceful in the extreme. They are viviparous, the embryo being nourished at a later stage of development by a creamy fluid secreted by the lining of the maternal uterus. See **Aetobatus, Myliobatis.**

Myliobatis   Myliobatidae
   aquila EAGLE RAY *c.* 1·8 m. (6 ft) long
The eagle ray is widespread in the e. Atlantic from British waters s. to Senegal, and in the Mediterranean and Adriatic seas. It has been recorded from S. Africa, probably erroneously.

It is a large, very graceful stingray with pointed tips to its pectoral fins, a pronounced head which stands clear of the disc, a small dorsal fin, a long serrated spine, and a whip-like tail. It is greyish brown above, yellowish below. It is an actively swimming fish, which moves with most graceful bird-like beats of its pectoral fins. For all that it feeds exclusively on the sea bed on molluscs and crustaceans, which are crushed whole in the mill-like teeth.

The young are born fully developed, in winter, in the Mediterranean, having been nourished before birth by secretions of the uterine membranes. It does not seem to breed in British waters where its presence is due mainly to n. migration during the warm seasons.

M. australis EAGLE RAY *c.* 1·2 m. (4 ft) wide
The Australian eagle ray is found in inshore waters of all the States of the continent. Its body shape is much the same as the other members of the family, as are its teeth, which are broad, flattened and arranged in rows, the centre row being several times the width of the others. Such teeth are clearly well adapted for crushing hard-shelled animals, and this stingray is said to be a pest in places where oysters or other shellfish are commercially produced.

In parts of Australia the eagle ray is very common and is often seen at the surface in shallow water. They are said to give good sport to the angler and underwater swimmer, and although they have a serrated tail spine they are usually regarded as harmless.

This eagle ray is usually green or olive with light blue spots and crossbands extending across the disc; occasionally bright yellow specimens are taken.

Mylocheilus   Cyprinidae
   caurinus PEAMOUTH 36 cm. (14 in.)
A slender-bodied dace-like fish with a small barbel at each corner of the small mouth, and a deeply forked tail. The dorsal fin is far forward, its origin in front of the pelvic fins. The back is brown or green, the sides silvery, with 2 lengthwise stripes, one from head to tail, the other from the eye to the vent. Breeding males have small white tubercles on the head, back, and anterior fins; their backs are dark green, the lateral stripes darker, and the lips and cheeks bright red.

The peamouth is found on the Pacific slope rivers of Canada and the U.S., n. to Vancouver Island, and e. to Alberta. It occurs in lakes and rivers forming large shoals, the young fish tend to stay in shallower water than the adults. It feeds on aquatic and terrestrial insects, plankton, and sometimes small fishes.

It spawns over gravel bottoms, usually in the outlet streams of small lakes, from April to July. The spawning fish form dense shoals and drop their grey-green eggs into the gravel. The eggs are not guarded.

It is one of the very few cyprinid fishes that can tolerate salt water, and its presence on Vancouver and other coastal islands is due to this tolerance. It is said to be a fair sporting fish on a fly.

Mylopharyngodon   Cyprinidae
   piceus BLACK AMUR 80 cm. (32 in.)
The black Amur is found, as its name suggests in the Amur basin, as well as continental China and Taiwan. It is a large fish, with a broad cylindrical body covered with large scales. Its dorsal and anal fins have few rays and are rounded. In colour it is very dark, almost black on the back, lightening to grey only on the belly.

Its crushing throat teeth are very powerful and its main food is said to consist of large freshwater molluscs, chiefly *Viviparus*, the shell of which it crushes in these teeth. Its eggs are said to be pelagic but its breeding biology is little known.

In Chinese rivers it is of great economic importance and substantial numbers are caught there for consumption.

Mylossoma   Characidae
   argenteum SILVER-DOLLAR FISH
20 cm. (8 in.)
This very lovely S. American characin is found in the s. part of the Amazon basin in the Rio Paraguay.

Its most notable feature is the rather high and rounded anal fin, which has scales well up onto the base. It is a plant-eating fish, which will also take a certain amount of animal food. It is a very attractive aquarium fish. **81**

Myoxocephalus   Cottidae
   aeneus GRUBBY, LITTLE SCULPIN
15 cm. (6 in.)
Found in coastal waters of Atlantic N. America from the Gulf of St Lawrence to New Jersey. In the N. of its range it is an abundant fish from low tide mark down to 27 m. (15 fathoms);

to the S. its range is deeper. It lives on a variety of bottoms, but is especially common in eel grass.

Like its relatives it is omnivorous and eats all kinds of bottom-living animals including worms, crustaceans, and fishes. It takes a baited hook freely, and is thus rather a nuisance to the dedicated sport fisherman on account of its size.

It is the commonest of the small sculpins on the Atlantic coast. It is distinguished by its short head spines, and few-rayed dorsal and anal fins.

Myrichthys   Ophichthidae
  acuminatus SHARPTAIL EEL 91 cm. (3 ft)
A beautifully coloured snake eel, found widely in the Caribbean region from Bermuda, Florida, s. through the W. Indies. It is a dark olive to purplish brown in colour, shading ventrally to white and with 3 rows of diffuse pale spots, each with a central yellow dot. Yellow spots also on the head. Otherwise it is typical of its family, being long and thin, with a sharp pointed tail. The vertical fins are low and poorly developed and the pectorals are absent. It is usually captured in sand or turtle grass beds, less often on reefs. It burrows in the sand and is rarely seen by the underwater swimmer.

Myripristis   Holocentridae
  amaenus 35 cm. (14 in.)
Found widely in the Pacific Ocean from Indonesia, New Guinea, and the Philippines, to Hawaii, and the Society Islands. The population living around the isolated se. Pacific island, Easter Island, has been described as subspecifically distinct, the major difference being that its members have more scales in the lateral line.

The species of *Myripristis* live on coral and rocky reefs in all tropical oceans, but they are most numerous in the Indo-Pacific. Most species are reddish in colour and they are often difficult to distinguish from one another.

In the Hawaiian islands they are valued food fishes and sell as menpachi for a high price. It is the commonest member of the genus there, living in inshore waters of 6–15 m. (4–8 fathoms). **222**

M. murdjan BLOTCH-EYE 30 cm. (12 in.)
Widely distributed in the Indo-Pacific and common in the Red Sea and along the E. African coast, found as far S. as East London in S. Africa. It occurs on the N. Queensland coast of Australia, and has been reported elsewhere in the Indo-Pacific.

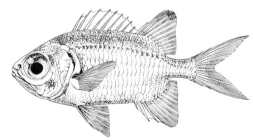

This genus resembles the squirrelfishes, but its members are deep-bodied and lack the heavy head spines which are so characteristic of the squirrelfishes. Fin spines are, however, well developed, and the eye is large. The blotch-eye is deep red in colour. **223**

Myroconger   Myrocongridae
  compressus 56 cm. (22 in.)
A little-known fish found first on the Island of St Helena in the S. Atlantic, and later at St Thomé, nearer the African coast. Very few specimens have ever been captured and its biology is unknown.

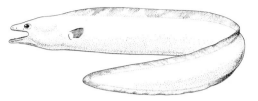

It has a rather deep, compressed body, with a moderately large head, jutting lower jaw, and a large mouth. It is scaleless, although under the throat it has traces of large scale pockets, regularly arranged and each about the size of the eye. In colour it is a uniform whitish.

MYROCONGRIDAE
A family apparently containing only one species of eel, which is known from the tropical Atlantic Ocean. It is conger-like in general appearance, with well-developed pectoral, dorsal, and anal fins. Its most significant external differences are the regularly arranged scale-pockets on the throat, and internally the very small openings of the gill slits into the throat. See **Myroconger.**

Mystus   Bagridae
  vittatus 21 cm. (8¼ in.)
Widely distributed from India and Burma to Thailand (where it is not particularly common), it occurs in both rivers and lakes. It is a popular aquarium fish, and makes an attractive pet fish.

Its colouring is variable, changing with locality and the condition of the fish. Its basic colour is pale silvery grey, with several pale blue or brown lengthwise bands of which the most constant is a double stripe arising just behind the head. The belly is shining white. It is distinguished by its long, low adipose fin and extremely long barbels from the upper jaw which reach to the anal fin, and the upper lobe of the tail being longer than the lower.

Myxine   Myxinidae
  glutinosa HAGFISH 61 cm. (2 ft)
Found on both sides of the N. Atlantic, and in Arctic Seas. On the N. American coast it is found as far S. as Cape Fear, N. Carolina, and s. Biscay in the e. Atlantic. Hagfish live in moderately deep water of 100–300 m. (55–164 fathoms) on soft muddy bottoms, in which they burrow with just the tip of the head showing. Their distribution is patchy, being confined to areas where the bottom is suitable. They are virtually blind, their eyes being hidden under skin and muscle. Although they feed on small marine worms and crustaceans, they are chiefly known as scavengers which attack helpless fish captured in set nets or on long-lines. Using its strong teeth the hagfish pierces the fish's skin and bores into the body, eating the flesh and eventually leaving only skin and bone. On account of this habit, their exceptionally slimy skin, and a generally un-

pleasant appearance, hagfish are heartily detested by fishermen where they occur in numbers as off Norway and Sweden.

Hagfish reproduce by laying large (2 cm., ¾ in.) oval eggs, enclosed in a tough shell with threads at each end which act as anchors in the mud. The adults are hermaphrodite, each possessing a single sex organ with male and female portions, but it seems that only one portion ever becomes functional in any individual.

MYXINIDAE
One of the 2 known living families of the class Agnatha, a class principally known from fossil forms. They have a cartilaginous skeleton, but no vertebrae, true fin rays, paired fins or scales. They lack jaws, but have a slit-like mouth, surrounded by barbels, and a strong tooth on the tongue. The Myxinidae do not have a gill cover like bony fish, and the gill openings vary in number from a single opening to 16 on each side. Marine fishes, they are found in the temperate and sub-tropical Atlantic, Indian, and Pacific oceans. See **Eptatretus, Myxine, Polistotrema.**

Myxodagnus   Dactyloscopidae
  belone DARTFISH 6 cm. (2½ in.)
Known only from the Bahamas and Puerto Rico. The only other members of the genus are found in the e. Pacific.

It is a long slender stargazer, sand-burrowing like its relatives and found in water less than 3·7 m. (2 fathoms) deep. It appears to be most common on sandy beaches with a light surf, although also found on rocks and marl bottoms.

It is almost colourless, the head is yellowish and there are brownish flecks on the back and near the base of the tail. The pectoral fin is conspicuously long.

N

NAKED SOLE see **Gymnachirus melas**

NANDIDAE
The family of leaffishes or nandids, a fascinating group of freshwater fishes with an interesting discontinuous distribution. The members of the family are found in n. S. America, w. Africa, India and se. Asia, and the E. Indies.

All are rather deep-bodied fishes with numerous spines in both dorsal and anal fins. The head is large, the mouth highly protrusible – all are predatory fishes, but most species are small (less than 20 cm. (8 in.)).

The family includes the remarkable leaffish, *Monocirrhus polyacanthus*, which mimics floating leaves in a very successful manner. See **Afronandus, Monocirrhus, Nandus, Polycentrus, Polycentropsis.**

Nandus   Nandidae
  nandus NANDUS 20 cm. (8 in.)
Widely distributed in the lowland freshwaters of India and Burma, and rarely reported from Thailand. It often occurs in brackish water.

It is a distinctive species with a rather elongate bass-like body, with a large head and well-developed, protrusible jaws, the lower jaw projecting. Its coloration is variable but is always unobtrusive, the back dark, the sides marbled with greens and browns; this colouring extends onto the fins.

It is a predatory species which is kept in aquaria, although usually on its own. Its habit of stalking prey from amongst vegetation accounts for its sombre, obliterative coloration.

NANDUS see **Nandus nandus**

Nannaethiops   Citharinidae
  unitaeniatus ONE-STRIPED AFRICAN CHARACIN 6 cm. (2½ in.)
A very widely distributed fish in w. central Africa found from the White Nile to the Niger basin. It is slender-bodied with a small mouth; the adipose fin is well developed, but the other fins are not notably large. Scales are moderately large, and the lateral line runs from head to tail in a straight line.

It is most attractive, olive-brown on the back, the belly and throat silvery with yellow tinges. A black streak runs from the tip of the snout through the lower edge of the eye to the tail fin and onto the fin rays. A bright gold line runs along the upper edge of this band. The fins are colourless or pink-tinged. The male is slimmer than the female, and at spawning time the upper lobe of the tail fin and the dorsal fin are bright red.

It is a hardy and peaceful aquarium fish, living close to the bottom and feeding on small bottom-living crustaceans, larvae etc. It scatters its eggs indiscriminately among plants and over the bottom sand when breeding.

Nannobrycon eques see **Nannostomus eques**

Nannocharax   Distichodontidae
  ansorgei 3·5 cm. (1½ in.)
This fish is found in w. Africa, in the basin of the upper Niger, and in the rivers of Portuguese Guinea, Sierra Leone, Senegal, and Gambia. It inhabits slow-flowing or still water, feeding mainly on bottom-living organisms. Its biology has been little studied in nature, but it has been kept as an aquarium fish recently with some success.

It is a slender fish, the body cylindrical in front and only slightly compressed towards the tail. It is covered in moderately small scales, each finely toothed on the free edge (ctenoid). The snout is pointed, the mouth is small and has only a single row of teeth, each of which has 2 cusps at its crown. **102**
N. taenia 6 cm. (2½ in.)
A small characin-like fish which is known only from the Congo River. It does not seem to be well known, although occasionally imported to Europe as an aquarium fish.

It is a rather slender fish with a cylindrical, compressed body. The snout is short, the mouth very small and set beneath the head, and each jaw has a single series of small, notched teeth, each with 2 cusps. **103**

Nannoperca   Kuhliidae
  australis PYGMY PERCH 7·5 cm. (3 in.)
A freshwater fish found in s. Australia in the states of S. Australia, Victoria, and New South Wales, in the cooler waters of the Murray-Darling system. It has been captured and kept as an aquarium fish, and proves to be very adaptable.

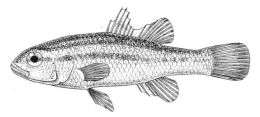

It is greenish above, lighter below, 2 faint stripes run along the body; the fins are reddish tinted. The singular shape of the dorsal fin is as distinctive as its 2 lateral lines.

Nannostomus   Lebiasinidae
  beckfordi GOLDEN PENCILFISH 6·5 cm. (2½ in.)
A very widely distributed fish in the freshwaters of n. S. America. It ranges from Guiana, the Rio Negro, and the lower and middle Amazon. In this vast area it shows some variation, and several subspecies have been described, based to some extent on colour differences.

It is a surface-living fish which feeds on insects at the surface film. It spawns among fine-leaved water plants after considerable display between rival males, and males and females. It is a popular aquarium fish, deservedly so as it is finely coloured and peaceful. **91**
N. eques TUBE-MOUTH PENCILFISH 5 cm. (2 in.)
The small mouth and the very distinctive lopsided tail of this species are diagnostic features Its habit of swimming at an oblique angle to the surface of the water, usually close to the surface, is also distinctive.

It is pale brown with 2 dark bands on each side, and a central band down the middle of the back. The band running from the tip of the snout becomes deep red along the body and eventually fills the whole of the lower tail lobe. A white crescent limits the red of the tail fin; the other fins are reddish, especially the anal fin.

This fish is common in the waters of the middle Amazon; its surface-living habit is possibly an adaptation to using the well oxygenated water at the air-water interface. It feeds on insects. It has been a popular aquarium fish for many years and is relatively easy to breed in captivity.

Some authorities place this fish in the genus *Poecilobrycon*, others in *Nannobrycon*.
N. marginatus DWARF PENCILFISH 4 cm. (1½ in.)
This is the smallest, and most popular in aquaria, of the pencilfishes. It is an extremely attractive species with an olive-green back, yellowish sides, and nearly white belly. Over this coloration it has 3 lengthwise dark brown to black bands, the middle one of which, the broadest, has a red stripe along its edge. The dorsal, pelvic, and anal fins are reddish with a dark edge.

Like other pencilfishes, this fish has a very distinctive night coloration, with a large dark blotch on the dorsal fin, and a small one on the gill cover.

Males have rounded anal fins with a black edge, while females have triangular light-edged fins.

It has been successfully bred many times in captivity, but tends to eat its eggs so the adults should be removed after spawning.
N. trifasciatus THREE-BANDED PENCILFISH 6 cm. (2½ in.)
This species is found in Guyana, the Rio Negro, and the Amazon. It is one of the few pencilfishes in which the adipose fin may be present, although in a substantial number of specimens it is entirely absent. Like other pencilfishes, this species has a distinct nocturnal coloration. It lives near the surface, feeding particularly on surface-living insects.
92

NANNYGAI see **Centroberyx affinis**

Narcine   Torpedinidae
  brasiliensis LESSER ELECTRIC RAY 46 cm. (18 in.)
This small electric ray is the most common member of the family in the tropical w. Atlantic. It is found commonly in inshore waters from s. Brazil to Florida and Texas, more rarely S. to n. Argentina and n. to N. Carolina. A closely related, if not identical species, *N. entemedor*, is known from the Pacific coast of Central America.

Within its range this small ray is found in shallow water down to 37 m. (20 fathoms) but often in the tidal regions, and many can be captured in beach seines. It burrows into the sand so that it is completely covered except for the spiracles and eyes. It feeds on worms.

This ray bears living young, in the cooler parts of its range in summer, but in tropical regions young may be produced all year round. The average length at birth is 11–12 cm. (4½ in.), and the litter number ranges from 4–15.

Like other members of the family this ray possess well-developed electric organs. Despite its relatively small size, the shock to a paddler is sometimes very severe, although no doubt it is more the suddenness of the shock than its power that is effective. The peak voltage has been measured as a modest 14–37 volts.

It is an attractively marked ray, medium brown on the back, with a number of irregularly shaped darker blotches, each ringed with dark brown spots. The underside is whitish. The disc is almost circular, the dorsal and tail fins moderately large. Its jaws are small, but equipped with very many rows of minute pointed teeth.

Narcine entemedor see under **Narcine brasiliensis**
NARROW-BANDED SOLE see **Aseraggodes macleayanus**
NARROW-BARRED SPANISH MACKEREL see **Scomberomorus commerson**
NASE see **Chondrostoma nasus**

Naso   Acanthuridae
  brevirostris UNICORNFISH 51 cm. (20 in.)
Widely distributed across the Indo-Pacific, the unicornfish is found from the tropical coast of e. Africa across to the Central Pacific and Hawaii.

It is dark greyish green with numerous vertical rows of small dots and lines on the sides. The dorsal and anal fins are greyish brown and the edge of the tail fin is green. Despite its scientific name, this unicornfish has the frontal horn well developed in the adult.

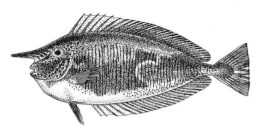

Even the young fish has a slight bump on the forehead; adults, however, develop a long spike in front of the eye. Its function is not known, and it would certainly handicap any fish browsing on a smooth surface as most of the relatives do. This species feeds on the larger leafy algae growing on dead coral or round the bases of live coral. It is most common in the sheltered reef areas at 5–45 m. (3–25 fathoms).

Members of the genus *Naso* have on each side of the tail 2 (occasionally 1 or 3) bony plates which bear fixed, forward-pointing spines. According to some reports these spines are covered with venom-producing tissue.

N. lituratus STRIPED-FACE UNICORNFISH
41 cm. (16 in.)
A distinctive Indo-Pacific species which can be identified by coloration alone.

It ranges from the E. African coast to Australia, the central Pacific and the Hawaiian Islands. It is often very common in reef areas where the water is relatively calm, and in moderate depths. It is usually seen in small roving schools swimming above the sea bed but diving occasionally to the bottom to feed amongst rocks and coral heads, cropping the larger leafy algae in considerably quantity.

Unlike most other members of the genus *Naso*, this species does not develop the frontal horn on the head with growth. Males develop long tail fin streamers. **445**

NATTERER'S PIRANHA see
Rooseveltiella nattereri

Naucrates Carangidae
ductor PILOTFISH, RUDDERFISH
61 cm. (2 ft)
The pilotfish appears to be cosmopolitan in its distribution and is found in all tropical and warm temperate seas, and as an occasional stray into cool temperate waters.

Its habit of 'leading' larger fishes and sailing ships, always staying in close proximity to them is well known, although, as they keep beneath rather than in front of the ships, they are perhaps more lead than actually piloting. As young fishes they shelter amongst floating weeds and often among the deadly tentacles of large jellyfishes. Adults seek the company of larger creatures, often sharks, turtles, and sailing ships. The association has not been explained satisfactorily; amongst the suggestions advanced are shelter in the shade of the larger object, increased possibilities for foraging on waste scraps from meals, and even the shark's excrement. It is possible too that the pilotfish acts as a cleaner of parasites from its host. In any event the bond is evidently a strong one for *Naucrates* have accompanied turtles wan-

dering as far as the inhospitably cold waters of England, far outside their normal range.

The pilotfish is rather elongate with a rounded body in cross-section; its fins are not very well developed and it has a keel on the sides of the tail.

Nautichthys Cottidae
oculofasciatus SAILFIN SCULPIN
20 cm. (8 in.)
Found from se. Alaska to California and confined to the Pacific coastline, from tidal waters to a depth of 109 m. (60 fathoms). It is most common in shallow waters and is often taken in shrimp trawls. Its food consists largely of shrimps. In calm conditions it swims very gracefully by wave-like movements of the dorsal fin.

It is distinguished by the very high spinous dorsal fin and the large branched tentacle above the eye. It is greyish brown above, cream on the belly, with several dark saddles

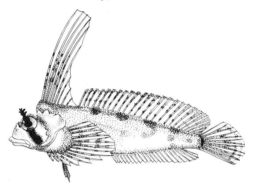

and spots on the fin. The tentacle is jet black, this colour running through the eye to the lower cheek.

Navodon Balistidae
ayraudi CHINAMAN or YELLOW
LEATHERJACKET 50 cm. (19¾ in.)
This species is widely distributed along the s. coasts of Australia. It occurs commonly in deep water off the coasts of W. Australia, S. Australia, and New South Wales. It is found in rocky and sandy habitats both inshore and offshore and occasionally in estuaries. In many areas it is common enough to be a pest to the line fisherman, shearing off lines and hooks with its sharp teeth. Its abundance and size, however, make it a marketable fish and substantial quantities are landed for the fish market. Its flesh is said to be white, tender and well flavoured.

It is relatively easily distinguished by its size – it is the largest of the Australian leatherjackets – and by its yellowish coloration, even the fins being entirely yellow. Its body is elongate, the dorsal spine small and sited just behind the eye, the dorsal and anal fins are placed opposite one another, both equal sized and with the front rays higher than the remainder.

Placed by some authors in the genus *Cantherines*.

NECK EEL see **Derichthys serpentinus**
NEEDLEFISH see Belonidae
NEEDLEFISH see **Hemiramphus far,
Petalichthys capensis**
NEEDLEFISH,
ATLANTIC see **Strongylura marina**
FLAT see **Ablennes hians**

NEEDLETOOTH SWALLOWER see **Kali normani**

NEENCHELYIDAE
A family of eels related to the Muraenesocidae but differing in that the internal openings of the gill clefts are very restricted. The body is scaleless, rounded and elongate, and the dorsal fin is placed well behind the pectoral fin.

Members of the family are known from the Red Sea and the Indo-Australian region, but they are little known and few specimens seem to have been reported. They are small eels, known to reach 21 cm. (8¼ in.) in length. See **Neenchelys.**

Neenchelys Neenchelidae
microtretus 18 cm. (7 in.)
A long slender eel with a rather sharply pointed snout, tubular nostrils at the tip of the snout,

and slit-like nostrils before the eye. The gill openings are small, as are the pectoral fins. The mouth is moderately large, with few, well-spaced slender teeth in the jaws. It is a uniform light brown.

This eel was described from a collection made in the Sudanese Red Sea in 1915. So far as is known it has not been collected there since, but related species have been taken in the Indonesian region.

Negaprion Carcharhinidae
acutidens see under **N. brevirostris**
brevirostris LEMON SHARK 3·4 m. (11 ft)
The lemon shark is a w. Atlantic species found from New Jersey to Brazil; it is common about Florida and among the Keys. Related species are found in other tropical seas, for example *N. acutidens* in the Red Sea and Indian Ocean, and *N. queenslandicus* on the Australian coast. All have a similar shape, with a short snout, a second dorsal fin almost as large as the first, and erect, symmetrical smooth-edged teeth.

The lemon shark is yellowish brown on the back, shading to pale yellow ventrally. It is essentially a shallow water shark and is often found close inshore, as well as in brackish creeks, and even fresh water. Its habit of living inshore has often brought it in contact with bathers, and there are a number of records of it attacking man (although many of these were the result of some provocation). Its habits also mean that it is suitable to keep in captivity and this is one of the few large sharks which has been kept successfully for experimental work in marine aquaria; it has thus unwittingly contributed much to knowledge of shark biology.
N. queenslandicus see under **N. brevirostris**

NEGRO, PEZ see **Astroblepus grixalvii**
NEHU see **Stolephorus purpureus**
NELMA see **Stenodus leucichthys**

Nemadactylus Cheilodactylidae
morwong MORWONG, BLACK PERCH
61 cm. (2 ft)
A fish of the se. coasts of Australia found

mostly off Tasmania, Victoria, New South Wales, and s. Queensland. It is mainly an off-shore species which is captured in some quantity by trawlers and is sold for food. It is said to be of good quality.

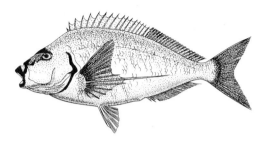

It is distinguished by the pectoral fin. It is purplish grey and each scale has a greenish spot, forming inconspicuous bands; a golden band runs from eye to mouth. The fins are mostly yellowish.

N. valenciennesi BLUE MORWONG
76 cm. (30 in.)
Found on the coasts of W. Australia, S. Australia, and New South Wales, in moderately shallow water inshore, but is more common offshore on sandy bottoms.

It is brightly coloured; bright blue above, lighter below, with clear yellow lines on the snout and radiating from the eyes. The soft dorsal fin is dark spotted.

This species has a very well developed single pectoral fin ray which attains almost the length of the head. The lower rays of the pectoral fin are long, well-spaced, and unbranched, and are separated by a deep notch from the upper part of the fin.

It is fished for commercially by trawlers. Its flesh is of good quality.

Nematalosa Clupeidae
come HAIRBACK HERRING, BONY
BREAM 25 cm. (10 in.)
Along the Queensland, New South Wales, and W. Australian coasts, this species inhabits coastal waters, estuaries, and freshwaters, and is found far inland in rivers. It is a common fish locally, and although eaten by many sea birds, including pelicans and shags, is not much eaten by man on account of its bony flesh. It is a mud-browser itself, feeding on the thin enriched film of detritus, nematode worms, small crustaceans, and other animals on the bottom, but taking in large quantities of mud in the process. Its stomach is muscular and gizzard-like, well suited for grinding and extracting food from the muddy residues. The shads with such a stomach, and there are several of them, are known as gizzard shads.

It is a very distinctive shad-like fish, with a deep body, short, small head, and a long thread-like extension to the last dorsal fin ray. It is greenish above, silvery below, with a dark blotch on the shoulder.

Nemateleotris Gobiidae
magnificus SPIKE-FINNED GOBY
6 cm. (2½ in.)
This strikingly coloured and very beautiful fish was first found in the vicinity of the Celebes; it has since been discovered in Micronesia and is evidently more widely distributed than records show. **432**

Nematobrycon Characidae
palmeri EMPEROR TETRA 6 cm. (2½ in.)
A native fish of the freshwaters of Colombia, but its biology and life style are not well known. It has been kept in aquaria but is not a widely distributed petfish.

Its body form and colouring are highly distinctive. The anal fin is very long-based, the dorsal fin high. Males have the centre rays of the tail fin prolonged into a spike. **82**

Nematocentrus Melanotaeniidae
maccullochi MCCULLOCH'S or DWARF
RAINBOWFISH 7 cm. (2¾ in.)
Restricted to the area of the Barron River, near Cairns in n. Queensland, and one of the most locally distributed of the rainbowfishes.

It is a moderately deep-bodied, compressed fish with 2 dorsal fins, the first having only 5–7 unbranched rays, the second being longer. The males are brilliantly coloured; the female is of lighter colour.

This rainbowfish has been kept and bred in aquaria. It is a peaceful, shoaling fish, but needs a well-lighted large aquarium. They spawn by shedding their eggs amongst the fine leaves of water plants; the eggs, which have thin filaments which tangle in the leaves, hatch in 7–10 days at 25°C. The young are dark coloured and continue to hang onto the plant leaves for a few days after hatching. **212**

NEMICHTHYIDAE
This, the snipe eel family, comprises a number of deep-sea eels, found mainly in mid-water in the open ocean. They are represented in all the major oceans.

They are long and slender, with very fragile bodies. All have long, thin beak-like snouts with minute teeth in the jaws. The dorsal and anal fins are well developed with long rays, tapering gradually towards the tail, but due to their fragile structure, whole undamaged specimens are rarely found. See **Avocettina, Nemichthys.**

Nemichthys Nemichthyidae
scolopaceus SNIPE EEL 1·22 m. (4 ft)
The snipe eel is probably the best known member of the family, because it is more abundant than other members, but also because it lives in less deep water and is thus caught occasionally in commercial fishing gear. It is very fragile and it is usually badly damaged on these occasions, although some specimens are recovered whole.

It is a long thin eel, with large eyes and very long beak-like jaws, lined with fine teeth. The dorsal fin begins close behind the head, and the anal only slightly posterior of that; the anal fin rays are longer than those of the dorsal fin. Its colour is dark, chocolate brown above and black ventrally.

It is not really a deep-sea fish, but lives in mid-depths in the ocean, probably never coming closer to the surface than about 366 m. (200 fathoms) and being on occasions caught at 1829 m. (1000 fathoms). Elongate leptocephalus larvae of this species are found nearer the surface, in 90 m. (50 fathoms) but only over deep water. Very little is known of the biology of the snipe eel.

NEMIPTERIDAE
A family of Indo-Pacific fishes, typically fish-like in shape, and related to the snappers (Lutjanidae). There are numerous species recognized, many of them used as food fishes locally. Most are brightly coloured inhabitants of shallow waters.

They have elongate, rather compressed bodies, fully scaled, the scales extending onto the head. The mouth is moderate in size, the jaws have teeth, in some species long and pointed in front. The dorsal fin is single, the front portion having numerous slender spines; the anal fin has 3 thin spines and then branched rays. See **Nemipterus, Scolopsis.**

Nemipterus Nemipteridae
delagoae 25 cm. (10 in.)
A species found on the e. coast of Africa from Delagoa Bay to Beira where it is described as not uncommon.

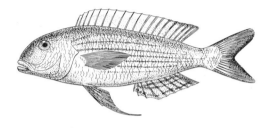

It is beautifully coloured, deep red above fading on the sides to pearly white below, the anal fin is pale blue with pearl like lines. As the late Professor J. L. B. Smith, who first described this fish, wrote, 'it is impossible to portray the delicate opalescence of the live fish'.

N. virgatus 40 cm. (16 in.)
A species widely distributed in the w. Pacific, from the coast of Japan, the E. and S. China Seas, the Philippines, and Java. It is an abundant fish on muddy bottoms at depths of 40–100 m. (22–55 fathoms).

It is a slender-bodied fish, rather elongate; the mouth is moderate with 4 pairs of canine-like teeth in the upper jaw. The dorsal fin is uniform in height, with 10 slender sharp spines. The upper lobe of the tail is very long and forms a filament.

Its coloration is basically red with yellow lengthwise stripes running from the snout to the tail.

It is an important food fish in Japan, where it is known as the itoyori; it is caught mostly on hook and line and is eaten fresh or pickled, cooked in many ways.

Neoceratias Neoceratiidae
spinifer 6 cm. (2½ in.)
A most striking-looking ceratioid angler, the female of which is the larger, black in colour, with long, many-rayed pigmented dorsal and anal fins. The jaws are large, the gape is enormous, and the surrounds of both jaws are studded with long, slender teeth. The eyes are small, and an illicium (fishing rod) is lacking. Males are parasitic when adult, although only one specimen is known. They are slender, the jaws have short teeth, eyes and olfactory organs degenerate.

NEOCERATIIDAE

A family of deep-sea anglerfish which apparently contains only the single genus and species. It has been found in the N. Atlantic, Indian Ocean, and W. Pacific, but is known from very few specimens, the greater number of which are larvae.

Parasitic adult males are characteristic of some families of deep-sea angler. It is a remarkable adaptation to life in the 3-dimensional vastness of the deep sea. Larval male anglers usually have well developed nasal organs, and an enhanced sense of smell, again an adaptation to this life. It must be presumed that female anglers have a characteristic scent. The parasitic male becomes wholly dependent on the female for life support. See **Neoceratias.**

Neoceratodus Ceratodontidae
forsteri AUSTRALIAN or QUEENSLAND
LUNGFISH 1·5 m. (5 ft)
This lungfish is the only species to be found in Australia, and its distribution is restricted to the Burnett and Mary rivers in se. Queensland. The species has been successfully introduced into a number of other rivers, amongst them the upper Brisbane, the Albert and Coomera rivers, and the Enoggera reservoir. There is a suggestion that they may even have been early introductions into the Mary River, and they have been released elsewhere in Australia.

The Queensland lungfish has become much rarer than it was soon after it was first discovered in 1870, and it is effectively protected by legislation. The introduction of the species outside its former very restricted range, is to some extent a conservation insurance.

This species lives in permanent waters and does not need to aestivate in mud-burrows in the same way as the African and the S. American lungfishes. However, it does breathe air.

It is essentially a carnivorous species and in captivity will eat nearly any form of animal food, only taking a little plant material. Spawning occurs from August to October in shallow water at a depth of about 1 m. (3¼ ft); the eggs adhere to the submerged vegetation and floating roots of water hyacinth. Observers have described how a pair of fish have been seen to swim to and fro through the weed at a set point one following the other for up to an hour during which spawning occurred.

This lungfish is occasionally referred to as the barramunda or Burnett salmon, the first of these names is undesirable due to the risk of confusion with *Scleropages* – the barramundi.

Neochanna Galaxiidae
apoda BROWN MUDFISH 13 cm. (5 in.)
The mudfishes (only 2 species are known, the other is *N. diversus,* the black mudfish) are found in a number of localities in New Zealand. The brown mudfish is best known from region of Lake Wairarapa, on N. Island but it occurs elsewhere in scattered areas there, and on S. Island in muddy creeks, ditches and

ponds. Their principal interest is the modification of the body for a burrowing life style in mud. They also can aestivate during dry seasons, burrowing deep in the mud and by lying quiescent when the water in the pool has dried up, surviving for several months.

The brown mudfish has been bred in aquaria when the eggs were deposited above the water level on the sides of the glass. This suggests that the mudfish may actually leave the water to deposit its eggs amongst damp vegetation at the waters' edge, or possibly that it normally spawns amongst vegetation at flood level, the eggs developing but not hatching until the next rains.

N. diversus see under **N. apoda**

Neocyttus Oreosomatidae
rhomboidalis SPIKY DORY 30 cm. (12 in.)
The first described specimen of spiky dory was found in S. African waters in 1097 m. (600 fathoms); it was later found in some numbers off the coasts of Tasmania, S. Australia, and W. Australia. It is probably widely distributed between these areas. It is usually taken at depths of 640–823 m. (350–450 fathoms).

It is rather distinctive with a deep, compressed body, a moderate sized extensible mouth, and relatively large eyes. The dorsal and anal fin spines are very heavy but not long. The body and cheeks are covered with small rough-edged scales. It is silvery, with dark fins.

Neogobius Gobiidae
melanostomus 25 cm. (10 in.)
This goby inhabits the Black and Caspian seas, including the Sea of Azov. It is one of the more valuable commercially exploited gobies, and large numbers are caught annually in the U.S.S.R. and used for food.

The female does not attain as great a size as the male, but they reach sexual maturity at 2 instead of 3 years. It spawns at the end of April, the male becoming almost black in colour; he guards the eggs when they are shed on hard substrates. This goby species feeds mainly on molluscs, and to a less extent on crustaceans. **435**

Neolebias Citharinidae
ansorgei ANSORGE'S CHARACIN
3·5 cm. (1½ in.)
This very small African characin is one of a genus very abundant in central and w. tropical Africa. It is a dull greeny brown on the back, the sides are pale green, tinted with a blue opalescent sheen. The underside is yellowish. Along each side a wide dark, but variable band runs from the head to the base of the tail fin, and above it a bright green stripe. At the base of the tail fin there is a green, yellow-edged vertical bar. The fins are pale red, except in the male during breeding when they are blood red in colour.

It is a most attractive aquarium fish, although rather retiring and shy by nature. It lives close to the bottom most of the time, often hiding beneath the plant roots. The male displays to the female by quivering his fins and body before her, until she follows him into a thick clump of water plants. Some 300 eggs

may be laid; these hatch in 20–24 hours at a temperature of around 25°C.

NEON
TETRA see **Paracheirodon innesi**
TETRA, BLACK see **Hyphessobrycon herbertaxelrodi**

Neopercis Mugiloididae
sexfasciata 15 cm. (6 in.)
This sandperch is found in the w. N. Pacific around the Japanese coast and in s. Korean waters. It is a shallow water, inshore species, found in from 1–10 m. (½–5 fathoms) of water. It is locally exploited (with related species) as a food fish in Japan.

It is distinguished by having the 2 dorsal fins continuous, the last ray of the first dorsal being almost the same height as the rays of the second dorsal. It is greyish-red above, with 6 dusky bars on the head and back, those on the body being V-shaped. A rounded spot on the upper base of the tail fin.

NEOSCOPELIDAE

A family containing a few species of lantern-fish-like fishes, found in deep water of all the tropical and warm temperate oceans. Superficially they resemble lanternfishes which either lack light organs completely, or if they are present they are scattered one per scale, especially on the underside. They also have a rather pointed head and a generally slender shape. In most species the first dorsal fin is well forward along the back and is separated from the adipose fin. See **Neoscopelus.**

Neoscopelus Neoscopelidae
macrolepidotus 25 cm. (10 in.)
Widely distributed and probably cosmopolitan in warm temperate and tropical seas, this fish is best known from the Atlantic, from Madeira S. to s. Africa. It is superficially like a lanternfish and clearly closely related to that family. Its most important distinguishing features are the forward placing of the rayed dorsal fin, vertically above the pelvic fins, and the presence of a small luminous pore on each scale

of the lower sides and belly. In coloration it is silvery with a pinkish sheen, the fins are pink, and around the photophores it has a violet tint. It seems to occur as deep as 914 m. (500 fathoms) but is more usually taken nearer the surface.

NEOSTETHIDAE

A small family of mainly freshwater fishes found in the Malaysian and Thailand region. Its members are closely related to the Phallostethidae, but differ in the arrangement of parts of the singular copulatory organ of the male.

The members of the family are slender-bodied with a rather long anal fin. The first dorsal fin is composed of 1–2 short slender spines separated by a space from the second dorsal. The pelvic fins are absent. In both sexes the urogenital opening is far forward, virtually on the throat. See **Neostethus.**

Neostethus   Neostethidae
   lankesteri 3 cm. (1¼ in.)
Found in brackish water in the Muar River, Johore, and the Island of Singapore and apparently not found again in this area since it was first described in 1916, although other forms are found there.

Like other members of this family this is a small, slender, elongate fish which is found in brackish and salt water. It is colourless in life, almost invisible in the water, only the sheen of the eye and body cavity being visible.

Adult males have an elongate organ arising beneath the head which comprises elements of ribs and pelvic fin skeleton. This complicated organ is believed to be used for grasping the female while the male fertilizes the eggs. The first dorsal fin is composed of one minute ray.

Neotoca   Goodeidae
   bilineata TWO-LINED NEOTOCA
6 cm. (2½ in.)
A rather deep-bodied toothcarp, the head is flat, the mouth horizontal, with the dorsal fin near the mid-point of the body. The tail fin is square cut, the pectorals and pelvics rounded. The male is distinguished by the modified first 6 anal rays which form a small lobe used for internal fertilization of the eggs. The males grow to 35 mm. (1½ in.), females are larger.

In colour, a grey-green with a brownish tinge; a narrow black streak runs from the mouth to the tail, with dark bars across the tail, and a black crescent shaped spot on the tail base. A greenish stripe beneath the dark line.

This fish is native to the rivers of Central Mexico, mainly those in volcanic areas especially the Rio Lerma, and the lowland rivers of Jalisco and Tepic. It has been kept as a pet fish successfully and breeds readily in captivity, producing broods of up to 40 young at a time.

NEOTOCA, TWO-LINED see **Neotoca
   bilineata**

Nerophis   Syngnathidae
   lumbriciformis WORM PIPEFISH
15 cm. (6 in.)
A small pipefish found on the Atlantic coast of Europe from s. Scandinavia, and the British Isles s. to Morocco. It is widely distributed on rocky shores, hiding under stones at low tide, and more often cunningly concealed amongst the stiff brown fronds of seaweeds, a habitat in which it is almost impossible to detect.

It is thin and wormlike, with a short snout and rounded body. Only the dorsal fin is developed, the other fins are absent. Males have a double groove on the belly to which the large eggs adhere until hatched; this species has no broodpouch. Egg-carrying males are found from June to August.

Its colouring is variable with habitat, sometimes almost black, more often dark olive with a series of white bars on the head and throat.

Nesiarchus   Gempylidae
   nasutus 130 cm. (51 in.)
A N. Atlantic species which is widely distributed in tropical and warm-temperate areas,

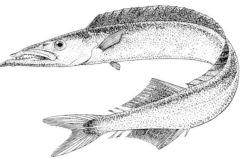

and is occasionally captured as far N. as Iceland and the Norwegian coast. It is a dark brown or black with violet tints on the sides.

It lives near the surface and down to depths of 1200 m. (655 fathoms). Adults are usually found in deeper water than the young fish. Its food consists of practically any deep-water fish species, squids, or crustaceans it encounters.

NESSORHAMPHIDAE
A family of bathypelagic eels found in the warmer parts of the Atlantic, Pacific, and Indian oceans. They are very slender-bodied, almost round in cross-section in front but flattened towards the tail; the snout in particular is long, flattened, slightly bulbous at the tip where the anterior nostrils are situated. See **Nessorhamphus.**

Nessorhamphus   Nessorhamphidae
The species illustrated in colour has not been identified. **25**
N. ingolfianus 25 cm. (10 in.)
Many thousand specimens of this deep-sea eel have been captured by research vessels, but the great majority of them are larval or adolescent forms; the adults are rarely caught. The larvae are typical eel leptocephali in form, but have a pointed snout with long sharp teeth turned outwards from the jaws. The adult is a long slender eel found between 731–1829 m.

(400–1000 fathoms). It appears to be relatively scarce even at this depth judging from the number captured. It is brownish in colour with a blue tinge, and the elongate snout with a slightly swollen tip is very conspicuous. It is believed to spawn at or near the surface in spring and early summer in the region of the Sargasso Sea in the Atlantic. Little is known of its biology apart from the observation that it eats small crustaceans.

NETTASTOMATIDAE
A family of deep-sea eels containing around 15 species. They are long-bodied, very fragile and scaleless. Their jaws are long and thin; the mouth is large, with small sharp teeth in bands; the fins are low, and they have no pectoral fins.

Members of the family are found in all temperate and tropical seas, but they mostly live in very great depths. See **Venefica.**

Nettodarus   Dysommidae
   brevirostris FACCIOLA'S EEL
26 cm. (10¼ in.)
This deep-sea eel has been found mostly in the Mediterranean at depths of 400–600 m. (219–328 fathoms), although as a single specimen has also been taken from off Miami, Florida in 351 m. (192 fathoms), it is evidently more widely distributed than had been thought. It is brown coloured, with a pale dorsal fin and a dark edge along the rear of the anal fin.

Its jaws are moderate, and well armed with large canine teeth and smaller teeth at the sides of the lower jaw. Large teeth are also present in the roof of the mouth. The most obvious distinguishing character is the bulbous snout which is ornamented with fleshy lobes and papillae. The nostrils are large and surrounded by fleshy tubes.

Little is known of the life history. The very depths at which it lives making the capture of adult specimens difficult. Its larvae are believed to be a long, sharp-snouted leptocephali with protruding, telescopic eyes (described as *Leptocephalus telescopicus*) from the Mediterranean.

NEW ZEALAND
   GRAYLING see **Prototroctes
   oxyrhynchus**
   SMELT see **Retropinna retropinna**

Nezumia   Macrouridae
   stelgidolepis CALIFORNIA RAT-TAIL
47 cm. (18½ in.)
A rat-tail from the e. Pacific, found on the continental shelf offshore of California. A few specimens have been captured in water as shallow as 91 m. (50 fathoms) but most have been taken between 291–640 m. (160–350 fathoms). It is a moderately common species taken mostly with bottom trawls and traps. Little is known of its biology.

Its body shape is typical of the rat-tails; the first dorsal fin is high and triangular with a serrated fin spine. The scales are moderate in size, finely serrated, and firmly attached. In colour it is dusky overall, darker over the ventral surface. The generic name *Nezumia* is from the Japanese *nezumi* – a rat.

NIBE see **Nibea mitsukurii**

Nibea   Sciaenidae
   mitsukurii NIBE 61 cm. (2 ft)
A Japanese species of croaker found in the Sea of Japan, along the Pacific coast and in the Yellow Sea. It is most common to the S. of its range and is found in shallow water on muddy bottoms. The young fish are found in estuaries; adults from the shore line to 37 m. (20 fathoms).

It is a valuable food fish, caught mostly with shore seines and trawls. Its flesh is tasty, especially in winter, and is eaten raw or prepared in several ways.

It is rather elongate, with the characteristic long second dorsal fin and small anal fin of the family. It differs, however, in having the first dorsal joined at the base to the second dorsal. The teeth in the jaws are all small. Light grey above, pale below with dark brown bands running obliquely across the back.

NILE

BICHIR see **Polypterus bichir**

MOUTH-BROODER see **Sarotherodon niloticus**

PERCH see **Lates niloticus**

PUFFERFISH see **Tetraodon lineatus**

NINE-SPINED STICKLEBACK see **Pungitius pungitius**

NINGU see **Labeo victorianus**

N'KUPE see **Distichodus mossambicus**

Noemacheilus Cobitidae

A genus of loach. Besides *N. barbatulus* a further species has been illustrated in colour. **152**

N. barbatulus STONE LOACH 12 cm. (4¾ in.) A widely distributed loach found from England (and Ireland by introduction), across Europe and n. Asia to s. Siberia and Korea. A number of local sub-species have been described.

The stone loach is an inhabitant of clear streams and rivers, especially those with a stony bottom. It is also found in the inshore region of lakes, and occasionally in lowland rivers. It is a relatively inactive fish during daylight, usually lying hidden under stones, but it becomes active at night or in dull light. Its life is spent on the bottom, and its food consists of bottom-living invertebrates. It spawns in April to May, the eggs being adhesive and usually placed on the underside of stones and boulders, although sometimes shed on plant roots. Males are slimmer than females, and have pointed larger pectoral fins, with a thickened second fin-ray.

The stone loach makes an interesting, if not very active, aquarium fish. They are tolerant of most conditions, except de-oxygenation, and are easy to feed. It is sometimes used as a bait fish for anglers, but its greatest significance for fisheries probably lies in being an occasional food item for predatory fishes, and as a competitor in salmon or trout streams with the fry of those fishes. **151**

NOMEIDAE

A small family of mainly tropical and warm temperate oceanic fishes which occur in all the large deep-ocean basins of the world. They are closely related to the blackfishes (family Centrolophidae) and the butterfishes (family Stromateidae), but are distinguished by having 2 dorsal fins, teeth in the jaws, and well-developed pelvic fins which are retained in the adult. Like their relatives they possess a thick-walled, toothed sac in the pharynx.

Most, if not all, members of the family pass through a planktonic early life, several of them being well-known for their association with jellyfishes or floating algae. Adult specimens are mostly mesopelagic or bathypelagic and little known, possibly because they are too active as swimmers to be caught other than occasionally. In some areas, such as off Japan and off Madeira they are caught and marketed for food, but in general their occurrence is too infrequent to make them anything but occasional food items. See **Ariomma, Cubiceps, Nomeus, Psenes.**

Nomeus Nomeidae

gronovii MAN-O'-WAR FISH, BLUEBOTTLE FISH 22 cm. (8½ in.)

The man-o'-war fish has long been known for its association with the large siphonophore *Physalia,* the Portuguese man-o'-war. This medusa has long trailing stinging tentacles hanging beneath its float amongst which this small fish lives. The association is usually referred to as commensalism but the true nature of the relationship has not been studied in detail. The fish is certainly relatively immune to *Physalia* toxin, but not entirely so, and *Nomeus* has from time to time been observed to browse on its host's tentacles and body. The association is formed when the fish is very young (c. 1 cm.), and specimens of 15 cm. (6 in.) have been found with *Physalia,* but they were not fully adult. The only adult known was taken in a bottom trawl in the Caribbean sea which suggests that the planktonic phase may end when the fish nears maturity. Further observations are needed, however.

The young fish is very distinctive. Its back is bright blue above, blotched and spotted with blue on the lower sides. The tail fin is very long and forked, the pelvic fins are large and black. The only known adult was a uniform dark brown in colour.

The man-o'-war fish is a wide-ranging species in all the major oceans in tropical seas. It is widespread in both the Indian and Pacific oceans, but appears to be restricted to the w. Atlantic and Caribbean (even though *Physalia* is common enough in the tropical e. Atlantic).

NORMANICHTHYIDAE

A family of marine fishes which contains only the single species, found in the S. Pacific.

It is said to be allied to the sculpins (family Cottidae) which are abundant in the N. Hemisphere, the suborbital bones being well developed to form an almost complete bar across the cheek. Other internal characters are said to support this view, but if it is correct then it must be emphasized that *Normanichthys* is the only member of the cottid group to have a scaly body. See **Normanichthys.**

Normanichthys Normanichthyidae

crockeri 11 cm. (4½ in.)

Found in the e. S. Pacific off the Chilean coast. It appears to live in moderately shallow coastal waters, the original specimens being captured in 37 m. (20 fathoms) by beam trawl, while others were taken around a submerged light in Valparaiso Bay. Nothing appears to be recorded of its biology.

It is distinguished by its many spined first dorsal fin, and by the complete scalation of the body, and most of the head. This also distinguishes it amongst the cottid fishes, which are scaleless.

NORTH PACIFIC BLUE-FIN TUNA see **Thunnus orientalis**

NORTHERN

ANCHOVY see **Engraulis mordax**

BARRAMUNDI see under **Scleropages leichardti**

BROOK LAMPREY see **Ichthyomyzon fossor**

CAVEFISH see **Amblyopsis spelaea**

KINGFISH see **Menticirrhus saxatilis**

PIKE see **Esox lucius**

REDBELLY DACE see **Phoxinus eos**

REDHORSE see **Moxostoma macrolepidotum**

RONQUIL see **Ronquilus jordani**

SCULPIN see **Icelinus borealis**

SEA ROBIN see **Prionotus carolinus**

SQUAWFISH see **Ptychocheilus oregonensis**

WHITING see **Sillago sihama**

WOLFFISH see **Lycichthys denticulatus**

NOTACANTHIDAE

The family of marine spiny eels, some inhabitants of the deep-sea, other living in only moderate depths. All share an elongate body form, rather blunted but protuberant snout, with the small-toothed jaws on the underside of the head. Like their relatives the halosaurs, they live on the bottom, browsing on the animals living there, in a head-down posture. They have a long anal fin composed of spines and soft rays, the spines anteriormost. Their dorsal fins are, however, a long series of sharp, but short spines quite unconnected by any membrane. They lack a tail fin, although in such elongate fishes it is not uncommon for an individual to lose its tail tip in life, and to grow what appears to be a tail fin from the elements of the anal fin.

Members of the family are known from the Atlantic, Indian, and Pacific oceans. Some attain a length of 122 cm. (4 ft), most are much smaller. See **Macdonaldia, Notacanthus.**

Notacanthus Notacanthidae

chemnitzii SPINY EEL 122 cm. (4 ft)

Most of the food of this fish is composed of large pink, actinarian sea anemones, and it is obvious that to feed on such bottom-living animals the fish must browse head down and tail up over the sea bed.

This spiny eel is moderately frequently captured in the n. Atlantic, off Iceland and in the Barents Sea, as well as off the Grand Bank and in Greenland waters, usually in depths of

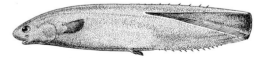

around 183 m. (100 fathoms), and in the e. Atlantic at least is not uncommonly caught by commercial trawlers. Although specimens with nearly ripe eggs have been taken in late autumn in Icelandic waters, nothing is known of their breeding or life history.

Nothobranchius   Cyprinodontidae
guentheri 7 cm. (2¾ in.)
Widely distributed in E. Africa, it has been found in freshwaters, and slightly brackish localities in Zanzibar, Tanzania, and Kenya. It has recently been introduced to India and the Solomon Islands as a potential predator on malaria-bearing insect larvae. It has also long been established as an aquarium fish in Europe.

As in other members of the family, the male is both larger and brighter coloured than the female.

It is a rather quarrelsome fish in the aquarium, but is suitable if kept in pairs. It breeds readily, laying its eggs on the bottom of the tank; the eggs hatch in 3 to 6 weeks at temperatures around 25°C. **202**
N. taeniopygus 5 cm. (2 in.)
Widely distributed in e. Africa, from Uganda near Lake Victoria and the Aswa River, in Tanzania, and along the Kafue River, Zambia. It was originally described from Lake Tschia in the Victoria-Nyanza area. In all these areas it lives in swamps and temporary streams. It breeds during the rainy season, drought-resistant eggs being deposited in the mud in which they remain during the dry season (the adults are unable to survive). With the rainy season the eggs complete their development and the young hatch. The young fish require 6 to 8 weeks to become full-grown, the eggs 8 to 10 weeks to develop. This fish is thus a true 'annual', and its breeding cycle beautifully adapted to the seasonal cycle.

As in other toothcarp species the males are brightly coloured, the body and fins reddish flecked with greeny blue, and an orange band along the anal fin. The female is a dull blue-grey.

The young fish feed on Protozoa, and the adults on small crustaceans and insect larvae. In places where it occurs commonly it is a useful biological check on the larval stages of the malaria carrying mosquito.

Notograptus   Notograptidae
guttatus SPOTTED EEL BLENNY
13 cm. (5 in.)
A long eel-like blenny found on the coasts of N. Queensland, Torres Strait, and the N. Territory of Australia. It is a little-known species which lives in shallow water down to a depth of 16·5 m. (9 fathoms).

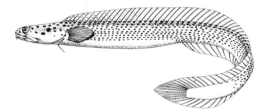

It is brightly, and unmistakably coloured, reddish brown background with numerous small blue spots and blue ocelli on the back and sides, becoming fainter posteriorly. The dorsal fin has blue spots along its length.

NOTOGRAPTIDAE
A small family of blenny-like fishes, related to the Congrogadidae, and confined to the waters around the tropical Australian coasts. Two species are recognized, both long, thin, eel-like fishes whose bodies are covered with small scales. The dorsal and anal fins are composed of slender pointed spines each with a short filament attached, except for the last 2 rays which are branched. See **Notograptus.**

Notolepis   Paralepididae
rissoi 30 cm. (12 in.)
This barracudina is worldwide in its distribution, being found in the Pacific, Indian, and Atlantic oceans. Although it appears to be most common in the temperate and tropical regions of these oceans, it has been found, particularly the large adults, in cooler water nearer the polar seas. Its habit of coming into cooler seas, where it is often found in shallow water, has meant that it is one of the better-known of the barracudinas. So familiar was it to the Greenlanders that they even had a local name for it.

Normally, however, it is found only in the open ocean in mid-depths of about 80–200 m. (44–109 fathoms). It is believed that the N. Atlantic population spawns in spring and summer to the S. of Ireland and W. of Biscay. It is entirely carnivorous, feeding on fish and shrimps. It is extensively eaten by larger fishes especially cod (in the N.), tuna, and even seals.

NOTOPTERIDAE
A small family of freshwater fishes found in tropical Africa and SE. Asia. They are generally known as featherbacks on account of the small, feather-like dorsal fin on the back (although *Xenomystus* lacks this fin). They are immediately distinguished by the very long anal fin, confluent with the tail fin, and arising close behind the pelvic fins, by the moderate sized mouth with many small teeth, and by their small scales.

The featherbacks swim by a gentle undulating motion of the anal fin, equally well forward or backward. They are not very active fishes, by day hanging at an angle close to the surface and under vegetation, and by night swimming restlessly over the bottom. See **Notopterus, Xenomystus.**

Notopterus   Notopteridae
chitala FEATHERBACK 87 cm. (34 in.)
This featherback is widely distributed in India and e. to Malaya, Thailand, and Java, Borneo and Sumatra. It is found in rivers, swamps, and canals and is a valuable food fish throughout the area. It is often seen at the surface, splashing as it rolls over, exposing its silvery flanks. Possibly this happens when it comes to the surface to gulp air, for it can use atmospheric oxygen for respiration.

Young specimens are relatively slender, brown fishes with a series of bands across the body, and wavy lines on the lower fin. Adults are hump-backed, dull on the back, but mainly silvery-sided.

It is a carnivorous fish, feeding on insects, shrimps, and particularly small surface-swimming fishes. It spawns in May to July (in the Ganges area), the eggs being laid on fallen trees and branches in the water. They are guarded entirely by the male who drives off predators, and fans them to free them of sediment and to keep them aerated. In Thailand, fisheries workers have for many years cultured this fish by driving stakes into the bed of rivers on which they will spawn. Here the fish is so valued for food that living specimens are transported hundreds of miles in water-filled barges to market.

Notorynchus   Hexanchidae
maculatus BROAD-SNOUTED SEVEN-GILLED SHARK *c*. 3 m. (10 ft)
Broad-snouted seven-gilled sharks are widely distributed but are best known in the Indo-Pacific, where they are known under several names. *N. maculatus* is found along the Pacific coast of N. America; *N. cepedianus* is the name by which the same species is known off s. Australia. It normally lives offshore and is seldom caught in coastal waters, although in San Francisco Bay a shallow water nursery ground exists where young sharks can be caught in numbers, the smallest being only 63 cm. (25 in.) long. This shark, which is distinguished by its 7 gill slits and wide head, is a sluggish species which nevertheless has a reputation for being pugnacious and potentially dangerous. This reputation has probably been earned by its fierce snapping and wild struggling when captured.

N. cepedianus see **N. maculatus**

Notothenia   Nototheniidae
coriiceps 61 cm. (2 ft)
A widely distributed Antarctic fish which has been found virtually all round the continent. Some confusion exists regarding the standing of this species and recently it has been divided into 2 subspecies, *N. c. coriiceps* which is found in the subantarctic and around the convergence of Antarctic and oceanic water, and *N. c. neglecta* which is found within the coolest polar seas.

Its colouring varies remarkably; the very young are pelagic in habitat, bright blue above, with silvery sides and belly, and a large black blotch on each pectoral fin. Immature fish are reddish, with paler bars, and a dark patch across the back of the head and gill covers. Adults are mainly brown with reddish or green tinges.

This nototheniid feeds mainly on algae, gastropod molluscs (winkles and others), amphipod and isopod crustaceans, and worms. It breeds in January, in depths of 100–200 m. (55–109 fathoms).

NOTOTHENIIDAE
This family is confined to the waters of the Antarctic, and are the most numerous and biologically dominant group of fishes. Some 68 per cent of the Antarctic fish fauna is composed of nototheniids.

The Antarctic cods, as they are sometimes called, are a diverse family. Most are bottom-living, sedentary fishes feeding on invertebrates and occasionally algae. Some live in close association with the sea ice, but only one has adapted to life in mid-water, and another is found living intertidally in the subantarctic region.

Body forms vary considerably. Most are rather elongate with a thickset anterior body, all have 2 dorsal fins, most have scaly bodies, and 2–3 lateral lines.

The Antarctic cods are an important link in the food chains of the region, they are eaten by most penguins, seals, and cetaceans. See **Dissostichus, Harpagifer, Notothenia, Pleuragramma, Trematomus.**

Notropis   Cyprinidae
  atherinoides EMERALD SHINER
10 cm. (4 in.)
A small N. American freshwater fish distinguished by its colour, and by its rather large scales, a long anal fin and the dorsal fin placed behind the pelvic origin. It is iridescent, with a silvery green to bluish green back, whitish below. It has a distinct emerald green stripe running along the side, and a narrow green stripe along the back.

It is very widely distributed in N. America from the Mackenzie River system, e. to the Appalachian mountains and s. to Alabama and Texas.

It is a pelagic shoaling fish found in lakes and large rivers and sometimes encountered in huge shoals. It feeds mainly on zooplankton, particularly the larger organisms, but the young feed heavily on planktonic plant matter before graduating onto animal plankton.

It is an extremely important fish in the overall economy of these waters, converting small animals and plants into forage for many large fish species. Not surprisingly it is a favoured bait used by anglers.

N. lutrensis RED SHINER 7 cm. (2¾ in.)
A very beautiful and lively little minnow which is widely distributed in the central region of the U.S., being found in S. Illinois to S. Dakota, to New Mexico and Texas. It is very abundant in clear small streams.

The males are brilliant steel-blue, the lower parts silvery and they have a violet crescent across the back with a red mark following, and an orange belly. The fins are reddish, the anal and tail fin being blood red. Females are greenish. **132**

Noturus   Ictaluridae
  gyrinus TADPOLE MADTOM 10 cm. (4 in.)
This little catfish is found from Saskatchewan, the Dakotas, through the Mississippi River system to Alabama and Texas, and

along the Atlantic coast rivers of Ontario and New York, New Hampshire, Massachusetts s. to Florida. It is a characteristic species of quiet and slow-running rivers, and is particularly abundant in lakes and their outlets, as well as small ponds and backwaters of streams. It distinctly prefers a soft muddy bottom with abundant vegetation. It is said to nest in small, hollowed-out cavities.

The madtoms are distinguished by having a very long, keel-like adipose fin which is continuous with the upper base of the tail. They also possess venom glands at the base of the pectoral spines, and can inflict very painful wounds. In this species the pectoral spine is only slightly serrated along its edge; its jaws are equal. It varies from dull golden yellow to olive-grey.

NUMBFISH see **Hypnos monopterygium**
NURSE, GREY see **Odontaspis arenarius**
NURSE
    HOUND see **Scyliorhinus stellaris**
    SHARK see **Ginglymostoma cirratum**

Nystactichthys   Congridae
  halis GARDEN EEL 51 cm. (20 in.)
This garden eel is found in the Caribbean, from Florida, the Bahamas, and the W. Indies. It has a close relative in the tropical e. Atlantic. It lives in clusters in the sand, each eel in its own burrow, and all evenly spaced through a considerable area. Normally a community or 'garden' as it has been termed, can be seen with the front two-thirds of their bodies out of the burrow, swaying gracefully with the movement of the water, and feeding on planktonic organisms passing in the water. On the approach of danger those eels nearest the threat retire slowly, deep into their burrows, the whole community retreating a little depending on their proximity to danger.

The garden eel is coloured to suit these habits. The front two-thirds of the body is dark brown, the last third pale, the whole has fine orange spots scattered over it. The body is very long and thin, the fins barely distinguishable, the pectoral fins are small, and the tail ends in a hard fleshy knob with no fin rays present. The mouth is small and oblique, and the eyes moderately large.

O

OARFISH see **Regalecus glesne**
OCEAN
    PIPEFISH see **Entelurus aequoreus**
    POUT see **Macrozoarces americanus**
    SUNFISH see **Mola mola**
OCEANIC
    BONITO see **Katsuwonus pelamis**
    HALFBEAK see **Euleptorhamphus viridis**
    PUFFER see **Lagocephalus lagocephalus**
    WHITETIP SHARK see **Carcharhinus longimanus**

Ocyurus   Lutjanidae
  chrysurus YELLOWTAIL SNAPPER
76 cm. (30 in.)
An inhabitant of the tropical Atlantic said to have been taken from the Cape Verde Islands in the e. Atlantic, but in the W. found from New England and Bermuda to s. Brazil. In the Gulf of Mexico and the Caribbean it is a common fish close to the reefs in open water. It is often seen close to the bottom where it eats bottom-living crustaceans and small fishes, but it is most typical of the mid-water zone between the reef and the surface. Its food is mostly animal plankton and small fishes.

It is fine food fish, and gives good sport to the angler, weighing 2·3 kg. (5 lb.).

Typically for an open water snapper it is slender-bodied and has a low dorsal profile. Its coloration is striking; a deep yellow stripe running from snout to the tail, broadening so that the whole tail and tail fin are yellow. The back is greyish blue with yellow blotches, the belly and sides below the yellow stripe are silvery.

ODACIDAE
A small family of wrasse-like fishes found only in the cooler seas of Australia and New Zealand. Their closest relatives are probably the wrasses (Labridae) but they share many features with the parrotfishes (Scaridae). The mouth is not protractile in the members of this family, and the teeth are lightly fused together to form a flat plate-like cutting edge. The dorsal fin has numerous slender spines in the anterior portion. See **Haletta, Olisthops, Siphonognathus.**

ODONTASPIDIDAE
This family (formerly known as the Carchariidae) contains a small number of typical sharks. All have 5 gill openings, 2 dorsal fins, with long slender, smooth-edged teeth usually with small cusps at the base. See **Odontaspis.**

Odontaspis   Odontaspididae
  arenarius GREY NURSE 4·6 m. (15 ft)
The grey nurse is found in Australian seas, but it is closely related to other odontaspids found elsewhere. It has a rather heavy shape, with large fins, 5 gill slits and long slender teeth which, on the lower jaw, are protuberant. It is greyish above, white below.

Like its relatives it lives close to the bottom in inshore waters being often found as shallow as 1·8 m. (1 fathom). No doubt this is why it is so often involved in attacks on man, for in Australian waters it is frequently implicated and is considered to be a dangerous shark. Its normal diet is fishes of various sorts.

O. ferox RAGGED-TOOTH SHARK 4 m. (13 ft)
This shark is widely distributed in the Mediterranean and in the adjacent Atlantic along the Portuguese and N. African coasts, as well as Madeira. It is also found on the Pacific coast of the U.S. It is a dull grey on the back, whitish on the belly, with black edges to the ventral fins. The upper jaw teeth each have 2 basal cusps each side. Not particularly common, its biology is little known, despite the fact that it was first discovered as long ago as 1810 by the French naturalist Antoine Risso. It is one of the potentially dangerous sharks of European waters.

O. taurus SAND TIGER or SHARK
3·2 m. (10½ ft)
The sand shark is widespread in the Atlantic Ocean, and although it was first described from the Mediterranean in 1810 it seems rare there, but is common from N. Africa s. to the Cape. In the w. Atlantic it occurs from the Gulf of Maine to Brazil. It is very common in in-

shore waters off the s. States and the Caribbean. It is a voracious shark feeding on any suitably sized fishes, and sometimes attacking and ruining fishermen's catches as they are being hauled in the net. Many of the fishes on which it preys are valuable sporting and food species, and large shoals of sand sharks must make heavy depredations on the fish population locally. On the American coast it is not regarded as a shark dangerous to man, but it has a sinister reputation on the African coast.

It is a uniform brown or grey-brown with irregular yellow-brown spots on the rear of the body and fins. The dorsal fins are both much the same size as the anal and pelvic fins. The sand shark has numerous long thin, pointed teeth in its jaws, each of which has a cusp at the base each side. In the lower jaw the teeth project forward and literally hang over the chin.

The sand shark gives birth to litters of only 2 pups after a gestation period of 12 months. They are comparatively large at birth, 76 cm. (30 in.), and have enormous bellies containing the yolk of the unfertilized eggs which they actively eat whilst in the maternal oviducts. **2**

Odonus   Balistidae
niger TRIGGERFISH, REDFANG
51 cm. (20 in.)
Widely distributed in the tropical Indo-Pacific, from the Red Sea and E. African coast to the E. Indies and through the w. and central Pacific. It is moderately common in inshore waters on the edges of reefs and over rough ground in depths of 10–35 m. (5–19 fathoms).

It is a very distinctive species, notably on account of the reddish teeth in the upper jaw (red with a yellow base in the lower jaw). After death it appears to be plain black. Large specimens develop long outer tail fin rays. **474**

OGCOCEPHALIDAE

A most bizarre group, the batfishes, related to the anglers and frogfishes, and sharing many of their features. Like them the pectoral fins are well developed and set on elbow-like stalks. The body is flattened, rounded or triangular in shape (viewed from above), the tail is moderately long. No spines in the fins, the dorsal and anal fins only small, and the spinous dorsal ray is reduced to a short rod with a small lure at its tip, sited under the pointed snout. This lure is supposed to be used for attracting prey towards the fish. The mouth is small.

Relatively small in size, they are distributed worldwide in deep oceans in temperate regions, and in shallow water and ocean deeps in the tropics. They have no commercial value, but are often sold as curios, sea-dragons and the like, and dried with small pebbles inside as rattles. See **Halieuta, Halieutichthys, Ogcocephalus, Zalieutes.**

Ogcocephalus   Ogcocephalidae
nasutus SHORTNOSE or REDBELLIED
BATFISH 28 cm. (11 in.)
The most common batfish in the W. Indian region, found in shallow water from the shore-line to 91 m. (50 fathoms) in the Caribbean Sea from Florida and the Bahamas to Guyana. It is a sluggish fish living on flat bottoms of sand, coralsand, mud, or turtle grass, and can be picked up by hand.

It moves slowly over the bottom, crawling

on its pelvic fins, supported also by its tail. Despite its slowness and sluggish behaviour it eats a remarkably varied assortment of molluscs, fishes, crustaceans, and worms.

It is rather triangular when viewed from above, only the fairly slender tail lying outside the triangle. The snout is pointed and the eyes are lateral, the pectoral fins are prominent and are placed on limb-like stalks, while the body is enveloped in a hard rather spiny carapace. It is dusky above, brown or red ventrally, with dark pectoral fins.

O. vespertillo LONG-NOSED BATFISH
23 cm. (9 in.)
A w. Atlantic species which is known from Brazil, n. to Cuba, the Florida Keys, and very rarely as a wanderer to the vicinity of New York.

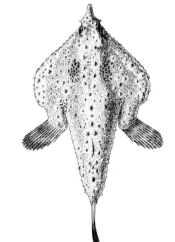

Its body form is distinctive of the group. It is greyish brown on the back, occasionally with dark spots; sometimes the belly is coppery red in colour.

Its name *vespertillo* is a recognition of its bat-like shape.

OGREFISH, FANGTOOTH see **Anoplogaster cornuta**
OIL SHARK see **Galeorhinus zyopterus**
OILFISH see **Ruvettus pretiosus**
OLD WIFE see **Balistes vetula, Enoplosus armatus, Spondyliosoma cantharus**

Oligocottus   Cottidae
maculosus TIDEPOOL SCULPIN
9 cm. (3½ in.)
The tidepool sculpin is distinguished from other N. American Pacific species by the forked preopercular spine each side of the head, the fine papillae on the back and sides of the head and the lateral line. It is widely distributed on the shore-line between the Bering Sea and n. California.

It is extremely abundant in shallow waters especially in tide pools on rocky shores. It breeds in winter, the pale greenish blue eggs being deposited on a rocky surface where they are fertilized by the male, who grasps the fe-

male with one pectoral fin. Males are distinguished by the long anal spines, and by an orange spot on the front of the dorsal fin.

Oligoplites   Carangidae
saurus LEATHERJACKET 30 cm. (12 in.)
This is one of the relatively few fishes to occur on both the Atlantic and the Pacific coasts of America; in the former it extends from the Gulf of Maine to Uruguay, and throughout the Gulf of Mexico and the Caribbean. It is a relatively small schooling fish which swims near the surface, commonly in turbid areas and in estuaries. It leaps clear of the water at times.

Its body is long and slender, the head small, and the mouth oblique and large. The dorsal and anal fins are long, and the rays low, each one separated as a small finlet. It is greenish on the back, silvery on the sides and with a bright yellow tail fin.

Olisthops   Odacidae
cyanomelas HERRING CALE 46 cm. (18 in.)
Found on the coasts of Australia, but only really common in the cooler, s. regions. It lives mainly in areas where algal cover is dense, and feeds entirely on plant matter.

The sexes are differently coloured. The female is brown above, lighter below with orange and yellow bars on the head; the male is bluish black above, lighter below with a broad blue bar on the head and others on the fins.

From the accounts of male fishes with female coloration it might be inferred that sex change occurs with growth in this species, as it does in the related wrasses (Labridae).

Olyra   Olyridae
burmanica 10 cm. (4 in.)
A small, rather slender catfish found in the rivers and streams of Burma. It is a secretive

species living under rocks in relatively fast-running water. It is dark brown.

OLYRIDAE

A family of small Asiatic catfishes found in e. India and Burma. Several species are known, all have a low, rather elongate body, the head depressed and flattened but covered with soft skin. The first dorsal fin is rounded but without a spine, the adipose fin is long and low, as is the anal fin. The barbels are 8 in number, the posterior barbel on each side being long. See **Olyra.**

OMOSUDIDAE

A family which is believed to contain one species only, a very distinctive fish with a massive head. Its general body shape is compressed from side to side, it is moderately long-bodied but with small to very small fins, and a low adipose fin close to the tail. It is an open ocean fish, which is best known from descriptions of larvae and juveniles, the adults being very active predators which apparently have little trouble in evading towed nets (most large specimens have been recovered from the stomachs of even larger, faster, predatory fish). See **Omosudis.**

Omosudis   Omosudidae
   lowei 23 cm. (9 in.)
This fish is most striking, with a brassy iridescence, dull brown on the back shading through silvery-bronze, and with the jet black stomach showing through the skin. It lacks light organs, but it has been suggested that the general shininess of its skin reflects light from other organisms thus breaking up its outline, confusing predators and prey alike.

It is distributed widely in the warmer regions of the 3 oceans, although apparently rare in the central and e. Pacific. Most records of the species are from the tropical Atlantic from the Gulf of Mexico e. to Madeira and the Gibraltar region. It is an open ocean fish found from near the surface down to 1300 m. (710 fathoms). In general, the young fish are found nearest the surface, and migrate vertically downwards in daylight, and towards the surface at night. As they grow they are found in increasing depths, and the adults are probably most common at and below the lowest depth noted above.

Omosudis is an active predatory fish, even eating prey larger than itself. It is well equipped for catching active fishes and squids, particularly with its large jaws and powerful teeth; its stomach is an extensible sack, while its slender yet rather broad tail denotes a powerful swimmer. Its food seems to be most commonly deep water squids, but it eats large numbers of lanternfishes, hatchetfishes, and other fish. In its turn it is eaten by other fish, and most of the large adults discovered have been taken from the stomachs of larger predators, especially tunafish and lancetfishes.

Ompax   Ceratodontidae
   spatuloides CASTELNAU'S FISH
46 cm. (18 in.)
This singularly interesting fish was first reported to live in a single water hole in the Burnett River, Queensland. The first and only described specimen was eaten for breakfast by its discoverer, a museum worker, who was

prompted by its curious appearance to have a drawing of it made after it was consumed. The drawing was submitted to the naturalist F. de Castelnau who published a description of it and named it formally in 1879.

It was recognized, with some scepticism, in subsequent accounts of Australian freshwater fishes, as a member of the lungfish family. Not until 1930 was the truth anonymously revealed that it had been manufactured from the head of a lungfish (some authors suggest a platypus), the body of a mullet, and the tail of an eel.

Ompok   Siluridae
   bimaculatus 46 cm. (18 in.)
Found in Java, Borneo, and Sumatra to Malaya, Thailand, and Indo-China, and w. to Burma and e. India. This catfish is reasonably common throughout its range, but its body form changes considerably and this has led to confusion. It is a relatively important food fish in some areas. It is also kept as an aquarium fish when young; large specimens are apt to be quarrelsome.

It is almost transparent when young, but older specimens develop a bluish sheen on the back and sides.

It is a lively, diurnal fish for the aquarium but one which must be kept in a small shoal; solitary specimens seem to pine. **154**

ONAGA see **Etelis carbunculus**

Oncocottus   Cottidae
   quadricornis FOUR-HORNED SCULPIN
36 cm. (14 in.)
Distributed as an inshore marine and estuarine fish throughout the Arctic Ocean and found in the White Sea, the Barents Sea, and the coasts of Arctic America, Labrador, and Greenland. It is also found in the Arctic N. Pacific. In addition it occurs widely in freshwater lakes in N. America, Europe, and Asia. These freshwater populations are regarded as relicts of immediately post-glacial flooding by the sea which brought them to habitats which became landlocked.

On account of the diversity of habitats, and their isolation from one another, many of these populations differ from one another and from the marine form. Several of these are regarded as subspecifically distinct.

The marine populations live in coastal waters, some also enter estuaries. They spawn in late autumn or winter and the young hatch in the spring. Lake populations usually live in very deep-water lakes, apparently at all depths close to the bottom down to 400 m. (219 fathoms). They are said to spawn in summer, but their life style is virtually unknown.

Oncorhynchus   Salmonidae
   gorbuscha PINK or HUMP-BACK SALMON
76 cm. (30 in.)
The pink salmon is easily distinguished from its Pacific relatives by the oval black spots on back and tail fin. At spawning time the males are particularly distinctive with dark backs, red sides, and a most remarkable humped back, as well as more usual male salmon features like elongate hooked jaws, and large teeth.

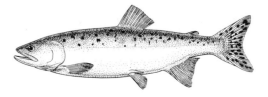

It is found naturally in the n. Pacific, along the American coast from California to the Bering Strait and the Mackenzie River, and on the Asian coast N. to the Lena River. It has also been introduced to the Atlantic, in Newfoundland waters, and the White Sea, on the nw. coast of the U.S.S.R. From one, or both, of these introductions specimens have spread as far as Iceland and the British Isles.

The pink salmon does not migrate far upriver to spawn, 160 km. (100 miles) upstream being the maximum in large rivers. It spawns in small streams in autumn in a redd cut on rough gravel, and the eggs hatch from December to February. The fry migrate downstream within days of emerging from the gravel in which they laid concealed after hatching. Adults die after spawning. The young return to the river to spawn after 2 years.

The pink salmon is a relatively small fish, usually weighing about 2·7 kg. (6 lb.). Despite this it is of considerable value as a food fish in the N. Pacific, particularly on the Asian coast although N. American catches are considerable.

O. keta CHUM SALMON 100 cm. (39 in.)
The chum salmon is widely distributed in the n. Pacific Ocean. On the American coast it is found from California n. to the Bering Strait, and on the Asian coast from Korea N. to the Arctic Ocean. This salmon is found in the Arctic Ocean both on the n. Canada and U.S.S.R. coasts. It is distinguished from the other Pacific salmons by the lack of dark spots on its back and fins. In the breeding season males are very distinctive, dark above and dusky below with blotchy red colouring and distinct greenish bars on the sides. Females are similar but with less red. Spawning males have a rather deep body, hooked jaws and large teeth.

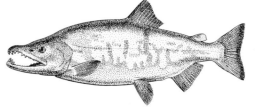

Like other salmons, the chum is migratory, entering rivers in July, and passing far up into their headwaters to spawn in September or October. Their eggs are shed in redds excavated in gravel in riffles and the young fish lie hidden in the gravel for some time after hatching. On emerging they begin to move downstream usually at night. The chum salmon spends very little time in freshwater, for they reach the sea in their first year and return to spawn after 3 to 5 years. The adults die after spawning.

Chum salmon are a valuable economic resource and large numbers are taken annually. They are particularly important to local fisheries on the n. Canadian coast and form a major part of winter food stores for man and dog. It is sometimes known as the dog salmon.

O. kisutch COHO SALMON 96 cm. (38 in.)
The coho salmon is found in the coastal and freshwaters of the N. Pacific basin. On the American coast from Baja California (where it is rare) and Monterey Bay n. to Alaska, and on the Asian coast from Hokkaido N. to the Anadyr River, n. U.S.S.R. It does not range so widely across the open sea as do other Pacific salmon, being found mainly in inshore waters. On the other hand it ascends rivers for great distances to breed, over 2400 km. (1150 miles) up the Yukon River, for example.

The mature coho enter rivers in late June, July, or August, usually when they are in their third or fourth year. They work their way upstream, until in about November they reach the spawning areas in small streams running into the larger rivers. The female excavates a redd or nest in a riffle area of gravel in which she and one male (occasionally 2) will breed. The eggs are buried in the gravel by later excavation of redds upstream. The adults die after spawning.

The eggs hatch in 6–8 weeks, but the larvae lie quiescent in the gravel for 2–3 weeks after hatching. For a while they form small shoals in the shallow margins of the river, but soon assume individual territories in pools and slow-flowing reaches. Many migrate to the sea in their second year, in some rivers not until their third year.

Young coho feed on aquatic and flying insects while in freshwater; in the sea they eat fish, crustaceans, and squids and grow rapidly.

It is a rather deep-bodied salmon which is distinguished from its congeners by the scattering of small black spots on the back and upper tail fin. At spawning time the back and belly become dark, the head bluish green, and a bright red line develops along the sides in males. The spawning males develop hooked jaws, and the teeth are larger.

The coho is one of the less valuable Pacific salmons although it is good food and preserves well in cans. On the other hand it gives good sport for the angler trolling or fly fishing. Coho have been introduced to the Great Lakes with every sign that they will produce a viable population.

The coho is sometimes known as the silver salmon.

O. nerka SOCKEYE SALMON 84 cm. (33 in.)
KOKANEE 41 cm. (16 in.)
The sockeye salmon is found in the N. Pacific and rivers entering it. On the American coast it occurs from California n. to Alaska, and on the w. coast from Hokkaido, Japan, n. to the Anadyr River, U.S.S.R. It is found in coastal waters and far out at sea, as well as in rivers and associated lakes as migratory fish. In a number of lakes it is found as a non-migratory fish spending all its life in freshwater maturing in its fourth or fifth year; these fish are known as kokanee, and were at one time considered to be a distinct species. They are usually relatively small, and except locally as in Japan, have little commercial value. The migratory sockeye salmon on the other hand is a very valuable fish especially on the American coastline.

The migration from the sea starts in June and continues through the summer. It is particularly attracted to rivers in which there are lakes, for it spawns in the brooks and streams running into the lake as well as on the

shores of the lake. The female digs a redd in coarse gravel, often in a riffle in the stream, after fertilization the eggs are covered by the female digging upstream. The adults die after spawning. The eggs hatch in 6–9 weeks, and the fry move into the neighbouring lake in which they live for 1 or 2 years before migrating to the sea. While in freshwater they feed on planktonic crustaceans, once in the sea their food is principally euphausiid crustaceans.

The sockeye salmon lacks distinct black spots on the back and sides. At spawning the males are bright red on the back and deeper red on the sides; the females are similarly coloured but the male has a hooked lower jaw and a moderately humped back. All Pacific salmon have more rays (13–18 in this case) in the anal fin than do the Atlantic salmon.

O. tshawytscha CHINOOK SALMON
147 cm. (58 in.)
The chinook, or king salmon (an alternative name is quinnat) is distinguished from its Pacific relatives by the dark spots on the back, dorsal fin, and the entire tail fin. In addition, the flesh of the jaws at the base of the teeth is black. It is widely distributed in the N. Pacific from s. California to Alaska, and on the Asian coast from Hokkaido to the Anadyr River, U.S.S.R. Within this area it enters large rivers to spawn, often travelling far upstream (in the Yukon River it may be found 2012 km. (1250 miles) from the mouth).

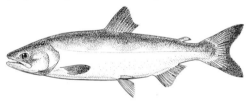

The run of the migratory fish starts in late May and is at its peak in June. Spawning takes place in late July and August. The female digs the redd in a riffle area and is accompanied by one dominant and several other males. The eggs are laid in the redd and fertilized by the dominant male and such of the others as can get close enough. Some chinook males become sexually mature at 10 cm. (4 in.) and are not migratory.

The eggs hatch in 7–9 weeks, and the young fish stay in the gravel for a further 2–3 weeks. The fry school at first but later become territorial and distribute themselves along the river. They spend 2–3 years in freshwater before moving downstream to the sea, often tail-first and at night. They grow very rapidly in the sea on a diet of anchovies, herring, squid, and crustaceans. The male chinook matures after 2–3 sea years, the females after 4–5, when they return to the rivers to spawn. Most chinook die soon after spawning, although some spent fish have been caught in the mouth of the river but no instances are known of a fish spawning twice.

The chinook is a valuable commercial species, second only to the sockeye salmon. Most are caught in the mouths of rivers as they

begin to migrate, but of recent years the high-seas gill-net fishery has become very important. They are eaten fresh, dried, or canned and have for long been one of the important food fish for the native peoples of the Pacific coast. Exceptionally large chinook may weigh 45 kg. (100 lb.), the average migrating fish weigh about 9 kg. (20 lb.), and ocean-caught fish are about 4.5 kg. (10 lb.). A juvenile is illustrated.

ONE-FINNED SHARK see **Heptranchias perlo**
ONE-SIDED LIVEBEARER see **Jenynsia lineata**
ONE-SPOT LIVEBEARER see **Phalloceros caudimaculatus**
ONE-STRIPED AFRICAN CHARACIN see **Nannaethiops unitaeniatus**

Oneirodes   Oneirodidae
  acanthias 20 cm. (8 in.)
A round-bodied, deep-sea angler with the typical large mouth and teeth of the group, and a rod on the snout at the tip of which a luminous, branched lure is placed. The body is black, but the fins are colourless. It has been found in the e. N. Pacific between the Bay of Alaska and Baja California, at depths of 366 m. (200 fathoms) and more.

This is one of the few ceratioids which is well-known from adult females; relatively few larvae have been caught. The males are large-headed, smaller, toothless, and are free-living. Most oneirodids feed on crustaceans.
O. carlsbergi 20 cm. (8 in.)
Known from relatively few female specimens taken in widely separated areas, including the S. Pacific, the S. China Sea, the Gulf of Panama, and the NE. Atlantic. All these specimens were captured by the Danish research vessel *Dana*.

It is a rounded bodied fish, darkly coloured with short-based dorsal and anal fins. The fishing rod is long and angled sharply with a broad tip, presumed to be luminous in life. The tip is branched, the posterior part being very long. **185**

ONEIRODIDAE
A family of deep-sea anglerfishes which contains about 15 genera. Many of them are known from only 1–2 adult specimens, and some only from larval fishes. Members of the family occur in the Atlantic, Pacific, and Indian oceans.

As a group they have no obvious external characters in common, the distinguishing features being based on internal structure. Like other ceratioid anglerfishes, the females are larger than males, and are equipped with luminous fishing lures on a cartilaginous rod on the snout. The males are free-living. See **Lasiognathus, Oneirodes, Thaumanichthys.**

OPAH see Lampridae, Veliferidae
OPAH see **Lampris guttatus**
OPALEYE see **Girella nigricans**

Opeatogenys   Gobiesocidae
  gracilis 2.5 cm. (1 in.)
A little known clingfish which appears to be confined to the Mediterranean. It was first described from Nice by the Italian naturalist

Canestrini; it has also been found in the Adriatic and off Messina, Sicily, so it is evidently well distributed.

This species is distinguished from the other clingfishes by having a strong, sharp spine in the anterior gill cover.

Ophicephalus Channidae
africanus AFRICAN SNAKEHEAD
32 cm. (12½ in.)
Found in w. Africa from Lagos to the Cameroons, this snakehead is typical of the family in body form and colouring. It can be distinguished by the series of dark chevron-shaped bars running along the back and sides, and by the black line which runs from the tip of the snout through the eye to the rear of the head.

It has been kept in aquaria in Europe, and the young fish make interesting if unspectacular pets.

O. micropeltes 1 m. (3¼ ft)
This is the largest of all the snakeheads, the biggest specimens attaining 1 m. in length and a weight of about 20 kg. (44 lb.). It is valued as a food fish, and is marketed alive, its ability to survive out of water being due to its accessory air-breathing organs at the back of the gill chamber. It is a voracious predator and eats all manner of fishes, frogs, snakes, and insects, which inhabit the rivers, swamps and pools with it. It has some reputation as an angling species.

Its geographical range is wide for it is found from India, Burma, Malaya, Vietnam, Thailand, and Cambodia. In Thailand at least it is more often found in the larger rivers than are the other snakeheads.

It is distinguished from other members of the family by its small, numerous scales, and its brown coloration with 2 narrow parallel black stripes running along the sides with a red interspace. **237**

O. obscurus 51 cm. (20 in.)
This snakehead is widely distributed in central Africa, from the White Nile to W. Africa. It appears to be the most common member of its family in Nigeria, and it is abundant in commercial catches especially where swampy conditions are found.

The accessory breathing organ enables it to live in oxygen-poor regions such as swamps and ditches, for it keeps coming to the surface to gulp air. Young specimens, which are more colourful, are often kept in aquaria. Adults are aggressive predators and this makes them unsuitable as pet fish. **238**

O. striatus 1 m. (3¼ ft)
The most widely distributed of the Asiatic snakeheads for it is found from Sri Lanka and India throughout the E. Indies and SE. Asia to China and the Philippines in rivers, canals, lakes, ponds, swamps, and ditches. On account of its abundance and its size it is of considerable economic importance, the more so as it can breathe atmospheric oxygen by means of its additional respiratory chamber and thus lives for a long time out of water.

It lives in swamps and waters in which dissolved oxygen levels are low, and burrows into the mud during droughts, surviving as long as its skin and the surrounding mud are still moist. Dr Hugh M. Smith records that in Thailand they are captured in times of drought by fishermen who cut the mud away in layers until the fish is exposed. It is a highly valued food fish in Thailand.

This snakehead prepares a nest by both parents biting off vegetation in a roundish area in shallow water near the margin of a lake or canal. The eggs float at the surface in this cleared area, hatching within three days. For the first weeks of life the young spend much of their time at the surface. At around 5 weeks they can stay on the bottom at will but still tend to return to the surface to breathe. At 9 weeks they are entirely bottom-living. The male fish guards the eggs and early young most carefully. **239**

OPHICHTHIDAE

A family of eels, often referred to as snake or worm eels, which are found in shallow water in all tropical and warm temperate seas. Most of the members of the family have a sharp pointed tail which is free of the dorsal and anal fins. A few members do have a tail fin, however. They are slim-bodied and by preference bury themselves tail-first in sand, or mud bottoms. For this reason they are rarely seen. They are mostly nocturnal in habit, and although occasional specimens can be attracted to lights at the surface, they are exceptionally difficult to catch, firstly on account of their length, and secondly because their questing tails immediately detect any hole in a net large enough to offer the chance to escape.

As a group they are mostly small, and many species are brightly banded or spotted. It is one of the largest and most variable of eel families. See **Ahlia, Ophichthus, Ophisurus, Myrichthys, Sphagebranchus.**

Ophichthus Ophichthidae
ophis SPOTTED SNAKE EEL 1·4 m. (4½ ft)
An eel reported from a number of localities in the Caribbean region, from Bermuda, and Florida, s. to Brazil. Like other snake eels it is a burrowing animal, frequently seen with only its head protruding diagonally from the sand. It does not have a permanent burrow (as do the garden eels), but bores tail-first into the bottom wherever it is suitably soft. Other than sightings of partially buried snake eels, most are seen at night when they occasionally come to surface lights.

The spotted snake eel is a relatively stout-bodied member of the family, but it has a typical pointed tail. Its colour is tan, shading to white on the belly with 2 rows of conspicuous dark brown, rounded blotches along the upper sides and small dots between them.

OPHICLINIDAE

A small family of scaled blennies, related to the clinids (Clinidae). Probably no more than 6 species exist, all found in the waters of S. Australia and New Zealand. They all have small scales on their bodies, the dorsal and anal fins having spines only along their length, both being joined to the tail fin by a membrane.

Known as snake-blennies, all the known

species are long and slender, with long many-spined dorsal and anal fins. See **Ophiclinops, Ophiclinus.**

Ophinclinops Ophiclinidae
pardalis SPOTTED SNAKE-BLENNY
8 cm. (3¼ in.)
A little-known snake-blenny from the coast of S. Australia, found also in St Vincent Gulf. Its body form is particularly eel-like, and the dorsal fin very long, containing 52 sharply pointed spines. The pelvic fins are well developed but typically blenny-like, while the pectorals are minute.

It is brownish with numerous light spots and dark flecks on the back and sides, and a heavily pigmented spot on the gill cover.

Ophiclinus Ophiclinidae
gracilis BLACK-BACKED SNAKE-BLENNY
6 cm. (2½ in.)
A slender, eel-like fish; its coloration is variable, brownish above, yellowish below, with a brown band running from the snout along the upper sides.

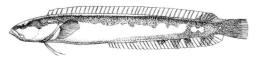

This snake-blenny occurs in shallow water along the coasts of S. Australia, New South Wales, and Tasmania.

OPHIDIIDAE

A small family of very varied, and successful fishes, the brotulids and the cusk-eels, which some workers consider should be separated into 2 families. Both groups are rather slender-bodied, the brotulas having a broad head and high body. Neither has spines in its fins, the dorsal and anal being long and in some genera joined to the tail fin. Brotulas have long, slender pelvic fins beneath the rear of the head, but the cusk-eels have similar pelvic fins under the throat.

Brotulas occur in a wide variety of habitats, from the deep sea (where some sightless species are found) to the seashore, and in places, freshwaters, again where some cave-dwelling forms are blind. Some forms are egg-layers, others are ovoviviparous, producing fully-formed young at birth.

The cusk-eels are mostly small, an average length being around 30 cm. (12 in.), some reach a considerable size, up to 1·5 m. (5 ft). Many of them are burrowing animals, boring tail-first into crevices, the sea bed, or turtle grass.

Both brotulas and cusk-eels are secretive animals, difficult to catch by reason of the places in which they live. No doubt many species are still waiting to be described, and for many of those that are known, the life history is vague. See **Genypterus, Lucifuga, Otophidium, Parophidion, Stygnobrotula, Typhliasina.**

Ophioblennius Blenniidae
atlanticus REDLIP BLENNY 12 cm. (4¾ in.)
A very distinctive fish on account of its high steep facial profile, dark coloration, and bright orange-red lips and dorsal fin edge. The body colour varies between olive to light grey but is usually dark brown.

The redlip blenny ranges from N. Carolina and Bermuda through the Caribbean and Gulf of Mexico, in which area the subspecies *O. atlanticus macclurei* occurs. *O. atlanticus atlanticus* is found in the tropical e. Atlantic, Ascension Island and the Brazilian coast.

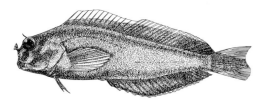

The adults are extremely abundant on rocky or coral bottoms down to a depth of 7·6 m. (4 fathoms). The eggs are laid in or on coral and are guarded by the male. The young fish are pelagic, pale stream-lined fishes with large curved canines in the jaws, and are very different in appearance from the adults.

Ophiodon Hexagrammidae
elongatus LINGCOD, CULTUS COD
c. 1·5 m. (5 ft)
Found along the Pacific coast of N. America from Alaska to Baja California. Its habitat is rocky areas from below low tide level to a depth of 304 m. (167 fathoms). To the S. of its range it is only found in deep water.

It spawns in winter to early spring, the female depositing her eggs in large pinkish masses on the rocky substrate. After they are fertilized the male guards them until they hatch, fanning them with his pectoral fins, and driving off intruders by fierce rushes. The adult lingcod feed almost entirely on fishes and squids; as young they eat crustaceans and small fishes. They are preyed upon by sharks, and possibly by sea lions.

Lingcod are important commercial and sporting fish. They are fished for with trawls and lines, and the fish are sold fresh. The flesh is very good eating, although in some specimens it is green tinted. Sports fishermen take large numbers along the Californian coast. Some doubt exists as to the maximum size attained, a record of 1·5 m. and 31·8 kg. (70 lb.) has been doubted, but females with a dressed weight of 45 kg. (100 lb.) have been reported, which suggests that it is an underestimate if anything.

It is distinguished by its slender body shape, large mouth with large caniniform teeth. The coloration is usually greenish brown, with dark blotches, but when fresh it has golden spots on the sides.

Ophistosternon Synbranchidae
infernale BLIND SWAMP-EEL
32 cm. (13 in.)
A most interesting fish found only in the Hoctun Cave, Yucatan, Mexico. It is presumed to live in the deep crevices of the pools in this cave and other subterranean water bodies.

It is an extremely slender-bodied fish. The eyes are totally covered by skin, and the dermal sense organs are well developed. Pigment is almost totally lacking in the skin although faint brown pigment cells are present.

This blind synbranchid eel is presumably derived from the surface living *Synbranchus marmoratus* which is found in Mexico and elsewhere in Central America. Another blind synbrachid, *Monopterus boutei* has been described from W. Africa.

Ophisurus Ophichthidae
serpens SANDSNAKE 2·3 m. (7½ ft)
This eel is widely distributed, being found from the Mediterranean, in the e. Atlantic from Portugal to S. Africa, and widely in the Indo-Pacific. In the Mediterranean and n. Atlantic it is found in moderately deep water, over sandy and muddy bottoms in which it is presumed to bury itself. In tropical areas it is found in shallow water, burying in mud and sand and even entering estuaries. It has been observed to lie buried with only its head protruding.

The head differs from most of its relatives; its jaws are long and thin with sharp teeth, long and fang-like in front, unequal in size posteriorly. These are clearly the teeth of a fish which eats active, soft-bodied prey.

The sandsnake has been found mummified within the body of a larger fish, having been swallowed entire, and then bored its way through the gut wall with the sharp tail. Seabirds are reported to eat them occasionally. They struggle fiercely when caught, and bite if handled, usually escaping thereafter!

Opisthonema Clupeidae
oglinum ATLANTIC THREAD HERRING
31 cm. (12 in.)
The thread herring is one of the easily distinguished herring-like fish of the Atlantic coast of America, for the last ray of the dorsal fin is prolonged into a thread usually about as long as the fish is deep. Otherwise it is a deep-bodied herring with the dorsal fin placed well towards the snout, and a low anal fin. Its coloration is blue above, silvery below, the tips of the dorsal and tail fins are black, and the scales on the back have a dusky centre forming broken streaks.

This fish is found from s. Massachusetts, s. through the Caribbean to Brazil. They are mainly tropical and subtropical fish which spread n. during the warmer months. Along the n. part of their range they are rather scarce and seasonal.

Their food consists of small organisms such as copepods and other animal plankton strained from the water through the fine mesh of their gill rakers. Being surface-living, shoaling fish they are vulnerable to a variety of predators, especially bluefish, weakfish, and Spanish mackerel; pelicans also feed on them. They are marketed in small numbers in the W.

Indies, but their food value is said to be poor, the flesh being dry and bony.

OPISTHOPROCTIDAE
A family of relatively small, bathypelagic fishes found in tropical and temperate waters throughout the oceans. In many respects they share the features of the black-smelts (Bathylagidae) and the argentinids, but they have digressed in a most singular manner with the development of the eyes. In opisthoproctids the eyes are tubular, so that they stand out, focusing above or in front of the head. Most have binocular vision as a result. Moreover many species have light organs within the orbit, and one at least is known to be able to cover the light organ apparently at will – a useful ability to save blinding itself. In body form some of the members of the family are probably the most bizarre of all mid-water fish. See **Dolichopteryx, Macropinna, Opisthoproctus, Winteria.**

Opisthoproctus Opisthoproctidae
grimaldii 6 cm. (2½ in.)
This bizarre, tubular-eyed fish has been found in a number of localities in the warm e. Atlantic, near the Azores, Canary Islands, and the Gibraltar region; it has also been found off the Bahamas. No doubt it is widely distributed in the tropical N. Atlantic. It is a pelagic species found in depths of 200–600 m. (109–327 fathoms). It appears to feed on the tentacles and stinging cells of siphonophores, jellyfish-like organisms common in the open sea.

Its body form defies description, the general colour is silvery, peppered with dark spots on the back. The belly is flattened, and forms a so-called sole, silvery coloured but overlain with clusters of dark pigment cells. The eyes of this fish are tubular, and look directly upwards; the lenses are coloured pale green. In life it must have adequate binocular vision, and the eyes' vertical view is possibly correlated with the shiny, flat belly of the fish, allowing species recognition, without attracting the attention of laterally sighted predators.

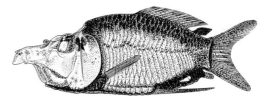

Another species, *O. soleatus*, is widely distributed in the tropical and temperate N. Atlantic and N. Pacific. It differs by lacking a recognizable anal fin, and by being dark coloured.

O. soleatus see under **O. grimaldii**

OPISTOGNATHIDAE
A small family of shallow-water, tropical marine fishes found in the w. Atlantic, and the Indian and Pacific oceans. The jawfishes or smilers are remarkable little fish with very pronounced large jaws which give them their names. Most species are rather slender with well developed, long-based dorsal and anal fins. Some forms live in burrows drilled vertically, lined with small shells, into which they enter tail first. The males of some species

incubate the eggs in their mouth. See **Mero-gymnus, Opistognathus, Tandya.**

Opistognathus Opistognathidae
aurifrons YELLOWHEAD JAWFISH
10 cm. (4 in.)
Found in shallow water off the Bahamas, Florida, and some W. Indian islands. It is one of the most colourful members of the family. The jaws are massive, with long curved fangs in the lower.

The jawfish has the habit of living in burrows excavated in sand, the walls being lined with shell fragments and small stones. It emerges from this burrow to feed, snapping at passing animal plankton in the water just above the entrance to its burrow, to which it returns if disturbed. At night it seals the entrance to the burrow with a small stone or shell and stays within.

The male carries the eggs in his mouth, leaving them in the burrow when he is actively feeding. **415**
O. nigromarginatus 20 cm. (8 in.)
An Indian Ocean species which is found from the E. African and Red Sea coasts to India and Sri Lanka. It is a brown fish, marbled with yellowish brown; a pronounced elongate black spot running along the centre of the front dorsal fin, and a rounded blotch on the tail fin are characteristic.

In this species the upper jaw bones are enormously developed, so that the whole mouth will hinge forward to open tremendously wide. It is presumed that this enables it to eat large food items but this is by no means certain.

OPLEGNATHIDAE
A small family of spiny-finned fishes found in the temperate and tropical regions of the Indo-Pacific. The members of the family are relatively deep-bodied, with a low spinous dorsal fin, and a high soft-rayed dorsal and anal. Their most remarkable feature, however, is that in the adult fish the teeth become fused together to form a parrot-like beak (they are often known as parrotfishes) but are not closely related to the true parrotfishes (family Scaridae). See **Oplegnathus.**

Oplegnathus Oplegnathidae
conwayi PARROTFISH, BASTARD GALJOEN, KNIFEJAW 91 cm. (3 ft)
Widely distributed in the s. Indian Ocean from the coasts of S. Africa and s. Australia.

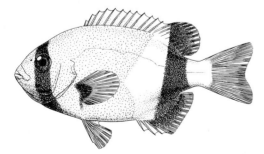

It is found mostly in shallow water, and down to a depth of 110 m. (60 fathoms). It is essentially a rock-living species which scrapes its food from the hard surfaces with its strong parrot beak.

Adults are dusky overall, but have a reddish sheen when live. Young fish are golden yellow with 2 dark stripes, one running across the head and eye, the other across the rear-end of the body.

Occasionally caught by anglers, but not a major sports fish. Its flesh is good.

Opsanus Batrachoididae
tau OYSTER TOADFISH 38 cm. (15 in.)
It is found in shallow waters along the e. seaboard of N. America from Cape Cod to Cuba, occasionally straying as far N. as Maine. It is commonest on sandy or muddy bottoms, hiding amongst eel grass. It eats a wide variety of invertebrate animals and many small fishes.

They have considerable noise-producing ability and grunt loudly if handled and at night naturally. They spawn in summer, the large eggs (5 mm. in diameter) being laid in cavities under stones, in old tin cans, or discarded shoes. The male guards the nest for the 3 weeks of incubation. The skin is scaleless and covered with thick mucus.

ORANGE-FINNED CHARACIN see
Creatochanes affinis
ORANGE-SPOT SURGEONFISH see
Acanthurus olivaceus
ORANGE-SPOTTED FILEFISH see
Cantherhines pullus
ORANGE-THROATED DARTER see
Etheostoma spectabile

Orcynopsis Scombridae
unicolor DOG-TOOTH or SCALELESS TUNA, PLAIN BONITO 1·5 m. (5 ft)
The dog-tooth tuna is distinguished from other members of the family by its apparently scaleless body (the corselet scales are minute), and by having well-spaced, conical, 'dog teeth' in the jaws. It also has patches of minute teeth on the tongue. The spiny dorsal fin has 11–14 fewer rays than its relatives.

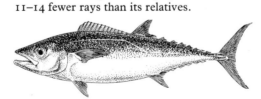

Its back is steel blue, the sides lighter, fading to silvery on the belly. There are no darker spots or lines on the body, although the fins are dusky.

It is a little-known species which is found in all the tropical oceans, and extends rarely into cool temperate seas. It is a fish of the high seas which comes into inshore waters adjacent to the open sea in warm seasons and is then occasionally captured by commercial or game fishermen. It is too sparsely distributed to make a significant fishery.

Considerable confusion surrounds the naming of the dog-tooth tuna. For long the Indo-Pacific form was given the name *Gymnosarda nuda,* but it is now generally regarded as conspecific with the Atlantic *O. unicolor.* Some workers still treat the 2 as distinct; some prefer to use the genus name *Gymnosarda* rather than *Orcynopsis.*

ORE see **Allocyttus verrucosus**

ORECTOLOBIDAE
A family of relatively small, shallow-water sharks, most species of which are found in the Indo-Pacific and Red Sea. They are rather heavy-bodied with rounded fins, 5 gill slits, and a fleshy feeler or barbel at the nostril edge which is connected to the mouth by a shallow groove. Often with conspicuous colour patterns. See **Crossorhinus, Ginglymostoma, Orectolobus, Stegostoma.**

Orectolobus Orectolobidae
maculatus WOBBEGONG 3 m. (10 ft)
The wobbegong, a name adopted from the aboriginal tongue, is widespread on all Australian coasts except for the n. states, where related species are found. It is basically a dull brown, ornamented with a beautiful pattern of light-edged spots and bars. Living in shallow

water, especially in caves and hollows in the reef, it is not infrequently encountered by swimmers. Although it is not rated as aggressive, it is dangerous if disturbed or attacked and has inflicted severe injuries at times.

OREO, OX-EYE see **Allocyttus verrucosus**

Oreodaimon Cyprinidae
quathlambae 9 cm. (3½ in.)
This little fish was first described in 1938 from a high altitude locality, 1615 m. (5300 ft), on the Upper Umkomazana River, Natal. In this river trout had been introduced and it was thought that they had exterminated this interesting species (which had originally been described in the genus *Labeo*). However, late in 1970, another population was discovered in the Drakensberg Mountains, again at a high altitude. Here also trout had been introduced and there is reason to fear that this rare fish is possibly preyed upon by the trout. Another, and probably more serious threat is the silting up of the river bed and changes in the flow, caused by over-grazing of the borderlands of the stream.

Oreodaimon is thus still threatened with extinction.

OREOSOMATIDAE
A small family of marine fishes, worldwide in distribution, and many of them found in the deep sea. As a group they are usually regarded as rare fish, few species are known from many specimens.

They have certain features in common with the dories (family Zeidae) most notably an oblique protrusible mouth, and spines in the dorsal, anal, and pelvic fins. They have large eyes, and rather compressed bodies. The body is scaly, but those scales on the sides are easily dislodged.

The juvenile fish are covered with distinctive bumps which are gradually lost as the fish grows. See **Allocyttus, Neocyttus.**

ORFE see **Leuciscus idus**
ORNATE
  ANGELSHARK see **Squatina tergocellata**
  COWFISH see **Aracana ornata**
ORTMANN'S DWARF CICHLID see
  Apistogramma ortmanni

Oryzias   Oryziatidae
  celebensis CELEBES MEDAKA 5 cm. (2 in.)
Found only in the flowing streams of the Celebes. It has been imported as an aquarium fish to Europe but has not survived for many generations in captivity. The male has elongate rays in both dorsal and anal fins.

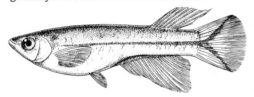

The male is greyish green with a brassy sheen by reflected light. A narrow dark line runs along the side and branches at the tail. The female is greyish, with a fainter dark marking.
O. latipes RICEFISH, JAPANESE MEDAKA
4 cm. (1½ in.)
Inhabits the paddy fields of lowland Japan, but has for many years been kept as an aquarium fish.

It is a slim-bodied fish with a flattened head and an almost straight dorsal profile; the dorsal fin is placed far back near the tail fin. The anal fin is long-based, with about 19 rays. The wild form is olive-brown, with a silvery belly, but the cultivated forms are rose pink with golden bellies. Males have a pointed dorsal fin, in the female it is rounded.

To keep it successfully in captivity a medium sized aquarium is required, well planted with vegetation, and with very slightly salt water. The breeding process is interesting; pairing takes place amongst the plants, the female carrying the eggs for a while in a mucus sheath on her belly but later transferring them to the plants. The eggs hatch after 10–12 days, and the fry are very small at first.

ORYZIATIDAE
A small family of egg-laying toothcarps found in se. Asia and n. to Japan. They are surface-living fishes, found in pools in the flood plains of lowland rivers, along the coastal marshes, and less commonly in inland waters. All are useful destroyers of mosquito larvae.

The members of the family were for long placed in the family Cyprinodontidae. They differ, however, in having a non-protrusible upper jaw and no teeth on the vomer. See **Oryzias.**

OSMERIDAE
The true smelts of the family Osmeridae are small relatives of the salmons and trouts, and like the members of Salmonidae have a small adipose, rayless fin on the back. The smelts are found in the N. Hemisphere, in the n. Atlantic, Arctic and, most particularly, the N. Pacific oceans, and in the river basins feeding these seas. Most are small fish which are often numerically very abundant. Some are fished for commercially by man, but most species, because of their size and abundance, are basic to many of the food chains of larger animals in n. waters.

Most of the species are rather fragile, silvery fish with easily detachable scales. Some are freshwater inhabitants but the majority live in the sea or are anadromous. See **Hypomesus, Mallotus, Osmerus, Thaleichthys, Spirinchus.**

Osmerus   Osmeridae
  dentex ASIATIC SMELT 41 cm. (16 in.)
The Asiatic smelt is widely distributed in the Asiatic U.S.S.R., and in the Pacific and Arctic ocean drainages of N. America. It is closely related to the European smelt which it much resembles, and according to many workers is but a subspecies of the latter. A second N. American smelt, the rainbow smelt, (*O. mordax*) which again may be no more than subspecifically distinct, is found in the e. region of N. America and in the Pacific and Atlantic oceans. *O. mordax* was introduced in 1912 into the Great Lakes (other than Lake Ontario to which it was native) and now supports a flourishing fishery, although its numbers fluctuate remarkably.

This smelt is anadromous, but many land-locked populations are known in isolated lakes. In the rivers and coastal waters of the U.S.S.R. it is a valuable commercial fish.
O. eperlanus SMELT, SPARLING
30 cm. (12 in.)
The smelt is a small European migratory fish found from Biscay to the Baltic Sea, and the White Sea. It is moderately common, if locally distributed, in coastal waters especially in estuaries, and migrates up rivers to spawn in freshwater although still in the tidal influence. It spawns in the spring; the eggs are shed over gravelly and sandy bottoms, and stick to the stones at first. Later the egg case breaks and the egg is left, toadstool-like, supported on a stalk. In time the stalk detaches and in its later stages of development the egg floats in the water suspended by a parachute of outer membrane.

Smelt are slender silvery fish with an olive-green back, large jaws, and a small adipose fin on the back. When fresh they are characterized by a strong cucumber-like odour, and make delicious eating.

It is a predatory fish, the young eat small crustaceans and the larger adults mainly fish. The migratory race grows moderately fast, but some populations found permanently in freshwater lakes, in Scandinavia notably, are slow growing and short lived. These land-locked populations are the descendants of migratory smelt which entered the lakes during changes of sea level relative to the land soon after the last Ice Age.
O. mordax see under **O. dentex**

OSPHRONEMIDAE
The small family which includes the gourami, a food fish of some importance and widely distributed from India through Asia to China and the Philippines.

It is closely related to the aquarists' gouramis which, however, belong to a separate family, Belontiidae. Like them it has an accessory respiratory organ above the gills on each side, and builds a floating bubble nest in which the eggs are laid.

The true gourami has a short spine in each pelvic fin and a very long second pelvic fin ray. The dorsal fin is short and is placed far back. See **Osphronemus.**

Osphronemus   Osphronemidae
  goramy GOURAMI 61 cm. (2 ft)
The gourami is believed to have been originally distributed in Java, Borneo, Sumatra, and other E. Indian islands. It is a valued food fish in Asia and was widely spread for culture at an early date and introduced to China, the Philippines, mainland SE. Asia, Sri Lanka and India. It is now almost impossible to be certain of its original range. It lives indifferently in ponds, swamps with open water, in streams and rivers, but nowadays is mainly cultured in fish ponds.

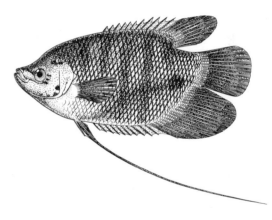

Large specimens may weigh several pounds, and grow very thick and heavy around the head and anterior body. Their flesh is said to be of good quality, although when taken from muddy ponds and having been poorly fed, is not always of a high standard. Its chief advantage as a food fish is that, due to its ability to breathe air while kept moist, it lives for a long time and stays fresh when marketed. This ability has also contributed to its widespread, man assisted, distribution.

Small specimens make pleasant aquarium fishes, the young fish being brownish red with irregular dark cross bands and a pale bordered, rounded blotch on the rear edge of the anal fin. The fins are bluish with the exception of the pelvics which are bright orange. Adults often become very dark, and eventually have a typical and not very beautiful swollen head region.

They breed by producing a nest of bubbles in which the eggs and larvae are kept afloat and guarded by the male.

It is usually immediately distinguished by its size, by the length of the pelvic fin ray which fin also has a spine, and by the posterior position of the dorsal fin. Males have pointed dorsal and anal fins.

Osteocheilus Cyprinidae
hasselti HASSELT'S BONY-LIPPED BARB
32 cm. (12½ in.)
This barb and its relatives are found in the E. Indian islands and rivers of the adjacent mainland. This species is common, and the most widely distributed of the group, and is found in Java, Borneo, Sumatra, most of Malaysia, and Thailand. It is found mostly in rivers and streams, less often in lakes. It is locally an important food fish, and fetches a good price.

Small specimens are particularly beautiful and are often kept in aquaria. They are olive-green on the back, with creamy sides and white belly, and have 6–8 rows of dark spots, one spot to each scale along the sides. It is a moderately deep-bodied fish, with a long, many-rayed and rather high dorsal fin. The mouth is distinctive in this and its relations, being protrusible with deeply fringed lips, while the lower jaw has a sharp scoop-shaped bony cutting edge.

It is an active shoaling fish which feeds on algae, will eat other plants, and can be fed on lettuce and live food in the aquarium.

OSTEOGLOSSIDAE

A small family of very distinctive, but rather primitive fishes with an interesting distribution. All are found only in fresh water, 2 species in tropical S. America, one in tropical Africa, and 2 in the Malayan-Australian region.

In general, these fishes are rather elongate, with large, bony scales, and a scaleless bony head. Their pectoral and pelvic fins are small, the dorsal and anal fins long, low and composed entirely of soft rays. The swim-bladder is large, its lining richly supplied with blood vessels, and it is connected to the pharynx. It can serve as a lung to utilize atmospheric oxygen. See **Arapaima, Heterotis, Osteoglossum, Scleropages.**

Osteoglossum Osteoglossidae
bicirrhosum ARAWANA 1 m. (3¼ ft)
The arawana is distinguished by the prominent barbels at the tip of the chin, by its steeply angled mouth, its large scales, and long anal fin which runs along the rear half of the fish, almost joining the tail. It is found in tropical S. American fresh-waters, Guyana and the Amazon basin. It is not such a large fish as its relative in the area, the arapaima (*Arapaima gigas*).

It is often found in large shoals in still water, in shallow reedy backwaters and lakes. It has the distinctive habit of swimming very near the surface film in a leisurely and graceful way. It is believed to be a mouth-brooder as it has a large pouchlike fold between the lower jaw bones, similar to the known mouth-brooder the Malayan *Scleropages*.

It is an interesting and rather well coloured species which is often kept in large aquaria. **30**

Ostracion Ostraciontidae
cubicus 46 cm. (18 in.)
A widespread Indo-Pacific species which occurs from the Red Sea, and E. African coast, e. to the Philippines, the Marshall Islands, and Hawaii. In many areas it is extremely common around coral reefs, in clear sandy areas, and even in sea grass areas.

It is yellowish brown to dark brown in colour, the hexagonal carapace plates each with a white centre, while the fins are all yellow. The young often have dark brown spots on the back and sides, and these persist in adults on the bases of the fins.

Its coloration is, however, very variable, as is its body form with growth, and some authors have concluded that this species and *O. tuberculatus* are identical, if representing the extremes of the single species. **481**

O. cyanurus 15 cm. (6 in.)
A species of boxfish found only in the Red Sea where it is apparently moderately common amongst the coral and in sandy patches between reefs.

It is a brightly coloured species, although its coloration tends to be rather variable. Small black spots are scattered over the sides of the head (in the female) the body, and the fins. Males have a convex snout (in the female it is hollow), lack the spots on the cheek, and have a dusky edge to the tail fin. **482**

O. diaphana see **Lactoria diaphana**
O. lentiginosum BOXFISH, TRUNKFISH
23 cm. (9 in.)
An Indo-Pacific species apparently of wide distribution, and originally described from the coast of India. This name has long been in use for the male of the species, while females were usually referred to as *O. sebae*; many authors now consider that both are identical with *O. meleagris*, also widely distributed in the Indo-Pacific. The confusion over the naming of the species of boxfish in particular stems from the description of so many specimens, dried, and brought to Europe in the 18th century by seafarers and often without locality – a habit still persistent in the present century.

It is often brilliantly coloured and can be seen swimming in leisurely manner in shallow water around reef-edges and in clear areas between. This is one of the Pacific boxfishes which is known to produce a toxic substance when alarmed or excited. **484**

O. meleagris 16 cm. (6¼ in.)
An Indo-Pacific species of wide distribution, the limits of which are not entirely certain on account of confusion with the related and possibly identical species, *O. lentiginosus*. Like that species it is heavily spotted with white dots on the back, the sides with yellowish dark edged ocelli, and the ventral surface is plain in males. Females have smaller spots on the back, those on the belly forming sinuous white lines. The male has a dark, often bluish, background colour; the female is light, even yellowish. **483**

O. sebae see **O. lentiginosum**
O. tuberculatus BLUE-SPOTTED BOXFISH
46 cm. (18 in.)
Wide ranging in the tropical Indo-Pacific, from the E. African coast and Zanzibar to the E. Indies, tropical Australia, the Philippines, and the w. Pacific. In many areas it is abundant, occasionally thrown ashore in numbers after storms, more often seen swimming slowly in reef-areas, feeding on bottom-living invertebrates. **485**

OSTRACIONTIDAE

The members of this family are probably the most bizarre of all fish groups, as they include the trunkfishes, boxfishes, or cowfishes. They are plectognaths, related to the pufferfishes, and rather more distantly to the triggerfishes (families Tetraodontidae and Balistidae).

Their most immediate feature is the heavy 'shell' that encloses the body, often symmetrically patterned and ridged, but complete except where the mouth, eyes, gill openings, vent, and fins protrude. The fins are much reduced in size and are all broad and rather paddle-like in appearance. They move by sculling movements of the pectoral, dorsal, and anal fins, normally only swim slowly, but can find a burst of speed by lashing the broad and flexible tail from side to side. Mostly they live quietly close to the sea bed secure in their suit of armour. Some boxfishes also secrete a toxic substance when alarmed, which at close quarters (as in an aquarium) will kill other fishes and themselves eventually. This presumably is also a deterrent against large predators. The toxin is produced particularly by the membranes round the mouth.

They are worldwide in their distribution in tropical seas, in some areas very common. Probably fewer than 50 valid species exist, most small fishes up to 30 cm. (12 in.) long, although some reach double that length. Few have any economic importance, although they are eaten locally, as they are regarded as the cause of fish poisoning or ciguatera, which may be the result of contamination with their own toxin producing membranes. See **Aracana, Lactophrys, Lactoria, Ostracion, Rhinesomus, Strophiurichthys, Tetrosomus.**

Otocinclus Loricariidae
maculicaudata 6 cm. (2¼ in.)
Found only in the s. branches of the Amazon, in se. Brazil. It is a fish of small rivers, and quiet waters which feeds on the fine algae growing on rocks and submerged vegetation, by browsing with its fine-toothed sucking mouth. Like other members of the family it adapts well to life in the aquarium and may live for years. It has the typical body form of the genus. **170**

Otolithes Sciaenidae
ruber LONGTOOTH or SNAPPER SALMON, SILVER JEWFISH 91 cm. (3 ft)
Widely distributed in the central tropical Indo-Pacific, from E. Africa to India and the E. Indies. In many areas very abundant in coastal waters and an important food fish. Grows to a weight of about 7 kg. (15 lb.).

It is a long-bodied fish, with a pointed head and large jaws with 2 well-spaced large canine-like teeth in each jaw. Each lateral line scale has much-branched tubules.

It is reddish above, silvery on the sides, sometimes yellowish ventrally.

Otophidium Ophidiidae
taylori SPOTTED CUSK-EEL 36 cm. (14 in.)
Widely distributed on the American Pacific coast from Oregon s. to Baja California. Along this coast it lives at depths between 18–242 m. (10–133 fathoms), usually hidden in the bottom in burrows or in crevices in the sea bed. When alarmed it burrows tail-first with remarkable ease, if undisturbed it emerges from the burrow and balances vertically on the last quarter of the tail. The late Dr Earl S. Herald first described this habit in captive specimens in the Steinhardt Aquarium, California, and related how even when pushed with a stick the fish curved its body towards the vertical.

This cusk-eel feeds on a wide range of small fishes, crustaceans, and octopuses; it is eaten by several larger predatory fishes as well as the California sea lion.

It has the typical slender body of all cusk-eels, the long dorsal and anal fins meeting at the tail; the pelvics are 2-rayed, the first ray shorter than the second, and are placed just behind the chin. It is light brown in colour, light ventrally, with dusky blotches on the back and dark edges to the vertical fins.

OTUNO see **Diplomystes viedmensis**
OUANANICHE see **Salmo salar**

OWSTONIIDAE
A small family of rather small marine fishes found in the Indo-Pacific. They have an elongate, compressed tapering body running into a rounded tail. The body is covered with minute scales, the lateral line rises sharply from the head and runs along the dorsal profile of the body. The eye is large.

These small fishes have, since their discovery, presented something of a puzzle to the systematist as to their correct relationships. Most of the described species are known from only 1–2 specimens, and they are usually regarded as rare. They are at present aligned with the bandfishes (family Cepolidae). See **Parasphenanthias.**

OX-EYE
OREO see **Allocyttus verrucosus**
TARPON see **Megalops cyprinoides**
OX-RAY see **Mobula diabolus**

Oxuderces Oxudercidae
dentatus 9 cm. (3½ in.)
A fish which was described from near Macao in the China Sea in the report on the voyage around the world in the French ship *La Bonite* in 1836 and 1837. It has not been encountered subsequently.

There seems to be considerable doubt as to whether it is a valid species, and if it is, where it should be placed in the systematic arrangement.

It was described originally as greeny-brown above and on the sides, white ventrally; the fins are greyish.

OXUDERCIDAE
A family which contains the single species described. It appears to have been based on a single specimen, which was not well described. The species has not been reported since. Its standing as a family is open to very serious doubt. See **Oxuderces.**

Oxycirrhites Cirrhitidae
typus 10 cm. (4 in.)
A hawkfish found only in the E. Indies and off Mauritius, although related species have been described from the Pacific around the Philippine Islands and on the Baja California coast.

This genus is distinguished by its acutely pointed snout. In other external features it resembles its relatives in having cirri on the

anterior membrane of the dorsal spines as well as on the anterior nostril.

O. typus has the snout particularly prolonged, with small pointed teeth in the jaws. The body and tail have oblique and lengthwise dark lines crossing each other. **391**

Oxygaster Cyprinidae
oxygastroides GLASS BARB 20 cm. (8 in.)
The glass barb is widely distributed in the Indo-Australian Archipelago, being particularly common in Java, Borneo, and Sumatra. It is the most abundant member of the family in Thailand. It is moderately deep-bodied, with a very small dorsal fin and a long, many-rayed anal fin. It is yellow-brown above, the sides are silvery with a greeny-blue tint, and the belly is white. A brilliant shining broad silvery stripe runs along the side, with a dark edge above it. The fins are colourless. The young fish are colourless and almost translucent, and are known to aquarists as glass barbs.

On account of its abundance in its native area this species is frequently captured and is conspicuous in the commercial catch.

It is a surface-living shoaling fish which is relatively hardy and omnivorous.

Oxymonacanthus Balistidae
longirostris BEAKED LEATHER-JACKET 8 cm. (3¼ in.)
A most attractive little inhabitant of the reefs and inshore waters of the e. Indian Ocean and w. Pacific. The extremities of its range seem to include Mauritius, the Queensland coast of Australia, and the Philippines. It lives amongst corals on the edges of reefs close to deep water.

Members of this genus are small, have an elongate body form, with a pointed snout. The dorsal spine is rough-edged and set immediately above the eye, the dorsal and anal fins are low and of equal size. **475**

OXYNOTIDAE
A small family of deep-water sharks, closely related to the family Squalidae. Like that family its members have a spine in each dorsal fin, and they lack an anal fin. They are distinguished by the greatly heightened back, by the coarseness of the dermal denticles ('skin teeth'), and by the characteristic teeth rows in the upper jaw, 6 or more rows each of increasing number from the front being functional.

Oxynotids are known from the e. N. Atlantic and Mediterranean, off Venezuela, and from Australian and New Zealand waters. See **Oxynotus.**

Oxynotus Oxynotidae
centrina see under **O. paradoxus**
paradoxus 90 cm. (35 in.)
A little known inhabitant of the deep waters of the e. Atlantic, from off the Hebrides s. to Morocco. It is usually found in depths of 180–550 m. (100–300 fathoms), and is regarded as

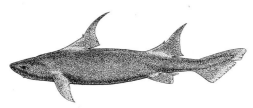

rather rare, although no doubt it is more common than the few records available make it appear.

The most noticeable feature of this shark is the heavy skin teeth which give its dark brown hide a thorny texture of painful roughness.

A second representative of the family occurs in European waters of rather more s. distribution, also found in the Mediterranean. This is the humantin, *O. centrina*, which rarely occurs in British waters.

OYSTER
BLENNY see **Petroscirtes anolius**
TOADFISH see **Opsanus tau**

P

Pachymetopon Sparidae
grande BLUE HOTTENTOT, JOHN BROWN, BRONZE BREAM 61 cm. (2 ft)
A s. African endemic sea bream found only from the Cape of Good Hope to Madagascar in rocky areas and in shallow water. It feeds mainly on plant matter and has flattened incisor teeth to enable it to browse on small algae.

It is one of the very important angling fishes of the area, being difficult to hook but fighting gamely. It is frequently caught on rocky shores. Its flesh is highly thought of for food. Apparently sensitive to cold, large numbers are from time to time washed ashore dead following upwelling of cold, deep water.

It is deep-bodied, almost oval in body shape. The head is iridescent blue, while the body is deep bronze, darker on the back.

Pachypanchax Cyprinodontidae
playfairi 10 cm. (4 in.)
Found along the tropical Indian Ocean coast of Africa. It was first discovered in the Seychelle Islands, and was subsequently found in Zanzibar, and along the E. African coast to Madagascar. It lives in fresh and slightly brackish water.

The males are pale brown above, greeny-blue on the sides with rows of red spots. The fins are clear yellow. Females are dull brown, olive on the sides with yellow fins. It is a rather thickset fish, especially at the head end.

Young fish, in particular, are popular aquarium fishes, the adults are quarrelsome. They are bottom spawners; the eggs hatch in 10–12 days. **203**

Pachystomias Melanostomiatidae
microdon 21 cm. (8¼ in.)
This scaleless dragonfish is known from very few specimens indeed, but they show that it is widely distributed. Most have been found in the tropical N. Atlantic, but one specimen is known from the Pacific Ocean, NW. of Australia. The depth range of the species may be as great as 4465 m. (2440 fathoms).

It is a short-bodied species, notable for its proportionately large head and eye. It is distinguished by its large, elongate double light organs under the eyes. These are part of a large mass of apparently luminous tissue in the roof of the mouth. The fish is otherwise velvety brown to black, but its light organs vary from rosy to red, with some greenish.

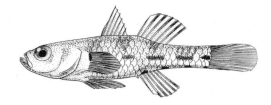

PACIFIC

- ANGELSHARK see **Squatina californica**
- BARRACUDA see **Sphyraena argentea**
- BLACK-SMELT see **Bathylagus pacificus**
- BUTTERFISH see **Peprilus simillimus**
- ELECTRIC RAY see **Torpedo californica**
- HAGFISH see **Polistotrema stouti**
- HAKE see **Merluccius productus**
- HALIBUT see **Hippoglossus stenolepis**
- HERRING see **Clupea pallasi**
- LAMPREY see **Entosphenus tridentatus**
- OCEAN PERCH see **Sebastes alutus**
- POMPANO see **Peprilus simillimus**
- SAND-DAB see **Citharichthys sordidus**
- SANDFISH see **Trichodon trichodon**
- SARDINE see **Sardinops caeruleus**
- SAURY see **Cololabis saira**
- SPINY LUMP-SUCKER see **Eumicrotremus orbis**
- TARPON see **Megalops cyprinoides**
- TOMCOD see **Microgadus proximus**
- PACU see **Colossoma nigripinnis**
- PADDLEFISH see Polyodontidae
- PADDLEFISH see **Polyodon spathula**
- PADDLEFISH, CHINESE see **Psephurus gladius**

Pagellus Sparidae
bogaraveo RED SEA BREAM 51 cm. (20 in.)
A European fish, widely distributed from the Canary Islands and N. Africa, the Mediterranean, and along the European Atlantic coast to Norway. It is not common however, N. of the English Channel and w. Ireland. It lives in water of 150–300 m. (82–164 fathoms) as an adult, but the young are found in much shallower water inshore, usually on sandy and muddy bottoms.

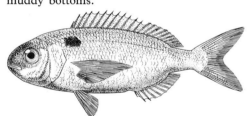

Its food is varied, the young fish eating small crustaceans, the larger ones eating many benthic invertebrates and fishes. This is the only sea bream to be commercially exploited in n. Europe, considerable quantities being taken by trawlers in the deep water to the SW. of Britain. Many are caught by anglers; this fish grows to 4 kg. (8¾ lb.). Its flesh is extremely good eating.

In the seas of Europe it is immediately distinguished by its pinkish coloration, the sides being silvery but the fins are red. A distinct black blotch on the upper side behind the head is best developed in adults.

Pagrus Sparidae
auriga 80 cm. (31½ in.)
A species which is widely distributed along the tropical and warm temperate e. Atlantic coast, and in the Mediterranean. In the Atlantic it ranges from Angola to the Portuguese coast, and is found in moderate depths of 20–60 m. (11–32 fathoms) mainly on rocky and broken ground.

It feeds on hard-shelled invertebrates, mainly molluscs with occasional crustaceans included in its diet. It has some value as a locally important food fish. **302**

PAICHE see **Arapaima gigas**
PAINTED
- GOBY see **Pomatoschistus pictus**
- MACKEREL see **Scomberomorus regalis**
- MORAY see **Gymnothorax pictus**
- SWEET-LIPS see **Plectorhynchus pictus**
Palaeodenticeps tanganikae see under Denticipitidae
PALING see **Anguilla mossambica**

Pallasina Agonidae
barbata TUBENOSE POACHER
13 cm. (5 in.)
A very slender, elongate poacher, with 2 rather small dorsal fins. It is grey to brown, heavily spotted with black, paler underneath; the fins are all spotted.

It is found along the N. Pacific coastline of America from Oregon to the Gulf of Alaska. It lives in shallow water usually on sandy bottoms or amongst eel grass. Its biology is little known.

PALMER see **Lates calcarifer**
PALOMETA see **Trachinotus goodei**

Palunolepis Cheilodactylidae
brachydactylus BUTTERFISH, STEENKLIPVIS 41 cm. (16 in.)
Found only around the coast of S. Africa in shallow water among algae in which it lies concealed. The young are very common in intertidal pools.

These fishes grow through a varied metamorphosis, the young (to about 5 cm., 2 in.), in length) being deep-bodied and silvery with a blue back and yellowish fins. At this stage it lives pelagically in the inshore sea, but once it comes inshore it becomes greenish brown

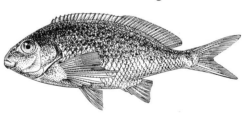

above, silvery below, and the pectoral fin rays become elongate. With some variation this is the colouring of the adult.

PANCAKE BATFISH see **Halieutichthys aculeatus**
PANCHAX,
- BLUE see **Aplocheilus panchax**
- DWARF see **Aplocheilus blocki**
- GREEN see **Aplocheilus blocki**

Pandaka Gobiidae
pygmaea PYGMY GOBY 11 mm. (½ in.)
Best known as one of the claimants for the title of the world's smallest fish (and the smallest vertebrate). Fully grown it reaches a maximum length of 11 mm. (½ in.), although mature specimens of 7.5 mm. (5/16 in.) have been reported.

It is an inhabitant of the freshwater lakes and streams of the Philippine region.

A rather slender-bodied goby, the head and

nape are scaleless. It is yellowish with dusky spots on the back and sides. A distinct black spot is present at the base of the tail fin.

Pangasianodon Pangasiidae
gigas MEKONG CATFISH 2.5 m. (8 ft)
This giant catfish is confined to the Mekong river system and is thus found in the larger rivers running through Thailand, Laos, Cambodia, Vietnam, and parts of China. During the rainy season it is found mostly in the lower reaches of the rivers, but runs upstream to spawn when flood conditions cease. It spawns in lakes and in the upper reaches of the major tributaries.

In body form it closely resembles other catfishes of this family but is distinguished from the other genera by having only one pair of barbels (on the angle of the upper jaw), the eye placed low down on the head, and by the lack of teeth. These are characters of the giant

specimens, and no juveniles have been described; it is possible that these features are the consequence of age, and young specimens have more typical characters of *Pangasius*.

The giant Mekong catfish is celebrated in ethnological and exploratory literature of the area. It is a valuable food fish, and has been for many years, but it is susceptible to overfishing so that with increased fishing pressure large specimens have become relatively rare.

PANGASIIDAE

A group of catfishes widely distributed in Asia, and closely related to (identical with, according to some authors) the African Schilbeidae. They are freshwater fish. Their general shape is flattened anteriorly with a small dorsal fin, an adipose fin, and an anal fin, short by schilbeid standards, but many-rayed. They have fewer barbels and no nasal barbels; one species only has maxillary barbels. See **Pangasianodon, Pangasius, Silonia.**

Pangasius Pangasiidae
pangasius PUNGAS CATFISH 120 cm. (4 ft)
Widespread in India, Burma, Java, and Thailand. It inhabits large rivers, estuaries and still-water pools in the flood plains of the rivers. It is said to be nocturnally active, scavenging for food on the bottom, and eating refuse and bottom-living invertebrates. For this reason it has a reputation as a 'foul-feeder' and in some areas is shunned as food. Elsewhere, however, it is a first rate food fish, commanding a ready sale, and having very white, good textured flesh. In Java it is an important food fish.

It is a slender-bodied catfish, with a broad

depresssed head and rather deep belly. A strong spine in the dorsal, and pectoral fins, a rather elongate anal fin, and a forked tail, help to distinguish it, as do the short barbels around the mouth. The back is dusky green, white below, with a purplish sheen on the sides; the fins pinkish or yellow, the ventral fins are clear in colour.

P. sanitwongsei 3 m. (9¾ ft)
This enormous catfish is found in Thailand, in the basin of the Menam Chao Phya, but is largely confined to the main river and its larger tributaries, although young specimens are found in the smaller rivers. It is a striking-looking fish, typically catfish in general build but with short barbels around the mouth, a short-based dorsal fin, moderately large adipose fin, and a deeply forked tail. The anterior rays of the dorsal, pectoral, and pelvic fins are greatly elongate, and the pectoral spines are very well developed. It is deep brown above, light below with a conspicuous white spot behind the head.

It is used widely for food in Thailand, but has a reputation for feeding on unsavoury refuse and thus is not highly esteemed. It has, however, considerable fisheries value, and there is evidence that fishing had reduced the stocks of large fish, for at one time specimens up to 3 m. (9¾ ft) were fairly frequent, but few fish of more than 2 m. (6½ ft) length have been taken more recently.

The late Hugh M. Smith, who first made known this huge fish, reported that a large specimen entangled in a cast net had with its pectoral spine inflicted a deep and fatal wound in the side of the fisherman struggling to pull it ashore.

Pantodon Pantodontidae
buchholzi BUTTERFLYFISH 10 cm. (4 in.)
The butterflyfish is found in the rivers of tropical W. Africa, in the Niger and Congo basins. It is found in still waters, often the stagnant, weedy backwaters of rivers, but also in ponds and ditches. It feeds mainly on flying insects and small land-living animals (chiefly insects) which fall into the water, although slow-flying insects are said to be captured also. The butterflyfish's habit of hanging motionless below the surface film is clearly part of this 'wait and see' way of life. However, it is well known as a leaper out of the water, and is capable of gliding short distances in the air, supported by the large pectoral fins.

The fins are most remarkable in this fish. In addition to hanging motionless in the water, it is frequently seen in shallow water to use its long fin rays as stilts on which it stands for long periods.

The eggs and fry float at the surface, but although many butterflyfish have been kept in aquaria, very few have bred successfully, and the young are particularly difficult to rear. **31**

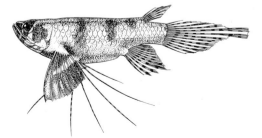

PANTODONTIDAE
A family which contains a single species, and which is related to the bony tongues, or Osteoglossidae. The single member is, however, externally very dissimilar to its relatives, except that its mouth is relatively large and angled nearly vertically. It is found in freshwater in tropical w. Africa. See **Pantodon.**

Panturichthys Heterenchelidae
fowleri see under **P. longus**
longus 1·5 m. (5 ft)
This eel is the largest known of the family. It is found in inshore waters along the W. African coast of Cameroon and the Congo. Relatively few specimens are known, and this species is said to be rare, but this is more likely to be due to the difficulty of catching a large eel buried in sand. It lives in depths of up to 15 m. (8 fathoms).

Its body is reddish brown, long and almost worm-like, with a blunt tail. Its head is pointed, jaws relatively small, and the eyes small and covered with skin. Its teeth are well developed, in the front of the jaws small, conical, and moderately sharp, while in the sides of the lower jaw and the roof of the mouth they are large, rounded, and blunt – obviously suited to crush hard-shelled prey.

A related species, *P. fowleri* lives in the e. Mediterranean.

PAPANOKO see **Cheimarrichthys forsteri**

Paracheirodon Characidae
innesi NEON TETRA 4 cm. (1½ in.)
This characin is probably the best known and most widely kept of the whole family, and deservedly so for its beauty and brilliant colours surpass all other fishes. Its natural range is in the upper region of the River Amazon, on the Brazilian-Peruvian borders in the area of Letica. It was first made known to aquarists in 1936, when it was named *Hyphessobrycon innesi*, thus associating with this living jewel the name of William T. Innes, the American pioneer of tropical pet fish and author of several text-books on the subject.

The coloration of this fish is its most striking feature. An electric green stripe runs from the eye to the level of the adipose fin, below it and starting as a tapering stripe at the dorsal fin is a gleaming red band. Both males and females have this colouring, and there is no difference between the sexes except that mature females are plumper.

The neon tetra can be induced to spawn given the right conditions. These consist of a well-planted aquarium, soft, slightly acid water and a temperature up to 24°C. The eggs are clear and are shed amongst the plants, they hatch after 24 hours and the fry hang by their snout on vegetation or stones. They become active after 4–5 days.

Paracirrhites Cirrhitidae
Besides the 2 species illustrated and described a further species is illustrated but has not been identified. **393**
P. arcatus HAWKFISH 15 cm. (6 in.)
A widely distributed species in the Indo-Pacific, which has been recorded from the E. African coast to Hawaii and the central Pacific. It appears to be locally rare in some areas, but this may be due to the fact that without scuba-

swimming gear it is not easy to see, and still less catch these fishes. In the Marshall Islands it is said to be moderately common on reefs where coral growth was abundant and wave-action strong.

It is a distinctive species, basically reddish in colour with an ovoid or V-shaped mark behind the eye white-edged round a dark line. Sometimes this mark is red edged, and at others it is solidly white. **392**
P. forsteri 25 cm. (10 in.)
A widespread species in the Indo-Pacific, found from the E. African coast to the central Pacific. It was originally described from specimens collected in the Marquesas Islands by the Forsters, father and son, during Captain Cook's second voyage round the world.

Most strikingly-coloured, it is essentially a reef fish found in moderately deep water between 3–18 m. (3–33 fathoms). It is found on coral and rocky substrates. **394**

PARADISEFISH see **Macropodus opercularis**
PARADISEFISH, COMB-TAILED see **Belontia signata**

Parailia Schilbeidae
longifilis 10 cm. (4 in.)
A slender African catfish, found in the basin of the Congo. It is almost transparent, but has a yellowish tinge, and numerous, irregular black pigment spots scattered over the body and fins. Despite this the vertebral column and viscera can be clearly distinguished through the body.

It is distinguished by its coloration, by the complete absence of a dorsal, or adipose fin, long anal fin, forked tail, and very long barbels, all about equal length.

Its behaviour is particularly interesting. It is normally only active in the half-light, in brightly lit places it takes refuge under roots or lies immobile on its side on the bottom. It is an attractive aquarium fish but prefers a shaded situation.

PARALEPIDIDAE
The barracudinas are a large family of oceanic and mid-water fishes with elongate slender bodies and rather pointed heads. The head is long in relation to the body. The maximum length attained by these fish is around 1 m. (3¼ ft), but the great majority of species are less than 30 cm. (12 in.) in length.

Their bone structure is thin and the bones are fragile, a means of reducing body weight adopted by many fish in the oceans. They can be considered to be a very successful group in the deep-sea and they occur in great numbers. Many species feature as important links in the food chains of the deep-sea. While they are most abundant in the tropical and temperate parts of all the oceans, they also occur in Arctic and Antarctic seas. They are all predatory. See **Lestidium, Notolepis, Paralepis, Sudis.**

Paralepis Paralepididae
atlantica KRØYER'S BARRACUDINA
56 cm. (22 in.)
This is one of the most widely distributed barracudinas for it is found in all the major oceans, including the polar seas. It is the most common of the family in the N. Atlantic and is occasionally found, no doubt by accident, in

the N. Sea and the English Channel in shallow water. Normally, however, it is an open ocean species found in mid-depths. Large adults are most frequent in the n. parts of its range in the Atlantic but the young fish are found in the region of the Sargasso Sea – where breeding evidently takes place.

This fish is carnivorous, it feeds to a great extent on small fishes and euphausiid shrimps. In turn it is eaten by a large number of predatory fishes, blue shark, marlin, various tuna, as well as whales. In life it is a bright iridescent silver overlain by dark spots.

Paralichthys Bothidae
californicus CALIFORNIA HALIBUT
1·5 m. (5 ft)
A Californian flatfish which is most common along that coast although captured as far N. as Oregon. It is found on sandy bottoms from 18–36 m. (10–20 fathoms), but occasionally it is found down to 91 m. (50 fathoms). It feeds almost entirely on fishes, especially anchovies, and in turn is eaten by electric rays, sea lions, and various kinds of cetacean.

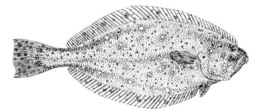

It is a very large fish. There are reports of specimens weighing over 32 kg. (70 lb.) but the authenticated maximum weight is 28 kg. (61½ lb.). Its flesh is firm and white and very good eating. It is exploited commercially along the Californian coast and a variable catch is made annually. It is also a much favoured fish amongst anglers and skin-divers both of whom take a considerable number each year.

This flatfish belongs to the group of left-eyed flounders but almost half of any population will be found to be reversed (i.e. their eyes will be on the right side). It is dark brown and speckled, the mouth is large and has large teeth, and it has a strongly curved lateral line above the pectoral fin.

P. dentatus SUMMER FLOUNDER 1 m. (39 in.)
The summer flounder is found along the Atlantic coast of the U.S. from Maine to S. Carolina. It is an extremely common fish in inshore waters in bays, harbours and along open coasts, but in such shallow water these are mostly young fish. Large specimens live offshore from 15–18 m. (8–10 fathoms) in summer, and between 45–146 m. (25–80 fathoms) in the winter. An onshore migration as the shoal waters warm up in summer is a feature of all age groups of this fish.

It is a large fish averaging at a maximum around 7 kg. (15 lb.), but the maximum weight appears to be 11·8 kg. (26 lb.). It is an important fish both to the sport fisherman and to commercial fishermen. The flavour of its flesh

is good and large quantities are taken by trawling in deep-water, and of younger fish in various nets inshore.

It is predatory feeding actively in mid-water as well as on the bottom. It feeds on smaller fishes of various kinds, squids, shrimps and other crustaceans, and molluscs. It is often seen pursuing small shoals of fish right up to the surface.

Like other members of its family, its eyes are on the left of the head, its jaws are large, and well equipped with teeth. Its body form is rather slender, but thickset. Coloration is very varied and always a match for the sea bed. Its upper side is brown or greyish with scattered small darker spots on the body only; it is white below.

P. olivaceus HIRAME 80 cm. (31½ in.)
The hirame is the most well-known of the flatfishes in the nw. Pacific. It is the most popular and high-priced food fish to be caught in Japanese waters, although its range extends from the Kurile Islands to Hong Kong. It lives in moderately deep water in winter, moving inshore to about 20 m. (11 fathoms) in summer to spawn. It is caught in gill nets and trawls and is a valuable commercial fish.

The eyes are on the left side of the head, the jaws are large and symmetrical with a single series of strong caniniform teeth. The body is elongate and eliptical. It is dull brownish with dark blotches and smaller white spots; the eyeless side is white with yellow streaks along the bases of the fins.

Parapercis Mugiloididae
nebulosus BAR-FACED WEEVER
30 cm. (12 in.)
Known best from the Queensland, New South Wales, and W. Australia coasts but also recorded from off S. Africa. It is found in depths of 20–55 m. (11–30 fathoms).

It is a brightly coloured fish. Its upper body overall is bright red to orange, ventrally it is creamy-yellow. The head is marked with

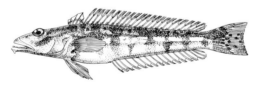

radiating lines from the eye to the snout. The fins are yellowish with an orange edge and the tail is blue spotted.

Paraplagusia Cynoglossidae
unicolor LEMON TONGUE-SOLE
33 cm. (13 in.)
An Australian species which is found from S. Queensland down the coast of New South Wales, and at Lord Howe Island. It is a common sole in shallow water on sandy bottoms and is frequently captured in shore-seines.

The members of this genus are similar to *Cynoglossus* species in having their eyes on the left side, their body scales are toothed both sides, and they have 2–3 lateral lines on the eyed side and none on the blind side. The lips of the eyed side are fringed with fine tentacles.

This species is pale yellowish brown on the left side with lighter yellow or milk-white blotches; bluish-white on the blindside.

Parapriacanthus Pempheridae
The identification of fishes of this genus is difficult for they have been little studied, so the colour transparency has not been named to species. **309**
P. beryciformes 8 cm. (3 in.)
Widespread in the w. Pacific and found from Japan to the Marshall Islands. It is said to be a pelagic species which in the latter locality were only caught at night when attracted to lights. It is a translucent pink when alive.

Parascyllium Scyliorhinidae
variolatum VARIED CATSHARK
91 cm. (3 ft)
The varied catshark is common in shallow water along the coasts of S. Australia, Victoria, and Tasmania. It is found down to a depth of about 165 m. (90 fathoms) usually on sandy bottoms.

Its slender body, with rounded dorsal fins placed far back, is typical of the sharks of this family. Its colouring, however, is remarkable for it has a broad black collar dotted with white spots around the neck behind the eyes. Elsewhere it is a light brown with scattered light blotches, while the fins have dark brown blotches and light dots.

This catshark is placed in the genus *Hemiscyllium* by some workers.

Parasphenanthias Owstoniidae
weberi 28 cm. (11 in.)
Found off the Indian Ocean coast of Africa, and discovered so far from Zanzibar to Natal. It inhabits moderately deep-water down to a depth of 366 m. (200 fathoms).

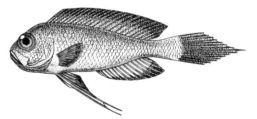

It is medium brown overall, with faint bars along the sides. The dorsal fin is pink with an elongate blotch at its anterior end. Its body shape is distinctive.

Virtually nothing is known of its biology.

Parazen Parazenidae
pacificus 14 cm. (5¼ in.)
A small species of dory-like fish which was originally described from the waters off the Japanese coast in 1935, but was then captured in the Caribbean off Cuba in 1955. The specimens from the Atlantic basin appear to be the

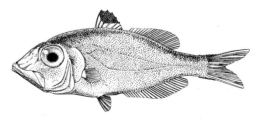

same as the Pacific form, or at most subspecifically distinct. They were caught at depths of 457–512 m. (250–280 fathoms) although off Japan it is taken at around 146 m. (80 fathoms).

PARAZENIDAE

A small family related to the Zeidae and Macrurocyttidae, and possibly not truly distinct from them. Only one species has been placed in the family, found in the w. N. Pacific and in the tropical Atlantic.

The single species is small, relatively slim-bodied, slightly compressed, with a large, protrusible mouth, and a large eye. The tail fin is forked, the pelvics are placed well forward on the belly and contain one unbranched and 6 branched rays. Its body is scaly, the scales weakly toothed and easily detached. Two lateral lines on each side which commence together at the head, diverge, and then meet again at the rear end of the second dorsal fin. See **Parazen.**

Parexocoetus Exocoetidae
  brachypterus SHORT-FINNED OR SAILFIN FLYINGFISH 20 cm. (8 in.)
A worldwide species found from the E. African coast and the Red Sea to the Indo-Australian region, and in the tropical Atlantic.

It is distinguished by its short pectoral fins, which are only about twice the length of the head. Its coloration is also distinctive, dark blue above, silvery below, with an intense dark patch at the top of the dorsal fin; the pectoral fins are dusky, especially in the young.

It is found mainly in the open ocean at the surface but occurs occasionally in inshore waters.

Parodon Parodontidae
  buckleyi 13 cm. (5 in.)
Described from specimens captured at Canelos, e. Ecuador by a Mr Clarence Buckley in 1880, but it does not seem to have been caught since. The possibility that this and other species are synonyms of a more widely distributed species, *P. suborbitale*, the valadora of Venezuelan waters, has been suggested. The 2 species are very similar.

Both are slender fish, brownish above, yellowish on the belly with a lengthwise brown line running along the sides. The dorsal fin and the anal fin are short-based, and the adipose fin is small. The teeth in these fishes are reduced in number, much flattened into broad incisors, and in *P. buckleyi* each tooth in the

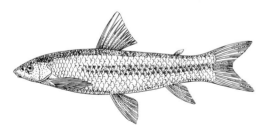

upper jaw has about 20 small lobes along the cutting edge. Teeth like this would be eminently suitable for browsing on algae growing on stones.
P. suborbitale see under **P. buckleyi**

PARODONTIDAE

A small family of characin-like fishes found in n. S. American freshwaters. As a group they are little-known, and it is far from certain as to how many species or even genera should be contained within the family, and a recent sur-

vey by the French ichthyologist, Dr J. Géry suggests that the group has only subfamily status within the family Hemiodidae.

These fishes have a blunt snout and inferior mouth, a rather slender body with a short dorsal fin and a small adipose fin. They are mainly bottom-living fishes of rivers and lakes. See **Parodon.**

Parophidion Ophidiidae
  schmidti DUSKY CUSK EEL 11 cm. (4¼ in.)
Found from Bermuda and the Bahamas, Florida to Jamaica and along the Gulf of Mexico coast. It is widely distributed and in places common. In the Bahamas it is usually in water of less than 3 m. (2 fathoms), occasionally down to 7·6 m. (4 fathoms). It frequents turtle grass beds and sandy bottomed, sheltered bays.

It is pale brown in colour, darker on the back than the sides. Long and slender in shape with the low dorsal and anal fins joined to the tail fin. The pectorals are broad, but the pelvics double thread-like, both rays being of equal length, and placed on the throat.

Parophrys Pleuronectidae
  vetulus ENGLISH SOLE 57 cm. (22½ in.)
An e. N. Pacific species found between Baja California and w. Alaska. It lives between the surface and 550 m. (300 fathoms), although it is most abundant in 73–128 m. (40–70 fathoms), and it moves into shallower water in spring and into deeper water with the onset of winter. Very young fish are often found in tide pools. Its food consists mainly of clams and their siphons, other molluscs, marine worms, and crustaceans.

It is a popular food fish, and large quantities are caught by both Canadian and U.S. fishermen. In some densely populated areas the English sole suffers from a myxosporidian disease which makes the flesh soft and 'milky', but although it destroys its market value and palatability, it is not rendered toxic.

The English sole is a rather slender-bodied flatfish with its eyes on the right side of the head. The head and jaws are pointed, the mouth rather small, and the lateral line almost straight, but with a curving branch running forward to the eyes and thence along the edge of the dorsal fin. It is uniformly brown on the eyed side, yellowish white on the left side of the body.

PARR see **Salmo salar**
PARROTFISH see Oplegnathidae, Scaridae
PARROTFISH see **Oplegnathus conwayi, Scarus sordidus**
PARROTFISH,
  BLUE see **Scarus coeruleus**
  MOTTLEFIN see **Scarus croicensis**
  QUEEN see **Scarus vetula**
  RAINBOW see **Scarus guacamaia**
  REDFIN see **Sparisoma rubripinne**
  STRIPED see **Scarus croicensis**
  YELLOWTAIL see **Sparisoma rubripinne**

PATAECIDAE

A small family of little-known fishes, known as prowfishes, found in Australian waters, particularly in the cooler, s. regions. They are distinguished by the body shape which is high in front, tapering towards the tail, by the very long dorsal fin which is continuous (in most

species) with the tail, and by the absence of the pelvic fins. The body is scaleless, the skin often being covered with warty growths. See **Aetapcus, Pataecus.**

Pataecus Pataecidae
  fronto RED INDIAN FISH 23 cm. (9 in.)
A most striking-looking fish with an extremely high profile, the body tapering from head to tail and being deeply compressed. The common name of this fish is derived from the high dorsal fin which resembles the head-dress of an American Indian chief! Its life-colour is scarlet or brick red, in some specimens with 4 black spots on the sides.

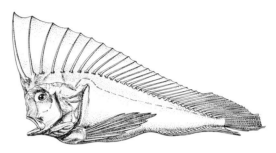

It has been recorded from the coasts of W. Australia, S. Australia, New South Wales, and Queensland but does not appear to be common off any of these states. Its biology is virtually unknown.

PATI see **Luciopimelodus pati**
PAVITO see **Cynolebias belotti**
PEACOCK FLOUNDER see **Bothus lunatus**
PEAMOUTH see **Mylocheilus caurinus**
PEARL
  BLENNY see **Entomacrodus nigricans**
  DACE see **Semotilus margarita**
  DANIO see **Brachydanio albolineatus**
  GOURAMI see **Trichogaster leeri**
  PERCH see **Glaucosoma scapulare**
PEARLEYE, BERMUDA see **Scopelarchus sagax**
PEARLFISH see Carapidae
PEARLFISH see **Echiodon drummondi**
PEARLFISH, ARGENTINE see **Cynolebias belotti**
PEARLSIDES see **Maurolicus muelleri**
PEARLY RASBORA see **Rasbora vaterifloris**

PEGASIDAE

A small family containing only 5–6 species of curious little fishes. For a long time they were placed in close association with the pipefishes and seahorses, a relationship suggested by the hard bony external skeleton, tubular snout and small mouth. Another school of thought placed them with the scorpionfishes on account of their similarity to the flying gurnards and poachers (Dactylopteridae and Agonidae). Modern concepts suggest that the latter placement is well founded, but to indicate their distinctness they are placed in a separate order, Pegasiformes.

The sea moths are found only in the warmer parts of the Indo-Pacific, from the E. African coast to Hawaii. They are all small, with armoured bodies, produced snouts, and large pectoral fins which spread out into moth-like wings. Their biology is little known. See **Acanthopegasus, Eurypegasus, Pegasus.**

Pegasus   Pegasidae
volitans WINGED DRAGON 14 cm. (5½ in.)
Widely distributed in the Indo-Pacific from
the E. African coast to n. Australia and the
Philippines. It is brownish in colour, sometimes spotted, the fins with darker spots. A long
slender fish, the anterior part of the body is
flattened from above, but the tail gradually
tapering, with a short spine at the edge of each
body ring. The pelvic fins are composed of 2
separate rays, the pectorals long, and laterally
expanded. The snout is moderately long.

It is said to be blood-red in colour but to
have blue eyes. This species was one of the
first known in Europe usually obtained as
pinned dry specimens in Chinese insect boxes.
It is said to have been used dried in Chinese
folk medicine.

Pegusa   Soleidae
lascaris SAND or FRENCH SOLE
36 cm. (14 in.)
A European sole which ranges as far N. as the
British Isles, S. to Morocco and the Canary
Islands, and in the w. basin of the Mediterranean. In British waters it occurs but rarely
N. of the English Channel. It occurs on sandy
bottoms in shallow inshore water in 6–48 m.
(3–26 fathoms), but it comes inshore in summer and migrates offshore in winter.

It is distinguished by its sole-like appearance, the tail being distinct from the dorsal
and anal fins. The underside of the head is
thickly covered with sensory papillae and the
anterior nostril is conspicuously swollen to
form a distinct rosette. Its right (eyed) side is a
warm brown with irregular darker blotches on
the body, and dark lines on the fins. The pectoral fin on the eyed side has a conspicuous
black blotch, ringed with creamy white, at its
far end. The blind side is white.

The sand sole is good eating but only along
the Spanish and s. Biscay coasts is it common
enough to be commercially exploited.

PELAGIC ARMORHEAD see **Pentaceros
richardsoni**

Pelates   Theraponidae
quadrilineatus TRUMPETER PERCH,
CROAKER 20 cm. (8 in.)
A widespread species in the Indo-Pacific,
ranging from e. Africa to n. Australia, China
and s. Japan. Like other members of the family
it is common in inshore waters but also found
in estuaries in abundance. It is particularly
common on algal or plant-covered sand flats.

When removed from the water it emits a
series of croaks or grunts, this habit giving it
its vernacular names.

It is a slender-bodied fish, greeny brown
above, light below, with 4 deep brown lengthwise stripes, and a dusky patch on the shoulder.

Pelecus   Cyprinidae
cultratus ZIEGE 51 cm. (20 in.)
The ziege is a pelagic, shoaling fish of the fresh
and brackish waters of the Baltic States and
and in the region of the Black and Caspian
seas. It is found mainly in the lower reaches of
rivers and their estuaries penetrating out to
sea into partly salt water. It feeds on flying
insects, surface-living insect larvae, and small
fishes; in brackish water it eats mainly the fry
of herring.

The 2 centres of distribution are well separated and this fish is most abundant in the
Black and Caspian sea basins, where a commercial fishery exists for it. Its scales are said
to be used for making *essence d'orient*, the
shiny basis for the artificial pearl industry. Its
flesh is eaten smoked.

The ziege is greenish on the back, brilliantly silvery on the sides, with clear fins.

Pelmatochromis   Cichlidae
In addition to the 3 species already illustrated
in colour, another, unidentified species is
shown. **369**
P. buettikoferi 13 cm. (5 in.)
An African cichlid which is found in the region
of Liberia and Sierra Leone. In many respects
it is similar to other unspecialized cichlids,
and the major difference between this genus
and others is internal, in that it has a papillose
pad on each side of the pharynx which shows
as a large protuberance in front of the gills
when the gill cover is raised.

This species is distinguished by the very
short lower (posterior) lateral line, by its
square-cut tail fin, and by the shortness of the
snout which is equal to the eye diameter. An
indistinct dark smudge on the back below the
junction of the spiny and soft rayed dorsal fins,
and round light spots on the membrane of the
soft dorsal fin, serve to distinguish it from the
approximately 25 other species in this genus.

It breeds in a saucer-shaped depression in
the river bed, some 60–100 cm. (23–39½ in.)
with smaller pits within it. It has become relatively common in aquaria in Europe. **370**
P. 'camerunensis' 10 cm. (4 in.)
A small species of African cichlid which has
been imported to Europe as an aquarium fish
since 1962. It is closely related to, if not a form
of *P. pulcher* a species found in s. Nigeria, but
it appears to differ from that species in a number of ways, and as a consequence has been
named *P. 'camerunensis'* in aquarium literature. According to the German authority,
Professor Gunther Sterba, it does not originate
in the Cameroons, but in the dense forests of
S. Nigeria.

The male is very boldly coloured at spawning time; the ventral surface and lower gill
covers being red, the mouth blood-red. A distinct line runs along the sides from mouth to
tail fin, and 3 light bars cross the back. The
pelvic fins are reddish with a light blue edge.
372
P. guentheri 16 cm. (6¼ in.)
Widely distributed in W. Africa from Ghana to
Gabon, it is a very successful species found in
a wide range of habitats, both in rivers and
swamps, in forests and the savannah, usually
on muddy bottoms in which it grubs in search
of its food.

It is distinguished by its moderately deep
body, long snout and large head. Males have a
bright red spot on the gill cover, while the females have a pink belly and a line of dark spots
along the base of the spiny dorsal fin.

It is a mouth-brooder, the males carrying
the eggs for the 11–13 days it takes for them

to develop, but either parent may pick up the
fry if danger threatens. **371**
P. pulcher see under **P. 'camerunensis'**

PEMPHERIDAE
The sweepers, a small family of mainly Indo-
Pacific fishes, found entirely in tropical and
warm-temperate seas. They are typically
shoaling fishes of reefs and coastal waters;
most are small. A number of species are found
in the tropical w. Atlantic.

Generally they are deep-bodied fishes with a
large eye, a short, but high dorsal fin placed
well forward on the back, and a long anal
fin. See **Liopempheris, Parapriacanthus,
Pempheris.**

Pempheris   Pempheridae
schomburgki GLASSY or COPPER
SWEEPER 15 cm. (6 in.)
A w. Atlantic species, recorded from Bermuda,
Florida and the Bahamas, s. to Brazil. It is a
common fish along reefs and around coral
heads and large shoals can be seen in caves or
under overhangs by day. They emerge at
night to feed on animal plankton over and
near the reef. It is found from 0·6–15 m.
(⅓-8 fathoms) deep.

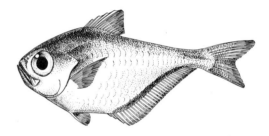

It is coppery red overlying a silvery background, while the head has bluish reflections.
A bright red stripe along the base of the anal
fin. Young fish are almost transparent but
their vertebrae are coloured strongly with red
and black – hence glassy sweeper.

PENCILFISH,
  DWARF see **Nannostomus marginatus**
  GOLDEN see **Nannostomus beckfordi**
  THREE-BANDED see **Nannostomus
    trifasciatus**
  TUBE-MOUTH see **Nannostomus eques**
PENGUINFISH see **Thayeria boehlkei,
  Thayeria obliquua**
PENNANT TREVALLY see **Alectis ciliaris**

Pentaceros   Pentacerotidae
richardsoni BOARFISH, PELAGIC
ARMORHEAD 53 cm. (21 in.)
Widely distributed in the Indo-Pacific. First
reported from the Cape of Good Hope, most
specimens have been found in New Zealand
waters and in the N. Pacific, both around
Japan and along the N. American coast.

It appears to be an open ocean fish, most
captures having been made in gill nets or near
the surface far from land. Little is known of its
life history and biology.

It is bluish brown on the back, lighter on the
belly. The head is marked with reddish brown.
The fin membranes are bluish black.

PENTACEROTIDAE
A small family of Indo-Pacific species found
mainly in temperate waters, around s. Africa,

in the N. Pacific, and around s. Australia and New Zealand.

The members of the family are all deep-bodied, strange-looking fishes, with a protruding snout, a small mouth, and fine teeth in the jaws. The bones of the head have rough ridges. The body is covered with small toothed scales. The dorsal fin in particular is high and composed of very long, strong spines and long branched rays. See **Histiopterus, Pentaceros, Zanclistius.**

PENTAPODIDAE

A small family of Indo-Pacific marine fishes which are related to the sea breams (Sparidae) and the scavengers (Lethrinidae). Some authors lump its members with one or both of these families.

The pentapodids have a rather deep-bodied form compressed from side to side, the dorsal fin is long, the anterior spiny portion composed of 10 spines, the anal with 3 strong spines. The head is scaleless in front, the eye noticeably large. Teeth in the jaws moderate, usually rather long and curved, sometimes flattened. See **Gnathodentex, Monotaxis.**

Peprilus   Stromateidae
   alepidotus HARVESTFISH 29 cm. (11½ in.)
A very deep-bodied member of the genus, with long-based dorsal and anal fins, the anterior rays of which curve outwards to form a long lobe. Its coloration is metallic blue above, silvery below.

The harvestfish occurs along the Atlantic coast of America, from Chesapeake Bay to Florida, and the Gulf of Mexico. The related *P. paru* occurs from the W. Indies, and Central American coast, to Brazil, and less commonly to Argentina. The young are often found with the stinging jellyfish *Chrysaora* and as they grow, feed on these and other medusae extensively, although the adults feed on other animals as well.

As with other butterfishes, this species is a valuable food fish where it is locally common enough to be fished for commercially.
P. paru see under **P. alepidotus**
P. simillimus PACIFIC POMPANO or
BUTTERFISH 25 cm. (10 in.)
An inhabitant of the Pacific coastline of N. America, this butterfish is found from British Columbia to Baja California. It is found in small, tightly-packed schools in inshore waters. Its food consists of small crustaceans mostly, but no detailed data are available. In turn the butterfish is eaten by a number of fish predators.

It is a moderately important commercial fish, caught mostly in purse-seine nets and sold as fresh fish. It fetches a high price and its flesh is of good quality. The butterfish is also taken in some numbers by anglers fishing from piers and inshore boats.

Its deep, compressed body, long pectoral fins, long-based but low dorsal and forked tail are distinctive, as is its metallic silvery coloration, iridescent blue above, silver ventrally.
P. triacanthus BUTTERFISH, DOLLARFISH, HARVESTFISH 30 cm. (12 in.)
The butterfish is found off the Atlantic coast of N. America from about 48°N. in the Gulf of St Lawrence to an area off s. Florida. It occurs off Newfoundland, Nova Scotia, and the Gulf

of Maine usually only in late summer and autumn. It is usually found in small schools often close inshore in bays and estuaries, and fairly near the surface. Recent studies have shown that there are 2 forms of this species, one in deep water over a muddy bottom, the other in shallows over sand. The former tends to be more elongate, and to have numerous spots on the body.

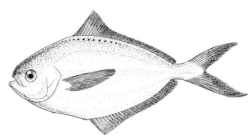

The butterfish is distinguished from other fishes in the area by its bluish back and silvery belly, its rather deep but thin body, the long soft-rayed dorsal and anal fins, and the total absence of pelvic fins.

It feeds on small fishes, squid, crustaceans, and ctenophores (sea-gooseberries) have been found in their guts on occasions. The young are sometimes found in association with the jellyfish *Cyanea*; the relationship is casual, but they are more commonly found with the stinging medusa, *Chrysaora* on which they occasionally feed.

It is an important food fish on the Atlantic coast, its flesh being fatty, oily, and deliciously flavoured. They are captured in a variety of ways, especially in fixed nets and seines, and many are caught on lines by anglers. Considerable quantities are landed all along the coast.

Perca   Percidae
   flavescens YELLOW PERCH 53 cm. (21 in.)
A native of central N. America, from the upper Mackenzie River basin e. to Nova Scotia, S. on the Atlantic coast to South Carolina. It also is found throughout the Great Lakes and in the upper Mississippi system. It has been widely introduced elsewhere in Canada and the U.S.

The yellow perch is closely related, and externally indistinguishable from the Eurasian *Perca fluviatilis*. Many taxonomists treat it as a subspecies only, *P. fluviatilis flavescens*. Its biology is virtually identical.

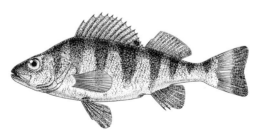

The yellow perch is a favourite amongst anglers in N. America, and in Canada, at least, is commercially fished. Its flesh is white, firm, and well flavoured.
P. fluviatilis PERCH 51 cm. (20 in.)
Widely distributed in Europe, from Ireland (where it was introduced), s. Scotland and England across the U.S.S.R. to Siberia. Outside this area it has been introduced to Australia, New Zealand, and s. Africa, its sporting

reputation and palatability making it a desirable fish in the eyes of English settlers.

It is a very distinctive species, relatively deep-bodied with a high, spiny dorsal fin quite separate from the second fin. The body is a deep olive-green, bronze on the sides with broad, vertical black bars on the back and sides. A black spot on the end of the spiny dorsal fin; the pelvic, anal, and lower tail fins are orange.

The perch is essentially a lake, and slow flowing river fish, more at home amongst vegetation, or lying close under fallen trees, landing stages, or submerged tree roots. It is a predator all its life, feeding on insect larvae and crustaceans when young, and on fishes as it grows larger.

It spawns in late April and May; the eggs are laid in long threads which are wound in and out of weeds or twigs in the water. Growth rates vary from water to water, and the perch easily becomes stunted, for example, when too many fish compete for limited food and living space. The females usually grow faster than the males, and most very large perch are female. The maximum weight recorded is around 4·75 kg. (10½ lb.), although few fish exceed 2·3 kg. (5 lb.).

It is a popular angling fish and in inland Europe is commercially important as a food fish.

Percalates   Serranidae
   colonorum ESTUARY PERCH
58 cm. (23 in.)
Found in freshwaters and in estuaries of rivers in Australia, in S. Australia, Victoria, New South Wales, Queensland, and Tasmania. It has been introduced to W. Australia, and spread within its native range. It lives mainly in the lower reaches of rivers, only a little above areas of tidal influence and is believed to migrate downstream to spawn in brackish water. Its status has been severely affected by drainage works, and dams constructed in the lower reaches of rivers. It gives some sport as an angling fish, but is not highly rated as food.

Its body form is typical of the basses, the dorsal fin having especially long and strong spines; the head and body are fully scaled. It is olive-green above with reddish tints, yellowish to white below.

PERCELLE, FIVE-STRIPED see **Cheilodipterus quinquilineatus**
PERCH see Centropomidae, Percidae
PERCH see **Perca fluviatilis**
PERCH,
   BLACK see **Nemadactylus morwong**
   BLUE-BANDED SEA see **Lutjanus kasmira**
   CHINESE see **Siniperca chuatsi**
   CLIMBING see Anabantidae
   CLIMBING see **Anabas testudineus**
   CRESCENT see **Therapon jarbua**
   DUSKY SEA see **Rhacochilus vacca**
   ESTUARY see **Percalates colonorum**
   GIANT see **Lates calcarifer**
   GOLDEN see **Plectroplites ambiguus**
   KELP see **Brachyistius frenatus**
   LAKE ALBERT see **Lates albertianus**
   NILE see **Lates niloticus**
   PACIFIC OCEAN see **Sebastes alutus**
   PEARL see **Glaucosoma scapulare**
   PILE see **Rhacochilus vacca**
   PIRATE see **Aphredoderus sayanus**

PYGMY see **Nannoperca australis**
RUBBERLIP SEA see **Rhacochilus toxotes**
SADDLE-TAILED SEA see **Lutjanus sanguineus**
SAND see Mugiloididae
SEA see Embiotocidae
SEA see **Morone americana**
SHINER see **Cymatogaster aggregata**
SILVER see **Bidyanus bidyanus**
SIX-LINED see **Helotes sexlineatus**
SPOTTED CLIMBING see **Ctenopoma acutirostre**
STRIPED see **Helotes sexlineatus**
TAIL-SPOT CLIMBING see **Ctenopoma kingsleyae**
TRUMPETER see **Pelates quadrilineatus**
WHITE see **Morone americana**
YELLOW see **Perca flavescens**
YELLOW-MARGINED SEA see **Lutjanus vaigiensis**

Percichthyidae see Serranidae

PERCIDAE

A family of freshwater fishes naturally distributed in the N. Hemisphere, but which have been introduced in parts of the S. Hemisphere (such as Australia, New Zealand, and s. Africa). The members of the family have a well-developed spiny first dorsal fin (which is usually separate from the second dorsal), they have 2 spines in the anal fin, and fully scaled bodies, each scale bearing fine teeth. The body shape is rather variable, most species are rather elongate rounded fishes; some, such as the perches, the walleye and zander are more compressed laterally. See **Aspro, Etheostoma, Gymnocephalus, Perca, Stizostedion.**

PERCOPHIDIDAE

A small family of deep-water fishes, best known from the Indian and Pacific Oceans, although also found in the Atlantic. Most of the known species are small, 25 cm. (10 in.) seems to be an average maximum length.

They resemble the sandperches (Mugiloididae) in several respects, but have the lower jaw projecting beyond the upper jaw, and the lateral line curves down behind the pectoral fin. These fishes always have 2 well-developed dorsal fins. See **Bembrops.**

PERCOPSIDAE

A small family containing only 2 representatives, both small freshwater fishes found in N. America. They appear to occupy a position intermediate between the soft-rayed and spiny-finned fishes, for they have spines in the fins and an adipose fin. The body is covered with rough, toothed scales, and the jaws are provided with teeth. See **Percopsis.**

Percopsis   Percopsidae
omiscomaycus TROUT-PERCH
20 cm. (8 in.)
A very distinctive small fish, easily distinguished by its slender body, dorsal (and anal) fin with slender spines as well as branched rays, and an adipose fin.

The back is silvery with a purplish tinge, the sides transparent, but the whitish lining to the body cavity shows through. A line of dusky blotches along the sides, another on the upper back.

The trout-perch is well distributed in N. America, across Canada from the Pacific drainage to the e. seaboard of the U.S., including the Great Lakes, and from W. Virginia, the Mississippi and the lower Missouri. It is typically an inhabitant of the backwaters of large muddy rivers and shallow lakes. It feeds on aquatic insects, small crustaceans, and molluscs. Spawning occurs in late spring and early summer, the eggs sink to the bottom to which they adhere.

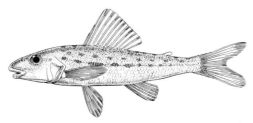

Of no direct importance either commercially or as a game fish, the trout-perch is of some value as a forage fish for lake trout and other larger fishes.

P. transmontana SANDROLLER 10 cm. (4 in.)
Found only in the Columbia River system of w. N. America. Like the other member of the family it has a short dorsal fin with spines in front of the branched rays, together with a small adipose fin. The body is covered with rough, toothed scales.

It is locally abundant in sandy or weedy lagoons and backwaters in the larger rivers of the system.

It is a pale, smutty green; the sides have 3 rows of oblong blackish spots, the back has similar spots, the most conspicuous being at the front and back of the dorsal fin base. A dusky spot on the gill cover; a silvery band runs along the sides.

Periophthalmus   Gobiidae
koelreuteri MUDHOPPER, CLIMBING-FISH 14 cm. (5½ in.)
An Indo-Pacific species of wide distribution. It appears to be common from E. Africa and the Red Sea to Micronesia and Polynesia, in suitable habitats. It is most common on intertidal muddy areas, particularly in mangrove swamps, up the exposed roots of which it climbs. Its agility on the mud is remarkable, it can leap in almost any direction if approached, and will take shelter in a crab burrow or crevice if it cannot reach the water. When undisturbed, however, it raises itself up on pelvic and pectoral fins, and moving each alternately wriggles forward across the mud.

Its coloration is brownish, lighter below, the lower sides with light spots. The fins are usually light spotted.

Periophthalmdon   Gobiidae
barbarus see **P. schlosseri**
schlosseri MUDSKIPPER, MUDHOPPER
28 cm. (11 in.)
A wide-ranging, Indo-Pacific species which occurs from the E. African and Red Sea region, around India and the Malayan region to Australia. It lives mainly in brackish water at the mouth of rivers and in mangrove swamps, and is frequently very abundant. Like the other mudskippers it is most frequently seen actually out of water, sometimes well away from it, basking on mud flats or on tree roots. Its agility is such that it can avoid most predators by active leaps to regain the water.

Its body form is similar to its relatives. The head is deep, with a steep profile, the eyes placed on the top of the head on raised bumps, viewing laterally, and clearly possessing good all-round vision. The first dorsal fin is high, especially anteriorly. The pectorals are angled downwards and are used to support the body, as do the pelvics which are almost separate from one another.

There are numerous variations in colour and markings. The body is usually brown or greyish, with pale blue spots overall. The dorsal fins have a bluish patch but a dark edge.

The species *Periophthalmodon* is distinguished by having 2 rows of teeth in the upper jaw (*Periophthalmus* has one). The nomenclature of these fishes is much confused; this species is often named *P. barbarus*.

Peristedion   Triglidae
cataphractum see under **P. miniatum**
miniatum ARMOURED SEA ROBIN
36 cm. (14 in.)
This most remarkable looking fish is native to the e. coast of N. America, from the edge of Georges Bank (Gulf of Maine) to S. Carolina. It is found offshore only on the lower edge of the continental shelf in depths of 91–366 m. (50–200 fathoms). It is a bottom-living species which appears to feed entirely on crustaceans.

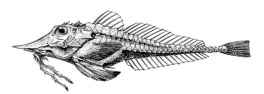

In colour it is bright crimson above and below. Its body form is quite distinctive, being heavily armoured over the head and with large strong scales on the body.

A similar species *P. cataphractum* is found in the Mediterranean and adjacent Atlantic.

PERLON see **Heptranchias perlo**
PERMIT see **Trachinotus falcatus**

Peronedys   Peronedysidae
anguillaris EEL BLENNY 11 cm. (4½ in.)
A slender, eel-like fish which possesses typical paired, two-rayed blenny-like pelvic fins. The eel blenny is rarely found and appears to be confined to the coastline of S. Australia. Its biology is unknown.

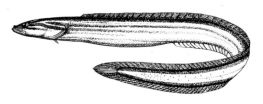

It is dark brown overall, the sides paler with a pinkish tinge. The upper parts of the head and body have lighter yellowish bands running in lengthwise stripes, fading towards the tail.

PERONEDYSIDAE

A family of doubtful status represented by a single species found on the S. Australian coast. It is closely related to the Notograptidae, but differs notably in lacking pectoral fins, and having very large gill openings. See **Peronedys.**

Perryena Congiopodidae
leucometopon WHITE-NOSED PIGFISH
16 cm. (6¼ in.)
This small species is little-known and has so far occurred only on the s. coasts of Australia.

It is a striking species, with a deep compressed body, a concave forehead and produced snout the tip of which is roughened. The body is scaleless and the sides have thin vertical depressions, one per lateral line pore.

It is deep brown, the forehead and snout white, bordered by a black band.

PERUVIAN LONGFIN see **Pterolebias peruensis**

Pervagor Balistidae
spilosoma 13 cm. (5 in.)
A native species to the Hawaiian Islands, which at times appears to be extremely abundant although not common every year. It is a small fish found in moderate depths and feeding on small benthic outgrowths.

This genus is distinguished by having a well developed pelvic spine with a movable, spiny knob at its end. The dorsal spine is moderately well developed but does not fit into a groove when depressed; it is sited over the middle of the eye and has 2 rows of small spines on its front surface.

This fish is yellow with black spots, the head with dark longitudinal lines. The tail is bright orange with a dark border. **476**

PESCADINHA see **Sillago sihama**
PESCE VIOLINO see **Rhinobatos rhinobatus**

Petalichthys Belonidae
capensis NEEDLEFISH 38 cm. (15 in.)
A fish which has only been reported in the waters off s. Africa, from the Cape to Natal. It is an inshore needlefish which is occasionally stranded, and sometimes enters estuaries.

The body is very thin and elongate, rather compressed. The dorsal and anal fins are moderately long. Teeth in the jaws well developed, but none on the palate or vomer; gill rakers well developed. In colour it is silvery, a bright stripe along the sides, bluish on the back.

Petenia Cichlidae
spectabilis 14 cm. (5½ in.)
The genus *Petenia* was named for the area and lake of Petén in n. Guatemala and its members are found widely in Central America and n. S. America.

This species has been found in the River Amazon at Gurupa and Obidos. It can be distinguished by the extremely fleshy, thick lips and protractile premaxillary (upper jaw) bone, the teeth in the outer row enlarged, curved, and sharp, with smaller teeth behind. It is relatively deep-bodied, but its body is plain coloured in contrast to the bars most species of this genus display. **373**

Petitella Characidae
georgiae 4 cm. (1½ in.)
A small characin which was first imported to Europe as an aquarium fish thought to be *Hemigrammus rhodostomus*, but was later discovered to be a distinct species. It is close to that genus in appearance, and in colour, although it lacks the red snout, but differs in having only a single series of teeth in the upper jaw and by the shape of the jaw bone.

This species was originally collected in the region of Iquitos, in the Loreto District of Peru, and near the village of Lagunas in the same area. **83**

PETO see **Acanthocybium solanderi**
PETRALE SOLE see **Eopsetta jordani**

Petrocephalus Mormyridae
bovei 51 cm. (20 in.)
A native of the lower Nile, Senegal, and Gambia rivers of Africa. This fish and its relatives are round-headed mormyrids, the snout being shiny, white and almost transparent (hence *Petrocephalus* or stone-head). Like their relatives they are capable of giving off weak electrical discharges as a means of navigation in the murky water in which they live.

The young have a black dorsal fin and a dark band across the back in front of the dorsal base.

This species has been kept in aquaria, but it is a rather fragile, easily damaged fish. **36**
P. catostoma 15 cm. (6 in.)
This mormyrid is widely distributed in the rivers and lakes of e. and s. Africa, from the upper Victoria Nile s. to Natal. It is a small species rarely found longer than 9 cm. (4 in.) although some larger ones have been reported.

It is a deep-bodied, rather compressed fish, with a smoothly rounded snout, and a mouth, curiously ineffectual in appearance, on the underside. Its dorsal and anal fins are relatively short, the anal being longer. In males the base of the anal fin is wavy in shape, and the fin rays are longer than in the female. Its usual colour is dark brown above, silvery underneath.

It is said to live amongst rocks and weeds in fast flowing rivers, presumably helped by its small size to shelter out of the mainstream behind the boulders and stones and to feed on the small animals sheltering there.

Petrochromis see under **Petrotilapia tridentiger**

Petromyzon Petromyzonidae
marinus LAMPREY, SEA LAMPREY
90 cm. (35 in.)
Coastal waters both sides of the N. Atlantic, and the w. Mediterranean, also in freshwaters of the Atlantic coasts of Europe and N. America. The lamprey is a migratory fish which leaves the sea to spawn in freshwater, usually far up the rivers on stony bottoms where a nest some 15 cm. (6 in.) deep and 60–90 cm. (2–3 ft) wide is hollowed out by the adults moving the stones with their sucker mouths. The larva, blind, toothless, and wormlike, lives buried in muddy silt downstream of the spawning site for 4–6 years, after which it changes into a toothed, sighted adolescent and migrates to the sea. During its larval life (the larva is known as an ammocoete, or pride) it feeds on microscopic plankton, and detritus filtered from the mud. Once fully grown it becomes parasitic on other fishes, fastening on to its prey by its sucker disc, and rasping away skin, scales, and flesh with its teeth. Glands in the mouth produce a secretion which prevents clotting of the blood of the prey, which is sucked dry of most of its body fluids. Death frequently results from lamprey attacks, if not directly, then from secondary fungal and bacterial infections of the wound. Lampreys attack a wide variety of marine and freshwater fishes. The marks of their suckers are frequently found on sperm whales, and basking sharks (although they do not puncture the skin).

After the cutting of the Welland Canal the lamprey gained access from the sea to the Great Lakes of N. America, and established a virtually landlocked population spawning in the tributary rivers and migrating to the lakes as if they were the sea. The effects on the commercial and sport fishing was disastrous, and the lake trout and other valuable fishes declined dramatically. Because of the serious economic loss an intensive research programme was undertaken, and considerable success achieved in controlling the lampreys in the lakes.

Lampreys can be eaten, and tradition has it that the English King Henry I died from eating a surfeit of them. Their appearance is not, however, attractive. Pollution of river estuaries and interruption of their spawning migration by weirs and dams in rivers have greatly reduced their numbers so that today in large areas of their range they are relatively rare fish.

PETROMYZONIDAE
One of the 2 families of the class Agnatha. Primitive fishes without true jaws, but with sucking mouths and rasping teeth; they also lack scales, paired fins, and true fin rays. Respiration is by means of a series of openings from separate gill pouches. There are few living representatives. See **Entosphenus, Geotria, Ichthyomyzon, Lampetra, Petromyzon.**

Petroscirtes Blenniidae
anolius OYSTER BLENNY 7·5 cm. (3 in.)
A common species in the W. Pacific and particularly well distributed on the coasts of S. Queensland and New South Wales. It is well known for its habit of living inside the shells of dead oysters. The eggs are laid in small clumps on the inside roof of the shells.

It is strikingly marked, nut brown in colour with silvery stripes on the head and body. The fins are orange edged. Large specimens have long rays in the posterior end of the dorsal fin and a fleshy crest on the head.
P. temminckii 10 cm. (4 in.)
A small blenny which has been found in a number of areas in the E. Indies and around the Philippines. Members of this genus are tropical Indo-Pacific blennies, distinguished by having the gill membranes attached to the throat so that the gill opening is reduced to a small pore, the teeth are moderate in size, fixed in the jaw and with an enormous canine each side in the lower jaw. This species lacks any tentacle above the eye, usually a conspicuous feature of blennies. **425**

Petrotilapia Cichlidae
tridentiger 15 cm. (6 in.)
A species of cichlid fish found only in Lake Nyassa where it is common in shallow water at the edges of the lake especially close to rocks.

It is distinguished by the very remarkable dentition, the teeth in both jaws forming a broad band, but each tooth is composed of a long slender shaft, curved at the tip to form a flat, 3-lobed cutting edge. This extraordinary dentition is almost exactly repeated in the Lake Tanganyika genus *Petrochromis*.

In other respects it is a rather slender-bodied, but a broad-headed typical cichlid. **374**

Petrus Sparidae
rupestris RED or YELLOW STEENBRAS
1·8 m. (6 ft)
A native sea bream of S. Africa, occurring from the Cape to Natal. It is found among reefs or rocks in deep water and occasionally enters large estuaries.

It is a very large fish, inshore specimens weighing up to 68 kg. (150 lb.), but rumours speak of fishes offshore that attain a weight of several hundred pounds. It is also rumoured to attack men swimming in the water. It is a favoured angling fish, taking fish baits eagerly and fighting well; its massive dog-teeth in the front of the jaws are capable of snapping off incautious fingers, so it has to be handled with care.

Commonly taken in trawls and its flesh is said to be excellent but the liver should not be eaten as it causes poisoning with subsequent loss of skin and hair.

It is a rather elongate fish with a pointed head and large jaws. Its colouring is greenish brown on the back with orange reflections on the sides and a yellow belly. The lower fins are orange.

This species is placed by many authors in the genus *Dentex*.

PEZ NEGRO see **Astroblepus grixalvii**

Phaeoptyx Apogonidae
conklini FRECKLED CARDINALFISH
9 cm. (3½ in.)
Known from Bermuda, the Bahamas, Florida, and the W. Indies. It is one of the commonest species in this area. It is found from just below the shore-line to depths of 23 m. (12 fathoms); in the Bahamas it is most common on patch reefs at depths of 12–18 m. (7–10 fathoms).

The body is pinkish or red, with the centre of each scale picked out with dark speckles. Smudgy dark bars run across the bases of the second dorsal, tail, and anal fins, and the tail fin has dark-edged rays.

Phago Ichthyoboridae
loricatus PIKE CHARACIN 15 cm. (6 in.)
The members of this genus are found in the rivers of tropical W. Africa. They are very distinctive in body form being elongate, with long snouts and large jaws, the upper of which can move upwards.

P. loricatus is found in the basin of the River Niger. Its body is covered with large, finely toothed scales which are very hard, almost forming an armour. The tail fin is forked, other fins are rather small and rounded, and the adipose fin is very small. Teeth in the jaws are small, and arranged in 2 rows, none is conspicuously enlarged.

It is dark brown on the back, reddish brown on the sides with 2–3 lengthwise bands, the middle one of which is the most pronounced.

The dorsal and tail fins are crossed by several dark bars.

It is a predatory fish, feeding on young fishes and occasionally insect larvae. It lives close to the bottom, hiding beneath roots and in the vegetation. It requires a high temperature (26–28°C.) to thrive. Although it has been kept in aquaria its shy nature hardly makes it a distinguished pet fish.

Phagoborus Ichthyoboridae
ornatus 18 cm. (7 in.)
A long, slender garfish-like species with very elongate jaws and large teeth. It is found in the central basin of the Congo. Its body is completely covered with scales, and the lateral line runs from head to tail. The dorsal fin is placed behind the mid-point of the body, the adipose fin is distinct.

The snout is long, but not so long as in the related genus *Phago*; in *Phagoborus* the teeth are in a single row along the edges of the jaws. They are sharp and conical, and those in the front of the jaws are notably long.

Its back is grey to reddish brown, the sides silvery green and the belly white. Three indistinct darker olive bands run along the side, and the tail is barred with dark brown. Large fish are said to have several black lengthwise stripes along the body.

Little seems to be known of its biology in nature, it has been kept in aquaria occasionally. It feeds almost exclusively on small fish (as might be expected from the shape of its teeth) with occasional insect larvae also taken.

Phalloceros Poeciliidae
caudimaculatus CAUDO, ONE-SPOT LIVEBEARER 5 cm. (2 in.)
Widely distributed in e. S. America, S. of the equator. It is found in the regions of Paraguay, e. Brazil, Uruguay, and Argentina, in the coastal belt and inland. It lives in streams, ditches, and pools, often in brackish water near the coast, but slightly distinct forms live in mountain streams and springs.

The male is dark olive-green above, the sides yellow, the belly light; on the tail a dark comma-shaped spot beneath the dorsal fin. The fins are yellowish with a black border. The female is similar but lacks the black edge to the dorsal. Very many colour varieties of this attractive fish occur in nature or have been bred by aquarists. It does not require very high temperatures to survive (18–20°C.). The female produces 20–80 young in broods at intervals of 5–6 weeks.

PHALLOSTETHIDAE
A remarkable family of small fishes found in the fresh and brackish waters of the Philippines, Malaysia, and Thailand. A number of species are known, each inhabiting different habitats from the lower mountain slopes to the estuaries.

They superficially resemble miniature grey mullets, but also have characters of the cypri-

nodonts, and are today placed close to the latter and the Atherinidae. Much confusion as to their family placement has existed in the past.

They are rather slender fishes with a fully-scaled body, a small second dorsal fin, and a rather long anal fin. The first dorsal fin is reduced to a single short spine. The pelvic fins are absent, but part of the pelvic skeleton in the male is adapted, with other bony elements, into a long, very elaborate copulatory organ, placed just behind and beneath the head. The urogenital opening of the female is covered by a shield-like scale also on the throat. See **Phenacostethus.**

Phenacostethus Phallostethidae
smithi 2 cm. (¾ in.)
Found in Thailand, apparently abundantly in the vicinity of Bangkok, but no doubt commonly elsewhere. Its discoverer, Hugh M. Smith, the distinguished American student of the fishes of that area, recorded it as abounding 'in fresh-water pools, ditches, and smaller canals in the Bangkok region, living in water that is nearly always muddy or turbid.'

It lives in small scattered schools near to the surface and feeds on planktonic microorganisms. Its back is a dusky olive, and it has a glistening yellow area on the top of the head, but the body is quite transparent, and the internal organs can be clearly distinguished from the side.

Smith observed that spawning was protracted, and continued through the rainy season, from May to December. This fish is oviparous, the complicated genital structures of the male are said to be used as clasping organs to ensure fertilization of the eggs as they are laid in the muddy water.

PHOLIDAE
A small family of fishes found in the cooler seas of the N. Hemisphere, and particularly well represented in the N. Pacific. Most of the members of the family are elongate, compressed, slender fishes, with long-based, wholly spiny dorsal fins. They all have small pectoral fins, but the pelvic fins are minute, placed almost on the throat and each is composed of a single spine and a ray. Some forms lack pelvic fins completely.

The gunnels are inhabitants of inshore waters and several species occur in inter-tidal habitats. They are all small, and none have commercial or sporting value. They are, however, often very common and play an important part in the ecology of intertidal and shallow water habitats by predation and in acting as intermediate hosts for seabird parasites. See **Pholis, Xererpes.**

Pholidichthys Microdesmidae
leucotaenia 9 cm. (3½ in.)
For over a century this small fish was known only from a specimen described by the Dutch naturalist and surgeon Pieter Bleeker in 1856. This specimen was taken at Buru in Indonesia.

Recently it has been discovered elsewhere in the Indonesian area, and specimens have been imported to Europe for exhibition in public aquaria.

It is distinguished by its long narrow body, the dorsal fin originating close behind the eyes and being joined to the tail fin (as is the anal fin). The teeth in the jaws are large, conical and lie in 4 overlapping rows. The bold coloration is also distinctive.

Its biology is virtually unknown, it is believed to burrow or hide in crevices. **438**

Pholis Pholidae
gunnellus BUTTERFISH, GUNNEL
25 cm. (10 in.)
The butterfish is widely distributed in the cool temperate N. Atlantic. In the E. it is found from the Brittany coast of France, around the British Isles and n. to the White Sea. In the w. it occurs from Labrador to Massachusetts. It occurs around Iceland and in s. Greenland.

It is best known as a shore-fish, and is very common in intertidal habitats throughout its range, although it occurs down as deep as 80 m. (43 fathoms). On the shore it lives amongst boulders, and in crevices especially in the kelp (*Laminaria*) zone. It spawns in mid-winter; clumps of eggs are deposited amongst stones where they are guarded by the parents. Egg-masses, about the size of a walnut can often be found on the low shore.

The food of the butterfish is varied and includes small crustaceans, worms, and occasionally molluscs. It is often eaten by seabirds, particularly gulls, and other fishes. Near seabird colonies its skin is often covered with black spots, the encysted form of the parasitic worm, *Cryptocotyle* which infests birds.

It is distinguished by its colouring, usually warm brown on the back with a line of prominent black spots, each ringed with white, running along the base of the dorsal fin.

P. ornata SADDLEBACK GUNNEL
30 cm. (12 in.)
Widely distributed in the N. Pacific from n. California through Oregon, Washington, and British Columbia to the Bering Sea and the Sea of Japan. It appears to be moderately common throughout its range, found mostly in depths of 18–37 m. (10–20 fathoms). It is reported to feed on molluscs and small crustaceans.

In body form it is closely similar to other members of the family. Its pelvic fins are short and placed well forward on the throat. It is olive-green to brown on the back, yellowish or orange on the belly. A series of dark V-shaped markings runs along the back from head to almost reach the tail; a similar series of open bars on the lower sides.

Photoblepharon Anomalopidae
palpebratus 8 cm. (3¼ in.)
A small fish found in E. Indian seas. It lives a short distance offshore, in water 4–5 m. (2–3 fathoms) deep, usually singly or in pairs around rocks and coral heads. It is active at night, and only comes to the surface occasionally.

It is a rather stout-bodied fish with high dorsal and anal fins, and a forked tail. Its body is fully scaled.

This fish has for long been known as a light-producing species and the mechanics of its light organ are of considerable interest when compared with its close relative *Anomalops*. Both species have an oval, broad bar beneath the eye which is attached at the front edge by cartilage. The outer-facing side is cream coloured, the rear wall is dense black. This organ is richly supplied with blood vessels, and its hollow polygonal tubes contain symbiotic bacteria which produce light when well supplied with oxygen. In order to control the light given off by the bacteria, this fish has a black tissue which covers the eye literally like a curtain from below. In *Photoblepharon* the light can thus be flashed off at will, as it is at longish intervals.

The function of the luminous glands is unknown, possibly it is to attract prey or to help navigation in the dark. The fishermen of the Banda Islands remove these organs and use them as a lure on the hook; they remain luminous for hours and are said to attract many fishes.

Phoxinus Cyprinidae
eos NORTHERN REDBELLY DACE
76 mm. (3 in.)
A small minnow-like freshwater fish, widely distributed in the n. U.S. in the Atlantic states, and in Canada. Its distribution is remarkably discontinuous and it is believed that the species must have survived in more than one refuge in glacial times.

It is a rather plump little fish with small fins and a small, steeply-angled mouth. Its body is covered with very small scales and only few pored lateral line scales are present. It is dark olive to dark brown, white or cream on the belly, with 2 lengthwise stripes, the lower of which runs from head to tail. In the spawning season the males are brilliantly coloured with red and yellow.

It is principally a plant-feeder, eating filamentous algae, and occasionally invertebrates. Its intestine is long and coiled – a sure indicator of a herbivore. It is most abundant in the swampy margins of small lakes. It is said to shed its eggs in the filamentous algae in which it is often found, a small shoal darting from one algal clump to another laying eggs in each.

P. phoxinus MINNOW 13 cm. (5 in.)
The minnow is widely distributed through Europe and Asia, from the British Isles e. to Siberia, n. to within the Arctic Circle, and s. to the Pyrenees, and the Black Sea. It is typically an inhabitant of cool, running water, such as small streams, although it is very adaptable and can be found in large, slow flowing lowland rivers and lakes as well. It is usually found in small shoals feeding on a wide variety of small bottom-living insects, crustaceans, and occasionally fish fry. In suitable streams it becomes an abundant fish and is often found in huge shoals numbering thousands of fish. Because of its size and usual abundance it is an important fish in the economy of streams, being eaten by a wide range of fish-eating birds, and other fishes, such as trout, perch, pike, and eels.

It is a small fish, rather cylindrical in body shape, with a small head and mouth. Its scales are very small. Its coloration is always attrac-tive, although variable with locality, usually the back and sides are olive-brown with a rich golden sheen on the sides shading to yellow on the belly. There is a series of dusky blotches on the sides often merging into a dark stripe. In the spawning season the males are brilliantly coloured, with reddish orange on the belly, fading to orange on the tail, the head is covered with large white tubercles, and the edges of the pectoral and pelvic fins are light.

PHRACTOLAEMIDAE
A most interesting family of African freshwater fish, represented by a single species. Its nearest relatives seem to be the fishes of the family Kneriidae also found in Africa. See **Phractolaemus.**

Phractolaemus Phractolaemidae
ansorgei 15 cm. (6 in.)
This fish is found in muddy, weedy waters in the river basins of the lower Niger and the Congo Rivers in W. Africa. It appears to be a rather uncommon fish and relatively little is known about its biology, although occasional specimens have been exhibited in aquaria. In the wild it lives in heavily turbid water close to the bottom, sucking up small invertebrates with its remarkable tubular mouth. In captivity it has been reported to eat bottom-living worms and dead water-fleas.

It is a very unremarkably coloured species being uniformly grey above, light brown on the sides, and pale ventrally. Its fins are dark. Males are distinguished by a cluster of spiny whitish tubercles on the head around the eyes, and in two major rows along the side of the tail from the region of the anal fin to the tail fin.

It is rather slim in build with a small down-turned head. Its body is covered with large scales and all its fins, except for the tail fin are small. The mouth is small and except when feeding is retracted into a narrow opening at the upper front of the head, it is, however, capable of extension into a long tube.

Phractolaemus is able to use its large swim-bladder as an accessory breathing organ.

Phrynelox Antennariidae
striatus STRIPED ANGLER 18 cm. (7 in.)
Widely distributed in the Indo-Pacific, from the coasts of s. Africa, the Indo-Malayan region to the Queensland and New South Wales coasts of Australia.

Its colour is brownish or yellowish with black parallel stripes radiating from the eye and breaking up into spots. Fins spotted. The lure on the fishing rod is deeply divided. Like other frogfishes this species lays eggs in broad sheets of jelly. It stalks its prey slowly over the sea bottom wriggling its worm-like lure enticingly until a prey fish is within snapping distance.

Phtheirichthys Echeneidae
lineatus SLENDER SUCKERFISH
76 cm. (30 in.)
A little-known suckerfish probably found in

most tropical seas except for the e. Pacific. It is, however, rarely seen or captured. Most specimens that have been examined have been found on such fishes as garuppa (*Promicrops lanceolatus*) and barracudas (*Sphyraena* spp.).

It is closely related to the large shark sucker, *Echeneis*, but differs essentially in having few bony plates in the sucker disc (10 at most). It is extremely elongate; brown above, sharply margined on the side by its light belly.

Phycodurus Syngnathidae
eques LEAFY SEADRAGON 30 cm. (12 in.)
Found only in the waters of S. Australia, this species represents the most extreme development of concealing camouflage adopted by the family. Shorn of its leafy skin appendages the fish is of basic pipefish pattern with a moderate snout, and rather deep, compressed, angular body. The head, body, and tail are covered with a large number of branched leafy appendages, each variable in shape.

It is light brown with thin white transverse lines on the trunk, with black and white lines radiating from the eyes.

Little seems to have been recorded of its biology. On the S. Australian coast it is not common, but is much prized for the marine aquarium. Its extravagant ornamentation is presumably a concealing device when living amongst algae which suggests that it is a shallow-water species.

Phyllopteryx Syngnathidae
taeniolatus WEEDY SEADRAGON
46 cm. (18 in.)
Found only in the waters of New South Wales, Victoria, Tasmania, and particularly common on the coasts of S. Australia. For all that, little seems to have been recorded of its life history.

As in all pipefishes the male carries the eggs on a soft area of skin beneath the tail; up to 120 eggs have been found on a single male.

Its body form is very distinctive, long and compressed. Long leafy flaps of skin project from the body and tail, and it must be assumed that the seadragon lives amongst algae and that these flaps resemble the plant fronds.

It is olive on the back; the sides are lighter with a network of dark lines, and 7 broad bands on the trunk. The leaf-like appendages are purple with a dark edge.

Physailia Schilbeidae
pellucida AFRICAN GLASS CATFISH
10 cm. (4 in.)
A singularly striking catfish, almost transparent and entirely colourless so that its vertebral column, swimbladder, and main blood vessels can be clearly seen. It has 4 pairs of long, almost equal-length barbels, a long anal fin, a minute adipose fin on the back but no true, rayed, dorsal fin.

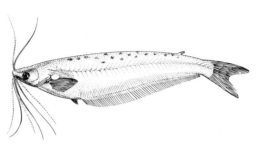

It is a lively aquarium fish, very active, and swimming in small shoals. It has the habit of resting in a tail-drooped position at a slight angle to the bottom.

It is found in the basin of the upper Nile.

Physiculus Eretmophoridae
bachus RED COD 46 cm. (18 in.)
Well distributed in the waters of New Zealand, and reported from Tasmanian waters, and doubtfully from S. Australia. It occurs in shallow water of 16 m. (9 fathoms) down to 187 m. (102 fathoms). It was first captured on Captain James Cook's second voyage round the world, although the descriptions prepared by the naturalist J. R. Forster were not published until 1801.

A slender-bodied fish with a short barbel on the chin, 2 dorsal fins, the first of which is short, and a single long anal fin, similar in shape and length to the second dorsal. Reddish green above, pink below, with a conspicuous dark spot at the base of the pectoral fin. The body turns reddish after death. Although not a prime food fish, the red cod is caught in some numbers, and is used for food.

PIMELODIDAE

A family of freshwater catfishes confined to S. America except for some forms which are found as far N. as Mexico and the larger Caribbean islands. The members of the family are mostly long-bodied, scaleless catfishes with 3 pairs of long, slender barbels on the lips; spines are present in the dorsal and pectoral fins, and a long adipose fin is present. The anal fin base is usually short.

Most pimelodids are nocturnal or crepuscular fishes, feeding by their extraordinarily sensitive barbels. One, *Typhlobagrus kronei*, is a totally blind cave species and found only in the Cavern das Areias, São Paulo, Brazil. Numerous species have been described in this family. See **Luciopimelodus, Microglanis, Pimelodus, Rhamdia, Sorubim.**

Pimelodus Pimelodidae
ornatus 13 cm. (5 in.)
Well distributed in the freshwaters of S. America, this catfish has been found in the Amazon basin, the Rio Negro, Rio Paraguay, and the Para.

A well distinguished species notable for the shortness of the dorsal and pectoral spines, and the rather high adipose fin.

Occasionally imported for the aquarium.
166

Pimelometopon Labridae
darwini 76 cm. (30 in.)
A wrasse endemic to the Galapagos Islands, which is found in the kelp beds in rocky areas amongst the islands. It probably feeds on slow-moving benthic organisms such as sea urchins, molluscs in general, and crabs.

Members of this genus are distinguished by their forward-pointing curved anterior teeth in the jaws. They also have a conspicuously rounded nape, giving them a bump-headed look. The closest relative of this Galapagos wrasse seems to be the California sheephead, *P. pulchrum*. **410**
P. pulchrum see under **P. darwini**

Pimephales   Cyprinidae
  promelas FATHEAD MINNOW 9 cm. (3½ in.)
A small minnow, widely distributed in e. N. America, from the s. rivers of the Great Slave Lake E. to New Brunswick and S. along the Mississippi and Missouri systems to Tennessee and Mexico. It is a stout-bodied fish with a blunt snout and rounded head. Its mouth is strongly oblique, and has no barbels. Its scales are moderate in size, but the lateral line rarely extends beyond the dorsal fin origin.

There are marked sexual differences in external appearance in the breeding season. The males develop large tubercles on the snout and lower jaw, and a spongy pad forms on the back, while the dorsal fin becomes thickened. The head and back becomes dark except for the light coloured tubercles. Females and non-breeding males are olive above, pale below, with a dark stripe along the side.

The fathead minnow lives in muddy streams and lakes, it feeds on bottom-living organisms and takes in considerable quantities of mud in doing so. It spawns from April to mid-August; the eggs are deposited under plant leaves, or in excavations under stones, as well as on clear vertical or horizontal surfaces. The male guards the nest. Males are usually larger than females, an unusual situation amongst cyprinids.

The fathead minnow is widely used by anglers as a bait fish and its present distribution owes much to man in the release of unwanted live bait.

PINE-CONE FISH see Monocentridae
PINE-CONE FISH see **Monocentris japonicus**
PINK SALMON see **Oncorhynchus gorbuscha**
PINK-TAILED CHARACIN see **Chalceus macrolepidotus**
PINKEAR see **Melanotaenia fluviatilis**
PIPEFISH see Syngnathidae
PIPEFISH,
  BLUE-STRIPED see **Doryrhamphus melanopleura**
  GHOST see Solenostomidae
  GHOST see **Solenostomus cyanopterus**
  GREAT see **Syngnathus acus**
  OCEAN see **Entelurus aequoreus**
  SARGASSUM see **Syngnathus pelagicus**
  SNAKE see **Entelurus aequoreus**
  WORM see **Nerophis lumbriciformis**
PIPEHORSE see **Amphelikturus dendriticus**
PIRACATINGA see **Luciopimelodus pati**
PIRANHA see **Pygocentrus piraya**
PIRANHA,
  NATTERER'S see **Rooseveltiella nattereri**
  RED see **Rooseveltiella nattereri**
  SPOTTED see **Serrasalmus rhombeus**
  WHITE see **Serrasalmus rhombeus**
PIRARUCU see **Arapaima gigas**
PIRATE PERCH see **Aphredoderus sayanus**

PIRAYA see **Pygocentrus piraya**

Plagiotremus   Blenniidae
  townsendi 5 cm. (2 in.)
This blenny is found in both the Gulf of Aqaba, close to the Red Sea, and in the Persian

Gulf. It is one of a trio of blenny species which form a remarkable complex of mimics, based on *Meiacanthus nigrolineatus*, a fish which is relatively immune from predators. *Plagiotremus townsendi* mimics the colouring of this species, being essentially blue anteriorly and yellow on the body and tail, with black marks along the back.

It employs its resemblance to the harmless but inedible *Meiacanthus,* to approach closely to larger fishes which it then attacks, tearing off epidermis and scales. Stomachs of specimens examined always contained fish scales and mucus, which seem to form its diet.

PLAICE see **Pleuronectes platessa**
PLAICE, AMERICAN see **Hippoglossoides platessoides**
PLAIN BONITO see **Auxis thazard, Orcynopsis unicolor**
PLAINFIN MIDSHIPMAN see **Porichthys notatus**
PLANER'S LAMPREY see **Lampetra planeri**
Platacidae see Ephippidae

Platax   Ephippidae
A genus of batfishes. Besides the 2 colour illustrations there is a further colour picture of a species of *Platax* not identified. **312**

Platax orbicularis

P. orbicularis ROUND BATFISH, BATFISH
32 cm. (13 in.)
An Indo-Pacific species found widely in the e. Pacific but also occurring around India, across to the Red Sea and e. Africa. The precise identification of the batfishes is not always clearcut due to the changes in body form and colouring with growth. This species is similar to other batfishes described.

The young fish are said to bear a striking mimetic resemblance to floating *Rhizophora* and *Hibiscus* leaves. Often with the yellowish leaves they drift on their sides, head inclined to the bottom, but sculling themselves by means of their colourless pectoral fins. It is said that when pursued they adopt this mimicry and sink to the seabed like a waterlogged dead leaf, but other observers have noted that when a mimicking batfish is approached too closely it will swim off rapidly in an upright posture. **313**

P. pinnatus ANGELFISH, SEABAT, BATFISH
76 cm. (30 in.)
An Indo-Pacific species, found widely from the coast of E. Africa and the Red Sea to the E. Indies, Australia and the Philippines. It is said to grow to a weight of around 22·7 kg. (50 lb.); although its flesh is palatable it is not highly esteemed but it is caught, mostly in nets, occasionally on lines.

It is deep-bodied with very high and well developed dorsal and anal fins, the pelvic fins are also long. The length of the rays of these fins decreases with age, but even in old fishes they are remarkably well developed.

Young fish are yellowish or orange with bold vertical dark stripes. The colouring becomes more uniform with age although the dark bars are still faintly discernible. Juveniles of this species are black with the outline of the fins bright orange. They are remarkably similar in coloration to turbellarian flatworms and nudibranch molluscs, which are known to be distasteful, if not toxic, to fishes. Moreover, the young fish swims on its side gently undulating its long fins in the same swimming movements of either model and thus improves still further on the mimicry. **314**

Platichthys   Pleuronectidae
  flesus FLOUNDER 51 cm. (20 in.)
A European flatfish of wide distribution. Its range extends from the White Sea and n. Norway s. to the Mediterranean, where it is found in the w. basin only, the Adriatic and the Black Sea. It is extremely abundant in the Baltic Sea. The flounder is the only European flatfish to penetrate into freshwater although this is essentially a habit of the n. parts of its range. Practically any tidal river or sea loch in the British Isles and northern Europe will contain small flounders living in apparently fresh water, although they return to the sea to breed.

It is easily distinguished, the back is usually dark greyish brown, often with pale orange spots and darker patches; the underside is dead opaque white. Along the front part of the lateral line, and at the base of both dorsal and anal fins between the rays there are small spiny prickles – which alone serve to distinguish it.

The flounder is found in the sea from the shore-line down to 55 m. (30 fathoms), but is most common close to the shore. It feeds mainly on molluscs, worms, and crustaceans, and it is a predator of commercially valuable shell fishes, such as cockles and shrimps. Locally it is used for food, being particularly exploited in the Baltic Sea, but its flesh is soft and rather insipid and in the British Isles is not highly considered. It is a popular anglers' fish, mainly because it is found close inshore and can weigh up to 2·5 kg. (5½ lb.).

In some regions as many as a third of the flounders examined will be sinistral (i.e. eyes on the left side), in other areas this proportion is less. **468**

P. stellatus STARRY FLOUNDER 91 cm. (3 ft) This very distinctive species is easy to identify on account of the broad bands on the dorsal, anal, and tail fins, the eyed side being otherwise brown. The body is also liberally covered with sharp thorn-like spines in the skin. Although it belongs to the right-eyed flatfish family about 60 per cent are sinistral on the American coast and up to 100 per cent are so in Japanese waters.

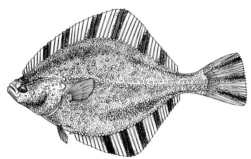

It is widely distributed in the N. Pacific ocean, in the E. ranging from s. California to Alaska, in the Bering and Okhotsk Seas, and sw. to Japan and Korea. It is mainly found in shallow water but ranges down to 275 m. (150 fathoms). It is particularly abundant in inshore coastal waters including bays and estuaries and even penetrates into rivers.

It eats a wide range of worms, crustaceans, molluscs, brittle stars and fishes. It appears to have few predators other than those which eat pelagic young fishes generally. It is a popular sport fish along the Californian coast and large numbers are caught annually. It is also caught commercially throughout its range, although on the American coast it is not so heavily exploited as it is on the Asiatic shores of the N. Pacific.

PLATY see **Xiphophorus maculatus**
PLATY, SWORDTAIL see **Xiphophorus xiphidium**

PLATYCEPHALIDAE
A moderately large family of marine fishes found widely in the Indo-Pacific, and tropical e. Atlantic. The flatheads are very distinctive relatives of the scorpion fishes, and have a very flattened forepart of the body and head, bodies covered with small dense scales, and 2 dorsal fins.

Most are found as typical inhabitants of sandy and muddy seas, lying buried in the bottom. They are important commercial fishes in many parts of the Indo-Pacific. See **Platycephalus, Thysanophrys.**

Platycephalus   Platycephalidae
  fuscus DUSKY FLATHEAD 1·2 m. (4 ft)

Widely distributed around the coasts of Australia, and found on the coasts of practically all states including Tasmania. It is especially an estuarine species and is found on shallow tidal flats on open muddy bottoms in which it burrows so that only its eyes show. It is a moderately important food fish, its flesh being firm, white, and of good flavour. It is taken on lines, in seines and in gill nets. The largest flathead in Australian seas, big specimens may weigh as much as 14·5 kg. (32 lb.), an average weight would be 6·8 kg. (15 lb.).

Its food is varied and consists mainly of small fishes, crustaceans, worms, and molluscs.

The dusky flathead is distinguished partly by its size, but also by its scaly head and relatively small eyes (the space between the eyes being larger than the width of the eye). In colour it is usually brown above, white below, the sides mottled, and the fins with brown spots.

P. indicus RIVER GURNARD, SAND GURNARD 1 m. (39 in.)
Widely distributed throughout the Indian Ocean, and extending to the Indo-Australian archipelago. It is found mainly in shallow water on sandy bottoms, and is quite common in estuaries. It is a valued food fish throughout its range, and is caught on lines, and in beach seines. Its flesh is very good eating.

Its body form is typical of the flatheads. It can be distinguished by its smooth lateral line, small eyes, wide interorbital space, and lack of skin flaps above the eye. It is light brown above with many small darker spots, almost white beneath.

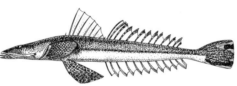

In s. Africa this, and other species, are usually known as rivergurnard or sandgurnard. **254**

Platyrhina   Platyrhinidae
  limboonkengi see under **P. sinensis**
  sinensis CHINESE GUITARFISH
68 cm. (26¾ in.)
In shape this guitarfish resembles a ray. It is widely distributed in the sea of Japan, the Yellow Sea, and along the Pacific coast of Japan and Chekiang Province, China.

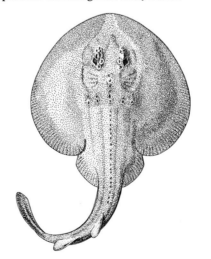

A related species *P. limboonkengi*, which differs in several ways, notably in the wider spacing of the dorsal fins, is known from Amoy, China.

PLATYRHINIDAE
A family containing 2 species both found in the w. N. Pacific, along the coasts of China and Japan. By some authors this family is considered to belong to the Rhinobatidae, but its members differ from that family in that the rostral cartilage does not extend to the tip of the snout, which is therefore more rounded, and because the pectoral fins are better developed. See **Platyrhina.**

Platytroctes   Searsidae
  apus 19 cm. (7½ in.)
Platytroctes apus was first captured in mid-Atlantic by the *Challenger* Expedition of 1872–6 at a depth of 2744 m. (1500 fathoms).

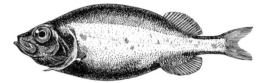

Since then it has been caught in a number of places in the e. Atlantic from off the coasts of Portugal S. to the Cape Verde Islands. It has also been found in the Indian Ocean, in the Arabian Sea at 1353 m. (740 fathoms). It has been taken down to 4900 m. (2677 fathoms), although young and adult specimens have been taken in mid-water, so there is reason for thinking that this fish, like other searsiids, is an inhabitant of the middle layers of the sea rather than the sea bed (as are the related Alepocephalidae).

Its colouring is described as translucent with the muscles visible through the skin. The head and back are tinted pinkish grey, the fins are darker, those on the back black.

PLECOGLOSSIDAE
A family which contains only a single species, found in the coastal and freshwaters of the w. N. Pacific seaboard. It is an interesting family which is clearly closest to the smelt family (Osmeridae) or the Salmonidae, having characters in common with both. It is now recognized as distinct, chiefly on the grounds of its unique dentition. The teeth are feeble, flat, broad, and movable, and lie in a fold of skin in the jaws. There are 3 folds of skin forming pouches between the lower jaws. See **Plecoglossus.**

Plecoglossus   Plecoglossidae
  altivelis AYU 30 cm. (12 in.)
The ayu is, and has been for many years, the most highly esteemed freshwater food fish in Japan. It is the subject of extensive and valuable fisheries. Although it is best known as a Japanese species, the ayu is widely distributed in the maritime countries of the w. N. Pacific being known from Manchuria, China, Korea, and Formosa.

It is migratory, breeding in freshwater. After hatching, the fry move downstream to the sea in which they overwinter, returning in the spring until sexually mature in the autumn when they spawn and return to the sea. Many

ayu spawn this once only, but some live on to spawn for 2–3 years in succession. They spawn in gravel bottomed, small streams, usually at night. Each female sheds about 10,000 eggs, each about 1 mm. in diameter, which hatch in 10–20 days at temperatures of 15–20°C.

Land-locked, dwarf populations of ayu are known in Japan and elsewhere. Those in Lake Biwa, Japan, locally named koayu, live in a sandy shored, rather infertile lake, are stunted and few grow longer than 10 cm. (4 in.). These fish have been transplanted to richer lakes and rivers and have grown to normal ayu size.

The ayu is rather smelt-like in appearance. Its colour is olive, fading on the belly to white, an elliptical orange mark behind the head and yellowish fins.

Although ayu are nowadays captured using nets and traps, and the stock is strictly conserved, they are the traditional subject of the famous fishery using cormorants. The bird is tethered to a fishing boat on a long leash, and has a metal ring fastened around its throat. It is trained to catch the migrating ayu, which it does with alacrity. On returning to the boat the cormorant is forced to part with the fish, although later the band is removed and it is rewarded with some less valued fish.

Plecostomus
Loricariidae
commersonii VIEJA 53 cm. (21 in.)
Widely distributed in S. America, in n. Argentina, Uruguay, Paraguay, and s. Brazil. It is found in rivers such as the Rio de la Plata, Rio Paraguay, Rio Paraná, and the Rio Uruguay. It is most common in the lower reaches of these rivers even penetrating to estuarine regions. It spawns in the spring. The young fish feed on algae growing on vegetation or hard substrates; adults also eat plant matter but worms and crustaceans as well.

Young fish are popular as aquarium specimens, their ability to clean algae from the glass sides being appreciated.

Members of this genus are distinguished from other loricariid catfishes by the absence of heavy scutes on the underside. Otherwise they are typical loricariids with a hard bony head, and large scales, heavily ridged along the back and sides. The dorsal fin is high and well-developed, the anal is small, and a small adipose fin is present with a roughened spine in front. It is dull coloured, grey-brown on the back, with dark spots, the underside pale green-yellow.

Plectorhynchus
Pomadasyidae
pictus PAINTED SWEET-LIPS 66 cm. (26 in.)
Widespread in the tropical Indo-Pacific, from the Red Sea and E. Africa e. to the E. Indies, n. Australia, Polynesia, the Philippines, and to the Sea of Japan. In many areas an abundant fish and a valuable food fish. It is encountered in inshore waters, along the clear edges of reefs and in sandy-bottomed bays.

Its coloration is variable with age, the young being brightly marked, yellowish with chestnut brown to black lengthwise bands from head to tail, the lowest one the widest. The upper bands merge at the end of the dorsal fin. Adults are greenish brown with small brown spots especially on the head and fins.

Plectroplites
Serranidae
ambiguus CALLOP, GOLDEN PERCH
76 cm. (30 in.)
Widely distributed in freshwater in Australia, and found in all states except Tasmania. It is very abundant in the Murray-Darling river systems, and occurs in the Clarence and Richmond rivers of New South Wales, and the Fitzroy of Queensland. It has been introduced fairly widely elsewhere and is mainly an inhabitant of the warm, sluggish, lowland reaches. It is a good sporting fish, and a valued food fish which may grow to a weight of 23 kg. (50 lb.).

It spawns with seasonal flooding, the planktonic eggs being spread widely by flood water.

The coloration is distinctive, being olive-green to dark green above shading to gold on the sides and belly. It is a very deep-bodied, perch-like fish with a small head and steep forehead.

Plectropomus
Serranidae
maculatus 16·5 cm. (42 in.)
Widespread in the tropical Indo-Pacific from E. Africa to the central Pacific. It is found mainly on reefs.

It exists in 3 colour forms (2 are shown here), one primarily reddish, the other light with brown bars across the back. Some authors, however, consider that 2 species are involved.

It is a fine food fish. **263, 268**

PLESIOPIDAE
A small family of tropical Indo-Pacific fishes found mainly in shallow water inshore on rocky grounds and coral reefs. They are distinctive small fishes with rather stout bodies, fairly large scales and a lateral line divided into 2 parts, the anterior following the back profile to the second dorsal fin, the posterior running along the mid-side of the body. The head is blunt and rounded, the mouth is rather large. Most species are dark in colour.

The family is closely related to the Grammidae, Pseudochromidae, and others, all forming a group perhaps close to the sea basses Serranidae. See **Plesiops**.

Plesiops
Plesiopidae
The species illustrated in colour has not been identified. **273**
P. nigricans 25 cm. (10 in.)
Widely distributed in the Indian Ocean and the w. Pacific, from the Red Sea and E. African coast to the Marshall Islands. It is common on the n. coasts of Australia where it has been called the blue-spotted long-fin.

It lives in reef areas, amongst stones and corals; in the New Hebrides it has been recorded as living concealed under boulders at low tide, apparently surviving with very little

water as long as it can burrow into wet sand. Juveniles of 5 cm. (2 in.) are very common around reefs, the normal maximum size appears to be 18 cm. (7 in.).

Its colouring is dark but striking, mostly dark brown but each scale having a blue spot, with similar spots on the shoulder and head and a black, blue ringed blotch on the gill cover. The fins are almost black, but the dorsal fin has a dark blue edge, and the remaining fins are edged with light blue.

Pleuragramma
Nototheniidae
antarcticum 20 cm. (8 in.)
This is the only member of the nototheniid family to have adopted a pelagic way of life. It is found virtually all round the Antarctic continent at depths of 150–500 m. (82–273 fathoms). It is the dominant mid-water fish over the continental shelf, at least in the Ross Sea, and judging by records of its distribution, all round the continent in addition.

The young have been found both inshore and in the open sea, at the surface down to 80 m. (44 fathoms). Both young and adults have many times been reported in the stomachs of seals and penguins.

It is a slender fish, with a protruding lower jaw and wide gape. The body is covered with firm, cycloid scales; there are 3 lateral lines. The skeleton is very feebly calcified, presumably a density-reducing device to conserve energy in this pelagic, mid-water fish. It is silvery on the sides, the back dusted with dark spots giving a bluish colour; the fins are pale.

Pleuronectes
Pleuronectidae
platessa PLAICE 91 cm. (3 ft)
The plaice is the most important flatfish in the fisheries of Europe. It ranges from the Barents Sea, and n. Norway s. to s. Spain and throughout the w. Mediterranean. It is a widespread fish on the shallow continental shelf.

It is found often in very shallow water, young specimens slipping away beneath the feet of surf paddlers and occasionally being found in sandy shore pools. It ranges down to 120 m. (66 fathoms) but is most common between 27 and 73 m. (15–40 fathoms). The largest specimens are usually found in these greater depths.

It is a well-known food fish easily distinguished by its warm brown colouring with very distinct orange spots on the eyed side, and clear white on the other. Its skin is smooth without the rough scales of the dab or the prickles at the base of the fin rays in the flounder. It is fished for throughout its range, but the greatest numbers are taken in the North and Irish seas, although important fisheries exist in Icelandic waters and to the far N.

Anglers also catch large numbers of plaice, and specimens in excess of 3 kg. (7 lb.) have been recorded.

The plaice feeds on a wide range of bottom-living invertebrates. The large specimens eat molluscs of various kinds, crustaceans, and worms. The species involved varies with the size of the fish for the large fish tend to live in deeper water and eat larger prey. Large plaice even eat fishes, particularly sand-eels. Plaice tend to feed less in the cooler months of the year, and are more active during daylight than at night-time.

They spawn in late winter and early spring; the eggs float at the surface at first but gradually sink. The larva at hatching is about 6·5 mm. long, and feeds, after its yolk is absorbed, on diatoms and crustacean larvae. They metamorphose to bottom-dwelling young fishes at a length of around 1 cm. ($\frac{1}{2}$ in.). Growth depends very largely on temperature and food supplies and tends to be better in richer areas, such as the North Sea, than in Icelandic waters for example. At the n. extremities of its range the plaice is very slow-growing and can support only a relatively small fishery.

Plaice are not often found as reversed specimens (in contrast to the flounder); the 2 species do, however, occasionally hybridize. The hybrid progeny is intermediate physically between the parent species and is locally fairly common at times.

PLEURONECTIDAE
The family of flatfishes which includes the important N. Atlantic food-fishes such as the plaice, halibut, dab, and flounder. Members of the family are found in the Atlantic, Indian, and Pacific oceans but are best represented in the cool temperate waters of the N. Atlantic and N. Pacific while many of the species found in tropical waters are found in relatively deep water.

The members of the family are dextral flatfishes, that is they have both eyes on the right side of the head (except in abnormal reversed specimens – which in some species are quite common). The dorsal fin runs from the front of the head, at least beginning at the level of the eye; the mouth is always at the tip of the head, in some species it is large but in many it is quite small.

As with other flatfishes the larva is a normal fish larval shape, with eyes placed each side of the head. At a late stage of development one eye (in the case of this family the left) migrates around the dorsal surface of the head to come to lie beside its fellow on the opposite side. Eye migration is usually completed by the time metamorphosis is complete and the fish begins to live on the sea bed. In flatfishes the cranium and head bones are skewed as a result of the eye moving, the optic nerves are crossed, some species have jaws with larger teeth on one side than the other, and differences in the development of nostrils and pectoral fins are observable. Once the transformation is complete the side of the fish with both eyes is coloured, the other side is usually white (although abnormally it may be wholly or partly coloured) and in *Reinhardtius* both sides are coloured although the blind side is less dark than the other. See **Ammotretis, Atheresthes, Eopsetta, Glyptocephalus, Hippoglossoides, Hippoglossus, Lepidopsetta, Limanda, Liopsetta, Microstomus, Parophrys, Platichthys, Pleuronectes, Psettichthys, Pseudopleuronectes, Reinhardtius, Samaris.**

Pliotrema Pristiophoridae
warreni SAW SHARK 91 cm. (3 ft)
Found only on the S. African coast, from the Cape along the Indian Ocean coast to beyond Delagoa Bay. It is quite commonly taken by trawlers in 37–366 m. (20–200 fathoms), and the flesh is said to be of excellent flavour.

This is a slim-bodied shark with well-developed fins and a long, saw-like snout with sharp, unequal teeth along its edges. At birth, for this species is viviparous, the teeth are folded down under the skin so that in the process of birth no injury is caused to the mother. The newly born young often have additional teeth on the underside of the snout which are lost after birth.

This is the only known member of the genus, which differs from the other saw sharks in that it has 6 gill-slits, not 5, on each side.

PLOTOSIDAE
A family of catfish, most of the members of which are marine or estuarine, although some species live in freshwater. The number of forms is not large. All have elongate, scaleless bodies, body armour is reduced, and the first dorsal fin is placed close behind the head, being fronted by a strong spine. The pectoral fins have a sharp spine and several rays. A second dorsal fin is present and is continuous with the tail and anal fins. The mouth has several barbels around it.

The family is confined to the Indo-Pacific basin. See **Cnidoglanis, Plotosus, Tandanus.**

Plotosus Plotosidae
anguillaris see **P. lineatus**
lineatus BARBER-EEL 30 cm. (12 in.)
Widespread in the Indo-Pacific from E. Africa and the Red Sea to Sri Lanka and SE. Asia. It is particularly abundant about reefs, in harbours and estuaries, dense shoals of young fish can be observed in such areas moving as if one entity. The young are also found solitary in tide-pools and under algae. The barbed spines of the dorsal and pectoral fins inflict most painful and dangerous wounds.

Young specimens have 2 bright yellow or whitish-blue bands running lengthwise. Adults are dull brown on the back, fawn towards the belly which is often white.

In s. Africa (where it is said to grow to 75 cm. 29$\frac{1}{2}$ in.) in length, its flesh is said to be excellent eating. In other areas it is not much esteemed. It has been kept as an aquarium fish, and will live in marine, or if acclimated carefully, in freshwater aquaria.

This species is frequently known as *P. anguillaris*. **165**

PLUNDERFISH see **Harpagifer bispinis**
POACHER see Agonidae
POACHER,
DEEP-PITTED see **Bothragonus swanii**
STURGEON see **Agonus acipenserinus**
TUBENOSE see **Pallasina barbata**

Poecilia Poeciliidae
latipinna SAILFIN MOLLY 12 cm. (4$\frac{3}{4}$ in.)
Found in the e. states of America from Carolina to Yucatan, in coastal regions and near the mouths of rivers. It was first described from the New Orleans area, but its principal habitat is the Rio Grande between Mexico and Texas, in fresh and brackish water, pools and streams.

It is a strikingly beautiful fish with a long-based dorsal fin (13–14 rays). In the male the dorsal fin is high (about as high as the body is deep) and placed just behind the head. The back is olive brown in colour, the sides brownish shading to blue with a pearly iridescence

and several longitudinal bands of red, blue, and greenish spots. The dorsal fin is pale blue with rows of black spots and a yellowish border. The female is dull coloured and her dorsal fin is comparatively short.

The black mollies so favoured by aquarists are breeders' attempts to improve on nature by selective breeding. While striking in an aquarium, they are depressingly dull in comparison with the wild fish.

Mollies are easy to keep and breed and require a large tank, well heated and planted. A large female will give birth to 20 to 60 large (10–12 mm.) young, after a gestation of 8–10 weeks. Young and adults feed extensively on algae, and eat small crustaceans and insect larvae. **207**
P. reticulata GUPPY, MILLIONS FISH
6 cm. (2$\frac{1}{2}$ in.)
The guppy is a native of the N. of the Amazon region, in n. Brazil, the Guyanas, Venezuela, Barbados, and Trinidad. It has also been introduced to many tropical regions as a controller of the larval stages of malaria-carrying mosquitos, and is established in many areas. Elsewhere (as in the British Isles) it is locally established in artificially heated canals and rivers due to the release of pet fish. The guppy is probably the most popular tropical aquarium fish. Its tolerance of low temperatures and confined spaces makes it an ideal inhabitant of small aquariums although its prodigious reproductive capacity quickly leads to overcrowding.

In its natural habitat it lives in fresh and brackish waters, in streams, ditches, pools and even wells. It occurs in vast numbers (hence 'millions fish') in these habitats.

The rather large range of this little fish has resulted in considerable variation both in body form and coloration. Most of these variations have been selected for and intensified by breeders so that the guppy is now a highly variable species containing many extreme forms – some by no means as lovely as the wild fish.

In the wild forms, the males are small (up to 3 cm., 1$\frac{1}{4}$ in.), olive-green to brown above, with 2 moderate black eye-spots on the sides. The sides shimmer with metallic greens and blues. The fins are pale; the tail fin sometimes with touches of metallic colour. The females are mostly greyish brown on the back and sides, light, almost white, over the body cavity. Pregnant females (and adults almost always are) have a distinct, internal black spot behind the abdomen.

Its feeding habits are omnivorous. Guppies will eat fine green algae, insect larvae, small crustaceans, and the eggs and young of other fishes (and their own young in the absence of cover).

For many years the guppy was known as *Lebistes reticulatus*, but modern nomenclature suggests it is correctly bracketed with the mollies, and other fishes under *Poecilia*. Its name guppy originated with the Rev. J. L. Guppy of Trinidad who collected some of the earlier known material. **209**
P. sphenops MOLLY 12 cm. (4$\frac{3}{4}$ in.)
A very variable fish found over a wide area of Central America. Its range stretches from Venezuela, Colombia, and the Leeward Islands, n. to Mexico and Texas. It is very adaptable and is found in rivers, lakes, and streams, especially where they are brackish or estuarine.

It is a very beautiful molly, in the wild form

being olive-brown above, the sides bluish with several lengthwise rows of orange dots and 8–9 faint dark crossbars on the sides. The dorsal fin has black dots at its base, a broad band of orange and a black edge. Males grow to 8 cm. (3 in.), females to 12 cm. The female has a smaller dorsal fin, and is rather bluish in colour with rows of faint red spots.

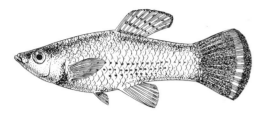

A popular aquarium fish, many spectacular varieties have been produced, amongst them the liberty molly. Black varieties are common.
P. velifera SAILFIN MOLLY 15 cm. (6 in.)
Found in freshwater and brackish lagoons, estuaries, streams, and pools near the coast in Yucatan in se. Mexico.

It is one of the largest molly species, and is very beautifully coloured. Its back is dark olive to blue, the sides are bluish green with pale spots, the throat and belly greenish and there are 3 or 4 dark bars on the lower flank. The dorsal and tail fins are bluish to pearly grey, with brilliant shining white spots and streaks. The dorsal fin of the male is huge, beginning above the back of the head, and with each ray very long. The female's fin is lower, and she is modestly coloured.

It is a popular aquarium fish, and numerous colour varieties have been bred. Its requirements are rigorous, however, and too cool water or an unclean tank quickly result in the death of the fish. **208**

POECILIIDAE

A large family of small fishes found naturally in the Americas, from the s. U.S., through Central America, and S. America as far S. as Argentine. They occupy a great diversity of habitats, from the slightly saline coastal marshes and river mouths to forest and mountain streams and pools, in general inhabiting those which are well covered with weed. Many of them feed on encrusting algae and plants, but almost all eat live food. Several species are particularly good destroyers of larval mosquitoes, and thus of direct importance as controllers of insect borne diseases. This ability has resulted in some species being spread worldwide as mosquito controllers (and many native fishes, some equally good mosquito eaters, have suffered as a result).

These fishes are toothcarps, that is they are in some ways similar to the carps but have well-developed small teeth in their jaws. They are all livebearers, giving birth to living young (a distinction from the egg-laying toothcarps – Cyprinodontidae). The anal fin of the male has either all its rays, or the first few rays, adapted as a movable, elongate tube, or gonopodium. This is used to transfer a spermatophore to the cloaca of the female. The liberation of sperm thereafter is slow and several generations of young can be produced from the one mating. Fertilization is thus internal; development continues in the ovarian cavity, and the young are born initially still in

the egg membrane, which bursts almost immediately. Technically this mode of development is known as ovoviviparity.

The structure of the male gonopodium is of critical value in the identification of these fishes and in understanding their relationships with one another. Individual mating also usually involves courtship behaviour and in most species the males are brighter coloured (and smaller) than the females and display repeatedly.

These colourful fishes are very popular with aquarists. Their lively behaviour, colouring, and in most forms tolerance of varying conditions make them ideal pet fish. See **Alfaro, Belonesox, Cnesterodon, Gambusia, Girardinus, Heterandria, Phalloceros, Poecilia, Xiphophorus.**

Poecilobrycon eques see **Nannostomus eques**

Pogonias Sciaenidae
cromis BLACK DRUM 1·8 m. (6 ft)
Native to the w. Atlantic and found from Argentina to s. New England, as well as in the Gulf of Mexico.

It grows to a huge size, a weight of 66 kg. (146 lb.) having been authoritatively reported from the Florida coast, while 27 kg. (60 lb.) fish are not exceptional.

It is distinguished by its short, deep body with a high arched back and flat belly. The snout is blunt, and the mouth is set low, while the chin bears a number of short barbels. Jaw teeth are small and pointed, but the pharyngeal teeth are flat, large and millstone like – clearly for crushing hard-shelled food.

It is silvery with bronze tinges on the back and upper sides.

POGY see **Brevoortia tyrannus**
POGGE see Agonidae
POGGE see **Agonus cataphractus**
POINTER,
  BLUE see **Isurus oxyrinchus**
  WHITE see **Carcharodon carcharias**
POLAR
  COD see **Boreogadus saida**
  SCULPIN see **Cottunculus microps**

Polistotrema Myxinidae
stouti PACIFIC HAGFISH 63 cm. (25 in.)
A marine fish found along the Pacific coast of N. America from s. California to se. Alaska. It is usually found on soft mud or clay bottoms, in which it burrows, in depths of 400–1000 m. (219–546 fathoms). In places it is relatively abundant and is caught in numbers in baited traps made out of iron drums pierced with holes, which permit access to the bait but retain the hagfish.

Like the N. Atlantic hagfish (*Myxine glutinosa*) it is a predator, which attacks larger fish and burrows into their bodies eating the tissues as it goes. The mouth is an oval slit, with 4 fleshy barbels, there are a further 4 barbels round the single nostril. The tongue has a heavy tooth plate, although like other hagfishes it has no jaws. The eyes are covered with thick skin and the Pacific hagfish is virtually blind, although it can scent food very acutely. It has between 10–14 gill openings along each side of the body. This species is sometimes placed in the genus *Eptatretus*.

POLKA-DOT RIBBONFISH see **Desmodema polystictum**

Pollachius Gadidae
pollachius POLLACK 130 cm. (51 in.)
A gadoid found in the European Atlantic and occasionally in the n. Mediterranean. It is found on the Norwegian coast s. to Spain and Portugal. Largely an inshore fish it is mainly found on rocky coasts or over rough grounds, swimming in shoals in mid-water. Large specimens are more solitary and are found in offshore waters. As an adult it is a fish eater, particularly sand-eels, sprats, herring, and small codfishes. Younger specimens eat small fishes and crustaceans.

It is not an important commercial fish although some are taken by trawl and on long lines. It is, however, a good sport fish and many are taken by anglers.

It is deep greeny-brown on the back, shading to yellowish on the sides, lighter ventrally.
P. virens SAITHE, COALFISH, POLLOCK
120 cm. (47 in.)
A N. Atlantic codfish, wide ranging in the e. Atlantic from the Barents Sea s. to Biscay, around Iceland, s. Greenland, and in the w. Atlantic from Labrador to N. Carolina. It becomes less common at the extremes of its range, but is very abundant elsewhere. It performs extensive seasonal migrations mainly to offshore spawning grounds in the winter; the young fish are common inshore (sometimes on the shoreline) in the following summer. It is usually encountered in small shoals, feeding on smaller fishes, especially codling, capelin, and sand eels, as well as many kinds of crustacean. The young fish feed mostly on small crustaceans and juvenile fishes. The saithe (pollock is its N. American name) is a valuable commercial fish. It is caught in large numbers in purse-seines, otter trawls, and on lines, and although not of the first quality its flesh is tasty and well flavoured, if slightly coloured. It is a popular sea angling species in Europe.

Its body form is typical of the family, with 3 dorsal fins, and 2 anal fins, short and small pelvics placed far forward on the belly. A very small barbel on the chin. The lateral line is almost straight, and light coloured. The body is a deep greeny-brown above, fading to yellowish on the sides and greyish on the belly. The fins are dark green. **189**

POLLACK see **Pollachius pollachius**
POLLAN see **Coregonus albula**
POLLOCK see **Pollachius virens**
POLLOCK, WALLEYE see **Theragra chalcogramma**

Polycentropsis Nandidae
abbreviata AFRICAN LEAFFISH
8 cm. (3 in.)
A species native to the rivers of W. Africa, the Lagos, Niger, and Ogowe included, but not the Congo.

It is very deep-bodied and compressed, with a large head and particularly long snout and large jaws. The spiny dorsal and anal fins are high and well developed, the soft fins and tail being small. Its coloration is dark, usually a blend of greens and browns, running into more or less distinct bars across the body. Its colouring and shape lead to it being well concealed amongst vegetation.

Its breeding habits are interesting. It builds a bubble-nest, usually just beneath the floating leaves at the surface. The female deposits her eggs amongst the bubbles, in a belly-upward posture, one at a time, and the male cares for the brood, keeping the nest together and the eggs in place. After they hatch he shepherds the young into a depression in the river bed. The brood size rarely exceeds 100. **353**

Polycentrus   Nandidae
schomburgkii SCHOMBURGK'S LEAFFISH
10 cm. (4 in.)
Found in the freshwaters of ne. S. America including the Guianas and Trinidad. In the latter it is usually known as king cascarob, or black cascarob, and it is very abundant in streams, dams, and pools.

Physically it is similar to the other members of the family, being laterally compressed, with numerous dorsal and anal spines. Its colouring is very variable, often pale grey but darkening to black or deep brown when excited. Silvery spots on the back and sides, and 3 dark stripes, usually with yellow edges radiating from the sides.

It received its name to commemorate its discoverer, the explorer of Guyana, R. Schomburgk.

Polydactylus   Polynemidae
approximans BLUE BOBO 35·6 cm. (14 in.)
Found in the e. Pacific from Monterey Bay to Peru, although not regularly common in the extreme N. of this range. The adult fish are found in shallow inshore water on sandy and muddy bottoms. It feeds mainly on crustaceans and occasionally fishes.

To the S. of its range it has some value as a commercial species, but in Californian waters its main use was as a bait fish for tuna lines, a use that has now largely died out. In body form it is much like the other threadfins except that it has a rather deep body and 6 free rays in each pectoral fin.

P. virginius BARBU 30 cm. (12 in.)
A moderately common species in the tropical w. Atlantic, it is found from New Jersey to Uruguay. Common throughout the W. Indies.

It is usually found on sandy flats, occasionally on muddy bottoms close to reefs; it also enters estuaries. In general it is grey-brown above, silvery on the sides and below; the edges of the ventral fins are white. In common with other members of the family, its lower, anterior pectoral fin rays are long, thin, and separated from one another.

Polymetme   Gonostomatidae
corythaeola c. 25 cm. (10 in.)
This bristle-mouth is widely distributed in the warmer Atlantic from off Portugal to the Gulf of Guinea, and from Florida to n. S. America, as well as in the n. Indian Ocean. It is most common between 300–500 m. (164–273 fathoms), although it has been taken at depths

of 740 m. (404 fathoms). It has mostly been found close to the sea bed, and does not seem to join in the vertical night-time migration so common in the deep sea. It is believed to eat fishes.

It possesses a small adipose fin (which its close relative *Yarrella* lacks). It also has on each side a double series of large conspicuous light organs on the belly, and a single series along the tail. Its head and belly are dull black, but its sides are faintly silvery.

Polymixia   Polymixiidae
japonica see under **P. nobilis**
nobilis STOUT BEARDFISH, BARBUDO
25 cm. (10 in.)
First described from deep water off Madeira in the e. Atlantic, this fish has been found subsequently from Newfoundland to Cuba and St Helena in the Atlantic, off Natal, Mauritius, and the Andaman Islands. A related, perhaps identical form has been described as *P. japonica* from the Sea of Japan.

It is probably widely distributed in all the tropical oceans at depths of from 183–640 m. (100–350 fathoms). Its long chin barbels suggest that it may be a near bottom dweller, but most of its relatives are mid-water fishes.

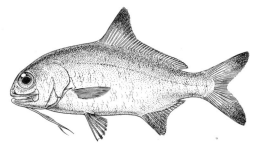

It is immediately distinguished by its rather deep fully-scaled body, by the long barbels under the chin, and its large eyes. Its coloration is variable, a soft violet brown on the back, the sides tinted with golden green, and reddish on the head. The tips of the tail fin, and the dorsal are distinctly black.

POLYMIXIIDAE
A small family of deep-water fishes distributed widely in the Atlantic Ocean, the N. Pacific, and parts of the Indian Ocean. Several species have been described, but it is probable that only one, or at the most 2, forms occur.

Its members are rather deep-bodied, with large eyes, and a pair of long, fleshy barbels beneath the chin. The body and most of the head is fully scaled, and both the dorsal and anal fins have stout spines and branched rays. See **Polymixia.**

POLYNEMIDAE
A group of marine fishes found in tropical seas around the world. They are usually found in inshore waters, and some species enter estuaries freely.

The threadfins are distinguished by their pectoral fins which are divided into 2 parts, the lower, anterior section comprising elongate rays. In the young they may be as long as the body, they become comparatively shorter with age. All the species have a prominent pointed snout, large, laterally-placed eyes, and ventral mouth. They are carnivorous and detect their prey at least partly by the sensory feelers of the lower pectoral rays.

Many of the threadfins are valuable food fishes in tropical waters. Although most species are rather small, one Indian form attains a length of nearly 2 m. (6½ ft). See **Eleutheronema, Polydactylus, Polynemus.**

Polynemus   Polynemidae
indicus BASTARD MULLET, DARA
1·2 m. (4 ft)
A threadfin which is found in the Indian Ocean and w. Pacific. It ranges from the E. African coast, around India, the E. Indies, and n. Australia. It is found mainly in inshore waters, usually in depths of less than 50 m. (27 fathoms), although occasionally found down to 70 m. (38 fathoms). It is found in river mouths but does not enter estuaries.

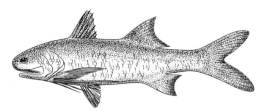

Like other threadfins it is carnivorous, feeding when young on planktonic organisms, but as it grows, eating first crustaceans and then fishes in considerable quantities.

It is one of the larger species of threadfin and especially in Indian waters is a valuable commercial species. It is captured both by trawling in offshore waters and by bottom-fishing gill-nets closer inshore.

It is distinguished by the extreme length of the tail fin lobes, by having only 5 free pectoral filaments which are rather long and reach to the anal fin origin. Its back is purplish and dark, the belly yellowish; the edges of the fins are dark.

Polyodon   Polyodontidae
spathula PADDLEFISH 2 m. (6½ ft)
The paddlefish has been described as a living plankton-net; it sweeps through the water with its lower jaw dropped down and the sides of the head swung outwards to form a giant funnel. Any planktonic organisms such as small crustaceans in the water are swept into its mouth and filtered out on its long dense gill rakers.

This species lived in the whole Mississippi system from N. Dakota to New York, and down to S. Carolina, but dams in the rivers, pollution, and over-fishing have restricted its range greatly in recent years. It was for a while heavily-exploited both for its flesh and for the sake of its roe, which although sometimes sold as caviar were also mixed with sturgeon eggs.

The paddlefish is found in the deeper waters of the Mississippi system. It breeds in the most turbulent regions of the river on stony or sandy bottoms in spring. The larva lacks the adult's prolonged snout, having merely a lump on its nose with minute barbels, at a length of 17 mm. ($\frac{3}{4}$ in.), but by the time it is 35 mm. ($1\frac{1}{2}$ in.) long it has grown a recognizable beak. By the time it is adult the snout occupies one third of its total length, and is a distinctive paddle shape, broader towards the tip than at the base. **16**

POLYODONTIDAE

A small family of archaic, sturgeon-like fishes which are known from only 2 living representatives, *Polyodon* in N. America, and *Psephurus* in China. Both are freshwater fishes, both have a typically sturgeon-like body, but have a very long snout. Their skins are smooth and they do not have bony plates on the sides as do true sturgeons, although both have ganoid scales on the tail.

Paddlefishes are known from the Eocene and Upper Cretaceous deposits of N. America. See **Polyodon, Psephurus.**

Polyprion Serranidae
americanus STONE BASS, WRECKFISH
2 m. ($6\frac{1}{2}$ ft)
Widely distributed in the Atlantic, mostly in tropical waters but occasionally drifting into the ne. Atlantic in summer-time. This is one of the few sea perches which is not confined to shallow inshore water.

Young specimens have a habit of closely following drift-wood, wreckage, or patches of algae floating at the surface. Occasionally they have been reported inside crates which they have entered when small but soon become too large to escape through the apertures. Large specimens are more normally free-living but very little is known about their biology. When fully grown they may weigh as much as 45 kg. (100 lb.).

The young and adults' feeding habits are little known. Probably they are fish-eating predators, stalking their prey in the shadow cast by their special flotsam which often serves as a focus for small fishes to collect around.

The wreckfish is distinguished by its massive heavy body, single long dorsal fin, pointed head, and generally spiny head. It is dull brown above, with yellowish sides.

POLYPTERIDAE

A small family of African freshwater fishes the members of which are divided into 2 genera. All are rather elongate, almost snake-like, and covered with an armour of hard, shiny, rectangular, ganoid scales. Their pectoral fins are fan-like, and have a fleshy stalk, while the dorsal fin is composed of a number of small fins, each containing one flattened stiff ray and a membrane. They have numerous resemblances to the primitive fishes now known only as fossils, amongst these is the presence of a swimbladder modified as an accessory breathing organ or lung. The swimbladder is double chambered, the right sac the larger; they unite and have a common entrance to the oesophagus. The polypterids rely to a great extent on their 'lungs' for oxygen. See **Calamoichthys, Polypterus.**

Polypterus Polypteridae
bichir NILE BICHIR 70 cm. (28 in.)
The Nile bichir is found, as its name suggests in the Nile, as well as Lakes Rudolf and Chad.

Like the other members of the family it mostly haunts the heavily weeded margins of lakes and rivers, and, as an adult, is predatory, feeding on fishes, and less often amphibians. It breeds during the rainy season, July to September, when the males develop a much enlarged anal fin. The larva has a special gland on the top of its head which secretes an adhesive mucus, presumably thus fastening it temporarily during later development to the underside of waterweeds. The larva also has an external gill each side of the head, and looks very similar to a newt tadpole.

The Nile bichir shares the characters of its family, heavy, ganoid scales, and a series of separate dorsal finlets. The polypterids have small but distinct pelvic fins. It has a higher number (14–18) dorsal finlets than most species, and the tip of the lower jaw projects. It is olive-green, fading to yellow on the belly. Young fish have a series of vertical bars and 2 lengthwise stripes.

P. delhezi 36 cm. (14 in.)
A polypterid found in the Upper and Middle Congo system, which is distinguished by its number of dorsal finlets (10–11) although these are typical in their shape. It is a yellowish brown with a series of prominent dark crossbars fading to irregular dark spots on the sides. The sides are yellowish, the underside white.

This is one of the more attractively marked members of the family and it is often kept in large aquaria. It tends to be pugnacious, however. In its native haunts it is not especially fished for although its flesh is quite edible. **17**

P. senegalus BICHIR 42 cm. ($16\frac{1}{2}$ in.)
The bichir (several species in the genus *Polypterus* share this name) possesses the typical features of the family, an elongate body, heavy ganoid scales, and a series of 8–11 separate fins along the back, each composed of a single slender spine and several rays supporting the fin membrane. It is a uniform olive-grey, although the young fish are said to be conspicuously marked with dark lengthwise stripes.

This species is found in some of the African Great Lakes (Albert, Rudolf, and Chad) and in their river systems, especially parts of the Victoria Nile and the Albert Nile, as well as the Senegal, Gambia, and Niger systems. In these areas it lives in the weedy margins of rivers and lakes, particularly where the vegetation is emergent. It feeds on small fish and frogs, and spawns during the rainy season, July to September, but little is known about its breeding biology. The larva has a single external gill each side of the head.

Pomacanthus Chaetodontidae
arcuatus GREY ANGELFISH 61 cm. (2 ft)
A w. Atlantic species found from the vicinity of New England to se. Brazil including the Gulf of Mexico and the Caribbean. It has been introduced to Bermuda and is common in much of the W. Indies and elsewhere in its range.

It is a deep-bodied fish, the back being steeply curved, while the lower front is equally steep. In the adult the front rays of both dorsal and anal fin are very elongate, but the tail fin is square cut.

The young fish are black with curved yellow bars across the head and body, while the tail fin is yellow with a rectangular mark in its centre. This juvenile colouring persists faintly

after the adult coloration has been attained. **342**

P. filamentosus 30 cm. (12 in.)
Said to be found in the w. Indian Ocean, this species was first described by the late Professor J. L. B. Smith, from Tekomazi Island (40° 40′E. 10°40′ S.), and many were seen about reefs among the islands in the n. parts of Mozambique. It was later reported from the Seychelles. It is clearly distinguished from the members of the group by the greatly elongated fin rays in the anal fin of adults.

P. imperator EMPEROR ANGELFISH
38 cm. (15 in.)
One of the most strikingly coloured angelfishes in the tropical Indo-Pacific. It is widely distributed, being found from the Red Sea, the E. African coast S. to Delagoa Bay, across the Indian Ocean, the E. Indies, n. Australia, Micronesia, Polynesia, and the Philippines. It is very abundant on reefs and around rocky areas, and is in places fished for as its flesh is said to be edible.

As an adult its colouring is very distinctive, being golden brown with many yellow lines running along its length, those above curving upwards. A large black patch surrounds the pectoral base and runs down to the pelvic fins, and on the head a deep green or brownish patch, bordered with blue.

The young fishes are strikingly different being basically black with alternating bluish and white stripes on the head and body. A small whitish circle on the tail. The changes in coloration with growth are shown in plates **343, 344, 345**

P. maculosus 21 cm. (8 in.)
A native of the Red Sea from whence it was first described by the Danish explorer Pehr Forsskål in 1775. It has also been reported from Zanzibar. By some authors this name has been regarded as a synonym of *Euxiphipops asfur,* but others have considered it to be distinct.

It is distinguished by the dull coloured body in adults and the scattered curved spots on the nape. A pale curved bar on the sides is entirely posterior to the level of the anal spines. Both dorsal and anal fin are rounded. In younger fish the light mid-lateral bar is well developed, while the very young are dark with 12 narrow blue cross streaks. **346, 347**

P. paru FRENCH ANGELFISH 41 cm. (16 in.)
An Atlantic species found from W. Africa, and the Cape Verde Islands in the E., and in the W. from Florida and the Bahamas to s. Brazil. It has been introduced to Bermuda.

In body form typical of the angelfishes, with a large curved spine on the lower edge of the preoperculum. It is deep-bodied, with long streamers on the second dorsal and anal fins when adult. The tail fin is convexly curved. In colouring it is very dark but the scales, from the pectoral fins back, have a golden yellow edge; the chin is light in colour and the base of the pectoral fin has a golden bar. Young fish are dark with vertical, curved yellow bars across the head and body. The tail fin is yellow with a large rounded dark central mark.

Young specimens are known as cleaners of other fishes, picking at infected wounds and parasites, and occupying locally dominant rocky prominences to which larger fish of varying species repair for cleaning. **348**

P. semicirculatus ZEBRA ANGELFISH
38 cm. (15 in.)

A widely distributed fish in the tropical Indo-Pacific, which ranges from the Red Sea and E. African coast, around India, and the E. Indies, to Australia and the w. Pacific. It is a common inhabitant of coral reefs in these areas.

It is well known for the striking colour changes through which the young pass. Juveniles at about 10 cm. (4 in.) are very dark blue or black with the fin edges deep blue, and the body striped vertically with distinct light bands alternately wide and narrow. Larger specimens are yellowish on the body, with the head a deep blue, and blue flecks on the back and sides. The fins are dark greyish blue with light flecks. **349**

POMACENTRIDAE

A large family of mainly small, often colourful marine fishes found worldwide in the tropics and temperate oceans. They are rather deep-bodied fishes with a moderate spiny dorsal and anal fin joined but anterior to the soft-rayed fins, the body scales extend onto the fin bases, and the lateral line is interrupted. They are also distinguished by having a single nostril each side of the head.

The damselfishes are mainly inshore, shallow-water species, found on reefs, on rocky grounds, while a few live in sea grass beds. Few have any economic importance but some species are locally very abundant and dominate the fish community in their area. They show very interesting behavioural adaptations in exploiting the varied habitats in which they live. They lay eggs in clusters on a rock face or crevice, which are usually guarded by the male.

Some species, the anemone fishes, have adopted a commensal relationship with large sea anemones, protected from the latter's stinging cells by their own mucus. Others apparently have less well developed relationships with stinging corals during their juvenile life. See **Abudefduf, Amphiprion, Chromis, Dascyllus, Eupomacentrus, Microspathodon, Pomacentrus.**

Pomacentrus Pomacentridae
pulcherrimus 9 cm. (3½ in.)
An inhabitant of the w. Indian Ocean; it is found from Bazaruto n. along the E. African coast and around the islands to and including the Seychelles. It is, however, nowhere abundant but gathers in small shoals in certain localities.

Its coloration is arresting being basically blue and yellow, but the proportion and tones of each vary. **390**

POMADASYIDAE

A large family of marine fishes found in tropical regions of all the oceans, a few extending to warm temperate zones. They are related to the snappers (Lutjanidae) but differ in having weaker dentition, no large canine-like teeth in the front of the jaws, and certain skeletal features of the head. Most are moderately slender-bodied fish with a high spiny dorsal fin continuous with the rayed dorsal fin.

They are known as grunts, from the very audible noises made both in and out of the water. They generate these noises by grinding their pharyngeal teeth together, the sound being amplified by the swim bladder.

Some grunts in the w. Atlantic display by facing one another and with wide open mouths pushing one another, an act often referred to as kissing, but its significance to the fishes is not really understood.

Grunts are essentially shallow-water fishes, abundant in inshore waters and on coral reefs, sometimes hundreds forming a single loose school. They are excellent food and sporting fishes. Recent research by Professor Carl L. Hubbs and Dr W. I. Follett has shown that the family name Haemulidae has priority and they recommend its use. See **Anisotremus, Gaterin, Haemulon, Plectorhynchus, Pomadasys.**

Pomadasys Pomadasyidae
hasta SILVER GRUNTER, SPOTTED JAVELIN FISH, GRUNTER BREAM
61 cm. (2 ft)
A very widely distributed Indo-Pacific species, found from the Sea of Japan, the S. China coast, the E. Indies, n. Australia, India to the Red Sea and E. Africa. As well as being found in coastal waters, both on reefs and over sandy bottoms, it enters estuaries and is found in almost fresh water. Throughout its range where it is common it is a valuable food fish.

Its common names in s. Africa (silver grunter) and Queensland (grunter bream) refer to the grunting noises made when it is caught which are presumably made underwater also.

It is a moderately deep-bodied species with strong, long spines in the dorsal fin, and an exceptionally strong second anal spine. It is coloured olive above, silvery on the sides, but each scale has a dusky spot to produce oblique lines. The dorsal fins have 3 rows of dusky spots; the ventral fins are yellowish.

POMATOMIDAE

A family containing the single species, the bluefish *Pomatomus saltatrix*. It is a rather sturdily-built, long-bodied fish with a single, low spiny dorsal fin in front of a much longer separate second dorsal. The tail is deeply forked, the head and body fully scaled, and the jaws large with strong teeth.

It is widely distributed around the world in tropical waters with the exception of the e. Pacific. See **Pomatomus.**

Pomatomus Pomatomidae
saltatrix BLUEFISH, TAILOR, ELFT
1·2 m. (4 ft)
A very distinctive fish as much for its habits as its shape and colouring, the latter blue-green above, paler below, has given it its common name. It is a widely distributed marine fish found in tropical and warm-temperate seas with the exception of the e. Pacific. In the Atlantic it is found regularly from Cape Cod to Argentina, and from Portugal to S. Africa. It is found almost everywhere in the Indian Ocean, and is well known off New Zealand and Australia.

It is a coastal fish, found offshore, in the open ocean, and least commonly, close inshore. It travels in schools which sometimes contain thousands of fishes. An active predator, the bluefish feeds on a wide range of smaller forage fishes, attacking in shoals and killing many more fish than it ever eats. To some extent it is migratory with the shoals of anchovies, sardines, shads, and mullet on which it feeds.

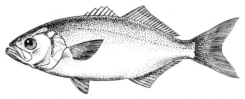

Throughout its range it is a valuable food fish. Although the flesh quickly becomes soft after capture, very fresh or smoked it is of fine flavour. It is also a prime sporting fish, ready to take a bait and fighting well once hooked. Large specimens have been reported to weigh 12·3 kg. (27 lb.); a more usual weight being around 4·5 kg. (10 lb.). Bluefish of up to 22·7 kg. (50 lb.) were reported off the Atlantic coast of N. America and the W. coast of S. Africa in the late nineteenth century before the stocks were exploited on a large scale. A juvenile is illustrated.

Pomatoschistus Gobiidae
pictus PAINTED GOBY 5 cm. (2 in.)
A European species found in the E. Atlantic from the English Channel and the Bay of Biscay, to the Norwegian coast (and apparently in the Adriatic Sea). It is a small fish, common in shallow water from low intertidal situations to 50 m. (27 fathoms) on gravelly grounds. Occasionally captured in intertidal pools on rocky shores where coarse sand forms the bottom. It is often abundant in eel grass beds.

It breeds in spring and summer; the eggs are laid in the cavity of empty bivalve shells, where they are guarded by the male. Particularly during the breeding season, the male's colours are heightened. **434**

POMFRET, ATLANTIC see **Brama brama**
POMMY SKATE see under **Raja whitleyi**

Pomoxis Centrarchidae
annularis WHITE CRAPPIE 51 cm. (20 in.)
Naturally distributed from the Great Lakes S. to the Gulf of Mexico and from Kansas to N. Carolina, and the se. States. It has been introduced to several states outside this range, such as Montana. It is typically found in turbid lakes, rivers, and their backwaters; as a consequence it is often released into small man-made ponds and reservoirs.

Its food consists mainly of small crustaceans but with growth it eats fishes increasingly. It spawns in shallow water, near to the bank, at depths of 1–2½ m. (3–8 ft). The male excavates the nest, and guards it with eggs or young in it. It is not a particularly large sunfish, few exceed 30 cm. (12 in.) in length, although the maximum weight attained is about 2·3 kg. (5 lb.). The small waters in which it lives frequently results in overcrowding, most of the population being stunted as a result.

This fish is distinguished particularly by its jutting lower jaw and large mouth.

The white crappie is one of the sporting fishes of the family, and its popularity is the reason for its man-assisted spread in the U.S. **282**

POMPADOURFISH see **Symphysodon aequifasciata**
POMPANO see Carangidae, Stromateidae
POMPANO,
 AFRICAN see **Alectis crinitus**
 PACIFIC see **Peprilus simillimus**

POMPANO DOLPHINFISH see **Coryphaena equisetis**

POND
  LOACH see **Misgurnus fossilis**
  SMELT see **Hypomesus olidus**
PONYFISH, PIG-NOSED see **Secutor ruconius**
POPE see **Gymnocephalus cernua**
PORBEAGLE see **Lamna nasus**
PORCUPINEFISH see Diodontidae
PORCUPINEFISH see **Diodon hystrix, Lophodiodon calori**
PORGY see Sparidae
PORGY, JOLTHEAD see **Calamus bajonado**

Porichthys Batrachoididae
  notatus PLAINFIN MIDSHIPMAN
38 cm. (15 in.)
Found widely along the Pacific coast of America from Sitka, Alaska to the Gulf of California. It is found exclusively on muddy bottoms into which it burrows in daytime; it hunts actively at night. It is found from the shore line (in the N. of its range) down to 300 m. (164 fathoms). It feeds on small crustaceans and fishes.

Its scaleless body is a purplish bronze above, yellowish below, with numerous rows of light organs on the underside. The head is broad and flattened, the eyes almost dorsal; it has a sharp spine on the upper gill cover each side.

The midshipman uses its light organs during courtship and will occasionally flash its lights when caught. They spawn on the sea bed, usually in crevices or on hard surfaces; the eggs are laid in a single layer and guarded by the male.

P. porosissimus ATLANTIC MIDSHIPMAN
30 cm. (12 in.)
Widely distributed on the American Atlantic coast, from Virginia and S. Carolina to Argentina, including the Gulf of Mexico and the Caribbean. It is found in inshore continental waters on sand or mud bottoms, occasionally amongst turtle grass.

In body form it is much like other members of the group, its head is broad and rather flattened, but its body is rather slimmer and less depressed. The most notable features are the rows of numerous, small light organs under the body. These are arranged in a definite pattern characteristic of the species. Another characteristic is its sound producing ability; choruses of midshipmen produce a variety of growls, grunts, and occasional whistle blasts. This is a natural phenomenon of the spawning season and other occasions; the fish also makes distinct grunts when captured.

PORKY see **Stephanolepis auratus, Stephanolepis cirrhifer**

Poromitra Melamphaidae
  crassiceps CRESTED BIGSCALE
15 cm. (6 in.)
Found in the e. Pacific from Alaska to mid-Chile offshore in deep water. It ranges in depth from 550 m. (300 fathoms) to 1830 m. (1000 fathoms), coming near the surface at night and

sinking to the depths in daylight. It frequents the open water of the deep-sea, and is not found on the bottom.

It is a deep-bodied fish with a large head and small eyes, and a single dorsal fin about the middle of the body. The skin is entirely black, the body covered with large thin paper-like scales which are extremely fragile. The head bones protrude through the skin and are thin and ridge-like with deep depressions under the skin between them.

PORT JACKSON SHARK see **Heterodontus philippi**
PORT-AND-STARBOARD-LIGHT FISH see **Cleidopus gloriamaris**
PORTUGUESE SHARK see **Centroscymnus coelolepis**

Potamotrygon Potamotrygonidae
  laticeps 61 cm. (2 ft)
One of the freshwater stingrays found in S. America which is distinguished by the internal skeletal feature of having a long bony process extending forwards from the anterior bone of the pelvic girdle. In most other respects it resembles the marine stingrays. This species has been found in Brazilian rivers.

Its disc is rounded but narrowing slightly posteriorly. The mouth is moderate in size, wholly ventral with numerous small black teeth. The tail has numerous rough spines in addition to the large 'sting'.

This species is sometimes placed in the genus *Disceus*. **10**

P. magdalenae RIVER RAY 30 cm. (12 in.) wide
This stingray is found in the rivers of n. S. America, especially in the Rio Magdalena of Colombia, and along the Venezuelan coastal plain. It occurs abundantly in rivers, lakes, and ponds of the Maracaibo Basin, partially burying itself on muddy or sandy bottoms.

It has an almost circular disc although the tip of the snout has a small button-like projection, the tail is longer than the disc although older specimens have usually lost the tip of their tails. The back is covered with minute spines, some larger ones along the mid-dorsal line, and the tail spine is relatively long and barbed on both sides. It is dark brown, often speckled with darker spots, and lighter blotches. Underneath it is white.

This ray is much dreaded by local fishermen, for if stepped upon in the water it throws its tail up over its back and jabs its spine with great force into the foot or leg of the unfortunate person. Serious wounds, severe pain, secondary infections, and occasionally death results from such a stab.

P. motoro RIVER RAY 30 cm. (12 in.) wide
A river ray found in the river system of the Paraguay, S. America, which apparently contains a number of other closely related species. It has an almost circular disc, with a thickset, tapering tail. Like its relatives it has a large, venom-laden spine in the tail, well clear of the body disc.

It lives partially buried in the sand, or mud of the shallows and backwaters of the river and its tributaries. It is ovoviviparous, the young rays being retained within the mother's body and nourished by a secretion from the uterine tissues. The breeding season starts in September or October and the young are born in

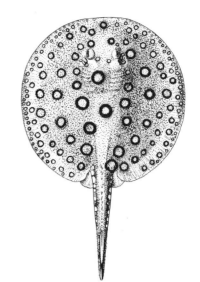

February, although the length of the gestation period varies with altitude and geographical area. **14**

POTAMOTRYGONIDAE
A small family of stingrays which is confined to the rivers and large lakes of central and n. S. America on the Atlantic and Caribbean watersheds, and rivers in W. Africa. They are purely freshwater inhabitants, many occurring over 1600 km. (1000 miles) up river from the sea.

The family is distinguished by its rounded disc, its moderately long thickset tail (longer than the disc is wide). They have a long, serrated spine on the tail, well away from the disc, with a lengthwise groove filled with venom-producing tissue on its underside.

The river rays are relatively small, rarely more than 30 cm. (12 in.) in diameter. Despite this they are much dreaded by local fishermen because of the severe injury and agonizing pain they can inflict with their tail spines. See **Potamotrygon**.

POUCHED LAMPREY see **Geotria australis**
POUT, OCEAN see **Macrozoarces americanus**
POUTING see **Trisopterus luscus**
POWAN see **Coregonus lavaretus**

Pranesus Atherinidae
  ogilbyi COMMON HARDYHEAD
17 cm. (6¾ in.)
A very abundant fish in shallow water on sandy flats, in bays and in estuaries on the n. coasts of Australia, New Guinea, and the Pacific Islands.

It is a rather deep-bodied species with a relatively large head. In either respects it shares the characters of the family of 2 dorsal fins, the first composed of several thin spines. Coloration: pale green above, each scale dotted with black, white below, and a silvery band running from head to tail.

Premnas see under **Amphiprion biaculeatus**
PRETTY TETRA see **Hemigrammus pulcher**

PRIACANTHIDAE
A small family of mainly tropical and subtropical fishes. Some species are shallow-living circumtropical fishes, assisted in their spread

by a prolonged pelagic larval life. Others are deep-water fish.

In general, they are deep-bodied with large eyes and heavily spined fins. Most of the species are bright red in colour. All have the pelvic fins joined to the body by a flap of skin. The shallow-water species are all nocturnal in their activity.

Few big-eyes grow larger than 60 cm. (2 ft); some species are of limited commercial importance. See **Priacanthus.**

Priacanthus Priacanthidae
arenatus BIG-EYE, CATALUFA
41 cm. (16 in.)
A native of the tropical Atlantic Ocean and the w. Indian Ocean. It is known from both sides of the Atlantic; in the W. from New England and Bermuda to Argentina, in the E. from Madeira to St Helena. It also occurs off the s. African coast. It lives in moderately deep water, from 15 m. (8 fathoms) and below, and is usually found in small schools over reefs. It is a nocturnal feeder.

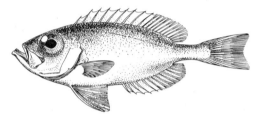

It is reddish overall, with the belly and sides slightly silver-tinted. The pelvic fins and the edges of the anal and tail fins are blackish.
P. hamrur SCAD, GOGGLE-EYE 41 cm. (16 in.)
Found in the central tropical Indian Ocean, and widely in the Pacific. It is common in the Red Sea, and on the E. African coast on reefs. It spends the daylight hours hiding in crevices or beneath overhangs, and only becomes really active at night. It lives in moderately deep water from 9–24 m. (5–13 fathoms).

Its coloration is red to purplish red, lighter below, the fins usually dusky, especially the pelvic fins which are mostly dark in colour.

Locally it is used as a food fish, as in Hawaii where it is known as alalaua. **283**

PRICKLEBACK, ROCK see **Xiphister mucosus**
PRICKLY
  LEATHER-JACKET see **Chaetoderma**
    pencilligera
  SCULPIN see **Cottus asper**

Prionace Carcharhinidae
glauca BLUE SHARK or WHALER
3·8 m. (12½ ft)
The blue shark is worldwide in its distribution, being found at the surface of the open sea in all tropical and sub-tropical regions and in temperate seas during the summer time. Summer time sees this shark abundant in the waters of New England and also on the W. coasts of the British Isles. Although attacks by it on man have not been proven, this is probably more on account of its preference for the open ocean (where swimmers are not usually encountered) than for any gentleness of disposition. Large blue sharks should be treated with great caution.

It is a graceful, slim shark, with long, rather pointed pectoral fins; brilliant indigo blue

above, its belly is by contrast snow-white in colour. Very often blue sharks can be seen swimming lazily at the sea's surface but they are powerful and active swimmers when roused by food. This consists of a wide range of schooling fishes, and squids, mostly those found near the surface. It scavenges occasionally, and being attracted by the flensing of whales at sea was a familiar sight to the warm-water whalers. It is well thought of as a sporting fish; the w. English Channel particularly attracts large numbers of sea anglers in search of this shark.

Prionodraco Bathydraconidae
evansii DEEP DRAGONFISH 16 cm. (6½ in.)
Widely distributed around the Antarctic Continent in moderate depths of 200–400 m. (109–219 fathoms). It is a long, very slender fish, with long many-rayed dorsal and anal fins, both slightly higher in front than to the rear. The lower jaw projects somewhat beyond the upper. The body is covered with 4 series of V-shaped plates, each with a sharp spine pointing backwards.

It is light brown, spotted in front with bars towards the tail; a round black spot on the front rays of the dorsal fin.

This fish was named for Edgar Evans, one of Scott's ill-fated companions to the S. Pole.

Prionotus Triglidae
carolinus NORTHERN SEA ROBIN
41 cm. (16 in.)
An abundant fish along the e. coast of N. and Central America; found from the Bay of Fundy to Venezuela. It is mainly a bottom-living fish (although occasionally specimens are captured near the surface) which lives on smooth hard grounds in depths of 9–73 m. (5–40 fathoms).

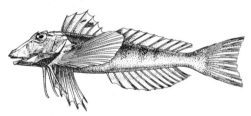

It feeds on a wide range of crustaceans, molluscs, worms, and small fishes. Spawning takes place from June to August, when the sea robin is noisier than at any other time, drumming loudly by vibrating its very large swimbladder.

It is usually greyish or reddish brown above with 5 dusky saddles across the back. Ventrally it is yellowish white. There is a small spot between the spines on the first dorsal fin.

Although occasional specimens are caught by trawlers and anglers, it is too small to be of interest either as a commercial or sporting fish.

Pristella Characidae
riddlei X-RAY FISH, WATER GOLDFINCH
4·5 cm. (1¾ in.)
This charming little characin is found in the lower regions of the River Amazon, in Guyana, and ne. S. America generally. It is reputed to

live as far down-river as to reach brackish water.

Its body is almost transparent, but in certain lights will reflect silvery, although the abdominal cavity is encased in silvery-white. Distinct dark spots on the shoulder and the middle rays of the dorsal and anal fins, which are otherwise tipped with very distinct white. The tail fin is reddish.

The sexes can be distinguished with some success. The male is generally slimmer than the female, and if viewed against the light the opaque body cavity tapers to point posteriorly. The female has a rounded end to the body cavity. **84**

PRISTIDAE
The sawfishes are familiar fish if only because the saw was a favourite curio or memento of a voyage in the tropics. The saw is formed by the enormously elongate snout equipped with large, blunt teeth along either side. These teeth are all of equal size (although they decrease in length towards the head). In this they differ from the saw sharks (Pristiophoridae) which have alternate small and larger teeth as well as long barbels under the snout. The sawfishes are rays, lacking such barbels and with their gill openings on the underside, not laterally placed.

Sawfishes are common in all tropical seas. They also penetrate rivers and can be found living in freshwater such as Lake Nicaragua in Central America. They are frequently very common in the mouths of large estuaries and although not dangerous intentionally, cause serious problems to local fishermen. See **Pristis.**

PRISTIOPHORIDAE
A family of small shark-like fishes, usually known as saw sharks, which have a long snout with sharply-pointed, uneven teeth along its edges. They differ from the sawfishes (Pristidae) in a number of ways notably in the possession of long barbels on the underside of the snout. Fossil forms are known from the Cretaceous period, but few representatives exist today. They are confined to the Indo-Pacific. See **Pliotrema, Pristiophorus.**

Pristiophorus Pristiophoridae
cirratus COMMON SAW SHARK 1·2 m. (4 ft)
This saw shark, which was the first of these curious sharks to be described, as early as 1794, is widely distributed in the s. Indo-Pacific. It

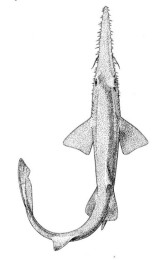

has been recorded off S. Africa but is common off the s. Australian States. The saw shark is a sluggish species which roots around in the bottom mud with its saw, detecting edible items by means of the very sensitive barbels on the snout. It eats a certain amount of bottom-living fishes, but its food mostly consists of invertebrates.

Its slender body and large dorsal fins show that it is more closely related to the sharks than any other fish group. The gill openings are at the side of the head, and it has no anal fin. The teeth in the saw alternate large and small. It is not regarded as dangerous to man but its saw can inflict nasty injuries if a live specimen is handled carelessly. The young are born well developed, but the teeth on the saw are folded within the skin until after birth.

In Australian waters this shark is commercially exploited, its flesh is of an excellent quality and is sold as fish fillets or under the name 'flake'.

P. nudipinnis SOUTHERN SAW SHARK
1·2 m. (4 ft)
A s. Australian species found in shallow water along the coasts of S. Australia, Victoria, s. W. Australia and Tasmania. It is usually captured by trawlers in depths of 37–165 m. (20–90 fathoms), although young specimens are frequently taken in much shallower water. It is

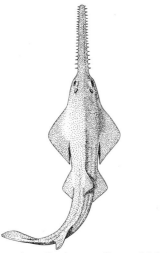

less common than *P. cirratus*, from which it is distinguished by the dorsal and pectoral fins being free of dermal denticles, and by the fewer rows of teeth in the upper jaw.

This saw shark has the prolonged snout of its family armed with numerous sharp teeth, alternately long and short. Like other members of the genus *Pristiophorus* it has 5 separate gill slits.

It is essentially a bottom-living fish which stirs up the sea bed with its toothed snout, doubtless maiming numerous hidden fishes with its sharp teeth. Food is detected by the elongate barbels under the snout. It is viviparous.

Pristis   Pristidae
  microdon SMALL-TOOTHED SAWFISH
4·6 m. (15 ft)
The small-toothed sawfish occurs in both the Atlantic and Indian oceans favouring shallow inshore tropical waters and estuaries. The Atlantic form is often referred to as *P. perotteti*. The small-toothed sawfish is fairly common in freshwater; Lake Nicaragua holds a population, thought to be non-migratory, and it is

also found in the River Zambezi although believed to come and go between the sea and the river fairly regularly. They penetrate at least 322 km. (200 miles) upstream into completely freshwater. Unidentified sawfishes, possibly this species, have been found in the Walsh River of N. Queensland at least 241 km. (150 miles) from the sea.

The small-toothed sawfish is distinguished from other species by its relatively few, widely-spaced saw teeth (only 17–21 pairs).

Like other sawfishes this is a bottom-living fish which feeds on small benthic organisms as well as fishes which it kills with its toothed snout.

P. pectinata GREATER OR SMALL-TOOTH SAWFISH 7·7 m. (25 ft)
This is the largest of the sawfishes, and it is found in all tropical oceans. It is perhaps best known from the w. Atlantic (from New York, where it is rare, to Brazil, including the Gulf of Mexico, and the Caribbean), and off the African E. coast. There is some doubt as to the size that this species attains, 7·6 m. (25 ft) appears to be a maximum length measured, but sawfish, probably this species, of 10·7 m. (35 ft) have been reported. Specimens of more than 5000 lb. (2268 kg.) in weight have been recorded.

Apart from its large size, this sawfish is distinguished by the large number, 24–32 pairs of teeth along its saw. It lacks a definite lower lobe in its tail, and its first dorsal fin is above the pelvic fins. In general terms its body is shark-like, except for the long saw-snout, the gill openings under the body, and the enlarged pectoral fins.

Sawfishes typically frequent shallow water, sometimes so shallow that their dorsal fins break the surface. They live on the bottom, rooting in the mud and sand with their saws for the small creatures, mostly invertebrates, that form their food. It is claimed that the sawfish feeds on shoaling fishes which it attacks indiscriminately by lashing its saw through the shoal, impaling and disabling the prey which are eaten later. This may be so, but the more usual use for the saw appears to be for stirring up the soft sea bed to disturb buried food organisms. This habit causes problems at times for undersea cables, especially in tropical estuaries, such as the Amazon where sawfish are abundant, for their teeth are often found embedded in the insulation, frequently being driven in with enough force to penetrate to the cable.

Although it has little commercial value and is not deliberately fished for it is occasionally caught in nets to which it does great damage. It is also feared by the fishermen, especially along the Indian coasts, for its slashing saw when captured can inflict the most fearful injuries.

P. perotteti see **P. microdon**
P. pristis SAWFISH 4·6 m. (15 ft)
This was the first sawfish to be named when the Swedish naturalist Linnaeus called it *Squalus pristis*, under the impression that it was a type of shark (*Squalus*). The sawfishes are, however, more nearly allied to the rays than the sharks.

It is found in the e. Atlantic, from Portugal to Angola on the African coast, and occasionally in the w. Mediterranean. It can be distinguished by its typical sawfish shape, and by

the few teeth on its saw, from 16–20 pairs only. The first dorsal fin is directly above the pelvic fins. Like most sawfishes, it is dull brown, sometimes sandy, although underneath it is creamy white. It is a bottom-living species feeding on benthic organisms, and fishes.

Like other sawfishes it is ovoviviparous; the eggs are retained within the mother's body while developing and the young hatch out shortly before birth. The saw teeth of the young are soft and flexible and covered with a gristly membrane which prevents injury to the mother. Litters of up to 23 have been reported in some of the larger species.

Prochilodontidae see under Curimatidae

Prochilodus   Curimatidae
  platensis SÁBALO, CURIMBATÁ
51 cm. (20 in.)
The sábalo is found in the rivers of central S. America notably the Rio Paraná, the Rio Uruguay, and the Rio de la Plata, although it occurs in most rivers in this general area. It is often very abundant, and forms a great part of the commercial food fish of the area. It is a migratory fish which runs upstream to spawn at temperatures between 14 and 18°C., usually at night during the full moon. The males move upstream first to running water, and they are said to attract the females to the spawning beds by grunting noises. The eggs wash downstream after spawning.

They are captured in set nets and traps, and during their migration by making fish traps of rocks built out into the river which can be sealed off when the fish are inside.

The sábalo is a mud and plant eater. Its finely toothed lips, extremely long intestine, and strong-walled stomach all testify to a diet of this nature.

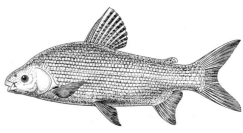

It is a deep-bodied fish, greeny grey on the back, silvery on the sides, with a yellowish tinge. The edges of the scales are dusky. Juveniles have dark bars on their sides, but these are lost with age.

Prognathodes   Chaetodontidae
  aculeatus LONGSNOUT BUTTERFLYFISH
9 cm. (3½ in.)
A native of the Caribbean from s. Florida and the Bahamas, s. through the W. Indies. It is a deep-water species, occasionally found on reefs in as little as 4·5 m. (2½ fathoms), but it only becomes common at a depth of 30 m. (16 fathoms) and extends down at least to 90 m. (49 fathoms) and more.

Its long snout is an adaptation to feeding on the small invertebrates living in the crevices corals, on the tentacles of tubeworms, and on the tubefeet and pedicellariae of sea urchins.

For long regarded as a rare fish mainly because it lived in deep water, now that its habitat is well known it is found to be common. It is even a popular pet fish for the marine aquarium. **350**

Promicrops lanceolatus see under
Phtheirichthys lineatus

Prosopium   Salmonidae
 cylindraceum ROUND WHITEFISH
51 cm. (20 in.)
The round whitefish is widely distributed in n. America, and the e. parts of the U.S.S.R. In America it is found from the Arctic Ocean drainages E. to Labrador along the Pacific coast rivers S. to n. British Columbia and across n. Canada to the Atlantic coast, New England and the Great Lakes with the exception of Lake Erie. It is one of the most widespread and abundant of the whitefishes, although its occurrence is 'patchy' in the SE. It is particularly found in streams and rivers, and when occurring in lakes, is usually confined to the inshore belt, and the mouths of tributary streams.

The round whitefish eats insect larvae and pupae, but has a considerable reputation as a feeder upon other fishes' eggs, particularly salmonids. It is even said to wait close to shoals of spawning shad in New England so that it can feed on their eggs.

It spawns in autumn along the shores of lakes and in streams where the current is moderate. Its eggs are shed indiscriminately over the gravel bed.

In Siberia this whitefish is of considerable economic importance and is fished for with traps at weirs and by gill netting. In the Great Lakes it was formerly fished in great numbers, and is still fished locally in Canada.

The small mouth, slender and rounded body of this whitefish is of distinguishing value, but precise identification depends on minute anatomical study.

Proterorhinus   Gobiidae
 marmoratus MOTTLED BLACK SEA
GOBY 11 cm. (4¼ in.)
Found in the Black Sea basin in brackish water and in the rivers running into this sea. It is found in the Danube as far as Austrian territory, as well as in the Soviet rivers D'neiper, Bug, and Don.

It is a distinctive species on account of its heavy head and anterior body, which gives the head profile a steep appearance. There is a pair of short thread-like barbels on the snout immediately above the upper lip. It is dull brown above with darker areas on the back and sides; the belly is light in colour. **433**

PROTOPTERIDAE
The family of the African lungfishes which are widely distributed in central tropical Africa in freshwater. With the S. American and Australian lungfishes (families Lepidosirenidae and Ceratodontidae) they form a group of literally 'living fossils' representing an order formerly abundant in the Devonian to Triassic periods.

Their common name refers to their most striking feature, the possession of an air-breathing organ which, unlike those of other fishes, really corresponds to the lungs of the higher vertebrates. In this family there is a pair of lungs which lie ventral to the gut and communicates with the oesophagus by a pneu-

matic tube. The lungfish is dependent on its lungs for survival although it also has normal, if poorly developed gills. Both in captivity, and in the wild, the fish needs to come to the surface to take a breath of air every half an hour or so.

The African lungfishes are also well-known for their ability to aestivate during the dry season, by burrowing deep into the mud forming a tube with a hollow at its end. Within this as the water drops the fish becomes inactive, curls up with its tail over its head, secretes a thick mucous cocoon around itself leaving only a small opening adjacent to the mouth. While the drought lasts the fish remains within the cocoon, protected from dessication by the mucous envelope, and breathing only by means of its lung. So efficient is its water conservation that fish in cocoons have been kept dry for 4 years and when flooded have emerged alive, if rather stiff and emaciated.

The African lunfishes mostly live in sluggish or stagnant water, often in swamps with low oxygen levels. They are always found in rather shallow water. They breed by laying their eggs in specially cleaned nests, which are guarded by the male. The young fish have external gills (and look remarkably like newt larvae or efts). Only 4 species are currently recognized.

Young specimens are often imported to Europe as aquarium fish, although when fully-grown they need very large aquaria! Throughout their range in Africa they are valued food fishes being caught both in nets or by spearing, and dug out of the mud while aestivating. See **Protopterus.**

Protopterus   Protopteridae
 aethiopicus LUNGFISH 2 m. (6½ ft)
Widely distributed in e. and central Africa, and occurring in the Nile, the Sudan, Lake Tanganyika, Katanga, Stanley Pool, the Victoria and Albert Niles, and lakes Victoria, Nabugabo, Edward, Albert, and George. Large fish live mainly in the shallow inshore regions of the lakes, and can be seen on a calm day coming to the surface regularly to breathe air, and diving after a short interval with a splash as its tail comes out of the water. As this species lives mainly in the permanent standing water of the lakes it rarely aestivates as the other members of the genus do. However, there is evidence that if it is trapped by receding water in the dry season it will burrow and survive in a cocoon in the usual way.

It breeds in a pit or hole cleared by the male. One or more female fish will lay eggs in the nest and then leave; the male guards the eggs for approximately 2 weeks to hatching and then the young fish for a further 5–6 weeks. The male both physically guards by chasing away other fishes, and will even attack a human intruder, and also aerates the eggs and young. By the time they leave the nest the young fish have well-developed external gills and are 3–4 cm. (1¼–1½ in.) long. Young fish, up to about 25 cm. (10 in.) in length can be found in the dense vegetation of inshore swamps and amongst papyrus roots. The young lose their external gills at about 15 cm. (6 in.) length.

This species is occasionally imported as an aquarium fish, but like the other lungfishes it is a rather dull, and lethargic pet! In Africa it is an important food fish locally (as in Lake George, Uganda). It is probably also of con-

siderable indirect importance as a predator on other fishes and by destroying fishes captured in gill nets.

Its food consists of various species of molluscs and crabs as well as fishes, amongst them cichlids (*Haplochromis*), and various catfishes (*Clarias, Synodontis*).

It is slaty-grey above, yellowish grey or even pink below, with numerous dark flecks over the back and fins, and dark lines where the sensory lateral line canals run.

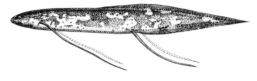

Its body shape is typical of the African lungfishes, rounded even thickset anteriorly, compressed at the tail. The pectoral and pelvic fins are long and filamentous. This species is distinguished by its relatively shorter head, and by having 35–41 pairs of ribs.

P. annectens LUNGFISH, MUDFISH
1 m. (3¼ ft)
A widely distributed African species found from Senegal and Nigeria, Lake Chad, and across to the Zambezi system. It is found in swamps, small creeks, and the marginal vegetation of larger waters. The areas in which it lives are likely to dry out partially during the dry season, and although some of the fish may find open water throughout the year, many aestivate in cocoons at the end of burrows.

This species spawns in swamps during the wet season, the male digging a shallow burrow in shallow water. The eggs are relatively few in number, whitish, and are about 4 mm. in diameter.

It is distinguished from the other species by its rather long head, by the dorsal fin being placed far back along the body, and by having 34–35 pairs of ribs. Young fishes are very dark, almost black in colour. Older fishes are lighter, the back grey-brown, sides paler with rows of dusky spots. The ventral surface is pale, yellowish, plain on the throat, but speckled on the belly.

Locally in Africa this species is fished for but certain tribes will never eat them. It is the most commonly imported lungfish in Europe.

Prototroctes   Aplochitonidae
 maraena AUSTRALIAN GRAYLING
30 cm. (12 in.)
The Australian grayling is patchily distributed from S. of Sydney, s. along the New South Wales, Victorian, and Tasmanian coastal rivers. It was formerly found in the Snowy River. Like its New Zealand congener, this fish has declined greatly with the advance of civilization.

It is a moderately stout-bodied fish with an adipose fin. Its body is covered with scales.

Its biology is little known, but it is believed to be migratory, spawning in freshwater rivers and dropping downstream to the sea soon after hatching. The chief threats to anadromous fishes are always pollution and obstructions in the river, and in the case of the Australian grayling it is probably the latter in the form of weirs and dams that have caused it to decline. Other factors, however, may have contributed such as the alteration of river flows by dams, the introduction of exotic species, and fishing pressure on local populations of marginal viability. The causes for its near extinction are not certain, but it is one of the native Australian freshwater fishes in danger of extinction.

P. oxyrhynchus NEW ZEALAND GRAYLING 25 cm. (10 in.)
The New Zealand grayling is probably extinct. It was an abundant fish in the later years of the 19th century in most coastal rivers, and was recognized as a good food and game fish. By the 1920s it was a rare fish, and the last specimens ever recorded were captured by accident during a demonstration of a Maori fish trap. Few specimens had ever been examined by fisheries workers and little is known of its biology. It is thought to feed on bottom detritus and associated fauna. It is just possible that small populations exist in some of the less exploited New Zealand rivers. It was a rather stocky fish, similar in a way to the European grayling but lacking the most obvious grayling feature, a long, high dorsal fin. Its dorsal fin is short with relatively few rays. It has been described as lacking any obvious markings, and being silvery to reddish brown in colour.

PROWFISH see Pataecidae
PROWFISH see **Zaprora silenus**
PROWFISH, WARTY see **Aetapcus maculatus**
PRUSSIAN CARP see **Carassius auratus**

Psenes Nomeidae
The species illustrated in colour has not been identified. **452**
P. pellucidus BLACKRAG, FLOTSAMFISH 51 cm. (20 in.)
A widespread fish which is found more or less evenly throughout the warm temperate Atlantic, and Pacific Oceans. It is best known from its juvenile stages, frequently found floating under or close to flotsam at the surface, and especially *Sargassum* weed. They are totally oceanic in habit and feed on a variety of planktonic food, copepods, amphipods, fish eggs and larvae. Adults feed on small fishes also, but they are mesopelagic or bathypelagic, rarely found at the surface and not often captured. It is a dark, sombre brown when adult. The adults and sub-adults are preyed upon by lancetfishes, tunas, and other species.

The juvenile is deep-bodied and coloured to match its well-lit surroundings. Adults become more elongate in the body, have 2 dorsal fins, and retain the pelvic fins throughout life.

Psephurus Polyodontidae
gladius CHINESE PADDLEFISH 7 m. (23 ft)
The Chinese paddlefish is known only from the lower reaches of the Yangtze River. Its huge body is typically sturgeon-like, except that it lacks large bony scutes along the sides. It possesses a very long bony snout which is

flattened, forming a sword-like blade. The mouth opens to an enormous capacity, but its principal food appears to be smaller fishes (not plankton as in the case of the American paddlefish).

Although the Chinese paddlefish is commercially exploited, and its flesh is highly valued as food, very little is known about its life history or spawning biology. Its present abundance in the Yangtze River is not known.

Psettichthys Pleuronectidae
melanostictus SAND SOLE 63 cm. (25 in.)
Found in the e. N. Pacific from s. California to Alaska, and in the Bering Sea. The sand sole is a shallow-water flatfish (but despite its name not a sole) which is widespread on sandy bottoms in 10–183 m. (5–100 fathoms).

It is an active forager on fishes, feeding on sand dabs, herring, and anchovies, as well as small crustaceans and bottom-living invertebrates.

The sand sole is a large-mouthed, amplytoothed flatfish with its eyes on the right side of the head. The first rays of the dorsal fin are elongate and free of the fin membrane. It is green to brown with fine black speckles on the eyed side of the head and body; dead white beneath.

Despite its moderate size and relative abundance this fish is not fished for commercially.

Psettodes Psettodidae
belcheri 51 cm. (20 in.)
Found only on the W. African coast, this flatfish is of relatively restricted distribution. It is a bottom-living fish found in moderately shallow water of from 18–91 m. (10–50 fathoms), although frequently leaving the seabed on feeding forays into mid-water.

Locally it is common and is exploited for food, but it does not make a great contribution to the fisheries of the area.

It is distinguished by its spiny rays in the dorsal fin, and by the large head with long curved teeth in the jaws. It is slimmer in body depth than the Indian Ocean species. Brownish or dark grey in colour, with variable small dark spots, those on the tail fin becoming larger and rounded.

It is named in honour of Captain (later Sir) Edward Belcher who collected the first specimens which were described in 1831.
P. erumei ADALAH, QUEENSLAND HALIBUT 64 cm. (25 in.)
An Indo-Pacific form which is found from the Red Sea and the Indian Ocean coast of Africa

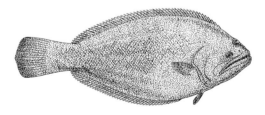

e. to the n. coasts of Australia, and into the w. Pacific. It lives in moderately shallow water from the shore-line down to about 91 m. (50

fathoms) although it is most common in depths of 29–54 m. (16–30 fathoms). In much of its range it is a common fish and is caught commercially on lines as well as in bottom-trawls. Its maximum weight is around 9 kg. (20 lb.).

It is distinguished from all other flatfishes by the spiny rays in the front of the dorsal fin. The eyes may be either on the left or right side.

Young fish are dark, almost black with 5 light cross bands each narrower than the interspaces. Adults are brown or greyish brown with 4 dark cross bands and dark edges to the fins.

PSETTODIDAE
A family of primitive flatfishes which contains only 2 species, one found off W. Africa, the other widely distributed in the tropical Indo-Pacific.

The flatfishes are believed to have been derived from basic perch-like fishes with spiny fins, and the members of this family are clearly close to the ancestral form. In these 2 species (alone of the flatfishes) the dorsal fin has the front rays spine-like, and the fin begins well back on the body. Also it seems a matter of chance which side of the body has both eyes, for as many dextral specimens (i.e. those with both eyes on the right) occur as do sinistral specimens.

Members of this family are thick-bodied, and the migrated eye is placed on the edge of the head not entirely lateral as in other flatfishes (see Pleuronectidae for an account of the migration of the eye). The jaws are large, similar in shape and size both sides, and the teeth are very large and some are barbed at their tips. Although found on the sea bed living in normal flatfish style these fishes also live in mid-water to a greater extent than many of their relations. See **Psettodes**.

Pseudaphritis Bovichtidae
bursinus CONGOLLI 36 cm. (14 in.)
Found in fresh and estuarine waters and the seas around S. Australia, Victoria, New South Wales, and Tasmania. Although it is a marine fish it is often found far inland in freshwater.

Its coloration is distinctive being dark blue above and silvery below, the 2 colours separated by a dark stripe. Dark blotches on the back and sides which extend down on to the lower sides. The fins are spotted.

The head and body have scales; 2 dorsal fins the first of which is placed behind the level of the head; a weak spine on the gill cover.

Pseudobagrus Bagridae
fulvidraco 32 cm. (12½ in.)
This catfish is found in the basin of the River Amur, and is thus found in n. China and se. Siberia. It is found mainly in the channels of rivers and lakes, in which it feeds on bottom-living insects, especially trichopterans and chironomids, molluscs, and sometimes fishes.

It spawns early in summer, the eggs being laid in shallow nests, excavated in the mud and clay bottomed river bed. The male, which is larger than the female, guards the nest and the larvae which hatch in about 2 days. It is a relatively important commercial species in the area.

This fish is distinguished from its local relatives by its large mouth, long barbels, and the serrated external edge to the pectoral fin spine.

Pseudobalistes   Balistidae
fuscus YELLOW-SPOTTED TRIGGERFISH
51 cm. (20 in.)
Widely distributed in the tropical Indo-Pacific, ranging from E. Africa, the Red Sea, across to n. Australia, and the Hawaiian Islands. It tends to live in moderately deep water on the outer side of coral reefs, but it seems is nowhere known to be abundant.

It is a variably coloured species, frequently described as greenish, and sometimes as bluish purple, with yellow spots on each scale, in most specimens forming a complex maze-like pattern of pale yellow lines. The lips and the tips of the pectoral and second dorsal fins are yellow. The outer ray of the tail-fin are very elongate in adults. The photographs show the juvenile, **477**, and an adult, **478**.

Pseudocetopsis   Cetopsidae
gobioides 15 cm. (6 in.)
A little-known small catfish known from the Upper Amazon, parts of Brazil, the Argentine, and the Rio Paraguay.

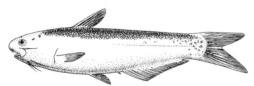

It is greyish on the back with clear flanks. The extreme third of the barbels darkly pigmented. Its body is cylindrical, the head slightly depressed; mouth small, barbel on the upper jaw small, the double pair under the lower jaw rather longer. The dorsal fin is short-based and triangular, the anal fin long-based and low. The tail is forked, each lobe being equal.

PSEUDOCHROMIDAE

A family of mainly small, colourful reef fishes widely distributed in the Indo-Pacific. They are slender-bodied, fully scaled, and with a long-based dorsal fin. The lateral line is divided into 2 parts, an upper row of scales parallel to the dorsal profile, and a short posterior section along the mid-side. The dorsal fin has only 3 spines, a character which distinguishes them from the sea basses (Serranidae) to which they and several other groups (Grammidae and Pseudogrammidae) are allied.

They are highly colourful little fishes and coloration has been used extensively to distinguish them from one another. See **Pseudochromis.**

Pseudochromis   Pseudochromidae
Two species are illustrated, but one has not been identified. **270**
P. fridmani 5 cm. (2 in.)
A brilliantly coloured species, widely distributed in the Red Sea including the Gulf of Suez, the Gulf of Aqaba, and Port Sudan; it ranges in depth from the surface to 60 m. (33 fathoms). It lives mainly in small holes in colonies on vertical rock faces or under overhanging rocks. This is a little-known species which was unknown to science until 1968 when it was first described. **269**
P. olivaceus 8·5 cm. (3½ in.)
A small fish found along the reefs of the Red Sea, the Gulf of Aden, and the Arabian Gulf. It lives down to depths of 20 m. (11 fathoms),

amongst rocks, coral fragments and coral heads. Young fish haunt the smaller crevices between the coral branches but adults are found in more open water, although they too will take shelter amongst coral branches. Adults are often found in pairs.

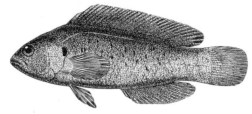

It is olive green overall, many of the scales edged with dark blue, and has a conspicuous dark blue, gold-edged spot on the gill cover. The fins are dull green but the edges of the tail are yellowish. The underside is yellowish.

Pseudocurimata   Curimatidae
gilberti SABALITO 20 cm. (8 in.)
The sabalito is widely distributed in the rivers of middle S. America, including the Rio Paraná, Rio Uruguay, and the Rio de la Plata. It is a silvery fish, rather dark on the back, with a dark spot on the base of the tail, apparently faintly continuing onto the middle rays of the tail fin. The upper sides have rows of dark spots Large specimens are, however, almost completely silvery. It is a deep-bodied fish, both dorsal and ventral profiles being high, the lower edge having a scaly keel. The body is covered with large scales.

It feeds extensively on plant material, although as some of its food is bottom living algae it also consumes quantities of mud and detritus. It is typically a fish of lakes and still back waters, although it is also found in rivers. It breeds in December and January in dense vegetation in still water.

It is a valuable commercial food fish in areas where it is common.

Pseudogramma   Pseudogrammidae
polyacantha 15 cm. (6 in.)
Widely distributed in the Indo-Pacific, from the Seychelles to Hawaii, and the Philippines. It is an inhabitant of reefs and rocks at depths of 1·8–9 m. (1–5 fathoms) usually living close to holes and hiding in them when disturbed. In the Marshall Islands it is described as being everywhere abundant on the lagoon and ocean reef in shallow water.

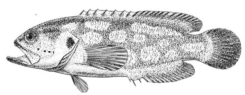

Its general coloration is dull brown, with a dark earlike mark on the gill cover. The sides are slightly reticulated in a light pattern. It is distinguished by the numerous spines in the dorsal fin, usually 7, sometimes 8.

PSEUDOGRAMMIDAE

A small family of tropical marine fishes found mainly in the Indo-Pacific, one species occurring in the w. Atlantic. Its members are all very small, and related to the sea basses (Ser-

ranidae). They appear to be closely related to the Pseudochromidae, and are grouped with those fishes by many authors. They differ from them mainly in having 6–7 sharp spines in the dorsal fin, and a longer based (16–17 rays) anal fin. See **Pseudogramma.**

PSEUDOPLESIOPIDAE

A small family of tropical Indo-Pacific fishes found from the E. African coast to the Philippines and the central w. Pacific. Their affinities lie with the Pseudochromidae and Plesiopidae, with the former of which both are often grouped in the single family. The members of this family differ in having in the anterior dorsal fin simple unbranched rays, not spines; the pelvic fins are very long, the eye is large and the body slender.

In general, they are little-known fishes; the species are frequently confused with one another. See **Chlidichthys, Pseudoplesiops.**

Pseudoplesiops   Pseudoplesiopidae
typus 6 cm. (2½ in.)
Reputedly widely distributed in the tropical Indo-Pacific and found from the Seychelles, the E. Indies and the Philippines. It is most abundant in shallow water on the edges of reefs, and is in places very common amongst the coral and algae.

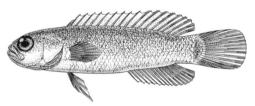

It is dull brown in colour, pale below, but there is a narrow dark ring around the eye. The fins are dusky. Its dorsal fin has 10 flexible, non-spiny rays, and 9–10 branched rays. The lateral line is in 2 sections.

Pseudopleuronectes   Pleuronectidae
americanus WINTER FLOUNDER
63 cm. (25 in.)
A widely-distributed N. American Atlantic species which is found from Labrador, the St Lawrence mouth, the coasts of Nova Scotia s. to N. Carolina and Georgia. It lives on soft mud to rather hard bottoms in relatively shallow water. Although it is most common in 2–37 m. (1–20 fathoms) it has been found down as deep as 143 m. (78 fathoms). Being northerly in distribution it tolerates low temperatures well and in the S. of its range migrates inshore towards cooler water – hence its name winter flounder.

As with most flatfishes its food is almost entirely bottom-living, principally small crustaceans, molluscs and marine worms. Adults are reported to bite off and eat the protruding siphon of the commercially valuable soft-shelled clam. The winter flounder is commercially exploited on a small scale, its flesh being marketed both fresh and frozen as well as used for animal feed.

This species is distinguished by its small mouth, eyes on the right side, and straight lateral line. Its colouring is variable, on the left (blind) side white – occasionally dusky, while the right side is muddy or reddish brown, sometimes mottled or spotted.

Pseudoraja   Pseudorajidae
  atlantica 48 cm. (19 in.)
This ray occurs in moderate depths off the
coast of tropical America. It was first described
from the area extending from the mouth of the
River Amazon to Nicaragua, but its range has
since been found to extend to the N. coast of
Panama and the area of Tobago. It is evidently
fairly common in this area in depths of 247–640
m. (135–350 fathoms).

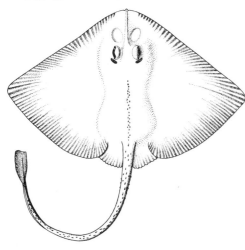

It is a distinctive, broad ray with sharply
pointed pectoral fins, and a short, rounded
snout. Some large males have strange knob-
like spines with radiating arms at the base on
the back.

PSEUDORAJIDAE
A small family of rays wich lack dorsal fins,
have no spine on the tail, but have a well developed tail fin. The pelvic fins are characteristic
with their reat margins being nearly straight
while the fin is rather large in relation to the
body disc, when compared with other rays.
The skin on the back is rough and thorny, and
one member of the family has a small fleshy
extension to its snout.
    The family is known from the tropical w.
Atlantic in moderate depths. See **Pseudoraja.**

Pseudorhombus   Bothidae
  arsius LARGE-TOOTHED FLOUNDER,
TAMPAR 38 cm. (15 in.)
Widely distributed in the tropical Indo-Pacific,
from the e. coast of Africa through the coastal
waters of the Persian Gulf and India to the n.
Australian coastline, China and the w. Pacific.
In much of this vast range it is one of the most
common flatfishes and is a valuable food fish.
It is found in shallow, inshore waters, and
estuaries and is taken in shore seines and by
angling; its depth range is from 1–55 m. (½–30
fathoms). Its flesh is very good eating.
    In this species the eyes are on the left side
and close together, the dorsal fin origin is in
front of the upper eye, the mouth is large with
the lower jaw prominent. It is brownish or
grey usually with darker spots and rings. A
dusky spot on the mid-line of the side behind
the pectoral fin and another nearer the centre
of the body. The head and fins are brown
spotted.

Pseudoscaphirhynchus   Acipenseridae
  kaufmanni FALSE SHOVELNOSE
STURGEON 51 cm. (20 in.)
A sturgeon-like fish which differs from the

other members of the family in its flattened,
shovel-like snout, by not having spiracles, and
by having rows of distinct, rather thorny
scutes. Three species are recognized, all confined to 2 rivers, the Syr-Darya and the Ama-
Darya in the se. U.S.S.R., which runs into
the Aral Sea. *P. kaufmanni* is easily distinguished from the others by the way its tail extends as a long filament.
    It is a non-migratory fish living permanently
in freshwater in the river. The young fish feed
on invertebrates, the adults mainly on bottom-
living fishes especially the local species of
loach and young barbel. It spawns in spring on
stony bottoms and the young stay in the channel of the river.
    This is locally an important commercial
fish, caught in nets and on baited hooks.

PSEUDOTRIAKIDAE
A family of little-known deep-water sharks
which contains 2 species so far found respectively in the N. Atlantic, SW. Indian Ocean,
and N. Pacific. Both species are rather stout-
bodied, with 5 gill slits, and relatively small
fins. Their most obvious character is the long
low first dorsal fin. See **Pseudotriakis.**

Pseudotriakis   Pseudotriakidae
  acrages see under **P. microdon**
  microdon FALSE CATSHARK
2·95 m. (9ft 8in.)
This deep water shark was first discovered off
Portugal in 1867, the second specimen was
found off Long Island, New York in 1883.
Since then other specimens have been found
off the Cape Verde Islands, off the W. coast
of the British Isles, Iceland, and the U.S.,
while off Japan a related species, *P. acrages*, is
known. About 20 specimens have been reported of *P. microdon*.

Most specimens have been caught in depths
of 305–1525 m. (167–833 fathoms) but the
New York specimen was actually washed
ashore dead. Its biology is virtually unknown;
its minute teeth suggest that it feeds on benthic
invertebrates. Only 2 young are born at a time,
and judging by the huge size of the eggs they
are relatively large at birth.

Pseudotropheus   Cichlidae
  auratus 10 cm. (4 in.)
A rather slender-bodied species with a very
distinctive colouring. The female's body is a
light golden brown, with 3 lengthwise dark
stripes each bordered with whitish bands and
the uppermost of which is on the dorsal fin. The
tail fin is boldly spotted on the upper half. The
male's colouring is bluish with black stripes.
    This species is a native of Lake Malawi, in
central Africa. It has been kept as an aquarium
fish for several years, and has been bred in
captivity. The female broods the eggs and
young in her mouth. **375**
P. zebra 15 cm. (6 in.)
A native of Lake Malawi, this fish has become
increasingly common in aquaria in Europe and
America. It feeds mainly on algae scraped off
the rocks, but will eat other food; it lives for
preference in crevices.

The male is bright blue with a darker lower
head, and numerous vertical stripes covering
the head and body. The posterior rays of the
anal fin have a number of rounded yellowish,
dark ringed spots. These are known as egg
spots, and it is conjectured that they resemble
the eggs of the fish thus causing mouth-brood-
ing females to pick at the 'eggs' and in doing
so inhale the male's sperm. **376**

Pseudupeneus   Mullidae
  auriflamma GOLDEN-BANDED GOATFISH
41 cm. (16 in.)
An Indo-Pacific species, found widely in the
Indian Ocean and Red Sea, which has penetrated through the Suez Canal and is now widespread in the e. Mediterranean. It has become
so common there that it is now being commercially fished for and is more important than
the endemic goatfishes. It is also a valuable
food fish in its native seas.
    It is found close inshore in shallow water,
usually over sandy and muddy bottoms. Its
back is reddish brown, the sides white and the
belly yellowish; 2 bright yellow lines on the
snout, a wide band of brilliant yellow from eye
to tail fin.
P. barberinus GOATFISH, RED MULLET
51 cm. (20 in.)
An Indo-Pacific species of wide distribution
in tropical regions. It ranges from the Red Sea
and E. African coast e. to the w. Pacific. It is
one of the largest known red mullets and is
locally a valuable food fish.
    In this genus the barbels are very long. This
species can be distinguished by its colouring.
306
P. fraterculus GOATFISH, SURMULLET
46 cm. (18 in.)
Widely distributed in the central tropical Indo-
Pacific from E. Africa around India and the E.
Indies. It is one of the largest of the goatfishes in the area, is very abundant, and a
valuable food fish. Like other members of the
family it lives in shallow inshore waters on
sandy and muddy bottoms.

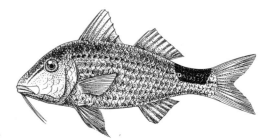

Its colouring is variable, but is basically reddish with dark edges to the scales, a purplish
band from eye to snout, the lateral line flanked
by golden spots, and a light golden patch on the
tail, followed by a dark saddle.
P. maculatus SPOTTED GOATFISH
28 cm. (11 in.)
Found in the w. Atlantic from New Jersey and
Bermuda to Brazil, including the Gulf of
Mexico, and the whole Caribbean. A common
species through most of this range, it is found
on reefs, and over the sand between reefs as
well as in turtle grass beds. It can be seen
foraging in shallow water stirring up the sea
bed to locate the small invertebrates on which
it feeds; it is often accompanied by small
wrasses which snap up unconsidered trifles.

It is capable of rapid changes of colour; mostly it is pale brown with 3 rectangular dusky patches on the upper side, but these can fade within seconds. Occasionally seen with reddish blotches overall, at other times greenish especially when living in turtle grass. **307**

Psilocranium   Cheilodactylidae
nigricans DUSKY MORWONG 41 cm. (16 in.)
Found on the coasts of W. Australia, S. Australia, Victoria, New South Wales, and Tasmania. It is an abundant fish in most of this range, living on rocky bottoms amongst dense algal covering. It is occasionally caught by anglers and spear-fishermen but is not commercially exploited.

It is distinguished amongst the Australian species by having the lower pectoral rays only slightly produced, and only the tips are free from the fin membrane. Adults are grey above, silver-grey below; the young fish are heavily blotched with greeny brown on the back and sides.

PSILORHYNCHIDAE

A small family of Asiatic small, loach-like fishes which have been recorded from the streams of NE. Bengal and Assam.

The body is rather high, but the belly and snout region are quite flat, the mouth is ventral, opens cross-wise and the lips are rather broad and covered with small pads, especially the lower lip.

This family is close to the homalopterid loaches (Homalopteridae). See **Psilorhynchus.**

Psilorhynchus   Psilorhynchidae
balitoria 5 cm. (2 in.)
Found only in the hill streams and rapids of the inland regions of NE. Bengal and Assam, this small fish is well adapted for life in fast-flowing rivers.

The mouth is wholly ventral with broad lips, which are covered with hard pores. The jaws have sharp, but not horny edges, and are toothless. Its build and especially the form of its mouth suggests that this is a fish which clings to rock faces, out of the main current, feeding on algae and anchored organisms.

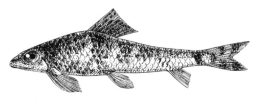

It is reddish brown in colour with irregular black blotches on the sides.

Psychrolutes   Psychrolutidae
paradoxus TADPOLE SCULPIN
6 cm. (2½ in.)
An inhabitant of the N. Pacific coast of America from Washington to the Bering Sea.

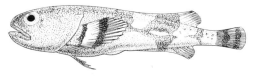

It appears to be fairly evenly distributed along the coast but on account of its size it is not often taken – its biology is little known. It inhabits water of moderate depths, from around 97–220 m. (53–120 fathoms).

It is distinguished by its tadpole shape, and by the loose skin on the body with scattered papillae. It is grey to light brown above with brown bands and blotches, and a prominent black bar across each pectoral fin.

PSYCHROLUTIDAE

A small family of marine fishes, best known in the N. Pacific. They are rather obscure sculpin-like species which are intermediate between the true sculpins (Cottidae) and the sea snails (Liparidae). They have a low first dorsal fin which is not differentiated from the second dorsal, with a loose, slightly prickly skin. Their biology is little known, all are small fishes. See **Psychrolutes.**

Pteraclis   Bramidae
aesticola see under **P. velifera**
carolinus see under **P. velifera**
velifera FANFISH 61 cm. (2 ft)
Found widely in the oceans of the S. Hemisphere and reported from off s. Africa and the SW. Pacific off Australia and New Zealand. It is probably common in moderately deep water in the open ocean but very few specimens have been reported, and the largest of these were stranded on the shore off New Zealand and S. Africa. Similar species are found in the tropical Atlantic (*P. carolinus*), and n. and se. Pacific (*P. aesticola*).

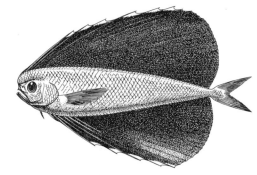

It is silvery overall, the fins dark blue with pale turquoise spots posteriorly, the eye is dark blue with a silvery iris.

Pterois   Scorpaenidae
antennata 23 cm. (9 in.)
Widely distributed in the Indian Ocean from the African coast, Mauritius, and the Seychelles, along the coasts of India to Singapore and well out into the w. Pacific including the New Hebrides, Solomon Islands, and Society Islands.

In common with other members of the family it is an inshore, shallow-water fish. Its swimming motion is graceful and its colouring distinctive; it also has venom-bearing tissue on the fin spines and despite its modest size wounds can be very painful. **244**
P. radiata TIGERFISH 15 cm. (6 in.)
This species is said to be found across the Indo-Pacific from the Red Sea and Zanzibar to Hawaii, but considerable confusion existed in identifying it which is reason enough for accepting records with caution. In the Marshall Islands, Dr L. P. Schultz, formerly of the U.S. National Museum, found that this was the commonest species of *Pteros*, and suggested that this applied to shallow reef areas of most coral atolls. It was most common where there were holes in coral growths or hiding places underneath coral blocks.

This species is similar to *P. antennata*, but the fleshy tentacle above the eye is plain black with white tip and margin. **245**
P. russelli BUTTERFLYFISH,
FIREWORKSFISH 30 cm. (12 in.)
Widely distributed in the Indo-Pacific from the African coast (Natal), Zanzibar and the Persian Gulf across to Singapore, Sumatra, and the Celebes. Its occurrence has not been positively confirmed from Australian waters.

Like the other *Pterois* species this is a beautiful and decorative fish with long fins. The scales are rather larger than in *P. volitans*. It is found in shallow inshore waters on and around reefs. **246**
P. volitans BUTTERFLYFISH, RED FIREFISH,
TURKEYFISH 38 cm. (15 in.)
Widely distributed in the Indo-Pacific, this species is positively reported from the E.

African coast to New Guinea and Australia, the Philippines and widely in the w. Pacific.

It is a very distinctive fish, positively identified by the length of the pectoral fin rays which are not branched, by having 10–12 branched rays in the second dorsal fin, and scattered spots on the tail. It is usually red or brownish red with numerous dark bands bordered with white. A large black blotch in the pectoral axilla has a distinct white spot in the centre.

It is a very colourful, reef-dwelling fish (although it is often found well away from reefs) of great beauty and eye-catching movement. It drifts along almost casually, immune to attack, for the brilliant colouring is clearly a warning that the spines are heavily equipped with venom producing tissue. Stings from these fish can be very painful.

The names listed above are used indiscriminately for all the *Pterois* species. **247**

Pterolebias   Cyprinodontidae
peruensis PERUVIAN LONGFIN
9 cm. (3½ in.)
A genus of killifishes which is widely distributed in n. S. America. This species is found in the upper Amazon in Peru, it is very attractively and distinctively coloured and has already achieved considerable popularity as an aquarium fish. Males have much longer fins than females.

This species has been bred in the aquarium, the eggs are laid amongst the bottom gravel to hatch in about 3 months. **204**

Pterophyllum Cichlidae
altum DEEP ANGELFISH 13 cm. (5 in.)
Confined to the Orinoco River system in S. America, this angelfish is one of the least well-known, and although it has been imported as an aquarium species it has not bred in captivity.

Its body form is typical of the group, the dorsal and anal fins being very well developed and elongate. The chief distinguishing feature is the steeply inclined head and back profile with the snout strongly concave. Its coloration is similar to the angelfish but it has brownish blotches on its sides.

P. eimekei see **P. scalare**

P. scalare ANGELFISH 15 cm. (6 in.)
A native of the Amazon basin where it frequents the well-weeded, slow-flowing regions. Its striking body shape are adaptations to life amongst water plants and fallen branches, and render it well-nigh invisible in the somewhat cloudy water it frequents. Its body is strongly compressed and little longer than deep.

A well-known aquarium fish, which has been much bred to give varied colour varieties. The well-known *P. eimekei* is considered to be a synonym. **377**

PTILICHTHYIDAE
A family which contains only the single species of quillfish. It is found throughout the N. Pacific from the Okhotsk Sea and the Kuril Islands to British Columbia and n. Washington. See **Ptilichthys.**

Ptilichthys Ptilichthyidae
goodei QUILLFISH 34 cm. (13½ in.)
This N. Pacific species is quite unmistakable with its tremendously elongate body, very long anal fin, many-rayed like the rather shorter dorsal fin. The lower jaw projects forward in front of the snout. The tail tapers to a fine filament. In colour very pale with a faint dark line along the belly. Some specimens have been reported to be greenish or yellow.

It has been taken occasionally at the surface attracted by lights at night, living in deeper water in daytime. It has been suggested that it burrows into the bottom mud, but its biology is virtually unknown.

Ptychocheilus Cyprinidae
lucius COLORADO SQUAWFISH
1·5 m. (5 ft)
The Colorado squawfish is the largest member of the family Cyprinidae to be found in N. American freshwaters. Specimens weighing as much as 36 kg. (80 lb.) have been reported, but the general weight of individual fish today is much lower. It is olive on the back, lighter beneath; young specimens have a black spot at the middle of the tail fin base, and a faint dark line along the sides.

This squawfish is confined to the Colorado River basin, but its range has shrunk with the development of the river by man. It seems that the impoundment of the water in reservoirs and dams has rendered much of the river unsuitable. It is an active predator which feeds entirely on fish. At one time it was an important food fish for the indigenous Indians of the

Colorado basin, and was also heavily utilized by white men when they arrived; they knew it as white salmon.

P. oregonensis NORTHERN SQUAWFISH
1·2 m. (4 ft)
The long, slender body, large mouth, elongate snout and absence of barbels helps to distinguish this squawfish, which differs from the Colorado squawfish by having slightly larger, and fewer (67–80) scales in the lateral line, and an average of 8 anal rays. It is found in the Columbia River basin of the Pacific NW., from the Pease River system in British Columbia s. and E. to Nevada tributaries of the Snake River.

It is primarily a lake-living fish although found in slow to moderate streams and rivers. They live for preference close to the bottom. Their diet is catholic, as young fish they eat insect larvae, plankton, and molluscs, but also take small fishes. As they grow they come to increasingly depend on fish. With their large jaws, sharp throat teeth, and predatory habits they occupy the same role as the pike does elsewhere. Their fish-eating habits have particular importance in areas where young salmon are released into the rivers and a measure of squawfish control is said to be required before stocking.

The northern squawfish offers good sport for anglers. It rises to a fly and fights well, and weighs up to 22·7 kg. (50 lb.). It was an important food fish for the Indians.

PUFFER,
  BANDTAIL see **Sphoeroides spengleri**
  OCEANIC see **Lagocephalus lagocephalus**
  SHARP-NOSED see **Canthigaster margaritatus**
  SHARPNOSE see **Canthigaster rostrata**
  SPINY see **Diodon holocanthus**
PUFFERFISH see Tetraodontidae
PUFFERFISH see **Amblyrhynchotes honckenii, Lagocephalus lagocephalus**
PUFFERFISH,
  COMMON see **Tetraodon cutcutia**
  NILE see **Tetraodon lineatus**
PUG, SPECKLED see **Tandya maculata**
PUMPKINSEED see **Lepomis gibbosus**
PUNGAS CATFISH see **Pangasius pangasius**

Pungitius Gasterosteidae
pungitius NINE-SPINED STICKLEBACK
6 cm. (2½ in.)
This is a wide-ranging stickleback found across the whole N. Hemisphere, from the British Isles and w. Europe, e. to n. Asia, and across N. America. It is found in the sea to the N. of its range, but is mainly a freshwater fish to the S. In Europe it is found as far S. as the Mediterranean; in N. America s. to New Jersey, Minnesota, and Michigan.

Morphologically it is similar to the more widespread 3-spined stickleback, the number of spines, 8–11, being an immediate distinguishing feature, although there are other distinctions between them. The nine-spined stickleback lives in densely weeded, often

almost swampy conditions, usually in small ponds and streams; it is rarely found in large rivers or open lakes. It builds its nest in the vegetation just above the bottom, plant fibres being cemented together with adhesive threads from the fish's urogenital aperture, and forming a bushy mass the size of a snooker ball. The male entices females into the nest, and oxygenates the eggs by fanning them and protects the young after hatching.

This stickleback is prey to fewer animals than the 3-spined species, but trout and charr do take them. It has no commercial value.

It is dark brown above, olive, or coppery on the sides; the eye and pelvic fin become blue or white in males in the breeding season.

Puntius see **Barbus**
PUPFISH see **Cyprinodon milleri**
PURPLE-HEADED BARB see **Barbus nigrofasciatus**
PUTITOR MAHSEER see **Barbus putitora**

Pygidium Trichomycteridae
itatiaye 15 cm. (6 in.)
A small catfish found in the rivers of e. Brazil, near Rio de Janeiro and the upper Paraná. It is a rather stout little fish. Dull coloured; the back brown, the belly yellowish, with a series of elongate blotches on the middle of the side, fins colourless.

This fish is mainly crepuscular, and lies buried under the leaves and vegetation during daylight. It has been kept in aquaria in Europe.

PYGMY
  BLACK-FACED BLENNY see **Tripterygion minor**
  DEVIL RAY see **Mobula diabolus**
  GOBY see **Pandaka pygmaea**
  PERCH see **Nannoperca australis**
  RASBORA see **Rasbora maculata**
  SHARK see **Euprotomicrus bispinatus**
  SUNFISH, EVERGLADES see **Elassoma evergladei**

Pygocentrus Characidae
piraya PIRANHA, PIRAYA 61 cm. (2 ft)
This is the largest of the piranhas, and it is widely distributed in the lower Amazon basin, especially the São Francisco River in e. Brazil. It is a very deep-bodied species, with a steeply rising back profile and a smoothly curved belly. The belly is edged with sharp toothed scales. The distinction of *Pygocentrus* from the other piranhas (*Rooseveltiella* and *Serrasalmus*) is mainly based on the fringed adipose fin in the former.

This, on account of its size and habits, is one of the more infamous characins known to popular writing. Many travellers' tales include an account of the ferocity by shoals of piranhas, and stories abound of large animals such as the Amazonian capybara, ponies, and alligators being stripped of their flesh within minutes of falling into the water. Its cutting teeth, mounted on strong jaw bones, meet exactly, and can slice flesh as neatly as a surgeon's scalpel. Even captured piranhas need handling with care, and apparently dead fish can still snap effectively. Despite this, this species has been kept in captivity, although it is suitable only for the largest aquariums, and in S. America it is captured for food. **85**

Pygoplites   Chaetodontidae
diacanthus 25 cm. (10 in.)
A widely distributed Indo-Pacific tropical fish which is found from the Red Sea, Zanzibar, Mauritius, Melanesia, Polynesia and n. to the Philippine Islands. In many areas it is a common, even abundant reef fish, and locally it is caught and landed for consumption.

Its colouring is very variable with age. The young fish has a large dark eyespot on the upper edge of the soft dorsal fin; this disappears with age. Adults are pale brown with yellowish tints, but the body is vertically divided by 9 light blue cross-bands which have narrow black edges. The rear end of the gill cover and the subopercular spine are pale blue. The number of the vertical blue and black stripes increases with age. **351**

Pylodictis   Ictaluridae
olivaris FLATHEAD CATFISH 1·5 m. (5 ft)
Widely distributed in e. N. America from S. Dakota and the tributaries of Lake Michigan and Lake Erie s. through the Mississippi system to Alabama, the Arkansas River in Oklahoma, and ne. Mexico. It is essentially a fish of large, lowland rivers, bayous, and lakes in the flood-plain of these rivers. The young are often found in shallow water under stones in riffles.

Its flattened head and anterior body give it a strikingly different appearance from any other large N. American catfish. It is yellowish in colour, mottled irregularly with brown and dark green, lighter below.

This is one of the larger American catfishes said to reach a weight of 45·4 kg. (100 lb.), although specimens up to 18·2 kg. (40 lb.) are more frequently recorded.

Pyramodon   Pyramodontidae
punctatus 18 cm. (7 in.)
A slender-bodied fish with a long compressed tail; pelvic fins well developed and sited on the throat region in advance of the pectorals, the vent below the front half of the pectoral fins. It is described as olivaceous in colour, powdered with little dark spots.

The first specimen of this species to be described was captured on Captain Scott's expedition in the *Terra Nova*, 7 miles (11·2 km.) E. of Cape North, New Zealand, in 172 m. (70 fathoms). It was taken on a sandy bottom.
P. ventralis 19 cm. (7½ in.)
A species close to the brotulids and pearl-fishes known so far only from the original specimen which was taken in a beam trawl near Doworra Island, in the E. Indies, at a depth of 375 m. (205 fathoms) on coral sand.

It is a long, thin species and the only known specimen was said to have a distended stomach due to the remains of a fish within. This fish was originally thought to belong to the pearl-fish family (Carapidae) but is now placed co-equal with that group and the brotulids.

It is brownish, the belly silver, except over the gut which is black.

PYRAMODONTIDAE
A family of little-known fishes related to the Ophidiidae. Its members have been found in the vicinity of New Zealand and the E. Indies (Doworra Island) in moderate depths.

Its members are distinguished by their scaleless, elongate body, the tail tapering to a fine point, and the vent below the pectoral fins which are large. Pelvic fins are well developed. See **Pyramodon.**

Pyrrhulina   Lebiasinidae
brevis SHORT PYRRHULINA 9 cm. (3½ in.)
A slender-bodied fish found in the Amazon, and the Rio Negro in S. America. Its fins are rather elongate (when compared to related species), and its body is slightly stouter. Its back is brown to bronze, the sides being lighter with a bluish tinge and the belly is pinkish. A distinct dark band runs from the lower jaw, through the eye, and along the side of the body. The sides have 4 rows of bright red spots, and the dorsal fin has a dusky mark near the leading edge.

The sexes differ in colour and in minor features. The females have yellowish fins, but the males have reddish fins, and the dorsal, anal, and pelvic fins have dark edges. Males also have a rather longer upper tail fin lobe, than do females.

It has been kept in aquaria with some success. It is an active, surface-living species, which is said to breed by laying its eggs on large submerged leaves.
P. vittata STRIPED PYRRHULINA 7 cm. (2¾ in.)
A slender-bodied characin-like fish from n. S. America, which like other members of the family lacks an adipose fin. Its fins are rounded, but with a forked tail. Its coloration is typical, greenish brown above, the sides lighter, and ventrally whitish with a pink flush. The edges of the scales are dark tinged, and the body has a lacy appearance. A sharply defined dark stripe runs from the mouth, through the eye to the gill cover, and it has several rounded dark blotches along the sides. The dorsal fin has a round, large black blotch in its middle.

The striped pyrrhulina has been found in the Amazon near Santarem, and the Rio Tapajoz. It is a lively, peaceful fish for the aquarium, and relatively easy to breed.

Males are distinctly more red coloured than the females, and the upper tail fin lobe is longer.

PYRRHULINA,
SHORT see **Pyrrhulina brevis**
STRIPED see **Pyrrhulina vittata**

Pythonichthys   Heterenchelidae
microphthalmus SMALL-EYED EEL
50 cm. (19¾ in.)
A little-known burrowing eel found on the w. coast of Africa from Morocco to Angola. In life it is a beautiful, uniform rose pink, due to the colour of the blood in capillaries beneath the near transparent scaleless skin.

As its name implies its eyes are very small, and are partially covered with skin. They are

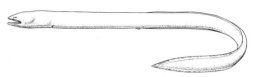

probably capable of no more than discerning daylight from night. It is interesting, however, that the nostrils of this eel are well developed, and the posterior nostril is internally equipped with an elaborate labyrinth. Little is known of its diet; it can be presumed to feed mainly on hard-shelled, slow-moving animals.

Q

QUEEN
  ANGELFISH see **Holacanthus ciliaris**
  PARROTFISH see **Scarus vetula**
  TRIGGERFISH see **Balistes vetula**
QUEENFISH see **Chorinemus lysan**
QUEENSLAND
  HALIBUT see **Psettodes erumei**
  LUNGFISH see **Neoceratodus forsteri**
QUILL-BACK ROCKFISH see **Sebastes maliger**
QUILLBACK see **Carpiodes cyprinus**
QUILLFISH see **Ptilichthys goodei**
QUINNAT see **Oncorhynchus tshawytscha**

R

RABBITFISH see Chimaeridae, Rhinochimaeridae, Siganidae
RABBITFISH see **Chimaera monstrosa, Siganus oramin**
RACEHORSE see **Congiopodus torvus**

RACHYCENTRIDAE
A family containing the single species, *Rachycentron canadum*, the widespread tropical marine predator, the cobia.

Its elongate cylindrical body has a series of separate dorsal spines on the back before the well-developed second dorsal fin. The adult has a deeply-forked tail, although in the young fish the central rays are longest.

It is placed close to the Pomatomidae and the Echeneidae, the family of shark suckers. See **Rachycentron.**

Rachycentron   Rachycentridae
canadum COBIA, SERGEANTFISH, RUNNER 1·8 m. (6 ft)

Found in tropical regions of the Atlantic, Indian, and Pacific oceans except that it does not occur in the e. Pacific. Its coloration is distinctive, in the adult the back and sides are brown, sharply divided by silvery bands, and the belly is yellowish.

The cobia is a fish of the open sea, occasionally coming into inshore waters and even estuaries. It grows to a large size, weights of up to 68 kg. (150 lb.) have been reported, and it is a fine game and food fish.

It is mainly a fish-eater, but also eats crabs with appreciation, and is in parts of n. Australia known as 'crab-eater' from this habit. It also eats squids and shrimps.

RADIICEPHALIDAE
A family of ribbonfish-like fishes found only in the Atlantic Ocean in warm water zones. It is close to the crestfishes (Lophotidae), and is long and thin-bodied, deeply compressed, tapering towards the long thin tail. The forehead is high, the dorsal fin runs from above the eye to the tail fin, the anal fin is greatly reduced. See **Radiicephalus.**

Radiicephalus   Radiicephalidae
elongatus 76 cm. (30½ in.)
A long slender, silvery fish with a deeply compressed body. Its body form is similar to the oarfish, and other ribbonfishes, but its tail is very narrow, it has a short anal fin, and its skin is covered with fine, rectangular divisions.

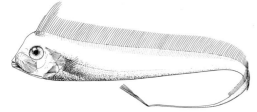

The first specimen known to science was one captured by a commercial fisherman from Portugal fishing off Morocco in 1917. No more were found until 1966 when 3 were caught by a research vessel off Morocco, the Canaries and the Azores. Subsequently it has been captured close to the equator in mid-Atlantic.

Little is known of its biology. Lanternfishes have been found in its gut, and it may hunt these by sight (its large eyes being apparently very effective). It is found in the upper mesopelagic zone, between 250–600 m. (136–328 fathoms). Its body cavity contains a 'brown sac' and this ribbonfish may well be able, like the crestfishes (Lophotidae), to eject a cloud of ink in order to confuse predators.

RAGFISH see **Icosteus aenigmaticus**
RAGGED-TOOTH SHARK see **Odontaspis ferox**
RAINBOW
    DARTER see under **Etheostoma spectabile**
    PARROTFISH see **Scarus guacamaia**
    RUNNER see **Elagatis bipinnulata**
    SMELT see under **Osmerus dentex**
    TROUT see **Salmo gairdneri**
    WRASSE see **Coris julis**

RAINBOWFISH see Melanotaeniidae
RAINBOWFISH see **Heteroscarus acroptilus, Thalassoma lunare**
RAINBOWFISH,
    CELEBES see **Telmatherina ladigesi**
    CRIMSON-SPOTTED see **Melanotaenia flaviatilis**
    MCCULLOCH'S see **Nematocentrus maccullochi**

Raja   Rajidae
australis see under **R. whitleyi**
batis SKATE 2·4 m. (8 ft)
This is the largest member of its family in the e. Atlantic. Its range is from the Arctic Ocean, s. to Madeira and the Mediterranean. It is a deep-water species and in consequence is not found inshore or in the shallower seas (or only rarely). Its normal depth range is 30–600 m. (16–328 fathoms).

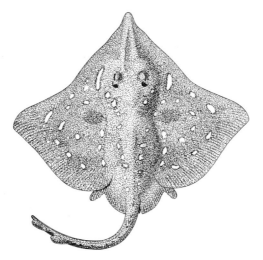

It is a valuable commercial species, although most of the 'skate' sold in the U.K. is composed of other species of the genus. It feeds on a large variety of fishes, including dogfishes and rays, as well as crabs, lobsters, and octopuses.

Its back is olive-grey or brown, ventrally it is blue-grey or ashy with very conspicuous lines of black pores.

R. binoculata BIG SKATE 2·4 m. (8 ft)
The big skate is a species confined to the e. Pacific from s. California to the Gulf of Alaska. It is one of the largest skates known, specimens of 1·8 m. (6 ft) weighing around 91 kg. (200 lb.), and on the Canadian market it is a valuable food fish, its pectoral fins being sold (as skate wings) in large quantities.

It is a long-snouted species, so the front margins of its disc are concave in outline. It has a line of large spines along the mid-line of the back, 2 dorsal fins, and a distinctive indentation in the outer edge of each pelvic fin. Its back is a dull olive-brown or grey, with lighter spots scattered, and 2 very distinctive eyespots, dark-centred with a light ring and then a dark ring, one on each pectoral fin.

The big skate seems to breed throughout the year, with a seasonal increase during the warmer months. The egg cases are large, about 30 cm. (1 ft) in length.

R. clavata ROKER, THORNBACK RAY 85 cm. (34 in.)
This is the most common of the rays in inshore waters of Europe. Its range extends from Norway and Iceland (where it is uncommon), s. to Madeira and the Mediterranean. It fre-

quents a wide variety of grounds from mud, sand, shingle, and even rocks, as well as depths 1·8–60 m. (1–33 fathoms). In the shallowest waters it is often the newly-hatched young that are most common, but occasionally quite large adults are taken. The adult females come close inshore to lay their egg-capsules in winter.

These capsules are brown, about 8 cm. (3 in.) in length with a horn of roughly equal length at each corner. The case, when the young has hatched, is often found amongst the jetsam of the shore and is known as a mermaid's purse (although this name can be applied to the egg case of other rays).

The roker (a name most used along the E. Anglian coast, England) is one of the mainstays of the inshore fisherman, and forms a large part of the 'skate' sold in English markets. Large numbers are also caught by anglers and it is rated as a good sporting fish, especially as good specimens can weigh up to 17 kg. (37 lb.). **8**
R. erinacea HEDGEHOG or LITTLE SKATE 53 cm. (21 in.)
The hedgehog skate is common in the nw. Atlantic, along the seaboard of N. America from N. Carolina to Nova Scotia and the s. Gulf of St Lawrence. It is found on sandy and gravelly bottoms, less often on mud and rocks, and in depths down to about 33 m. (18 fathoms) although its depth range extends to 146 m. (80 fathoms). It feeds on a wide range of crustaceans, worms, bivalved shells, squids and fishes.

It breeds over the whole year, but there are 2 peaks for egg laying, during October-January and June-July. The eggs are laid in amber- or golden-coloured cases, which darken with age, with long slender horns at each corner. The young skate hatches in 6–9 months and is nearly 10 cm. (4 in.) long.

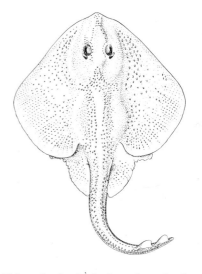

Although the hedgehog skate is the most common skate on the American Atlantic coast it is not fished for to any great extent. It is distinguished by the rounded corners of the pectoral fins and snout; its back is also densely thorny. It is greyish to light brown with rounded darker spots on the back, and white or pale grey ventrally.
R. laevis BARNDOOR SKATE 147 cm. (58 in.)
The barndoor skate is found along the Atlantic seaboard of N. America from the Grand Banks of Newfoundland and the s. Gulf of St Lawrence to N. Carolina. Within this range it occurs over the whole width of the continental

shelf from the shore line down to 430 m. (235 fathoms). It lives on sandy or gravelly grounds although in deeper water it is often found on mud.

It is typically skate-shaped with a rather long pointed snout, almost rectangular body disc and a slim tail with 2 dorsal fins. It is distinguished from other skates in the area by the absence of prickles on the mid-part of the disc, and by the 3 rows of thorns along the tail. It also has small black spots or short streaks marking the under-side which is otherwise whitish. The upper surface is brown with darker marks.

The barndoor skate feeds mainly on larger crustaceans including lobsters, crabs, and shrimps, but a large quantity of fish is eaten. It breeds along its whole range; its eggs are deposited mainly in winter although the young do not hatch until early summer. The young are approximately 18 cm. (7 in.) long at hatching. The egg cases from which they hatch are yellowish brown about 13 cm. (5 in.) long, with additionally a short horn at each corner.

The barndoor is one of the skates to be commercially fished in N. America, the fleshy parts of the pectoral fins only are marketed as 'skate saddles'.

R. montagui SPOTTED RAY 75 cm. (30 in.)
The spotted ray is widely distributed in British waters and along the European Atlantic and Mediterranean coasts. It is usually found in moderately deep water from 60–120 m. (33–66 fathoms) on sandy and even rocky bottoms.

In colour it is a warm brown, heavily scattered with small black spots, which do not extend to the edges of the disc. The skin is almost smooth except for the front of the disc, but it has a densely packed line of small spines along the mid-line of the back and tail.

This ray feeds mainly on crustaceans, although large specimens eat fishes in some number as well as the larger crabs, prawns, and shrimps. It breeds in English waters during early summer, and the young ray hatches from the egg case in 5–6 months.

This ray was named for Col. George Montagu, one of the most able English naturalists of the early 19th century. Montagu first described it from the Devon coast but mistakenly identified it with another named form.

R. naevus CUCKOO RAY 70 cm. (28 in.)
One of the most prettily marked of the European rays, its back is a light fawn to grey-brown with 2 distinct, black and yellow marbled rings, one on each pectoral fin. Its coloration also serves to distinguish it from all other rays in European coastal waters. It is found from Scotland s. to N. Africa, and in the Mediterranean, in moderately deep water of 20–150 m. (11–82 fathoms).

In British waters it is relatively common and is caught on long lines and in trawls, making some contribution to the total landings for food. Anglers also catch numbers of them.

It lays its transparent amber-coloured egg capsules in spring. The capsule measures about 6 cm. (2⅓ in.) in length, and has a long horn at each corner, one pair being longer than the other.

R. ocellata WINTER SKATE, EYED SKATE
1 m. (39 in.)
The winter skate is found in the w. N. Atlantic from n. Nova Scotia and the Newfoundland Banks to n. N. Carolina. This skate is found on sandy and gravelly bottoms, from the shore line to depths of 91–110 m. (50–60 fathoms), although it seems most common around 73 m. (40 fathoms). The shallow water stock tends to migrate shorewards at the onset of winter, withdrawing again to cooler deeper water in summer.

It is a common skate which is fished for commercially to a limited extent, only the thick fleshy parts of the pectoral fins being marketed. It breeds throughout its range; the eggs are laid in greenish or brownish cases, in summer and autumn. The egg case is between 55–85 mm. (2¼–3½ in.) in length with a horn at each of its 4 corners. The young hatches at a length of about 12 cm. (4¾ in.). Adults prey heavily on crabs and shrimps, but eat other invertebrates, as well as fishes.

The winter skate is distinguished by 1–4 white-edged dark spots on its back which is otherwise light brown with dark spots; its ventral side is whitish. Its snout is blunt and the corners of the disc rounded; it is heavily covered with thorns on the back and tail which has 4–6 irregular rows of curved spines along its length.

R. richardsoni RICHARDSON'S SKATE
145 cm. (57 in.)
This moderately large skate is known from deep water off the coast of New Zealand, s. of Ireland, and off Newfoundland. It was first named in 1961 from New Zealand waters, but its discovery elsewhere within a decade suggests that it may be worldwide in its distribution. The depths at which it lives, 2000–3000 m. (1093–1639 fathoms), are little explored for bottom-living fishes, and most of those that have been caught have been taken on specially set deep-water lines.

It is a long-snouted species with fine prickles in the skin on both sides of the body. Its eyes are very widely spaced. It is light brown above, lighter below, but the underside of the tail is the same colour as the back.

R. whitleyi MELBOURNE SKATE 1·5 m. (5 ft)
The Melbourne skate is well distributed on the coasts of S. Australia, Victoria, and New South Wales. It is found in relatively shallow water for such a large species.

Like other members of the family it is oviparous, its eggs being rectangular and enclosed in a capsule described as silky green in colour. It is distinguished from its few relatives in Australian waters by its long snout, and its light prickling of the front part of the disc.

A closely related, if not identical skate from s. Queensland waters is the common skate, or Pommy skate (*Raja australis*) which has similar coloration of olive to grey-brown above and light spots. The underside is greyish with numerous black pores. It is a valued food fish where common which on account of its resemblance to the English skate (*R. batis*) is locally known as 'Pommy skate'.

RAJIDAE

The family of the skates and rays, a group of bottom-living cartilaginous fishes widely distributed in temperate and cold waters, and mainly in deep water in the tropics. A very large number of species are known. They are distinguished by their flattened body shape, with a quadrangular disc formed laterally by the enlarged pectoral fins, and a well developed but thin tail. The tail fin is small, as are the dorsal fins. In many species the skin is rough with small spines. Most species have weakly developed electric organs. All have large spiracles through which they pass water in respiration, and 5 ventral gill slits. Fertilization is internal but the eggs are laid protected in a horny capsule.

The names skate and ray are more or less interchangeable, there is no biological basis for dividing them. In practice it is convenient to use the word skate for the larger species, while retaining ray for the smaller members, but 'skate' is used in the U.K. for any rajid sold as food. See **Dactylobatus, Raja.**

Ranzania   Molidae
   laevis SLENDER SUNFISH 80 cm. (31 in.)
As distinctively shaped as the other members of the family, this species is characterized by its mouth, the lips extending over the teeth and the mouth opening in a vertical plane.

It is an oceanic species found in all tropical and temperate seas, but apparently nowhere abundant. Its biology is virtually unknown, too few specimens have ever been available to study critically and most of those have been stranded or captured in shallow inshore waters, an alien habitat. It will probably be found to live in the upper 200 m. (109 fathoms) of water in the open sea, and to feed on jelly-fishes and ctenophores.

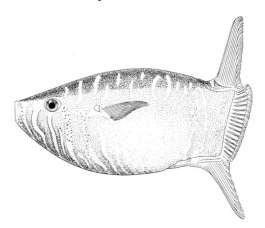

Its coloration is striking, deep blue on the back, gleaming metallic on its sides, with brilliant silvery black-edged stripes across the head, curving onto the belly, and fainter stripes near the tail region.

It never attains the size of the other ocean sunfishes, its maximum weight is probably never in excess of 11 kg. (25 lb.).

Rasbora   Cyprinidae
   borapetensis 5 cm. (2 in.)
This rasbora was discovered in 1934 in Thailand. It was found in Bung Borapet, and probably occurs in the rivers adjacent to this large artificial lake. It is, like others of its genus, a shoaling fish found mainly near the surface. Since its discovery it has been imported occasionally, but it has not yet been known to have bred in captivity. It feeds freely on small crustaceans and mosquito larvae in the aquarium.

Its body form is similar to other rasboras, but its lateral line is short. **133**
R. einthoveni BRILLIANT RASBORA
9 cm. (3½ in.)
This is a widely distributed rasbora in the

Indo-Australian Archipelago, being found in Malacca, Singapore, the islands of Malaysia, and Thailand. It is a typical member of the group. Its back is greenish brown or olive in colour; the sides and belly are silvery. A deep green or black slightly curved line runs along the sides, edged above by a reddish golden line. The fins are clear coloured.

A popular aquarium fish, the brilliant rasbora is relatively easy to keep and induce to spawn.

R. heteromorpha HARLEQUINFISH, RED RASBORA 4·5 cm. (1¾ in.)
This is one of the most popular of the rasboras for the aquarium and it has been imported now for many years, as well as being successfully bred in captivity. Its breeding habits are interesting in that, following a brief courtship display by the male, the female selects a firmly attached broad-leaved water plant and lays her eggs on the underside. A relatively high temperature, of 24–28°C. is necessary for successful spawning.

This is a shoaling fish found alike in streams and lakes of the Malayan Peninsula, e. Sumatra, and Thailand. **134**

R. kallochroma RED-EMBER RASBORA 10 cm. (4 in.)
A beautiful species of rasbora the native range of which is Malaya, Sumatra, and Borneo. It is a little-known species whose habits and habitat are still largely unknown. It has been imported and kept in aquaria in Europe. **135**

R. lateristriata YELLOW RASBORA 12 cm. (4½ in.)
A widespread species in the islands of the E. Indian Archipelago and in Thailand, where it inhabits the cool, clear, swiftly-flowing streams in the mountain foothills. It is common in waterfall pools in certain areas. Its choice of such streams is reflected in the tolerance it shows to low temperatures in the aquarium. **136**

R. maculata PYGMY or SPOTTED RASBORA 2·5 cm. (1 in.)
This, as its name suggests, is a diminutive species of rasbora which is sexually mature at a length of less than 2 cm. It is an attractive aquarium species, living in shoals and being moderately hardy. It does best in aquaria planted with peaty bottom soil, no doubt a reflection of its chosen habitat of small ponds and ditches. It is a native to Sumatra, Singapore, and the s. Malayan Peninsula. Females are deeper-bodied, and slightly less colourful than the males. **137**

R. vaterifloris PEARLY RASBORA 4 cm. (1½ in.)
A rather deep-bodied rasbora with well developed, high dorsal and anal fins. It has been imported to Europe quite commonly and survives in aquaria for a long time; it has been bred in captivity.

Its native range is in mountain streams in Sri Lanka, being originally found in the streams in the Ratnapura district. **138**

RASBORA,
   BRILLIANT see **Rasbora einthoveni**
   PEARLY see **Rasbora vaterifloris**
   PYGMY see **Rasbora maculata**
   RED see **Rasbora heteromorpha**
   RED-EMBER see **Rasbora kallochroma**
   SPOTTED see **Rasbora maculata**
   YELLOW see **Rasbora lateristriata**

Rasborichthys   Cyprinidae
altior 9 cm. (3½ in.)
This genus shows many of the features of the rasboras and the barbs. It is deep-bodied as are the latter, but has no barbels. Its dorsal fin is high, its anal fin many-rayed. Two species are known in the Sumatra, Borneo, Singapore region of which *R. altior* is confined to Singapore Island where it is common in pools, reservoirs and their tributary streams.

It makes a peaceful aquarium fish, easy to feed, and breed. Its habit of swimming in a tight shoal makes it particularly attractive. **139**

RASCASSE see **Scorpaena porcus, Scorpaena scrofa**
RASPHEAD ROCKFISH see **Sebastes ruberrimus**

Rastrelliger   Scombridae
kanagurta LONG-JAWED MACKEREL 30 cm. (12 in.)
An Indo-Pacific species of wide distribution which is found from the E. African coast, throughout the Indian Ocean to n. Australia and the w. Pacific. It occurs in the Red Sea and is one of several fish species to have penetrated into the Mediterranean *via* the Suez canal.

It is a rather deep-bodied mackerel distinguished mainly by its stout body, moderate scales, long jaw, the lower projecting, and by 2 small keels either side of the tail fin lobes. Its colour is bluish above, green-tinged in front with a row of faint dusky spots along the dorsal profile. The sides and belly are silvery, the fins mainly yellowish.

It has some local value as a food fish but is not specially fished for. It does, however, form a major component of the diet of some of the large Indian Ocean tuna and is thus of considerable indirect importance.

RAT-TAILS see Macrouridae
RAT-TAIL, CALIFORNIA see **Nezumia stelgidolepis**
RATFISH see Chimaeridae
RATFISH see **Chimaera monstrosa, Gonorhynchus gonorhynchus, Hydrolagus colliei**
RAVEN, ATLANTIC SEA see **Hemitripterus americanus**
RAY see Anacanthobatidae, Pseudorajidae, Rajidae
RAY,
   BUTTERFLY see Gymnuridae
   BUTTERFLY see **Gymnura natalensis**
   COW-NOSED see Rhinopteridae
   COW-NOSED see **Rhinoptera bonasus**
   CUCKOO see **Raja naevus**
   DEEP-SEA ELECTRIC see **Benthobatis marcida**
   DEVIL see Mobulidae
   DEVIL see **Mobula mobular**
   EAGLE see Myliobatidae
   EAGLE see **Myliobatis aquila, Myliobatis australis**
   ELECTRIC see Torpedinidae
   ELECTRIC see **Torpedo nobiliana**
   FIDDLER see **Trygonorhina fasciata**
   GIANT DEVIL see **Manta birostris**
   LESSER BUTTERFLY see **Gymnura micrura**
   LESSER ELECTRIC see **Narcine brasiliensis**

PACIFIC ELECTRIC see **Torpedo californica**
PYGMY DEVIL see **Mobula diabolus**
RIBBONTAIL see **Taeniura lymma**
RIVER see **Potamotrygon magdalenae, Potamotrygon motoro**
SHARK see **Rhina ancylostomus**
SHOVEL-NOSE see **Rhinobatos armatus**
SMOOTH BUTTERFLY see **Gymnura micrura**
SPOTTED see **Raja montagui**
SPOTTED EAGLE see **Aetobatus narinari**
THORNBACK see **Raja clavata**
TORPEDO see Torpedinidae
WHITE SPOTTED see **Rhynchobatus djeddensis**
RAY'S BREAM see **Brama brama**
RAZORBACK SUCKER see **Xyrauchen texanus**
RAZORFISH see **Centriscus scutatus**
RED
   BANDFISH see **Cepola rubescens**
   BARB see **Barbus conchonius**
   COD see **Physiculus bachus**
   EMPEROR see **Lutjanus sebae**
   FIREFISH see **Pterois volitans**
   HAKE see **Urophycis chuss**
   INDIAN FISH see **Pataecus fronto**
   IRISH LORD see **Hemilepidotus hemilepidotus**
   GURNARD see **Chelidonichthys kumu**
   LIZARDFISH see **Synodus synodus**
   MULLET see Mullidae
   MULLET see **Mullus surmuletus, Pseudupeneus barberinus**
   PIRANHA see **Rooseveltiella nattereri**
   RASBORA see **Rasbora heteromorpha**
   SEA BLENNY see under **Ecsenius gravieri**
   SEA BREAM see **Pagellus bogaraveo**
   SEA-HARDER see **Emmelichthys nitidus**
   SHINER see **Notropis lutrensis**
   SNAPPER see **Lutjanus argentimaculatus, Lutjanus sebae, Sebastes ruberrimus**
   SOLDIERFISH see **Holocentrus rubrum**
   STEENBRAS see **Petrus rupestris**
   TETRA see **Hyphessobrycon flammeus**
   TONGUE-SOLE see **Cynoglossus joyneri**
RED-BAIT see **Emmelichthys nitidus**
RED-BELLIED FUSILIER see **Caesio erythrogaster**
RED-EAR SARDINE see **Harengula humeralis**
RED-EMBER RASBORA see **Rasbora kallochroma**
RED-EYED CHARACIN see **Arnoldichthys spilopterus**
RED-NOSED TETRA see **Hemigrammus rhodostomus**
RED-PHANTOM TETRA see **Megalamphodus sweglesi**
RED-SPOTTED
   COPEINA see **Copeina guttata**
   HAWKFISH see **Amblycirrhitus pinos**
RED-STRIPED BUTTERFLYFISH see **Chaetodon lunula**
RED-TAILED BLACK SHARK see **Labeo bicolor**
REDBELLY DACE, NORTHERN see **Phoxinus eos**
REDBREAM see **Chrysophrys auratus**
REDEYE TRIPLEFIN see **Enneanectes pectoralis**
REDFANG see **Odonus niger**
REDFIN
   PARROTFISH see **Sparisoma rubripinne**
   PICKEREL see **Esox americanus**

REGALECIDAE

A family of extremely elongate marine fishes which are found worldwide in tropical or temperate seas. Numerous names have been proposed for apparently differing forms but there is probably only one species.

The body is ribbon-shaped, the sides very compressed. The dorsal fin origin is above the eyes, the first rays are very elongate, and the fin continues the whole length of the body; the tail fin is rudimentary or absent. The mouth is very protractile, and is of characteristic formation. See **Regalecus.**

Regalecus   Regalecidae
glesne OARFISH, KING-OF-THE-HERRINGS
7 m. (23 ft)
This most remarkable fish is found worldwide in temperate and tropical seas. It is probably best known from specimens in the New Zealand-Tasmania region, and from the e. N. Atlantic, but most have been cast ashore after storms or found in shallow water. Thus this huge fish is mainly known from disabled or sick specimens found out of their normal environment. Healthy fish are presumed to live in deep water and to be able to outswim trawls or other catching apparatus.

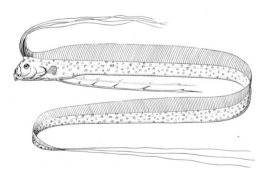

It is presumed to be a mesopelagic fish found in the deep sea at depths of 300–600 m. (164–328 fathoms). Larval specimens are sometimes captured in mid-water trawls and near the surface, and the young fish are occasionally found in the stomachs of deep-feeding tunas and lancet fishes.

Little is known of its biology; specimens caught in Californian waters have contained large quantities of euphausiid crustaceans (krill).

It is a most distinctive fish with its silvery body and deep red fins. The dorsal fin has an anterior section of high fin rays each with a flap of skin at the tip, and the pelvics are very long with skin flaps at the tip. So many oarfishes have been found with substantial parts of their tails missing that it appears to be almost an expendable organ.

Reinhardtius   Pleuronectidae
hippoglossoides GREENLAND or BLACK
HALIBUT, GREENLAND TURBOT 102 cm.
(40 in.)
A cold-water flatfish found in the seas of the far N. In the Atlantic, throughout the Arctic Ocean and Norwegian Sea, s. to the Faeroe-Shetland ridge but rarely beyond it, and in the w. Atlantic Ocean from Greenland, and Newfoundland, s. to New Jersey. In the N. Pacific basin it is found in both the Bering and Okhotsk seas, s. to Japan and to California. In both oceans there are records of specimens occurring far to the S. of the normal range, due presumably to isolated wanderers being caught in deep cold water.

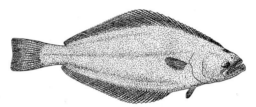

It is found only in deep cold water, usually in depths of 250–1600 m. (136–875 fathoms) although to the N. of its range it can be found in shallower water. It is a very active predator, unlike most flatfishes, habitually quitting the seabed to hunt in mid-water and even at the surface. Its food consists mainly of prawns, shrimps, fishes, and squids.

This species is one of the few flatfishes to have a heavily pigmented blind side to its body. The eyed side is dark brown almost black, but the left side is a dull olive-green. No doubt this is equally due to the fish's habit of foraging in mid-water, and to the placing of the upper eye on the extreme edge of the head where it must have a greater angle of vision than normal in flatfishes.

The Greenland halibut is heavily exploited by the natives of that land, and is commercially fished for in both Atlantic and Pacific Oceans but it is a relatively poor fish when fresh, its flesh being watery and insipid. It attains an average weight of about 10 kg. (22 lb.).

Remora   Echeneidae
australis WHALESUCKER 51 cm. (20 in.)
Probably worldwide in its distribution, but little known on account of the paucity of specimens correctly identified. This species has been found attached to the hides of cetaceans only. It seems to be unselective in its choice of host having been reported from blue whales and porpoises.

It is a very short-bodied, stout fish with a very large adhesive disc on the top of the head, with between 25 and 27 laminae. It is dark grey to brown above, darker on the lower surface. The dorsal and anal fins are rather small.
R. remora REMORA, SHORT SUCKINGFISH,
SHARKSUCKER 46 cm. (18 in.)
Very widely distributed in tropical and warm temperate seas, attaching itself to various species of mainly offshore sharks. Many of these perform long migrations and consequently remoras are found in temperate seas, such as those of Britain by virtue of the fact that the host travelled there. This species is usually found attached to the skin of its host, and feeds extensively on the parasites which are likewise attached. It is a relatively common species.

This species is distinguished by its uniform colour, dark brown above and below, its rounded rather thickset body, and by the numerous laminae (14–20) forming the sucking disc.

REMORA see Echeneidae

Retropinna   Retropinnidae
retropinna NEW ZEALAND SMELT
10 cm. (4 in.)
This is a slender-bodied fish, found in rivers (often far from the sea) and in estuaries in New Zealand. It is almost transparent, but in salt water the back may be dark, and it has a pearly iridescent stripe along the sides.

This, the common smelt of New Zealand, spawns from November to April in the lower reaches of rivers close to the sea's influence, and the fry may live in the estuary before returning to freshwater.

As in other smelt species the head and trunk of the males are covered with a rash of pearl organs or nuptial tubercles, most obvious around spawning time, but giving the fish a rougher texture at all times. The male also has a longer anal fin. Both sexes have a small adipose fin between the tail fin and the dorsal fin, a rounded snout, and an absence of large teeth in the mouth.
R. semoni AUSTRALIAN SMELT 10 cm. (4 in.)
This smelt occurs along the e. coastal rivers of Australia as far N. as the Fitzroy River, and throughout the Murray-Darling river system. It has been introduced to Tasmania. It is mainly a freshwater fish but has been found in salt water at the mouth of streams.

It spawns in spring at a temperature of 15°C.; the eggs are adhesive and sink to the bottom of the stream. They hatch in about 9 days, and measure about 5 mm. at hatching. They become sexually mature at one year of age, the male can be distinguished as its head and trunk are covered with small pearl organs or nuptial tubercles. Both sexes are colourless with a few black specks along the back.

RETROPINNIDAE

The members of this family are often known as smelts; their external appearance, as well as the habits of some, are similar to the N. Hemisphere smelts (Osmeridae). They are confined to the waters around s. and e. Australia, Tasmania, and New Zealand. Some species are found in the sea and migrate into freshwater to breed; others are found established permanently in freshwater rivers and lakes. They are variable in body form, depending on climatic and physical features of the locality in which they live, and consequently much confusion has occurred in their taxonomy; even now further advances in knowledge of their relationships with one another will probably be made.

All are rather slender fishes, with a small head and mouth. The dorsal and anal fins are placed far back near the tail, and they all possess an adipose dorsal fin near the tail. All have small scales on the body. See **Retropinna.**

Rexea   Gempylidae
   solandri KING BARRACUTA, HAKE
1·3 m. (52 in.)
A species reported only from the region of s. Australia and New Zealand. In the seas of the former it occurs around Tasmania, New South Wales, and Victoria. It is essentially a midwater, pelagic species occasionally taken by trawlers, but most often captured by lines.

At one time it was a very important commercial species, but after 1880 it virtually disappeared from the fishery and very few specimens were captured. Its flesh is said to have a fine texture and flavour.

It is a rather stout-bodied fish with a long spiny dorsal fin, short second dorsal and anal fin, large head with very large teeth. It is deep blue above, silvery below with a dark patch on the anterior membrane of the first dorsal fin.

Rhabdosargus   Sparidae
   globiceps WHITE STUMPNOSE,
GO-HOME FISH 51 cm. (20 in.)
One of many species of sea breams which are found only in the waters of s. Africa, this species ranges from Natal to the Cape, where it is very common. It is mostly found in sandy areas but the young fish penetrate into estuaries.

It has powerful rounded or oval molar teeth in each jaw but flattened cutting teeth in front. It is mainly silvery, bluish on the back with darker crossbars on the upper sides.

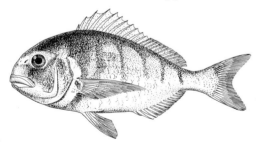

The white stumpnose is an important commercial fish in S. Africa, taken by nets and lines mostly inshore at night. It is also a fine sporting fish. Its flesh is well flavoured. Its local name 'go-home-fish' is bestowed on account of the belief that when this fish is about all others will disappear.
R. sarba YELLOW-FIN OR SILVER BREAM,
TARWHINE 40 cm. (16 in.)
Widespread in both the Indian and Pacific oceans, found from the Red Sea and E. African coast, around India, the E. Indies, n. Australia, and n. to Japan. It is abundant in shallow inshore waters, on sandy and rough bottoms, and in clear patches between reefs.

Throughout its range it is an important food fish and large numbers are caught by anglers. In S. Africa it is especially regarded as an angler's fish and is said to grow to 11·3 kg. (25 lb.) – at which weight the length is much greater than 40 cm.

The jaws have powerful rounded molars in the sides. It is bluish on the back, each scale

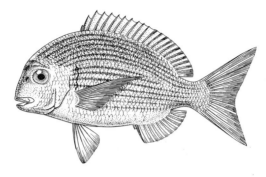

has a gold centre giving an impression of yellowish lines; the belly and lower fins are deep yellow.

Rhacochilus   Embiotocidae
   toxotes RUBBERLIP SEAPERCH
46 cm. (18 in.)
A Californian species found, according to Dr John E. Fitch and Dr Robert J. Lavenburg, from the Little River, Mendocino County to Cape Colnett, Baja California. It is one of the largest members of the family, and is fished for commercially as well as for sport. It is an inshore fish, found over kelp-beds, in harbours and bays, around jetties, and just outside the surf zone of beaches.

Like other members of the family it is viviparous, the females giving birth to young during April to June, these are about 9 cm. (3½ in.) long at birth.

It is distinguished by its thick fleshy lips, and relatively short dorsal spines.

Rhamdia   Pimelodidae
   sapo BAGRE SAPO 41 cm. (16 in.)
Widely distributed in the central region of e. S. America, particularly in Argentina, Uruguay, and se. Brazil. It is found in both lakes and rivers but favours rivers with very slight currents.

Its body form is typically pimelodid, flattened from above in front, compressed laterally posteriorly. The dorsal fin is moderately high and rounded, the adipose fin long; a strong, serrated spine in the pectoral fins. Two pairs of shortish barbels on the lower jaw, a pair of very long barbels on the upper jaw. Colour, deep olive with dark spots on the back and upper sides, lighter below.

The bagre sapo is a moderately important food fish in parts of its range and is captured on lines. Its flesh is white. Small specimens are imported as aquarium fish.
R. vacca PILE PERCH, DUSKY SEA PERCH
38 cm. (15 in.)
Found along the w. seaboard of the U.S. and Canada, between s. California and se. Alaska. It is very common in shallow inshore water, but in the n. of its range in winter it moves into deeper water. It is most familiar living around wharves, harbours, and in the surf zone of bays. It is a popular sporting fish for the shore angler.

It is dark brown above, silvery on the sides, with dusky blotches running down the sides. A distinct black spot behind the mouth.

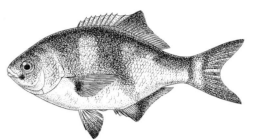

RHAMPHICHTHYIDAE
Knifefishes related to the Gymnotidae and like them widely distributed in the freshwaters of lowland S. America. A number of species are known, and several genera are recognized, all characterized by having the upper jaw overlapping the lower, and by the lack of a dorsal filament and a tail fin. All members of the family have a thread-like tail, without the anal fin rays reaching to the tip. In other respects they closely resemble the gymnotids, notably in the extremely long anal fin which originates in the region of the pectoral fins.

They are mostly fishes living in murky still waters, with muddy bottoms. Most species are nocturnal and conceal themselves during daylight under vegetation. Their eyes are poorly developed, but they possess electrical organs by which they can set up a weak field around about, and navigate and find food in this way. See **Eigenmannia, Hypopomus, Rhamphichthys, Sternopygus.**

Rhamphichthys   Rhamphichthyidae
   rostratus BANDFISH 137 cm. (54 in.)
This most striking knifefish is one of several species which has a long, trunk-like snout, ending in a small mouth. Its body form is otherwise as in its relatives, the dorsal, tail, and pelvic fins being lacking, and the anal fin long. The anal fin commences under the throat and continues to within a head-length of the tip of the tail.

It is widely distributed in ne. S. America from the Guianas s. to the Rio de la Plata. It lives in the smaller and more open streams, but is occasionally taken in larger rivers. It can be found (in daytime at least) under the roots of plants growing in the water, at night it forages for the mud-inhabiting insect larvae and worms on which it feeds. It is a highly regarded food fish in areas in which it is common; it has also been imported as an aquarium fish.

It is a medium brown in colour with blotches of dark brown and black on the back, and mottling of brown on the sides. The ventral surface is creamy white.

Rhaphiodon   Characidae
   gibbus 33 cm. (13 in.)
A most striking fish which is of wide distribution in the region of the Amazon and extends as far N. as Guyana rivers.

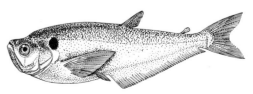

Its body shape is quite unmistakable, so much so that the distinguished American ichthyologist C. H. Eigenmann wrote, 'a fantastic fish, the appearance of which suggests a "grafting" of two types, one type being represented from the head to behind the shoulder-girdle, the other from behind the shoulder-girdle to the tail.' The body is deeply compressed, the scales minute, and overall, silvery except that it has a large dark spot just behind the head.

This fish was formerly placed in a family of its own, the Cynodontidae. Recently, however, the French student of the characoid fishes, Dr Jacques Géry has suggested that, with the genus *Hydrocynus*, it forms a subfamily Rhaphiodontinae within the Characidae.

Rhina   Rhynchobatidae
   ancylostomus SHARK RAY, MUD SKATE
2·75 m. (9 ft)
Widely distributed in the Indo-Pacific from the E. African coast across to Australia and in the Pacific. It differs from the other members of the family by its wide head and bluntly-rounded snout, the pectoral fins also are relatively small. In colour it is dull brown, lighter below, sometimes with whitish dots and spots. A series of ridges on the head have large bony tubercles; the teeth in the jaws are flattened and rounded.

It is a very large fish, specimens of 125 kg. (275 lb.) having been captured. It is not, however, deliberately fished for either by anglers or commercial fishermen. Despite its rather repulsive appearance its flesh is good to eat.

The mud skate lives in shallow water, feeds on crabs and shellfish, with which its teeth are well equipped to deal.

RHINCODONTIDAE
A single member of this shark family is known, the huge *Rhincodon typus*, the whale shark, the largest fish in the world. See **Rhincodon**.

Rhincodon   Rhincodontidae
   typus WHALE SHARK 18 m. (60 ft)
The whale shark is found in all tropical seas. It is said to feed exclusively on small planktonic animals, but one reliable report refers to small tuna being injested while the shark was feeding on smaller fish. Whale sharks are seen mostly at the surface of the sea, and there have been a

number of incidents in which they have been rammed by vessels.

Their gigantic size has led to occasional exaggerations but there is little doubt that they grow to a length of 15·2 m. (50 ft), and even occasionally to 18 m. (60 ft). Their weight has been less reliably measured but the maximum is probably close to 20 tons (20·3 tonnes). The whale shark is the largest living fish.

Despite its size its natural history is very little known. A chance capture by a shrimp trawler in the Gulf of Mexico in 1953 of a comparatively huge egg case, 30 cm. (12 in.) long, was for a long time the only known evidence that this shark lays eggs. The unhatched embryo, although well developed, measured 36 cm. (14 in.) overall. Young whale sharks are otherwise unknown.

Rhinecanthus   Balistidae
   aculeatus BLACK-BARRED TRIGGERFISH
30 cm. (12 in.)
A widely distributed tropical Indo-Pacific species found from the E. African coast, throughout the Indian Ocean and w. Pacific to the Hawaiian Islands. In Hawaii it is known as humuhumu – well known in island songs.

Its coloration is very variable, greenish in background above, white below, with 4 alternating broad and narrow stripes running across the side. A patch of spines on the sides of the tail are set in an elongate black oval surrounded by blue. A dark bar running across the side of the head.

The late Professor J. L. B. Smith in his book on the sea fishes of s. Africa reports that this triggerfish 'sleeps soundly on its side at night. Makes a whirring noise when startled.'
R. assasi 20 cm. (8 in.)
A triggerfish endemic to the Red Sea and first described by Pehr Forsskål in 1775 from Djedda; 'azzazi' is its local name. In most of the Red Sea they are abundant, living under stones, in crevices in the coral which they excavate completely by themselves, or by enlarging a smaller crevice. They are aggressive fish, fighting between themselves, by means of tail blows which brings the sharp spines along the sides of the tail into play. It eats a variety of food but prefers living prey, killing and feeding on any smaller fish they can capture. **479**

Rhinesomus   Ostraciontidae
   reipublicae TURRETFISH 23 cm. (9 in.)
An Australian species, found only in the area of New Guinea, Queensland, New South Wales, and Lord Howe Island. It is reported to be a pelagic species (in a group which is almost entirely bottom-living) but this may be due to the number that are stranded after storms. On the other hand the Queensland prawn-trawlers which operate in moderate depths catch numbers of this boxfish which suggests a benthic, deep-water species.

It is dull brown with milky-blue spots over

the body. It is distinguished from the other members of the family by the upward pointing spine above each eye, 2 low spines on the midline of the back, and 3 spines along the lower edges of the carapace, although it does not have a spine at the lower rear corner of the box. Its biology is little-known.

Rhinhoplichthys   Hoplichthyidae
   haswelli DEEP-SEA FLATHEAD
43 cm. (17 in.)
Widely distributed on the more s. coasts of Australia, and reported from W. Australia, S. Australia, Victoria, and New South Wales. It has been reported in the Great Australian Bight. It is a deep water form which is taken only at depths of 137–1463 m. (75–800 fathoms) and is not well known. It is said to be good eating.

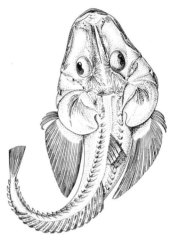

It is pinkish above, white below, the back rather mottled.

Rhinichthys   Cyprinidae
   cataractae LONGNOSE DACE 15 cm. (6 in.)
A long slender freshwater fish of N. America, the longnose dace is distinguished by its long projecting snout, by the presence of a barbel, and by the absence of a groove between the upper lip and the tip of the snout. It is olive or dark green, lighter below, and with an indistinct dark lengthwise stripe from the gill cover to the base of the tail fin. Males during the spawning season have a rather heightened colour, as well as small whitish tubercles on the top of the head, pectoral and pelvic fins.

It is very widely distributed, virtually across the whole of the n. U.S., and all Canada except for the Arctic regions.

It is mainly a bottom-living river fish, living amongst crannies in the river bed in a swift current, although the younger specimens are often found close inshore under stones. It sheds its eggs in clumps under stones; they are guarded by one parent. They hatch in 7–10 days at 16°C. The young are pelagic after about 7 days and live at the surface of the stream's backwaters.

RHINOBATIDAE
A family of ray-like fishes found in shallow seas in tropical and warm temperate regions the world over. In many respects they appear to be intermediate between the rays and the sharks, for the body is rounded and elongate although the pectoral fins are broad and well developed. The gill openings, 5 each side, are

placed ventrally, and all the family have flattened, tapering snouts. Their body shape suggests a number of their vernacular names, like guitarfishes, fiddle sharks, and shovel-nose sharks.

They are bottom-living fish, feeding on crustaceans and molluscs mainly, and their closely packed small teeth are well adapted for such prey. See **Rhinobatus, Trygonorhina.**

Rhinobatus   Rhinobatidae
  armatus SHOVEL-NOSE RAY 2·1 m. (7 ft)
The shovel-nose ray is the most common member of the family in n. Australian waters, and is found throughout the E. Indies to India. It is a shallow water form frequently found in estuaries and even in freshwater. Young specimens are rated as good food fish and it is frequently marketed in N. Australia and Queensland.

Like all its family it is a bottom-living fish and is dull coloured, usually a light brown, and well adapted to match the colour of the sea bed. Its teeth are blunt with an indistinct ridge, suggesting that its food is mainly crustaceans.
  R. cemiculus see under **R. rhinobatus**
  R. halavi see under **R. rhinobatus**
  R. lentiginosus SPOTTED or ATLANTIC GUITARFISH 76 cm. (30 in.)
This is the commonest of the guitarfishes found in the w. Atlantic; it has been reported in the area from Yucatan to Cape Lookout, N. Carolina.

Its body shape is typical of the group, and the snout is blunt-tipped and long, forming a triangle with the pectoral fins which are rounded at the base. A small cluster of tubercles on the snout tip. It is dull brown, with a dense covering of small white spots. Underneath it is creamy white.

A bottom-living fish, found most commonly in bays and estuaries where it finds the small crustaceans on which it feeds. Occasionally forages in the breakers, and on the Florida Keys and beaches it can be seen at the water's edge, its dorsal fins breaking the surface while it hunts down its small, burrowing prey.
  R. rhinobatus 1 m. (39 in.)
The only guitarfish to be found at all commonly in European seas. It is found through-

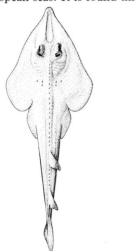

out the Mediterranean (although it is rare in the n. parts of that sea), and in the e. Atlantic from Angola to the s. Bay of Biscay, where again it is rare. It possesses the typical pointed snout, and fiddle-shaped body (its Italian name is Pesce violino) common to the family.

Its dorsal and tail fins are well developed. In colour it is a dull grey-brown unrelieved by markings; the undersurface is white.

This guitarfish is ovoviviparous, the young are born in spring from February to July. It is a sluggish fish found most commonly half buried in sandy or muddy grounds. It feeds on the small crustaceans and molluscs common in such habitats.

The Mediterranean contains one other native guitarfish R. cemiculus, which apart from its rather larger head and more produced snout differs in the shape of its nostril valves. It lives in deeper water than the other species and appears to be confined to the s. coast of the Mediterranean. A third species, R. halavi, has been reported from the e. Mediterranean and has immigrated from the Red Sea via the Suez Canal.

Rhinochimaera   Rhinochimaeridae
  atlantica 136 cm. (54 in.)
This long-snouted chimaeroid was first discovered off the coast of SW. Ireland, during fishery explorations by the R. V. *Helga* in 1908 in depths of 1225–1408 m. (670–770 fathoms). None have been captured so far S. since, although it has been taken off the W. coast of Scotland, off Iceland, and off the N. American coast. Its biology is unknown, except for the obvious fact that it is an inhabitant of the lower continental slope.

The genus *Rhinochimaera* is distinguished from *Harriotta* by smooth dental plates in the roof of the mouth, and by the upper edge of tha tail being armed with spiny denticles, many of them having 2 points.

In addition to the species in the Atlantic, another occurs off Japan (R. pacifica), and an egg case possibly belonging to the genus was dredged up in the Bay of Bengal many years ago.
  R. pacifica see under **R. atlantica**

RHINOCHIMAERIDAE

A family of chimaeroid fishes or rabbitfishes which are found in deep water in the n. Atlantic, off S. Africa, and also off Japan. It is quite possible that the family will be found to be represented elsewhere in the cool oceans at appropriate depths.

Like other chimaeroids these combine certain shark-like features with those of bony fishes, the cartilaginous skeleton, and paired pelvic claspers of males being shark-like. They also have a cartilaginous gill cover over the single external gill opening – a feature of bony fishes. A characteristic of the rhinochimaeroids is their long, pointed snout, but they also have a single rod forming the male's clasper (not 2–3 as other families). They all lay eggs. The shape of the egg capsule is elongate with a large ribbed flap down each side. See **Harriotta, Rhinochimaera.**

Rhinonemus   Gadidae
  cimbrius FOUR-BEARDED ROCKLING 41 cm. (16 in.)
Distributed on both sides of the Atlantic, this

rockling is found from the nw. Gulf of St Lawrence to N. Carolina in the w. Atlantic, from Iceland and n. Norway to the English Channel. It is also found in the w. Baltic.

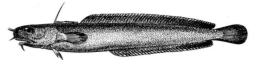

It is a long slender fish with barbels on the tip of the lower jaw, tip of the snout, and on each anterior nostril. The dorsal fin is long, and preceded by a series of short low rays and a single long ray. It is sandy or reddish brown, lighter on the belly, with dark patches at the end of the dorsal and anal fins. This rockling is a bottom-living animal, found between 50–550 m. (27–300 fathoms) although mostly in the shallower depths to the N. It feeds almost entirely on crustaceans, especially shrimps and isopods but also eats marine worms. It spawns in late spring and summer; the eggs and young are pelagic.

It has no fisheries or sporting value.

Rhinoprenes   Rhinoprenidae
  pentanemus THREAD-FIN SCAT
15 cm. (6 in.)
A very striking scat-like fish with a deep body, compressed and almost quadrangular outline. The body is covered with small scales but the most characteristic features are the very elongate second dorsal spine, the fourth ray of the pectoral, and the first pelvic ray, while the snout is peculiarly blunt.

It is known only from the muddy bottoms of the river mouths in the Gulf of Papua. Many of its pecularities are thought to be adaptations to life in the heavily silted muddy water, the enlarged nostrils, and very long fin

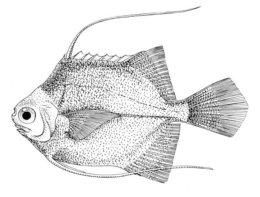

rays being obvious sensory adaptations. This very interesting species, which is thought to be allied to the scats (family Scatophagidae), was discovered only as recently as 1964.

RHINOPRENIDAE

A family created to contain the single species *Rhinoprenes pentanemus*. This is a small, scaly-finned fish found in the mouths of rivers in the New Guinea area. It is closely related to the scats (family Scatophagidae), but differs in having a blunt, pig-like snout, rather well-developed nostrils, and several long thread-like fin rays. See **Rhinoprenes.**

Rhinoptera   Rhinopteridae
  bonasus COW-NOSED RAY 71 cm. (28 in.)
wide – possibly much more
This ray is found along the coastal waters of

the American Atlantic from New England to mid-Brazil, although its occurrence in the Caribbean seems to be sporadic and there may be 2 centres of population N. and S. of the Equator. To some extent it seems to be migratory for schools containing between 4000 and 6000 individuals have been seen, and photographed, from an airplane off Florida. It is a moderately large ray with pointed pectoral fins and a blunt snout. The snout region is characteristic in the family being divided into 2 lobes above and below while the upper and lower surfaces are separated by a deep groove. The tail is moderately long, and possesses both dorsal fin and serrated spine. It is described as plain brownish above, whitish beneath.

The teeth of these rays are notable in that they are flattened with interlocking sides forming a mosaic in both jaws. Such powerful crushing teeth imply a diet of hard-shelled animals, and in N. American waters they are known to feed almost exclusively on crabs, lobsters, oysters, clams, and other molluscs. These rays expose the buried shellfish with the beating of their powerful pectoral fins and have been seen in compact shoals working over the mollusc-rich sand or mud. They are powerful swimmers and are frequently seen in mid-water in large shoals.

R. marginata *c.* 1 m. (3¼ ft) in length
This cow-nosed ray does not differ greatly from the w. Atlantic species *R. bonasus*. It is said to be distinguished by having teeth in the jaws arranged in 9 distinct series, and by having a roughened patch of skin teeth on its back, but it is a little-known and poorly studied species.

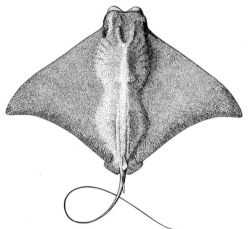

It was first described in 1817 in the published scientific reports of Napoleon's expedition to Egypt, by one of the naturalists who accompanied him, Geoffroy Saint-Hilaire. Since then it has been reported at isolated places along the s. coast of the Mediterranean, in the Straits of Gibraltar and in the adjacent Atlantic. It probably occurs s. to W. Africa.

RHINOPTERIDAE
A family containing a single genus of closely similar rays, related to the eagle rays. These, the cow-nosed rays, have rather pointed pectoral fins and a blunt head which protrudes from the outline of the disc. The snout is divided into a double fleshy lobe. They have a relatively long tail, with a dorsal fin, and one or more serrated spines close behind that fin; they lack a tail fin.

They are active, swimming rays, which move most gracefully by beating their powerful pectoral fins. They are, however, dependent on bottom-living molluscs and crustaceans for their major food items. Like the stingrays they are ovoviviparous the young being nourished at first on the yolk of the egg, but later receiving nourishment from the secretions of the maternal uterine lining.

The cow-nosed rays are found in the coastal waters of the tropical and warm-temperate regions of all the oceans. They are all of medium size. See **Rhinoptera.**

Rhodeus   Cyprinidae
   amarus BITTERLING 9 cm. (3½ in.)
The bitterling is a small fish, rather deep-bodied and plump, possessing moderately large scales, but a lateral line which extends only to the first 5–6 scales. It is very beautifully coloured, the back is greenish brown, the sides are silvery, and have a blue-green stripe which begins just beneath the dorsal fin and continues to the tail fin. In the spawning season the colours of the male are heightened, the sides become iridescent, the throat and belly orange-red, and the fins reddish.

It is widely distributed in n. and e. Europe, from n. France and Germany across to the Black and Caspian Sea basins. A separate population (the subspecies *R. amarus sericeus*) is found in n. China. Both subspecies live in densely weeded regions of small lakes and ponds, and slowly flowing rivers. They feed on plants and small invertebrates. It can survive rather poor conditions of oxygenation.

The breeding habits of the bitterling are of the greatest interest. The presence of swan mussels (*Anodonta cygnaea*) is essential, and at spawning time the female develops a long-egg-laying tube with which the eggs are deposited within the mussel. The male releases his sperm into the inhaling siphon of the mussel to fertilize the eggs. The eggs develop within the mussel, leaving it after 2–3 weeks (about 2 days after hatching). The mussel is unharmed. The advantages of this relationship obviously lie in the protection the young fish and developing eggs derive, they also have a well oxygenated micro-habitat in which to develop, and may avoid the worst effects of droughts for mussels move into deeper water as pools dry up.

Rhodichthys   Cyclopteridae
   regina 30 cm. (12 in.)
Found only in the Arctic seas, in the W. from Baffin Bay and the Davis Strait, and in the E., N. of Novaya Zemlya. It is only found at great depths from 1308–2416 (715–1320 fathoms) on muddy bottoms at nearly freezing temperatures. It is not an entirely bottom-living species, for some specimens have been captured in mid-water, and it feeds on planktonic and bathypelagic crustaceans.

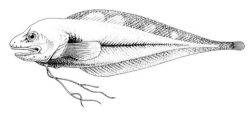

It is a rather slender-bodied form with a broad head. The sucking disc on the underside is completely lacking, and there are long branched pectoral rays on the throat. Its body is pinkish in colour but almost transparent; the body cavity is dark blue.

RHYACICHTHYIDAE
A family of specialized goby-like fish, represented by a single species found in freshwaters in the E. Indies and the Philippines.

In body form and behaviour it is very similar to the homalopterid loaches (family Homalopteridae) which also live in hill streams, an interesting example of convergent evolution, for they are not related. See **Rhyacichthys.**

Rhyacichthys   Rhyacichthyidae
   aspro LOACH-GOBY 23 cm. (9 in.)
The loach-goby is widely distributed in rivers and streams of the E. Indies (notably Java, Sumatra, Bali, Celebes, New Guinea) and also occurs in the Philippines and the Solomon Islands. It lives in freshwater often far up the head waters of the streams where the gradient is steep and the current fast. Its flattened head and forebody, and the widely-spread pelvic fins and flat belly form a suction device to help the fish maintain station in the running water. The mouth is curved, rather horse-shoe shaped and although placed at the end of the head is ventral.

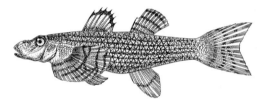

It is brown to yellowish, with dark blotches on the back and sides. The first dorsal fin has a dark band near the base of the rays and a dark margin; the second dorsal has several dark bars; and the pectoral fins are dark flecked.

RHYNCHOBATIDAE
A small family of guitarfishes which differ from the Rhinobatidae in a number of details of anatomy. For example the rhynchobatids have a distinct lower tail fin lobe, and the first dorsal fin is placed over the pelvic fins; in addition the pectoral fins are widely separated from the pelvic fins. Some authorities, however, consider that this family should be included in Rhinobatidae.

Its members are mainly Indo-Pacific in distribution, one species lives on the African coast. They are large fish of rather elongate body shape, flattened ventrally. Some species have a long, shovel-like snout. See **Rhina, Rhynchobatus.**

Rhynchobatus   Rhynchobatidae
   djeddensis SHOVELNOSE, SAND SHARK
3 m. (10 ft)
A giant guitarfish of the Indo-Pacific, which is found from s. and e. Africa, and the Red Sea, across to Australian waters. This is a famous big game fish for anglers in these areas, especially on the Natal coast of S. Africa, on the New South Wales coast, and the mouth of the Brisbane River. Specimens up to 227 kg. (500 lb.) in weight have been caught, with a bottom-hugging fish like this a feat of both skill and physical strength.

It is greyish or light brown with scattered

white spots on the back – hence its name in Australia of 'white-spotted ray'.

This ray lives in relatively deep water except that during the warmer season of the year it comes into shallower water. It feeds on bottom-living crustaceans, squids, and molluscs.

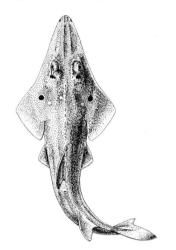

In its turn it is said to have well flavoured flesh, reminiscent of prawns, although it is not commercially exploited regularly.

RIBBON CONGER see **Taenioconger chapmani**
RIBBONFISH see **Lepidopus caudatus**
RIBBONFISH, POLKA-DOT see **Desmodema polystictum**
RIBBONTAIL RAY see **Taeniura lymma**
RICE EEL see **Monopterus alba**
RICEFISH see **Chologaster cornutus, Oryzias latipes**
RICHARDSON'S
  TOADFISH see **Sphoeroides hamiltoni**
  SKATE see **Raja richardsoni**

Richardsonius   Cyprinidae
  balteatus REDSIDE SHINER 18 cm. (7 in.)
A small, rather plump minnow-like fish from the freshwaters of n. America. Its principal distinguishing features are a rather long anal fin, and the dorsal fin placed far along the back, almost over the anal fin. Its back is dark olive or brown, the belly silvery, with a dark streak from head to tail and a lighter line above this, and reddish marks around the gills. The breeding male is brilliant with gold and crimson on the head, fins and sides.

It is well distributed in river basins of the Pacific coast, from the Columbia River, n. to the Mackenzie River in British Columbia. Within its range it may be abundant in lakes, ponds and slow rivers. It feeds on a wide variety of prey, including aquatic and terrestrial insects, plankton, and small fishes. It is essentially a shoaling species, found in shallow water in daytime and in deep water at night. It spawns from April to July, on gravelly bottomed riffles or rivers running into lakes. The eggs are small and yellow and fall in amongst the stones (those that do not are quickly eaten by the adults). The young hatch in 3–7 days in 21°–23°C.

The redside shiner is an important fish in the food-chain, eating many small invertebrates and being eaten by larger fish. It has been introduced to a numbers of waters as a forage fish for planted trout.

RING-TAILED PIKE CICHLID see **Crenicichla saxatilis**
RIPPON FALL'S BARBEL see **Barbus altianalis**

Risor   Gobiidae
  ruber SMALLMOUTH or TUSKED GOBY
3 cm. (1 in.)
Found only in the Caribbean and adjacent regions, it apparently ranges from the Bahamas and Florida, S. to Surinam including the Gulf of Mexico. It is a sponge-dwelling goby which inhabits at least 3 species of massive sponge, and often lives in numbers within the single specimen. It occurs commonly in depths of 3–15 m. (2–8 fathoms), but has been found in the shore zone and at depths of 183 m. (100 fathoms).

Its habit of living in association with sponges has resulted in a number of modifications of body form and structure. The body is scaled only in its latter half, and the peculiar mouth and dentition are distinctive. The mouth is small with well-developed lips, while the paired front teeth are long and pointed, and curve outwards so that they point forwards. The function of this peculiar dentition is not known; it has been suggested that it may be employed to open wider the gaps in the sponge walls to obtain hidden invertebrates.

It is usually dark coloured, often with a purplish cast. Some specimens are yellow. The coloration is believed to vary with the colouring of the host sponge.

RIVER
  BARB, INDIAN see **Cyclocheilichthys apogon**
  CARPSUCKER see **Carpiodes carpio**
  GURNARD see **Platycephalus indicus**
  RAY see **Potamotrygon magdalenae, Potamotrygon motoro**
  ROMAN see **Lutjanus argentimaculatus**

Rivulus   Cyprinodontidae
  hartii HART'S RIVULUS, LEAPING GUABINE 10 cm. (4 in.)
A widely distributed fish in the freshwaters of e. Colombia, Venezuela, Guyana, and the s. Caribbean islands of Tobago, Grenada, and Trinidad. It is found mainly in streams and rivers, but also is common in pools and ponds. It is the largest of the rivuline toothcarps in the Americas and is locally used as a food fish. It has also been kept in aquaria successfully. It has a habit of leaping clear of the water – hence its Trinidad name.

The male is brown on the back, its sides yellowish green and belly yellowish. Each scale on the sides has a red centre and green stripes form between the rows. The female is reddish brown above, lighter on the sides with rows of coppery spots. The fins are yellow to reddish, the anal becoming red with age.

R. strigatus HERRINGBONE RIVULUS
5 cm. (2 in.)
Widely distributed in the streams of the central Amazon region, extending s. to n. Argentina. It is one of the most strikingly coloured and graceful members of the family.

In males the back is olive to brown, the flanks are deep blue, the underside orange. The head and sides have rows of small red dots which to the rear take the form of chevron (hence herringbone) markings. The fins are

yellowish or light green, with rows of red spots, and the tail fin has an orange border. The female is paler, but has faint markings resembling those of the male.

It has been kept as an aquarium fish but it is difficult to breed in artificial conditions. When it does it has been found that as many as 80 per cent of the offspring are males.

RIVULUS,
  HART'S see **Rivulus hartii**
  HERRINGBONE see **Rivulus strigatus**
ROACH see **Rutilus rutilus**
ROBALO see Centropomidae
ROBUST BOXFISH see **Strophiurichthys robustus**

Roccus   Serranidae
  saxatilis STRIPED BASS 127 cm. (50 in.)
This is the famous game fish of the American Atlantic and Pacific coasts. Commonly called striper, this refers to one of the obvious external characters of the species, the 7–8 close-set dark sooty stripes running along the upper sides. The back is dark olive-green to blue, paling on the sides to a whitish belly.

It is found along the Atlantic coast from the St Lawrence River to n. Florida, and along the coasts of Louisiana and Alabama. In the late 19th century it was introduced to the Pacific coast and is now found from Washington to California.

It is mainly an inshore fish, found in the surf, along estuary shore lines, shallow bays, and rocky headlands. It is a very active predatory species which feeds on a wide variety of smaller fishes and crustaceans; its prey increasing in size as it grows. It grows to a large size, fishes up to 22·7–31·7 kg. (50–70 lb.) having been captured.

The striped bass enters estuaries to spawn, and actually sheds its eggs at the extreme tidal limits or in running fresh water. The spawning season is from late April to early June.

It is extremely valuable as a sporting fish, it fights well and reaches a large size. Some are also caught by commercial fishermen, but the landings are not very important.

ROCK
  BEAUTY see **Holacanthus tricolor**
  COD, LUNAR-TAILED see **Variola louti**
  COOK see **Centrolabrus exoletus**
  EEL see **Scyliorhinus canicula, Squalus acanthias**
  FLATHEAD see **Thysanophrys cirronasus**
  HIND see **Epinephelus adscensionis**
  PRICKLEBACK see **Xiphister mucosus**
  SALMON see **Lutjanus argentimaculatus**
  SKIPPER see **Alticops periophthalmus**
  SOLE see **Lepidopsetta bilineata**
  WHITING, BLUE see **Haletta semifasciata**
ROCK-COD, BLUE-SPOT see **Cephalopholis miniatus**
ROCK-SUCKER see **Chorisochismus dentex**
ROCKCOD see **Sebastes levis**

ROCKFISH,
   QUILLBACK see **Sebastes maliger**
   RASPHEAD see **Sebastes ruberrimus**
   YELLOWEYE see **Sebastes ruberrimus**
ROCKHEAD see **Bothragonus swani**
ROCKLING,
   FIVE-BEARDED see **Ciliata mustela**
   FOUR-BEARDED see **Rhinonemus cimbrius**
ROCKSPEAR see **Synodus synodus**
ROCKWEED GUNNEL see **Xererpes fucorum**
ROCKY see **Clinus superciliosus**

Roeboides Characidae
   guatemalensis GUATEMALA GLASS-CHARACIN 10 cm. (4 in.)
The glass-characin is found in Central America, widely distributed especially in rivers flowing into the Caribbean. The members of the genus *Roeboides* are very distinctive, slender-bodied fish with a very long anal fin of an even height. Its body is translucent, pale yellow in colour with small shining, silvery dots, and a broad band of dull metallic sheen runs along the sides. A conspicuous dark spot near the upper base of the tail fin. Males have a noticeably pointed dorsal fin.

It is an interesting fish which normally swims in a head-down inclined plane. It is often kept in aquaria although it needs large, rather open, aquarium conditions. They are reputed to be peaceful with other fish only being rather snappy when fed. Despite this, this along with other *Roeboides* species, is a scale eater, the larger specimens eating nothing but scales which they dislodge from other fish. Smaller specimens eat insect larvae as well as fish scales. The specialized dentition of these fishes becomes pronounced with age. They have large teeth on the outer edges of the jaws.

ROKER see **Raja clavata**

Roloffia Cyprinodontidae
   liberiens CALABAR LYRETAIL
6 cm. (2½ in.)
Found in the coastal swamps near Monrovia, Liberia, W. Africa, from whence the first specimens to be described originated. It has also been found along the coast of Calabar (and this population was known as *Aphyosemion calabricum*).

This species spawns near the bottom; the fry emerge from the eggs within 12–14 days of laying, an unusually short period. It is a rather timid, easily startled fish, which when alarmed will leap out of the aquarium. It is relatively easy to breed, and has made a popular aquarium species.

Females are dull coloured. The males are greeny-blue with a network of dark red spots. The tips of the dorsal, anal, and tail fins are produced, and each fin has a deep red bar running along the blue-green of the rays; the tail fin is edged with sulphur yellow. **205**

ROMAN, RIVER see **Lutjanus argentimaculatus**

Rondeletia Rondeletiidae
   bicolor 10 cm. (4 in.)
This whalefish was originally found in the Atlantic Ocean, but has since been taken in the Indian Ocean and W. Pacific, and there seems

little doubt that it will be found to be world-wide in distribution, in depths of 700–2000 m. (383–1092 fathoms). It is bathypelagic in habit. It is a dark brown in colour, the tips of the fins light. The jaws are well provided with

minute densely packed teeth, and the skin is smooth except that the sides have a number of vertical rows of papillae. Well spaced, larger papillae follow the mid-side of the body.

RONDELETIIDAE
A family of whalefishes containing the species *Rondeletia bicolor*. Unlike most of its relatives (see Cetomimidae) this species has distinct, if small pelvic fins, but its most distinctive feature is the numerous vertical rows of small papillae along the sides. The usual hollow and very conspicuous lateral line is not present.

The family appears to be distributed world-wide, although as it is relatively infrequently captured there are too few data for this to be certain. See **Rondeletia**.

RONQUIL, NORTHERN see **Ronquilus jordani**

Ronquilus Bathymasteridae
   jordani NORTHERN RONQUIL
17 cm. (6¾ in.)
Found along the Pacific coast of N. America from Monterey Bay, California to the Aleutian Islands and the Bering Sea. It is found in inshore waters at depths of 18–165 m. (10–90 fathoms) close to the bottom. It spawns in March, and the larvae are found close inshore at the surface, feeding on crustaceans and other planktonic forms.

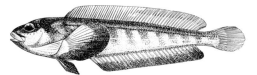

It is a well distinguished fish with small, cycloid scales which extend onto the cheek, and by having the first 20–30 rays of the dorsal fin long and unbranched. Males are orange in colour with faint dusky bars on the upper sides; females are orange-brown.

Rooseveltiella Characidae
   nattereri NATTERER'S or RED PIRANHA
30 cm. (12 in.)
Widely distributed in n. S. America, including the Amazon basin, the Orinoco, and the Paraná systems. This seems to be one of the most common and widely spread piranhas, and it is the species most often seen in public aquaria.

In body shape it is typical of the piranha (see *Serrasalmus* and *Pygocentrus*), a group which some ichthyologists consider deserves to be placed in a separate family, the Serrasalmidae.

The genus *Rooseveltiella* is distinguished by having teeth on the palate. It is very deep-bodied and thickset, with a serrated edge to the belly. Its coloration varies with its environmental conditions, but a good specimen should be blue-brown on the back, the sides pale brown shading to light olive and speckled silvery. The belly and ventral fins are bright red; the tail and dorsal fins are dark, the former being pinkish in front of the black edge.

It is a wholly predatory species, eating fish, and other invertebrates which it tears at with its sharp interlocking teeth. This species is one of the several piranhas which has been reported to attack man and other large animals. **86**

ROSADO, BAGRE see **Hypophthalmus edentatus**
ROSE-BELLIED SIPHONFISH see **Siphamia roseigaster**
ROSE-COLOURED CURIMATOPSIS see **Curimatopsis saladensis**
ROSEMOUTH, BLACKBELLY see **Helicolenus dactylopterus**
ROSY
   BARB see **Barbus conchonius**
   BLENNY see **Malacoctenus macropus**
   TETRA see **Hyphessobrycon rosaceus**
ROUGH
   DAB, LONG see **Hippoglossoides platessoides**
   HOUND see **Scyliorhinus canicula**
   ROUGH-HEAD GRENADIER see **Macrourus berglax**
ROUGHTAIL GOBY see **Evermannichthys metzelaari**
ROUGHY see **Trachichthys australis**
ROUGHY, DARWIN'S see **Gephyroberyx darwini**
ROUND
   BATFISH see **Platax orbicularis**
   HERRING see **Etrumeus teres**
   WHITEFISH see **Prosopium cylindraceum**
RUBBERLIP SEAPERCH see **Rhacochilus toxotes**
RUBY, BLACK see **Barbus nigrofasciatus**
RUDD see **Scardinius erythrophthalmus**
RUDDERFISH see Kyphosidae
RUDDERFISH see **Naucrates ductor**
RUFF see **Arripis georgianus**
RUFF,
   BLACK see **Centrolophus niger**
   TOMMY see **Arripis georgianus**
RUFFE see **Gymnocephalus cernua**
RUMMY-NOSED TETRA see **Hemigrammus rhodostomus**
RUNNER see **Elagatis bipinnulata, Rachycentron canadum**
RUNNER, RAINBOW see **Elagatis bipinnulata**
RUSSIAN STURGEON see **Acipenser gueldenstaedti**
RUSTY DAB see **Limanda ferruginea**

Rutilus Cyprinidae
   rutilus ROACH 46 cm. (18 in.)
The roach is an extremely abundant and widespread freshwater fish in Europe and w. Asia. Its range extends from England e. to central U.S.S.R., and s. from northern Sweden to the Black and Caspian Sea basins. It is basically a fish of well weeded, lowland lakes and rivers, where it occurs in shoals. It is, however, very adaptable, and can tolerate low oxygen con-

ditions, as well as warm temperatures, and moderate pollution, and consequently is often found in only marginally suitable waters. Its popularity with anglers in the British Isles has meant that it is widely introduced to all kinds of waters, and within recent historic times it has been introduced to Ireland.

Its food varies with locality, and the size of the fish. Young roach feed on copepods and other small crustaceans, insect larvae, and plant matter; larger fish eat larger crustaceans, molluscs, and plants. In winter feeding drops off with lower temperatures and the roach shoals usually retire to deeper water. They breed in spring and summer, later in cooler areas and cold seasons, spawning in shallow weedy areas, or on a stony bottom. The males arrive at the spawning site a few days before the females, and spawning activity with much thrashing of the water continues for up to a week. They are not infrequently joined on the spawning beds by other cyprinid fishes, bream and rudd notably, the resulting progeny being hybrids intermediate in body form and colouring between the parents.

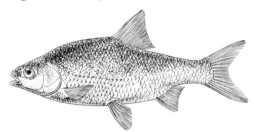

The roach is a beautifully coloured fish, distinguished by the forward position of the dorsal fin, above the pelvic origin, by its rather ventral mouth, and by the lack of a sharp keel behind the pelvic fins.

By its very abundance throughout Europe it is an important fish. It is eaten by many predators, such as herons, otters, pike, perch, and zander, in its turn it preys on numerous invertebrates. It serves as an intermediate host to a number of parasitic worms, notably the cestode, *Ligula*, and the eye fluke, *Diplostomum*, which later are parasites of fish-eating birds.

Although in the British Isles its chief value is an angling fish, in Europe it is locally commercially important as human food. Caught on a large scale in e. Europe in seines, traps, and stake nets it is marketed as fresh fish, smoked, or salted. **140**

Ruvettus Gempylidae
pretiosus OILFISH, ESCOLAR 1·8 m. (6 ft)
Worldwide in its range, probably most abundant in tropical waters but ranging into temperate seas regularly. In the Atlantic, for example, it has been found as far N. as Britain and off Newfoundland. It is a striking fish, its long body rounded in cross-section and powerful-looking, violet or purplish brown, fading to dull brown after death.

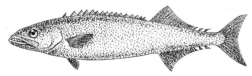

It is an active predator feeding on a wide range of fishes. It is usually captured at depths of 183–550 m. (100–300 fathoms). Large specimens weigh in excess of 45 kg. (100 lb.).

Despite its size it is not greatly valued as a food fish. Its flesh is very oily, and the oil has a purgative effect. It is sometimes called the castor-oil fish.

Rypticus Grammistidae
saponaceus SOAPFISH 30 cm. (12 in.)
The soapfish is widely distributed in the Atlantic Ocean, being found in the E. on the tropical African coast, St Helena, Ascension Island, and in the W. from Bermuda, Florida

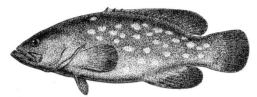

to Brazil, and throughout the W. Indies. It is brown or greyish brown, with irregular blotches of light grey on its back and sides. Its skin is very slimy, the mucus produced being toxic to other fishes in captivity, and is certainly a deterrent to predators. It earns the name soapfish from the frothy suds-like feel of water in which it is placed.

The soapfish lives in shallow water, preferring a bottom of rough rocks and sand. It usually takes refuge in crevices between the rocks during the day and is active mainly at night. It feeds equally on crustaceans and fishes.

S

SABALITO see **Pseudocurimata gilberti**
SÁBALO see **Prochilodus platensis**
SABLEFISH see **Anoplopoma fimbria**
SABRE see **Sternopygus macrurus**
SABRE-TOOTHED FISH see Evermannellidae

SACCOPHARYNGIDAE
Related to the Eurypharyngidae, this is the largest family of the gulper-eels, formerly placed in the order Lyomeri. These are the largest of the group, some attaining a length of 180 cm. (71 in.). They have been found mainly in the Atlantic, but are also known from the Indian and Pacific oceans, as bathypelagic fishes in considerable depths.

They are elongate fish, the tail being longer than the body, with large jaws which are capable of being swung forward to form an enormous gape. The jaws are not so large as in the Eurypharyngidae. The eyes are set near the tip of the snout. This group also has the dorsal fin originating well back nearer the vent than the snout, and moderate teeth in the jaws. See **Saccopharynx.**

Saccopharynx Saccopharyngidae
ampullaceus WHIPTAIL GULPER
137 cm. (54 in.)
This gulper eel has been taken only in the N. Atlantic to date. The first specimen was captured in the Davis Strait, near Greenland – this is the largest specimen that has been captured – subsequently it has been taken off Portugal, and in the Madeira-Azores region. Most of these specimens were found near the surface, but there seems reason to suppose that the usual depth for the species is around 2000

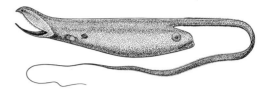

m. (1093 fathoms). Fewer than 25 whiptail gulpers have been reported as captured, and only 5 have been assigned to this species. Consequently it is a little-known fish.

SADDLE STARGAZER see **Gillellus rubrocinctus**
SADDLE-TAILED SEA PERCH see **Lutjanus sanguineus**
SADDLEBACK GUNNEL see **Pholis ornata**

Sagamichthys Searsidae
abei 33 cm. (13 in.)
This species is one of the most abundant searsid fishes. It is found throughout the N. Pacific Ocean and in the e. S. Pacific, in mid-water between 200–1000 m. (109–546 fathoms), rising to the upper of these levels at night. It feeds extensively on small crustaceans.

It is light grey-blue in colour with a jet black shoulder organ, and several large cross-wise light organs on the belly. As a young fish the tail is unpigmented but as it grows it gradually becomes dark, and light organs develop on the head. The shoulder organ contains light-producing cells which are discharged through the tube opening above the pectoral fin.

SAILFIN
CHARACIN see **Crenuchus spilurus**
FLYINGFISH see **Parexocoetus brachypterus**
MOLLY see **Poecilia latipinna, Poecilia velifera**
SCULPIN see **Nautichthys oculofasciatus**
SAILFISH **Istiophorus platypterus**
SAILFLUKE see **Lepidorhombus whiffiagonis**
ST PETER'S FISH see **Zeus faber**
SAITHE see **Pollachius virens**

Salangichthys Salangidae
microdon GLASSFISH 10 cm. (4 in.)
The glassfish is a small, very slender salmon-like fish. The males differ from females by having a relatively deeper body, longer pectoral fins and a series of large scales around the

base of the anal fin. The body is transparent and glassy, except for 2 rows of black dots along the belly.

It is widely distributed in the w. Pacific, from Japan, Korea, to the coasts of the U.S.S.R. It is found in the sea, but migrates into estuaries to spawn in April and May. The eggs are very characteristic having a mass of branched threads at one end which adhere to stones, drift-wood and vegetation. The glass-fish matures at the end of its first year, and all the mature fish may die after spawning.

Although not of prime importance as a commercial fish, small, locally valuable fisheries for glassfish exist all along its area of abundance. In Japan particularly it is fished for by various methods, and as shirauwo is eaten as a delicacy in a variety of ways.

Saliota   Eretmophoridae
australis 38 cm. (15 in.)
A deep-sea cod found in the Antarctic regions of S. America. It has been found in the Patagonian-Falkland Islands region, the Straits of Magellan and s. Chile.

It is similar in body form to the rock cods (*Physiculus*) of New Zealand and s. Australia but differs in having a patch of small teeth on the roof of the mouth. It is greeny-brown in colour, lighter ventrally.

This fish is frequently captured in trawls on the continental shelf at depths down to 250 m. (137 fathoms). It is not fished for commercially but represents a potential food resource.

Salminus   Characidae
maxillosus DORADO *c.* 76 cm. (30 in.)
The dorado is one of the finest game fishes of the S. American continent which fights well, and often weighs up to 22·7 kg. (50 lb). Several species of *Salminus* are known, most of which have the colloquial name dorado, but this species is found throughout the Paraná and Uruguay rivers, especially in fast-flowing water, in riffles or in the broken water ahead of rocks or obstructions in the river. Usually they are found in gravel bottom areas, but the smaller fish occur in soft-bottomed slow-flowing areas. Its biology has not been fully studied; it probably spawns in the fast water after an upstream migration of adults, the eggs dropping into the gravel and washing downstream.

The dorado is very beautifully coloured, deep golden, darker on the back but bright on the sides, with rows of scales bearing dark dots, forming broken stripes. The fins are bright red except for the tail fin which has a black bar across it. Its body is typical of the tetras in shape, but massive when compared with the minute aquarium species.

Salmo   Salmonidae
clarki CUTTHROAT TROUT 1 m. (39 in.)
The cutthroat trout is well distributed along the Pacific coast rivers of N. America from California n. to Prince William Sound in Alaska. Migratory cutthroat are found in the n. parts of its range. Away from the coastal rivers and

lakes it is represented in the headwaters of the Missouri, Columbia, Saskatchewan, and Fraser rivers by the Yellowstone cutthroat trout (*S. clarki lewisi*). Both forms of the cutthroat trout have been artificially spread by angling interests.

In body shape it is a typical trout, rather slender and with a short head. It has teeth along the mid-line of the roof of the mouth. Its colour is rather silvery with rounded black spots on the back, fins, and head. Under the head in the throat region it has very conspicuous orange or red blotches in parallel grooves; these give it the name of cutthroat trout.

Cutthroat trout spawn in spring and early summer in shallow streams. River-living trout migrate into smaller streams, and the lake trout enter tributary rivers to spawn. The eggs are buried in redds, deep in the gravel. It feeds on a wide variety of crustaceans and insects, including flying insects.

It is a fine sporting fish, growing in some lakes to a weight of 8 kg. (17 lb.) although in others, it is much smaller. Taken on fly or by trolling it is widely accepted as one of the best angling fishes of w. N. America.

S. gairdneri RAINBOW or STEEL-HEAD
TROUT 122 cm. (4 ft)
The rainbow trout is too well-known to require any description, but the dense small dark spots on the back and sides as well as on the dorsal and tail fins are as distinctive as the rainbow colour of the band along the sides. Its coloration is, however, very variable depending on its habits and size, the migratory anadromous form in particular differs in that its back is dark blue and the sides and belly are silvery.

This variability has caused a good deal of confusion with local names, two local variants being the shasta trout and the kamloops trout. The steel-head trout, long thought to be distinct, is the migratory anadromous form of the rainbow, bearing the same relationship as sea trout do to brown trout.

Its native range is on the Pacific slopes of N. America from NW. Mexico, and California n. to Alaska. It is probably identical to the species known as *S. mykiss* on the Asiatic coast of the Pacific. On account of its fighting qualities, and its generally good growth rate even in only moderately productive waters, the rainbow trout has been widely introduced in almost all temperate parts of the world. It is intensively farmed for stocking purposes and for food in Europe, N. America and elsewhere.

The rainbow feeds almost exclusively on insect larvae, molluscs, and crustaceans. Only large fish eat fishes to any extent, although some eat Pacific salmon eggs and fry. In N. America they spawn in early spring, the female excavating a redd in a gravel area at the top of a riffle. The eggs are shed and fertilized in the redd and covered over as the female parent, or another, excavates another redd upstream. The eggs are large (3–5 mm. in diameter), and non-migratory fish rarely contain more than 2000; the big steel-head trout often holds up to 7000 eggs. The eggs hatch in the gravel after about 2 months, and the young fish live in the riffle for the first months of their life, dropping down to deeper pools or lakes for the winter. The steel-head grows to a much bigger fish, up to 16 kg. (36 lb.) in weight, than the ordinary rainbow. **37**

S. mykiss see under **S. gairdneri**

S. salar SALMON, ATLANTIC SALMON
c. 1·5 m. (5 ft)
The salmon is essentially an inhabitant of the N. Atlantic. On the w. side it is found from Labrador and the rivers of Greenland s. to the Connecticut River (and at one time to the River Hudson). On the European coast from the Arctic Ocean coast of Russia s. to n. Spain. It also occurs in the high seas of the N. Atlantic but was until recently rarely caught there. Although it is widely distributed, and in places moderately common, the salmon is much diminished in abundance. Pollution and obstruction of the lower reaches of rivers and overfishing have combined to extinguish it in some areas.

The salmon is anadromous, that is it enters rivers to spawn in the headwaters, later returning to the sea. The adults enter the rivers at varying times, in some rivers in early spring, in others in summer, all spawn in the winter after migrating upstream for as much as 320–480 km. (200–300 miles) in large rivers. The female excavates a redd in the gravel bed in a moderate current and depth, in which the eggs are laid to be fertilized simultaneously by the male. The eggs are shed in several spawnings during a day or two, and are eventually buried by the further digging of redds upstream. The eggs hatch in the following spring having over-wintered in the gravel, but the fry lies quietly amongst the stones for a further 6 weeks until the yolk of the egg is completely used up. Once it becomes active it begins to feed on small crustaceans, and later insect larvae and other small animals.

Later in its life the young salmon, now known as a parr, with 8–10 blotches on its sides feeds on a wide variety of insect and crustacean life. At some time between their second and sixth year (depending on the river), the young salmon changes in colour, becoming silvery, and moves downstream during April to June. As a smolt it spends some while in the estuary acclimatizing itself to sea water, and feeding on marine crustaceans and fishes, before moving into the open sea. After 1–4 years the salmon returns from the sea to the natal river to spawn; those that return after only one year are known as grilse.

During the sea-dwelling phase the salmon ranges far across the Atlantic. Many travel to the Norwegian Sea, others to the region of Greenland, both evidently areas offering rich feeding, for they grow fast in the sea. Unlike the Pacific salmons which die after spawning, some Atlantic salmon as kelts recover from the fatigue of migration and spawning with its resulting loss of condition and its infections. Some even spawn 3 times. However, a proportion of the adult population always dies after spawning. A curious feature of the salmon's breeding biology is that a number of male parr become sexually mature without moving to the sea, and frequently join in the spawning act on the redds.

In the sea salmon mainly eat fish and crustaceans, the list of prey species being very long. In turn, they are eaten by a number of predators, pollack, coalfish, sharks, and seals (the latter especially pick them out of nets). As young fish they are preyed upon by kingfishers, diving ducks, herons, and cormorants, as well as fish-eating mammals and other fishes.

Man is possibly the greatest threat to the salmon. With pollution, river development, and dams he has barred many salmon runs, and he catches the adult fish in estuarine nets as it returns to spawn. Sport fishing in freshwater is well known. More recently, high seas fisheries have been developed using floating nets which catch very large numbers of salmon in their sea-going phase. Whether the stocks can withstand this additional strain is a matter of doubt.

In several Canadian lakes there are landlocked salmon, which migrate from river to lake as if the latter was the sea. This is the ouananiche, a name borrowed from the local Indian dialect, and a famous game fish. Another landlocked salmon is the e. American sebago salmon, found in Sebago and other lakes and their associated rivers. This has been widely cultured and introduced in the e. U.S.

S. trutta TROUT 140 cm. (55 in.)
The trout is essentially a European fish, found in the sea from the White Sea s. around Iceland and the British Isles, to n. Spain, and as a freshwater fish within that area and in the Mediterranean borderlands E. to the Black and Caspian seas. The migratory phase (the sea trout) is found only in n. waters, but soon after the last Ice Age it is believed to have occurred in the Mediterranean basin from which higher temperatures later drove it, leaving its non-migratory successors well distributed there.

Trout can be distinguished from salmon by a number of characters: the upper jaw bone is long and extends past the eye, the body in front of the tail fin is thickset and deep, and the edge of the tail fin is straight or only slightly concave. In coloration the trout is very variable. Sea trout are very silvery with a few scattered black marks on the back and sides; the brown trout is heavily dark spotted on a variable greeny brown back, and silvery sides.

The two forms also differ considerably in habits. Both spawn in freshwater in redds cut in gravelly shallows in winter. The eggs hatch in early spring, and after a short period spent in the gravel the fry distribute themselves away from the spawning site. Sea trout spend from 1–5 years in freshwater (longest in the N.) before migrating to the sea. While in freshwater they feed on insect larvae, flying insects, crustaceans, and as they grow, increasingly on fishes, the same diet as the growing brown trout. The sea trout stays at sea from 6 months to 5 years growing rapidly in the food-rich environment. On its return to the river sea trout are usually distinctive by their large size and silvery colour.

The brown trout stays in freshwater all its life, it does not pass through a silvery smolt stage, and generally spawns at an earlier age. They never attain the size of the sea trout, and indeed the maximum size of the brown trout is governed by the food available per mouth in its particular environment. Thus many food-poor mountain lakes, or small streams, contain

small brown trout of 15 cm. (6 in.) which are fully mature. Fortunately in larger lakes and rivers the trout has a greater potential growth than this. Some brown trout living in large lakes grow almost as large as the sea trout, and indeed migrate to and from the lake as if it were the sea.

The trout is too well known as an angler's fish to require much description of the methods by which it is taken. For its size it is a game fighter, and its edible qualities give it additional value. Many are stocked in artificial and natural waters to improve angling. It was for its angling potential that the trout was introduced to many areas outside its original range. N. and S. America, New Zealand, Australia, S. Africa, India, and the E. African highlands are some of the areas in which it is now established, often to the detriment of the native fauna.

SALMON see Salmonidae
SALMON see **Salmo salar**
SALMON,
  ATLANTIC see **Salmo salar**
  AUSTRALIAN see **Arripis trutta**
  BEAKED see **Gonorhynchus gonorhynchus**
  BURNETT see **Neoceratodus forsteri**
  CAPE see **Atractoscion aequidens**
  CHINOOK see **Oncorhynchus tshawytscha**
  CHUM see **Oncorhynchus keta**
  COHO see **Oncorhynchus kisutch**
  HUMP-BACK see **Oncorhynchus gorbuscha**
  KING see **Oncorhynchus tshawytscha**
  LONGTOOTH see **Otolithes ruber**
  PINK see **Oncorhynchus gorbuscha**
  ROCK see **Lutjanus argentimaculatus**
  SEBAGO see **Salmo salar**
  SILVER see **Oncorhynchus kisutch**
  SNAPPER see **Otolithes ruber**
  SOCKEYE see **Oncorhynchus nerka**
  WHITE see **Ptychocheilus lucius**
SALMON
  BASS see **Argyrosomus regius**
  HERRING see **Chanos chanos**
SALMON-TROUT see **Arripis trutta**

SALMONIDAE

Members of this family include such well-known fishes as the salmons, trouts, charrs, the whitefishes and the graylings (both the latter are often recognized as separate families, Coregonidae and Thymallidae, respectively). All are slim, predatory fishes, most of which possess an adipose, or rayless fin on the back between the rayed dorsal and the tail. The pelvic fins are placed about midway along the body, and the pectorals are low on the body. The salmons and their relatives have well-developed teeth in the jaws, on the vomer, and the palatines, a short dorsal fin and small scales, while the coregonines have very small or no teeth, large scales, and a short dorsal fin, and the graylings large scales, moderate teeth, and a long dorsal fin.

The family is widely distributed in the freshwaters of the temperate N. Hemisphere, although some species have been introduced elsewhere. Many are migratory species spending a considerable part of their lives in the sea and returning only to freshwater to spawn. As a family they are immensely important to com-

mercial fisheries. In addition, they are important members of aquatic ecosystems in boreal freshwaters. See **Brachymystax, Coregonus, Hucho, Oncorhynchus, Prosopium, Salmo, Salvelinus, Stenodus, Thymallus.**

Salvelinus   Salmonidae
  alpinus ARCTIC CHARR, CHARR
96 cm. (38 in.)
The Arctic charr is circumpolar in its distribution, being found landlocked in mountainous districts in the British Isles, Europe, n. U.S.S.R., and the n. regions of N. America. It is also anadromous in near-Arctic seas, spending much of its life in the sea but returning to freshwater to spawn. In the s. parts of its range it is only found in cool, deep lakes, in which it has survived since the later stages of the last Ice Age when migratory charr inhabited the sea in these latitudes. Due to the long isolation of many of the lake populations they have diverged in many cases to be quite dissimilar to one another, and to the migratory form. Many such populations have been named as distinct species or subspecies with consequent and unnecessary confusion of the nomenclature. Some of these lake populations are dwarf races, the mature adults are less than 20 cm. (8 in.) long, but the migratory charr grow very large, a weight of 12 kg. ($26\frac{1}{2}$ lb.) being not uncommon.

The charr is carnivorous, eating small fishes, molluscs, and midge larvae when well grown, although the young eat large quantities of small crustaceans, especially the freshwater shrimp. This is largely a matter of opportunity as the young fish are usually found in small rivers and streams, while the adults inhabit lakes. Lack of suitable food is undoubtedly the cause of the stunting of some lake populations, where in a generally food-poor environment they prey on small, planktonic crustaceans and insect larvae all their lives. The migratory charr, however, benefit by the richer feeding in the sea where they eat mainly crustaceans and fishes.

Migratory charr breed in rivers on gravelly beds, the male establishing a territory in which the female excavates a redd or nest. The eggs are fertilized in the redd the female driving them down between the stones by flapping movements of her tail, and then covers them by digging upstream. The males often stay around the nest. Most lake populations spawn in similar situations in affluent streams, but some spawn in deep water on the lake bed, usually in spring. The majority however, spawn in autumn, and the eggs incubate overwinter.

The Arctic charr is a valuable food and sporting fish. Many of the local populations are fished for and, being good eating, form local delicacies, such as the potted charr of Lake Windermere, in the English Lake District. In Arctic Canada the charr is of considerable importance to Eskimos, who fish for it all the year round, both for their own consumption and latterly for shipment frozen as a delicacy to the S. Clearly salmonid in appearance the charr can be distinguished from its relatives by its small scales and by the large round pinkish spots on its back and sides. The word charr was originally spelled thus by the earliest English naturalists, a later spelling as char, is sometimes used but it is an undesirable alteration.

S. fontinalis BROOK TROUT or CHARR 86 cm. (34 in.)

The brook trout, or brook charr as it is better named as it belongs to the charr genus *Salvelinus*, is native to ne. N. America. Its original distribution was S. from Hudson Bay, Labrador, Newfoundland, through the Great Lakes region to the upper Mississippi system, and headwaters of the Appalachian mountain rivers. It has been widely introduced to rivers throughout the temperate zones of the world, and is found in Europe in a number of places, S. Africa, and elsewhere. Anadromous fish are found along the n. Pacific coast-line.

It is a fish of cool clear streams, rivers, and lakes, feeding on insects of all kinds, and as adults on small fishes. It spawns in autumn usually in smaller rivers and streams than other charr. A typical salmonid redd is dug by the female flexing her body and driving into the stones. The eggs are rather large (about 5 mm., ¼ in., in diameter), and a large female may contain as many as 5000. They are covered over after spawning is completed, and overwinter in the gravel.

The brook charr is one of N. America's prime game fish. It takes a lure readily, and fights well once hooked. In addition, its rapid growth-rate in warmer latitudes, when sufficiently fed, makes it an ideal species for hatchery work and stocking in put-and-take angling waters. **38**

S. malma DOLLY VARDEN 127 cm. (50 in.)

The Dolly Varden is closely related to the Arctic charr, and it has been said to be merely a subspecies of that fish. However, recent opinion is that they should be regarded as distinct. Its back and sides have numerous small, round spots, usually yellow, orange, or pink, each smaller than the pupil of the eye. This bright, polka-dot appearance was the cause of its common name, a name used by Charles Dickens in *Barnaby Rudge* for a young lady who favoured brightly coloured dresses.

It is found in freshwater on both sides of the N. Pacific Ocean, from Korea N. to Siberia and on the American coast from the Sacramento river system and Nevada. In the S. of this range most Dolly Varden populations are non-migratory, to the N. anadromous fish are found which breed in freshwater and migrate to the sea to feed and grow.

Large Dolly Varden are mainly fish-eaters, although the young ones eat insect larvae, crustaceans, and molluscs, particularly bottom-living forms. Although alleged to eat young salmon and salmon eggs there is little evidence that they are serious predators. Dolly Varden spawn in the autumn, the eggs are large (*c*. 5 mm., ¼ in., in diameter) and overwinter before hatching.

Perhaps inferior to trout as a game fish, the Dolly Varden is nonetheless a favoured angling fish. Its pink flesh is excellent eating.

S. namaycush LAKE TROUT 122 cm. (48 in.)

The lake trout is widely distributed in freshwaters in n. America from Alaska to the Labrador area, S. to n. New England, the Great Lakes basin, the upstream lakes of the St Lawrence and Hudson rivers, and of the n. part of the Mississippi river system. Outside that area it has been widely distributed especially in the W. For example, Lake Tahoe, Cali-

fornia was stocked with lake trout in 1895 and it is now well established there and is said to have exterminated a native form of the cutthroat trout.

It is a most beautiful fish with a dark green to grey back, shading gradually to a pale belly, white or faintly yellowish. The head, back and sides are thickly covered with light spots, rather irregular in size; the pectoral, pelvic, and anal fins are orange with a white leading edge.

The lake trout is one of the most important commercial freshwater fishes of N. America. Its flesh is excellently flavoured and commands a high enough price to be flown out from the near Arctic lakes. The fishery in the Great Lakes was of vast importance until it was ruined by the invasion of the parasitic lamprey (see *Petromyzon marinus*). Moreover the sporting qualities of this trout are so good that sport-fishing centres are now established in n. Canada with the anglers being flown in.

The lake trout is usually credited with being an inhabitant of deep cold lakes, which it is in the S. of its range, but to the N. it is found in shallow tundra lakes and rivers. Its food consists of fishes, especially ciscoes, whitefish, and sticklebacks, insects, crustaceans, and plankton. In many deep lakes it feeds on the postglacial relict shrimp *Mysis*. Many smaller lake trout are eaten by large ones. They spawn in the shallows of lakes over a gravel bottom. The males arrive on the spawning ground first and clear it of leaves and silt, but do not make a redd as so many salmonids do. The eggs are shed loosely over the gravel. They spawn in late summer or autumn, the eggs (which are 4–5 mm. in diameter) overwinter to hatch in the early spring. Growth in s. lakes is fairly rapid, but in the relatively food-poor, cold n. lakes it is slow, taking up to 9 years to grow to 2·3 kg. (5 lb.) and 17 years to attain 9 kg. (20 lb.). With such a slow growth rate careful management is needed if the stock is not to be over-fished.

Although widely known as the lake 'trout' it is actually a charr (genus *Salvelinus*) not a true trout (genus *Salmo*).

Samaris Pleuronectidae **cristatus** 18 cm. (7 in.)

An inhabitant of the tropical Indo-Pacific which is found from s. Africa to Sri Lanka, the Andaman Islands, the E. Indies to China. It is always found in moderately shallow water around 55 m. (30 fathoms).

This is one of the few genera of this family to be found in tropical waters. They have no commercial value.

Its body-form is striking, the body is elongate and compressed, both the mouth and head are small. The dorsal fin begins in front of the upper eye, which is on the right side of the head, and the first 13–14 dorsal rays are very long and form a crest. Both the pelvic and pectoral fin rays are also long. It is brown with darker patches.

SAND

DIVER see Trichonotidae
DIVER see **Synodus intermedius**
FLOUNDER see **Scophthalmus aquosus**
GURNARD see **Platycephalus indicus**
LANCE see Ammodytidae
LANCE, AMERICAN see **Ammodytes americanus**

PERCH see Mugiloididae
SHARK see **Odontaspis taurus, Rhynchobatus djeddensis**
SOLE see **Pegusa lascaris, Psettichthys melanostictus**
STARGAZER see Dactyloscopidae
STARGAZER see **Dactyloscopus tridigitatus**
STOMPKOP see **Sparodon durbanensis**
TIGER see **Odontaspis taurus**
TILEFISH see **Malacanthus plumieri**
WHITING see **Sillago ciliata**
SAND-DAB, PACIFIC see **Citharichthys sordidus**
SAND-EEL see Ammodytidae
SAND-EEL see **Ammodytes tobianus, Gonorhynchus gonorhynchus**
SAND-EEL,
EUROPEAN see under **Ammodytes americanus**
GREATER see **Hyperoplus lanceolatus**
SAND-SMELT see Atherinidae
SAND-SMELT see **Atherina presbyter**

Sandelia Anabantidae **capensis** CAPE KURPER 21 cm. (8¼ in.)

This small member of the climbing perch family is confined to the rivers of the S. coastal plain of S. Africa. It is quite isolated from its nearest relative, *Ctenopoma multispinnis* in Lake Ngami. Like others of the family it has an accessory breathing organ inside and above the gill chamber each side, and it can survive in poorly oxygenated water. The breathing organ is, however, relatively simple when compared to those of other anabantids.

It feeds indiscriminately on insects, insect larvae, and fishes (in the case of large specimens). It spawns during spring and early summer in shallow quiet water, the eggs being shed and fertilized, sink to the bottom. The male is said to guard the eggs.

It is a rather slender-bodied, compressed fish, with long-based dorsal and anal fins. The lateral line is formed in 2 sections. Coloration is yellowish brown with numerous black speckles and bars; a dark spot on the edge of the gill cover.

The genus *Sandelia* was named by Castelnau in 1861 after Sandeli, the chief of the Gacha branch of the Xhosa tribe.

SANDFISH see **Crapatulus arenarius** and see under **Arctoscopus japonicus**
SANDFISH,
BELTED see **Serranus subligarius**
PACIFIC see **Trichodon trichodon**
SANDROLLER see **Percopsis transmontana**
SANDSNAKE see **Ophisurus serpens**
SANDY DOG see **Scyliorhinus canicula**

Sanopus Batrachoididae **splendidus** 20 cm. (8 in.)

This beautiful toadfish is known from the coast of Mexico. It has recently been discovered by underwater divers, and the striking photographs by Herr Hans Flaskamp were taken before this species had been described as new to science. They were taken on the W. coast of the island of Cozumel, where this fish is evidently very common.

Hans Flaskamp found them living under rocks or in small caves in the coral on sandy bottoms in depths of 9–25 m. (5–14 fathoms).

They normally lie with their heads at the entrance to the cave into which they retire if disturbed. **180**

SAPO, BAGRE see **Rhamdia sapo**
SAPO
   BOCON see **Amphichthys cryptocentrus**
   CANO see **Thalassophryne maculosa**

Sarda   Scombridae
   australis see under **S. sarda**
   lineolata see under **S. sarda**
   orientalis see under **S. sarda**
   sarda BONITO, ATLANTIC BONITO
91 cm. (3 ft)
An Atlantic species which is found from the Cape of Good Hope across to the S. American coast and n. to s. Scandinavia and Nova Scotia. At these extremities of its range, however, it only occurs seasonally and then rarely. It is common in the Mediterranean.

Similar species occur in the Indian Ocean (*S. orientalis*) and the Pacific (*S. australis* and *S. lineolata*). All species of *Sarda* are valuable commercial fishes, the flesh light coloured and very suitable for canning. Few of them exceed a weight of 7 kg. (15 lb.).

The Atlantic species is a strong, swift, open sea predator, travelling in compact schools and feeding on a wide range of herring-like and other fishes, and squids. They have the rather distinctive habit of regularly jumping clear of the water when in pursuit of their prey. The shoals are usually found offshore by 25–32 km. (15–20 miles).

It is fished for commercially wherever it is common, often by means of trolled lines, or purse seines. Anglers catch numbers also and it has the reputation of being a hard fighter.

The bonito is distinguished by its rather slender shape and by its large mouth the hind edge of which reaches beyond the eye. Its back is steel blue with numerous oblique dark lines; the sides and belly are silvery.

Sardina   Clupeidae
   pilchardus PILCHARD, SARDINE
25 cm. (10 in.)
The pilchard is distinguished from most of its European relatives by having raised ridges on its gill cover, and by its large scales. It is rather round-bodied by comparison with other members of its family, but has their typical coloration, greeny olive on the back shading to golden silvery sides and belly.

The pilchard is most abundant in the Mediterranean and on the Atlantic coast of s. Europe, s. to the Canaries. It becomes less common in the e. Mediterranean, is rare in the Black Sea, and in the Atlantic, although it occurs n. to the s. coasts of England and the North Sea where it is variable in numbers with periodic climatic changes.

It is a shoaling pelagic fish, found from the surface to a depth of about 55 m. (30 fathoms), although coming nearer to the surface at night. It spawns in spring and summer in British

waters, but practically all year round in the Mediterranean. The young form shoals close inshore in bays and estuaries in their first year, moving offshore to spawn in their second year.

The pilchard is a valuable food fish, and essential to the economy of many fishing communities along the French, Spanish, and Mediterranean coasts. The young fish particularly are exploited, and sold canned in oil or sauces as sardines. The English Channel fishery concentrated especially on catching the adult fish, which were sold as pilchards. Because of their oily flesh they do not keep well enouth to be marketed fresh, other than locally, so the traditional preservation was to salt them in barrels; this later gave way to canning. This fishery has slowly declined over the years.

SARDINE see Clupeidae
SARDINE see **Sardina pilchardus,**
      Sardinops ocellata
SARDINE,
   GOLDEN see **Sardinella aurita**
   PACIFIC see **Sardinops caeruleus**
   RED-EAR see **Harengula humeralis**
   SURF see **Iso natalensis**

Sardinella   Clupeidae
The species illustrated in colour has not been identified. **28**
S. aurita GOLDEN SARDINE 38 cm. (15 in.)
This sardine is found in the Mediterranean, and rarely in the Black Sea, as well as in the Atlantic from Portugal s. to Angola. It is a shoaling fish of coastal waters, which occurs in great abundance in the s. part of its range, but is limited in the N. to seasons which are warmer than usual.

The golden sardine is slim-bodied, oval in cross-section, but with a distinct scaly toothed keel along the belly. Its scales are moderate in size and less easily detached. It is bluish above, silvery beneath with a golden stripe along the side, and a dusky spot on the upper gill cover.

It is a valuable food fish off the N. African coast.

Sardinops   Clupeidae
   caeruleus CALIFORNIAN PILCHARD,
PACIFIC SARDINE 41 cm. (16¼ in.)
This pilchard is found from s. Alaska to Cape San Lucas and throughout the Gulf of California. It is the fish that was the mainstay of the gigantic Californian pilchard fishery, best known for the canned product. The first cannery was set up in 1889 but the catch expanded tremendously during the First World War, fluctuating between 600,000 and 4 million pounds annually before then, but reaching totals of 1·5 thousand million pounds in the period between the World Wars. The fishery crashed tragically after 1944 and has virtually failed due to the scarcity of the fish. There seems little doubt that overfishing was the basic cause for this decline, although suggestions have been made that it may also have been in part due to natural fluctuations in numbers due to climatic changes.

In its days of abundance the sardine was found off the Californian coast in shoals estimated to contain 10 million or more fish. Such vast shoals had a tremendous impact on the other marine inhabitants of the area. They are themselves filter-feeders straining off minute

plants and animals from the surface of the sea through their fine sieve-like gill rakers. At various stages of their life cycle they are the prey of other marine animals, as eggs they are eaten by arrow worms, as larvae by other fishes, and jelly-fishes. The adults are prey to most larger fishes, tuna, barracuda, and sharks, while whole communities of birds, such as pelicans, gulls and cormorants, and sea lions, porpoises, and other cetaceans depend on the presence of the sardines.

The Californian pilchard is similar in build to the other pilchards. Its back is greeny-blue, its sides silvery with a line of rounded black spots behind the head. Like its relatives it is round-bodied and plump, with a dorsal fin placed well forward on the back. It has large, fragile scales on its body, none on its head, and raised ridges running obliquely across the gill covers.

It is a prolific spawner, each female producing between 100–200 thousand eggs annually. The eggs are shed at night near the surface and float at the surface until hatching takes place about 3 days later.

Some authors consider that this and the 2 succeeding species, being closely related, should be considered as subspecies of the s. Pacific *S. sagax*.

S. neopilchardus AUSTRALIAN PILCHARD
28 cm. (11 in.)
This is the species of pilchard found along the s. coast of Australia, and off Tasmania and New Zealand. Its biology is much like the other species, for it is found in large shoals near the surface feeding on planktonic organisms. It is also migratory as are the other species.

In colour it is dark blue above changing suddenly to silver on the sides, it has a row of rounded dark spots along each side at the level of the eye, and each scale on the back has a dusky centre. The tips of the dorsal and tail fins are dusky. In all respects it is similar to the other pilchards in the genus differing only in small anatomical features.

This is the most common of the Australian herrings, and is already fished for in a minor way. There is little doubt that the pilchard is one of the great underexploited fishery resources of s. Australian waters, which will become of commercial importance in time.
S. ocellata SARDINE, PILCHARD, SOUTH AFRICAN PILCHARD 30 cm. (12 in.)
In shape and colouring a typical pilchard. The body is rather elongate, the head moderately large. Scales large and easily detached. The mouth is moderately large with no teeth in the jaws, but the gill arches have a dense mesh of long gill rakers through which the planktonic food is sieved. It is bluish green on the back, silvery on the sides and belly with a golden line between these 2 colours, and close behind the head a line of rounded dark spots. The tail fin and pectorals are yellow tinted.

This pilchard is found in the waters of s. Africa. It is closely related to the s. Australian, and Pacific American pilchards, and some authors recognize them at the most as sub-specifically distinct. In s. African waters they are found from the shore line to water of 183 m. (100 fathoms) depth, but their occurrence is seasonal within coastal waters, there being an inshore migration in autumn. Spawning mainly takes place in spring and summer. The young fish drift inshore from the spawning grounds, and locally bays and shallow water are important nursery grounds.

This pilchard feeds, like its relatives, on plankton. A very large amount of their food is diatoms and plant plankton; of the animals eaten copepods are the most important. In its turn the pilchard is preyed upon by numerous animals. Their planktonic eggs are eaten by pelagic molluscs, later larvae and young fish are preyed on by squid, scad, and seabirds. The latter, particularly the Cape cormorant, Cape gannet, and Cape penguin, take millions of young and adult pilchards annually (the total was estimated at 61,600 tons annually in S. African waters).

The pilchard fishing industry of S. and SW. Africa began in the 1940s, and expanded at a rapid rate after the Second World War. Despite conservation measures there is evidence that the stock has been overfished and that the level of landings will start to fluctuate, before falling severely. The landings in S. Africa in the 1960s reached 400 thousand metric tons, and in SW. Africa rose to 650 thousand. Much of this catch was used for fish meal, and oil extraction, although canned pilchards are also produced.

S. sagax see under **S. caeruleus**

SARGASSOFISH see **Histrio histrio**
SARGASSUM
PIPEFISH see **Syngnathus pelagicus**
TRIGGERFISH see **Xanichthys ringens**
SARGO see **Anisotremus davidsoni**

Sarotherodon Cichlidae
alcalicus see under **S. grahami**
amphimelas see under **S. grahami**
galilaeus GALILEE CICHLID 40 cm. (15 in.)
Widely distributed from Israel and Jordan (as its name suggests, it is found in Lake Galilee), through the Nile to range over the whole of E. and Central Africa as far as Liberia.

Its body form is typical of the group. The mouth is small, with minute teeth, and the gill rakers are fine, thin and numerous. Its food is mostly plant plankton although small crustaceans are also eaten. In coloration its body and fins are uniformly silvery grey, often with 3–5 dark bars across the back and sides.

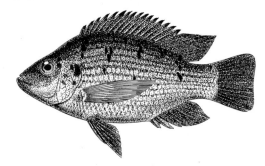

Both male and female brood the small olive-green eggs in the mouth; in the n. parts of its range it is usually the male which broods the eggs, towards the S. it is usually the female.

It is a good food fish throughout its range, and is also kept in aquaria.
S. grahami GRAHAM'S CICHLID 10 cm. (4 in.)
A most interesting dwarf cichlid species which lives only in the alkaline springs of the margins of Lake Magadi in Kenya. These are warm water springs, around 36°C. at source, and the water is highly alkaline (ph c. 10.5). Lake Magadi lies just below the equator (1°43′S) in the Great Rift Valley. The fish browses on the algae, eating occasional invertebrates in the algae, around the cooler margins of the springs, so much so that the algae growing in the warmer-water area is noticeably more luxuriant. The fish tolerates temperatures of up to about 41°C.

Males prepare a shallow nest up to 15 cm. (6 in.) wide and 7 cm. (3 in.) deep in the gravel, algae, or soft bottom, which they defend actively. After the eggs are laid they are brooded by the female in her mouth. The males are sexually mature at 3.5 cm. (1½ in.), and females at 2.5 cm. (1 in.), but the smaller females produce very many fewer eggs than the large ones. The fry are free-swimming at about 1 cm. (½ in.), when they are released by the female in shallow-water nursery areas.

Graham's cichlid is similar in body shape to many of the *Tilapia* species; males can, however, be identified by their conspicuously white lower lips, while the upper lip is grey-mauve. The head is largely bluish mauve, the body greyish.

Other, and similar species live in soda lakes in the Rift Valley, *S. alcalicus* in Lake Natron, and *S. amphimelas* in Lake Manyara. *S. grahami* has recently been recognized as a subspecies of *S. alcalicus*.
S. mossambicus MOZAMBIQUE CICHLID, BREAM 36 cm. (14 in.)
Found in E. Africa, and s. to the Zambezi River and Port Alfred in S. Africa. It occurs in freshwater in the tropical parts of its range, but to the S., where temperatures are lower, it is increasingly found in brackish water.

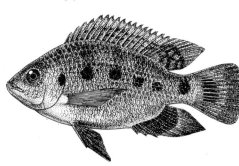

Coloration varies greatly in this species with the breeding season. Males become deep black, the lower part of the head white, and the fins have a reddish margin when spawning; the mouth and snout region becomes swollen and thickened. Females are greyish-yellow with several black blotches on the sides.

It is a mouth-brooder in which the female takes the eggs into her mouth as soon as they are laid.

This species is a valuable food fish in its native range and has been introduced elsewhere for pond culture. In s. Africa it is also well-liked as an anglers' fish.
S. niloticus NILE MOUTH-BROODER 50 cm. (19½ in.)
A widespread species in Africa, found from E. Africa across to the Congo and Nigeria, and

extending n. along the Nile to Syria, and Israel. It is one of the larger cichlid species, and specimens of up to 6.4 kg. (14 lb.) have been reported. In many areas it is a valuable food fish, and its range has been extended by stocking dam-pools and ponds.

Its food is mainly plankton, but this species is very adaptable and it also eats insects and crustaceans as well as blue-green algae.

It is a mouth-brooder in which the female carries the eggs.

Sarpa Sparidae
salpa SAUPE, BAMBOOFISH 46 cm. (18 in.)
Found widely in the e. Atlantic from Biscay to S. Africa where it extends into the s. Indian Ocean. It is found throughout the Mediterranean. It is particularly associated with rocky areas in shallow water of less than 15 m. (8 fathoms). It feeds by scraping algae and diatoms off the rocks and larger seaweeds. It is always recognizable by its habit of swimming in a tight-packed shoal. **303**

SAUPE see **Sarpa salpa**

Saurida Synodontidae
undosquamis LIZARDFISH, SPOTTED-TAILED GRINNER 51 cm. (20 in.)
This is one of the largest lizardfishes, and it is very widely distributed in the Indo-Pacific, from the coast of Africa across to the E. Indies, Australia, the Philippines, and N. to Japan. Partly because of its size, it is one of the few members that are used for food, but it is not

an important food fish except locally. It is a moderately deep-water species found at depths of 30–40 m. (16–22 fathoms) and usually on muddy bottoms.

It has the typical lizardfish body shape, and is grey-brown in colour, light ventrally with a row of rounded spots along the sides.

The large slightly curved jaws are the origin of the Australian vernacular grinner for the lizardfishes in general.

SAURY see Scomberesocidae
SAURY,
ATLANTIC see **Scomberesox saurus**
PACIFIC see **Cololabis saira**
SAW
SHARK see Pristiophoridae
SHARK see **Pliotrema warreni**
SHARK, COMMON see **Pristiophorus cirratus**
SHARK, SOUTHERN see **Pristiophorus nudipinnis**
SAWAL see **Eleutheronema tetradactylum**
SAWBELLY see **Alosa pseudoharengus**
SAWFISH see Pristidae
SAWFISH see **Pristis pristis**
SAWFISH,
GREATER see **Pristis pectinata**
SMALL-TOOTH see **Pristis pectinata**
SMALL-TOOTHED see **Pristis microdon**
SCABBARDFISH see Trichiuridae
SCABBARDFISH see **Lepidopus caudatus**

SCABBARDFISH, BLACK see **Aphanopus carbo**
SCAD see Carangidae
SCAD see **Priacanthus hamrur, Trachurus trachurus**
SCAD,
BIG-EYE see **Selar crumenophthalmus**
YELLOWTAIL see **Trachurus maccullochi**
SCALDFISH see **Arnoglossus laterna**
SCALED BLENNY see Clinidae, Ophiclinidae
SCALELESS
CATFISH see Mochokidae
TUNA see **Orcynopsis unicolor**
SCALYHEAD SCULPIN see **Artedius harringtoni**

Scaphirhynchus Acipenseridae
platorynchus SHOVELNOSE STURGEON
1 m. (3¼ ft)
This shovelnose sturgeon is found in the Mississippi River system of N. America. It was very abundant in all the major rivers in this system, such as the Ohio, Illinois, Wabash and Cumberland rivers, but has declined in numbers over the past century due to a variety of causes. It was formerly fished for extensively, its flesh used for food, and the female's eggs for caviar.

It is found only in freshwater, and does not migrate to the sea, although the adults make seasonal migrations upstream during the spring to spawning grounds. It is distinguished by its broad flattened snout, long barbels, and lack of a spiracle.

Scardinius Cyprinidae
erythrophthalmus RUDD 46 cm. (18 in.)
The rudd is a freshwater fish widely distributed in Europe, from the British Isles e. to the Caspian basin, and from the S. Baltic S. to Italy. Within this area it undoubtedly has been greatly spread by man (as in the case of Ireland where it is not native).

The rudd is an inhabitant of shallow, warm lakes, or deep, slow-flowing lowland rivers. It is a shoaling fish feeding on aquatic insect larvae, crustaceans, and some plant matter. Its steeply angled mouth especially suits it to taking insects at the surface of the water. It spawns in April to June, depending on the water temperature; the small eggs stick to water plants and hatch in 3–10 days. After hatching the fry hang passively on the water plants until their yolk in the yolk-sac is consumed.

The rudd is a popular angling fish in the British Isles. Young specimens make good aquarium pets. Being relatively hardy it is often introduced to all kinds of small waters, often unsuitable ones, and proliferates to form a numerous, stunted population. It also hybridizes with other cyprinids to the confusion of amateur taxonomists! **141**

SCARIDAE

A family of marine fishes found in tropical and warm-temperate seas. The parrotfishes are most closely related to the wrasses (Labridae) but differ from them in the shape of the teeth which are fused together to form a beak-like edge to the jaw. In the back of the throat they also have large, very distinctive grinding teeth, fused on bones, one below, 2 above.

Parrotfishes are active in daylight and are herbivorous. Their normal feeding behaviour is to scrape algae and coral from coral reefs, leaving distinct scars in the coral growth. The coral and algal mixture is crushed into a fine state in the pharyngeal mill, and the indigestible sand excreted. Parrotfishes are probably one of the most important biological factors in the wearing down of coral reefs and the production of sand.

Several species have been found to sleep at night, wedged into crevices; others are known to secrete around their bodies a veil-like cocoon of mucus. Lying in this sleeping-bag they are presumed to be safe from night-hunting predators such as moray-eels.

Parrotfishes are well-known for their brilliant colours. Many of the earlier descriptions of species were based on colour, but only relatively recently has it been widely accepted that males are frequently a totally different colour from females of the same species. Reversal of sex from female to male is known in this group. See **Bulbometopon, Heteroscarus, Scarus, Sparisoma.**

Scarus Scaridae
coeruleus BLUE PARROTFISH
1·2 m. (4 ft)
A beautifully coloured parrotfish which when adult is deep blue with a pink band on the lower jaw. The young are striped, but later become bluish with a yellow patch on the head. Adults, possibly only the males, develop a pronounced bump on the upper snout.

It is a w. Atlantic species found from the Carolinas and Bermuda to s. Brazil, including the Gulf of Mexico and the Caribbean. It is common around reefs and on coral sand, the larger specimens being found in deeper water. This species has been observed to secrete a mucous envelope at night in which it sleeps.
S. croicensis STRIPED or MOTTLEFIN
PARROTFISH 28 cm. (11 in.)
A w. Atlantic species found from Bermuda, Florida, and the Caribbean to Brazil. In much of this area it is the most common parrotfish. It is a small species which is found in large shoals on, or close to, the reef.

In common with a number of other parrotfishes this species shows interesting spawning behaviour. Some males which are distinguished by their blue-green and orange colouring, spawn individually with striped females, but other males with the colour striped like the female, spawn in shoals. The blue-green and orange so called terminal males, are believed to have resulted from sex-changed females. The illustration shows a young fish in its mucous cocoon. **414**
S. ghobban 91 cm. (3 ft)
Widespread in the Indian and Pacific oceans from the Red Sea and E. African coast to the central and w. Pacific. It is a very variable

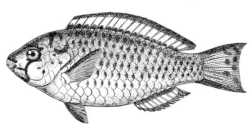

species, although the background is usually light orange or yellowish, with deep blue markings on the scales and fins, those on the scales forming broken vertical bars.

Throughout its range, and no doubt due to its variable colouring, this species has been described more than a dozen times as separate species.
S. guacamaia RAINBOW PARROTFISH
1·2 m. (4 ft)
A w. Atlantic species found from Bermuda and Florida, throughout the Caribbean to n. Argentina. It is a common fish in the W. Indies although in shallow water they are mostly of moderate size, the really large specimens (up to 20 kg. (44 lb.)) are found only in deep water. It is mainly a reef species, coming so far inshore that at times schools of them may be seen with their backs breaking the surface. Some individuals have been reported to produce mucus sleeping-cocoons at night.

It is a large, heavy-bodied parrotfish. Large males are usually bronze coloured anteriorly, greenish to the rear. When young it is pastel orange and green.
S. sordidus PARROTFISH 100 cm. (39 in.)
A widely distributed tropical Indo-Pacific parrotfish, the range of which extends from the Hawaiian Islands, through the central and w. Pacific Ocean, the Indian Ocean, to the e. coast of Africa, and the Red Sea. It is probably the most abundant parrotfish in the whole of its range, and locally, as in the Red Sea, it is very common.

As with other members of the genus its colouring varies with age. The young are reddish brown and rather drab; sexually mature males are a beautiful blend of greens and blues, with reddish stripes on the belly and a red bar along the dorsal fin base. **413**
S. vetula QUEEN PARROTFISH 61 cm. (2 ft)
Known from Bermuda, the Bahamas and Florida S. to the Caribbean Sea. It is a reef species which in the W. Indies is moderately common, often seen in small schools comprising 3–4 females and one male. They feed unselectively on coral growths and algae; algal strands have been found growing on the beak-teeth of large specimens. It is known to secrete a mucus envelope in which it sleeps at night.

Females are drab bluish-brown, with a pale band running along the lower side. Males are greeny-blue, the scales with yellow centres, and distinct yellow lines running from the mouth to the eye.

SCAT see Scatophagidae
SCAT see **Scatophagus argus**
SCAT,
AFRICAN see **Scatophagus tetracanthus**
THREAD-FIN see **Rhinoprenes pentanemus**

SCATOPHAGIDAE

A small family of Indo-Pacific fishes, found in inshore waters, estuaries and brackish waters. Most are small, silvery, deep-bodied fishes, few of which are used for food, but they have become popular as aquarium fishes – usually known as 'scats'.

They have a high dorsal profile, a well developed spiny dorsal fin separate from the soft-rayed dorsal fin. The anal fin has 4 spines. The body is covered with minute, embedded scales which extend onto the head and body. See **Scatophagus, Selenotoca.**

Scatophagus   Scatophagidae
  argus SPOTTED BUTTERFISH, SCAT,
ARGUS 31 cm. (12½ in.)
Widely distributed in the tropical Indo-Pacific in the sea, brackish water and freshwater, from India and E. Africa, throughout the E. Indies to the W. Pacific islands. It is an abundant fish which eats plant matter and bottom detritus; they are often found in great numbers around the outfalls of sewers and have the reputation for feeding of faeces (*Scatophagus* literally

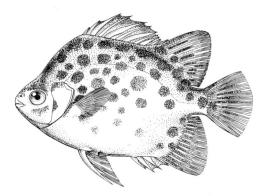

means dung-eater) and as a result in many areas they are not regarded as fit for food. Elsewhere it is regarded as a good food fish while fresh.

It is bluish grey, olive above and silvery or yellowish on the belly, the sides marked with scattered round or oval blotches. A dark bar running through the eye, another through the rear of the head while the bases of the second dorsal, tail and anal fins are conspicuously dark. Young fish have the sides marked with dusky bars.

It is a popular aquarium fish in marine or brackish water. Very lively and peaceful when young, and relatively easy to keep.
S. tetracanthus AFRICAN SCAT 18 cm. (7 in.)
An Indian Ocean fish found from E. Africa to the E. Indies, n. Australia and New Guinea. Very common in inshore waters, estuaries, and in freshwater in lower reaches of rivers.

A popular aquarium fish best kept as young in a marine or brackish aquarium. It is distinguished by its high rays in the front part of the second dorsal and anal fins, and by its pattern. Bold black-brown bands run across the back and upper sides which are otherwise yellowish or silvery. The young fish have dark bands running to the belly; in adults they end on the sides. The fins are yellowish or light brown.

SCAVENGER see Lethrinidae
SCAVENGER see **Lethrinus miniatus, Lethrinus nebulosus**

Schedophilus   Centrolophidae
  medusophagus CORNISH BLACKFISH,
BARRELFISH 58 cm. (23 in.)
Known only from the Atlantic Ocean and the Mediterranean although related species are found worldwide in tropical and warm temperate seas. The juvenile occurs frequently in association with jellyfishes and flotsam, feeding on the medusae and small crustaceans. It is deep-bodied, greenish brown above and

lighter below. Adults are dull brown in colour with a violet sheen over the body cavity. Large specimens live in the bathypelagic and meso-pelagic zones of the open sea, and are relatively common off the W. coast of the British Isles. Their bodies are laterally compressed, flabby, and very fragile. Examination of the gut contents shows that adults eat bathypelagic medusae (especially *Atolla*). They are very fragile; few undamaged specimens have become available for study.

SCHELLY see **Coregonus lavaretus**

Schilbe   Schilbeidae
A genus of freshwater catfish, found in Africa. The species illustrated in colour has not been identified. **156**
S. mystus BUTTERFISH 36 cm. (14 in.)
A small catfish distinguished by its short, few-rayed dorsal fin, a long anal fin, extending almost to the deeply forked tail fin, and by its 4 pairs of short barbels around the mouth. The genus *Schilbe* lacks an adipose fin.

This species is widely distributed in African rivers, including the Nile, the rivers of W. Africa, the Congo, and Zambezi, and in the lakes of Africa. It is found in open shallow water and is an active gregarious species feeding on small fishes and insect larvae. It spawns during the flood season.

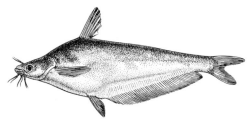

It has some local value as a commercial fish and its flesh is very palatable. It is also commonly kept as an aquarium fish. It is silvery-grey, rather darker above, with a dark blotch behind the gill cover on the sides. The young have 3 lengthwise dark bands.

SCHILBEIDAE

A family of catfishes found in the freshwaters of Africa, being distributed over nearly all the continent with the exception of the arid regions, and also found in Asia. Its members bear a superficial resemblance to the silurid catfishes, having a scaleless body, moderately elongate and compressed, and a very long anal fin. Some have a short dorsal fin, in others it is absent; some have an adipose fin. Generally they have 4 pairs of barbels. See **Etropiella, Eutropius, Parailia, Physailia, Schilbe.**

Schindleria   Schindleriidae
  praematurus 2·5 cm. (1 in.)
Found widely in the tropical Pacific. First recorded from the Hawaiian islands, where it is said to be probably the commonest fish, it has subsequently been taken off Samoa, Tahiti, New Guinea, the Tasman Sea, and around Bikini. It is a surface-living fish, very abundant in many areas and attracted to a light at night.

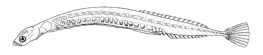

Its body is transparent, and the developing large eggs can be clearly discerned through the body wall. The skeleton is poorly developed, and is represented by a series of scarcely connected, slightly calcified larval structures. The best developed are the finely-toothed premaxillary bones in the upper jaw.

SCHINDLERIIDAE

A very curious family of minute fishes found in tropical waters of the Pacific Ocean. The 2 species placed in the family are slender-bodied and transparent, possessing many larval features although they may be sexually mature, a phenomenon rare in fishes and known as neotony.

Their placement in the systematic order has varied with the views of individual workers. Originally they were placed by their discoverer Dr Otto Schindler amongst the halfbeaks (family Exocoetidae), but they are now placed in a separate suborder, close to the sand-eels (Ammodytidae) and gobies (Gobiidae). See **Schindleria.**

Schizothorax   Cyprinidae
  argentatus MARINKA 51 cm. (20 in.)
A genus of cyprinid fishes represented by numerous species in the lakes and river basins of Central Asia, and s. to China and Vietnam. They form a rather distinct group of barbel-like fishes, but are distinguished by possessing a row of distinctly larger scales along the base of the anal fin. The body is covered with small scales but is sometimes naked.

S. argentatus is one of several species inhabiting the waters of the s. U.S.S.R., but is confined to the basin of the Lake Balkhash in Kasakhstan (to the N. of the Himalayas). It lives both in the rivers and the lake but migrates to rivers to spawn, which it does on gravelly bottoms in shallow water well upstream in spring. It feeds primarily on vegetation and has the appropriately long gut of a herbivore, in this case 3–5 times the length of the body.

It is of some commercial importance in the lake, being caught in fyke nets and seines. It is frequently dried for consumption, but the unshed eggs of this fish are highly poisonous.

SCHOMBURGK'S LEAFFISH see **Polycentrus schomburgkii**
SCHOOL SHARK see **Galeorhinus australis**
SCHOOLMASTER see **Lutjanus apodus**
SCHWANENFELD'S BARB see **Barbus schwanenfeldii**

Sciaena   Sciaenidae
  umbra CORB, BROWN MEAGRE
70 cm. (27½ in.)

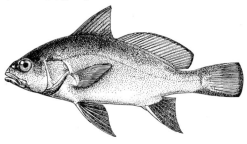

A Mediterranean species, occurring throughout that sea, and present in the Black Sea and the e. Atlantic from s. Biscay to Senegal. It is, like other croakers, a coastal species, found in small schools in 5–20 m. (3–11 fathoms). They can usually be found on rocky bottoms, often at the mouth of a cave or crevice, and amongst *Posidonia* beds. It is nocturnally active, feeding on crustaceans, molluscs, and occasionally fishes.

It is not often caught, except sometimes on a line, but its flesh makes very good eating. It is a beautiful browny-bronze on the back with golden reflections, ventrally it is light, but all the fins are dark.

SCIAENIDAE

A large family of mainly marine fishes found in all tropical and most temperate oceans. Numerous species are known, probably around 200, all but a few found in salt or estuarine waters.

The croakers or drums are distinguished particularly by their ability to produce sound; nearly every species has an elaborate swim-bladder which acts as a resonating chamber amplifying the noises produced by the adjacent muscles. Sound production is voluntary, it increases in the spawning season and after sunset, and croakers kept in an aquarium gradually cease to make noises as they become familiar with their surroundings. Many croakers live in murky estuarine habitats where visibility is poor, so a navigation system based on the production of sound and good hearing is not unexpected.

They are distinguished as a group by having 2 dorsal fins, the first just meeting the base of the second which is very long and many rayed; they also have a short-based anal fin with only 2 spines. The lateral line runs from the head to the tail and continues onto the tail fin rays. Chin barbels, or elaborate pores are present on the lower jaw, and the otoliths or earstones are well developed. Many of these features are obvious developments of a sensory nature. See **Aplodinotus, Argyrosomus, Atractoscion, Cynoscion, Equetus, Johnius, Menticirrhus, Nibea, Otolithes, Pogonias, Sciaena.**

Scleropages Osteoglossidae
formosus 90 cm. (35½ in.)
An Asiatic member of the family found widely in Banka, Borneo, Malaya, Sumatra, and Thailand. It is olive to brown, the sides silvery with a dark spot on each scale.

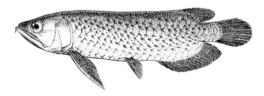

Where it occurs it is fairly common in streams, canals, and swamps, and is caught for food by various means. Large specimens are said to attain a weight of 7·2 kg. (15¾ lb.), and their flesh is well flavoured. It is a predatory species feeding on insects when young, and on fishes as an adult. Despite this, the female carries the large eggs in her pouch-like throat after they are laid. They are relatively few in number.
S. jardini see under **S. leichardti**

S. leichardti SPOTTED BARRAMUNDI
90 cm. (35½ in.)
The bony-tongued fishes are represented in the freshwaters of tropical Australia by the barramundi. Recently the existence of 2 Australian species has been recognized, the spotted barramundi (*S. leichardti*) which occurs in the Fitzroy River system, and the northern barramundi (*S. jardini*) in the n. rivers of Australia, Papua and W. Irian. Most of the earlier reports of this fish referred to them by the former name.

Both species are found in relatively slow-flowing rivers, especially in oxbow lakes and billabongs. They eat small fish, frogs, crustaceans, and insects, but the spotted barramundi is said to feed more at the water's surface than its relative. The spotted barramundi is a mouth brooder, the female carrying her unhatched eggs and later newly hatched young in a pouch within her mouth. The diameter of the eggs is about 10 mm. (½ in.), and they take an estimated 10–14 days to hatch; the newly hatched fish are 35 mm. (1½ in.) in length.

The spotted barramundi has the typical features of its family, a moderate anal fin, short dorsal, and large scales. It is said to provide good sport for the fly fisherman, attaining a weight of at least 4 kg. (8¾ lb.), and has palatable flesh.

Scolopsis Nemipteridae
temporalis BARRED-FACE SPINE-CHEEK
43 cm. (17 in.)
Widely distributed in the Indo-Pacific, but best known along the Queensland coast and the Great Barrier Reef where it is common. It is distinguished by the rather small scales on the body, and by its markings of 3 light bands across the snout, and a dark ring present on the top of the head. Like other members of the genus it has a sharp spine immediately beneath the eye.

It is widely used as a food fish but is not especially sought after.
S. vosmeri WHITE-CHEEKED MONOCLE-BREAM 25 cm. (10 in.)
Found in the Indian Ocean from the E. African coast, around the coast of India to the E. Indies. It is very common in coastal waters, around reefs, and rocky areas, and is used to some extent as a food fish.

The sharp spine on the bone beneath the eye is characteristic of this genus. This species is rosy pink in coloration, with a very distinctive white band across the gill covers, and a blood red spot behind. The dorsal and anal spines are bright red, the fins yellowish.

Scomber Scombridae
colias see **S. japonicus**
japonicus SPANISH or CHUB MACKEREL
40 cm. (15¾ in.)
This mackerel is cosmopolitan in its range in tropical and warm temperate seas. It is well known in Japanese waters and the N. Pacific generally, especially off California. It also occurs commonly in the S. Hemisphere. In the Atlantic it was long regarded as a separate species, *S. colias,* but recent research has suggested that the 2 forms are identical. In the N. Atlantic it occurs in British waters rarely, and N. to the Gulf of St Lawrence. In the N. Pacific it ranges from Alaska to Mexico.

It is a schooling fish which is sometimes

found close inshore. It feeds upon such small fishes and crustaceans as are numerous in the locality. In turn it is fed upon by a large series of predators, including fishes, seals, porpoises, and seabirds. Man takes a heavy toll, and the Californian mackerel fishery appears to have succeeded in reducing the population to an uneconomic state. In Japan it is one of the most important food fishes, consumed fresh or canned (as is the Californian catch).

The Spanish mackerel (as it is known in the U.K.) has a swim bladder. It is blue above with faint wavy dark lines on the back. The sides and belly are silvery with numerous rounded dusky spots.
S. scombrus MACKEREL, ATLANTIC MACKEREL 56 cm. (22 in.)
The mackerel is a N. Atlantic species which occurs on both sides of the ocean, and also in the Mediterranean and Black Seas. In European waters it ranges from N. Africa n. to central Norway and around the British coast; in the w. Atlantic it is found from Labrador s. to N. Carolina. In neither region is it particularly abundant at the n. extremity of its range.

It is a relatively small member of the family, which includes the giant tunas, averaging a weight of 1 kg. (2·2 lb.), with occasional specimens attaining 1·8 kg. (4 lb.). What it lacks in size, it makes up in numbers for it is frequently encountered in huge schools. It is a surface-living fish found mainly off the coastline facing the open sea. They are highly migratory, making inshore migrations and moving N. with the rise in temperature in summer, and returning in winter. They spawn in summer in a prolonged season which may start in May and go on until September. Average sized female mackerel each produce about half a million eggs which float at or near the surface. The eggs hatch in 2–5 days depending on temperature. The early growth of mackerel is fast and yearlings are around 24 cm. (9½ in.).

The mackerel is an extremely important food fish and is used fresh or frozen, but does not keep well fresh. It is caught on lines baited with feathers, gill netted, and purse seined. The fishery, however, tends to fluctuate, some good years being succeeded by very poor years, due to factors not fully understood. In addition, mackerel are favourite prey for many of the large tuna, and other large fishes and sharks.

The mackerel is a brilliantly beautiful fish. Its resemblance to the tunnies is striking, like them it has a series of finlets following the dorsal and anal fins. It differs, however, in having widely spaced dorsal fins, in lacking a groove for the reception of the spiny dorsal, and although having small keels at the base of the tail fin lobes it does not have a lateral keel at the side of the tail. **451**

SCOMBERESOCIDAE

A small family of oceanic surface-living fishes known as sauries. They are all slender-bodied, elongate fishes with a rather pointed head (and in some forms long beak-like jaws), the tail is forked, and behind the normally rayed dorsal and anal fins a series of small finlets continue to the tail.

One species or another may be often very abundant seasonally and they have been commercially exploited locally, but their greatest value seems to be as a food fish for the valuable tunas and billfishes.

Four species are recognized. The family is distributed in all 3 oceans, mostly in temperate regions where they appear to take the place of the flyingfishes of the tropics. Some species do, however, live in tropical seas. See **Cololabis, Scomberesox.**

Scomberesox　　　　　Scomberesocidae
　　saurus SKIPPER, ATLANTIC SAURY
46 cm. (18 in.)
A long slender-bodied fish, with thin beak-like jaws, a series of small finlets behind the dorsal and anal fins, and a forked tail. The lateral line runs along the belly, a typical adaptation to life at the surface of the sea. The skipper is widely distributed in the N. Atlantic, from the Gulf of Maine s. to the W. Indies and across the ocean to the Mediterranean and the Canary Islands. This warm temperate area is the breeding region from which, with seasonal warming of the ocean and under the influence of oceanic currents, it extends n. to Nova Scotia, and Norway and Iceland. After strong penetration of these ne. regions in some years, large numbers are trapped in the North Sea and become stranded. These n. excursions are principally feeding migrations.

In the S. Hemisphere it is distributed circumglobally in temperate waters off s. America, S. Africa, s. Australia, and across the Pacific to the American continent.

The eggs of the skipper are spherical and small, with long filaments; they float at the surface. The young at first have jaws of unequal length, but at around 15 cm. (6 in.) they are fully developed. The food of the skipper is principally small crustaceans and small fishes. It is eaten by tuna, marlin, and many other fishes, and when pursued by predators, shoals leap out of the water in 'cascades'. It is not infrequently found on the low decks of ships at night, having presumably leapt aboard in escaping from predators, or possibly having been attracted by lights.

On account of its abundance and importance as a prey for other fishes it has considerable indirect value. It is exploited directly in small quantities, but outside its spawning range the skipper is too sporadic in occurrence to be regularly fished for.

Scomberomorus　　　　　Scombridae
　　cavalla KING MACKEREL, KINGFISH
165 cm. (65 in.)
A w. Atlantic species found from N. Carolina to Rio de Janeiro, and throughout the Caribbean. Occasionally it wanders as far N. as s. Massachusetts and the Gulf of Maine. Like the other members of the genus it is found in small schools or singly, usually on the seaward

side of reefs or offshore. It is always on the move, hunting schools of smaller fishes.

It is a good food fish and is captured throughout its range. Occasionally its flesh has proved toxic when eaten. It is also a good game fish, specimens weighing up to 36 kg. (80 lb.) having been caught by anglers.

It is distinguished by its plain colouring, deep blue above, silvery below. The dorsal fin is blue. The lateral line drops abruptly below the second dorsal fin.

S. commerson NARROW-BARRED SPANISH MACKEREL, BARRACUTA, KATONKEL, SERRA 230 cm. (90 in.)
This species is widely distributed through the tropical Indo-Pacific. It is believed to occur at least seasonally between the Red Sea and E. African coast, throughout Indo-Australian waters to China and Japan. This enormous range and its popularity as a food and game fish are responsible for the numerous vernacular names applied to it, only a few of which are listed above.

In many areas it is a valued food fish. In Queensland for example, it is the most important fish to be landed, caught particularly between August and December when the fish are schooling in numbers outside the reef. Here it is thought that outside this season the schools break up and the mackerel scatter into the open sea to feed. The schools reassemble early in the year and move along the open water outside the reef as the water warms. Its migrations are clearly seasonal wherever it occurs and are presumably governed by water temperature.

Although most of the commercially caught fish are around 11 kg. (25 lb.) occasional specimens weighing as much as 59 kg. (130 lb.) are reported. It is a highly popular angling fish throughout its range.

This species is distinguished by its elongate body-shape, the snout is pointed, the teeth large. The lateral line bends downwards abruptly below the end of the second dorsal fin. The back is deep blue, the sides and belly silvery, with numerous wavy, vertical lines which increase in number with age. A juvenile is illustrated.

S. maculatus SPANISH MACKEREL
1·2 m. (4 ft)
Found in the tropical Atlantic, in the W. from Maine to Brazil, including the Caribbean and Gulf of Mexico, although it is not common in either area. In the tropical e. Atlantic it is very common off the W. African coast and seems to be the only member of the genus found there. It is found mainly in open water, migrating seasonally coastwise and occasionally entering estuaries.

It is a relatively small species, most specimens captured being around 2 kg. (4½ lb.) but occasional fish weighing 9 kg. (20 lb.) are reported. It is caught for food locally and despite its size is a good sporting fish.

Its body shape is similar to the other members of the genus. It differs in having a gently downcurved lateral line below the second

dorsal. Its back is deep blue, the sides and belly silvery but the sides are liberally marked with rounded yellow to orange spots – not elongate as in *S. regalis.*

S. regalis CERO, PAINTED or CERO MACKEREL 1·8 m. (6 ft)
An inhabitant of the tropical w. Atlantic, where it has been recorded from New England s. to Brazil, and throughout the Gulf of Mexico and the Bahamas. If not the most common of the Spanish mackerels to be found in the W. Indies, it is the most frequently seen and captured for it comes close inshore over the reefs, feeding on the small schooling clupeoids and atherinid fishes. It is usually encountered singly but may be found in small schools.

The cero is a fine food fish and is locally captured in some quantities. It is also a good angling fish, mostly weighing up to 4·5 kg. (10 lb.) but occasional specimens up to 16 kg. (35 lb.) have been caught.

It is deep blue on the back, silvery on the sides and belly. The lower sides are sprinkled with oval yellow to bronze spots, which form darker streaks higher up the body. The lobe of the first dorsal fin is black. The lateral line curves gently downwards beneath the second dorsal fin.

SCOMBRIDAE
The family of the tunnies, tunas, and mackerels, a large group of marine fishes found mainly in tropical and warm waters of the world with some species entering cool temperate seas often seasonally. They are widely distributed pelagic fishes, usually making migrations, sometimes of great distances. They are active predatory fishes, swift and powerful swimmers which feed in schools on small fishes, such as various sardine or herring-like fish and squids, while the smaller members of the family are selective plankton feeders.

Most species are commercially exploited. Heavy fishing for the large, open-ocean tunas is a phenomenon of the last 2 decades, and there is evidence that in some areas tuna stocks have been quickly overfished. Elsewhere, as in the Mediterranean and off the Californian coast, various species of tuna have been fished locally for many years. Mackerels too are the subject of large local fisheries. The flesh of the tunas and mackerels is dark and rather oily. Generally it is best canned, although if consumed fresh it is palatable, but it does not keep. Most of the extensive fisheries for the larger members of the family are producing fish for canning and byproducts. Tunas are also famous sporting fish the world over.

Members of the family all have similar body forms. They are rather spindle-shaped, round-bodied in cross-section with a pointed snout, deep mid-section and tapering tail. The mouth is moderately large, teeth usually well developed (in the Spanish mackerels, very large). The first dorsal fin is composed of stout, well-spaced spines, but slots completely into a groove on the back. The second dorsal and anal fins are well developed and comprised of densely packed rays, followed by a series of finlets. The tail-fin is broad, and high – a high aspect ratio tail – which provides tremendous motive power in swimming. Scales are small to minute in the scombroids but most have a corselet of larger scales over the shoulder region. The tail has conspicuous ridges along the sides. The muscles of the tail region are richly supplied with blood vessels, which give the flesh its dark colour, and also aid in the carriage of nutrients and waste products from use. The body temperature of these fishes is usually higher than that of the surrounding water, and the tunas are one of the few fish groups which could be called 'warm-blooded'. The whole structure of the scombroid body is thus an adaptation to powerful and prolonged swimming. There can be few more efficient swimmers in the seas.

Tunny is the usual British-English usage; tuna is used in other English-speaking areas. See **Acanthocybium, Auxis, Euthynnus, Gasterochisma, Katsuwonus, Orcynopsis, Rastrelliger, Sarda, Scomber, Scomberomorus, Thunnus.**

SCOPELARCHIDAE
A family of small to moderate sized fishes the members of which are rather long-bodied, and have large mouths. They are found in the open sea from the surface to 2380 m. (1300 fathoms), but show some vertical zonation so that only the larvae and youngest juveniles are near the surface, and the adults are found in the deepest water. They are clearly fast swimming, active fishes, and the adults are rarely caught, nor are they often found in other fishes' stomachs.

The family is widely distributed, virtually worldwide in temperate and tropical waters, including the Mediterranean and Red Sea. See **Scopelarchus.**

Scopelarchus　　　　　Scopelarchidae
sagax BERMUDA PEARLEYE 13 cm. (5 in.)
This species has so far been discovered only in the waters off Bermuda in the open ocean. It has been taken in depths of 366–1830 m. (200–1000 fathoms), but relatively few specimens are known. Most of its teeth are short and sharp, but the lower jaw has a number of much longer, slender and depressible teeth. The

eyes of this species (and of the whole family) are distinctive, for they are elongate, telescopic, and directed upwards, with a protoberant lens. It has a conspicuous large, 'glistening spot' on the side, which may be a light organ in life. When living it is brassy, iridescent in colour. It is an active predator feeding on small fishes and mysid shrimps.

SCOPELOSAURIDAE
A small family widely distributed in the tropical and temperate regions of the 3 major oceans, although occasional specimens have been found in cooler regions. They are all slender-bodied, rather pike-like in appearance with a moderately long head. They have soft-rayed fins, and an adipose fin, and moderately large, easily detached scales. Their eyes are large.

Relatively few specimens have been described, and of those that have few were caught in nets. It is thought that the adults are powerful, darting swimmers easily able to dodge slow-moving trawls. See **Scopelosaurus.**

Scopelosaurus　　　　　Scopelosauridae
smithi 21 cm. (8¼ in.)
This fish has been found only in deep water in the tropical and warm temperate Atlantic Ocean. It was originally described from off the coast of Brazil, and was subsequently found off Madeira. The later capture of larvae suggests that it is widespread in the Atlantic Ocean.

It is a slender fish with large eyes, and a large mouth. The pupil is distinctly eliptical with a prominent lens-less space. It is distinguished by having 55–56 vertebrae as well as by the number of gill rakers. It is described as a deep purplish black in colour.

SCOPHTHALMIDAE
A family of flatfishes which includes the turbots, brills, and topknots, many of which are important and valued food fishes. In this group, during development of the larva, the right eye migrates over the top of the head and comes to rest at the level of, and fairly close to, the left eye. The members of the family thus have both eyes on the left side. (Occasional reversed specimens are reported.)

Most of the members of this family are deep-bodied fishes with well developed pelvic fins, that on the blind side being the same size as the other, both are broad-based. They are found only in the N. Atlantic and Mediterranean. See **Lepidorhombus, Scophthalmus, Zeugopterus.**

Scophthalmus　　　　　Scophthalmidae
aquosus WINDOW-PANE, SAND FLOUNDER
46 cm. (18 in.)
A w. Atlantic flatfish found from S. Carolina n. to the Gulf of St Lawrence. It lives in shallow water down to a depth of 73 m. (40 fathoms) mostly on sandy bottoms, but it is most common in the region of the lower shore line down to 46 m. (25 fathoms).

Once well grown the window-pane feeds mainly on fishes, and a wide range of species are taken. Young specimens feed mostly on crustaceans, especially shrimps and mysids, but young fishes are likely to be eaten at any time.

This species has been exploited as a food fish from time to time but it is not commercially important.

S. maeotius BLACK SEA TURBOT
85 cm. (33 in.)
A native to the Black Sea which is also found in the adjacent Mediterranean. It is widely distributed in the Black Sea and lives down to depths of 100 m. (54 fathoms), although in the summer months it comes close inshore to feed and spawn. Its food consists mainly of small fishes especially young mullet, and anchovies, sprats, and whiting. Its fecundity is high, females produce between 3 and 13 million eggs depending on their size.

It is locally an important food fish, well flavoured and growing to a weight of 15 kg. (33 lb.). It is caught on set lines, in traps, and by trawling.

Physically it is very similar to the European turbot but its body is broader and heavier. The bony tubercles of the eyed side are larger and more pronounced and the blind side has a large number of small tubercles.

S. maximus TURBOT 1 m. (39 in.)
A European fish, the turbot is found from the N. of England and Ireland, s. to the N. African coast and throughout the Mediterranean. Occasionally it ranges further N. but the effective limits of its distribution are the Baltic, N. and Irish seas.

Scales are absent over the body but there are irregularly scattered large bony tubercles on the body and smaller ones on the head. Its colour is variable but always an excellent match for the sea-bed, usually it is sandy brown with larger spots and blotches.

It is an inshore flatfish found from the lower tidal limits to a depth of 80 m. (44 fathoms). Adults are usually found just offshore but the young are taken in only a few inches of water and even in sandy-bottomed tide pools. Although turbot are found on sand, they are more common on shell gravel and fine gravel. Large turbot eat smaller fishes almost exclusively; they are active predators capable of catching most of the smaller species with which they live, most notably sand-eels, sprats, and whiting. The young eat crustaceans, particularly shrimps, but from an early age begin to feed on fishes.

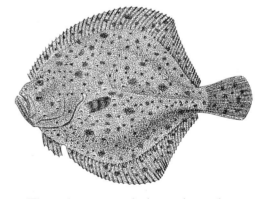

The turbot spawns during spring and summer (the later further N.). It is enormously fecund, females producing between 5 and 10 million eggs. The eggs and early larvae are pelagic, and the young fish have a distinct swim-bladder at first; by the length of about 2·5 cm. (1 in.) it assumes a bottom-living life, its eye has completed its change over from right to left, and the swim-bladder is lost. Growth thereafter is slow in the n. areas it inhabits, in Scandinavian waters a 5-year-old fish may be only 20 cm. (8 in.) long, but to the S. it is relatively rapid.

The turbot is an important food fish in European waters. Its flesh is rated by many gourmets as the finest of all sea fish and it always commands a high price. It is caught on lines and by trawl but in the heavily fished waters in which it lives it is constantly threatened by over-fishing. On the other hand its growth-rate in warm water, and the high price it fetches have suggested that it might be a suitable subject for marine culture and a good deal of research has been undertaken into this possibility. It is also popular with anglers, and said to attain a weight of 25 kg. (55 lb.).

S. rhombus BRILL 61 cm. (2 ft)
Found in the seas of Europe from the Mediterranean and the e. Atlantic from N. Africa n. to the British Isles and the N. Sea basin. It occurs on the s. coasts of Norway and Sweden but here, as in Scottish waters, it is rare. Like the turbot it is a shallow-water flatfish found close inshore and usually on sandy bottoms although sometimes on mud or gravel. Very young fish can be found in intertidal sandy pools but the usual depth for adults is between 9–73 m. (5–40 fathoms).

It is a fish-eating species, feeding mainly on benthic or near-bottom living fishes; some small squids and shrimps are also eaten. Invertebrates are probably more important in the brill's diet than in the turbot.

It spawns in spring and summer, the eggs and larvae (which hatch at about 4 mm. length) are pelagic. The young fish metamorphose at 20–35 mm. ($\frac{3}{4}$–$1\frac{1}{4}$ in.) and take to life on the sea bed. They are particularly common inshore at a length of about 5 cm. (2 in.).

The brill can be distinguished from the turbot by the presence of scales on the body which are embedded ventrally. The body is rather broad and relatively heavy, but is more elliptical than that of the turbot. The front rays of the dorsal fin are deeply divided and are free of the fin membrane for a great part of their length.

The brill is a good food fish although lacking the quality of the turbot. Locally it is fished for and marketed but it is not a particularly valuable commercial species. Some are caught by anglers.

Scorpaena   Scorpaenidae
plumieri SPOTTED SCORPIONFISH
43 cm. (17 in.)
A widely spread scorpionfish which is found in the w. Atlantic from Massachusetts to Rio de Janeiro, throughout the Caribbean, and from the S. Atlantic islands of St Helena and Ascension. It is abundant on coral or rocky bottoms, living in almost perfect concealment amongst algae, turtle grass, and other marine growths. It is found in shallow water.

In colouring it is very variable, usually shades of brown, red and green on the head and body, but a broad pale bar on the tail is followed by a darker bar and a succession of light and dark bars on the tail fin.

When alarmed this fish spreads its pectoral fins outwards to display the striking black and white pattern of the axillary region. This is presumed to be a warning coloration. As with most scorpionfishes the fin and head spines are believed to be sheathed in venomous tissue. **248**

S. porcus RASCASSE 25 cm. (10 in.)
A relatively small species which is widely distributed in the Mediterranean Sea and the Black Sea, as well as in the e. N. Atlantic from Madeira to n. Biscay. It is essentially a shallow water, even littoral fish often found hiding amongst weed-fringed rocks in only a few feet of water. Its coloration is varied, usually darkish, but it is always so good a match for

its surroundings as to be well-nigh invisible.

It breeds in April to May in the Mediterranean; the eggs are shed in a mass of jelly-like mucus.

It is more common than the other scorpaenids in shallow water in the Mediterranean and is thus more frequently encountered by the diver or angler. It forms the basis of the famous French fish soup *bouillabaise*.

It is distinguished from the other members of the family in the area by the relatively small head, small body scales, and relatively few lappets of skin on the head. The long dorsal spines have venom glands on their sides and a puncture wound from the spine can be very painful. **250**

S. scrofa RASCASSE 50 cm. ($19\frac{3}{4}$ in.)
Best known as a Mediterranean sea fish, the rascasse is found throughout that sea and in NE. Atlantic from the English Channel to Senegal. Its occurrence N. of Biscay is excessively rare and is probably due to the accidental carriage of young fish in ocean currents.

It is most common in depths of 20–110 m. (11–60 fathoms) on rocky, algal-covered grounds, but is occasionally found on sandy bottoms. It breeds from May to August (Mediterranean); the eggs are laid in a mass of mucus on the sea bed.

One of the features which helps to identify this species is the numerous lappets of skin on the head, and to a less extent on the body scales, particularly the lateral line.

This rascasse is less commonly caught by fishermen than the shallow-water species *S. porcus,* but it is used for food to a certain extent, and as an ingredient in the s. French *bouillabaisse.* **249**

Scorpaenichthys   Cottidae
marmoratus CABEZON 76 cm. (30 in.)
This is one of the largest members of the family. The maximum length attained is not known certainly and weights are even more doubtful, a maximum of 11·3 kg. (25 lb.) is reported. A certain quantity of cabezon is caught by commercial fishermen annually and is marketed fresh but the catch is incidental to more valuable fisheries. It is moderately popular sporting fish on the Californian coast. Its roe is said to be poisonous.

Its range extends from Alaska to Baja California. In the N. it is found in only moderately deep water but to the S. its depth range extends to 183 m. (100 fathoms). It is most common on rocky bottoms, but does inhabit sandy and muddy grounds, as well as kelp beds. It spawns from November to March, usually at communal nesting sites; the eggs are laid in large masses on the rocks and guarded by the males.

They feed on a large variety of crabs, molluscs, and smaller fishes. Apart from man they have few predators.

The cabezon is distinguished by its heavy

body, the broad tentacle above the eye, the double dip in the dorsal fin, and the white patches on the otherwise greeny-brown body.

SCORPAENIDAE
The family of the redfishes and scorpionfishes, distributed worldwide except in the Antarctic region. All are marine fishes many found in temperate and cool temperate areas, while others are abundant in tropical seas. They have a general perch-like appearance with strong dorsal fin spines, numerous and long spines on the head, and fully-scaled bodies. It is a large family of mainly bottom-living fishes. All have a characteristic bony plate or stay running across the cheek from the eye to the gill cover (a feature they share with the gurnards, Triglidae, and other relatives).

Many of the scorpionfishes are important food fishes, others are well armed with venom glands on the spines. Many, if not most, are primarily red in coloration. See **Amblyapistus, Dendrochirus, Helicolenus, Inimicus, Pterois, Scorpaena, Scorpaenodes, Scorpaenopsis, Sebastes, Sebastichthys, Sebastodes.**

Scorpaenodes   Scorpaenidae
caribbaeus REEF SCORPIONFISH
10 cm. (4 in.)
Found only along the American coast from Florida to Panama, and in the Bahamas. It is said to be the commonest of the scorpionfishes in the Bahamas in shallow water, being found from a depth of about 15 m. (8 fathoms) to the tide line, in a variety of habitats, including turtle grass, shells, sand and coral.

Distinguished from its relatives in this area by the dusky black spot at the end of the first dorsal fin, and the 13 dorsal spines; it has 18–20 rays in each pectoral fin.

Scorpaenopsis   Scorpaenidae
gibbosa see under **S. diabolus**
diabolus SCORPIONFISH 25 cm. (10 in.)
A small fish widespread in the Indo-Pacific faunal region, and well known from Hawaii. The members of this genus are small and difficult to distinguish from one another. Much confusion has existed between this species and *S. gibbosa,* but a recent revisionary study by the distinguished American ichthyologists William N. Eschmeyer and John E. Randall has shown that *S. diabolus* has a longer snout, and wider interorbital region than *S. gibbosa,* and usually has 18 rather than 17 pectoral rays.

At rest it is very difficult to distinguish amongst the rocks and marine growth, but when it moves the violent reds and yellows on the insides of the pectoral fin are startling, and presumably serve as warning colours. It is presumed rather than proven, that the spines on the head and dorsal fins are venom laden, as are those of many of its relatives. **251**

SCRAWLED

COWFISH see **Lactophrys quadricornis**
FILEFISH see **Aluterus scriptus**

SCULPIN see Comephoridae, Cottidae, Icelidae

SCULPIN,

BUFFALO see **Enophrys bison**
COMB see **Icelinus borealis**
FOUR-HORNED see **Oncocottus quadricornis**
LITTLE see **Myoxocephalus aeneus**
LIVEBEARING see **Comephorus baicalensis**
LONGWING see **Cottocomephorus comephoroides**
NORTHERN see **Icelinus borealis**
PRICKLY see **Cottus asper**
POLAR see **Cottunculus microps**
SAILFIN see **Nautichthys oculofasciatus**
SCALYHEAD see **Artedius harringtoni**
SILVER-SPOTTED see **Blepsias cirrhosus**
SLIMY see **Cottus cognatus**
TADPOLE see **Psychrolutes paradoxus**
TIDEPOOL see **Oligocottus maculosus**

SCULPTURED SEA-DRAGON see **Acanthopegasus lancifer**

SCYLIORHINIDAE

This is one of the larger families of sharks comprising some 60 species. All are small, mainly shallow water species, with dorsal fins placed far back along the back, and long tails with only the upper part of the tail fin developed. They are primarily bottom-living species. All lay eggs encased in brown leathery coverings, rather slender in shape and with a tendril at each corner for attachment to weeds. Many catsharks or dogfishes are beautifully marked and coloured. See **Apristurus, Cephaloscyllium, Galeus, Haploblepharus, Hemiscyllium, Holohalaelurus, Scyliorhinus.**

Scyliorhinus   Scyliorhinidae
canicula DOGFISH 76 cm. (30 in.)
The dogfish is one of the most common small sharks in British seas. It is also found from Norway s. to N. Africa and in the Mediterranean. It is a relatively small species which rarely attains a weight greater than about 4 kg. (8·8 lb.), but despite this it is one of the more familiar species to sea anglers. Large numbers are also caught by commercial fishermen and it forms part of the total of small sharks sold as 'flake' or 'rock eel' in British fish shops. Few biology students at senior schools can have avoided knowledge of its anatomy for it has long been a fish for dissection.

It lives on all types of coast but mainly over sandy or gravel bottoms in depths of between 18–110 m. (10–60 fathoms) although it can occasionally be found in only 2 or 3 m. (1–1½ fathoms) of water. It is a bottom-living shark which feeds on crustaceans, molluscs, and fishes, the latter chiefly bottom-living forms like gurnards, dabs, and gobies, but occasionally surface-living species such as pilchards and mackerel are eaten.

When a living specimen is handled it often winds its body around one's hand, the rough teeth in the skin scraping the knuckles painfully. Its skin was at one time used for shagreen, an abrasive like sandpaper. This rough skin earned this shark its name 'rough hound'; it is also known as the sandy dog, or lesser spotted dogfish.

The dogfish lays eggs in horny, brown, oblong capsules, each 5 cm. (2 in.) long. They have extremely long tendrils at each corner which wind amongst the sea weed in which they are laid. The young shark hatches about 9 months after the egg was deposited, and measures 10 cm. (4 in.). Egg laying appears to continue for most of the year, particularly during the winter and spring; the eggs are deposited in pairs. **5**

S. retifer CHAIN DOGFISH 43 cm. (17 in.)
Found along the e. coast of N. America, between N. Carolina, Virginia to Nantucket, the chain dogfish is caught between 73–228 m. (40–125 fathoms). The pattern of narrow black stripes on the back and sides have a chain-like look which gives it its common name. Its background colouring is reddish brown. Its teeth are small and close-packed, as befits a bottom-feeder living on small invertebrates and fishes.

S. stellaris NURSE HOUND 1·5 m. (5 ft)
The nurse hound is a common shark of the shallow waters of the e. Atlantic, found from the Shetlands, s. to Spain and the Mediterranean. It is one of the largest of the catsharks (family Scyliorhinidae).

Like other members of the family it is slender-bodied, with rather small fins, the dorsals placed far back near the tail. Its colouring is unremarkable being basically a sandy brown background with small dark spots heavily scattered over the back and sides. Ventrally it is whitish or cream coloured.

The nurse hound is most common on rough or rocky grounds, and is not infrequently caught in lobster pots. Anglers catch considerable numbers also, and as large specimens weight up to 9 kg. (20 lb.), it is fairly well considered as a sport fish. Although it can be captured in water as shallow as 2 m. (1 fathom) it is most abundant in deeper water of 20–60 m. (11–33 fathoms).

It feeds on a wide range of marine animals, principally invertebrates such as crabs, and squids, but also eats many bottom-living fishes.

Few other fish have as many local names in the British Isles – bull huss, bounce, and large spotted dogfish being the most frequently used alternatives.

Scytalina   Scytalinidae
cerdale GRAVEL DIVER 15 cm. (6 in.)
Found on the e. N. Pacific coast from central California, through to British Columbia the Aleutian Islands and the Bering Sea. It is found in tide pools and on gravel and coarse sandy beaches in which it burrows. Its rather secretive habits have prevented it from being well known.

Its body-shape is distinctive. It is brownish purple or pink above, lighter below, with faint darker speckles and bands of colour.

SCYTALINIDAE

Found in the NE. Pacific, this family is represented by a single species, the gravel diver, *Scytalina cerdale*. It is closely related to the gunnel and snake-blenny families (Pholidae and Stichaeidae).

It can be distinguished by its elongate shape, by the equally long dorsal and anal rays which are confluent with the tail fin, and contain only rays, not spines. Pelvic fins are absent and the pectorals are very small. See **Scytalina.**

SEA

BASS, GIANT see **Stereolepis gigas**
BASS, WHITE see **Cynoscion nobilis**
BARBEL see **Tachysurus feliceps**
BREAM see Sparidae
BREAM see **Seriolella brama**
BREAM, RED see **Pagellus bogaraveo**
BULLHEAD see **Taurulus bubalis**
CARP see **Dactylosargus arctidens**
CATFISH see **Arius felis**
CHUB see Kyphosidae
CHUB see **Ditrema temmincki**
HEN see **Cyclopterus lumpus**
LAMPREY see **Petromyzon marinus**
MOTH see Pegasidae
MOTH see **Europegasus draconis**
PERCH see Embiotocidae
PERCH see **Morone americana**
PERCH, BLUE-BANDED see **Lutjanus kasmira**
PERCH, DUSKY see **Rhacochilus vacca**
PERCH, RUBBERLIP see **Racochilus toxotes**
PERCH, SADDLE-TAILED see **Lutjanus sanguineus**
PERCH, YELLOW-MARGINED see **Lutjanus vaigiensis**
RAVEN, ATLANTIC see **Hemitripterus americanus**
ROBIN see Triglidae
ROBIN, ARMOURED see **Peristedion miniatum**
ROBIN, NORTHERN see **Prionotus carolinus**
SCORPION see **Taurulus bubalis**
STICKLEBACK see **Spinachia spinachia**
SNAIL see **Liparis liparis**
TROUT see **Cynoscion regalis**

SEA-BREAM, BLACK see **Spondyliosoma cantharus**
SEA-HARDER, RED see **Emmelichthys nitidus**
SEABAT see **Platax pinnatus**
SEADEVIL, WARTED see **Cryptopsarus couesi**
SEADRAGON,

LEAFY see **Phycodurus eques**
SCULPTURED see **Acanthopegasus lancifer**
WEEDY see **Phyllopteryx taeniolatus**

SEAHORSE see Syngnathidae
SEAHORSE see **Hippocampus kuda**
SEAHORSE,

DWARF see **Hippocampus zosterae**
EUROPEAN see **Hippocampus ramulosus**
SHORT-SNOUTED see **Hippocampus hippocampus**

SEARCHER see **Bathymaster signatus**

SEARSIDAE

This is a moderate sized family of generally small deep-sea fishes found in all the oceans, except for the sub-polar seas. The family is characterized by having a tube-like projection behind the gill cover and above the base of the pectoral fin. The tube connects with a darkly-pigmented sac containing a mass of connective tissue and small cells which are believed to give rise to larger loose cells. These, when ejected through the tube into sea water, burst, giving a fiery display of blue-green sparks sufficient to leave a glow lasting for a second or two.

The family is closely related to the smooth-heads (Alepocephalidae). See **Platytroctes, Sagamichthys.**

SEBAGO SALMON see **Salmo salar**

Sebastes Scorpaenidae
alutus PACIFIC OCEAN PERCH
46 cm. (18 in.)
Found on the Pacific coast of N. America from s. California to the Bering Sea. The ocean perch is an abundant fish and an important commercial species in the n. parts of its range; most of the catch is taken in trawls but a proportion is caught on lines. It lives in depths of 73–640 m. (40–350 fathoms). In addition to its direct commercial value it is said to be an important food of fishes such as halibut and albacore.

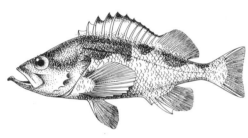

This redfish is distinguished by the lower jaw being very long and having a pronounced knob at the end, a flat interorbital space, by its deep red coloration, and broad back saddles on the back.
S. levis COWCOD, ROCKCOD 94 cm. (37 in.)
A distinctive scorpaenid fish found only along the Californian coastline. Adults live in moderate depths of 154–244 m. (83–133 fathoms), although young fish are found in shallower water. It is usually found on rocky areas, and feeds on fishes, crustaceans, and squids.

Like all members of the genus, its eggs are internally fertilized and are carried inside the female until ready to hatch. They are released as very early larvae, and up to 2 million may be produced at a single spawning.

The cowcod is a notable sporting fish and large specimens, which may weigh as much as 13 kg. (28 lb.), are great favourites with anglers. Some are also landed by commercial fishermen. It is identified by the light coloured body with several broad dusky bars, and the deep cheek between the eye and the upper jaw.
S. maliger QUILL-BACK ROCKFISH
61 cm. (2 ft)
Widely distributed along the American coast of the N. Pacific, it ranges from s. California to the Gulf of Alaska. It lives from the shore line when young, down to depths of 275 m. (150 fathoms). The adults are always found in deeper water. It is fished for commercially but the chief claim to fame of the quill-back rockfish is as a sporting fish; it fights well on light tackle.

It is immediately distinguished from its relatives in the same region by its high spines in the first dorsal fin, with the membrane attached to the back of the previous spine. Its

yellow to brown coloration with orange spotting is equally distinctive.
S. marinus REDFISH 81 cm. (32 in.)
The redfish inhabits the cold waters of the N. Atlantic. On the European coastline it occurs down as far S. as the Scottish and Swedish coast, usually as young fish in moderately deep water, and in the w. Atlantic it is found s. to the deep, offshore waters of New Jersey. Its n. range includes the waters of the continental shelf into Arctic seas.

It is a very valuable commercial fish, large numbers being caught by vessels from all N. Atlantic countries. In Canada and the U.S.S.R. much of the catch is filleted and sold fresh or frozen, but in the British Isles it is processed into various ready-to-cook packs mostly on account of the conservative tastes of the consumer and the fresh fish trade. Its flesh is white, well-flavoured and good food.

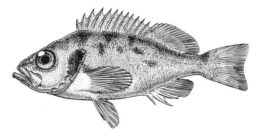

Redfishes are typically deep-water fishes living on the edges of offshore banks and the continental shelf in depths of 110–640 m. (60–350 fathoms). During daylight they live close to the sea bed, on rocky or muddy bottoms, but at night-time becoming pelagic. They are predators, eating fishes and euphausiid shrimps and other crustaceans. In turn they are eaten by halibut, Greenland halibut, large cod, and sperm whales.

The redfish, like many of its relatives, is viviparous, the fry being retained within the ovary until the yolk is absorbed. At birth they are about 8 mm. (¼ in.) long, and are pelagic. A relatively large number, 25,000–40,000, are produced by a large female each year.
S. paucispinis BOCACCIO 89 cm. (34 in.)
Widely distributed along the Pacific coast of N. America, the bocaccio has been found between Alaska and Baja California. While the young fish are often caught in the surf zone, adults are usually found in depths of 76–228 m. (40–125 fathoms) on a sandy or rocky sea bed.

The bocaccio is a voracious predator and as an adult feeds on a wide variety of fishes. In turn it is eaten by many animals including whales, sea lions, sharks, and man. Some are captured by sports fishermen but the great majority are taken by commercial fishermen along with related species of rockcod.

Its colouring is olive-brown, lighter below. The head is pointed with a long lower jaw, and lacks many of the spines so typical of this group of fishes.
S. ruberrimus RASPHEAD or YELLOWEYE ROCKFISH, RED SNAPPER 91 cm. (3 ft)
Widely distributed in the N. Pacific and found from s. California to the Gulf of Alaska. It is common along the coast, especially in the n. parts of its range, and is found in depths of 55–275 m. (30–150 fathoms). It is a valuable commercial fish and is caught in trawls and on long-lines often incidental to other species. Its flesh is of high quality.

It is distinguished from the great number of other rockfish in the area by the many points on the central spine of the preoperculum, and by the roughened head bones. It is bright red in colour.

Sebastichthys Scorpaenidae
capensis JACOPEVER 40 cm. (16 in.)
A moderately deep-water fish of the S. Atlantic, best known from the Atlantic coast of S. Africa but extending to Tristan da Cunha and Gough Island. It is usually found in depths of

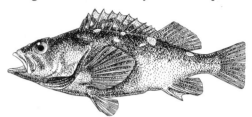

37–274 m. (20–150 fathoms) although the young can be found closer inshore and in shallower water. It is typically a species from the lower continental shelf and is found on the sea mounts in this region.

It is a deep browny red on the back, fading on the sides to a rosy colour. A few irregular light spots on the back.

It is a relatively common species which is commercially exploited, being caught mostly on lines and less often in trawls. It is moderately valuable as a food fish and may well become more so in time.

Secutor Leiognathidae
ruconius SLIMY, SOAPY, PIG-NOSED PONYFISH 12·7 cm. (5 in.)
Widespread in the tropical Indo-Pacific, from the E. African coastline to Queensland on the Australian coast, where it is commonly caught by trawlers, and thence to the Philippines and E. China Sea. It is found in shallow water over sand and mud as well as in estuaries.

It is a very deep-bodied little fish, with a steeply oblique small mouth which when extended forms a long horizontal tube. Few, weak teeth in the jaws. It is silvery-blue, slightly brown above, but with a series of darker flecks on the upper sides. The high front part of the dorsal fin is dark.

Selar Carangidae
crumenophthalmus BIG-EYE SCAD, GOGGLE-EYE JACK 61 cm. (2 ft)
Reported from tropical and subtropical waters around the world, in the w. Atlantic it is found from Nova Scotia to Rio de Janeiro and throughout the Caribbean. It is an active schooling fish, usually found over shallow reefs, and inshore where the water is cloudy. It is often captured from the shore by beach seine, and by anglers. In the Indo-Pacific it is commercially exploited.

It receives its name goggle-eyed jack from the size of the very large eyes, which are almost covered by thick adipose tissue. Its body is relatively elongate, a well developed first dorsal fin, scutes along the side of the tail, and a deep groove on the side beneath the pectoral fin.

Selene Carangidae
vomer LOOKDOWN 30 cm. (12 in.)
Found in the tropical Atlantic, on the w. coast

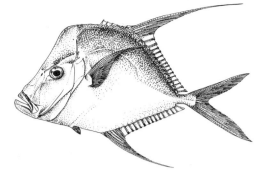

of Africa in the E., and in the W. from New England and Bermuda S. to Uruguay including the Gulf of Mexico. It is a shallow water species found over soft sandy and muddy bottoms. It is caught occasionally by anglers, more commonly in seines and trawls and is said to be a good food fish. It is silvery in colour, and its body form is quite distinctive.

Selenotoca Scatophagidae
multifasciata SOUTHERN BUTTERFISH
41 cm. (16 in.)
An Australian species, found on all coasts except for the S. It is very common particularly in shallow water in estuaries and enclosed bays, especially over sand and sandy-mud. Large numbers are captured in seine nets in these habitats, but they are not favoured as food due to prejudice connected with their congregating around sewers. They feed on vegetable detritus and plant matter mainly.

Like other scats it is a good aquarium fish, but is not widely available in Europe. It is distinguished by the uniform height of the second dorsal and anal fins, and by its markings; dark bars run across the back and sides and end in lines of spots on the belly. The background colour is olive on the back, yellowish-silver on the sides and belly.

Semotilus Cyprinidae
margarita PEARL DACE 15 cm. (6 in.)
A widely distributed N. American freshwater fish, found from the lower Sass River in the Canadian N.W. Territory, e. to Nova Scotia, and S. to Virginia, Wisconsin, and n. Montana. Within this range it has been divided into 2 or more subspecies, one of which occupies the Alleghany region.

It is a small fish, superficially resembling the Old World minnow, with its small scales, and blunt-snouted appearance. It usually has a weakly developed barbel at each corner of its mouth. It is dark brown on the back, silvery on the belly with a dark lateral stripe.

The pearl dace is found in a wide variety of lakes and streams. It eats insects both aquatic and terrestrial, as well as animal plankton and occasionally small fish. It spawns in shallow water over a gravel or sandy bottom, and the males show strong territorial behaviour over their patch of the stream bottom, driving other males away but encouraging females. The males are distinguished by white tubercles on the head.

Pearl dace are important food fish for the larger predators in the area. They are also used by anglers as bait.

SERGEANT BAKER see **Aulopus purpurissatus**
SERGEANT MAJOR see **Abudefduf saxatilis**

SERGEANTFISH see **Rachycentron canadum**

Seriola Carangidae
dorsalis YELLOWTAIL 1·5 m. (5 ft)
Found in the e. Pacific along the Californian and Mexican coastline, s. to n. S. America. It is probably conspecific with the Australian yellowtail, *Seriola grandis*, and like that species grows to a considerable weight, specimens in excess of 45 kg. (100 lb.) have several times been reported.

Like other large seriolas it is an active predator, eating almost anything that comes its way; squids, sardines, mackerel, and swimming crabs are possibly its chief food. It is eaten by large sea bass, and occasionally sea lions.

The yellowtail is commercially important, most are taken in Mexican and s. waters in purse seines, and off California in gill nets and on lines. It is mostly eaten fresh, some is canned or smoked. It is as a sportfish that the Californian yellowtail is best known. Most are taken offshore but good catches can be made in inshore waters.

S. dumerili GREATER AMBERJACK 1·8 m. (6 ft)
Known from the tropical and warm temperate Atlantic, it is widely distributed, in the W. from New England to Brazil, and in the E. from the Mediterranean and adjacent Atlantic and S. to the W. African coast. It is closely related to other large *Seriola* species in tropical regions and may prove to be identical with them.

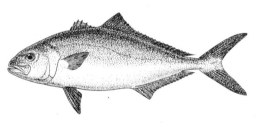

It is the most common species in the tropical w. Atlantic and is frequently found in inshore waters. It is found mainly at the surface, but occasionally ventures into deeper water. In general it is a roving predator that feeds extensively on fishes.

The greater amberjack is a fine sporting fish; anglers have taken specimens weighing up to 80 kg. (177 lb.). It is edible but in some areas in the W. Indies it causes ciguatera, fish poisoning passed on in the food chains of the reef, and it is always suspect as food.

It has 10–13 gill rakers on the lower limb of the first gill arch. Its back is green or blue, silvery to white below, a diagonal dark band runs through the eye to the nape.

S. grandis KING AMBERJACK, YELLOWTAIL KINGFISH, YELLOWTAIL 1·8 m. (6 ft)
Widely distributed in the s. Pacific, and found around the coasts of Australia, especially those of Queensland, New South Wales, and S. Australia. It is possibly conspecific with the Californian yellowtail, *Seriola dorsalis*, and the S. African amberjack, *S. lalandi*.

On the Australian coastline it is common, being found in schools in inshore waters and even enters estuaries. It is a very popular sporting fish, fighting well and taking a bait freely. It attains a weight of 68 kg. (150 lb.). Large specimens have rather tough, coarse flesh, but the young fish are edible and are marketed in

numbers. They are caught on trolling lines and by seine netters.

S. lalandi see under **S. grandis**

Seriolella Centrolophidae
brama WAREHOU, SEA BREAM
76 cm. (30 in.)
A species found in the temperate waters of Australia and off New Zealand. Related and often similar fish are found throughout the S. Hemisphere in coastal waters. In New Zealand waters it is common and fished for locally (warehou is the Maori name).

Unlike most centrolophids, this genus is found in shallow inshore waters; the warehou inhabits kelp beds at depths up to 73 m. (40 fathoms). The young occasionally enter estuaries.

It is distinguished by its rather compressed, elongate body, short-spined dorsal fin, and long soft-rayed dorsal (much longer than the anal). It is deep purple above, silvery below, scattered dusky patches on the back, and a dark blotch at the back of the head. The fins are all dusky.

SERPA TETRA see **Hyphessobrycon serpae**
SERRA see **Scomberomorus commerson**

SERRANIDAE
A family of mainly tropical marine fishes, although some species are found in temperate seas, while others have evolved a tolerance for brackish water and some are known only from freshwater. They are mostly marine fishes of bottom-living habits, although some are active surf species; almost all live in inshore waters. In general they are large predatory fishes, some reputedly growing to, but not accurately weighed, 453 kg. (1000 lb.).

In general, they are rather heavy-bodied fishes with heavy heads and wide mouths. They have 2 dorsal fins, the first composed of strong spines; the 2 fins are frequently not differentiated by a division in the outline. They all have 3 strong spines in the anal fin. Most have fully scaled bodies, and the lateral line is continuous from head to tail. Many serranids are hermaphrodites. In some species eggs and sperm develop simultaneously in the same fish, and in one species self-fertilization took place in an aquarium (this is not to suggest that this is a normal occurrence, or that it happens in other species). More usually, fishes are females when young, and change to males when larger.

Several genera (among them *Dicentrarchus*, *Morone*, and *Roccus*) are now placed in the family Percichthyidae, following the recent studies of the distinguished American ichthyologist Dr William T. Gosline. See **Alphestes, Anthias, Cephalopholis, Dicentrarchus, Epinephelus, Hypoplectrus, Maccullochella, Morone, Mycteroperca, Plectroplites, Plectropomus, Percalates, Polyprion, Roccus, Serranus, Siniperca, Stereolepis, Variola.**

Serranus Serranidae
subligarius BELTED SANDFISH
15 cm. (6 in.)
Found only on the coast of Florida this small sea bass is fairly common on rocky bottoms in shallow, inshore waters of 2·4–20 m. (1–11 fathoms).

It is apparently truly hermaphrodite, sexually mature at only 3 cm. (1¼ in.), at which length eggs and sperm are present in the gonads. In the aquarium it has been possible to fertilize the eggs with sperm from the same individual, but in the wild it is unlikely that this happens; there probably exists some physical or behavioural blockage to render self-fertilization unlikely. Spawning takes place in small shoals.

Serrasalmus   Characidae
rhombeus WHITE or SPOTTED PIRANHA
36 cm. (14 in.)

This is one of several species of piranha, fierce flesh-eating S. American characins, and probably the best known (if least understood) of all characid fishes. The white piranha is well distributed in the Amazon basin and in S. America. When young it is light in colour, dark grey or olive on the back, with the sides lighter. Large dark spots are scattered on the back and sides, and the tail fin is reddish with a dark margin. With age this species may become wholly black. The jaws are illustrated.

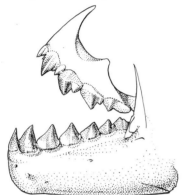

Its body form is much like that of other piranhas being deep, with a steep profile to the back which slopes off gradually, while the belly is deepest at the base of the anal fin. It is a stocky fish, with a toothed edge to the belly, most pronounced behind the pectoral fins.

This species is sometimes kept in aquaria, but it needs a lot of space as it is nervous and, like other piranhas, tends to be aggressive.

Serrivomer   Serrivomeridae
parabeani THREAD EEL 61 cm. (2 ft)

A species of bathypelagic eel found in the Atlantic, Pacific and Indian oceans (although some authorities regard the forms found in the last 2 as distinct). In the Atlantic it has been captured in a number of areas and it is obviously widely distributed. It has been found mainly in depths of 1000–3500 m. (547–1913 fathoms), although the deepest recorded catches were at 4500 m. (2460 fathoms).

Partly due to the depths at which these eels live, and their generally fragile build, undamaged specimens are rarely found, and those only by well-equipped oceanographic expeditions. They are believed to swim in groups, feeding on shrimps and occasional deep water fish, such as lanternfishes, and

themselves being preyed upon by larger fishes. A number have been found in the stomachs of codfish in the N. Atlantic.

SERRIVOMERIDAE

A family of little-known deep-sea eels which have been found in the n. Atlantic, and in the Indian and Pacific oceans. They are bathypelagic in habit.

The members of the family are long, slender eels of moderate length, with a fine tapering tail and slender jaws, silvery with dark speckles. The dorsal fin origin is well back along the body behind the anal fin origin. See **Serrivomer.**

SEVEN-GILLED
  SHARK see **Heptranchias perlo**
  SHARK, BROAD-SNOUTED see
    Notorynchus maculatus
SEVRUGA see **Acipenser stellatus**
SHAD see **Alosa sapidissima**
SHAD,
  AMERICAN see **Alosa sapidissima**
  BLACK-SPINED see **Caspialosa kessleri**
  HICKORY see **Alosa mediocris**
  TWAITE see **Alosa fallax**
SHANNY see **Blennius pholis**
SHARK see Alopiidae, Carcharhinidae, Cetorhinidae, Chlamydoselachidae, Dalatiidae, Echinorhinidae, Heterodontidae, Hexanchidae, Isuridae, Mitsukurinidae, Odontaspidae, Orectolobidae, Oxynotidae, Pseudotriakidae, Rhincodontidae, Scyliorhinidae, Sphyrnidae, Squalidae, Triakidae
SHARK,
  BASKING see **Cetorhinus maximus**
  BLACK see **Morulius chrysophekadion**
  BLUE see **Prionace glauca**
  BONNETHEAD see **Sphyrna tiburo**
  BRAMBLE see **Echinorhinus brucus**
  BROAD-SNOUTED SEVEN-GILLED see
    Notorynchus maculatus
  BULL see **Carcharhinus leucas**
  COBBLER CARPET see **Crossorhinus
    tentacularis**
  COMMON SAW see **Pristiophorus
    cirratus**
  COW see **Hexanchus griseus**
  DUSKY see **Carcharhinus obscurus**
  DWARF see **Squaliolus laticaudus**
  ELEPHANT see **Callorhinchus milii**
  FIDDLE see Rhinobatidae
  FRILLED see **Chlamydoselachus
    anguineus**
  GHOST see **Callorhinchus milii**
  GOBLIN see **Mitsukurina owstoni**
  GREAT HAMMERHEAD see **Sphyrna
    mokarran**
  GREENLAND see **Somniosus
    microcephalus**
  GUMMY see **Mustelus antarctica**
  GURRY see **Somniosus microcephalus**
  HORN see **Heterodontus francisci**
  LEMON see **Negaprion brevirostris**
  LEOPARD see **Triakis semifasciata**
  MACHEREL see **Lamna nasus**
  NURSE see **Ginglymostoma cirratum**
  OCEANIC WHITETIP see **Carcharhinus
    longimanus**
  OIL see **Galeorhinus zyopterus**
  ONE-FINNED see **Heptranchias perlo**
  PORT JACKSON see **Heterodontus
    philippi**

  PORTUGUESE see **Centroscymnus
    coelolepis**
  PYGMY see **Euprotomicrus bispinatus**
  RAGGED-TOOTH see **Odontaspis ferox**
  RED-TAILED BLACK see **Labeo bicolor**
  REEF WHITETIP see **Carcharhinus
    albimarginatus**
  SAND see **Odontaspis taurus,
    Rhynchobatus djeddensis**
  SAW see Pristiophoridae
  SAW see **Pliotrema warreni**
  SCHOOL see **Galeorhinus australis**
  SEVEN-GILLED see **Heptranchias perlo**
  SHARP-NOSED MACKEREL see **Isurus
    oxyrinchus**
  SHOVELHEAD see **Sphyrna tiburo**
  SHOVELNOSE see Rhinobatidae
  SIX-GILLED see **Hexanchus griseus**
  SMOOTH HAMMERHEAD see **Sphyrna
    zygaena**
  SOUPFIN see **Galeorhinus zyopterus**
  SOUTHERN SAW see **Pristiophorus
    nudipinnis**
  SWELL see **Cephaloscyllium ventriosum**
  THRESHER see **Alopias vulpinus**
  TIGER see **Galeocerdo cuvier**
  WHALE see **Rhincodon typus**
  WHITE see **Carcharodon carcharias**
  ZEBRA see **Stegostoma fasciatum**
SHARK RAY see **Rhina ancylostomus**
SHARKNOSED GOBY see **Gobiosoma
  evelynae**
SHARKSUCKER see Echeneidae
SHARKSUCKER see **Echeneis naucrates,
  Remora remora**
SHARP-NOSED
  MACKEREL SHARK see **Isurus oxyrinchus**
  PUFFER see **Canthigaster margaritatus**
SHARPNOSE PUFFER see **Canthigaster
  rostrata**
SHARPTAIL
  EEL see **Myrichthys acuminatus**
  MOLA see **Masturus lanceolatus**
SHASTA TROUT see **Salmo gairdneri**
SHEEPHEAD, CALIFORNIA see under
  Pimelometopon darwini
SHEEPSHEAD MINNOW see **Cyprinodon
  variegatus**
SHEMAIA see **Chalcalburnus chalcoides**
SHINER,
  EMERALD see **Notropis atherinoides**
  RED see **Notropis lutrensis**
  REDSIDE see **Richardsonius balteatus**
SHINER PERCH see **Cymatogaster
  aggregata**
SHINY LOOSE-JAW see **Aristostomias
  scintillans**
SHIP see **Acipenser nudiventris**
SHIP STURGEON see **Acipenser nudiventris**
SHIRAUWO see **Salangichthys microdon**
SHORE
  CLINGFISH see **Lepadogaster
    lepadogaster**
  EEL see **Alabes rufus**
SHORT
  PYRRHULINA see **Pyrrhulina brevis**
  SUCKINGFISH see **Remora remora**
SHORT-FINNED
  EEL see **Anguilla australis**
  FLYINGFISH see **Parexocoetus
    brachypterus**
SHORT-NOSED GARFISH see **Hemiramphus
  quoyi**
SHORT-SNOUTED SEAHORSE see
    Hippocampus hippocampus

SHORTFIN MAKO see **Isurus oxyrinchus**
SHORTHEAD REDHORSE see **Moxostoma macrolepidotum**
SHORTNOSE
　BATFISH see **Ogcocephalus nasutus**
　GAR see **Lepisosteus platostomus**
　GREENEYE see **Chlorophthalmus agassizi**
SHORTSPINE TAPIRFISH see **Macdonaldia rostrata**
SHOVEL-NOSE RAY see **Rhinobatos armatus**
SHOVEL-NOSED CATFISH see **Sorubim lima**
SHOVELHEAD SHARK see **Sphyrna tiburo**
SHOVELNOSE SHARK see Rhinobatidae
SHOVELNOSE see **Rhynchobatus djeddensis**
SHOVELNOSE
　STURGEON see **Scaphirhynchus platorynchus**
　STURGEON, FALSE see
　Pseudoscaphirhynchus kaufmanni
SHRIMPFISH see **Aeoliscus strigatus**
SIAMESE FIGHTINGFISH see **Betta splendens**
SICKLEFISH see **Drepane punctata**

SIGANIDAE

The family of rabbitfishes or spinefeet, found widely in the tropical Indian and Pacific oceans in inshore waters. They are so-called because most have a rounded blunt snout and rabbit-like appearance of the jaws (but should not be confused with the chimaerid rabbitfishes – family Chimaeridae).

Closely related to the surgeonfish family (Acanthuridae), the rabbitfishes have more (7) spines in the anal fin, have 2 spines (the outer rays) in each pelvic fin, have a forward-pointing spine in front of the dorsal fin, and lack the characteristic tail spines of the surgeonfishes. Their fin spines are sharp and strong, and can inflict painful wounds, the mucus from the base of the spine is said to contain a venomous agent.

Most rabbitfishes are reef fishes feeding on algae and often coming into very shallow water. Locally they are exploited (especially in Asia) as valued food fishes; elsewhere there is considerable reluctance to eat them.

Although the family is naturally confined to the Indo-Pacific at least one species, *Siganus rivulatus*, has penetrated from the Red Sea through the Suez Canal and is now locally common in the e. Mediterranean. See **Lo, Siganus.**

Siganus　　　　　　　　Siganidae
　corallinus CORAL SPINEFOOT
30 cm. (12 in.)
A widely distributed species found in the tropical e. Indian and w. Pacific oceans. Its range stretches from the Seychelles to the Philippines, but it is best known in the E. Indian region.

Identification of the rabbitfishes rests very largely on coloration although it is known that their colouring is very variable. It would not therefore be very surprising if a thorough revision of the group resulted in considerable changes in the names in use and a reduction in the number of the present very numerous species. **449**
S. oramin RABBITFISH, SLIMY, SPINY
36 cm. (14 in.)

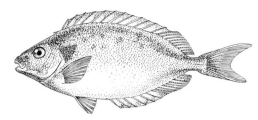

Widely spread in the Indian Ocean from E. Africa to India, Sri Lanka, and the E. Indies, this fish is locally common in inshore waters. It is particularly abundant about reefs and in quiet weedy bays. Its food consists mainly of algae.

A distinctive species which is olive-green, brownish above with many small, pale rounded spots. Frequently it has a round dark patch at the upper edge of the gill opening, another above the eye. Said to be delicious eating, fresh or smoked.
S. virgatus BLUE-LINED SPINEFOOT
25·4 cm. (10 in.)
An Indo-west Pacific species which is well known in inshore waters of s. India and Sri Lanka, but ranges through the E. Indies to China, Japan, the Philippines and n. Australia. It lives mostly on the edges of reefs and areas of broken rock, feeding on the fine algae growing there. **450**
S. vulpinus see **Lo vulpinus**

SILLAGINIDAE

A small family of purely Indo-Pacific species, found from E. Africa to China and Japan. They are probably best-known in Australian seas where they are important food and sporting fishes and are generally called whitings (not to be confused with the European whiting – family Gadidae).

They are elongate, rather cylindrical-bodied fishes, covered with small scales. They have 2 dorsal fins, the first containing slender spines, the anal fin is moderately long and has only 2 weak spines in front. See **Sillaginoides, Sillago.**

Sillaginoides　　　　　Sillaginidae
　punctatus SPOTTED WHITING
69 cm. (27 in.)
An abundant food fish off the s. coasts of Australia; it is scarce or absent on the tropical coasts. In S. Australia and off Tasmania it is one of the most important commercial fishes; it is found in moderate depths on sandy bottoms. It is an omnivorous predator eating a wide range of invertebrates, especially crustaceans, and fishes.

It is captured mostly by hand lines for the commercial fishery. It is also a popular sporting fish especially in W. Australia.

Its back is light brown, the sides and belly almost white, and small black spots scattered densely over the back and upper sides.

Sillago　　　　　　　　Sillaginidae
　sihama SMELT, PESCADINHA, NORTHERN
WHITING 30 cm. (12 in.)

Widely distributed in the Indo-Pacific, from the Red Sea to the s. parts of the E. African coast – where it is known as smelt, or in the Portuguese-speaking regions as pescadinha – to Australia. It is taken in sandy regions, in estuaries, and in bays; it sometimes skips along the surface of the water when disturbed. It is delicious eating, and is a locally valuable food fish.

Long, and slender-bodied, with a rather high first dorsal fin. It is uniform greenish olive with an indistinct silvery line on the side.
S. ciliata SAND WHITING 46 cm. (18 in.)
An e. Australian species, the sand whiting is found mainly along the coasts of Queensland and New South Wales. It is one of the most important food fishes in the former state, being caught in shallow bays and in shoal water by line and net fishermen. It is mainly confined to sandy areas.

Its body form is the same as the other members of the family. Its background colouring is a uniform light brown with no dark blotches, except for an intense black spot at the base of the pectorals.

SILOND CATFISH see **Silonia silondia**

Silonia　　　　　　　　Pangasiidae
　silondia SILOND CATFISH 1 m. (3¼ ft)
An Indian catfish found mainly in the lower Ganges, and although reported from Burma and elsewhere probably confined to that river. It is a large species, reported as attaining a length of 1·8 m. (5·8 ft), but due to fishing pressure rarely now exceeding half that. It is a good food fish and large numbers are caught and marketed. It also has some reputation as an anglers' fish.

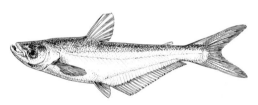

It is believed to breed during the rainy season after an upstream migration to the upper tributaries. Young fish are very common in the swollen rivers, and are frequently found living in pools, and waterways in the flood plain. They feed mainly on invertebrates; large specimens eat fishes. Its jaws have abundant, curved teeth.

SILURIDAE

A family of catfish confined to the freshwaters of Europe (2 species), and Asia, as far E. as China, and Japan. As a group they are easily distinguished by the lack of an adipose fin, by lacking a spine in the dorsal fin (which is usually very small, sometimes absent), and by its very long anal fin which is occasionally joined to the tail. It possesses such typical catfish characters as a flattened head, long barbels around the mouth (those on the upper jaw being especially long), and a scaleless skin.

Some silurids are small, popular aquarium fishes growing to around 7 cm. (3 in.) in length; others, including the European *Silurus glanis*, are huge, occasionally up to 3 m. (10 ft) long. See **Kryptopterus, Ompok, Silurus, Wallagonia.**

Silurus Siluridae
  glanis WELS, EUROPEAN CATFISH
3 m. (10 ft)
The wels is found in central and e. Europe, and across the s. regions of the U.S.S.R. including the basins of the Black, Caspian, and Aral seas. Although it is occasionally found in brackish water in the Baltic and Black seas, it is mainly a fish of large rivers and lakes. It has been introduced to s. England without spreading greatly.

Like many other catfishes it is chiefly nocturnal, keeping close to the bottom during daylight and hiding under tree roots, or in hollows. It feeds on larger fishes mainly, but is known to eat frogs, crayfish, occasionally water voles and ducklings. As the wels, when fully grown, may weigh 200 kg. (440 lb.) there are few aquatic organisms which it cannot tackle. The largest recorded specimen, captured in the River Dneiper, was 5 m. (16 ft) long and weighed 306 kg. (674 lb.). In e. Europe it is an important commercial fish, usually captured in traps, but also on lines with baited hooks. The flesh of small specimens is tasty, and glue is made from the swim-bladder and bones. In places it is farmed, being fed on the unwanted and unsaleable fish species, such as silver bream in the stock ponds. It is a singularly unprepossessing fish. **155**

SILVER
  BREAM see **Blicca bjoerkna,
    Rhabdosargus sarba**
  CARP see **Hypophthalmichthys
    molitrix**
  DORY see **Cyttus australis**
  DRUMMER see **Kyphosus sydneyanus**
  GAR see **Strongylura marina**
  GRUNTER see **Pomadasys hasta**
  HATCHETFISH see **Gasteropelecus levis**
  JENNY see **Eucinostomus gula**
  JEWFISH see **Otolithes rubber**
  MINNOW see **Micralestes acutidens**
  PERCH see **Bidyanus bidyanus**
  SALMON see **Oncorhynchus kisutch**
  TOADFISH see **Lagocephalus scleratus**
SILVER-BANDED SWEETLIPS see **Gaterin
    diagrammus**
SILVER-BIDDY, LINED see **Gerres oyena**
SILVER-DOLLAR FISH see **Mylossoma
    argenteum**
SILVER-DOLLAR, SPOTTED see **Metynnis
    maculatus**
SILVER-SPOTTED SCULPIN see **Blepsias
    cirrhosus**
SILVERBELLY see Gerridae
SILVERSIDE see Atherinidae
SILVERSIDE,
  ATLANTIC see **Menidia menidia**
  HARDHEAD see **Atherinomorus stipes**
SILVERSPOT see **Threpterius maculosus**

SIMENCHELYIDAE
An eel family containing only one species although in the past others have been described. This species is distinguished by its small mouth and rather snub-nosed appearance, the jaws are small with flattened teeth, the pectoral fins are moderate in size. Although generally eel-like, with long dorsal and anal fins, it is rather heavy-bodied; the gill openings are small and situated close to the throat.

Found in the deep water of the Atlantic, and

the w. Pacific (off Japan). See **Simenchelys.**

Simenchelys Simenchelyidae
  parasiticus SLIME or SNUB-NOSED EEL
61 cm. (2 ft)
The slime eel has been found in a number of places on the continental slope and the shelf of offshore banks in the N. Atlantic, from Long Island to the Newfoundland Banks, and off the

Azores, as well as off S. African coasts, and in the W. Pacific off Japan. It is locally abundant in these areas, and will probably be found elsewhere. It occurs mainly between 700–1400 m. (382–765 fathoms), although occasionally it has been taken as deep as 2620 m. (1432 fathoms).

It is partly parasitic in habit, burrowing into the bodies of other, larger fishes. From this habit numerous specimens have been found within the body of commercially caught deep water fish, such as halibut. In all probability it also scavenges for its food to some extent for it can be captured in numbers in baited traps set in deep water. It is extremely slimy, and drips with strings of mucus when pulled out of the water. The correlation between this habit and sliminess in this fish and the hagfishes (see Myxinidae) is remarkable.

Siniperca Serranidae
  chuatsi CHINESE PERCH 1 m. (39 in.)
Found only in the freshwaters of China and the River Amur along the Russian borderlands. It is a moderately important food fish locally, for it grows to a large size, well grown specimens weighing up to 8 kg. (17½ lb.).

It is a predatory species which when adult feeds mainly on fishes, but the young eat invertebrates. It spawns in the larger rivers in summer, the adults and young fish being widespread later in the year but mostly congregating into the deeper river channel in winter.

It is mainly dark greeny-brown with a characteristic pattern of light patches.

Siphamia Apogonidae
  roseigaster ROSE-BELLIED SIPHONFISH
7·5 cm. (3 in.)
Found in estuaries, harbours, and close inshore on the coasts of Queensland and New South Wales. This is one of a dozen or so Indo-Pacific members of this genus in which a brilliant silvery gland is present running from beneath the tongue to the belly and along the lower side of the tail almost to the tail fin. It is a reflecting organ for a bioluminous gland in the thorax region.

It is mainly nocturnal in habit, and the Australian ichthyologist, Tom C. Marshall records that in the Brisbane River it is commonly caught at night by prawn trawlers.

The male of this species broods the eggs in its mouth; they are distinguishable from females by the deeper, wider head.

It is silvery white above, pale rose on the sides; the head and back are lightly spotted with black.

SIPHONFISH, ROSE-BELLIED see **Siphamia
  roseigaster**

Siphonognathus Odacidae
  argyrophanes TUBEMOUTH
42 cm. (16½ in.)
A most striking wrasse which has much of the external appearance of a pipefish. Its body is long and thin, not much more than the thickness of a man's finger. It is dark green above, emerald green on the sides, with a series of reddish spots on the belly.

It is a common inhabitant of rich algal areas on the coasts of W. and S. Australia, and Victoria.

SIPHONOPHOREFISH see **Kasidoron edom**

SISORIDAE
A small family of catfishes found in the freshwaters of Asia. They differ from the bagrids by the absence (or when present, the slenderness) of dorsal fin spines, and by having very thick-based barbels, especially the pair at the angle of the mouth; the adipose fin is present but mostly not well developed. They are greatly flattened from above, the lower surface being flattened, and in some forms corrugated, while the first pectoral rays are large and thickened. These adaptations are an aid to living in the fast currents of mountain streams, a habitat favoured by many species in the family. See **Bagarius, Glyptothorax.**

SIX-GILLED SHARK see **Hexanchus griseus**
SIX-LINED PERCH see **Helotes sexlineatus**
SKAAMHAAI see **Holohalaelurus regani**
SKAAMOOG see **Haploblepharus edwardsi,
  Holohalaelurus regani**
SKATE see Rajidae
SKATE see **Raja batis**
SKATE,
  BARNDOOR see **Raja laevis**
  BIG see **Raja binoculata**
  COMMON see under **Raja whitleyi**
  EYED see **Raja ocellata**
  HEDGEHOG see **Raja erinacea**
  LITTLE see **Raja erinacea**
  MELBOURNE see **Raja whitleyi**
  MUD see **Rhina ancylostomus**
  POMMY see under **Raja whitleyi**
  RICHARDSON'S see **Raja richardsoni**
  WINTER see **Raja ocellata**
SKELLY see **Coregonus lavaretus**
SKILFISH see **Erilepis zonifer**
SKIPJACK TUNA see **Katsuwonus pelamis**
SKIPPER see **Scomberesox saurus**
SKIPPER, ROCK see **Alticops
  periophthalmus**

SLANGETJIE see **Halidesmus scapularis**
SLEEPER see Gobiidae
SLEEPER, FAT see **Dormitator maculatus**
SLENDER
  FILEFISH see **Monacanthus tuckeri**
  SNIPEFISH see **Macroramphosus gracilis**
  SUCKERFISH see **Phtheirichthys lineatus**
  SUNFISH see **Ranzania laevis**
SLICKHEAD see Alepocephalidae
SLIME
  EEL see **Simenchelys parasiticus**
  HEAD see **Hoplostethus mediterraneus**
SLIMY see **Leiognathus equula, Secutor ruconius, Siganus oramin**
SLIMY SCULPIN see **Cottus cognatus**
SLIPPERY see **Gadopsis marmoratus**
SLIPPERY DICK see **Halichoeres bivittatus**
SLIPS see **Solea solea**
SLOANE'S VIPERFISH see **Chauliodus sloani**
SMALL-EYED EEL see **Pythonichthys microphthalmus**
SMALL-HEADED CLINGFISH see **Apletodon microcephalus**
SMALL-MOUTHED WRASSE see **Centrolabrus exoletus**
SMALL-TOOTH SAWFISH see **Pristis pectinatus**
SMALL-TOOTHED SAWFISH see **Pristis microdon**
SMALLEYE SQUARE-TAIL see **Tetragonurus cuvieri**
SMALLMOUTH
  BASS see **Micropterus dolomieui**
  BUFFALO see **Ictiobus bubalus**
  GOBY see **Risor ruber**
SMELT see Mugiloididae, Osmeridae, Retropinnidae
SMELT see **Osmerus eperlanus, Sillago sihama**
SMELT,
  ASIATIC see **Osmerus dentex**
  AUSTRALIAN see **Retropinna semoni**
  BLACK see Bathylagidae
  NEW ZEALAND see **Retropinna retropinna**
  PACIFIC BLACK see **Bathylagus pacificus**
  POND see **Hypomesus olidus**
  RAINBOW see under **Osmerus dentex**
SMOLT see **Salmo salar**
SMOOTH-HEAD see **Alepocephalus rostratus**
SMILER see Opistognathidae
SMILER, HARLEQUIN see **Merogymnus eximius**
SMOOTH
  DOGFISH see **Mustelus canis**
  FLOUNDER see **Liopsetta putnami**
  HAMMERHEAD SHARK see **Sphyrna zygaena**
  HOUND see **Mustelus asterias, Mustelus mustelus**
  STARGAZER see **Kathetostoma averruncus**
  TRUNKFISH see **Lactophrys triqueter**
SMOOTHHEAD see Alepocephalidae
SNAIL,
  SEA see Cyclopteridae
  SEA see **Liparis liparis**
SNAILFISH, BLACKTAIL see **Careproctus melanurus**
SNAKE
  BLENNY see Ophiclinidae

BLENNY see **Lumpenus lumpretaeformis**
BLENNY, BLACK-BACKED see **Ophiclinus gracilis**
BLENNY, SPOTTED see **Ophiclinops pardalis**
DRAGONFISH see **Stomias colubrinus**
EEL see Ophichthidae
EEL, SPOTTED see **Ophichthus ophis**
MACKEREL see Gempylidae
MACKEREL see **Gempylus serpens**
PIPEFISH see **Entelurus aequoreus**
SNAKEFISH see **Trichiurus lepturus, Trachinocephalus myops**
SNAKEHEAD see Channidae
SNAKEHEAD, AFRICAN see **Ophicephalus africanus**
SNAPPER see Lutjanidae, Sparidae
SNAPPER see **Chrysophrys auratus, Lutjanus kasmira, Lutjanus vaigiensis**
SNAPPER,
  BLOOD-RED see **Lutjanus sanguineus**
  GREY see **Lutjanus griseus**
  MUTTON see **Lutjanus analis**
  RED see **Lutjanus argentimaculatus, Lutjanus sebae, Sebastes ruberrimus**
  WAIGEU see **Lutjanus vaigiensis**
  YELLOWTAIL see **Ocyurus chrysurus**
SNAPPER SALMON see **Otolithes ruber**
SNIPE EEL see Nemichthyidae
SNIPE EEL see **Avocettina infans, Nemichthys scolopaceus**
SNIPE-EEL, BOBTAILED see **Cyema atrum**
SNIPEFISH, SLENDER see **Macroramphosus gracilis**
SNOEK see Gempylidae
SNOEK see **Thyrsites atun**
SNOOK see Centropomidae
SNOOK see **Centropomus undecimalis**
SNUB-NOSED EEL see **Simenchelys parasiticus**
SOAPFISH see Grammistidae
SOAPFISH see **Rypticus saponaceus**
SOAPFISH, GOLDEN-STRIPED see **Grammistes sexlineatus**
SOAPY see **Leiognathus equula, Secutor ruconius**
SOCKEYE SALMON see **Oncorhynchus nerka**
SOLDIERFISH see Holocentridae
SOLDIERFISH,
  CROWNED see **Holocentrus diadema**
  RED see **Holocentrus rubrum**
SOLE see Soleidae
SOLE see **Solea solea, Synaptura marginata**
SOLE,
  BLACK see **Synaptura orientalis**
  DOVER see **Microstomus pacificus, Solea solea**
  ENGLISH see **Parophrys vetulus**
  FRENCH see **Pegusa lascaris**
  LEMON see **Microstomus kitt**
  NAKED see **Gymnachirus melas**
  NARROW-BANDED see **Aseraggodes macleayanus**
  PETRALE see **Eopsetta jordani**
  ROCK see **Lepidopsetta bilineata**
  SAND see **Pegusa lascaris, Psettichthys melanostictus**
  THICKBACK see **Microchirus variegatus**
  YELLOWFIN see **Limanda aspera**
  ZEBRA see **Gymnachirus melas**

Solea   Soleidae
  solea SOLE, DOVER SOLE 51 cm. (20 in.)
The most common member of the family in European waters and the most valuable of the group. Its range extends from Norway and the Faeroes (where it is relatively rare) s. to the African coast and throughout the Mediterranean. It is widely distributed both in inshore and offshore waters (although not in deep water), and is very adaptable, being found in river mouths in a few metres of water down to depths of 73 m. (40 fathoms). Young specimens are particularly common close inshore, often being taken in intertidal sandy pools; the largest fish live offshore.

It is migratory in a sense, moving into shallow water in spring and summer, and offshore with winter-time cooling of the sea. In the North Sea, where it is practically at the n. limit of its range, it tends to congregate into the rather few deeps in winter, and in severe winters many will be killed by the cold in this relatively shallow sea. The Silver Pits in the central North Sea are said to have earned this name because of the vast numbers of soles congregated in a particularly cold winter.

The sole is found on sand, mud, and even fine gravel. During daylight it lies buried with only the eyes and gill cover exposed. At night-time, or during very dull days it is active, and large specimens are not infrequently seen swimming at the surface of the sea. The best catches of soles are usually made at night.

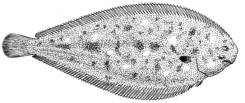

In spring and early summer the adult fish gather on offshore sandy banks to spawn. The eggs and early larvae are pelagic, but at a length of 1·5 cm. ($\frac{2}{3}$ in.) they metamorphose and begin to live on the sea bed. By this length they have usually been swept into inshore waters.

The sole feeds on a wide range of bottom-living organisms, principally marine worms, small crustaceans and molluscs. Large specimens eat brittlestars and small fishes.

The sole is well known as a food fish and its flesh is highly rated. As it is probably best when kept for a few days it can be widely distributed to inland markets. Its popularity as a restaurateur's fish, usually as Dover sole, wherever the fish was caught, is well known. Most soles are taken in otter trawls, less often in seines; a few are caught by anglers but rarely deliberately so. The young fish are often called slips.

SOLEIDAE
The family of true soles, a group of flatfishes of worldwide distribution in tropical and temperate seas. Like other flatfish families (see Pleuronectidae and Bothidae) they pass through an early planktonic larval stage when their eyes are normal, one on each side of the head. As they develop one eye migrates around to join its fellow on the other side of the head, and at metamorphosis the young fish lies on the seabed on its blind side, the other side being coloured to match the substrate and bearing both eyes.

The soles are dextral, that is they have both eyes on the right of the body (very rarely abnormal, reversed specimens are found). They are distinguished in other ways such as by having the preoperculum covered by skin and not free. The dorsal fin begins on the snout and runs to the tail but is not joined to the tail fin, or if it is then the junction is marked by a notch. The anal fin is similarly separate, and the tail fin is rounded.

Most soles are purely marine fishes, usually found living in shallow, continental shelf waters; a few forms are found in deep water. Others are found living in freshwater mainly in tropical regions.

Many of the soles are valuable commercial fishes. Most of the N. American 'soles' are not true soles but belong to the families Bothidae, Scophthalmidae, and Pleuronectidae. See **Aseraggodes, Buglossidium, Gymnachirus, Microchirus, Pegusa, Solea, Synaptura.**

SOLENETTE see **Buglossidium luteum**

SOLENOSTOMIDAE

A small family containing at the most half a dozen species found only in shallow water in the Indo-Pacific. These fishes have been called the ghost pipefishes because of their similarity to and affinity with the true pipefishes and sea horses. The snout is prolonged into a tube, with a small mouth, in typical pipefish style, but the body is short, thickset, and craggy with large well-developed fins. See **Solenostomus.**

Solenostomus   Solenostomidae
cyanopterus GHOST PIPEFISH
17 cm. (6½ in.)
Widely distributed in the Indo-Pacific from E. Africa to the Indo-Australian region and beyond. It lives amongst algae in shallow reef areas, and although it may be locally common it is not often found and almost nothing is known of its biology. Its drab brown and green colouring makes a perfect concealment amongst algae.

In contrast to the situation in pipefishes and sea horses, where the male fish carries the eggs after fertilization, in the ghost pipefish the female cares for the eggs. Females have the outer margins of the pelvic fins joined to the body to form an open ended pouch. On the inside, short filaments extend from the fins and serve as attachments for the eggs. The young, after hatching, live independently of the mother.

Somniosus   Dalatiidae
microcephalus GREENLAND or GURRY
SHARK 6·4 m. (21 ft)
This giant amongst its family is widely distributed in the n. Atlantic inside the Arctic Circle, and s. to the Gulf of Maine and s. England. Its teeth are small, close set and so strongly oblique that the side of the tooth

forms the cutting edge. In colour it is grey-brown, lighter underneath.

Although the Greenland shark appears to be sluggish, in its habits it eats a large number of active fishes; it also eats seals, porpoises, seabirds, and squids. It was well known as a scavenger around Arctic whaling stations and gorged itself on floating whale carcases. In its turn it was fished for, particularly off Greenland, for the sake of its abundant liver oil, chiefly for fuel oil, and its flesh dried as dog food; fresh it is an intoxicating poison to dogs and man.

The Greenland shark is frequently found at the surface but also at depths up to 600 m. (330 fathoms). It is a live-bearing shark, the young in litters of up to 10, are born at a length of at least 40 cm. (15½ in.), and probably much larger.

Sorubim   Pimelodidae
lima CUCHARON, SHOVEL-NOSED
CATFISH 61 cm. (2 ft)
Widely distributed in the freshwaters of ne. S. America, from Venezuela, Colombia, the Amazon basin, and N. of Argentina.

A nocturnal and crepuscular fish, which during daylight lies hidden amongst debris on the river bed. It eats small fishes and crustaceans, although in aquaria it can be fed on small worms. **167**

SOUPFIN SHARK see **Galeorhinus zyopterus**
SOUTH AFRICAN
  AMBERJACK see under **Seriola grandis**
  PILCHARD see **Sardinops ocellata**
SOUTH AMERICAN LUNGFISH see
    Lepidosiren paradoxa
SOUTHERN
  BLUE-FIN TUNA see **Thunnus maccoyii**
  BUTTERFISH see **Selenotoca
    multifasciata**
  CAVEFISH see **Typhlichthys
    subterraneus**
  SAW SHARK see **Pristiophorus
    nudipinnis**
  STINGRAY see **Dasyatis americana**
SPADEFISH see Ephippidae
SPADEFISH see **Chaetodipterus faber**
SPANGLED EMPEROR see **Lethrinus
    nebulosus**
SPANISH
  HOGFISH see **Bodianus rufus**
  MACKEREL see **Scomber japonicus**
  MACKEREL, NARROW-BANDED see
    Scomberomorus commerson
  TOOTHCARP see **Valencia hispanica**

SPARIDAE

The family of sea breams, porgies, and snappers, marine fishes found around the world in tropical, warm temperate, and temperate seas. They are the most abundant in the tropical Atlantic, Indian and W. Pacific oceans, but very few species occur in the e. Pacific. Several hundred species are properly placed in this family.

Most of them are deep-bodied fishes, fully scaled on body and head except for the snout. The mouth is usually large and the teeth coni-

cal, or canine-like, in many species with rounded molars in the rear of the jaws. Some breams, however, have chisel-like cutting teeth in the front of the jaws.

They are very important food and game fishes throughout their range; most are moderately small but some grow to as heavy as 45 kg. (100 lb.). See **Acanthopagrus, Calamus, Chrysophrys, Cymatoceps, Dentex, Lithognathus, Pachymetopon, Pagellus, Pagrus, Petrus, Rhabdosargus, Sarpa, Sparodon, Spondyliosoma.**

Sparisoma   Scaridae
rubripinne YELLOWTAIL or REDFIN
PARROTFISH 45 cm. (18 in.)
A common species in the tropical w. Atlantic from Massachusetts to s. Brazil, and off the W. African coast. It is a very abundant species in the Caribbean, possibly the most common of the group in shallow water. Dr John E. Randall, formerly of Puerto Rico, reports that if pursued it sometimes swims into the foaming swirl of waves breaking on the reef and disappears. Its ability to change colour rapidly to match its background is remarkable.

Supermales, fish which have changed from females into breeding males, are greenish overall with a black blotch at the base of the pectoral fin. Females and normal males are nondescript brown with bluish flecks and red ventral fins. The supermales spawn singly with females, drab coloured males and females spawn in large schools.

SPARLING see **Osmerus eperlanus**

Sparodon   Sparidae
durbanensis MUSSEL CRACKER, SAND
STOMPKOP, STEENBRAS 114 cm. (45 in.)
An endemic species to the se. African coast, where it is found from the Cape of Good Hope to Natal. Found in very shallow water on sandy and muddy-bottomed areas, and occasionally even enters estuaries.

It is one of the best known anglers' fishes in S. African seas, taking almost any bait and fighting well; it grows to a weight of 18 kg. (40 lb.). Its flesh is good but young specimens are best flavoured.

The mussel cracker can be distinguished from other sea breams in the area by its dentition. In the front of the jaws there are 2 huge rather flattened teeth, a smaller tooth outside each; the sides of the jaws have huge rounded and flattened molar teeth. The jaws are immensely strong as are the muscles which activate them. The diet of this fish is mainly hard-shelled bottom-living animals.

SPECKLED PUG see **Tandya maculata**

Sphaeramia   Apogonidae
nematoptera 7 cm. (2¾ in.)
A shallow water cardinal fish which appears to be confined to the E. Indies; it was originally described from the Philippine Islands. Like many of its relatives it has been recorded as brooding its eggs in its mouth. **284**
S. orbicularis 7 cm. (2¾ in.)
A native of the tropical central Indo-Pacific, occurring on the E. African coast as far S. as Mozambique, where it is said to be particularly common in mangrove swamps.

It is distinguished from most cardinalfishes

by its generally silvery body, greeny brown on the back, with a dark cross-stripe running from the front of the spiny dorsal fin to the belly. The back and sides are dark spotted. The young fish are transparent. **287**

Sphaerichthys   Belontiidae
  osphronemoides CHOCOLATE GOURAMI
6 cm. (2½ in.)
This gourami gets its popular name amongst aquarists from the deep brown colouring of its back, upper sides, and fins. The sides have a faint greenish sheen with several variable pale yellow transverse bars. Its body is deep and compressed, the head pointed, and a single ray in each pelvic fin is very long. Males have higher fins with a pointed dorsal.

It is native to the freshwaters of Sumatra and the Malaysian region, living in the smaller waters, ditches, and pools. It was imported to Europe as an aquarium fish some years ago but has proved rather delicate in constitution. Unlike many of the labyrinth fishes which are bubble-nest makers, this species broods its young and early larvae in the mouth of the male fish.

Sphagebranchus   Ophichthidae
  ophioneus SURF EEL 43 cm. (17 in.)
A Caribbean species, found from Bermuda, the Bahamas, Florida, S. to the Greater Antilles. Its gill openings are ventral and small, and the eyes are minute. It is flesh pink or paler and apart from the slight swelling around its head, it is perfectly worm-like.

It is very abundant in sandy banks in the surf zone where the waves break. It seems particularly to favour coasts facing the open sea. It is rarely found in depths greater than 3·5 m. (2 fathoms).

Sphoeroides   Tetraodontidae
  hamiltoni RICHARDSON'S TOADFISH,
COMMON TOAD 14 cm. (5½ in.)
A species found in the vicinity of New Zealand, in Polynesia, and around most of the Australian coastline. T. C. Marshall, in his work on the fishes of the Great Barrier Reef records it as being extremely common all along the coasts of Queensland and New South Wales, and that it is frequently seen swimming along the shore in very shallow water. This species has on some occasions been so abundant that it blocks the sea-water intakes of oil-refineries along the Australian coast.

It is a typically rounded pufferfish, short-bodied and robust, with rounded fins; short spines cover the whole body except for the chin and lower tail. Its colour is brownish with numerous close-set dark brown spots. Larger dark brown blotches on the sides; ventrally it is white.
S. rubripes MAFUGU 70 cm. (27½ in.)
A species found around the whole of the Japanese islands. It is very common especially in the s. parts of the islands.

It is a robust, rounded species with short

rather pointed dorsal and anal fins, and a rounded tail fin. Apart from the head and tail, the whole body is covered with short prickles. It is dark brown with a bluish tinge about it, fading to white on the belly. Above each pectoral fin and at the base of the dorsal fin there is a large, rounded white-ringed black blotch.

In Yamaguchi Prefecture this species is used to make a famous pufferfish dish. It has, however, to be properly prepared as the liver, gonads, and blood are very toxic and almost certain death follows if they are eaten.
S. spengleri BANDTAIL PUFFER
30 cm. (12 in.)
Found in both the e. and w. Atlantic, this species has a wide range in shallow inshore water less than 7·6 m. (25 ft). In the w. Atlantic it is found from New England and Bermuda to s. Brazil; in the E. from the Azores, Madeira, the Canaries, and Cape Verde Islands (where it is common). Its choice of habitats is varied, but it seems most abundant on sea grass beds, although also found on patch reefs, in tidal creeks, and amongst algal covered rocks.

It is a rather elongate species with a blunt head and moderately large eye. It is distinguished from its relatives in the area by the row of rounded large, dark blotches along the lower sides, from chin to tail, and by the barred tail. Its back is greenish grey; its belly whitish.

Sphyraena   Sphyraenidae
An unidentified member of the genus is illustrated. **396**
S. argentea CALIFORNIA or PACIFIC
BARRACUDA 1·2 m. (4 ft)
An e. Pacific species, this barracuda has been reported from the Alaskan coast to Baja California, but it is common only along the Californian coast.

It is found in small schools in shallow inshore waters, and young ones often enter estuaries and bays. Like other members of the family, it is a voracious predator and eats large quantities of smaller fishes. It is an important sporting and commercial fish on the Californian coast, large numbers being caught by anglers in inshore waters while the commercial fishery is conducted with gill nets and hook and line. It is equally important as a commercial fish on the Mexican coast.
S. barracuda GREAT BARRACUDA
1·8 m. (6 ft)
Widely distributed in all tropical seas except for the e. Pacific, but best known in the w. Atlantic and Caribbean. It occurs there from off New England to s. Brazil, throughout the W. Indies and the Gulf of Mexico. It lives in a variety of habitats, the larger specimens often keeping station close to a coral head, or patrolling the edge of a reef, while young ones are usually found inshore often in not more than a foot or two of water on sandy or weedy bottoms.

At all ages it is a solitary species, except that from time to time large schools have been observed, and these may be spawning aggregations.

Its food varies with its habitat, but is almost entirely fish. Large specimens eat grunts, pufferfish, jacks, and sea basses, and no doubt, through some of these fish the toxin which causes the flesh of the barracuda to become poisonous is passed on. Dr John E. Randall,

who investigated the occurrence and causative factors of fish poisoning, suggests that this species is the prime agent of ciguatera in the Floridan and W. Indian region.

The great barracuda is also dangerous to man because of its large jaws and sharp teeth. Some 30 odd cases are known of attacks on humans in the W. Indies, most have involved attacks on bathers in murky water, or when barracudas have been provoked. Any kind of commotion in the water, such as a splashing bather, a flashing object, or freshly speared fish, is likely to provoke an attack.

Not surprisingly, such a large predatory fish is much prized as an angling species. A long-standing world record for a rod-caught fish in 1932 is 168 cm. (66 in.) long and weighed 46·7 kg. (103 lb.).

The length which this species attains has been much discussed. Reports of specimens of 4·6 m. (15 ft) in the 18th century, and later accounts of 2·4 m. (8 ft) long sightings are either due to exaggeration, or, possibly due to greater longevity and thus length, when man's fishing pressure was less. It probably attains a maximum of 1·83 m. (6 ft) today.
S. guachancho GUAGUANCHE 61 cm. (2 ft)
Best known in the w. Atlantic where it occurs from New England to Brazil, including the Caribbean and Gulf of Mexico. It has been reported also in the e. tropical Atlantic.

It occurs mainly in small shoals in turbid water along silty shores, although it is also found close to the bottom in harbours and clear water bays. It is a good sporting fish taken both with artificial lures and live bait, and is considered to be the best flavoured barracuda for eating purposes. Its flesh has not been reported as poisonous.

Its body colouring is olive green above, silvery, with a faint golden stripe, along the sides. The edges of the anal, pelvic, and tail fins are dark. A juvenile is illustrated.

SPHYRAENIDAE
The family of the barracudas, a group of predatory marine fishes found throughout the tropical and warm temperate seas of the world. Most species are found in inshore shallow waters and some enter estuaries.

In general they are all closely similar, having a long, rather slender body with a pointed snout, large jaws which are very well equipped with formidable teeth. They possess 2 well-separated dorsal fins, the first containing 5 spines only. The body is closely covered with small scales.

Barracudas are well-known for their rapacious habits, and even the smaller species are formidable predators on smaller fishes. The w. Atlantic species *Sphyraena barracuda*, which grows to a considerable size, is greatly feared as a dangerous fish to fishermen and bathers. Its large size and huge teeth, as well as its habit of attacking in clouded water, makes it more dreaded than any shark in the W. Indies. Moreover its flesh is frequently poisonous if eaten in this area. See **Sphyraena.**

SPHYRNIDAE

A small family of sharks the members of which are distinguished by the remarkable flattened appearance of the head which gives them the name hammerhead or bonnethead. The eyes and nostrils are spaced widely apart at the extreme edges of the head. They are tropical and temperate ocean sharks, some of which reach a large size.

The function of the flattened head is uncertain. Various suggestions have been advanced, amongst them that advantage is gained by spacing out the sensory organs, that it acts as a bow rudder thus improving manoeuverability, or that it simply compensates for the small forward lift of the pectoral fins. See **Sphyrna**.

Sphyrna   Sphyrnidae
mokarran GREAT HAMMERHEAD SHARK
6·1 m. (20 ft)
The great hammerhead is circumtropical in distribution; in the Atlantic it ranges from N. Carolina to Brazil, and off W. Africa, n. to Spain and, rarely, the Mediterranean. In the Indo-Pacific it occurs from the Red Sea and the E. African coast to Australia, and the Philippines. It is distinguished from the other hammerheads by its large size, by the indentation on the leading edge of the snout's midline, and by its serrated teeth.

It is an active, strong-swimming shark, which feeds on fishes, including stingrays. It is found in inshore waters rather more than on the high seas and is frequently reported from estuaries. It must be regarded as one of the dangerous species of shark.

S. tiburo BONNETHEAD SHARK,
SHOVELHEAD SHARK 1·5 m. (5 ft)
The bonnethead shark differs from the other hammerhead sharks by virtue of the smoothly rounded front of its narrow hammer head. Its shape viewed from above is similar to a shovel blade. In colour it is grey, or grey-brown above, paler below, occasional specimens marked with rounded dark spots on the sides.

Two subspecies are recognized: *S. tiburo tiburo* in the w. Atlantic from New England to s. Brazil, and *S. tiburo vespertina* on the Pacific coast from S. California to Ecuador.

Hammerhead sharks appear to migrate in large shoals with the seasonal warming of the sea in higher latitudes. The bonnethead has also been observed to form dense shoals although it is not proven that they are migratory.

A relatively small shark, it is not rated as being particularly aggressive or dangerous to man.

S. zygaena SMOOTH HAMMERHEAD SHARK
4·3 m. (14 ft)
This hammerhead shark is found in tropical and warm temperate areas of the Atlantic, Indian, and Pacific oceans. In the Atlantic it is found from Nova Scotia and Portugal (although it has rarely been reported from the

British coast) to Argentina and S.W. Africa. It ranges into these higher latitudes only during summer.

It feeds on fishes, especially on rays, including stingrays, but also scavenges when in inshore waters. This species is considered dangerous to man, and has been involved in a number of unprovoked attacks on swimmers. It also makes a nuisance of itself at times by attacking hooked and netted fishes. It was fished for commercially in Mexico and the U.S. for the Vitamin A content of its large liver, but this fishery died with the synthesising of the vitamin in the late 1940s. **6**

SPIKE-FINNED GOBY see **Nemateleotris magnificus**
SPIKY DORY see **Neocyttus rhomboidalis**

Spinachia   Gasterosteidae
spinachia SEA or FIFTEEN-SPINED
STICKLEBACK 19 cm. (7½ in.)
A European marine stickleback which is found only from Biscay n. to n. Norway, and in the Baltic. It is widespread around British

coasts. In the sea it is confined to the shore line and inshore waters and is found only where there is sufficient growth of small algae. It occurs, sometimes abundantly, in estuaries.

Like other sticklebacks the male builds a nest from fragments of algae and plants held together with mucus. The nest is about the size of a man's fist, and in it successive females lay their eggs which are guarded by the male.

Its food is composed of small crustaceans and young fish. Despite its size this stickleback is said to live for only 1–2 years. Its colouring is variable, usually medium brown with darker bars, the belly being silvery white.

SPINE-CHEEK, BARRED-FACE see **Scolopsis temporalis**
SPINED LOACH see **Cobitis taenia**
SPINEFOOT see Siganidae
SPINEFOOT,
    BLUE-LINED see **Siganus virgatus**
    CORAL see **Siganus corallinus**
SPINY see **Siganus oramin**
SPINY
    BATFISH see **Halieutichthys aculeatus**
    DOGFISH see **Squalus acanthias**
    EEL see Lipogenyidae, Mastacembelidae, Notacanthidae
    EEL see **Notacanthus chemnitzii**
    LUMPSUCKER, PACIFIC see **Eumicrotremus orbis**
    PUFFER see **Diodon holocanthus**
SPINY-CHEEKED ANEMONEFISH see **Amphiprion biaculeatus**
SPINYFIN see **Diretmus argenteus**
SPLITLURE FROGFISH see **Antennarius scaber**

Spondyliosoma   Sparidae
cantharus BLACK SEA-BREAM, OLD
WIFE 30 cm. (12 in.)
A European Atlantic species, found from the Canary Islands and N. Africa, n. to the British

Isles and less commonly to Norway. Large specimens are most common in moderately deep water around wrecks and close to rocky outcrops, young ones are often found on sandy bottoms and amongst sea grass at depths of 15 m. (8 fathoms).

It feeds on a wide variety of bottom-living invertebrates and fishes. The black bream is one of the few breams to lay its eggs in a hollow excavated in the sea bed; the male hollows out the sand and guards the eggs.

It is not a large species, reaching about 1·4 kg. (3 lb.) in weight, and although not commercially fished for, is a popular angling fish. **304**

SPOTFIN
    BUTTERFLYFISH see **Chaetodon ocellatus**
    HOGFISH see **Bodianus pulchellus**
SPOTTED
    BARB see **Barbus binotatus**
    BATFISH see **Zalieutes elator**
    BUTTERFISH see **Scatophagus argus**
    CATFISH see **Anarhichas minor**
    CLIMBING PERCH see **Ctenopoma acutirostre**
    CUSK-EEL see **Otophidium taylori**
    DANIO see **Brachydanio nigrofasciatus**
    DOGFISH, LARGE see **Scyliorhinus stellaris**
    DOGFISH, LESSER see **Scyliorhinus canicula**
    EAGLE RAY see **Aetobatus narinari**
    EEL BLENNY see **Notograptus guttatus**
    GOATFISH see **Pseudupeneus maculatus**
    GUITARFISH see **Rhinobatos lentiginosus**
    HEAD-STANDER see **Chilodus punctatus**
    JAVELINFISH see **Pomadasys hasta**
    MORAY see **Gymnothorax moringua**
    PIRANHA see **Serrasalmus rhombeus**
    RASBORA see **Rasbora maculata**
    RAY see **Raja montagui**
    RAY, WHITE see **Rhynchobatus djeddensis**
    SCORPIONFISH see **Scorpaena plumieri**
    SILVER-DOLLAR see **Metynnis maculatus**
    SNAKE-BLENNY see **Ophiclinops pardalis**
    SNAKE EEL see **Ophichthus ophis**
    WEEVER see **Trachinus araneus**
    WHITING see **Sillaginoides punctatus**
SPOTTED-TAIL FLOUNDER see **Engyprosopon grandisquama**
SPOTTED-TAILED GRINNER see **Saurida undosquamis**
SPRAT see **Sprattus sprattus**
SPRAT,
    BLUE see **Spratelloides robustus**
    CASPIAN see **Clupeonella delicatula**

Spratelloides   Clupeidae
robustus BLUE SPRAT 10 cm. (4 in.)
The blue sprat is very common in the inshore waters of the s. states of Australia. It is a small fish found in dense shoals in shallow inlets and bays. It also occurs in numbers offshore where it is preyed upon by tuna and Australian salmon and a large variety of sea birds.

It is a typical herring-like fish, elongate with a dorsal fin set well forward along the back; it differs from the sprats and herrings of the N. Hemisphere by having a smoothly-rounded belly, without a keel of sharp scales. It is a blue colour above, silvery on the sides and ventrally, with a dark curved patch at the base of the tail.

Sprattus   Clupeidae
    sprattus SPRAT 14 cm. (5½ in.)
The sprat is widely distributed in European in-shore waters. It is found from the Norwegian coast s. to the n. Mediterranean and the Black Sea. It is also found in the Baltic Sea.

This is a small, shoaling fish with a greenish back and silvery sides. Its scales are thin, moderate in size but very easily detached. Its body is flattened, forming a sharp keel under the belly, which with the formation of the scales has a saw-toothed edge with pungent qualities.

The sprat is typically a coastal fish, living just offshore during the warmer months of the year, when it spawns; it moves inshore in the winter. The eggs of the sprat float at the surface of the sea. The young fish are found close inshore in winter, in dense shoals, often mixed with young herring. In certain areas of the British coast, especially the larger estuaries, they are caught and sold as whitebait. Elsewhere the sprat is subject to important fisheries, many tons are caught annually in the North Sea and processed for fish meal or oil. Some are used fresh as food, others are canned, and the Norwegian fjord stocks are particularly exploited, canned in oil as brislings.

SPRAYING CHARACIN see **Copeina arnoldi**
SPRINGER see **Heteromugil tricuspidens**

Springeria   Anacanthobatidae
    folirostris 62 cm. (24½ in.)
A little known deep-water skate, from the n. half of the Gulf of Mexico, this species was described first in 1953, when the genus was named after the distinguished American ichthyologist Stewart Springer. Its most noticeable feature is the extreme length of the snout, produced almost to a needle-like point with leaf-like extensions either side. Mature males have a patch of conspicuous thorns in the middle of each wing, while their clasper tips are branched and spiny. In colour it is ash grey or light brown, sometimes with dark patches; the snout is black edged.

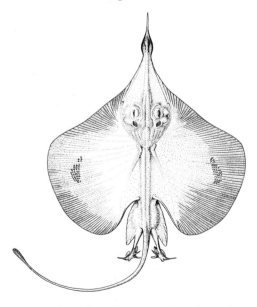

It has been found on a number of occasions in depths of 300–512 m. (164–280 fathoms). Relatively few specimens are known.

SPURDOG see **Squalus acanthias**

SQUALIDAE
A family which is represented by a variety of mainly small sharks. All have a sharp spine in front of each dorsal fin, all also lack an anal fin. Other than that they are typically shark-like in character with sharp teeth and 5 gill slits. They are worldwide in distribution, several species inhabit the deep oceans, and some are relatively important fish to the fisheries of the world. See **Centrophorus, Centroscyllium, Centroscymnus, Deania, Etmopterus, Squalus.**

Squaliolus   Dalatiidae
    laticaudus DWARF SHARK 15 cm. (6 in.)
possibly to 23 cm. (9 in.)
The dwarf shark is the smallest of all sharks, the largest known specimen being just 15 cm. in length. It is known from relatively few specimens since it was first caught off the island of Luzon in the Philippines in 1908. The larger specimen caught then was a sexually mature male, also the largest reported. Other specimens have been taken from Japanese waters.

There seems to be good reason to suspect that the dwarf shark found in the Atlantic, off Madeira and Biscay, and described as *S. sarmenti* is identical with the Pacific species.

Some of these specimens were taken in relatively shallow water, 300 m. (164 fathoms), but others were caught as deep as 914 m. (500 fathoms). Evidently the species has a wide vertical range; it probably makes diurnal vertical migrations in the open sea from the depths in which it normally lives.

It is described as jet black in colour with white fins. Its body is slim and the fins are very small. This would suggest that it is not a very powerful swimmer but as it is nearly neutrally buoyant in the sea it is able to move considerable distances vertically and horizontally with the minimum of energy.
S. sarmenti see under **S. laticaudus**

Squalus   Squalidae
    acanthias SPURDOG, SPINY DOGFISH
120 cm. (4 ft)
The spurdog is widely distributed in the n. Atlantic being found on the e. side from Norway to the N. African coast, as well as the Mediterranean, and on the w. side from W. Greenland to Florida. The N. Pacific contains a spiny dogfish believed now to be identical.

The spurdog is dull grey with distinct white spots; the belly is cream. Over its whole range it is an abundant species in inshore waters, although it has been found down to depths of 950 m. (520 fathoms). This is a shark which is frequently encountered in huge shoals, very often containing one sex only. The shoals are migratory, apparently capriciously so, for the ground which contained thousands one day may have none the next. To some extent migrations are related to the breeding cycle, for the females come into shallow water to give birth to their young.

The size of the litters may be from 4–11, and the young sharks are 20–33 cm. (8–13 in.) at birth. Gestation in this species is very prolonged, from 18–22 months. Sexual maturity is not attained by the males until 11 years and by females until 19–20 years of age. This combination of late sexual maturity, small litter size, and long development within the mother

has made the spurdog particularly vulnerable to fishing pressures. In Europe it is widely eaten (it forms the 'flake' or 'rock eel' of British fish shops) and it was observed that after some years of exploitation the catch became sharply reduced.

It still forms a valuable fishery in Europe although some conservation of the stock is required. On the U.S. coasts, however, it is not exploited and indeed is regarded as a severe threat to better fishing. Large shoals of spurdogs make great inroads into valuable fish stocks, such as herring, young haddock, and cod, and long-lining and sometimes trawling become impossible when these sharks are in the area.

The spines in the dorsal fins can inflict serious wounds, worsened by the venom injected into the wound from the spine's basal tissue. This risk of injury makes the spurdog even less appreciated in areas such as the U.S. where sharks rank low as food.
S. kirki WHITE-SPOTTED DOGFISH
106 cm. (42 in.)
Found on the s. coasts of Australia and around New Zealand, the white-spotted dogfish is closely similar to, if not identical with, other spurdogs off S. Africa and s. America. It is a slim-bodied species, with well developed spines in its dorsal fins, a large tail but no anal fin. It is greyish above, creamy white below, with conspicuous but irregularly spaced white spots on the back.

It is a viviparous shark, the female producing small litters at extended intervals (as does its n. relative *Squalus acanthias*). It is harmless to man but causes a good deal of damage to his food fishes where it is present in sufficiently large numbers.

SQUARE-TAIL, SMALLEYE see
    Tetragonorus cuvieri

Squatina   Squatinidae
    californica CALIFORNIAN MONKFISH,
PACIFIC ANGELSHARK 91 cm. (3 ft)
This angelshark is found along the Pacific coast of N. America from Alaska to Lower California. It is a bottom-living shark found in shallow water, which chiefly feeds on invertebrates, sea urchins, crabs, and especially molluscs.

In contrast to other members of this family the Californian monkfish is an egg-laying species. The eggs are protected in a horny capsule.
S. squatina MONKFISH 183 cm. (6 ft)
The monkfish is common in the e. Atlantic from the coast of n. Scotland s. to the Canary Islands, and in the Mediterranean. To the N. of this range, around the British Isles and in the North Sea it is most common in summertime, evidently as a result of northward migration.

It is the largest of the angelsharks, big specimens weighing as much as 32 kg. (70 lb.) having been caught from time to time. It is not an aggressive species, although, on account of its size and its sharply-pointed teeth, live specimens are handled with care. It is a bottom-living fish which, despite its cumbersome appearance, is an active swimmer, its food consists of benthic organisms chiefly flatfishes and rays, but it also eats crustaceans and molluscs. It is a live-bearing shark, the litter size ranging between 9–16 young which are born in summer.

As a common shallow-water species in European seas it was well known to the earliest naturalists. However, dried specimens, sometimes mutilated, were more familiar to them than the living fish and on account of this fancied resemblances to human faces were described. The 'monkfish', 'angelfish', and even 'bishopfish' were all names used for this species by mediaeval writers, and the two former are still in use. Although it has no commercial importance today, and few anglers deliberately fish for it, the monkfish was at one time of value for its tough, denticle covered skin which was used as ornamental shagreen or leather.

S. tergocellata ORNATE ANGELSHARK
51 cm. (20 in.)
A little-known angelfish of the seas of s. Australia which has been found off W. Australia, S. Australia, and New South Wales. It is most common in the Great Australian Bight where it is trawled in depths of 130–365 m. (70–200 fathoms). Like the other members of the family it is bottom-living, and also gives birth to fully-formed young.

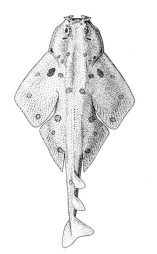

This is one of the more colourful of angelsharks, yellowish brown above with small blue spots and large brown rings and spots over the body and fins.

SQUATINIDAE
The family of angelsharks appear to be intermediate in many ways between the true sharks and the rays. The mouth is placed at the end of the body, the gill openings are on the side of the fish, the dorsal fins are well developed, and they swim by movements of the tail, all shark-like features. They also possess very broad pectoral fins, a pair of large spiracles, and internally their hearts are like those of rays. The balance, however, is towards the sharks.

They are relatively small sharks, the largest growing to around 1·8 m. (6 ft). They are confined to warm temperate oceans and are found along both coastlines of the N. Atlantic, off S. Africa, Australia, Japan, Korea, and the Pacific coastline of N. America. See **Squatina.**

SQUAWFISH,
    COLORADO see **Ptychocheilus lucius**
    NORTHERN see **Ptychocheilus oregonensis**
SQUEAKER see Mochokidae
SQUETEAGUE see **Cynoscion regalis**
SQUIRE see **Chrysophrys auratus**
SQUIRREL HAKE see **Urophycis chuss**
SQUIRRELFISH see Holocentridae
SQUIRRELFISH see **Adioryx xantherythrus, Holocentrus ascensionis**
SQUIRRELFISH,
    DUSKY see **Adioryx vexillarius**
    LONGJAW see **Flammeo marianus, Holocentrus ascensionis**
STAR-EATER see Astronesthidae
STAR-EATER, BLACK see **Astronesthes niger**
STARGAZER see Uranoscopidae
STARGAZER see **Ichthyscopus lebeck, Kathetostoma laeve, Uranoscopus scaber**
STARGAZER,
    SADDLE see **Gillellus rubrocinctus**
    SAND see Dactyloscopidae
    SAND see **Dactyloscopus tridigitatus**
    SMOOTH see **Kathetostoma averruncus**

Starksia Clinidae
ocellata CHECKERED BLENNY 5 cm. (2 in.)
Found in the w. tropical Atlantic and the Caribbean. Its range extends to N. Carolina, the Bahamas, s. to Brazil, and includes most of the W. Indian islands. It occurs in rocky and coral reef formations at depths of 1·5–18 m. (1–10 fathoms), and is particularly common amongst algal-covered rocks and in broken coral. Occasional specimens have been found living in burrows in sponges.

It is a rather stout-bodied blenny, its body covered with scales except ventrally. Its coloration is brownish, sometimes nearly uniform, at others boldly chequered with brown. It always has a series of white-centred dark rings on the cheeks and the base of the pectoral fin. Mature males have a distinct genital papilla, joined to the first 2 rays of the anal fin, the latter being separated from the fin.

STARRY FLOUNDER see **Platichthys stellatus**
STARSNOUT, GREY see **Bathyagonus alascanus**

Stathmonotus Clinidae
stahli EELGRASS BLENNY 3·5 cm. (1½ in.)
A Caribbean species which is widely distributed between the Bahamas and Florida, along the Central American coast to Venezuela, and throughout the W. Indies. In some areas it is said to inhabit sea grass beds, but in the Bahamas its preferred habitats are sponges, dead corallines, or amongst the gaps in the many-branched *Porites* coral.

It is a distinctive scaled blenny, very elongate in shape with a long dorsal fin, composed of spines only and joined to the tail fin. A large, club-shaped tentacle over the eye, another on the nape. The body scales are relatively large. Its usual colour is greenish with lighter blotches on the sides, and reddish on the fins.

This species was once found on the Welsh coast of the British Isles, said to have been re-covered from the stomach of a sea stickleback, *Spinachia spinachia*. Its occurrence there has never been satisfactorily explained and remains one of the minor mysteries of ichthyology.

STEEL-BLUE APHYOSEMION see **Aphyosemion gardneri**
STEEL-HEAD TROUT see **Salmo gairdneri**
STEENBRAS see **Sparodon durbanensis**
STEENBRAS,
    BLACK see **Cymatoceps nasutus**
    RED see **Petrus rupestris**
    YELLOW see **Petrus rupestris**
    WHITE see **Lithognathus lithognathus**
STEENKLIPVIS see **Palunolepis brachydactylus**
Stegophilus insidiosus see under Trichomycteridae

Stegostoma Orectolobidae
fasciatum ZEBRA SHARK 3·4 m. (11 ft)
Found throughout the warmer waters of the Indo-Pacific, from e. Africa eastwards. The zebra shark is heavy-bodied with a seemingly over-long tail; it is light sandy brown with darker bars across the back. The juveniles are most heavily marked. It is a sluggish species, feeding mainly on crustaceans and molluscs; it seems to be harmless to man. This is an egg-laying shark; the egg cases are brownish and oblong with curved sides, and have 2 tufts of dense fibres attached to one side.

STELLATE STURGEON see **Acipenser stellatus**

Stenodus Salmonidae
leucichthys INCONNU, NELMA
150 cm. (59 in.)
The inconnu is a predatory whitefish widely distributed across Eurasia and the nw. regions of N. America, along the Arctic Ocean basin. Two subspecies are recognized, the Caspian nelma (*S. leucichthys leucichthys*) and the Siberian and n. American inconnu (*S. l. nelma*). The former is confined to the Caspian basin, spawning in the rivers Volga and Ural, sometimes as much as 3000 km. (1875 miles) from the Caspian. It is extremely important to the fisheries of that sea, taken mainly during its migration. The population is maintained by natural spawning and by hatchery rearing of eggs and fry, but the nelma is also threatened by increasing pollution and industrial use of the water in the spawning rivers.

The inconnu is most abundant in the large, muddy rivers and associated lakes within the Arctic Circle. In many rivers they are migratory, the adults moving up from the estuary to spawn in freshwater, and returning later to the sea. Elsewhere, and especially in lakes, it is not migratory. The inconnu spawns in autumn on gravelly areas far upstream; the numerous eggs are scattered between the stones. The young may spend 1–2 years in freshwater before migrating to the sea.

At first young inconnu feed in plankton, but later they feed on small bottom-living animals, and by their second year they are fish-eaters. Like the adults they eat large quantities of smaller fishes, sticklebacks, minnows, whitefish, and young chinook salmon.

Inconnu are fished for wherever they occur.

Many are taken while migrating, but others are caught in gill nets in lakes, and by angling. They offer very good sport as large specimens can weigh up to 28 kg. (62 lb.), and in Siberia fish as heavy as 40 kg. (88 lb.) have been taken. Its flesh is said to be good eating.

The inconnu is unlike any other whitefish in the shape of its mouth which is large and wide, extending back to beyond the eyes. It is also rather slender. The name inconnu is said to have been given it by early French-speaking explorers in n. Canada, it was literally the 'unknown' fish, for it is not found to the S.

STEPHANOBERYCIDAE
A small family of deep-sea fishes which have been captured in the tropical regions of the Atlantic, Pacific, and Indian oceans. Very likely they are widely distributed but very rarely caught.

It is distinguished from its nearest relatives (families Gibberichthyidae and Melamphaeidae) by having the pelvic fins comprising 5 soft rays, placed well back, in lacking a distinct series of spiny fin rays on the back, and particularly in having small, toothed scales with heavy backward-pointing spines. See **Acanthochaenus.**

Stephanolepis   Balistidae
  auratus PORKY, FILEFISH 25 cm. (10 in.)
A s. African species found on the E. coast from Knysna to Beira, and particularly common in shallow bays. It is common in inshore waters over sand and amongst algae. Large specimens are often caught and marketed locally, but there is no regular fishery.

It is a deep-bodied fish, highly compressed and with a deep flap on the belly. It is basically greenish, yellow ventrally and with yellow fins.
S. cirrhifer FILEFISH, PORKY 25 cm. (10 in.)
A common species in the nw. Pacific where it occurs in the E. China Sea, around Japan, and Korea. It is the commonest of the monacanthid plectognaths (see Balistidae) in these waters and is commercially fished. Its flesh is said to be very tasty and the liver is good to eat, although the fish has to be skinned before cooking due to the rough, finely toothed scales in the skin.

It breeds from June to August, the young fish being particularly abundant in the surface waters, floating with algae. At a length of about 3 cm. (1¼ in.) they begin to live on the bottom in inshore weed beds, feeding on small crustaceans and benthic organisms, while the large fish are most common at depths of 10–30 m. (5–16 fathoms).

This filefish is deep-bodied with a prominent flap of skin beneath the belly strengthened by a stout spine which just protrudes through the skin. The second dorsal ray is elongate in mature males, the dorsal spine is slender and barbed on front and back. It is dull grey with dull brown blotches on the sides.

Stereolepis   Serranidae
  gigas GIANT SEA BASS 2·1 m. (81 in.)
As its names suggest this is a literal giant amongst sea basses. It is found on the Pacific coast of Mexico and California, and has also been captured on the Asiatic coast of the Pacific. It lives in inshore waters, the adults just below kelp beds on rocky bottoms in depths of 30–46 m. (16–25 fathoms), while the

young fish are found amongst the kelp in depths of 12–30 m. (7–16 fathoms).

It is a huge fish. The largest authenticated weighed 253 kg. (557 lb.), but there is reason to believe that it may exceed 272 kg. (600 lb.). The American ichthyologists, John E. Fitch and Robert J. Lavenberg, report that these large specimens are of considerable age. They cite a 197 kg. (434 lb.) specimen of 72–75 years, and a 145 kg. (320 lb.) fish of around 50 years of age. It becomes mature as 11–13 years (a weight of around 23 kg., 50 lb.), and spawns through the summer in shallow water.

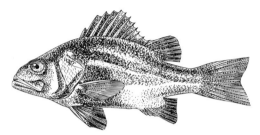

It is wholly predatory; the young fish feed on anchovies and the larger fish eat a wide variety of fishes and crustaceans. It is a fine sporting fish, taken on lines and by spear fishing; it is also fished for commercially mainly to the s. of its range. Because of fishing pressures of various kinds large specimens have become scarce and controls are exerted on the number taken by sports fishermen.

It is distinguished by its size, by the relatively short-based dorsal fin. Its body is deep and heavy, brick red when young, browner as it grows older with irregular rows of dark spots on the sides.

STERLET see **Acipenser rutheneus**

STERNOPTYCHIDAE
The marine hatchetfishes are a very distinctive group, characterized by their body shape, laterally compressed to form a sharp edge below the belly and with a thin tail, seemingly the handle of the hatchet. They are all small and rather silvery in colour, with characteristically arranged clusters of large light organs on the underside. Hatchet fishes are taken in the open sea from the surface down to depths of possibly 3658 m. (2000 fathoms), although they seem to be most abundant between 914–1829 m. (500–1000 fathoms). They are worldwide in distribution in the deep oceans, and by their numbers make a substantial contribution to the diet of other fishes. See **Argyropelecus, Sternoptyx.**

Sternoptyx   Sternoptychidae
  diaphana 5 cm. (2 in.)
This hatchetfish is widely distributed in both the Atlantic, Indian, and Pacific oceans. It is found in deep water between 182–1829 m. (100–1000 fathoms) although occasional specimens have been reported to have been taken down to 3083 m. (1686 fathoms).

It has the body shape typical of its family, thin and compressed with a sharp belly and a narrow tail. The mouth is strongly oblique, and the eyes are lateral (not upward turned as in *Argyropelecus*). As in other species it is silvery coloured, dark on the back, and has numerous small oval light organs on the belly and under the tail in short clusters. This

species is characterized by having a thin, transparent bony blade projecting out of its back just in front of the dorsal fin.

Sternopygus   Rhamphichthyidae
  macrurus SABRE, CUCHILLA 91 cm. (3 ft)
The knifefish is found in the ne. part of S. America, the Guianas, the Amazon, and

Orinoco basins, and the Rio Magdalena. Living specimens are quite translucent, so much so that the backbone and internal organs can be seen; the muscles are clear and show only a red colour where blood vessels pass through them. A scattering of blue colour cells, the pale yellow skin, and clear fins mean that the fish is almost invisible in cloudy water. It is widely distributed in streams, trenches, ditches, and the backwaters of rivers in open savannahs and in plantations, appearing to prefer dark coloured water. Like other knifefishes, it is mainly crepuscular, foraging at night. When young it feeds on small crustaceans and insect larvae. As it grows its diet changes to include larger organisms such as shrimps, and fishes. However, the most important food item at all ages is adult insects, many of which are flying terrestrial forms.

This fish is eaten in many parts of its range. Its flesh is said to be of good flavour and firm.

STICHAEIDAE
A moderately large family of marine fishes, widely distributed in the cool temperate seas of the N. Hemisphere. The family is most varied in the N. Pacific although a number of species occur in the N. Atlantic basin.

They are long rather slender fishes, with flattened bodies and small scales, rarely scaleless. The dorsal fin is composed of spines only and runs from just behind the head to the tail. Some species lack the pelvic fins, in others they are well developed and have branched rays. Their nearest relatives are probably the scaled blennies (Clinidae). See **Anoplarchus, Chirolophis, Delolepis, Lumpenus, Xiphister.**

STICKLEBACK see Gasterosteidae
STICKLEBACK,
  BROOK see **Culaea inconstans**
  FIFTEEN-SPINED see **Spinachia spinachia**
  FOUR-SPINE see **Apeltes quadracus**
  NINE-SPINED see **Pungitius pungitius**
  SEA see **Spinachia spinachia**
  THREE-SPINE see **Gasterosteus aculeatus**

Stigmatogobius   Gobiidae
  sadanundio 8 cm. (3 in.)
A native of Asia from India and Sri Lanka, e. to the Malay Peninsula, Sumatra, Java, Borneo, to the Philippines. Although occasionally found in the sea it is most common in low salinity estuaries and freshwater.

It is a rather stout-bodied goby, with a fully-scaled body, and well developed dorsal, anal, and tail fins. The scales extend forward onto the head, the first being a very large single median scale just behind the eyes.

This goby is frequently kept in tropical aquaria, in freshwater to which a little salt has been added. **436**

Stizostedion   Percidae
  lucioperca ZANDER, PIKE-PERCH
1 m. (39 in.)
The zander is native to the rivers of central and n. Europe, being found in the basins of the Baltic, Black, and Caspian seas. It has been widely introduced in w. Europe, and is now present from the Dutch and French rivers eastwards. It has even been liberated into the rivers of e. England.

It thrives in large lakes and big, slow-flowing rivers, particularly favouring murky water. It is entirely a fish-eater once past its earliest life stages, and there are few species that it will not eat. Even the deep-bodied bream *Abramis brama* (normally relatively immune from predation once well grown) will be attacked.

It spawns in spring, from April to June on hard gravel, or clay bottoms; the eggs are placed in a cleared nest, where they are guarded by the male. Breeding adults will make considerable migrations to reach these regularly-used breeding areas.

In central Europe it is a commercially valuable species; it is caught on lines, in seines, and trap nets. In the U.S.S.R. considerable effort has been expended on conserving the species and maintaining stocks for fishery purposes. In w. Europe it has some reputation as a sporting fish, and in England it will no doubt be further liberated in misguided attempts to 'improve' the angling. Its real value as a food fish is not appreciated in Britain.

S. vitreum WALLEYE 91 cm. (3 ft)
Widely distributed in the central and e. parts of N. America from the Mackenzie River system, the Hudson Bay drainage system, e. to Quebec, and S. to N. Carolina in the coastal rivers, and to Georgia in the Mississippi system. In Canadian waters the walleye has been distinguished as the yellow walleye, *S. vitreum vitreum*, distinct from the Great Lakes blue pike, *S. vitreum glaucum*.

The walleye prefers clear water in hard-bottomed lakes and rivers. It is usually found in moderately deep water of between 5–10 m. (3–5 fathoms), although in the s., warmer parts of its range it moves into deeper water in the summer. Its food consists of a wide variety of native fishes, but it also takes some insects and crustaceans. Growth rate and size attained vary with the water in which it is living. The largest walleyes are found in the S. It is reputed to grow to a maximum weight of 11 kg. (25 lb.), but a good average is around 5 kg. (11 lb.), at which length it is likely to be around 15–16 years old.

The walleye is a prized food fish, its flesh being well flavoured, white and flaky. It is commercially very valuable in inland areas of N. America. It is also a good sport fish, the possibility of a large specimen making it particularly valued.

Stolephorus   Engraulidae
  heterolobus 9 cm. (3½ in.)
A widespread Indian Ocean anchovy which was first reported from the Red Sea, although later found in the E. Indies and to the N. of Australia. Like other members of the family it is a planktonic schooling fish of considerable commercial value, and prey to many larger fishes and birds.

It is slender-bodied with thin fragile scales over the whole body. **29**

S. purpureus NEHU 10 cm. (4 in.)
An anchovy of great abundance in Hawaiian waters, it resembles most of its relatives by its characteristic head shape, with a projecting snout and enormous mouth.

It is the most important bait for tuna fishing in the Hawaiian Islands, and forms a considerable part of the natural diet of tuna and other fishes and birds in the area. It feeds on planktonic crustaceans, fish larvae and other small animals.

The nehu is found very commonly in estuaries and water of low salinity, tidal inlets, and in shallow coastal waters. It spawns throughout the year, the eggs floating near the surface and developing quickly. Growth is very rapid and the young may attain 5 cm. (2 in.), and be functionally adult within weeks of hatching.

Stomias   Stomiatidae
  colubrinus SNAKE DRAGONFISH
41 cm. (16 in.)
This dragonfish is well known from the waters of the e. Pacific, from the W. coast of Central America S. to Peru, and across to the Galapagos Islands. It is also found in the Atlantic in the tropical region and as a rare wanderer further N. It lives in much deeper water than its relatives, having been found most commonly at around 1200 m. (656 fathoms). It is said to inhabit rather colder water than its relatives, such as are found at these depths, and its presence in shallower water is probably due to up-welling of cold deep water.

It has a luminous bulb on the end of a chin barbel which is about the length of the head. It is black in colour, with iridescent sides, and many small luminous glands along the sides.

STOMIATIDAE
The dragonfishes are a moderately small family living in deep water in all the seas of the world, although they are most common in the tropical and temperate regions. Their depth range is from close to the surface to depths of as much as 2000 m. (1094 fathoms), although their centre of vertical distribution appears to lie around 300–500 m. (164–273 fathoms).

All have long, slender bodies with rows of hexagonal pigmented areas, covered by scales along their sides. The dorsal and anal fins are set close to the tail fin; they do not have an adipose fin. By comparison with their long bodies, the dragonfishes have short heads, and the eye is set well forward so that the snout is very short. Their jaws are long, and free to swing open to form a capacious gape, with large, rigid fang-like teeth in both jaws. They are well supplied with light organs along the sides and beneath, and a large light organ behind the eye. All dragonfishes have a long chin barbel, variously branched at its swollen tip and equipped with luminous tissue, which serves to attract its prey. See **Stomias.**

Stoneiella   Loricariidae
  leopardus 14 cm. (5½ in.)
A very striking catfish, closely related to *Plecostomus* species, and externally similar to them. Its body is relatively short and thickset, the head depressed with a rather pointed snout, the cheeks and gill covers with short spines. Scales on the body are large, ridged and scute-like, but they are lacking on the underside. The most notable feature of this fish is its high dorsal fin, the rays being particularly elongate.

Pale to dark brown on the back and sides with numerous black blotches; underside yellowish.

This fish, occasionally kept in aquaria, originates in the Novo River in Brazil.

STROMATEIDAE
A distinctive family of deep-bodied fishes which lack pelvic fins when adult. In keeping with their deep, compressed bodies the dorsal and anal fins are well developed and often high; the tail fin is forked. Their nearest relatives are the blackfishes (family Centrolophidae) and

like them they have a distinct pharyngeal sac with hardened papillae on the inner wall. This feature appears usually to be associated with a diet of soft-bodied animals like jelly-fishes.

The stromateids live in shallow, inshore waters in tropical and warm temperate regions around both coasts of America, and from the Mediterranean along the African coast to the Indian Ocean thence coastwise to Japan. They are not found around the oceanic islands or around Australia. Many of the species are of considerable commercial importance. The flesh of these butterfishes or pompanos is of excellent quality. See **Peprilus, Stromateus.**

Stromateus   Stromateidae
    fiatola BUTTERFISH 50 cm. (19 in.)
Widely distributed in the e. Atlantic from the N. African coast to S. Africa. It occurs commonly throughout the Mediterranean. Off the W. African coast it is common in depths of 12–50 m. (6–27 fathoms) and is found on both hard and soft bottoms down near the edge of the continental shelf. Juveniles, however, are pelagic fishes and often found associating with medusae.

It is a valuable food fish wherever it can be caught in numbers, its flesh being delicate and tasty, although it does not keep well.

It is a very striking-looking fish, deep-bodied and compressed with long-based, but low dorsal and anal fins, and a forked tail fin. In the juvenile small pelvic fins are present; these decrease in size as the fish grows and are absent in the adult. It is iridescent green or blue above, silvery ventrally. The young have several dusky vertical bands across the back and sides, while adults have round or oblong, yellowish to black spots on the upper surface of the body.

Strongylura   Belonidae
    marina SILVER GAR, ATLANTIC
NEEDLEFISH 1·2 m. (4 ft)
Widely distributed in the w. Atlantic from Maine to Texas, including the Gulf of Mexico where its range overlaps that of the related timucu, *Strongylura timucu*. In body-form it is typical of the family, with a long bill, armed with sharp teeth, and a long slender body but rounded in cross-section.

It is a voracious predator, eating fishes, squids, and invertebrates. It is found mainly at the surface but comes inshore, and even into river mouths, in which it spawns. The eggs are small spheres with many long filaments.
193
S. timucu see under **S. marina**

Strophiurichthys   Ostraciontidae
    robustus ROBUST BOXFISH 25 cm. (10 in.)
A deep water boxfish, related to *Aracana* and the other deep-bodied, rounded-carapace cow-fishes, which is known from a number of localities in the Indo-Pacific. It has been reported from several places in the Pacific Ocean, the tropical coasts of Australia, the Solomon Islands, and off s. Africa. It is a deep water species living in depths of 18–274 m. (10–150 fathoms) and for this reason is rarely captured, except when local fisheries (as the Queensland prawn trawlers) reveal it in numbers. It is probably very widely distributed, and common.

As with its relatives in the *Aracana*-group,

the dorsal, anal, and tail fins are free from the carapace, but this species has several bony plates on the tail. A distinct ridge runs along the belly, and the carapace is rough to the touch and composed of heavy hexagonal plates. It is yellowish brown with dark spots on the back and sides.

STUMPNOSE, WHITE see **Rhabdosargus**
    globiceps
STURGEON see Acipenseridae
STURGEON see **Acipenser rutheneus,**
    Acipenser sturio
STURGEON,
    ATLANTIC see **Acipenser sturio**
    FALSE SHOVELNOSE see
        Pseudoscaphirhynchus kaufmanni
    LAKE see **Acipenser fulvescens**
    RUSSIAN see **Acipenser gueldenstaedti**
    SHIP see **Acipenser nudiventris**
    SHOVELNOSE see **Scaphirhynchus**
        platorynchus
    STELLATE see **Acipenser stellatus**
    WHITE see **Acipenser transmontanus**
STURGEON POACHER see **Agonus**
    acipenserinus

Stygnobrotula   Ophidiidae
    latebricola BLACK WIDOW 7·5 cm. (3 in.)
Evidently widely distributed in the Caribbean but only taken at a few points between the Bahamas and Curaçao. It is a deep-bodied, broad-headed species, with a blunt snout, and conspicuously down-turned corners to its mouth. It is distinguished also by being one of the few shallow-water brotulas with a deep-brown body and blackish fins.

It is a live-bearing species, the fertilized eggs developing inside the female until the young are fully formed. In the Bahamas it haunts the hollows and crevices of coral heads. Here and elsewhere it has been observed living in shallow-water caves near the shore-line keeping close to the roof and sides of the cave.

STYLOPHORIDAE
A remarkable family of fishes which has been for long allied, rather tentatively, with the dealfishes (Trachipteridae). Relatively few specimens have ever been described. They are slender, moderately deep-bodied, with a small, but very protractile mouth, and large eyes. The dorsal fin runs along the length of the body; the anal fin is short, while the tail fin is composed of 2 parts, the upper 5 rays directed obliquely upward and the lower 2 rays in the form of long trailing filaments. The eyes are remarkable, being cylindrical and directed forwards, in effect telescopic. See **Stylophorus.**

Stylophorus   Stylophoridae
    chordatus 25 cm. (10 in.)
An intriguing fish first found at the surface between the islands of Cuba and Martinique, and described by the one-time British Museum zoologist George Shaw in 1791. This original specimen was 55 cm. (22 in.) long, of which 30 cm. (12 in.) was the very elongate lower tail rays; it was described as silvery, with deep brown membranes round the head. For more than a century this was the only known specimen, but in 1908 a specimen was reported from the area of the Galapagos Islands; later specimens were taken in the central Atlantic.

This fish is believed to live at depths of 500–700 m. (273–383 fathoms), and the post-larvae nearer the surface. Probably it is distributed worldwide in tropical, deep oceans, but very few specimens have ever been captured. Its habits are virtually unknown; it is presumed to swim slowly, its small mouth and

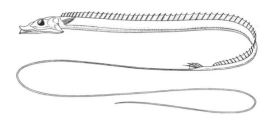

highly protrusible jaws suggesting a diet of slow swimming crustaceans. Its remarkable, long, tubular, telescopic eyes presumably give binocular vision and their development indicates that it lives in the moderately lit zone of the oceans.

SUCKER see Catostomidae
SUCKER,
    CORNISH see **Lepadogaster**
        lepadogaster
    HARELIP see **Lagochila lacera**
    HUMPBACK see **Xyrauchen texanus**
    LONGNOSE see **Catostomus catostomus**
    RAZORBACK see **Xyrauchen texanus**
    WHITE see **Catostomus commersoni**
SUCKERFISH see **Echeneis naucrates**
SUCKERFISH, SLENDER see **Phtheirichthys**
    lineatus
SUCKINGFISH, SHORT see **Remora remora**

Sudis   Paralepididae
    hyalina 40 cm. (16 in.)
This barracudina, although typical in many respects of its family, does differ from most of its relatives, notably in the shape and structure of the head. To all practical purposes, however, it is a paralepid with a rather deep, heavy head, and rather long fins, especially the pectoral fins. It is a scaleless species, except for 2 series of scales along the lateral fin.

Originally known only from the Mediterranean, where it was first described by the extraordinary polymath S. C. Rafinesque-Schmaltz in 1810, it has been found in both the e. and w. tropical Atlantic. Adults have rarely been seen, most of the specimens known are juveniles and post-larvae. Beyond a knowledge of the growth stages of this fish nothing is known of its biology. It is apparently a carnivorous fish of the open sea, found down to depths of 700 m. (383 fathoms).

SUMATRA BARB see **Barbus tetrazona**
SUMMER
    FLOUNDER see **Paralichthys dentatus**
    HERRING see **Alosa aestivalis**
SUNFISH see Centrarchidae, Molidae
SUNFISH see **Cetorhinus maximus,**
    Masturus lanceolatus, Mola mola
SUNFISH,
    BLACK-BANDED see **Enneacanthus**
        chaetodon
    BLUESPOTTED see **Enneacanthus**
        gloriosus
    DWARF see **Elassoma evergladei**
    EVERGLADES PYGMY see **Elassoma**
        evergladei

GREEN see **Lepomis cyanellus**
LONGEAR see **Lepomis megalotis**
MUD see **Chaenobryttus gulosus**
OCEAN see **Mola mola**
SLENDER see **Ranzania laevis**
SURF
   EEL see **Sphagebranchus ophioneus**
   SARDINE see **Iso natalensis**
SURFPERCH see Embiotocidae
SURFPERCH, BARRED see **Amphistichus argenteus**
SURGEONFISH see Acanthuridae
SURGEONFISH,
   BRISTLE-TOOTHED see **Ctenochaetus strigosus**
   FIVE-BANDED see **Acanthurus triostegus**
   ORANGE-SPOT see **Acanthurus olivaceus**
SURMULLET see **Pseudupeneus fraterculus**
SWALLOWER see Chiasmodontidae
SWALLOWER,
   BLACK see **Chiasmodon niger**
   NEEDLETOOTH see **Kali normani**
SWAMP-EEL, BLIND see **Ophistosternon infernale**
SWAMPFISH see **Chologaster cornutus**
SWALLOWTAIL see **Trachichthodes lineatus, Trachinotus russelli**
SWEEPER see Pempheridae
SWEEPER,
   COPPER see **Pempheris schomburgki**
   GLASSY see **Pempheris schomburgki**
SWEET WILLIAM see **Galeorhinus galeus**
SWEETLIP EMPEROR see **Lethrinus chrysostomus**
SWEETLIPS,
   PAINTED see **Plectorhynchus pictus**
   SILVER-BANDED see **Gaterin diagrammus**
SWELL SHARK see **Cephaloscyllium ventriosum**
SWORDFISH see **Xiphias gladius**
SWORDFISH, BROAD-BILL see **Xiphias gladius**
SWORDTAIL see **Xiphophorus helleri**
SWORDTAIL
   CHARACIN see **Corynopoma riisei**
   PLATY see **Xiphophorus xiphidium**

Syacium   Bothidae
micrurum CHANNEL FLOUNDER
30 cm. (12 in.)
A tropical Atlantic species, said to be found in the E. from the Cape Verde Islands, the Nigerian coast and W. Africa generally, and in the W. from Bermuda, the Bahamas to Brazil. It lives in shallow water on mixed sand and turtle grass bottoms, burying itself in the loose sand.

The eyes are close together and are placed on the left side of the head; the mouth is moderately large, and the lateral line is almost straight. Its body is light brown with irregular darker markings, mostly brown rings with a dark spot at the centre of the ring. The mid-line of the left side has a series of 3–4 dusky blotches; the fins are flecked with dark marks.

Symbolophorus   Myctophidae
californiensis 13 cm. (5 in.)
Found in the e. Pacific Ocean, offshore from n. British Columbia to the Californian region, this is one of the more common lanternfishes off the Californian coast, judging by the number of larvae taken there by fishery research vessels. As larvae they are often distinguished

by their size alone for they do not change to the adult shape and develop light-organs until they are 24 mm. (1 in.) in length. As larvae their eyes are eliptical in shape and stand out on short but distinct stalks.

In body form it is a typical member of its family, relatively slender in shape with a large head, rounded snout and big eyes. Its tail fin is distinctive because all the rays, including the outermost ones are soft and flexible. Its precise identification is a matter of placement and number of light organs on the body. It spawns in spring and summer, and feeds almost exclusively on small crustaceans.

Symphurus   Cynoglossidae
arawak CARIBBEAN TONGUEFISH
45 mm. (1¾ in.)
A recently discovered Caribbean species, this miniature tongue-sole was described jointly in 1965 by Dr C. R. Robins and Dr John E. Randall, both distinguished explorers of the fauna of this region. It has been found at depths of 3–23 m. (1½–12½ fathoms), around the Bahamas, the Cayman Islands, Haiti, Puerto Rico, the Virgin Islands, and Curaçao. Like others of this genus it lives partially hidden in fine sand.

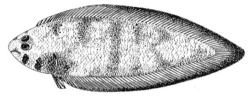

Although its identification is based largely upon fin ray counts, 11–14 in the tail fin, 69–75 in the dorsal, 56–61 in the anal fin, it is also distinguished by its small size and markings.

S. plagusia BLACKCHEEK TONGUEFISH
20 cm. (8 in.)
Widely distributed along the Atlantic coast of the U.S., this tongue-sole has been found from New York, s. to Florida and the Bahamas. It also occurs in the Gulf of Mexico. It is particularly abundant over sandy bays and in estuaries in depths of 2–25 m. (1–13 fathoms). It is probably most common around 10 m. (5 fathoms) of water.

Its body shape is typical of the group, being broadest at the front of the body and tapering to a point at the tail. Its dorsal fin runs round to the very front of the snout, its eyes are small and close-set, and its mouth is twisted. Its colouring is an unremarkable light brown, with dusky markings, and in most specimens a sooty black spot on the cheek. The right (blind) side of the head and body are uniformly pale.

Symphysodon   Cichlidae
aequifasciata DISCUS, POMPADOURFISH
15 cm. (6 in.)
This species exists in a number of colour varieties which the American ichthyologist Dr Leonard P. Schultz chose to differentiate with subspecific names. *S. a. aequifasciata* is greenish in colour and is known as the green discus; *S. a. axelrodi* is brownish and is the brown discus (this is the form illustrated), and *S. a. haraldi* is the blue discus. The necessity for subspecific names for such differences is doubtful.

This discus is widespread in the Amazon

basin inhabiting similar habitats to the angel-fishes (*Pterophyllum*). It is a very popular aquarium fish, although rather delicate to keep and requiring ample space. It prefers a well planted, and rather shaded aquarium. It has been bred in captivity, the young being nourished on the parents' body slime as in *S. discus*. **378**

S. discus DISCUS 20 cm. (8 in.)
A S. American species which is found in the River Amazon, Rio Negro, Rio Cupai, and other tributaries of the larger rivers. Its natural habitat is amongst the heavy vegetation and fallen trees of river back waters and pools.

It is a most beautifully coloured fish and is deservedly popular as an aquarium species. It is, however, a rather delicate fish, which requires quiet, well-shaded and densely planted aquaria in which to thrive. It has been bred in captivity.

The eggs are shed in areas of cleaned gravel on the bottom, and the newly-hatched young are transferred to adjacent water plant leaves. Within 3 days the young fish are able to swim freely and attach themselves to the body and fins of one of the adults. The fry feed on the slime secreted by the skin of the parents, both of which care for the young, in turn. Some aquarists have succeeded in rearing the young without the presence of the parents but the latter are usually more successful. **379**

Sympterichthys   Brachionichthyidae
verrucosus WARTY ANGLERFISH
5 cm. (2 in.)
This small anglerfish or frogfish is very similar to the members of the family Antennariidae, but the second and third dorsal rays are united to form a small fin instead of being free.

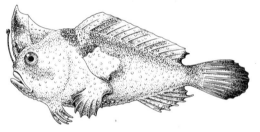

Found only off the coasts of S. Australia and New South Wales. Nothing is known of its habits.

Synanceia   Synanceiidae
horrida STONEFISH 61 cm. (2 ft)
This stonefish is widely distributed in the w. Pacific and Indian Ocean, and is found on the coasts of India, n. Australia to China and the Philippines.

It is an inshore species found in the intertidal areas and down to a depth of 10 m. (5 fathoms). Although most are reported on coral reefs it also occurs on shallow mud-flats and in estuaries. It is expert in hiding itself in whichever habitat it is living, and its dorsal spines are equipped with venom spines. As with its relative (*S. verrucosa*) stings are painful and can cause death.

Its colouring is drab, usually brownish above, with grey mottling; the inside of the mouth is light. This species is identified by the deep saddle-like depression behind the eyes which results in the eyes being rather elevated.

S. verrucosa STONEFISH, DEVILFISH
30 cm. (12 in.)
An Indo-Pacific species of wide distribution, which has been found from the e. coast of Africa and the Red Sea, to n. Australia, and the Philippines as well as many of the island groups of the w. Pacific. It is an inhabitant of shallow water, especially in coral areas in which it lies hidden in a crevice and is perfectly concealed by its colouring and shape. The art of animal camouflage is probably at its peak with the stonefishes, their rough, craggy head and body form a perfect match to their surroundings.

If trodden on, the sharp spines of the dorsal fin are erected and penetrate deeply into the foot, injecting some of the venom from the venom glands at the base of the spine. The envenomed wound is agonizingly painful in its early stages but numbness sets in later, and unless treatment is effective death may follow.

In some cases where fatality has been avoided, the limb has become gangrenous and required amputation. Numbers of cases of stonefish stings have been reported and due to the wide range of the species they are a relatively frequent occurrence.

This species is distinguished by the deep almost cubic pit behind each eye, and the concave interorbital space. Its colouring is variable, mostly drab but with occasional flashes of scarlet. **253**

SYNANCEIIDAE
The family of the stonefish, and other related scorpionfishes, found in the tropical Indo-Pacific in shallow inshore waters. They are amongst the most bizarre looking of all the scorpionfishes, with their scaleless bodies, depressed head and eyes often protuberant. Some have rough warty skins, others are smooth with fleshy appendages.

The dorsal spines are strong, very sharp and equipped with venom-producing glands; they can inflict an agonizingly painful wound which can result in crippling injury or death. See **Synanceia.**

SYNAPHOBRANCHIDAE
A family of deep-water eels, found in all the major oceans, except in polar regions. In many respects they appear intermediate between the congers and the morays. They are typically eel-shaped with long, rather pointed heads and long jaws, rows of fine teeth in the jaws, and small gill openings placed close together on the underside of the throat. They all have pectoral fins.

Members of this family live in the deep sea, many of them in depths greater than 1000 m. (547 fathoms), and some below 3000 m. (1640 fathoms). They probably live on, or close to the ocean floor as adults and immature fish, but their larvae are typical leptocephalus forms

living near the surface. See **Ilyophis, Synaphobranchus.**

Synaphobranchus Synaphobranchidae
bathybius 62 cm. (25 in.)
An elongate deep-sea eel, found in the Pacific and Indian oceans. It inhabits the deep abyssal plain of these seas, being found in depths of between 3000–3700 m. (1640–2022 fathoms). The first known specimens of this species were taken in mid-Pacific at 3750 m. by the British oceanographic expedition on H.M.S. *Challenger*, which sailed in 1872.

In colour it is uniform brown. It has long jaws with fine teeth, and rounded teeth in the roof of the mouth. Its dorsal fin originates just behind the head and joins the anal fin around the tail tip. Its gill openings lie close together and beneath the throat.
S. kaupi KAUP'S DEEP-SEA EEL
80 cm. (31½ in.)
This species is found in the Atlantic Ocean, from the Greenland area, S. to Brazil, and from off Ireland to s. Africa. It is probably equally common across the whole of the Atlantic basin wherever the depth is suitable. Its centre of distribution is believed to be between 800–2000 m. (437–1093 fathoms), but specimens have been taken below 3000 m. (1640 fathoms).

It is a dusky brown eel with dark fins. The head is slender and the jaws long, but its teeth are small and close set, with larger conical teeth on the roof of the mouth.

Synaptura Soleidae
marginata SOLE, TONG 41 cm. (16 in.)
Found only on the Indian Ocean coast of Africa from Knysna to Delagoa Bay in shallow water from 36 m. (20 fathoms) to the shoreline. It moves close inshore into the intertidal region during summer months and can be speared in numbers with a 4–5 pronged fish spear as it lies in the sand. Its flesh is good eating.

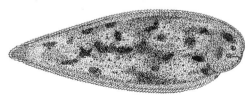

Brownish in colour, well speckled with dark spots, most regular on the fins.
S. orientalis BLACK SOLE 35 cm. (14 in.)
A wide-ranging Indo-W. Pacific species which is found on the coasts of Queensland and New South Wales, through the e. Indian Ocean and n. to China. It is a plentiful fish in parts of this range and is extensively caught in shore seines and by shallow-water trawling. It is very good eating.

Like most soles it lies buried in the sea bed, in this case in muddy estuaries and muddy sand. It feeds on a wide range of bottom-living invertebrates, mainly worms, and small crustaceans.

It is very dark brown, almost black at times but with small creamy-white spots on the eyed side. The blind side is whitish, sometimes clouded with pale yellow. Its eyes are on the right side of the head, its body is very wide, and the dorsal and anal fins are confluent with the tail fin, although separated by a slight notch.

SYNBRANCHIDAE
Widely distributed freshwater fishes found in n. S. America and Central America, W. Africa, and Asia including the Indo-Australian archipelago.

All the members of the family are superficially eel-like in appearance but they are not related to eels. They are slender-bodied, lack both pectoral and pelvic fins, have no fin rays in the dorsal and anal fins, which are reduced to low ridges running along the body to join up with the tail fin. There is a single slit-like opening on the underside of the head which serves as a common gill-opening for the branchial apparatus.

They are air-breathing fishes which often live in stagnant water, absorbing oxygen by gulping air at the surface and holding it in the gill pouch or in a specialized portion of the hind gut. In drought conditions some species burrow into the mud and aestivate.

Some of the species in this family are hermaphrodite. In certain areas all the young fish are females but some as they grow develop male gonads and become functional males. In other areas, in the same species males and females are distinguishable from the earliest ages. See **Monopterus, Ophistosternon, Synbranchus.**

Synbranchus Synbranchidae
marmoratus 1·5 m. (5 ft)
Widely distributed in n. S. America and Central America, from the Argentine to Mexico. It has been reported also from Cuba. It lives in slow-flowing rivers, backwaters and lagoons in which most of the time it lies buried in the soft muddy bottom. During the summer it buries itself and may spend the dry season inactive, but from March to November it is found in open water. Locally it is fished for commercially at this time.

This species has a single gill slit under the head which is not divided internally by a septum into 2 chambers. The whole of the gill chamber is distensible and can be filled with air at the surface. This fish can travel far overland, and will live for a long time out of water.

Its live coloration is very variable, but is usually dark brown or grey-brown with black spots scattered over the back and sides. The belly is yellowish.

Synchiropus Callionymidae
splendidus MANDARINFISH 8 cm. (3 in.)
Found in inshore waters of the Philippine Islands, and on the coral reefs of N. Queensland. This striking dragonet has achieved considerable popularity as an aquarium fish both in Europe and the U.S. For all that, little is known of its life history beyond the fact that it is a bottom-living fish which lies concealed by rocks or coral in depths of around 7 m. (4 fathoms). Observers have noted that it gives off copious mucus from the skin which smells strongly and has a bad taste; it is suggested

that the brilliant coloration is an advertisement of a noxious taste. **430**

SYNGNATHIDAE
The family of the seahorses and pipefishes, worldwide in its distribution in tropical and warm-temperate oceans. Most species are found in inshore waters and shallow seas down to depths of at most 90 m. (50 fathoms), although 1–2 species are found at the surface of the open ocean, and a number of pipefishes have colonized freshwaters.

All the members of the family have segmented bodies, formed by a bony armour beneath the skin. All have tubular snouts with a small mouth, and characteristic tufted lobed gills. Because of the general rigidity imposed by the body armour, body movement is minimal, and locomotion is effected by means of gentle wave-like motion of the fins. It follows that all the pipefishes and seahorses are slow-moving animals, adept at concealing themselves, and living a low-key existence, preying on small planktonic crustaceans, and animal larvae. They are, however, a successful fish family in that they are widely spread and numerous species exist. See **Amphelikturus, Dorichthys, Doryrhamphus, Dunckerocampus, Entelurus, Hippocampus, Nerophis, Phycodurus, Phyllopteryx, Syngnathoides, Syngnathus.**

Syngnathoides Syngnathidae
biaculeatus 25 cm. (10 in.)
An Indo-Pacific species of wide distribution which is found from the Red Sea and e. coasts of Africa to Australia, China, and Japan. It has a very characteristic body shape, with the tail shorter than the body, without a tail fin and capable of wrapping itself around an object. The body is triangular in cross-section, the back narrow and the belly broad. In the male the belly is covered with soft skin on which the eggs are deposited and where they develop not covered by any skin fold.

It is pale green or brown, sometimes with brown spots. It is a relatively sedentary pipefish and lives in shallow water amongst algae. Reputedly, it was valued to a considerable extent in China as medicine.

Syngnathus Syngnathidae
acus GREAT PIPEFISH 30 cm. (12 in.)
This species is the largest of the common European pipefishes and it is found from the Norwegian coast s. to Portugal. It also occurs throughout the Mediterranean and the Adriatic where the populations differ slightly from the Atlantic form and have been recognized as distinct subspecies. It is also reported in s. African waters.

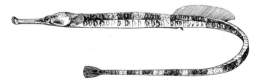

It lives mainly on sandy and muddy bottoms in moderately shallow water down to depths of 15 m. (8 fathoms) but rarely shallower than 3 m. (1½ fathoms). It is not normally found between tide marks. It is occasionally found in estuaries. Its food consists mainly of small crustaceans, mostly copepods, amphipods, and larval decapods, but some young fishes are eaten as well.

Breeding takes place from May to August at which time most mature males will have enlarged brood pouches containing developing eggs. The broodpouch in this genus is a double fold of skin arising from the sides of the anterior tail and meeting in the mid-line. The young, when finally released from the pouch, are perfectly formed and about 30 mm. (1¼ in.) long.

This pipefish is a warm brown above, creamy below.

S. pelagicus SARGASSUM PIPEFISH
16 cm. (6½ in.)
Recorded from the surface waters of the open seas in the Atlantic, Mediterranean, Indian, and w. Pacific oceans. It is only found in the tropical and warm-temperate zones; in the w. Atlantic, for example, it is recorded from the Gulf of Maine to n. Argentina including the Gulf of Mexico. It is usually found living in the floating sargassum seaweed.

It is slender-bodied with distinct tail and pectoral fins, its tail rings are rather rounded and number 33–34. Its live colours are variable but it is usually dark greeny-brown, with the sides marked with white lines, one per segment, margined with black.

S. pulchellus 15 cm. (6 in.)
Found in W. African freshwater and brackish water habitats, especially in the Congo and Ogowe areas. It has been imported to Europe for keeping in aquaria and has proved very successful as a pet fish.

As with other members of the genus *Syngnathus* the tail fin is well developed, the body is hexagonal in cross-section, and the male has a post-anal brood pouch with fleshy skin-folds in which the eggs develop. **236**

S. rousseau CARIBBEAN PIPEFISH
22 cm. (8½ in.)
Found on sandy bottoms especially those on which turtle grass is abundant; less often amongst algae. It is confined to the Caribbean Sea, s. to Surinam.

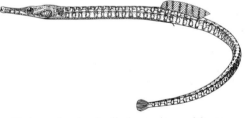

It is a slender-bodied species, with conspicuous tail and pectoral fins; the snout is long. Its colouring above is light brown, the belly creamy with numerous small white spots spreading upwards on the sides.

SYNODONTIDAE
The lizardfishes found in shallow tropical and warm-temperate seas in all oceans belong to this family. They deserve this common name as they look singularly reptilian with heavy shiny scales on the body, a broad bony head, pointed snout, and long jaws. The jaws are armed with long sharp teeth in dense rows. They have a single, rayed dorsal fin almost midway along the back, and most have a small adipose dorsal fin close to the tail. The pelvic fins are large.

Their lizard-like appearance is heightened by the general habit of these fishes of lying close to the bottom, propped up at an angle on their pelvic fins.

All lizardfishes have rather unusual planktonic post-larvae, dissimilar to the adults in body form, being very elongate, scaleless, and transparent. They have obvious and distinctive black blotches on the belly and sides, and sometimes on the back; the shape, number, and position of these are important identifying features. See **Bathysaurus, Saurida, Synodus, Trachinocephalus.**

Synodontis Mochokidae
alberti 16 cm. (6½ in.)
Found only in the freshwaters of the Congo, and not well known even there. In body form it is typical of its family, a high dorsal fin, a long adipose fin, and heavily armoured head. In this species, however, the dorsal spine is not serrated on the front edge, and the barbels, which are simple, are very long. It is a popular aquarium fish. **159**

S. batensoda 25 cm. (10 in.)
Fairly widely distributed in central and w. Africa, from the Nile basin, Lake Chad, Senegal, Nigeria, and the Gambia River.

It is a short deep-bodied *Synodontis*, which has a rather high adipose fin, and much branched (feathered) barbels on the lower jaw, while the barbels on the upper jaw have only a slight membrane attached to one side. Sooty black on the belly, the sides and back are brownish grey; the tail and anal fins are spotted.

This species frequently swims upside-down (hence the reversal of the normal colouring). It is found chiefly in swamps, and feeds mainly on insect larvae and plankton. It is also said to eat mud, which seems improbable.

In Nigeria this is the most important member of the family as a commercial fish; it is locally valuable elsewhere. Small specimens are imported as aquarium fish.

S. flavitaeniatus 19 cm. (7½ in.)
A catfish which is found widely distributed in the River Congo basin, being found both in the main river and its tributaries.

In body form it is typical of most of the African *Synodontis* species, but it has a pair of large barbels on the upper jaw which have fine branches running along the outer edge. **160**

S. nigriventris UPSIDE-DOWN CATFISH
6 cm. (2½ in.)
A catfish which habitually swims with its belly upwards. This habit is common in the family as an occasional posture but in *S. nigriventris* it is its normal position. The usual obliterative coloration pattern (dark on the back, light on the belly) is reversed.

This habit is presumably due to its stable diet of encrusting algae growing on the undersides of leaves of water plants. It has a rather restricted distribution being found in streams in central Congo. It has been widely imported to both Europe and the U.S. as an aquarium fish, and is deservedly popular. **161**

S. schall 40 cm. (16 in.)
Widely distributed in Africa, from the Nile to Senegal and Nigeria, Lake Chad, Lake Albert and Lake Rudolf. In body form typical of all *Synodontis* species, except that in this case the

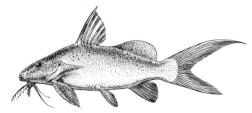

maxillary barbel is long, and single, while those on the lower jaw have short branches. The bony plate behind the head is long and pointed. Adult fish, which may weigh more than 1 kg. (2·2 lb.), are olive brown above, lighter below, with irregular spots on the body; young specimens are marbled with brown, and have yellowish markings on the head.

This catfish is found in both deep and shallow water in Lake Albert. Its food consists of molluscs, insect larvae, and small fishes. It is often imported as an aquarium fish.

Synodus Synodontidae
A genus of lizardfish found in shallow tropical seas. The illustrated specimen has not been identified. **46**
S. intermedius SAND DIVER 45 cm. (18 in.)
A sand diver is a typical member of the family, with a rather slender, rounded body, a moderately large head with long, many-toothed jaws. It is a yellowish brown with dark bars across the back and sides; faint yellowish lines run lengthwise along the body, and it has pale orange marks between the bars. The ventral and tail fins are pale orange.

It is one of the largest lizardfishes and the most abundant species in the W. Indies. It ranges in the w. Atlantic from Bermuda, and the Carolinas, S. to Brazil and is found throughout the Caribbean and the Gulf of Mexico. It is common in shallow water on sandy bottoms close to boulders or reef formations. It has the habit of propping itself up on its pelvic fins, darting away if disturbed and burrowing swiftly in the sand.
S. lucioceps CALIFORNIA LIZARDFISH
63 cm. (25 in.)
This lizardfish is known only from the Californian area, and it is the only member of the family common there, although other species are found in the e. Pacific S. of California. It is also one of the largest of the family, attaining a weight of about 1·8 kg. (4 lb.).

It is a moderately deep-water fish found between 18–46 m. (10–25 fathoms), although young fish live near the surface in the plankton over deep water. It is believed to spawn during the summer months, when adult fish have been observed to congregate on sandy patches. It is largely a fish-eater, although occasionally it takes small squids.

In body shape it is much like other lizardfishes, the sharply pointed, rather triangular head, and large shiny scales being distinctive. Its jaws are long, and possess many needle-sharp teeth. It is dull brown.
S. synodus RED LIZARDFISH, ROCKSPEAR
32 cm. (13 in.)
The red lizardfish is an Atlantic species, found on both sides in coastal waters. In the w. Atlantic it is common from Florida and the Bahamas, throughout the Gulf of Mexico and the W. Indies to Uruguay. In the Bahamas it is the most common member of the family, and although it is sometimes found in shallow

inshore water, it is most abundant in deep water close to reefs and coral heads.

It is a rather heavy-bodied lizardfish, light olive-brown, with a series of dark green-brown bars across the back and sides. Ventrally it is a silvery white, but the tail fin is marked with reddish bands. This fish usually has a small dark spot on the tip of the snout.

T

Tachysurus Ariidae
feliceps BARBEL, SEA BARBEL
51 cm. (20 in.)
A marine catfish found around the coasts of s. Africa, especially in estuaries. Its coloration is variable, mainly bronzy brown with some iridescent sheen, lighter on the belly.

It is moderately stout-bodied in form with a flattened head, a high dorsal fin which is armed with a stout serrated spine, as are the pectoral fins. It has an adipose fin; the tail fin is forked.

Like other members of the family, the male of this species incubates the eggs in its mouth, and the young fish for a short while. The spines on the fins are covered with a toxic mucus and wounds can be painful and even dangerous.

Tachysurus is used by some authors in preference to *Arius*.

TADPOLE
CLINGFISH see **Arcos macrophthalmus**
MADTOM see **Noturus gyrinus**
SCULPIN see **Psychrolutes paradoxus**

Taenioconger Congridae
A genus of garden eel. The species illustrated has not been identified. **23**
T. chapmani RIBBON CONGER
70 cm. (27½ in.)
An eel which is found only in the vicinity of the Philippine Islands, although a similar species has been found in the Gulf of California. It is probably a burrowing species but no observations are available on its life history.

It is very long and slender, the eyes relatively large but said to be covered by skin, the mouth oblique, and the tail blunt. Unlike several of the burrowing eels, it has well developed pectoral fins.
T. digueti GARDEN EEL 91 cm. (3 ft)
A species found in the Gulf of California at depths of 3–41 m. (2–22 fathoms) on sandy bottoms. This garden eel lives in colonies, each individual in its own burrow, well spaced away from its neighbour. Divers have recorded them in daylight lying with the head and forebody protruding from 20–40 cm. (8–16 in.) above the sand, but as they are approached sliding down into their burrow.

They are only found where the current is moderate and they feed by snapping up individual planktonic organisms as they drift on the current. The eye is moderately large, as in the mouth, and there is no doubt that they pick their food out by sight. At night they retreat into their burrows.

Taeniodes Gobioididae
cirratus 30 cm. (12 in.)
Found in the Indo-Pacific, allegedly from Zanzibar, India and across to the Philippines

and Japan, although there is the possibility that other species have been involved in some of these records.

It is a striking-looking fish with a very elongate eel-like body. The dorsal fin runs from just behind the head and is joined to the tail fin; the first 6 rays are unbranched and well-spaced the remainder are branched. The head is broad, the lips thick and the lower lip fringed with distinct short barbels. The eyes are minute, almost certainly the fish is blind, and the sensory canals on the head are well developed. It is a pale flesh colour in life.

It is usually found in shallow, inshore waters, often in estuaries buried in burrows in soft mud.

Taeniophorus Eutaeniophoridae
festivus 7 cm. (2¾ in.)
This is an extremely slender-bodied member of a slim-bodied family. In the larval stage this fish has an enormously long streamer from the middle rays of the tail fin. Despite the small size of the specimens known, and their general immature appearance, it has not so far proved possible to allocate them to any other known fish family. They may well prove to be the young of some other fish.

All the specimens have been taken in the open sea, and have been distributed over all the major oceans in the tropical zone, except for the e. Pacific Ocean. It is believed to feed entirely on copepod crustaceans.

Taeniura Dasyatidae
lymma RIBBONTAIL RAY 2·4 m. (8 ft)
This distinctive stingray occurs through almost the whole tropical Indo-Pacific including the Red Sea. The tail, which is longer than the body, is flattened and ribbon-like, with 2 (sometimes one) long spines.

On the n. Australian coast this is a common stingray in shallow water and the lagoons of the reefs. It feeds on a variety of crustaceans and worms. It is not particularly heavy for its elongate body and tail account for its considerable length. It is, however, a dangerous species for its long tail spines are placed well along its muscular tail. **11**

TAIL-LIGHT FILEFISH see **Cantherhines pullus**
TAILSPOT CLIMBING PERCH see **Ctenopoma kingsleyae**
TAILOR see **Pomatomus saltatrix**
TAIMEN see **Hucho taimen**
TAKABE see **Labracoglossa argentiventris**
TALANG see **Chorinemus lysan**
TALKING
CATFISH see **Acanthodoras spinosissimus**
GOURAMI see **Trichopsis vittatus**
TAMPAR see **Pseudorhombus arsius**
TANDA-TANDA see **Lutjanus kasmira**

Tandanus Plotosidae
tandanus FRESHWATER CATFISH
61 cm. (2 ft)
Found only in the freshwaters of S. and e.

Australia; it occurs in the Murray-Darling River system as well as in some rivers in Victoria, New South Wales, and Queensland.

The arrangement of fins is typical of the family, and the sharp spines of dorsal and pectoral fins can inflict painful wounds. It is dull brown or olive-green above, paler on the belly; the upper surface is mottled.

It makes an excellent pet fish for the aquarium, and its flesh is said to be good to eat, but

not often marketed on account of its unhandsome appearance.

Tandya Opistognathidae
maculata SPECKLED PUG 43 cm. (17 in.)
A Pacific species which has been found in Australian tropical waters of N. Queensland and the N. Territory, as well as the Aru Islands. It is reddish brown, spotted with dark blue on the body, smaller spots on the head; a large dark spot beneath the pectoral fins. Like the other members of the family its jaws are very large.

This species was long ago reported by native pearl-fishers to make burrows in the sand amongst sea-fans from which it darted out to seize food items, returning to its burrow after each sally. This behaviour corresponds to that observed in related species in the W. Indies.

TANG see Acanthuridae
TANG,
 BLUE see **Acanthurus coeruleus**
 CONVICT see **Acanthurus triostegus**

Tanichthys Cyprinidae
albonubes WHITE CLOUD MOUNTAIN MINNOW 4 cm. (1½ in.)
A very beautiful little fish which originated in China, in Canton Province near the White Cloud Mountains – hence its name. It is also said to have been named for a local boy scout called Tan!

It is a relatively hardy fish able to withstand considerable variation in temperature. It spawns in captivity, shedding its eggs on plants; it is not infrequent for the adults to eat their eggs however well they are fed. **142**

TAPER-TAIL ANCHOVY see **Coilia quadragesimalis**
TAPIRFISH, SHORTSPINE see **Macdonaldia rostrata**

Taractes Bramidae
asper 45 cm. (18 in.)
A little-known bramid which is probably worldwide in its distribution. Larvae and young fishes have been found in the tropical Atlantic (off the W. Indies), the Indian Ocean (off Madagascar), and the Pacific (California, Formosa and the Philippines). Adults are more rarely seen, but have been found widely in the N. Atlantic and N. Pacific. The young differ so markedly from the adults that for long the 2 were regarded as different species. An adult is illustrated.

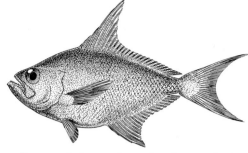

It seems to be nowhere abundant and relatively few specimens have been captured.

This species retains the juvenile spiny scales in part throughout life. Its body form is distinctive; its coloration generally warm brown with a golden or coppery sheen on the sides.

TARARIRA see **Hoplias malabaricus**

Tarpon Megalopidae
atlanticus TARPON 2·4 m. (8 ft)
This famous marine game fish of the tropical Atlantic is probably one of the best known of anglers' fishes. It is found on both sides of the Atlantic, along the American coast from Nova Scotia to Brazil and in the Gulf of Mexico, but it is not often seen n. of N. Carolina.

It is a huge fish, specimens of more than 2·4 m. which weighed around 159 kg. (350 lb.) have been reported.

In colour the tarpon is silvery with big irregular scales, and a dark blue back. Other distinguishing features include the jutting lower jaw and the elongate last ray of the dorsal fin.

The tarpon breeds well out to sea, and is an incredibly prolific fish, a 6 ft (1·8 m.) long female containing about 12 million eggs. The larvae are thin and transparent, totally unlike the adult, and drift into inshore waters before they change into recognizable young tarpon. They live in the littoral zone, often in salt marshes, swamps, and estuaries. Often such areas are lacking in dissolved oxygen and the young fish can be seen at the surface gulping, a direct connection leading from the gullet to the swimbladder which is modified for breathing air. Such a habitat, unpromising as it sounds, has the advantage of being relatively free of predators. Adult tarpon tend to live near the open sea.

TARPON see **Tarpon atlanticus**
TARPON,
 OX-EYE see **Megalops cyprinoides**
 PACIFIC see **Megalops cyprinoides**
TARWHINE see **Rhabdosargus sarba**
TASSEL-SNOUTED FLATHEAD see **Thysanophrys cirronasus**
TASMANIAN
 CLINGFISH see **Aspasmogaster tasmaniensis**
 TRUMPETER see **Latris lineata**

Taurulus Cottidae
bubalis SEA SCORPION or BULLHEAD 17 cm. (7 in.)
A European marine sculpin, which is found

along the coast of nw. Europe from Biscay to Norway. It is essentially an inshore and littoral fish, but is virtually confined to rocky shores and dense algal cover. It feeds on a wide variety of crustaceans, polychaete worms, and fishes.

It spawns in early spring from February to April; the eggs are deposited in clumps in rock crevices and other sheltered places.

This is the commonest marine bullhead in Europe. It is identified by its very long spine on the preoperculum and the small fleshy flap on the corner of the upper jaw. The body is scaleless but the lateral line is spiny. Its coloration is cryptic, usually greens and browns depending on the area in which the individual is living.

Telmatherina Atherinidae
ladigesi CELEBES RAINBOWFISH
7 cm. (2¾ in.)
Found only in the freshwaters of the Celebes, and the interior of Macassar.

The body is elongate and rather compressed; 2 dorsal fins, the first composed of short slender spines, the second of long rays which in the male are very elongate and have tattered-looking fin membranes. The male's anal fin rays are elongate too. It is an extremely attractive fish which has become a popular aquarium species in Europe. It needs a large aquarium with plenty of sunshine and fine-leaved plants. Spawning takes place after vigorous driving by the male, the eggs being shed on the plants. The young hatch out in 8–11 days and generally keep near the surface. **215**

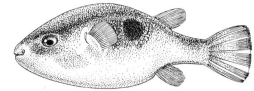

RED-PHANTOM see **Megalamphodus sweglesi**
ROSY see **Hyphessobrycon rosaceus**
RUMMY-NOSED see **Hemigrammus rhodostomus**
SERPA see **Hyphessobrycon serpae**
TWO-SPOT see **Astyanax bimaculatus**
YELLOW see **Hyphessobrycon bifasciatus**

TETRAGONURIDAE

A small family of oceanic fishes found in tropical and warm-temperate seas. The family is widely distributed in the w. Mediterranean, Atlantic, Pacific, and Indian oceans. Three species only are recognized but the characters that distinguish them are variable and more species may need to be acknowledged in time. The family is related to the Stromatiidae and Centrolophidae.

The tetragonurids are very distinctive. They have a long, cylindrical body with an elongate tail, the body is covered with large, rough-keeled scales which form distinctive keels at the base of the tail fin. The snout is large, the head profile curved, the jaws having very specialised knife-like teeth. See **Tetragonurus**.

Tetragonurus   Tetragonuridae
  cuvieri SMALLEYE SQUARE-TAIL
61 cm. (2 ft)
A widely distributed oceanic fish found in the Mediterranean, the e. Atlantic, the N. Pacific, and off Australia and New Zealand. Despite its wide distribution its biology is not well known. The young fish are known to associate with medusae, and occasionally other planktonic animals. Adults are free-swimming oceanic fishes, but at all ages they feed on jellyfishes and comb-jellies (ctenophores). Its flesh is claimed to be poisonous in the Mediterranean due to the venom of ingested medusae but this has been disproven in other areas.

The square-tail is frequently eaten by tuna and other fishes and other specimens have been taken at the surface in gill-nets. Adult fish are probably bathypelagic, and their sombre coloration appears to support this.

It is immediately distinguished from all but its closest relatives by its body form, especially the long, narrow tail and the heavy keeled scales laid down in a regular spiral about the body.

Tetraodon   Tetraodontidae
  cutcutia COMMON PUFFERFISH
15 cm. (6 in.)
Native to the freshwaters and slightly brackish waters of India, Burma, and the Malaysian Archipelago. It is a common fish in many of the larger rivers and backwaters of this area, feeding on bottom-living invertebrates and occasionally small fishes. It is strikingly coloured and has been imported to Europe as an aquarium fish for a long time.

The skin is leathery and lacks any skin spines. Its back is dark green, the sides yellowish to grey, and the belly white; the back is patched with irregular golden yellow blotches.

It inflates itself very readily when disturbed,

forming an almost spherical body. This species is one of the few pufferfishes which has been bred in captivity. The male and female are said to circle one another on the bottom, the female eventually shedding her 200–300 clear eggs on the gravel. They are guarded by the male who literally lies on them to conceal them from predators. They hatch in 6–8 days and the young are still sheltered by the male in a shallow trench for a further period.

T. lineatus NILE PUFFERFISH 40 cm. (16 in.)
Widely distributed in the Nile, and represented in w. Africa by several, possibly sub-specifically distinct forms, amongst them *T. l. strigosus* of the Niger basin. These forms are all much alike, round-bodied, with small rounded fins, and the body except for the snout covered with minute spines. Like all pufferfishes it can inflate itself with water or air into a nearly spherical shape, disallowing the tail.

It is dark grey or yellowish brown on the back, white or yellow on the belly, with 6 or more dark oblique bands running across the upper side and back. The fins are yellow.

This species is often imported to Europe as an aquarium fish and makes an engaging, but rather quarrelsome pet-fish. In Africa, large specimens are often eaten, care being taken to avoid the poisonous entrails, although dark rumours abound that its liver is used as a poison, and the dried skin used for covering drums.

T. mbu 75 cm. (29½ in.)
A pufferfish found in freshwater in the Middle and Lower Congo River. It has become quite popular as an aquarium fish, although only small specimens can be kept satisfactorily.

It is a long, rather slender-bodied fish, with a narrow tail and long tail fin; the body except for the underside of the tail and head is closely set with small spines. Small specimens are yellowish to orange with large black to dark brown blotches, and 1–2 lengthwise bands on the tail. Adults are the same colour but the blotches break up into dense spots and a maze of brown wavy lines, tending to run lengthwise down the tail. The underside is clear yellow.

As with marine species this fish inflates itself with air or water. It feeds mainly on snails and other invertebrates. **494**

T. miurus 10 cm. (4 in.)
A small species found in freshwater in the Middle and Lower Congo river in W. Africa. It is occasionally kept in aquaria and makes an interesting, if not very active, pet fish.

Its habits are dissimilar to other freshwater pufferfishes in that it is cryptically coloured, changing its background colour to suit the colour and texture of the river bed. It is relatively flattened from above and buries itself in the soft mud bottom where it lies in wait for passing small fishes, on which it pounces, frequently biting them in half.

It can be identified by its flattened back, with eyes pointing upwards, the snout being tuberous, the head is broad and flattened. Its colouring is indescribable, but the underside is usually clear and the back spotted. **495**

TETRAODONTIDAE

The family of the pufferfishes, also called toad-fish, or toados in Australia, tobies in S. Africa, fugu in Japan, and often just puffers elsewhere. They are able to inflate themselves with either air or water like a balloon; air-filled they float helpless at the surface. Most species also have plentiful spines buried partially in the skin, which, when they are inflated, stick out like a minor pin-cushion. It is curious too that a group with 2 such well-developed defensive devices should also be acutely poisonous if eaten, but none of these deterrents is wholly effective, for many do get eaten by other fishes.

Their use as food for humans is restricted by their toxic properties. It is established that the gonads (especially when nearly ripe), the liver, the gut, and blood are especially toxic and that the flesh of many is wholesome, but occasional cases of poisoning occur when only the flesh has been eaten so there is always an element of risk. However, in Japan the various fugus are particular delicacies and many are eaten, prepared by specially trained cooks who are required to give proof of their skill in preparation. This notwithstanding, most of the research into the causes and effects of tetrotoxin poisoning has been undertaken in Japan.

Pufferfishes are found in all tropical and warm temperate seas, and have invaded freshwaters in many parts of the world (being the only group of plectognath fishes to have done so). Most are stout-bodied, rounded fishes with small fins, moderately large eyes, and small slit-like gill openings. The great majority are well-covered with spines in the skin, a few species are naked, but a number have clear patches of skin. All have 4 teeth in the jaws (hence *Tetraodon*) the pair in each jaw forming a parrot-like beak.

Pufferfishes in general are shallow water inshore fishes, found around reefs, in sea grass beds, and in estuaries. A few are found living a pelagic life. They are not powerful swimmers, but propel themselves by means of gently waving dorsal, anal, and sometimes pectoral fins. They would seem stately fish if it were not for their clownish habits of puffing themselves up to twice life-size. See **Amblyrhynchotes, Arothron, Canthigaster, Lagocephalus, Sphoeriodes, Tetraodon, Torquigener.**

Tetrapturus   Istiophoridae
  albidus WHITE MARLIN 2·5 m. (8 ft)
The white marlin is well known in the coastal waters of the w. Atlantic and ranges as far N. as Nova Scotia and s. to Brazil. In this area it is a well-known sporting fish. A very similar, if not identical fish, is caught occasionally on the N. African and Spanish coasts and, exceptionally, as far N. as Biscay, and it seems reasonable to conclude that it is found throughout the tropical Atlantic.

It is a slender-bodied marlin with a relatively low body weight, which may attain around 70 kg. (154 lb.). It is caught in numbers on the American coast, as far N. as New York and Massachusetts each summer. Its presence there is due to a warm-season n. migration some 1·6–40 km. (1–25 miles) offshore.

It is distinguished by its relatively small size, by the rounded lobe of the first dorsal fin and its curved pectoral fins. Its back is medium blue, the sides conspicuously lighter and the belly white; faint lighter blue bars run across the back and upper sides.

T. audax STRIPED MARLIN 3 m. (10 ft)
The striped marlin is found throughout the warmer waters of the Indian and Pacific oceans. It ranges from the E. African coast all the way across to the w. coast of America, and from Japan to New Zealand. It is possibly more common in the warm-temperate rather than the tropical waters.

Like most members of the family it feeds primarily upon fishes, with squids occasionally abundant in its diet. The fishes it eats are mainly those which are locally abundant, pilchards, flying fishes, and sauries (*Scomberesox*) being especially favoured. Specimens are occasionally captured which have been feeding on numerous species of deep water fish, evidently its depth range is considerable.

The striped marlin is one of the most valuable of the family to the world's fisheries. Its flesh is of very good flavour and as in the Indo-Pacific it is the most common billfish it is widely fished for. As a sport fish it is well regarded, although it is not one of the very heavy species (maximum weights approach 226 kg. (500 lb.)); it fights well and leaps spectacularly.

It is typically dark steely-blue on the back and top of the head fading to white below. The sides of the body are marked with a variable number, around 15, of prominent white or pale blue vertical stripes. The fins are dark except for the first dorsal and anal, which are in life cobalt blue.

Tetrosomus Ostraciontidae
gibbosus BOXFISH 30 cm. (12 in.)
An Indo-Pacific species of wide distribution being found in tropical waters from the Red Sea, Zanzibar, the E. African coast across to Japan and the Philippines. It is a shallow-water fish found on reefs and in sea grass beds in considerable numbers.

It is distinguished from other boxfishes by the high pointed ridge on the back which terminates in a blunt compressed spine, it also has a pair of upward-pointing spines on the front of the head, and 5 blunt, curved spines along the lower ridge of the body. Its colouring is very variable, usually brownish with light spots at the centres of the hexagonal body plates; the fins are usually clear or faint brown. **486**

Thalassoma Labridae
bifasciatum BLUEHEAD WRASSE
15 cm. (6 in.)
An abundant fish in the w. Atlantic where it is found from Bermuda, Florida, and the Bahamas s. to the S. American coast. It is found in the S. in the Gulf of Mexico and the W. Indies where it is one of the most abundant reef fishes. It feeds on a wide variety of small bottom-living animals, zooplankton, and at times on the external parasites of other fishes.

This wrasse occurs in 2 very distinct colour phases. Most specimens are yellowish, the upper half of the body being yellow, the lower half white; a distinct dark spot is present on the front of the dorsal fin. A small proportion of the population has a bright blue head, a double black saddle mark on the back, greenish body and long tail fin rays. These are males,

and it is suggested that they may be sexually reversed females, for their spawning behaviour differs from the yellow males in that they spawn individually with a single female while yellow phase fish spawn as a group. Only the yellow fish pick parasites. **411**

T. lunare RAINBOWFISH, MOON WRASSE
25 cm. (10 in.)
A widespread Indo-Pacific species, found from the E. African coast across to n. Australia and the w. Pacific. It is found in small schools in tidal pools and in deeper water off the reef edge.

Its colouring is remarkable although very variable. The most common colour form has the head a rich violet with several lengthwise green stripes; the body is a dark greenish blue, each scale edged with a vertical red line. The fins are orange and blue except for the tail fin which is yellowish. **412**

Thalassophryne Batrachoididae
maculosa VENOMOUS TOADFISH, SAPO CANO 19 cm. (7½ in.)
The venomous toadfish is one of several species (2 genera) of this family of bottom-living, inshore fishes found in the tropical waters of both coasts of Central and S. America. They have the most highly developed stinging apparatus in the fish world, the 2 dorsal fin spines and the spines on the gill covers being hollow and leading directly to the venom glands. These fish lie buried in sand, sometimes with only the eyes exposed and are thus likely to be trodden upon by bathers or fishermen. Wounds from the spines cause severe pain.

This species is known only along the Caribbean coastline of S. America from Trinidad w. in depths of 30–60 cm. (1–2 ft) down to 182 m. (100 fathoms). It is a relatively small member of the family, with a flattened head, and broad fleshy pectoral fins. The venomous dorsal spines are well developed. Its coloration is variable with age, but is usually dull brown, with numerous spots and blotches.

Thaleichthys Osmeridae
pacificus EULACHON, CANDLEFISH
30 cm. (12 in.)
A small fish, distinguished by its large mouth, short pectoral fins, and curious concentric striations on the gill covers. It is bluish brown dorsally, whitish ventrally, with unspotted fins. The eulachon is found on the w. coast of N. America from California n. to the Bering Sea and the Pribiloff Islands.

It is an anadromous fish, spending most of its life in the coastal waters, but running up rivers for a short distance to spawn. The eggs are shed over sand or gravel, and have a double covering, the outer of which adheres to the bottom, breaking soon after but forming an anchor for the inner membrane to which it is fastened. The young move out to sea soon after hatching.

The eulachon is a very important link in the food chains of the e. N. Pacific. They feature in the diet of salmon, sturgeon, and seals, and locally they are caught for human food. The name eulachon is a Chinook Indian name, and it is called candlefish, for the Indians used to use them lighted and tied to a stick as candles; so oily is their flesh that they burn steadily when dried.

Thaumanichthys Oneirodidae
plagidostomus 8·5 cm. (3½ in.)
Apparently widely distributed in the Indian and Atlantic oceans although known only from 6 specimens. Adult females are quite distinctive, having a flattened compressed head, and and very thorny skin. In this species the luminous lure is minute and placed below the protruding upper jaw in the mid-line directly in front of the mouth. As in other deep-sea anglers the mouth is large and well-equipped with teeth.

Larval specimens have been described as having rounded bodies and thin, gelatinous skin, the underlying tissue being pigmented. Immature males have larger nostrils than the females.

Thayeria Characidae
boehlkei PENGUINFISH 8 cm. (3 in.)
This characin always swims with its head pointing obliquely upwards. It is kept in aquaria, and has been known to spawn in captivity. It is said to spawn in twilight, the brownish eggs being scattered over the gravel. They hatch in 18–24 hours at a temperature of 26°C. It is a renowned jumper, capable of leaping well clear of the aquarium if it is not kept covered. **87**

T. obliquua PENGUINFISH 8 cm. (3 in.)
All the members of the genus *Thayeria* which are commonly kept as aquarium fishes have a lengthwise dark stripe along the tail extending onto the lower tail fin.

The penguinfish occurs widely in the lower Amazon basin. It has long been a popular aquarium fish, and adds considerable interest due to its habit of adopting an inclined, head upwards, posture. It has been bred in captivity, the female producing upwards of 1000 brown eggs, which hatch after only 12 hours. The eggs are scattered over the bottom of the aquarium, which should be densely planted. The sexes appear to be identical. **88**

Theragra Gadidae
chalcogramma WALLEYE POLLOCK
91 cm. (3 ft)
A N. Pacific codfish of wide distribution from central California n. through the Bering Sea, in the Sea of Okhotsk, and the Sea of Japan. It is not especially associated with the sea bed as are other cods, but is found from the surface to around 366 m. (200 fathoms) mainly in midwater. It feeds on a wide variety of invertebrates, particularly crustaceans, and small fishes, including young salmon.

It is a rather slender-bodied fish with a large head, 3 widely spaced fins on the back, and 2 anal fins. The eye is relatively large, the lower jaw prolonged, and the chin barbel is very short. It is olive-green to brown above with numerous blotches; ventrally lighter.

The walleye pollock forms a valuable fishery, used for fish meal, industrial products, and for food. It appears not to be much appreciated as a food fish on the American coast, but Russian, Japanese, and Korean landings are very heavy, and have greatly increased in recent years.

Therapon   Theraponidae
 bidyanus see **Bidyanus bidyanus**
 jarbua TIGERFISH, CRESCENT PERCH,
ZEBRAFISH 30 cm. (12 in.)
This is one of the most widely distributed and
better known members of the family. It is
found from the Red Sea and E. coast of Africa
to n. Australia, the Philippines and s. China.
It is abundant in marine habitats in inshore
waters, but is equally at home in estuaries and
extends into almost freshwater.

It is a very active fish, schooling when young
but more solitary as an adult. It is a popular
salt water aquarium fish, very tough and
peaceable when young, but inclined to be
aggressive as it grows. It is predatory, the
larger fishes eating any small fish available.

The colour pattern of dark curved lines
along the back and sides makes it very distinctive. Its background colour is brownish grey,
the sides silvery.

It is used as a food fish in Japan, but rarely
elsewhere. It is well-known for its ability to
produce quite loud noises with its swim-
bladder.

THERAPONIDAE
A family of fishes similar to the sea basses (Serranidae) and widely distributed in the Indo-
Pacific from the E. African coast and the Red
Sea, to Australasia, and the w. Pacific islands.
Mostly fishes of a moderate size are found in
the sea, although many species penetrate into,
or live entirely in, fresh water. Some grow to
a moderate size and are locally valuable food
fishes, others are small and popular in marine
aquariums.

They are distinguished from the sea basses
by the number of dorsal spines (11–14), the
small mouth, and numerous teeth, each tri-
lobed or serrated, in fixed rows in the jaws. See
Bidyanus, Helotes, Pelates, Therapon.

THICK-LIPPED
 GOURAMI see **Colisa labiosa**
 MULLET see **Crenimugil labrosus**
THICKBACK SOLE see **Microchirus**
    variegatus

Thoracocharax   Gasteropelecidae
 stellatus 7 cm. (2¾ in.)
The flying hatchetfishes of the genus *Thoracocharax* are distinguished from the other genera in the family by differing tooth formation,
by the larger scales with radiating lines, and
by the greater number of dorsal and anal fin
rays. Otherwise they have a similar body form,
an almost straight dorsal profile, and a deeply-
curved belly. The pectoral fins are large and
well developed, and an adipose fin is present.

This species is yellowish to pale olive, with a
brilliant silvery sheen. The fins are clear, with
the exception of the front of the dorsal fin
which has a dark blotch.

It is distributed from Central Brazil to the

Argentine. It appears to be common in these
regions and has been imported as an aquarium
fish.

THORNBACK RAY see **Raja clavata**
THREAD
 EEL see **Serrivomer parabeani**
 HERRING, ATLANTIC see **Opisthonema**
    oglinum
THREAD-FIN
 BUTTERFLYFISH see **Chaetodon auriga**
 SCAT see **Rhinoprenes pentanemus**
THREADFIN see Polynemidae
THREADFIN, GIANT see **Eleutheronema**
    tetradactylum
THREE-BANDED
 BULLFISH see **Heniochus permutatus**
 PENCILFISH see **Nannostomus**
    trifasciatus
THREE-FIN BLENNY see Tripterygiidae
THREE-SPINE STICKLEBACK see
    Gasterosteus aculeatus
THREE-SPOT
 ANOSTOMUS see **Anostomus**
    trimaculatus
 DAMSELFISH see **Eupomacentrus**
    planifrons
 GOURAMI see **Trichogaster**
    trichopterus

Threpterius   Chironemidae
 maculosus SILVERSPOT 33 cm. (13 in.)
Found on the coasts of W. and S. Australia in
relatively shallow water. It is found mainly in
rocky areas, amongst algae, and is occasionally
known, with its relatives, as a kelp-fish.

Its body is bright red, the sides being
covered with dark brown spots and blotches;
the dorsal fin with broken light and dark bands.
A brilliant silver spot on the extreme edge of
the gill cover.

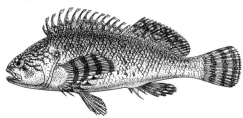

This fish can also be identified by the numerous dorsal spines, 14 in number, with deeply
notched fin membranes; the spines have a deep
groove each side.

The silverspot is occasionally caught by
anglers but has no great value as a game or
food fish.

THRESHER SHARK see **Alopias vulpinus**

Thrissocles   Engraulidae
 setirostris WISKERED ANCHOVY
20 cm. (8 in.)
Members of the genus *Thrissocles,* the wiskered anchovies, are found in the warmer waters
of the Indo-Pacific. *T. setirostris* is widely distributed in the Indian Ocean from e. Africa,
across the E. Indies and in Australian waters.

All the anchovies have overhanging snouts
and long jaws, but in the wiskered anchovy
the upper jaw bone is enormously prolonged
so that its tapering hind end reaches half-way
along the body. It is a greenish yellow in
colour, silvery below but without the prominent silvery side-line of other anchovies.

It is said to make excellent eating and good
bait for other larger fishes.

THUMB, MILLER'S see **Cottus gobio**

Thunnus   Scombridae
 alalunga ALBACORE, LONG-FINNED
TUNNY 130 cm. (51 in.)
The albacore is worldwide in its distribution
in tropical and warm-temperate seas; it also
occurs seasonally in cooler waters. Like many
other tunas it travels in large schools, usually
close to the surface and offshore over the continental shelf. It prefers to stay in the blue

water of the open sea rather than venture into
the silt-laden greenish inshore water. It feeds
on a wide range of surface and mid-water
fishes, including the saury (*Scomberesox*),
clupeoids, and lanternfishes. It also eats squids
and crustaceans in numbers.

In many parts of its range it is immediately
distinguishable by the extreme length of the
pectoral fin (which reaches beyond the anal
fin), but where it occurs it can be confused
with the big-eye tuna, *T. obesus*, small specimens of which have a longish pectoral fin. The
albacore, however, has a slightly shorter head
(it ends before the level of the first dorsal
spines), and the vent is round. Its body is also
deepest at around the mid-point.

Its back is deep blue with bronze tints,
shading to yellowish-blue on the sides, and
cream ventrally. The fins and finlets are dark
except that the trailing edges of the tail fin and
the small finlets are light. There are no conspicuous dark markings on back and sides.

The albacore is possibly the most valuable
commercially exploited tuna. It is captured
virtually throughout its range and although the
best-known and most valuable fishery is that
off California, many minor fisheries exist such
as the French one in the Bay of Biscay. Its
flesh is of very good quality and is canned extensively. Albacore are also famous angling
fishes which attain a weight of 23 kg. (50 lb.)
regularly, although a specimen of 43 kg. (95
lb.) is on record from a commercial longliner.
T. albacares YELLOW-FIN or ALLISON
TUNA 2 m. (6½ ft)
The yellow-fin tuna is a cosmopolitan species
in tropical and warm temperate seas. It occasionally enters cooler waters (one was found
on the N. Wales coast in 1972 – the first
reported from British waters), but is generally
found in water temperatures of 22°–28°C.,
although it can tolerate temperatures as low as
14°C.

It is extensively exploited in the high seas
tunny fishery and recent investigations sug-

gest that some areas (for example parts of the Indian Ocean) have been substantially overfished. It is a migratory species, seasonal in its movements, swimming near the surface especially in the warm season. It is also one of the few large tuna to come close inshore. It feeds on surface-living fishes especially *Scomberesox* and flying-fishes, but also eats many squids and pelagic crustaceans.

Its identification at certain ages is difficult, for the big tunnies are superficially very similar. Its coloration is blue-black on the back, a golden band runs along the midside, but ventrally the body is silvery. The second dorsal, anal, and the finlets behind both fins are strikingly lemon yellow. In large specimens the second dorsal and anal are conspicuously long, forming long curved lobes. Young fish do not have this feature and their identification depends on a combination of rather long pectoral fins, a slightly more slender shape, and lack of striations on the liver. Because of the changes in body form the yellow-fin tuna has been given many scientific names; its synonymy is very involved.

T. maccoyii SOUTHERN BLUE-FIN TUNA 2·4 m. (8 ft)
A large blue-fin tuna which is probably found across the whole of the s. Indo-Pacific. It was first described from Australia where it is well-known as very common around the s. states. More recently it has been found off S. Africa on the Indian Ocean coast, and can be presumed to occur in intermediate seas.

It is closely similar to the Atlantic blue-fin but differs in having many fewer gill rakers (31–40, mean 33·7) on the first gill arch. In general it is otherwise identical with the Atlantic species but has no yellow on the dorsal and anal lobes, although the finlets are usually bright yellow.

Like other large tunas it is an extremely powerful migratory fish which may be found seasonally close to the continental coastline. It is very common off s. Australia and is a potentially valuable fishery resource.

T. obesus BIG-EYE TUNA, BIG-EYE 2·4 m. (7¾ ft)
A large tunny found around the world in tropical and seasonally in warm-temperate seas. Like most of the other members of the genus it is strongly migratory and schools are suspected of travelling hundreds, possibly thousands of miles to seasonal feeding grounds. It is seasonal in its occurrence throughout its range, although it appears to tolerate a rather wide range of temperatures from 13°–27°C.

It feeds on crustaceans, mainly prawns, squids, and whatever fishes are locally common, including sardines, scombroids, hake, and deeper-water fishes. It ranges into deep water during daylight, coming nearer to the surface at night.

It is a very important species to the high-seas tuna fisheries. Caught on floating long-lines and in purse seines, this large species, which may weigh up to 200 kg. (440 lb.), is now fished in almost all seas.

Its identification presents difficulty as there are several other large tuna which resemble it at various growth stages. Its pectoral fin is moderately long (but except when young never as long as *T. alalunga*) and reaches to the level of the second dorsal fin. The body is deepest just behind the head. One of the surest ways of identifying *T. obesus* is that the liver has numerous striations on the ventral surface. Its back is dark blue above, its belly light, neither being marked with dusky lines or blotches.

T. orientalis NORTH PACIFIC BLUE-FIN TUNA 1·5 m. (5 ft)
Widely distributed in the N. Pacific, and the commonest of the large tuna off the Japanese and Korean coast. It also occurs off Hawaii and the n. coasts of Australia, but due to persistent misidentification with *T. maccoyii*, its precise range is difficult to establish. Many authors refer to it by the name of *Kishinoella tonggol*.

Like its relatives it is a migratory, open-seas predator, which ranges the N. Pacific and approaches the coast (although it is rarely found inshore) during the warm season. It feeds on a wide range of fishes including mackerel, flying fishes, and anchovies, and also eats squids and crustaceans.

It has considerable commercial value, especially in Japan where it has long been fished for with long lines, set nets, and recently purse seines, and floating nets. Most productive are warm, still, dark nights when the tuna are close to the surface. Its flesh is eaten raw in Japan; elsewhere it is usually canned.

T. thynnus TUNNY, BLUE-FIN or ATLANTIC BLUE-FIN TUNA 4 m. (13 ft)
The blue-fin tuna is probably the world's largest bony fish although records of maximum length and weight are difficult to verify due to their sheer size. Lengths of 4·26 m. (14 ft) have been reported, as have weights of 907 kg. (2000 lb.).

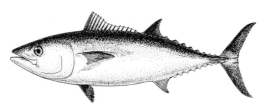

The blue-fin is widely distributed in the Atlantic Ocean; closely related forms occur in the Indian and Pacific oceans. The Atlantic species mingles with one of these only in the region of S. Africa. Its range encompasses the whole of the tropical and warm temperate region, and tuna migrate seasonally into the cooler areas, such as the Norwegian Sea, and off the Nova Scotia coast. It is a strong, swift swimmer which makes vast migrations; fishes tagged off the American coast have been caught in European waters, and there is no reason to doubt that a proportion of the population regularly crosses the N. Atlantic; migrations into S. African waters are equally possible. A substantial migration occurs from Spanish waters, if not the Mediterranean, into the North Sea and Norwegian waters, going N. about the British Isles, and at various periods extensive fisheries existed in both areas. The Norwegian fishery was based on young fish and increased to substantial proportions in the 1960s but crashed suddenly, quite possibly due to overfishing, for the same population was exploited in s. European waters.

Young blue-fins travel in large compact schools near the surface; the adults tend to be solitary or form small schools. They feed indiscriminately on whatever shoaling fish is most abundant locally, most often clupeoids, gadoids, and myctophids, but substantial numbers of squids are eaten, and the young prey on crustaceans. When feeding, blue-fin tuna can be seen breaking the surface with their backs, and the prey-fish leaping, usually accompanied by flocks of fish-eating birds.

Wherever it occurs the blue-fin tuna is fished for either commercially or for sport. In many regions it is a valuable species usually used for canning although locally as in the Mediterranean it is often eaten fresh.

The blue-fin tuna is described as dark blue on the back, white or silvery on the belly, in life separated on the sides by a golden stripe. The second dorsal fin is dark at its base, reddish above this; the anal fin is similar with a white base. The finlets are bright orange-yellow with a dark edge. A juvenile is shown.

The Atlantic species is distinguished from the Indo-Pacific species (which some workers regard only as subspecies) *T. maccoyii*, and *T. orientalis*, by the high number of gill rakers (34–44, mean 38·8) on the first gill arch. From other large tunnies it is distinguished by its short pectoral fin which reaches only to the level of the eleventh or twelth dorsal fin spine, and by having relatively short lobes to the second dorsal and anal fins.

Thymallidae see under Salmonidae

Thymallus   Salmonidae
arcticus ARCTIC GRAYLING 61 cm. (2 ft)
The Arctic grayling is widely distributed across w. N. America and the n. Asian landmass. In effect it is found from the central regions of the U.S.S.R. e. to the Pacific, and in N. America from Alaska across to Lake Superior in n. Michigan. Here, however, it is now extinct, and the pattern of its distribution has been confused by introductions, transplantations, and local extinctions elsewhere.

Like its European counterpart, it is a fish of cold, clear water usually living in small shoals. To a great extent it feeds on insects flying close to the surface but its feeding habits are variable and it will feed on whatever insect larvae, crustaceans, or small fish happen to be abundant. It spawns in late spring, usually in streams over a gravel bottom; the eggs hatch within 3 weeks at normal summer temperatures.

It is closely similar to the European grayling with a high and long dorsal fin, an adipose fin, a small mouth with small teeth in both jaws. Its back is dark blue, the sides are grey with scattered black spots. The dorsal fin is flecked with orange and green; the fin and the body colours are greatly heightened in the spawning season.

The Arctic grayling is a good sporting fish, taking a fly eagerly and is moreover, good to eat. It makes a considerable contribution to the economy of the primitive peoples bordering the Arctic Ocean as food for men and dogs.
T. thymallus GRAYLING 46 cm. (18 in.)
The grayling is a European fish found N. of the Pyrenees, from e. England (although introduced elsewhere) across Europe, including Scandinavia, to the Ural and Volga rivers in the U.S.S.R. It is mainly a river fish, particularly found in cool, clear, swift and unpolluted rivers, but it will live in large lakes. It is often found in large shoals, but in spring time it is more usual to see them in pairs, the male

noticeable by its higher dorsal fin and brighter colours. Grayling spawn during March to May, laying their eggs in gravelly shallows, even as shallow as 15 cm. (6 in.) of water.

Grayling eat a variety of aquatic organisms, particularly insects and insect larvae, crustaceans, and molluscs. It is accused of feeding on trout eggs, but where this happens it is usually where competition for insufficient living space occurs following introduction of one or both to an unsuitable stream. They also eat terrestrial organisms such as woodlice and spiders which fall into the stream.

It is very distinctive with its high, many-rayed dorsal fin, and the small adipose fin close to the tail. In coloration it is equally unmistakable being silvery on the sides, greyish on the back, but with many horizontal delicate violet stripes along the sides.

The grayling is a good angling fish and fine food, but too often neglected in favour of trout. It attains a weight of about 2·27 kg. (5 lb.).

Thyrsites Gempylidae
atun BARRACOUTA, SNOEK 137 cm. (54 in.)
A valuable food fish in the S. Hemisphere, especially around the coast of s. Africa (where it is known as snoek) and s. Australia (barracouta – not to be confused with barracuda – see family Sphyraenidae). It also occurs off New Zealand, and S. America. It is a migratory species travelling in great schools through the oceans and usually arriving in numbers off the coasts at around the same time each year. Shoals sometimes enter estuaries, but most are found in open water close to the ocean or in the larger bays. They are usually found at the surface or close to it but sometimes they are encountered in deeper water. It is steel blue above, silvery below; the fins are dark.

In both S. Africa and on parts of the Australian coast it is an extremely valuable food fish. In Australia the most important fisheries are in Victoria, New South Wales and Tasmania. Most are caught on hooks in various ways although an increasing number are taken in Danish seine nets. Its flesh is of high quality as human food both fresh or smoked, and is greatly appreciated.

Its food consists mainly of small fishes and euphausiid crustaceans (such as the krill on which whalebone whales feed). It is a rapacious predator which feeds on a large range of smaller species.

Thyrsoidea Muraenidae
macrura LONG-TAILED EEL *c.* 3·7 m. (12 ft)
This large eel is found in shallow water in the tropical Indo-Pacific, from the E. African coast across to the Australian coast including the Great Barrier Reef area. It often enters estuaries and may be found well up rivers.

It is certainly the longest eel known. A specimen from Queensland measured one inch short of 13 ft (4 m.), and bêche-de-mer fishermen on the Barrier Reef claim to have seen specimens of 6 m. (20 ft). Although it is formidably long, it is not especially massive, for it is thin-bodied. Neither is it very aggressive

although if provoked or cornered it can be dangerous.

In colouring it is a uniform brown, often olive-brown. The gill opening is only just larger than the eye and is placed well along the body. Its teeth are small and conical in both jaws, with some larger depressible fangs in the front of the upper jaw.

Thysanophrys Platycephalidae
cirronasus ROCK or TASSEL-SNOUTED
FLATHEAD 38 cm. (15 in.)
An Australian flathead, found most commonly on the coasts of S. Australia and New South Wales, and extending occasionally into Queensland. It lives mostly among rocks, well concealed by its colour amongst the algae.

Its body form is typical of the family, the head being pointed but flattened as is the anterior part of the body. In this fish the head is scaleless, although the body is encased in rough-edged scales, those of the lateral line being larger than the remainder. It is reddish brown with several broad darker cross bars on the back, and many smaller light spots and blotches.

TIDEPOOL SCULPIN see **Oligocottus maculosus**
TIGER, SAND see **Odontaspis taurus**
TIGER
    BARB see **Barbus pentazona, Barbus tetrazona**
    BOTIA see **Botia macracantha**
    MULLET see **Mugil argenteus**
    SHARK see **Galeocerdo cuvier**
TIGERFISH see **Hoplias malabaricus, Hydrocynus vittatus, Pterois radiata, Therapon jarbua**
TIGERFISH, GIANT see **Hydrocynus goliath**

Tilapia Cichlidae
sparrmanii BANDED BREAM
18 cm. (7 in.)
A species native to the Orange River system, the Zambezi system and elsewhere in s. Africa. It is one of the few cichlids to occur as far S. as Cape Province and was early discovered by explorers there (it is named for the Swedish naturalist, Anders Sparrman who visited the Cape in 1772–76).

Unlike its relatives, now placed in *Sarotherodon*, it is not a mouth-brooder. The male selects a spawning site which is guarded and cleaned of silt, usually at the base of a rock or rooted plants. The eggs are laid in the nest and are fanned by both adults. On hatching the young may be moved to a second nest, carried in the mouth, but they are not retained in the mouth for any length of time.

The adults are omnivorous, feeding on aquatic plants, zooplankton, insect larvae, and worms.

TILEFISH see **Lopholatilus chamaeleonticeps**
TILEFISH, SAND see **Malacanthus plumieri**

Tinca Cyprinidae
tinca TENCH 64 cm. (25 in.)
The tench is very easily distinguished from its relatives by its thickset, heavy body and head, by its rounded fins, and above all by the very small scales. The skin gives off copious mucus and tench are always slimy, and slippery to hold. In colour it is usually dark, green or brown, only slightly lighter on the belly. Some ornamental varieties are bright yellow or orange in colour.

Tench are fishes of still waters found mostly in lakes, and slowly flowing lowland rivers. They are typical inhabitants of marshes and ox-bow lakes, and are well adapted to such waters which often become poorly oxygenated. Tench are said to overwinter in cold areas by burying themselves in the bottom, and it is true that they become very inactive in winter.

They feed on bottom-living organisms especially insect larvae, small crustaceans, and molluscs. They breed in spring and summer, when the water temperature has reached 18°C. after a long hot spell. In cool summers in n. Europe they may fail to spawn. Their small green eggs adhere to submerged vegetation over which they are shed.

The tench is an important food fish in many parts of e. Europe. Elsewhere it is well regarded as an anglers' fish, and young ones make good aquarium fish. It is widely distributed throughout Europe and w. U.S.S.R and has been introduced to Australia, New Zealand, the U.S., and elsewhere. **143**

TITTEYA see **Barbus titteya**
TOAD,
    COMMON see **Sphoeroides hamiltoni**
    GIANT see **Lagocephalus scleratus**
TOADFISH see Batrachoididae, Tetraodontidae
TOADFISH see **Antennarius hispidus, Arothron hispidus**
TOADFISH,
    BANDED, see **Torquigener pleurogramma**
    OYSTER see **Opsanus tau**
    RICHARDSON'S see **Sphoeroides hamiltoni**
    SILVER see **Lagocephalus scleratus**
    VENOMOUS see **Thalassophryne maculosa**
TOADO see Tetraodontidae
TOADO, WEEPING see **Torquigener pleurogramma**
TOBY see Tetraodontidae
TOBY see **Arothron aerostaticus, Arothron hispidus, Lagocephalus lagocephalus, Zanclus cornutus**
TOLSTOL see **Hypophthalmichthys molitrix**

Tomeurus Poeciliidae
gracilis EGG-LAYING TOPMINNOW
3 cm. (1¼ in.)
A small toothcarp which is found in freshwater in Guyana, Brazil, and Venezuela, living in shallow muddy creeks off the larger rivers and streams.

The mouth is large and nearly vertical with small conical teeth. The anal fin is relatively small, but in the male the first 3 rays form a very long intromittent organ, the tips divided into thorn-like prongs. The presence of this organ was at first thought to imply that this species was a live-bearing toothcarp, and it was grouped with the other live-bearers. It is now known, however, that the female lays one large, shelled egg at a time from which soon hatches a fully formed fish.

Apart from a silvery lengthwise line and silver tissue over the body cavity this fish is almost transparent.

Tomicodon Gobiesocidae
fasciatus BARRED CLINGFISH 5 cm. (2 in.)
Widespread on the tropical American Atlantic coast, from the Bahamas to s. Brazil, including the coast of Central America. It is a shallow-water form, living on, and under, rocks rather than coral. It is found in intertidal pools and down to about 6 m. (3 fathoms).

It is a slender-bodied clingfish, not notably flattened above and below, but it has the typical scaleless skin, single short dorsal fin, and sucking disc on the belly.

TOMMY RUFF see **Arripis georgianus**
TOMCOD,
    ATLANTIC see under **Microgadus proximus**
    PACIFIC see **Microgadus proximus**
TOMPOT BLENNY see **Blennius gattorugine**
TONG see **Synaptura marginata**
TONGUE-SOLE see Cynoglossidae
TONGUE-SOLE,
    LEMON see **Paraplagusia unicolor**
    LONG see **Cynoglossus lingua**
    RED see **Cynoglossus joyneri**
TONGUEFISH,
    BLACKCHEEK see **Symphurus plagusia**
    CARIBBEAN see **Symphurus arawak**
TOOTH-BRUSH LEATHERJACKET see
    Acanthaluteres guntheri
TOOTHCARP see Cyprinodontidae, Goodeidae, Jenynsiidae, Oryziatidae, Poeciliidae
TOOTHCARP, SPANISH see **Valencia hispanica**
TOPE see **Galeorhinus australis, Galeorhinus galeus**
TOPER see **Galeorhinus galeus**
TOPKNOTS see Scophthalmidae
TOPKNOT see **Zeugopterus punctatus**
TOPMINNOW see Cyprinodontidae
TOPMINNOW see **Lucania goodei**
TOPMINNOW,
    BLUE-FIN see **Lucania goodei**
    DWARF see **Heterandria formosa**
    EGG-LAYING see **Tomeurus gracilis**
    PIKE see **Belonesox belizanus**
TOR MAHSEER see **Barbus tor**

TORPEDINIDAE

The family containing the electric rays, sometimes known as torpedo rays. Its members are flattened rays, with cartilaginous skeletons, soft, usually naked, skins, and with a thick tail clearly divided from the pectoral fins. In general they have small eyes (some forms such as *Benthobatis* are blind) and small mouths. All have well developed electrical organs in the disc; some of the larger ones can give a disabling electric shock, painful even to man. All are ovoviviparous.

The electric rays are found in all tropical, sub-tropical, and temperate seas. They are sluggish and bottom-living, and the majority are found in shallow inshore waters; others are found in depths up to 1060 m. (580 fathoms). See **Benthobatis, Diplobatis, Hypnos, Narcine, Narke, Torpedo.**

Torpedo Torpedinidae
    californica PACIFIC ELECTRIC RAY
91 cm. (3 ft)
Widely distributed along the Pacific coast of N. America from s. British Columbia to s. California. This species is typical of its family, with a broad, almost round disc, stout tail with 2 dorsal fins, and a broad tail fin. It is also a sluggish species, lying partially buried in the sand and mud well concealed by its coloration.

It has well developed electrical organs with which it captures its prey, and which also must act as defensive weapons against enemies, including man.

T. nobiliana ELECTRIC RAY, TORPEDO, ATLANTIC TORPEDO 1·8 m. (6 ft)
This is one of the largest electric rays known. Specimens of nearly 6 ft have been reported on occasions, as have weights of up to 50 kg. (110 lb.). Its disc is smoothly rounded, almost circular, with a rather stout tail, a large tail fin and 2 dorsal fins, the second much smaller than the first. Its eyes are small, placed together and just in front of the spiracles, which have smooth edges. In colour it varies from a slate grey, through browns to almost black on the back; underneath it is a creamy white, the edges of the disc and tail being dark tinted.

This torpedo is widely distributed in the Atlantic; in the E. from w. S. Africa along the African coast to Scotland, and in the W. from s. Nova Scotia to N. Carolina. It is also found in the Mediterranean. To the N. of its range it is relatively rare and probably only occurs as a result of n. migration during the summer.

It is ovoviviparous; the young are born at a length of about 25 cm. (10 in.) in summer, usually offshore. Newly born young have been found in British waters.

This electric ray has been found to eat a variety of fishes. They are captured by the ray springing on them and wrapping its pectoral fins around the fish, simultaneously discharging its electric organs. If not killed, the prey fish is stunned by the shock and can then be eaten by the ray. For its size it has a small mouth with tiny teeth, and even the largest electric ray could not capture an actively swimming fish in its mouth unaided.

The electric shock is powerful enough to throw a man to the ground but fortunately this species is rarely found in depths of less than 9 m. (5 fathoms) so bathers rarely encounter it. Spear fishermen and, less often, anglers, catch this fish and may suffer the consequences of a severe shock. The voltage produced by this species varies from 170 to 220, but weakens quickly after repeated discharges or if the ray is captured in a net.

T. torpedo 60 cm. (24 in.)
This electric ray lives in the Mediterranean and e. Atlantic from s. Biscay s. to Angola. It is strikingly marked, with a warm sandy brown back with 5 distinct blue spots, ringed with black and then white or cream. They are symetrically arranged and must serve the function of warning colours.

This ray lives, usually buried under a light sprinkling of sand, in depths down to 50 m. (27 fathoms), and it is not often found in less than 4 m. (2 fathoms) of water. It produces living young; pregnant females are found in the Mediterranean from March to September. The size of litter depends on the size of mother and varies from 3 to 21. The young are born at a length of about 8 cm. (3 in.), usually in autumn.

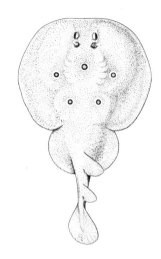

The electrical properties of the torpedoes have been recognized in literature since the time of Aristotle (who knew the Mediterranean species) and because of this unusual property they were frequently used in early medicine. These kidney-shaped organs are composed of modified muscle tissue; they consist of small individual electric plates which are vertically stacked to form columns which may number up to 1000 per pectoral fin (the number varies with the species). Most of the electric plates are connected in parallel, and the combined current of these plates in the many columns can amount to a powerful shock, in one species of up to 220 volts.

TORPEDO see **Torpedo nobiliana**
TORPEDO, ATLANTIC see **Torpedo nobiliana**
TORPEDO RAY see Torpedinidae

Torquigener Tetraodontidae
    pleurogramma BANDED TOADFISH, WEEPING TOADO 22 cm. (8½ in.)
Known only from the coasts of Australia, New Guinea, and Lord Howe Island. In Australia it is found all round the coastline being particularly common off the s. states. It occurs in shallow inshore waters and at depths down to about 55 m. (30 fathoms).

Its body is moderately elongate, but not grossly rounded as in some toadfishes. The lateral line is single and runs along the side of the tail as a raised ridge. The dorsal and anal fins are moderately high. It is light green or grey above with a dark brown network and 4 broad cross bars.

The flesh of this species is thought to be toxic, but the internal organs are certainly highly poisonous.

TORRENTFISH see **Cheimarrichthys forsteri**
TORSK see **Brosme brosme**
TOVIRA CAVALLO see **Apteronotus albifrons**

Toxotes Toxotidae
chatareus ARCHERFISH 25 cm. (10 in.)
Widely distributed in coastal waters from India to n. Australia, and the Philippines. It is found in inshore waters, brackish river mouths, and in Australia far up rivers into entirely freshwater. In this area fishes from 2·5 cm. (1 in.) upwards are found and it is suggested that they breed in freshwater. Nothing is, however, known of the breeding habits of any archerfish. Its habit of spitting water to obtain insect food is the same as that described for *T. jaculator*.

It is distinguished by having 5 spines in the dorsal fin, the head is not so pointed, and the scales are smaller. Rounded dark blotches on the back, rather than bars, distinguish it from the other archerfish described. **310**
T. jaculator ARCHERFISH 23 cm. (9 in.)
A widely distributed fish in the Indo-Pacific region. It is a native of the inshore waters, estuaries, and lower reaches of rivers from India, Burma, Malaya, the E. Indies, S.E. Asia, n. Australia, and the Philippines.

This remarkable fish is well-known for its ability to spit drops, or a stream of water at insects near the water's edge, a habit that has been known for many years (first described in 1764) although as it was at first attributed to the butterflyfish, *Chelmon rostratus*, it was disputed by many scientists until the present century. In fact, the archerfish can spit drops of water with great accuracy at 1 m. (3¼ ft) distance, and after a few ranging shots can hit a small target at 3 m. (10 ft). The propulsion is mainly provided by sudden compression of the gill covers, water being held in the pharynx, and the mouth cavity being restricted to a narrow tube by pressure of the tongue on the roof of the mouth. The roof of the mouth has a deep groove which forms the tube, and the tip of the tongue acts as a valve and stopper. The force of the water drops, at short range, strike a person's face with a stinging sensation.

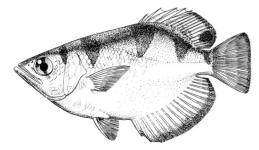

This modification, remarkable as it is, is supplemented by a precision of vision which not only requires the fish to see potential prey but can make the necessary corrections to range to allow for the bending of light rays at the air-water interface. The eyes of archerfishes are large and very mobile and certainly permit binocular vision forwards and above.

The archerfish feeds mostly on insects and arthropods which it knocks into the water from overhanging vegetation, or which, such as spiders and caterpillars, are hanging on webs. Occasionally it will knock flying prey down by spitting, but almost as often it leaps and seizes it in its jaws; it also takes aquatic insects and crustaceans in the water.

It swims at or close to the surface of the water most of the time, protruding its mouth tip whilst swimming and so leaving a slight wake as it passes. Most of the waters in which it lives naturally are very turbid, and it has been suggested that the brilliant gold flecks on the sides of the young fish are an adaptation to enable them to maintain contact within the loose school. Young fishes of up to 2·5 cm. (1 in.) in length begin to obtain their food by shooting water, but it is not until they are half-grown that they become proficient at it.

In Thailand, the late Hugh M. Smith reported that it was occasionally caught by angling, and was a good food fish. It is often imported as an aquarium specimen, the young fish being most suited to captivity, and can be fed so as to display its water spitting abilities. **311**

TOXOTIDAE
The Asiatic family of archerfishes, which regularly spit water drops at insects on vegetation near the water or shoot down flying insects. Several species are found in coastal waters of Asia, and their range extends from the Philippines and Australia, throughout the Indo-Australian archipelago to Burma and India. Some of them enter estuaries and are found in freshwater.

All have the same general body shape, a flat back, deeply curved belly profile, and a pointed snout; their eyes are large. A single dorsal fin, the first portion composed of 4-5 slender spines; 3 spines in the anal fin; both fins are placed well back along the back. See **Toxotes**.

Trachichthodes Trachichthyidae
lineatus SWALLOWTAIL 36 cm. (14 in.)
A common fish in deep water off the coasts of W. and S. Australia. It is found in depths of 131–256 m. (72–140 fathoms), and is clearly abundant in places for a catch of 320 kg. (700 lb.) was made in one haul of the net by a survey ship. It is caught and marketed in small numbers.

It is a relatively slender fish with a large eye, moderately large mouth and the body fully scaled. Its coloration is striking, a deep crimson with each scale light centred; the fins are red.

TRACHICHTHYIDAE
A family of marine fishes of rather distinctive appearance and worldwide in their range. Some are deep-water fishes found only in the open ocean, but others are found in shallow inshore waters.

All have very deep, compressed bodies, a large head which has many ridges, and hollow glandular areas which contain copious mucus canals. The pelvic fins are placed well forward on the belly and have a single large, sharp spine. The dorsal and anal fins both contain sharp spines and branched rays. Body scales are usually large, rough-edged, and spiny on the belly. See **Gephyroberyx, Hoplostethus, Trachichthodes, Trachichthys.**

Trachichthys Trachichthyidae
australis ROUGHY 15 cm. (6 in.)
Widely distributed in Australian waters, especially to the S., although occasional specimens straggle into tropical n. waters. It inhabits rocky reefs in shallow water, and is occasionally taken on hook and line, or in craypots. Its small size precludes its being used as food.

Like its deep-water relatives it is compressed and deep-bodied, with a large head, and oblique mouth with a big eye. The scales are rough edged, and the belly has a line of sharp scutes along it (hence roughy). Its coloration is reddish brown, with a dark bar on the gill covers, and dark brown on the fins except for the pectorals, although there is a white band at the dorsal and anal base.

TRACHINIDAE
The family of the weeverfishes, a small group of marine fish found on the coasts of Europe and as far S. as W. Africa. They are distinguished by a rather elongate body, together with a deep, but compressed head. The mouth is strongly oblique, and the eyes placed almost on the top of the head. The body is fully scaled, the scales arranged in diagonal rows.

Their most notable feature is the small, spiny dorsal fin, black in colour, and containing venom-producing tissue, as do the spines on the gill covers. Wounds from either set of spines are incredibly painful, disabling in the short term, and may lead to permanent injury due to secondary infections. The habit of all the weevers is to lie buried in sand, with only the eyes and spiny dorsal fin exposed. In British waters the most common species is the weever, *Trachinus vipera*, which lives in very shallow water. It is occasionally trodden upon by bathers. The most effective treatment for weever stings is to soak the affected area in as hot water as can be borne by the patient. See **Trachinus.**

Trachinocephalus Synodontidae
myops LIZARDFISH, SNAKEFISH
37 cm. (15 in.)
The lizardfish is almost cosmopolitan in its distribution, being found in the warmer waters of the Atlantic, Indian, and e. Pacific. In the Atlantic it is found on both sides, from the coast of Massachusetts s. throughout the W. Indies to Brazil, and from w. to S. Africa.

It is a typical lizardfish in body form, with heavy almost shiny scales, a moderate head, large mouth, and eyes on the top and at the front of the head. It is distinguished from its relatives by its long anal fin. Its coloration is pale, alternate broad stripes of blue and yellow in life. It has been recorded from close inshore to water as deep as 387 m. (212 fathoms), although it is most abundant in depths of 37–91 m. (20–50 fathoms) usually on sand, shell, rock, or mud. It is said to burrow in soft bottoms, lying with only its eyes exposed. It has no particular value as a food or game fish, and only occasionally features in the diet of other fishes.

Trachinotus Carangidae
falcatus PERMIT 109 cm. (43 in.)
Found in the tropical Atlantic, but best known in the w. Atlantic where it ranges from Massachusetts to Brazil, including the Gulf of Mexico. It occurs on sandy flats and reefs from about 1·5–30 m. (1–17 fathoms), the adults being found in deeper water where they feed principally on molluscs, sea urchins, crustaceans, and occasionally, fishes. The young fish eat small crustaceans mostly and live in shallow water in bays and coves.

It is an excellent sporting fish, growing to a weight of about 23 kg. (50 lb.). Its flesh is excellent food, but the larger specimens are less well flavoured than moderately young ones. The young are found in small schools; the adults are mainly solitary.

When young the body is deep, and the dorsal and anal fin lobes very long; with age the body lengthens relative to the height and the fins are less high. The young are almost all silvery with a grey-blue back and dark fins; adults are blue overall, lighter on the belly and with a triangular yellow patch before the anal fin. The fins are dark.

T. goodei PALOMETA 50 cm. (20 in.)
This deep-bodied, very graceful fish is found in the w. Atlantic from Bermuda and New England to Argentina, including the Gulf of Mexico and the Caribbean. It is in places extremely common, particularly in shallow to moderately deep water around reefs. It is most abundant along sandy areas, and may at times circle around the feet of bathers presumably picking up disturbed crustaceans and molluscs on which it feeds. It is almost invariably found in schools.

It is a very handsome fish, silvery above and on the sides, yellowish ventrally. The long lobes to dorsal and anal fins are black, as are the outer tail-fin rays.

T. russelli SWALLOWTAIL, DART, MOONFISH, LADYFISH 61 cm. (2 ft)
Found widely in the tropical Indo-Pacific from the E. African coast to Queensland, New South Wales, and the w. Pacific. It is found in inshore waters, even coming into the surf zone to feed. It is considered to be a good sporting fish on light tackle, and is caught in great numbers on the Australian and S. African coasts. It is of moderate quality as a food fish.

Like other members of the genus it is deep-bodied, flattened from side to side, with very high lobes to the second dorsal and anal fins; a series of short isolated spines forms the first dorsal fin. The tail is deeply forked. Its back is deep blue, the sides silvery to white, a series of 6–7 oval dusky blotches along the sides, the tips of the fins are deep blue.

Trachinus Trachinidae
araneus SPOTTED WEEVER 25 cm. (10 in.)
Found exclusively in the Mediterranean, which sea has the greatest wealth of weever species. It is found in moderately shallow water, and is usually seen lying half buried in sand, especially close to rocks or amongst sea grass beds.

Its body form is similar to the other weever species. It can be distinguished by having the first part of the spiny dorsal fin black, and by the series of rounded black blotches on the sides of the fish.

As with other weevers, the gill cover spines and the dorsal fins are equipped with venom-producing issue.

T. draco GREATER WEEVER 41 cm. (16 in.)

Distributed from the Norwegian coast, s. around Europe to Morocco, and in the Mediterranean. It is found in moderately deep water, 30–100 m. (16–55 fathoms) and is rarely found in shallower water. It burrows into sand and feeds more on small fishes than its relatives, although it also eats some crustaceans and other benthic invertebrates.

It is grey-brown on the back, yellowish on the belly and sides; dark lines follow the oblique rows of scales. The top edge of the dorsal fin only is dusky.

This weever is sold for food on the European market, especially in Belgium and in the Mediterranean countries. The venomous spines are removed by fishermen on capture.

T. vipera WEEVER, LESSER WEEVER
14 cm. (5½ in.)
Found along the coasts of Europe from n. Scotland s. to Morocco, and throughout the Mediterranean. It is easily distinguished by its rather short stout body, which is laterally compressed, and the oblique scale rows on the body. It is yellow-brown on the back and sides, with darker spots and blotches on the back; ventrally it is creamy or yellow. The first dorsal fin is conspicuously black.

The weever is a bottom-living species found in depths between low-water mark and 50 m. (27 fathoms), although possibly most common in 1–5 m. (½–3 fathoms) of water. It is confined to sandy areas, beaches and offshore banks, in clean sand in which it lies buried with only the top of the head visible. It is commonly caught in shore seines and shrimp nets, and its venom-laden spines are an ever present hazard to the fisherman. A number of cases of bathers being stung are reported each year in Britain. The venom-laden spines are on the gill covers and the first dorsal fin. Stings are extremely painful, and although bathing with hot water brings relief, medical assistance should always be sought.

The spines are purely defensive. Its food consists of small fishes and crustaceans of various kinds. It becomes active in search of food at night.

TRACHIPTERIDAE
A small family of slender-bodied marine fishes related to the opah and oarfish. Like these groups, the mouth and jaws are very distinctively formed, and the mouth is protrusible. The body, while moderately deep, is very compressed and narrow, the dorsal fin runs along the whole length of the body from the head rearwards. The anal fin is absent, but the tail fin is composed of several long rays upturned in a fan-like shape.

All the members of the family are silvery coloured, mesopelagic fishes. They are found in the Atlantic, Pacific, and Indian oceans.
See **Desmodema, Trachipterus, Zu.**

Trachipterus Trachipteridae
arcticus DEALFISH 2·5 m. (8½ ft)
Widely distributed in the e. N. Atlantic from

Madeira and off the African coast, n. to beyond the Arctic Circle, w. to Greenland. Most dealfishes are taken at or near the surface or are stranded on shores after storms, but in some years schools numbering several hundred have been seen off the n. coasts of Iceland. It is a mesopelagic fish living in depths of 183–914 m. (100–500 fathoms), although it has been taken near the surface on occasions. It feeds on a wide variety of fishes, squids, and crustaceans. Its body form is typical of the family. It is silvery with 1–5 rounded dark spots along the upper sides.

Trachurus Carangidae
mccullochi YELLOWTAIL SCAD
33 cm. (13 in.)
A small species of scad found on the coasts of W. Australia, S. Australia, Victoria, and New South Wales. It is very common in the estuaries and coastal waters of the e. states. Although caught by anglers it has no commercial value.

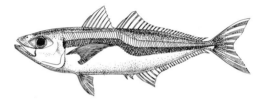

Its body form is typical of the many species of *Trachurus*, the horse mackerels or scads, the long curved row of modified scales, which become spiny towards the tail being distinctive of the group. It is yellowish green above, silvery below.

T. symmetricus JACK MACKEREL
76 cm. (30 in.)
Found in the e. Pacific from British Columbia s. to Baja California and far out into the open sea. It is a surface-living pelagic species, feeding mostly on crustaceans, squid, and many kinds of smaller fishes. It takes its place in the food chain of the sea by falling prey to sealions, porpoises, swordfish, many seabirds – and man.

Jack mackerel are popular sporting fish caught in inshore waters in numbers. They grow to about 2·3 kg. (5 lb.). They are also commercially exploited on a small scale all along the N. American coast. It is distinguished in its natural range by having a series of bony scutes along the sides of the body, large in front then smaller, but finally increasing in size. A small finlet at the end of both dorsal and anal fins.

T. trachurus SCAD, HORSE MACKEREL,
MAASBANKER 41 cm. (16 in.)
Distinguished within its range by the complete, curved row of bony scales running from head to tail, by the 2 anal spines, and by the separate spiny dorsal fin. The scad is grey-blue with greenish tints, the sides silvery, the belly white.

It is widely distributed in European seas, in the Atlantic from s. Norway to N. Africa, throughout the Mediterranean and Black seas. It is also found off s. Africa. It is a shoaling fish, the young found in shallow water over sandy bottoms; the adults in deep water, up to 100 m. (55 fathoms).

The very young are frequently found swimming amongst the trailing tentacles of several species of large jellyfishes, a habit common in this family.

It is not a particularly important species commercially although some fishing for processing as fish meal is undertaken. In the Mediterranean it is used as a food fish. Off S. African coasts, however, large numbers are captured and marketed fresh, canned, or smoked, and the maasbanker is a valuable commercial species.

Trachyrhynchus   Macrouridae
   trachyrincus 51 cm. (20 in.)
A European rat-tail of wide distribution, from the Faeroe-Shetland ridge, and Rockall, s. to the Mediterranean and N. African coast.

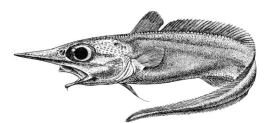

It is found on the lower continental shelf most commonly at depths of 550–730 m. (300–400 fathoms) although occasionally captured down to 1100 m. (600 fathoms). It is a bottom feeding species.

It is distinguished by the very prolonged and angular snout. The body scales are heavy each with one or more stout spines, the largest scales lie along the base of the dorsal fin.

Trematomus   Nototheniidae
   bernacchii 35 cm. (13 in.)
An Antarctic cod which is distributed all around the shelf of Antarctica. It occurs there in depths down to 700 m. (383 fathoms). It feeds mainly on bottom-living invertebrates especially polychaete worms, molluscs, and isopod crustaceans; to a lesser extent it eats amphipod crustaceans.

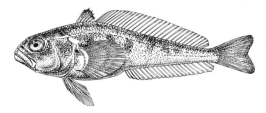

This fish is reddish-brown, the sides having brown or near-black spots and bars. The dorsal and anal fins are brownish, the pectoral fin is clear except that at the base there are 3 black marks which are characteristic of the species.

TREVALLE, DEEP-SEA see **Hyperoglyphe antarctica**
TREVALLY,
  GOLDEN see **Caranx speciosus**
  GREAT see **Caranx sexfasciatus**
  PENNANT see **Alectis ciliaris**

TRIACANTHIDAE
The triple-spines, a family of plectognath fishes with some of the features of their nearest relatives the triggerfishes (family Balistidae). Like them, the front teeth are separate and not fused into a beak-like form, they also have several well-developed spines in the anterior dorsal fin, and the body is covered with hard, rather spiny scales.

This family is distinguished by possessing well developed pelvic fins, usually only a strong spine, but in some species a small ray is also present. They are widely spread in the Indian and Pacific oceans where several species occur in shallow water, and in the deep sea. In the tropical Atlantic they are represented only in deep water. This group are the only plectognaths to be found in deep water. See **Atrophacanthus, Triacanthus, Tydemania.**

Triacanthus   Triacanthidae
   brevirostris 26 cm. (10½ in.)
A species of plectognath fish widely distributed in the Indian Ocean and w. Pacific. Its range includes the waters of s. Japan, China, and Korea, the Philippines, Malaysia and the E. Indies, and around the whole Indian subcontinent to the Persian Gulf. The Indian Ocean form was formerly recognized as a distinct species, *T. indicus,* and was distinguished by its slightly longer snout.

T. brevirostris is a common inshore fish which enters estuaries freely and tolerates low salinity conditions. It is particularly common in the coloured, silt-laden estuaries of rivers and over sandy or muddy bottomed bays.

It is easily distinguished from other plectognaths by its high first dorsal fin, and by having long spines in each pelvic fin which lock into position pointing obliquely outwards.

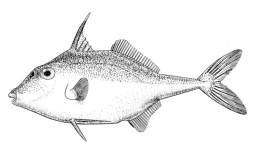

It is grey-blue on the back, pale below with a silvery cast over all the body. A black spot lies at the base of the spiny dorsal fin; the other fins are yellowish.
T. indicus see under **T. brevirostris**

TRIAKIDAE
This is a relatively small family of sharks, none noted for its size or dangerous habits, indeed some are used by man for food. They are slender-bodied with well-developed fins, 5 gill-slits, and small flattened teeth arranged to form a crushing mill in the jaws. The family is confined to shallow seas, but lives in both temperate and tropical climates. All its members bear living young, most simply retaining the fertilized egg within the mother's body while the young shark develops, although in some species the yolk sac forms a placental connection with the mother. See **Mustelus, Triakis.**

Triakis   Triakidae
   semifasciata LEOPARD SHARK
1·5 m. (5 ft)
The leopard shark is so called because of its striking colour pattern, black saddle marks and blotches along the sides over a light tan background. It is found along the Pacific coast of N. America from Oregon to Lower California. It is a harmless blunt-toothed species, although there has been one case of a small specimen attacking a skin diver, without causing injury.

It is easily kept in captivity because it is not very demanding of the quality of the water in which it lives. For this reason most large public aquaria keep this active shark for long periods. It is also easy to obtain for the young sharks can easily be caught on the shallow nursery grounds like those in San Francisco bay. Like others of the family it gives birth to living young.

TRICHIURIDAE
A moderately small family of marine fishes of worldwide distribution in tropical and temperate seas. In general they are inhabitants of the surface and mid-waters, some being found as deep as 914 m. (500 fathoms).

All the 30 or so members of the family have long slim, compressed bodies, with heads and jaws elongate and the latter armed with formidable dagger-like teeth. The dorsal fin origin is close behind the head and the fin runs the whole length of the back or almost so; the anal fin in contrast is poorly developed. Many species have a small tail fin, in others the body ends in a point. Pelvic fins are lacking.

Most of the trichiurids, which are known variously as scabbardfishes, cutlassfishes, hairtails, or frostfish, are moderately large (up to 1·5 m. (5 ft)). Some are exploited locally as food fish, and their flesh is of good quality. See **Aphanopus, Lepidopus, Trichiurus.**

Trichiurus   Trichiuridae
   lepturus HAIR-TAIL, ATLANTIC
CUTLASSFISH, SNAKEFISH 1·5 m. (5 ft)
A most striking fish which is plain silvery all over, the edges of the fins are yellowish green, and the tips of the jaws are dusky. This colouring, its shape and large teeth make it quite unmistakable.

It occurs throughout the Atlantic (and a closely related species, *T. savala,* is found in the Indian and Pacific oceans). It is more common in tropical and warm-temperate seas than elsewhere but does extend n. into cooler temperate waters occasionally (for example the Gulf of Maine, and off s. Britain). Normally it lives in the upper layers of the sea being found from the surface to 350 m. (191 fathoms). Occasionally it enters shallow water, and is stranded on shore. In some areas (as in s. Africa) it is often found close inshore, probably due to the close proximity of deep water and local vagaries of ocean currents.

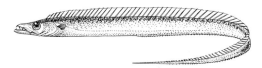

It is a good food fish, although the flesh is sparse. In tropical regions it is captured in very large numbers for local markets.
T. savala see **T. lepturus**

Trichodon   Trichodontidae
   trichodon PACIFIC SANDFISH
30 cm. (12 in.)
Native to the N. Pacific, and found from n.

California along the Pacific coast to Alaska, the Aleutian Islands to Kamchatka. Its normal life-style is to lie buried in sand in very shallow water. It has been found in the gut of chinook salmon.

It is quite unmistakable in appearance, the upturned jaws with terminal mouth, and deeply fringed lips being distinctive. It is drably coloured, light brown above, silvery below, dark on the sides with irregular darker patches.

TRICHODONTIDAE

A small family of marine fishes found only in the N. Pacific Ocean. They bear a superficial resemblance to the weeverfishes (Trachinidae) in having a deeply curved ventral profile, a long anal fin, and broad pectoral fin. The mouth is almost vertical and opens on the top surface of the head.

Both the 2 known species are small, 30 cm. (12 in.) seems to be a maximal length. One of the 2 species is an important food fish in Japan. See **Arctoscopus, Trichodon.**

Trichogaster Belontiidae
leeri PEARL GOURAMI 11 cm. (4½ in.)
Found in the Malaysian region, Thailand, Sumatra, and Borneo. It is relatively common in the well-weeded swamps and lowland waters, often living in water that is poorly aerated. It feeds mainly on vegetable matter and insect larvae.

It is a delightful aquarium fish, peaceful and relatively undemanding. It builds a large bubble nest in which the eggs develop and are guarded by the male.

The pearl gourami is distinguished by the features of all gouramis, deep body, compressed, with a long anal fin, and very long pelvic fin rays. The back and upper sides are pale green with a strong pearly sheen on the sides, the back and fins have pearl-like spots. Ventrally it is orange or pinkish, including the pelvic streamers.

T. microlepis MOONLIGHT GOURAMI
15 cm. (6 in.)
This gourami is a native of Cambodia and Thailand, where it is recorded mostly in the central region. Like other members of the genus it is a bubble-nest breeder, blowing masses of glutinous bubbles to form a large, spreading nest. The eggs, once fertilized are spat into the nest and hatch there guarded by the male.

It lives in areas where submerged vegetation is dense but dissolved oxygen may be low, and gulps air at the surface for transfer to the accessory breathing organs in each gill chamber.

This is an excellent, but not readily available aquarium fish. Rather slim-bodied, with very small scales, and a dorsal fin with only 3–4 spines – this species is quite distinctive. The colouring is plain being bluish silver, the young often with faint rows of dark spots. Males have orange-red pelvic fins.

T. trichopterus THREE-SPOT GOURAMI
15 cm. (6 in.)
A native fish in the Indo-Australian Archipelago, the Malayan peninsular, and S.E. Asia generally. In Thailand it is widely distributed and found in weedy habitats in streams, canals, ditches, lakes, ponds, and swamps. Like many other labyrinth fishes, this gourami is equipped with an accessory breathing organ in a chamber above the gills and is also a bubble nest builder. The eggs in this species are small and numerous.

It is a very beautiful aquarium fish, deep-bodied with a long-based anal fin, relatively short dorsal, and extremely long pelvic fin rays. The 'three spots' of its name lie at the tail base, at mid-body above the pectoral fin, and the eye represents the third spot.

TRICHOMYCTERIDAE

A family of small, rather slender-bodied catfishes found in ne. S. America. They are almost loach-like in appearance, with scaleless skins, short-based, rounded dorsal and anal fins, no adipose fin, rather short barbels around the mouth in 3 pairs. Most of the species whose habits are known, appear to be crepuscular or nocturnal and lie buried during daylight in the sand of sand bars, or in the leaf-litter and fallen tree branches. Some, such as *Stegophilus insidiosus*, are parasitic and live in the gill chambers of larger catfishes; others are known to be scale-eaters of larger fishes. See **Homodiaetus, Pygidium, Vandellia.**

TRICHONOTIDAE

The family of sand divers, a small group of Indo-Pacific marine fishes. Most are small, the largest reaching a length of 18 cm. (7 in.). They are elongate, almost sand-eel like, with scaled bodies and 2 dorsal fins the first of which has 3–7 rays, the second is long-based and many-rayed. Most sand divers live buried in sand, only making short forays to feed. Most species have rather specialized protuberant eyes which afford them some degree of binocular vision. See **Trichonotops.**

Trichonotops Trichonotidae
marleyi 18 cm. (7 in.)
Known only on the Indian Ocean coast of s. Africa from Delagoa Bay to Durban. Its biology is unrecorded but there is little doubt that it shares the sand-burrowing habits of its relatives.

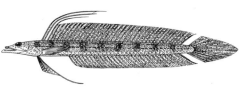

It is a striking looking fish with extremely high dorsal fin, and 2 long separate dorsal rays. Its colouring is light brown with a dense covering of pale blue spots, and blackish dots on the body and fins.

Trichopsis Belontiidae
vittatus TALKING or CROAKING GOURAMI
6·5 cm. (2½ in.)
This species is found from Java, Sumatra, Borneo, Malaysia, and se. Asia. It abounds in small well-weeded streams, as well as ponds, and even occasionally in high altitude streams.

Like other labyrinth fishes, it lives in poorly oxygenated waters and makes frequent visits to the surface to fill its accessory breathing organ with atmospheric oxygen. The fish makes a high-pitched croaking noise, amplified possibly by the accessory breathing organ, but its precise mechanics are doubtful.

Males have a dusky spot above the pectoral fin, a longer more pointed anal fin, and heightened colouring at the anal base. It is a popular aquarium fish, but difficult to get to breed. **459**

TRIGGERFISH see Balistidae
TRIGGERFISH see **Balistes carolinensis, Melichthys niger, Odonus niger**
TRIGGERFISH,
BIG-SPOTTED see **Balistoides conspicillum**
BLACK see **Melichthys ringens**
BLACK-BARRED see **Rhinecanthus aculeatus**
GREY see **Balistes carolinensis**
QUEEN see **Balistes vetula**
SARGASSUM see **Xanichthys ringens**
YELLOW-SPOTTED see **Pseudobalistes fuscus**

Trigla Triglidae
kumu see **Chelidonichthys kumu**
lucerna TUB or YELLOW GURNARD
61 cm. (2 ft)
This is the commonest large European gurnard. It ranges from the coasts of Norway (occasionally), commonly round the British Isles to the N. African coast, the Mediterranean, Adriatic, and Black seas. It is also reported on the w. coast of S. Africa.

It is a moderately shallow water fish found most commonly in depths of 50–150 m. (27–82 fathoms) although young fish usually live in shallower water. It is normally found on sandy or muddy bottoms. Its food is mainly bottom-living crustaceans, molluscs, and occasionally fishes.

The tub gurnard (gurnet is an old-fashioned variation) is easily distinguished by the brilliant colouring. The lowest 3 pectoral rays are isolated from the fin and form efficient food locators, as well as serving as props on which the fish rests.

This species is commercially fished for in some areas and it is also of value to the sea angler, for it can weigh up to 5 kg. (11 lb.). **252**

TRIGLIDAE

The family of gurnards or sea robins, a group of marine fishes of worldwide distribution in tropical and temperate seas. Most are rather small fishes, species exceeding 60 cm. (2 ft) are exceptional. The head is covered with thick, heavy bone, while the body may have either scales or thin plates along it. Pectoral fins are large, the lower rays separated from the fin and capable of bending forwards to act as finger-like feelers searching the bottom for food.

The group are well known sonic performers, quite loud noises being produced under stress, and low-level sound is clearly part of their normal life. The sound is produced by the action of muscles on the very large swim-bladder.

All the gurnards are bottom-living fishes of coastal waters. See **Chelidonichthys, Eutrigla, Peristedion, Prionotus, Trigla.**

Trinectes Achiridae
maculatus HOGCHOKER, DWARF
FLOUNDER 20 cm. (8 in.)
Found off the Atlantic and Gulf coasts of N. America, the range of the hogchoker extends from Massachusetts Bay to Panama. It is a coastal species, very common in bays and estuaries even when the water is only brackish. It feeds on marine worms and small crustaceans; fragments of algae have also been found in its stomach. It spawns in late spring and early summer.

The hogchoker gets this name from the extremely rough, hard scales which were said to choke hogs which fed on discarded soles on the beach. Nevertheless its flesh is delicious eating, and although too small to be commercially exploited makes a local delicacy.

It is distinguished by its broad body, the eyes on the right side of the head, with the dorsal fin origin in front of the snout. The very rough scales are also distinctive. It is dark grey to deep brown with a varying number (around 8) of rather indistinct, narrow dark cross bars.

Juveniles will tolerate water of very low salinity and are often kept in aquaria, even being imported to Europe as pet fish.

Triodon Triodontidae
bursarius 45 cm. (18 in.)
A little known fish which is distributed apparently widely in the tropical Indo-Pacific. It has occurred in areas as far apart as Mozambique and Japan, as well as such localities as Mauritius, India, Sumatra, Ceram, the Philippines, and Korea, but nowhere does it appear to be common and little is known about it.

Its appearance is most striking, particularly in the large flap of loose skin on the belly, which is not inflatable (as in the pufferfishes) but which can be expanded in the longitudinal

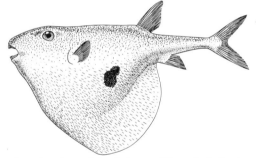

plane by the pelvic skeleton. The whole body is covered with long, thin, spiny scales which give it a coarse sand-papery feel. It is light sandy brown with a large rounded black blotch on the lower side which is surrounded by a bright yellow ring.

TRIODONTIDAE
A family containing a single species of plectognath fish. Its body is in some respects like that of the related elongate pufferfishes but the ventral surface is a huge compressed flap supported anteriorly by a long thin bone formed by the pelvic fin skeleton. The teeth in the jaws form a beak, the lower teeth being fused in the mid-line the upper with 2 separate teeth. See **Triodon.**

TRIPLE-SPINE see Triacanthidae
TRIPLE-TAIL see **Lobotes surinamensis**
TRIPLEFIN, REDEYE see **Enneanectes pectoralis**

TRIPODFISH see **Benthosaurus grallator**
Triportheus elongatus see **Chalcinus elongatus**

TRIPTERYGIIDAE
A moderately large family of scaled blenny-like fishes found mostly in tropical and warm temperate seas. Most are shallow-water forms living close to the substrate, usually coral or rocks, and diversifying to inhabit very localized and specialized depth ranges and habitats.

The three-fin blennies, as they are known, are distinguished by having 3 dorsal fins, the first and second of which are composed of slender spines. Most of the species show striking sexual differences in coloration; males frequently have dark heads, black in some forms, red in others. All are closely scaled, most species having ctenoid (toothed) scales over the whole body. All species are small, none has sporting or food value. See **Enneanectes, Tripterygion.**

Tripterygion Tripterygiidae
In addition to the illustrated *T. xanthosoma*, there is a colour picture of an unidentified species. **426**
T. minor PYGMY BLACK-FACED BLENNY
5 cm. (2 in.)
A Mediterranean species which appears to be widely distributed at least on the n. coasts of the w. Mediterranean and in the Adriatic. It is found in moderately shallow water of 2–15 m.

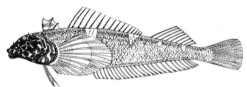

(1–8 fathoms) in crevices and on the roof of underwater caves where red algae and sponge growths are dominant. It is often found in the same habitat, side by side with the similarly coloured blenny, *Blennius nigriceps*.

This three-fin blenny is a bright red in colour with triangular light bars or spots along the back. In males the head is conspicuously black with whitish lines running across it, but the dark area only extends to the base of the first dorsal fin.

T. varium MOTTLED BLENNY 7·5 cm. (3 in.)
A very common species of three-fin blenny in the waters of New Zealand. It is an inshore species found usually where water movement is rapid and vigorous.

This was one of the earliest known New Zealand blennies and for years other species were confused with it. However, due to recent work by scuba-diving biologist, Gordon Anderson, the remarkable wealth of species of tripterygiids in New Zealand seas has been revealed, Numerous species adapted to many habitats live there of which the mottled blenny is one common inshore form.

Its colouring is very varied, basically greenish-brown with dark cross bars, but in the breeding season the male is deep black overall with a pale blue edge to the dorsal fin.

It spawns in late June with considerable display of colours and fins. The eggs are deposited in a single layer over a clean rock face, the pair staying together for a few days although only the male guards the eggs during their later development.

T. xanthosoma 9 cm. (3½ in.)
Found in the Mediterranean, and apparently widely distributed. This species has for many years been confused with the other Mediterranean species (it is close to *T. tripteronotus*) and has only recently been distinguished from them.

It lives in rather deeper water, from 10–40 m. (5–72 fathoms) and is found on exposed rock faces usually in partially shaded situations. Males are immediately distinguished by their bright orange-yellow coloration and black faces. Other morphological differences are confined to slightly more scales and fin rays. This species is thus separated from its nearest relatives by ecological, and possibly behavioural barriers, while still being morphologically almost identical. **427**

Trisopterus Gadidae
luscus BIB, POUTING 41 cm. (16 in.)
An extremely common inshore fish of the European coastline. It occurs from the Swedish coast to the Mediterranean, and along the N. coasts of that sea. It is particularly common on sandy bottoms as a juvenile, but the adults are found round rocks and underwater obstructions. Although the young are common in inshore waters, older fish are found down to 100 m. (55 fathoms).

It feeds mainly on shrimps, small squids, and sometimes small fishes. It is not of commercial importance, but by its very abundance makes a considerable impact on the food chains of inshore waters. Some are caught by anglers. **190**

TRITOLO see **Characidium fasciatum**

Tropheus Cichlidae
moorii 15 cm. (6 in.)
A species found only in Lake Tanganyika in e. Africa. It is confined to rocky regions of this lake and is apparently never found more than 1 m. (39 in.) away from the rocks.

Within the lake it exists in several forms, the most notable of which are the individuals which are brownish black in colour. In other parts of the lake it is black overall with a wide, vertical orange band running across the dorsal fin, back and sides. This form is most commonly imported as an aquarium fish. **380**

TROUT see Salmonidae
TROUT see **Aplochiton zebra, Salmo trutta**
TROUT,
  BROOK see **Salvelinus fontinalis**
  CORAL see **Cephalopholis miniatus**
  CUTTHROAT see **Salmo clarki**
  INDIAN see **Barilius bola**
  KAMLOOPS see **Salmo gairdneri**
  LAKE see **Salvelinus namaycush**
  RAINBOW see **Salmo gairdneri**
  SEA see **Cynoscion regalis**
  SHASTA see **Salmo gairdneri**
  STEEL-HEAD see **Salmo gairdneri**
  YELLOWSTONE CUTTHROAT see **Salmo clarki**
TROUT-PERCH see **Percopsis omiscomaycus**
TRUMPETER,
  BASTARD see **Latridopsis forsteri**
  TASMANIAN see **Latris lineata**
TRUMPETER PERCH see **Pelates quadrilineatus**

TRUMPETFISH see Aulostomidae
TRUMPETFISH see **Aulostomus maculatus,
Aulostomus strigosus**
TRUNKFISH see Molidae, Ostraciontidae
TRUNKFISH see **Lactophrys trigonus,
Masturus lanceolatus, Mola mola,
Ostracion lentiginosum**
TRUNKFISH,
BUFFALO see **Lactophrys trigonus**
SMOOTH see **Lactophrys triqueter**

Trygonorhina   Rhinobatidae
fasciata FIDDLER RAY 1·2 m. (4 ft)
A common ray in Australian waters although
probably more abundant off the s. states than
elsewhere. It is chiefly found on sand-flats, in
estuaries, and in inshore waters but has been
trawled down to 110 m. (60 fathoms). It is
adept at burying itself in the sand and gravel,
and swims slowly by undulations of its pectoral
fins, although when threatened it uses its tail
as its main propulsive force.

The fiddler ray is rather blunt-snouted and
the outline of the disc is almost circular. The
tail is rather short and the dorsal fins comparatively small. It is dark brown with a bluish
grey pattern, bordered by dark brown or
black, the pattern being very pronounced. A
related species, *T. melaleuca* from S. Australia
is yellowish brown round the disc, with a dense
black marking over the back.

The fiddler ray is ovoviviparous, that is the
eggs are retained within the mother's body and
hatch there shortly before the young are born.
T. melaleuca see under **T. fasciata**

TRYPAUCHENIDAE
A small family of goby-like fishes confined to
the Indo-Pacific region. The members of the
family are long-bodied fishes, the body compressed and covered with small to moderate
scales. The dorsal fin is simple and long, joined
to the tail fin at its extremity, which in turn
is joined to the almost as long anal fin. The head
is scaleless, deep and compressed with a low
fleshy crest on the nape. There is a pit, opening to a cavity at the upper edge of the gill
opening. The eyes are minute and rudimentary.

Most of the species whose habits have been
noted have been found to live in burrows in
muddy or shingle bottoms in estuarine and
intertidal areas. Live colours are usually pinkish, which with the reduction of the eye
suggests that they are effectively blind fish
showing the typical reduction of pigment
associated with burrowing fishes. See **Ctenotrypauchen**.

TUB GURNARD see **Trigla lucerna**
TUBE-MOUTH PENCILFISH see
Nannostomus eques
TUBEMOUTH see **Siphonognathus
argyrophanes**
TUBENOSE see Aulorhynchidae
TUBENOSE see **Aulorhynchus flavidus**
TUBENOSE POACHER see **Pallasina
barbata**
TUBESNOUT see Aulorhynchidae
TUBESNOUT see **Aulorhynchus flavidus**
TUNA see Scombridae
TUNA,
ALLISON see **Thunnus albacares**
ATLANTIC BLUE-FIN see **Thunnus
thynnus**

BIG-EYE see **Thunnus obesus**
BLUE-FIN see **Thunnus thynnus**
DOG-TOOTH see **Orcynopsis unicolor**
LITTLE see **Euthynnus alletteratus**
NORTH PACIFIC BLUE-FIN see **Thunnus
orientalis**
SCALELESS see **Orcynopsis unicolor**
SKIPJACK see **Katsuwonus pelamis**
SOUTHERN BLUE-FIN see **Thunnus
maccoyii**
YELLOW-FIN see **Thunnus albacares**
TUNNY see Scombridae
TUNNY see **Thunnus thynnus**
TUNNY, LONG-FINNED see **Thunnus
alalunga**
TURBOT see Scophthalmidae
TURBOT see **Balistes vetula,
Scophthalmus maximus**
TURBOT,
BLACK SEA see **Scophthalmus
maeotius**
GREENLAND see **Reinhardtius
hippoglossoides**
TURKESTAN CATFISH see **Glyptosternum
reticulatum**
TURKEYFISH see **Pterois volitans**
TURRETFISH see **Rhinesomus reipublicae**
TUSKED GOBY see **Risor ruber**
TWAITE SHAD see **Alosa fallax**
TWO-LINED NEOTOCA see **Neotoca
bilineata**
TWOLINE EELPOUT see **Bothrocara
brunneum**
TWO-SPOT
LEBIASINA see **Lebiasina bimaculata**
TETRA see **Astyanax bimaculatus**

Tydemania   Triacanthidae
navigatoris 7 cm. (2¾ in.)
A small, apparently deep-water plectognath
found in the w. Pacific Ocean in the Madura
Sea, off the Philippines, and off Japan. Relatively few specimens have ever been captured
and its biology is virtually unknown. It has
been caught at depths of 290 m. (159 fathoms).

It is slender-bodied with conspicuously
large pelvic and dorsal spines, the largest of
which have pronounced barbs along their
length. Its eye is large and its lips thick and
heavy, with the lower jaw protuberant. The
body is covered with small, spiny edged scales.

TYGUM see **Mugil argenteus**

Tylobranchus   Curimatidae
maculosus 15 cm. (6 in.)
This species is found in freshwater near the
coast of Guyana and the Rio Negro. It is a
moderately slender fish, cylindrical in body
shape anteriorly but compressed towards the
tail. It is rather similar to the head-standers,
and it has their habit of posing in an oblique
head-down attitude, but it differs in many
ways, most notably in having an elongate,
rather pointed anal fin.

It is a warm brown, the sides yellowish, and
the belly white. A dense black line runs from
the tip of the snout along the length of the fish
to the end of the tail fin. Parallel to this stripe
are 2–3 rows of dark dots; the dorsal fin has a
dark apex. The remaining fins are yellowish.

Tylosaurus   Belonidae
acus see under **T. crocodilus**

crocodilus HOUNDFISH 1·5 m. (5 ft)
Worldwide in its distribution, this needlefish
shows slight differences of body form in the
various areas in which it is found, and has been
given a number of different scientific names. It
is well known in the tropical Atlantic, in the W.
from Bermuda to Brazil, including the Gulf of
Mexico, and in the E. in the Gulf of Guinea.

It closely resembles the other Atlantic
houndfish, *Tylosaurus acus*, but is stouter-
bodied, and of more solid appearance. The
snout is relatively shorter also, and there are
differences in the numbers of dorsal fin rays
and vertebrae (80–84 in this species). It is also
usually green on the back, and silvery white
on the sides. The scales and bones are tinged
with green.

It is the largest of the needlefishes and is
found inshore, on flats in coastal waters. It
feeds mainly upon fishes which it catches
cross-wise in its long jaws and then dextrously
manipulates into a head forward position before swallowing. This species has been called
the 'living javelin' because of its habit of leaping from the water and skittering across the
surface when disturbed by a passing row boat
or by bright lights. Persons fishing, or merely
rowing by have been occasionally severely injured when hit by the acutely pointed beak.

Typhliasina   Ophidiidae
pearsei 9 cm. (3½ in.)
A blind cave fish found only in Balaam Canche
Cave, near Chicken Itza, Yucatan, Mexico. It
was originally discovered in small pools between 70–80 m. (230–263 ft) from the mouth
of the cave, habitats it shared with blind crustaceans and another fish, the synbranchid
Ophistosternon infernale.

It is a remarkable looking fish with a large,
heavy broad head, high back, and gradually
tapering tail. The dorsal and anal fins are long,
but just fall short of the tail fin; each pelvic is a
single long ray. The eyes are minute, but completely covered by skin. The head is well supplied by large sensory cavities beneath the skin,
and small papillae are scattered over the head.
In life these fishes are translucent white,
pinkish at the rear end, but the tone of white is
variable.

Typhlichthys   Amblyopsidae
subterraneus SOUTHERN CAVEFISH
7 cm. (2¾ in.)
Found over a wide area of limestone caves
from ne. Oklahoma, s. Missouri, n. Arkansas
to central Kentucky, Tennessee, and n. Alabama.

Distinguished by the lack of pigment overall, the colouring being pale pinkish yellow (although specimens kept in the light develop a
dusky colouring on the body). The eyes are
absent, it has no pelvic fins, and few (a short
row) papillae on each half of the tail fin. The
head and body are covered with short lines
of papillae, which have a sensory function.
These fish are very sensitive to movements in
the water or vibrations of the aquarium. Like
other members of this family this cavefish is
believed to have achieved its wide distribution

by travelling through subterranean connections between caves.

Typhlogobius Gobiidae
californiensis BLIND GOBY 6 cm. (2½ in.)
As its name suggests this species is found on the coast of California. It lives its entire life in burrows dug in gravel by the ghost shrimp *Callianassa*, and its eyes have degenerated so that the fish is effectively blind. During its early life, the young goby is pigmented and the eyes are functional. As an adult, in addition to being blind, the body is a pale pink colour, all pigment having been lost.

The fish is wholly dependent on the shrimp for existence, if the shrimp dies the blind goby cannot survive unless it can find another host.

U

Uaru Cichlidae
amphiacanthoides 25 cm. (10 in.)
Found in the Amazon and Guiana regions, in association with the other cichlids (*Pterophyllum* and *Symphysodon*).

It is a pleasant species for the aquarium and fairly popular but it is difficult to get to spawn. It is distinguished by its body shape and coloration which varies from yellowish to brown, with 3 large blotches on the sides, the middle one of which is very large and wedge shaped. The juvenile is overall blackish.

It spawns inside cavities (in the aquarium a flower pot is often provided) and its spawning behaviour is much like the angelfishes, *Pterophyllum* spp. **381**

Umbra Umbridae
krameri EUROPEAN MUDMINNOW
13 cm. (5 in.)
This little fish is the only representative of the family in European freshwaters. It occurs in the basins of the Danube and Dniester rivers, both of which flow into the Black Sea. It lives in overgrown ponds, swamps, and streams, feeding on bottom-living insect larvae, crustaceans, and molluscs. It can survive long periods when oxygen levels are near zero in the shallow, heavily silted water in which it lives.

It spawns in late spring; the eggs are deposited in a hollow in the bottom which the female guards and keeps clean, as well as removing infected or dead eggs. The male is smaller than the female.

It is a stout-bodied fish with rounded fins, the dorsal is well back and sited above the pelvic fins. It is covered with small scales which extend on to the head and cheeks. It is greenish brown, with faint darker bars on the sides; lighter below.

U. limi CENTRAL MUDMINNOW 15 cm. (6 in.)
The central mudminnow is widely distributed in the central region of N. America, through almost the entire Great Lakes region to Quebec, and the upper Mississippi basin. It is found in silt-bottomed lakes and ponds, typically in spring-fed, well silted, and rather stagnant pools. It burrows into the mud and silt, and in severe winters can survive in waters where all other fishes are killed, for it can tolerate low oxygen conditions and low temperatures without difficulty.

It is a carnivorous fish, but catholic in its tastes, for it eats almost any kind of insect larvae and small crustaceans. It spawns in spring; the eggs are laid in the vegetation amongst which the adults live. The males at the breeding season have an iridescent stripe along the anal fin.

It is a short, rather stout little fish with moderately large scales. As in other members of the family the dorsal and anal fins are placed close to the tail. The pelvic fins are set low down and far back also. In colour it is conspicuous, a dull brown on the back, mottled sides and yellowish underneath. It has a dark bar at the base of the tail fin.

U. pygmaea EASTERN MUDMINNOW
7·5 cm. (3 in.)
This is the smallest of the N. American mudminnows and it is confined to the lakes and pools of the e. seaboard of the U.S. from New York to Florida. This species has been introduced to Europe and can be found in parts of Germany, France and Holland.

In biology it is much like its counterpart in the central states, being found in very silted, densely weeded pools. Like the others it is reported to survive being frozen solid in the winter's ice, and this is possible provided the body fluids have not frozen. It certainly can survive in very cold stagnant conditions such as occur when heavy snow lies on the ice, conditions which kill most fish.

It is a short-bodied little fish, with a blunt snout and moderately large scales. Its colouring is unspectacular except that it has a dark bar at the base of the rounded tail fin.

UMBRIDAE
A small family of N. Hemisphere freshwater fishes, best represented in n. America. They are closely related to the pikes (family Esocidae) but unlike them are small fishes at most 20 cm. (8 in.) long. They have a number of features in common, however, most noticeably in the rearward position of the single dorsal and anal fins. They have moderately large scales with a distinctively etched surface, and are rather short-headed, stout-bodied little fishes. All are capable of surviving under adverse conditions, both of low oxygen levels and temperatures, and some have the reputation of surviving being frozen in the winter's ice. See **Dallia, Umbra.**

UNICORNFISH see **Naso brevirostris**
UNICORNFISH, STRIPED-FACE see **Naso lituratus**
UPSIDE-DOWN CATFISH see **Synodontis nigriventris**

URANOSCOPIDAE
The stargazer family, a group of marine fishes found in tropical and warm temperate seas in all oceans of the world. They are all rather similar, with a heavy, broad, deep body, and a rather slender tail; the small eyes are placed on top of the head, hence the name stargazer. Pectoral fins are well developed and broad, mouths vertical and capacious in this group.

Stargazers are equipped with a heavy spine on the upper gill cover, grooved, with a venom gland at the base. They also possess well developed electric organs behind the eyes; some species are capable of generating up to 50 volts. These are formed from modified eye muscles.

Most stargazers are found buried in sand with only the top of the head exposed. The anterior nostril connects directly to the mouth and thus permits respiratory currents to flow to the gills even when the fish is buried. The electric organs are probably a sensory system to detect approaching prey rather than defensive in nature. See **Ichthyscopus, Kathetostoma, Uranoscopus.**

Uranoscopus Uranoscopidae
scaber STARGAZER 30 cm. (12 in.)
A European species found in the e. Atlantic from Portugal to Senegal, and throughout the Mediterranean. Its habit is to lie buried in sand, in from 3–15 m. (1½–8 fathoms) of water with only the top of the head visible. The lower lip has a stalked flap which can be folded out and vibrated, acting as a lure to small fishes on which it feeds. Its electrical powers are quite extensive, and may assist in stunning prey at close quarters. On land a lively fish can give the incautious hand a sharp electrical jolt. **416**

UROLOPHIDAE
Stingrays distinguished by their short tails with a distinct tail fin; the tail is usually shorter than the body. The disc is smoothly rounded, rather longer than wide. All the members of the family are relatively small, the largest only 76 cm. (30 in.) in length. They are found in shallow coastal waters from tidal levels down to about 73 m. (40 fathoms) usually buried in sand. They are capable of inflicting serious wounds with their tail spine, a serrated dagger close to the tail fin.

The family ranges from the w. Pacific, from Japan, Australia, and the E. Indies, along the American Pacific coast from California to Chile, and the warm Atlantic N. American coastline including the Caribbean. See **Urolophus.**

Urolophus Urolophidae
jamaicensis YELLOW-SPOTTED
STINGRAY 67 cm. (26 in.)
A small stingray found in the w. tropical Atlantic from the s. Caribbean to Florida, occasionally to N. Carolina. It has been recorded from many of the Caribbean islands, and was first described from Jamaica in 1725.

Its disc is nearly round although the snout is slightly pointed, the tail is shorter than the disc and has a distinct tail fin at its extremity. It also possesses a venomous spine near the end. It is densely spotted with yellow dots on a variable dark background, with larger pale blotches around the disc; ventrally it is yellowish white.

This stingray is confined to shallow water usually on sandy or muddy bottoms. It buries itself in the sea bed by flapping its pectoral fins, and is said to feed on the small shrimps, fishes, and worms it disturbs. Because of its shallow water habits it is very common in harbours and bays and is a hazard to the bather and fisherman in its area. It gives birth to live young in litters of 3–4.

U. testaceus COMMON STINGAREE
76 cm. (30 in.)
An Australian species widely distributed in shallow water, down to about 128 m. (70 fathoms) from Queensland to New South Wales, Victoria, and S. Australia.

This species can best be distinguished from other stingrays by examination of the lobes of its nostrils. It is a cinnamon brown above with the edges of the disc light; the lower surface is white. The tail usually has a very small dorsal fin at the spine level.

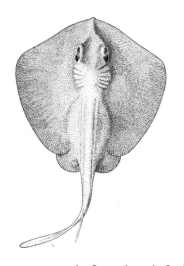

Common on sandy flats where it feeds on hard-shelled bottom-living prey such as crustaceans and molluscs, and itself spends much of the time partially buried in the sand.

Urophycis   Gadidae
chuss SQUIRREL or RED HAKE 76 cm. (28 in.)
Widely distributed in the n. W. Atlantic from s. Labrador, the Gulf of St Lawrence, the Grand Banks to Virginia. The larvae are pelagic floating at the surface, but the young fish and adults are found both inshore and offshore, down to a depth of 320 m. (175 fathoms). The younger fish are more common in shallow inshore waters than the adults. It is found on soft bottoms, chiefly gravelly or shelly grounds.

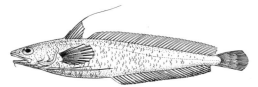

Its food consists very largely of crustaceans; copepods and amphipods when young, prawns and shrimps when larger. Small fishes are also eaten, and rarely molluscs and worms.

The squirrel hake is reddish or olive-brown on the back and sides, ventrally yellowish.

Fished for commercially; although the flesh is rather soft, it is sold fresh, as well as canned and salted. Small ones are used for fish meal. These N. Atlantic hakes should not be confused with the true hakes (family Merlucciidae).

U. tenuis WHITE HAKE 127 cm. (50 in.)
A gadoid found in the w. N. Atlantic from the Gulf of St Lawrence s. to N. Carolina. It occurs from the lower tide mark down to depths of about 1000 m. (545 fathoms). In general smaller specimens are found in shallow water; the large ones, mostly found on the continental slope, may weigh up to 18 kg. (40 lb.).

With the squirrel hake it forms a moderately important fishery in which the 2 are rarely distinguished. Substantial arguments have been advanced suggesting that the white and squirrel hakes are identical. It is extremely similar externally, differing mainly in having smaller scales and a slightly longer jaw which extends to behind the eye rear margin.

V

Valencia   Cyprinodontidae
hispanica SPANISH TOOTHCARP
8 cm. (3 in.)
This is one of the few toothcarps native in Europe; it is found along the Mediterranean coastline of Spain (and possibly part of Greece). It lives in freshwater and slightly brackish water in pools and ditches of coastal marshes. Development of the Spanish coastline, and drainage of swamps has destroyed much of the available living space of this fish, and it is further threatened by the introduced predatory *Gambusia affinis*.

Fortunately it has long been kept in aquaria and it makes an undemanding and lively pet fish. Adult males are quarrelsome, but pairs of fish live harmoniously and breed freely. The eggs are laid on water plants, and hatch in 11–14 days at 20–22°C.

This fish is distinguished from the other European toothcarps by its single-cusped, conical teeth. It is rather slender and compressed with small, yellowish fins. Males are greenish or greeny-brown, with numerous broad black bars on the sides. Females are grey-brown with faint bars.

Vandellia   Trichomycteridae
cirrhosa CANDIRÚ 2·5 cm. (1 in.)
A minute catfish, almost transparent in life, although sometimes with a yellowish tinge, but with large dark eyes. Although slender-bodied it is capable of considerable distension for its habit is to feed by sucking the blood from other fishes until sated, then to burrow into the sandy bottom. It is reported to enter the gill chambers of larger fishes and to suck blood from their gills.

The candirú is infamous from its occasional habit of penetrating into the urethra of any bather foolish enough to urinate in the water, with painful and sometimes fatal consequences for both bather and fish. It has been suggested that it is attracted to the stream of urine by its resemblance to the current from the gill opening of a large fish.

Its appearance is very specialized, the fins are small and rounded, the gill covers have distinct spines, and the mouth is small. It appears to be well distributed in the Amazon region. Other, similar catfishes are also known as candirú.

VARIED CATSHARK see **Parascyllium variolatum**

Variola   Serranidae
louti LUNAR-TAILED ROCK COD
91 cm. (3 ft)
Widely distributed from the Red Sea and E.

African coast to India, n. Australia, and in the w. Pacific to the Marshall Islands.

This rock cod is found on coral reefs, but in the deeper lagoon areas it is both more common and larger. It is a fine game fish and makes very good eating.

VEILFIN see **Caristius macropus**

Velifer   Veliferidae
hypselopterus 30 cm. (12 in.)
An intriguing fish long known in Japanese waters from whence it was first described in 1850, and where it is evidently fairly common. It has more recently been found off Madagascar. Very probably it is relatively common in moderately deep water in the Indian and Pacific oceans.

It is pale silvery grey with about 8 darker bands across the back and sides. These are most distinct in the young.

VELIFERIDAE
A small family of marine fishes related to the opah and dealfishes (families Lampridae and Trachipteridae). Like these fishes they have a small but very protractile mouth. Members of the family are rather deep-bodied, compressed fishes, usually with high, many-rayed dorsal and anal fins. The body is covered with thin easily shed scales, those along the front of the dorsal fin forming a characteristic sheath.

Members of this family have been found off Japan, off s. Africa, and Australia. See **Velifer.**

VELVET-BELLY see **Etmopterus spinax**
VELVETFISH see **Aploactisoma milesii**
VENDACE see **Coregonus albula**

Venefica   Nettastomidae
proboscidea 1 m. (3¼ ft)
A deep-water eel, brownish in colour. Relatively few specimens have been found, and the biology of the species is practically unknown.

It has been reported in the tropical Atlantic, where it was first found at a depth of 2200 m. (1200 fathoms) off Morocco, and in the Arabian Sea at 1893 m. (1035 fathoms). Other records of captures are only slightly shallower.

VENOMOUS TOADFISH see
Thalassophryne maculosa
VIEJA see **Ancistrus cirrhosus,
Loricaria parva, Plecostomus
commersonii**

Vimba   Cyprinidae
vimba ZAHRTE 50 cm. (20 in.)
This bream-like fish is found in the Danube
basin, and in rivers running into the Black and
Caspian seas. It is also found in a quite separate
area, in n. Germany and around the Baltic
Sea. This disjunct distribution is shown by
some other European fishes and is believed to
be due to separation during the Ice Age of one
population into distinct stocks.

The zahrte (the name is German but is
widely used throughout Europe) is a reddish
brown on the back, fading to rosy yellow on
the belly. The fins are dark brown on the back,
reddish ventrally. Its general body shape is of a
rather slim bream, a longish snout, moderately compressed body, and a many-rayed anal
fin.

It is typically an inhabitant of the lower
reaches of rivers, and part of the year of the low
salinity areas of the sea. It is to some extent
migratory, moving upstream to spawn in late
spring and summer in well-weeded, shallow
water on stony bottoms. Most of its life, however, it is found over mud feeding on bottom-
living insects.

The zahrte is of some commercial value as a
food fish in e. Europe.

Vinciguerria   Gonostomatidae
attenuata 4·5 cm. (1¾ in.)
This is a pale brown fish, almost transparent,
but with a double row of large, rounded light
organs on the belly, and a single row along the
tail, on each side. Its eye is large, and to some
extent tubular. Like other bristle-mouths its
very large jaws are lined with fine teeth.

It occurs in the Mediterranean (where it
forms virtually a dwarf race, maturing at 30
mm. (1¼ in.)), and across the tropical Atlantic
to Bermuda. It is found in depths of between
200 and 800 m. (110 and 440 fathoms), the
young stages in shallower water, as a mid-
water inhabitant of the deep sea. It is occasionally found at the surface at night, and it may
well make regular daily vertical migrations. It
appears to be moderately common in the deep
sea, and is believed to be one of the important
forage fishes for larger predators.

The name *Vinciguerria* commemorates the
work of the Italian naturalist Decio Vinciguerra, active in the 19th century.

VIOLET GOBY see **Gobioides broussonetti**
VIOLINO, PESCE see **Rhinobatos rhinobatos**
VIPERFISH see Chauliodontidae
VIPERFISH, SLOANE'S see **Chauliodus
sloani**
VIVIPAROUS BLENNY see **Zoarces
viviparus**

W

WAHOO see **Acanthocybium solanderi**
WAIGE SNAPPER see **Lutjanus vaigiensis**

Wallagonia   Siluridae
attu MULLEY 2 m. (6½ ft)

A huge catfish found in the freshwaters of Java,
Sumatra, Thailand, Indo-China, Burma, Sri
Lanka, and India. It is one of the largest members of the family, specimens of 2 m. not being
rare, although due to their slim build they are
not particularly heavy, weighing around 55 kg.
(120 lb.).

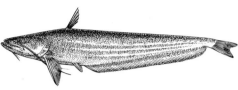

It is a valued food fish in many parts of its
range although in places it is not eaten on
account of its allegedly unclean feeding habits.
It is a voracious predator which feeds extensively on fishes, and can be a pest in cultivated
fisheries. The mulley is also a valued angling
fish, being caught on live bait, or on a trolled
spoon.

It is light green, with golden-cream sides,
and a pinkish flush on the gill cover. The anal
and tail fins are grey.

WALLEYE see Percidae
WALLEYE see **Stizostedion vitreum**
WALLEYE, YELLOW see **Stizostedion
vitreum**
WALLEYE POLLOCK see **Theragra
chalcogramma**
WARBONNET, DECORATED see **Chirolophis
polyactocephalus**
WAREHOU see **Seriolella brama**
WARMOUTH see **Lepomis gulosus**
WARTED SEADEVIL see **Cryptopsarus couesi**
WARTY
ANGLERFISH see **Sympterichthys
verrucosus**
DORY see **Allocyttus verrucosus**
PROWFISH see **Aetapcus maculatus**
WATER GOLDFINCH see **Pristella riddlei**
WEAKFISH see **Cynoscion regalis**
WEATHERFISH see **Misgurnus fossilis**
WEEDFISH see **Fucomimus mus**
WEEDFISH, CRESTED see **Cristiceps
australis**
WEEDY SEADRAGON see **Phyllopteryx
taeniolatus**
WEEPING TOADO see **Torquigener
pleurogramma**
WEEVER see Mugiloididae, Trachinidae
WEEVER see **Trachinus vipera**
WEEVER,
BAR-FACED see **Parapercis nebulosus**
GREATER see **Trachinus draco**
LESSER see **Trachinus vipera**
SPOTTED see **Trachinus araneus**
WELS see **Silurus glanis**
WHALE SHARK see **Rhincodon typus**
WHALEFISH see Barbourisiidae,
Cetomimidae, Rondeletiidae
WHALER, BLUE see **Prionace glauca**
WHALESUCKER see **Remora australis**
WHIFF see **Lepidorhombus
whiffiagonis**
WHIPTAIL GULPER see **Saccopharynx
ampullaceus**
WHITE
AMUR see **Ctenopharyngodon idella**
BREAM see **Blicca bjoerkna**
CLOUD MOUNTAIN MINNOW see
Tanichthys albonubes

CRAPPIE see **Pomoxis annularis**
HAKE see **Urophycis tenuis**
MARLIN see **Tetrapturus albidus**
MULLET see **Mugil curema**
PERCH see **Morone americana**
PIRANHA see **Serrasalmus rhombeus**
POINTER see **Carcharodon carcharias**
SALMON see **Ptychocheilus lucius**
SEABASS see **Cynoscion nobilis**
SHARK see **Carcharodon carcharias**
STEENBRAS see **Lithognathus
lithognathus**
STUMPNOSE see **Rhabdosargus globiceps**
STURGEON see **Acipenser
transmontanus**
SUCKER see **Catostomus commersoni**
WHITE-CHEEKED MONOCLE-BREAM see
Scolopsis vosmeri
WHITE-NOSED PIGFISH see **Perryena
leucometopon**
WHITE-SPOTTED
BUTTERFLYFISH see **Chaetodon kleinii**
DOGFISH see **Squalus kirki**
RAY see **Rhynchobatus djeddensis**
WHITEBAIT see **Atherina breviceps, Clupea
harengus, Sprattus sprattus**
WHITEFISH see Salmonidae
WHITEFISH see **Lactarius lactarius,
Lithognathus lithognathus**
WHITEFISH,
EURASIAN see under **Coregonus
clupeaformis**
HUMPBACK see **Coregonus clupeaformis**
LAKE see **Coregonus clupeaformis**
ROUND see **Prosopium cylindraceum**
WHITESTAR CARDINALFISH see **Apogon
lachneri**
WHITETIP
SHARK, OCEANIC see **Carcharhinus
longimanus**
SHARK, REEF see **Carcharhinus
albimarginatus**
WHITING see Sillaginidae
WHITING see **Menticirrhus saxatilis,
Merlangius merlangus**
WHITING,
BLUE see **Micromesistius poutassou**
BLUE ROCK see **Haletta semifasciata**
NORTHERN see **Sillago sihama**
SAND see **Sillago ciliata**
SPOTTED see **Sillaginoides punctatus**
WIDOW, BLACK see **Stygnobrotula
latebricola**
WIFE, OLD see **Enoplosus armatus**
WINDOW-PANE see **Scophthalmus aquosus**
WINGED DRAGON see **Pegasus volitans**
WINTER
FLOUNDER see **Pseudopleuronectes
americanus**
SKATE see **Raja ocellata**

Winteria   Opisthoproctidae
telescopus 13 cm. (5 in.)
This tubular-eyed fish is rather slender-
bodied, with a pointed snout and small mouth.
Its scales are large but fragile. The eyes have
large lenses, and are mounted in a tube, facing
forwards and upwards. The living fish must
have efficient forward binocular vision, but
the precise value of this has not been deter-
mined. It has been suggested that it aids in
finding food in the water above the fish, and
alternatively that better than usual visual
powers may help a feeble swimmer to escape
predators.

First described from off the tropical W. African coast, but extremely few specimens have been collected and its biology is almost unknown. **39**

WISKERED ANCHOVY see **Thrissocles setirostris**
WITCH see **Glyptocephalus cynoglossus**
WITCH FLOUNDER see **Glyptocephalus cynoglossus**
WOBBEGONG see **Orectolobus maculatus**
WOLF HERRING see **Chirocentrus dorab**
WOLF-EEL see **Anarhichthys ocellatus**
WOLFFISH see Anarhichadidae
WOLFFISH see **Anarhichas lupus**
WOLFFISH, NORTHERN see **Lycichthys denticulatus**
WORM EEL see Moringuidae, Ophichthidae
WORM
    EEL see **Moringua macrochir**
    EEL, KEY see **Ahlia egmontis**
    PIPEFISH see **Nerophis lumbriciformis**
WORMFISH see Microdesmidae
WRASSE see Labridae
WRASSE see **Anampses caeruleopunctatus, Achoerodus gouldii**
WRASSE,
    BALLAN see **Labrus bergylta**
    BLUEHEAD see **Thalassoma bifasciatum**
    CUCKOO see **Labrus mixtus**
    GIANT see **Cheilinus undulatus**
    HUMP-HEADED MAORI see **Cheilinus undulatus**
    MOON see **Thalassoma lunare**
    RAINBOW see **Coris julis**
    SMALL-MOUTHED see **Centrolabrus exoletus**
WRASSE BLENNY see **Hemiemblemaria simulus**
WRECKFISH see **Polyprion americanus**
WRYMOUTH, GIANT see **Delolepis gigantea**

X

X-RAY FISH see **Pristella riddlei**

Xanichthys   Balistidae
  ringens SARGASSUM TRIGGERFISH
25 cm. (10 in.)
The Sargassum triggerfish is so called on account of the habit of its young of floating under bunches of *Sargassum* weed at the surface of the sea. Adults are found in the open sea and in moderately deep water of 30 m. (16 fathoms) or more along the seaward edge of the bank. Beyond this depth it is moderately common in the Caribbean.

This species is said to be circumtropical in the Atlantic, Indian, and w. Pacific oceans; however there is some uncertainty about the identity of the specimens reported outside the Atlantic. In this ocean it is found from the Carolinas and Florida s. through the Caribbean to the S. American coast.

Its background colour ranges from brown, through violet and green, to yellow. The 3 slender lengthwise stripes beneath the eye are reddish or black. **480**

Xenetodon   Belonidae
  cancila 32 cm. (12½ in.)

A freshwater member of a mostly marine family, widely distributed throughout India, Sri Lanka, Burma, the Malayan Peninsula, and in Thailand. It is a surface-living fish found both near the coast and far inland, and eats a wide variety of small fishes and even amphibians.

It is relatively stout-bodied with long, well toothed jaws. Males have the dorsal and anal fins deeply concave and edged with black. The back is grey-green, a shining stripe runs along the side, usually black edged, although sometimes reddish tinted. Minute black spots over the back.

This fish is kept in aquaria, but as it is an excellent leaper the tank has to be carefully covered.

Xenocara   Loricariidae
  dolichoptera BLUE-CHIN XENOCARA
13 cm. (5 in.)
An interesting catfish, native to the Amazon and the Guianas, which has often been imported as a pet fish for the aquarium. Its colour is striking, dark brown to grey-brown above, with bluish sheen, ventrally paler. Fins blue-black, the tail fin and dorsal with a pale blue edge. Young fishes are noticeably more blue spotted.

It has the typical depressed head and body of the loricariid catfishes, with very large scute-like scales on the back and sides (absent ventrally). The dorsal fin is high, an adipose fin is present. Males have many long, stout tentacles on the snout and head; females have many fewer, shorter tentacles.

XENOCARA, BLUE-CHIN see **Xenocara dolichoptera**

XENOCEPHALIDAE
A family which contains a single species, and that known from a single specimen. Although originally placed amongst the cod-like fishes it is now aligned with the blennies. However, its systematic position remains unclear, and there is every possibility that the only known specimen was a damaged or aberrant specimen of some other fish. See **Xenocephalus.**

Xenocephalus   Xenocephalidae
  armatus
The only known member of the family and a species based on a single specimen collected in New Ireland, in the New Guinea region, sometime prior to 1858. The validity of the family is doubtful.

Described as having a large head, covered with bony plates each armed with spines; the body is small with a single dorsal fin. The head plates are yellowish brown, the skin between them blackish; body dark brown with black spots, gold below. Fins yellowish white; eye golden yellow.

The length of the only specimen is unknown; it appears never to have been figured.

Xenoconger   Xenocongridae
  fryeri 45 cm. (17¾ in.)
A long, thin-bodied scaleless eel, which lacks

both pectoral and pelvic fins. The snout is broad and flat, the nostrils lateral, and the anterior one has a small flap on it.

Known only from a single specimen found in a large pit in the rock, cut off from the sea although full of seawater, from Assumption Island in the Indian Ocean. Nothing is known of its life history or habits.

XENOCONGRIDAE
A little known family of small eels which, until collecting with fish poison on a large scale was widely practised, were mostly known from their oceanic larval stages, and isolated captures of adults. One of the best known species is the Mediterranean *Chlopsis bicolor*, first described from Sicily by Rafinesque in 1810. It grows to 25 cm. (10 in.). Although few adult specimens have been taken, its larvae are exceptionally abundant in the Mediterranean.

The xenocongrids can be recognized by a combination of characters. They are scaleless, with the vent well forward along the body, the front nostrils are near the end of the snout, but the rear nostrils are either inside the mouth or on the upper lip. Most species have no pectoral fin, in those that do it is very small and often no more than a flap of skin. The gill slits are small rounded openings.

Members of the family are found mostly in tropical waters, although a few occur in warm temperate seas. A number are found in the central and w. Pacific, others in the e. Pacific and around the W. Indies, the Indian Ocean, and the Mediterranean. See **Kaupichthys, Xenoconger.**

Xenodermichthys   Alepocephalidae
A genus of smooth-heads. The species illustrated in colour has not been identified. **45**
X. socialis 15 cm. (6 in.)
This deep water smooth-head is found in the Atlantic Ocean from the Grand Banks in the W. to the region of s. Africa. It is a rather slender fragile fish with a completely scaleless body, and soft, deep violet to black skin. It is

also distinguished by the small, raised light organs on the ventral surface of the head and body (few of the members of this family have light organs). It is extremely common in depths of 366–732 m. (200–400 fathoms).

Xenolepidichthys   Grammicolepidae
  dalgleishi 12 cm. (5 in.)
An apparently rare, deep-water oceanic fish which was first reported off the S. African coast in depths of 128–457 m. (70–250 fathoms). A number of specimens have been found in that area in the catches of special research boats, and isolated specimens have been washed ashore after storms. It has also been captured off the Philippine Islands, and in the Caribbean off British Honduras (at 885 m. (484 fathoms)).

It is a deep-bodied fish, with a large eye and small mouth. The dorsal and anal spines are long, extremely elongate in the young, having a long filamentous tip. In colour it is mainly silvery, the younger specimens have round dark, irregularly spaced spots.

Xenomystus Notopteridae
nigri FALSE FEATHERBACK 20 cm. (8 in.)
Although it has the characteristic appearance of its relatives, namely a long anal fin, compressed body, and a moderately large mouth, it differs from them by completely lacking a dorsal fin. It is dull brown, or grey, sometimes with faint stripes, and paler on the lower head and belly.

The false featherback is widely distributed in tropical w. Africa, from the upper tributaries of the Nile to the Congo, and Liberia. It lives in large slow-flowing rivers, backwaters and pools, often overgrown and low in dissolved oxygen, like its relatives it has a swim-bladder connection to the pharynx and can utilize atmospheric oxygen.

It is often kept in aquaria. It feeds on plant material, insects, and crustaceans. **32**

Xenopoecilus Adrianichthyidae
poptae 20 cm. (8 in.)
A strikingly interesting fish found only in Lake Posso, in the n. interior of the island of Celebes in the E. Indies.

The mouth is horseshoe-shaped, large and rather oblique, with numerous fine teeth on the jaws. Head and body are covered with scales.

This fish is caught for food on hooks in depths of 12–15 m. (6–8 fathoms) from November to January. At this season, it is spawning; the young fish hatch directly the eggs are shed (and, it is said, follow their mother!). In the spawning period the hatched egg cases float on the surface of the lake in characteristic fashion.

Xenophthalmichthys Argentinidae
danae 8 cm. (3 in.)
This slender-bodied argentine is known from less than a dozen specimens. It is extremely thin and elongate, with fragile fins, dark brown with a brassy sheen on the sides and belly, and silvery gill covers.

Its most remarkable feature is its large eyes set on a short stalk; they project from the outline of the head and are forwardly directed. The living fish must have good binocular vision forward, as well as vision above, below, and to the sides. Unfortunately nothing is known of its biology. The only known specimens came from deep water in the tropical Atlantic; a related species has been described from the Indian Ocean.

Xererpes Pholidae
fucorum ROCKWEED GUNNEL
23 cm. (9 in.)
Found on the coast of the e. N. Pacific from Baja California, Oregon, Washington, n. to British Columbia. It lives in shallow inshore water, mostly amongst fucoid algae, occasionally in intertidal situations. Its food is said to consist principally of small crustaceans and molluscs.

Its body form is similar to that of other members of the family, being long, thin, and deeply compressed. This species, however, totally lacks pelvic fins. It is most easily distinguished by its plain colouring, bright green to red with at the most a line of dusky spots on the sides and a dark bar through the eye.

Xiphasia Blenniidae
setifer HAIR-TAILED BLENNY
61 cm. (2 ft)
A singularly shaped blenny, with a very elongate eel-like body, and long, many-rayed dorsal and anal fins which are joined to the tail fin. The central rays of the tail fin are very elongate and hair-like. Its most striking character is the long, curved, pointed teeth in the back of the lower jaw, with a slightly smaller pair in the upper jaw.

The function of these teeth is unknown; the lower jaw has to be swung down through 90 degrees to expose the tips. They are formidable weapons and have been alleged to be equipped with venom organs at their bases. South African ichthyologist, Professor J. L. B. Smith, recounted that pearl-divers in the Pacific describe an eel-like creature of large size, which is said to attack men with great ferocity and to cause their death; his conjecture that it could be this species sounds reasonable.

It is widely distributed in the Indo-Pacific but is known from relatively few specimens.

Xiphias Xiphiidae
gladius SWORDFISH, BROAD-BILL
SWORDFISH 4·9 m. (16 ft)
The swordfish is of cosmopolitan distribution in temperate and warm-temperate seas. Its occurrence in the cooler regions is clearly governed by water temperature as around such areas as the British Isles it occurs only in summer and late autumn, and then only in seasons when oceanic currents have brought warm water further N. than usual. Most swordfishes reported have been seen, and sometimes harpooned, while lazing at the surface, but they also occur quite commonly at depths of 610 m. (334 fathoms) and have been seen from submersible vehicles and photographed at these depths. They appear to be attracted particularly to areas at the heads of submarine canyons.

Although swordfish do occur in numbers in certain localities they do not form regular schools. They are active strong swimmers which feed on almost any smaller fish numerous in their area, including mackerel, members of the herring family, argentines, rat-tails, and other fish from deep water. They also eat large quantities of squids and these may be their normal diet in deep water. They are so active that, other than man, only certain large sharks and cetaceans can prey on them. A mako shark of about 330 kg. (730 lb.) caught off the Bahamas was found to contain a 55 kg. (120 lb.) swordfish complete with sword. Swordfishes are, however, often infested with external parasites and frequently carry sucking-fish or remoras (family Echeneidae).

Man takes a heavy toll of swordfish wherever they occur. In the Mediterranean fishing for this species has been prosecuted for thousands of years, and off the coasts of Europe it is a relatively uncommon fish, due perhaps to the constant fishing pressure. On the N. American Atlantic coast it has been fished fairly intensively since colonial days but only in the middle of the present century has it been particularly in demand. On average perhaps 20,000 fish are landed a year which is an appreciable tonnage.

On the Pacific coast appreciation of swordfish as food showed a similar progress this century. In the early 1920's and before, there was practically no market for it, but its popularity increased and in 1948 (the most successful year) the Californian catch was 1·1 million lb. Most of them are taken offshore off the coast of California.

The discovery of mercury in swordfish flesh in the 1970s led to controls being placed on its sale in the USA (and this affected the fishery). More recent studies have shown that high levels of mercury in its flesh are not necessarily connected with industrial pollution; high levels have been found in museum specimens collected many years ago.

The swordfish is well known for its reputed habit of thrusting its sword into the hull of wooden ships. This is not normal behaviour! Most cases have involved fish harpooned from fishing boats which have retaliated in kind. A few authentic *Xiphias* attacks have been substantiated (many reports refer to billfish species), usually by the discovery of the broken sword in the ship's timbers. A recent report, however, is of an attack on the Woods Hole Oceanographic Institute's submersible *Alvin* at 600 m. (330 fathoms), the swordfish wedging its sword so tightly into a seam that it could not withdraw it.

XIPHIIDAE
The family which contains the single species, the swordfish, *Xiphias gladius*. Its appearance is unmistakable, the long snout, flattened above and below, which gives it its vernacular

name being sufficient identification. It can be distinguished from the marlins and sailfish by the shape of the sword, by lacking pelvic fins, teeth, and body scales. It has 2 dorsal fins when adult (in the young it has a single continuous fin, the middle of which disappears with age). Like its relatives, the tunnies, it has a strong keel either side of the tail. Rarely abundant anywhere; in some areas small fisheries for it exist. See **Xiphias.**

Xiphister Stichaeidae
mucosus ROCK PRICKLEBACK
51 cm. (20 in.)
Distributed along the Pacific coast of N. America from s. California to s. Alaska. It is a common fish in intertidal situations, found from mid-shore to depths of around 18 m. (10 fathoms). Its food consists mainly of algae.

Its body form is slender and compressed, the head, eye, and mouth are small. Its body is fully scaled, but it has no pelvic fins. It is greenish brown with dusky white bars near the tail; 3 dark-bordered light bands run from the eye across the cheek and gill cover.

Xiphophorus Poeciliidae
helleri SWORDTAIL 12 cm. (5 in.)
This very familiar and popular aquarium fish originates from the general area of Mexico and Guatemala. It is found both in springs and streams in the mountainous regions, and in streams, rivers, lagoons and swamps in the coastal plain. Within this very large range numerous forms exist differing mainly in response to special habitats, in colouring, number of scales, development of the 'sword', and body shape. Four subspecies are currently recognized but many have been described.

The typical form has a ground colouring of pale olive-brown, green along the side with a central stripe of orange sometimes flanked by red. This lateral stripe continues along the prolonged lower edge of the tail (the sword). The centre of the tail may be orange, red or green. The female's colouring is rather more subdued, and they lack the characteristic tail sword.

Very many variations on this basic coloration have been produced by selective breeding for the aquarium.

Swordtails are relatively undemanding fishes, they are lively, hardy, and mature males excepted, peaceful. They will eat live foods of all kinds and will accept dried foods.

Change of sex is not unusual in this species. A fully productive female will cease bearing young, and gradually change in coloration and grow a sword to become fully functional male in a matter of months. Sex change from male to female is not recorded. **210**

X. maculatus PLATY 6 cm. (2½ in.)
Found widely distributed along the Atlantic slopes of Central America, from n. Honduras, Guatemala to s. Mexico. It is an inhabitant of the coastal plain and is found in swamp pools, ponds, and lakes, and occasionally in the slower-flowing streams and rivers. It is established well inland as a result of flooding carrying it to new habitats.

The most common is the usual wild form – dark olive on the back, the sides bluish tinged, the belly yellowish; it also occurs in nature in red and black, or black chequered forms. Two round black blotches on the tail. Males have a

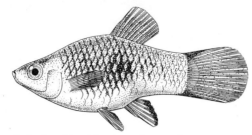

dark shoulder blotch and sometimes up to 4 faint bars; the tail and anal fins have a pale bluish edge. Females, which are larger than males, have colourless fins.

Platies are relatively easy to keep; they require medium hard water and a temperature of 20–25°C. The aquarium should be well planted, and they feed on algae as well as live and dried food. The gestation period is 4–6 weeks, the female may produce between 10–80 young in a brood (according to her size). They measure 7–8 mm. at birth. Aquarists have developed the colour variations to an extreme.
X. xiphidium SWORDTAIL PLATY 5 cm. (2 in.)
A platy which originates in Mexico, and which has achieved some success as an aquarium fish since its first introduction in the 1950s. It was originally described from the vicinity of the Rio Purificacion in the vicinity of Ciudad de Victoria, Tamaulipas, Mexico.

The male is smaller than the fully grown female, and has a broad but short prolonging of the lower tail fin rays forming a short sword.
211

Xyrauchen Catostomidae
texanus RAZORBACK or HUMPBACK
SUCKER 61 cm. (2 ft)
The razorback sucker is very restricted in its range being found only in the Colorado River and Gila River basins in w. N. America. It is, in general, a typical sucker, its body covered with small scales, the head naked, with a blunt snout, ventral mouth but with only moderately enlarged lips. It is atypical when adult only in body form, the back being very high and sharp-edged, hence humpback sucker. Older specimens show this at its most extreme.

Although it is found in lakes its most typical habitat is in the swift water of the main rivers, and its peculiar body shape can be seen to be an adaptation to life in running water, the flattened head and belly and the inverted keel of the back presenting little resistance to the flow of the water.

Its food consists of vegetable matter and debris from the bottom. It spawns in shallows over clay and pebble bottoms in small groups.

Large razorback suckers weigh up to 4.5 kg. (10 lb.). They were at one time an important resource for Indians living near the Colorado River.

Y

Yarrella Gonostomatidae
blackfordi 32 cm. (12½ in.)
This species has been found on both sides of the tropical Atlantic, off the African coast in the E., and in the Gulf of Mexico and the Caribbean in the W., mainly in depths be-

tween 380–500 m. (207–273 fathoms). Although nothing is known for certain of its habits, it is believed to live close to the bottom, to form shoals of moderate size, and to eat crustaceans.

Yarrella blackfordi is uniform blackish with most of the fins dusky, but it is very fragile and few undamaged specimens have been seen. It is an elongate fish, with a long-rayed anal fin. Its jaws are large and fringed with minute bristle-like teeth. The underside of the fish is lined with rows of small, reddish light organs.

The name *Yarrella* commemorates the 19th century English naturalist William Yarrell.

Z

Zalieutes Ogcocephalidae
elator SPOTTED BATFISH 15 cm. (6 in.)
An extremely oddly shaped fish even in this family of bizarre fishes. From above it looks strikingly like the head of an arrow with a short tail. Pectoral fins are wide and angled out, the tail fin is well developed; all other fins are minute. The eyes are large, placed close together, and are laterally sited. It feeds on tiny crustaceans and fishes.

This batfish ranges from the Californian coast to Panama, in the e. Pacific. It lives in depths of up to 45 m. (25 fathoms), usually over sandy or muddy bottoms. It is occasionally caught incidentally in fishing nets, or picked up by skin divers, but other than as a curiosity, it has no commercial value.

Zanclistius Pentacerotidae
elevatus BLACK-SPOTTED BOARFISH
30 cm. (12 in.)
Found in the coastal waters of s. Australia, and recorded frequently from Tasmania and S. Australia. It is found only in moderately deep water where it is taken commonly by trawling.

The adults have the strikingly concave snout with a pronounced bump on the nape; in juveniles it is smoothly concave from snout tip to dorsal origin. The body is silvery grey in colour with broad vertical dark bands on the body and a black spot at the end of the soft dorsal.

Zanclus Acanthuridae
canescens see **Z. cornutus**
cornutus MOORISH IDOL, TOBY
18 cm. (7 in.)
A very lovely and distinctive fish in the Indo-Pacific region, from the E. African coast across

both oceans to the Central Pacific, including the Hawaiian Islands. Its coloration is so bold and body form so distinctive that there are few fish with which it could be confused except for the butterflyfishes of the genus *Heniochus*, which have no black on the tail fin.

It is a shallow-water reef species found as shallow as 1·5 m. (1 fathom) and often in schools.

When young these fishes have a knife-like spine behind each corner of the mouth. These drop off when the fish is between 8–10 cm. (3–4 in.) long. With age a pair of horn-like pro-

tuberances grow in front of the eyes and gradually increase in size. These changes in body form resulted in the young and adults being described originally as 2 species (the young being *Z. canescens*), a confusion which has persisted in some areas until recent years.

A legend persists in some books that this fish is regarded with great respect by some orientals and if one is captured it is returned to the water with some ceremony. Its common name Moorish idol is said to refer to this. **446**

ZANDER see Percidae
ZANDER see **Stizostedion lucioperca**

ZANIOLEPIDIDAE
A family of fishes containing very few species. Its members are closely related to the greenling family (Hexagrammidae), and were for long included within it. It is confined to the e. N. Pacific.

It differs externally from the greenlings by having rough-edged scales set firmly in the thick skin, which gives the skin a rough sandpapery feel. It also has several sharp, closely spaced spines on the preoperculum. Like the greenlings it has a single nostril each side and is generally compressed anteriorly. See **Zaniolepis.**

Zaniolepis Zaniolepididae
latipinnis LONGSPINE COMBFISH
30 cm. (12 in.)
A widely distributed fish along the N. American Pacific coast from s. California to Vancou-

ver Island. It is found in moderately deep water down to depths of 110 m. (60 fathoms). It feeds mainly on crustaceans.

It is immediately distinguished from the greenlings (family Hexagrammidae) by the thickened first rays of each pelvic fin, and by the first 3 dorsal spines which are extremely long (the second the longest) and free from the fin membrane. The scales are toothed and feel rough. Its colouring is variable but is usually greenish-brown with indistinct dark spots on the body, and dark bars running along all the fins. A dark stripe runs across the snout.

ZAPRORIDAE
A family which is represented by a single species of fish, the N. Pacific prowfish, *Zaprora silenus*. It is regarded as being related to the sea catfishes (Anarhichadidae) and snake blennies (Stichaeidae), although its systematic position was for long a matter of uncertainty. See **Zaprora.**

Zaprora Zaproridae
silenus PROWFISH 88 cm. (34¾ in.)
Widely distributed in the N. Pacific from California n. along the American coast to Alaska and the Aleutian Islands, and along the Asian

coast and islands to Kamchatka and Hokkaido. It appears to be a rare fish throughout its range. The adults are bottom dwelling in depths of 91–457 m. (50–250 fathoms). Larvae and juveniles are bathypelagic or pelagic in habitat, and the latter have been found to associate with large orange jellyfish, *Cyanea*.

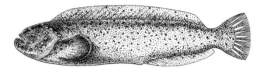

It is dark green or brown above, and sides shade to tan on the belly. It has irregular dark spots overall, those on the head being large; the head and pectoral fin bases are often yellowish.

It has no sporting or commercial value, although its flesh, which is said to be sometimes reddish, is mild and tasty.

ZEBRA
ANGELFISH see **Pomacanthus semicirculatus**
DANIO see **Brachydanio rerio**
EEL see **Echidna zebra**
FIREFISH see **Dendrochirus zebra**
SHARK see **Stegostoma fasciatum**
SOLE see **Gymnachirus melas**
ZEBRAFISH see **Therapon jarbua**

Zebrasoma Acanthuridae
flavescens see under **Z. scopas**
scopas 15 cm. (6 in.)
A widely distributed tropical Indian Ocean and w. Pacific species found from E. Africa to the E. Indies, thence to the Philippines, Solomon Islands and Marshall Islands. It is found in or close to deep water, but in some areas occurs in shoal water close to reefs.

The ground colour is usually dark brown but varies in occasional specimens to yellowish green. This species is distinguished by having only 4–5 spines in the dorsal fin.

A bright yellow member of this genus, *Z. flavescens* is found in the Hawaiian Islands. Some authorities have suggested that it is no more than subspecifically distinct. **447**
Z. xanthurum 19 cm. (7½ in.)
A surgeonfish which has been reported from a rather restricted area of the Indian Ocean. It has been recorded from Sri Lanka, the Gulf of Aden, and the Red Sea. It is the largest member of the genus which is distinguished from *Acanthurus* species by having only 4–5 spines in the dorsal fin (instead of 8–9 spines).

Its body form is similar to the surgeonfishes, including possessing 4 distinct tail spines. Its body colour in the Sri Lankan region is described as wholly black with a bright golden-yellow tail, and yellowish pectoral fins. **448**

ZEIDAE
A rather small family of characteristic appearance found in temperate and warm-temperate seas. Several species are found in shallow water only; others are found at considerable depths.

They all have deep, compressed bodies, with a deep head, a large protrusible mouth, and often large eyes. The general impression they give is of fishes habitually living in a state of deep gloom! Several of the species in this family have small scales; others are scaleless except for large scaly plates flanking the fins. The anal, dorsal, and pelvic fins have strong spines as well as long rays. See **Cyttus, Zenopsis, Zeus.**

Zenopsis Zeidae
nebulosus MIRROR DORY 46 cm. (18 in.)
Widely distributed in the Indo-Pacific, although never particularly abundant except locally. It has been reported from the S. Australian coast, also Tasmania, Victoria, and New South Wales, and in the e. Pacific off California. Off New Zealand and Japan it is fished for commercially at depths of 128–220 m. (70–120 fathoms).

It is a bright silver with a faint dark blotch on each side. In body shape it is much like other members of the family, deep and compressed with a large, extensible mouth. The first dorsal fin has strong spines, the anal has 3 short spines only, with both fins composed of soft rays.

Z. ocellata AMERICAN JOHN DORY
61 cm. (2 ft)
Found on the Atlantic coast of N. America, from the Newfoundland Banks, Nova Scotia, to Chesapeake Bay. It occurs mainly in offshore waters of about 91–137 m. (50–75 fathoms), and is fairly frequently taken in the trawl at these depths, although it seems to be moderately uncommon in general.

It differs from the European John dory (*Zeus faber*) by having a shallower head, with a more concave dorsal profile. The dorsal fin has long, stout spines preceding the soft rays, and has 3 anal spines in the anal fin. Also the bony plates along the base of the dorsal and anal fins are larger, but have smaller spines than in the European form. Its colouring is silvery overall with a number of irregularly arranged dark spots on the sides.

Zeugopterus Scophthalmidae
punctatus TOPKNOT 25 cm. (10 in.)
Found only along the European Atlantic coast from Norway to the Bay of Biscay and within that area confined to rocky areas so that its effective range is along the w. British coast and the French Atlantic coast. Elsewhere it seems very rare. It lives in shallow water from the low shore line down to 30 m. (16 fathoms), although those living in shallow water are mostly immature. It clings to rocky surfaces by creating a suction disc of its body, and although not difficult to dislodge is exceedingly

hard to see by reason of its near-perfect colour match to its background.

It is distinguished by its wide body, large jaws, and well-spaced eyes. The dorsal fin origin is in front of the eyes, and both this and the anal fin continue ventrally under the tail to form a small lobe each side. The body is fully scaled, those on the eyed, coloured side being rough to the touch. **465**

Zeus Zeidae
faber JOHN DORY 66 cm. (26 in.)
This remarkable looking fish is easily distinguished by its deep body and compressed head, and wide, spacious mouth with steeply-angled jaws. The dorsal fin is composed of long, strong fin spines, with a second, soft-rayed fin; the anal fin has a similar formation with 4 strong spines.

The dory is found in the e. Atlantic from N. of Scotland, s. to the S. African coast, as well as in the Mediterranean. A very similar species, *Z. japonicus*, is found in the Indo-Pacific. The 2 scarcely differ morphologically.

The John dory is essentially a solitary fish usually found in inshore waters of less than 200 m. (109 fathoms). It is often taken in trawls over soft-bottomed areas, but is also captured on rocks. Some have been found floating underneath flotsam just offshore. It appears to be a rather feeble swimmer covering distances by drifting in the ocean currents, and it catches its prey, mostly small fishes and crustaceans by stealth. Its approach is slow and head on, and when it is close to its prey the vast mouth drops downwards drawing in the food item with great rapidity.

The flesh of the dory is white, firm, and excellently flavoured. By some gourmets it is said to be the best eating of all European fish, but around the British Isles it is too uncommon to form large landings. It is occasionally taken by anglers.

The black thumb-prints on the sides have given rise to the legend that the dory bears the thumb marks of the Apostle Peter who took the tribute money from the mouth of a fish. It is occasionally called St Peter's fish in English or its equivalent in other European languages. **224**
Z. japonicus see under **Z. faber**

ZIEGE see **Pelecus cultratus**
ZINGEL see **Aspro zingel**

Zoarces Zoarcidae
viviparus EELPOUT, VIVIPAROUS
BLENNY 46 cm. (18 in.)
A widely distributed species in n. European coastal waters, it is found from the White Sea, and n. Norway to the e. English Channel and the W. coast of Scotland. It is also found in the Baltic. It is an abundant fish in shallow water, to 40 m. (22 fathoms) in the s. parts of its range, but becoming more common on the shore to the N. It is frequently found on muddy bottoms and on rocky shores. Its colouring is variable, usually dull brown with golden tints, lighter ventrally.

Its diet is varied, being mainly crustacean, with some small fishes, molluscs, and worms.

It is well known as a live-bearing fish; the eggs are fertilized internally and develop within the ovary to be expelled as miniatures of the adult (about 4 cm. ($1\frac{1}{2}$ in.) long). The number

of young depends on the size of the female fish, from 9–132 have been recorded, with averages between 30–70.

ZOARCIDAE
A family of cool temperate to cold water fishes found only in the sea. They live from the shoreline down to considerable depths, and are represented by numerous species in both Arctic and Antarctic Seas. Most are moderately small.

The eelpouts are all relatively slender fishes with the dorsal and anal fins meeting to fuse with the tail. Pectoral fins are generally broad and well developed, the pelvics small and placed well forward on the head region. The head is usually broad and rather flattened, with thick lips and a protuberant upper jaw. Some species give birth to living young, for example, the European eelpout, *Zoarces viviparus*. See **Bothrocara, Gymnelis, Lycodes, Macrozoarces, Melanostigma, Zoarces.**

Zu Trachipteridae
cristatus 1 m. (39 in.)
Probably worldwide in distribution but certainly found in the Mediterranean, warm e. Atlantic, off S. Africa, New Zealand, Japan, and California.

It is brilliantly silvery except for 5–6 brown blotches; the dorsal fin is reddish, the tail fin black. A juvenile is illustrated.

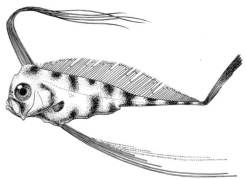